Beeing inforced (through the grievous visitacion of
Gods heavie hand, vpon your Highnes poore Cittie of Lon=
don) thus long (& yet longer like) to deferr the Impres=
sion of my slender Labours (long-since meant vnto your
Maᵗⁱᵉ) I thought it more then tyme, by some other
meane, to tender my humble Homage to your Highnes.
But wanting both leasure, in my self, &(heere in the Country)
such helps, as I could haue wished, To copie the entire
Worke (woorthie your Maᵗⁱᵉˢ reading) I was faine, thus
soudainlie to scribble over this small Parte: That (in
the mean time) by a Parte, I might (as it wear) giue
your Highnes Possession of the Whole; vntill it shall
please the Almightie, in his end his Mercie to giue an
end to this Lamentable Affliction; wᶜʰ for his deir Sonns
sake I most earnestlie beseech him: & ever to protect your
Sacred Maᵗⁱᵉ & all your Royal ffamilie, vnder the winges
of his gracious ffavour.

Your Maiestis

most humble Subiect,

& devoted Servant,

Josuah Sylvester.

THE
COMPLETE WORKS

OF

Joshuah Sylvester

FOR THE FIRST TIME COLLECTED AND EDITED:
WITH MEMORIAL-INTRODUCTION, NOTES AND ILLUSTRATIONS,
GLOSSARIAL INDEX, &c. &c. PORTRAITS, AND FACSIMILES, &c.

BY

The Rev. ALEXANDER B. GROSART, LL.D., F.S.A.

ST. GEORGE'S, BLACKBURN, LANCASHIRE.

IN TWO VOLUMES.

VOL. II.

AMS Press, Inc.
New York
1967

AMS PRESS, INC.
New York, N.Y. 10003
1967

Manufactured in the United States of America

CONTENTS OF VOL. II.

*** *Notes and Illustrations are added at the close of each of the above sections.*

ILLUSTRATIONS IN VOL. II.

URANIA,

OR, THE

HEAVENLY MUSE.

D.O.M.S.

GUILIELMO SALUSTIO
POETARUM FACILE PRINCIPI,
SCRIPTORI MIRABILI, PIO
MIRABILIUM ASSERTORI,
PRÆCONI VIRTUTIS DULCI

DOCTOQ.

CUJUS MONUMENTA DOCUMENTA
POSTERIS FUTURA SUNT:
QUI MUSAS EREPTAS PROFANÆ
LASCIVIÆ SACRIS MONTIBUS
REDDIDIT, SACRIS FONTIBUS
ASPERSIT, SACRIS CANTIBUS

IMBUIT,

VIRO VERE NOBILI, MORTALI-
BUS EXUVIIS SPOLIATO,
IMMORTALITATIS
COMPOTI.

A.MM.PP.

---

*H*Is, fateor, nemo exuviis inscribere honorem,
  Aut Pater Aonii debuit ipse chori :
Gratia sed quoniam taciti propè nulla doloris,
  Neu videar mæstas non maduisse genas ;
Audiat ecce gemens etiam me turba gementem ;
  Ecce, meus vano munere peccet amor.
Et titulus saltem esto, BONA SUPER AETHERA FAMA
NOTUS, EGET NULLO, QUI JACET HIC, TITULO.

Jac. Lectius.

TO

MY EVER-MOST

HONOURED MISTRESSE,

MISTRESSE ESSEX, WIFE TO THE

Right worthie, *William Essex* of Lamborn, Esquire ;
and eldest Daughter of the right valiant, and
Nobly-descended Sir *Walter Harecourt*
of Stanton-Hare-court, Knight
Baron of Ellen-Hall.

*W*It's Beatue's, Vertue's *perfect Quintessence*
  (*Yet grac't in* Soule *with more Divine* perfec-
tion)
Grace, with a glance of your milde Eye's reflection,
This humble Pledge of Zeal *and* Reverence :

Which (as the Stork, *for gratefull recompence,*
Where shee hath bred, one of her Birds bestoweth)
My thankfull Muse (*who you like* Duty *oweth*)
Here consecrates *to your dear excellence.*
Dear ESSEX *here (to make your* Faith *apparant*
Unto the Faithfull, and confirm the same)
Embrace (I pray) the Faith of ABRAHAM
Offering his Isaac (*on th' Almightie's warrant*) :
So shall th' Imputer *of his* Righteousnesse
Impute you yours ; and your young Isaac's *blesse.*

———————————— Your Vertue's

———————— ever-vowed Servant,

———————— JOSUAH SYLVESTER.

❧ TO VERTUES

PATTERNE, AND BEAU-

TIES PARAGON, MISTRESSE

JONE ESSEX : now Wife to the right worthie *William Anderson*, Esquire (second Sonne
of the late Lord *Anderson*) and only Sister
of the Honourably-descended WILLIAM
ESSEX of Lamborn ESQUIRE.

*U*RANIA (*noblest of the learned* NINE)
  Comming from Heav'n, to call my Muse from
    Earth,
From Love's loose Sonnets, *and lascivious Mirth ;*
In sacred WEEKS *to sing the Works divine :*
Of all the Nymphs extract from mortall Line,
  For sweet Companion picks you only forth
  (*As best resembling her self's grace and worth*)
  Dear Beautie's best, Wit's wonder, Vertue's shrine.
Sweet, heav'nly temper of a humane soule
  (*Whose lovely smiles set coldest hearts a-fire :*
  But, instantly, with modest brow's controule
Th' aspiring hope of any bold desire)
  Daign t' entertain in your milde gracefull manner
  This Heav'nly Mayd, the mirrour of your Honour.

Your Vertue's

---

humble Votary,

JOSUAH SYLVESTER.

URANIA,

Or, The

HEAVENLY MUSE.

1

S Carce had the *Aprill* of mine Age begun,
  When brave desire t' immortalize my Name,
Did make mee (oft) Rest and Repast to shun,
In curious project of some learned *Frame*.

2

But, as a Pilgrim, that full late doth light
Upon a crosse-way, stops in sudden doubt ;
And, 'mid the sundry Lanes to finde the right,
More with his Wit than with his Feet doth scout :

3

Among the many flowry paths that lead
Up to the Mount, where (with green Bayes) *Apollo*
Crowns happy Numbers with immortall meed,
I stood confus'd, and doubtfull which to follow.

4

One while I sought, the *Greekish-Scœne* to dress
In *French* disguise : in loftier stile anon
T' imbrew our Stage, with Tyrants' bloudy Gests,
Of *Thebes*, *Mycœna*, and proud *Ilion*.

5

Anon, I sacred to th' *Aonian* Band
My Countrie's Storie ; and, condemning much
The common error, rather took in hand
To make the *Mein French*, then the *Sein* be *Dutch*.

6

Anon, I meant with fawning Pen to praise
Th' un-worthy Prince ; and so, with gold & glorie,
T' inrich my Fortunes, and my Fate to raise,
Basely to make my *Muse* a Mercenarie.

7

Then (gladly) thought I, the Wag-Son to sing
Of wanton *Venus ;* and the bitter-sweet,
That *Too-much Love* to the best Wits doth bring ;
Theam, for my Nature and mine age, too-meet.

8

While to and fro thus (tossed by *Ambition*)
Yet un-resolved of my Course, I rove ;
Lo, suddenly a sacred Apparition ;
Some Daughter (thinke I) of supernall *Jove*.

9

Angelicall her gesture and her gait ;
Divinely-sweet her speech and countenance ;
Her *Nine*-fold Voice did choicely imitate
Th' harmonious Musick of Heav'n's nimble Dance.

10

Upon her Head a glorious *Diadem*,
Seven-double-folded, moving diversly ;
And on each fold sparkled a precious Gem,
Obliquely turning o're our heads on high :

11

The first of *Lead*, the second *Tin* (mee thought)
Third *Steel*, the fourth of yellow *Gold* was cast,
The fift of pale *Electrum* seemed wrought ;
Sixt *Mercurie ;* of *Silver* was the last.

12

An *Azure Mantle* on her back shee wore,
With art-less Art, in orderly disorder ;
Flourisht, and fill'd with thousand *Lamps* & more,
Her sacred Beauty to set forth and further.

13

Here flames the *Harp*, there shine the tender *Twins :*
Here *Charles his Wayn*, there twinkling *Pleiades :*
Here the bright *Balance*, there the silver *Finns :*
And thousand *Stars* more then I can express.

14

I am URANIA (then aloud, said shee)
Who humane-kinde above the *Poles* transport,
Teaching their hands to touch, and eyes to see
All th' enter-course of the *Celestiall Court*.

15

I quint-essence the Soule, and make the *Poet*
(Passing himselfe) in a Divine Discourse
To draw the deafest, by the ears unto-it ;
To quicken stones, and stop the Ocean's course.

16

I grant, My learned Sisters warble fine,
And ravish millions with their *Madrigals :*
Yet all, no lesse inferiour unto mine,
Then Pies to Syrens, Geese to Nightingals.

17

Then take Mee (BARTAS) to conduct thy Pen,
Soar up to Heav'n ; Sing me th' Almightie's praise :
And tuning now the *Jessean* Harp again,
Gaine thee the *Garland* of eternall *Bayes.*

18

I cannot (grief-lesse) see my Sister's wrongs
Made Bawds to *Lovers*, in deceitfull faynings,
In forged sighes, false tears, and filthy songs,
Lascivious shews, and counterfeit complaynings.

19

Alas ! I cannot with dry eyes behold
Our holy Songs fould and profaned thus
To grace the grace-lesse ; praising (too-too bold)
Caligula, *Nero*, and *Commodus.*

20

But, most I mourn, to see rare *Verse* apply'd
Against the Author of sweet *Composition :*
I cannot brook to see Heav'n's King defy'd
By his own Souldiers, with his own Munition.

21

Man's eyes are sield-up with *Cimmerian* mist :
And, if ought precious in his Life he reach,
Through sundry hands, by the Heav'ns' bountie is't :
But God, himselfe, the *Delphian* Songs doth teach.

22

Each *Art* is learn'd by *Art :* but POESIE
Is a meer *Heav'nly gift :* and none can taste
The Deaws wee drop from *Pindus* plenteously,
If *sacred Fire* have not his breast imbrac't.

23

Thence is't, that many great *Philosophers*,
Deep-learned *Clarks* (in *Prose* most eloquent)
Labour in vain to make a gracefull *Verse*,
Which many a Novice frames most excellent.

24

Thence is't, that yerst, the poor *Meonian* Bard,
Though Master, means, and his own eyes he misses,
Of Old and New is for his Verse preferr'd,
In 's stout *Achilles*, and his wise *Ulysses.*

25

Thence is 't, that *Ovid* cannot speak in *Prose :*
Thence is 't, that *David* (Shepheard, turned *Poet*)
So soon doth learn my *Songs :* and Youths compose
After our *Art*, before (indeed) they know it.

26

Dive day and night in the *Castalian* Fount,
Dwel upon *Homer* and the *Mantuan Muse ;*
Climb night and day the double-topped Mount,
Where the *Piërian* learned *Maidens* use :

27

Read while thou wilt, read over every Book
In *Pergamus*, and in the famous City
That her great name, of *Alexander* took ;
Still ply thy Pen, practise thy language (wittie) :

28

Take time enough, choose seat and season fit,
To make good *Verse ;* at best advantage place thee :
Yet worthy fruit thou shalt not reap of it,
For all thy toil, unlesse *Minerva* grace thee.

29

For, out of Man, Man must him all advance,
That time-proof *Poems* ever hopes to utter ;
And extased (as in a *holy Transe*)
Into our hands his *Sensive part* must put-her.

30

For, as a humane Furie makes a man
Lesse then a man : so *Divine-Fury* makes him
More then himselfe ; and sacred *Phrenzie* then
Above the heav'ns' bright flaming arches takes-him.

31

Thence, thence it is that divine *Poets* bring
So sweet, so learned, and so lasting *Numbers ;*
Where Heav'n's & Nature's secret works they sing,
Free from the power of *Fate's* eternall slumbers.

32

True *Poets*, right are like winde-Instruments,
Which full, do sound ; empty, their noise surceases.
For with their *Fury* lasts their Excellence ;
Their *Muse* is silent, when their *Fury* ceases.

33

Sith therefore *Verses* have from Heav'n their spring,
O rarest spirits ! how dare you (damned scorners)
Profanely wrest, against Heav'n's glorious King,
These sacred gifts given from your lives' adorners ?

34

Shall your ingratefull Pens be always waiting,
As Servants to the *Flesh*, and slaves to *Sin ?*
Will you your *Volumes* evermore be fraighting,
With *Dreams* and *Fables*, idle *Fame* to win ?

35

Still will you fill the World with *Love-sick* groans?
Still will you fawn on Fooles, and flatter Evill?
Still will you parbreak loathsome passions?
Still will you make an Angell of a Divell?

36

Still will you comment on this common Storie?
And (Spider-like) weave idle Webs of folly?
O! shall wee never hear you sing the glory
Of God, the great, the good, the just, the holy?

37

Is 't not enough, that in your soules, yee feel
Your *Paphian Fire?* but every Brothel-Lover,
T' inchaunt the wanton with his wanton stile,
Must (Strumpet-like) his lustfull flame discover?

38

Is 't not enough, that you your selves doe wallow
In foul delights? but that you must intice
Your heed-lesse *Readers*, your loose Race to follow;
And so for *Vertue*, make them fall to *Vice?*

39

Tunes, Notes, and *Numbers* (whence they do transfer
Th' harmonious powr that makes our *Verse* so pleasing)
The sternest *Catoes* are of force to stir,
Man's noblest spirits with gentle *Fury* seazing.

40

And, as a Seal printed in wax (almost)
Another Seal; a learned *Poet* graveth
So deep his passions in his Reader's Ghost,
That oft th' Reader th' Author's form receiveth.

41

For, *Verse's* vertue, sliding secretly
(By secret Pipes) through th' *intellectuall Notions;*
Of all that 's pourtraid artificially
Imprinteth there both good and evill motions.

42

Therefore did *Plato* from his *None-Such* banish
Base *Poêtasters*, that with vitious verse
Corrupted manners, making vertue vanish;
The wicked, worse; and even the good, perverse.

43

Not those that car'd to match their gracefull Phrazes
To grave-sweet matters: singing now the praise
Of justest *Jove;* anon from error's mazes
Keeping th' unsteady, calling back the straies.

44

O profane Writers! your lascivious Ryme
Makes our best *Poets* to be basely deemed
As Jugglers, Jesters, and the scum of Time;
Yea, with the Vulgar, lesse then these esteemed.

45

You make chaste *Clio*, a light wanton Minion;
Mount *Helicon*, a Stews; your ribaldrie
Makes prudent Parents (strict in their opinion)
To bar their Children reading *Poëtrie*.

46

But, if you would (yet at the last) inure-yee
Your *Gnidian Idols* in the dust to trample,
And rouz the *Genius* of your *sacred Furie*,
To shew the World some holy *Work's* example;

47

All would admire your Rymes, and do you honour,
As *Secretaries* of the Heav'nly Court;
And *Majestie* would make you wait upon-her,
To manage Causes of the most import.

48

The chain of *Verse* was at the first invented
To handle onely sacred Mysteries
With more respect: and nothing else was chanted
For long time after in such *Poêsies*.

49

So did my *David* on the trembling strings
Of his divine *Harp* onely sound his *God:*
So milde-soul'd *Moses* to *Jehovah* sings
Jacob's deliv'rance from th' *Egyptian's* Rod.

50

So *Debora* and *Judith*, in the Camp;
So *Job* and *Jeremy*, in cares oppressed;
In tune-full *Verses* of a various stamp,
Their joyes and sighs divinely-sweet expressed.

51

And therefore *Satan* (who transforms him slily
T' an Angel of the Light, the more t' abuse)
In 's Oracles and Idols speaking wily,
Not common Prose, but curious *Verse* did use.

52

So the fond *made-Priests* of *Apollo* sung
His *Oracles* in sweet *Hexameters;*
With doubtfull Riddles from a double tongue,
To haplesse-hopefull, conquered Conquerers.

53

So th' ancient voyce in *Dodon* worshipped:
So *Æsculapius, Hamon*, and the fair
And famous *Sibyls* spake and prophesied
In *Verse:* in *Verse* the Priest did make his prayer.

54

So *Orpheus, Linus,* and *Hesiodus*
(Whereof the first charm'd stocks and stones, they say)
In sacred *Numbers* dar'd (to profit us)
Their divine secrets of deep skill convay.

55

O ! you that long so for the *Laurell Crown*,
Where 's possible a richer Theam to take
Then his high praise, who makes the Heav'ns goe round,
The Mountains tremble, and dark Hell to quake?

56

This *subject* is a deep, broad, bound-lesse Ocean,
Th' aboundant *Horn* of *Plentifull* discourse ;
The Magazin of wealth for Wit's quick motion ;
Of divine Eloquence th' immortall source.

57

Base Argument, a base stile ever yeelds :
But (of it selfe) a lofty *subject* raises
Grave stately words, and (of it selfe) it gilds
It selfe ; and crowns the Author's Pen with praises.

58

If then you would survive your selves so gladly,
Follow not him who burnt (to purchase fame)
DIANA'S Temple : neither him that madly,
To get renown, a *Brazen Bull* did frame.

59

Imploy no more th' *Elixir* of your spirit
On *Cytheréa* and her winged Son.
How better never to be named were-it,
Then named (blamed) for a mischief don ?

60

Wee, *Thrice three Sisters of Parnassus Hill,*
Bee *Virgins* all : your *Pallas* self is so ;
So is that sacred *Tree-turn'd Lady* still,
From whose pure locks your still-green *Laurels* grow.

61

Then, consecrate-mee (rather) your Wit's miracles,
To sacred Stories : spend your Eloquence
In singing loud those holy Heav'nly *Oracles ;*
Pour there your Soule's pure pretious quint-essence.

62

Let CHRIST (as *Man-God*) be your *double Mount*
Whereon to Muse ; and, for the winged hoove
Of *Pegasus*, to dig th' immortall Fount,
Take th' *Holy-Ghost*, typt in a *Silver-Dove.*

63

Excelling Works preserve the Memory
Of those that make them : The *Mausolean* Toomb
Makes *Artemisia, Scopas, Timothie,*
Live to this day, and still in time to come.

64

Name-lesse had *Hiram* been, but for his ayd
Towards God's *Temple* built in *Israel :*
And, but for God's *Ark*, in dark silence laid
Long since had been th' *Hebrew Bezaleel,*

65

Then, sith these great and goodly *Monuments*
Can make their makers *after death abide ;*
Although themselves have *Vanished* long since,
By Age, and Rage, Fire, Arms and Storms destroy'd :

66

O think (I pray) how-much-much greater glory
Shall you attain, when your Diviner quality
In sacred strains shall sing th' *Almightie's Story ;*
Sith from immortall things springs immortality.

67

I know you 'll answer, that the *Ancient Fictions*
Are (even) your *Song's* soule : and that every *Fable*
Ay breeding other, makes by their commixtions
(To vulgar ears) your *Verse* more admirable.

68

But, what may be more admirable found
Then *Faith's Effects ?* Or what doth more controul
Wit's curious pride? or with more force confound
The reach and reason of a humane soule ?

69

I 'ld rather sing the *Towr of Babylon*,
Then those *three Mountains,* that in frantick mood
The *Giants* pil'd to pull *Jove* from his Throne :
And *Noah's*, rather then *Deucalion's* Floud.

70

I 'ld rather sing the sudden *shape-depriving*
Of *Assur's* Monarch, then th' *Arcadian* King :
And the *Bethanian Lazarus* reviving,
Then valiant *Theseus'* Sons re-sobering.

71

Th' one onely doth delight their ears that hear it ;
The other tends to profit in some measure :
But, onely *Hee the Laurel Crown doth merit,*
Who wisely mingles profit with his Pleasure.

72

As sweetest walks are by the water side,
And safest swimming neer the flowry shore :
So, prudent Writers never doe divide
Knowledge from Mirth, Mirth from Instruction's lore.

73

Such shall you be, if such a taske you take :
For, teaching others you your selves shall learn-all
Rules of good life ; and happy so shall make,
As is your subject, your own Songs eternall.

74

Abandon then those *Old-wive's-Tales* and Toyes ;
Leave the *Blinde Lad*, who but the blinde abuses ;
And onely, addle, idle hearts annoyes.
Hence-forth no more profane the *Sacred Muses.*

75

But (O !) in vain, in vain (alas !) I plain-mee ;
Some subtle Aspicks, to eschew my Charming,
Stop their dull ears ; some *Epicures* disdain-mee
And my advice, and scoff my zealous warning.

76

Some, for a season, listen to my Laws ;
But soon *Relapse*, through the World's sorceries :
And this discourse (which but the Vertuous draws)
Enters at one ear, out at th' other flies.

77

Alas ! I scarce see one (nay, none at all)
That Courts not *Venus*, or corrupts not more
His golden *Honey* with profaner *Gall :*
Although this Age of happy Wits have store,

78

But thou, my Darling, whom before thy birth,
The *Sacred Nine*, that sip th' immortall spring
Of *Pegasus*, predestin'd to set forth
Th' Almightie's glory, and his praise to sing :

79

Although their Subject seem a barren soyl,
Which finest Wits have left for fallow fields ;
Yet, doe thou never from this task recoyl :
For, *what is rarest, greatest glory yeelds.*

80

Faint not (my-*Salust*) though fell *Envie* bark
At the bright *Rising* of thy fair *Renown ;*
Fear not her Malice ; for, thy living *Work*
(In spight of spight) shall not be trodden down.

81

That *Fame's*-foe Monster, is much like a Curr,
That fiercely barks at every new-come Guest ;
But, once-acquainted, after doth not stur,
Saving at strangers ; fawning on the rest.

82

Or, like a thick, dark, pitchy Cloud of smoak,
That round-about a kindling Fire suppresses
With waving smother, the new Flame to choak :
But, as the *Flame* augments, the *Fume* decreases.

83

Wherefore (my dear) that *sacred Path* pursue,
Where none but heav'n-blest happy spirits can pase :
And here I swear, that shortly for thy due,
Among best Wits thou shalt have worthy place.

84

With these sweet accents (grac't in utterance)
URANIA holding in her Maiden hand
A glorious Crown, rapt-up in *sacred Transe*,
My prostrate soul, prest to her high Command.

85

Since when, alone *that Love* my heart hath fired ;
Since when, alone that Winde my sails hath spread :
O happy ! might I touch that *Crown* (desired)
But with my hand, not put it on my head.

86

Now out of zeal *to your dear* Name *and* You
(*Dear* noble Name, *that I must ay affect :*
And whose Disasters *I must ever rue*)
This MONUMENT *of Honour I erect*
To you (*sweet* ESSEX) *as your* Vertue's *due,*
For an eternall token *of respect :*
Where, your great worth, *and my* good-will *shall stand*
Inrowld for ever with URANIA'S *hand.*

FINIS.

NOTES AND ILLUSTRATIONS.

PAGE 2, col. 1, l. 32, '*Mrs. Essex*'—see our Memorial-Introduction on this 'fair lady' and her family: col. 2, ll. 1-2, '*Stork*'
—a still quick myth : l. 17, '*Mrs. Jone Essex*'—see as *supra*.
URANIA —St. 1, '*Aprill of mine age*'—see Glossarial Index,
s.v., for parallels : St. 4, '*Gests*'=actions, as Gesta Romanorum :
St. 5, '*sacred*' = consecrated : St. 7, '*Wag-Son*' = Cupid : St.
13, '*silver Finns*' = Pisces : St. 27, '*of Alexander took*' =
Alexandria in Egypt : St. 35, '*parbreak*' = eructate : St. 40,
'*Ghost*' = spirit, soul : St. 46, '*Gnidian idols*'—see Glossarial
Index, *s.v.* : St. 52, '*fond*' = foolish : St. 74, '*Blinde Lad*' =
Cupid.

G.

THE TRIUMPH
OF FAITH;

Former-ly
DEDICATED,
and now againe,
FOR EVER
Consecrated to the
gratefull Memorie *of*
the first kinde Fosterer of
our tender Muses, my never-
sufficiently-Honoured dear Uncle
W. PLUMB, *Esq.*

For whose dear Bones wee would a Toomb advance
Of Gold, and Silver, and CORINTHIAN Brasse,
With Ivorie Pillars mixt with Jett and Rance,
Rarer and richer then th' old CARIAN'S was ;

But, sith the most of our poore Meanes (alas !)
Not the least part of that Rich Pride affords ;
For want of Wealth, wee build a Toomb of Words :

    * *   *Which* (*though it cost lesse*) *shall out last*   * *
    * *   *The proud cloud-threatning Battlements,*   * *
    * *   *Th' aspiring Spires by* NILUS *plac't,*   * *
    * *   *And Hell-deepe-founded Monuments.*   * *

For greedy waste of Hours, that all things else devours,
Spares the sweete Maides of sacred HELICON :
And those faire Ladies, to their Friends alone,
This precious Gift doe give, Still (after Death) to Live.

47

THE TRIUMPH
OF FAITH.

To Guy de Faur, Lord of
Pibrac; W. Salustius du BARTAS.

I Hate those Satyrs, that the best still bite,
 I hate the shamelesse Pens that sooth the vicious :
 For these be flatterers, and those malicious :
But, wise is hee can hit the Mean aright.
 I pinch not oft, nor doe I often praise :
Yet, must I needs praise the praise-worthy still :
I cannot hold my free and forward quill
From those whom Heavn adorns with speciall rayes.
 Now all that God doth by retail bestow
On perfect'st men, to thee in grosse hee gives :
Therefore my Muse thy praise so often drives,
For Dutie's sake, but not to flatter so.
 Our Age's wonder ! when thy tongue (refin'd
By vse and Art) in our King's name dilates
With Counsails, Germane or furr'd Polish States,
The sweet tongu'd Cyneas thou dost make us minde.
 In privie counsell, when our miseries
Thou dost be-moan, most Nestor-like thou art :
And when, in Paris Parliament, thy part
Of Lawes thou Plead'st, thou seem'st to Scævolize.
 Thy Latin Prose doth match smooth Salust's stile
And when thy Pen distils the Nectar sweet
Of Helicon (where all the Muses meet)
Me thinks I read sweet Virgil all the while.
 In honour of these gifts, this gift I bring,
Small for my paines, great for the argument :
But if the Heav'ns had richer treasure lent,
Thy New-yeer's gift should be som better thing.

THE TRIUMPH

OF FAITH.

CANTO I.

1

N Eer th' hour that *Erycin' Aurora* cals,
　　And shee the Sun ; sad *Morpheus*, entring in
Through 's horny gate, to shew me did begin
A sacred Virgin's stately TRIUMPHALS.

2

Then *Faith* (for so shee hight) bids with celerity,
Of Pen and Paper that I make provision
To write the summ of this celestiall Vision,
To be recorded unto all Posterity.

3

I know my task to be impossible :
I know, in this, man's eyes are beetle-blinde :
His ears quite deaf ; clean voyd of sense his minde ;
But, hardest things *Faith* makes most possible.

4

Eternall Sun, O scatter with thy Light
All misty clouds, that make me not to see
Thy health-full Face : and give true *Faith* to me ;
Since Faith, sans *Faith*, cannot be known aright.

5

FAITH sits triumphant in a Carr of gold,
Of *Tubal's* making ; where blew Saphires shine,
Rich Diamonds, and many Rubies fine,
And if ought else Earth doth more costly hold.

6

Her glorious Charret's rowling wheels are like
The holy wheels the great *Ezechiel* saw :
For, one self-spirit, self-winde, and will doth draw
Their restlesse courses, equall, both alike.

7

The Bird that led the *Roman* Standards out :
The Bird, that fixtly can oppose his eyes

Against the greatest light in all the skies ;
High through the air, draws this rich Coach about.

8

Faith flaunts it not in silver, silk, nor gold,
Nor precious scarlet of the *Tyrian* Dy,
Nor paints her face to hide deformity ;
But, as shee is, shee doth her self unfold.

9

Her body (that all bodies doth disgrace)
Like *Juno's* Bird is full of watchfull eyes,
Whose holy glances pierce the lofty skyes,
Pierce Air, and Heav'n, and see God face to face.

10

Sh' hath many sweet and flowing tongues to praise
The Lord of Hoasts : sh' hath strong and mighty wings
(Passing the swiftness of all earthly things)
That in a moment up to Heav'n her raise.

11

Her glorious head is compast with a Crown,
Not made of Olive, Pine, or Laurell bough ;
Nor Parsly Wreath, which *Grecians* did alow
Th' *Olympian* games for signals of renown :

12

But, of fresh Roses pluckt from Honour's Tree,
That never shrink for Winter's chilling frost,
That wither not when *Titan* parcheth most :
For, by the Lord they ever wat'red be.

13

Now, stain-lesse *Truth* for Standards doth display
Two Testaments : next, *Courage* marshals right
Th' undaunted Troups that are prepar'd to fight
Under her Colours, into battell-ray.

14

Then, *Constancy* bears a two-edged Blade,
And *Patience* an impenetrable Shield ;
Whose brightnesse hath inforc't more monsters yeeld,
Then that which of grim *Gorgon's* head was made.

15

Next, *Charity*, that kindly doth prefer
Her neighbour's good before her own utility :
Repentance, Hope, and hearty-milde *Humility*,
Doe flank the wings of *Faith's* triumphant Carr.

16

For, *Faith* (indeed) without her Maids were vain.
But, as the Sun can never lack his light,
Nor Fire want heat : so (if wee mark aright)
Faith cannot want these Hand-maids in her train.

17

Before this Coach there is a Beldam gon,
That seems (at first) fairer then *Helen* was :
But neerer view'd, shee is more foul (alas !)
Then fell *Meger', Alect'*, or *Tesiphon.*

18

Shee never goes (like *Faith*) with open face,
But seeks for masks, vizards, and garments gay ;
For cloak on cloak to keep the light away,
Of her loath'd limbs to hide the foul disgrace.

19

Sh' hath tongues (like *Faith*) with which shee boldly chats,
Blaspheming Heav'n with filthy vanities ;
Sh' hath eyes (like *Faith*) but yet (alas !) those eyes
See cleer by night, by day are blinde as Bats'.

20

Sh' hath wings (like *Faith*) with which shee soars on hy :
Like *Icarus* shee proudly mounts aloft
(Forgetting that her feathers are so soft)
Till *Phœbus'* force her waxen wings doth fry.

21

Shee (whom, *sans* reason, men have *Reason* hight)
Since first, in Fire, the Lord the Air inclos'd ;
In Air the Sea, in Sea the Earth dispos'd ;
Hath with milde *Faith* maintain'd continuall fight :

22

Now, arming Kings, and putting in their brains,
That nothing lesse beseems their Royall State
Then under *Faith* their Scepters to abate ;
Then to endure her gentle-ruling reans.

23

Another-while, shee puffs with pois'ny-pride
(Whom their disciples onely Doctors deem)
Such as (I grant) have spent much oyl, and time,
To draw men's soules from the true way, too wide.

24

Yet still, the Lord (who still upholds the just)
Hath still the case of holy *Faith* maintain'd ;
Hath still so well her holy side sustain'd,
That still her Foes lye groveling in the dust.

25

A thousand Princes, bound in fetters fast,
Before her march, that her milde yoke disdain'd,
That all the Earth with bloud of Saints distain'd,
And Christ his Church with Fire and Sword did waste.

26

Hee that (the first) in this world's Pupillage,   Cain.
Brain'd his owne brother, leads this bloudy crew :
Then th' hardned Tyrant, that did dare pursue   Pharaoh.
Through the Red-Sea God's chosen Heritage.

27

Then saw I him that *Zachary* did stone ;   Joash.
Athaliah, Ahab, wicked *Abian,*
Occazias, Amon, Ahaz, and *Joram :*
Then all that sate on the *Samarian* Throne.

28

I saw *Senacherib*, and Him whose Grace   Nebuchadnezzar.
Was turn'd to grasse ; proud *Haman*, and withall
Brave *Holophernes*, and who on the Wall   Baltsazar.
Read how his Kingdom to the *Medes* should passe.

29

Annas and *Caiaphas*, and him that set   Antiochus
His hatefull Idoll in the holy Place ;   illustris.
Which five *Jew*-brethren bravely did deface :
All these too-late, in sad repentance fret.

30

The Tyrant too, that (at our Saviour's birth)   Herod.
In Cradles kill'd so many Innocents :
And that vile Judge, whose seared conscience   Pilat.
Condemn'd the guilt-lesse Judge of all the earth.

31

That viperous Monster (of mankinde the shame)   Nero.
Who Mother, Wives, Brethren and Sisters slue ;
Then from a lofty Towr did laugh to view
Rome's glittering Spires all on a burning flame.

32

With *Seventh Severus* came accompanied :
Jule, Maximin, with fell *Maximian,*
Cruell *Gallerian*, fond *Domitian,*
That (god-lesse) would like God be honoured.

33

Then saw I him that served *Sapores*
For foot-stool base : I saw *Valerian,*
Decius, Lecinus, and *Hostilian ;*
And fell *Maxentius*, marching next to these.

34

I saw great *Trajan*, learn'd *Aurelius,*
And learned *Dioclesian :* all which three
Among wise *Cæsars* might well praised bee,
Had they not been 'gainst Christians barbarous.

35

Anastasius.
Eumeves.

Justin,' The'dorus, Constantinus' Sonne,
Heraclius, Valence, Constance, Manuel,
And that *Bizantian* Prince, that did mis-tell
A four-fould Essence in the onely ONE.

36

Then (*Goths* and *Vandals, Gens'ric, Trasimond*)
Honorius, Theodorus, Totilas,
Alaricus, and *Rhotoris* (alas!)
Who *Rome* and *Africk* with *Saints*' bloud have drown'd.

37

But who is this, that, loaden so with chains,
By thousand hang-men racked with dispight,
By thousand Furies tortur'd day and night,
For god-lesse deeds receives so righteous pains?

38

Sergius a Nesto-
rian *Monk holp*
Mahomet *to make*
his Alcoran.

'Tis *Mahomet,* who more by *Mavor's* Art,
Then 's *Alcoran* (Bird of a Frier's nest)
Hath all subdu'd the wealthy golden East,
And won withall the triple world's best part.

39

I see Prince *Saladine,* of match-lesse force,
But th' *Alcoran* too-deeply favouring :
Haly the *Caliphe,* and the wanton King
That did our Maids on *Edesse* Altars force.

40

With wrath and woe old *Ottoman* opprest
Too-late repentance in his face presents ;
And *Mahomet* the second much laments
That hee the *Greekish* Empery supprest.

41

Bajazeth.

So the proud scorn of (scourge-Turk) *Tamberlaine,*
That in an yron Cage was cooped straight ;
And hee that first presum'd to passe the Streight
Which *Europ's* bounds divides from th' *Asian.*

42

Mahomet 3

Then hee that quittance did with *Scythia* cry,
And over Sea his Scepter rais'd again ;
And *Amurath,* that did repell amain
Vincenslaus, that first had made him fly.

43

Orcan (the *Phrygian's* fear) and *Calipine,*
Who foil'd *Sigismond's* hoast, his Father fear'd ;
And *Bajazeth,* that, being haughty rear'd
By *Germain Tropheis,* did their peace repine.

44

Selim 1.

Solyman.

Hee that his Sire and Brother put to death,
Is with a Cable kill'd ; his Son that quail'd
Th' *Hungarian* King, and *Rhodes* and *Bud* assail'd,
With trembling fear now quakes like Aspen leaf.

45

And neer this *Solyman* there doth remain *Selim.*
An empty room for him that yet survives ;
Who (by our King's strange jars) so richly thrives,
That (proud) hee threats both *Germany* and *Spain.*

46

O Wretched Christians ! while your civill rage
'Gainst your owne hearts doth arm your proper hands :
O see you not the *Turks* invade your Lands,
And safely spoyl the Lord's choice heritage ?

47

The discord grown 'twixt the *Bulgarian* King,
And th' Eastern *Cæsar,* even the Bridge it was
For hate-Christ Turks the *Hellespont* to passe,
And so in *Greece* a *Pagan* Scepter bring.

48

The discord of two brethren *Morea* lost ;
And (O !) I fear lest Christians home-bred fraies
(Dejecting quite Christ's Name, and all his praise)
Bring Turks to land in farthest Western Coast.

49

Forget then, Christians, your un-Christian jars
(Your civill strife for wagging of a straw)
Joyn hearts and hands, and all joynt weapons draw
In *Faith's* defence to fight *Jehova's* wars.

50

In *Asi'* and *Egypt* make your forces knowne :
Recover *Gaza, Antioch, Ascalon,*
Tyre, Sidon, Joppa, and King *David's* Throne,
And *Famagosta,* lost a year agon.

CANTO II.

1

THough bloudy Tyrants had in every age
    Busiris Altars Bulls of *Phalaris,*
Gemonid Ladders, making Land and Seas,
And fire, and air, racks of their beastly rage :

2

Yet could they never wound the Church so much,
As have the Writings of the worldly Wise,
Which on men's soules doe felly tyrannize ;
The tortures, onely did the bodies touch :

3

These *Sages,* puft with self-conceited pride,
Dare to controule th' Almightie's match-lesse work ;
Where mystike Secrets from our senses lurk,
The search whereof the Lord hath us deni'd.

4

And though the spred of our too-feeble wings
Scant raise us from the ground, they mount aloft
Even up to Heav'n ; where they doe measure oft
(By their Wit's compasse) God's eternall things.

5

Their knowledge is but meerly ignorance :
They lose the Truth in seeking it too much ;
For, Truth doth still conceal her self from such,
And to the humble doth her self advance.

6

Truth alwayes dwels within the holy Tables
Of God's live word ; not in our wanton brain ;
Which daily coining some strange Error vain,
For Gold takes Lead, for Truth electeth Fables.

7

Long time their reasons were with Reason rife,
To wrack the Church, and *Faith* to ruinate ;
But, now I see they doe detest, too-late,
Their former errors and their former life.

8

In formost rank, march all *Gymno-sophists*,
Follow'd by all the cunning *Persian Mages*,
The old *French Druids*, learned *Chaldé-Sages*,
And flow'r of all the *Brachoman-sophists*.

1. The ancient
Sages of the
World.

9

Pythagoras, Zeno, Xenophanes,
Parmenides, merry *Democritus,*
Empedocles, and sad *Heraclitus,*
Architas, Naucides, Nausiphanes.

2. Philosophers,
Greek and Latin.

10

Brief, all the Doctors of the *Latin* Sect,
Tearing their Tresses, melting into tears,
Beating their breasts, detest those dreams of theirs :
And so the greatest of the *Greeks* Elect.

11

Anaximander, Anaximenes,
Mylesian *Thales, Anaxagoras,*
Gnaw'n with continuall care, cry out (alas)
On their own Errors ; and so *Socrates.*

12

Cleanthes and *Chrysippus* next to these,
With *Zeno* (*Stoicks*) that have often strai'd :
And next, the *Cyniks* (all as ill-appai'd)
Diogenes, Crates, Antisthenes.

13

There, the grand Patrons of each *Academ,*
Plato, Speusippus, and *Zenocrates,*
Clytomachus, Crantor, Carneades ;
And hee that labours to conciliate them.

14

There mourns in vain *Pirrhon* (Son of *Plistarchus*)
That (fond) beleeves not what his ears doe hear,
Eyes see, nose smels, tongue tastes & hands do bear :
Then *Timon, Hecaté,* and *Anaxarchus.*

15

There, the *Stagyrian* (that, with learned vein,
In 's Works includes the *Encyclopedy*)
Sorry t' have led so many souls awry,
With *Strato, Theophrastus* doth complain.

Aristotle.

16

There, carnall *Epicurus* wails with tears,
And *Metodorus :* next to whom there came
Both *Aristippi, Aretas,* that same
Vile wretch that coin'd a worser Sect then theirs :

17

I mean that Monster *Theodorus* hight,
Who shame-lesse saies, There is no God at all :
And that the Wise may (when occasions fall)
Be Liar, Traitor, Theef, and Sodomite.

18

Alas ! how true the Proverb proves too-plain,
Saying, *Bad weeds grow every-where apace :*
But, wholsom herbs scant spring in any place
Without great labour, and continuall pain.

19

O *Grecians'* Bane, thy mortifying Mores
To grow in *Rome* the swelling Seas have crost ;
From *Rome* too-soon over the *Alps* have past
As far as *France,* and all her neighbour shoars.

20

Thy deadly Plant now buds on Justice Throne,
In Christian Camps, & Courts of Christian Kings ;
In Church and Chair, and every-where so springs,
That with thy thistles all is over-grown.

21

But, now return wee to our task again :
All these Wise-men, of *God* have false defin'd,
Of *Chiefest-good, Soules,* or wrong place assign'd
Where (dead) wee feel or end-lesse peace or pain.

22

Those that (since Christ, true Son of righteousness,
On our *Horizon* brought the daie's broad light)
Have led men's soules in dark eternall night ;
Feel torments worthy of their wickedness.

3. Deceitfull
Sophists, & Apos-
tates, open Ene-
mies to Christ.

23

Next *Symmachus Porphirius* marcheth first :
Lucian, and *Celsus,* then whose hardned heart
The Gospel (knowne) did labour to subvert ;
And *Julian* also, of all *Cæsars* worst :

24

Who, knowing well that tortures were but vain
To force the Saints from the right Faith to stray ;
(By sugred stile) studies another way,
Turns truth to lies, and lies to truth again.

25

4. Cabalists, and Talmudists, Rab-bies.

Next, I perceive the Circumcised Crew
Of *Cabalists*, and burly *Talmudists*,
Troubling the Church with their mysterious Mists ;
Who, wel-nie dead, 'gainst CHRIST do spet and spew :

26

Much like to Snakes, that wagg their sting-less sting,
When as (their heads and bodies being slain)
They threat their Foes with force-lesse fury vain,
And to their Graves their Thirst of vengeance bring.

27

5. Turkish Doc-tors.

Now come the Doctors of the *Alcoran ;*
Who, mingling poison, by their subtil gloze,
The World's blinde eyes with darker Clouds inclose ;
They shew their sorrow by their saddest mone.

28

6. Heretikes old & new.

But, who are these that wear *Faith's* Livery,
And bear the badge of *Faith's* best Souldiers ;
And yet are loaden with such bolts and bars ;
And so despised of *Faith's* company ?

29

These (if I erre not) are the *Heretikes*
Who (pusht by proud and curious spirits) do blend
Both Heav'n and Earth, and busily contend
To lead the World in crooked paths and Creeks.

30

Now, as soft windes, with straight constrained breath
(Through chinks and crannies stealing privily)
Hurt more our health, then boist'rous blasts that fly,
And roule (abroad) the stones upon a heath :

31

And as the Foe, that shakes the Citie's wals
With thundring shot, is not so dangerous
As a lewd Burgesse, false and mutinous,
That in the Town stirs-up domestick brauls :

32

So *Pagans, Turks, Jews*, do not damnifie
The Faith, like these : their open violence
May be avoided : but false fair-pretence
Is hardly scaped with much jeopardy.

33

They make (like us) a fair religious show :
They have (like us) one Church, one FAITH, one Lord :
They read (like us) one Bible, and one Word :
So sly they are God's Church to over-throw.

34

In foremost rank, here goe the *Sadduces,*
That doe deny Angels and Resurrection ;
Both Spirits of grace, and also of rejection :
Then th' *Esseans* foul, and Formall *Pharisees.*

35

Simon Magus. Nicolaus, Author of the Sect of the Nico-laits.

Next, that Deceiver, that devised first
Church-chaffering : and after him ensues
That Marriage-Foe, who brutishly renues
Pluto's (not *Plato's*) *Common*-Law accurst.

36

Cerinthus next, all bruis'd, and bleeding fresh,
Of Beam-pasht wounds that brain'd him suddenly ;
When in the Baths (profane) hee did deny
Christ's holy God-head, hidden in our flesh.

37

For having likewise warr'd against the same
God-head of th' onely *Man-God ; Ebion,
Paul, Samyan, Photin, Carp'crate, Artemon,*
Shew by their looks their sorrow and their shame.

38

There mourns that *Manes*, who did fondly fain
Two divers gods, Authors of Good and Ill :
There *Valentin* the ayr with cries doth fill,
Who did deny that bodies Rise again.

39

Cerdon (great Patron of the Stoïcall)
Marcion, Menander, piteous Moan doe make :
There sighs *Apelles ;* saying, Christ did take
Not (simply) flesh, but flesh fantasticall.

40

There goes *Basilides*, who canoniz'd
Cyrenean Simon in our SAVIOUR's stead ;
Montanus there (a frantick head indeed)
Who guiltlesse Children kill'd and sacrifiz'd.

41

There, *Titians, Encratits, Severions,
Sabellians* too, which (seeking th' unitie
In God's great Essence) lost the Trinity ;
Abhor'd too-late their fond conclusions.

42

There, th' *Alexandrian* Priest, that yerst did void
His entrails at the stool, whose Heresie
(Witching well-neer th' Earth's University)
With Sword & Schism the World so much annoi'd.

43

Sadly beholds sad-marching *Macedonius*
And *Eunomus,* who at the first had sown
His poys'ny seeds ; but after, of their owne
They gathered tw' other Sects erroneous.

44

Bizantian Nestor, and (our own) *Pelagius,
Libian, Donatus, Luciferians,
Eutichians* fond, and fond *Priscillians,*
All frown and fret for inward grief outrageous.

45

Shall I conceal *Servetus*, and the train
Of those *Deïsts* that in *Sarmatia* swarms :
And (Kingling) *Muncer*, that with frantick arms,
Founds hundred sorts of Anabaptists vain ?

46

Both *Syrtes* sands I might as eas'ly number,
As number those, whose sweet inchanting Writs
With Error's dregs have drenched wanton Wits,
Chiefly 'n this Age, which all corruptions cumber.

47

For, Satan now him so insinuates
In faithlesse hearts, that ween themselves be wise,
That so foul Error can he not devise,
But shall be backt by strong associates.

48

7. Antichrist & the Schismaticks.

I see the Beast that bears the purple Whore
(Great Anti-Christ usurping pow'r Divine)
Set on Seav'n Hils ; who with her whoredom's wine
Makes drunk the Princes that her Seat adore.

49

And (last of all) I see the *Schismatiks*,
Which (renting Christ's unseamed coat in twain)
Trouble the Church-peace with contentions vain ;
Follow too neer the steps of *Hereticks*.

Canto III.

1

Great Sire's great Son ! O live, God's lively face,
Wisedome conceived of the onely Wise :
To us giv'n Giver ; First and Last : born twice ;
Once, in full Time ; once out of all Time's space.

2

Beam of that Sun which fils the world with Light :
Life of our life, our death's death, Stinger's sting :
Our perfect, wise, just, holy, valiant King,
Word, that no word can full expresse aright :

3

O Lord, draw, draw me, draw me from this throng,
Whose feet and hands are bold to war with Thee :
For, with dry eyes I can them never see,
Nor without griefe recite them in my Song.

4

Ah ! I am out ; now (my dear God) I goe
From *Babel* to *Jerusalem*, the Land
Of Life, Saints' House, and holy Ark, to stand
Against all Seas, and all rough storms that blow.

5

Lo here these Champions that have (bravely-bold)
Withstood proud Tyrants, stoutly consacring
Their lives and soules to God, in suffering :
Whose names are all in Life's fair Book in-roul'd.

6

All-hail, Saint-Souldiers, let us once imbrace :
O valiant Knights ! let mee your hands and brows
Adorn with Palms, and with *Apollo's* boughs :
Let present honours former shames deface.

7

Come, sacred Kings ; O holy Princes, come :
Come to this Triumph, Lords, whose valiant hands
Have Satan's kingdome sought to bring in bands,
And in your Crowns giv'n *Faith* the chiefest room.

8

Hee that (the first) *Isaac* infranchised,   Moses.
Leads by the hand that Duke, whose faithfull word   Iosua.
Stopt *Phœbus*' Coursers, and whose conquering
Subdu'd the *Land* the Lord had *Promised*.

9

Hee, that, but armed with an Asse's bone,   Samson.
Slew thousand Foes, *Sangar*, *Othoniel*,
Ahod and *Jeptha*, *Barac*, *Samuel*,
And (th' Heathen's scourge) triumphant *Gedeon*.

10

That great King-Prophet, Poet, Conqueror,   David.
Sweet Psalmograph : *Asa*, that Idols brake :
Hee, that made all the Idol-Altars quake ;   Iosias.
And (after) did the Paschall Lamb restore.

11

Jehosophat, *Joathan*, *Azarias* ;
And hee, whose life the Lord did dis-abbridge,
Whom Heav'nly arms, from *Assur* did unsiege ;
The most religious, match-lesse *Ezechias*.

12

Wise *Mardochey* ; and the five *Maccabees* ;
All, the right heirs of heart and zeal paternall,
Receive their guerdon from the great Eternall,
And up again their stooping Standards raise.

13

Before these Warriours, and the Royall Band,
March holy Fathers, that with vertue rare,
And holy Doctrine, did the Divell dare ;
Foiling the force of his infernall hand.

14

Enos, by whom this World's great Architect   Henoch.
Was call'd upon, leadeth (religious) :
That holy Father God took-up from us :
And hee, whose ship did save the World Elect.   Noah.

15

Then *Sem* and *Japheth* ; and great *Abraham*,
The Faithful's Father ; and his faithfull Son :   Isaac.
And then his Nephew, that saw Angels run
Both up and down from Heav'n to th' earthly frame.   Iacob.

16

Aaron, Eleazer, Phinees full of zeal,
Good *Joyada,* and hundred priests select ;
That were by Heav'n, by zeal, and Church, elect
To keep the Law the Lord did once reveal.

17

Zacharias.
Ioseph.
Simeon.

His Father who was sent to sweep the way
Of sweet *Messias ;* then the man suppos'd
To be his Sire ; then, Hee that him inclos'd
In 's joyfull arms, and sung a Swan-like Lay.

18

Then *Barnabas, Titus,* and *Timothy,*
(*Paul's* famous Friends, Sin's fierce and deadly Foes)
And hee that did, by *Sol's* Eclipse, suppose
Some greater Sun to be eclips't then hee.

19

Then (this brave *Triumph* to adorn the more)
All on a row a hundred Prophets come ;
Which have so sure foretold the things to-come,
As if (indeed) they had been done before.

20

Elias.

Elizeus.

There first coms hee, that in the Coach of fire
By God's strong Spirit was rapt above the Air :
And then his Servant, that was made his heir
Of cloak and knowledge, as hee did desire.

21

Nathan.

Ionas.

Hee that reprov'd old *Isha's* Sceptred Son
For double fault ; *Amos, Ezechiel,*
Joel, Semayah, Abdiah, Daniel ;
And hee that three dayes in the Sea did won.

22

Zachariah.

With these I see the Son of *Barachy,*
Both *Michais, Baruc, Jehu, Jeremias :*
Agg', Abacuc, Nahum, and *Sophonias,*
Ahias, Hose, Esdras, Malachy.

23

The glorious troup that march before this troup,
Are martyrs all, who (full of constant zeal)
Their faith infract with their own blouds did seal,
And never did to any Tyrant stoop.

24

Their blessed bloud is like the morning deaw,
To make more fertil all the Churche's field :
These are the weapons that inforce to yeeld
The furious Foe (examples not a few).

25

For, as a fruit-Tree lopped in *December,*
For one old Trunk, many new twigs returns,
Which Nature kindely with sweet fruit adorns :
So, one sole martyr many doth engender.

26

First, *Abel* goes, then *Joyad's* zealous Son,
That neer the Altar (constant) yeelded breath :
The next goes hee *Manasses* put to death ;   Esay.
Then hee, whose head th' incestuous Dancer won.   Iohn Baptist.

27

Next *Salone* and her Sons, who rather chose
To crosse the King then God, strengthning each other
Even in their death : Sons worthy such a Mother,
And Mother worthy of such Sons as those.

28

That *Proto-Martyr,* the young faithfull *Steven,*
Whom th' hatefull *Jews* with hellish rage did stone ;
Who, dying, saw Christ Jesus on his Throne,
Leads those that for like cause their lives have giv'n.

29

Som, smeard with hony, for the Flies were feasts ;
Som, men did eat, som were on Gridirons broil'd ;
Som, nail'd on Crosses ; som, in Cauldrons boil'd ;
And som were throwne to most devouring beasts.

30

After the Champions of this humble Troup,
I see fair *Sara, Rebecca, Rachel :*
Then *Debora,* stout *Judith,* and *Jahel,*
Who (Faith's Viragos) their proud Foes did stoop.

31

Then shee that (rais'd to royall state and stile)   Hester.
Preserv'd her people ; in a ranke shee goes
With *Naomi, Ruth,* and the Dame that chose   Susanna.
Rather to dy then Nuptiall bed defile.

32

From these, mine eye no sooner traverseth,
But I discerne three Ladies zealous-led,
That sought their living Lord among the dead :
Then *Anna, Martha,* and *Elizabeth.*

33

But, my weak eyes cannot endure to gaze
On beaming beauties of that *Mother-Maid,*   The Virgin Mary.
Who Sire-lesse bore her Sire, yet ever-Maid ;
Of Faith and Love th' inimitable maze.

34

This, this (my *Muse*) this is th' *Aurora* clear
Which brought the Sun to light the World unkind ;
A Virgin pure in body and in minde,
Christ's Mother, Sister, Spouse, and Daughter dear.

35

God's holy Temple, and the happy stair
Whereby the Heav'ns came downe to dwell with Earth :
Rich-fraighted Ship, Vessell of rarest worth,
Where *Phœbus* hid his beams most bright and fair.

CANTO IV.

I

I Thought t' have been now at my Race's end,
  T' have (though unworthy) born away the prize :
But I fall short, my task doth longer rise ;
For, halfe the *Trophè* is yet hardly penn'd.

2

Before *Faith's* Coach, born in convenient heighth,
Are curious Tables drawn by cunning hand ;
Where (after guise of warlik Romans) stand
The Victories of never-conquer'd *Faith*.

3

Ios. 6. 20.
2 Kin. 18. 13.
2 Chr. 32. 20.
Esay. 37. 21.

Here, *Jericho's* cloud-kissing Tow'rs doe fall,
Batter'd alone by *Faith's* great Ordinance :
A count-lesse hoast of craking Idolants,
By *Esay's* Faith is here confounded all.

4

Exod. 7. 8. 9.

Dan. 6. 12.

By Faith meek *Moses* with a zeal-full ire
Arms smallest Worms the *Egyptian* King to vex ;
Daniel, by Faith, fierce Lions' fury checks,
And quenches Dragons' hot impoisoning fire.

5

Acts 28. 5.

Ionas 2. 3.

Here, *Paul* by Faith, fears not (in *Mitylene*)
The deadly sting of th' ugly Viper-Worm :
Here, myching *Jonas* (sunk in sudden Storm)
Of his Deliverance findes a Fish the mean.

6

Then, in another Table, that was fram'd
By Art, exceeding Art ; I did espy
Pale Death, blithe Health, and frail Infirmity,
That had by Faith a thousand times been tam'd.

7

Num. 12. 10.
2 King 6. 14. 17.

Moses, by Faith, doth *Myriam* leperize :
By Faith, *Elisha* (curing *Naaman*
The *Syrian* Prince) strikes instantly his man
With his Disease, for Bribing Covetize.

8

1 Kin. 13. 4.

A man of God, by Faith, first strangely dri'd,
Then heald again that King's unholy hand ;
Who made ten Tribes of God's (then) chosen Land
From God, and from their lawfull Prince to slide.

9

Acts 13. 11.

Acts 15. 5. 16.

By Faith, Saint *Paul* stark-blinded *Elymas ;*
By Faith, Saint *Peter* (full of just disdain)
With sudden death did smite those perjur'd twain,
That durst dissemble with the Spirit of Grace.

10

Tob. 11. 11.
Acts 5. 6. & 14. 10.

By Faith, young *Toby* kindely doth restore
His Father's sight : by sacred Faith likewise,
Two crooked Cripples are made straight to rise ;
In *Lystra* th' one, th' other at Temple dore.

11

By Faith, Saint *Paul* did a rich *Maltois* cure
Of grievous Flix, that him afflicted sore :
By Faith, Saint *Peter* likewise did restore
A Palsie-sick, that eight years did indure.

Acts 21. 8.

Acts 9. 34.

12

By Faith, Saint *Paul* did *Eutichus* re-live :
By Faith *Elias* rais'd the *Sareptite ;*
Elisha raised the young *Sunamite :*
At *Joppa*, *Peter Dorcas* did revive.

Acts 20. 10.
1 Kin. 17. 21.
2 Kin. 4. 33.
Acts 9. 40.

13

Then in another picture I did view
The foure first bodies of this massie Globe ;
Green-gowned *Tellus*, *Vulcan* Scarlet-robe,
Py'd-mantled *Juno*, *Neptune* clad in blew.

The foure
elements.

14

Elisha's Faith brought, from the loftie skies,
Bright fiery Charrets 'gainst the *Syrian* hoast ;
Elias' Faith (scorning the *Ba'l*-Priests' boast)
Fir'd without fire his moated Sacrifice.

2 Kin. 6. 17.

1 Kin. 18. 38.

15

By Faith three *Hebrews*, cast in seaven-fold flame
By a proud Prince, escape the raging Fire :
(Their very garments sent-lesse and entire)
While their Tormentors perish in the same.

Dan. 3. 27.

16

Moses, by Faith, makes Fire from Heav'n to fall
In th' *Hebrew* hoast ; those wretches to consume,
Whose profane hands, with profane Fire and Fume,
God's holy Altar had polluted all.

Rev. 10. 21.
Num. 16. 35.

17

Moses, by Faith (heard by the God of pow'r)
Compels the Mountains' burly sides to shake ;
Commands the Earth to rent, and yawn, and quake
To swallow rebels, and them quick devour.

Num. 16. 30.

18

Moses, by Faith, divides the Sea in twain,
When *Israel* came out of *Egypt* Land :
Then in the Desart's dry and barren sand,
From flinty Rocks doth plenteous river strain.

Exod. 14. 21.

Exod. 17. 9.

19

Moses, by Faith, converts to foul black bloud
The Crystall Current of the seaven-fold *Nile :*
By Faith again, hee makes (another while)
Those stinking waters, holsom, sweet and good.

Exod. 7. 20.

Exod. 15. 25.

20

Thrice, silver *Jordan* did it selfe divide,
To give safe passage to God's dear-belov'd :
Once by the Faith of valiant *Joshua* prov'd ;
Elias once : once by *Elisha* tri'd.

Ios. 3. 16.
2 K. 2. 8. 14.

21

The zealous *Thisbit* did by Faith seal-up
The Heav'n's wide windows, that their fell no Raine
In seav'n-six months ; and then by Faith again
(To drench the dry Earth) set them all wide-ope.

1 Kin. 18. 41.

22

Likewise by Faith, the nimble-winged train,
That cleave the Air, are to our service set ;
The Rav'ns are made to bring *Elias* meat,
The Dove serves *Noah*, Quails for *Moses* rain.

1 Kin. 16. 6.
Gen. 8. 11.
Exod. 16. 13.

23

O ! who is able Faith to countermand ?
If Faith doe force all-taming yron yeeld !
If Faith make yron float on *Neptune's* field !
If that *Elisha's* Faith strong steel command !

2 Kin. 6. 6.

24

Faith hath not onely pow'r on things terrene,
Both high and low ; but oftentimes doth force
God's justice too, and somtimes seems (perforce)
God's purposes to change and alter clean.

25

The *Ninivits*, by Faith (repenting) shun
Their overthrow, that *Jonas* threatned neer ;
And *Ahaz'* Son by Faith adds fifteen year
To his short life, that seem'd already done.

Ionas 3. 10.

2 Kin. 20. 10.

26

Now, if the Giver of this Faith (wee see)
Seem to incline and bow unto her still,
As bound and ready to obey her will ;
What marvell is 't if Angels be not free ?

27

The Angels serve in *Ezechias'* pay ;
By Faith, they bring the *Thisbit* needfull Cates,
By Faith, they ope for *Peter* prison gates,
By Faith, to *Jacob* they direct the way.

2 Kin. 19 35.
1 King 19.
Acts 12. 7.
Gen. 32. 1.

28

About twelve paces past these former Pomps,
Full many sacred Minstrels sound on hye
Triumphant Faith's great name and dignity ;
Tuning aloft their Clarions, Flutes and Trumps.

29

Mark, Mathew, Luke, and (the Lord's dearest) *John,*
Christ's Secretaries, winde with such a brest
Their warbling Cornets, that from East to West
Through all the world their sacred sound is gon.

30

Both *Jameses,* one the Son of *Zebedeus,*
Th' other *Alpheus, Thomas, Simon, Andrew,*
Peter, Matthias, Philip, Bartholemew,
Paul (Gentiles' Doctor) with the good *Thaddeus,*

31

Sound with so sweet accord their Sagbuts long,
And their shrill Fifes (heard from the North to *Nile*)
As if one Spirit did fill them all the while,
And one same hand had set their holy Song.

32

While thus my spirit this strange discourse did cumber,
Rare-builder *Prognè*, earlier then the rest,
Beginning th' out-most of her curious nest,
Brake, with her pratling, my deep-pleasing slumber.

33

Sorry to be sudden wakt, I would
I were a Dor-Mouse for a hundred year ;
That I might sleep full twenty Lustres here,
To shun the woes that waking I behold.

34

For now (alas !) waking (with griefe) I see
Babel triumphing over *Sion* still :
And on the Good th' Ungodly work their will :
The Wicked prais'd, the Righteous scorned be.

35

I see (alas !) in these lamented Times,
Men's greatest zeal in bloudy murder stands,
Profane our hearts, and so profane our hands :
Bare Christian name serves but to cloak our crimes.

36

Incest 's a sport, and Murder Man-hood thought :
Disloyalty a speciall Vertue deem'd :
And Perjury sound Policy esteem'd :
Medea's Arts, and *Sodomie* are taught.

37

Maidens be bold, and Wives be impudent,
Princes are Tyrants, People full of rage :
This Age is sink of every former Age,
Receiving each Sin's ugliest excrement.

38

But, my swolne brest, shut-up thy sighs' sad gate ;
Stop, stop, mine eyes, the passage of your tears ;
Cast-off, my heart, thy deep-despairing fears ;
That which most grievs me, most doth consolate.

39

No, no : my Dream is true ; soon shall wee see
Faith's glory shine.   Satan (perceiving nie
His pride's Eclipse) his greatest force doth try
To stop great *Faith's* triumphant Victory.

40

Sure, if my Card and Compasse doe not fail,
W' are neer the Port : where (danger being past)
Wee need not fear the billow, nor the blast
Of blustering windes, nor Seas that can assail.

41

Our beastly Manners, like *Gomorrha's* guise :
The troubled Seasons : Wars domesticall :
The threats of Heav'n : are the fore-runners all
Of CHRIST that coms to hold His last Assize.

42

That drad-desired Day shall soon appear,
Christ coms the Rav'ns from Swans to set a-side :

The tares from wheat : and Goats from Lambs divide :
And this brave *Triumph* (that I sing) is neer.

43

O Father ! while this *Triumph* I expect,
Waiting to see the Wicked's utter Fall,
And thy just Scepter Ruling over all ;
Let lively *Faith* my *Reason* still direct.

NOTES AND ILLUSTRATIONS.

Page 9, line 12, ' *W. Plumb* '—see our Memorial-Introduction on this uncle of Sylvester : l. 14, ' *Corinthian brasse* ' = an amalgam, on which see full note in Glossarial Index : l. 15, ' *Rance* ' = a kind of marble : l. 22, ' *Spires* ' = pyramids.

P. 10. On *verso* of this page is a large woodcut of a conventional representation of the ' Day of Judgment ' above and of the ' Resurrection ' below, with these texts : ' Be thou faithfvl vnto the death : and I wil give thee a crowne of lyfe ' (Revelation ii. 10), and ' We mvst all appeere before the ivdgment seat of Christe ' (Romans xiv. 10). There are similar woodcuts elsewhere in the folio ; but none have merit claiming reproduction. They seem to have been blocks in hand used in different books.

P. 11, st. 1, ' *Erycin* ' = Venus : st. 9, ' *Juno's Bird* ' = peacock : st. 13, ' *battell ray* ' = battle-array.

P. 13, st. 40, ' *Empery* ' = empire. So in Milton : st. 44, ' *Cable* ' = rope, *i.e.* hanged : st. 48, ' *fraies* ' = frays, contests : st. 50, ' *Famagosta* '—in now much-spoken-of Cyprus. I found it recently ruinous and mean ; but with pathetic traces of former splendour.

P. 14, st. 8, ' *Mages* ' = Magi ; st. 12, ' *ill-appai'd* ' = ill content ; see Glossarial Index, *s.v.* : st. 19, ' *Mores* ' —see Glossarial Index on this ambiguously used word.

P. 16, st. 5, ' *consacring* ' = consecrating : st. 10, ' *Psalmograph* ' = Psalm-writer — an anticipation of modern coinages, *e.g.* telegraph, photograph, etc. etc.

P. 17, st. 21, ' *won* ' = dwell : st. 23, ' *infract* ' = un-broken : st. 33, ' *maze* ' = wonder.

P. 18, st. 3, ' *craking* ' = bragging, boastful : st. 5, ' *myching* ' = truant : st. 11, ' *Flix* ' = flux : st. 17, ' *quick* ' = living.

P. 19, st. 31, ' *Sagbuts* ' = sackbuts.   G.

TETRASTICA.

Or,

THE QUADRAINS

OF GUY DE FAUR,

Lord of Pibrac.

Tranſlated

BY

Josuah Sylvester.

Acceptam refero.

TO THE RIGHT
EXCELLENT AND MOST
HOPEFULL YOUNG
Prince, HENRY.

A*Fter so many golden Rules of* State,
    Religious *Lessons,* Morall *Precepts grave,*
As in your Father's * ROYALL-GIFT *you have;*
These seeme superfluous, or to come too-late:
Yet,'tis no error to re-iterate
    The Voyce of Wisedome *to the tender Ear*
    Of Princes (*chiefly*) *such as* You, *that bear*
    The Hope *and* Hap *of* Europe *in your* Fate.
And, though You *want not these weak helps of ours*
    To consummate Your *Self in* Excellence :
    Yet may those Subjects, *which shall once be* Yours,
Draw vertuous Wisedome, *and all duty hence,*
    If you but daign with your dear Name *to grace-it,*
    Which (*Load-stone-like*) *shall draw them to imbrace-it.*

JOSUAH SYLVESTER.

THE QUADRAINS

OF PIBRAC.

I

DIEU tout premier, puis Pere & Mere Honore.
Sois juste & droict : & en toute saison
De l'innocent pren en main la raison :
Car Dieu te doit la-haut juger encore.

First, honour God, and then thy Parents dear :
Be True and Just : and see thou never grudge
The Innocent oppressed cause to clear ;
For, one-day God shall also be thy Judge.

2

Si en jugeant la faveur te commande,
Si Corrompu par or ou par presens,
Tu fais justice, au gré des Courtisans ;
Ne doute point que Dieu ne te le rende.

If gold and bribes corrupt thy conscience,
If fear or favour in thy Judgement sway-thee,
If thou respect the Person's difference ;
Be sure that God will in the end repay-thee.

3

Avec le jour commence ta journée :
De l'Eternel le sainct nom benissant :
Le soir aussi ton labeur finissant,
Love-le encor', & passe ansi l'année.

Begin thy Daie's-Work when the Day begins,
First blessing God's thrice-blessed Name (devout)
And then at Evening, when thy labour ends,
Praise him again ; so bring the Year about.

4

Adore assis (comme le Grec ordonne)
Dieu en courant ne veut estre honoré :
D'un ferme cueur il veut estre adoré,
Mais ce cueur lá il fault qu'il nous le donne.

Adore thou sitting (as the Greek doth bid)
For, running prayer is preposterous :
With stedfast Heart God will be worshipped,
But such a heart Himselfe must give to us.

5

Ne va disant, ma main a faict cest œuure ;
Ou ma vertu ce bel œuure a parfaict :
Mais dis ainsi, Dieu par moy l' œuure a faict :
Dieu est l'autheur du peu de bien que i'œuure.

Say not, My hand this Work to end hath brought ;
Nor this my vertue hath attained to :
Say rather thus ; This, God by me hath wrought :
God's author of the little Good I do.

6

Tout l'Univers n'est qu'une cité ronde ;
Chacun a droict de s'en dire Bourgeois,
Le Scythe & More autant que le Gregeois,
Le plus petit que la plus grand du monde.

The World is all but a round Citie like,
Where each may right be said a Citizen :
As well the rude Barbarian as the Greek,
As well the meanest as the mightiest men.

7

Dans le pourpris de ceste cité belle
Dieu a logé l'homme comme en lieu sainct,
Comme en un Temple, ou luy mesmes s'est peinct
En mil endroicts de couleur immortelle.

In this fair Citie's goodly Wals God planted
And placed man as in a Sanctuary,
Where Hee, Himselfe in thousand parts hath painted
With lively colours that doe never vary.

8

Il n'y a coing si petit dans ce temple,
Ou la grandeur n'apparoisse de Dieu :
L'homme est planté justement au milieu,
Afin que mieux par tout il la contemple.

There's not a nook so small in all this Temple,
Wherein God's Greatnesse doth not plain appear :
Which that wee might the better all contemple,
Hee placed man just in the middle here.

9

Il ne scauroit ailleurs mieux la cognoistre
Que dedans soy, où, comme en un miroir,
La terre il puet & le ciel mesme voir :
Car tout le monde est compris en son estre.

Yet can hee no where better know the same
Then in himselfe, wherein hee may behold
(As in a Glasse) Earth, Water, Air, and Flame :
For, all the World, his Essence doth infold.

10

Qui a de soy perfaicte cognoissance
N' ignore rien de ce qu' il fault scavoir :
Mais le moyen asseuré de l'avoir,
Est se mirer dedans la Sapience.

Who of himselfe hath perfect Knowledge gain'd,
Ignoreth nothing that hee ought to know :
But the best means whereby it is attain'd,
Is oftentimes to Wisdom's Glasse to goe.

11

Ce que tu vois de l'homme n'est pas l'homme,
C'est la prison où il est inserré :
C'est le tombeau où il est interré,
Le lict branlant où il dort un court somme.

That which thou seest of Man, it is not Man :
'Tis but a Prison that him captive keeps :
'Tis but a Toomb where hee's interred (wan)
'Tis but a Cradle where a while hee sleeps.

12

Ce corps mortel, où l'œil ravi contemple
Muscles & nerfs, la chair, le sang, la peau,
Ce n'est pas l'homme : il est beaucoup plus beau,
Aussi Dieu l'a reservé pour son temple.

This mortall body, where the ravisht sense
Sees sinnews, flesh, bones, muscles, bloud and skinne,
It is not Man : Man's of more excellence,
As the fair Temple *that God dwelleth in.*

13

A bien parler, ce que l'homme on appelle,
C'est un rayon de la divinité :
C'est un atome esclos de l'unité :
C'est un degout de la source eternelle.

Rightly to speak, what man wee call and count,
It is a beamling of Divinity :
It is a dropling of th' Eternall Fount :
It is a moatling hatcht of th' Unity.

14

Recognoy donc (homme) ton origine :
Et brave & haut dedaigne ces bas lieux,
Puis que fleurir tu dois la hault és cieux,
Et que tu és une plante divine.

Then know (O Man) thine own Originall,
And, brave-ambitious, scorn base Cells of Earth ;
Sith thou shalt flourish in Heav'n's glistring Hall,
And art (indeed) a Divine Plant by Birth.

15

Il t'est permis t'orgueillir de la race,
Non de ta mere ou ton pere mortel :
Mais bien de Dieu ton vray pere immortel,
Qui t'a moulé au moule de sa face.

Well maist thou vaunt thee of thy glorious Race :
Not from thy mortall Parents either Line,
But from thy true immortall Father's Grace,
Who by the modell of His Face, made thine.

16

Au ciel n'y à nombre infini d'Idées,
Platon s' est trop en cela mesconté,
De nostre Dieu la pure volonté
Est le seul moule a toutes choses nées.

There's not in Heav'n a number infinite
Of bright Idéas (Plato *did mistake) :*
God's onely will (the onely Rule of Right)
Was th' onely mould of all that Hee did make.

17

Il veut, c'est faict : sans travail & sans peine
Tous animaux, jusqu'au moindre qui vit,
Il a crée, les soustient, les nourrit,
Et les defaict du vent de son aleine.

Hee Will'd, and it was done : Hee (without pain)
All kinde of Creatures (to the least that is)
Created, feedeth, and doth still sustain :
And re-dissolves them with that breath of His.

18

Hausse tes yeux : la voute suspendue,
Ce beau lambris de la couleur des eaux,
Ce rond parfaict de deux globes jumeaux
Ce firmament esloigné de la veüe :

Lift up thine eyes : The hanging Vault *above,*
The goodly Seeling *of a* Watry *hew,*
The perfect Orb's Twin-Globes *that ever move,*
The spangled Firmament *so far from view :*

19

Brief, ce qui est, qui fut, & qui peut estre,
En terre, en mer, au plus caché des cieux,
Si tost que Dieu l' a voulu pour le mieux,
Tout aussi tost il a receu son estre.

All (to be briefe) past, present, and to come,
In Earth and Sea, and Air, (beyond your seeing) ;
So soon as God thought good, each in their room
Immediatly received all their Beeing.

20

Ne va suivant le troupeau d' Epicure,
Tropeau vilain, qui blaspheme en tout lieu,
Et mescroyant ne cognoit autre Dieu,
Que le fatal ordre de la nature.

Shunne Epicures' *profane and filthy Sect*
(*Bold Mis-creants blaspheming every way*)
The which no God acknowledge nor respect,
Save onely Nature *and her* fatall *Sway.*

21

Et ce pendant il se veautre & patroüille
Dans un bourbier puant de tous costez :
Et du limon des sales voluptez
Il se repais, comme une orde grenoüille.

And in the mean-while (*like the grunting Hog*)
Lie always wallowing in the stinking Mire :
And feed on filth (*like to the loathsom Frog*)
Voluptuous filth of every Flesh-desire.

22

Heureux qui met en Dieu son esperance,
Et qui l'invoque en sa prosperité,
Autant où plus qu' en son adversité
Et ne se fie en humaine asseurance.

Happy whose hope on God alone relies :
And who on Him in either Fortune call,
As well in calmes as in Calamities,
And put no trust in humane helps at all.

23

Voudrois tu bien mettre esperance seure
En ce qui est imbecille & mortel ?
Le plus grand Roy du monde n'est que tel,
Et a besoign plus que toy qu'on l'asseure.

Canst thou assure thy hopes on worldly things,
Frail mortall things (*I pre-thee tell mee, how*) ?
Such are the greatest of all earthly Kings,
And have more need to be secur'd then thou.

24

De l'homme droict Dieu est la sauuegarde,
Lors que de tous il est abandonné,
C'est lors qu'il est moins il se trouue estonné,
Car il scait bien que Dieu lors plus le garde.

God is the just-man's Anchor and his Ayd,
His sure Defence, when all the World forsakes-him :
And therefore, then is hee the least dismai'd ;
Knowing, that God then most to safe-guard takes him.

25

Les biens du corps, & ceux de la Fortune,
Ne sont pas biens, a parler proprement :
Ils sont subjects au moindre changement,
Mais la vertue demeure tousiours une.

The goods of Fortune *and the* Body (*call'd*)
They are not goods, if wee them rightly name :
For, to least changes they are ever thrall'd :
But Onely Vertue *still persists the same.*

26

Vertu qui gist entre les deux extrémes
Entre le plus & le moins qu'il ne fault ;
N'excede en rien, & rien ne luy default :
D'autruy n'emprunte, & suffit à soy-mesmes.

Vertue, between the two extremes that haunts,
Between too-mickle and too-little sizes :
Exceeds in nothing, and in nothing wants :
Borrows of none : but to it selfe suffizes.

27

Qui te pourroit, Vertu, voir toute nue,
O qu' ardemment de toy seroit espris ?
Puis qu'en tout temps, les plus rares esprits
T'ont faict l'amour au travers d'une nue.

O Vertue ! *could wee see thy naked face*
How would thy sacred Beauties sweetly mad-us ?
Sith rarest Wits (*rapt with a* Seeming Grace)
Have in all Ages courted (*even*) *thy Shadows.*

28

Le sage fils est du pere la joye :
Or, si tu veux ce sage fils avoir,
Dresse le jeune au chemin du devoir :
Mais ton exemple est la plus courte voye.

The Parents' comfort is a prudent Sonne :
Now, such a Sonne if thou desirest ay,
Direct him young in Dutie's race to run :
But, Thine Example is the neerest way.

29

Si tu es né enfant d'un sage pere,
Que ne suis tu le chemin ja battu ?
S'il n'est pas tel, que ne t'efforces tu,
En bien faisant, couurir ce vitupere ?

If thou be borne Son of a prudent Sire,
Why tread'st thou not in his fair beaten Trace ?
If otherwise : why dost not thou desire
(*By vertuous Deeds*) *to cover this Disgrace ?*

30

Ce n'est pas peu, (naissant d'un tige illustre)
Estre esclairé par ces antecesseurs,
Mais c'est bien plus luire à ses successeurs,
Que des ayeux seulement prendre lustre.

'Tis no small Honour, from illustrous Line
To be descended by our Predecessours :
But 'tis much more, then by their light to shine,
Our selves to shine unto our own Successours.

31

Jusqu'au cercueil (mon fils) veuilles apprendre,
Et tien perdu le jour qui s'est passé,
Si tu n'y as quelque chose amassé,
Pour plus scavant & plus sage te rendre.

Cease not to learne untill thou cease to live :
Think that Day lost, wherein thou draw'st no Letter,
Nor gain'st no Lesson, that new grace may give,
To make thy Selfe Learneder, Wiser, Better.

32

Le voyageur qui hors du chemin erre,
Et esgaré se perd dedans les bois,
Au droict chemin remettre tu le doibs :
Et s'il est cheu, le relever de terre.

If any stranger in his journey stray
Through doubtfull Paths (as happens now and then)
Direct him rightly in his ready way ;
And if hee fall, soon help him up again.

33

Ayme l'honneur plus que ta propre vie :
I'entens l'honneur qui consiste au devoir
Que rendre on doit (selon l'humain pouuoir)
A DIEU, au Roy, aux Loix, à sa Patrie.

Thine Honour more then thine own Life respect,
Th' honour (I mean) which each man's duty drawes
(To th' uttermost w' are able to effect)
To GOD, our King, our Country, and our Laws.

34

Ce que tu peux maintenant, ne differe
Au lendemain, comme les paresseux :
Et garde aussi que tu ne sois de ceux
Qui par autruy font' ce qu'ils pourroient faire.

What (now) thou canst, defer not till to morrow,
Like selfe-lame Sloath (of foulest sins the Mother) :
Nor be like those who others' hands do borrow,
And what themselves might doe, will doe by other.

35

Hante les bons, des meschans ne t'accointe,
Et mesmement en la jeune saison,
Que l'appetit pour forcer la raison
Arme nos sens d'vne brutale poincte.

Frequent the good, fly from ungodly folke,
Especially in thy Youth's tender season,
The while outrageous appetites provoke,
And arme thy sense against the sway of Reason.

36

Quand au chemin fourchu de ces deux Dames
Tu te verras comme Alcide semond,
Suy celle-la qui par un aspre mont
Te guide au ciel, loing des plaisirs infames.

When to the double way of those two Dames
(Alcides-like) thou shalt be summoned,
Follow thou her who far from glorious shames,
Over steep Mountains up to Heav'n doth lead.

37

Ne mets ton pied au travers de la voye
Du pauure aveugle : & d'un piquant propos
De l'homme mort ne trouble le repos :
Et du malheur d'autruy ne fay ta joye.

Set not thy foot to make the blinde to fall ;
Nor wilfully offend thy weaker Brother,
Nor wound the Dead with thy Tongue's bitter gall :
Neither rejoyce thou in the fall of other.

38

En ton parler sois tousiours veritable,
Soit qu'il te faille en tesmoignage ouyr,
Soit que par fois tu veuilles resiouir
D'un gay propos tes hostes à la table.

Let thy discourse be true in every Word,
Whether as publike Witnesse thou be prest
To clear a Question : whether, at thy Boord
With pleasant chat thou cheer thy welcome Guest.

39

La Verité d'un Cube droict se forme,
Cube contraire au leger mouuement :
Son plan quarré jamais ne se dement,
Et en tout sens à tousiours mesme forme.

The Truth resembles right, the right Cube's Figure,
(The Cube, contrary to light instability)
Whose quadrat flatnesse never doth dis-figure ;
Whose solid Forme admits no mutability.

40

L'oyseleur caut se sert du doulx ramage
Des oysillons, & contrefaict leur chant :
Aussi, pour mieux deceuoir, le meschant
Des gens de bien imite le langage.

The crafty Fowler, to beguile the Birds,
Deceitfully their own sweet Notes doth faine :
So subtle Mates doe counterfeit the words,
And simple guise of honest men and plaine.

41

Ce qu'en secret lon t'à dit ne revelle :
Des faicts d'autruy ne sois trop enquerant.
Le curieux volontiers tousiours ment :
L'autre merite estre dict infidele.

Reveale not what in secret hath been told
Nor busily of Others' things inquire.
Th' inquisitive can hardly Counsell hold :
The carry-tale is commonly a Lyer.

42

Fa pois egal, & loyale mesure,
Quand tu deurois de nul estre apperceu :
Mais le plaisir que tu auras receu,
Ren le tousiours auecques quelque usure.

Make alwayes equall weight and lawfull measure,
Though none could spy, thy dealing to discover :
But where thou hast received any pleasure,
Restore it still with some advantage over.

43

Garde, soigneux, le depost à toute heure :
Et quand on veult de toy le recouurer,
Ne va subtil des moyens controuuer,
Dans un palais, à fin qu'il te demeure.

Keep carefully what thou hast tane in charge :
And when the Owner shall demand-againe-it,
Deny it not ; neither with conscience large
By subtle Law-tricks strive thou to detaine-it.

44

L'homme de sang te soit tousiours en haine :
Hue sur luy, comme fait le berger,
Numidien sur le Tigre leger,
Qu'il voit de loing ensanglanter la plaine.

Hate evermore the bloudy homicide ;
Hunt him with hue and cry : as Shepheards hunt
The Lybian *Tygre which they have espy'd,*
Spoyling his Prey, and rioting upon-'t.

45

Ce n'est pas tout ne faire à nul outrage :
Il faut de plus s'opposer a l'effort
Du malheureux, qui pourchasse la mort,
Ou du prochain la honte & le dommage.

'Tis not enough that thou do no man wrong :
Thou even in others must suppresse the same ;
Righting the Weake, against th' unrighteous Strong,
Whether it touch his Life, his Goods, or Name.

46

Qui a desir d'exploiter sa proüesse,
Domte son ire, & son ventre ; & ce feu
Qui dans nos cueurs s'allume peu a peu,
Soufflé du vent d'erreur & de paresse.

Whoso the Fame of Valour doth desire,
Must tame his Anger and his Belly both,
And that heart-swelting, Marrow-melting Fire,
Blown by the winde of error and of sloath.

47

Vaincre soy mesme est la grande victoire :
Chacun chez soy loge ses ennemis,
Qui par l'effort de la raison soubmis,
Ouurent le pas a l'eternelle gloire.

Our-own-Self's Conquest is the most victorious :
For in our Selves ambush our greatest Foes ;
And th' onely way to make us ever glorious,
Is by stout Reason still to vanquish those.

48

Si ton amy a commis quelque offense,
Ne va soudain contre luy t'irriter,
Ains doucement, pour ne le despiter,
Fay luy ta plainte, & recoy sa defense.

If so thy Friend have done thee some Offence,
Fall not out flat, nor urge him with abuse ;
But milde and meekely, without insolence,
Make thy complaint, and take thou his excuse.

49

L'homme est fautif : nul viuant ne peut dire
N'auoir failly : és hommes plus parfaicts,
Examinant & leurs dicts & leurs faicts,
Tu trouueras, si tu veux, a redire.

All men are faulty : none alive can say,
I have not Erred ; even the Perfectest,
If thou his Life in word and deed survay,
Thou shalt perceive hee hath Perfection mist.

50

Voy l'hypocrite auec sa triste mine,
Tu le prendrois pour l'aisné des Catons,
Et ce pendant toute nuict à tastons
Il court, il va pour tromper sa voysine.

See th' Hypocrite's severe and Saint-like guise,
Whom th' elder Cato *thou wouldst think for Life ;*
Yet in the darke hee groaping hunts and hies
T' entice and trap his honest Neighbour's Wife.

51

Cacher son vice est une peine extréme,
Et peine en vain : fay ce que tu voudras,
A toy au moins cacher ne te pourras,
Car nul ne peult se cacher à soy mesme.

'Tis a most busie, yet a boot-lesse paine,
To hide one's fault : for doe the best thou can
Thou canst not hide it from thy Selfe (though faine)
For who can hide him from himselfe (O Man) !

52

Aye de toy plus que des autres honte ;
Nul plus que toy par toy n'est offensé :
Tu dois premier, si bien y as pensé
Rendre de toy à toy-mesme le compte.

More of thy Selfe, then others be asham'd,
Thy Selfe art most wrong'd by thine own offence :
And of thy Selfe, thy selfe first, (Selfly-blam'd)
Must give account to thy Selfe's Conscience.

53

Point ne te chaille estre bon d'apparence,
Mais bien de l'estre à preuue & par effect :
Contre un faulx bruit que le vulgaire faict,
Il n'est rempart tel que la conscience.

Care not so much to seem in outward show,
As to be good indeed, and in the proofe :
For from false rumours which the Vulgar blow,
A Selfe cleer Conscience is Defence enough.

54

A l'indigent monstre toy secourable,
Luy faisant part de tes biens à foison :
Car Dieu benit & accroit la maison
Qui a pitie du pauure miserable.

Relieve the needy, after thine ability,
And in their wants participate thy store.
For, God doth blesse with Plenty and Tranquillity
The House that pities the distressed Poore.

55

Las ! que te sert tant d'or dedans la bourse,
Au cabinet maint riche vestement,
Dans tes greniers tant d'orge ou de froment,
Et de bon vin en ta cave une source ;

What boot thy bags to be so cramm'd with Coyne ?
Thy Ward-Robe stuffed with such store of Change :
Thy Cellars filled with such choyce of Wine ?
And of all Graines such Plenty in thy Grange ;

56

Si ce pendant le pauure nud frissonne
Deuant ton huys : & languissant de faim,
Pour tout en fin n'a qu'un morceau de pain,
Ou s'en reuá sans que rien on luy donne?

If all the while the naked Poore (halfe dead
With cold and hunger) shiver at thy Gate ;
And at the length gets but a peece of bread,
And many times (perhaps) but hardly that ?

57

As tu, cruell, le cœur de telle sorte,
De mespriser le pauure infortuné,
Qui, comme toy, est en ce monde né,
Et, comme toy, de Dieu l'image porte?

Hast thou a heart so cruell, as to scorne
Th' unhappy Poore, that at thy beck doth bow ;
Who like thy Selfe into this World is borne,
And bears God's Image even as well as Thou ?

58

Le malheur est commun à tous les hommes,
Et mesmement aux Princes & aux Roys :
Le sage seul est exempt de ces loix :
Mais où est-il, las, au siecle où nous sommes ?

Misfortune is a common lot to all ;
Yea, even to Princes, Kings, and Emperours :
Onely the Wise are freed from her thrall,
But O, where are they, in this age of ours ?

59

Le sage est libre enferré de cent chains,
Il est seul riche, & iamais estranger :
Seul assuré au milieu du danger,
Et le vray Roy des fortunes humaine.

The wise man's free, among a thousand chaines,
Hee's only Rich (content with his estate)
Only secure in Dangers, eas'd in paines ;
Only true King of Fortune and of Fate.

60

Le menasser du Tyran ne l'estonne :
Plus se roidit quand plus est agité :
Il cognoist seul ce qu'il a merité,
Et ne l'attend hors de soy de personne.

Hee is not daunted with a Tyrant's threat,
But by his Trouble grows more strong and hard :
Knows his own merit, looks not from the Great
For Recompence ; Vertue's her own reward.

61

Vertu és mœurs ne s'acquiert par l'estude,
Ne par argent, ne par faueur des Roys,
Ne par un acte, par deux, ou par trois,
Ains par constante & par longue habitude.

True morall Vertue cannot purchast be
By Study, Treasure, or the grace of Kings :
Nor by one action, nor by two or three :
But long-long practice her perfection brings.

62

Qui lit beaucoup, & jamais ne medite,
Semble à celuy qui mange avidement,
Et de tous mets surcharge tellement
Son estomach, que rien ne luy profite.

Who readeth much and never meditates
Is like a greedy Eater of much Food,
Who so surcloyes his stomach with his Cates,
That commonly they doe him little good.

63

Maint un pouvoit par temps devenir sage,
S'il n'eust cuidé l'estre jà tout à faict.
Quel artisan fut onc maistre parfaict,
Du premier jour de son apprentissage?

How many might (in time) have wise been made
Before their time, had they not thought them so ?
What Artist e'r was Master of his Trade,
Yer he began his Prentiship to know ?

64

Petite source font les grosses Rivieres :
Qui bruit si hault à son commencement,
N'a pas long cours, non plus que le torrent
Qui perd son nom ès prochaines fondrieres.

From smallest Springs, the greatest rivers rise :
But those that roar so loud and proud at first,
Runne seldome farre, but soon their glory dyes
In some neer Bogg, by their selfs'-furie burst.

65

Maudit celuy qui fraude la semence,
Ou qui retient le salaire promis
Au mercenaire : où qui de ses amis
Ne se souvient si non en leur presence.

Cursed is hee that doth defraud the seed :
Or who detains the Hireling's promis'd right :
Or who (ingratefull for the kindest deed)
Thinks never of his friends but in their sight.

66

Ne te parjure en aucune maniere,
Et si tu és contrainct faire serment,
Le ciel ne jure, où l'homme où l'element,
Ains par le nom de la cause premiere.

Forsweare thee not, what ever cause be given :
And if for ought thou needs an Oath must take,
Swear not by Man, nor by the Earth, nor Heav'n,
But by his sacred Name who all did make.

67

Car Dieu qui hait le parjure execrable,
Et le punit comme il a merité,
Ne veult que lon tesmoigne verité,
Par ce qui est mensonger où muable.

For God who doth all Perjury detest,
And justly plagues it as most execrable,
Would not wee should the constant Truth contest
By any thing that's false or alterable.

68

Un art sans plus, en luy seul t'exercite :
Et du mestier d'autruy ɪʃe t'empescant,
Va dans le tien le parfaict recherchant :
Car exceller n'est pas gloire petite :

To some one Art apply thy whole affection ;
And in the Craft of others seldome mell :
But in thine own, strive to attain perfection :
For, 'tis no little honour to excell.

69

Plus n'embracer que lon ne peut estraindre :
Aux grands honneurs convoiteux n'aspirer :
User des biens, & ne les desirer :
Ne souhaiter la mort, & ne là craindre.

T' embrace no more then one can manage fit,
Not to the top of Greatnesse to aspire :
To use the World, and yet not covet it :
Neither to dread Death, neither death desire.

70

Il ne fault pas aux plaisirs de la couche,
De chasteté restreindre le beau don :
Et ce pendant liurer à l'abandon
Ses yeulx, ses mains, son oreille, & sa bouche.

We must not Chastitie's fair Gift restrain
Onely to th' actuall Pleasure of the Night :
And in the mean while not a whit refrain
Our heart, our hand, our tongue, our ear, our sight.

71

Ha le dur coup qu'est celuy de l'oreille !
On en devient quelque fois forcené :
Mesmes alors qu'il nous est asséné
D'un beau parler plein de doulce merveille.

O what a hard blow is a box on th' Eare !
Som-time it drives men even besides their Wit ;
Especially when (stunned as it were)
With the sweet wonder of smooth words, 'tis smit.

72

Mieulx nous vaudroit des aureillettes prendre,
Pour nous sauver de ces coups dangereux :
Par la s'armoient les Pugiles valeureux,
Quand sur l'aréne il leur falloit descendre.

'Tis therefore best our tender Ears to arme,
To shun the danger of those deadly blowes :
Warie Ulysses so eschew'd the Charm
Of those soule-rapting Impes of Acheloes.

73

Ce qui en nous par l'oreille penetre,
Dans le cerveau coule soudainement,
Et ne scaurions y pourvoir autrement,
Que tenant close au mal ceste fenestre.

What ere it be that enters by the Eare,
Immediatly into the Brain doth creep ;
And th' onely mean to shun the mischiefe there,
Is the Ear's Casement, ever close to keep.

74

Parler beaucoup on ne peut sans mensonge,
Ou pour le moins sans quelque vanité
Le parler brief convient à verité,
Et l'autre est propre à la fable & au songe.

Much talke is seldome without Lyes among,
Or at the least without some idle bables :
Unto the truth, brief Language doth belong :
And many words are fit for Dreams and Fables.

75

Du Memphien le grave contenance,
Lors que sa bouche il serre auec le doigt,
Mieulx que Platon enseigne comme on doit
Reueremment honnorer le silence.

Th' Egyptian's grave aspect and sober brow,
When his fore-finger seales his lips so sure;
Better than Plato, doth instruct us how
To honour Silence with devotion pure.

76

Comme lon voit, à l'ouurir de la porte
D'un cabinet Royal, maint beau tableau,
Mainte antiquaille, & tout ce que de beau
Le Portugais des Indes nous apporte :

As at the Opening of the Cabinet
Of some great Prince, many rare things wee see,
Rich Monuments, and all that fair and neat,
From either Inde Portugals bring, or wee :

77

Ainsi des-lors que l'homme qui medite,
Et est scauant commence de s'ouurir,
Un grand thresor vient à se descouurir,
Thresor caché au Puis de Democrite :

So when the Wise and Learned doth begin
T' open the organs of his plenteous Wit;
A wondrous Treasure suddenly is seen,
A Treasure hidden in th' Abderian's Pit :

78

On dict soudain, voilà qui fut de Grece,
Cecy de Rome, & celà d'un tel lieu,
Et le dernier est tiré de l'Hebrieu,
Mais tout en somme est remply de sagesse.

And Standers by, say by and by, This came
From Greece, from Rome That, That from such a Place,
And (lastly) That from th' Hebrew : and the same
And all the rest most full of Prudent grace.

79

Nostre heur, pour grand qu'il soit, nous semble
    moindre :
Les ceps d'autruy portent plus de raisins :
Mais quant aux maulx que souffrent nos voysins,
C'est moins que rien, ils ont tort de s'en plaindre.

Our Goods (how ever great) the least do seem,
Our neighbours' fields still bear the better Grain :
But others' harmes wee alwayes light esteem ;
Tush, they are nothing : why should they complain ?

80

A l'enuieux nul tourment ie n'ordonne,
Il est de soy le juge & le bourreau :
Et ne fut onc de DENYS le Toreau
Supplice tel, que celuy qu'il se donne.

To th' Envious-man no Torment I assigne ;
For, Judge and Hang-man to himselfe he is :
And there's no Denis Bull, nor Rack (in fine)
So fell a Torture as that Heart of his.

81

Pour bien au vif peindre la Calomnie,
Il là faudroit peindre quand on là sent :
Qui par bonheur d'elle ne se ressent,
Croire ne peult quellé est ceste Furie.

To pourtray Slaunder, to the life, behooves
To do 't in th' instant while one feeleth her :
For who so happy that her never prooves,
Can scarce imagin what shee is, or where.

82

Elle ne faict en l'air sa residence,
Ny soubs les eaux, ny au profond des bois :
Sa maison est aux oreilles des Roys,
D'où elle brave & flestrit l'innocence.

Neither in th' Ayre hath shee her residences,
Nor in the wilde Woods, nor beneath the Waves :
But shee inhabits in the ears of Princes,
Where th' innocent and honest shee depraves.

83

Quand une fois ce monstre nous attache,
Il scait si fort ses cordillons nouër,
Que bien qu'on puisse en fin les desnouër,
Restent tousiours les marques de l'attache.

And when this Monster hath once chaunc't to trap-us,
Her spightfull Cords shee can so closely knit,
That though at last wee happen to un-wrap-us ;
The print thereof still in our Fames will sit.

84

Judge, ne donne en ta cause sentence :
Chacun se trompe en son faict aizément :
Nostre interest force le jugement,
Et d'un costé faict pancher la balance.

Never give Sentence in thy proper cause :
In our own case wee all erre easily :
Our interest our partiall judgement draws ;
And ever makes the balance hang awry.

85

Dessus la loy tes jugemens arreste,
Et non sur l'homme : elle sans affection ;
L'homme au contraire est plein de passion :
L'un tient de Dieu, l'autre tient de la beste.

Upon the Law thy Judgements alwayes ground,
And not on Man : For that's affection-less ;
But Man in Passions strangely doth abound :
Th' one all like God ; th' other too-like to Beasts.

86

Le nombre sainct se juge par sa preuue,
Tousiours egal, entier ou departy :
Le droict aussi en Atomes party,
Semblable à soy tousiours egal se treuue.

The sacred Number proveth alwayes even,
Whether divided or intire it be :
So Justice (*shar'd in Atomies*) *is given*
Still like it selfe, in just equality.

87

Nouueau Ulysse appren du long voyage
A gouuerner Ithaque en equité :
Maint-un a Scylle & Charybde euité,
Qui heurte au port, & chez soy faict naufrage.

Learn by long Travell (as Ulysses *conned*)
To govern right thy native Ithaca :
Many have Scylla *and* Charibdis *shunned,*
That (after) have at home been cast-away.

88

Songe long temps auant que de promettre :
Mais si tu as quelque chose promis,
Quoy que ce soit, & fust ce aux ennemis,
De l'accomplir en deuoir te fault mettre.

Before thou promise, ponder what and why :
But having promis'd, what-soever ' t were,
Yea, were it to thy greatest Enemy,
Thou must perform, thy tongue hath ty'd thee there.

89

La loy soubs qui l'estat sa force a prise,
Garde là bien, pour goffe qu'elle soit :
Le bonheur vient d'où l'on ne s'appercoit,
Et bien souuent de ce que l'on mesprise.

Maintain those Lawes (however rude and plain)
Whereby before thy Common-wealth hath thriv'd :
Good fortune oft coms by the meanest mean :
How, or from whence sometimes is scarce perceiv'd.

90

Fuy jeune & viel de Circe le bruuage :
N'éscoute aussi des Sirenes les chants,
Car enchanté tu courrois par les champs,
Plus abruty qu'une beste sauuage.

In youth and age shunne Circe's *banefull Bowle,*
Lend not thine eare to Sirens' *wanton Notes :*
Lest thou (inchanted in thy sense and Soule)
Become more brute then Hogs, and Dogs, and Goats.

91

Vouloir ne fault chose que l'on ne puisse,
Et ne pouuoir que cela que l'on doit,
Mesurant l'un & l'autre par le droit,
Sur l'eternel moule de la Justice.

Wee must our Will *still limit with our* Power,
And bound our Power *within the Lists of* Law ;
Measuring both, and what so else is our,
By the Right *line th' eternall* Just *did draw.*

92

Changer à coup de loy & d'ordonnance,
Et faict d'estat est un poinct dangereux :
Et si Lycurgue en ce poinct fut heureux,
Il ne fault pas en faire consequence.

A sudden Change *in any mighty* State,
Is full of Danger unto each Degree :
And though Lycurgus *found it fortunate,*
No consequent can that Example be.

93

Ie hay ces mots, De puissance absoluë,
De plein pouuoir, De propre mouuement :
Aux saincts Decrets ils ont premierement,
Puis à nos loix, la puissance tolue.

I hate these phrases : Of Power *absolute :*
Of full Authoritie : Full proper motion.
The Divine Lawes they have trod under foot,
And humane-too ; for private men's promotion.

94

Croire leger, & soudain se resoudre,
Ne discerner les amis des flateurs :
Ieune conseil, & nouueaux seruiteurs,
Ont mis souuent les haults estats en pouldre.

Not right-descerning friends from flatterers,
Light-crediting, and sudden Resolution,
Young giddy counsell, and new Servitors,
Have often caus'd the highest States confusion.

95

Dissimuler est un vice servile,
Vice suiuy de la desloyauté :
D'où sourd és cueurs des grands la cruauté
Qui aboutit à la guerre civile.

Dissimulation is a servile vice,
A vice still followed by Disloyalty,
Whence in great hearts doth cruelty arise,
Which alwayes ends in Civill Mutiny.

96

Donner beaucoup sied bien à un grand Prince,
Pourueu qu'il donne à qui l'à merité,
Et par proportion non par equalité,
Et que ce soit sans fouler sa Province.

Nought more beseemes a Prince then Liberality,
So it be given to those that merit well,
By due proportion, not by just equality,
And without burthen to the Common-weale.

97

Plus que Sylla c'est ignorer les lettres,
D' auoir induit les peuples à s'armer :
On trouuera les voulant desarmer,
Que de subjects ils sont deuenus maistres.

'Tis to be more then Sylla *Letter-lesse,*
To hurry Armes into the Vulgar's hand :
For, when again you think them to suppresse,
In stead of Subjects they will All command.

98

Ry si tu veux un ris de Democrite,
Puis que le monde est pure vanité :
Mais quelque fois 'touché d'humanité,
Pleure noz maux des larmes d'Heraclite.

Sith all the World is nought but meerly vanity,
Laugh if thou list like blythe Democritus :
Yet sometimes toucht with tender-soul'd humanity,
Weep for our woes with sad Heraclitus.

99

A l'estranger sois humain & propice,
Et s'il se plainct incline à sa raison :
Mais luy donner les biens de la maison,
C'est faire aux tiens, & honte & injustice.

Be kinde to strangers, and propitious,
And to their cause thy willing eare incline ;
But to bestow thy Goods out of thy House,
Is shame and wrong unto thy selfe and thine.

100

Ie t'apprendray, si tu veux, en peu d'heure,
Le beau secret du breuuage amoureux :
Ayme les tiens, tu seras aymé d'eux :
Il n'y a point de recepte meilleure.

Ile teach you here (if any list to prove)
A passing Love-drink, any heart to get ;
Love vertuously, and be assur'd of Love :
And this (beleeve-it) is the best Receipt.

101

Crainte qui vient d'amour & reverence,
Est un appuy ferme de Royauté :
Mais qui se faict craindre par cruauté,
Luy-mesme craint, & vit en deffiance.

The fear that springs from Love and Reverence,
A firme support to Royall Greatnesse gives :
But he that makes him fear'd for Violence,
Himselfe fears most, and in distrust still lives.

102

Qui scauroit bien que c'est qu'un Diadéme,
Il choisiroit aussi tost le tombeau,
Que d'affeubler son chef de ce bandeau :
Car aussi bien il meurt lors à soy mesme.

Hee that knew right what were a Diadem,
As soon would seek in a cold Toomb to lie,
As girt his Temples, with that glorious Gem :
For, then begins hee to himselfe to dye.

103

De jour, de nuict, faire la sentinelle,
Pour le salut d'autruy tousiours veiller,
Pour le public sans nul gré trauailler,
C'est en un mot ce qu'Empire i'appelle.

For, day and night to stand as Sentinel ;
For publike good ingratefull toyle to take ;
Incessantly to watch for others' weal :
This is, to Raigne, *if wee it rightly take.*

104

Je ne veis onc prudence auec ieunesse,
Bien commander sans auoir obey,
Estre fort craint, & n'estre point hay,
Estre Tyran, & mourir de vieillesse.

I never saw Wisedome and Youth, but two :
Nor him Command well, that had not obay'd :
Nor any fear'd, that was not hated too :
Nor Tyrant, aged in his Toomb be layd.

105

Ne voise au bal qui n'aymerà la danse,
Ny au banquet qui ne voudra manger,
Ny sur la mer qui craindra le danger,
Ny à la Cour qui dirà ce qu'il pense.

Come not at Revels, who delights not Dance :
Nor on the Sea, who fears rough waves and winde :
Nor at a feast, who a good stomack wants :
Nor at the Court, who means to speak his minde.

106

Du mesdisant la langue venimeuse,
Et du flateur les propos emmielez,
Et du moqueur les brocards enfielez,
Et du maling la poursuite animeuse :

The soothing honey of smooth Parasites :
The poys'ny Tongues of slaunderous Sycophants :
The jeering Buffon that the best still bites :
The brazen-face of begging Cormorants.

107

Hayr le vray, se feindre en touts choses,
Sonder le simple àfin de l'autraper,
Braver le foible, & sur l'absent draper,
Sont de la Cour les œillets & les roses.

To gull the Simple ; and the Weake to brave :
To hate the Truth ; to halt in every thing :
To under-mine : The Absent to deprave :
These are the Flowers that in the Court *doe spring.*

108

Adversité, desfaueur, & querelle,
Sont trois essais pour sonder son amy :
Tel a ce nom qui ne l'est qu'à demy,
Et ne scauroit endurer la coupelle.

An Enemy, Misfortune, and Disgrace,
Are three Essayes to prove if Friends be loyall :
For many have the Name, and bear the face,
That are not so, if they be put in triall.

109

Ayme l'estat tel que tu le vois estre :
S'il est royall, ayme la Royauté :
S'il est de peu, où bien communauté,
Ayme l'aussi, quand Dieu t'y à faict naistre.

Commend the State where-under born you are :
If it be Royall, love the Royalty ;
If of the Best, or meerly Popular ;
Allow of either where thy Lot shall be.

110

Il est permis souhaiter un bon Prince ;
Mais tel qu'il est, il le convient porter :
Car il vault mieux un tyran supporter,
Que de troubler la paix de sa Province.

'Tis lawfull (where they want) to wish good Princes :
But men the while must beare them as they are.
'Tis better beare a Tyrant's insolences,
Then to disturb the Common-weal with War.

111

A ton Seigneur & ton Roy ne te iouë :
Et s'il t'en prie, il t'en faut excuser :
Qui des faveurs des Roys cuide abuser,
Bien tost, froissé, choit au bas de la rouë.

Sport not too boldly with thy Lord and King ;
And though hee bid thee (if thou canst) refuse :
From highest Fortunes sudden down they ding
Who doe presume a Prince's grace t' abuse.

112

Qui de bas lieu (miracle de Fortune)
En un matin t'és haulsé si avant,
Penses tu point que ce n'est que du vent,
Qui calmera, peut estre, sur la brune :

Thou (Fortune's wonder) that from lowest place
Dost in a morning to the top attain :
Suppose it but a winde that blew a space
Which yet yer night (perhaps) will calme again :

113

L'estat moyen est l'estat plus durable :
On voit des eaux le plat pays noyé,
Et les haults monts ont le chef foudroye
Une petite tertre est seur & agreable.

47

The meane Estate is the most permanent :
We see the Vales with every shower are drown'd ;
And Mountain tops with every Thunder rent :
But Little Hils are pleasant, safe, and sound.

114

De peu de biens nature se contente,
Et peu suffit pour vivre honestement,
L'homme, ennemy de son contentement,
Plus a, & plus pour auoir se tourmente.

Nature's with little pleas'd : enough's a Feast :
A sober life, but a small charge requires :
But Man, the Author of his own un-rest,
The more he hath, the more he still desires.

115

Quand tu verras que Dieu au ciel retire
A coup à coup les hommes vertueux,
Dy hardiment, l'orage impetueux
Viendra bien tost esbranler cest Empire.

When thou shalt see th' Almightie take from hence,
By one and one the Vertuous of the Land,
Say boldly thus ; These are the Arguments
Of some drad Tempest of his Wrath at hand.

116

Les gens de bien ce sont comme gros termes,
Ou forts piliers, qui servent d'arcs-boutans,
Pour appuyer contre l'effort du temps
Les haults estats, & les maintenir fermes.

For, Vertuous men are even the Buttresses,
The mighty Columnes, and the Arches strong,
Which against all Time's fellest outrages
Support a State, and doe maintain it long.

117

L'homme se plaint de sa trop courte vie,
Et ce pendant n'employe où il devroit
Le temps qu'il a qui suffir luy pourroit
Si pour bien vivre auoit de vivre envie.

Man doth the shortnesse of his Life repine ;
Yet doth not duly spend nor rightly drive
The Time he hath : which might suffice his minde,
If, To live well, he did desire to live.

118

Tu ne scaurois d'assez ample salaire
Recompenser celuy qui t'a soigné
En ton enfance, & qui t'a enseigné
A bien parler, & sur tout à bien faire.

Thou hardly canst sufficiently requite
Him, who thy Child-hood hath been Tutor to ;
Nor him, that hath instructed thee a-right,
Both well to speake, but chiefly well to doe.

119

Es jeux publics, au theatre, à la table,
Cede ta place au viellard & chenù :
Quand tu seras à son age venù,
Tu trouueras qui fera le semblable.

In Theaters, at publike Playes and Feasts,
Give alwayes place unto the hoary head :
So, when like age shall silverize thy Tresse,
Thou shalt by others be like-honoured.

120

Cil qui ingrat enuers toy se demonstre,
Va augmentant le loz de ton bien fact :
Le reprocher maint homme ingrat a faict :
C'est se payer, que du bien fair monstre.

Who, for thy friendship shows himselfe ingrate ;
Unwillingly extols thy Benefit :
But to up-braid one, makes a Man ingrate ;
Who vaunts his kindnesse, payes himselfe for it.

121

Boire, & manger, s'exercer par mesure,
Sont de sánté les outils plus certains :
L'excez en l'un de ces trois, aux humains
Haste la mort, & force la nature.

To eate, and drinke, and exercise in measure,
Three props of Health, the certainest shee hath :
But the excesse in these (or other pleasure)
Enforceth Nature, and doth hasten death.

122

Si quelque fois le meschant te blasonne,
Que t'en chaut il ? helas, c'est ton honneur :
Le blasme prend la force du donneur :
Le loz est bon, quand un bon nous le donne.

If evill men speak somtimes ill of thee,
What need'st thou care ? alas ! it is thy praise :
Blame, from the Author takes authority,
And 'tis a good report that good men raise,

123

Nous meslons tout, le vray parler se change
Souuent le vice est du nom revestu
De la prochain' opposite vertu :
Le loz est blasme, & le blasme est loüange.

Wee all confound ; true Language is trans-formed :
Vice oftentimes puts-on the Vertue's name
Next opposite ; 'Tis Forme to be de-formed :
Blame is a Praise : and Commendation Blame.

124

En bonne part ce qu'on dit tu dois prendre,
Et l'imparfait du prochain supporter,
Couurir sa faulte, & ne la rapporter
Prompt à louër, & tardif à reprendre.

Of what is spoken, ever make the best :
Beare the defect of Neighbour and of Friend :
Cover their fault ; publish it not (at least) :
Ready to praise, and slow to reprehend.

125

Cil qui se pense & se dit estre sage,
Tien le pour fol, & celuy qui scauant
Se faict nommer, sonde le bien auant,
Tu trouueras que ce n'est que langage.

Hee that esteemes and vaunts himselfe for wise,
Think him a foole : and him that doth assume
The name of Learned, whoso soundly tries,
Shall finde him nothing but bare words and fume.

126

Plus on est docte, & plus on se deffi
D'estre scavant : & l'homme vertueux
Jamais n'est veu estre presumtueux.
Voila des fruicts de ma Philosophie.

The better Learned, learn the more their want,
And more to doubt their owne sufficiencie :
And vertuous men are never arrogant :
These are the Fruits of my Philosophy.

FINIS.

NOTES AND ILLUSTRATIONS.

No. 8, ' *contemple* ' = contemplate. No. 29, ' *Trace* ' = track, foot-prints. No. 31, ' *no Letter* '—the old classical artist-saying. No. 39, ' *quadrat* ' = arranged in squares. No. 51, ' *paine* ' = painstaking, as before. No. 62, ' *sur-cloyes* ' = over-cloys, as ' surcharge,' etc. No. 68, ' *mell* ' = mix. No. 72, l. 4, ' *Impes* '—see Glossarial Index, *s.v.*, for a full note. No. 80, ' *Denis Bull,*' *ibid.* No. 82, ' *depraves* ' = depreciates. No. 91, ' *Lists* ' = bounds or boundaries. No. 113, ' *meane* ' = medium.—G.

SONNETS

Upon

THE LATE MIRA-
CULOUS PEACE
IN FRANCE.

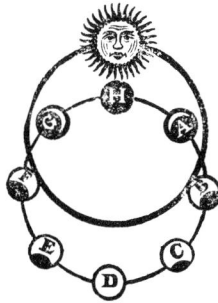

Acceptam refero.

TO THE MOST
HONOURABLE, LEARNED,
AND RELIGIOUS GENTLEMAN,

Master *Anthonie Bacone.*

B*Ound by your Bounty and mine owne desire,*
To tender still new tribute of my zeale
To you (your Countrie's watchfull Sentinel,
Whose wisedome, ours and other States admire)
Lo, here I tune vpon mine humble Lyre
Our Neighbour Kingdome's vn-expected weale,
Through sudden ceasing of War's *enter-deale;*
As Celtike *Muses to my Muse inspire,*
Miraculous the Work; and so his wit
That firstly sung this sacred MIRACLE :
A gracious Theame (If I dis-grace not it)
That your grave eyes may daigne for spectacle.
What e'r it be, accept it as a due,
From him whose all doth all belong to You.

JOSUAH SYLVESTER.

NOTES AND ILLUSTRATIONS.

Page 36, '*Anthonie Bacone*'—see our Memorial-Introduction: l. 11, '*enter-deale*' = intercourse. Sonnet 3, l. 14, '*all heale*' = all health : Son. 8, '*fine*' = end : Son. 9, l. 12, '*mel*' = honey : Son. 12, l. 8, '*Mausole*' = mausoleum : l. 10, '*raps*' = rapts : Son. 14, l. 8, '*boany*' = bony : Son. 20, '*Imps*'—see Glossarial Index, *s.v.*, as before : Son. 25, l. 12, '*ure*' = use : Son. 26, l. 5, '*fine*' = end, as before.—G.

TO THE FRENCH KING,

HENRY THE FOURTH.

SONNET I.

HEnry, triumphant though thou wert in war,
   Though Fate & Fortitude conspir'd thy glory,
Though thy least Conflicts well deserve a Story ;
Though *Mars* his fame by thine be dark'ned far ;
Though from thy Cradle (Infant Conquerour)
   Thy martiall proofs have dimm'd *Alcides'* praise ;
   And though with Garlands of victorious Bayes
Thy Royall temples richly crowned are :
Yet (match-less Prince) nought hast thou wrought so
   glorious
   As this un-lookt-for, happy PEACE admired ;
   Whereby thy self art of thy selfe victorious :
For, while thou mightst the world's throne have aspired,
   Thou by this *Peace* thy war-like heart hast tamed :
   What greater conquest could there then be named ?

SONNET 2.

But what new Sun doth now adorne our Land,
   And gives our skie so smooth and smiling cheer ?
   For, 'tis not *Phœbus ;* else his golden brand
Shines brighter now then 't hath don many a year.
Sweet Angel-beauty (sacred *Peace*) heav'n's present ;
   Is't not the Rising of thy new-com star,
   Wᶜʰ makes the Air more cleer, the Spring more
   pleasant,
   Zephyre more calm, & *Flora* merrier ?
Ah, I perceive the *Olive, Dove,* and *Bow,*
   Divine presages that the Floud abates
   (The dismall floud where bloud and tears did flow)
And *Janus* now locks-up his Temple gates :
   Justice and *Faith* doe kindely kisse each other :
   And *Mars* appeas'd, sits down by *Cupid's* mother.

SONNET 3.

Fair fruitfull Daughter of th' Omnipotent,
   Great Umpire that dost either World sustain,
   Without whose help all would return again
   (Like hideous *Chaos*) to confusion bent.
O Mother of the living, second Nature
   Of th' Elements (Fire, Water, Earth, and Air)

O Grace (whereby men climb the heav'nly stair)
   Whence void, this world harbours no happy creature.
Pillar of Lawes, Religious Pedestall,
   Hope of the godly, glory of th' immortall ;
   Honour of Cities, Pearl of Kingdoms all ;
Thou Nurse of Vertues, Muses' chief supportall ;
   Patron of Arts, of Good the speciall spring :
   All hail (dear *Peace*) which us all heale dost bring.

SONNET 4.

Com forth (dear *France*) frõ thy dark Cell of mone,
   Com (as new-born) from War's unkindly quarrels ;
   Turn tragick Cypresse to triumphant Laurels ;
   Change black to greene, and make thy Grave a
   Throne.
Let *Ceres* dwell upon thy Desart Plain,
   Bacchus, and *Dian,* on thy Hils and Groves,
   Pomona in Gardens, *Pan* among thy Droves,
   Secure all Roades, and ope all Gates again.
Resume (O Cities) Rule and Reverence ;
   Revest (yee States) your Robes of dignitie ;
   Rise-up (yee Ruines) in fair Battlements ;
Come *Muses, Pallas, Themis, Mercurie,*
   Restore us Laws, Learning, and Arts, and Trade :
   And let our Age, a golden Age be made.

SONNET 5.

Most Christian Kingdom, thou wert ne'r so near
   Drown'd in the deep Gulphs of thy Civill war,
   As in the tempest of this later Jar,
   Which past conceit of calming did appear.
When all the Windes adversly armed were,
   (Tho selfly-foes, yet friends to work thy wrack)
   Thy Ship a helm, thy selfe a heart didst lack,
   On troubled waters tossed here and there :
Then from above (O bountie most admired !)
   Saint *Hermes* shin'd : whose gentle light presageth
   That then the anger of the Heav'ns asswageth.
O happy PEACE ! lesse hoped then desired :
   O grace much honour'd ! little yet conceiv'd ;
   O blessed guile, that thus our sense deceiv'd !

S o n n e t 6.

Who could expect (but past all expectation)
   So sudden order from so sad confusion?
   So loyall friendship, from false emulation?
   So firm possession, from so fierce intrusion?
Who could expect (but past all likelihood)
   From such a storm, such and so sweet a calme:
   From *France* her cinders, such a *Phœnix*-brood;
   Pandora's box to yeeld so rare a balme?
Who could expect (but past all humane thought)
   So frank a freedom from a thrall so late,
   Or certaine Rudder of so rent a State?
True *Æsculapius*, thou alone hast wrought
   This Miracle, not on *Hyppolitus*,
   But on this Kingdome, much more wonderous.

S o n n e t 7.

Th' unlook't-for working of all things almost,
   Inconstant-constant, in succession strange,
   Amazeth those whose wits wee chiefly boast,
   To see this sudden un-expected change.
Each feels th' effect, but none the cause descries
   (No though hee have with stars intelligence):
   God to himselfe reserves such Mysteries,
   Disposing Kingdomes by his Providence:
O end-lesse Bountie! In the midst of Broyles
   He gives us Peace, when War did us inflame;
   And reaves the mischiefe we pursu'd yer-whiles:
But, this doth most extoll his glorious Name,
   That when most sharply this extremest Fit
   Strove to be cure-lesse, soon hee cured it.

S o n n e t 8.

Some reasoned thus; No violence can last:
   Revolted Subjects, of themselves will quail:
   Just Soveraigntie can never be displac't;
   And lawfull Princes first or last prevail:
But who could think, that the conjoyned powers
   Of *Spain* and *Rome*, with an exceeding number
   Of rebell Cities, and false States of ours,
   So weak a King so little should encumber?
Others discoursed in another sort,
   While all things sorted to another end
   Then their imaginations did purport:
That earth may know, it cannot comprehend
   The secret depths of Judgements all-divine,
   No: there's no ground, beginning, midst, nor fine.

S o n n e t 9.

Admire we onely God's Omni-potence,
   His deep-deep Wisedome, and his Mercy dear.
   For, with these three, he hath surmounted here
   Our hatefull foes, our hopes, and all our sense:
His power appears upon our Lord and King,
   As yerst on *David:* for they both attain

By war-like broyls their pre-appointed Reigne;
   Strangers, and Subjects, and selves conquering:
His prudence shines, when to preserve us thus,
   All humane wit his Wisedome doth convince:
   His gracious bounty in our bounteous Prince.
O various wonders! mel delicious
   Flows from a living Lion; *Mars* is quiet,
   Valour relenting, Conquest void of riot.

S o n n e t 10.

This was no action of a humane hand
   But th' onely work of the great Thunderer,
   Who (wise-directing all the things that are)
   In us divinely works his own command.
Some men, unwilling, benefit their Land,
   Or unawares their Countrie's good prefer;
   Another motions Peace, but mindeth War,
   And Peace succeeds what-ever drifts with-stand.
Th' Arch-Architect, the matchlesse Artizan
   All instruments unto good uses proves:
   Man's but a wheel, wch that great Mover moves,
Each gracious gift in that first cause began:
   Each good's a gleam of that first light alone,
   If ill approach us, onely that's our own.

S o n n e t 11.

If God dart lightning, soon hee deaws down rain;
   A dreadfull Judge, and yet a gentle Father:
   Whose wrath slow-kindled is soon quencht again,
   To move us sinners to repent the rather.
'Gainst hel-bred *Hydra*, heav'n-born *Theseus* brings
   The great *Alcides'* arm and armory:
   Of greatest Ill, a greater Good there springs;
   And Mercie still doth Rigour qualifie.
Ah *France*, so many Monsters to suppresse,
   Thou hadst great need of Royall fortitude,
   Else hadst thou been an *Africk* Wildernesse.
O happy lost Realme! for, it hath ensu'd,
   That now thy gain is more, in restauration,
   Then was thy losse in all my desolation.

S o n n e t 12.

But, if I sing great *Henrie's* fortitude;
   Shall I not then be blam'd for over-daring?
   If over-slip it, then be taxt for fearing,
   Of silent dread, and dumb ingratitude?
What ere befall, my youth-bold thoughts conclude
   (Like *Icarus*) my nimble *Muse* to rayse:
   And if I fall in such a Sea of praise,
   What rarer *Mausole* may my bones include?
A sacred rage of some sweet-furious flame,
   Will-nill-I, raps mee boldly to rehearse
   Great *Henrie's* Tropheis, and his glorious name.
Then roule thou Torrent of my tender Verse:
   Though his high Theam deserve a consort rather
   Of all the Muses, and all Musick's Father.

Sonnet 13.

Great Prince not pleas'd with a vaine vertue-seeming :
  Great Victor, prone to pardon humblnes,
  Happy, all Hap Heav'n's onely gift esteeming ;
  Warrier, whose wars have wrought his countrie's
    PEACE :
Noble by deeds, and noble by descent ;
  Ancient *Achilles*, youthfull *Nestor* sage,
  Whose ripe-experienc't courage confident,
  To knocks knits counsail, and gives rule to rage.
As hard in toyle, as in compassion soft :
  Inur'd to that, by nature born to this ;
  Who sheds no bloud, but sheddeth tears as oft,
  Who never fights but still the Field is his.
    So like to *Mars*, that both in loves and wars,
    Bellona and *Venus* take him still for *Mars*.

Sonnet 14.

A spirit, to vertues cheerfully addrest ;
  Apt to all goodnesse, to no ill inclin'd ;
  Quick to conceive, ingenious to digest ;
  Whose tongue is still true trumpet of the mind :
A bodie, resting when it hath no rest ;
  A waxen mildnesse in a steely minde ;
  A soule tra-lucent in an open brest,
  Which others' thoughts through boany wals can finde ;
Whose front reflects majesticall-humilitie,
  Whose grave-sweet look commandingly-intreats,
  Which in one instant fear and love begets :
A King still warring to obtain tranquillitie.
    To save his Country, scorning thousand dangers ;
    Mirror of *France*, and miracle of Strangers.

Sonnet 15.

If that, before thee fall rebellious Towers ;
  If battered Wals, before thy Souldiers, loose ;
  If hugest Rocks be pierced by thy powers ;
  If 'gainst thine Armes, no armour be of proofe ;
If that our fields flow with *Iberian* bloud ;
  If that thy Camp compos'd of many a *Cæsar*,
  Can by no dismall dangers be withstood ;
  Jousting with Gyants, as it were at pleasure :
If lofty Mountains to thine homage vaile ;
  If Valleys rise to bulwark thee about ;
  If for thy sake, Rivers doe flow and fail ;
'Twas neither Canons, nor our conflicts stout,
    Nor strength, nor stomack got these victories :
    No, 'twas thy presence (*Henry*) and thine eyes.

Sonnet 16.

They be to blame then, that thy boldnesse blame,
  For having put thy selfe so oft in danger :
  Sith against Rebels and against the Stranger,
  Thy looks, like lightning, did thy troups inflame.
France fought before, all bloudy, faint, and lame,
  Craving thine ayd to venge her hatefull wrong ;

When, like a Lion to preserve her yong,
  Thou laydst about thee to redeeme the same.
Then hadst thou cause to hazzard so thy life
  (In extreme perils, extreme remedies.)
  But spare thee now, thy State is free from strife :
Soveraigne, our safety in thy safety lies.
    Codrus could keep his, onely by his death :
    Thou thine, alone by thine own living breath.

Sonnet 17.

What wreath were worthy to become thy crown,
  What *Carr-triumphant* equall with thy worth,
  What marble statue meet for thy renown,
  Thou that hast rais'd the Lilly of the earth ?
What honourable Title of Addition
  Dost thou deserve, who (joyning might with mild-
    nesse)
  Hast sav'd this great Ship from a sad perdition,
  Nigh lost in th' Ocean of warr's civill wildnesse ?
O modern *Hercules* (thy Countrie's Father)
  Hope not of us thy just deserved meed :
  Earth is too base, in Heav'n expect it rather.
Our Laurels are too-pale to crown thy deed,
    Who thus hast salv'd the universall Ball :
    For, th' health of *France* imports the health of all.

Sonnet 18.

Pardon mee (*Henry*) if Heav'ns silver raine,
  Dewing the pearls, impearle mine humble laies :
  And if my Verse (voyde both of price and paine)
  Presume thy Vertues passing-price to praise :
Pardon (great King) if that mine Infant Muse
  Stutter thy name ; and if with skill too scant
  I limne thee here, let zeal my crime excuse ;
  My steel's attracted by thine Adamant.
For as the Sunne, although hee doe reflect
  His golden Rayes on grosser elements,
  Doth never spot his beautifull aspect :
So, though the praises of thine Excellence
    Doe brightly glister in my gloomy stile,
    They nothing lose of their first grace the while.

Sonnet 19.

Now, sith as well by conquest as succession
  France is thine owne ; O keep it still therefore.
  'Tis much to conquer : but, to keep possession
  Is full as much, and if it be not more.
Who well would keep so plentifull a portion,
  Must stablish first the heav'nly Discipline ;
  Then humane Lawes, restraining all extortion ;
  And Princely wealth with publike weale combine.
A Prince's safety lies in loving People :
  His Fort is Justice (free from stratagem)
  Without the which strong Cittadels are feeble.
The Subjects' love is wonne by loving them ;
    Of loving them, n'oppression is the triall :
    And no oppression makes them ever loyall.

SONNET 20.

Bold *Martialists*, brave Imps of noble birth,
  Shining in steel for *France*, and for your King :
  Ye sons of those that heretofore did bring
  Beneath their yoake the pride of all the earth.
It is an honour to be high-descended ;
  But more, t' have kept one's Country & fidelity :
  For our own Vertues make us most commended :
  And Truth 's the title of all true Nobility.
Your shoulders shoar'd up *France* (even like to fall)
  You were her *Atlas; Henry, Hercules :*
  And but for you, her shock had shaken All ;
But now shee stands stedfast on Civill PEACE :
  Wherefore, if yet your war-like heat do work,
  With holy Arms go hunt the hatefull *Turk.*

SONNET 21.

But you that vaunt your antike Pedigrees,
  So stately timbring your surcharged shields,
  Perking (like Pines above the lower Trees)
  Over the Farmers of your neighbour fields ;
Is 't lack of love, or is it lack of courage,
  That holds you (Snaile-like) creeping in your houses,
  While over all your Countries Foes do forrage,
  And rebell out-rage every corner rouses ?
If no example of your Ancestors,
  Nor present instance of bright-armed Lords,
  The feeble temper of your stomach stirres ;
If in your lives yee never drew your swords
  To serve your King, nor quench your Countrie's
    flames,
  Pardon me, Nobles, I mistook your names.

SONNET 22.

You sacred Order, charg'd the Church to watch,
  And teach the holy Mysteries of Heav'n,
  From hence-forth all seditious plots dispatch,
  And (Father-like) to all be alwaies even.
Though superstition stirre to strife again ;
  Revolt 's a mischiefe evermore pernicious :
  Pluck up abuses, and the hurtfull grain
  Sprung from the ignorant and Avaricious.
Avoyd Ambition (common cause of strife)
  Your reverend Robe be free from stains of bloud,
  Preach holy Doctrine, prove it by your life :
Fly idlenesse, choose exercises good ;
  To wit, all works of lively faith and piety.
  So, to your Fold shall flock the best Society.

SONNET 23.

You grave assembly of sage Senators,
  Right Oracles, yee *Ephori* of *France ;*
  Who, for the State's and Justice' maintenance,
  Of Sword and Balance are the Arbitrers :
That from hence-forth (against all Enemies)
  Our PEACE may seat her in a settled Throne ;

Represse the malice of all mutinies,
  W^{ch} through th' advantage of these times have grown.
At a low tide 'tis best to mend a breach,
  Before the flood returne with violence ;
  'Tis good in health to counsaile with a Leach ;
So, while a People 's calme from insolence,
  'Tis best that Rulers bridle them with aw ;
  And (for the future) curb the lewd with law.

SONNET 24.

People, lesse settled then the sliding sand ;
  More mutable then *Proteus*, or the Moone ;
  Turn'd, and return'd, in turning of a hand :
  Like *Euripus*, ebbe-flowing every Noone.
Thou thousand-headed head-lesse Monster-most,
  Oft slain (like *Antheus*) and as oft new rising,
  Who, hard as steele, as light as winde art tost ;
  Chameleon-like, each object's colour prysing :
Unbinde thy blinde soule, ope thine inward sight ;
  Be no more tinder of intestine flame :
  Of all fantastick humors purge thy spright :
For, if past-follies urge yet griefe and shame,
  Lo (like Oblivion's law) to cure thy passion,
  State-stabling *Peace* brings froward minds in fashion.

SONNET 25.

Engins of *Vulcan*, Heav'n-affrighting wonders,
  Like brittle glasse the Rocks to cindars breaking ;
  Deafning the winds, dūbing the loudest thūders ;
  May ye be boūd a thousand years from speaking.
Ye hate-peace Hacksters, flesht in Massacres,
  Be ye for ever banisht from our soyle ;
  Ye steeled Tooles of slaughter, wounds, & wars,
  Be you condemn'd to hang, and rust a while :
Or (not to languish in so fruit-lesse rest)
  Be you transform'd to husband furniture,
  To plow those fields you have so oft deprest :
Or (if you cannot leave your wonted ure)
  Leave (at the least) all mutinous alarmes,
  And be from hence-forth Justice' lawfull Armes.

SONNET 26.

O *Paris*, know thy selfe, and know thy Master,
  As well thy Heav'nly as thine Earthly guider :
  And be not like a Horse, who (proud of Pasture)
  Breaks Bit, & Reans, & casts his cunning Rider,
Who nill be Subjects, shall be slaves in fine :
  Who Kings refuse, shall have a Tyrant Lord :
  Who are not mov'd with the milde rods divine,
  Shall feel the furie of Heav'n's venging Sword.
Thy greatness stands on theirs that wear the crown,
  Whereof, th' hast had now seventy (saving seven).
  Think one sufficient soon to pull thee down :
Kings' greatness stands on the great King of Heav'n.
  Knowing these two, then (*Paris*) know thy selfe,
  By War's afflictions, and by PEACE's wealth.

SONNET 27.

Swell not in pride, O *Paris* (Princely Dame)
 To be chiefe City, and thy Soveraign's Throne :
City? nay modell of this Totall Frame,
 A mighty Kingdome of thy selfe alone.
The scourge that lately with paternall hand
 For thine amendment did so mildly beat-thee,
 If any more against thy Kings thou stand,
 Shall prove that then God did but onely threat-thee.
Wert thou a hundred thousand-fold more mighty,
 Who in th' Olympike court cõmands the thunders,
 In his least wrath can wrack thee (most almighty)
Thebes, Babel, Rome, those proud heav'n-daring wonders,
 Low under ground in dust and ashes lye :
 For earthly Kingdoms (even as men) doe dye.

SONNET 28.

But, O my sorrows ! whither am I tost ?
 What ? shall I bloudy sweet Astræa's Songs?
 Re-open wounds that are now heal'd almost,
 And new-remember nigh-forgotten wrongs?
Sith stormes are calmed by a gentle Starre,
 Forget wee (Muse) all former furie-moods,
 And all the tempests of our Viper-Warre ;
 Drown wee those thoughts in deep-deep *Lethè* flouds.
O but (alas) I cannot not-retaine
 So great, notorious, common miseries,
 Nor hide my plaint, nor hold my weeping rain :
But 'mid these hideous hellish out-rages,
 Ile show and prove by this strange spectacle,
 Our civill Peace, a sacred Miracle.

SONNET 29.

As hee that scap't from Ship-wrack on a plank,
 Doubts of his health, and hardly yet beleeves
 (Still faintly shivering on the fearelesse bank)
 That (through that fraile help) certainly he lives :
As hee that new freed from strange servitude,
 Returnes again to tread his native allies,
 Seems still to fear his Patron's rigour rude,
 And seems still tugging, chained in the Gallies :
So alwayes, ruth, ruine, and rage, and horror
 Of troubles past doe haunt mee every-where,
 And still I meet Furies and ghastly Terror :
Then, to my selfe thus rave I (rapt with feare)
 From pleasures past, if present sorrow spring,
 Why should not past cares present cõfort bring ?

SONNET 30.

Wee must not now upbraid each other's crimes
 Committed wrongly in the time of warre ;
 For wee have all (alas) too oftentimes
 Provok't the vengeance of the Lord too far :
Some robbing Justice under mask of Reason ;
 Some blowing coles, to kindle-up Sedition ;

Som 'gainst their King attempting open Treason ;
 Some Godding *Fortune* (Idol of Ambition).
Alas, wee know our cause of maladie,
 All apt t' accuse, but none to cleanse th' impure ;
 Each doth rebuke, but none doth remedie :
To know a griefe, it is but halfe a cure.
 Is it our sins ? let's purge away that bane ;
 For what helps Physick, if it be not tane ?

SONNET 31.

Who cloake their crimes in hoods of holinesse,
 Are double villaines : and the Hypocrite
 Is most-most odious in God's glorious sight,
 That takes his name to cover wickednesse.
Profane Ambition, blinde and irreligious,
 In quest of Kingdoms, holding nothing holy,
 Thinkst thou th' Eternall blinde (as thou in folly)
 Or weake to punish Monsters so prodigious ?
O execrable vizard, canst thou hide thee
 From th' All-pierce Eye ? Are treason, rape
 murder,
 Effects of Faith, or of the Furie's-Order ?
Thy vaile is rent, the rudest have descri'd the

SONNET 32.

'Tis now apparent to each plaine Opinion
 Thy hot Devotion hunted but Dominion.
'Tis strange to see the heat of Civill brands.
 For, when wee arme us brother against brother,
 O then how ready are our hearts and hands,
 And Wits awake to ruine one another !
But, come to counter-mine 'gainst secret treason,
 Or force the forces of a stranger foe,
 Alas, how shallow are wee then in reason,
 How cold in courage, and in camping slow !
France onely strives to triumph over *France :*
 With self-kill Swords to cut each other's throat.
 What swarms of souldiers every where do float,
To spend and spoyle a Kingdom's maintenance ?
 But, said I Souldiers? ah, I blush for shame,
 To give base Theeves the noble Souldier's name.

SONNET 33.

Is 't not an endlesse scandall to our dayes
 (If possible our heires can credit it)
 That th' holy name of Peace, so worthy praise,
 Hath been our Watch-word for a fault unfit ?
That the pure Lilly, our owne native flower,
 Hath been an odious object in our eyes ?
 That Kingly Name, & King's heav'n-stablisht power,
 Hath been with us a marke of treacheries ?
T' have banisht hence the godly and the wise,
 Whose sound direction kept the State from danger ;
 Yea, made their bodies bloudy Sacrifice ?
And (to conclude) seeking to serve a Stranger,
 T' have stabb'd our own ? but (O Muse) keep that in :
 The fault 's so foul, to speak it were a sin.

Sonnet 34.

I waile not I so much war's wastefull rigours,
  Nor all thy ruines make mee halfe so sorrie,
  As thy lost honour (*France*) w_{ch} most disfigures,
  Losing thy loyalty, thy Native glory.
From *Moores* to *Muscovites* (O cursed change !)
  The *French* are called, *Faith-lesse Parricides.*
  Th' yerst most Prince-loyal people (ô most strange)
  Are now Prince-treachers more then all besides:
With us, *Massacres* passe for Pietie ;
  Theft, rape, & wrong, for just-attain'd possessions :
  Revolt for Merit, Rage for Equitie :
Alas, must wee needs borrow the transgressions
  And imperfections of all other nations,
  Yerst onely blamed for inconstant fashions?

Sonnet 35.

Not without reason hath it oft been spoken,
  That through faire Concord little things augment,
  And (opposite) that mightiest things are broken
  Through th' ugly Discord of the discontent.
When many tunes doe gently symphonize,
  It conquers hearts, and kindly them compounds ;
  When many hearts doth gently sympathize
  In sacred friendship, there all blisse abounds.
Alas, if longer wee divide this Realme,
  Loosing to every Partizan apart ;
  Farewell our Lillies and our Diadem.
For though it seem to breath now somwhat peart,
  Our sins (I feare) will work worse after-claps :
  And there 's most danger in a re-relapse.

Sonnet 36.

O, how I hate these partia-lizing words,
  Which show how wee are in the Faith devised :
  Is 't possible to whet so many swords,
  And light such flames 'mong th' In-one-Christ-bap-
      tized :
Christians to Christians to be brute and bloudy,
  Altars to Altars to be opposite ;
  Parting the limmes of such a perfect body,
  While *Turks* with *Turks* doe better far unite?
Wee, in our truth finde doubts (whence follow schismes)
  They, whose fond Law doth all of lies consist,
  Abide confirm'd in their vaine Paganismes.
One nought beleeves, another what him list :
  One over-Creeds, another Creeds too-short ;
  Each makes his Church (rather his Sect) a-part.

Sonnet 37.

Put off (dear *French*) all secret grudge and gall,
  And all keen stings of vengeance on all parts :
  For if you would have PEACE proclaim'd to all,
  It must be first faire printed in your hearts.
Henry the mildest of all Conquerors
  (Your perfect Glasse for Princely clemencie)

Hee, to appease and calme the State from jars,
  For his friends' sake, hath sav'd his enemie.
Let 's all be *French*, all subjects to one Lord ;
  Let *France* from hence-forth be one onely State ;
  Let 's all (for God's sake) be of one accord.
So (through true zeale Christ's praise to propagate)
  May *the most Christian King* with prosp'rous power
  On *Sion* wals re-plant our Lilly-flower.

Sonnet 38.

O Christian cor'sive ! that the *Mahomite*
  With hundred thousands in *Vienna* plaine,
  His mooned Standards hath already pight,
  Prest to joyne *Austria* to his *Thracian* Reigne :
Malth, Corfu, Candie, his proud threats disdaine ;
  And all our *Europe* trembles in dismay ;
  While striving *Christians* (by each other slaine)
  Each other weakning make him easie way.
Rhodes, Belgrade, Cyprus, and the Realms of *Greece*,
  Thrall'd to his barb'rous yoke, yet fresh-declare,
  That while two strive, a third obtains the fleece.
Though name of *Christian* be a title faire ;
  If, but for Earth, they all this while have striv'n,
  They may have earth, but others shall have Heav'n.

Sonnet 39.

May I not one day see in *France* againe
  Some new *Martellus* (full of stout activity)
  To snatch the Scepter from the *Saracen*,
  That holds the Holy Land in strait captivitie?
May I not see the selfe-weale-wounding Launce
  Of our brave Blouds (yerst one another goring)
  Turn'd with more valour on the *Musulmans*,
  A higher pitch of happy prowesse soaring?
But who (deare *France*) of all thy men at armes
  Shall so far hence renew their ancient Laurels :
  Sith here they plot thine and their proper harms?
I rather feare, that (through their fatall quarrels)
  That hate-Christ Tyrant will in time become
  The Lord and Soveraigne of all *Christendome.*

Sonnet 40.

Mid all these mischiefes, while the friend-foe strangers,
  With us, against us, had intelligence ;
  Henry our King, our Father, voyds our dangers,
  And (ô heav'ns wonder) planteth *Peace* in *France.*
Thou Judge that sitt'st on the supernall Throne,
  O quench thy furie, keep us from hostilitie :
  With eyes of mercy look thou still upon
  Our PEACE, and found it on a firme stability :
Sith (in despight of discord) thou alone,
  Inward and outward, hast thou salv'd us (Lord)
  Keep still our *France* (or rather Lord thine own)
Let Princes love, and live in just accord :
  Dis-arme them (Lord) or if Armes busie them,
  Be it alone for thy *Jerusalem.*

FINIS.

⁎⁎ See Notes and Illustrations on page 36.—G.

A

DIALOGUE

Upon The

TROUBLES

PAST;

BETWEENE

Heraclitus and Democritus,

The weeping and the laughing

Philofophers.

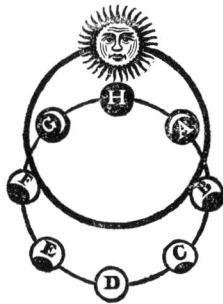

Acceptam refero.

A

DIALOGUE.

Heraclitus.

ALas! thou laughst, perhaps not feeling well
   The painfull torments of this mortall Hel :
Ah ! canst thou (tear-lesse) in this yron Age,
See men massacred, Monsters born to rage?

Democritus.

Ha ! but why weep'st thou ? wherefore in this sort
Dost thou lament amid this merry sport?
Ha ! canst thou chuse but laugh, to see the State
Of men's now-follies, and the freaks of Fate?

Heraclitus.

Hee hath no heart that melts not all in tears,
To see the treasons, murders, massacres,
Sacks, sacrileges, losses, and alarmes
Of those that perish by their proper armes.

Democritus.

Who all dismaied, swouneth suddenly
To heare or see some fained Tragedie
(Held in these dayes, on every Stage as common)
Is but a heartlesse man, or but a woman.

Heraclitus.

O ! would to God our Countrie's Tragick ruth
Were but a fable, no effected truth :
My soule then should not sigh to anger Heav'n,
Nor for her plagues my tender heart be riv'n.

Democritus.

I take the world to be but as a Stage,
Where net-maskt men do play their personage :
'Tis but a mummerie, and a pleasant show ;
Sith over all, strange vanities do flow.

Heraclitus.

Those vanities I have in detestation,
As cursed causes of God's indignation ;
Which makes mee alwaies weep, sith on the earth
I see no object for the meanest mirth.

Democritus.

Thus, from one Subject sundry sequels spring
As diversly our wits conceive a thing.
I laugh to see thee weep ; thou weepst to see
Mee laugh so much, which more afflicteth thee.

Heraclitus.

Laugh while thou list at mortall miseries,
I cannot chuse but even weep out mine eyes :
Finding more cause for tears in bloudy slaughter
Then for thy sense-less ill-beseeming laughter.

Democritus.

Melt thee, distill thee, turne to wax or snow ;
Make sad thy gesture, tune thy voyce to woe ;
I cannot weep, except sometimes it hap
Through laughing much, mine eyes let fall a drop.

Heraclitus.

I weep to see thus every thing confused,
Order disordred, and the Lawes abused ;
Justice reverst, and Policie perverted ;
And this sick State neer utterly subverted.

Democritus.

I laugh to see how Fortune (like a ball)
Plaies with the Globe of this inconstant All ;
How shee degradeth these, and graceth those ;
How whom shee lifts-up, down again she throws.

Heraclitus.

I raine down Rivers, when against their King
Cities rebell, through Subjects bandying :
When Colledges (through Armes) are reft of Art :
When every Countie Kingdomes-it a-part.

Democritus.

I burst with laughter, when (confounding Stat
I see those rebels hunt their Magistrate ;
When I heare Porters prate of State-designes,
And make al common, as in new-found *Indes*.

Heraclitus.

I weep to see God's glory made a vaile
To cover who his glory most assayle :
That sacred Faith is made a maske for sinne,
And men run head-long to destruction's ginne.

Democritus.

I laugh (with all my heart) at the transforming
Of Juggling *Proteis*, to all times *Conforming* :
But, most I laugh, t' have seen the world so mad
To starve and die, when those damn'd *Atheists* bad.

Heraclitus.

I weep (alas) to see the people weep,
Opprest with rest-lesse weight in danger deep ;
Crying for PEACE, but yet not like to get-her,
Yet her condition is not greatly better.

Democritus.

I laugh to see all cause of laughter gone
Through those which (yerst thou saidst) have caus'd
    thy mone :
Noting th' old guise, I laugh at all their new :
I laugh at more, but dare not tell it you.

Heraclitus.

Some sorrows also I in silence keep ;
But in the Desart, all my woes shall weep :
And there (perhaps) the Rocks will help me then ;
For, in these dayes they are more milde then men.

Democritus.

Ile dwell in Cities (as my *Genius* guides)
To laugh my fill ; for, smiling PEACE provides
Such plenteous store of laughing-stuffe to fill me,
That still Ile laugh, un-lesse that laughing kill me.

FINIS.

AN ODE OF

THE LOVE

AND

BEAUTIES

OF

ASTRÆA.

Acceptam refero.

TO THE MOST

MATCHLESSE

Faire and Vertuous

M. M. H.

Tetrastichon.

THou, *for whose sake my freedome I forsake ;*
Who, murdring mee dost yet maintain my life :
Here, vnder PEACE, *thy beautie's Type I make,*
Faire, war-like Nymph, that keepst mee still in strife.

An Ode to Aftræa.

Sacred PEACE, if I approve thee,
 If more then my life I love thee,
Tis not for thy beauteous eyes :
Though the brightest Lamp in skies
In his highest Summer-shine,
Seems a sparke compar'd with thine,
With thy paire of selfe-like-Sunnes,
Past all else-comparisons.

'Tis not (deare) the dewes Ambrosiall
Of those prettie lips so Rosiall,
Make me humble at thy feet :
Though the purest honey sweet
That the Muse's birds do bring,
To Mount *Hybla* every spring,
Nothing neere so pleasant is,
As thy lively loving kisse.

'Tis not (Beautie's Emperesse)
Th' Amber circlets of thy tresse,
Curled by the wanton windes,
That so fast my freedome bindes :
Though the precious glittering sand
Richly strow'd on *Tagus*' Strand,
Nor the graines *Pactolus* roll'd,
Never were so fine a gold.

'Tis not for the polisht rowes
Of those Rocks whence Prudence flowes,
That I still my sute pursue :
Though that in those Countries new
In the Orient lately found
(Which in precious Gemmes abound)
'Mong all baits of Avarice
Be no pearles of such a price.

'Tis not (Sweet) thine yvorie neck
Makes me worship at thy beck ;
Nor that prettie double HILL
Of thy bosome panting still :
Though no fairest *Læda's* Swan
Nor no sleekest Marble can
Be so smooth or white in showe,
As thy Lillies, and thy Snowe.

'Tis not (O my Paradise)
Thy front (evener than the yce)
That my yeelding heart doth tye
With his milde-sweet Majestie :
Though the silver Moone be faine
Still by night to mount her waine,
Fearing to sustain disgrace,
If by day shee meet thy face.

'Tis not that soft Sattin limme,
With blew trayles enameld trimme,
Thy hand, handle of perfection,
Keeps my thoughts in thy subjection :
Though it have such curious cunning,
Gentle touch, and nimble running,
That on Lute to heare it warble,
Would move rocks, and ravish Marble.

'Tis not all the rest beside,
Which thy modest vaile doth hide
From mine eyes (ah too injurious !)
Makes mee of thy love so curious :
Though *Diana* being bare,
Nor *Leucothoë* passing rare,
In the Crystall-flowing springs
Never bath'd so beauteous things.

What then (O divinest Dame)
Fires my Soule with burning flame,
If thine eyes be not the matches
Whence my kindling Taper catches ?
And what *Nectar* from above
Feeds and feasts my joyes (my Love)
If they taste not of the dainties
Of thy sweet lips' sugred plenties ?

What fell heat of covetize
In my feeble bosome fries ;
If my heart no reckoning hold
Of thy tresses' purest gold ?
What inestimable treasure
Can procure me greater pleasure
Then those Orient Pearles I see
When thou daign'st to smile on me ?

47

What ? what fruit of life delights
  My delicious appetites
  If I over-passe the nests
  Of those apples of thy brests?
What fresh Buds of scarlet Rose
Are more fragrant sweet then those,
Then those Twins thy Straw-berry teats,
  Curled-purled Cherrylets?

What (to finish) fairer limne,
  Or what member yet more trimme,
  Or what other rather Subject
  Makes me make thee all mine object ?
If it be not all the rest
By thy modest vaile supprest ;
(Rather) which an envious cloud
  From my sight doth closely shroud.

Ah 'tis a thing more divine,
  'Tis that peere-lesse Soule of thine,
  Master-peece of Heav'n's best Art,
  Made to maze each mortall heart.
'Tis thine all-admired wit,
Thy sweet grace and gesture fit,
Thy milde pleasing courtesie
  Makes thee triumph over mee.

But, for thy fair Soule's respect,
  I love Twin-flames that reflect
  From thy bright tra-lucent eyes :
  And thy yellow locks likewise :
And those Orient-Pearly Rocks :
Which thy lightning smile un-locks :
And the *Nectar*-passing blisses
  Of thy honey-sweeter kisses.

I love thy fresh rosie cheek,
  Blushing most *Aurora*-like :
  And the white-exceeding skin
  Of thy neck and dimpled chin,
And those Ivorie-marble mounts
Either, neither, both at once :
For, I dare not touch to know
  If they be of flesh or no.

I love thy pure Lilly hand
  Soft and smooth, and slender : and
  Those five nimble brethren small
  Arm'd with Pearl-shell helmets all.
I love also all the rest
By thy modest vaile supprest ;
(Rather) which an envious cloud
  From my longing sight doth shroud.

FINIS.

SONNET 1.

SWeet mouth, that sendst a muskie-rosed breath ;
  Fountain of *Nectar*, and delightfull Balm ;
  Eyes cloudy-clear, smile-frowning, stormy-calm ;
  Whose every glance darts mee a living-death :
Brows, bending quaintly your round Ebene Arks :
  Smile, that then *Venus* sooner *Mars* besots ;
  Locks more then golden, curl'd in curious knots,
  Where, in close ambush, wanton *Cupid* lurks :
Grace Angel-like ; fair fore-head, smooth, and high ;
  Pure white, that dimm'st the Lillies of the
    Vale ;
  Vermilion Rose, that mak'st *Aurora* pale,
Rare spirit, to rule this beautie's Emperie :
  If in your force, Divine effects I view,
  Ah, who can blame me, if I worship you ?

SONNET 2.

Thou, whose sweet eloquence doth make me mute ;
  Whose sight doth blind me, & whose nimbleness
  Of feet in dance, and fingers on the Lute,
  In deep amazes makes mee motion-lesse :
Whose only presence from my selfe absents mee ;
  Whose pleasant humors, makes mee passionate ;
  Whose sober moods my follies represent mee ;
  Whose grave-milde graces make mee emulate ;
My heart, through whom my heart is none of mine ;
  My All, through whom, I nothing doe possesse,
  Save thine *Idæa*, glorious and divine :
O thou my Peace-like War, and War-like PEACE,
  So much the wounds that thou hast given mee
    please,
  That 'tis my best ease never to have ease.

EPIGRAMS

AND

EPITAPHES

UPON

Warre and Peace.

Upon the League.

FRance, without cause thou dost complaine
    Against the *League* for wronging thee.
Sh' hath made thee large amends again,
With more then common usurie :
For, for thy one King which shee slew,
Sh' hath giv'n thee now a thousand new.

Upon the taking of Paris.

1

When *Paris* (happily) was wonne
    With small or no endangering,
    Such sudden common joy begunne,
    That one would say (t' have seen the thing)
Th' King took not *Paris, Paris* took the King.

2

O rarest sight of joyfull woe,
    Adorned with delightfull dread ;
    When *Henrie* with one self-same show,
    Conquer'd at once and triumphed !

3

Sith thee from danger and distresse to free,
The King thus took, or rather entred thee ;
Paris, it was not in stern *Mars* his Month,
But in the month that milde ASTRÆA own'th.

Upon the fall of the Millar's bridge.

1

The Millars, in the River drown'd,
    While *Paris* was beleaguerd round ;
    To dye were all resolv'd in minde,
    Because they had no more to grinde.

2

Then was their fittest time to dye,
    Because they might intend it best :

But their intent was contrarie,
    Because they then liv'd so at rest.

3

As, after long sharp famine, some (forlorn)
Of surfet Die, their greedinesse is such :
This Mill-bridge, having fasted long from Corn,
Is drown'd (perhaps) for having ground too-much.

Upon the recoverie of Amiens.

1

I know not which may seem most admirable,
To take or re-take such a Citie's force :
But, yet I know which is most honourable,
To take by fraud, or to re-take by force.

2

Eachwhere they sing a thousand wayes
    The glory of this enterprise,
    But yet of all their merry Layes,
    The best is still in the Re-prise.

3

Hernand was happy by this Enterprise,
To take so soon our *Amiens* without blow :
More happy yet, to dye yer the Reprise,
Else had he dy'd for shame to leave it so.

Upon the Reduction of Nantes.

Nantes would not yeeld so soon (they sayd)
Nor be recovered so good cheap :
And yet, for all defence it made,
'T was made to make the *Britton* Leap.

Upon PEACE.

1

Souldiers, late prest, are now supprest :
Crost and cashierd from further pay :
Yet will they (in this time of rest)
Take up their lendings by the Way.

2

This PEACE (it seemeth) doth not sound
To all the world ; for, every-where
More Sergeants now doe goe the Round
Then Souldiers yerst accustom'd were.

Upon Captaine Cobler.

A merry Cobler left the Wars,
To turn unto his Occupation :
And, asked by his Customers
The reason of his alteration :
'T hath pleas'd (quoth hee) the King t' ordain
That each his office take again.

Upon Warre.

Here, under this huge heap of stones
Lately enterr'd lyes cruell WARRE :
Pray God long rest her soule and bones :
Yet there is nothing worse for her.

Upon Rowland Rob-Church.

Here lyeth *Rowland*, that was lately slaine,
In robbing of a wealthie Chappell, spy'd :
Yet I beleeve he doth in Heav'n remain,
Sith onely for the Churche's Good hee dy'd.

Upon Captaine Catch.

Here under, Captain CATCH is layd,
Who six times chang'd from side to side :
Of neither side (it seem'd) affraid.
He wore a white Scarfe when hee dy'd :
Yet some suspect (and so doe I)
For his inconstance shown before,
That to the Black-band hee did fly :
But now he can revolt no more.

Upon Sir Nequam Neuter.

Here lyeth hee, who the more safe to prey
On both sides ; *Neuter*, between both abode :
Whither his Soule is gone, I cannot say,
Sith hee was not for Divell, nor for God.

Pax omnibus una.

FINIS.

A l'honeur de la Paix, chantee par
Monsieur du NESME, & rechantee en
Anglois par Monsieur
SYLVESTRE.

S*Ans Paix rien ne subsiste : en Paix tout croist & dure :*
  Dieu maintient par sa Paix le beau Grand Univers
  Et le Petit, bastis de membres si divers,
  Touts s'entr'aydans l'un l'autre en commune facture :
Elle unit a son Dieu l'humaine creature :
  Elle emplit de Citez les Royaumes deserts :
  Elle bride les fols, & rend les champs couverts
  De biens donans plaisirs, vesture, & nouriture.
Envoy-la donc (O Dieu) à nos Princes & Roys,
  En nos maisons, en nous ; & fay que de une voix
  Nous suivions les accords de ton Nesme admirable :
Lors (à jamais) seras loûé de nos Gaulois
  Par ses chants tout-divins : & Sylvestre, en Anglois
  Redoublera ce loz d'un stile inimitable.

R. CATELLE.
I'attens le temps.

THE

PROFIT OF

IMPRISONMENT.

A PARADOX,

WRITTEN IN FRENCH

BY

Odet de la Nove, Lord of *Teligni,* being
Prisoner in the Castle of
TOURNEY

Translated

BY

JOSUAH SYLVESTER.

Acceptam refero.

TO HIS LONG
APPROVED FRIEND,

M. R. Nicolson,

J. S.

Wisheth

Ever all true Content.

TO thee (*the same to mee as first I meant*)
   Friend to the Muses, and the well-inclin'd,
Loving, and lov'd of every vertuous minde :
To thee the same, I the same Song present
(*Our mutuall love's eternall Monument*)
   Wherein, our Nephews shall here-after finde
   Our constant friendship how it was combinde
   With linkes of kindnesse and acknowledgment.
Accept againe this Present in good part,
   This simple pledge of my sincere affection
   To Tangley *Thee, and thy* Soon-calm-in-heart
(*Perfect good-will supplies all imperfection*).
   Chameleons *change their colour ;* Guile *her game :*
   But (*in both* Fortunes) *Vertue's still the same.*

A SONNET OF
The
AUTHOUR TO
HIS BOOK.

THe Bodie *over-prone to* Pleasures *and delights*
   Of soft, fraile, dainty flesh, *and to selfe-*ease *addicted,*
   Abhors Imprisonment, *as a base paine inflicted*
   To punish the defaults of most unhappy wights.
The Soule, *as much surpriz'd with love of heav'nly sights,*
   And longing to behold the place that appertains-her,
   Doth loath the Bodie, *as a* Prison *that detaines-her*
   From her high happinesse *among the blessed sprights.*
Then sith both Bodie *and* Soule *their bondage never brook,*
   But Soule *and* Bodie *both doe love their* libertie :
   Tell, tell me (*O my Muse*) *who will beleeve our Book ?*
Hee that hath learn'd a-right both these to mortifie,
   And serve our Saviour Christ *in* bodie *and in* spirit,
   Who both from thrall *hath* freed *by his owne onely merit.*

A PARADOX,

That Adverſitie is more neceſſarie

Than Prosperitie ; and that, of all Afflictions, Close-
Prison is most pleasant, and most
Profitable.

Ow-ever fondly-false a vaine Opinion seeme ;
If but the Vulgar once the same for right esteem,
Most men account it so : so (in absurdest things)
Consent of Multitude exceeding credit brings.
Nor any mean remaines when it is once received,
To wrest it from the most of erring mindes deceived.
Nay, whoso shall but say, they ought to alter it,
Hee headlong casts himselfe in danger's deepest Pit.
    For never nimble Barke that on adventure runs
Through those blew bounding Hils where hoary *Neptune* wuns,
Was set upon so sore with never-ceast assault,
Maintain'd on every side by winds, and waters salt,
When, raging most, they raise their roughest tempest dreaded ;
As th' Idiot Multitude, that Monster many-headed
Bestirs it selfe, with wrath, spight, furie, full of terror,
'Gainst whatsoever man that dares reprove her error.
Who undertakes that taske, must make account (at first)
To take hot Wars in hand, and beare away the worst.
Therefore a many Works (worthy the light) have dyed
Before their Birth, in breasts of Fathers terrified,
Not by rough deeds alone ; but even by foolish threats :
Yet onely noise of words base cowards onely beats.
    Then feare who list (for mee) the common Peoples cry,
And whoso list be mute, if other minded : I
(Scorning the feeble force of such a vain indeavour)
Will freely (spight of feare) say, what I censure ever :
And, though my present State permit mee not such scope,
Mine un-forbidden pen with Error's pride shall cope.
Close Prison (now a-daies) th' extremest miserie
The world doth deem, I deem direct the contrarie :
And there-with-all will prove, that even *Adversities*
Are to be wished more than most Prosperities.
And, for *Imprisonment*, though that be most lamented,
Of all the griefes wherewith men feare to be tormented ;

Yet, that 's the State most stor'd with pleasure and delight,
And the most gainfull too, to any Christian wight.
A *Paradox*, no doubt more true, than creditable ;
The which my selfe sometimes have also thought a fable,
While guilefull vanities, fed not, but fill'd my minde,
For strengthning sustenance, with un-substantiall winde.
    I hated Death to death, I also did detest
All sicknesse and disease that might a man molest,
But most I did abhorre that base esteemed state,
Which to subjection's Law our selves doth subjugate,
And our sweet life enthrals unto another's will :
For, as my fancy wisht I would have walked still.
Death (thought I) soon hath done, and every griefe besides,
The more extreme it is, the lesser time abides :
But now, besides that I esteem'd the Prisoners' trouble
Much worse, me thought the time his martyrdom did double.
So that, to scape that scourge, so irksome to my heart,
I could have been content t' have suffer'd any smart.
    Lo, by blinde ignorance how judgments are mis-led ;
Now that full thirty months I have experienced
That so-much-feared ill, 'tis now so us'd to mee,
That I (a Prisoner) live much more content and free,
Then when as (under cloak of a false freedome vain)
I was base slave (indeed) to many a bitter pain.
    But now I see my selfe mockt every-where almost,
And feeble mee alone met by a mighty hoast
Of such, as (in this case) do not conceive as I,
But do esteem themselves offended much thereby.
    And therefore (Father dear) this weak abortive Childe,
For refuge runs between th' arms of his Grand-sire milde.
If you accept of it, my labour hath his hire :
For, carelesse of the rest, all that I here desire,
Is onely that your selfe (as in a Glasse) may see
The image of the estate of my Captivity :
Where, though I nothing can availe the Common-weale,
Yet I availe my selfe (at least) some little deale ;

Praysing th' all powerfull Lord, that thus vouchsafes to poure
Such favours manifold upon mee every houre ;
Whereof, your self (yer while) so sweet sure proof have tasted ;
In cruell bitternesse of bands that longer lasted :
Now, I beseech his Grace to blesse mine enterprise,
My heart and hand at once to governe in such wise,
That what I write, may nought displeasing him containe :
For voyd of his sweet ayde, who works he works in vaine.
Within the wide-spred space of these round elements,
What-ever is indu'd with living soule and sense,
Seeks (of it selfe) selfe-good ; this instinct naturall
Nature her selfe hath graven in hearts of Creatures all :
And of all living things (from largest to the least)
Each one to flie his ill doth evermore his best.
Thereof it comes (wee see) the wilde horse (full of strength)
Tamely to take the bit into his mouth at length ;
And so, by force wee tame each most untamed beast,
Which, of it selfe, discreet, of evils takes the least :
And though that that which seemes to be his chiefe restraint
Hee often-times despise, that 's by a worse constraint :
As, when the Lion fierce, fear-lesse pursues the shining
Of bright keen-piercing blades, and 's royall crest declining,
Full of the valiant fire, that courage woonts to lend,
Runnes midst a million swords, his whelpings to defend ;
More fearing far that they their liberty should lose,
Then on himself the smart of thousand wounding blowes.
　But, all things have not now the selfe same goods and ils ;
What helpeth one, the same another hurts and kils :
There 's ods between the good that savage Beasts doe like,
And that good (good indeed) wch soul-wise man must seek :
When Beasts have store of food ; and free from foes annoy,
Smartlesse, and sound, and safe, may (as they list) injoy
Their fill of those delights, that most delight the sense ;
That, that 's the happinesse that fully them contents :
But reasonable soules (as God hath made Mankinde)
Can with so wretched good not satisfie their minde.
But, by how much the more their inly sight excels
The brutish appetite of every Creature else,
So much more excellent the good for which they thirst.
Man of two parts is made : the body is the worst,
The Heav'n-born soule the best, wherein man's blisse abides ;
In body that of beasts, nought having else besides ;
This body stands in need of many an accessorie,
To make it somewhat seem : the soule receives this glory,
That selfly shee subsists, and her aboundant wealth
(Unlike the bodie's store) is ever safe from stealth.
　Our body took his birth of this terrestriall clod :
Our spirit, it was inspir'd of th' inly breath of God ;
And either of them still strives to his proper place,
This (earth-born) stoops to Earth ; that flies to Heav'n apace.
But, as the silly Bird, whose wings are wrapt in lime,
Faine, but in vaine, attempts to fly full many a time :
So, our faire soule, surcharg'd with this foule robe of mud,
Is too-too often held from mounting to her GOOD.
Shee strives, shee strikes, somtimes shee lifts her up aloft :
But as the worser part (wee see) prevaileth oft,

This false fraile flesh of ours, with pleasure's painted lure,
Straight makes her stoop againe down to the dust impure.
　Happy who th' honour hath of such a victorie :
Hee crowns his conquering head with more true Majestie
Then if hee had subdu'd those Nations by his might,
Which doe discover first *Aurora's* early light,
And those whom *Phœbus* sees from his *Meridian* Mount,
Th' *Anti-podes*, and all ; more then the sand to count.
For, small the honour is to be acknowledg'd King
And Monark of the World, one's self un-mastering.
　But, each man on his head this Garland cannot set,
Nor is it giv'n to all this victorie to get.
Onely a very few (God's deare belov'd Elect)
This happy Goale have got by Vertue's live effect :
The rest, soon wearie of this same so painfull War,
Like well of Heav'n, but love the Earth above it far :
Some drunk with pois'ny dregs of worldly pleasure's brute,
Know where true good consists, but never doe ensue 't :
Some doe ensue the same, but with so faint a heart,
(That at the first assault they doe retire and start :)
Some, more courageous, vow more then they bring to passe
(So much more easie 'tis to say, then doe, alas) ;
And all, through too-much love of this vain world's allurements :
Or too-much idle feare of sufferings and endurements :
Meere vanities, whereto the more men doe incline,
The farther-off they are from their *chiefe good* divine.
　Therefore so many thinke themselves so miserable :
Therefore the ayre is fill'd with out-cries lamentable
Of such as doe disdaine the thing that better is,
To entertaine the worse, with forfeit of their blisse :
Therefore wee see those men that riches doe possesse,
Afflicted still with care : and therefore heavinesse
Abandons never those, that, fed with honour's fill,
Fawn upon Potentates, for flitting favours still.
And cause (God wot) they have, to be at quiet never,
Sith their felicitie is so uncertaine ever.
Neither are Kings themselves exempted from vexation,
How-ever Soveraigne sway they bear in any Nation :
For, now they wish to win, anon feare losse no lesse.
Yea, though (for Empire) they did this wide world possesse,
Not one of them, withall, could full contented be :
For, how man more attaines, the more attempteth hee.
Who, therefore, covets most such soon-past goods uncertain,
Shall n'er enjoy the joy of goods abiding certaine :
But, whoso seeks to build a true content, to last :
On else-what must else-where his first foundation cast
For, all here below are apt to alter ever ;
Here 's nothing permanent : and therefore whosoever
Trusts thereto, trusteth to a broken staffe for stay ;
For no earth's vanitie can blesse a man for aye.
Wee must (to make us blest) our firme assurance found
Else-where then in this World, this change-inthralled ground :
Wee must propose our selves that perfect, perish-lesse,
That true unfained good, that good all danger-lesse
From th' unjust spoyle of theeves, which never, never stands
In need of guard, to guard from Souldiers' pilling hands.

Now, 'tis with spirituall hands, and not with corporall,
That wee doe apprehend these Heav'nly treasures all :
Treasures so precious, that th' onely hope to have-them
In full fruition once, with him that frankly gave-them
Fils us with every joy, our sorrows choaks and kils,
And makes us feele, amid our most tormenting ills,
A much more calme content, then those that every day
On this fraile earth enjoy their heart's wish every way.   190
It 's therefore in the spirit, not in the flesh that wee
Must seek our *Soveraigne Good* and chiefe felicitie.
Th' one is not capable of any injury :
The other 's thrall to th' yoke of many a miserie :
Th' one end-lesse, ever-lasts : th' other endures so little,
That wel-nigh yer 't be got, 'tis gone, it is so brittle.
For, who is hee that now in wealth aboundeth most,
Or, hee that in the court Kings' favours best may boast,
Or, hee that 's most with roabes of dignitie bedight,
Or, hee that swimmes on Seas of sensuall sweet delight, 200
But is in perill still to prove the contrarie,
Poore, hated, honour-lesse, and full of miserie?
But, one, that scorning all these rich proud pomps &
    pleasures
About him, *Bias*-like, beares alwayes all his treasures,
Ev'n, like to him, can leave his native Countrey sackt
Without sustaine of losse ; and, with a mind infract,
Ev'n vanquished bereave the Victor's victories,
Who, though his Land he win, cannot his heart surprise.
Let exile, prisonment, and tortures great and small,
With their extremest paines at-once assaile him all :   210
Let him be left alone among his mighty foes,
Poore, friendlesse, naked, sick (or if ought worse then
    those)
Hee doth not onely beare all this with patience,
But taketh (even) delight in such experience,
Regarding all these griefes, which men so much affright,
As Baby-fearing buggs, and scar-crowes voyd of might :
Hee chooseth rather much such excercise as these,
Then mid the flesh-delights to rust in idle ease.
But, verie few there are, that thus much will admit :
Nay, few or none there are that eas'ly credit it ;   220
The most part, taking-part with common most conceit,
Yet they have heard of this, sustaine the tother straight :
Not seeking, that themselves shun and refuse as ill,
What unto other men, for good they offer still.
Not one of them will brook his Son in sloath to lurk,
But moves and stirs him up incessantly to work :
Forbids him nothing more than sin-seed idlenesse :
Nor any pleasure vaine permits him to possesse
(For well hee knows, that way to vertue doth not lead, 229
But thither-ward who walks, a path of paine must tread) :
If hee offend in ought, he chastens and reproves him,
In so much sharper sort by how much more hee loves him.
Thus handleth man the thing that most hee holdeth
    dear,
Yet thinks it strange himselfe should be so handled here.
May we not rather think wee are belov'd of God,
When as wee feele the stripes of his just gentle rod ?
And that, whom here hee lets live as they list in pleasure,
Are such as least hee loves, and holds not as his treasure ?

For so, not of our slaves, but of our sonnes elect,
By sharp-sweet chastisements the manners wee correct. 240
In very deed, God doth as doth a prudent Sire,
Who little careth what may crosse his child's desire,
But what may most availe unto his betterment :
So, knowing well that ease would make us negligent,
Hee exercises us, hee stirs us up, and presses :
And, though wee murmur much, yet never more hee ceases,
Hee chastens, hee afflicts : and those whom most he
    striketh,
Are those whom most he loves, and whom he chiefly liketh.
No valiant men of warre will murmur or mislike,
For being plac't to prove the formost push of pike :   250
Nay, rather would they there already front the foe,
With losse of dearest bloud, their dauntlesse hearts to
    show.
If any exploit approach, or Battell-day draw nigh,
If ambush must be laid, some stratagem to trie ;
Or, must they meet the foe in eager skirmish fell,
Or for the sleepy hoast all night keep sentinell :
From grudging at the paines, so far off are they all,
That blest they count themselves ; therefore their Generall
Imployes them often-times, as most courageous ;
And, them approv'd, he plants in places dangerous :   260
But, no man makes account of such as shun the charge
Whose pain is not so small as their discredit 's large.
All of us (in this world) resemble Souldiers right,
From day-break of our birth even to our dying night :
This life it is a war wherein the valiantest,
With hottest skirmishes are ever ply'd and prest :
Whom our grand-captaine most sets-by, hee sets a-frunt
The foreward, as most fit to beare the chiefest brunt.
Cares, exiles, prisonments, diseases, dolours, losses,
Maimes, tortures, torments, spoiles, contempt, dishonors,
    crosses,   270
All these are hard exploits, and full of bickrings bold,
Which hee commits to those whom hee doth dearest hold :
But, leaveth those behinde for whom hee careth little,
To stretch themselves at ease amid their honours brittle,
Their pomps, their dignities, their joyes, their gems, their
    treasures,
Their dainties, their delights, their pastimes, and their
    pleasures ;
Like coward Groomes that guard the baggage and the
    stuffe,
While others meet the foe, and shew their valour's proofe.
But have not these (say some) in these afflictions part ?
No ; but of punishment they often feele the smart.   280
Afflicted those we count, whom chastenings tame, and
    turne ;
The other punished, that at correction spurne :
The first (still full of hope) reape profit by their rods ;
The latter (desperate) through spight wex worse by ods.
Boy-stragglers of a Camp, so should be punisht then,
Being naked forc't to fight with troupes of armed men,
Who cannot reap nor reach the pleasure, nor the meed,
Nor th' honour incident for doing such a deed :
To such praise-winning place, brave Souldiers gladly run
Which as a dangerous place these faint-hearts sadly shun

What Warriour in the world, that had not rather try 291
A million of extremes (yea rather even to die)
Than with disgracefull spot to stain his Honour bright
In these corporeall Wars?   Yet in the ghostly fight
(Of glorie carelesse all) wee shun all labour's pain,
To purchase with reproach a rest-nest idly-vain.
Vertue is not atchiev'd by spending of the year
In pleasure soft, sweet shades, doun-beds, and dainty
     cheare:
Continuall travell 'tis that makes us there arrive,
And so by travell too, Vertue is kept alive: 300
For, soon all Vertue vades without some exercise;
But being stirr'd, the more her vigour multiplies.
     Besides what man is hee, that feels some member rotten,
Whereof he feares to die, but causeth straight be gotten
Some Surgeon, that with sawe, with cauter, or with knife,
May take that part away, to save his threatned life:
And suffers (though with smart) his very flesh and bones
To be both sear'd, and saw'd, and clean cut-off at once?
But to recure the soule (the soule with sin infected)
All wholesome remedies are hated and rejected: 310
With the Physician kinde th' impatient Patient frets,
Nor to come neere him once his helpfull hand hee lets:
Wee are halfe putrefied, through sin's contagious spot,
And without speedie help the rest must wholly rot:
Cut-off th' infected part, then are wee sound and free,
Else all must perish needs, there is no remedie.
     Most happy they, from whom in this fraile life, the
          Lord
(With smart of many paines) cuts-off the paines abhord
Of th' ever-never death, wherein they lye and languish,
That here have had their ease and never tasted anguish. 320
     But many, which as yet the adverse part approve,
Conceive (if not confesse) that it doth more behoove
By faintlesse exercise faire Vertue to maintaine,
Than over-whelm'd with Vice, at rest to rust in vaine.
But yet th' extremitie of suffrings doth dismay-them,
The force whereof they feare would eas'ly over-lay-them:
They love the exercise, the chastnings likewise like them,
But yet they would have God but seld' and softly strike-
     them;
Else are they prest to run, to ruine, with the Divels,
They are so sore afeard of false supposed evils: 330
Most wretched is the man that for the feare of nifles,
All lively-breathing hopes of happie goodnesse stifles.
Of nifles, Sir, say they? seeme all their bitter crosses,
As nothing? nor their paines, nor lamentable losses,
That daily they endure? were not the wretches blest,
If from their heavie loade their shoulders were releast?
     Who is not happy (sure) in miserie and woe,
No doubt prosperitie can never make him so:
No more than hee that 's sick should finde more ease upon
A glorious golden bed, than on a wooden one.   340
Man harbours in himselfe the evill that afflicts-him,
And his own fault it is, if discontentment pricks-him:
And all these outward ills are wrongfully accused,
Which flesh and bloud doth blame; for, being rightly used,
They all turn to our good: but whoso takes offence
Thereby, hath by and by his just rough recompence:

For neither in their power, nor in their proof the same
Are evils in effect, but in conceit and name:
Which when we lightly weigh, the least of us surmounts them,
Nor hurt they any one, but him that over-counts them. 350
     Neither ought that (indeed) for evill to be rated,
Which may by accident be unto good translated:
For ill is ever ill, and is contrarie ever
Directly unto good, so that their natures never
Can be constrain'd to brook each other, neither yet
Can th' one be ever turn'd to th' other opposite:
But, plainly wee perceive, that there 's no languor such,
But long continuance and custome lighten much;
Familiarizing so the Fit, that how-so fret it,
Ev'n in the extremitie one may almost forget it.   360
What better proofe of this then these poore Gally-slaves,
Which, having been before such Rogues and idle Knaves,
As shunning services to labour were so loth,
That they would starve and die rather then leave their
     sloth;
But being us'd a while to tug the painfull Oare,
Labour that yerst they loath'd, they now desire the more:
Or those that are assail'd with burning fever-fit,
Ev'n then when least of all they dread or doubt of it:
Who carefully complaine, and cry, and rave, and rage,
Frying in inward flames, the which they cannot swage; 370
Yet, if it wex not worse, the daintiest bodie makes it:
In eight dayes as a Use, and as a trifle takes it:
Or, those that have somtimes the painfull rack indured,
Who without charge of paine being a while inured,
The paine that did constraine them to bewaile and weepe,
Seemes them so easie then, they almost fall a-sleepe.
     All are not evils then, that are surnamed so,
Sith evill never can his nature mingle, no;
Nor turne it into good; whereas wee plainly see
On th' other side, that these are changed suddenly.   380
And, were they ills (indeed) sith they so little last,
Were 't not a very shame to be so much agast?
     But here again (say they) th' one's nature never taketh
The other's nature on, but still the stronger maketh
His fellow give him place, and onely beareth sway
Till that, return'd againe, drive it againe away.
     Nay, that can never be: for never perfect good
Can by his contrary be banisht (though withstood):
For, good is ever good, and wheresoe'r it goe
Evill doth ever strive, but with too strong a foe.   390
There is no reason then, these, good, or ill to call,
That alter in this sort, and never rest at all:
Neither to blesse or blame them for the good or ill
That ever in her selfe our soule concealeth still.
     For, if that from without, our bale, or else our blisse
Arrived; evermore withall must follow this,
That alwayes, unto all, selfe ill, selfe paine, would bring:
Selfe good, one selfe content: but 'tis a certaine thing,
They are not taken for their qualitie and kinde
But rather as th' effects of men are most inclin'd.   400
     One, losing but a Crown, hath lost his patience quite:
Another having lost five hundred in a night,
Is never mov'd a jot, though (having lesse in store,
Then th' other hath by ods) his losse might grieve him more.

One, being banished, doth nothing but lament,
Another (as at home) is there as well content.
And, one in prison pent, is utterly dismay'd :
Another, as at home, lives there as well appaid.

    Needs must wee then confesse, that in our selves doth
        rest   409
That which unhappieth us, and that which makes us blest :
In us (indeed) the ill, which of our selves doth grow ;
And in us too the good, which from God's grace doth
    flow,
To whom it pleaseth him : true good that none can owe-yet,
Save those on whom the Lord vouchsafeth to bestow-it :
And that the bitter smart of all the paines that wring-us,
From nothing but our sin, receiveth strength to sting-us,

    Yea, surely in our selves abides our miserie :
Our Grand-sire *Adam* left us that for legacie,
When hee enthrall'd himselfe unto the Law of sinne,
Wherein his guiltie heires their griefe-full birth begin.   420

    The Lord had giv'n to him a nature and a feature,
Perfect, indeed, and blest above all other creature :
And of this Earthly world had stablisht him as King,
Subjecting to his rule the reanes of every thing :
His spirit within it selfe no selfe-debates did nurse,
Having no knowledge yet of better nor of worse :
His body ever blithe and healthfull felt no war
Of those foure qualities that now doe ever jar :
Nor any pois'nie plant, nor any Serpent fell,
Nor any noysom beast could hurt him any deale :   430
Hee might, without the taste of bitter death attaine
Unto the haven of Heav'n, where all true Joyes doe raigne.
And, had hee not misdone, hee might have well bequeath'd
The same inheritance to all that ever breath'd :
How happy had hee been, if hee had never eaten
Th' unlawfull fatall Fruit that double death did threaten ?
O that hee never had prefer'd the Serpent's flatter
Before th' eternall Law of all the World's Creator.

    You shall bee (said the Fiend) like supreme Deities :
This sweet fruit's sugred juice shall open both your eyes 440
Which now your tyrant God (envying all your blisse)
Blinds with a filmie vaile of black Obscurities,
Lest that you should become his equals in degree,
Knowing both good and ill, as well as ever hee.

    Poore *Eve* beleeves him straight, and Man beleeves his
        Wife,
And biteth by and by the apple asking-life :
Whereof so soon as hee had tasted, hee begins
(But all too-late alas) to see his cursed sinnes.

    His eyes (indeed) were ope, and then hee had the skill
To know the difference between the good and ill :   450
Then did hee know how good, good was when hee had
    lost-it,
And evill too hee knew (but ah too dearly cost-it)
Leaving himselfe (besides the sorrow of his losse)
Nothing but sad despaire of succour in his crosse.

    Hee found himselfe falne down from blisse-full state of
        peace
Into a civill warre where discords never cease :
His soule revolting, soon became his bitter foe.
But (as it oft befals that worst doe strongest grow)

Shee is not eas'd at all by th' inly striving jarres,
Which doe annoy her more then th' irefull open warres. 460
Wrath, hatred, envie, feare, sorrow, despaire, and such ;
And passions opposite to these, afflict as much,
Distracting to and fro the Princesse of his life,
In restlesse mutinies, and never-ceasing strife.
Then th' humor-brethren all, hot, cold, and wet, and dry,
Falne out among themselves, augment his miserie.
So that (by their debate) within his flesh there seeded
A harvest of such weeds as never can be weeded.
All creatures that before (as Subjects) did attend him,
Now, 'mong themselves conspire by all meanes to offend
    him :   470
In briefe, Immortall borne, now mortall hee became,
And bound his soule to bide Hel's ever-burning flame,
Leaving his wofull heires (even from their birth's beginning)
Heires of his heavie paine, as of his hainous sinning.

    So that, in him, the Lord condemned all mankinde,
To beare the punishment to his foule sinne assign'd :
And none had ever scapt had not the God of grace
(Desiring more to save, then to subvert his race)
Redeem'd us by the death of his deare onely Sonne,
And chosen us in him before the world begun :   480
Forgiving us the fault, and with the fault the fine ;
All save this temporall death, of *Adam's* sinne the signe.

    Now in the horror of those ease-lesse, end-lesse paines,
It may be rightly said, that evill ever reignes :
That's evill's very selfe ; and not this seeming-woe,
Whereof the wanton world complaineth daily so.

    Liv'd wee ten thousand yeares continually tormented
In all fell tortures strange that ever were invented,
What's that compar'd to time that never shall expire,
Amid th' infernall flames, whose least-afflicting fire   490
Exceedeth all the paines, all mortall hearts can think ?
Sure, all that wee endure, till *Lethé* drops wee drink,
Is all but ease to that : or if it be a paine,
'Tis in respect of that a very trifle vaine.

    But, were't a great deale worse, why should wee evill
        name
That which wee rather finde a med'cine for the same ?
Health, wealth, securitie, honour and ease doe make us
Forget our God, and God for that doth soone forsake us ;
Whereas afflictions are ready meanes to move us,
To seek our health in him that doth so dearly love-us. 500

    'Tis true indeed : (say some) that benefit they bring-us,
But yet the smart thereof doth so extremely wring-us,
That th' evill which they feele that doe indure the same,
Makes them esteeme it just to give it that for name.

    Man's nature, certainly (it cannot be deni'd)
Is thrall to many throes, while here on earth wee bide
In body and in soule : the troubled soule sustaines
A thousand passions strong, the bodie thousand paines :
And that's the wretched State, the which yer-while I
    said,
Was justly due to us, when *Adam* disobay'd.   510

    But, hee that's once new-borne in Jesus Christ by faith,
Who his assured hope in God sole settled hath,
Who doth beleeve that God gives essence unto all ;
And all sustaineth still : that nothing doth befall

But by his sacred will, and that no strength that striveth
To stop his just decrees, can stand, or ever thriveth ;
Not onely doth accept all paines with patience,
The which hee takes for due unto his deep offence :
Nor onely is content (if such be God's good pleasure)
To feele a thousand-fold a much more ample measure, 520
But even delights therein ; and voyd of any feare,
Expects th' extremitie of all assaults to beare :
Whether almightie God abate their wonted vigor
Or (that his may not feele their crosses' cruell rigor)
Doe wholly arme them with new forces for the nonce,
To beare the bitter brunt : or whether both at once.
    And, to approve this true ; how many daily drink
Of torment's bitter Cup, that never seem to shrink ?
Alas, what sharper smart ? what more afflicting paines ? 529
What worser griefe then that, which eas-lessly sustaines ?
Hee that by some mischance, or else by martiall thunder,
Unhappily hath had some maine bone broke in sunder ?
What torment feeleth not the sore-sick deep-diseased ?
One while with cruell fit of burning Fever seised :
Another while assail'd with Cholick and with Stone,
Or with the cure-lesse Gout, whose rigour yeelds to none ?
Or thousand other griefes, whose bitter-vexing strife
Disturbs continually the quiet of our life ?
Yet notwithstanding this, in all this painfull anguish
(Though the most part repine, and plain, and mourn, &
    languish,   540
Murmuring 'gainst the Lord, with male-contented voyce)
Some prayse his clemencie, and in his rods rejoyce.
    How many such (deare Saints) have fell tormentors seene
To die between their hands, through moodie tyrants' teen,
So little daunted at their martyrdome and slaughter,
That in th' extremitie they have expressed laughter ?
How many at the stake, nay, in the very flame,
Have sung, with cheerfull voyce, th' Almightie's praise-full
    name ?
Yet were they all compact of artirs and of veines,
Of sinnews, bones, and flesh : and sensible of paines 550
(By nature at the least) as much as any other,
For being issued all from one selfe earthly mother.
    What makes them then to finde such extreme smart so
    sweet ?
What makes them patiently those deadly pangs to meet ?
No doubt it is the Lord, who first of nothing made-us,
Who with his liberall hand of goodnesse still doth lade-us,
Some more and other lesse : and never ceaseth space
From making us to feele the favours of his grace.
Accurst are they (indeed) whom hee doth all abandon
To doe their Lust for Law, and run their life at randon : 560
Accurst who never taste the sharp-sweet hand of God :
Accurst (ah, most accurst) who never feele his rod.
Such men (by nature born the bond-slaves unto sin)
Through selfe-corruption, end worse then they did begin :
For, how they longer live, the more by their amisse,
They draw them nearer Hell, and farther off from blisse.
Such men within themselves their evil's spring containe :
There is no outward thing (as falsly they complaine)
Cause of their cure-lesse ill : for good is every thing,
And good can (of it selfe) to no-man evill bring.   570

    Now, if they could aright these earthly pleasures prize
According to their worth, they would not in such wise,
For lack, or losse of these (so vaine and transitorie)
Lament so bitterly, nor be so sadly sorrie.
But over-loving still these outward things unstable,
To rest in true content an houre they are not able,
No, not a moment's time, their feare doth so assaile them :
And, if their feare fall true, that their *good-fortune* faile them,
Then swell their sullen hearts with sorrow till they burst,
And then (poor desperate soules) they deem themselves
    accurst ;   580
And so (indeed) they are : but yet they erre in this,
In blaming other things, for their owne selfe-amisse ;
Other indifferent things, that neither make nor marre,
But to the good, bee good ; to th' evill, evill are.
Is 't not great foolishnesse, for any to complaine
That somthing is not done, which doth him nought con-
    straine ?
Sith, if hee use the same, soule-health it hurteth not :
Or, if hee doe not use 't, it helpeth not a jot.
    But needs must we complaine (say some) for we have
    cause :
Then at your perill be 't ; for, that which chiefly drawes 590
You thereto, 'tis in truth your brutenesse in mis-deeming
Things evill, that are good (for sense-contrarie seeming) :
And, while that in the darke of this foule error's mist,
Your drowsie spirits doe droope, alas what marvell is 't
If evill follow you, and (if injurious) still
To others you impute your selfe-ingendred ill ?
    Happy are they to whom the Lord vouchsafeth sight
To see the lovely beames and life-infusing Light
Of his sweet sacred Truth ; whereby we may perceive
And judge a-rightly, what to love and what to leave.   600
Such men within their soules, their goods have wholly plac't ;
Such goods, as never fire can either burne or waste :
Nor any thiefe can steale, nor Pirat make his prey ;
Nor usurie consume, nor Tyrant take away ;
Nor time's all-gnawing tooth can fret away nor finish,
Nor any accident of sad mischance diminish.
For it is built on God, a Rock that ever stands :
Not on the vanities of these inconstant sands,
Which are more mutable then winde, and more unstable,
And day by day doe make so many miserable.   610
    O, to what sweet content, to what high joyes aspires
Hee, that in God alone can limit his desires !
Hee that in him alone his hopes can wholly rest,
Hee that for onely end, waits for the wages blest,
Wherewith he promiseth for ever (sans respect
Of their selfe-meriting) to guerdon his elect ?
    What is it can bereave the wealth of such a man ?
What is it that disturbe his perfect pleasures can ?
What is it can supplant his honours and degrees ?
Sith all his treasures, his delights, his dignities,   620
Are all layd up in Heav'n, where it were all in vaine
For all the sons of earth to warre with might and maine.
    No doubt (will some man say) each Christian doth aspire
(After their bodie's death) to those dear treasures higher,
That are reserv'd in Heav'n, whereof the sweet possession
Fears not the violence of all the world's oppression :

But, while that here below this fraile flesh-burden tyes-him,
But the bare hope hee hath : which how can it suffice-him
Against the sharp assaults of passions infinite,   629
Whose glad-sad crosse conflicts afflict him day and night?
    Needs must I grant (indeed) that the same perfect joy
Wee cannot perfectly upon this earth enjoy :
But, that that hope alone doth not sufficiently
Blesse his life where it lives (for my part) I deny.
Some doe not feare (wee see) to spend their stock and store,
To undertake the taske of many travels sore,
To hazzard limmes and lives, in service of some Lord ;
Depending oft upon his foole-fat-feeding word ;
Or waiting else (perhaps) without all other hold,
Untill it please himselfe his franknesse to unfold ;   640
Not reaking all their paine, they are so inly pleas'd
With hoped benefit, whereof they are not seaz'd?
And, shall th' assured hope of ever-blisses then,
For which wee have the word, not of vaine mortall men,
That teach their tongues to lye ; but of the highest God,
The God of truth, Truth's selfe, where truth hath still
    aboade :
Shall that, I say, not serve to settle our faint hearts,
Against (I will not say) like dangers and like smarts :
But 'gainst these petty griefes, that now and then doe
    pain-us,
No more like those then Heav'n neer Earth that doth
    sustain-us?   650
Ah, shall wee then despise all trouble and vexation,
Supported by a prop of doubtfull expectation?
And, while for earthly things wee can indure all this,
Shall wee not doe as much for an immortall blisse?
    Indeed not of our selves : for, selfly nought wee can ;
But God (when pleaseth him) doth give this strength to
    man,
Whereby hee standeth stout ; even like a mighty rock
Amid the mounting waves, when *Eole* doth unlock
Sterne *Auster's* stormie gate, making the waters wrastle,
And rush with wrathfull rage against the sturdy Castle, 660
While it (for all the force of their fell furie shown)
Is not so much as mov'd, and much lesse overthrown.
    So fareth such a man : for, if from high degree,
Hee suddenly doe slide to live contemnedly
With the vile vulgar sort ; That cannot make him waver :
For well hee is assur'd, that God's high holy favour
Depends not on the pomp, nor vain-proud state and port,
That for the grace of Kings adorns the Courtly sort.
    If hee be kept in bands, thrall to the tyrannies
And extreme cruell Lawes of ruthlesse enemies,   670
Both voyd of helpe and hope, and of all likelihood
Of being ever free'd from their hands'-thirsting bloud ;
In spight of them, hee knowes that one day hee shall dye,
And then hee shall enjoy an endlesse *Libertie.*
    If hee be forc't to flie from his dear Countrey-clime,
In exile to expire the remnant of his time,
Hee doth suppose the World to be a Countrey common,
From whence, a tyrant's wrath (till death) can banish no
    man.
    If that hee must forsake his Parents and his Kin,
And those whose amitie hee most delighteth in ;   680

Hee knowes that where hee finds a man hee finds a kins-man:
For, all mankind is come from one selfe Father (sin's-man).
    If (being spoyl'd of wealth, and wanton-pampering plentie)
Hee finde upon his boord two dishes scant of twentie,
And to his back one coate to keepe the cold away,
Whereas hee had before, a new for every day ;
Hee learneth of Saint *Paul,* who bids us be content
With food and furniture to this life competent :
Sith nothing (as saith *Job*) into this World wee brought,
Nor with us when wee die can wee hence carrie ought.   690
    If hee be passing poore, and in exceeding lack
Of every needfull thing for belly and for back,
Hee learneth of the Sonne, that God the Father heedeth
To give to every one (in time) the thing hee needeth :
And that the fowles of Heav'n, and Cattell small and
    great,
Doe neither sow nor reape, yet finde they what to eate :
Yea, that the *Lillies* faire, which grow among the grasse
Doe neither spin nor work, and yet their garments passe
(For colour and for cost, for Art and Ornament)
The glorious *Salomon's* rich roabes of Parliament.   700
    If so that hee be sick, or wounded in the arme,
In body, back, or breast, or such like kinde of harme :
If in extremitie of angrie paine and anguish,
Enfeebled still by fits, hee bed-rid lye and languish :
If all the miseries that ever martyr'd man,
At once on every side afflict him all they can :
The more that hee endures, the more his comforts grow,
Sith to his wretchednesse hee sooner comes to know ;
That from world's vanities hee may himselfe advance,
Which hold all those from Heav'n, that still delight that
    dance :   710
Hee fears not those at all that with their utmost might,
Having the bodie slaine, can doe no farther spight :
But onely him that with ten thousand deaths can kill
The soule and bodie both for ever if hee will :
Hee knowes it is their lot that seek to please their God,
To bee afflicted still with persecution's rod :
So that, what-ever crosse, how-ever sharp, assaile-him,
His constant heart's content and comfort cannot faile-him.
    But, hee must bye (say you). Alas, can that dismay?
Where is the Labourer (that having wrought all day   720
Amid the burning heat, with wearinesse opprest)
Complaines that night is come when hee shall goe to rest?
The Merchant that returnes from some farre foreine Lands,
Escaping dreadfull rocks, and dangerous shelfs and sands,
When as hee sees his ship her home-haven enter safe,
Will hee repine at God, and (as offended) chafe
For being brought too soon home to his native soil,
Free from all perils sad that threaten Saylors' spoyle?
He knows, from thousand deaths that this one death doth
    lose-him,
That in Heav'n's ever joyes, he ever may repose-him : 730
That he must bring his bark into this Creek, before
In th' everlasting Land he can set foot a-shoare :
That he can never come to incorruption,
Unlesse that first his flesh doe feele corruption :
So that, all rapt with joy, having his help so readie,
This ship-wrack hee escapes, as on a rock most steddie.

But more (perhaps) than death the kind of death dis-
   mayeth,
Which serves him for a bridge that him to Heav'n con-
   vayeth.
Whether hee end his daies by naturall disease :
Or in a boystrous storme doe perish on the Seas :   740
Or by the bloudy hands of armed foes be slaine :
Or by mischance a stone fall down, and dash his braine :
Or by the murdering ball of new-found earthly thunder,
Dy day or else by night his bones be pasht a-sunder :
Or burned at a stake, or bitterly tormented
By cruell slaughter-men, in tortures new-invented :
Alas, alas ! for that, much lesse than least hee careth :
For, as a man falne downe into a Pit, hee fareth ;
Who, if hee may be drawn up from the noysome place,
Where Adders, Toades, and Snakes, craule over feet and
   face,   750
Respects not, whether that hee use a silken scaine,
Hemp-rope, or chain of gold, so hee get up againe :
Even so, so hee may come to his desired blisse,
The manner and the meanes to him indifferent is :
As for the differing paine (if any him doe torture)
If it be violent, hee knowes it is the shorter :
But be it ne'r so long, long sure it cannot last
To us whose post-like life is all so quickly past.
   Now, such a man, in whom such firme contents doe
   hyve,
Who can denie to be the happiest man alive ?   760
And who so impudent, that dareth now professe
That this world's fained sweet (whose unfain'd bitternesse
Brings, to this very life, full many torments fell,
And after dingeth down to th' endlesse pain of hell)
Should be preferr'd before these seeming-sowrs, that make us
Taste many true-sweet sweets yer this dead life forsake us,
And after, lift us up to that same blessed joy,
That evermore shall last, exempt from all annoy.
So few there will be found (as I suppose) so deeming,
As many which (more fear'd with these ils falsly-seeming, 770
Than inly falne-in-love with Heav'n-joyes' excellence)
Approving this estate, fly't as the pestilence.
   And yet, in this estate is sound felicitie
(As far forth as it may, amid the vanite
Of this fraile fading World, where each thing hourly
   changes) :
For, never from it selfe true happinesse estranges :
It never doth decay, it never doth decrease :
In spight of angry warre, it ever lives in peace :
Maugre poore want, it hath ten thousand kinds of wealth :
Amid infirmities it hath continuall health :   780
Inviron'd round with woe, it doth rejoyce and sing :
Depriv'd of dignities, it 's greater then a king :
It sits secure and safe, free from heart-pining fears :
For, ever with it selfe it all deare treasures beares.
Not needing any ayde of men-of-armes to watch them,
Nor fearing fraud, nor force of any foe to catch them.
   Whereas, wee dayly see so many men, whose minde
To transitorie trash of worldly wealth inclin'd,
In their abundance beg, and in their plenty poore
(For who hath had so much, that hath not wished more?) 790

No treasure can suffice the gulfe of their desire ;
Yea, make them Emperours, yet will they more aspire ;
Peace cannot pacifie the fell rebellious broyle
That in their troubled soule doth ever burne and boyle.
For every short content of any false delight,
A thousand bitter throes torment them day and night.
All their estate doth stand abroad in hands of strangers :
Therefore, the more their wealth, the more their daily
   dangers,
The more their miseries, because the more they need
Much strength and many men unto their hoords to heed ; 800
Dreading (with cause) lest craft, or cruelty, or either
Bereave them of their blisse, and treasure both together.
   Needs must wee then confesse, that in adversitie
There is more happinesse than in prosperitie ;
Sith that the mind of man so soone it selfe betrayes
Unto the guilefull snares that worldly pleasures layes
Which make us at the last head-long to Hell to runne :
All which, adversitie doth make us safely shunne,
   But, here it may be askt, if pleasure, state, and store
(Plunging us in the Pit of vices more and more)   810
Be subject so to make us more and more accurst,
Must wee esteme that griefe (which sense esteemeth worst)
More fit to better us, and bring us unto blisse,
Then those whose smarting sting is not so strong as this ?
Sure, sith that in our selves our cause originall
Of blisse and bale wee hide, it matters not at all :
For, still the faithfull man one and the same remains,
Whether the griefe be great or little hee sustains ;
Sith how so e'r it be, hee takes occasion thence,
To seek in God alone, his comfort and defence.   820
But for because our soule (the while shee doth consort
With this grosse fleshly lump) cannot but in some sort
Suffer as sensible, yea, oftentimes so far,
That her best functions all, lesse apt and able are,
Then else at other times ; I doe suppose the proofe
Of one, then other ill, availes more in behoofe.
   That this is so, wee see a sick man oft to finde
Such joyfull quietnesse, and comfort in his minde,
That hee esteems himselfe the best content-alive :
But yet the sharp disease (which doth his health deprive) 830
With-holdeth in some sort his senses and his wit,
That freely other-where hee cannot use them fit.
And so it fares with him, that (through-resolved well)
Endures the cruell strains of any torture fell.
   Now, for the banisht man, the changing of his dwelling
Never disturbs, his joy.   And hee whose wealth excelling
Turns in a trice to want by whatsoever chance,
His courage never shrinks, nor yet his countenance.
   So that in their content, all foure are all a-like.
A-like rejoycing all in their affliction's eke :   840
A-like contemning all world's pompous vanities :
But, the two last have odds in their extremities ;
In that, without impeach, they may apply their minde
To many goodly things, wherein great joy they finde
(I mean, when each distresse offends a man alone,
Not when hee is assail'd at once of every one.)
   Yet, perill 's quickly past, danger endureth not,
Exile so easie growes that it is soon forgot,

The greatest losse that is, wee minde not many houres :
For, thousand accidents distract this soule of ours, 850
Which cannot in such sort the senses still restraine,
But that they will goe feed on many objects vaine ;
Whereby at un-awares shee oftentimes, surpris'd,
Is over-reacht by those, whose rigour shee despis'd :
And so, the pleasant taste shee doth untimely misse,
Wherewith affliction sweet doth season here her blisse.
So that, some other state (wherein our soule lesse fed
With sundry objects vain, shall be more setteled)
May rightly be prefer'd to these which make her stay,
And stumble often-times, unto her owne decay. 860
And therefore I maintaine *Close Prison* to be best
Of all afflictions that may a man molest ;
Considering, all defects to other crosses common,
In this are seldome found, and almost, felt of no man.
 For *Prison* is a place where God sequesters men,
Farre from the vile prospect of vanities terrene,
To make them thence withdraw their hearts, and to confesse
That in his grace alone consists their happinesse.
It is a learned Schoole, where God himselfe reads clearly
True wisdome's perfect rules, to those hee loveth dearly. 870
 There th' understanding (free, amid the many chains,
That binde the body fast) findes out a thousand meanes
To learne another day to be more apt and able
(According to our place) for uses serviceable,
To profit publike-weal : for evermore wee ought
(In seeking selfe-gaine) see that common good be sought.
Knowledge is onely learn'd by long exercitation :
For which, what fitter meane then such a sequestration,
Where each man, undisturb'd, through diligence may
 grow,
According to the gifts that gratious Heav'ns bestow : 880
One, in ability to rule a lawfull State,
The vertuous to advance, and vicious to abate :
Another, from the Tombe to fetch Antiquity,
Another to discerne the Truth from Sophistry :
Another (by the feats of elder men at Armes)
To frame wise Stratagems for wofull war's alarmes :
For, Souldiers oftentimes may more experience get
By reading, then they can where Camp and Camp is met.
And (briefely to conclude) some, gravely to advise,
Some, bold to execute, as each man's calling lies : 890
But most of all, to search within the sacred Writ,
The secret mysteries to man's salvation fit.
 A world of vanities (that doe distract us here,
During our *Libertie*) in Durance, come not neere :
The wall that lets our leggs from walking out of door,
Bounding us round about within a narrow floor,
Doth guard us from the gall that Sathan (spring of spight)
Mingles among the sweets of this vain world's delight.
If hee be happier man that liveth free from foes,
Then hee whom angry troops of enemies inclose, 900
Much more the Prisoner then of his high blisse may boast
For being so far off from such a hugie hoast
Of hatefull foes so fierce in malice and in might,
Himselfe so faint and weake, and so unfit to fight.
For hee, and wee (God wot) in stead of standing to-it
(How-ever in a vein, wee vaunt that wee will doe-it)

When 't commeth to the brunt wee cannot brook the
 field,
But either fly like hares, or else like cowards yeeld.
 The sundry objects fond, which make us soon forget
Each other chastisement, in this doe never let. 910
For turn wee where wee list, and looke which way wee
 will,
At all times to our sight one thing is offred still :
Whether on pavement, roof, or wall, wee cast our eye,
Alwayes of our estate an Image wee descrie :
And so it also fares with our news-greedie eare,
One very sound resounds about us every where :
Where-ever hearken wee, wee heare of nought but foes,
Our keepers commonly are not too-kind, God knowes :
By the least noyse that is, continually they tell
In what estate wee stand, and in what house wee dwell. 920
So that incessantly our hearts are lift on high,
Som-times to praise the Lord for his benignitie,
Who doth not punish us after our foule offence,
Though by a thousand sinnes wee daily him incense :
Som-times to magnifie his admirable might,
Which hath our feeble hearts with such great force bedight,
That wee, in stead of griefe, or grudging at the pains
Of sharpest chastisements, whereof the world complains,
Leaving this loathed Earth, doe mount the highest place,
Where (through true faith) wee taste his honey-sweeter
 grace : 930
Somtimes to give him thanks for all the wealth exceeding,
Which from his liberall hand wee have to help our needing :
And to be short, *sans* cease to meditate on all
The countlesse benefits that from his goodnesse fall
Not suffering any houre to passe away for nought
Without exalting him, in deed, or word, or thought.
 Yet, doth the world esteeme this, a most hard estate,
And him that feels the same, it counts unfortunate :
But I would gladly see some other state wherein
(With such commoditie) so much content is seen ; 940
Wherein lesse hinderance, and lesse incomb'rance lyes,
To make men misse the path unto perfection's prise.
 Sure sir (will some man say) you set a good face on-it,
One might at length convert, commenting so upon-it,
The cruell'st Prison-house into a Mansion faire,
Where 't were not hard to live content, and voyd of care.
You take your *Pris'ner* for a practive man of Art :
But such as those (God knows) you finde the fewest part,
You fain him to be friend to solitude and quiet :
But the most part are prone to revell and to riot. 950
One must be free from noyse that meanes to studie well :
Whereof, who can be sure in such a servile Hell ?
Besides, hee must have Books, and Paper, Pen, and Inke,
All which in *Prisoner's* hands are seldome left I thinke ;
So that you doe not faine your gail so good and gainfull,
As to finde out the same is difficult and painfull.
 I answer in a word (if any so shall wrangle :)
I doe not bound all blisse within so straight an angle
I say, great happinesse and heart-reviving joy
Followes th' afflicted sort in every sharp annoy : 960
But that there is no crosse that doth so much availe,
To make us fit to help our neighbour, as the gaile,

Wherein the God of grace at his good pleasure gives
Meanes to effect the same, unto the least that lives.
　But be it so, in bands, that nothing learne wee can,
Tis to be learn'd enough to be an honest man :
And this is th' onely Schoole, wherein th' Arch-master
　　teacheth,
Himselfe by secret means, rules that the rudest reacheth.
Th' advice of such a one more profit doth impart,
Then of the wicked sort with all their curious Art.　　970
　Concerning solitude, although that commonly
Our nature be inclin'd unto the contrarie ;
There the assistant grace of God wee chiefly finde,
Who changing of our place doth also change our minde.
　For beeing free from noyse, and for obtaining tooles
To help our knowledge with, as in all other Schooles ;
God ever cares for those that feare his name for love :
And, if that any such, such inconvenience prove,
If any money need, or else (through ample distance)
Be destitute of friends, hee gets them (for assistance)　　980
The favour of their foes, whose hearts hee handles so
(How ever they intend his children's overthrow)
That his, of what they need have evermore enough,
According as hee knowes to be to their behoofe.
　Now say, that wee consent (say some) that this is true :
But what if somewhat worse then all this worst ensue ?
What, if hee be inforc't his Country to forsake ?
What, if continuall fits his sickly body shake ?
What, if hee lose at once his wealth and reputation,
Repleat on every side with every sharp vexation ?　　990
Can hee still keep his joy, and can hee still retain
Such meanes to profit still, for all his griefe and pain ?
Concerning his content, it 's alwayes all a-like,
Whether that every griefe particularly strike ;
Or, whether all at once hee feel their utmost anger :
And if hee be surpris'd with so extreme a languor
That (as I said before) the spirit it inforce
(Through suffering of the smart that doth afflict the corse)
To leave his Offices, so that hee cannot write,
Nor reade, nor meditate, nor study nor indite ;　　1000
It is so quickly past, that in comparison,
Regarding so great good, 'tis not to thinke upon.
For, by a mighty griefe our life is quickly ended ;
Or els, by remedie it selfe is soon amended :
And, if it be but mean, then it is borne the better,
And so unto the soule it is not any letter.
Besides, wee must conceive, our spirit (as opprest
With fainting wearinesse) somtimes desireth rest
To gather strength againe, during which needfull pawse
Wee are not to [be] blam'd, sith need the same doth
　　cause :　　1010
So, that the time that 's lost while such sharp pangs doe
　paine,
May be suppos'd a time of taking breath againe.
　In prison (to conclude) a man at once may trie
All manner of extremes of earthly misery :
In which respect (perhaps) the worse some deem of it,
Being (as 't were) the Butt that all men strive to hit ;
But, I esteem the same the perfecter for that :
For, if one crosse alone can make us elevate

Our groveling earth-desires from cogitations base,
To have recourse to God, and to implore his grace,　　1020
Seeking in him alone our perfect joy and blisse ;
Much more shall many griefs at once, accomplish this.
For many can doe more then one (without respect) :
And still, the greater cause the greater the effect.
　Indeed (say other-some) these reasons have some reason :
But, then whence comes it, that so many men in Prison
(With hundred thousand pains, pincht and oppressed sore)
In stead of bettering there, wax worser then before :
In stead of sweet content, doe still complaine and crie ;
In stead of learning more, lose former industry ?　　1030
Though (in appearance great) your saying seem but just,
Yet plain experience (sure) wee think is best to trust.
　That hidden vertue rare, that so great good atchieves,
Lies in the Prisoner's heart, not in his heavy Gyves ;
The good grow better there, the bad become the worse :
For by their sinne they turne God's blessing into curse.
And that 's the cause the most are male-content and sad :
Sith evermore the good are fewer then the bad.
　But, wherefore doth not God to all vouchsafe his grace ?
Proud earth-worms pawse wee there : let 's fear before his
　　face,　　1040
Admiring humbly all his holy Judgements high,
Exceeding all too far our weake capacitie.
The Potter's vessell vile, doth us our lesson show,
Which argues not with him why hee hath made it so :
Much lesse may wee contend, but rather rest content
With that which God hath given.　Hee is omnipotent,
All gracious, and all good, most just, and perfect wise.
On some, hee pours a Sea of his benignities,
On some a shallow Brook, on other some a Floud :
Giving to some, a small ; to some, a greater good :　　1050
As from eternity hath pleas'd th' Almighty Spirit
To love men more or lesse, without respect of merit.
　For my part, should I live ten *Nestors* yeers to passe,
Had I a hundred tongues more smooth then *Tully's* was,
Had I a voice of steel, and had I brazen sides,
And learning more then all the *Heliconian* guides ;
Yet were I all too-weake to tell the many graces,
That in ten thousand sorts, and in ten thousand places,
Ten hundred thousand times hee hath vouchsafed mee
(Not for my merit's sake, but for his mercy free) :　　1060
But yet, 'mong all the goods that of his liberall bounty
I have receiv'd so oft, none to compare account-I
With this *Close prisonment*, wherein hee doth with-draw-
　　mee
Far from the wanton world, and to himselfe doth draw-
　　mee.
　I posted on apace to ruine and perdition,
When by this sharp-sweet Pil, my cunning kinde Physician
Did purge (maugre my will) the poysony humour fell
Wherewith my sin-sick heart already 'gan to swell.
I lookt for nothing lesse then for their miseries,　　1069
And paines that I have prov'd : the world's vaine vanities
Had so seduc't my soule with bait of sugred bane,
That it was death to mee from pleasure to be ta'en :
But (crossing my request) God (for my profit) gave
Mee quite the contrary to that which I did crave.

So that, my body barr'd from freedom false and small,
He set my soule at large, which unto sinne was thrall :
Wounding with musket-shot my feeble arme, hee cur'd
The festring sores of sinne, the which my soule endur'd :
Tripping mee from the top of some meane dignity,
Which drew mee up to climbe the mount of vanity,   1080
Hee rais'd mee from the depth of vice's darksom Cell,
The which incessantly did ding mee down to hell :
Easing mee (to conclude) of all the griefe and care,
Wherewith these false delights for ever sauced are,
Hee made me finde and feel (amid my most annoyes)
A thousand true contents, a thousand perfect joyes.
    But som (perhaps) amaz'd, will muse what kinde of
        pleasure
Here I can take, and how I passe my time and leasure :
For, in soule idlenesse, to spend so large a time,
It cannot be denied to be a grievous crime.   1090
    First in the morning, when the spirit is fresh and fit,
I suck the honey sweet from forth the *sacred Writ*,
Wherein (by faith) wee taste that true celestiall bread,
Whence our immortall soules are ever onely fed :
Then search I out the sawes of other sage Divines
(The best here to be had) among whose humane lines,
Supported by the grace of God's especiall power,
I leave the thorne behinde, and pluck the healthsom flower.
Somtimes, I doe admire, in books of Heathen men,
Grave-sayings, savouring more a sacred Christian pen,   1100
Then many of our age, whose bold unlearned pride
Thinking to honour God, hath err'd on every side :
Sometimes when I observe in every ancient story,
Such vertues presidents, trim paterns of true glory,
I wofully bewaile our wretched wicked dayes,
Where vertue is despis'd, and vice hath all the praise.
Oft I lament to see so many noble Wits
(Neglecting God's high praise, that best their learning fits)
To sing of nought but lies, and loves, and wanton Theames,
False sooth-sin flatteries, and idle Fairy dreames.   1110
Then, turning toward those, that fill'd with holier flame,
For onely object chuse th' Eternall's sacred Name ;
These chiefly I admire, whose honourable brows
Disdain the fained crown of fading *Laurel* boughs :
Then full-gorg'd with the Sweets of such a dainty feast
(Prickt forward with desire to imitate the best)
Oft-times I exercise this Art-lesse Muse of mine
To sing in holy Verse some argument divine.
One while to praise my God for all received good :
Another while to beg, that in his deare Son's bloud   1120
My black sins hee will wash, and that hee will not waigh
At his high Justice beam, how I have gon astray.
Sometimes, these wretched Times to pity and deplore,
Wherein the wicked ones doe flourish more and more.
Sometimes, to wail the State of sad distressed *Sion*
Imploring to her aid the Tribe of *Judah's* Lion.
If any other Theam at any time I take,
Yet never doth my Verse the settled bounds forsake
That Verity prescribes, nor now no more disguise
The ugly face of sinne with mask of painted lies.   1130
And though that (heretofore) I also in my time
Have writ Love's vanities in loose and wanton rime :

'Twas as a whetstone that, whereon I whet my stile,
Yer it were ably-apt ought graver to compile :
Yet I repent thereof : for, wee must never tend
To bring by evill means a good intent to end.
    When as my weary spirits some relaxation aske,
To recreate the same, I take some other taske :
One while upon the Lute, my nimble joints I plie,
Then on the Virginalls : to whose sweet harmonie   1140
Marrying my simple voyce, in solemne Tunes I sing
Some Psalme or holy Song, unto the heav'nly King.
So that, the idlest houre of all the time that flies
So fast, is never free from some good exercise :
Wherein I joy as much, as ever I have done
In the most choise delights found underneath the Sun.
    But, you can never walke, nor goe to take the aire,
Nor once looke out of doore, be weather ne'r so faire ;
But there in solitude you leade your life alone,
Barr'd from the fellowship of (almost) every one :   1150
Which doubtlesse (at the least) must grieve you, needs, I
    thinke.
A man that never thirsts hath never need of drinke :
So, though I be bereft these other things you speake-of,
I misse nor minde them not as things I never reake-of,
For, I have School'd my heart since my captivitie,
To wish for nothing els, but what is granted mee :
And, what is granted mee, contents mee passing well.
In each condition doth some contentment dwell.
But men of differing states have difference in delights,   1159
What pleaseth common eyes, that irketh Princes' sights,
What rashlings doe delight, that sober men despise,
What fooles take pleasure in, doth but offend the wise,
What prosperous people loath, afflicted folke will love,
And what the free abhorre, that prisoners will approve :
But all have equally indifferent power to make
Them equally content, that can them rightly take :
For, whoso presently himselfe can rightly beare,
Hath neither passed ill, nor future ill to feare :
Th' one, which is now no more, ought now no more
    affray-us,
Th' other which is not yet, as little can dismay-us.   1170
For, what no essence hath, that also hath no might :
And that which hath no power, can doe a man no spight :
Besides, sith this our life is but a pilgrimage,
Through which wee daily passe to th' heav'nly heritage ;
Although it seeme to thee that these my bands doe let-
    mee,
Yet haste I to the goale the which my God hath set-mee,
As fast as thou that runn'st thy selfe so out of breath
In posting night and day, by dales, and hills and heath.
    If thou have open fields, and I be Prisoner ;
T' importeth mee no more, then to the Mariner   1180
Whether hee goe to Sea shipt in some spacious Arke,
Or else (a lesser scope) aboord some lesser barke.
Nay, here the least is best ; sith this vast Ocean wide,
Whereon wee daily saile, a thousand rocks doth hide,
'Gainst which the greater ships are cast-away full oft ;
While small boats (for the most) float over, safe, aloft.
    Then may I well conclude with reason and assurance,
That there 's no better state then to be kept in durance.

47

A sweeter kinde of life I never prov'd then there :
Nor was I ever toucht with lesser griefe and care.   1190
If that I care at all, it is for others' cause,
And for the miseries this time's corruption drawes :
But, being well assur'd that nothing here betideth
Against God's ordinance and will, that all things guideth :
And knowing him to be good, just, and most of might,
I gladly yeeld my selfe to th' order hee hath pight.
For hee it is, that now makes mee accept so well
And like of this estate which others hate as Hell :
Hee 'tis, that heretofore vouchsaf't mee like reliefe,
When as I was opprest with a more grievous griefe :   1200

Hee 'tis from whom I hope in time to-come no lesse,
Although a hundred-fold were doubled my distresse.
Yea, hee it is that makes mee profit every day ;
And also so content in this estate to stay,
That of my libertie I am not now so faine
To think by libertie a happier life to gaine :
For, I were well content no more from hence to go,
If I might profit most my friends and countrey so.
   Now here I humbly pray (expecting such an end)
The Lord still towards mee his favour to extend ;   1210
And that hee will vouchsafe still to allot like grace,
To all that for like cause are handled in like case.

FINIS.

NOTES AND ILLUSTRATIONS.

DEDICATION TO 'M. R. NICHOLSON'—see our Memorial-Introduction on this 'approved friend.'
Line 6, '*Nephew*' = descendants.
  ,, 11, '*Tangley Thee*'—see Glossarial Index, *s.v.*
PARADOX, line 5, '*mean*' = medium.
Line 10, '*wuns*' = wons, dwells.
  ,, 37, '*creditable*' = credible.
  ,, 94, '*whelpings*' = little whelps.
  ,, 107 and 118, '*inly*' = inward.
  ,, 143, '*brute*' = bruit ?
  ,, 144, '*ensue*' = pursue.
  ,, 206, '*infract*' = unbroken.
  ,, 216, '*buggs*' = bugbears.
  ,, 267, '*a-frunt*' = a-front.
  ,, 301, '*Vades*'—see Glossarial Index, *s.v.*
  ,, 330, '*nifles*' = trifles.
  ,, 408, '*apaid*' = satisfied, rewarded.

Line 410, '*unhappieth*' = an odd coinage.
  ,, 424, '*reanes*' = reins.
  ,, 437, '*flatter*' = flattery.
  ,, 544, '*teen*' = rage.
  ,, 560, '*randon*' = random.
  ,, 641, '*reaking*' = recking, reckoning.
  ,, 642, '*seaz'd*' = legal term of possession.
  ,, 744, '*pasht*' = dashed.
  ,, 751, '*scaine*' = skean, skein.
  ,, 833, '*well*' = will—by stress of rhyme.
  ,, 895, '*letts*' = hinders.
  ,, 947, '*practive*' = practical.
  ,, 990, '*Repleat*' = replete.
  ,, 1016, '*Butt*' = mark.
  ,, 1082, '*ding*' = knock down.
  ,, 1154, '*recke-of*' = reck, reckon.
  ,, 1196, '*pight*' = placed, pitched.—G.

OF THE WORK,

AUTHOUR, AND

TRANSLATOR.

L O here a MONUMENT admir'd of all
 That weigh the *compass, weight,* and *height* of it ;
O'r-topping *Envie's* clouds, and ever shall
Sith built by deepest *Art,* and highest *Wit.*

The BASE that bears it, is the WORD that stands
True GROUND of highest *glorie, truth,* and *grace :*
The BUILDING rear'd by two rare *heads* and *hands*
(Divinely holp) to glorifie that BASE.

Here *French* and *English,* joyne in friendly fight
(On even *Ground*) to prove their utmost power ; 10
Who shew such equall *Skill,* and equall *Might,*
That hard it is to say who's conqueror.

But, *English* bound to foot it like the *French*
And offer nought, but what shall like her foe,
It is as glorious seld to take a Wrench,
As being free, to give an overthrow.

If *French* to *English* were so strictly bound,
It would but passing lamely strive with it ;
And soon be forc't to lose both *grace* and *ground,*
Although they strave with equall *Skill* and *Wit.* 20

Besides, all *Prose* is easier to translate
Then *Verse ;* and easier low, then lofty *Lines :*
Then, these LINES, reaching to the top of STATE
Are hard'st of all : yet none of all declines.

O faire *Translation* then, with smoothed face,
Goe forth t' allure TIME'S *Turns,* to turn Thee o'r :
So shall they in thy folds unfold thy *grace ;*
And grace thee with Fame's glory more and more.

Ovid me

If * Hee, that churn'd the Cream of *Poetry,*
To honied *Butter,* that the *Muses* feeds, 30
Divined truly, it should never die ;
Then, what shall *This,* that far the same exceeds ?

Hee labour'd *Lines,* wch though they doe endure
All turns of *Time,* yet was their stuf profane :
But these are drawn of STUF more heav'nly pure,
That most shall shine ; when those are in the wane.

Hee, though his *Braines* (profanely) were divine,
And glorious *Monuments* of art compos'd,
Was yet exil'd for many a looser *Line,*
That made them wantons, chastely else dispos'd : 40

But, thou (*clear* BARTAS, his dear SYLVESTER,
Whose *Lines* do lead to VERTUE'S only gaine,

And with sweet *Poesies* strew'st the way to her)
How should the *World* remunerate thy paine ?

And, if *from heart's aboundance tongues do speak ;*
And what we most affect, wee most doe minde :
It argues, thou this *Argument* didst seek ;
Sith, in thy *Soule* before, thou didst it finde.

So, BARTAS was but Mid-wife to thy *Muse,*
With greater ease to utter her *Conceits ;* 50
For whose dear birth, thou didst all ease refuse,
World's-weale, and (being a *Merchant*) thy *Receits.*

This *pain* so pleas'd thy labouring *Thoughts,* that thou
Forsook'st the *Sea,* and took'st thee to the *Soile,*
Where (from thy royall *Trade,*) thou fell'st to plow
Art's furrows with thy *Pen,* that yeeld but toyl.

This stole thee from thy selfe, thy selfe to finde
In sacred *Raptures* on the *Muses'* Hill :
And, went'st out of thy *Body* with thy *Minde,*
More freely so, to use thy *Wit* and *Will.* 60

And (O !) how haplesse had wee *Britains* been
(Sith here is stor'd such sweet Soule-*ravishments*)
Hadst thou not made them to us clearly seen :
Who give thee for it praising *Discontents ?*

If so great *Art* and *Grace,* finde nought but *fame*
Of famous *Men* for grace ; the *Presse* shall be
Prest but for *Vice's* Service (Source of *shame*).
So *Times* to come, in *Print* our shame shall see.

But O ! be 't far from this so famous Isle
For *Armes* and *Learning,* either to neglect ; 70
Sith it doth grace and glorie quite exile,
And is the cause of many a bad effect.

O terrene Gods, as yee to State aspire,
Lift *Learning* up with you ; especially
If matcht with *Wisedome,* and divine desire :
So shall yee twice be like the DEITY.

And, weigh what pow'r the PENS of such possesse
(Of such ; for others will but gild your *Crimes*)
Their PENS eternise can your worthinesse :
And make yee glorious, past succeeding *Times.* 80

But you doe justly to neglect and scorn
The cursed crue, that doe the Muse abuse :
For, they your praises to dispraises turn ;
As Vice, in praising VERTUE'S grace, doth use.

Their wine-driv'n brains, involv'd in follie's cloud,
Fly here, and there (and where not?) with a trice :
And, though both beggars base, yet passing proud ;
Constant in nothing but inconstant Vice :
   Making loose lines (forsooth) their *Scala Cœli,*
A *Taverne* for a Temple to adore ;   90
Their onely god, their guts, their beastly Belly,
To whom they offer all their slender Store.
   The *Lands* of such, are odious like their Lives :
They (*Pitch*) pollute what-ere they doe but touch ;
Whose glory to the foulest shame arrives :
Then, well you fence your fame to keep off such.
   But they whose lives, and lauds, and lines are SOURCE
Of Moral vertue, running by each stone
(Men high, and hard, that let them in their Course)
To Seas of glory, like clear *Helicon ;*   100
   O ! these ye should support, and still receive
Into the Ocean of your bound-lesse love :
For these (like truest Friends) will take, and give
No more but what true *Vertue* shall approve.
   If these should pine away through your neglect,
Your memories shall dye, or live with shame ;
Sith such a Muse is the chiefe *Architect,*
To reare, from *Earth* to *Heav'n,* a lasting NAME.
   Achilles' fame, with him, had been interr'd,
Had HOMER'S lines not ty'd it to the *Stars :*   110
And, of *Æneas* wee had never heard,
Had *Virgil's* STRAINS not been his *Trumpeters.*
   One of the NINE had bin our *Warwick's* GUY,
(The NINE, whose *worth* all *Times* so much commend ;)

And so disrankt great BULLEN'S GODFERY
Had hee but had a TASSO for his friend.
   LAURA had ne're so greenly growne above
Her *Peers,* as now she doth, to after-times,
Had she not had a PETRARCH to her Love ;   119
Which made her mount, with NECTAR-dropping *Rimes.*
   No, no : ye cannot but out-live your Fame,
If ye uphold not FAME's best Notaries :
If these ye scorne, your glory is but game ;
For, when ye die, in game your glory dies.
   And, though blest PEACE hath turn'd our Spears to
      spades,
Let it not turn our *pens* to *ploughs,* or worse ;
By *Learning* some should live as some by Trades,
In blessed STATES, that would incurre no curse.
   Where Vertue is not rais'd, and Vice supprest,
There all to Vice will run ; and so to wrack :   130
For, there the worst shall lord it ore the best ;
And where that is, all goes to utter sack.
   Reward, and *Punishment* (like *Armes* of Steel)
Doe still uphold each KING-upholding STATE :
For, neither wants, but it begins to reel ;
But, both imploy'd, stands sure in spight of *Hate.*
   Then may thy HOPES, wing'd by thy vertuous
      Muse,
Dear *Sylvester,* expect some cherishment,
In this blest *State ;* that still those *Armes* will use,
To stay her *Grace,* and grace her *Government :*   140
   But, if thy *paines* acquire but pure *renowne,*
   Thou art *Christ's* Image, crost for *Glorious* crown.

Beneficium dando accipit, qui digno dedit.

The unfained lover of thine Art, honesty, and vertue,

JOHN DAVIES *of Hereford.*

FINIS.

NOTES AND ILLUSTRATIONS.

Line, 44, '*remunerate*' = recompense : l. 129, '*rais'd*' = praised.   This is included in our collective edition of John
Davies of Hereford.—G.

A BRIEFE INDEX,

EXPLAINING MOST OF THE

hardest words scattered through this whole
Worke, for ease of such as are least exercised
in these kinde of readings.

A

Bysse, a gulfe or bottomlesse pit.

Abderian and *Abderite*, Democritus, the laughing Philosopher of Abdera, a Citie in Thracia.

Aben-Roes, a learned Philosopher of Corduba, sprung from Arabian parents.

Abidus, Leander's Towne.

Academian Shades, Plato's school.

Acheron, a river in Hell.

Aconite, Libbard's (or Wolfe's) bane.

Achilles, the most valiant Captaine of the Myrmidons.

Adonis, a most beautifull young man, beloved of Venus.

Adrian } *Sea*, the gulfe of *Venice.*'
Adriatike

Æson, the father of *Jason*, made young again by the skill of Medea.

Ætheriall, heavenly.

Æsculapius, an excellent Physician, father of Apollo.

Africa, the South-quarter of the World.

Ajax shield, a proverbe, for a sure defence.

Aiguescald, a bath in Gasconie.

Alarbies, and *Arabians*, wilde and upland *Arabian* theeves.

Albion, England, the Ile of great Britaine.

Alcesté, the most chaste and loving wife of Admetus, that gave her owne life to save her husband's.

Alcides, Hercules: *Alcides spires*, Hercules' Pillars: *Alcides grief*, the falling Sicknesse.

Alcmæna, Hercules' mother.

Alcaron, the Turk's Law and Religion.

Aleband, a Citie in Caria, of old famous for the best bow-strings.

Alecto, look *Furies*.

Alexander's Altars, were at the foote of the Ryphean Mountains.

Almicantharats, and *Almaderats*, Arabian names of Circles, which are imagined to passe through every degree of the Meridian, Parallel to the Horizon up to the Zenith.

Alhidade, a Rule on the back of the Astrolabe to measure heights, breadths and depths.

Amafrosse, gutta serena, a disease in the Sinnewes of the Sight.

Amalthean Horne, plenty of all things.

Amblygone, a flat Triangle.

Ambrosia, the Gods' meat.

American, the French disease, brought first from the Indies to Naples, from thence to France, &c.

Amia, a fish like a Tunny, found in the Sea neere Constantinople.

Amphitrite, the Sea.

Amphisbæna, a Serpent having a head at both ends.

Amphion, the author of Harmony and builder of Thebes.

Amiclean Harp, Arion, the Lesbian harper.

Amyot, a learned French-man, translator of Plutark, and other Greek Authors.

Ancossa, a bath in Gasconie.

Andromeda, the wife of Perseus, (with her husband, father and mother) turned into a Star.

Androdus, a Romane slave gratefully requited of a Lion.

Anoreixia, a queasinesse of stomach.

Antheus, Antenor's sonne, beloved and unwillingly slain by Paris.

M. *Anthony*, competitor with Octavius and Lepidus for the Romane Empire.

Antiperistasis, incounter of contraries, or contrarie-circumstance.

Antipodes, those people that dwell directly under us.

Antartike, Southerne.

Aonian band, the Muses.

Apelles, an excellent Painter.

Apium rise, a kinde of Crowfoot that kils men with laughing.

Appianus' way, one of the broadest wayes in Rome.

Apollo, the Sun, the god of Musicke and Physicke.

Apoplexie, a kinde of dead palsie.

Apoge, the point farthest from the Center of the earth.

Arabians, people of Asia, inhabiting betweene Judea and Egypt, rich in aromaticall spices and sweet odors.

Arcadian scout, Mercurie.

Arcenal, an Armorie or storehouse.

Archelaus, a King much praised by Plutarch and others for wisedome and temperance, and for delight in husbandry.

Archimedes, a famous Mathematician of Syracusa.

Architas, a noble Philosopher of Tarentum.

Arion, a famous Harper and lyrike Poet, born at Methymna in the Ile of Lesbos.

Arne, a River in Italy.

Arcenik, orpine : supposed okar.

Artemisia, Queene of Caria, wife of Mausolus.

Artemisian stem, Mugg-wort.

Armorik, Britain in France.

Armados, Spanish Armies, or great ships of Warre.

Artik, Northern, or of the North.

Aristotle, the most famous Philosopher of Stagyra.

Asia, a third part of the world, in former times most famous for Learning and Religion ; but now for the most part miserably yoaked under the Turk's tyranny.

Asylum, a refuge or defence.

Assur, one of the Sons of Sem : also the Countrey of Assyria.

Astaroth, an Idol of the Philistines.

Astræa, Justice.

Astrolabe, an instrument to gather the motion of the Stars.

Asthma, short-windednesse.

Attalus, a wealthy King of Pergamus, delighted in the countrey life.

Atlantik Sea, is the Mediterranean, or a part thereof.

Atlas, a King skilfull in Astronomy, therefore fained to bear up Heaven : it is also a Mountaine in Barbary.

Athenian Sage, Socrates.

Attik Muse, Xenophon.

Atheists, those that acknowledge no God, infidels.

Aurora, the morning.

Auster, the South-winde.

Avernus, Hell.

Avicen, a learned Philosopher and Physician, borne at Sevil, of Arabian stock.

Aziminths, great Circles meeting in the Zenith, or verticall Point.

Anian, a Streight, or narrow Sea between Asia and America : as yet little discovered.

Aglaia, look *Graces*.

Ætna, a burning Mountaine in Sicilia.

Asphaltis, *Mare Mortuum*, the stinking lake, where Sodom and her execrable sisters stood.

Annals, Histories from year to year.

Arch Colonel, usurped for the Generall, or chiefe Captain of the Hoast.

Anathem, execration, curse, excommunication.

Anatomie, the incision or cutting up of the bodie of Man or Beast, as Surgeons doe, to see the parts.

Amphitrionide, Hercules, begotten by Jupiter on Alcmena, the wife of Amphitryo.

Attick, a Province of Greece ; wherein stood the City of Athens.

Atropos, looke *Parcæ*.

Allecto, looke *Furies*.

Assabine, Jupiter, with the Assyrians.

Architrave, the crowne or chapter of a Pillar : also a principall beam in any building.

Arabian bird, the Phœnix.

Argolian showers, Jupiter's golden Raine in the lap of Danäe, daughter of Acrisius, King of the Argives, Argolikes, or Argolians.

Ægisthus, look *Clytemnestra*.

Aspiks, venomous little serpents.

Anchises Pheer, is Venus, on whom he begat Æneas.

Abramide, of the race of Abraham.

B

*B**Altik Ocean*, the Danish Sea.

   Baignere, a Bath in Gasconie.

Bandans, the Ilanders of the Moluques, rich in excellent spices.

Bachanalian Froes, Women-Priests of Bacchus the god of Cups.

Bardes, ancient Poets and Sages.

Barege, a Bath in Gasconie.

Barr-Geese, and *Barnacles*, a kinde of fowles that grow on rotten Trees and broken ships.

Bek, a Phrygian word signifying bread.

Belgian, of the Neather-lands.

Belgrade, a Towne in Hungary, taken by the Turk.

Bellona, goddesse of warre.

Belus Sonne, Ninus, first King of Assyria, supposed to be inventer of Navigation.

Bitumen, a kinde of oylie, slimie, gummie, or clammy Clay.

Bizantium, Constantinople.

Brontes, one of Vulcan's Forgemen.

Briareus, a Gyant with 100. hands.

Brutus, heires, Englishmen, Britains.

Bacconi, Poisonie confections, Italian figs.

Bon-jours, Good-morrowes.

Bonarets, a kinde of Beast-plants.

Boôtes, a little star in the North Pole neer to *Ursa minor*, used for the North.

Boreas, the North-winde.

Bosphores, two Straights, so called of an oxe's wading over : the one sirnamed Thracian, the other Cimmerian.

Boulime, a hungry or greedy disease in a cold stomach.

Bucephalus, the courageous Horse of Alexander the Great.

Busiris, a most cruell Tyrant of Egypt, which used to sacrifice st[r]angers to Jupiter.

Butrick, a learned and eloquent Germane (of late dayes) Counseller to Cassimirus.

Bombards, great ordnance.

Bubastik, that is, Egyptian.

Bethel, a Mountaine in the South Confines of Israel, where Jeroboam set up one of his Calves.

Birdene, a Wildernesse in the West of Egypt.

Babels, indeed Bables, idle Monuments of Pomp and Plentie.

Beelzebub, the god of Acheron, the Prince of Divels.

Brachmans, Indian Philosophers : Moderne writers call them Bramines.

Bigaurian Hils, part of the Pyrene Mountaines between France and Spaine.

C

*C*Abalistik*, mysticall Traditions among the Jewes Rabbins.

Cæsars, Emperours, so called from Caius Julius Cæsar the first Emperour.

Cadmus, sonne of *Agenor*, who slew a serpent, and pulling out his teeth, sowed them in the ground, whereof instantly there sprung-up ready armed men.

Cairo, a Citie in the midst of Egypt, of old called Babylon, and thought one of the greatest in the world.

Calamarie, a fish that may well be called the Sea-Clark, being furnished with necessaries for a scribe.

Callicrates, an excellent Carver, especially in small works.

Calpe, a Mountaine within the Straights of Gibralter, just opposite of *Abila :* these two are called the Pillars of Hercules.

Cannibals, people in the South part of America that eat Man's flesh.

Candia, an Iland in the Mediterrean Sea, subject to the Venetians.

Cana, a Towne in Galilee where Christ wrought his first miracle, at a marriage.

Cantharus, a fish of admirable chastity.

Capharean Rock, a most dangerous and Rockie Coast of Eubœa, now called Negropont.

Carpese, a venomous plant, whose Juice causeth deep sleep, and so strangleth the Patient.

Carinthia, a Dutchie belonging to the Dukes of Austria.

Carraques, great Spanish vessels.

Caligula, a most wanton and wicked Emperour of Rome.

Cassagale, the City Quinzay, in the East Indies.

Cassiopeia, Mother of Andromeda.

Castalian Well, Springs, Fount ; Springs at the foot of Parnassus sacred to the Muses.

Cathay, a large Countrey in East Asia fronting on the Sea, now called Cambula.

Cataract, a violent fall of any water, causing a deafnesse with the noyse, also a disease in the Eye distilling a tough humour like gelly.

Catiline, a factious Citizen of Rome, famous for his dangerous conspiracy against his Countrey.

Cato, a reverend and renowned Romane both for his temperate life, and resolute death.

Caudrets, a Bath in Gasconie.

Caucasus, a very high Mountaine that divides Scythia from India.

Ceres, Goddesse of Harvest, Inventresse of Tillage and of the use of Corne, somtimes used for the Earth.

Cephalus, the husband of Procris, the minion of Aurora.

Centaures, halfe men, halfe horses, begotten by Ixion on a Cloud.

Cerastes, a Serpent of sundry colours, with horns like a Ram.

Cerathus, a River in Candie from whence comes the best Malmsie.

Cerbas, a Tree in the Indies, of 15. fadome about.

Cerberus, the three-headed dog of Hell, the Porter there.

Celtike, a part of France.

Chaos, a confused heap, the matter of the World before it received form.

Chaldea, the Countrey wherein Babylon stood : where were great Astronomers, Magicians, and Southsayers.

Charles Martell, K. of France, overthrew 400000. Turks neer unto our Tours.

Chermez, the graine wherewith Scarlet and Crimson are died.

Chimeras, strange Fancies, monstrous Imaginations, Castles in the Aire.

Cincinnatus, one called from the plough (all dustie and almost naked) to the Romane Dictatorship.

Cimmerians, people far North, that are thought never to see the Sun.

Cittadel, a Castle built with a small Garrison to keep a great Town in awe.

Cirques, round Lists to behold publike Races.

Chus, Æthiopia.

Clio, one of Muses, reciting the glorious Acts of Worthinesse.

Clitus, one of Alexander's greatest Minions whom yet in his drunkennesse hee slew.

Cocos, an admirable Nut brought from the Indies.

Cocytus, a River in Hell.

Colchos, Medeas Countrey, from whence Jason fetcht the Golden Fleece.

Codrus, a King of Athens, that gave his owne life for the safeguard of his Countrey.

Colonies, numbers of People sent to inhabite some new conquered Countrey.

Colures, two Circles in Heaven, wherein the Sun-stops are caused. [qu. spots?]

Cochenel, grain wherewith Purple is dyed.

Colosses, huge Statues erected in honour of any person.

Columbus, a Genoese, discoverer of America for Ferdinando, K. of Castile.

Comitiall-Ill, the Falling sicknesse.

Commodus, a most vicious Emperour.

Cones, geometricall figures, broad beneath, and sharpe above, with a Circular bottome.

Concentrick, having one common center.

Copernicus, a learned Germane, that maintained the Heavens to stand still, and the earth to turne round about.

Corvinus, a Romane Orator, that after a great sicknesse forgat his owne name.

Corfu, an Iland in the Ionian Sea, subject to the Venetians.

Critik, and *Criticall*, sharp censurers : all dangerous dayes for health, observed by Physicians.

Crescent, the Moon increasing.

Ctesiphon, the builder of Diana's Temple at Ephesus.

Ctesibes, an excellent inventer of water engines.

Cubes, geometricall figures foure-square, like a Die.

Cucuio, a strange bird in new Spain.

Cupid, the bastard of Mars and Venus, the little god of love.

Curius, a Citizen of Rome, famous for frugality and temperance, who delighted rather to command the rich, then to be rich.

Cylindres, geometricall figures round and long consisting from top to toe of two equall parallel Circles.

Cyclops, Gyants with one eye, working in the Forge of Vulcan.

Cyprus, a fruitfull Iland in the gulf of Issa, formerly subject to the Venetians, but now usurped by the Turk, anciently consecrated to Venus.

Cynthia, *Phœbe*, *Diana*, the Moon.

Cetherea, Venus.

Cynosure, seven stars in the North Pole, the North Pole, the North-star.

Cimbrians, the people of Denmarke and Norway.

Cyrus, the great King of Persia ; conquerour of the Medes, and after slaine by Tomyris, Queen of the Massagets.

Charites, looke *Graces*.

Clotho, looke *Parcæ*.

Chamosh, Idoll of the Moabites.

Chyron, a centaur, an excellent both Physician and Musician, the Master of Achilles.

Cornaline, looke *Onyx*.

Clarian, Lot-guider.

Cornich, looke *Frize*.

Crisis, the dangerous, or (as Physicians call it) criticall day for any disease.

Clide, a River running by Dombertan in Scotland.

Cyclades, floating Ilands in the Ægean Sea.

Cedron and *Kedron*, a brook in Judea.

Civik-Garland, a crowne or chaplet of Oaken sprigs, given to honour him that had rescued a City.

Clytemnestra, wife of Agamemnon, whom, with the helpe of her Adulterer Ægisthus, in a sleevelesse shirt shee murthered.

Cypris, sap, seed of generation.

Castor and *Pollux*, Twins begotten on Leda, by Jupiter in the shape of a Swan : and supposed Sea-Gods favourable to Saylors.

Crimsin Gulf, the red Sea.

Cecropian, that is, Athenian : of Cecrops, first King of Athens.

Cineas, a Thessalian, exceeding eloquent, and of admirable memory, Embassador from King Pyrrhus to the Romans.

Carthaginian, of that famous City of Affrica, built by Dido, and by Haniball undone.

Cadmean, by some writers used for Carthage.

Coronan, that is, Lacedemonian : for Corone was a City of the Messenians, who were subject to that State.

Cest, in Latin *Cestus* and *Cestum*, the Bride's Girdle, which the Bridegroome took off at night.

Coloquintida, a kinde of wilde Gourd that purgeth Choler.

Chrysocolle, Boras, Gold-soder.

Cibele, look *Rhea*.

D

*D*Amon, the most faithfull friend of Pythias, both disciples of Pythagoras.

Danae, daughter of Acrysius, who kept her lockt in a brazen Tower ; Jupiter rayned himselfe in a Golden shower into her lap.

Danubius, the greatest River in Europe, called also Isther.

Dardane Ants, Indian Emmets.

Darius, a King of Persia, vanquished by Alexander the great.

Delian Twins, the Sun and Moon.

Delian Princesse, Diana.

Delos, an Iland, one of the Cyclades, which for a long time floated as hidden in the Sea, and after suddenly appeared.

Delphian Oracle, the Oracle of Apollo, at Delphos.

Delphos-God, Apollo.

Democritus, the laughing Philosopher of Abidus.

Demosthenes, the best Orator of the Grecians.

Denis, or Dyonisius, a Tyrant of Syracuse.

Deucalion, sonne of Prometheus, who with his wife Pyrrha, escaped the Floud and (as the Poets faine) restored the world.

Diabete, a disease, when one cannot hold his water.

Diapason, a concord of all.

Diarrhea, a Laske or loosenesse of the Belly.

Diameter, a strait line dividing any figure into equall parts, passing through the middle point of any figure.

Dialect, a forme of speech divers from others in any language.

Diana, the Goddesse of virginity, the Moon.

Dircean wals, Thebes.

Disenteria, the bloudy-flux.

Dodochædrons, figures of the twelve Angles.

Druides, ancient learned Priests and Sages of France : supposed to have first issued out of this Ile of Britaine.

Dombertan, a Towne in Scotland.

Dagon, the Idol of the Philistines.

Demam, Possessions of inheritance, time out of Minde continued in the occupation of the Lord.

Duel, single Combat.

Demi-Gods, look *Heroik*.

Dorik musicke, soft and effeminate musicke, here opposed to the Phrygian, which was more lofty and full of life, and fitter to stirre up a courageous spirit.

Dan, a Towne in the North frontier of Judæa, where Jeroboam erected his other Calfe.

Ditthyrambik, a Song in the honour of Bacchus.

E

ECliptik line, a great Circle in the middle of the Zodiake, thorough which the Sun runneth his proper course in 365. dayes.

Egyptian floud, the river Nilus.

Electrum, Amber.

Electra, one of the sisters of Phaeton, who incessantly weeping for her brother's fall, was turned into a Tree that droppeth Amber.

Elixir, an Arabian word, signifying Quintessence, the Philosopher's stone.

Elysium, the fained Paradise of heathen Poets.

Eldebag, a learned Arabian Satyricall Poet.

Embrion, the Childe in the Mother's wombe before it have received shape.

Encyclopædie, that learning which comprehendeth all liberall Sciences.

Endymion, a young shepheard, the favorite of Cynthia.

Engastromith, one possessed, which seemes to speake in his belly.

Empiema, an impostume in the brest.

Enyon, the same that Bellona, sister to Mars, and Goddesse of Battaile.

Enthousiasmos, poeticall furie.

Eoan Monarch, Alexander the great.

Eolian scouts, the windes.

Ephemerides, Day-books, Registers, Journals.

Ephesian Temple, the Temple of Diana in Ephesus.

Ephesian moan, Heraclitus, weeping at the world's miseries.

Ephori, a kinde of Magistrates, Protectors of the people.

Epidemik-ills, Universall diseases.

Epicicle, a lesser Circle, whose center is in the circumference of a greater.

Epicurus, a Philosopher that placed man's felicity in the pleasures of the Sense, beleeving no God but Fortune.

Epilepsis, the falling-sicknesse.

Epithalamie, a nuptiall song.

Epitaph, a funerall song, or an Inscription on a Toomb or Grave.

Epithets, additions to Nounes, expressing some quality.

Epitomé, an Abridgement.

Epirus, a Countrey in Greece (now called Albania) famous in late times by the noble exploits of G. Castriot (sir-named Scanderbeg) against the Turk.

Equinoctiall, a Circle in Heav'n, through which when the Sun passeth, the dayes and nights be of equall length.

Erœtrian soyl, medicinable earth, brought from Eretrea.

Erebus, a river in hell : Hell.

Erithrean Deep, the red Sea.

Erynnis, one of the Furies.

Eridanus, a figure in Heav'n : the river Po, in Lumbardy.

Eurus, the East-winde.

Euripus, a narrow Sea ; which ebbeth and floweth seven times in 24. houres.

Euphrates, one of the Rivers of Eden, that runs through Babylon.

Europa, Christendome, or this Western part of the world.

Eccentrick, that hath his centre wholly separated from the Centre of the Earth.

Erisipiles, hot and red swellings, called S. Anthonie's fire.

Ericina, Venus.

Euphrosyne, look *Graces*.

Euphorbium, a certain medicinable Plant found and named by Euphorbus, King Juba's Physician.

Ethnick, see *Pagan*.

Entidorian.

Etesian gates, Easterly windes.

Ephod, a linnen garment worn by the Priests and levites of Israel.

Edom, and Idumea, a part of Palestine.

Eleutherian, Deliverer.

Epicarpian, Fruit-keeper.

F

FAbricius, a famous Romane, contemner of Riches, and in extreme poverty most puissant for vertuous valour and integritie.

Faustina, a most lascivious Empresse, wife to Marcus Aurelius, and daughter of Antonius Pius.

Fez, a Kingdome in Barbary.

Finland, a Dukedome under the King of Sweden.

Flamine, a Sacrificer, or high Priest, among the Heathen.

Flavio, Melphio a Neapolitan, inventer of the needle in the Mariner's compasse, and the use thereof.

Foix, a Country belonging to Navarr, neer the Pyren Mountaines.

Flora, a fair and rich harlot, which made the People of Rome her Heir : in respect whereof, they made her goddesse of Flowrs, and kept yearly Feasts in honour of her.

Furies, 3. (viz.) Alecto, Megera, and Tesiphone (sometimes called also Persyphone) which are said to bee tormentors of the damned in Hell, wittily fained to expresse the fear and fury of a guilty conscience.

Frize and *Cornich*, the crests, furniture and finishing at the upper end of a Column.

Farfalla, a Candle-Fly.

Fergusius, Evenus, Donaldus, famous ancient Kings of Scotland.

Fanes, Temples, consecrated Places.

Funambulant, a Rope-walker.

Feretrian, Peace-bringer, or dread striker.

G

GAlen, a famous Physician, borne at Pergamus, whose learned workes through all ages have been honoured.

Galenite, one skilfull in Physick, wherein Galen excelled.

Ganges, a great River in India.

Gaules, the ancient name of Frenchmen.

Genius, a man's spirit, or naturall instinct or inclination.

Gemonide, and *Gemonian* Ladders : a place in Rome from whence condemned persons were throwne downe.

Ghihon, one of the Rivers in Eden.

Gnidion, Idols, Venus and Cupid : for in Gnidos shee was worshipped.

Gonorrhea, a foule and involuntary Flux of seed, the Running of the Reins.

Gordian knot, a knot thought impossible to be undone, wherewith Gordius had fastned his Ox-yoke in the Temple of Apollo.

Gorgons, ugly hellish monsters, in forme of scaly Dragons, with crooked teeth, one eye, yron talons, and mighty wings.

Graces, look *Charites*.

Gymnosophists, Philosophers of India ; so called, because they went naked.

Groon-land, an exceeding cold Countrey, butting upon the Sea beyond Izeland.

Grave, is as much as an Earle with us ; but in this place used for the Generall and Governour JOSUA.

Galactite, a kinde of white Marble, or Alabaster.

H

HAlcion, a little water-bird thought to be the King's fisher.

Harpies, ravenous Birds, with faces like women.

Hecatombes, Heathen Sacrifices, wherein were offered an hundred Beasts.

Hebe, Jove's cup-bearer : the goddesse of youth.

Heber, of whom the Hebrews and Hebrew tongue are so called, the great-great-Grand-Childe of Sem, the Son of Noah.

Hecuba, the frantike and dis-figured, old withered wife of Priamus King of Troy, and here opposed to the fresh, young, beautifull Helena, the fatall Prize of their Son Paris.

Helicon, a Mountaine sacred to Apollo and the Muses.

Helena, the wanton wife of Menelaus, cause of the tedious siege, and finall sacke of Troy.

Hemisphear, halfe the compasse of Heav'n which wee behold.

Hercules, the most renowned Monster-Tamer of Thebes.

Hermes, Mercury.

Hero, the faire Sestian Nun, for whose sake Leander was drowned in Hellespont.

Heroës, halfe Gods, excellent men for valour and vertue.

Herophilus, a very ancient Physician.

Herodotus, an eloquent Greeke Historiographer.

Hesiodus, an ancient Greek Poet.

Hesperian Plant, golden fruit-trees guarded by a Dragon which was slain by Hercules : but here it is used for the Sugar Cane, a richer Plant then those (fained) golden fruits.

Hexameters, verses of six feet.

Hiades, 5. stars (some hold seven) in the Head of the Bull.

Hiëro, a King of Sicilia (after Agathocles) greatly delighted in husbandry.

Hiëroglyphicks, secret Cyphers, strange characters, mysticall writing by sundry forms of things.

Hiram, King of Tyrus, remembred in the Scripture for sending Timber and workemen to Salomon, to the building of the Temple in Jerusalem.

Homer, so called for his blindnesse, the most excellent of all the Greeke Poets.

Horizon, a Circle dividing the halfe-spheare of the firmament, which wee see over us, from the other halfe under us, which wee see not.

Hun, furious Attyla, who surnamed himselfe the scourge of God, and terrour of the World.

Hyantian Fount, springs sacred to the Muses.

Hydrantik braule, Musicke artificially made with the fall of waters.

Hyæna, a horrible Beast that counterfeiteth man's voyce.

Hydrargire, quick-silver.

Hydra, a Serpent with 50. heads slain by Hercules.

Hybla and *Hymetus*, } Mountaines abounding in Bees and Honey.

Hymen, the god of Mariage.

Hyperborean, above or beyond the blowing of the North-winde.

Hypocrates, a most excellent Physician.

Hypolitus, the Sonne of Theseus, who shunning the wanton inticemens of his step-dame Phædra, was (through her false accusations) torne in pieces.

Hyren, a faire Greeke Maiden-Captive, on whom Mahomet the second extremly doated.

Hesperus, the Evening-star, the Evening.

Helleborus, an herb, whereof be two kindes, supposed our Ling-wort and Bears-foot.

Heroïk, noble ; but anciently appropriate to those which were counted Demi-gods, supposed to bee borne and begot of a heavenly and an earthly Parent : as Æneas, of Venus and Anchises.

Hebridian Wave, the Sea about the Iles Hiberides, to the North from Ireland.

I

J Anus, an ancient King of Italy; whom, in respect of his wisedome and providence, they figured with two faces, as looking back into things past and foreseeing things to come.

Jaffa, (anciently *Joppa*) a notable Haven-Town in Syria, where they land that travell to Jerusalem.

Iapetus, a Thessalian, more famous by his two sonnes (Prometheus and Epimetheus) then for any great worth of his owne.

Jason, captain of the Argonautes, who by the favour of Medea, surmounting all dangers, brought home the Golden Fleece.

Ibis, a certaine high Bird, with a long Bill and stiffe legs, worshipped by the old Ægyptians.

Ibnu-farid, a learned Arabian, not much knowne in these parts.

Iberians, Spaniards.

Icarus, the sonne of Dedalus, who presuming to flee, was drowned in that Sea, which after bore his name.

Ichneumon, Pharaoh's Ratte: a little Beast, enemy to the Crocodile.

Idalian Fire, the burning desire of Love.

Idea, an Image or Patterne of things conceived in the Fancy.

Idioma, a proper and peculiar forme of speech.

Jessean Harp, the Holy Musicke of David, the Son of Ishai, commonly called Jesse.

Iliaca Passio, a kinde of Colicke.

Ilium, and *Ilion :* Troy.

Imaus, a hill in India, part of Caucasus.

Impartiall Maids, the fatall Sisters, Clotho, Lachesis, and Atropos.

Ile of Iron, or *Isola di Ferro*, one of the fortunate Ilands now called Canaries.

Incubus, a disease oppressing the stomach in our sleepe, which the ignorant have thought to bee a sprite: it is commonly called the Night-Mare.

Individuum, a body that cannot bee divided.

Jove's Bird, the Eagle.

Iris-bow, the Rainbow.

Juno's Bird, the Peacock.

Isleban, glory of Wittemberg: Martin Luther.

Isthmus, a narrow-strait of Land betweene two Seas.

Isther, Danubius.

Ithacan, Ulysses, the prudent husband of the most chaste Penelope.

Jupiter, the chiefe God of the Pagans.

Jubile, a year of libertie and release, which was every fiftieth year.

Justinian, a learned Emperour, Compiler of the Civill lawes.

Juturna, the North part of Scotland towards the Orcades.

Jaboc, a little brooke running into the river Jordan.

Isis, the wife of Osiris, both Idols of the Egyptians.

Juadan.

Jove, Jupiter, chiefe of the Heathen gods.

Juno, the Sister and wife of Jove: Goddesse of Dominion and Wealth, and supposed helper to women in travaile: sometimes taken for the Aire.

Iris, the Rain-bow.

Japhean, (or Jaffian) Seas beating upon the Coast of Zabulon towards Tyre and Sidon, on the farthest North of Judea: here opposed to Tygris in Mesopotamia, the farthest South of the same.

Jaffa, of old called Joppa.

Isaacians, children of Isaac, Israelites.

Izeland, an Iland in the farthest North towards Groonland.

Jebusites, the Heathen inhabitants of Jerusalem, before it came to the possession of the Israelites.

K

K Aros, a drowsie and stupifying disease in the head.

Kennet, a pleasant River running thorough Barkshire, neer unto whose flowry banks, our callow Cignets had their nest.

L

L Acedæmon, (called also Sparta) a City and a common-wealth, most famous and flourishing under the Lawes of Lycurgus.

Laconia, the Country where that City stood.

Lachesis, looke *Parcæ.*

Læda, the Wife of Tyndarus, who, by the help of Jupiter's Swan, layd two egges, whereof were hatched double Twins: of the one Pollux and Helena, of the other Castor and Clytemnestra.

Latmos, a Hill in Ionia, where Cynthia is said to have embraced her deare Endymion.

Latona, the Mother of Diana and Apollo.

Latonian Twinnes, those children of hers, the Sunne and Moone.

Lais, a beautifull and costly harlot of Corinth, frequented by many Gallants of Greece.

Lee, a neat little Towne in Essex, in the mouth of the Thames.

Leander, a young man of Abydus, beloved of Hero, drowned in Hellespont while he was swimming to her.

Lers, a River of France of most strange quality.

Lethé, a River in Hell which causeth forgetfulnesse.

Lethargie, the sleepy disease.

Lestrigons, a cruell people of Campania in Italy, which were said to feede on Man's flesh.

Lyguria, the Territory of Genoa.

Lycurgus, the famous Law-maker of the Lacedemonians.

Lemnos, Vulcan's Iland, now called Salamine.

Limbo, Hell.

Linus, an excellent ancient Musician, Master of Orpheus.

Linx, a beast of exceeding quick and piercing sight.

Leucippus, a Philosopher that imagined infinite worlds.

Leucothoe, a Sea goddesse.

Liquor-God, Bacchus.

Lopez, a late Jew-Spanish Physician, executed for infinite treasons against this State.

Lotos, an admirable plant, strangely sympathizing with the Sun.

Lucania, a Province of Italy, now called Basilicata.

Lucina, Juno and Diana, supposed of old to be assistant to women in their travell.

Lucretia, the chaste wife of Collatinus, ravished by Tarquin.

Lucretius, a very ancient Latine Poet.

Luna, the Moon.

Lupercales, Sacrifices and Feasts solemnized to Pan.

Lyceum, the School of Aristotle.

Legislator, a Law-maker, or a Law-giver.

Lesbian Squire, the Lesbians were so perfect workmen, that they made Rules and Squires by their Worke, and not their Worke by the Rule.

Loumond, a great lake in Scotland, where they say, their is a floating Iland.

Lucifer, the Prince of the proud Angels that fell from Heaven : The Divell, also the morning star.

Locusts, a kinde of Grashoppers.

Libanus, and Libanon, a Mountaine in Syria, famous for the fairest Cedar trees.

M

*M*Adera, one of the Canaries, from whence come excellent Sugars.

Malta, an Iland in the Mediterranean Sea, where the knights that were of Rhodes, now keep their residence.

Manie, a disease in the head, causing madnesse.

Martian-field, a field betweene Tyber, and the City of Rome, where they used to behold the fight of condemned men with wilde beasts.

Mars, the god of war.

Mark Pole, a notable Venetian Navigator and discoverer.

Maiz, Indian wheat.

Mausole, a sumptuous Toombe, built by Artemisia, Queene of Caria, for her husband Mausolus.

Marcellus, a most noble Romane Captaine, Conquerer of Syracusa, and five times Consull.

Mahomite, the Turkish Emperor, worshipping Mahomet.

Mantuan Muse, the Poet Virgill.

Massacres, horrible murders.

Medea, a sorceresse, or (as some call them) a cunning-woman.

Meanders, crooked turnings, so called of the River Meander, for his exceeding crookednesse.

Medices, the late Queene mother of France, of the House of Florence.

Medusa's Tresse, a head with snake-like hairs, turning the beholders into stones.

Mein, a River in Germany, whereon stands Frankfort, the famous Mart of the World.

Meonian Bard, Homer.

Mecænas, a noble Roman, and liberall favourer of Virgill.

Megera, one of the Furies.

Melt, an admirable Tree in Mexico, a mighty kingdome of America.

Memphians,
Memphites, } Ægyptians.
Memphists,
Memphitists,

Mercury, one of the Planets, the god of wit, eloquence, invention, and subtilty, and the messenger of the gods.

Mercuriall, (as it were) a Chancery, controuling and revoking false judgements of inferiour Courts.

Meridian, the South circle.

Metaphoras, borrowed speeches.

Metempsychosis, transmigration of soules from one body to another : after Pythagoras.

Metaphysicall, supernaturall.

Milo, a man of prodigious strength, that carried a Bull on his back, killed him with his fist, and ate him up in one day.

Mince, a river neere Mantua, where Virgil was borne.

Minerva, the same that Pallas : goddesse of wit and war.

Moly, an herb brought from Heaven by Mercury to Ulysses, supposed to be our Rue, or herb-grace.

Moloch, the Idoll of the Ammonites.

Moluques, rich Ilands in the East Indies, plentifull in all kinde of excellent Spices and other Treasures.

Moors, the people of Æthiopia, subjects of Prester John.

Morpheus, the god of dreams.

Mummie, a drug, taken for part of ancient imbalmed bodies.

Musculus, a little fish most officious to the Whale.

Musulmans, Arabians.

Mycæna, Agamemnon's kingdome.

Midas, a wealthy King of Phrygia, whose touch (by the grant of Bacchus) turned all things into Gold : so that at last his gold-turned meat in his mouth choaked him.

Myrmecides, a cunning and curious carver in small works.

Myron, an excellent statuarie, or Image-maker.

Mounte-banks, Jugglers.

Meroe, an Iland in the River Nilus.

Mages, Sages, Wise-men, Southsayers.

Morisco and *Mattachine*, Antike and fantastike dances.

Moderatrix, a Regent or Governesse.

MAGNIFICENCE, Greatnesse, State, Glory, Pomp.

Munificence, bounty, liberality.

Medals, Images of wood, stone, or metall.

Musaik worke, a kinde of painting so curiously shadowed, that it seems in some places imbossed, in some carved, in some in-laid, in some graven, &c.

Meteors, or *exhalations*, strange apparitions of comets, or other figures in the Air.

Megaria, where flourished the Philosopher Euclides, in the same time that Socrates in Athens.

N

N*Acre*, the Pearle-shell, or mother of Pearle.

Nadir, the point directly under us, just opposite to the Zenith or point verticall.

Natolia, Asia minor, now wholly under the Turk.

Nectar, the drink of the gods.

Neptune, the Sea.

Nephelean, Crook-horn, the signe Aries.

Nepenthe, an herb which being steeped in wine, is thought to expell sadnesse.

Nereus, the Sea.

Nero, a most cruell Emperour of Rome, the Monster of Nature, and shame of Mankinde.

Nestor, a wise and eloquent Greek, who being nie 300. years old, came to the siege of Troy.

Nile and *Nilus*, the famous River of Egypt, used often for Egypt it selfe.

Nimrod, the builder of Babel, the first ambitious usurper of soveraignty.

Niphates, a Mountaine from whence the River Tygris hath his source.

Nitre, a light, white, spongy matter, much like salt, which some have (falsly) thought to be salt-peter.

Noremberg, a City in Germany, especially famous for curious handy-crafts.

Nubian, of a Kingdome fronting on the South of Egypt.

Numidian, people of a part of Affrica, accustomed to live continually in the fields with the flocks, and heards, removing often for fresh pastures.

Numa Pompilius, 2ᵈ· from Romulus King of the Romans, and their first Law-giver.

O

O*Bsequies*, funerall ceremonies.

Ocean and *Oceanus*, the Sea.

Oedipus, a Riddle-reader of Thebes.

Oedems, thin, waterish, and flegmatike swellings.

Olympius, an Arrian Bishop, stroke dead with Lightning for blaspheming the Deity of Christ.

Olympus, a very high hill fronting on Macedonia : it is often used for Heaven.

Ophthalmy, a disease in the Eye through inflamation of the uttermost tunicle.   .

Optick sinnew, is that which brings sight unto the Eye,

Orgies, sacrifices to Bacchus.

Oracles, Mysteries of the Heathen gods, delivered by diverse meanes and in divers manners.

Orion, a tempest-boading star.

Orpheus, an excellent Poet and Musician of Thrace.

Oromene, a Mountaine in India, full of salt-quarres.

Ortygion Delos, a floating Iland, where Diana and Apollo were borne.

Orithyas love, Boreas, the North-winde.

Ottoman, the first Emperour of Turks.

Ovid's heirs, wanton Poets.

Oxygone, a sharp-Triangle.

Omer, a certain measure among the Hebrews.

Ophir, supposed to be Peru.

Onyx, a red pretious stone fit for Seals.

Orient, the East Sun-rising clear.

Oran, a Port-Towne in Barbary, within the Streights of Gibraltar.

P

P*Actolus*, a River in Lydia, which (after the washing of King Midas) is said to have golden sands.

Pallas, the goddesse of Arts and Wisedome.

Palæmon, a Sea-god, called also Melicertes.

Palestine, Judea, the holy Land, first called Canaan.

Pan, the god of Shepheards.

Pandects, Bookes treating of all manner of Arguments.

Panchaian Fumes, Incense.

Pannonia, Hungary and Austria.

Panope, a Sea-Nymph.

Pandora, fained (by Hesiodus) to bee the first woman, and made by Vulcan : indued by all the gods with severall excellent gifts, but afterward by Jupiter (in displeasure) sent to her spouse Epimetheus, with a Box full of all manner of miseries.

Paphos Archer, Cupid, the little god of love.

Paphian Fire or *shot*, } his Arrowes.

Parrhasius, a most excellent Painter of Ephesus.

Parthians, a people of Asia, excellent Archers, and notorious enemies to the Romans.

Paros, an Iland in the Archipelago (which divideth Europe and Asia minor) wherein is excellent white Marble or Alabaster.

Parcas, Parcæ, (*à non parcendo*) the Destinies, or three Fatall Sisters, (viz.) Clotho, Lachesis, and Atropos : death it selfe, the inevitable end of all.

Parallels, lines every where like distant.

Paradox, an argument maintained contrary to the common and received opinion.

Pegasus, the flying Horse of Bellerophon, which straining to flee up to Heaven, with his hoofe raised the top of Helicon, whence immediately gushed out a spring, which therefore is called Hypocrene.

Penelope, the most chaste Wife of the wandring Prince Ulysses.

Peneian Vale, is Tempe, a most pleasant valley in Thessaly, on the verge of the River Peneus.

Pentheus, a young Prince, who for contemning the drunken feasts of Bacchus, was by his owne mother (*Agave*) murdered.

Peripneumony, the Impostume of the Lungs.

Perige, that point of Heaven wherein the Sun (or other Planet) is nearest to the Centre of the Earth.

Persiphone, or *Proserpine :* the Queene of Hell and Horror.

Perseus, a most triumphant champion, that rescued Andromeda from the Sea-monster : who for his prowesse is both by Poets and Astronomers magnified as a god, and placed among the Stars.

Parnassus, the Mountaine of the Muses.

Persian Monarke, with the Heaven of glasse, was Sapores.

Peru, one of the largest and richest parts of America.

Phaeton, the Sonne of Phœbus, who presuming to guide his father's Chariot, set the world on fire, and fell himselfe headlong into the River Eridanus.

Phœbus, the Sun.

Phalaris, a most cruell Tyrant of Agrigent.

Phalec, the son of Heber.

Pharos, a Lanthorne-Tower to beare a light for the guide of Sailers in a haven by night : also an Iland.

Phlegon, one of the horses of the Sun's Chariot.

Phlegeton, a River in Hell, taken oft for Hell it selfe.

Philtre-charm'd, inchanted with love-potions.

Phantick, such as are haunted with strange and illuding visions.

Philirian Scout, the signe of Sagittarius.

Philometor, an ancient King of Egypt, much given to husbandry, and delighting in the country-life.

Phlebotomy, bloud-letting.

Phlegmons, hot and red inflammations of bloud.

Phrygian Skinker, the signe Aquarius.

Phrixus' Sister was Helle, drowned in Hellespont, which of her is so called.

Phrenzie, a most violent and dangerous disease of the braine.

Phthisick, the consumption of the Lungs.

Phthiriasis, the louzie disease.

Pica, the longing disease of women with childe.

Physon, one of the Rivers in the garden of Eden.

Pigmes, little people of the North a cubit high.

Pyrene, a Princesse from whom Pyrene Mountaines (which divide France and Spain) are so called.

Pindus, a Mountaine sacred to the Muses.

Pierian Maids, the Muses.

Pirrhon, (reade *Pirrho*) a Philosopher alwayes doubtfull of all thing, yea even of those subject to our senses.

Plato, Prince of the Academicks, sir-named divine, and indeed the most neere approaching Divinitie of all the Heathen.

Pleiades, the 7. stars.

Plessis, a noble learned Frenchman of our time, a notable defender of the truth of Christian religion against all Jewes, Turks, Pagans, Papists, Atheists, and Infidels whatsoever.

Pluto, the god of Hell and of riches, the Divel and all.

Po, the River that watereth Lumbardy, the garden of Italy.

Polipes, a subtle Fish called a Many-feet, or Pourcontrell.

Polymnia, manifold memory, in variety of knowledge.

Poles, the imagined Hinges of the Heavens, whereon the World is turned, commonly used for Heaven.

Poëtasters, base, counterfeit, unlearned, witlesse and wanton Poets, that pester the world, either with idle vanities, or odious villaines.

Porphiry, Marble.

Porus, a King of India of huge stature, overcome by Alexander.

Polygamie, the having of many wives.

Polypheme, a huge and cruell Gyant, with one eye in his forehead.

Pomona, goddesse of fruits.

Pontik heath, Pontus is a region in Asia minor, fronting Eastward upon Colchis.

Progne, Pandion's daughter, sister of Philomele, and wife of Tereus, transformed to a swallow.

Proteus, a Sea-god that taketh on him all shapes.

Problems, mathematicall propositions, referred especially to practice.

Prometheus, is fained to have made the first man, and to have stollen fire from heaven to put life into his creature.

Pryenian Sage, Bias.

Ptolemeus Philadelphus, most famous for his learning and love to the learned, and especially for his noble Librarie erected in Alexandria.

Pyramides, exceeding huge and high Spires, built by the Kings of Egypt for fond and idle ostentation of their riches and pride.

Pyrausta, a fire-flye, or winged worm, breeding and living onely in the fire.

Python, a horrible Dragon slaine by Apollo.

Pagan, Heathen, an Infidell, uncircumcised, unbaptized, that knowes not God.

Phidias, a famous carver in wood and stone.

Persyphone, look *Furies*.

Pirenes, look *Bigaurian*.

Phrygian Musick, look *Dorik*.

Pellean Prince, Alexander the Great borne in a City of Macedonia called Pella, as was also Philip his father.

Panomphean, all-hearing.

Phryxian, fugitive.

Proselite, a stranger new-converted to our faith and fashion.

Pharan, a City between Egypt and Arabia : also a Wildernesse which the Israelites passed in their Pilgrimage to Canaan.

Pharus, look *Pharos*.

Pyrrhus, a valiant King of the Epirots, a notable Enemie to the Romans.

Passe-Lamb, the Paschall Lamb.

Pelusian Foord, Nilus, the great River of Egypt.

Pythian Knight, is Apollo, sir-named Pythias, for slaying the dreadfull Serpent Pytho.

Parian Rocks, Mountains of white Marble or Alabaster, in the Ile of Paros.

Patagons, Indian Canibals, such as eat man's flesh.

Posthumus, one borne after his Father's death.

Prodigies, extraordinary and miraculous accidents.

Picts, ancient Inhabitants of a part of Scotland.

Para-Nymphs, Bride-dressers, too curious prankers of themselves.

Pyrrhik Galiard, a kinde of dancing in armour, invented by Pyrrhus.

Porphire, a kinde of red Marble.

Plynth, a part of the Base of a pillar, flat square like a tile.

R

R *Abbines*, great Doctours among the Jewes.
  Rabican, the name of a gallant horse in *Orlando Furioso*.

Regulus, a noble Consull, and resolute Captaine of the Romans in the Punick-war.

Remora, a little fish (which some call a Suck-stone) that suddenly stoppeth a ship under all her sails in her full course.

Rendezvous, an appointed place of meeting.

Rome's Dragon, the Pope.

Ryphean Wood, Forrests of Scythia.

Rhea, the same that Cybele, Vesta, Tellus, the Earth.

Rheubarb, an excellent root, and very pretious for the purging quality.

Rubrick, the Titles and Directions in the old Psalters, or service-Bookes : so called, because they are written or printed in red Letters.

S

S *Aba*, chiefe City of the Sabæans in Arabia, abounding in Cinnamon, Cassia, Frank-incense and Myrrhe.

Salamander, a spotted beast like a Lizard, whose extreme coldnesse quencheth the fire.

Salmoneus, a King, that with certaine violent engins counterfeited Thunder.

Salust, a notable Romane Historiographer, also the sir-name of our noble and renowned Author Du BARTAS.

Samian wise, Pythagoras.

Sardanapalus, a most effeminate King, the last of the Assyrians.

Sargus, a Fish strangely lustfull.

Saturn's door, the end of Time.

Saturnalls, Feasts kept in December in the honour of Saturn.

Satyres, nipping Poesies, that reprove vice sharply without respect of persons.

Scaliger Josephus, now living, a Frenchman, admirable in all languages, for all manner of learning.

Scipio, (sir-named Affrican) a most wise, valiant, and vertuous Captaine of the Romans, who, being ill requited for infinite honourable services, sequestred himselfe to a Country-life.

Schirrhes, a kinde of hard (yet pain-lesse) swellings in the flesh.

Scolopendra, a certaine fish that casteth forth her bowels, to clear them from the hook.

Scopas, a notable Architect, imployed in the building of Mausolus' Tomb, which is numbred among the seaven wonders of the world.

Syrtes, dangerous sands in the Lybian Sea.

Serhan Forrests, (now Cathay and Cambalu) are in Asian Scythia, abounding in the best Silks.

Serranus, a worthy Roman fetcht from his plough to the Dictatorship, which was (for the time) an office of King-like Authority.

Sentinel, a scout, or Night-watch in a Camp or Town of Garrison.

Seraphin, an Angell.

Sein, the river of Paris.

Shynar, or *Sennaar*, the Plain where Nimrod built the Tower of Babel.

Sibels, Prophetesses : Varro remembers ten of them.

Semiramis, the proud and wanton Queene of Babylon, wife of Ninus.

Sirius, the Dog-star, at whose rising the Dog-dayes always begin.

Skink Alexandrian, a kinde of Serpent, a land-Crocodile.

Skinker, the signe Aquarius.

Sol, the Sunne, one of the 7. Planets.

Solides, 5. regular bodies or figures Geometricall (viz.) the Circle, Cube, Pyramide, Cilinder, and Dodochædron.

Sostrates, a notable Architect, builder of the Lanthorn-Tower in the Ile of Pharos.

Stagyrian, Aristotle, there borne.

Stix,
Stigian strand, } Hell.

Steropes, one of Vulcan's Cyclops.

Stoiks, severe Philosophers, pretending to condemne all passions : and esteeming all things to be ordered by an inevitable necessity of Fate or Destiny.

Strymon, a River betweene Macedon and Thrace.

Suisses, (wee call them Swizers) the war-like people of the Cantons of Helvetia.

Sulphur, Brimstone.

Starre-ship, Argos, a Signe or Constellation in Heaven, supposed to have been the Ship that Jason and his fellowes fetcht the Golden Fleece in.

Synonimas, words of the same signification.

Symbolize, to resemble or agree.

Sympathy, consent or resemblance of quality.

Symphony, consent of time or harmony.

Symmetry, proportion of parts betweene themselves, and to their whole.

Syracusa, a great, wealthy and wanton City in Sicilia.

Syrens, Mer-Maids.

Satyr, a wilde wood-monster, halfe-man, halfe-goate : also a kinde of nipping Poesie, reproving vice impartially.

Salem, Jerusalem.

Spartans, look *Lacedæmon*.

Sina, or *Sinai*, a Mountain in Arabia, the same that Horeb, where the Law was given to Moses.

Salamina, an Iland and City in the Euboike Sea, now called the Gulf of Negropont.

Stentorian, Homer reports him to have had the voyce of fiftie men.

Signories, Lordships, Dominions.

Sues, a Port in the East part of Egypt upon the red Sea.

Seir, a Mountaine in Idumæa, betweene Asphaltis and Egypt.

Siddim, the place where Lot, with the Princes of Sodom, was taken prisoner, by Chedor-Laomer.

Sanctum Sanctorum, the inmost Sanctuarie, the Holy of Holies, where onely the high Priest might enter once a yeare,

Stratian, War-like.

Scammonie, alias *Diagrydium*, an herb purging Choler mightily.

T

Tagus, the River Lisbone in Portugall.

Tanais, a mighty River dividing Asia from Europe.

Tantalus, a King of Phrygia, whom they fained to stand in Hell up to the chinne in water, and to have delicate Fruits dangling over his upper lip, yet can touch neither ; either to ease his hunger, or allay his thirst.

Tambut, a Countrey of the Negros, which is a part of Affrica, extending to the uttermost bounds thereof towards the South and East.

Taprobane, an Iland under the Equinoctiall (now called Sumatra) situate betweene Malca and Java Major, above 450. leagues long, and above 120. broad : abounding in Gold, and very plentifull in other excellent commodities.

Tarentum, a famous City in Calabria.

Tarnasser, is in the East Indies, neere the gulfe of Bengala.

Thebes, a City in Bœotia where Hercules was borne it was first builded by Cadmus, but more beautifully restored by Amphion.

Thetis, the Sea.

Themis, Justice.

Thersites, the foulest Lubber in all the Grecian Campe, whom Achilles slew with his fist.

Theseus, for valour, another Hercules : but most famous for his kinde and constant friendship to Pirithous.

Thisbe's Tree, the Mulbery.

Thule, an Iland beyond the Orcades, the farthest north that was known to the Romans, and therefore then called *Ultima Thule*.

Timanthes, one of the most excellent of the ancient Painters.

Tindarides, Castor and Pollux.

Tygris, a river in Asia, passing by the East of Mesopotamia, through Armenia & Media.

Titan, the Sun.

Tirrhenian, the Tuscan Seas.

Tyrians, Merchant men of Tyrus, a City of Syria, anciently flourishing in trade, and famous for the excellent purple-Die.

Tivoli, a village neer Rome, where the Cardinall of Ferara hath a sumptuous house of pleasure, furnished with infinite Curiosities.

Torpedo, the Cramp-fish.

Tresor trove, Gold, Money, or other riches found under ground.

Troglodytes, a people of Æthiopia, that dwell under ground, go naked, and eat Serpents.

Tropiks, two great Circles in heaven in equal distance from the equinoctiall, the one called the Tropik of Cancer, the other of Capricorne, at which the Sun turneth either higher (having been at the lowest) or lower (having been at the highest) whereof they are so called.

Trytons, Neptune's Trumpeters.

Tuscan, Italian.

Tyber, the River of Rome.

Typhis, the Master or Captaine of the Ship Argos, that sailed with Jason to Colchis for the Golden Fleece.

Tymothy, an excellent carver that wrought on Mausolus' Tomb.

Typhon, a huge Giant, that indevoured to pull Jupiter out of heaven.

Type, a figure or stamp of any thing.

Tesiphone, or *Thesiphone*, one of the Furies.

Tropheis, glorious Monuments erected in honour of some famous victorie.

Timotheus Milesius, an excellent musician, that flourished under Philip of Macedon and Alexander his son.

Theory, Contemplation, Study.

Tully, Cicero, the Prince of Roman Orators.

Thalia, look *Graces* and *Muses*.

Tabernacle, properly a Tent or Pavilion.

V

Valois, one of the royal families of France extinguished in the late Henry the third (slain by a Friar before Paris) who in his Monsieurship (with his mother and the Duke of Guise) had been too busie an Actor in the bloudie Massacre.

Venus, the goddesse of Love and Beauty, also one of the Planets.

Venus Escuage, Knights (or nights) service to ladies.

Venerean mirth, Idem.

Ver, the Spring.

Vertumnus, an imagined god of the Romans that took on him all shapes.

Vespucio, Americus Vespucius, a Florentine, first discoverer of America, of whom it was so called.

Viginere, a learned French-man of late times, translator of Cæsar, Livius, and other Latine Writers.

Vienna, a City in Austria, where usually the Emperour keeps his court.

Urania, one of the Muses, especially handling heavenly things, therefore called the heavenly Muse.

Urim and *Thummim*, two words graven in the Breast-plate of Aaron, signifying Illumination and Integrity.

Ulysses, the Politick Prince of Ithaca, husband of Penelope.

Vulcan, the god of fire and forge-men.

Uranoscopus, a Fish alwaies gazing up to heaven.

X

X*Anth,* called also *Scamander,* the River of Troy : there is also an Iland in the Archipelago so called.

Xenian, hospitious, milde-entertainer.

Z

Z*Ebut,* an Iland in the West Indies, exceeding rich in Gold, Sugar, and Ginger.

Zenith, the point verticall, the point of heaven right over our heads : the contrary point is called Nadir,

Zeno, the chief of the Stoïcke Philosophers.

Zeuxis, a most cunning and exceeding rich Painter.

Zodiack, a biaz or sloaping Circle in the heavens, wherein are the twelve Signes thorow which all the planets passe.

Zones, imagined Circles, dividing the world into five parts.

Zopyrus, a Persian that strangely dis-figured himselfe to doe his Prince an important service.

Zephyrus, the West, the West-winde.

F I N I S.

LITTLE
BARTAS:
OR, *BRIEFE*
MEDITATIONS
ON
The Power,
Providence, Greatnes,
AND,
Goodnesse of God,
IN THE
CREATION;
Of the World, for *Man:*

Of Man,
For HIMSELFE.

Translated; and dedicated

To The

Most Royall Ladie,
ELIZABETH.

BY

JOSUAH SYLVESTER.

TO THE MOST ROYALL

LADY ELIZABETHA INFANTA

of England; Princesse PALATINE
of RHINE.

SWeet Grace of GRACES, Glory of Your Age,
    Lustre of VERTUES (Morall and Divine)
    Whose Sacred Raies (already) far out-shine
Your Princely State, Your Royall Parentage;
Here, to your HIGHNES (with all Good-Presage,
    Congratuling Your little PALATINE)
    I consecrate This LITTLE-One of Mine,
    To serve Your Self first; then Your Son, for Page.
Your gracious Favours to my former Brood,
    So binde my Thoughts, so bolden my Desires,
    To shew Mee gratefull, as I know You good;
That Thus to You, This LITTLE Mine aspires:
    Little in Growth, yet of so great a Spirit,
    As (happily) Your Grace's grace may merit.

———————————————————————————To your Highnesse service,

———————————————————————————Duely and Truely devoted,

———————————————————————————JOSUAH SYLVESTER.

Sou haits
Royaux & Loyaux

Au Roy.

AInsi, l'Ancien des Temps, d'Ans, d'Honneurs, & Bonheurs,
    Comblant ce Chef Royall; couronne voz Labeurs:
    Qui, pour le Droict des Roys, d'un Glaive tout divin,
    Combattez l'Antichrist, & son grand BELLARMIN.

Au Prince Charles.

AInsi, le Tout-puissant, de sa main de PANDORE,
    Face d'un Charle-moindre, un Charle-magne encore;
    Qui, suivant Voz Vertuz, derive, perennel,
    Saincts-Sages-Preux STUARTS au Sceptre paternel.

Aux Princes Palatins.

AInsi, le Ciel benin de ses Tresors benisse,
    L'Hymen heureux & sainct de FRED'RIC & d'ELIZE;
    De sorte, que d'Iceux, leurs Filz & leurs Neveuz,
    Nous naissent desormais des EMPEREURS heureux.

Aux Anglois & Allemans.

AInsi, Lions ANGLOIS & Aigles d'ALLEMAGNE
    (Triumphants, pour la Foy, de ROME & de l'ESPAGNE)
    Terrassent coup à coup les Lunes du TURQUOIS,
    Pour planter tout par tout les Lauriers de la CROIX.

LITTLE BARTAS.

If wanton Lovers so delight to gaze
  On mortall Beautie's brittle little blaze;
  That, not content with (almost) daily sight
Of those dear Idols of their Appetite;
Nor with th' Idëas which th' Idalian Dart
Hath deep imprinted in their yeelding hart;
Nor with their Pictures (with precisest charge)
Done by De-creets, Marcus, or Peak, at large
(And hang'd of purpose, where they most frequent,
As some faire Chamber's choicest Ornament)   10
They must have Heliard, Isaac, or His Sonne,
To doe, in Little, what in Large was done;
That they may ever, ever bear about
A Picture's Picture (for the most, I doubt):
Much more should those, whose Soules, in Sacred Love,
Are rapt with Beautie's-Proto-Type above
(Sith, heer, they cannot see th' ORIGINALL;
Nor, in themselves, now, finde his Principall)
Thirst for Their Object; and [much lesse content
With th' ample Table of the Firmament,   20
And various Visage of this goodly Globe,
Wherein, they see but (as it were) His Robe
Embrodered rich, and with Great Works embost,
Of Pow'r, of Prudence, and of Goodnesse, most;
Yet, so far-off, so massy, so immense,
As over-swaies Their weak Intelligence:
Or with that lesser Tablet of their owne
(The Little-World, wherein the Great is show'n)
Which, neer and dear, though still about they bear,
Such Clouds of Passion are still crowding there,   30
That seld or never can they ought perceive
Of those pure Raies it did at first receive]
Long for their Long-home, past the Gates of Grace,
To see their Love, in Glory, face to face.

  Till when; awhile to entertain them here
With Prospects fittest Their faint Thoughts to cheer
(In stead of That Great Universall Table,
Made in Six Dayes, with Art so admirable;
And, by My BARTAS, in His Weeks divine,
So large and lively drawn in every line)   40
Du-VAL, and I (too short of Isaac's Art)
Have Thus Essaid to play the Limner's part,
And draw in little (like a Quintessence)
That goodly Labour's glorious Excellence;
For ease of Such, whom Publike Charge denies
Leasure to view so large Varieties:
And Such whose Means may not afford their Minds
So costly Pleasures of so Gainlesse kindes:

And (lastly) Such, as, loving BARTAS best,
Would glad and fain still bear Him in their Brest,   50
Or in their Bosom, were Hee Pocket-fit,
As well Hee might; would Printer's Gain permit.
  Now therefore, Thou, All-forming ONELY-TRINE,
As, in the Large, Thou led'st His Hand and Mine;
Lend likewise here Thy gracious Help agen,
To guide aright my Pencil and my Pen;
To sute my Colours, sweet my Shadows, so,
That This my little, Thy Great Works may show.
  And grant, the while, I be not like the Hand
Which at S. Albons, in the Street, doth stand   60
Directing Others in the ready Way;
But, void of minde, it Selfe behinde doth stay:
Nor, like a Buoy, which warneth from a Shelf;
But lies still wallowing in the Sea, it Selfe.

Supernall Lord, Eternall King of Kings,
  Maker, Maintainer, Mover of All things,
How infinite! how excellently-rare!
How absolute Thy wondrous Works they are!
How-much Their Knowledge is to be desir'd!
How, THOU, in All, to be of All admired!   70
  Thy glorious Pow'r so suits thy gracious Will:
Thy sov'rain Wisedome meets thy Goodnesse still:
Thy Word effects thy Work; and, void of Pain,
Turns round the Heav'ns, & doth the Earth sustain.
  Thy Spirit, infallible and infinite,
Filling the World (yet not contain'd in it)
By Pow'r and Presence, all, in All things dwels;
In Essence though, the Heav'n of heav'ns excels.
  Eternally, before All Form began,
Thou, onely God, wert in Thy-self, even than,   80
As absolute; as after all the Term
Of All thy Works: They, changeful All; Thou firm.
  The Revolution of This ample All,
Heav'n's hight, Stars' light, the Ocean's floud & fall,
To all Mankinde, in some wide, make Thee known;
But adde not Thee more Glory to Thine own.
  To make a World, or mar it, Thou art free.
All coms and goes by Thy divine Decree.
Thou, at Thy pleasure, hast made All of Nought:
All at Thy pleasure, shall to nought be brought.   90
  Thy Name is (right) I AM: for without Thee,
Is None: all beeings of thy BEEING be:
All perfect Unity, proper Existence,
Is onely found in Thine owne sacred Essence.
  Although the World a goodly Piece appear,
'T hath, to Thy Greatnesse, no Proportion neer:

'Tis but a Point to Thine immense Infinity.
Then, what (alas !) is Man to Thy DIVINITY?
Yet hast Thou Him a Tongue and Reason giv'n ;
And Eyes erected towards Thy glitt'ring Heav'n,　100
To read and ruminate Thy Wonders there ;
And afterwards proclaim them every-where.

The Heav'ns declare Thy Glory, and they preach
To Man, Thy *Works*, Thine *Excellence* in Each :
The Elements accorded Discords sound
How good for us thy goodly *Works* are found.

The radiant Stars, in their eternall Sway,
Th' alternate Changes of the Night and Day,
The birth of beasts, the growth of plants, each hour,
Teach every where Thy Providence and Pow'r.　110

From THEE, the Sun receives his Beauty bright,
And Soveraigne Rule of Each celestiall Light ;
Whose Yearly Course, in certain Circuiting,
Makes Winter, Summer, Autumn, and the Spring.

Be 't cloudy, cleer, Eclipse, or Night, or Day ;
His lovely brows are equi-lucent ay :
And, whether swift and soft Hee seem to wend,
His Speed is such, Wee cannot comprehend.

Though us Hee warm, yet is himselfe not hot ;
Though red, or pale, Hee seem, yet is Hee not :　120
Though small to us, His Orb is eight-score times
And six, as big as All our Earthly Climes.

Did not Hee draw moist Vapours from below,
To drench our fields ; here, nothing green would grow :
Did not Hee dry excessive Show'rs again,
Wee could not sow, or mow, our Grass, nor Grain.

Thou, Lord, by Him, work'st all this Alteration,
And causest so all Creatures' generation :
Prankest the Earth in diverse-Flowred hew ;
And yearly, almost, mak'st the *World* anew.　130

Thou hast dispos'd His oblique Body so,
That Rise hee, Set hee, be hee High, or Low ;
His Noon 's perpetuall : and hee makes at once

Day, Night ; $\left.\begin{array}{l}\text{Summ}\\\text{Wint}\end{array}\right\}$ er : frying, freezing Zones.

When low to Us, to Others hee is high ;
When Others see not, Wee behold his Eye ;
When here hee Sets, hee rises other-where ;
When here direct, hee looketh glancing there.

When som, in Summer, hear sweet Nightingales,
Then som, in Winter, hear but blustring Gales ;　140
Som see but Buds, when som supply their Granges :
Each-where, the Sun thus Seasons contre-changes.

When here, ther springs both leaf & gras together,
Else-where the Meads do hang their heads and wither :
So, in their turns, so in their times, he measures
His Gifts to all ; and all partake his Treasures.

In brief, each change of short, long ; Day & Night ;
Of Seasons, Times, Turns, and Returns of Light ;
Which, in a whole Year, every-where hee forms :
That, in the whole *World*, daily hee performs.　150

So that, drad Lord, were not Thy sacred Lore,
Man, above All, would likely Him adore,
(As som have done) ; but Supreme Reason showes,
That all His Glory unto Thine hee owes.

Things finite have Beginning and Beginner ;
Things mov'd, a Mover (as the wheel, the Spinner) :
Effects, their finall Cause ; and (formerly)
Elder then Time, Nature or Faculty.

Even Thee the *Cause* of *Causes :* Sourse of All :
First, and *Last, Mover ; Prime*, and *Principall :*　160
Infallible, involuble, insensible,
All *Self-comprising*, else incomprehensible :
Immense, Immortall, absolute Infinity,
Omnipotent, Omniscient, DIVINITY.

Even Thee, in Whom alone begins all *Good*,
And all returns into thy bound-lesse Floud.

By Order then of thy Decrees divine,
Th' hast set the *Sun* o'r all the *World* to shine,
And (as the Subjects lightly suit their King)
With his fair Light, t' enlighten every thing.　170

His goodly Face, th' ungodly ever fly,
Seeking for *Night's* black horrid Canapy
To cover Theft, Rape, Incest, murder too,
And all foul *Sinnes*, which, in the Dark, they doe.

By Him *Wee see thy Works* in their Propriety ;
Discern their Beauties, learn their vast variety :
Where, without Him, the *World* would all return
To th' old first CHAOS, or in Blindnesse mourn.

By Him, Wee calculate our Grandsires' Dates,
Th' Increase of Kingdoms, and Decay of States :　180
By Him, Thou measur'st, Lord, to Us and Ours,
Yeers, Ages, Seasons, Months, Daies, Minutes, Hours.

All Wits admire th' immense and wondrous way
His great bright Body circuits every Day :
The more his Orb is from the Centre far,
The longer Daily his great Journies are.

Besides his Daily Course, his Coursers drive
One of three hundred threescore Daies and five,
Five Hours, three Quarters : of which Over-plus,
In every fourth Year, growes a Day with us.　190

Yet, Whoso would the Year exactly rate,
In five-score-five Years, must one Leap abate :
And, in threescore, for th' Error ready past,
Should no Bissextile in our Bookes be plac't.

But though Wee erre, Hee never erres at all :
Nor, Since Thou didst him in his State install,
Hath Hee mist Moment of the Task hee ought :
Though hee have seen Men fail and fall so oft.

Above all Creatures, Hee retains, of Thee,
Som-thing conform to Thine *Eternity :*　200
For, though Hee see our hourly Changes here,
His Light and Beauty still the same appear.

How many Changes hath Hee seen on Earth !
Kings, Kingdoms, States ; their buriall, & their
　　birth ;
Rising and falling of triumphant Races ;
Raising and Razing of Renowned Places?

How often hath Hee seen Empires reverst ?
Rich Cities sackt ? Rare Common-weals disperst ?
Fields turn'd to Flouds, and Seas return'd to Sands,
While stedfast Hee between his Tropiks stands?　210

Him, just betwixt Six Wand'rers hast thou plac't,
Which prance about Him with unequall haste :

All which, without Him, could no Light reflect,
As is apparent by the Moon's defect.
　By His Aspect, her owne shee daily makes :
She, Wax-less, Wane-less, doth both wane & wax :
And, though to Us Shee seem a Semi-Ray,
Her full round Face doth never fall away.
　By his fair Beams, as well by Day as Night,
The full whole Halfe of her thick Orb is bright :　　220
And, as Shee draws neer or far-off from Him ;
So more, or lesse, Our Half is cleer or dim,
　Her upper Half is full in her Coition,
Her lower Half is in her Opposition :
Her other Quarters other Forms expresse ;
And, up or down-ward, shew Her more or lesse.
　When We see little, then the Heav'ns have store :
When Heav'ns see little, then have Wee the more :
Neerer the Sun, the lesse Shee seems in sight ;
Turning her Horn, still to her Opposite.　　230
　At Even, Increasing, Shee the Sun succeeds ;
At Morn, Decreasing, Shee his Car preceeds :
So that, each Month the Sun environs Her,
On every side His Splendor to confer.
　Her silver Light then onely faileth her
When th' Earth's between Them (in Diameter) :
Which Masks her Beauty with a sable Cloud,
From Sight of Him, her Brother Golden-brow'd.
　Good Lord, what changes dost thou work by these
Varieties ; in Air, in Earth, and Seas !　　240
Fair, or foul Weather ; Winde, or Wet, or Thunder ;
To dry, or drip ; or cool, or warm Here-under.
　If shee but Smile the fourth day, 't will be fair ;
If then Shee blush, wee shall have blustring air :
If then her brows be muffled with a Frown,
Most of that month shall sad tears trickle down.
　Thus doth the Vigour of the Signs superiour
Rule in the Vertues of these things inferiour :
But All are govern'd by Thy soverain Might :
O ! happy Hee who understands it right.　　250
　Thrice happy Hee, who sees Thee every-where :
In Heav'n, and Earth, in Water, Fire, and Air :
Who, due admiring Thy wise Works (of Yore)
Thee above All, Thee onely, doth adore.
　Who knowes Thee so, so needs must love Thee
　　too ?
And, with his Will, Thy sacred *Will* would doe :
Still lifts his eyes to Heav'n-ward, to contemple
The stately Wonders of Thy starry Temple :
　Admires the set and measur'd Dance of Thine
All-clasping Palace, Azure crystalline,　　260
Rare-rich imbost with glittering Studs of Gold ;
And, more admires, the more Hee doth behold.
　'Tis a wondrous thing to see That mighty Mound,
Hinge-less and Ax-less, turn so swiftly round ;
And th' heavy Earth, prop-less (tho downward tending)
Self-counter-poiz'd, 'mid the soft Air suspending.
　On th' ample Surface of whose massie Ball
Men (round about) doe trample over all,
Foot against Foot, though still (O strange effect !)
Their Faces all be towards Heav'n erect.　　270

　Those dwelling under th' *Equinoctiall*, they
Have, all the Year long, equall Night and Day :
Those neer the *Tropiks* have them more un-even ;
The more, the more that they are Nor-ward driven.
　But those, whose Tents to either Pole are neer,
Have but One Night, and One Day, in a yeer :
Yet All well compast by due ruled Rite,
Neither, then other, hath more Dark or Light.
　Thus have thy Works, O All-disposing *Deity*,
Som-what conform, for all their great variety :　　280
Which Harmony, amid so diverse things
In All, aloud Thy wondrous Wisdom rings.
　But, specially, wee wonder at the Place
Which here thou hast bestow'd on *Adam's* race :
To see our selves set on so Round a Ball,
So firmly hang'd just in the mid'st of all.
　For, This our Globe hangs Prop-less in the Air ;
Yet, but thy *Self*, can nothing shake or sway-her :
No roaring Storm, nor rumbling Violence,
Can move the *Centre's* sad Circumference.　　290
　Which, whoso should oppose in Disputation,
Might be convinc't by easie Demonstration :
So, far doe they from Sense and Reason erre,
Who think the Heav'ns stand, and th' Earth doth stir.
　The Parts and Whole of same-kind bodies, have
Same or like Motions ; be they light, or grave :
Upward, or downward ; round or overthwart :
Needs must the Totall move as doth his Part.
　So, if wee see the Sun and Moon to veer ;
Their Ample Heav'ns have even the like Career :　　300
But, who hath seen a Selfly-turning Stone ?
How then should *Earth* turn her whole lump alone ?
　Let 's therefore, boldly, with old Truth affirm,
That th' Earth remains unmoveable and firm :
And (if wee credit the Geometer)
Three thousand leagues is her Diameter :
　This Measure of her vast thick Depth, is found
By th' admirable Compasse of her Round ;
Which hath, by Test of Art's Experiments,
More then nine thousand leagues Circumference.　　310
　Yet, learned Mappists, on a Paper small,
Draw (in Abbridgement) the whole Type of all ;
And, in their Chamber (pain-lesse, peril-lesse)
See, in an hour, and circuit, Land and Seas.
　This mighty Globe is but a Point, compar'd
With th' upper Globe : yet on his Point are shar'd
Millions of millions of Man-kinde, which plow
With Keel and Coulter its Twin Back and Brow.
　Man, placed thus, in This Mid-Point, so even,
Sees alwaies Halfe of God's great Hall of Heav'n :　　320
Th' other 's beneath him ; yet abides not there
But in a Day doth to him all appear.
　Ah, Soveraign Artist ! O how few of us
Know right the Place where Thou hast plac't us thus !
Alas ! how many know not, to what end
Thy gracious Wisdome did them hither send !
　Yet, giving Man a quick Intelligence,
Thou sett'st him just in the World's Midst ; that,
　　thence

Seeing thy Wonders round about him so,
Knowing himself, hee might Thee better know.　330
　By th' usuall Circuit of the Heav'nly Ball,
The Stars appear unto us (almost) all ;
That Wee in time, observing all their Figures,
Might contemplate their Courses, Natures, Vigors.
　To view the Stars, is honest Recreation :
To search their Course, deserveth Commendation ;
So wee beware, with some presuming Sects
To pick things future out of their Aspects.
　Wee must renounce That Error's patronage,
That what som Dreamers by our Births presage,　340
Must needs betide us ; tying to their Lawes
Our nature, govern'd by a Higher Cause.
　Perhaps the Signes some inclination bring,
Inducing hearts to some Affectioning :
But, by God's grace, well may wee vary that ;
As, never forc't by necessary Fate.
　For, sure if Man, by strong Necessity,
Doe any Ill, ill meriteth not Hee :
Did Stars constrain us, neither Vertue, then,
Nor Vice, were worth Praise or Reproof in Men.　350
　If any way the Will of Man be free,
On These Effects what Judgement's ground can be ?
What Certainty can from the stars be knowne
Of Weal, or Woe, Life, Death, or Thrall, or Throne ?
　When Kings are born, many are born beside :
Must all be Destin'd to be Kings, that tide ?
Oft, many at-once are hang'd, or drown'd, or
　　slain :
Did all at-once their groaning Mothers pain ?
　Who can conceive, that such or such Aspect
Is good, or bad ; boads Life, or Death's Effect ?　360
Who can produce so sure Prognostications
Of our frail Life, so full of Alterations ?
　Certain's that Art which shews the daily Course
Of restlesse Stars, their Influence and Force :
But, Divination's an uncertain Skill,
Full of fond Errour, false, and failing still.
　What booted, Lord, our humblest Vows to Thee,
Were their Conclusions certain Verity ?
Disastrous Fate would mate us with Despair,
And frustrate all religious Faith and Prayer.　370
　Were it their Sayings, were right certain true,
Then of necessity must all ensue :
But, if Events their Verdicts often thwart,
False is their Aim, and fallible their Art.
　Observe the Works those subtill Authors write ;
Th' are so ambiguous, or so false out-right,
That if somtimes som truth they chance to hit,
They 'll counterpoiz a hundred lies for it.
　Too-busie-bold with Thee, Lord, they presume ;
And to themselves Thine Office they assume,　380
Who, by Star-gazing, or ought else below,
Dare arrogate the Future to foreknow.
　Wee hardly see what hangeth at our Eyes :
How should wee read the Secrets of the Skies ?
None knowes To-morrow what betide him shall :
How then fore-tell Yeers' Fortunes yer they fall ?

　Then leave wee all to God's high providence ;
Not list'ning for To-morrow-Daies Events :
Better then Wee, He knowes what 's meet to send.
Then fear wee nothing, but Him to offend,　390
　O ! Thou All-knower ! Nothing more doth thrust
Proud Man from Thee then this Ambitious Lust
Of knowing All : for, by that Arrogance,
In stead of Knowledge, got Hee Ignorance.
　Man nothing knowes, nor nothing comprehends,
But by the Power which Thy pure spirit him lends.
If then, Thy Wisdom have so bounded His ;
Why would Hee hold more then His Measure is ?
　Let 's humbly stoop our Wits, with all Sincerity,
Unto thy *Word :* there let us seek the Verity ;　400
And all Predictions that arise not Thence,
Let us reject for impious Insolence.
　Let us repute all Divination vain,
Which is derived from man's fuming brain,
By Lots, by Characters, or Chiromancy ;
By Birds, or Beasts, or damned Necromancy.
　Let 's also flee the furious-curious Spell
Of those Black-Artists that consult with Hell
To finde things lost ; and *Pluto's* help invoke
For hoorded Gold, where oft they finde but smoke.　410
　Hee 's fond that thinks Fiends in his ring to
　　coop :
Or in a knife them by a Charm to hoop.
Such as have try'd those courses, for the most,
Have felt in fine Their malice, to their cost.
　Woe, woe to them that leave the living God,
To follow Fiends, and Mountibanks abroad ;
Seeking for light, dark, dreaming Sorceries,
And, for the Truth, th' erroneus Prince of Lies.
　Condemning therefore all pernicious Arts,
Let 's be contented with our proper Parts :　420
Let 's meekly seek what may be safely knowne,
Without usurping God's peculiar Owne.
　W' have Stuffe enough (besides) our time to spend,
And Our short life can hardly comprehend
The half of half the Wonders licenst us
To search, and know, and soberly discusse.
　The smallest Garden usually contains
Roots, Fruits and Flowrs, sufficient for the pains
Of one man's life, their natures to descry :
When will hee know all Creatures' property ?　430
　Earth 's but a Point, compar'd to th' upper Globe ;
Yet, who hath seen but half her utter Robe,
Omitting All her Inwards, All her Water ?
When shall wee then see All this vast Theater ?
　What here wee see, wee see is Exquisite :
What 's This to That so far above our Sight ?
Excelling fair, what to our Eye is sensible ;
Even to our Soule, the rest 's incomprehensible.
　Who then can vaunt himselfe Omniscient ?
More then All, sin-lesse, Pure and Innocent ?　440
As none 's all-guiltlesse, in thy glorious Eyes,
There 's none all-knowing thy high Mysteries.
　Yet must wee praise and glorifie thee fit,
For that wee know ; and for our good by it :

There is no Pleasure can be comparable
To Contemplation of Thy Wondrous Table.
  Thereon the more wee muse, the more we may ;
So our Delight, Desire encreaseth ay
Of finding Thee : and that divine Desire,
Calming our Cares, quencheth our fleshly Fire.   450
  All other Pleasures have Displeasures mixt :
Joyes meet annoyes, and smiles have tears betwixt :
Yea, all Delights of Earth have ever been
Fellow'd or follow'd, by som tragick Teen.
  But, who of Thee, and Thine, contemplates ever,
Scapes all the Fits of th' hot-cold cruell Fever
Of Fear, of Love, of Avarice, Ambition,
Which haunts all others, with small Intermission.
  Man, labour-lesse, receives a rare Delight,
When hee observes the settled Order right,   460
Whereby all Creatures (with, or wanting Sense)
Subsist, through thine Unchanging Providence.
  What more content can Wee have here below,
More high, more happy? then, but This to know
(This certain Sum) That, when This world began,
Thou mad'st Man for Thy-Self, and All for Man?
  Th' Horse was not made to glorifie thy Name,
Nor th' Elephant to magnifie the same :
Man, onely Man, hath mem'ry, voyce and wit
To sing thy Praise, and sound thy Glory, fit.   470
  And, to serve Thee, as Hee is sole ordain'd ;
So, to serve Him, Thou hast the rest derrain'd :
All things that flee, that walk, that craul or swim,
Yea, Heav'n and Earth, and All, are vow'd to Him.
  For Him, the Earth yeelds Herbs, Trees, Fruits, &
    Flowrs,
(To sundry purpose, and of sundry powrs)
Corn of all kindes, in Vallies far and wide
(For Bread and Drink) and dainty Vines beside.
  For him, the Rocks a thousand Rivers gush :
Here, rouling Brooks ; There silver Torrents rush ; 480
Indenting Meads and Pastures, as they passe,
Whose smiling Pride peeps in their liquid Glasse.
  For Him, the Mountains, downs, & Forrests breed
Buffs, Beefs, Sheep, Venzon ; and the lusty Steed
To bear him bravely thorough thick and thin,
And silly Worms, his Silken Robes to spin.
  For Him, the Bullock bears his painfull Yoak :
For Him, the Weather wears his curled Cloak ;
For Him, the Birds their brooding-chambers build :
For Him, the Bees their Wax and Honey yeeld.   490
  For Him, the Sea doth many millions nurse ;
With whom, the Air helps both his panch & purse :
The Fire 's His Cook, to dresse th' abundant Cheer
Which Air, and Sea, and Earth, doe furnish here.
  Yea, Dragons, Serpents, Vipers venemous,
Have Fel, Fat, Bloud ; or somwhat good for us ;
In Leprosie, or Lunacie apply'd :
And Triacle is also hence supply'd.
  Hee (briefly) Hee hath use of all that is ;
Winnes the most savage of the Savages :   500
None so fierce Lyon, but to tame hee wonts ;
Nor Elephant so high, but that hee mounts.

And makes, besides, of his huge Bones and Teeth,
Hafts, Boxes, Combs, and more then many see'th.
Nay, more ; for Him, the fell *Monocerote*
Bears in his brow a soveraine *Antidote.*
  Yea, many soverain Remedies Hee findes,
For sundry Griefs, in Creatures of all kindes.
All (in a word) wilde and domestick too,
Som way or other him som service doe.   510
  For food, Hee hath the flesh of Beasts and Birds :
For clothes, the Fleece, the Hair & Hide of Heards :
For house, each Quarr, and every Forrest offers :
For mettals, Mines furnish his Camp and Coffers.
  For Him, the jarring Elements agree ;
Fire cleers the Air : Air sweeps the Earth wee see ;
Earth bears the Water : Water (moistly milde)
Cools Fire, calms Air, & gets the Earth with-child.
  So, All is made for Man ; and Man for Thee :
To love, and serve and Laud thy Majesty ;   520
Thee above all, Thee onely to obey :
With thankfull soule walking Thy sacred way.
  This doth He well, that yeelds his Will to thine ;
Full of desires, if not of deeds divine :
Striving to stop, under the Spirit's awe,
The members' stubborn and rebellious Law.
  For, Man consists of discordant accords
(What the great World, the little World affords.
There heav'n & earth ; here earth & heav'n there
    are :
There War and Peace ; Here also Peace and War.) 530
  Hee hath a heav'nly soule, an earthly Sheath :
That, soars above ; This ever pores beneath :
That, lightly wing'd all creatures comprehends :
This, leaden-heeld, but to corruption tends.
  The Spirit oft against the Flesh doth fight ;
And somtimes, vanquisht by his Opposite,
Is carried Captive with the most dishonor,
After his Foe ; and forc't to wait upon-her ;
  Till rouz'd again, and raised by Thy Grace,
His striving Will recovers wonted place ;   540
With better watch, and braver resolution,
To stand it out untill his dissolution.
  Survaying then both heav'n and earth about,
Hee bringeth in what hee hath seen without ;
And marking well th' Effects of natures visible,
Ascends by those unto their cause invisible.
  For, but two Organs hath our soule whereby
To finde and know th' eternall Majesty :
Faith which beleeves the sacred *Word* of God ;
And *Reason*, reading all his *Works* abroad.   550
  Those Wonders send us, to their Author over ;
Those certaine Motions, to their certaine Mover :
Then *Faith* conducts us, where our *Reason* leaves ;
And, what th' eie sees not, that our *Faith* conceives.
  Faith, firm and lively, doth our soules perswade,
That Thy high pow'r of nothing, all hath made :
Thine ESSENCE is eternally-Divine :
The *World* beginning had, and shall have fine.
  Wee must not say, *Of Nought is formed Nought*
(Although to Man it may be justly brought.)   560

47

Th' eternall Spirit can all of nought produce ;
And instantly, to nothing all reduce.
   Nor may wee aske, *What th' eviternall-One,*
That space-lesse Space could find to doe alone.
His Trine-One-Selfe to know and to partake,
Is (Countless) more then Thousand *Worlds* to make.
   A passing Artist is no lesse compleat,
Then in composure, in his rare Conceit :
For, in the Knowledge, Art's perfection lyes ;
And, *Works* deferr'd vail not the *Work-man's* Prize. 570
   The minde's not idle, though the Hand awhile
Use neither Pen, Pencill, nor Gouge, nor File.
The Mind 's before the Work ; and works within,
Upon th' *Idea* yer the Deed begin.
   Would wee not say, the *World* were God indeed,
If from no other it did first proceed?
Eternall, onely is God's proper tearm ;
Alone, preceeding Time, exceeding Term.
   The *World* supports not Thee, nor Thee supplies :
Thou dost Thy-Self sustain, Thy-Self suffice : 580
And grosly erres who-ever shall suppose,
Thee, Infinite, within a *World* to close.
   And, as wee may not match the heav'n's extense
Unto Thy Circle, infinite, immense :
No more may wee to Thine eternall-age,
Compare the *World's* short, brittle little age.
   Before all time, Thou *Everlasting-One*,
Decree'dst in time to make the Sun and Moone.
The *World's* few dayes and ill (with little cumber)
Thy sacred Book will teach us soon to number. 590
   What Book, what Brass, what marble ought can
     show
But of an hundred thousand years ago?
Had Man been here, from an eternall Line,
Here must have been (sure) some perpetuall Signe :
   Of years, Millions of Millions must have past
From th' endlesse Clue of th' eviternall-Vast :
In all these years, of all that did survive,
Of all their acts, could none to us arrive ?
   Wee hear (and often) of the *Babylonians,*
Medes, Persians, Grecians, Romans, Macedonians : 600
But, where 's the Nation whose renowned glory
Hath liv'd an hundred thousand years in story?
   Seek all (*Greek, Latin, Hebrew*) Authors round,
Of All, will Moses be the Senior found :
Who (To his times) in expresse tearms hath cast
Th' age of the *World*, with the *Descents* that past.
   Now from his dayes to ours, what years amount,
Wee may with ease within few hours account ;
And, adding Both, soon by the totall finde
Th' age of the *World*, and of our crooked kinde. 610
   Five thousand years, five hundred, forty eight,
This yeer are past ; since first this *World* took date :
Since all the Heav'ns, Fire, Water, Air, and Earth,
Had, by thy Word, their being and their birth.
   Then was the *Heav'n's* Azure *Pavilion* spred,
And with *Spur-Royals* spangled over-head :
Then those twin-*Princes*, with their train of *Light*,
Began their Kingdoms over day and night.

   Then was the Air, the Earth, and Sea repleat
With birds, and beasts, and fishes, small and great : 620
With plants, & trees, and fruits ; each yeelding seed
To propagate their Kinds that should succeed.
   Then (lastly) *Man* thy *Master-piece* of Art,
Thou did'st appoint to his Imperiall part ;
Innobling him with *Sense* and *Reason's* light,
And in his *Soule*, graving *Thine Image* right :
Gav'st him *Possession* of this earthly Throne,
And gracious *Promise* of the heav'nly One :
Immortall Soule, thou daign'st him to inspire,
Equall (almost) to thine owne heav'nly Quire. 630
   And, as thy Spirit all other Spirits excels
(Angell, or other that in body dwels :)
So doth his body all else bodies passe
For comely forme, and for Majestick face.
   All creatures else low on the ground doe pore,
And groveling feed : but (as was toucht before)
Man hath an *Upright* and a stately *Stature*,
With head aloft, agreeing to his nature ;
   Which properly is to behold the Skies,
To lift to Thee his heart, his hand, his eyes ; 640
And by his Soule's discursive pow'r to peiz
Things past, and present, and of future dayes.
   For, onely Man can measure, number, waigh ;
True, False, Good, Evill : know, cast, sound, survay.
Man onely hath an in-reflecting Knowledge
Of his owne selfe (from Nature's onely *Colledge :)*
   Knows his own fact, his form, his load, his
     strength ;
Knows that he lives, knows he must die (at length :)
And, that a ruled sober life and sage,
Preserves his health, and may prolong his age : 650
   Knowes how to finde ease in his owne disease ;
And, if need be, his neighbour to appease :
And for himself and others, make of flowrs,
Fruits, herbs and roots, Unguents of passing powrs.
   But none so powrfull (when his Term is spent)
As can his owne or others' death prevent :
For, our short Date (*Childe-age*, or *Wilde-age*) ends ;
And now but seldome to *Old-age* extends.
   Yet what is *Old-age* to Eternity ?
To Man, expecting Immortality, 660
What is't to live some three or fourscore yeer ?
Or yet ten more (in Languor) linger here?
   Of all our time-past underneath the Sunne,
Nothing remains, save good or evill done :
Hundreds of years, once past, are lesse (in Summe)
Then a few daies, or a few hours to-come.
   For, to say truth, of Times three pointed Powrs,
Only the Present (instant) Point is ours.
W' have of the Past, but vain imagination ;
Of that To-com, but doubtfull expectation. 670
   But, to th' Eternall, are all times alike
Instant, and present, dead as well as quick ;
Ay is To-day with Thee : Lord, in Thy sight,
Both Past and Future are even equall bright.
   Though in times, terms, the heav'ns revolved be ;
A thousand years are but one day with Thee :

And shortest moment of one onely day
With Thee is as a thousand years (for ay.)
But, our set dayes, to us are long, or short ;
As them good accidents, or bad consort :   680
Sobriety and Peace prolong our life :
Which is abbridg'd by Surfet and by Strife.

Excess or cares, now so cut-off our lives,
That of a thousand, not a man arrives
Neer to the Tythe of the admired age
Of those that liv'd in *Nature's Pupillage :*

Eight hundred years, nine hundred, some, some
   more ;
In minde and body, full of Nature's store ;
To stock the earth with Issue rationall,
And learn the course of heav'n's Star-spangled ball : 690

Which first of all, Their long observance found :
Then by degrees, they taught their heirs the ground :
And wee, from them (so eas'd of end-lesse pain)
Derive that Art, wee could not else attain.

In their long age they learn'd heav'n's full Careers
(Not to be compast in our span of years)
Whence one of them might in his life know more,
Then in our dayes, successively, a score.

Of their so long age who so doubtfull is,
Let him but looke in sacred *Genesis :*   700
Where *Moses* mentions divers famous men
So old ; and shews their years as ours were then.

Th' all-drowning-floud-year did 12. months contain,
And every month did his due daies retain :
Which made up one year of that *Patriarch,*
Who liv'd sev'n fifties, having left the *Ark,*

And was six hundred when hee came aboord :
Teaching his Sons his wondrous skill, by word.
See, see, (alas !) how our unhappy life
Is now abbridg'd, and charg'd with mischiefs rife. 710

Had wee not pleasure in thy works, O God,
Soon must wee sink under the heavy load
Of Cares and Crosses (in a thousand things)
Which this our wretched, sad, short, Way-fare brings.

O ! let us therefore bend our best and most
To magnifie Thee, Lord, in all thine Host :
And so contempling all thy goodnesse giv'n,
With true content, begin (in earth) our heav'n.

Man knowing Thee, knows all that can be known :
And having Thee, hath all that is, his owne : 720
To long for Thee, is endlesse joy, internall :
Dispos'd to Thee, to dye, is life eternall.

Not knowing Thee ; to Live, is daily Dying :
To rest without Thee, is continuall flying :
But all extremes of torments passing measure,
In Thee, and for Thee, are exceeding Pleasure.

Yet, no man ought to offer wilfull force
To his own Self ; nor his owne soule divorce :
But patiently attend thy cheerfull Call ;
Then, to Thy hands gladly surrender all. 730

Nor may wee ween our souls (as beasts) to dye ;
And with our bodies vanish utterly :
Death 's but a passage from a life of pains,
Unto a life where death-lesse joy remains.

W' have, after death another life to see :
As after Storms, a calme and quiet Lee :
As, after Sicknesse, Health : as, after Durance,
Sweet Liberty, with Saf'ty and Assurance.

Two Contraries, oppos'd, in their Extreme,
Have this unfailing property in them : 740
That th' one 's *Privation* is the other's *Ens :*
So, death concluding, doth our life commence.

For, on each-other Contraries depend,
Chain'd (as it were) unto each other's end ;
Day after Night : Attonement after Strife ;
And, after mortall Death, immortall Life.

Our soule 's immortall then (wee must infer-it)
Having beginning of th' Immortall Spirit :
And they are brute (as beasts) that do contend,
That with our bodies, soules for ever end. 750

If there be God immortall, All-scient,
All-mighty, just, benign, benevolent ;
Where were his wisedom, goodnesse, justice, power.
If Vice Hee damne not, nor give Vertue Dower ?

Here, for the most, the godly suffer still :
Th' ungodly here have most the winde at will :
Shall they not one-day change their difference ?
And one-day look for diverse recompence ?

Here, proud, rich, mighty ; meek, poor, weak, op-
   presse :
Lions kill Lambes ; Fox strips the Fatherlesse : 760
O ! is there not another life imperible,
Sweet to the guiltlesse ; to the guilty terrible ?

Who, for Thy sake their lives have sacrific'd ;
In all the torments Tyrants have devis'd ;
O ! how unhappy were they, were there not
Crowns kept with Thee, for their eternall lot !

Then were wee beasts, or worse then beasts, indeed :
For Hee were best that could the worst exceed.
Then *Let us eat, drink, dally,* might wee say :
If after this, there were no Shot to pay. 770

But leaving now that song of *Sensuality,*
Beleeve wee firm our blessed *Immortality ;*
Blessed for those, that in Perseverance,
To Thee alone (Lord) their whole hopes advance.

Blessed for those, who in sincere Humility,
Acknowledging, as knowing their Debility :
Through th' old corruption of all *Adam's* race ;
Them-selves distrusting, onely trust thy *Grace.*

Thou Lord (alas !) know'st all our Imperfections,
Our vain Desires, our mutable Affections, 780
How prone wee are to fall ; how wilde, how wood,
Pursuing evill, and eschewing good.

Th' incessant sway of our continuall ill,
Requires the grace of thy prevention still ;
And th' odious fruits our Nature wonts to breed,
Lord, of Thy mercies have continuall need.

Of frailty therefore, when our foot shall slip,
Or sway, or stray, or turn-awry, or trip ;
Yer flat wee fall, vouchsafe thy helping hand,
To raise us, then ; and make us, after, stand. 790

For, without Thee, our Force is Feeblenesse ;
Our Wisdome Folly, Will is Waywardnesse :

Our Knowledge Ignorance, our Hope Despaire ;
Our Faith but Fansie, and our All but Aire.
　Without Thee, Lord, meer Idols are wee all ;
W' have Eyes, but see not ; Feet, but cannot craul :
Ears, but wee hear not ; Senses without sense :
Soules without soule ; without intelligence.
　Without Thee, all our Counsels and Designes
Are but as Chaffe before the boyst'rous Windes ;　800
Our preparations quickly come to nought ;
Our enterprises vanish with a thought.
　Without Thee, boot neither our foot, nor horse ;
From Thee alone all things derive their force :
Thou onely givest Vertue, Wisdome, Wealth,
Peace, Honour, Courage, Victory and Health.
　Thou holdst the hearts of Princes in thy hand,
Their strength, and state is all at thy command :
No chance of war, no pow'r, no policy ;
But, changelesse, Thou giv'st losse or Victory.　810
　By Thee *Kings raign :* bound equally to all
To weigh just Justice both to great and small ;
To reach the good their Scepter's helpfull vigour ;
And teach the lewd their sword's severest rigour.
　Who them reject, or their just Lawes repugne ;
Thine honour, and Thine ordinance impugne.
They owe their Subjects justice and defence ;
Their Subjects Them, honor, obedience.
　Each ought to pay Them (in degree and manner)
Tribute, where Tribute ; Honor, to whom Honor ;　820
And to the people, They their best protection,
And each his Owne ; without mis-fond affection.
　And thinke themselves (the while) thy Subjects too,
And bound the more thy sacred Lore to doe :
To shew the more their vertue's excellence,
The more their charge is, and their eminence.
　Justice due Dooms slackly to execute,
Makes some disloyall, others dissolute ;
Some too out-ragious, in wrongs greedinesse,
Others (on th' other side) in all Excesse.　830
　'T hath oft been seen (*and in our times and
　　climes*)
Good Princes smart for wicked people's crimes :
And sometimes also, for their Princes' sin,
Subjects are plagued outward and within.
　But, O ! how highly happy is the Land
Where a just Prince doth Prudently command !
And where the people in a Love-bred awe,
Pay willing service, and obey the Law.
　O happy ! both, People and Prince (in fine)
Where both obey thy sacred Lawes divine :　840
Who grately using blessings great and small ;
Acknowledge Thee Owner and Lord of All.
　Of Thee, in Fee, all Princes of the earth
Hold their Estates, Goods, Honors, Beeing, Birth ;
And, without Thee, can neither keep, nor get,
Least point of honor, nor of earth least bit.
　Their *Arcenals*, without Thee are but vain,
Their hoords of Treasure, and their heaps of Grain :
'Tis vaine without Thee, to affie in force
Of Men, Munition, Champions, Charrets, Horse.　850

　Without Thee, Order is dis-order'd soon,
Valour soon vanquisht, Policy undone,
Number but Cumber : and a multitude
Of beaten Souldiers, beaten by few rude.
　Thou, at thy pleasure, mak'st the deepest sea
Divide it selfe, to give thy servants way ;
And suddenly, againe it selfe to close,
To over-whelm Thine and their stubborn foes.
　Thou from the rock mak'st plenteous rivers spout,
For Thine to drink in sandy desarts' drought.　860
And there, from heav'n send'st them exceeding store
Of Quails, for meat, till they can eat no more.
　Thou fed'st them there, with Angels' bread (awhile)
And gav'st them then a milk & hony soile :
There, without stroak to conquer in the field ;
And mine-less make their tumbling wals to yeeld.
　To shew the use and pow'r of humble prayer ;
And how to Thee behooves us still repaire ;
While heart and hands *Moses* to heav'n doth
　　strain,
Renowned JOSUAH conquers in the plain.　870
　Thou, at thy pleasure, mak'st the Sun to stay ;
And without night, to make one double day ;
To give thy servants compleat victory ;
And ever-raze their foes' foul memory.
　Thou to expresse thy pow'r (in *Gedeon's* Raign)
Hast by three hundred, six-score thousand slain ;
And by one man, one Goad-groom (Silly *Sangar*)
Destroy'dst six hundred in religious anger.
　Thou canst in one a thousand's strength compress,
And place it strangely in his slender Tresse ;　880
Which cut, hee lost, and then re-grown, re-gain'd ;
And dying, more then living, foes hee brain'd.
　Thou turn'dst to grasse a King of *Babylon :*
And set'st a Shepheard on a Regall Throne.
Thou slew'st a Gyant, by a gentle Lad,
Who, for a *Pistoll*, but a Pebble had.
　How many troubles had that Prophet-Prince !
For happy service, hatefull recompence ;
Through hill and dale, hunted from place to place :
Yet still preserv'd by thine assisting grace ;　890
　And set, at last, upon his Master's Throne,
Subduing all civill and forrain foen :
Then, in Thine honour warbles many-a Psalm ;
And hoary, leaves his Son, his Kingdome calm.
　By thee, his Son, renowned *Salomon*,
Obtain'd the Name of *Wisdome's Paragon :*
For, asking only That, Thou gav'st him wealth,
Honour and peace withall, and pow'r and health.
　And, as good Princes thus Thou dost advance ;
So bring'st thou down fell tyrants' arrogance :　900
Such as, transported in their Pride extreme,
Dare wrong thy Saints, or thy drad Self blaspheme.
　Senacherib must this confesse, and rew,
With nine-score thousand which thine Angel slew,
Of his proud Hoast ; besides th' unkindly slaughter
Of his owne Selfe, by his owne Sons soon after.
　So that *B'al*-blinded, bloud-soild, sin-soild Pair
(In whose sad dayes the zealfull *Thesbit's* pray'r,

For sev'n six months, seal'd-up thy heav'nly deaws)
Thy pow'r, truth, justice, in their judgement shews. 910
   Oft-times, thy hook hales moody Tyrants back ;
Oft-times themselves by their own swords to wrack :
Sometimes, by Women's weake unwarlike hands,
Thou conquer'st Captains, & confound'st their bands.
   Yea, Lord, at all times, in extremest straights,
Thy sacred Arme, or secret Army waits,
To succour Thine (from famine, sword, and fire :
And all the plots that foes or fiends conspire)
   And them so daily, to supply, support
(Their wants, their weaknesse) in so various sort, 920
That all thy wonders of this kinde to count,
Even past examples, past all numbers mount.
   But, All thy mercies, unto all, and each
Of thine elect ; what words, what thoughts can
    reach !
What thou hast said, and done unto Thy *Vine*,
Thy *Love*, thy *Dove*, that little flock of thine !
   To whom thou spakest divers waies of old ;
In Visions, Dreames, Types, Figures manifold ;
By Priests and Prophets ; sealing oft thine Oracles
Of wrath, or mercy ; with respective miracles. 930
   And last of all, when Time's full term was run,
Sent'st us from heav'n Thine owne and only SON ;
Whom co-eternall God Thou didst ingender,
Thine owne *grav'n Image*, Thine owne glorie's splendor ;
   Th' eternall Word, by whom, when all began,
Thou madest All ; and since, re-madest Man :
The *Mediatour*, and the *Umpire*, giv'n
To reconcile revolted earth to heav'n.
   Who to impart to us his Immortality,
Took part with us in this our fraile Mortality ; 940
And, in all things (except all sin alone)
A perfect Man, put all our Nature on.
   Borne in the world, to make us born a-new :
In poverty, us richly to endue :
Humbling himself, that wee might raised be :
In servant's form, to make us ever free :
   Came down to earth, us up to heav'n to mount :
Was tempted here, our tempter to surmount :
Dy'd to destroy the strength of death and sinne ;
And rose againe, our righteousnesse to win. 950
   How oft did hee visite the poore and sick !
Cure the Distracted, and Paralitique ;
Restore the Blinde, Deaf, Dúmb, and Dead revive ;
And Satan's Captives from his rage reprive !
   How many Idiots did hee make excell
The *Wisest Masters* in all *Israel!*
How many rude, plain, silly fisher-men,
Rare pow'rfull Preachers ; fishers (then) of Men !
   How many sin-sick did hee inly cure ;
And deep soule-wounded binde-up, and assure ! 960
How many Proud, Loose, Cruell, Covetous,
Made hee Meek, Modest, Gentle, Bounteous.
   By him, dear Father, come wee Thee to know,
Thy *Word*, thy *Will;* to frame our own Will so :
By Him alone, Wisedome wee seek and find :
In cares and crosses, to confirme our mind.

   By Him alone, Thy sacred truth wee learn
From suttlest errors cleerly to discern :
By Him all clouds of darknesse are dispell'd ;
Idolatry and Heresie refell'd. 970
   By Him, wee pray to Thee, and what wee crave
In lively faith, wee are assur'd to have :
Heav'n's kingdom first, soule's feast, and bodie's food,
Grace, Comfort, Peace, and every needfull Good.
   By Him, be wee Thy Children of Adoption,
Co-heires of heav'n, and vessels of Election :
Becomming Man, Hee is become our Brother ;
So, happy wee, have also Thee our Father.
   By Him, of Thee, thine holy Spirit wee have ;
Which in our hearts thy Law doth lively grave : 980
The Comforter, the Spirit of truth, of love,
Of Pow'r, of Peace, of Wisdome from above :
   The Spirit, which stayes us, when in storms wee
    ride;
And steers us steddy in our calmer Tyde :
Which kils the flesh, and chils insatiate fires ;
To quicken soules, and kindle heav'n's desires :
   Which brings the straies home to Thy holy Fold,
Gives Stutters Tongues, & makes the bashfull bold ;
Opens the Sense of sacred Mysteries ;
Gives form or life to every thing that is. 990
   In Him, Thou built'st Thy heav'n of heav'ns excelling,
Thy Court prepar'd for Saints' eternall dwelling :
In Him Thou mad'st the World and All to move
In every part, as doth it best behoove.
   Hee, to the fainting heart new heart procures,
Confirms the feeble, fearfull soules assures ;
Gives faith and hope, love, grace and godly zeal.
Happy those soules where hee delights to dwell.
   For, Those Hee fils with his aboundant treasures,
In divers manners, and in divers measures : 1000
As diversly befits thy Churche's state,
To *Plant*, or *Prune*, or *Prop*, or *Propagate*.
   To some hee gives a cleer, quick apprehension :
To som, deep judgement ; som, divine invention :
To som, the door of gracefull Eloquence ;
To som, the store of Wisdom's excellence :
   Som, to interpret with divine dexterity
The sacred secrets of th' eternall Verity :
Som (School-lesse, Schollers ; Learned, studi-lesse)
To understand and speak all Languages ; 1010
   Som (to confirm their Office, and Thine Oracles)
To work strange Wonders, great & many Miracles ;
Revive the dead, recover native evils,
Cure all Diseases, and even cast out Devils.
   Such are th' effects, works, vertues, gifts, & graces,
Which by degrees, in divers times and places,
Thy holy Spirit to silly men hath giv'n ;
From them, to Thee, to raise our hearts to heav'n.
   And as in our fraile bodies (through variety
Of members fitted into one Society) 1020
One very soule doth actions different,
Some more, some lesse, noble or excellent :
   So in the mystick body of Thy Sonne
(Where many Members' Love unites in One)

Thine owne One Sp'rit, works actions admirable,
Among themselves more or lesse honourable.

Yet orderly, each his owne Rank observes ;
And properly, each his owne office serves :
Nor boasteth any, other not to need :
For oft the least, the most of all doth steed.　　1030

Therefore the stronger must the weak support :
The safe and sound, cheer the afflicted sort :
The rich and mighty, not despise Inferiours ;
Neither the mean, envie or hate Superiours.

Were All a Head, in this faire frame of *Man ;*
Where were the Foot, the Hand, the Stomack than ?
Were All a Tongue, where should the Eye becom ?
Were all an Eye, where should the Ear have room ?

O Spirit Eternall ! which hast all compos'd ;
In Number, Measure, Order, All dispos'd :　　1040
Make Charity Us (mutuall members) move ;
Unite our Spirits in thy perpetuall Love.

Quench all contentions, errours, heresies,
Which o're our mindes and bodies tyrannize :
Quench all concupiscence, and foule desire,
Which both our bodie's and soule's death conspire.

Vouchsafe our souls rest, without Schismick
　　　strife ;
Our bodie's health, through chaste and sober life.
What could we ask ? what should we rather crave,
Then in sound bodies as sound soules to have ?　　1050

Sound is the body kept, by keeping chaste,
With mod'rate exercise, and mean repast :
Sound is the soule, which resteth (sober-wise)
Content in Thee, un-vext in vanities.

Sound is the soule, free from all self-sedition
Of Pride, Hate, Envie, Avarice, Ambition,
And all the crowd of Man's concupiscence ;
Binding His will to Thy obedience.

Who is so bound (Thy Servant) is most free :
Most rich, who leaves all riches else, for Thee :　　1060
Most easie rests, who most for Thee endures :
Most self-distrusting, most Thy strength assures.

So Thee to Serve, is even to *Reign :* in brief,
So to obey, is to command in chief.
To walke thy wayes, is onely *Liberty.*
To learn Thy *Learning* ENCYCLOPEDIE.

O ! happy those that stand in such a state,
And in Thy Statutes alwaies meditate :
Or, if they slip, or trip, or faile or fall,
Return betimes, and for Thy mercy call.　　1070

For, though thy Law in fiery thunder giv'n,
Threat still the stubborn, with revenge from heav'n,
Thy gracious Gospel offers pardon free,
To humbled soules that sigh in faith to Thee.

And Thou, who wilt not sinners die, but live,
Hast promis'd all, so suing to forgive.
This Word is truth : Thy promise to fulfill,
Thou (God of truth) hast ever Pow'r and Will.

O ! bounteous Thou, which dost so oft repaire
Our broken soules, and keep'st them from despaire :　1080
And blessed wee, whose faith in Love's Physicion,
Assures our hope of all our sins' remission.

Who-so hath sorrow for his sinfullnesse,
Purpose to mend, desire of holinesse,
Trust in Thy mercy ; hath no need to doubt
But by Thy grace his sins are wiped out.

O Cordiall word ! O comfortable breath !
Reviving soules, even in the gates of death !
From jawes of hell, raising our hope to heav'n !
Therefore, dear Lord, to Thee all praise be giv'n.　1090

Who shall acuse us now, if Thou acquight ?
God being with us, what can us affright ?
Our faith in Thee (O !) what can shake, or shock :
So surely fixt upon so firme a Rock ?

What shall divide us, Lord, from love of Thee ?
Shall shame ? shall sorrow ? shall adversity ?
Shall famine ? plague ? war ? wealth, or want ? (in sum)
Shall life ? shall death ? things present, or to come ?

Stay, stay us, Lord, and steel our feeble hearts
Against the sting of temporary smarts :　　1100
Draw, draw our soules neer to thy self, O Lord,
With powrfull touches of Thy Spirit and Word.

Guide, guide our steps still in Thy gracious way,
During our durance in this house of clay :
That when this Prison shall be broken down,
Wee may with thee receive a glorious Crown.

So shall wee ever, with a voice divine,
Sing *Haleluiahs* to th' ETERNALL TRINE :
Record Thy mercies, which all thoughts surmount :
And thus the glory of Thy deeds recount :　　1110

S Upernall Lord, Eternall King of Kings,
　Maker, Maintainer, Mover of All things,
How infinite ! how excellently-rare !
How absolute Thy Works, thy wonders are !
How-much Their Knowledge is to be desir'd !
How, THOU, in All, to be of All admir'd !

F I N I S.

NOTES AND ILLUSTRATIONS.

Page 84, ' *Lady Elizabeth Infanta* ' — see Memorial-Introduction on this 'fair' and unfortunate lady : l. 10, ' *bolden* ' =
embolden.
　LITTLE BARTAS : l. 8, ' *Marcus or Peak* '—see Glossarial
Index, *s.n.* : l. 11, ' *Heliard* ' = Nicholas Hilliard, the famous
goldsmith and portrait painter : B. 1547 : D. 1619 : ' *Isaac* ' =
Isaac Hilliard, the equally famous miniature painter—of whom
and his father, see our Memorial-Introduction—see also l. 41 :
l. 116, ' *equi-lucent* ' = equal-lucent, *i.e.* always lucent : l. 257,
' *contemple* ' = contemplate, by stress of rhyme, but see l. 717 :
l. 290, ' *sad* ' = heavy, solid : l. 367, ' *booted* '= advantaged : l.
411, ' *fond* ' = foolish : l. 432, ' *utter* ' = outer or upper : l. 454,

' *Teen* '= rage : l. 472, ' *derrain'd* ' = de-reigned, *i.e.* subordin-
ated : l. 434, ' *Buffs* '= buffaloes : l. 488, ' *Weather* ' = sheep, so
named : l. 496, ' *Fel* '=skin : l. 505, ' *Monocerote* '—see Glossarial
Index, *s.v.* : l. 513, ' *quarr* '=quarry : l. 558, ' *fine* '=finis, end :
l. 741, ' *Ens* '=being : l. 745, ' *Atonement* '=agreement, at-one-
ment, not the theological sense : l. 751, ' *All-scient* ' = all-
knowing : l. 761, ' *imperible* ' = imperishable ?—see Glossarial
Index, *s.v.* : l. 781, ' *wood* ' = mad : l. 841, ' *grately* ' = gratefully : l. 849, ' *affie* ' = enter into affiance or alliance : l. 866,
' *mine-less* ' = without gunpowder blasting : l. 892, ' *foen* ' =
foes—note form : l. 908, ' *Thesbits* ' = Tishbite's : l. 1047,
' *Schismick* ' = schismatic.—G.

Micro-cofmo-graphia:

THE

LITTLE-WORLDS

DESCRIPTION;

OR,

THE MAP OF MAN

(From *Latin Saphiks* of that Famous, late,

Preacher in London, M^r. HENRY

SMITH.)

Translated;

AND

Dedicated

To the Right Honourable,

HONORIA,

Lady Hay,

BY

JOSUAH SYLVESTER.

TO

THE RIGHT-RIGHT

HONOURABLE

HONORIA,

Wife of JAMES, Lord HAY, Sole Daughter
and Heire of EDWARD Lord DENNY.

E *Qually* bound, *in humble* Gratitude,
　To two dear Equals (*to You equall Dear*) ;
　Unable (yet) with Both *at once to* cleer,
　Unwilling *yet, with* Either *to be* rude :
Faine would I crave *to have my* Bond *renew'd*,
　For a more Happy, *or more* Hopefull *Year*,
　When gracious Heav'n *shall daign* to *set me* freer
　From old cold Cares, *which keep my* Muse *unmew'd*.
Would You *be pleas'd* (Madame) *to interpose*
　Your gentle breath, *I would not doubt to* speed :
　Such vertue hath Your Vertue *still with* Those.
Therefore in Hope *of* Your *kinde* Help (*at need*)
　This simple Pledge *I* Offer *at Your* Feet ;
　Altar of Love, *Where* both *Their* Vowes *do meet*.

———————————————————————Your Honourable Vertues

————————————————————————————humble Votary

——————————————————————————JOSUAH SYLVESTER.

THE MAP OF MAN.

I *Sing not, but (in sighes abrupt)*
  Sob-out the State of MAN, corrupt
    By th' old Serpent's *banefull breath ;*
Whose strong Contagion still extends
To every creature that descends
  From th' Little World *of Death.*
Drad-dear Creator, *new-create*
Thy Creature : Saviour *expiate*
  This, *and all our Owne* Addition :
O sacred Spirit, *Our Spirits renew ;*   10
Informe, reforme, and tune Mee true,
  To condole our sad Condition.
In earth Man wanders (Pilgrim-wise)
Hopes, doubts ; desires, faints, freezes, fryes ;
  Crossed, tossed to and fro :
Hee turnes, hee windes ; hee findes no good :
Hee ay complaines that Evill's floud
  (Farre and wide) doth over-flow.
His Birth (in sinne) begins in tears :
His Life is rife in pains and fears ;   20
  Will-hee, nill-hee, spoyling sport :
His Death with groans, in doubtfull case,
Sends him, God knowes, unto what place :
  Blest none rest, but in the Port.
The Flesh against the Spirit rebels :
The Spirit againe the Flesh repels :
  Ever striving, never still :
And suddenly, while these contend,
Their common Foe, the cursed Fiend,
  Findes advantage Both to kill.   30
Earth (Step-dame-like) sharp Rods doth yeeld,
To scourge her Sonnes : the Sea is fill'd
  (Both above and under too)
With hideous Horrors, past report :
Th' Air whirling in tempestuous sort,
  Beats, and threats All to undoe.
The Countrey's rude, and foe to Fame ;
The Court more brave, and more to blame ;
  Painted Faces, graces fain'd :
The Citie (There, O ! bad 's the best)   40
Seat of deceit, and Miser's nest ;
  Gold their God, ungodly gain'd.
Jarre at the Barre : Stews at the Stage ;
In Way-fare, Theeves : in War-fare, Rage ;
  Noyse abroad : Annoyes at home :
In Churches, Purchase-Profanation,
Fiends seeming Saints ; Abomination :
  Every-where, no feare of *Doome.*

The Throne 's not given unto the Just :
The faithfull is not put in trust ;   50
  Prophets are not held for true :
Nor loyall lov'd, nor learned grac't,
Nor weary eas'd, nor Worthy plac't :
  Nor hath any here his due.
The impudent, the insolent,
The foole, the friend in complement,
  And the sly, wee see (by proofe)
Held eloquent, magnanimous,
Right pleasant, kinde, ingenious ;
  And the Wealthy wise enough.   60
Reward is heard : words are but winde :
Each Art is long ; Life short confin'd :
  Might makes Right in every Cause.
Physick is vile, and vilely us'd ;
Divinity disdain'd, abus'd ;
  Under-foot men tread the *Lawes.*
The Rich with rage, the Poore with plaints,
With hate the Wise, with scorne the Saints,
  Evermore are curstly crost :
With painfull toile the Private-man,   70
The Nobler states with envie wan,
  Without end are torne and tost.
If good, hee fares no better for 't ;
If bad, no worse they him support :
  Fortune serveth all alike.
Though shee simper, though shee smile,
Though shee laugh outright awhile,
  Shee is alwayes slippery-sleeke.
Who lately served, Lords it now :
Who lately becked, now doth bow :   80
  Valleys swell, and Mountains sink :
Who lately flourisht, now doth fade :
Who late was strong, now feeble made,
  Feeding Worms, in Dust doth stink.
So Lowly rests : so, Lofty rues,
Say that one might his fortune chuse,
  Under Heav'n to have his will ;
'T would be a doubt among the Wise,
Whether it better were to rise
  To high state, or to sit still.   90
Phant'sie conceives, Reason receives,
Passion repugnes (and patience reaves).
  What I wish, What I desire,
I see : and Sense importunes so,
I covet, I commend it too :
  Then againe it doth retire.

47

Sense, whither now ? 'Tis griefe to see
What flits so fast so suddenly.
  Reason, whither roams thy reach ?
What hurts, were better still be hid,   100
And still unknowne : O ! ill-bestid !
  Poor in store, in Wealth a wretch,
When Fortune comes, shee meanes our Wrack.
And when shee goes, shee breaks our back :
  Comming, going, all is one.
For, what shee gives shee takes away,
Unkinde and blinde, inconstant ay ;
  Frank to few, and firme to none.
Oft have I canvas'd, whether's Case
Is Worst ; the Fall'n, or th' ever-Base :   110
  Yet, scarce can I it decide.
The Fall proves plainly for the first :
Want pleads, that ever-Want is worst ;
  Partiall to their proper side.
It irks the Fall'n to have been High ;
Th' ay-Poor could wish hee had been By :
  Either other's state would glad.
If even in gladnesse sadnesse grow,
Were not I somewhat glad also,
  How extreme should I be sad !   120
If Care wee take, it Health impaires :
If not, it takes us un-awares :
  Whether should wee seek or shun ?
Whether (to passe unto the next)
The good or bad be most perplext,
  Is another Question.
The Guilty suffers for his fault :
The Guilt-lesse doubts no lesse assault
  By Mis-fortune : both desire
To live on earth, to draw this breath ;   130
Both feare to dye ; and after death,
  Torment of eternall Fire.
Hence, slow daye's labour wears us thin :
Hence, lightly, nightly fears begin :
  Hence, rathe Rising, and late Rest :
Hence, toughest storms, and roughest streams :
Hence, griping Cares, and ghastly Dreams,
  Waking, sleeping, doe molest.
Winter's too-cold : Summer's too-hot ;
Autumne too-moyst (which breeds the Rot)   140
  All the hope is in the Spring.
The lively Spring is lovely faire :
But if keen yce, then chill the Aire,
  Little pleasure doth it bring.
Seas drowne the Vales ; the Winds do heave
The Hils to heav'n ; the Rocks they cleave.
  Bold Ambition stands amaz'd,
Expecting where to build a Fort
So strong, and rampyr'd in such sort,
  That it never may be raz'd.   150
Peace is too-drown'd in lust and sloth :
Warre is too-drunke with bloud and wrath ;
  That, too-gaudie : This, too-grim.
Men's mindes are all so delicate,
So soft, and so effeminate,
  Small things, all things, grievous seem.

Either the Head doth alwayes ake,
Or Palat slip, or Palsey shake,
  Or our Belly roars within ;
Or else with Choler wee abound,   160
Or else with Phlegm, or else (unsound)
  Tumour's humours, scald our skin.
What dread of Death, What greedy Lust,
What Surfeit, Sloth, and Deeds unjust,
  Daily plunge in perils rife ;
What sword consumeth every houre,
And what the Plague doth quick devour,
  Lengthens Physick, shortens life.
Where's now *Æneas* ? Where's his Son ?
Where's *Hercules* ? Where's *Salomon* ?   170
  Where is *David* ? Where is *Saul* ?
Where's *Cyrus*, *Cæsar*, and the rest ?
Ah ! Hee and They are all deceast :
  I must follow : so must all.
Hark : Thou, whom most the People hailes ;
The wisest erres : the justest failes ;
  Strongest limpeth now and than :
The humblest swels ; the sobrest sips :
The holyest sins ; the wariest slips :
  God is fault-lesse ; never, Man.   180
Too-curious or too-carelesly,
Too-lavish or too-slavishly,
  By the Foole or by the Knave ;
Too-craking or too-cravenly,
Too-hatefull or too-gratefully :
  Haste or waste marrs all wee have.
Ambition's end is Rule and Reigne :
Crueltie's Conquest : Guile's is Gaine,
  To grow rich by hook or crook ;
Juggling, and struggling, strife in all :   190
No Triumph without Fight will fall ;
  War-lesse, none for Peace may look.
Wee think, but never can intend,
Good thoughts well to begin ; or end
  If perhaps they be begun :
Or, if wee end them, never finde
(How-ever rare, in any kinde)
  Recompence when wee have done.
Our heart it hath an in-borne Guest,
Will-ill (it hight): it posteth prest   200
  To the Tongue, ill words to vent :
Desire, then rushes to ill Deeds :
Vengeance anon the Fact succeeds :
  Thus comes Ill to punishment.
If safe, this Snake, wee choak or charm ;
Within, againe wee hug it warm,
  Daring, doubting, up and downe ;
Till Lust, as lighter, up doth surge ;
And th' horror of the fearfull scourge,
  Fall, as heavier, to the ground.   210
Come flesh, be frolike, take delight,
Let 's revell now : 't will once be night :
  Shall a little Gout, or Colick,
Or sudden Qualm, or sullen Care,
Or addle fit of idle Feare
  Mar thy mirth ? Come Flesh be frolick,

What seeks, wee shun ; What shuns, wee seek :
What helps, wee loath ; What hurts, wee like !
   Bird in hand wee leave for bush.
For, what wee want wee panting crave ;   220
And loosely lavish what wee have :
   Brag of that should make us blush.
With-child with mirth, wee bring-forth scorn ;
Wee bring up Furie ; over-born
   (Mov'd and moving) either way :
Too-sorry, or too-merry mad :
The happy Meane is never had,
   While wee wretches here doe stay.
Wee reigne and serve ; wee want and flow :
Wee joy and mourne : wee freez and glow :   230
   Vowes wee make and break (together) :
Wee build and batter ; joyne and jarre :
Wee heap and scatter ; make and marre :
   And wee flourish, and wee wither.
Wee look to Heav'n, and leap to Hell :
Our Hope and Fear (by turns) rebell ;
   Plunging down, or puffing-up :
Please would wee faine, but finde demurre ;
Please might wee well, did Will concurre :
   Sloth doth stay, and Lust doth stop.   240
So still wee stand, and whine the while ;
Nought labour boots, nor love, nor wile :
   All is lost, when 'tis too-late.
Evils to th' evill and the good
Are dayly sent : and if with-stood
   Wee but faster foster *Fate.*
I will at once give-over quight
Both to be wicked and upright,
   To doe either right or wrong :
For, goods well-gotten, grow but thin,   250
Get hardly up, come slowly in :
   And th' ill-gotten last not long.
What shall I doe ? If I forbear
My cause-lesse Foe, I blush, I fear
   His Despight and my Disparage.
If to revenge mee, I resolve ;
It satisfies, when I revolve
   None's all-faultlesse, in all Carriage.
When I have spar'd, I wish t' have spoke :
And when I speak, I would revoke ;   260
   Better pleas'd t' have held my peace :
Would God I could (as Wiser-ones)
Both speak and hold my peace at once ;
   So to live at quietnesse.
Deare Minde, how dost Thou ? Frayle and sick,
My Flesh implores thy succour quick :
   Canst ? O ! canst thou cure her griefe ?
O ! daign (I pre-thee) then with speed
To help thy servant now at need ;
   Send her Reason for reliefe.   270
For, *Faithfull* Minde's firm Resolution
Cures oftentimes th' ill Constitution
   Of a body sick-inclin'd :
But, then the Body (late deplor'd
For weak estate) to health restor'd,
   Grows a burthen to the Minde.

O Sin-bred hurt ! O in-bred Hell !
Nor full, nor fasting, never well ?
   Never sound ? what shall I say ?
Once all was well, and would be now   280
Better then ever, if that Thou
   Cursed sin wert quite away.
But now (alas !) all mischiefe lyes
In Ambush with all miseries,
   Man's Confusion to conspire :
Desire and *Feare* at-once torment :
Fear is a Tyrant ; Mal-content,
   And insatiate is *Desire.*
Who fears? who mourns? who wants? who wanders?
Ah ! onely Men (Wils ill-Commanders).   290
   Man alone abounds therein.
Loud Lamentations, lasting Terrors,
Heart-wounding Wants, and wilfull Errors,
   Had not been, had Man not been.
Here Pestilence, there Hunger's Jaw ;
Here Drink, there *Duel,* there the Law,
   Snatches one or other hence.
Here crosse, there care : or (better blest)
Who hap these Haps to scape the best,
   Age devoures without dispense.   300
Perpending This in minde perplext,
The miserable (Envie-vext)
   Cryes, *O Beasts, O Fowles, O Fish!*
You happy, harmlesse, stormlesse things,
Precise in *Nature's* Lessonings,
   Live you long : You life may wish.
But, I think, better not be borne ;
Or, born, hence quickly to returne
   To our Mother's dusty lap ;
Then living, daily here to dye,   310
In cares, and feares, and miserie,
   By Mis-heed, or by Mis-hap.
While hunger gripes mee gut and gall,
While burning thirst for drink doth call,
   While for cold I quake : alas !
In languor long I linger-on.
O ! happy Those, whose Woes, whose Mone,
   Ridding quick doth quickly passe.
The Stout, the Coward, and the Meek,
All skirmish under *Fortune* like,   320
   Striking all with Mischief's ay ;
The Stout repugns, the Patient prayes,
The Hare-like Coward runs his wayes ;
   Fortune differs not, but They.
Too-peevish This, Too pleasant That,
(Too-fierce, or too-effeminate)
   Golden Mean can hardly stand
Betwixt these Two Extremes, upright ;
'Tis worn so weak, and waigh'd so light :
   Error playes on either hand   330
Wedlock, with Wife and Children clogs :
The Single-Life, Lust's heavier Logs :
   (Rare's the Gift of *Continence*).
The Young-man stalks, the Old-man stoops,
That over-dares, This ever droops :
   Th' Infant craules through Impotence.

Masters taxe Servants, proud, slut, slow ;
Servants, Churle Master, Mistresse Shrow :
  Either Other's Fault can finde.
The Daughter thinks her Mother froward ;   340
Mother her Daughter deems un-toward :
  Kit (they say) will after kinde.
Princes doe envie Subjects' Wealth ;
Subjects doe envie Princes' Health :
  Each doth envie other's Good ;
All, all doe envie *Learning's* Honour
(If any be confer'd upon her)
  O ! ô wicked, wretched Mood !
The Souldier likes the Rustick's Calm ;
The Clowne affects the Souldier's Palm :   350
  Thus doth *Envie* inly fret-her :
Our Pastures parch, our Heards be poore ;
Our Neighbour thrives in every store :
  Others' Crop is ever better.
Fond Lovers languish at their eyes :
The Wrathfull fosters and defies
  Frenzies, Furies, (wayward Elves :)
What need yee call for Whip or Scourge ?
Their punishment what need wee urge ?
  Their Selve's-errors scourge themselves.   360
Fear hunts the Coward at the heel ;
The Cruell, still revenging steel ;
  Ruine Him that Ruine seekes ;
Heavy Revenge on haynous Crimes :
Yea, in the sin, the Plague, some-times ;
  Heav'n's just hand so justly strikes.
Sorrow and Shame, for what is past ;
Care, of the present ; Fear (fore-cast)
  Of the danger yet to-come ;
Make all false pleasures shorter seem,   370
And sharper too in pain extreme,
  Then even Paine it selfe to some.
If I be merry, I am mad
(Say the Severe :) if Sober-sad,
  Merry Greeks mee Meacok call.
Is 't possible for any-Man,
At-once to please (do what hee can)
  God, Himselfe, the World, and all ?
Who *Greatnesse* hautily affects,
Who *Great things* happily effects ;   380
  That is hated, This envi'd :
But, hoping *Greatnesse*, who so haps
To faile (or fall in After-claps)
  Him the Vulgar dare deride.
VERTUE is vanquisht by her foes,
Whose Triumph even their Fore-head showes,
  'Tis a shame to be ashamed ;
But shall I tell (and tell thee true)
Thy Fate (the fruit that shall ensue
  Shame-lesse shamefull life untamed) ?   390
This Fate then falls to be Thine owne,
Such shalt thou reap as thou hast sowne :
  Wages like thy Work expect.
Who here their Dayes in evill spend,
Shall suffer evills, without end ;
  Such is *Minos'* Doom direct.

Then, swagger, stagger, spend and spoile ;
Steal and conceale, and keep a coile.
  Quickly shalt thou all forgoe ;
Kill, conquer, triumph : down againe   400
Shalt thou be cast ; bouz, beat, disdaine :
  Th' End 's at hand, and comes not slow.
The wise bewaile men's follies rife,
And faine would cure their vicious life
  With *Receits* of heav'nly Skill :
But sin-sick Fooles (what-ever prick,
Benum'd by Custome) lethargike,
  Care not, fear not, feel no ill.
Who knoweth much, much ill hee knowes :
Who little reaks, much good forgoes.   410
  Hence perplexed doubts hee casts ;
What is great Knowledge ? What so much
Of Learning ? or of Book-skill such ?
  But great Blazes, and light Blasts ?
While *Plato*, sportive, doth despise,
The sullen *Cynik's* Sloven-guise :
  Hee as fast (on th' other side)
Doth *Plato's* pomp as much condemn
And trample-on : Were both of them
  (Who can tell mee ?) Wise, or Wide ?   420
Democritus, here, laughs a-good :
Heraclitus, there, weeps a floud.
  Glad and sad would mend us faine :
But now, so stubborn-stiffe is Man,
That Tears, nor Tunes, nor ought else can
  Faults restore, nor Fates restrain.
Sloth nere wanteth Want for Mate ;
Thrift, Sweat and Labour macerate ;
  Either in their issue languish :
So, Health is never without sin,   430
Nor Sicknesse without paine with-in :
  Outward Ache, or inward Anguish.
Service is to th' lofty minde
A Curb, a Spur to th' abject Hinde ;
  Seld or never stoops the Will :
The Vulgar voice, the Common cry
Is, *Welcome, Welcome, LIBERTY ;*
  Good for good, but ill for ill.
A griefe it is alone to be ;
But more, to have ill company :   440
  More or lesse (alas !) by This,
Appeareth plaine, when all is done,
(As Proofe hath found) that under Sunne,
  Here 's no full, no perfect *Blisse*.
Who never yet himselfe could please,
What can content ? What use ? What ease ?
  What availeth Wealth at will ?
Needy and naked here I live :
To die, it doth mee nothing grieve ;
  But to perish, and live still.   450
I look to heav'n and there (alas !)
With feare I see my Judge's Face,
  Auditing my summes of sin :
I thinke of Hell, and then I burne
Like *Ætna :* then to earth returne,
  Cares and Fears there never lin.

This feel I, thus I justly fare :
O Man ! learne quickly, and have care
  Sacred Duties to observe,
This life is rife in troubles sore :   460
But yet (alas !) a Million more
  Our Rebellion doth deserve.
Much like, or worse then *former* Age,
The *future's* Face wee may presage :
  Better seldome comes, they say.
Now right, now wrong ; now Good, now ill ;
Now Fiend, now Friend ; now Good, now Will,
  Seem to have alternate Sway.
Nothing is *gratis* given nor got :
Each labours more or lesse (God wot)   470
  With the hand or with the head :
None without Art or Vertue thrive ;
Nor Art, nor Vertue all atchieve :
  Onely, these, not alwayes sped,
What should I seek or sue for much,
To live at Rest ? Content is Rich.
  Fortune often is too-free,
And often kils where shee 's too-kinde :
But, had wee once an equall Minde
  Wee should all contented be.   480
But every one is too-secure,
In sunny Dayes ; and in obscure.
  Too-dejected in Desire :
Hence, over-faint, or over-full ;
Too-pyned, or too-plentifull,
  Fry wee all with inward Fire.
Now, Dust her dustie Brood expects :
Come, Earth to Earth (of either Sex).
  Pleasure trembles at her Call ;
Cryes-out of Haste, complains of Heav'n :   490
But Paine and Sorrow (narrow-driven)
  Are well pleas'd, and eas'd withall.

Who gives mee grace to gush-out Tears,
And lends mee space to poure forth Prayers ;
  Yet, both seeming to neglect?
'Tis God the dreadfull, Sinners' Scourge ;
The gracious God, which oft doth purge
  Ills with Pils, in his Elect.
Behold mee, Thou that didst bestow
Thy Son on Mee ; Forgive mee, Thou   500
  That didst suffer for my Sin :
Assist and stay mee evermore
Thou, Thou that here so oft before,
  In my brest a Guest hast bin.
Regard us, Lord, unworthy though ;
Thy Glory seek, thy Mercy show ;
  Enemies approach apace :
Wee faile, wee fall, wee cannot stand,
Our Foes will have the upper hand ;
  But Thou help us with thy Grace.   510
Witnesse my Self that here lie slain,
But, by Thy Touch reviv'd again ;
  Glad to live, to live to Thee :
And yet desire to be dissolv'd
(When my due Date shall be revolv'd)
  As more happy far for Mee.
Shew mee the *Holy Land*, which flowes
With Milk and Hony (*Saints' Repose*)
  Traine mee in the new commerce,
In the New Art of *Better Life :*   520
Then fare-well *Muses*, fare-well Strife :
  In Thy Courts I will converse.
I cannot strike Apollo's *string,*
Study for Heav'n and timely ring
  Sacred Aaron's *golden Bell ;*
Nor sing at-once the Thespian *Songs,*
And serve my Countrey, as belongs :
  Therefore, MUSES, *here Fare-well.*

FINIS.

NOTES AND ILLUSTRATIONS.

PAGE 96, '*Honoria, wife of James, Lord Hay.*' See our
    Memorial-Introduction on this ' fair lady.'
Line   8, '*unmew'd*' = unrenewed—as the eagle after
    moulting.
  ,,   12, '*condole*' = lament.
  ,,   46, '*Purchase-Profanation*' = simony.

Line 135, '*rathe*' = early—fine example of this word.
  ,, 184, '*too-craking*' = too boastful.
  ,, 375, '*meacock*' = effeminate fellow.
  ,, 401, '*bouz*' = drink to excess.
  ,, 410, '*reaks*' = recks.
  ,, 456, '*lin*' = cease.—G.

CERTAINE EPIGRAMS OF
The same Master *H. S.*
Tranſlated ; and Dedicated
To my dear-affected, due-respected,

Dᴿ. Hall, and Dᴿ. Hill.

I Owe you Each *a larger Summe :*
  Why bring I then to Both *a crumme ?*
To shew you Both, *my* Shifts, *to live,*
Even faine to Borrow, *what I* Give :
But Better so, then (blushlesse) steale
Others' Conceits ; *or Debts* conceale.
  Till more my Might, divide *this Mite :*
A Larke *(they say)* is worth a Kyte.
Some Greater, greater things present,
Of lesser Worth, *or worser* meant ;
God measures *not our* Work, *but* Will :
Doe You *the* like : *and* love *mee still.*

J. S.

---

1. Of a King.

Extirp, extoll ; know, keep ; love, learne (from High)
Bad, Good ; Thy Self, The Lawes-path ; Peace, to Dye.

2. Of a Lawyer.

Live just (Justinian) *still : shield, shun, suppresse ;*
Good-men's Good-cause, Bribes, Brawling-Peevishnesse.

3. Of a Physician.

Hee that can Cure the Sick, and keep the Sound,
Shall be My Leach (Whether Hee Kill, or Wound).

4. Of a Divine.

Know God ; know'n, teach Him ; as thou teachest, tread :
So shall thy Flock be as well taught, as fed.

5. Of a Judge.

Both blinde and lame I judge Thee best to make ;
Lest that thine Eyes mis-give, thy Hand's mis-take.

6. Of a Husbandman.

Good-morrow bids the Cock, th' Owle bids Good-night,
To Countrie-Cares : I bid, God *speed them right.*

7. Of a Captaine.

In War and Peace, Christ *is the sole Commander,*
To lead *to God-ward : follow still His Standard.*

Of all the Seven.

So Rule, Plead, Practise, Preach, Doom, Delve, Direct ;
Climes, Causes, Cures, Christ, *Crimes, Turves, Troops*
select.

FINIS.

NOTE.

Last line ' *Turves* ' = turfs. See No. 6, Of a Husbandman.—G.

THE

MAIDENS

BLUSH;

OR,

JOSEPH,

MIRROR

Of Modeſtie, Map of Pietie,

Maze of Deſtinie,

Or rather,

DIVINE PROVIDENCE,

From the Latine of *Fracaſtorious*,
Tranſlated ;

AND

Dedicated

To the High-Hopefull

CHARLES,

Prince of Wales,

BY

JOSUAH SYLVESTER.

TO THE HIGH HOPEFULL

HAPPY PRINCE Charles, PRINCE

Of Wales, Duke of Cornwall,

and Earle of Chester.

A Mong the Preace that to Your Presence flowes,   [= press.
    With joy-full Honours, as this time requires ;
    Instead of costly Suits, of curious showes,
Of precious Gifts, of solemne Panegyres :
Accept a Heart which to Your Highnesse *owes*
    Whole Hecatombes of Happy-most Desires ;
    Praying All prosperous to your blowing Rose,
In All, to equall or excell Your Sire's :
That in All Vertues *of a Prince complete,*
    All Princely Glories *may attend you still :*
    All that may make a King *as Good as Great :*
All Joseph's *blessings (from th' Eternall Hill)*
    Whose Happy Legend *comes to gratulate*
    Your High Creation, *and Your* Birth-daye's *Date.*

Prince Arthur's Castle, chiefest Art's chast Lure ;
Now, Now, or Never, Daign my Heart's last Cure.

L Ike sad Arion *on his* Dolphin's *back,*
    Amid the Ocean of my Carefull Feares,
    Nigh stript of all, Now stept in hoary haires ;
Sit (I poore Relique, of Your Brother's *wrack.)*
My Harp-strings quaver, while my Heart-strings crack :
    My Hand growes weary, and my health it wears ;
    To stir Compassion in some Powerfull eares,
    At last to land mee, and supply my lack.
You, You alone (Great Prince) *with Pitie's grace*
    Have held my Chin above the Water's brinke :
    Hold still, alas ! hold stronger or I sinke.
Or haile mee up into some safer place,
    Some, Privie-Groom, *some Room within your Doores :*
    That, as my Heart, my Harpe may all be Yours.

——————————————————— In Effect, as in Affection, To your Highnesse

————————————————————— service, Ever humbly devoted ;

———————————————————————Josuah Sylvester.

THE MAIDENS
BLUSH; OR
JOSEPH.

C Haste *Muse* of *Muses*, that in sacred Layes,
   With streins unwonted, dost delight to raise
From black *Oblivion's* sad and silent Tents,
Th' Heroick Gests and Noble Monuments
Of antike *WORTHIES*, and their fames revive
Through every Age to all that shall survive ;
Now, Now revolve th' Authenticall *Records*
Of th' *Holy Nation*, whom the Lord of lords
Chose for his owne, (Whose Line directly came
From Princely Loins of faithfull *ABRAHAM*) :   10
And sweetly tun'd to th' sacred voyce of Truth,
Sing That Religious, That rare-Modest *Youth*
(Good *Isaac's* Grand-child, and great *Jacob's* Son)
Whom *God* indu'd, by *Dreams*, of things yer done
To tell the issue : Tell, O ! tell Thou All
That Hee indur'd through swelling Envie's Gall ;
Till at the last, triumphing of his Foes,
Through *Pharao's* grace to Princely Place hee rose
(As *Egypt's* Viceroy) ; by divine Decree
Fore-sent a Friend and Founder there to be   20
Of th' happy People and the holy Seed,
From whence should hope of future Life proceed ;
And whence *Salvation* should be freely given,
Through th' heav'nly Key that should re-open *Heaven.*
   And, O ! Thou Glory of Great STUART'S stem,
Great Jacob's *Heire,* Great-Brittain's *Joy and Gem,*
CHARLES, King of Hopes, and hopefull Prince of
   Men,
My great Mecœnas, *to encheere my Pen,*
Assist Thou also : and with gentle Gales
Of Help-full Favour, fill my Hopefull Sailes :   30
That, maugre Envie's *Rock and* Fortune's *Storm,*
My sacred Voyage I may safe perform,
To th' onely glory of my Ghostly Guide,
His Churche's Profit, and Your Praise beside ;
While under JOSEPH'S Wondrous Temperance,
His Pietie, His Prudent Governance,
I prophecie Your Princely Vertue's Crop
(Your Parents' Prayer, and Your People's Hope)

God say Amen. But, Tide for none doth stay :
I must aboord, I must mine Anchor waigh.   40
Away to Sea ; the Winde is wondrous good :
Spread all our Canvas, O how swift wee scud !
Through all the Western, and the Mid-land Seas,
Arriv'd already to descry (with ease)
The Coast of *Joppa*, and *Samarian* Hills,
With wealthy *Sichem's* goodly Groves and Fields.
Already (running 'twixt his winding banks)
Jordan begins to wash our wel-come Planks,
Where *Hebron's* valley our glad Welcome sings,
And even *Mount Tabor* with the Eccho rings.   50
   Th' Old Serpent knew (for, much to know is
   given
Unto that Hell-god, by the God of Heaven)
It was decree'd by everlasting Date,
And promised, that there should propagate,
From *Abraham's* happy Stock, a holy Stem
Which should confound th' Infernall Diadem.
In doubt whereof, perplext and vexed sore,
His Jealousie of *Jacob* grew the more,
The more hee envies *Sichem's* Shepheard-Prince
As well because, with duer Reverence   60
Did None observe and serve th' Eternall Lord,
Nor juster liv'd, nor righter him ador'd ;
As for the goodly blessings of his bed,
(Twelve lusty Sons) likely alone to spread
Into a People holy and devout.
   Therefore hee labours, and hee layes-about,
With all the Engines of his hellish Hate,
That, That dear Issue to exterminate.
Especially, that lovely Lad (whose Birth
Had happy Stars, presaging holy Worth ;)   70
JOSEPH, the darling of his Father's age,
Borne of his (first-lov'd) second marriage :
Whom, *Nature-grac't*, the *Graces* nurtur'd fine
In liberall Arts, and love of Law divine ;
Inspir'd his Soule with skill of future things ;
His minde aspiring with celestiall wings :

To elders modest, to his equals milde,
With *Piety* and *Prudence* past a Childe.

Now, as from flow'rs whence Bees their honey make,
The loathsom Spider doth his poyson take ;　　80
Hence did the Fiend in th' other Brethren hatch
Close deadly Hate, him harm-lesse to dispatch :
Nor would Hee let the first occasion slip,
That might advance his wily workmanship :
For, for the most, to each man's Inclination,
Hee knowes in time, to offer his Temptation.
It hapned then, upon a Summer's day,
When as the Sun had with his parching Ray
Driv'n all the Brethren all their flocks to drive
To the coole Covert that the Woods would give ;　　90
Them-selves set round under a shady Oake,
Young JOSEPH thus gently the rest bespoke :

Brothers, I'le tell you my strange dream to night ;
Heare it, I pray you (what ere meane it might,
It was an odde one.)　Early when the Stars
Were all call'd in (excepting *Lucifer's*,
Daye's daily Usher) slumbring sweet this morne,
Mee thought Wee all were in a field of corne,
All binding Sheaves ; and when wee each had One,
My Sheafe, mee thought, stood bolt upright alone,　100
And all your Sheaves did instantly incline,
And lowly bow their bended tops to mine.
Then *Judah*, nettled with no little hate
Against the Lad, began him thus to rate :
Why, saucy Boy, What phant'sies dost thou
　　fable?
Is this your Dreame, you deem so admirable ?
Hath not perhaps some Spirit inspir'd you so ?
No doubt there hath : the spirit of Wine I trow.
But, pray, what *Augure* doth your wonder bring ?
That you (belike) shall of us all be King.　　110
Good King of crickets, line thy Crown with baies,
Lest drunken Vapors some Rebellion raise.

The rest concurr'd to gird the harmlesse Boy
With slouts and shouts of *O God give you joy :
God save your Grace, your Majesty to come ;*
And tell, in Scorne, their Father all the summe.

Hee, good old man (not without *God* within),
Hee ponders all that hee had heard and seen ;
As if discerning somewhat in the Lad
Of higher straine, then every stripling had :　　120
Yet to conceale it from the rest hee seems,
And bids the Boy beware of guilefull *Dreams.*

But, Hee, to whom GOD greater Honors meant,
Soon after dream'd of graver Argument.
Him seem'd, that, set in stately Eminence,
Before his Feet, with humble Reverence,
The Sun and Moon and Eleven Stars hee saw,
Stooping unto him with obsequious awe.
Which well recording (for by heav'nly grace
That Gift hee had) within a little space　　130
Hee tels his Brethren o his second Transe :
Who, re-incenst with ragefu Arrogance,
Soon shew their Father, with his fatall *Dream,*
Their rancor, spleene, and cank'red spite extreme.

Jacob at first, amazed, calls his Son ;
And, as interp'ring, thus to chide begun :
What ! Sirra ; shall I, and your Mother too,
And all your Brothers bow our Necks to you ?
Shall you be mounted on your Chaire of State,
And Wee come All base Beggars to your Gate ?　　140
If such a folly hath befum'd your brain,
And fill'd your phant'sie with presumption vain,
With idle Hopes : away with those Conceits,
Trust not to *Dreams*, list not to such Deceits
So reason-lesse, ridiculous, and light ;
Monsters, *Chimæra's*, shadows of the Night :
Which (if not good) it is not *God* doth send,
But som Illusion of the subtle Fiend,
To train our Weakenesse to some sinfull Trap ;
Or, to betray us to some dire mis-hap :　　150
As from his Cels false Oracles hee wrests,
From flight of Birds, & Tripes of mangled Beasts.

Hast thou not heard of *Belus, Anubis,
Ops, Hecatè,* and other *Dëities,*
Whom the blinde *Heathen* in their Temples have,
Frequent their Altars, and their Rites observe ;
Waiting their Altars with the humblest Awe,
All which is hatefull to our *Holy-Law ?*
Therefore be Wise : and look henceforth wee hear
No more such *Dreams* of such phantastike gear.　　160

Hee, thus dismist, the rest hee milde bespake
To calme their storme, and kindly bade them take
The Flocks to Field, and drive them soft and fair
To *Sichem* Woods, to feed in cooler aire.

Their Father's bidding they eft-soones obay'd
(Young JOSEPH yet at home with him hee staid)
Passing the fruitfull Vales and flow'ry Greens
Of plenteous *Hebron,* to those shadie Screens.

But, nor the Verdure of those Hills nor Dales,
Nor song of Birds, nor shade of Woods, nor Gales　170
Of whisp'ring Winds, could kill or cancell quite,
Those odious *Dreams* they dream-on day & night :
Rather, they gather daily more disdain,
Sharpen their Envie, give their Rage the rain,
With Threats and Vows ; while th' evill spirit too
　　nigh,
Still stirs and spurs their hatefull Jealousie.

Now, twice the Sun had run his Journy swift,
When the next morning they prepare to shift
To *Dothan's* pleasant Downs for fresher Feed,
And to be further off from home (indeed) ;　　180
And so the longer ere they could revert ;
Which they even loath'd, and hated at the heart.

Wherefore (night after night, day after day)
When, past their wont, their Father saw them stay ;
In musefull care his JOSEPH calls hee quicke,
And bids him thus ; I pre-thee Boy go seeke
Thy Brethren out (on *Sichem* Downes they feed,
Or neer about) and bring mee word with speed,
What uncouth Reason of their stay there is :
My minde mis-gives mee somewhat is amisse　　190
With them, or with their Cattle : hye thee Lad.

Away scuds JOSEPH (no lesse swift then glad)

As far as *Sichem :* but there looking round,
Neither his Brethren, nor the Flocks hee found.
Perplexed then, hee calls them one by one ;
Hoaw, Brothers ! *Reuben ! Levi ! Simeon !*
Then, whoops and hallooes with a treble throat,
So loud and shrill, that, to his warbling Note
With doubled *Ecchoes,* Woods and Caves reply :
But not a Brother answers Eare or Eye.   200

By chance, a Wood-man that an Oak did shrowd,
Hearing the Lad, and knowing, call'd him loud,
And told him thus ; I heard your Brethren say
They would to *Dothan :* Thither, that 's the way ;
There shall you finde them with their Cattle safe,
In better Pasture then is here by halfe.
Thanks thinks the Lad : and *Sichem* out of sight,
As swift as Roe hee runs to *Dothan* right.

When, from a Hill, his hatefull Brethren spi'd
Him yet far-off : O ! yonder comes (they cry'd)   210
Our King to-come, whom both the Sun and Moon,
And all the Stars must serve and worship soon.
Wee, wee base Hinds, born but for Heards &
      Neat,
Drudging all day in the Sun's scorching heat,
Lodging all night in holes or hollow Trees,
Clad but in Lether, or in coursest Freeze,
And meanly fed with Bread and water most ;
While hee is set-up with his Sod and Roast,
His Messe of Goat's-milk, and his fill of Wine,
In change of Coats, pranked and painted fine ;   220
Snoring all night upon his ease-full bed,
Where, from the Forge of his phantastike head,
Hee feignes these *Dreams* in meer disdain of us :
But, Brethren, shall wee, shall wee suffer thus
Him and his Scorning ? Shall wee be so blinde
T' indure him still, till grown a man, his minde
Grown big withall, and bearing proud upon
His Father's fondnesse, Hee supplant anon
Our Haps and Hopes, usurping All our due,
And so (in fine) fulfill his *Dreams* too-true ?   230
O ! Wee are Buzzards, Blockheads, Cowards all,
Why rather here, where none descry us shall,
Where all things sort, where hee is come so pat,
Shall wee not kill him, and make sure for that ?
For, in this Pit wee may him deep interre,
And say (at home) some hungry Wolfe or Beare
(Whereof the Desarts, not far off, have store)
Him quick devoured, and to peeces tore.

While these dire Counsels they together cast,
Reuben (who all in years and pity, past)   240
Cry'd, GOD defend, O Brethren, GOD defend,
Against our Brother wee should so offend ;
O ! in his bloud doe not your hands imbrue,
Lest Heav'n's drad Vengeance that dire fact pursue
On Us and Ours. Though no man witnesse be,
GOD, GOD himselfe is witnesse, and doth see
And heare us all : from him is nothing hid ;
Hee 's all an Eye that never closeth Lid.
But, if you needs will of the Lad be quit,
Sanz bloud or slaughter, put him in this pit,   250

There leave him to his Fate. This hee advis'd,
That, rescu'd thus from present death devis'd,
Hee, late at night returning to the Cave,
Might hale him up, and th' harmlesse strippling
      save,
To bring him safe unto his aged Sire,
And calme at length his Brethren's envious Ire.

Their Elder's Words them All a little mov'd,
And his advice they all at once approv'd :
Him down unslain, into the pit to slide,
His worse or better Fortune to abide.   260
Then *Reuben* said ; Be Witnesse GOD for mee,
How clear I am from this your Cruelty :
And as hee spake, him from them far withdrew
Into the Woods to wait what would ensue.

By This, was JOSEPH (full of lively cheer
For having found them) even arrived neer :
When, fell and furious, they inclose him round,
Lay hands on him, his tender hands they bound,
With braving Threats ; Now shall you see (say they)
Your *Dreams* fulfill'd : Must not wee all obey   270
Your Mightinesse ? *Our sheaves must stoop to you :*
Yea, *to your State, Sun, Moon, and Stars must bow.*

Wondring & frighted with their uncouth guise,
In vein (alas !) in vain hee calls and cries
To them for pity of his Innocence ;
While inly Rage, with more Impatience,
Still egg'd them on, with fell *Erynnis* brands :
And hellish *Pluto* (who too-ready stands,
Weening to crosse the *Destinies divine*)
Doth all their Edge 'gainst him alone incline.   280

When he perceiv'd (poor Boy !) no vows, no tears
Could mollifie those stony hearts of Theirs
To hold their hands, already heaving him
With violence unto the Dungeon's brim ;
His eyes lift up towards th' *Emperiall Pole*
Thus loud hee groaned from a grieved soule :

Great GOD of *Abr'am, Is'ac, Jacob* too,
Who kennest all things, and canst all things doe ;
If I sincerely have ador'd thee still ;
If I have gladly done my Parent's Will ;   290
If I have lived pious and upright ;
Lord looke upon mee in this wofull plight.
Or, if it please thee, that I here expire ;
Yet spare, O Lord, O spare mine aged Sire.
And, O ! my Brethren (whom, with due respect
Of Eldership, I ever did affect)
How-ever Mee you pity not, I pray
Pity our Father (lest untimely gray
His hoary head come to the grave for griefe)
Let not him heare it : rather say some Theefe,   300
Or knot of Theeves, Mee (by the way) bereft ;
That some false hope may of my life be left,
To lengthen his : though here alas ! I lye
Dead in these sands, and hid from any eye :
And as hee spake, his tears so fast did fall,
They stopt his speech, and almost staid withall
His Brethren's rage ; till Ruth-lesse *Issachar*
Re-fand the fire. Nay having gon thus far,

Wee may not now, Wee cannot safe desist ;
For why ? whereon I need not now insist ;   310
Your selves (said hee) can quickly ghesse, I trow,
Mischiefs enow, if now wee let him goe.
Let us therefore go on as wee decreed,
Let 's let him down. Hereto they all agreed,
With heart and hand, and did it instantly ;
And then remorselesse, on the Grass hard by
Made no more bones, but sate them down to dinner :
O ! the dull Conscience of a hardned sinner !
    But, from th' *Emperial*, through th' *Ætherial*
        Pole,
GOD looking down upon the harmlesse Soule,   320
In tender pity, and eternall love
Towards his Owne, among the Troops (above)
Of winged Heralds that are ever prest,
Expecting gladly his Divine Behest,
To one hee beckens, and hee bids him Thus ;
Right Trusty, hy thee quickly down from us,
Toward *Samaria*, well thou knowest where,
And whom thou know'st one day ordain'd to bear
A glorious Part, in honourable Place,
Good *Is'ac's* Grand-Child, now in piteous case,   330
Crying for succour from a dark deep Cell,
Against his Brethren's envious Furie fell :
Goe comfort him, poor heart ; but in what kinde
I need not say. Thou seest, thou know'st my mind.
    So, with his gratious All-directing Nod,
Th' Angell, dismist, in th' instant spreads abroad
Æthereall wings on his Aëreall sides,
And through the woundlesse Welkin swifter glides
Then *Zephyrus ;* or, than (when mounted high
With many Turnes, and towring in the Skie)   340
The stout *Ger-Faulcon* stoopeth at the *Herne*,
With sudden Souse, that many scarce discerne :
Such was the speed of this Celestiall Bird
(To prosecute, and execute the Word
Of his great Master) towards *Dothan* Down,
Alighting first upon *Mount Tabor's* Crown,
Amaz'd to see his Groves so sodain green,
And Lawns so fresh, with flow'ry tufts between.
The Hill-born *Nymphs* with quav'ring warbles sing
His happy *Well-come ;* Caves and Rocks doe ring   350
Redoubled Ecchoes ; Woods and Winds withall,
Whisper about a joyfull Madrigall.
But th' Heav'nly Herald from the Mountain eying
The Vale about, sees there the Brethren lying
Along the Grasse, and busie at their Vittle,
And from a Hill (thence distant but a little)
Th' *Arabian* Merchants with their Camels, hard
(As God would have it) driving thither-ward :
Thence instantly hee casts his gentle Eye
On wofull JOSEPH ; and immediately   360
Descending swift, stands on the dungeon's brim,
Now shining bright with sudden light from him.
Wherewith the Lad at once dismai'd and joy'd,
The sacred Torch-man (to that end imploy'd)
In lovely Shape, with sweet and lively grace,
Thus cheers the Lad (himselfe a Lad in Face).

Feare not, dear JOSEPH, dear to God above :
Thy Father's God, who All doth guide and move,
Hath sent mee hither from his heav'nly Throne,
To comfort and confirm thee, in thy Mone.   370
First, Hence thou shalt be freed : yet, behold,
Twice, as a Slave, thou shalt be bought and sold,
Transferr'd to *Memphis*, and for many a year
Shalt live a Servant and a Pris'ner there.
But if thou still have in abhomination
Strange Women's Love, and strange gods' adoration :
If still with all thy strength, with all thy heart
Thou serve the Lord, and from him never start :
If in his Wayes thou walk, and doe his Will,
Hee will be with thee, for thee, in thee still :   380
So that where-ere thou goe, what-ere thou doe,
Favour and Fortune shall attend thee too.
And that thou maist with greater confidence
Contemne thy wrongs, and trust his Providence ;
Know for a certain, hee hath destin'd thee
A high Estate, and glorious Emperie ;
And time will com, when thou with me shalt view
Thy former *Dreams* in every part prove true ;
When as thy Brethren with selfe-guilty brow,
And thy good Father shall before thee bow :   390
When thy Compassion, paying good for ill,
Shal save their lives, yet meant thee first to kil :
Shall feed their mouthes that thought thee once to
        sterve,
And buy them seats that sold thee forth to serve ;
And not alone receive themselves to grace,
But them and theirs within thy Kingdome place ;
That grown at length in number like the sand,
Thence the Almighty with a mighty hand
(In spight of *Envie* and *Ambitious* sway)
May bring them dry-shod through the crimson sea, 400
Directed safe in all their uncouth Way,
By Fire by Night, and by a Cloud by Day ;
Through the dry *Desart*, plentifully fed
With Quails from Heav'n, & *Manna* (Angels' bread)
Into a Land where milk and hony flow ;
The happy signe of happier substance though :
Where, in due Time (O haste yee Times away.)
A *Golden Age* shall see a *glorious Day*,
A *Day* full oft to be fore-typ't, fore-told,
Fore-promised by Prophets manifold ;   410
When from the Bosome of th' Eternall SIRE,
Th' Eternall SON (What may wee So admire !)
(The Spirit *o're shadowing of a Virgin-Mother*)
Shall take man's Nature, and become your Brother ;
Old Adam's Guilt, and Your's to expiate,
And wide re-open Heav'n's long-locked Gate :
Concluding here, to Heav'n the Angell hy'd.
    JOSEPH, though first distract and stupefi'd
With such a glory (and confus'd a-space)
Him re-collects, and re-erects his Face ;   420
Inly rejoycing, deeply rumining,
All in his minde maturely pondering.
And future Hopes confirm him passing strong,
'Gainst present fears, and all his Woes and Wrong ;

That cheerly thus, with heart and hands erect,
His holy vowes hee doth to Heav'n direct :
　Great King of kings, that rulest All-abroad ;
My Father's, Grandsires', and Great-grandsires' God,
Almighty Guide and Guard, still gratious be
To Us and Ours, whose trust is all in Thee.　　430
Especially, thy Favour, Lord I crave
Towards my Father, ready for the Grave :
And as for mee ; how-ever please thee, deale
Mee sowre or sweet, or send mee woe or weale ;
It shall be welcome, and I well content.
Onely dear Father, if that death prevent
Mine eyes (unworthy) of that wished Day,
That long long-hoped, happy *Holy-Day*,
When from thy Throne (whose glory hath no end)
Thine onely *Son* shall into *Flesh* descend ;　　440
At least vouchsafe mee, though in shadow dim,
As in a glasse to see and knowledge Him ;
And (thorough Faith) to feel the *saving Savour*
Of this thrice-sacred, gratious, pretious *Laver :*
So, with an inward and deep sigh, hee ceast.
　The while, *Arabians* (Merchants of the East)
With Camels loaden with their Countrey Ware,
Myrrhe, Storax, Incense, the most choyce and rare,
Comming from *Madian*, towards *Ægypt* bound,
Were passing by, where on the grassie ground,　　450
The Shepheard Brethren sate to eat and talke :
And busie yet, their Teeth and Tongues did walk,
Till on the sudden they descry'd the men.
Whence *Judah* thus begins : O Bretheren,
Behold how God doth better far provide,
Then wee could plot (more safe for either side).
For, to these merchants if wee sell the Lad,
First, a good peece of money will be had ;
Next, of our Brother's bloud wee shall be cleer :
And last of all, be sure no more to hear　　460
Or news, or noise, or name of JOSEPH here,
Whether to *Memph's* or *Marmorid's* they wend.
Therefore forthwith one to them let us send,
The mart to offer, and the price to make,
As of a Slave ; and bring their answer back.
　They all agree, and one is sent away
To drive the Bargaine ; while the rest assay
About a Tree-trunk fastning fit a rope,
And letting 't down to hale their Brother up.
And up hee comes as fresh as Mayey-Rose,　　470
Or Daffadill that in a Garden growes :
As lively Form as yerst, as lovely Face,
Singing with signes of GOD'S assisting Grace.
　By this, the merchants with their Broker came,
To see the Ware ; and did so like the same,
They stood not hucking, of the price to bate
(So good, and so good cheap, who would not ha 't !)
But, who would ween (*good God !*) that ever Hee,
That was præ-destin'd to such dignitie,
To whom such Wealth and Honour should befall,　　480
Should thus be sold, and for a price so small?
Save that my *Saviour*, Heire of Heav'n and Earth,
That *God*-begotten, holy *Virgin's*-Birth,

Whom Angels serve, whom Cherubins adore,
To *Jews* his *Judas* sold for little more ;
(Woe to His Soule, Woe to my Sins therefore !)
As, *Twenty Pence*.　O base and cursed Thrall !
　But, both sides pleas'd, *Joseph* must suffer all,
Now must hee mount on his new master's pack
Upon his Camel's double-bunched back,　　490
To trot to *Nile*-ward (never heard-of *Nile*) :
As proud and glad of such a Load, the while
His gentle Beast, now easiest of the Troop,
Aptest to stop, humblest at need to stoop
To this new Rider, with a cheerfull Neigh,
Lifts light his feet, and still hee leads the way.
　Well : Now the Brethren have their Brother rid,
How shall his Fate, how shall their Hate be hid ?
Who to their Father the sad news shall bring ?
This is the doubt : This they are hammering.　　500
In fine, they jump ; first to send home his Coat
(For they had stript him) and in bloud of Goat
Deep dipping it, *Dan* is instructed fit
In this sad manner to deliver it
To aged JACOB, doubting nothing lesse,
Then His mis-hap, or their so Hatefulnesse.
Father (said *Dan*) ranging within a Wood,
Our Cur did find this Coat, thus stain'd with bloud.
Not knowing therefore, whence, nor whose it is,
Nor how it came, wee thought it not amisse　　510
To shew 't you first, and after hearken further,
As you think fit, in case of Maime, or Murder.
　But, Father *Jacob* had no sooner spy'd
The spotted Coat, with bloud and dirt bedy'd,
But, drown'd in Tears, hee teares his hoary haire,
With Ashes sprent, and rent his garments there,
And cries, Alas ! dear JOSEPH, staffe and stay
Of all mine Age, so sudden ta'n away !
O ! O ! My Son, Who? How? What did befall,
To murder Thee, to murder Mee withall?　　520
Doubtlesse, no Man : some savage Beast it was,
Som hungry Boare, some hairie Beare, alas !
Where are your Brethren?　Quickly all of you,
Through all the Woods, go take a thorow view :
You may perhaps at last yet light on him,
Or finde at least som Part, som mangled Lim,
Som wofull Relique, which I pray bring home,
That I may give it his last Rites, a Tombe :
Or rather, let mee goe my selfe to seeke,
And finde my dead Son, or a Death, his like :　　530
And saying so, downe in a swoune hee slid,
With much adoe to be recovered.
　On th' other side, sad *Reuben* towards night,
When th' Evening Star began to twinkle bright,
When Sheep and Shepheards to their Cotes were gone
All but himself, himself comes all alone
Unto the Cave, and calling twice or thrice,
Why ! *Joseph, Joseph ;* when as none replyes,
Dismaid, and doubting, lest in their disdaine,
His Brethren there the silly Lad had slaine ;　　540
Hee makes a shift to cut an Holmen Pole,
And by that help, gets downe into the hole,

Lookes round about ; but finding nothing there,
Gets up againe, as full of griefe and feare :
Then hopeless, leaves that search to seek the others ;
And by the Sheep's track, tracking of his Brothers,
Soon findes them out ; and out of them will know
Both how, and where, they JOSEPH did bestow.
They tell him truely how it did befall.
A little eas'd (though little pleas'd withall)   550
To heare the Lad was yet alive and safe
(Though for his thraldome hee did inly chafe)
Hee thus advises ; Brethren, let us hye
Home to our Father, and our best apply
To comfort him ; Let us informe him this
That the *Arabians* (as their manner is)
Spying the Lad alone upon the Way,
Pursu'd him, took him, stole him quite away ;
And while hee struggled from them to have got,
With a light hurt hee bloudied all his Coat.   560
Which let some Shepheard's boy or other bring
(As having found it) to aver the thing ;
For there be many can affirm (no doubt)
They lately saw *Arabians* here-about.
This fitted thus, together home they goe,
And doe their best to cheer their Father's woe.
But though perhaps with som small hope reliev'd,
Perpetually (alas !) hee mourn'd and griev'd,
Nor could the Torrent of his tears retain,
Nor outward Solace inly entertain ;   570
But day and night a bitter life hee led,
Mostly alone, although alive, as dead.
Mean-while, the Merchant well content and glad
Holds on his Journey, bears away the Lad ;
Wondring to see all things so sute his will,
Weather so temp'rate, and the Windes so still,
The Wayes so dust-lesse, and so dirtlesse faire,
The Sun so friendly, and so fresh the Aire ;
Above their wont : for, having Heav'n to friend,
With JOSEPH, *Graces, Hope,* and *Hap* do wend.   580
Now, having past *Judæa's* confines quite,
From a steep Hill, they have anon the sight
Of stately *Memphis'* lofty Tow'rs and Walls,
With glitt'ring roofes of high and sumptuous Hals.
Amid a rich and pleasant Plaine, repleat
With goodly Heards of Cattell, Sheep, and Neat,
With goodly Corn-fields, here and there between :
And, neer the City, on a spacious Green,
They might behold, as in som Martiall Muster,
Thousands of Youth in severall Troops to cluster ;   590
Attending all, som manly Exercise ;
Some, light and speedy, running for a prize :
Some, strongly active, wrastling for a fall,
Some, hurling Sledges, till they sweat withall :
Some, on swift Horse-back to out-swim the wind ;
Some, to shoot backward at their foes behinde :
Some, with their Launches ready coucht in Rest,
Wheeling about, to charge in Flank or Breast :
Some, at the Tilt, in strong and steady course,
To break their Staves, or bear down man and
    horse.   600

Wheron th' *Arabians*, with th' *Is'acian* Lad,
(Now very neer) stood gazing, as right glad,
And almost greedy of so various sorts
Of Manly Proems, of so warlike sports.
An *Eunuch* of the Kings, one much esteem'd,
And master of those Martiall Games (it seem'd)
Seeing those Strangers, with so much delight
Stand still so long in viewing all the Sight,
Sends to invite them kindly to com neer ;
And then perceiving that they Merchants were,   610
Began to ask What Ware, what rare device,
They had to sell ? Nothing, said they, but Spice,
And this young Lad ; Whom, if Your Lordship
    like,
Accept as Yours, and freely, wee beseek ;
Or, if you nill accept him *gratis,* prize
As please your selfe ; your favour shall suffize.
Yes, said the *Eunuch,* I accept your Love,
And of Your Present I so well approve,
And prize it so, You could not bring mee better :
The more my hope, the more am I your debter,   620
Such grace his face presageth to my minde ;
So shall you never mee ungratefull finde,
Said *Potiphar :* and then hee takes the Lad ;
And, causing him to be right seemly clad,
In Silken suit, gives him a Livory
Of Purple, guarded with Embroderie.
Then on a goodly Horse hee sets him up,
The stillest, yet the stateliest in the troup.
JOSEPH right joyfull, from a bashfull Brow
Returnes dumbe *Homage,* with a gracefull Bow   630
Unto his Lord : then, re-erect, appears
Taller and trimmer then were all his Peers.
Him, home before (thus furnisht) with a Guide,
Sends *Potiphar* unto his lovely Bride.
Now *Hesperus* the Evening on did bring ;
When, leaving Fields, the youthfull troops do ring
About their Captain, and attend, in State
To guard him home triumphant to his Gate.
And lovely JOSEPH, having had by this
A view of his faire *Lady-Misterisse ;*   640
And of his Office, tutured at large,
What him belong'd in his *Lord's Chamber* charge,
Him humbly ranked (of his owne accord)
Among his fellows to go meet his Lord.
As burnisht Gold amid a heap of Sand,
Or Orient Pearle among the Pebble Strand,
Such seemed Hee, among ten thousand Squires,
Whom men and matrons, young and old admires :
His pase so grave, his Face so gracious,
His eyes and Feet still so officious   650
About his Lord, as fixed still on Him,
With steady Looks, and with as ready Limbe :
No lesse within doores then hee was without,
Active and apt in all hee went about ;
On all occasions, in what-ever kinde,
Of bodie's labour, or of birth of minde.
But above all, his faithfull diligence,
And mature Wisdome in all managements,

So well accepted and admired are,
That not alone unto his trusty Care   660
His Lord committed what before hee had :
But over All, him onely *Steward* made.
For, *Potiphar* perceiv'd that under him,
What-ere hee had did thrive and prosper trim :
His Fields and Flocks more fruitfull then before ;
His Favours greater, and his Honours more :
All which inspired by some secret Test,
To this young JOSEPH hee ascrib'd, as Blest.
And th' *Oracles* of *Egypt*, then a-foot,
Seem'd even to point at, and perswade unto 't.   670
  There was a *Peach*-Tree growing then amid
God-Camosh Temple, to him consacred,
Which, brought from *Persia* long agoe, they say,
When *Isis* yerst did all the World survay,
By her own hand was planted, for Posterity,
To be a famous Monument of Verity.
Hereon, arriving from far wanderings,
Bright-shining *Apis* with change-colour'd wings,
Faire *Apis* settled ; after whom did muster
A mightie Swarm, which hung all in a Cluster   680
Upon one Bough. This wonder blown abroad
Among the *Bards*, they vouch that it did boad,
Some stranger should from forrein parts arrive ;
And after him, a mighty people hyve ;
Through whom the house of *Potiphar* should
     rise
To wondrous Wealth and goodly dignities.
Weening therefore these *Augures* all fulfill'd
In JOSEPH now, him every one well-will'd,
Him every one accordingly respected,
Him every one for this the more affected.   690
  But, fair *Iëmpsar* (wife of *Potiphar*)
Above the rest, his Parts did high prefer ;
Him more then All shee inly did admire,
And still beholds him with a young desire.
Yet, ignorant what furie would ensue
The pleasing Passion shee did so pursue ;
What wily *Godling* to beguile her, sought
To snare her freedome in a servile thought ;
As yet shee vented neither Sigh nor Teare :
All yet was sweet, no bitter Fit, no Feare.   700
  Which th' envious Prince of *Styx* and *Acheron*,
Malignant Father of confusion,
Man's deadly Foe, observing ; and beside,
That *Isaac's* seed still happy multipli'd ;
In fell despight and full of desp'rate rage,
Hee calls a bird of his infernall Cage,
A cruell Harpy, full of wicked Wile,
A thousand wayes the wisest to beguile.
Goe, hye, saith Hee, my darling, hye thee quick
To faire *Iëmpsar ;* shee is *Phant'sie-sick*   710
Already : Therefore so insinuate,
That more and more thou her intoxicate :
Breathe in her bosome, blow-in new infection,
Kindle the Tindar of her light affection,
To such a flame, that neither Gods nor men
May be of pow'r to put it out agen :

And doe the best (for that I most desire)
If possible, set JOSEPH (too) a fire :
But if on him, thou nothing canst prevaile,
Return to her, her Phant'sie re-assaile,   720
Fill her with Phrenzie, and with furie double
Still burn her fell, till all her Friends shee trouble :
Till with disgrace, disdain'd, and desperate,
Shee turn her dear Love to as deadly Hate :
Till then, desist not ; but persist and ply
To play thy Part with Art and Subtilty.
  Hee, glad and ready for the worst of Ills,
With *Stygian* puddle halfe a Viall fills,
Blending some bitter, sharp-sweet wine withall.
Then snatching quick one of the snakes that craule 730
About *Alecto's* grim and ghastly Browes,
Away hee hyes to *Potiphar* his House,
Within his bosome hiding what hee had,
And formally just in the Form him clad
Of *Iphicle*, the Lady *Iëmpsar's* Nurse ;
With better credit, to beguile the worse.
Then to her Lady having made a Duck,
Sweet *Madame* (said shee, fie on all ill luck)
What sad disaster, what misfortune rife,
Hath made poor JOSEPH weary of his Life?   740
My selfe, of late have seen him oft, forlorne
Sit sole and sighing, and have heard him mourn,
Wishing for Death. And when I sought to know
The secret cause of his exceeding woe :
O ! Mother (said hee) or whether I conceale it
Needs dye I must, or whether I reveale it.
Inquire not therefore ; for, 'tis better end,
With my sad life my sorrow's cause unkend.
  Not so, my Son (said I) for oft a wound
Discover'd, is recover'd, and made sound ;   750
Which, hid a while, would gangrene to the bone :
Tell boldly (Lad) art thou in love with none?
If that be cause of thy distresse ; Why Boy
Be of good cheer, Thou shalt thy Dear enjoy,
Hope well, and have well : So shalt thou ; or else
I 'll charme *Love's Passion* with some stronger spel.
  With bashfull Blush, then said hee, Yes, I love :
Be witnesse, *gods*, how earnest I have strove
To strangle it ! How I have labour'd long !
How loth (alas !) my Lord in thought to wrong !   760
More wishing Death : Death, now make good my
     triail :
Happy were I to live and dy so loyall.
And, saying so, on his fair Cheeks hee pours
A Sea of Tears, in Pearl and Crystall showrs :
So that I see, without quick Remedy,
For love of you, *Madame*, the Youth will dy.
  Alas ! then said the Lady, Woe is mee
For his Misfortune and his Misery ;
To mee right tragick is the tale you tell :
For, truth to say, I love him but too well,   770
And would enjoy him if I could or durst ;
But, O ! I cannot : O ! I may not : first,
For sacred Lawes, for *Hymen's* secret yoke,
(Which never any yet, unpunisht, broke)

For fear of danger, and dis-honour's brand,
And dreadfull vengeance of my Husband's hand.
  Why, my dear Daughter, damned Nurse replies,
The gods do laugh at Lovers' injuries :
And with thy Wedlock thou maiest well dispense,
On so good ground of so great consequence,   780
As is the saving of a Life so young,
So innocent, that never yet did wrong ;
Unlesse it be a wrong to love too much,
Or dy for love. (Who would not die for such?)
Lovers must dare, and Wise-men must not dread
The worst of dangers that is threatened :
For, even the gods have Lovers in their guard,
And *Love* and *Pity* they will still reward.
I have a *Water* of a soverain use
(Th' extracted Spirit of many a *Chimick-Juice*)   790
Which inly ta'n in a perplexed Case,
Expels the Doubt, and shews *Truth's* naked Face :
That, far from *Ambage*, th' undistract affection
May of the better freely make election.
If therefore, *Madame*, yet you stand divided,
What Part to take ; to have your doubts decided,
I 'll give it you : and, as shee spake, shee gave
The hellish *Philtree*, made of *Stygian* wave.
  Thanks, dearest Mother, said her Ladiship :
And, taking all, not with a fearfull sip,   800
But full Carouse, lifting her hand on hy,
Quaft off the poison, drew the goblet dry.
  This done, the *Dæmon*, with a Beldam's face,
Tow'rds *Joseph's* chamber hies with hobbling pase ;
Where hee was praying, and devoutly praysing
The God of gods, for his so gracious raising :
But when the false Fiend in his Portall spi'd
A heav'nly Warder (both his Guard and Guide)
With threatfull brandish of a shining Blade,
More speed then good, headlong hee downward
      made   810
In dreadfull Maze ; and, as the foulest Fowle,
Transforms him quick into a *Scrieching-Owle*,
Night's horrid Monster, hov'ring long aloof,
At last pearcht on *Iëmpsar's* Chamber roof :
  Wretched *Iëmpsar*, having quaffed up
The brim and bottome of the *Stygian* Cup,
Now all alone, shee feels her all a-fire,
Bloud, bones and Marrow, burning in desire ;
Sad, silent, sighing : in a wondrous Fit ;
And all for *Joseph*, nigh beside her wit :   820
Now on her bed shee fals, and by and by
Flings up again ; and to and fro doth fly
From place to place ; soon weary of the best,
Runs every where, and no where findeth rest ;
Like one whose brest a burning Fever fryes,
Or whom some Serpent's sting doth agonize.
At last shee breaks out ; and Alas ! quoth Shee,
What, what is this that thus tormenteth mee ?
O ! is it Love? or was it not the Drink
I took right now? No : it is Love I think,   830
'Tis surely Love, Love in extremity,
And but fair JOSEPH gently help, I dye.

Then help, Sweet-heart, come, be thou boldly mine :
Come be my Love, and I will still be thine.
Both living loving, wee 'll die guiltlesse both
Of either's bloud : Be witnessee gods how loth
I would incur so fell, so foul a stain,
To kill such Lover with unkinde disdain.
Duly and truly, while I ought and could,
I served *Hymen*, till (alas !) controul'd   840
By higher Godheads more Imperiall Right :
Hee favour mee, as now I feel his might
Far, far exceed weak Woman's opposition :
Hee will no doubt ; and daign us both Tuition.
Sith wont, himselfe, to love, hee as a Lover
Will pity Passions and our pleasures cover.
  Thus having said, impatient of delay,
Efren shee calls (*Efren* a Maid, that aye
Us'd, as most trusty, diligent and charie,
Her Mistresse Errands to and fro to carry)   850
Goe quickly *Efren*, seek mee JOSEPH out,
And if the businesse hee is now about
Be not too earnest, and too instant too,
But what hee may as well hereafter doe,
Bid him forth-with to come and speak with Mee.
  Wing'd with her words, about it strait runs shee,
And after summons, JOSEPH comes anon
Up to his *Lady ;* who then all alone,
First with a Blush, and bashfull glance among,
From quiv'ring bosome with a shiv'ring tongue,   860
Thus breaks the Yce (still bidding him com neerer)
Dear, my dear *Joseph*, then mine owne Eyes dearer ;
Shall I intreat thee, what I might command,
To answer truely what I shall demand ?
  Madame, said hee, Should I be false to you ?
What ere it be, I sweare to tell you true.
  I hear (quoth shee) that thou art deep in Love :
If it be true (thou must thy Truth approve)
Thou maist not hide it ; though my selfe were shee,
For whom thou suff'rest, thou must tell it mee :   870
Confesse it freely : and I must confesse
As much to Thee ; for, Thee I love no lesse :
So, loving Both, wee shall have mutuall Fewell,
Nor thou to Mee, nor I to Thee be cruell.
Joyne hands, joyne hearts, how happy manifold !
How great ! how grac't ! how will I heap thee
      gold !
Thus shee protests, and with a sudden kisse
Upon his Lips shee seales her Promises.
  Hee, red for shame, selfe-sadly ruminates
His heav'nly Angels' sacred *Caveats*   880
Against temptation and Attempts unjust,
Of Idols' service, and unlawfull Lust :
Internall praying for supernall Strength,
In modest manner Thus replies at length :
  Madame, what ever of my Love you hear,
How-ever fervent, or how deeply-dear ;
If you have heard it as (perhaps) impure,
Unchaste, unhonest Love ; I you assure
None love I so : nor wish I (I protest)
So to be lov'd : and of my Lady, least.   890

My Lord, you know, hath nothing from mee kept,
I all command, onely your selfe except :
And shall I then, disloyall, Traitor prove
Unto my Lord ; and to my *God* above?
No, *God* forbid : No ; rather let mee dye ;
And in the sands unburied ever lye,
A prey to Birds and Beasts : and as hee spake,
Her and her Chamber did hee quick forsake.

Shee, seeing then her Hopes so sudden dasht,
Her selfe deluded ; as with Lightning flasht,   900
Stands first a while moveless, amaz'd and mute ;
Then grindes a Groan, and many sighes pursue't ;
Then wrings her hands, falls backward on her bed,
Distract in minde, her colour pale and dead.

All which observed by that *Divell-Owle*,
Upon the Roofe, hee putteth off the Fowle,
And re-puts-on Nurse *Iphicle* a space,
To see *Iëmpsar* in so piteous Case.
Alas ! quoth shee, What ailes my Lady deer?
My tender Nursling, what hath hap'ned here?   910
Why are you daunted and dejected so?
Be of good Cheer ; be of good comfort : Lo,
I, I am here ; look on mee, look, my Lamb,
Your help at need, your loving Nurse I am.

At name of Nurse, her somwhat shee erects,
And with these Taunts a frowning glance reflects :
Nurse, once a Nurse, or Mother more then Nurse,
But now a Step-dame, or some Furie worse.
Thou, thou hast kill'd mee, thou hast quite undone me :
Thou told'st mee *Joseph* was enamour'd on mee   920
Deep, to the Death ; and when I come to prove him,
Alas ! hee loves not, nor will let me love him :
Nay, Prayers, Proffers, Presents cannot move him.
Thou, thou hast made mee make my selfe a mock,
To shame my Name, to stain my House and Stock,
To wrong my Lord, to break my Faith, to fall ;
Thou wert the Author, thou the cause of all.
What wanteth more, but with a murd'rous blade,
This guilty Soule to send to endlesse shade?

False *Iphicle* doth her as sharp reprove :   930
Ah, foolish woman, unexpert in Love :
What wonder was it, if a bashfull boy,
Untrain'd, untoucht (as Virgin) first were coy
To heare of Love ; a Novice, yet, a Stranger ;
Doubtfull of you, perhaps ; fearfull of danger :
'Twas not the course : you have miscarried it.
Then be not heartlesse, neither hopelesse yet ;
For I will once more undertake the matter,
I 'll chide his rudenesse, and instruct him better
How to behave him : Have you Patience   940
But for three dayes, and on the fourth from hence
Will reigne a gracious Star, whose milde Aspect
On Love and Lovers gently doth reflect ;
Under whose Radiance, in Conjunction sweet,
Hymen and *Cupid* in one instant meet.

With these her Words *Iëmpsar* part re-chear'd,
Her sinking heart again a little rear'd :
Then Goe, said shee, the Gods grant better speed :
And that wee may the better now succeed,

Wee will the while the sacred Pow'rs implore,   950
Frequent their Altars, and their Shrines adore.

Next morning therefore, by what time the Sun
With glitt'ring Rayes had gilt the *Horizon*,
Iëmpsar decks her,—goodly to behold,—
In Scarlet, set with Jewels and with Gold
(But much more goodly for her lovely grace,
And native Beauties of her Forme and Face)
And to the Temple with a Train shee tends,
Of Matrons, Maidens, Servants, Nighbours, Friends.

Among the rest the Steward also went,   960
Faire-featur'd JOSEPH, with his Eyes down bent,
As inly pitying with a griefe unshown,
His Ladie's Passions as hee did his own :
For, hee suppos'd her gaite to Church had bin
To seek for Mercy and forsake her sin :
But, nothing lesse ; Shee all the gods requires,
To friend her love, and further her desires ;
And so the next day, and the next ensuing,
And every day still greater Gifts renuing,
The reaking Entrailes of her Offrings viewing.   970
But, when the fourth, long-wished wel-com day
Tytan 'gan burnish with his burning Ray,
Haile, happy day (said shee) haile holy Lights,
That favour Lovers, and that love delights :
And by your pow'r and gracious Influence,
Preserve the World's perpetuall Increments.
And then shee sends for the beloved Lad :
Who, selfely good, suspecting nothing bad,
Supposing now his Misteresse' minde reclaim'd,
At least from daring what before shee aim'd,   980
Comes instantly : Shee, by the Nurse seduc't,
Presuming All to her content conduc't ;
No sooner spies him, but shee springs for haste,
About his neck her Iv'ry Armes shee cast :
Shee holds him, hugs him, saying, Welcome Mine,
Mine, Mine thou art, and I am onely thine :
Then, Why delay wee? Why defer wee thus
Our joynt-delights, sith none can hinder us?
Why burn wee day-light? Hence with fear and sloth,
Let's mixe our loves. This bed will serve us both.   990
Shee leaps upon't ; and like a nay-lesse Wooer,
Holding his Cloak, shee puls him hard unto her.

The goodly Youth. as beautifull as blamelesse,
Amaz'd, asham'd, to see his Lady shamelesse,
Replies, Alas ! (Thus sharp reproving her)
Late Noble Wife of Noble *Potiphar*,
What mood, what madness hath obdur'd your mind,
To dare these Pranks, uncomly and unkinde?
To shame your Selfe, your Sex, your House, your State,
To wrong my Lord, and mee unfortunate?   1000
These are the fruits of easefull Idlenesse,
Of wanton Pride, of wastefull Pamprednesse :
From whence the Fiends (our foes) advantage cull,
To kill our Soules, and fill our Sins-sack full :
For, 'tis not *Iphicle*, your Nurse, your Friend,
As you suppose : no, 'tis a hellish Fiend,
A Hag, a Furie sent from Sulph'ry *Styx*,
That thus deludes you with deceits and tricks :

Shee dar'd, and did attempt to tempt mee too ;
But, God forbad : shee mee no hurt could doe.   1010
I saw her shrinking out as I came in :
I know the fained forme shee masketh in :
I feele the Sulph'ry fume, the filthy Sent
Shee left behinde her, when away shee went.
    Hee having spoken from behinde the dore,
The subtle Fury (lurking there before)
With sudden rush did crush the posts in sunder ;
And comming in, fills all with feare and wonder ;
When ghastly squinting, griezly, Thus shee spake
With hellish voyce : Indeed you doe mistake,   1020
False, *Iphicle* I am not ; I am one
Of th' odious Sisters, sent from *Acheron :*
I'll make you prove it now : then forth shee drew
A pois'nous Snake, and it at JOSEPH threw :
But th' Heav'nly Warder still repell'd it back,
And all th' endeavours frustrate still did make :
Unable therefore Him to hurt at all,
Towards *Iëmpsar* doth it softly craule,
With slippery windings, wriggling to and fro :
Into her skirts at length it twineth so,   1030
That up it creeps, and quick into her gets,
Gnawes all her bowels, and despitefull spets
His hellish poison in her inmost heart.
    The Lad, thus frighted, quick away did start,
To his owne Chamber : and perplext in minde,
Forgetfull hee had left his cloak behinde.
    Seeing him fled, and feeling in her wombe
The fretting Venome ; wholly overcome,
In ragefull fury, suddenly shee falls,
And, *Help, Help, Help,* with a loud Cry shee calls, 1040
So loud and shrill, that all the Court it heard,
And all the house, and neighbours neer, it scar'd ;
As if within had been som sudden fire
Which instantly would to the roof aspire.
Help, Women, Help, quick, quickly. O ! the
        Slave,
The Jew, the Rascall, the young Hebrew Knave,
Even now (O Gods !) finding mee here alone,
(O the bold Villaine ! Hath the like been know'n ?)
Dar'd t' have defil'd great *Potiphar* his Bed ;
And, but my Nurse mee timely rescued,   1050
Had ravisht mee (O, horrid thing to think !) :
But hearing Help, away the slave did slink,
And left, for haste, his cloak behind him here.
With Hue and Cry, pursue him far and neer,
Lay hold on him, and lay him fast in Hold ;
And let my Lord of his abuse be told.
    Thus fell *Iëmpsar* her complaint prefers,
All which, and more, false *Iphicle* avers,
And aggravates, adjudging him exempt
From pitie, fit to hang for such attempt   1060
So insolent, so impudent ; and whets
The hearers hearts. Then close away shee gets,
Unseen, and *Owl-like* in a Cloud involv'd,
Her borrow'd Body into Air dissolv'd :
Descending swift from whence shee came, to tell
Her good-ill service, and successe, in Hell.

Poore JOSEPH then his fellowes felly seaze ;
And, hasty, hurry him tow'rds Little-Ease :
Fain would hee speak, but none would hear a
        word ;
None, none at all, and least of all his Lord,   1070
Whom the Report already had incenst ;
Yet not with Death to have him recompenc't :
But, in a Dungeon (worse then Death) to dwell,
For worst Offendors the most loathsom Cell ;
There, kept close Pris'ner to be barely fed
With puddle-water, and with barly-bread.
    But, better kept by his supernall Keeper
(Yet, more his dear, the more their woes be deeper)
A winged Watch-man shining heav'nly bright,
Is sent to JOSEPH (when the first sad night   1080
With sable Courtain had beclowded all)
Who entring (through the Wicket and the Wall)
Into the Prison, with a new-come Ray
Lightning the dungeon, driving Night away,
With spirituall Comforts, and with speeches kind,
Cancels his fears, and well confirms his minde.
    This, from a Tow'r th' Egyptian Keeper spy'd :
Som God, som God is in the Light hee cry'd.
I know, such Splendor, and the speech I heard,
If it be God it must be needs inferr'd   1090
This Lad is guiltlesse of the crime pretended.
For, Innocence just *JOVE* hath ay defended.
Thenceforth to JOSEPH bare hee great respect,
A kinde of Reverence, with a kinde Affect ;
Took off the Irons from his hands and feet ;
Fed, lodg'd him better, made his Prison sweet ;
Visits him oft, intreats him friendly fair,
With loving Comforts, lets him take the Air.
    Now, twice four Roundles *Phœbe* had compleat,
When on suspicion of some treacherous feat   1100
Of pois'ning *Pharao's* Bread (as went the Fame)
Two were committed from the Court (by name
The Kings chiefe Baker, and chiefe Butler, too)
To the same Gaole where JOSEPH hath to doe.
For, now his Keeper trusted him so deep,
Hee made him Keeper, and of nought took keep.
    In short time after, Either, in one night,
Dreamed a Dream ; whence the next morrow light,
Pain'd and perplexed, what they might portend.
Too sadly serious seem'd they to perpend.   1110
Which JOSEPH noting ; Gentlemen, I pray,
How hap (quoth hee) you are so sad to day ?
    To night (said they) wee dreamed each a Dream,
But none wee finde that can interpret them :
And that's our trouhle. Can you tell them mee ?
Come let mee heare them, if you can, quoth hee ;
It may please God wee may have sight therein.
Right gladly, said the Butler, I'll begin.
Mee thought I saw a green and goodly Vine,
With three fair Branches, budding, blowing fine ; 1120
Then flowring fresh, then swelling Clusters blush,
Whose spumy Juice in *Pharao's* cup I crush ;
Which with my hand into his hand I raught,
Whereof the King took-in his wonted Draught.

Then, thus the Lad : I'll tell your Dreams portent.
First, by that goodly Vine your Life is Meant ;
The Buds, Flow'rs, Fruits, be fruits your self have
    bore,
Your Services, your Vertues here-tofore,
Which shall be guerdon'd, you restor'd to grace ;
The three fair Branches are but three dayes space, 1130
When in your wonted manner you shall bring
The wonted Cup unto your Lord the King.
Then, when with *Pharaoh* you shall gracious be
(If I be worthy) but remember mee,
And that unworthy I am here detain'd.

    The Baker, hearing This thus right explain'd,
Said, Let mee also, if you please, I pray,
Report my Vision ; and your Verdict say.
Mee thought I had three Baskets on my head :
Two full of Flow'r, the third of finest bread, 1140
Made with most Art and Cunning that I might ;
But, all anon the Birds devoured quite.
Then said the good Interpr'er : Things to come
Are known to GOD ; Men often faile in some :
Yet, what I ghesse and gather of this matter,
I'll tell you true ; I cannot, may not, flatter.

    That which you saw the Baskets filled with,
Of divers kindes, your Life betokeneth :
The Flow'r your former, simple and sincere ;
The Bread, your later, compound (as it were) 1150
Of all deceits, Theft, Plotting, Poysoning,
Treason, and all discover'd to the King ;
Who, for reward of these foule Crimes, by Law
Will hang you up : and then the Birds you saw
Rav'ns, Vultures, Eagles, Kites, and carren Crowes,
Shall eat your Carcasse, peck your Eyes and Nose.
Within three dayes, your Baskets number notes :
Yet I may erre, and you may change your Lots.
For, God doth change, when men doe change from ill :
His mediate Work, not his immediate Will. 1160

    This past, their Parts, Both, divers pondering,
On the third day came Warrant from the King,
To clear and to declare the Butler Quit,
And hang the Baker, at first sight of it.

    Accordingly, from Prison both are brought ;
But, to a divers End, with divers thought :
Th' one with reproach, th' other with good report ;
Th' one to the Cart, th' other to the Court ;
Th' one to the Gallowes, the other to be grac't
Of Prince and Peer, and in his room re-plac't ; 1170
With Caps and Claps, with cheerfull shouts and songs
Welcom'd, rewarded, honor'd for his wrongs.

    Thrice through the *Zodiak* had *Hyperian* pranc't,
And fourthly now his fiery Teem advanc't,
When quiet stretcht upon his Ivory bed,
In sweetest sleep, well toward morning-sted,
To mighty *Pharaoh* the Almighty sent
A double *Dream*, of so deep Consequent,
That wondring much, the King awoke withall,
Conceiving it some high *Prognosticall*. 1180

    Wherefore, forth-with he summons far and wide
Through *Ægypt* and *Chaldæa*, from each side,

All that had knowledge in *Astrologie*,
Cunning in Spels, or skill in Prophecie ;
Or could fore-tell by Magick from below ;
Or from above, by Oracles fore-show ;
Or by in-sight of sacrificed Heards,
By Fire, by Water, or by flight of Birds,
Or by their songs ; by Sand, by *Geomancy* ;
Or by what-ever *Heathen* Feat or Phant'sie. 1190

    Then swarm'd the Court with Sages of all sorts,
Of divers habits, and of divers ports.
Som on their heads wore hornes, hairy and horrid,
Som wth thick Turbands did surroūd their forehead,
Som with high Miters, som with trailing whoods,
Som with rich Garlands set with precious Studs ;
But, broad long-bearded all adown their Chin,
With sad aspect, and of a sallow skin.

    Whom when before him *Pharaoh* had admitted,
Hee tells his *Dreams :* first then (as him befitted) 1200
Propoundeth Honours and rich Recompence
To whomsoever shall expound the sense ;
And sets them dayes, & nights, & times, and houres,
To bring their Answer : But, (beyond their pow'rs)
Daies, nights, times, hours, they break ; none doth
    appeare
T' explaine the *Dream*, or the Kings doubt to clear :
Neither their Spheres, Spels, Circles, Sorceries,
Birds, Beards, nor Miters could decypher This.
Angry therefore, and thence-forth grieving deep,
The King would heare none, but did private keep. 1210
The Butler then remembring (at the last)
During his Durance what before had past,
(Which hitherto,—as Courtiers yet, for most,
Good turnes receiv'd,—hee had forgot, or crost)
How truly JOSEPH by their Dreams did tell,
What to the Baker and himselfe befell ;
Fell on his knees, and cryes unto the King,
Pardon, my Liege, my stolid lingering
To tell your Highnesse, in this manner mov'd,
What (late) in prison I both saw and prov'd. 1220
Your Majesty (no doubt) remembers yet
Your Baker and my selfe you did commit
To your High Marshals Tower ; where then wee found
An Hebrew Youth, a Pris'ner (on false ground,
As may be ghest) late Page to *Potiphar*.

    Both grown in time with him familiar,
Both of us dreamed in one very night ;
Both of our Dreams to Him wee did recite ;
Both hee expounded ; and both did succeed
To both of us, as hee of both did reed. 1230

    To mee, said hee, Thou shalt in three dayes space
Returne to Court, recover Place and Grace :
But, to the Baker ; Thou (said hee) that day
Shalt be hang'd up, for rav'ning Birds a Prey,
Unlesse thy faults thou canst so quick repent,
That change of life thy threatned death prevent :
(For, God doth change, when men do change from Ill :
His mediate Work, not his immediate Will.
All which for True, before your Eyes is cleer ;
The Baker hang'd : and I your Butler, here. 1240

Upon my Life, my Lord, your hidden Dream
That Lad will read : he hath som Spirit supreme.
  Herewith the King re-cheer'd, and inly glad,
Commands him straight, Go, quickly fetch the Lad,
And in Our Name him instantly inlarge.
  Forthwith hee hies him to performe his charge ;
Gets forth the Pris'ner, shifts him, suits him prest,
Of his owne cost, and hath him barb'd and drest ;
And then conducts him, bashfull, to the King ;
Who well beholds the Lad, likes every thing ;   1250
Then questions thus : They tell mee, Youth, that you
Interpret Dreams ; now, tell mee, Tell they true ?
  My gracious Lord, said JOSEPH, God alone
Immediately knowes dreams ; and other none,
Save onely such, to whom that sacred Gift
Th' Almightie daignes : I may my prayer lift
Unto my God for you, my Lord, and shall :
It may be, Hee will grant this grace withall :
For, ay with speciall care hee guides the things,
That 'long to Kings ; as onely King of kings.   1260
A while then inly did hee meditate :
Then prayes the King his Visions to relate.
  Mee thought, said *Pharaoh*, by *Nile's* bank I stood,
And suddenly from out the silver Floud,
Came seven fair Kine ; which ranging far and wide,
Fed in the Meads along the Rivers side,
On ox-lips, Cowes-lips, Trifole and the rest ;
Which for the Altar fat our Beasts the best.
  Scarce had I turn'd mine eye, when on the shore,
Me-thought in th' instant came up seven Kine
    more,   1270
With staring haire, too-weak to stand alone,
Ill-favour'd, lank, and leane, bare skin and bone ;
As, poorly fed, with Holly, Broom, and Heath,
Anatomies, or living forms of Death.
  Amaz'd with this, yet was I more anon,
When these (mee thought) for hunger set upon
The former seven, and so to work did fall,
That suddenly they had devour'd them all.
  Here-with I waked : and anon agen
Sweet slumber caught mee, and I dreamed then   1280
I saw seven goodly full faire Ears of Corne,
Rise from one straw, scarce able to be born :
And by and by, seven other Ears there sprung
Light, chaffie, blasted, thin and closely clung ;
Which in like manner greedily did eat
And quick consume the seven full Ears of Wheat.
  These were my *Dreams*, which I have oft propounded
To many, yet by none can be expounded.
Now, if for Thee this Honour be reserv'd,
If Thee alone my deeper *Dreams* deserv'd ;   1290
Then, happy Youth, rejoyce with all thy heart,
Eternall Fame shall trumpet thy Desert :
And with reward wee shall so richly store thee,
That in all Ægypt none shall be before thee.
  Great King, said *Joseph*, both your *Dreams* be one,
Sent down from God, to be reveal'd by none
(How-ever wise, how-ever full of Parts,
How-ever compleat in all depth of *Arts*)

Save by some Vessell of his owne election,
To whom hee daignes the grace of his direction :   1300
And therefore could your Sages nothing show,
Not knowing God, though all things else they know.
Know this, O King : God by this Vision sends,
To let you know what shortly hee intends.
  Your seven fat Bullocks are seven fruitfull years,
Which through all Ægypt shall oreflow your shiers ;
While *Nile*, far fatter then to-fore he wont,
Shall farther spread his slimy sweat upon't ;
When happy *Memphis* shall such plenty see,
That your old Barnes shall all too little be :   1310
Your Ricks, your Garners, and your Bartons all,
Too narrow for your Crops, too short, too small :
And, to confirme it, that it shall be so,
Your seven full Ears but the same thing fore-show.
Now be you pleas'd my great and gracious Prince,
To hear the rest with heed and patience :
For, seven poor years these seven rich years shal
    follow,
Whose Penury their Plenty soon shall swallow ;
When *Nile* shall shrink into his Channell, nye
Leaving the Ridges and the Furrows dry ;   1320
Fields scorched, parched, burned even to dust,
Both Solstices like deawlesse and adust :
No Torrents gushing from the Mountain tops,
Nor (under *Cancer*) on the *Æthyops*
Any return of Winter's Moist again,
Nor any help of sweet and timely Rain :
So that the Husband cannot plough his Land :
Or if hee could, hee should but plough the sand,
And cast his Seed amid the flame to burn,
Without all hope of any Crops return,   1330
Or of increase : but rather prest for need,
To quit his Plough, and on his Oxen feed.
Your seven leane Bullocks, and seven slender Ears,
Devouring, shew these seven devouring years.
This is your dreame, O King ; and doubled thus,
That more assured, more solicitous,
More speedily you may provide before
(Thus warn'd by God) a salve unto this Sore.
  Which, how to doe (of mee if you demand) :
I would advise you first through all the Land,   1340
To build new Garners, long and large enough,
From time to time to store up all the stuffe,
That may be spared throughout all your State,
During those years of Plenty fortunate ;
Allowing onely for each Housholds need,
And for their Land a Competence of Seed.
  You must have also Treasure ready still
To buy this store, if well proceed you will.
And to this end, let there a man be sought
Discreet and wise, to wield it as it ought.   1350
Let him have pow'r as in your Royall Name,
Through all your Kingdome to dispose the same ;
And underneath him to subordinate
Sub-Officers, to serve him and the State.
  Thus JOSEPH counsell'd : and the while the King,
With silence, all maturely pondering,

At last breaks out in joyfull admiration :
There is (no doubt) a Divine inspiration
In this young man ; Without a spirit Divine,
Of future things, none could so deep define :   1360
There is none like him, none to match him neer,
In all *Chaldæa*, nor in *Ægypt* here.
   Then, on his neck, shedding a showre of Joy,
The King imbrac't, and kindly grac't the Boy ;
Then, thus bespake him : Seeing God hath giv'n
Thee this to know, and to fore-shew from Heav'n ;
I know not one so wise and so discreet,
Nor for this Office then thy self more meet.
Thee, next to Mee, shall all my people serve,
And call thee Saviour ; Thou dost them preserve. 1370
   Then, on his back a purple robe hee dons,
Embossed round with rich and Orient Stones ;
About his neck a massie Chaine of gold,
And on his finger (as they wont of old)
A royall Signet, a most precious Ring ;
(Not to be worne by any but the King,
Or his Vice-gerent, whom hee doth esteeme
And will have deemed *Second unto Him*)
Which *Pharaoh* there then plucked from his own,
To put on JOSEPH'S, that hee might be known   1380
To be the *Second to Himselfe*, in all.
Then, on a Steed, the second in his Stall,
(Or second Chariot) in his solemne Pompe
He makes him ride ; and with the sound of Trumpe
Proclaimes, before him that they bow the knee
To his Vice-gerent, to this *Second Hee*,
To this Preserver of their State ; or rather
To this (adopted Sonne) their Countries Father ;
This Prince of worth, this more then man, this
    miracle,
This happy, holy, Heav'n-inspired Oracle ;   1390
Who, the Kings Dreame in time interpreting,
Had sav'd themselves, their Country & their King.
   With all these honors, and with wealth confer'd,
With all applause good JOSEPH is prefer'd
To rule all Ægypt : which with great dexterity,
Wisdome and worth, care, courage, and Sincerity,
Hee executes : And first, his Circuit rides
Ore all the Land ; Barnes every where provides,
Which in those plenteous years he fils with Store
Of every kinde. And, sith it is no more   1400
Vertue to purchase then preserve what's got,
Hee slips no time, but prudenly doth plot
To kill all Vermine, cut off all excesse
Of Gluttony and beastly Drunkennesse ;
Abates their needless beasts, Dogs, Mules, & Horse,
Rids idle Rogues and Vagrants that be worse
And rather buyes in from the Coasts about,
Then by a Licence lets a Corne go out.
Thus hee proceeds : and GOD so blest his hand,
That all things prosper'd over all the Land.   1410
   There was a City call'd *Heliopolis*,
(Whose Surname from the Sun derived is)
Whose Prince (a Priest too, to *Apollo's* Grace)
Had one faire daughter (faire indeed of Face

And outward Feature ; but, much more divin'd
For inward Beauties, Graces of the minde)
Whom *Phœbus* oft consulted with, had show'n
Not to be match to any of their Owne :
But by a higher Fate reserv'd to be
A Strangers Bride, with Greater dignity   1420
To raise her Name, and honour her Posterity.
This Oracle at JOSEPH points in Verity,
Thinks *Phœbus* Priest and great King *Pharaoh* too :
And to this end th' *Isa'cian* Prince they wooe.
When Ægypt now seven happy years had had,
All plentifull, all prosperous and glad ;
It pleas'd the King, with Royall Pompe and State,
These Nuptiall Bands to knit and consummate
With sumptuous feasts ; and (to prolong their joyes)
With Tilts, & Tourneys, Dances, Maskes, & toyes, 1430
So long, that now the seven rich years at last,
Were ended all, and all their plenty past.
   And now, *Sol's* Palfreys, having past the Twins,
Where posting hotly towards *Cancers* Innes,
When the Ægyptians could no more perceive
Nile's over-floud, nor any mud to leave ;
But pure, unpuddled on the sand to slide,
And in his Bottom him well-neer to hide :
Their whilome fertill soyl now serely rives,
Yawnes wide for thirst, no hope of Harvest gives : 1440
If any seed be sown, it never springs,
Or never buds, or never bears ; or brings
Unhappy Darnell, or Dry Poppy seed,
Or is devour'd by Vermins hungry breed.
So that they live of former Years remains,
Which hardly yet the first hard Year sustains ;
But men are fain to Grasse and Rats to fall,
To harmlesse Creatures, unclean Beasts and all.
   Then, to the King, City and Countrey fly
To sue for comfort, and to seek supply :   1450
Hee to his *Vice-roy* JOSEPH them refers ;
Hee instantly to under-Officers,
Who (by his order) furnisht all their wants,
At equall price : yet do so high advance
The King's advantage, that from far and nye
The Wealth of all runs to his Treasurie ;
His Checquer's full : yet had they past (alas !)
Scarce four hard years, and had three more to pass.
What shal they do, poor souls? How will they shift ?
Now nothing have they, but their bare Lands left : 1460
Those they would sell ; but, who (alas !) should
    buy?
None hath the Purse, except the King. They try
The Prudent *Vice-roy :* who approves the thing,
Bargains and buys a fift part for the King.
   This Famine raging fiercely every where,
Fame bruits abroad (which came to *Jacob's* eare)
That yet in Ægypt they were stor'd so well,
That they had Corne enough, and some to sell :
Old *Isr'el* therefore calling up his Sons,
You see, saith hee, our short provisions :   1470
You see how like wee are to starve and pine,
And perish all, without the hand Divine :

I heare there's Corne in Ægypt to be bought ;
Mee think ere now, you should your selves have thought
It time to go : Go get you quickly thither,
Take Coyne and Sacks : goe hye you altogether,
Save *Benjamin.*   The other Ten agree,
And, furnisht fit, set forth immediately.
   Arrived in Ægypt, they eftsoons enquire
The great *Corne-Master ;* lowting low, desire   1480
Corn for their money.   JOSEPH knows them brim
To be his Brethren : but they know not him.
Hee well remembers their unkindness past,
(And wrong receiv'd draws strong revenge too fast.)
Yet, for God's sake, his Father's, and his Brother's
(Young *Benjamin's*) hee spareth all these others ;
And speaks to them, but strangely and austere :
Whence? what are you? you (Sirs) that cluster there?
   My Lord, your Servants are one *Jacob's* Sonnes ;
We come from *Canaan* (where our Father wonnes) 1490
Compell'd by Famine (which there rageth sore)
To seek your Favour : of your happy store,
To daign us for our money what you may.
Our Father hath great houshold to defray,
Himselfe, Eleven of Us, our Little Fry,
Shepheards and Bondmen a great Company :
And therefore hither are wee come, my Lord,
To crave the help your Favour may afford,
To save so many lives, that may be able,
And shall be willing (som way serviceable)   1500
To thank your Lordship : for, our Father reigns
As King in *Sichem,* and hee stocks the Plains
With goodly flocks of many thousand Sheep,
And store of Cattle of all kinds doth keep :
Vouchsafe us therefore of your Corn, wee pray,
That wee may live, what ever price wee pay :
For, wee come hither, not to beg, but buy.
   To buy? said JOSEPH ; nay, I doubt to spy :
Spyes are yee all ; so many sturdy Clownes
To troup at once through all our Forts and Townes, 1510
To view and to survay our strength and store,
And so the weaknesse of the Land explore.
Yee tell mee of your Father and your Brother :
But I beleeve neither the one, nor other :
Where's your Commission? Where's your Father's
   Test?
Why came not that one Brother with the rest?
Or why came you so many?   It is clear
You come to spy : and you shall buy it dear.
Thus, though his heart doth melt, his bowels yerne ;
Hee faines him fierce, and bears him roughly sterne. 1520
   They, prostrate all, beseech him not suspect
Them any such.   Our comming was direct.
Wee swear (say they) : The witnesse wee implore
Of th' onely God our Father doth adore,
Our Father sent us ; Famine drove us hither ;
For Corn wee come : and that wee come together,
Our need, our number, and our distance crave
At once as much as wee at once can have ;
Our other Brother is but yet a Lad
(And all the comfort that our Father had)   1530

Too young to travell such a journey yet ;
Which upon us our Father laid, more fit.
Wee thought on no Commission : for, indeed,
In such a case wee thought there none should need.
Be good unto us, good my Lord, wee pray,
Pity our Father, and (if pity may
Pierce you at all) pity our Brother's case,
Pity our Babes, the hope of all our race.
   'Twixt over-joy'd, his eies will needs run over ;
Which, yet a while, he turns aside to cover :   1540
Then thus returns ; your cunning answer showes
That you are false.   Truth needs not such a Glose :
I am resolv'd : and can beleeve no other.
By th' life of *Pharaoh,* till you fetch your Brother
You shall not hence ; one Hostage shall remaine,
The rest shall goe well loaden home with graine :
This favour will I doe, expect no other,
Nor move me more, untill you bring your Brother,
To testifie your Stories are not lies :
Else by the life of *Pharaoh* you are Spies.   1550
(Here, Sirra, Marshall, take them to your charge,
Look none of them be let to goe at large)
Ile give you three daies Respit to revolve ;
Then let mee heare what herein yee resolve.
   They (inly prickt in their owne conscience
For cruelties committed now long since,
'Gainst this their unknown Brother, now a Prince)
Among themselves debating what was best
(Seeing the *Vice-Roy* did so deep protest)
Thought most expedient, and resolve in briefe,   1560
To send home Nine, loaden with such reliefe,
To fetch their Brother ; leaving one behinde :
Which Part by lot, to *Simeon* was assign'd ;
Whom they for Hostage to the Prince present,
(Upon the third day) with their full intent.
Then he commands their Sacks with Corn be fill'd :
They pay for it, but, secretly hee will'd,
That each man's money should againe be put
Into his Sack, and then the Sack re-shut.
   So now their Hostage in safe custody,   1570
They lade their Asses, and full heavily
Leave Ægypt and their Brother ; hying home,
Unto *Samaria :* where no sooner come,
But, their old Father, forthwith missing one,
Cryes, Where's your Brother?   Where's my *Simeon ?*
What, is hee sick, or dead (I doubt mee rather)?
Neither, said *Juda,* dead, nor sick, good Father :
Hee's well in health, but doth for pledge remaine
In Ægypt, till we all go back again,
And bring with us our brother *Benjamin :*   1580
For, such conditions must wee enter in,
Or else we could have brought you nothing thence.
   The Man wee dealt with, a great Man, a Prince,
Next to the King, at our arrivall there,
Askt many questions, whence, and what wee were :
Whether wee had a Father, or a Brother,
In what estate, how old ; and many other.

Wee doubting nothing, told him truely all :
Then, more austere, and more Majesticall,
Now I perceive (saith hee) that you are Spyes,   1590
And all your Answers are so many Lyes :
You come but to survay our strength and store,
To finde our weaknesse, and our wants explore :
Yee tell me of your Father and your Brother :
But, I beleeve neither the one, nor other :
Where's your Commission? Where's your Father'sTest?
Why came not that one Brother with the rest?
Or why came you so many? It is clear
You come to spy : and you shall buy it dear.

   Wee answer'd for our selves the best wee could : 1600
All would not serve : Th' issue was this ; we should
Leave one for Hostage, and the other Nine
Should bring home Corn, and bring him *Benjamin,*
Or never to returne unto that place,
Or never dare to look him in the Face :
For, by the life of *Pharaoh,* wee were Spyes,
(That is his Oath) and all our Words were Lies.
Good Father *Jacob,* having heard all this,
With many a sigh (as Sorrow's manner is)
Is there, saith hee, under the Heav'n's bright Eye, 1610
Another Father so distrest as I ?
One Sonne is lost ; another pris'ner left
In a strange Land ; another now bereft
(By your device, or your advice at least)
And all of you (I doubt mee) all the rest
To be extinct, while I survive in feares
Of so bad news to come to my sad eares.
First would to God (so God were not displeas'd)
My dayes were ended, and my sorrows eas'd.
Thus speaking wept hee, and thus weeping spake. 1620
His Sons with Comforts seek his Care to slake,
Saying, The godly should not fear so deep,
Sith God his Servants will more safely keep.
Then to their sacks ; Each having his unknit,
Each findes his money in the mouth of it.
Amazed all : sad *Jacob* thereupon,
Sons, Sons (said hee) there lackt but this alone :
This is enough to kill all hope (as vaine.)
For, if to Ægypt you returne againe,
The mighty man that fain'd you Spies before, 1630
Will find you Theeves now ; & what need he more,
Having so sifted and so sought your Coat,
To finde a hole, that hee might cut your throat?
No, no (I sweare) my *Benjamin,* my Boy,
Mine onely Comfort left, mine onely Joy,
I will not hazzard on so tickle ground :
You, you shall goe that are so promise-bound,
If you think good, and God will have it so :
And when you are determined to go,
I'll give you all the golden good I have, 1640
Jewels and Coyne, your Brother to un-slave
And save your selves ; and to bestow in Corne,
If God be pleased that you shall returne.
On th' other side, against his Father's feares,
Sad *Judah* thus intreats him, even with Tears :
   Deare Father, heare us first ; and then I pray
Have care of us, and of your selfe this day.

For, how shall wee unto that Man returne,
Who solemnly hath by his *Pharao* sworne?
Except wee bring our Brother *Benjamin,* 1650
Nor wee, nor hee that is there cooped in,
Shall be dismist : nor shall wee have the grace
To hear his voyce, or ever see his face ;
Where, God hee knowes, what shall of us become :
And how much better shall you be at home?
How will you live? Where will you have to feed
This multitude, if there wee do not speed?
Father, for God's sake follow my advice :
Upon my perill, stand not off so nice.
This Lad will save both us, and you, and all ; 1660
And on my life, no hurt shall him befall :
Two tender pledges leave I here of mine ;
If hee miscarry, let them pay the Fine.
   Then doubt not, Father, lay your feare aside,
And prudently for you and yours provide.
That thus our money was return'd ; no doubt,
By his direction it was brought about :
But for a pit-fall, or for Pity rather,
It is uncertain : this is certain, Father,
Hee is reported, over all that Coast, 1670
To be a good man, and a godly-most ;
And, if the Whole be partly ghest by Part,
Wee saw some tokens of a tender heart :
For, while to him wee there did sad relate
The sad distresses of our present state,
Of You, and of our Brother, and our Brats ;
Our miseries hee so compassionates,
That hee even wept : which though hee thought to hide
And turn'd away, yet many of us spy'd.
Wherefore, good Father, let us lose no time ; 1680
Prolong no longer, neither doubt the Clime,
Nor feare the man, nor faint for anything ;
Wee shall be safe under th' Almighties wing.
   This urg'd with tears ; the Old man overcome,
Cryes, Go on God's name, God re-guide you home :
Go when you will, and with you take the Lad,
And some best Presents that may here be had
In this hard time : *Mirrhe, Storax, Almonds, Hony,*
Gumme, Cinnamon, and therewith, double mony,
Both for the former, which you brought againe 1690
And for the New, if Now you shall obtaine.
And Wee the while, will pray and pay our vowes,
To th' everlasting Patron of our house,
The *Lord of Hoasts,* our Father's God and ours,
To prosper and protect you with his pow'rs.
Blushing *Aurora* sweetly peeping out,
When *Sol* againe had brought his Teem about,
The Father and the Sonnes, together all,
All up and ready, on their knees doe fall
In due Devotion, as they daily wont : 1700
Then to their Breakfast (not to dwell upon't)
Furnisht of what their Journey did require,
Gifts, money, *Benjamin.* Their tender Sire,
Weeping, Him kissing, and imbracing, thus
Bids sad *Adieu :* Dear Son, Ay prosperous
Thy journey be. If Fates thee safe restore,
Then wish I life ; for tears hee could no more,

Then to the rest ; imbracing, blessing all,
While all for blessing, on their knees, do call.
   They to their long-hard journey settling them,   1710
Leaving *Samaria* and *Jerusalem ;*
Past *Idumæa's* Palmy Groves, and past
Syrbonian Moors, Arabian Desarts vast ;
At length arrive on *Egypt's* wealthy Coast,
And reach at last their *Memphis* wished most.
Whom gladly JOSEPH entertaineth there,
And instantly lets out his Prisoner.
   Admitted then to gracious Audience,
Thus *Reuben* spake : When wee, right Noble Prince,
Returned home, had to our Father done   1720
Your high Commands, touching his younger Son,
Whom you required to be hither brought ;
Opening our Sacks to shoot the Corn wee brought,
In every Sack wee found our severall summe
(Which God he knows, we know not how should come.)
Our Father hearing what was com to pass,
And, seeing it, deep-sighing, cry'd, Alas !
Alas ! My sonnes, I see som sad Mis-hap
Hangs over us : and all our old good-hap
Is crost and cancell'd. Sees Heav'n's glorious eye 1730
Another Father so distrest as I ?
Twelve sonnes I had, and one (alas !) is lost :
Another Pris'ner in a forrain Coast ;
Another, now (mine onely comfort left)
Surrepted Thus, and You withall bereft :
And all of you to goe I wot not whither
(Made theeves) perhaps to perish all together.
   We comfort, We thus press with all our pow'rs ;
O Father trust our Father's God and ours.
And for the man that now in Ægypt swayes   1740
Hee is most just, most gentle. Him they praise
For their Preserver, and their Father there
Pious and pure : then, What is thence to feare ?
   Wonne with our words, at last with much adoe,
Hee granted us to bring his Darling too.
Go then, said hee, God to and fro direct you ;
And with his wings of Favour still protect you.
Take with you *Benjamin ;* and take withall
(Such as your Countrey yeelds) these Presents small,
Gumme, liquid *Storax,* bitter *Almonds, Hony,*   1750
Mirrhe, Cinnamon : take also double mony,
To pay both for the Corne you had before,
And for as much as now you shall bring more :

And to that just Man (as you say) commend
Mee and my Sonne ; pray him to stand a friend,
To pity Him, and You, and Mee, and All :
So all goodhap to Him and You befall.
   While this he spake, The Prince with much adoe
Refraining tears, cries, Welcome all of you,
Your Selves, your Presents, and your Brother here, 1760
Who quits you from suspect : Be of good cheer,
Goe wash your weary Limbs from soyl and sweat,
And soon I pray come sit with mee at meat.
   Thus said the Prince. The Servants, som prepare
Bath for their feet ; som Vessels, som their Fare ;
Buttry and Pantry, som ; som spred the Table ;
And other-som as busie in the Stable.
Him-self the while dispatcht affaires of State,
Heard Suits for food, appointed each their Rate ;
And then returns unto his Guests again ;   1770
Shows them his stately House, his Stuffe, his Train ;
His gold and silver Plate, ingrav'n, imbost,
Couches and Carpets of a wondrous Cost ;
And round about, most sumptuous to behold,
Deep Arras Hangings, all of silke and gold,
Of sundry Stories there so lively wrought,
That almost living were the Figures thought ;
Such sprightly Postures, and so speaking Gestures,
So native Visages, so nat'rall Vestures.
   Faith-famous *Abra'm* after Heav'n's behest,   1780
Leads here his *Isa'c* to be kill'd as Beast.
The Lad here loads the Asse with Holmen sprayes :
The Father makes the Pile : Hereon hee layes
His bond-led, blind-led Son : his hand heav'd up,
An Angell holds, and there is held a Tup.
   There, *Jacob,* flying his rough Brothers' wrath,
Hyes him amaine towards his native Path,
His Father's ancient Seat, and happy Realm,
Betwixt swift *Tigris,* and th' *Euphratean* stream ;
There, at a Well his Uncle's Daughter aides,   1790
Drawing up Water for the tender Maids ;
There on the Downs he tends their Father's sheep,
Serving for *Rachel* double Prentice-ship.
   While *Isr'el's* glad Sons (at this Wealth amaz'd)
Now full of hope, on these things greedy gaz'd,
Great JOSEPH calls (for Supper was gone up)
Come, give us Water : it is time to sup :
Then, tall, hee sets him in his Ivory Chaire,
And bids them sit, and treats them wondrous faire.

Here, Death preventing Fracastorious,
This late begun, Hee left un-ended Thus.

FINIS.

NOTES AND ILLUSTRATIONS.

Verse-dedication to '*Prince Charles,*' etc. = Charles 1st.
See Memorial-Introduction : l. 1, '*Preace*' = press : l. 4,
'*Panegyres*' = panegyrics, *r.g.* : '*Prince Arthur's Castle,*'
etc. : l. 4, '*Your Brother's wrack*' = Prince Henry—see
Memorial-Introduction.
   The Maiden's Blush ; or Joseph, l. 4, '*Gests*' = deeds, *e.g.*
Gesta Romanorum : l. 218, '*Sod*' = sodden or stewed meat ?
l. 317, '*made no more bones*' = difficulty ; but see Glossarial
Index, *s.v.* : l. 421, '*rumining*' = ruminating : l. 476, '*huck-
ing*' = huckstering, bargaining : l. 500, '*hammering*' = plan-
ning, plotting, but see Glossarial Index, *s.v.* : l. 501, '*jump*' =
agree : l. 541, '*Holmen*' = holly ? So l. 1782 : l. 626,

'*guarded*' = faced or trimmed : l. 667, '*Test*' = testimony or
witness. So ll. 1515, 1596 : l. 737, '*Duck*' = obeisance : l.
793, '*Ambage*' and l. 801, '*Carouse*'—see Glossarial Index,
s.v. : l. 997, '*obdur'd*' = hardened : l. 1067, '*felly*' = fiercely :
l. 1068, '*Little Ease*' = prison : but see Glossarial Index, *s.v.* :
l. 1099, '*Roundles*' = rounds : l. 1123, '*raught*' = reached :
l. 1140, '*Flow'r*' = flour : l. 1176, '*morning-sted*'—see Glossarial Index, *s.v.* : l. 1189, '*Geomancy*'—see Glossarial Index,
s.v. : l. 1230, '*reed*' = read, interpret : l. 1311, '*Bartons*'—
see Glossarial Index, *s.v.* : l. 1439, '*serely*' = sered, blighted
like autumnal leaves : l. 1481, '*brim*'—see Glossarial Index,
s.v.—G.

THE
PARLIAMENT
OF
VERTUES ROYALL;
(Summoned in France, but affembled in England)

FOR

Nomination, Creation, and Confirmation

OF

The moſt Excellent Prince

PANARETUS.

{ A Præsage of Pr. DOLPHIN ;
A Pourtrait of Pr. HENRY ;
A Promise of Pr. CHARLES ; }

Tranſlated,

AND

Dedicated

TO HIS HIGHNES,

BY

JOSUAH SYLVESTER.

To the Honourable, Sir *Robert Carie*: Sir *James*
Fullarton: Sir *Robert Carr*: Sir *David Foulis*:
Master *Thomas Murray*.

GRave *Guides* and *Guards* of Hopefull CHARLES *his*
   Wayn,
Lest I incurr the least of Your Disdaine ;
If, without leave, I (over-rashly rude)
Usurpe Your Rooms, or on Your Rights intrude ;
I humble crave your *Licence;* and your *Loves*,
For my *Addresse*, when my *Accesse* behooves.
  I know the *Field* of his Young HIGHNES' heart
So duely *till'd* by your deep *Care* and *Art*
(Adding his Father's *Royall Golden Writt;*
And goodly *Practise* to demonstrate it :
His (late) rare *Brother's* Pattern, of Renowne :
With Honest *Quin's* new-cast *Prince-worthy Crowne:*
And *holy Promptings* of that reverend Payre,
Milborne and *Hackwill*, from the *sacred Chaire*)
That little needs Hee the *Stagyrian's* store,
The *Corduban's*, or th' *Attick-Muse* his Lore :
Much lesse (alas !) my silly *Muse's* Myte,
With *borrowed Feathers* to advance his Flight.
  Yet, sith, too often, to a tender Ear,
Too-serious *Lectures* sound but too-severe ;
Especially, to *Prince's* dainty Taste,
They seeme but harsh, and will not downe in haste

(As wholesom'st Dishes, if but homely drest,
Some queasie Stomacks hardly can digest) :
Let mee presume (with your good leaves) a while
To imitate *Physicians'* honest Guile ;
Who, oft, in *Sugar* sheathe their bitter *Pills,*
The better so to *Cure* unwilling *Ills;*
When wayward *Patients* for the *Sugar's* sake,
Take-in their *Health*, which else they would not
   take.
  Sad Rules of *Patience, Abstinence, Austeritie,*
Humilitie, Frugalitie, Sinceritie,
Religion, Labour, Care of *Common-wealth,*
And *Many*, meet for *Prince* and *People's* Health ;
Which hardly can, in their *Owne Likenesse*, sink
In *Youth-full* mindes (scarce in their Eares, I think)
How gravely oft, with greatest Diligence
Prest, and imprest with *Tullian* Eloquence :
Sweetly *disguis'd*, in artificiall Sutes,
Dancing the *Measures* after *Delphian* Lutes,
Washed in *Nectar*, wrapt in sugred *Verse*,
Enter more easily, and more deeply pierce.
  This I endeavour ; and to this Intent
  I summon CHARLES to *Vertue's* PARL'AMENT.

TO THE HIGH-HOPEFULL
CHARLES, *Prince of Great-*
Brittaine.

WHere *witty* Bertault (*in his* Fancy) *meant*
   But a faint Præsage *of His Prince of* France ;
Our Hopes of Ours *the better to advance,*
Wee *have presum'd to* call *a PARLIAMENT ;*
Where Royall Vertues *from* Olympus *sent,*
By severall ACTS *of sacred Ordinance,*
Conform, confirm Your *future* Governance ;
So please it Heav'n Your heart *and* hand *consent.*
O ! please it Heav'n, You *may be blessed Thus,*
These Works *to imitate, These* Acts *to act ;*

To prove Your selfe, This same *PANARETUS,*
When future Age shall see our Hopes *in* Fact.
Which, while I pray ; sweet Prince, in humblest sort
I cite Your HIGHNES to This Soveraign Court.

_____ To your Highnesse Service

_____ humbly devoted,

_____JOSUAH SYLVESTER.

TO THE RIGHT HONOURABLE

Lords *Spirituall and Temporall;*

The Knights and Burgesses of the

Lower-*House:*

And to all generous and ingenuous Readers.

PResuming all your Lordships will appear,
  Not by your *Proxies*, but in person, here ;
And in your turnes say (Every-one) *Content*,
To every *Act*, in *Vertue's* PARLIAMENT ;
I humbly bring You every-one A *Briefe*
Of every *Bill ;* or, at the least, *the Chiefe.*

An *Act against* Duels, *desperate* Combats *and* Roaring Boyes.
An *Act for better* Execution *of the former Act.*
An *Act against* Hypocrisie.
An *Act against* Superstition.
An *Act against* Abuses *in the Courts of* Justice.
An *Act for some* Mitigation *of the former Act.*
An *Act for due* Execution *of* Justice *in generall.*
An *Act against* Persian *State, in proud* Retired-nesse.
An *Act against profuse* Prodigality.
An *Act of exceeding* Love *and excellent* Resolution.
An *Act of rarest* Pietie *in a Prince.*

An *Act for* Imitation *and* continuance *of the former Act.*
An *Act for right* Imployment *of Publike and Private* Treasure.
An *Act against* Ingratitude.
An *Act against* King-Killers, Powder-Traitors, *and their Abetters.*
An *Act for* Clemency, *and against* Impunitie.
An *Act for* Propagation *of Princely* Pietie.
An *Act against the* Mitred Monarchy.
An *Act of* Admiration.
An *Act for* Reading of Histories.
 An *Act against* ignorant *and ignominious* Chroniclers.

THese All are *Publike Acts ; Private* this *Session*
  Hath passed None ; but in the next *Impression*,
Your *Acts of Bounty*, and the rest of *Marke*,
Shall be recorded,

> *By your under-Clarke*,
> JOSUAH SYLVESTER.

（decorative border）

NAMES OF THE NOBLES IN

This *Parliament,*

Interpreted.

PANARETUS :	*AL-VERTUOUS.*
Andria :	*Prowesse.*
Phronesia :	*Prudence.*
Pistia :	*Fidelitie.*
Eumenia :	*Clemencie.*
Evergesia :	*Liberalitie.*
Hypomoné ; ⎱	⎰ *Patience.*
Cateria : ⎰	⎱ *Constancie.*
Aletheia :	*Truth.*

Dicea :	*Justice.*
Eusebia :	*Pietie.*

Interpretation of other terms used in This *Parliament.*

Dysidiamoné :	Superstition.
Eridea :	Contention.
Merimné :	Carefull vexation.
Dapania :	Charge or cost.
Adicia :	Injustice.
Oval.	Crowns for unbloudy Victors.

PANARETUS.

YEARS timely Turnes unto a Lustre run,
 Brought forth at last the long-long wished Sun,
Whereon our hopes our just desires pursu'd,
To see our PRINCELING with a *Name* indu'd
(*Which since* WEE *saw, or heard that happy sound,*
Saturn's slow Teem had trotted twice the Round)
When, lo, Th' *Etern All-Maker's* Majesty,
Quick-darting down his All-discerning Eye,
Whereby his goodnesse all his Works doth guide ;
And seeing prest the sacred Pomp and Pride   10
As in so solemne Mysteries is wont)
T' adorn the *Altars* and the hallowed Font ;
In th' instant summons with a gracious beck
Nine nimble Scouts, which scudding light & quick,
Dispatch more speedy then a thought the things
Above injoyn'd them by the King of kings ;
Who with a mildly-most-majestick gest,
In heav'nly words, his pleasure thus exprest ;
 The young *French* DOLPHIN is even ready now
To take the *Name* my fore-Decrees allow :   20
A frequent *Name* of Kings, and famous farre ;
Wonders in *Peace*, Thunders in dreadfull *Warre;*
And one of them, more Excellent in *Grace*,
Among my *Saints* hath justly held a place.
But yet besides that *Name*, which *France* affects
For one Man's vertue, and for due Respects ;
Besides that *Name*, which onely men have giv'n,
I 'll give him one my Selfe as sent from Heav'n ;
And such a one, as one-day, by Events
Shall prove it a true *Præsage* of that *Prince;*   30
And, in *One Word*, mysteriously contracts
The *History* of his succeeding *Acts.*
 Go therefore, quickly from all Quarters cite
The rarest *Vertues*, and most requisite
For Royall bosomes, that did ever rest
Within the Closet of a Kingly brest.
Tell them, it is Our pleasure and *Decree*,
That to this *Prince* they all *God-mothers* be :
And Shee among them that is found most fit,
And best behooves in *Crowned soules* to sit,   40
Shall at the Font, her sacred *Name* impose ;
And from thence-forth inspire him, as hee growes,
With all her pow'rs ; to correspond the scope
And full Extent of that great Empire's Hope,
Whose *Limits* yet unlimitted appear ;
Where Sire and Son to mee are equall dear.

 I see th' *Ægean* streams, and *Thracian* strand,
Already trembling under his command :
And th' horned *Crescent* (which had scorn'd to vale)
Before the Beams of this new Sun growes pale.   50
 To greatest Ships (as Guides of all the Fleet)
The cunning'st Pilots evermore are meet :
Mine, most Immediate, seems the soverain care
Of *Soverain Kings* (who but my Subjects are) ;
And therefore, I, that have behight *This Lad*
An ampler Rule then ever Monarch had,
As, of the WORLD to make him *Emperour*,
I 'll have his *Vertues* equall to his pow'r :
I 'll make them so : and to approve it, all
The Earth's foure Corners I to witnesse call.   60
 This publisht thus : eft-soons the winged posts
Addresse them quick to these inferiour Coasts :
And (swift as arrow) hee that took to finde
Fair *Andria*, or great and goodly minde,
Among the many Idols of our dayes
That counterfeit her fashion and her phraze,
Spy'd her at last, for her here slight account,
Ready to leave us, and above to mount
A winged horse ; in hope else-where to get
A new Renowne, 'mid stranger Nations yet.   70
 Her Helmet (ever as her head shee stirs)
Seemed to twinkle with a thousand Stars :
A stately grove of Azure Plumes did wave,
And proudly shadow'd her gilt Armour brave :
The bright keen Blade that by her side shee wore,
Inur'd to bloud in Battels long before,
As it were, weary of that rusting rest,
And greedy longing for his wonted feast,
Seem'd male-content, and his proud sheath disdain'd
(The golden Prison that him still detain'd)   80
Whereon were grav'n (with *Art's* Art-passing strife)
By such a hand as could give Metall life,
The noblest feats of *Valour* (most extold)
In later Times, and in the Dayes of old,
Of greatest *Monarchs* that yet ever were,
Whose marks the World (unto this day) doth bear.
 There, by the Banks of *Granic* dy'd in graine
(As then : no Banks, but rather Hills of Slaine)
Philip's Great Son (in spite of multitude)
To his sole Scepter the whole World subdu'd.   90
There, valiant CÆSAR (*Rome's* first Emperour)
Quashing the Senat's and the People's pow'r,

And stopping all their Lawes to his Sword's Law,
Tramples the Trophies of his Son-in-Law ;
Who pale without, and all appall'd within,
Flyes from *Pharsalia*, and his hoast, unseen.

Why flyes Great *Pompey?* so (at once) to lose
Th' Honors so oft wonne from so many foes?
Because Thine fainted, must Thou faulter too !
O yes ; with *Cæsar* thou hadst here to doe.   100
There 's thy Excuse : & though Thou lost the Game,
Thy Victor yet some-what abates Thy Shame.

There (on the Chape of massie gold, unmixt
With other Metall plain or wrought betwixt)
Our own, Great HENRY, smear'd with bloud and
        dust,
Pursues th' *Ibereans* with keen fauchin just ;
And justly keening his courageous sp'rite
Against those daring *Demi-Moores* despite,
Beats out of breath the bravest of their Troup ;
Who, bleak for fear, begin to faint and droup :   110
The Gold, there loose, seems even to fly and (more)
Looks pale in faces full of pride before.
But Hee (well marked by his milk-white Plume)
With Kingly scorne, disdaining th' odious fume
Of vulgar bloud, in valiant Fury runns
Upon the proud Commanders, *Dukes* and *Donns*,
Who (either proud of Port, or rich Attire)
Had by his hand a sudden death for hire.
Their royall Pattern and all his Troups take-after
And of the rest they make a glorious Slaughter :   120
Whence streams of gore that to their Center scud,
—Met in a Ruby—make a Lake of bloud.
Such costly Sheath sheath'd in such workmanship
The sheen keen Blade on *Valour's* brawnie hip
(*Hung in an Azure Scarf, all over-sow'n*
With Crowned Swords, and Scepters over-thrown.)
A thousand other famous Battels fought
At sundry times, with cunning-cost were wrought
Within her Crimsin Bases, waving low
About her Calves, in Buskins white as snow.   130
Shee seem'd like *Pallas*, 'gainst the Giants prest ;
Or (on Mount *Ida*) against *Mars* addrest.

At sudden sight of Heav'n's bright Messenger,
In milder port shee straight composed her ;
And when Hee briefly to her heedfull thought
Had done the sacred Arrand that hee brought,
And (by the way) had question'd her (beside)
Whither her Haste was bent, shee thus reply'd :
Cœlestiall Herald, While th' Heroïck Prince,
Whose gentle Yoke his *Celticks* so contents,   140
Carv'd with his Sword a Statue to my Name,
To stand triumphant in the house of *Fame ;*
Nothing could hold me from his steps, a-part,
My hand did guide his hand, my heart his heart :
Yea, I was with him, nay, within him prest,
His spirit's familiar, and perpetuall guest.
But sithence *Peace* Him now hath quite disarm'd,
And keepeth *Mars* within her Temple charm'd ;
I did give way to my keen Sword's Request,
(Which can no longer lie and rust in Rest)   150

And, while his heart, now all in love with *Peace*,
Hath left his hand, for mee, no businese,
I meant to seek som other *Strand* for Stage
To act my Wonders, in Warre's dreadfull rage ;
That in brave Battels I again might reap
The Palms Hee wonted on my head to heap.

For, with the sparkles of my glorious fire,
Th' incensed brests of Younglings to inspire,
I can no more find in my heart ; sith they
So rashly rush to cast themselves away,   160
So oft, for Trifles (bred of idle breath)
So madly run to an untimely death ;
So daily sacrifice their Life and Soule,
In som so foolish Quarrels, som so foule,
That, in the issue (fatall for the most)
The Victor's Selfe may rather blush then boast ;
And such, as for such to usurp the Sword
(Besides the Conquest 's even to be deplor'd)
Is nothing else but to profane the same,
And to blaspheme mine Honour and my Name.   170
Not that I blame (where Bloud & Nature binds)
In point of *Honor* (Idol of brave mindes)
A Cavalier, so sensible of wrongs,
To hazzard Life and all that him belongs ;
Sith, void of Honour, hee is void of sense,
That holds not Life a deadly Pestilence.
But I would have them rightly learne before
(Not, of a heart meer valiant and no more ;
But of a heart valiant at-once and wise)
Wherein that point of precious Honour lyes,   180
For which, hee 's happy that his Life shall lose ;
And cursed hee that carelesse it foregoes.

For, such a cup-fume over-flowes the brain
Of such whose Soules this error entertain,
That One will ween his Honour interess't
To lose a Word, though spoken but in jest ;
Who never thinks it tainted with a Lye,
Nor toucht with base and wilfull Perjury,
Nor with his Treason, when for som pretence
Hee hath betraid his Countrey or his Prince,   190
Or yeelded-up som un-distressed Place,
Or fled the first to save a Coward's case.

So th' Hypocrite, through superstitious Error,
Thinks hee hath done som Sin of hainous
        horror,
When by mis-heed, or by mishap, hee coms
Un-hallow-washt, into the *Sacred* Rooms ;
Yet makes no Conscience, yet hath no Remorse
To have undone, or done to death, by force
Of un-just Doom, or fraud of Evidence,
A many poor and harmeless Innocents :   220
Nay, laughs at Widows' and at Orphans' tears,
By his deceit dispoyl'd of all was theirs.

Those valiant *Romans*, Victors of all Lands,
They plac't not *Honour* there where now it stands ;
Nor thought it lay, in making of the Sword
Interpreter of every private word ;
Nor stood upon *Puntilios*, for Repute,
As now a-dayes your *Duellers* pursue't.

But from their Cradle, train'd in Rules more fit,
They neither knew th' abuse nor use (as yet)   210
Of Challenges, Appells, and *Seconds*-aid.
But, when the Lawes their Bridle loose had laid,
For publike Glory 'gainst a publike Foe,
There Honour's point, there Valour's proof to show.
    But, when behoov'd, bravely and first to front
An Armie's force, or bear their sudden Brunt ;
Or, larded thick with darts, victorious, dy
Upon a Breach, or on a Rampire high ;
Or, leap alive into a yawning Hell,
To save their City from Infection fell ;   220
Liv'd never Men that lesser feared death,
More-daring Valour never yet had breath.
Witnesse (unto this day) th' undaunted hearts
In *Curtius, Decius,* and *Horatius* parts :
With many Worthies more, Immortaliz'd,
Which for their Countries have selves sacrific'd ;
And Whose brave deeds, whose honours, whose
        deserts,
Move more despair than envy in men's hearts :
For, dying so, Garlands and glorious Verse,
Not Cries and Tears, honour'd their happy Herse ; 230
Their Flower of Fame shall never, never shed,
Because their Death, their Country profited :
Wheras the death wch brings now brain-sick youth
Unto their Grave, deserves but Tears and Ruth :
Their Courage casts them even away, for nought ;
Without Memoriall, save a Mournfull Thought ;
Which banning but the fury that inflam'd-them,
Honours enough, if that it have not blam'd-them.
    O what a number of courageous Knights,
Abortively, have in these *Single Fights*   240
Lost the fair Hope the World conceiv'd of them,
Have idly frustred, of their Valours gem,
Their gracious Prince ; who justly might expect,
Against his Foes, their forward Worths effect ;
And, sacrilegious, to their Wrath have given
And heady Rage (whereby they have been driven)
The sacrifice, which (with more sacred zeal)
They ought to God, their King, their cōmon-weal !
    Ynow to make (could they return from death,
Such as they were, when here they lost their breath) 250
Not a Sole Squadron, but an hoast of men,
Whose Acts alone would furnish every Pen ;
An Hoast of *Hectors,* and *Achilleses,*
Cæsars and *Scipios,* who, by Land and Seas,
Following great HENRY for their Generall,
Mought (if hee would) have made him Lord of All ;
Where, now, they lie in an inglorious Toomb,
Longing for Light untill the Day of Doom ;
Or lower, in eternall Dungeons dwell,
With Ghosts and Shadowes skirmishing in Hell.   260
This mischief therefore, springing day by day,
And spreading so, as nought his course can stay ;
And seeing (too) mine Honour blurr'd with blame,
When these rash Mad-caps do usurp my name ;
To be from hence-forth, from the Rage exempt
Of such as turn my glory to contempt,

And thus deface my Vertues grace with Vice,
I hop't else-where some holier Exercise ;
And rather would, hearts so intemperous
Should not enjoy me, than imploy mee thus.   270
    Here *Andria* ceast : The Angell, gracefully,
Humours her Anger with this milde Reply :
Certes, fair *Nymph,* your Plant hath right & truth ;
But yet, excuse the boiling heat of Youth ;
Perhaps 'tis harder then you ween (precise)
To be at-once a *French-man, Young* and *Wise.*
This Evill from this in-born Errour springs,
That a *Brave Minde,* when wrong'd in any things
Hee weens himselfe (if so hee *Armes* professe)
Must no-where seek, but in his Sword redresse :   280
And that an Aye, a No, a Nod, a Nick,
'S enough t' offend a Noble sense and quick :
Pernicious Errour, which doth undermine
Both *Martiall* Thrones, and *Civill,* and *Divine!*
For, to no end the *Publike* Sword shall serve,
If every man may with his *Private* carve.
And then, in vain are Sovereign Princes Lawes,
When Subjects dare themselves decide their cause.
    But, I beleeve, This Madness will no more
Præcipitate their courage, as before.   290
The curb of Law, which by their prudent Prince
Is now new made against This Insolence,
Will bar their boldness, and (directing mean
How This deer Honour saved whole and clean ;
A gallant Spirit, wrong'd in any kinde,
May lawfully his Satisfaction finde)
Will binde their hands, & even glue-in their blades :
Till when some Foe their Common Right invades,
In forward Zeal of their dear Countrie's good,
It shall be honour (even) to dive in blood.   300
    Disposed therefore to expect Amends,
Dispatch the Order which Heav'n's Monarch sends ;
And goe not hence, where thou art so renown'd,
Till all the World be but This Empire's bound :
Were it for nothing but that *Rising Sun,*
Whereon all Eyes already have begun
(Both Friends & Foes) to fix their hopes and fears,
That brave *Young Prince,* who from his cradle
        bears
Thine Image in his eyes, and in his arms,
Thine Exercise in every kinde of Arms.   310
    Surely, said *Andria,* 't had been hard to finde
A stronger Charm here to arrest my minde
(Chiefly, here living my Soule's *Sympathy,*
His Father ; rather, that same other, I)
For, as in th' one I am a Miracle,
So will I be a match-less Spectacle
In th' other too, when to his Ancient Right
His daring Sword shall make his Claim by Fight ;
Whether his Armie's royall-Front aspire
Those craggy Hils whose name is ta'n from Fire ;   320
Or tend unto those fruitfull Plains which spred
Towards *Bôotes,* and *Hyperion's* Bed ;
Whose Princes, in their Fables Antique-fram'd
Counts among *Kings, Kings* among *counts* are nam'd.

After these words, pronounc't with voyce &
 gest,
As Oracles are wont to be exprest ;
Both took their flight through the thin crystall air,
Towards the place appointed for Repair
Of all the rest of *Royall Vertues* Band,
Which were convented by Heav'n's high command. 330
 Royall *Eumenia* was already come,
And simple-maner'd *Pistia* (thought by some
Long-since exiled from the World) ; and Shee
Who from afar doth all Events fore-see.
There was (apparent by illustrious things)
Fair *Euergesia*, Ornament of Kings,
And firm *Hypomonè*, with her Twin-sister
Crateria, and Shee whose Patron and Assister
Are often shent, *Alethia*, little known
To mortall men (no scarce among her own)   340
With vails and cloaks they do be-cloud her so,
Whose spotless Selfe should rather naked goe.
In brief, of all the *Vertues* summon'd here,
There wanted none but *Dicea* to appear :
And St. *Eusebia*, in her Shadows hid,
That long it was ere Her the Angel spid.
For, here among us a queint *Idol* haunts ;
Whose simple habite, whose sad countenance,
Whose lowly look, whose language mildly-meeke,
Whose zeal-like gestures, and whose postures like, 350
So counterfeit Her, with the Mask it makes,
That many times the wisest it mistakes.
 Youl'd think, her heart had onely God for Joy,
Her exercise onely to fast and pray ;
That shee abhors the World ; and, lodg'd therin,
Lives as the Fish that out of water bin ;
That burning zeal of Heav'n consumes her so,
That all seems bitter that shee tastes below.
Yet all the while, This hollow *Holy-Tricks*
Doats but of Honours, dreams of Bishopricks,   360
Thirsts for Promotion, thrusts for Primacy,
Hunts Glory still, yet seems it to defy.
Never does good but for som great applause,
Nor ever did good, for meer *Godnesse* cause.
 This Bane of Soules, and that same Foppery
(Of old) sirnamed *Dysidaimonie*,
Whose heart, deject with terrors over-strong,
To fear God's *Justice*, doth his *Mercy* wrong
(Right *Servile Fear*, with Errors foolifi'd)
Hath driven *Eusebia* hence, else-where to bide ; 370
Because th' one loves not, th' other mis-beloves
What best to fear, and least presume behooves.
 The Angell therefore ferrets every nook,
And narrowly her wonted haunts doth look.
In every Cloister, and in every Cell,
Where Folk beleev'd that shee did ever dwell :
Yet nothing findes hee of her, any-where,
Save som old track or footing here and there ;
No, though he visit the austerities
Of famous *Abbeies* and fair *Nunneries :*   380
But, in her stead, hee meeteth evermore
One of these Hags in every *Covent* Door,

Drest in a habite of so humble show,
That hard it was the difference to know.
 Yet, at the last, prying on every side,
Her, (as conceal'd) in a by-place hee spy'd ;
Where, with incessant tears, shee staid to rew
And to bewaile our Errors old and new ;
Amid an humble Troup, whom like Desire
To loath the World, and from it to retire,   390
Had made preferre a poor and mean estate,
Yea Want it self, in place so separate ;
Before the Wealth, the Honours and Delights,
Wherewith the World inveigles, as invites :
As choosing rather here to lose all These,
Then lose thereby their Soules' eternall Ease.
 In this sequestred place, prostrate in Praier
(Best *Antidote* 'gainst *Hope's pride* and *Despair ;*
The two grand poysons of Soules' Faculties)
The Angell found *Eusebia* on her knees.   400
Their talk was short, the Time importun'd so :
In briefe therefore hee doth his Message show,
Acquaints her quickly whence, and why hee
 came.
Then shee eft-soons consenting to the same,
Away they post in a swift Airie Coach
Towards the place where all the rest approach ;
The generall *Rendez-vous* for all this Act :
Where yet (alas !) the Lady *Dicea* lackt.
For, th' Angell, tasked to goe seek her forth,
Sees her no more conversing on the Earth,   410
Nor findes her sitting (as shee wont of-old)
On Princes' Thrones, and Prelates uncontroul'd ;
Nor among Magistrates, which are the Tongue
And life of *Law*, 't interpret Right and Wrong.
Where-at amazed, and desiring more
To sound what reason men could yeeld therefore ;
Assumes a body, bearing in his hands
A bagg of Writings and seem-Deeds for Lands :
Comes to a Hall, all full of Murmuring
Of people pricked with the angry sting   420
Of fell *Eridea*, who her Venome sheds
Even into Boores' and Paisants' hearts and heads,
By her keen fury (as with Brizes) stung ;
And by *Merimnè* and *Dapania* wrung :
 In this great Hall, unknown unto Repose,
Stalks that stern Furie, either among those
Of her owne Frye, or 'mong the wretched Crew
Whom her hard gripes had made (in vain) to rew.
A rank of Seats, each unto other fixt,
And every one a sundry Name affixt,   430
Bordred the Walls, smokie with age, and foule ;
Perches of many Plumie-pounced Fowle,
Whose nimble Quills have learn'd to fly for that
Rich Minerall, which makes men peace and prate.
There was no Order : a lowd-buzzing Presse
With whirling Eddies hurry'd without cease,
Full of all Sorts ; of Priests, of Gentlemen,
Merchants, Mechaniks, Grooms and Husbandmen :
Each justled other, crowding to and fro,
As here and there the stream did ebb and flow.   440

This yauld, that brawld, another beat the Barr ;
One woo'd the Judge, another urg'd him farr ;
This proves *Default*, That pleads a *Warrantie;*
This avoids *Witnesse;* That *Appeals* more high ;
Another, fleering, doth his adverse flowt ;
With Rod in hand the *Ushers* trudge about :
A world of *Lawyers* swarm'd ; yet som had leasure
(As least imploy'd) the Place's length to measure.
All boyl'd with *Discords;* one no sooner done,
But instantly another New begun ;   450
With such a Noyse as soundeth neer the Shoare
When towards a Storm, the Sea begins to roare.
    Hard-by this Ocean, which Night onely still'd,
Appear'd an Old-man (as one deeply ill'd,
And inly galled for som grievous losse)
With eyes lift-up, pale cheeks, and armes acrosse ;
Whom th' Angell spying, towards him hee speeds ;
And (seeming Mortall by his shape and weeds)
Good Father said hee (so to sound his minde)
Where might I (think you) Lady *Dicea* finde,   460
Whom I have sought already far and neer,
And surely thought now to have found her here?
    Dicea, my sonne, said the Old-man (well-nigh,
Gushing out Tears which stood in either eye ;
And sending forth a deep-fet sigh, before)
Dicea, alas ! is in the World no more.
That Fire which only Death hath pow'r to quench,
That fell Desire no Deluge else can stanch ;
The burning Thirst of Worldly goods and
        Gold,
And all Sins, taught to war against her, bold ;   470
Have forc't her to forsake this wretched Frame,
And fly again to Heav'n whence first shee came.
Or, if in Earth shee yet have any Stance,
'Tis with the *Cynois, Turks,* or *Scythians:*
But in this *Climate* hardly doth appear
Any small signe, to show shee hath been here.
Cruell *Adicea* in her Room is set :
Hate, Favour, Fraud, and Madame *Counterfeit*
(Out of all *Courts* hunting all *Conscience* quite)
Make of Right Crooked, and of Crooked Right.   480
Art and *Deceit* keep there their open Schooles :
Reason and *Law* are but the phrase of Fooles.
For *Law* and *Reason* are now waigh'd (by sleight)
In *golden Scales;* Where onely GOLD is waight.
    Thus, the old-man proceeding still complain'd ;
Till th' Angel, thus, his Blasphemies restrained :
Alas! good Father, your fresh Griefe (I see)
For some great suite, late lost unhappily,
From your sad lips this bitter language draws ;
Excusable (perhaps) for your Grief's Cause :   490
But th' eye of Passion ill discerns the truth.
    This having spoken ; the Celestiall youth
Turns to another, lesse disturb'd in minde ;
And likewise asks, where he might *Dicea* finde.
Hee more discreet, and milder-spoken, far,
Replyes ; My Son, sure very few there are
(Yea of the wisest, who best understand)
That easily can answer thy demand.

For one perhaps will think her to be there ;
Whereas, another (seeming wrong'd) will swear   500
By Heav'n, and all that in it Heav'n contains,
That not a spark nor mark of her remains :
Each holding her, present or absent, still
As his own cause hath thrived well or ill.
But I'll assure the (and past all Appeal)
That in this place shee doth not alwayes dwell.
Sometimes shee comes, and brings for companie,
Honour, and *Faith*, and old *Integritie:*
But the strange Tricks of a bold babbling Dame
Call'd *Quiddi-quirk*, as barbarous as her Name,   510
Molest her so, that soon they drive her hence ;
For, both at once have no-where Residence :
And *Plutus* too, her many-times dismaies ;
With that sweet Power whereby the world he
        swaies,
Causing her oft return with heavy cheer :
And that's the Cause shee staies so seldome here.
Oft have I seen her on the soveraigne Seat
In that high *Senate* whose *Edicts* compleat
Sway all the Kingdome ; and (if any where)
I sure beleeve, you yet shall finde her There,   520
If those Abuses whose bold Tyranny
From other Thrones have driven her openly,
Have not crept in by some close Golden Port :
But, far be that from such a reverend Court.
    Here ceased Hee : and instantly, withall
Losing his sight, the Angel leaves the Hall ;
His airie body to the air repaies.
And while hee takes to other Courts his waies,
Hee happily the wished *Lady* meets :
Who, inly joy'd (which outward gesture sweets)   530
Because in Judgement shee had overthrow'n
Wrong's proud support, & giv'n poor right his own,
Came from deciding of a Cause of waight,
Before the Peers and Counsell of Estate.
    But, her content was doubled when shee heard
Heav'n's sacred will (as th' Angel had averr'd)
And his high pleasure (whose Omnipotence
The Heav'ns adore) for *Surname* of the Prince :
With him therefore Her speedie shee directs
Towards the troupe which onely her expects.   540
    Now all these *Nymphs* assembled seemed prest
(All diversely with Joy and Hope possest)
To take their flight to that King-favour'd Place
Where (pre-ordained for this Work of grace)
They should impose the Royall Infant's Name,
The world's main hope (as most conceive the same)
When suddainly there did among them breed
A noble strife, which stay'd their forward speed ;
Through great desire to see the radiance
Of that young Sun which should enlighten *France*,   550
Hasted their haste : and though on every side
As welle the sacred Pomp as civill Pride,
The King himselfe, Princes and Princely Dames
Glittring in Gold, sparkling in pretious Flames,
And all the Court adorn'd in rich Array,
Seem as offended at the least delay.

But yet, because Heav'n's Monarch had decreed,
That of the *Vertues* Shee which should exceed,
As most conducing to Kings' happy state,
Should with her name this Princeling nominate ;   560
When one of those high Heralds urg'd them on,
Amorg themselves This to consult upon :
Consult? said *Andria :* Why consult about
A Point, whereof (I think) was never doubt?
Mine, Mine's this Honour : for, among us all,
Who more adorns a King's Memoriall,
Or better keeps a Scepter's Majesty
At his full height in Royall hands, then I?
I fill his name with Glory and Renown :
I make him fear'd abroad of every Crown :   570
I, with the terror of his Arms, deterr
Ambitious Tyrants that they dare not stir
Offensive War against Himselfe or His,
How ever spurr'd by Spite or Avarice ;
His famous Valour gaining This, for Meed,
That at the last hee seems it not to need :
Unlesse he list his conquests to extend
Throughout the World ; then is it I that bend
The proudest Mountaines under his command,
The strongest Holds I render to his hand :   580
I fill with feare, I chill with trembling Ice,
The boldest hearts of oldest Companies
That dare resist his quick and thick Alarms,
With th' onely lustre of his glittering Arms.
I often onely with his Trumpets sound
(Without a stroke) his Enemies confound :
And, dreadfull make the most redoubted here
Think it no shame to flee his fierce Career,
As if (no Steel, of proof to ward his blows)
'T were Rashness more then Valour to oppose.   590
    Such were of-old those hardy *Heroes* found,
For Prowess, Then for *Demi-Gods* renown'd :
Such, He whose shoulders shor'd *Olympus'* walls :
Such, He who conquer'd th' Empire of the *Gauls :*
Such, that great *Macedon :* and such (again)
Those famous *Paladines*, whose Fables vain
(Yet usefull Tales) th' old *Romans* fain to fit,
That even they seem by *Morpheus'* fingers writ :
But what they had *Ideally* from Art,
That *Really* I to a Prince impart.   600
    Who knows not that I, onely us'd in Field,
Serve all the *Vertues* both for Sword and Shield?
Your selves indeed seeme to agnize no less,
Although in words you shame it to confess.
For, when the Fury of War's dreadfull Showers
Begins to thunder neer your dainty Bowers,
All pale for fear, all trembling, all dismaid,
To Mee yee flee, to Mee yee cry for Aid ;
Under my wings yee creepe to keepe you sure ;
Where (& but there) you thinke your selves
    secure.   610
And, rather I, then Any (who expose
My Self alone against the Hail of blowes)
Begin Estates, beget and bring them forth,
And plant (in bloud) the Empires of the Earth.

Th' admired height of *Rome's* great Scepter yerst
(As that of *Greece*) was but My work at first ;
And that same Other famous, glorious throne,
Whose Greatness yet, doth in its Cinders groan.
For, though by War, with Fire and Sword, I waste
What Heav'n's Decree hath doom'd to be defac't ;   620
Even while I raze, I raise ; and, of the Rubble
Of petty States, I build one hundred double :
As horrid Dragons grow so hugely great,
Of many Serpents that alive they eat.
    You are indeed extoll'd (and worthily)
For knowing well, to use a Victory :
But, without Mee, You can have none to use ;
Without me then, your Knowledge nought accrues.
Therefore, your honour's less ; at least, 'tis such
As (at the best) on mine dependeth much.   630
    In brief, in all the sacred works wee doe,
Our Merit's divers, and our Honour too :
You rule the humble, I the proudest tame :
You adorn Kingdomes, and I conquer them :
You can direct, and I protect a Crown :
You do besiege, I dare assault a Town :
You shew the utmost of Man's Wit and Art,
I act your aimes with valiant hand and heart :
You (lastly) plot, in shady Chambers seel'd,
What I perform, abroad, in bloudy Field.   640
    But, in all these, I pass you All, as far,
As to subdue the stoutest Foes in War ;
To see about one (Lightning-like) to flash
Millions of Shot, Millions of Swords to clash ;
To hear no noise but Canons roaring Thunder,
Divorcing Soules from Bodies pasht in sunder ;
To march in bloud even to the knees ; and yet
In all undaunted, not dismai'd a whit ;
Is both more painfull and more Princely too,
Than clearing of a cloudy Fraud, or two ;   650
To shield by counsell Equity opprest ;
To gain the Fame of Wisedome with the best ;
To fast and pray, or give abundantly,
Or get the name of gracious *Clemency.*
    Then well fare *Valour :* and, long live the Story
Of Valiant Princes in the Fane of Glory :
No humane *Vertue* hides so well as I,
Obnoxious stains when Princes step awry ;
An ALEXANDER, ARISTIDES seems,
Because the splendor of my spreading beams   660
With radiant lustre dazles so the sight,
That nought is seen but great and glorious Light.
Where, if hee lack my Rayes, or my Renown ;
Boast hee of double or of treble Crown,
Be hee benign, be hee munificent,
Just, wise, religious, learned, eloquent,
Precise of Promise (both to Friend and Foe)
Princes abroad little regard him though ;
Yea, might he justly all (else) *Vertues* vaunt ;
Yet, wanting mee, hee seemeth all to want.   670
His hare-like heart at wars least noise doth
    quake,
And to his Beads hee doth him all betake :

His fear strikes fear in his best Refuges,
And his no-courage doth discourage His.
In brief, as blest with *Peacefull Vertues* rare,
Hee seems far fitter (in a time of War)
With *Keyes* and *Crosiers*, a POPE's Part to play,
Than *Sword* and *Scepter*, as a KING, to sway.
　As *Andria* had ended here her part ;
Shee, in whose School wee learn the heedfull art　680
Of never fondly undertaking ought ;
Soft, soft, said shee : To boast our selves, wee
　　ought
Not blame our Equals ; nor (with proud Exchange)
To our own Praises their Dispraises change :
Andria, I grant, Thy Merit's great ; but Mine
Is, if not greater, full as great as Thine ;
Sithens, to raigne in Soule of *Majestie*,
There is no *Vertue* to be matcht with Mee.
　For let a King be full of High-designes,
Let him be valiant as your *Paladines ;*　　690
Let him be gracious, just and liberall ;
True of his word, and so devout withall,
That at his Feet all Vices prostrate ly ;
If Mee hee lack, that am all *Vertues'* Eye,
Blind-fold hee uses (nay, well-neer abuses)
These divine Gifts, which bounteous Heaven infuses ;
And right resembles a fair Ship, for sea
Already rigd, and furnisht every way
With every Needfull : Men, Munition, Beef,
Beer, Biscuit, all : onely shee wants (the Chief,　700
The Life and Soule, the Sense, the Law, the Light
Whereby shee lives, moves, stirs, and steers aright)
A skilfull Pilot, with *Discretion's* hand
Her winged manage rightly to command
With hempen Rains, and wooden Bridle ; so,
That never wry shee sail, nor wrong shee row :
Without whose guidance, if the puffing gales
Into the Deep transport her huffing sails,
Shee runs at random, and with ruefull Knock
Soon splits her selfe upon some Shelf or Rock.　710
　Even so it fares with Princes when they make
Or Peace, or War, and not my Counsell take ;
Or, without mee, as it were blind-fold, use
Their other Gifts the gracious Heav'ns infuse :
They thrive so little, that (as in a Wrack)
Their own rich burden often breaks their back.
Their forward Valour but sad Fruit doth yeeld ;
They win the Victory, yet lose the Field :
They bravely fight, and yet are bravely foil'd :
Some Error still hath all their Actions spoil'd.　720
Their bounty bindes not, but unbindeth, hearts :
Their Clemency, much more than Rigor, smarts :
Their Zeal it selfe proves to themselves pernicious ;
And unto others, blinde and superstitious :
Their Vice and Vertues them so inter-nex,
That scarce can one distinguish their Effects.
　Not that *Ill* still is not *Good's* Opposite ;
But that, They, wanting Mee, their onely Light,
Doe (even) Good evill ; or do, out of season,
A Good, which is not good, done without Reason ;　730

And of fair *Vertues*, fruitfull Seeds of Glory,
Reap blasted Buds, which stain their goodly Story.
　What famous conquest ever yet was got,
Which to the Victor I prepared not ?
Thou fightest bravely and in Victories
Of bloudy blades, get'st the first Crown, for prize :
But I, by th' art of Providence dispose
To glorious issue thy courageous blows.
I wisely take the fit advantages.
Of Time and Place, to second Courages ;　　740
I skilfully the Squadrons range and ranke ;
I marshall them to shew their Front or Flanke
As best befits (by warlike Stratagem)
T' inclose their Foes, to clip, or curtall them ;
Or, brest to brest (as angry Lions wont)
With brave incounter, charge them full afront :
I, by an ambush, laid with lucky speed,
Opprest with number, help thee at thy need :
I many times prevent thy like mis-hap.
When seem-flee Foes would train thee to the trap :　750
I, to be brief, with ever watchfull brain
Assist, to make thy Valour never vain.
　But, if a Prince must needs want one of us,
And mought not be both *Wise* and *Valorous ;*
Sure, Reason would our glorious parts assigne ;
Thine, to brave Souldiers ; to great Captains,
　　Mine ;
Because, my Pow'rs are proper to command,
As thine to execute with hardy hand.
　But though our humours so far divers be,
Yet may wee Both, in one brave Spirit, agree :　760
And, for this age, wee need no Witnesse else
But famous HENRY, who in both excels ;
With so great Wisdome ruling on the Throne
Which with such Valour hee hath made his own :
His Victories, yet, making Men dispute,
To which of Us, they should them best impute.
　Yet hundred Laurels never widow-curst,
And hundred *Ovals*, which no skin have burst ;
Prove I have often Conquer'd without Thee,
But never wert Thou Victor without Mee.　　770
For, I have oft seen Armies dissiped,
And proud, strong Cities often rendered,
(Well mur'd, well manned, & well stor'd with food)
Without the spilling of a drop of bloud ;
Using no other than the ancient Wile
Of wasting fields ; where Publique losse (the while)
Return'd this Gain, to stoop by famine Those
Which could not else have been subdu'd by blows.
Besides th' off-cutting of All Passages,
As well of Succours as of Forrages ;　　780
Is even to conquer by uncasuall course,
Fight-lesse to fight, and without force to force.
　Great Captains therefore did Us never part :
Sith either, sole, is as a head-lesse Dart ;
Or (if not head-lesse) heed-lesse thrown (as ill)
From feeble Caster, without aim, or skill.
　'Tis said of *Pallas*, in the *Trojane* Broil,
That Shee in fight stern *Mars* himselfe did foil ;

To show how far *Wise-Valour* doth excell
A rash Excesse of *Courage* boiling fell ;   790
Whose fume-blind force, wanting Discretion's beam,
Resembles right a sightlesse *Polyphem.*

But, whether joynt or sever'd be our Pow'rs,
My Cunning still yeelds fairer fruits and flow'rs,
Then doth Thy Violence (though oft it spread
Bright vertuous rayes about Thy glorious head).
For, onely then are Thy stiffe arms imploy'd,
When stubborn war dares to have all destroy'd.
But, when sweet *Peace* fils crowns with Coronets,
Thou art lockt up in Princes' Cabinets ;   800
Among the Corselets, which now wariefi'd
Through love of *Peace*, they have new laid aside ;
Or those, which idlely (through time's alteration)
Hang by the Walls, both out of Use and Fashion.
But I, indifferent, serve in *War* and *Peace;*
I breed her, feed her, and her years increase,
By prudent Counsails, provident Decrees,
Kinde turnes, calme treaties (fitting all degrees) ;
In brief, by all means meet to render Kings
Mutually friends ; and rule their Underlings :   810
When to their States if happy fruits accrew,
Th' honour of all to Mee alone is due.

But, in the world, what State hath ever thriven ;
Or rather, which hath not to wrack been driven,
Where lackt My Conduct, and where onely *Chance*
Hath steer'd the course of Publique Governance?
What humane action, what design, what thought,
Without Mine aid hath ever come to ought?
What Private stock, what Publique stem of Bloud,
Without my rules hath sprung, or long hath stood? 820
All noblest arts, all nimblest works of worth,
Which humane brains conceive, and hands bring
       forth ;
Hold they not Mee for rich and fruitfull wombe,
From whence their births (both first & secōd) com?
The kindest Counsails, without Mine among,
May wee not call them Treasons of the Tongue ;
When blind and bad advice (though malice-lesse)
Ruins the Friend to whom it meant Redresse?

Nay nothing, nothing under Heav'n, may misse
The Minds-guide rayes of my Resplendencies :   830
I am the true Sun of all humane acts ;
Without Mee, *Fortune* all their praise exacts.
If ought I leave to *Fortune's* doubtfull deed,
I shall appear well set, though ill succeed :
But where my Scepter hath a soveraign sway,
Fortune's false Die hath little power to play.

Then, be 't on Cedar, with a Pen of Gold,
For *Memory* and *Glory* too inrol'd,
That *Of all Soule-adorning Giftes divine,*
The Majesty, the Monarchie is Mine :   840
That I, Their Queen, life of Their Lawes and spring,
Am, of all, VERTUES, *worthiest of a* KING.
To whom, I seem so much more requisite
(Being both his Guide and Eye to give him light)
As hath a Guide (so judge the most discreet)
More need of Eyes, then either hands or feet.

Here ceast *Phronesia : Andria* instantly,
Weening her wrong'd, seems willing to reply,
And to her Selfe already soft shee sayes,
Shee hath lesse skill in Phrases then in Frayes ;   850
But, to maintain the honour of her Cause,
Where need requires, not words but swords shee
       drawes.

Then St· *Eusebia*, joyntly raising fair
Her Soule's pure Zeal, and her sweet Voyce's air,
See, see said shee, how proudly insolent,
Vain men admiring, and too-confident
Of their fond *Wisdome*, and frail *Fortitude*
(Forgetting heav'n's quick Eye and Arm) conclude,
That their own strength, or their owne providence,
Hath foil'd their foes, or giv'n their own defence ;   860
As silly children (set on fourm or stool)
Whose hand are (first) held at the *Writing-School:*
Forming som Letter, vaunt it for their Owne,
And think their Art-lesse fingers skilfull growne.

But, O fond Mortals ! Neither is 't your Art
Of mystike State, nor your high hand and heart,
Which in your Borders Peace and Plenty brings,
Or ends your Battels in your Triumphings :
But Heav'ns Right-hand, invisibly address
To rescue You, death hath it selfe represt ;   870
Repell'd all Perils, put-by all Mis-haps
(Ready to quell you with tempestuous claps)
And then retorting all upon your Foes,
In lieu of *Laurels* (which they did propose)
Sends Terrors, Errors, or Disorders rife,
Or Mutinies, or other Civill strife,
Or other Mischief, which confounds their pow'rs
With their own swords, or maks them fall on yours :
So that your hands, victorious Thus, doe bear
Right glorious Palms, and Olives every where   880
Adorn your Coasts with their rich oily tresse,
And all with you is *Victory* or *Peace.*

Yet you, ingrate the-while, through blind Selfe-love,
Not seeing, that these Gifts come from above,
Sacrifice to your Selves, confer the honour
Of all, to all, save to their owne right Owner.

O cursed Soil ! O barren Sand and dry !
Not better'd ought by any husbandry ;
Hardned with Heav'nly dews, the more the worse :
More worthier nothing then a heavie Curse.   890
O wretch ! refer, refer aright, and bring
These sacred Streams birth to their sacred Spring,
That perfect Good, which can no more desist
To doe thee good, then thou him to resist.
Through all thy Province let his name be prais'd :
If to a Crown his favour have thee rais'd,
Rear Him on Altar in thy Soule anon ;
And, for Burnt-Offring lay thy heart thereon :
His pow'r (alone) adore, implore and trust ;
And in thy Selfe kill every kind of Lust :   900
So shalt thou not, what-ever Hap succeed,
Neither so much Courage nor Counsell need ;
For covering thee with his protecting hand,
Did all the World in Arms against thee band,

Besiege thee round, assault thee in such sort,
That nought could save thee ; neither force, nor fort :
Amid all dangers which might fright thee there,
Hee, hee would free thee from all cause of fear ;
And thine, preserv'd from death and deadly Foes,
Would be amaz'd to conquer without blowes.   910
Thy Prayers would put a hundred Hoasts to flight,
Had each a *Cæsar* to command them right :
Yet, fighting on thy knees, with arms acrosse,
Thou, thou (alone) shouldst conquer ; without losse.
Again, His Angell would assume the Sword
Wherewith somtimes th' *Assyrian* swarms he gor'd ;
Again, *Senacherib's* braving Blasphemies
Should finde a King, with water in his eyes,
To vanquish him with vows : and, as with charms,
Thou shouldst do more with Tears, then hee with
          arms.   920
    Why then thus vainly dare we here consult
Of other's Right, or of our Own insult ?
Shee, shee that gives to God (nay, giveth God)
On Her of right this Crown should be bestow'd ;
Sith, her possessing, they all Good possesse :
But, wanting her, All else is emptinesse.
    Let neither *Prowesse* then, nor *Prudence* ween
Her Selfe *King's Glory*, neither *Vertue's* Queen :
I have seen Valiant Kings, and Prudent too,
And such as knew in all turns what to doe,   930
And such whose Constance was incomparable,
Live wretchedly, and dy as miserable ;
Yet, never saw I but a happy end
Of Pious Princes, which on God depend ;
And in all doubts, all dangers (from their Birth)
Have (sacring unto Heav'n the thoughts of Earth)
With eyes ay-fixt on that *Sun's* sunny side,
Beleev'd his Love their guard, his Law their guide.
    Not that I would a Prince, secure and idle,
Should so let-goe his Empire's Rains and Bridle ;   940
To cast on God the Cares, the Managings,
And glorious labours that belong to Kings :
Nay, rather would I, that with Vigilance,
Constancy, Justice, Wisdome, Valiance,
And all else Vertues which his God hath giv'n,
Hee second still th' assisting hand of Heav'n :
Ay well assur'd, that God will not neglect
Just-armed Prayers of his own Elect.
But, to His onely Bountie must they give
Th' honour of all the fruits they shall atchieve   950
By their most noble Cares, most royall Pains :
Not to the depth of *Machiavilian* Brains,
Not to the vain Effort of humane force,
Nor martiall courage, mowing Men and Horse ;
Which in effect (how glorious Name it bear)
Is but a Publique (lawfull) Massacre.
    In brief, what Worth, or Wit in King may be,
Heav'n's King comands hee make Them wait on mee :
Make That, the Spur ; Me, Rain of each Intent ;
This, of his Counsail ; Mee the President :   960
Credit them often, Mee continually,
That they inspire his Heart ; his Judgement, I.

And, that in nothing They with Mee compare ;
Nor any else (how Royall) *Vertues* rare :
But make Mee sit in Honours fourm the first ;
Yea, without Mee, esteem his State accurst :
Hold Them for *helpfull*, Mee for *necessary* :
And firm beleeve, when Times are adversary,
Rather to faile, with *Prowesse* and *Policy*,
Nay fall, with All ; then flourish without Mee.   970
    Through such a *Faith*, that great *King-Prophet*
          yerst
With little force, so many Foes reverst :
So oft escap'd so many Snares of Death,
Which Envie's hand had set to stop his breath :
So fortunate, in every jeopardy,
Hee almost seem'd t' have wedded *Victory*.
    What Monarch would not gladly be the Heire
Of these high fortunes of His *Vertues* fair ?
Who would not purchase at the dearest rate
Of all his Pains, the glorious Praise hee gate ?   980
And yet, the *Vertue* which advanc't Him so,
And on his Acts such honours did bestow,
Was not his *Prowesse* (though hee durst enough)
Neither his *Prudence* (though of famous proof) ;
But his religious *Piety* and *Zeal*
To serve the Lord, the God of *Israel* :
Zeale, which, consuming him with heav'nly flame,
Made him to consecrate his Facts, his Fame,
Himselfe, his Sword, his Scepter, and his Song,
At th' Author's feet, to whom they all belong :   990
As still esteeming that hee held his Crown,
By his support who had it first bestow'n ;
Not by the Prowesse, or the Policy,
Of his owne darefull hand, or carefull eye.
    Let noblest Princes imitate this Part,
This pious zeale of his religious heart :
And let them know, that nor their Heed in sway,
Nor their Good-hap (wch seemst' attend them ay)
Their Knowledge, Courage, nor Victorious fame,
About their heads so glorious Garlands frame ;   1000
Neither from Heav'n so many blessings bring,
Neither so much doe magnifie a King,
Nor dignifie the Scepter in his hand
So many millions justly to command ;
As I, who, after this world's *Diadem*,
Find them a-new, in new *Jerusalem* :
That God himselfe vouchsafes to *watch* their state,
Becomes their *Counsell*, their *Confederate*,
Their Rock, their Refuge, from their Enemies,
And gets them daily glorious Victories :   1010
That, without Mee, no *Vertue* is complete ;
And that, in That which maketh truely Great,
I pass the rest, and all the best they can,
As far as God in Greatness passeth Man.
    Eusebia here concluding her discourse,
Dicea began her Title to enforce :
I have (said shee) long lent you ear a-like,
Yet from your Reasons and your Rhetorike
I gather nothing, from the most of you,
But Usurpations of mine honours due ;   1020

While mine own Nursling from my side you steal :
Wherein, with *Justice*, you scarce justly deal.

For, if of *Vertues* any worthy be
To raign, as Kings' eternall Companie ;
And with more lustre their great Names doe grace,
I, I am shee may justly claime that Place ;
As shee alone, who, by One duety, doo
Make happy Kings, and happy Subjects too :
Shee, that of all the graces from above,
Acquire them most their Peoples' hate or love :   1030
Shee that the Stock of Traytors doth extinguish,
She that good Kings from Tyrants doth distinguish :
Shee that to Each due recompence imparts
According to their good, or bad Deserts :
Shee without whom, the rife-full strife-full sound
Of *Mine* and *Thine*, would all the World confound.

Not that I am so inly blunt, or blinde,
As not to value *Valour's* valiant minde ;
Or not to see, What benefits to Kings
Sacred *Eusebia*, and *Phronesia* brings :   1040
But save *Eusebia* (whom I honour more
Than all the Greatnesse worldlings most adore)
Not one of you produceth her effects
So fortunate and free from all defects,
But oftentimes some evill them succeeds
Which equals oft their good, sometimes exceeds :
Much like some Herbs, of doubtfull fame and force,
Which cure one Grief, and cause perhaps a worse.

'T's a glorious Work triumphing worthily,
To win by force a famous Victory ;   1050
To flowr a field with dead, to swim in bloud,
To glass one's Valour in a Crimsin flood ;
But, what's all this, but a meer Massacre
Of furious Lions (not a humane War)
Unless the Right of the bright Sword Victorious,
Make the cause just, and the Effect as glorious ?
And are not those so bloudy Palmes (the while)
Gathered in countries ruin'd with the spoile
Of War's dire fire, flaming on every side
Of those sad fields, forsaken far and wide ?   1060
O bloudy *Vertue*, for Warre onely fit,
And for the Mischiefs that do wait on it !

Yet lest (alas !) her thirsty Steel should rust
Within her Sheath, too-long restrained ; must,
Must men wth tears see their dear countries spoil'd,
Their fields with heaps of slaughtred bodies pyl'd,
Their cities sackt, their houses all inflam'd,
Their treasures shar'd, their wives and daughters
    sham'd,
Their tender babes (which have no help but cries)
Brain'd, broached, broyl'd, in horrid Sacrifice ?   1070
Sure, Noble Furie of heroike hearts,
The hideous Stage whereon thou act'st thy Parts,
Is too-too-costly to a State ; too-dear
Are all thy Palms ; thy Glory walks too-neer
Deep Miseries, Pains, Perils, Dolours, Deaths,
And dire Events ; which not alone the breaths
Of Foes bereave, and Foraign States undoe ;
But wrack withall thine own Domesticks too.

For what Effects, but such nefarious things,
Have been the fruits of thousand *Valiant* Kings? 1080
Whose memories so ring of Battailes yet,
That even with bloud their Stories may be writ :
Leaving their Names, just Arguments of terror,
Loading the Earth with Monuments of horror,
Filling both Land and Sea, with Gore, with Gall,
And, to no purpose, topsie-turning all :
Sith all the gain of all their Victories,
Is but a fame of Valiant Robberies ;
Reproachfull praise to Soveraign Potentates,
To *Supreme Pastors*, to high Magistrates :   1090
Yet most of These have reapt no other fruit,
From bloudy labours, but this odious Bruit :
Whereas They should (onely) their Powrs imploy
To salve, to save ; and never to destroy.

One onely King (no further Name is need)
Justly constrain'd to arme, and mount his steed,
By force to enter to his own by Right :
Hath sacred all his Art, his Heart, his Might,
To's Empire's good : and, chasing War away,
Makes Peace approv'd his Valour's daughter ay ;   1100
The rest, still greedy of new *Isles*, new *Indes*,
Have rais'd such stormes wth their ambitious winds,
As in their own Seas have nigh sunk themselves,
And cast their Subjects upon Rocks and Shelves ;
Where (through more woes) they, even with tears,
    behold
How ill it is to have a King too Bold.

Now, for your Prudent (but meer Prudent) Kings,
Too much discourse, wch frō their judgement springs,
Oft makes them timorous, loth to take-in-hand ;
To lose their time, while waiting Time they stand ; 1110
And daring nothing, but Discoursing still,
To Erre, as much as those that dared ill ;
Or, makes them, more (in Worldly matters, here)
Subtile and sharp, than loyall and sincere.
So that as they of dangers heedfull are ;
Of Them, no lesse behoves it to beware.
I will not say that many times the grounds,
Whereon the world's blind, foolish wisdom founds,
Are contrarie unto the solid Base   1120
Which Heav'n's true wisedome every where doth place.
So that, one Thought never it selfe extends
(Nor can) at once, to two so divers Ends :
No more than can the sight of mortall eyes
In one same instant, Heav'n and Earth comprise.

What shall I say of Thee (and doe thee right)
Sweet St. *Eusebia*, God's own dear Delight ?
Thou fillest Kings, indu'd with thy desires,
With sacred fervour of Celestiall fires ;
Thou mak'st their Lives a lively speaking Law,
To rule their Subjects more by Love than Awe ;   1130
But yet, thou mak'st (if thou alone be theirs)
Them too-too-slack in other Kingly Cares ;
Too-mew'd in Peace, in War too-scrupulous ;
And think so much of Heav'n that Earth they lose.
And *Euergesia*, praising Thine Effects,
Amid the best well may wee doubt defects :

For, what in Kings more Heav'n-like seems to all,
Or God-like more, than to be *Liberall* ?
Yea, *Liberall* Princes seem even Gods on Earth,
Com-down from Heav'n to hunt despair and death, 1140
Care, Indigence, Incumber and the rest,
Where-with poor *Vertue* often is opprest.
Yea, even as Gods their names are honour'd here,
And for their Service nothing is too-deer.
(The ground of which so great Benevolence,
In some, is Hope ; in some Experience) :
So that all Vows, all Voices end in Them,
And as the Sun, Their Scepters brightly beam.
 Yet, oftentimes, those *Bounties* of thy hand
Prove *Publike Burdens*, bitter to a Land ; 1150
When fluent Princes (lest their Favours' source
Should be exhausted) have too-oft recourse
To Tributes, Imposts ; and some worse withall ;
Whence *Flowers* too few, too many *Thornes*
 befall :
And *Avarice* her selfe unjustly fills
With what *Profusion* over-fondly spills.
 Nor thou, *Eumenia*, though extoll'd so high
As liveliest Type of Heav'nly *Clemency*,
And onely Shield of such as dare infringe
My sacred Rules, to save them from Revenge : 1160
Thou canst not cleer thee from the confluence
Of Evils us'd to follow *Indulgence*.
For, by too-sparing, Thou dost vices spread ;
Thou losest sound, to save corrupt and dead :
And filling Cities with home Enemies,
Thy *Pardons* turn to publike *Injuries*.
 But I, by practice of unpartiall Rigor,
Maintain good Orders, keep the Laws in Vigor :
Make Kings at-once belov'd and feared too
(Feared, alone of those that evill doe) 1170
Their Subjects (set on happie Plentie's knee,
In their possessions from Oppressions free)
Blesse them, adore them, hold them (ever dear)
Their Countries' Fathers, nay their gods well-neer.
In brief, no Blessing can befall a Realm,
But theirs enjoy, from, by, or under Them.
For, as it is, of the *Wild-Ash-Tree*, said,
That th' onely savour, nay the onely shade,
Instantly kils (by strong *Antipathie*)
What ever Serpents underneath it lye : 1180
Such, to the Snakes of Vice, those Princes are
Which 'gainst *Injustice* have proclaimed War,
With no less Care to make my Rules to raign,
Than their own Scepters in their hands sustain.
Can no rebellion spring, at least, none speed
In their Dominions, neither Factions breed ;
Sith gracious Heav'ns vouchsafe them this accord,
For having us'd so equally My Sword
(To all degrees, in City, Field and Town)
In Civill War they shall not weare their Own. 1190
 Their People feeling in their happy Sway,
What Hap, what Rest, what freedome they injoy,
Deeming them as their gods, and meeting (rife)
Their length of Bliss by their dear length of Life,

Watch for their Safeties ; and can suffer nought
'Gainst them to be mis-done, mis-said, mis-thought ;
No more than 'gainst their Publique's Prospering
Whereof they hold their *Justice* onely Spring.
 For, of all rarest Vertues that may meet
In a just Prince, they onely take the sweet 1200
Of Mine Effects ; and of that *Equall Care*
Of not surcharging more than they may beare.
What boots it that their Majesties be *meek*,
Magnanimous, frank, pious, politique,
And of a sp'rit surpassing each Extreme ?
Misse they but Mee, they little reck of them :
They love them not, they listen far and neer
Some welcome newes of their wisht death to hear :
When, if they use My sacred Exercises,
Though they be stain'd (perhaps) with other vices, 1210
They hold them perfect ; and, in spite of Fate,
Even after death, their Names they celebrate ;
As living *Reliques*, still preserv'd above
In *Fame's* fair bosom, and their People's love.
Witness, unto this day that *Norman* Prince,
Brave *Rollo*, still belov'd (though dead long since)
Still call'd upon (as for His *just* Revenge)
When some new Wrong doth their old Right infringe.
 Henceforth therefore, O Princes, that desire
To have your Names to highest Fames aspire, 1220
To leave behinde you Monuments of Worth,
To give you Glories, after death, new Birth ;
Endeavour not to dazle proudest eyes
With Tow'rs of Marble mounted to the skies ;
Neither by War (whose Train is plague and dearth)
With fire and bloud to mingle Heav'n and Earth ;
To thousand Perils to expose your lives,
Whereby your greatness, not your goodness, thrives.
Onely, love *Mee ;* let *Mee* be reverenc't
Through all your lands, by all your hands defenc't : 1230
Let *Mee* sit by you on an Awfull Throne,
To daunt the Lewdest with my looks alone ;
And with my Sword still drawn to prune away
Luxuriant Twigs that break my *just* Array :
Let my *Tribunals* be the Poor's Refuges ;
Let thereon sit no mercenary Judges :
Let *Innocence* finde there her surest Fort ;
And who wants Right, there let him want support :
There let My *Balance* be impawn'd to none ;
But, as his Right is, let each have his own : 1240
In brief, with You let Mee be set so high,
That absolute as you doe Raigne, may I :
And I shall more enrich your lasting Stories,
Than all your golden Tow'rs, your conquering
 glories,
Your precious Gifts that with full hand you give,
Or ought besides, whereby your Names can live.
 Dicea as yet did her Discourse pursue
(Though milde *Eumenia*, loth to lose her due,
Loth longer to endure her Vaunts so high,
With open mouth was ready to reply ; 1250
And so her Sister *Euergesia* eek,
Some little choler colouring her cheek)

When from th' *Empyreall* (right *Imperiall*) Court,
Came a new *Nuntio* with a new Report ;
A trustie Truch-man of supernall Pleas,
Their gentle Jars thus gently to appease.

Immortall Beauties of past-humane Soules,
Hee, that both Globes in his own hand-gripe holds ;
Does you to weet, that his high pleasure is
(To quench for ever all your Differences)   1260
You All have th' honour to impose the *Name*,
To whom hee means such favour and such Fame,
PANARETUS (for an auspicious Signe
Y' have markt him all with all your Types divine)
That all transform'd into that *reverend* Clark,
Heav'n's hallowed Organ, for this sacred work ;
Eusebia, Thou (Whom hee resembles best)
Shalt *Name the Child*, in name of all the rest ;
After that Hee hath six times sounded tho
That other *Name* his *Nation* fancies so.   1270

Hy, hy yee then : Time calls you ; for the throng,
These Rites expecting, thinks each minute long.
And I, the while, with no lesse speed must spy
Th' Unholsome Den where *Pestilence* doth ly,
And in Heav'n's name, her straitely countermand,
That Shee presume not once to lift her hand,
Nor from her Quiver shoot one Arrow out
At any of the Royall Courtly Rout
Assembled for the sacred *Mysterie*,
During the Pomp of That *Solemnity*.   1280

Here-with the Angell henc't, and bent his flight
Tow'rds Our Sad Citie ; which then deeply sigh't
Under the furie of that Monster fell.
Hee found her out in a hot-humid Cell,
About to arm her, and to scout abroad,
Even towards the Place which now the Heav'ns for-
bode.

Foul seam-rent rags (wch som old Robe had bin)
Cas't here and there her yellow-sallow skin ;
Where-in hot fiery *Carbuncles* were fixt,
With poys'nie *Rubies*, here and there betwixt :   1290
A quench-lesse Thirst, with a continuall Feaver,
Broil'd in her breast, boil'd in her body ever ;
Her very breath was as a deadly stroak :
Her cursed Stance ready with stink to choak :
So close it was, that never Wind could fan,
Save th' unrefin'd autumnal *Affrican ;*
Whose noysom air a stuffing fog did pen
With musty Vapours of a moisty Fen.

All round about her, by her side did ly
All sorts of Fruits that soonest putrefie ;   1500
Millions of Milions ; Pears, Plums (passing numbers)
Most-humour-poys'ning, crudie-cold Cucumbers ;
Green Grapes ; and that soft *Persian* Fruit (so deer)
Banefull at home, and little better here.

The Angell, wonted to Heav'n's Blisse-full Hall,
Made little stay in this unholsome Stall :
But, loathing soon that thick contagious air,
Hee speedily dispatcht his Message there ;
And Heav'n-ward quickly from the *Furie* flew,
Whose horror yet so seem'd him to pursue,   1510

That hee had fainted to have been so nigh-her,
Had hee not felt him of th' immortall Quier.

Th' immortall *Sisters*, in one troup the while
(Which from their owners every Vice exile)
Transported swift upon a winged Cloud,
By their Arrivall make the Palace proud.

The pompous Scaffold, for this purpose rear'd,
Seem'd at their sight to tremble (as afear'd) :
The stately Towers of th' antique Edifice,
The massie Porch, and Arch, and Frontespice ;   1320
Seem'd round about to lighten smiling flames,
As at their Entrance to adore these Dames.

They, shuffling them (unseen) amid the throng
Of those *Good-great*, whom (as they past along)
A soft sweet Murmur, for their Vertues, blest ;
Served with Them (each in her office prest)
That goodly *Rising Sun*, whose Rayes, new spred,
So rathe a Spring of flowring Hopes have bred :
And, after both his favour'd *Names* were given,— 1329
The humane first, then that they brought frō heav'n, —
All, in a ring, about him did appear
(Under the form of som faire Princesse neer,
Or som great Prince then present there in view)
To doe his Name the honours justly due :
Each cheering Him to follow for direction
The Propertie Shee brings to Kings perfection.

Maist thou (said one, as his sweet Eyes shee kist)
Great-little Prince, be of the Heav'ns so blist,
That, though *Augustus* fortunes Thine surpasse,
Thy Fortunes yet may give thy Prudence place :   1340
Maist thou abound in royall Bountie so
(Another said) that *Trajane* thou out-goe :
May (said another : how my Hopes aspire !)
Thy Valour, one-day even excell thy Sire :
May there (said one) one-day appear in thee,
Thy Martiall father's match-lesse Clemencie ;
And, maist thou from thy Child-hood (said another)
Exceed in *Zeal* thy Mother and God-mother.
In brief (*Pandora*-like) each offered there
Their precious Gifts, in Præsage (as it were)   1350
Till with advantage gracious Heav'ns produce
Their *Wished Counsails* into act and use.

Grant, God Almighty, King of kings, that Hee
When on these Thrones his royall Turn shall be,
Hee may have care t' accomplish every-where
What all our Hopes have for him dar'd to swear ;
And what his Looks, Words, Maners, Motions,
seem
In every part to promise still for Him.

May Hee, his People tender, love, protect ;
Delight in *Justice*, yeeld them her Effect ;   1360
May hee forbear to over-charge their backs
With novell Tributes, or with needlesse Taxe :
And let them see that of all Titles given
To all the Kings that have been under Heav'n,
Hee holdeth *Good* the best ; better then *Glorious*,
Wars-thunderbolt, Earths-Terror, Great, Victorious ;
Whose loftie sound makes Princes oft become
Abroad more feared then belov'd at home.

High swells the Ocean, when the Moon's at full,
And with proud Billowes threats both hill & hull ; 1370
But sinks againe, and shrinks into his Bed,
When *Cynthia* mues her never-constant Head :
So (swelling proud ; so, surly-browd the while ;
So, temper-lesse ; tempted with Fortune's smile)
Ignoble Natures are too lightly pufft ;
And with her Frown as basely counterbufft.

Far other be his firm and generous Minde,
Whether his Fate be curst or be shee kinde ;
Yea, fawn-shee, frown-shee, (firm indeed to none)
Be Hee still like Himselfe, *The same, still one ;* 1380
Still bountifull, still milde-majesticall,
And still vouchsafing free Accesse to all :
So that no Bar (a *Barbarous* device)
But due respect doth sever Him from His.
For, be a Prince never so mighty *Great,*
If betwixt Him and His a Bar Hee set ;
At length hee sets one (which scarce ought repairs)
'Twixt their affections and his own affairs.
Leave hee to th' idle Pomp of *Prester-Jans,*
To miss-proud *Sophyes,* and soft *Asians,* 1390
That Care, to keep their tawny Majesties,
From Subjects' sight (save once a year or twice)
And let him daily (like the Sun) goe out
To cleer and cheer the cloudy World about ;
To doe the poor oppressed Widow right,
To help the Orphan, over-born by might ;
To ease the just sighs of sad Labourers :
And alwayes (like that best of Emperours)
Think That no Day, nor think it lost (for nought)
Wherein hee hath not som such action wrought ; 1400
Or that hee lives not then, or lives in vain ;
Or as a Subject, not a Soveraigne.

Consume not Hee in frivolous Expence,
What gold a just Love's gentle violence
Shall for his Succour (in extreme Affair)
Force his poor People from their hands to spare
(Nay, frō their mouths, nay rather frō their bellies)
Perhaps drawn-dry with Pump of former Tallies.
But rather, counting it (with som Remorse)
Not Gold, but Bloud ; may Hee with greater force 1410
Abhor to lavish, upon idle Vains,
His Subjects' soule, and th' humour of their Veins.

That great *King-Prophet* (so renown'd for Song)
Once for the water of a Well did long,
Which at the Postern of a Citie rose,
Amid an Hoast of his most deadly Foes :
Three of his *Worthies* (in despight of death)
Brake through their armie, even to underneath
The very wall whereas the Well did spring ;
Whereof they drew a portion for the King. 1420
Then, off again they bravely come their wayes
(Cover'd with wounds, but more with worthy praise)
And re-arriv'd in their own camp, their prize
Unto their Prince present in humble wise.
But Hee, bethinking through how many deaths
Those dreadlesse Champions had then fetcht their
　　breaths,

In fetching of that wished Water so ;
For all his thirst, hee would not drink it tho :
For, what is This (said hee) but the heart-bloud
Of these that thus have ventur'd for my good ? 1430
So to God's will, His, willing to accord,
Hee offers it on th' Altar of the Lord.

So, may our Prince another-day imploy
The publique Treasure, which with carefull Joy,
His loving Subjects shall (as ought the loyall)
Yeeld to support his Port and Charges royall.
May Hee present to th' in-sight of his Thought,
With how much Sweet and Sorrow it is bought :
What Rigor (used in his Name perhaps)
Extorts it from oppressed Widows' laps, 1440
From wretched Crafts-men, from hard-wracked Swains,
Whom Poverty at her own Messe maintains ;
And, in Compassion say (with tender grief)
This is my Subjects' bloud, my People's Life :
This must not then an idle Pomp and Play
(As water spilt) be spent and cast away.
Then (doubting lesse the damage then th' abuse)
Vow it to God, as to the rightfull Use.

And, 'tis to consecrate, and vow it right
(And in a fashion pleasing in God's sight) 1450
To poure it out in Royall (right) Expence ;
Either in War-works for his Realm's defence,
Or for his Honour : to all Times to seale
His King-like Bounty, Providence, and Zeale.

Close-fisted therefore may Hee never be
To the true *Seed* of sacred *Memorie ;*
To those whose lustre doth adorn Renown,
And honours Kings more then their orient Crown :
To stately Structures, speaking Eminence,
So as their Use match their Magnificence : 1460
To wall high-waies ; to heaw down harmfull ridges :
To parallel Eld's Aquæducts and bridges :
Found Hospitals, or to endow them founded ;
To stop Sea-Breaches where they have surrounded :
To fence with Peers and Piles of sundry sorts
From *Neptune's* furie his importing Ports :
To build fair Shops for th' *Helyconian* Looms,
T' advance their *Arts,* and give chiefe Parts chiefe
　　Rooms ;
And (as with living Nets) by Benefits,
To catch both *Valiant* Spirits and *Learned* Wits. 1470

Millions of Verse have sounded loftily
The Prudence, Prowesse, Pitie, Pietie,
And sacred Justice of our Soverain Sir,
As divers Gales their divers Sails did stir :
But not a Voice, in low or lofty vain,
Hath of his Bounty ever sung a strain :
Yet yeerly from his *liberall* hand doth come
A million (a more then Royall Sum)
Among those (happy) whom his goodnesse graces,
Or whom their own in his opinion places ; 1480
Which of his Predecessors (first or last)
In Gifts or Guerdons these fair limits past ?
Not one of them did ever reach so high ;
Yet Vulgar bruit (halfe false, halfe flattery)

Gives som of them the great and glorious Name
Of *Liberall* Princes, of illustrious fame.
And shall not wee then, bear through th' Universe
His worthy Praise upon the wings of Verse?
Shall not wee say that his renowned hand,
As worthily (in Peace) with bountie's band   1490
Can binde unto him whom hee worthy knowes,
As bravely conquer (in the Field) his Foes?
   Be mute that list, and muzzle they their stile,
On whom his Bounty never daign'd to smile
(Were 't throw their own mis-fate, in having none,
Or having Vertues, not to have them known).
But I, whose hap hath been to march with those
Towards whose laps his golden River flowes,
My Voice and Verse shall trump-it far and nigh
To modern ears, and to Posterity.   1500
And (without Flattery) say, that all the scope
Of Wishes waiting on our future Hope,
And all our Prayers for a compleat Prince
(As in the rest of Royall *Ornaments*)
Need of the Heav'ns no greater Hap require,
But that in This, the Son be like the Sire;
And that hee may (observing golden mean)
Give like a King that means to give again:
Yet, with such fervour to this glorious Part,
That still hee give lesse with his hand then heart.   1510
   Vouchsafe th' Eternall Destinies-disposer,
Kings' sole Advancer, and Kings' sole Deposer,
That maugre Tyrants' wrath, and Traytors' wile
(*Whose Master-peece wee Heer have seen yer-while*)
Hee may wax old (after his aged Sire)
In Peacefull Raign, untill his Raign expire:
And never but at Tilt, or Tourney, feel
The combrous burthen of a Case of steel;
Or, when just furie shall inflame his sp'rite
Against Usurpers of His ancient Right.   1520
But, whether law-lesse Need or Glories love,
Him drive or draw, his Force in Field to prove;
May Hee in Counsail, Courage, and Successe,
Match his great Parents' constant Happinesse,
So as there be no need to spur Him forth,
With brave remembrance of His matchless worth.
   But, *Laurell* burnt, crackles in vain; and of-it
Champing the leaf alone, makes not a Prophet,
If that his Tutors have not more to doe,
To hold him from, then to incite him to;   1530
To cool, then kindle, that courageous heat,
Which makes men fear no death, no dangers threat:
But, as once *Theseus*, ready to be kill'd,
Was known to be the King's son, that so will'd;
By his gilt Sword and Signe engrav'n thereon:
Hee shall be known to be His Father's Son,
By the exploits of His, in such a Rank,
As would have made the two first *Cæsars* blank.
   Be Hee Benign, so as his Indulgences
Breed not Bad-Boldnesse, Feed not Insolences;   1540
Like to some Winters, over-milde and warm,
Which neither kill the Weed, nor chill the Worm;

But breed the Plague, Pox, Murrain and the rest,
That rotten humours make, in Man and Beast.
   Not, but I know it far more honourable
To save then spill (in Cases tolerable)
Sith here a World of Dust-bred Creatures live,
Can reave Man's life, which onely God can give:
But too-oft Pardoning oft too-many draws
T' have need of Pardon, through contempt of Laws 1550
And Magistrates; whom the Audacious reak
But Bugs, and Bridles to base mindes and weak.
   In mildnesse then, be Hee so moderate
(For his own safety and the publique State)
That neither Horror taint his Executions;
Neither his Favours harbour Dissolutions:
And, too-remisse, by His too-oft Reprieves,
Turn Pitie's Temple to a Den of Theeves.
   May he fear God, love, worship, seek, & serve him,
Know, it's Hee sole doth stablish and preserve him: 1560
That Kings, as his Annointed, have Regard:
That but he guard them, little boots their Guard.
May hee beleeve His Word, honour, obey;
Take it for Compasse in this Worldly Sea,
Make it the Measure of Kings' Power, in all;
And counting That of Laws the principall;
Have it ay written in his heart's deep rooms;
But, as a Prince, not as a Priest becoms.
   Under th' old Law (now abrogate long since)
One might be both a *Pontife* and a Prince;   1570
For nothing seemed then to hinder them
From matching so Mitre and Diadem:
But now their Functions are divided far,
And Monkish Kings, now but contemned are:
There Man and Master but *Hail-fellow* is;
And Subjects play the Kings, where Kings play Priests.
   May Hee be loyall, constant in sincerity;
In soule, abhorring lies, and loving verity:
That as his Deeds shall (for the most) be Miracles,
So may his Words be altogether Oracles.   1580
   Th' Almighty grant, that during all His dayes,
All sparks be quencht which factions wont to raise;
For, for the most (to double Miserie)
There be two Kings where two great factions be.
But, if there should (which God forbid) succeed
Such Mischiefs here as here-to-fore there did;
May hee not want sound Counsail's happy Light,
To guide him in his Father's steps aright:
Who reaving th' eldest Emperours their Palms,
Suddenly turn'd such Tempests into Calms,   1590
By means so milde, that it was rather thought
By heav'nly Hap, then humane Wisdome wrought.
But, were it Wisdome, were it Happinesse,
Match Hee our *Wishes*, and His *Wise successe:*
Th' one of Himselfe, th' other from Heav'nly hand,
That Peace may prosper over all his Land.
   I know that Princes being born for th' Arts
Which Counsels, Camps, & danger's school imparts,
The Books most needfull and peculiar Theirs,
Are *Politiques*, of State and State-affaires.   1600

But, sith so few yeers doe our *Age* comprise,
That even the greatest of the greedy-Wise,
Should know but little, if no more they knew
Then from experience of one *Age* they drew :
That hee, at once, may see all Accidents
Of all *past Ages*, with his own's Events ;
May Hee propose and set before his eyes
The goodly Tables of all Histories ;
And there contempling all the true Records
Of other Monarchs, mighty States, and Lords, 1610
Observe their acts, their Counsells, their Discourse,
All (notable, or rare) in all their Course ;
Both what to follow there, and what to shun,
And whether Fame or Shame their lives have won :
May Hee there glasse himselfe, and mark it brim,
Whether the same shall not be said of Him.
For here, Our *Verses* smoothly sing and smile :
But *History* will *hisse*, in other stile :
And Kings that here have been compar'd to Gods
Entomed once, though under golden Clods, 1620
If in their lives they have deserv'd it, first ;
Shall have their Names torn, & their Fames accurst.
 What may I add unto These Wishes *more ?*
No more but this ; that All here wisht before,
And All presaged of the DOLPHIN *here,*
Concur in CHARLES : *that all his Parts appear*

A living Picture of all Parts of Worth
Of all those Worthies *Whence Hee takes his Birth :*
That gracious Heav'ns (*which promise even as much*)
In all these Vertues daign to make Him such, 1630
That really hee give royall Assent
To all the Acts *of Vertue's* PARLIAMENT :
That in his Tern, the Ages after Us,
May finde, and know him for PANARETUS :
And, sith That Name *must needs Immortall be,*
That no prophane hand blurr His History :
But some sweet Daniel, *or some sacred* Hall,
Or civill Hayward, (*milde-majestike all*)
With purest faith, *in a peculiar* stile,
A glorious Worke *of his great* Works *compile :* 1640
Or, if that any of more worthy Skill-is,
Be hee the HOMER *to This new* ACHILLES.
GREAT BRITAN'S *great hope of great hap to-come,*
Phœnix arising from a Phœnix dust :
In whom the heavens (*as mercifull as just*)
Restore our great losse in great HENRY'S *Tombe.*
 Long, long and Happy (*in thy* Brother's *roome*)
Succeed Thou CHARLES, *ever as Good as Great :*
Deriving, old, to thy old Father's *Seat,*
Wise, Great, Good STUARTS, *till the Day of Doom.* 1650
Which while I pray, sweet Prince vouchsafe a space
To read and rue Your humble Bead-man's *Case.*

FINIS.

NOTES AND ILLUSTRATIONS.

PAGE 122, *Verse-dedication,* 'Sir Robert Carie,' etc.
—see Memorial-Introduction on all the names herein ;
also Index of Names, *s.n.* : l. 15, '*Stagyrian's*' = Aristotle : l. 16, '*Corduban*' = Seneca.
 PANARETUS : l. 10, '*prest*' = prepared, ready : and
so *frequenter* : l. 17, '*gest*' = gesture, and so *frequenter :* l. 49, '*vale*' = stoop, lower : l. 103, '*Chape*'
—see Glossarial Index, *s.v.* : l. 106, '*fauchin*' = falchion : l. 107, '*Keening*' = sharpening, exciting : l. 136,
'*Arrand*' = errand : l. 227, '*Puntilios*' = punctilios :
l. 211, '*Appals*' = appeals : *ib.*, '*Seconds*' = in duels,
friends or supporters : l. 242, '*frustred*' = frustrated :
l. 248, '*ought*' = owed : l. 249, '*Ynow*' = enough ; l.
264, '*Mad-caps*'—a name utilised by Breton and Nash :
l. 269, '*intemperous*'—see Glossarial Index, *s.v.* : l. 281,
'*Aye*'—misprinted, '*Eye*' in the original : l. 330, '*convented*' =convened : l. 341, '*vails*'—misprinted '*nails*'
in the original : l. 382, '*Covent*' = convent—so still in
'Covent Garden' : l. 434, '*peace*' = at peace or friends :
l. 442, '*farr*' = fair : l. 510, '*Quiddi-quirks*'—from
'Quiddity' and 'Quirks' : l. 523, '*Port*' = gate : l.
577, '*list*' = choose, *frequenter :* l. 603, '*agnize*' =
acknowledge : l. 621, '*Rubble*' = loose refuse : l. 639,

'*seeled*' = ceiled : l. 681, '*fondly*' = foolishly : l. 705,
'*Rains*' = reins. So l. 940, *et alibi* : l. 708, '*huffing*'
—see Glossarial Index, *s.v.* : l. 744, '*curtall*' = transi-
tion form of our 'curtail' or shorten : l. 768, '*Ovals*'
—see Glossarial Index, *s.v.* : l. 771, '*dissiped*' = dispersed : l. 773, '*mur'd*' = walled : l. 781, '*uncasuall*'
= uncausal : l. 801, '*wariefi'd*'—see Glossarial
Index, *s.v.* : l. 936, '*sacring*' = consecrating : l. 1070,
'*broached*' = transfixed as on a spit : l. 1191, '*sacred*'
=consecrated. Cf. l. 936 : l. 1294, '*Stance*,' Cf. l. 1306,
'*Stall*,' and see Glossarial Index, *s.v.* : l. 1303, '*Persian Fruit*'—see Glossarial Index, *s.v.* : l. 1389, '*Prester-
Jans*' = Prester-Johns : l. 1411, '*Vains*' = vanities :
l. 1419, '*whereas*' = whereat : ll. 1413-32 = David and
the Well of Bethlehem : l. 1495, '*throw*' = through :
l. 1552, '*Bugs*' = bugbears—the use of this word in a
well-known Psalm has given a distinctive name to the
old English Bible in which it occurs : l. 1609, '*contempling*' = contemplating : l. 1615, '*brim*'—see Glossarial Index, *s.v.* : l. 1633, '*Tern*' = turn, term or reign ;
l. 1637, 'Daniel,' 'Hall,' 'Hayward'—see our Memorial-
Introduction, and Index of Names *s.n.*—G.

HEre (like LEANDER in the *Hellespont*)
    Tost in a Tempest in the darkest Night.
Distract with fears, divorced from the sight
Of my *High Pharus* which to guide mee wont :
Spying *Bôotes* in your HIGHNESSE Front,
For life I labour towards your hopefull Light
(May never Care beclowd that Beam so bright,
Come never Point of least *Eclipse* upon't) ;
Yet, though (alas !) your gracious Rayes have show'n
My wracked limbes a likely way to land :
Unlesse (by Others' Help, or by your Own)
The tender Pity of your Princely hand
        Quick hale mee out, I perish instantly,
        Hal'd in againe by *Six* that hang on *Mee.*

SIxe-times already, ready even to faint,
    With grievous Waight of guiltlesse Want opprest,
BARTAS and I have bow'd and vow'd our best
Before the *Altar* of our *Soveraign Saint :*
And yet, the Eare that heareth every Plaint,
The Heart that pities every poore Distrest :
Alone (alas !) seems deafe to my Request ;
And onely, is not mov'd with my Complaint.
Yet must I needs (NEED still importunes so)
Importune still, till some mild Soule relent :
But (under Heav'n no Help, no Hope, I know,
Save You alone my Ruine to prevent :
        You onely may, *Now* onely, if at all :
        Past Help, past Hope, If *Now* You faile, I fall.

Your Highnesse's
most humbly-devoted
and observant Servant,
JOSUAH SYLVESTER.

THE
SECOND SESSION
OF THE
PARLIAMENT
OF
VERTUES ROYALL,
(Continued by Prorogation)

FOR

BETTER PROPAGATION
of all true Pietie,

AND

Utter Extirpation

of

$\left\{\begin{array}{l}\text{ATHEISME, \& HYPOCRISIE;}\\ \text{AVARICE, \quad \& CRUELTIE;}\\ \text{PRIDE, \qquad \& LUXURIE;}\end{array}\right\}$

(From the Originall)
Tranſcribed,
AND
Inſcribed
To the High-Hopefull
CHARLES,
Prince of Great Britaine,
BY
JOSUAH SYLVESTER.

TO THE RIGHT HONOURABLE

Lords *Spirituall and Temporall;*

The Knights and Burgesses of the

Lower-*House;*

And to all generous and ingenious Readers.

YOur prest *Assistance*, and *Assistance* past,
  Vouchsafed, here, when you were *summon'd* last,
Binde and imbold mee once more to present
My humble *Briefs*, in form of PARLIAMENT ;
Hoping no lesse *Consent* of Your good-wills
In *Passing* These, then of Our former *Bils;*
So-much more *Need*-full in this *Weed*-full Time,
By How-much *Vice* doth over *Vertue* clime.

An *Act against* Atheisme *and* Irreligion.
An *Act of pious and humble* PATIENCE.
An *Act conformable to the former.*
An *Act confirming both.*
An *Act of humane* Frailty, *to teach the Best,* Humility.
An *Act of the* Weaker Vessell.
An *Act of* Imitation, *with better Application.*
An *Act* (*of many Branches*) *concerning the* Justice *of* GOD *in his* Judgements.
An *Act of* exhortation *to* Repentance *and* Humiliation.
An *Act against* Presumption *of our selves.*
An *Act touching* GOD'S Omnipotence, Omniscience, Al-regency, Al-sufficiency.
An *Act against* rash *and erroneous* Censures.
An *Act against* Partiality *in* Judgement, false Witnesse, Suborned *Evidence.*
An *Act, intimating the* Comfort *and* Confidence *of a good* Conscience.
An *Act averring the* shortness of Life, *and uncertaine Certainty of* Death.
An *Act against* Saducees *and* Epicures.
An *Act against* Puritanisme.
An *Act intimating the effects of an* evill Conscience.
An *Act against the* Security *and* Insolence *of fat and easefull* Epicures *and* Oppressors.
An *Act against* Hypocrites.
An *Act against* Bribery, Brokery, Usury.
An *Act against uncivill* Indiscretion *in visiting of* Friends, *Especially against* Aggravation of Griefs.
An *Act for our* Imitation.
An *Act against* Flattery.

An *Act of* Terror *to the* Wicked *in their sudden and fearfull* Fall, *Anno* 1615.
An *Act against* Ambition, *conformable to the former.*
An *Act against* Unkindnesse of *Kinsmen, Neighbours, Friend, Servants, Wives, &c.*
An *Act of lively* FAITH, *against all* Saducees, Epicures, Atheists.
An *Act of* Animadversion, *that wee stumble not at the Prosperity of the* Wicked.
An *Act for the* Last Assise, *and finall* Sentence & Execution *of the Ungodly.*
An *Act against* Merit *of* Works.
An *Act against* Works *of Supererogation.*
An *Act against the Children of* Darkness ; Murderers, Adulterers, Burglers, &c.
An *Act against all* greedy Wringers, Wrongers, Usurers, *and* Oppressors.
An *Act of* Meditation *on the manifold* Manifest Works of GOD, *mighty and marvelous.*
An *Act of* Invincible Faith *and* PATIENCE.
An *Act against* Tyrants, Extortioners, Rackers, *and All Unrighteous and Unrelenting* Rich.
An *Act, limiting Man's* Wit *and* Industry from *the illimitable* Wisdom, *and inimitable* Works of God.
An *Act against* loose *and* idle Education *of Youth.*
An *Act against* Wandring *and* Wanton Eyes.
An *Act against* Pride *and* Vanity *of all kindes.*
An *Act against* Cousenage, Concupiscence, Cruelty, Briberie.
An *Act against* Adulterie.
An *Act against impious and* imperious *Masters and Mistresses.*
An *Act against* dilatory *Almners, and solitary* Nabals.
An *Act against the* Uncharitie *of our Dayes, suffering so many Poor to dye without Doores.*
An *Act against all* Injury, Inhumanity, &c.
An *Act against* Avarice *and* Infidelity : Superstition *and* Idolatry, Sacriledge *and* Surcuidry.
An *Act against* insulting *over Miserie.*
An *Act against all manner of* Extortion *and* Cruelty.

An *Act touching the* right use *and happy* issue *of* Afflictions.

An *Act of the pronenesse of* Mercy *toward the* Penitent.

An *Act against* empty *and* idle FAITH.

An *Act* (*by implication*) *against the* Pope's *depriving
and depraving of* Princes.

An *Act containing a* Divine Lecture *of* Naturall Philosophy, *to the last Chapter : which is the* Last Act *of
This Holy* PARLIAMENT.

WHose severall *Acts*, of sweet and soverain *Use*
To cherish *Vertue*, and to check *Abuse*
(Too rough transcribed, by too rude a hand,
For so high *Statutes* of the HOLY-LAND)
Are here presented, as fit *Precedents*
Of sacred Rules for your High *Parliaments ;*
By (th' once least Moat in th' Upper-House's Sun).

Your Under-Clarke,

Unworthily Undon

(By over trusting to a starting *Bow-
Yer*-while too strong, to my poor Wrong and Woe)

JOSUAH SYLVESTER.

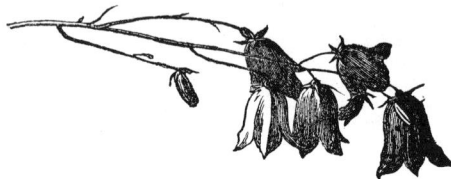

A

DIVINE AND TRUE

TRAGI-COMEDY;

IOB

TRIUMPHANT

IN

HIS TRIALL:

OR

THE HISTORIE

OF

HIS HEROICALL

Patience,

IN

A meafured

METAPHRASE.

*

*
To
AR-
THUR'S
CASTLE
(*call'd by*
ART'S CHAST LURE)
****

*
My
Hope
Heere
Hastneth,
For My
HEART'S LAST CURE.
****

Sir, You   A SWEET   A REAL   In My S^{t.}
have seen,   I D E A   A C T   o f   L E W I S
In my Pa-   O f——O u r   that—Ideal   Roy—All-
NARETUS,   hopes in You :   V I E V V E,   Vertuous.
Here (more HEROIK,   and more HOLY-True)
I bring Your Highness   (*Past all the Patterns*
Yet a Higher Peece   *of old Rome & Greece*)
Faith's PATIENT Champion, in His Triumph due.
Farre be His Crosses   *Neer be His Courses*
From my Prince, *I pray :*   (*As the most complete*
In sacred GRACES that beseem The GREAT)
Tow'rds God & Man ; in cleer or cloudy Day ;
So much more needfull   *By how much Satan*
In This Sin-full Age,   (*neer his end*) *doth rage :*
With Whom and His, the better Aye to wrastle,
Great *Michael* gard & strengthen ARTHUR'S CASTLE ;

Praies

Prostrate

JOSUAH SYLVESTER.

To   &
the   *Ho-*
Right   *norable*
Reverend   FATHER
G E O R G E   A B B O T,
Lord ARCH-Bishop
O F   C A N T E R B U R Y.
****

I N   Grate-full   H O N O R
Of your MANY *Giftes*
Of GRACE & NATURE
(*Apted to your Place*)
This DORIKE *Pillar*
My DEVOTION *liftes ;*
To shew Here——*After*
What Wee owe your Grace ;
Both,   for   your   Prudence,
And your Pious Zeale ;
Learning   *And*   Labour
In your Double Charge,
Swaying the CHURCH,
Staying the Common-Weale ;
Most STUDIOUS *Ever*
E I T H E R to Enlarge :
And   Last (not least) of all,
For CONSTANT *standing*
On Right's *weak Side,*
Against the Tide of wrong ;
When P H I L I S T I N E S,
And Daliladies *banding,*
With Armes or Charmes
Would binde or blinde the Strong :
In Honour of these Honours, this I bring
To Reverend ABBOT, & his Second ; KING.
VESTER—SYL—VESTER
Deditissimus.

TO THE RIGHT HONOURABLE,

the LORD ELESMORE, *L. High Chancelour of England,*

*THOMAS EGERTONUS: (*Anagramma*)

*NESTOR THEOMAGUS.

G*Rave;* *GOD-WISE NESTOR; *Never did a Name*
(*Save* A JUST MASTER) *better speak a man*
(*As Court and Councell, with Mee, witnesse can*)
Then doth Your Owne, in this Your Anagram.
Should I a Volume *of Your* Vertues *frame,*
Broad as my Brest, and Thicker then my Span;
Could I say More, more True, more Duely, than
The Character *concluded in* This *same?*
For, *Pious-Prudence *cannot but be* Just:
And Justice *cannot but be* Temperate:
And Temperance *from* Courage *issue must,*
So that your Name *doth your whole* Life *relate,*
So NESTOR-*like, for grace-full,* *Godly Sage,*
That Nothing wants, but (what wee wish) His Age.

Ex Animo exoptat
JOSUAH SYLVESTER.

TO THE RIGHT HONOURABLE,

WILLIAM HARBERT, *Earl of Pembroke,*

Lord Chamberlaine &c.

P*ATIENCE* prevailes (*when* Passions *are undon*)
This doth This Volume *truely intimate:*
So doth Your Vertue, *firm, and fortunate,*
Now cheer'd *with Radiance of our* Royall Sun.
O! long and Happy may Hee shine *upon*
So Noble *a Plant (mo Such to propagate)*
So Grace-*full,* Use-*full, both in* Court *and* State';
*Help-*full to all,* Hurt-*full at-all to None.*
Among Those Many *whom your* Worth *hath won*
(*Of either Sexe, of every Age, and State*)
With glad *Applauses to congratulate*
The Worthie Honour *of your* Charge *begun*
(*Though not, perhaps, so long and lowd, as* Many)
Accept my AVE, *as Devout as* Any.

Your Lordship's most obliged
JOSUAH SYLVESTER.

TO THE RIGHT HONOURABLE,

Sir EDWARD COKE, Knight; *Lord Chiefe Justice*

of England, and one of his Majestie's most Honourable

Privie Councell.

*EDWARDUS COCUS :

(*Anagramma*)

*SUCCEDO, ARDUUS.

*Ardy *and* Happy *may You long* Succeed,
 In all the Courses of your Christian Zeale,
 To scourge Abuse; and purge the Publike-Weale,
 Of vicious Humours, with auspicious Speed.
Hardy *and* Happy *Never more did need,*
 To meet with Malice, and with Might to deale;
 And sift the Drift the Serpent would conceale.
 How happy Heav'n You for these times decreed !
Hardy *and* Happy *may You still* proceed,
 Untill you finde, confound, and suffocate,
 The Viperous Vermin that destroy the State,
Hardy *and* Happy *be Your Minde and Meed*
 With GOD and Men : applauded and approv'd
 Of Prince and People ; of All Good, beloved :

—————————————————————————Ex Animo Exoptat

—————————————————————————JOSUAH SYLVESTER.

IOB TRIUMPHANT
IN HIS TRIALL.
The Proem.

A Solid Rocke, farre seated in the Sea
　(Where many Vessels have been cast away)
Though blackest Storms of blust'ring Winds do threat,
Though boysterous Rage of roaring Billowes beat ;
Though it be rak't with Lightning and with Thunder ;
Though All, at once assault, and Each asunder ;
With massie Bulk of it Selfs Marble Tower,
Still, still repels th' inevitable Stower ;
And seems still firmer, and more permanent,
The more the Tempest hath been violent : 10
Right so the Faithfull ; *in whose humble Brest*
Religious feare of GOD *is deep imprest :*
What-ever Stroak of Fortune *threat his State,*
What-ever Danger him discommodate,
What-ever Mischiefe that betide him shall,
What-ever Losse, what-ever Crosse befall :
Inflexible, invincible pursues
The sacred Footing he did ever use :
And ay more constant and confirm'd is Hee,
The more extreme his sad Afflictions be. 20
　If any Spirit inspir'd with holy-mood,
Carefully-Curious of the publike Good,
Would lively limne th' immortall Excellence
Of such a Patterne of such PATIENCE,
As neither Elements displaced quite,
Nor envious Starres, nor angry Foes' despight,
Nor all the Fiends' insatiate furie fell
(By fraud or force) could ever quail or quell :
'T were labour lost, to fable (Homer-like)
The strange long Voyage of a wily Greek ; 30
The Paines, the Perills, and extreme disease
That hee endured both by Land and Seas ;
Sith sacred Truth's *Heav'n-prompted Books present*
In Constant JOB *a worthier Argument.*
　Thou then, Urania, *to whom right belongs*
The sacred Consort of Celestiall *Songs,*
Tune Thou my Voice, Thou teach mee to record
Who did incite, what did invite the Lord,

With Miseries so rewfull and so rife,
So to disturbe his quiet happy life ; 40
What hainous Sin, what horrid high Offence,
Th' Almightie's vengeance mought so deep incense :
Or else what Cause, what Object else might stir-it.
Boiles there such wrath in an impassive Spirit ?

B *Ut, O Presumption ! Why have I begun*
　(Alas ! no Prophet, neither Prophet's *Sonne ?*
No Priest, *no* Levite ; *nay, no* Israelite
(Such as Nathaniell*) but a* Cananite
Full of corruption, foule of hand and heart)
To touch the ARK ? *to under-take* This *Part ?*
　Ah ! pardon Lord ; O ! purifie mee all
From all profanenesse ; from sin's bitter Gall :
And as yer-while it pleas'd thee to infuse
In mine un-schooled and unskilfull Muse
(By vertue of Thine All-sufficing Grace)
*Immediate pow'r du-*BARTAS *Track to trace :*
So as how-ever weak and Artlesse, I)
That Worke *findes* Welcome *with the gravest Eye :*
Now more good Lord, *my Wits and Words refine,*
To treat divinely Matters so Divine : 60
O ! sacred Spirit, now sanctifie my Stile
Let not my sensuall, thy pure Sense defile :
But tune mee right, to Eccho, *as belongs.*
Thy HUSSIAN'S *Sighs, and then thy* JESSEAN'S *Songs.*
And to that end, vouchsafe mee (at thy pleasure)
Lesse Need-full Life, in a lesse Care-full leasure.

CHAP. I.

N Eare where *Idumë's* dry and sandy Soil
　Spreads Palmfull Forrests, dwelt a man yer-while,
Of Life unblotted, and unspotted Fame ;
God-fearing, Just, Sin-flying JOB by Name. 70
　With due respect to Heav'n's and Nature's Law
In Wedlock's sweet Yoke did hee seemly draw :
Whence, by that Bounty, whose all blessings be,
Seaven Sons hee had, and lovely Daughters Three.

Great was his Substance : for, of fleecy Sheep
Upon the Downs seven Thousand did hee keep ;
Five hundred yoke of Oxen did hee owe ;
Five hundred Ass-shees, Camels six times so :
Great Train within doores, & great Train without,
Made him esteem'd through all the East about.   80

His Sons, by turns, their Sisters did invite
And feast each other, in a daily Rite :
JOB blest them every Even ; and every Morn
When first *Aurora's* rosie beames return,
The good Old-man, to GOD in humble-wise,
For each of them did offer sacrifice :
Lest they might have *mis-don, mis-said, mis-thought,*
Or (in their Feast) offended GOD by ought.

While hapy JOB thus brought the year about,
It came to pass one day when all the Rout   90
Of Light-full *Angels* did themselves present
Before the foot-stoole of th' *Omnipotent,*
There also came the Executioner,
Th' ambitious Prince, Malicious *Lucifer :*
With whom the Lord expostulating, thus
Said ; *Sathan,* say, Whence comest thou to Us?
I come, said Hee, from walking in and out,
And compassing the Earthly Ball about.
Hast thou not then survei'd my Servant JOB
(Reply'd the Lord) whose like in all the Globe   100
There is not found ; so full of loving-feare,
So faithfull, fruitfull, rightfull, and sincere ?

Is it for nothing, said the subtle Foe,
That JOB adores, and loves and fears Thee so ?
Hast thou not hedg'd him safe on every side ?
Hast thou not heapt him blessings far and wide ?
But, for a while with-hold thy Favour's stream,
With-draw thy hand, & hide thy bounteous beam,
Then shalt thou see (or double my disgrace)
Hee will anon blaspheme thee to thy Face.   110

Lo, said th' *Eternall,* from this instant how'r
All that hee hath is in thy hand and pow'r ;
All, but Himselfe, Himselfe I sole exempt.
Satan eft soons assumes his bold Attempt.

As all his Children were together met,
Their elder Brother's hearty Cheer to eat,
Came one to JOB running and breathlesse nigh,
Scarce could hee speake, yet weakly thus did
     cry,
Ah ! woe is mee to be the Messenger
Of so sad news as now I bring you, Sir,   120
As all your Oxen under painfull yoke,
Their pointed Journeys in your Fallowes broke ;
And as your Asses in the Meads did feed,
Sabéan Theeves came forth with furious speed
And tooke them all, and all your Servants slew,
I onely scap't, to come and tell it you.

While Hee yet spake, there came Another in,
Hared and hot, and thus did Hee begin :
Sir, From the heav'ns a sudden Fire did fall
Among your Sheep, and hath consum'd them all,   130
And slaine your Servants yer they could eschew ;
I onely scap't to come and tell it you.

While Hee yet spake, Another came, amaz'd
And sadly said ; Sir, while your Camels graz'd
In your own Pastures up and down the lands,
The proud *Chaldéans* in three armed Bands,
Surpriz'd them all, and all your Servants slew ;
I onely scap't to come and tell it you.

While Hee yet spake, Another came and cry'd
In piteous Fright (as if himselfe beside)   140
O, Sir ! your Sons and Daughters (all the rest)
Were met to day at my young Master's Feast,
Where, from beyond the Wildernesse anon
A sudden Whirle-wind rose and rusht upon
The corners of the house, and shooke it so
That instantly it fell from Top to Toe,
And with the fall them altogether slew ;
I onely scap't to come and tell it you.

Then starting up, JOB 'gan his clothes to rent,
Shaves his hoare haire, his head with Ashes sprent ;   150
As in a swoune falls to the ground with grones,
And sadly sighing, Thus himselfe bemones :
Ah ! Naked came I from my Mother's wombe,
Naked shall I returne unto my Tombe :
The Lord hath taken what himselfe hath giv'n :
Blessed be God, th' Almighty Lord of heav'n.
Yet did not JOB, for all that him mis-fell,
Murmur at God, nor inly sink or swell ;
Nor sin against th' eternall Providence,
But suffred all with humble *Patience.*   160

CHAP. 2.

ANother day, when all the sacred Bands
       Came all attending their high King's commands,
Came also Hee, whose Envie (since he fell
From heav'n) hath striv'n to hale down man to hell ;
With whom the Lord expostulateth thus :
Now *Satan,* say, Whence comest Thou to Us?
I come said hee from walking in and out,
And compassing the Earthly Ball about.
Then, hast thou found, replyes th' *Omnipotent,*
In all thy circuit, man more confident,   170
Or minde more constant, or more faithfull Soule,
Then JOB my servant : whom thine Envie foule,
Late urg'd my Leave by sharp assaults to try ?
How hast thou sped ? what hast thou got thereby ?

Alas, said hee, I reft him but the things
That fly from men with transitory wings ;
And therefore hee regards his losse the lesse :
But would thy pow'r him som-what neerer presse,
Would'st thou permit mee touch him to the quick,
I yeeld mee conquer'd if hee do not kick ;   180
If more hee serve, trust, pray, or praise thy Grace,
If hee, in fine, blaspheme not to thy Face.
Pinch but his body, and then *skin for skin,*
Hee'l winch without, and sudden flinch within.

Go Fiend, said God ; sith th' art so obstinate,
Fall on my JOB, him felly crutiate :
Touch not his Soule ; his Body onely touch.

Hence *Satan* hyes, glad that hee might so much.

Without delay then, with the most despight,
Hee sets on JOB ; and in most piteous Plight,   190
With ulcerous anguish fils his body so
That crusted all in Scabs from top to toe,
Amid the Ashes, sad and desolate :
Scraping his Sores with shels (or sherds) hee sate ;
Yet constant still, still calmely *Patient*,
Without a word of grudging Discontent.
  Then said his Wife, What helps Integrity ?
What boots it, Man ? Alas ! curse God and dye.
Goe, foolish Woman, the good man reply'd,
Thy rebell heart doth thy rash tongue mis-guide :   200
Shall wee, from God, of Good receive our Fill ;
And, at his pleasure, not partake of Ill ?
So JOB as yet, for all that him mis-fell,
Displeas'd not God, but bore it wondrous well.
  By this, the light-foot, feather-tongued Dame
Had far and wide spred and disperst the fame
Of JOB'S Mis-fortunes (from the first begun)
That Hee was halfe dead, and was whole undone.
  His Friends then, *Eliphas* the *Themanite*,
Bildad the *Shuite*, the *Naamathite*   210
Zophar (as others) hearing this report,
As soon as might be towards him resort ;
Resolv'd with Comforts, to relieve in part
Their Friend's Affliction, and asswage his smart.
  But, there arrived, at the very sight
Of his so wofull and so wretched Plight,
They all amaz'd, their Garments sadly tore,
Their heads with ashes all besprinkled o'r ;
And for seav'n daies and nights in sorrows drown'd,
Lay grieving, by him, groveling on the ground,   220
Without word speaking, lest untimely trouble
Amid his anguish should his Dolours double.

CHAP. 3.

I OB therefore straining his obstructed voice,
    Began Thus, sadly with a shivering noise :
O ! Woe be to the Day when I was born :
O ! be it ever of the Light forlorn :
O ! may it ever under Darknesse lye,
And never Sun vouchsafe it cheerful eye ;
Nor God regard it : let a deadly Shade
O'r-cloud it ay, as ever Dismall made.   230
  O ! woe be also to the Night Wherein
My Mother my Conception did begin :
Lightning and Thunder thrill it evermore,
Whirle-wind and Tempest may it ever roare :
Of Fogs, of Frosts, of Show'rs, of Snows, of Hail,
Of Mists, of Mil-dews may it never fail :
May it no more in *Calender* be plac't ;
But, from the Roll of Months and Years be rac't :
May th' Evening Stars be dark : No light returning :
May it no more see th' Eye-lids of the Morning,   240
Because it clos'd not, at my wretched Birth,
The fruitfull Dore that brought me weeping forth,
But let me passe unto this wofull Light,
To undergoe so miserable Plight.

O ! Why, when shapelesse in my Mother's Womb
I lay as dead, Why did not Death strike home ?
Why not (alas !) amid the bearing Throes,
When I began to feel Man's feeble woes ?
Why did the knees support mee ? Why the breast
Supply mee suck ? why was I swath'd and drest ?   250
Sith else (alas !) I had now lien at ease,
Had been at rest, had slept in quietnesse,
Among the high and mighty Potentates,
Kings, Counsellors, great Lords, and Magistrates,
Who in the World to leave their Names renown,
Have built them bowers wch others shall pul-down :
And those rich Princes that have heapt of-old
Their houses full of Silver and of Gold.
Or, Why (alas ! as an abortive Birth),
Was I not hid and buried in the Earth ?   260
There, Tyrants cease from their imperious Pride :
There, Vertuous Workers at their rest abide :
There, Pris'ners rest from their Oppressors' Braul :
There, Slaves are free from their fell Masters' Thrall :
There, High and Low (without Disdain, or Dread)
Rest all together in one Common bed.
  O ! wished Death (more to be wisht then Life)
Thou break'st the Force of Envie's Ingînes rife :
Thou cuttest-off our travail's tediousnesse :
Thou kilst our cares, Thou calm'st our most distress.   270
O ! to the wretched why is Light imparted ?
Why Life (alas !) unto the heavie-hearted ?
(Who longs for Death : and if it linger long,
Would fainer seek it then even Gold (among)
And gladder finde it (as of Joyes the Chiefe)
Within their grave to burie all their Griefe)
Especially, to Him whose Way is hid :
Whom God hath shut-up, stopt and streightened ?
Sith, yer I eate, My Sighs resell my Food,
My Roarings gush out like a raging Flood.   280
  For (though my Plenty never made mee proud ;
My Power imperious ; nor to pleasure bow'd :)
What most I doubted I endure, (alas !)
And what I feared is even come to passe.
For Care and Feare, I had no rest before ;
Yet Trouble 's come and trebbles more and more.

CHAP. 4.

I OB ceasing so ; began the *Themanite*,
    Inly perplex't, an Answer thus to dight :
If wee presume to comfort thee, dear Friend,
Will our Discourse (I fear it will) offend ?   290
Will thy Disease our kinde Good-wills disdain ?
But in this Case (alas !) Who can refrain ?
Who so hard-hearted, so uncivill-bred,
That can unmoved see thee thus bested ?
To see and heare Thee in this deep Distresse,
Who can keep silence ? Who can hold his peace ?
  Why ? Thou wert wont, in thy Prosperities,
To stay weak hands, and strengthen feeble knees ;
To counsell those that in their Course had stray'd,
To comfort those whom Crosses overlay'd :   300

Now that Mis-hap on thine own head hath hit,
Now that the Storm hath thine own vessell smit,
Now that the Case is thine, how art thou sunk
From thine own Succour! from thy self how shrunk!
　Where is, alas! where is Thy confidence,
Thy Constancy, thy Hope, thy *Patience*,
Thy Pietie, thy Faith, thy Fear of God,
And th' upright Path which thou hast ever trod?
　O! ponder this: who ever Innocent
Hath perished? Hath the Omnipotent　　　　　310
Eternall Justice ever plagu'd the Just;
Destroy'd the Righteous who him onely trust:
As I have seen Those that have plough'd and sow'n
Iniquity, reap suddenly their own;
When with the blast of God they blasted fall,
And with his breath are quick consumed all?
God, in his Fury starveth in distresse
The roaring Lion and the Lionesse;
Their rav'ning Whelps are scattered far away,
Their Teeth are broken, and they pine for Prey.　320
　I'll tell thee more: Once in a certain night,
Silent, I heard a Voyce, and saw a Sight.
(About the time when Sleep begins to seaze
Our drowzie Lids, our daily Loads to ease)
Amaz'd with feare my hair began to heave,
My heart to tremble, every part to leave
His proper Part; when to mine eyes a-space
Appear'd the Image of an unknown Face:
One stood before mee, whence (yet more dismaid)
I heard a *Voice*, and thus (mee thought) it said:　330
　Shall Man be juster then his God (said Hee)?
The Creature purer then his Maker be,
Behold, hee found not in his Angels bright
Firm Fëalty, but Folly in his sight;
How much more, then, in Those whose habitation
Is but of Clay, but Dust their best foundation?
Whose brittle Vessels here so little last,
That yer they know them they are often past:
Whose fickle Garment (how-so-ever loath)
Shall be destroy'd and done, before the Moath:　340
Whose doubtfull Dayes, yer they begin, be gone;
Cut down by death, when least they think thereon:
Whose Dignities (how-ever grac't, or great)
Shall die with them, and them the Worms shall eat.

CHAP. 5.

N Ow call thou loud, if any will reply:
　　Among the Saints where wilt thou turn thine eye?
Two sorts of Fooles (th' Idiot and Envious) die;
Of anger th' one, th' other of Jealousie.
I have beheld the Fool fair rooted yerst:
Yet have I soon his Habitation curst;　　　　350
Because his Children succour-lesse shall suffer
By *Justice*-Doom, and none shall Pitie offer:
Himselfe withall confounded void of Hope,
To gather-in his long expected Crop,
Which th' hunger-starved from the Thorns shall snatch;
The Thirstie shall his substance all dispatch;

A Misery, which God doth oft permit:
For, th' Earth it selfe is not the Cause of it;
Sith, were not Sin it should not barren be,
But, Man, for Sin, must toile him servily,　　　360
In Sweatfull Labour; born for labour's end
As properly as Sparkles to ascend.
　But were My Case, as Thine; in this Distresse,
Rather to God would I my selfe addresse:
Him would I seek, of Him would I enquire,
Whose works are great, whose wonders all admire;
Unspiable, Unspeakable by Man;
Immutable, Inscrutable to scan:
Who on the Earth the rain at pleasure pow'rs,
And in the Streets distils the liquid Show'rs:　　370
Who lifts the lowly up, brings down the lofty;
And rears sad Mourners unto Health and Safety:
Who dissipates the craftiest Policies;
And dis-appoints the Counsels of the wise:
Who takes the wariest in their proper wiles;
And wicked ones in their own guile beguiles;
So that they meet with darknesse in the day,
And, as at Midnight, grope at Noon their way:
But, Hee preserves the poor, from sword & tongue,
And cruell hands of Tyrants, prone to wrong:　　380
So that the Poor shall have their blessed Hope;
But wicked ones their cursed mouths shall stop.
　Lo, then, how happy hee whom God correcteth!
Repine not therefore that hee Thee afflicteth.
Hee wounds, and heals; hee strikes and hee restores:
Hee sendeth Plagues, and Plaisters for the Sores:
Hee in six troubles shall deliver thee;
And in the seaventh, thou shalt be danger-free.
Hee will preserve thee from fell Famine's rage;
And from the Sword of War thee dis-ingage:　　390
Thou shalt be safe from scourging tongs of momes,
Nor shalt thou fear Destruction when it comes:
Nay, thou shalt laugh at it, and Dearth deride;
Not dreading Beasts of fellest Pawes and Pride.
Stones, thorns, and thistles shall be friends with thee:
With thee the Beasts in constant league shall be.
And, as without, thou shalt have Peace within
Thy house; thou shalt behold it, and not sin.
Thou shalt perceive thy Seed's seed's seed to spread
As Grass in Fields, and Flowers in every Mead.　400
In a full Age to thine owne Grave shalt thou,
As, in due Time, Corne to the Barn or Mow.
Lo, this is Truth; and thus wee daily try-it:
Consider it, and to thy Selfe apply-it.

CHAP. 6.

J OB then reply'd: O! were my Sorrows waigh'd,
　　And with my Suffrings in just Balance lai'd,
They would exceed the Sea's wet Sands in poize:
Therefore (alas!) they swallow up my voice:
For the Arrows of th' Almighty, keen and quick,
Have thrilled mee, and still within me stick;　　410
Their Anguish makes my spirits faint and quail me.
Alas! the Terrors of the LORD assail mee.

Braies the Wilde Asse if hee have grass his fill?
Or lowes the Oxe if hee have fodder still?
Unsavory things who without Salt can eat?
In white of Eggs is there a taste of meat?
Yet am I fain, alas! and forc't (indeed)
Of what my soule abhorred most to feed.

O! that the LORD would daign mee my desire,
Grant mee my Longing, grant what I require : 420
Which is but This ; that Hee would end my dayes,
Let goe his hand, and let mee goe my wayes.
So should I yet have Comfort (though I burn
In bitter pangs of Death, I will not spurn,
Let him not spare mee) for yet doe not I
The holy Word of th' *Holy-One* denie.
But O! What Power have I to persist?
What may ensue, if I shall long subsist?
Am I as hard, as tough, as strong (alas!)
As strongest Stones? or is my flesh of Brass? 430
Nay, am I not already Impotent,
My spirits consumed, and my strength all spent?

In crosses, comforts should friends most afford :
But men (alas!) have left to fear the LORD.
My Brethren have deceiv'd mee as a Brook.
As rising Flouds, they have mee soon forsook ;
Which, foule and deep, in Winter all ore-flow,
Or, crusted thick with yce, no moisture show ;
Or else, in Summer, by *Sol's* thirsty ray
Are licked-up, and quickly dry'd away, 440
While Travellers to *Thæm'*, and *Saba* thought
To water there, and for their supper sought ;
But failing quite, and frustrate of the same,
They are confounded, and they blush for shame :
Even such are you, you see mee ill appay'd
In dismall plight, and you are all dismai'd :
Why are you so? when have I bid you bring,
Or out of yours, supply mee any thing?
Or crav'd of you auxiliarie bands
To rescue mee from foes, or tyrants' hands? 450
Shew mee mine Errour, where I have gone wrong :
Tell mee my Fault, an I will hold my tongue.
But, bold and free 's the speech of Innocence :
Which of you can reprove ; and what Offence?
Think you advantage of my words to have,
As if Affliction made mee wildely rave ;
Then on the Orphan doth your furie fall ;
You dig a Pit to catch your Friend withall.

Therefore, vouchsafe mee better to revise ;
Wrong mee no more : My words be neither lyes, 460
Neither my deeds (as you shall finde, I trust,
If you returne) in that behalfe unjust.
Complain I causeless? Doe I counterfait?
Is not my mouth with anguish all repleat?

CHAP. 7.

Hath not Man's warfare his set limits here,
  As hath the Hireling (by the day, or year)?
As toyled Servants for the Night attend ;
And weary Taskers for their Labour's end ;

So have I looked, but (alas!) in vain,
For end of Sorrows, and for ease of Pain. 470
Perpetually my fruitless Months proceed ;
My tedious Nights incessantly succeed :
No sooner laid down but I long to rise,
Tired with tossing, till the Morning spies.
My Flesh is clad with Worms, with excrement
Of lothsom dust, my Skin doth rot and rent :
My Dayes flit faster then the Shuttles slide
From Weavers' hands, whipping from side to side.

Consider, Lord, my Life is but a Blast :
Mine eye no more shall see the Goodnesse past : 480
Who now beholds mee, shall no more, anon :
If thou look-on Mee, I eft-soons am gone.
As clouds doe passe, and quite away doe flit,
Whoso descends ascends not from the Pit ;
Neither returns unto his wonted own ;
Nor of his place is any more be-known.

Therefore (alas!) I will not spare to speak :
I cannot hold, needs must I silence break,
Amid the anguish of my Spirit's distresse,
And in the depth of my Soule's bitternesse. 490
Am I a Sea? or Whale? that with a Guard
Thou girtest mee, and keep'st me in so hard?
If I have said, In Silence of the Night
(When drousie humour siels-up every Sight :
When all, above, in, under Air, Earth, Seas ;
In quiet Slumber seem to take their Ease)
It may be that my painfull Pangs shall cease :
It may be that my Passions shall have peace :
With fearfull Visions then thou dost affray mee,
With Dreams and Fansies dreadfully dismay mee : 500
So that my Soule had rather chuse (at once)
To die, then live in Durance of my Bones.
Wearie of life, live alwayes shall I not ,
Then leave mee, Lord, alas! my dayes are nought.

O! what is Man that thou extoll'st him so?
That Thou on Him dost even thy heart bestow?
That every Morning Him thou visitest?
And every Moment Him examinest ;
How is it that Thou leav'st mee not a little?
Alas! nor lett'st mee swallow-in my spettle? 510
O! Thou Preserver of Mankind, I know,
And I acknowledge I have sinn'd, but, O!
What shall I say? what shall I doe to Thee?
Why in thy wrath dost thou incounter Mee?
Why mak'st Thou mee (alas!) the mark and white
To thy Displeasure, in my Self's despight?
Remit, O Lord, what I have ill omitted :
Remove (alas!) what I have mis-committed.
For, now I goe down to the dust, to lie :
And, if Thou seek, to morrow, none am I. 520

CHAP. 8.

But *Bildad* then (loth longer to refrain)
  Said ; JOB, How long wilt thou this Plea maintain
With words, as high as Tempest's vehemence
Blow'n by the breath of thine Impatience?

Dar'st thou averre, that God doth Right subvert?
Or that th' Almighty Judgement doth pervert?
　　Though, Sith thy Sons had sinned them hee sent
To the due Place of their sinne's Punishment ;
Yet, If thou early unto God repair,
And to th' Almighty make thine humble Prayer,　530
If Thou be pure, and in his sight sincere ;
Hee will again awake to Thee : and rear
Thy ruin'd State ; thy righteous House restore
With Peace and Plenty, manifoldly more.
　　Ask of the Ages past : inquire (I pray)
Of th' Ancient Fathers (for, of yesterday
Wee Novices know nothing in effect ;
Our dayes are but a Shadow in respect)
Will not they teach thee (without wiles of Art)
And truly speak the language of their heart?　540
　　Can Rushes spring? are Sedges seen to grow,
Where is no moisture ; where no waters flow?
Say that they should : yet would they sooner wither,
Though never cut, then all else grass together.
Such is the way of all that God forget :
So failes the Hope of th' Holy-Counterfait :
His Hope shall be cut off : his Confidence
Like busie Spider's brittle Residence :
Hee shall be leaning on his House, but it
Shall not be able to support him : yet　　550
Hee shall hold fast, and thereon fix him sure ;
But that (alas !) shall never long endure :
As doth the Tree, which growing in the Sun,
O'r-spreds an Orchard with fresh Boughes, anon,
His happy Roots among the Fountains winding,
And round about the rockie banks them binding :
If from his Place to pluck it any ween,
It will deny ; as safe as if not seen :
Lo, by this means it will rejoyce, the while
That it may prosper in another Soile :　　560
So, God will never the Sincere reject,
Neither the wicked by the hand erect.
Till hee have fill'd thy mouth with merriment,
Thy lips with triumph (in intire content)
Thy Foes shall all be with confusion clothed,
Wrapped in shame, disperst, despis'd and loathed ;
Th' ungodly shall be razed to the ground,
Their Tabernacle shall no more be found.

CHAP. 9.

JOB then reply'd : I know, I grant you this ;
　　In God's respect, that no Man righteous is.　570
No : if Hee argue, if Hee question ;
O ! Who can answer of a Thousand one?
What heart so constant ! O ! what soule so cleer,
That dares for Just before that Judge appear?
Hee is All-prudent, and All-powerfull too :
Who thrives, that strives with what hee minds to doe?
Hee mounts the Vallies, & he vails the Mountains :
Hee shakes the Earth, hee opes and stops the Foun-
　　tains :
Hee bids the Sun shine, and forbids it soon :
Hee seals the Stars up ; hee conceals the Moon　580

Hee spreads alone the Heav'n's large Canapey :
Hee treads upon the bound-less ground-less Sea :
Hee makes *Arcturus* Star, the *Stormy youth,
The *Pleiades*, and *Climats* of the *South :*　　* Orion.
Hee worketh mighty things and manifold,
Miraculous and more than can be told :
Hee passeth by mee, and repasseth so,
Unseen of mee, and unperceived tho :
Hee, when him pleaseth, if a Prey hee take,
Who can compell him to restore it back?　　590
Nay : who so bold into his acts to pry?
Or, who dares question what hee doth, or why :
His anger is not stopt, nor stoopt a whit ;
But strongest helps are fain to stoop to it.
Then, how-much-lesse ; O ! how-much-lesse am I
Able (alas !) with Him my Case to try?
No, were I just, I were not absolute ;
But, to my Judge would I make humble Sute :
And, to my cry if hee reply, yet hard
Can I beleeve that hee my voyce hath heard.　　600
For, with a Tempest hee destroyes mee stern ;
And wounds mee Causeless (for ought I descern) ;
Nor suffers mee so much as breathe at all ;
But fils mee still with Bitterness and Gall.
　　If Strength wee speak of ; Who is strong but
　　　He?
If Judgement ; then, who shall mine Umpire be?
If I would justifie my Selfe (with him)
Hee by mine own mouth will mee soon condemn :
If I would plead mee perfect and upright,
Hee, Hee would judge mee wicked, in his sight,　610
Though I were perfect (to my Selfe) from Sin ;
Alas ! I know not mine own Soule within.
Therefore (thus vexed and perplexed rife)
I loath alas ! and I abhor my life.
　　Yet, grant I not, but that the Lord doth smite
(Which you deny) both wicked and upright ;
Else, when Hee strikes a People (old and young)
Would he seem smile at good men's stripes among?
Would Hee bestow upon th' ungodly most
Earth's Soveraintie, and let them rule the Rost ;　620
Would Hee permit prophane Bribe-blinded ones
With blunted Sword to sit on *Justice* Thrones ;
While that the Vertuous to the wall are thurst?
While th' Innocent are troden in the Dust?
For, who, but Hee, directs, acts, orders all
In all the world, whatever doth befall?
　　My Daies far swifter than a Poste have past ;
Past without sight of any Good (to-last) ;
As swiftest Ships, so have they slid-away ;
Or as the Eagle hasting to her prey.　　630
If that I say, I will forget my Greife,
Forgoe my wrath and yet re-hope Reliefe :
Ah ! then my Torments all afresh affright,
With terrours, lest Thou wilt not quit mee quight.
For, if I be Ungodly, all in vain
I cry to Thee, and to no end I plain :
Or, if Unguilty, clean, and white as Snow
(In mine own sight) in Thine I am not so ;

But in the sight of Thy pure Eyes, as soil'd,
And with the Garment that I weare defil'd.   640
    GOD is not Man, as I (in equall Sute)
That I with Him should argue or dispute :
Nor is there (should wee meet) a Moderator,
Twixt Him and Mee to arbitrate the matter.
Let Him leave-off his hold, take-off his rod,
Lay-off his awfull Majestie, as GOD ;
Then will I speak, and freely, void of Fear :
But, as it is, I must, I will forbear.

CHAP. 10.

A S dead alive, upon my Selfe I'll lay
    My sad Complaint ; and in mine anguish pray 650
Thus to the Lord : O Lord, condemne mee not :
But show mee, why thou huntest mee so hot.
Lord ! art thou pleased to oppresse mee thus ?
O ! dost thou judge as do th' Unrighteous
(Unheard, untry'd, and unsuspect) to trip
And cast-away thine own hand's Workmanship ?
See'st Thou, as Man ? or hast Thou carnall Eyes ?
Years as Man's years ? daies as Man's daies, who dies ;
That thus thou rack'st Mee, and protract'st Me still,
Searching and sifting to finde out mine Ill ?   660
I cannot sin, Thou know'st, but thou must see :
For, from thine hands can None deliver Mee.
    Thy hands have made Mee, all, and every part :
And wilt thou now thine own hand's work subvert ?
Remember, Lord, how frail and brittle stuff
Thou mad'st mee of (then use mee not so rough)
Even of the Clay, as is the Potter's Crust :
And wilt thou then re-crush mee into Dust ?
    Thou pour'dst me out as milk (within the womb)
Thou mad'st mee there, as Cheese, a Crud becom ; 670
With Skin and Flesh Thou cloth'dst mee fair & fit,
With Bones and Sinewes fast together knit ;
Inspir'dst mee Life and Soule, Reason and Sense ;
And still preserv'dst mee by thy Providence.
These Things as hidden in thy Bosome be :
But well I know, that it is so with Thee.
    If I have sinned, Thou wilt sift mee neer ;
And of my Guilt Thou wilt not hold mee cleer.
If wicked I have been ; then woe to mee :
If righteous ; yet still will I humble be ;   680
Though deep confounded and amazed much,
To see, and feel, my sad Affliction Such.
    But, be it more : come, Lion-like set on-mee :
Returne and show Thee marvelous upon mee ;
And so (indeed) Thou dost : for, Thou renew'st
Thy plagues on mee : and me more fierce pursew'st :
Changes of woes, Armies of pains extreme,
Afresh invade mee, and mee round behem.
    Then, why, (alas !) why didst thou bring me forth
From fruitfull Womb (being no better worth) ?   690
O ! that I there had perished unseen :
And that I were as if I had not been,
Brought from the womb (one tomb, unto another)
To Earth my Mother, from my Earthly Mother.

Is not my Glass neer out ? My Date neer done ?
O ! let him cease, and leave-off laying-on :
That I may take a little Comfort's breath,
Yer quite I goe to the dark land of Death,
A Land of Darknesse, Darknesse Selfe (I say)
And Shade of Death : where is no Light, no Day. 700

CHAP. 11.

T Hen answered *Zophar, the Naamathite ;*
    Should words prevail ? Shall prating passe for
        right ?
Should all be mute ? Shall no man dare reply,
To mock thy Mocks, and give thy Lie the Lie ?
For, Thou hast said (and that too-vehement)
My words, and deeds, and thoughts, are innocent ;
Pure in thine eyes.   But ! O that GOD would speak ;
That Hee would once His sacred silence break,
To shew thee Wisdom's secrets : Thou might'st see,
Thou merit's double what hee'layes on Thee ;   710
And surely know that (in his *Justice* strict)
After thy Sins, Hee doth not Sores inflict :
But seems to have forgotten, or forgiven
Thy Trespasses against himselfe and Heav'n.
    Canst Thou, by searching, GOD's deep counsell find ?
Conceive th' Almighty ? Comprehend His mind ?
Reach His perfection ? It doth Heav'n excell
In Height ; in Depth exceeds the lowest Hell :
Longer then Earth : larger then all the Seas.   719
O ! what ? when ? where ? How wilt thou measure these?
    If Hee cut-off, shut-up, collect, reject ;
Who can divert Him ? Who his Course correct ?
He knows vain men : he sees their harts yᵗ hard them
In Guiles and Wiles, and will not hee regard them ?
That foolish man, made wise, may be reclaimed ;
Born brute and dull, as an Asse Colt untamed.
    If therefore, by Repentance thou prepare
Thine humbled heart : if that, in hearty Prayer,
Thou stretch thine hands unto his Throne above :
Though thou hast sinn'd, if thou thy sin remove :   730
If thou remove it, and permit no more
Iniquity to dwell within thy Doore :
Then shalt thou, doubtlesse, free from fault & fear,
Settled and safe, thy Face again uprear :
Then shalt thou sure forget thy misery :
Or, but esteem it as a Stream past by :
Then all thy Dayes be then the Noon more bright ;
And thou shalt shine, as Morning after Night :
Then shalt thou rest secure and confident,
Hopefull and Happy, in thy proper Tent   740
In thine own Dwelling : where, for Eminence,
Sutors shall flock, with seemly Reverence.
    But, as for stubborne, wilfull Wicked-ones,
That still run-on in their Rebellions,
Their helps shall fail, and all their Hap shall fall ;
And as a Gasp, their Hopes shall vanish all.

CHAP. 12.

T Hen said the *Hussian :* You, undoubtedly,
    You are the Men : Wisdom with you must dy :

Yet, (would yee knew it) somwhat know I, too ;
I understand perhaps as well as you.   750
Nor will I yeeld you in this Jarre a jot :
What you have urg'd I know : and who doth not ?
  Yee say, I lie ; yee tell mee that I mock :
But I am made my Fellows' Laughing-stock :
Who calls on GOD, and whom Hee heareth prest,
Th' Upright and Just is (indeed) made a Jest :
And Hee that's going down (in state forlorn)
Like dying Lamp, is to the Rich a Scorn ;
While (for the most) Oppressors prosper, sure ;
And God-provokers, safely and secure,   760
Have in their hand (GOD in their hand hath put)
The Horn of Plenty, them at will to glut.
  Ask but the Beasts ; inquire of Earth, or Seas ;
Or Fowls, or Fish : for, which is it of These,
But knows, and shows, and plainly tells thee this ;
That GOD's their Maker : and of all that is :
That in his hand's the Life of all that lives :
That Hee alone, to all Men, breathing gives.
  Doth not the Eare try speeches (bad or good) ?
And, for it Selfe, the Palate taste the food :   770
So, Wisdome should be to the many-year'd ;
And Understanding to the hoary-hair'd.
  With him it is (with th' *Antientest of Dayes*)
With him is Counsell, Wisdom, Pow'r and Praise :
Lo, Hee destroyes, and no man can restore :
Whom Hee shuts-up, can be let out no more :
Hee stops the Streams ; then dry they up and shrink ;
Hee sends them forth ; then all the Earth they sink.
  With Him is Strength : with Him is all that is :
Who erreth, and who maketh erre, are His :   780
Hee doth distract the Counsellors of State ;
Hee makes the Judges as infatuate :
Hee breaks the Bonds of Kings' Imperiall aw ;
And brings them bounden under Others' Law :
Hee leads the Princes as a Captive prey :
Dismounts the Mightie ; and, with strange dismay,
Hee duls the Learned, dumbs the Eloquent,
And reaves the Judgement of the Ancient :
Hee powres contempt upon the Noble-born ;
Hee strips the Strong, Hee leaves the Stout forlorn :790
Hee deepest Secrets soon discovereth :
Hee brings to light the darkest shades of Death :
Hee multiplieth People ; and Hee mowes
Them down again (by Famin, Plague, or Blowes) :
Hee sends them forth in *Colonies* to spread ;
And brings them back (by wracke, lacke, sacke, or
        dread) :
Hee reaves the hearts of those that rule the Earth,
And maks them roam throw desart sands of dearth,
Where none goe by ; They grope as in the dark ;
They have no Light, no Sight ; no certaine Mark ; 800
They stray ; they stumble ; to and fro they wheele :
And Hee, Hee makes Them, Drunkard-like, to reel.

CHAP. 13.

ALL this my eyes have seen, my ears have heard :
   Al this my heart hath waigh'd & wel conferr'd.

So that, in This what you have known I knew ;
And am not herein to give place to You.
  But, as You wish, I also wish : O ! would
Th' Almighty pleas'd that I might be so bold
(In his own Presence, at his Bar to stand)
To plead with him the Cause I have in hand !   810
For, You, indeed, are too Sophisticall :
Silly Physicians, for my Sicknesse, all.
O ! that you therefore had still held you mute :
So might you still have held a wise Repute.
But, list you now unto my Arguing :
Mark well my Reasons, and the Proofes I bring.
  Will You speak falsly for th' Almighty Lord ?
Will you for Him pronounce a Guilefull word ?
Will you be partiall for His person's sake ?
Will you for Him, with Cavils under-take ?   820
Shall it avail you ? will Hee con you thank
At his great *Audit*, for this double Prank ?
(Or, ween you, smoothing, these Deceits to smother ?
Or, but to mock Him, as one Man another ?)
  No : you shall know, Hee will not brook nor bear it,
But chide you sharp ; how-ever secret were it.
Shall not the brightnesse of his Face affray you ?
His majestie with awfull Rayes dismay you,
Meer Earth and Ashes (daring thus to play)
Your best but Dust, your rest but Dirt and Clay : 830
Hold you your Tongues : no more your silence
        break :
But (at my Perill) give Mee leave to speak.
  Why should I teare mee (as one out of Sense)
With mine own Teeth ? or doe Selfe-Violence ?
No : should Hee slay mee, I would hope again
(Though in his sight I still my right maintain)
For, Hee himselfe will save and doe mee right ;
And cleer mee from your doom of Hypocrite :
Sith, in his presence Such can have no place,
Nor hope such help of his assisting Grace.   840
Give therefore eare unto my words ; and waigh
With due regard What I shall truely say.
Lo, here I stand, as ready to be try'd
(And well I know I shall be justifi'd)
Come, who will charge mee, and oppose my Pleas ?
(Alas ! I die, if now I hold my peace)
Onely, but spare mee in Two things : with-draw
Thy heavie hand ; with-hold thy glorious Awe
From frighting mee ; then, from before thy face
I shall not hide mee : nor betray my Case :   850
Then, at thy choice, be in this cause dependant
(I am indifferent) *Plaintif*, or *Defendant*.
  What, and How-many are my Sins (pretended) ?
Shew mee wherein, and how I have offended,
That Thou should'st shun, & turn thee from me so ;
And handle mee as thy most hated Foe.
Dost thou vouchsafe a wither'd Leaf to crush ?
Against dry Stubble dost thou daign to rush ?
That in so bitter and severe a stile
Thou dost endite mee ; and recite (the while)   860
My sins of Youth (them re-recording fresh,
With th' Heritage *inherent* unto Flesh) :

And putt'st my feet into the Stocks so strait ;
Watchest my wayes, and at my heels doth wait,
To finde some hole in my fore-acted Life
(Scourging mine Errors with thy Terrors rife)
While, rotten-like, it wasteth, as a Cloth
Grown full of holes and eaten by the Moth.

CHAP. 14.

MAn born of Man's and Woman's loynes, alas !
Hath but few daies, and those full sad, to pass.
Much like a Flower hee shooteth up and fades ;   870
Quickly cut down : hee vanisheth, as Shades ;
Of no continuance [here] Yet, dost thou daign
To frown at Such ? and strive with mee so vain ?
Who, from Pollution, can pure thing extract ?
O ! there is None ; none that is so exact.
Sith then his dayes thou hast determined ;
Sith that his Months with thee be numbered ;
Sith thou hast set the certain time hee has
(To Him uncertain) which Hee cannot passe ;   880
Forbear awhile, and from him look away,
Till (as the Hireling) hee hath done his Day.

For though a Tree be felled ; from the Root,
Yet is there hope that Branches will re-shoot :
Though in the Earth the Root be old and dry,
Though on the Earth the Trunk as dead doe lie ;
Yet, by the Sent of the neer-winding Floud,
It will revive, and, as a Plant, re-bud :
But Man (man's Body from his Soule bereft)
Man down and dead ; O ! what of Him is left ?   890

Sith as Sea-waters, past, re-passe no more ;
As rivers, dry'd, returne not to their Shore :
Man, dead-asleepe, shall never wake againe ;
Nor never rise, till Heav'n no more remaine.
O ! wert thou pleas'd, mee in my Grave to hide,
Untill thy Wrath were past and pacifi'd !
Or that there were some time, or term assign'd me,
When thou wilt cease ; and in thy mercy mind mee !
Or shall a Man *neer* dead, *here* live againe ;
Still living-dying in continuall paine ?   900
And shall I still, in this distressed state,
Wait, all the Dayes of mine appointed Date,
Untill my Change (my *Renovation*) come ;
When Thou shalt call mee ? nor shall I be dumb,
But answer thee : Then, then thou wilt approve
That thou the works of thine own hands dost love ;
Though now my steps thou numbrest so exact ;
Not'st all my Sins, and seem'st them to have packt
As in a Bagge, safe sealed ; yea, to add
New Trespasses unto the old I had.   910
So that, as Mountains, mouldring down to sink ;
As from their places shiver'd Rocks doe shrink :
As waters break the Stones ; as Show'rs surround
The dusty Earth ; Thou dost Man's hope confound ;
And tryumph'st ever over Him, dejected ;
Transform'd in face as from thy face rejected.
Nor knoweth hee, whether his dear Posterity
Shall poorly fare, or flourish in prosperity :
But, while his Soule his Body bears about,
That shall have Woe within ; and This without.   920

FINIS.

JOB.

THE SECOND BOOK.

CHAP. 15.

TO This of His (so hot and vehement)
  Thus *Eliphas* (in the same Element) :
Should one so wise (as thou dost vaunt thee here)
Discourse so vainly ? bring such idle gear ?
Vent from the Centre of a swelling brest
As noysom Gales as the unholsom East ?
Trifle the Time (about I wot not what)
In idle and unprofitable chat ?
Nay : nullifie Religious fear and *Pietie*,
Not praying to, but pleading with the *Deitie ?*   10
Which thine own mouth hath witnest too-too-far,
With subtill Cavils of a Sophister.
Yea, thine own mouth (not mine) shal thee convince ;
Against thy selfe thy lips give Evidence.
  Why Man ! wert Thou the first man on the earth ?
Or, wert thou borne before the Hills had birth ?
Hast Thou alone GOD's Secret understood ?
And hast Thou onely Wisdome, in thy Hood ?
What is't Thou knowest, that wee have not kend ?
What understand'st Thou, but wee comprehend ?   20
There are of Us as old as Thou ; or rather,
Some (I suppose) more ancient then Thy Father ;
And dost Thou slight our Comfort (godly sent) ?
Or hast Thou of thine Own more excellent ?
Why doth thy heart, and whither, thee transport ?
Why dost thou close thine eyes ? that in this sort
Thy Spirit turns (shall I say spurns ?) at GOD,
And from thy Lips spets words so bold and broad ?
  O ! what is man, that hee should clean exist ?
Or woman's Son, that hee should Just persist ?   30
Behold, hee found his Angels stood not sure :
Neither, the Heav'ns, in his pure sight, are pure :
Then, how much-more, before him, filthy stinks
Stock-stained Man, who Sin, as Water, drinks ?
  I'll therefore shew thee (hark, & mark me well)
What I have seen ; I will declare and tell
What, from their Elders, Sages yerst have know'n,
And to their Heirs successively have show'n.
Such as, indeed, have had the Helm in hand,
To steer their Own, and Strangers to with-stand.   40
  The wicked Man's in-labour, all his Life ;
In bitter Pains, in Pangs, in Passions rife :

Number of years are seldome his to sum ;
A Sound of Fears still in his ears doth hum ;
Or, if at all hee seem in ease to swim ;
The swift destroyer shall soon seize on him,
Hap-lesse, and hopelesse ever to recover ;
Seeing the Sword, him ever hanging over.
  Needy, indeed ; or greedy still of more
(Pining in Plenty, starving in his Store)   50
Hee wanders, seeking of his Bread about ;
In dread of want ; of a Black Day, in doubt :
Trouble and Anguish shall him deep affright ;
As royall Armies ready for the Fight.
  For, hee hath stretched his proud hand at Heav'n ;
And stubbornly hath with th' Almighty striv'n,
Running at him, rushing upon his Neck ;
Yea, on the Bosses of his shield so thick :
Because his Fat, his full broad Face doth cover ;
And lardy Collops on his sides hang over ;   60
And dwels in Houses, rather Towns of late
(By him) dis-patron'd and depopulate ;
By him, re-built, re-gilt, re-glost, re-glas'd ;
By him, re-*Named* (ready to be ras'd).
  Yet, shall not hee be rich, nor in Prosperity
Persist, nor leave Possession to Posterity :
Nor, out of Darknesse ever get shall hee ;
Nor ever other than inglorious be :
His branch shall wither, and with flame be wasted :
Himself shal, sodain, with GOD's Breath be blasted.   70
  Then, let not (hard-beleeving haut humanity)
O ! let not the Deceived trust in Vanity.
For, Vanity shall be his recompence :
Before his time shall hee be snatched hence :
His Spring shall never sprout, his Flowers shall fall,
His Fruit, yer ripe, shall be off-shaken all :
(As Grapes and Olives with untimely Frost)
The Lord shall shake them, and they shall be lost.
  For th' Hypocrites' Dissembling Congregation,
Shall be disperst, and brought to Desolation :   80
And suddenly shall Fire consume the Tents
Of *Bribery*, with all their Instruments.
For, They conceive but Mischief ; breed but Guile,
And bring forth vain Iniquity the while.

CHAP. 16.

Ee pausing here, JOB Thus replyes him, sad :
Yet more of This ? This have we often had :
You are indeed a sort of Visiters ;
A Crew of cold and wretched Comforters.
Shall idle, addle, airy, words surcease ?
Or what doth make you dare to dwell on these ?　　90
　　Could I, as you, if you were in my Case,
And I in yours ; your Soule in my Soule's place :
Could I, against you, words have multiply'd ?
Insulted on you ? at you shook my head ?
No : I should rather have raught you Relief,
And with my speeches have asswag'd your Grief.
　　But, though I plain, my Grief's not mitigated ;
Either, forbear I, what is it abated ?
For, hee hath wearied mee : Yea, Lord, thou hast
Spoil'd mee of all ; and laid mee wholly waste :　　100
The wrinkled Furrows on my brow and back
(Bare skin and bone) bear witnesse of my Wrack.
　　My Foe's fell wrath hath raakt and rent me sore :
Hee strives against mee ; and still angry more,
More eager still, gnasheth his Teeth upon mee ;
And with his eyes keen flashing frowneth on-me.
My Friends (alas !) they laugh at mee the while,
They buffet mee, and bitterly revile ;
They gape upon mee, and together gather,
Not to relieve mee, but to grieve mee rather.　　110
Thus hath God hemm'd mee with ungodly bands,
And turn'd mee over into wicked hands.
　　I was at ease ; when by the Neck hee took mee,
Brake mee a-sunder, and to shivers shook mee :
And (whether for Disport or for Despite)
Made mee his Butt, and set mee as his White.
His cunning Archers doe beset mee round ;
Hee cleaves my Reins ; and ruth-less, on the ground
Pours-out my Gall : with doubled blows he crushes,
And Gyant-like, upon mee fiercely rushes.　　120
　　I have in Sack-cloth sadly sow'd my Skin,
In Dust and Ashes have I humbled bin ;
I have (alas !) besmear'd my Face with Tears,
On mine Ey-lids death's Shade hath swom, in fears :
For no foule Sin, neither, for Fashion's sake,
To seem a *Saint :* pure Prayers did I make,
Pure and Sincere : else never may they come
In Heav'n, to have either regard or room.
Neither, O Earth ! if ever bloud I shed,
O ! let it not by thee be covered.　　130
　　But lo, my Witnesse is in Heav'n above ;
My Record there, my Conscience to approve.
My friends contemn mee, and condemn mee too :
But, drown'd in tears, to GOD appeale I doe.
O ! that one might (as Man with Man, in Sute)
That, Neighbour-like, one might wᵗʰ GOD dispute.
For the few dayes of my set number gone,
I goe the Way from whence return is none.

CHAP. 17.

Y Spirit's spent : my daies are don (& leave me)
The Grave's already ready to receive mee.　　140

Yet are there wᵗʰ me none but those that mock me :
Doth not mine eye still see them still provoke me ?
　　But, put mee in a Surety, give mee Pledge,
To answer mee what I shall then alledge.
Who'll undertake it ? who will give his hand,
That to the Triall thou wilt daign to stand ?
Sith Thou, O Lord, their hearts hast hidden quite,
From understanding, and from judging right ;
And therefore wilt not, for their Arrogance,
Admit of them, nor them so high advance.　　150
　　Not, that I would, they should have sooth'd mee
　　　　neither :
For such shall perish, and their Seed together.
But, to the Vulgar I am made a Song,
A Tale, a Tabret unto every Tongue
Through grief whereof, mine eye decayes & dims ;
And as a Shadow are my other Limbs).
The better sort amazed at my Plight ;
The Innocent, judge mee an Hypocrite.
Yet, shall the Righteous still hold on his Course ;
And the Sincere shall still adde force to force.　　160
　　Therefore, my Friends, return, recant, re-call
Your hard Opinions, and mis-Censures, all :
For, of you all, not one wise man I finde ;
Nor fit *Physician* for a troubled minde.
　　My Dayes are past ; and my Designes undone ;
Yea, even my hopes (my heart's Possessions) gone :
My Noon (alas !) is changed into Night :
Small ods there is 'twixt Darknesse and my Light.
What can I look for, but among the Dead
To make my house ? to have my Grave, for Bed ?　　170
For, to Corruption, thus aloud I call ;
Thou art my Father : to the Worms that crawl,
You are my Mother, and my Sisters all.
　　Where's then my hope ? how shall that Hap appear,
Which you yer-while did so re-promise, here ?
Those things with mee shall down into the Deep :
And, with my Dust, amid the Dust shall sleep.

CHAP. 18.

Hen said the *Shuhite :* Will you never cease
Your tedious Talking ? Never hold your peace ?
Forbear a while ; give eare a little now :　　180
Observe our Speech, and wee will answer you.
But, why, as beasts, are wee upbraided thus ?
And why so basely do you count of us ?
Hee, rather seems to be besides his Sense,
That wounds himselfe in his impatience.
　　Why ? Shall the Earth, for thy sake be forsaken ?
The Rocks remov'd ? and solid Hills be shaken ?
No, no : The Light of Wicked-ones shall out :
His Fiery Sparkle shall not shine about ;
Within his Doores shall Darknesse be for Light :　　190
With him, his Candles shall be quenched quite :
His Strength shall fail him (or be fatall to him) :
His Counsells cast him ; his owne Wit undoe-him :
For, his own Feet shall bring him to the Net
And willingly upon the Gin shall jet :

Him, by the heel the subtill Snare shall catch :
Him, shall the Theeves and Robbers over-match :
For him are laid the Meshes of Mis-hap ;
Trains on the ground, and in his wayes a Trap :
Him, on all sides, sad Terrors shall affright ;   200
And sudden drive him to his Feet, to flight :
His plenteous Store shall Famin soon devour :
Destruction's Sword shall hunt-him every-hower,
Consume his Sinews, and un-bare his Skin ;
And Pestilence (Death's Heir) shall rage within.
His hope shall hop without his expectation :
His confidence shall from his habitation
Be rooted out, and razed (as it were)
And bring him down to the drad king of Fear ;
Who ay shall dwell within his Tabernacle,   210
(Because not his, not his own Habitacle) :
Som secret harm, som flash, som Sulph'ry shower,
Shall sudden spread amid his cursed Bower :
His Roots below shall rot amid the Clay ;
His Boughs above be cut and cast away :
His Memory shall perish from the Earth ;
His Name here namelesse (as before his birth)
Hee shall be driv'n to Darknesse, from the Light ;
And forth the World hee shall be hunted quite.
Nor Son, nor Nephew shall he leave behind ;   220
Nor in his Houses any of his Kind.
So that, the Ages, present, and to come,
Shall stand amazed at his dismall Doom.
And this is sure the Lot, the heavy Load
Of wicked-ones, that fear not, know not GOD.

CHAP. 19.

IOB then reply'd : Alas ! how long will Yee
    Torment my Soule, with words ; & torture mee ?
Ten times yee have with too obdurate minde,
Reproacht mee This : uncivill and unkinde.
But, put the Case, that I have sinn'd, indeed :   230
Must not I bear it ? Then (alas !) what need
You load mee more ; and magnifie your wit,
To amplifie my Guilt, and Grief of it ;
Seeing you see that GOD hath cast mee down,
And wlth his Net hath compassed mee round ?
Lo, I cry-out of wrong and violence ;
Aloud I cry ; yet have no Audience,
Nor Ease at all : hee hath so hedg'd my way,
I cannot passe : My Paths, in stead of Day,
Are Dark beset : hee hath my Glory reft ;   240
And from my head hee hath the Crown bereft :
Hee hath destroy'd mee, every-way undone :
My hope, removed (as a Tree) is gone :
And more, his wrath against mee fiercely fryes ;
He reckons Mee among his Enemies.
His Troups assembled, march against Mee egre ;
And round about my feeble Tent beleguer :
Hee hath disperst my Brethren from mee far,
To Mee, my Kindred as meer Strangers are ;
My Neighbours fly mee ; my Familiar Friend   250
Hath now forgot mee (as if never kend) :

Nay : mine own Household ; men, maid-servants, all,
Count mee a Stranger, care not for my Call,
Nor will come at mee ; though I speak them fair :
Nay : to mine own wife (for the noisom air)
My Breath is strange, though I beseech her, sad,
By those dear Pledges wee together had.
The Basest scorn mee ; and when up I rise,
They spet their spite in bitter Obloquies.
Mine Intime-most, Those that I loved best,   260
Abhor mee all, and mee the more molest.
My Bones, in stead of flesh, cleave to my skin ;
And that not sound, save what my Teeth grow in.
Then pity mee, O ! pity mee, my Friends ;
Sith GOD on mee his heavy hand extends :
Ah ! Why doe you yet persecute mee, rough,
As GOD ? alas ! hath not my Flesh enough ?
O ! that my words (the words I now assever)
Were writ, were printed, and (to last for ever)
Were grav'n in Marble with an yron pen   270
With Lead in-yoated (to fill up agen).
I surely know that my Redeemer liveth :
And that Hee shall (This firm my Faith beleeveth)
In th' end of Time, return and rise from Dust
(*The First and Last*) *to judge and save the Just :*
And, that I shall, when worms have eat this Clod :
I shall awake, and in my flesh see God :
Yea, I shall see him with these Eyes of mine ;
And with none else : though now in Pains I pine.
The rather, therefore should you now retract,   280
And thus Your-selves discreetly now correct :
Why persecute Wee him ? Why hate Him, Wee ?
Sith This foundation is thus fixt in Mee,
Then, be you warn'd ; beware, and fear the Sword :
For wickednesse and cruelty [in word]
Incenseth Wrath : know, there shall Judgment com,
To doom them right, who Others (rash) misdoom.

CHAP. 20.

SCarce had hee done ; when the *Naamathite*
    Replies him thus : therefore my thoughts incite
My sudden Answer ; therefore am I spurr'd   290
(Regarding light thy sharp and shamefull Gird)
With speed to speak, unto the Point in hand,
What I conceive and rightly understand.
Know'st thou not this of old, through every age,
Since first on Earth began Man's Pilgrimage ;
That the triumphing of the wicked Sort,
The Joy of th' *Hypocrite* is ever short ?
Although to Heav'n hee mount his glorious top ;
Though to the Clouds his head be lifted up ;
Yet shall hee perish, as his dung, for ay :   300
And who hath seen them, shall ask, where are they ?
As Dreams forgotten, shall hee take his flight ;
Yea chas'd away, as Visions of the Night :
Th' Eye that hath seen him, shall not see him twise,
Nor shall his Places him againe revise.
His Children shall be fawning on the Poor,
And his Extortions shall to them restore :

His Bones are full of his Youth's sins (his Lust)
Which shall not leave him till he lye in dust :
Though to his Taste his Sin be passing sweet,   310
Though under-neath his Tongue hee cover it,
Though there hee spare it, and not spet it out,
Though on his Palate still it roule about ;
Yet is his meat turn'd, in his Bowells, all ;
And is, within him, as the *Aspic's* Gall :
H' hath swallow'd wealth, but God shall make him fain
To spue it out, to cast it up again :
Hee shall the *Aspic's* direfull Poison suck :
With Vipers' tongues hee shall be deadly stuck :
Hee shall not see the Oylie Rivers' Currents,   320
Nor Brooks of Butter, nor the Hony Torrents :
His Labour never shall regain his Losse :
Hee shall restore whom hee before did crosse :
The Restitution shall be all his state ;
Hee never shall digest, nor joy thereat ;
Because the Poor hee crushed, and forsook ;
And Others' houses violently took.
Sure hee shall have no quiet Calm within ;
Without, no Store of what hee joyeth in.
There shall be no Remainder of his meat ;   330
And his Reversions none shall wait to eat.
Nay : in his Ruffe, and at his greatest height,
Hee shall be stocked in full many a Strait :
Continuall hazzards shall him round enring ;
Each spitefull hand shall have at him a fling :
When hee is ready for his rich Repast,
On him will God his fiery Fury cast ;
Amid his Feasts his drad Displeasure thrilling
In stead of Food, his breast with horror filling ;
If hee escape the Sword ; from Bowes of steel   340
Steel-headed Arrowes shall him thorough thrill :
The naked Swords bright-shining terror shall
Peep through his bosom, creep through guts & gall.
Horrors shall haunt him : and so, hard-bestid,
From hiding him, all Darknesse shall be hid.
A Fire unblow'n him sudden shall consume :
And woe to them that tarry in his Room :
Heav'n shall discover his Iniquities,
And Earth for witnesse shall against him rise ;
All his Revenews, all his state, and stay,   350
Shall flow to Others in his wrathfull Day.
This is the Portion of the Wicked : This
His heritage by God appointed is.

CHAP. 21.

SO, *Zophar* ceast.   Then Job reply'd : I pray
   Hear heedfully what now I have to say :
Be this the Comfort you vouchsafe, alone ;
Let Mee but speak ; and afterwards, mock on.
  Doe I complain, or make my moan to Man ?
Why doe you crosse, or interrupt mee, than ?
If I have cause of Grief should not my spirit   360
Be mov'd withall ?   Can flesh and bloud forbear it ?
Behold mee well ; and be withall dismay'd :
And let your hand upon your mouth be layd.

Thought of the like (els-where) would mee affright,
And daunt my Flesh : how then, my present sight ?
  How comes it that the Wicked live, live long,
Grow rich, grow great ; wex eminent, and strong ;
They see their Children, and Grand-children, rife
Settled about them : In their House no Strife ;
No Feare ; no Foe : They feel not any Rod,   370
No stripe, no stroke, of the drad hand of God.
Their Bullock genders, and proves ever fit :
Their Heifer calves, and never casteth it :
Their little ones, like Lambkins send they out ;
Their Striplings play and skip, and daunce about ;
They tune their voice to sweetest Instruments,
Harp, Pipe, and Tabret ; to delight their sense :
In Wealth and Health they live ; scarce, ever, sick
Of long disease ; but to their Graves goe quick.
  Yet These are Those, that to th' Almighty say,   380
Depart from us ; wee will not learn thy Way :
Who is the Lord, that wee should him obey ?
What should wee profit, if to Him wee pray ?
  They have not sure the power in their own hand,
To get and keep their wealth at their Command.
Be therefore far, be ever far from Mee,
Their works, and words, and thoughts, Impiety :
Far be their Counsells ; far be all their Wayes :
And far the Peace of their so prosperous Dayes.
  And yet, how often is their Lamp put-out ?   390
How often are they compassed about
With swift Destruction ? In his Fury strict
How oft doth God their payment here inflict ?
How oft, as Straw before the winde, are They,
And as the Chaff with Tempest whift away ?
How oft doth God, in the Ungodly's sight,
For Their own Guilt, their own dear Issue smite ?
Or, lets Themselves here see Themselves undone ;
Drinking the hot Wrath of th' Almighty-one ?
For, what is it to Them ? or what care They   400
(Their mouths cut-off, their mouths once-stopt w^{th}
   clay)
What hap their house, what hazzard follow shall :
What weal or woe, unto their Heirs befall ?
  But herein, who God's wisdome shall impeach ?
Or, who shall him, that rules the highest, teach ?
One dyes at ease, in Strength's perfection growing ;
His brests with milk, his bones with marrow flowing.
Another dyes in anguish of his spirit ;
And never did good Day or Night inherit :
Both are, alike, layd in the Dust together ;   410
And Worms, alike, doe case and cover Either.
  Lo, I conceive your mis-conceits, from hence ;
Your mis-collections, and your wrested Sense :
For, where (say ye) where's now the Prince's Court ?
And where the Palace of the wicked sort ?
Have yee not asked those that travaile by ?
And doe yee, can yee, yet their Marks deny ?
That (for the most) the wicked most are spared,
Reprived here ; till that dread Day prepared
For dire Destruction : and then (for their Errors)   420
Shall be brought forth, in that *great Day* of Terrors.

For here so Mighty and so Great they are ;
Who to their face shall their Offence declare ?
Who dares disclose it ?   Who shall prosecute ?
And their due Sentence who shall execute ?
   Nay (notwithstanding) to their Grave in peace
They passe, with pomp of solemne Obsequies ;

Accompany'd, attended (in their kinde)
With Mourning Troups, before them and behinde :
Entomb'd among their Ancestors ; and rest   430
In gloomy Vales, as happy as the Best.
   How doe You then, Mee comfort, or confute ;
   While vainly thus, and falsly you dispute ?

FINIS.

JOB.

THE THIRD BOOK.

Chap. 22.

TH' old *Themanite*, as mov'd withall, replyes,
Can Man, to GOD (as to Him-selfe, the Wise)
Be profitable? any pleasure is't
Unto the Lord, if righteous Thou persist?
If Thou be just, if perfect and upright ;
Is GOD the better? Gaines th' Almighty by 't?
For fear of Thee, will Hee reprove thee (strict)
Enter in Judgement, and thee thus afflict?
Is not thy Sin great and thy Wickednesse ;
And infinite thy foule Unrighteousnesse?   10
    Yes : thou hast ta'n thy brother's Pledge for nothing,
And stripped even the Naked of their Clothing :
Thou hast not giv'n the wearie, Drink at need :
Nor to the Hungry, wherewithall to feed :
The Eminent and Mighty had their fill :
They held the Earth, and sway'd thee at their will :
But silly Widows hast thou empty packt ;
And th' arms of Orphans have bin crusht & crackt.
Thence is it now, that Snares beset thee round,
And sudden Fears thee trouble and confound :   20
Or a black Darknesse that thou canst not see ;
And a huge Deluge that o'r-whelmeth thee.
    Is not the Lord in th' High *Empyreall* Blisse?
Behold the Stars, how high their Distance is :
And then (saist thou) What can th' Almighty mark?
How judgeth Hee? What sees he through the dark?
Clouds cover Him from spying so far hence :
Hee walketh in the Heav'n's Circumference.
    But, hast not Thou observ'd the ancient Track
The wicked trod, to their untimely Wrack ;   30
Who, quick cut downe, supplanted where they stood,
Had their Foundations swallowed with the floud?
Who said to GOD, Depart from us ; and thought,
What can th' Almighty doe to us, in ought :
Yet, with good things Hee fill'd their habitations.
But, far from mee be their Imaginations.
    This see the Righteous ; safe the while, and glad :
And laugh at them, in their Destruction sad.
For, Wee shall stand : our Substance not decay :
But their remainder shall the Fire destroy.   40
    Therefore, acquaint thee, (and that quickly too)
With GOD ; make peace : & thou right wel shalt do ;

Receive (I pray thee) from his mouth Direction ;
And in thy heart lay-up his Word's instruction.
    If, to th' Almighty thou at-once return ;
Thou shalt be built-up : and shalt bravely spurn
Iniquity far from thy Selfe away ;
And from thy Dwellings put it far, for ay.
Then, as the dust thou shalt have Gold, at will ;
Pure *Ophyr* Gold, as Pebbles of the Rill :   50
Yea, the Almighty Thy defence shall be :
And store of Silver shall be still with Thee.
For, in the Lord thy Pleasure shalt thou place ;
And unto Him shalt thou lift up thy Face :
Him shalt thou pray-to ; Hee shall hear thy Layes,
And grant thy Sute ; and thou return him Praise :
Thou shalt decree, and Hee shall make it good,
(So thy good purpose shall not bee withstood) :
And on Thy Wayes, and in all Works of Thine,
His Light of Grace (and Glory too) shall shine.   60
Nay : when-as Others (as Thy selfe art now)
Shall be cast down ; re-comfort them shalt Thou,
And thus re-cheer them : Yet, yet may you rise,
For God will save such as have humbled eyes.
Yea : on the Noxious will hee pitie take,
For th' Innocent ; and spare them for thy sake.

Chap. 23.

THen answered JOB : Tho to this day my mones
    Right bitter be, my Grief exceeds my Grones ;
How is it then, that I, as yet, am held,
For having plain'd, as if I had rebell'd?   70
    O ! that I knew, that som would shew me, where,
I might goe finde my Soveraign Arbiter !
That I might speedy unto him repair ;
And even approach to his Tribunall Chair !
I would before him plead my just defence,
And fill my Mouth with pregnant Arguments.
Then would I know what should His answer be ;
And understand what Hee would say to mee.
Would hee oppose mee with his Power divine?
No : rather would hee steel and strengthen mine,   80
There might the Just in his just Plea proceed :
And I should ever from my Judge be freed.

47

But, Whether to the West I take my way ;
Or to the pearly Portall of the Day ;
Or, to the Norward, where hee worketh rife ;
Or, to the South, the Cell of blustring strife :
Whether I look before mee, or behinde ;
On This, or That side : Him I cannot finde.
　　Yet, knowes Hee well my Way.: and hath mee try'd :
And I, like Gold, shall come forth purifi'd.　　90
My Foot hath walked in his steps : His Way
Have I observed ; and not gone astray :
Nor have I started from his Precepts set,
But priz'd them more then my appointed Meat.
　　Yet, Hee persisteth in one purpose still.
Who can divert him ? Hee doth what hee will ;
And will perform what is of mee decreed ;
And many such things are with Him, indeed.
　　Therefore, before Him, am I wonder-smit :
Affraid of Him, when I consider it.　　100
For, GOD hath suppled and made soft my heart,
And deep perplext mee in my inward Part :
Because my Languors neither end, nor I :
Nor can I see, nor sound the Reason, Why.

CHAP. 24.

BUt, can it be, (how can it other be ?)
　　But that the Times of the Divine Decree
(Concerning Judgements more or lesse severe ;
When, why, & who, and how, and what, and where)
Hidden with GOD, and hidden from his Own ;
Should to the World, and wicked be unknown ?　　110
　　They shift the Land-marks frō their ancient seat :
They take by force men's flocks, to feed, or eat :
They drive away the silly Orphan's Asse :
They take for Pledge the Widow's Ox (alas !) :
They turn the Needy from their neerest way :
They make the Poor together hide them ay ;
Lo, like wilde Asses in the Wildernesse,
They ramp about their brutish Businesse :
Rising betimes for Boot (like Free-booters) :
The Desart Field yeelds Food for them and theirs.　　120
They reap them Each a Crop, from Other's Crop :
They gather Each a wicked Vintage up :
They cause the Naked without Clothes to lie,
Quivering for Cold, no Covering but the Skie ;
Washt with the Showers that from the Mountains shed ;
Embracing Clifts, for Shelter ; Rocks for Bed :
They pluck the Pupill from the tender Brest :
They take from Poor a Pawn of all their best ;
They leave them Naked ; Nay, the Hungry soule
Even of his Sheaf, and gleaned handfulls poule :　　130
Yea ; Labourers, that in Their service toyle ;
That tread their Wine-press, & that make their oile,
That trudge and drudge in their Affairs ; in fine
They let them starve, and even for thirst to pine.
　　The City groanes under their wicked Thrall,
Th' oppressed, slain, and wounded, cry, and call :
Yet, 'tis apparent (as the Sun is cleer)
GOD doth not alwayes smite (nor cite) them heer.

Yet, These are Those, that ay the Light abhor :
Know not their Way, nor keep, nor care it for :　　140
The Murd'rer rises (early) yer the Light ;
To kill the Poor : and robbeth (late) at night :
Th' Adulterer's Eye doth for the twy-light wait ;
And, muffled, saies, None sees my quaint Deceit :
They (Burglars) dig through houses in the Dark,
Which in the Day, they for their owne did mark.
But, Light they loath ; Morning to Them is death :
Death's Terror, Day ; which all discovereth :
On Waters swim they light and swift, for fear :
On Earth, as Vagrants, fly they here and there　　150
(Their cursed portion) every-where undone :
By-wayes they seek, and the High-waies they shun.
　　As Heat and Drought dissolve, & drink the snow ;
The wicked-One the Grave shall swallow so.
The Womb that bare him, shall him quite forget ;
And, to the Worm hee shall be wel-come Meat.
Hee shall, with Men, no more remembred bee :
But broken-off, as is a withered Tree.
Hee weds the barren that brings never forth ;
And, if a Widow, leaves her nothing worth.　　160
Yet, by his power, Hee drags the Mighty down ;
And none is safe, if Hee in Fury frown :
No ; though, with Presents they his Patience buy,
And build on it ; on Them hee casts an eye.
　　Such, for a little, are aloft : Anon
As low as Others ; as all others, gone :
Soon taken hence, shut-up, cut-off, and shorn
As (with the Haile) the tufted ears of Corn.
If thus it be not, who will (I desire)
Disprove my Speech ; and prove mee now a Lyer.　　170

CHAP. 25.

TO this, the *Shuite* answered shortly Thus :
　　Hee is Almighty, Dradly-Glorious ;
Whose Power imperiall, and All-humbling Aw,
Rules his High Places in most peacefull Law.
Is any number of His Armies known ?
What Light so bright, but His hath over-shone ?
How, then, may Man, wlth GOD, be just defin'd ?
Or, Hee be Clean, that 's born of Woman-kinde ?
Behold the Moon, before Him, is not bright :
Stars are not pure in his All-piercing sight.　　180
Then, How-much-less ? How-much-less man (alas !)
The Son of Man : a Worm, a Worthlesse Masse ?

CHAP. 26.

IOB, hereunto replyes incontinent :
　　Well have yee said ; but how Impertinent !
How hast Thou holp the weak and feeble wight ?
How fit defended him that hath no might ?
How sweetly taught the simple and unwise ?
How full declar'd the Matter, as it lyes ?
To Whom dost Thou this Speech of thine direct ?
What moves thee to it ? and to what effect ?　　190
　　For, I (for My part) know, that, Not alone,
Th' Eternall rules, on his supernall Throne

The things above, in their harmonious Course ;
But here below, the Better and the Worse.

Beneath the waters, dead things formed bin :
And, dumb (their own Inhabitants) within :
Hell is not hid from him : Destruction's Cave,
From his inspection can no Covering have.
Hee, th' ample heav'ns over the Void extends :
Hee, upon Nothing the sad Earth suspends: 200
Within his Clowds He bottles up the rain,
Which with its weight tears not the Clowds in twain :
Hee hath in-bow'd the fore-front of his Throne,
And spread his Clowdy Canapey thereon :
He hath begirt the Waters with a List
Shall ever last, till Day and Night desist.
The massie Pillars of the Pole doe shake
If hee but chide ; and at his check they quake.
Hee by his pow'r doth the deepe Sea divide :
His prudence smites her, in her fellest pride :   210
Hee by his Spirit, the Spangled Heav'ns hath drest
With glittering Signes ; the Serpent and the rest.

Lo, these are parcels of his wayes supreme :
But, O ! how little doe wee heare of him !
Who can conceive ! Who understands the Thunders
Of his more secret, and most sacred Wonders ?

Chap. 27.

WHile none repli'd, JOB gravely thus goes on :
    As lives the Lord, th' Almighty *Holy One*,
Who seems a space my *Verdict* to suppress,
Loading my soule with brunts of bitterness ;   220
While Breath is in mee ; till my Spirit, inspir'd
By God, be gone, and from mee quite expir'd ;
My Lips shall speak no wickednesse, no wile ;
Nor shall my Tongue deliver any guile.
No ; God forbid that I should justifie
Your rash mis-judgement.   Mine integritie
I 'll not abandon, to my dying day :
Mine innocence I never will betray :
My righteousnesse still will I fast retain ;
And, my cleer conscience, while I life maintain.   230
But, as the wicked, be mine enemies :
Those, as unrighteous, that against mee rise.

For what 's the hope of th' hollow Hypocrite
(Though hee hath heaped Treasures infinite)
When God shall take (in a disastrous day)
His Land (his Life) his Goods (his Gods) away?
Will God regard, or heare his howling Cry,
When hee is compast with Calamity?
Or, in th' Almighty can he comfort take ?
Will hee to God continuall Prayer make ?   240

I 'll show you, how the Almighty hand doth deale :
God's wonted course I will not now conceale :
Nay ; you your Selves, you all have seen it too ;
Why talke yee then thus vainly as yee do ?

This is, with God, the Portion and the Part
Of th' ungodly and the cruell heart :
This heritage shall impious Tyrants have
From the Almightie, This they shall receive :

If many Children hee shall leave behinde,
As many shall the Sword or Famine finde :   250
Or, if that any in Remain be left ;
They by the Plague, shall, unbewail'd, be left.

If hee have heaped Silver, as the dust :
And Clothes, as Clay ; hee may : but sure the Just
Shall 'joy his Silver, and his Treasures share ;
And weare his Ward-robe, how-so rich and rare.

If brave hee build ; it is but like the Moth
(On other's ground, as that in other's Cloth)
Soon dispossest : or, like a Watch-house, soon
To be set up, and suddenly pull'd down.   260

Such Rich, shall dye ; and lie without regard,
Ungather'd to his Fathers' Toomb prepar'd :
Nothing of him remaines in Memorie :
Hee vanisheth in Twinkling of an Eye.
Horrors shall seize him, as a Flood, with Fright ;
And as a Tempest hurry him by night.
An Eastern Storm him quite away shall chase ;
And as a Whirle-winde, hurle him from his place,
So pitilesse, in wrathfull Jelousie,
(While glad and fain hee would his fingers flie)   270
Will God pursue him ; and good men shall smile,
And clap their hands, and hiss at him the while.

Chap. 28.

SUre, there are Mines & veinlings (under ground)
    Whence Silver 's fetcht, and wherein Gold is found ;
Iron out of Earth, & out of stone the Brass
Is melted down (into a purer mass)
Beyond the bounds of Darkness Man hath pry'd
And th' excellence of under-ground descry'd :
The rarest stones, and richest minerals,
From deadly Damps, and horrid Darks hee hales :   280
And if some Torrent come there rushing in
(Such as no foot hath felt, no eye hath seen)
Hee can revert it, or divert it, soon,
Without Impeachment to his Work begun.

Earth's surface yeelds him corn & fruits for food ;
Her under-folds, some burning Sulphury flood :
Amid the Quars of stone are Saphires store :
Among the Dust, the precious Golden Ore
(Where never Bird, before did Path descry,
Where never Vulture cast her greedy eye,   290
Where savage Whelps had never-never trac't ;
Nor furious Lion ever by had past) :
On Cliffs of Adamant hee laies his hands ;
Their height and hardness hee at will commands ;
Slents them wth sledges, crops their clowdy crown :
Hee by the roots turns Mountains up-side down :
To let out Rills, he cleaveth Rocks in sunder :
His eye perceives all that is precious under :
Hee binds the Waters, that they shall not weep ;
And dives for Riches in the deepest deep.   300

All this, and more, hath Man.   But where is found
That soveraign Wisedome, sacred and profound ?
That understanding of the Waies divine,
Of God's supreme and secret discipline ?

Man knowes it not ; nor kens the worth of it :
It is not found in any living Wit.
The Deeps confess, the Sea acknowledgeth ;
'Tis not in mee ; nor with mee, th' other saith.
  Nor gold, nor silver, nor all gems that are,
Can purchase it, nor equall it by farre :   310
No wedge of *Ophir*, never so refin'd ;
No *Æthiopian Topaze, Pearle of Inde*,
No precious *Onyx*, neither *Saphire* pure
(*Corall* and *Crystall* passe I, as obscure)
No *Carbuncle*, no *Diamant* so rare ;
No One, nor All, with Wisedome may compare.
  But, whence is then, and where is to bee found
That sacred Wisedome, secret and profound ?
Sith it is hidden from all humane eyes,
And from the sight of every Fowle that flyes ;   320
Death and destruction say : Wee of the same
Have with our eares but onely heard the Fame.
  GOD, GOD alone doth understand its way ;
And knowes the place where it abideth aye.
For, hee, at once beholdeth all that is
In all the World : All under heav'n hee sees,
To poyze the Winds, and portion (at his pleasure)
Unto the Waters their due weight and measure.
  When for the raine hee stablist a Decree,
And for the Thunder's Lightning Mutinie ;   330
Then did hee see it, and fore-see it fit :
Hee numbred, pondred, and prepared it :
And unto Man this *Maxime* did apply ;
GOD's Fear is Wisedome and from sin to flie.

CHAP. 29.

JOB yet proceeded, and said furthermore,
  O ! were it with mee, as it was of yore,
In my fore-passed Months, my former dayes,
When God preserv'd me ; when with gracious rayes
His lightfull Lamp reflected on my head,
Whereby I walkt through Darkness, void of dread : 340
As in my younger times, when yet the Lord
Vouchsaft mee blessings of my Bed and Boord ;
When yet the Lord was with mee in my Tents,
And showred there his hidden Providence.
  When, where I went, my waies were bath'd in butter,
And Rocks about mee Rills of Oyle did gutter :
When I had gone unto the publike Gate
To take my place where all our Senate sate,
At sight of me, should yong men hide them thence,
And the elder sort stand up, for reverence :   350
Nobles were silent if I present were ;
And if I spake, they turn'd their Tongue to Eare :
And th' Eare that heard me blessed me : and th' Eye
That saw mee, witnest mine Integrity.
  For, I delivered every Poor opprest,
The Orphan and the Helplesse I redrest :
Hee blessed mee that was well-neer undon :
The Widow's heart I cheered : I put-on,
I put on *Justice*, as a seemly Gowne ;
It was unto mee as a Robe and Crowne.   360

I, as an Eye unto the blind became ;
And as a foot unto the Halt and Lame :
A Father was I to the Poor : and where
The Case was dark, I would discuss it cleer.
I also brake th' Oppressor's greedy Jawes,
And tooke the Prey out of his Teeth and Pawes.
  Then thought I, sure, to dye at home in rest :
And said, I shall with good long dayes be blest.
For, by the Waters was my Root out-spred :
Upon my top Heav'n's nightly Deaw was shed : 370
My Wealth increast, mine Honour daily grew,
My Bow of Health (my strength) did still renew.
  When I had spoken, every Eare was prest
To give mee Eare, and in my Counsels rest,
Without Reply : and as the later Rain
The thirsty earth, my Words they entertain.
If I had laught or smil'd on any neer,
They took no notice, nor would change my cheer.
I sate as Chief, I onely rul'd the roast,
Dwelt as a King amid an armed Hoast ;   380
And as a man, amid a mourning Rout,
That from his lips pours lively comforts out.

CHAP. 30.

BUt now (alas !) my Puisnès Mee deride :
  The meanest mock me ; Yea, and those (beside)
Whose ragged Fathers I refus'd to keep
My Shepheard's Curs, much more to cure my sheep.
For, to say truth, what service could they doe ?
So idle bred (both Young and Elder too)
Weak'ned with Sloth, and wicked Conversation ;
And waxen old, in wretched Desolation :   390
For Cold and Hunger wandring here and there,
With Mallowes fed, and Roots of Juniper :
Pursu'd as Theeves, hunted from place to place
With *Hue* and *Crie ;* and ever had in Chase ;
And therefore fain, for Shelter's sake, to creep
In Clifts and Caves ; in Rocks and Dungeons deep :
Among the Thornes and Thickets roaring rife ;
Wild Out-lawes, leading a most bestiall life :
The Breed of Fooles, the Fry of basest birth,
Of Name-lesse Men : indeed the Scums of Earth. 400
  And yet, to such am I now made a Song,
A Ballad, and a By-word in their tongue :
Yea, These despise mee, and despight mee too,
Spet in my Face, and make no more adoe.
Because the Lord my Bow-string hath unbent,
And slackt my Cord, therefore these insolent
Insulters now loose and let go the Raines
Of all Respect, unto their lewd disdaines.
  Now very Boyes doe take the Wall of mee,
Trip at my Feet ; and (in their Jollitie)   410
Mis-judge my Life, and of mee Rumors raise,
After their owne cruell and cursed Wayes :
They mar my Path that I have walked in,
Further my woes, and have no help therein :
As a wide Floud-breach, they have rushed on-mee,
And with the Ruines have roul'd-in upon-mee.

Terrors are turn'd upon mee, and pursue
My life as Winde ; my Weale, as Vapours flew :
Therefore my Soule, in sore afflictions vext,
Is poured out, and inly deep perplext.   420
    Dayes dark and irksome have upon mee seaz'd :
And in the night (when others most are eas'd)
My very bones within mee are opprest,
Nay, pierced through : my Sinnews take no rest :
My strange Disease, with angry violence
Of th' hot impostumes' loathsome Virulence,
Hath staind my garments : and with straining dolor,
About my neck it gripes mee as a Coller.
Laid in the Dust, I roule the Mire among :
Becomn, indeed, like Ashes, Dirt and Dung.   430
    To Thee I cry, to Thee the while I call ;
But, Lord, Thou hear'st not, nor dost heed at all.
Nay, thou art also cruell turn'd to mee ;
With hot Assaults, as on an enemy :
Thou lift'st mee up (as in a storm, the Stubble)
To ride a whirle-wind, while with Fear and Trouble
I faint, and fall (dissolved, as it were)
In deadly Swoun, hurry'd I wot not where :
But well I wot, Thou soon wilt bring mee home
To death, the House where all that live shall come : 440
Whither, thy Hand thou wilt no longer stretch ;
And whence, no prayers boot, nor need, to fetch.
    Did not I weep for others' wofulnesse?
Was not my soule griev'd at their poor distresse ?
When good I lookt for, evill came : when light,
A dismall darknesse, worse then blackest night.
My bowels boyled with continuall heat ;
A troublous time upon mee sudden set :
Not with the Sun, but sorrow black I turn'd :
Amid th' Assembly, loud I cry'd and mourn'd,   450
With hideous noyse (for horrid Anguishes)
As kin to Dragons, and to Ostriches.
My Harp is tuned to a heavy Tone ;
My Musick turned to the voice of mone.

CHAP. 31.

I Made a Covenant with my constant eyes,
    From gazing out on blazing vanities :
(Having my Choice, whereon my thoughts were staid)
Why should I once mis-think upon a Maid?
For, O ! for such, what Part, What Portion is
With God, above, in th' Heritage of blisse ?   460
Nay ; is there not destruction still behinde,
Strange Punishment, for wicked (of this kind)?
    Are not my Paths apparent unto God ?
Doth not hee see and summe the steps I trod ?
    If I have walkt in vanity and pride :
If unto fraud my foot have ever hy'd :
In his just Balance let him weigh mee right,
And hee shall finde mee by his Beam upright.
    If that my Steps have straid, or trod awry :
If that my heart have hearkned to mine eye ;   470
If to my hand hath cleaved any spot :
If bloud or bribes the same did ever blot ;

Then let mee Sow, and others eat my Crop ;
Yea, let my Plant be ever plucked-up.
If ever Woman have my heart beguil'd ;
Or I layd wait t' have Other's Wife defil'd ;
Let mine againe unto another grinde,
And mee be punisht in my sin's owne kinde.
For this is sure a high and hainous Crime,
To be condemn'd and punisht in the prime :   480
Yea, 'tis a fire, whose fury will not cease,
But ruine all, and root out my Increase.
    If ever I despis'd my Man, or Maid,
Debating with mee, and them over-waid ;
What shall I doe? What answer shall I make,
When God, as Judge, their Cause shall under-
    take ?
Did not one Maker them and mee create,
Of Matter like, in Manner like, and Fate ?
    If ever I deny'd the Poor's desire :
Or let the Widowe's longing hopes to tyre :   490
Or ever eat my morsels all alone,
And gave the Orphan and the needy none :
(Hee hath been with me from my child-hood bred
As with a Father : Shee, in Husband's sted,
Hath ever had my Counsell for her Guide,
My Pow'r for Guard ; my Purse her want supply'd).
    If I have seen or suffered any Poor
To lye and dye, Naked, or out of Door :
Nay, if his loynes be-blest not mee from harm,
Because my Fleece and Cottage kept them warm :   500
    If ever I, against the Impotent,
Poor, Father-lesse Friend-lesse Innocent
(For Fear or Favour, of a Friend or Foe,
For Gaine, or Grudge that I did ever owe)
Have lift my hand, or him in right withstood ;
Or, when I might have, have not done him good :
Then let mine Arme off from my shoulder fall,
And from the bone be pasht to powder all.
For, God's drad Judgements did I alwayes fear :
Whose Highness Wrath I could nor balk nor bear. 510
If I on Gold have fixt my Hope, or Heart ;
Or, to the Wedge have said ; My trust thou art ;
If I have joy'd for being growne so Rich ;
Or for my Hands had gotten mee so much :
    If, when I saw the Sun or Moon to shine,
My heart (intic't) in secret did incline
To th' idle *Orgies* of an Idolist ;
Or (*Heathen*-like) my Mouth my Hand hath kist ;
Or if, in Summer of my golden Dayes,
Or silver Night shining with prosperous Rayes,   520
My heart in private hath been pusht too-high,
Ascribing all to mine owne industry
(Which had been impious sacriledge and Pride :
For then had I the God of Heav'n deny'd) :
    If I rejoyc't at ruine of my foes,
Or have triumphed in their overthrowes ;
Or have so much as let my tongue to roule.
Or heart to wish a curse unto their soule :
Though oft my Servants in their rage extreme,
Would faine have beaten, nay, have eaten them :   530

If I have shut the Stranger out of door :
Or let-not-in the weary Pilgrim poor :
If I (like *ADAM*) have conceal'd my sin,
And closely cloakt my Wickednesse with-in :
(Although I could have over-born, with Aw,
Whole multitudes ; the meanest Groom I saw,
I feared so, I durst not wring, nor wrong,
Nor wrangle with : but kept my Tent & Tongue).
  O ! that I had an equall Arbiter,
(To heare, and waigh, consider, and confer).   540
Behold my Aime : th' Almighty I desire
(A certaine Signe of mine intent intire)
For, Hee, I Know, would sentence on my side ;
And witnesse for mee, that I have not ly'd.

  Then though against mee (in his fell despight)
Mine Adversary should a Volume write,
It, as a Robe, I on my Back would beare,
And as a Garland on my head it weare :
I would by piece-meale, shew my Conversation,
All so unlike to all his Accusation,   550
That cleering mee, it should him more convince,
To come and aske mee Pardon, as a Prince.
  But, if my Land against mee plead or plain :
Or, if my Furrowes cry-out, or complain :
If *Tithe-lesse, Taxe-lesse, Wage-lesse, Right-lesse*, I
Have eat the Crop, or caused the Owners dye ;
In sted of Barley, and the best of Corn,
Grow nothing there, but Thistles, Weeds & Thorn.

Here JOB *surceast.*

JOB.

THE FOURTH BOOK.

CHAP. 32.

HEre also ceast the Three fore-named Friends
From farther speech (as hopeless of their ends)
Sith JOB so stifly still maintain'd his right
Of righteousnesse, in his owne proper sight.
　　Then angry *Zeale* began to swelt and swell
In *Elihù* the sonne of *Barachel*,
The *Buzzite* born, and of the race of *Ram* :
Both against JOB began his wrath to flame
(Because, as tenour of his words imply'd,
Rather Himselfe, then God, he justify'd)　　　10
And also those his Foe-friends, for so strict
Condemning JOB, untry'd and unconvict.
　　His modestie him hitherto with-held,
As giving place to others of more Eld :
But, seeing JOB to a full period come ;
And th' other three without reply, as dumb ;
His *Zeale* burst out, and Thus in briefe began :
　　I must confesse, I am too-young a man
T' have interrupted you (so old) before
In this dispute ; and therefore I forbore :　　20
I was in doubt ; I durst not speak (till now)
My weake Opinion, and present it you.
For, dayes (thought I) and years can farther reach :
And long Experience Wisdome best can teach.
　　Men have a Soule, and Reason's light inherit :
But, Wisdome is inspir'd by th' *Holy-Spirit*
(Which bloweth where it will, and worketh free,
Nor ty'd to Age, nor to Authority) :
For, Great-men alwayes are not wisest found,
Nor the Ancient still the most profound.　　30
Therefore awhile to mee give eare, I pray ;
And let Mee also mine Opinion say.
　　I well observ'd your Words, with diligence
I scan'd your Reasons, markt your Arguments :
Yea, neer and narrow have I watcht and waigh'd
What Each of you, and All of you have said :
Yet is there None of you (apart, or joynt)
Convinces JOB ; or answers to the poynt :
Lest You should say ; We Wisdome compasse can,
God will evince him ; not the wit of man.　　40
For mee, mee yet hee never did gain-say :
Nor do I mean to answer him, your way.

Here-with amaz'd, they still continuing mute
Without Reply, or shew of more Dispute
(For I expected yet some speech from some :
I waited still ; and whenas none would come)
I will, said I, now prosecute my part,
To give my Censure from a single heart :
For, I am full of matter to the top ;
My spirit within mee, strains mee, stirs mee up :　　50
My brest is like a Wine-Butt, wanting Vent,
Ready to burst ; or Bottles like to slent.
I'll therefore speake, that I may yet re-spire ;
And ope my mouth, to fanne mine inward fire.
　　Yet none, I pray, from mee the while expect
Smooth soothing Titles ; personall Respect :
For, soothing Titles know not I to give ;
Nor should I, would my Maker let mee live.

CHAP. 33.

NOw therefore, JOB, hark with attentive heed
To all the Words that from me shall proceed :　60
For, what I speake, premeditated is ;
Nor out of Passion, or of Prejudice :
But most sincere and from a single heart,
Out of cleer Knowledge (without Clouds of Art).
　　One and the same, of the same masse of Mire,
Made mee, as thee ; and did my Spirit inspire :
Feare not therefore, if thou have ought to say ;
Oppose and answer : put thy Words in ray :
I am (according to thy wish) to plead
And parley with thee, in th' Almightie's stead :　　70
And yet, a man : My terrors shall not fright thee,
Neither my hand with heavy tortures smite thee.
　　Lo, Thou hast said (I heard and markt it well)
In mee, there none iniquity doth dwell :
I am Upright, and Clean, and Innocent :
Yet, as a foe, Hee is against mee bent :
Hee picks occasions to inflict mee Strokes ;
Sifts all my wayes, and sets mee in the Stocks.
And lo, in this, even in this saying so,
Thou art not Just : for (if thou knowst not) know,　80
That God is Greater then all men : then, Why
Striv'st thou with him ? whose supreme Soveraignty

Yeelds us no reason, nor account at all,
Of his high Counsels ; Why, or How they fall.
　For once, yea twice, to man th' Almighty speaks ;
Yet man perceives not (or it little reaks)
By Dream, or Vision of the night, in Sleep
Upon his bed ; or in some Slumber deep :
Then opens hee men's eares, and him revealeth,
And sweetly there their meet instruction sealeth ;　　90
To turn a man from his intended Ill,
And hide the Pride of his ambitious Will :
To keep his soule back from the brink of hell :
To save his life from death, and dangers fell.
　Sometimes, hee's also chast'ned on his bed,
With grievous Sicknesse, from the foot to head ;
Incessant burning in his bones and bloud :
So that he loatheth the most dainty food.
His flesh consumed, and his bones so high
That they appeare (as an Anatomie) :　　　　100
His Life and Soule draw neer unto the Pit,
(The Grave doth gape, and Worms do wait for it).
　If with him be a holy Messenger
(One of a Thousand) an Interpreter,
To shew to Man the *Justice* of his God,
In his Correction, with his sharpest Rod ;
And, rightly humbled, re-advance the Meek,
By Faith, above his righteousnesse to seek,
And pray to him ; Hee will propitious stand,
And to his Servant hee will thus command,　　110
Deliver him from going to the Grave,
I am appeas'd ; a Ransom found I have.
　Then, then a Child, shall fresher be his Flesh,
Hee shall returne unto his Youth a-fresh :
Then shall hee call on God, and God shall be
Right gracious to him : hee with joy shall see
His glorious Face.　For hee will render than
(Hee will impute) his righteousnesse to Man.
　Hee visits men ; and if that any say,
I have offended : I have gone astray :　　　120
I have mis-done : I have perverted right :
O! I have sinn'd, and had no profit by't ;
Hee will deliver from infernall Doom,
His Soule ; his Life from an untimely Toomb.
Lo, all these things doth God do, twice or thrice,
(Oft and againe) to man (too prone to Vice)
To re-reduce his Soule from Death's dark Night ;
To be enlightned with the living light.
JOB, mark it well, And harken farther yet
What I shall speak ; save when thou seest it fit,　　130
If ought thou have to answer, or object,
Speak on, in God's Name, for I much affect
To justifie and cleer thee (if I may) :
If otherwise, if nought thou have to say ;
List, and observe with silence, I beseech ;
And I shall teach thee Wisedome, by my Speech.

CHAP. 34.

S O, hee proceeded, and said furthermore :
　Heare mee, yee Sages ; men of skilfull lore :

For, as the Palate doth discerne of Food,
Th' Eare tryeth words (how they be bad, or good).　140
Let's then debate this matter among us ;
Examine it, and what is right, discusse.
　For, JOB hath said : *O! I am just, upright ;*
And yet (saith hee) *GOD hath bereft my Right.*
Should I belye my cause ? My thrilled Wound
Is past all Cure ; and yet no crime is found.
　What man, like JOB, himselfe so over-thinks ?
Who (wilfully) Contempt, like Water, drinks :
Who, with the wicked and ungodly walks,
Jumps, just with them, and in their language talks.　150
For, hee hath said ; *Man hath no profit by't*
To walk with God, and in him to delight.
　But, heare me now, all yee that understand ;
O! be it far from the All-ruling hand
Of *Justice* Selfe (th' Almighty God, most High)
To doe Injustice, or Iniquity.
No : Hee to Each man his owne Work repaies ;
And makes him finde according to his Wayes.
Undoubtedly, the *Lord of Hoasts*, the strong,
Nor hath, nor doth, nor will, nor can do wrong.　160
　Who hath to him charge of the Earth impos'd ?
And, Who but hee, hath the whole world dispos'd ?
If hee but please on man to set his minde,
To re-assume his Spirit, his Breath, his Winde,
All flesh at once (if hee but hold his breath)
Shall turn to Dust ; and perish all, in death.
　Now note thou this, if so thou hast a heart
To understand ; list what my words impart :
Shall he have Rule, that Judgement loathes and
　　　lacks ?
And for unjust, wilt thou the Justest tax ?　　　170
Beseems it Any to a King to say,
O! *thou art wicked* (in thy partiall Sway) ?
Or unto Princes (to upbraid them) thus,
You are ungodly, you are impious ?
Then, how much lesse to him that puts no Ods
Touching the persons of those earthly *Gods :*
Nor 'twixt the Rich and Poor, the Great and Small ;
For they (alike) are his owne hands-work, all.
　They (at his will) shall in a moment dye ;
Yea, even at midnight (unexpectedly)　　　180
The people shall be troubled and transported ;
And even the Princes, without hands subverted.
For, evermore his Eyes are open wide
On all men's Wayes, on every Step and Stride.
There is no Darknesse, nor no shade of Death,
For, Wicked-ones to hide them under-neath :
Nor, will hee Any yet so over-load,
That they may justly grudge, or plead with God.
　By heaps, will hee to pieces grinde the Great,
And (in their steed) set others in their seat :　　190
For, unto him their works are manifest ;
Night turn'd to Light : and they shall be supprest.
Them, as most wicked, smites hee (as it were,
In all men's sight, in open Theatre)
Because from him they did revolt and swerve ;
And would not any of his Wayes observe :

But caus'd the loud Cryes of the poor ascend
To Him, who alwayes doth their Cryes attend.
　When Hee gives Quiet, who dares be so bold
To cause Disturbance ; and, if hee with-hold　　200
His Countenance, Who then behold him can ;
Whether a People, or a Private man?
That th' Hypocrite no more may raigne (as King)
Nor, under him, the snared People wring.
　Us therefore thus beseems, to say to God :
I beare with Patience thy correcting Rod :
I will not murmur, nor burst out therefore ;
But sigh in silence, and offend no more :
Shew mee my sins I see not, nor perceive ;
And henceforth will I all unjustice leave.　　210
　Or, should it be after thy pleasure ay ?
No, will-thou-nill, Hee will (not I) repay.
Now, therefore speak thy Conscience seriously ;
And let the prudent mark and testifie,
That, void of knowledge, JOB hath mis-averr'd ;
And, wide of Wisdome, his Discourse hath err'd.
　Would therefore (Father) he might yet be tri'd ;
Sith for the Wicked hee hath so reply'd ;
For, to his sin hee doth rebellion add :
Claps hands at us, as hee the better had :　　220
And (too-too-pure in his too-prudent Eyes)
Against th' Almighty, Words hee multiplies.

CHAP. 35.

E *Lihù* speaking, Thus moreover said :
　　Think'st thou this right (if it be rightly waid)
Which thou hast spoken (or thy speech imply'd)
My Righteousnesse is more then God's (O Pride !
For, thou hast said, *What will it vantage mee,*
What shall I gain, if I from sin be free ?
　I'll answer thee ; and with thee All so dreaming :
Look up, and see the heav'ns above thee gleaming ;　230
Behold, how high : If therefore thou transgresse,
And multiply thy sin and wickednesse ;
What hurt dost thou to God? what detriment?
On th' other side, if thou be innocent,
If just ; what dost thou to his *Goodnesse* give?
Or, from thy hand, What, what doth hee receive?
Thy wickednesse may hurt a Man (like thee) :
Thy righteousnesse to Man may helpfull bee.
　For manifold and frequent Tyranny,
Oppressors make oppressed-ones to cry ;　　240
Yea, to cry-out for cruell Violence
Of Mighty-ones, of men of Eminence :
But there is none that saith (as due belongs)
Where's God *my Maker* (Who by Night gives songs,
Who teacheth us, hath us more Wisdome giv'n,
Than Beasts of earth, or to the Fowles of heav'n)?
There cry they oft ; but none doth heare or heed,
For, th' Evil's sake (who in all ills exceed)
For, Vanity, God doth not, hath not heard ;
Nor ever will th' Almighty it regard.　　250
　　Now, though thou saist, thou seest him not, hee's
　　　Just :
With him is judgement ; therefore in him trust :

For want whereof, his Wrath hath visited ;
Yet not so hot as thou hast merited.
Therefore doth JOB open his mouth in vain :
And voyd of knowledge, yet, yet, mis-complain.

CHAP. 36.

E *Lihù* said : A little suffer mee ;
　　For I have yet more to alledge to Thee,
On God's behalfe.　I'll fetch mine Arguments
From farre (confirm'd by long Experience)　　260
To justifie my Maker's *Holinesse,*
Give him his owne, and right his righteousnesse.
I'll speak no falshood, nor no fraud propound :
All my Discourse shall be sincere and sound.
　Lo, God is mighty ; yet doth none despise :
Omnipotent, Omniscient, Strong and Wise.
Hee spareth not the Life of wicked wights ;
But the Oppressed in their wrongs hee rights :
His eyes are never off the righteous sort :
Them on the Throne hee doth with Kings consort : 270
Them he advances ; and beyond all Term
Doth them establish, and them fast confirm.
　Or, if that ever fetters them befall,
Or, they be holden in affliction's thrall ;
Hee lets them see their works, their wickednesse,
Their wandring By-wayes, and their bold excesse :
And opens then their Eare to Discipline,
Commanding quick that they returne from Sin.
If they return, to serve and him obey,
Their dayes and years their happy spend shall they : 280
If not ; the Sword shall smite them suddenly ;
And in their wilfull Folly shall they dye.
　But Hypocrites, the men of double heart,
They heap-up wrath : they cry not when they smart.
They dye in youth ; their life among th' uncleane,
Most Insolent, most Impudent, Obscœne.
　Hee th' humble Poor in his affliction frees :
Their Ears hee opens, in calamities :
So would hee, thee from thy distresse have freed,
And brought the forth, far from the streits of need, 290
To spacious plenty ; and thenceforth thy Boord
Should with the best and fattest have been stor'd :
But thou, too-wicked-like, too-stiffe hast stood ;
As their presumptions seeming to make good ;
Not stoopt, but strutted in contesting pride :
Therefore, on thee doth judgement yet abide.
　Sith wroth hee is, beware to tempt him more ;
Lest with his stroke, hee sudden smite thee ore :
Or hisse thee hence with his Almighty breath :
Then can no Ransom thee redeem from death.　　300
Will hee regard thy Goods? or reak thy Gold?
Thy State, or strength (how much, or manifold)?
　Nor wish thou (hopelesse) for the (haplesse) night,
When from their place People are taken quite :
Beware, regard not thou iniquitie ;
Neither (alas !) through faint infirmity,
Chuse rather that, than thine Affliction's Part,
With humble Patience of a constant heart.

Behold, the Lord is, for his Pow'r supreme :
And, for his Prudence, Who doth teach like him ?   310
Who hath appointed unto him his way ?
Or, Who can tell him, *Thou hast gone astray ?*
    Rather, remember that thou magnifie
His publike works, apparent to our eye ;
So visible, that both the young and old,
Them from a-far do bright and brim behold.
    Lo, God is greater then wee comprehend :
Nor can the number of his years be kend.
Hee makes the thick exhaled Vapours thin,
That down again in silver Deaws they spin,   320
From strouting Clouds abundantly distilling
For th' use of man, the Plains with Plenty filling.
    Also, can Any understand th' extent
Of Clouds, or know the Rattling of his Tent ?
Behold, Hee spreadeth out his light there-over,
And even the bottom of the Sea doth cover.
For, by the same Hee worketh divers wayes,
Both to his *Justice* and his *Mercies*' praise :
That, through excesse, causing a fearfull Floud ;
This, temperate, producing store of Food.   330
Hee vailes the Light with Clouds that come between,
Forbids it shine, and lets it not be seen :
Boading a shower, or storm's approaching rage :
Which oft, even Cattell of the Field presage.

CHAP. 37.

Here-at, my heart trembles for inward fear,
    As if remov'd from its owne place it were :
Hark, hark with heed unto the hideous Noise,
The horrid Rumbling of his dreadfull Voice,
Which, with his Lightning, hee directeth forth,
Under whole Heav'n, and over all the Earth.   340
After the Flash, a Clash there roareth high ;
Hee thunders-out his Voice of Majestie :
And then no longer will hee keep them back,
When that is heard over our heads to crack.
    God with his Voice, doth thunder wondrously,
And works great things that wee cannot discry :
Hee bids the Snow to cover Hill and Plain ?
So, drizling Showers ; and so, his mighty Rain ;
Whereby, from field-works he seals up men's hands,
That they may know his Works, how he commands.   350
Then, to their Den the savage Heards doe hie ;
And for a season in their Covert lye.
    From Southern Chambers the hot Whirle-wind coms :
From Northern Cels, that which with cold benums.
The Frost is giv'n us, by the breath divine ;
When Crusts of Crystall spreading Flouds confine.
The blackest Cloud hee doth exhaust of waters :
And, his bright Cloud (the Lightnings shroud) hee
                                    scatters.
And (by the counsell of his Providence)
All This, by turns, in round Circumference   360
Is turn'd about : and ready at his Call,
Throughout the World, to doe his will in all.
For, Hee commands them, come for Punishment,
Or Love to His ; or else indifferent.

Harken to this O Job ; stand still and ponder
The Works of God, so full of weight and wonder.
Know'st thou (alas !) when hee disposed them ;
Or caus'd the Light out of his Lump to beam ?
Know'st thou the clouds just poize (the high or lower)
And wondrous works of the All-perfect Knower ?   370
How, when he calms the Earth with Southern puff,
Thy thinnest clothes thou findest warm enough ?
Hast thou with him, spread forth the spangled skie ?
That (liquid Crystall-like) strong Canapie ?
    If so ; then shew us, what to say to him :
For, what to say, we are (alas !) too dim.
Should I mis-speak, needs any him inform ?
Nay, should I not be swallowed up (in storm) ?
    None fixtly can (when clouds be cleer'd away)
Behold that bright and shining Lamp of Day.   380
From out the North stream goodly beams of gold :
With God is Light more bright by manifold,
More pure, more piercing, past a mortall eye ;
More dreadfull far.   His glorious Majestie
(*Dwelling above, in Splendors inaccesible*)
For us to find out, is a point impossible.
Hee's excellent in *Prudence :* passing *Strong :*
Plenteous in *Justice :* and doth no man wrong.
Therefore men fear him : Yet for their desert,
Regards not hee those that are Wise of heart.   390

CHAP. 38.

Then, drad JEHOVA from a Whirl-wind spake
    In sacred termes ; and thus with JOB hee brake :
Where ? Who is Hee, that (to himselfe so holy)
Darkens my Counsels, with contentious Folly ?
Come, gird thy loynes, prepare thee, play the man ;
I will oppose thee : answer if thou can.
    Why ? Where wert thou, tell (if thou know'st, dismaid)
When the foundations of the Earth I laid ?
Who marked first the Measures of it out ?
Or (canst thou tell) who stretcht the Line about ?   400
What Bases had it ; and fixt where-upon ?
Or, who thereof, laid the first Corner-stone,
When Morning Stars for joy together sang,
And all God's children cheerfull eccho rang ?
Or, who with Doore, shut-in the Sea so streight,
When from the womb it rushed with such weight ?
Whenas I made the Cloud a clowt for it,
And blackest Darkness as a swath-band fit :
And Cradled it in mine appointed place,
With Bars about, and Doores at every pace :   410
And said unto it, Hitherto extend ;
And farther, not : here thy proud Waves be pend.
    Hadst thou the Morning from thy birth, at beck ?
Mad'st thou the Dawn in his due place to break ?
That it might reach the earth's Circumference,
And that the Wicked might be shaken thence :
To stamp it (various, as the Potter's clay)
With many Formes, in manifold array,
When as th' Ungodly shall be all discry'd ;
That *Justice* hand may break the armes of Pride ?   420

Hast thou gone down into the Sea it selfe ;
Walkt in the bottom ; searched every Shelfe ;
Survai'd the Springs ? Or have the Gates of death
Been open'd to thee ; and those doores beneath
Death's gastly shadows ? Know'st thou (to conclude)
(Tell if thou know'st) the earth's just latitude ?
    Which is the way, where lovely Light doth dwel ?
And as for Darkness where hath she her Cell ;
That thou should'st both, in both their bounds comprise ;
And know their dwellings, and their Paths precise ? 430
Needs must thou know them : Thou wert born yer
    than :
No doubt thou wert, thou art so old a man.
    Hast thou the treasures of the Snow survai'd ?
Or seen the Store-house of my Hail (up-layd
And hid in heaps against the time of need)
For War-like battry, where I have decreed ?
    Which is the way whence Lightning flasheth out,
Scattring th' unhealthy Eastern Gales about ?
Who hath dispos'd the upper Spouts and Gutters,
Whereby the Aire his over-burthen utters ? 440
Or given the Lightning and the Thunder way,
To cause it rain on places parcht away ;
On Thirstie Desarts, where no people passe ;
On barren Mountains, to revive the grasse ?
    Had Rain a Father ? Or, begot by whom
Was pearly Deaw ? Or, from what pregnant Womb
Came crystall Yce ? Or, canst thou rightly render,
Who did the hard and hoary Frosts ingender,
When Waters creep under a stone-like cover,
And th' Ocean's surface is thick-glased over ? 450
    Canst thou restrain the pleasant influing
Of *Pleiades* (the Ushers of the Spring) ?
Or canst thou loose *Orion's* ycie Bands,
(Who rules the Winter with his chil Commands) ?
Canst thou bring forth (the soultry Summers Guide)
Bright *Mazareth* (or *Dog-star* (in his Tide ?
Or canst thou lead *Arcturus* (and his Train,
Th' *Autumnal* Signs) his Sons or *Charles his Wain ?*
Know'st Thou the Statutes of the Heav'n's above ?
Or canst thou (here) them in their order move ? 460
Wilt thou command the Clouds, & Rain shall fall ?
Will Lightning come, and answer at thy call ?
    Who hath infus'd Wisdome in th' inner part ?
Or Understanding who hath giv'n the heart ?
Who can sum-up the Clouds, or clear the Sky ?
Or ope Heav'n's bottles, when the Earth is dry ?
To steep the dust, and knead the clotted Clay,
Yerst over-baked with too-hot a Ray ?

CHAP. 39.

Wilt Thou go hunt, th' old Lionesse to help ;
    Or fetch-in prey to fill her greedy whelp, 470
When they are couchant in their Den, or watch
For passant Heards, their wonted Boot to catch ?
Who for the Raven provideth timely food ;
When as her hungry greedy-gaping brood,
Wandring about, and wanting what to eat,
Do (croaking) call, and cry to mee for meat ?

Know'st thou the time when mountain Goats and
    Hinds
Do yean & calve (according to their kinds) ?
Canst thou keep reckning of the Months they go,
And how their Burdens to their birth-time grow ; 480
When they but bow them, and forth-with let fall
Their tender fruit, and all their pains withall ?
    Who hath sent out the Wild Asse, free to feed ;
Or let him loose (from serving humane need)
Whose house and haunt I have ordaind expresse
Within the brackie barren Wildernesse ?
Hee scorns the Citie's multitude and noyse :
Hee reaks not of the yawning Driver's voyce :
The craggie Cliffs his shaggie Pastures been ;
Where off hee croppeth what hee findeth green. 490
    Will th' Unicorn thee willingly obay ?
Or, will hee come unto thy Crib for Hay ?
Will hee be brought to harrow or to plow ?
Or will hee bring thy Corn unto thy Mow ?
Wilt thou presume of him, for strength in fight ?
Or leane to him, thy labour to acquite ?
    Didst thou bestow the Peacock's goodly Fan ?
Or, gav'st thou Feathers to the Stork (or Swan) ?
Or, to the Ostridge her delicious Tress
(Th' ambitious badge as well of War as Peace) 500
Who layes her egges, and leaves them in the Dust,
To hatch them there, with radiant Heat adust,
Without her help, or heed ; lest tread or track,
Of Man or Beast them all to pieces crack :
Unkindest Dam, the labour of her wombe
That dares annull ; while Hers not Hers become :
So void I made her of intelligence,
And kinde instinct of Nature's influence :
Yet, with her wings and feet so fast shee skips,
That she the Horse and Rider both out-strips. 510
    Hast thou indu'd the Horse with strengthfull wonder,
And cloath'd his crest, and fill'd his brest with thunder ?
Canst thou affright him, as a Grass-hopper ;
Whose nostrils pride snorts Terrors every where ?
Hee pawes the Plain, hee stately stamps and neighs,
And glad goes-on against the arm'd Arraies,
Disdaining Fear. For, for the sword and Shield,
Dart, Pike, and Lance, Hee'll not forsake the Field,
Nor turn his back (how-ever thick they shiver)
Nor for the Crosse-bow, and the rattling Quiver. 520
Hee swallowes-up the Earth in furious heat ;
Nor will beleeve the sound of the Retreat.
Among the Trumpets, sounds his cheerfull Laugh,
Ha-ha-ha-ha : hee smelleth afar-off
The wished Battaile ; hears the thundring Call
Of proud Commanders ; and loud Shouts of all.
    Is't by thy wisdome that the Hawk doth mew,
And to the Southward spreads her winged Clew ?
Doth th' Eagle mount so high at thy behest,
And build aloft (so neer the clouds) her Nest ? 530
Shee dwels upon the Rock and ragged Cliffe,
And craggie places the most steep and stiffe :
From whence, about to seek her prey shee flyes ;
Which, from afar, her quick keen Sight espies :

Her young ones also, onely Bloud doe suck :
And where the slaine are, thither doe they ruck.

CHAP. 40.

M Oreover, yet, The Lord, proceeding, said
　　To JOB : Shall he that dares wth God to plead,
Teach him his part ? Let him (who God doth tax)
Here let mee hear the Answer that hee makes.　　540
　　JOB sadly then Thus humbly did reply :
O ! Lord, behold ; O ! most-most Vile am I.
What shall I answer Thee ? What shall I say ?
Onely, my hand upon my mouth I'll lay.
Once have I spoke, and twice ; and too-too-bold :
But now, for ever I my Tongue will hold.
　　Again, the Lord out of the Whirle-wind spake,
And said to JOB : Yes, yes ; thy Theam re-take :
Gird up thy loynes again, and play the Man :
I'll question thee : now answer, if thou can.　　550
　　Wilt thou make void my Judgements (just and hie) :
Condemning Mee, thy selfe to justifie ?
Hast thou an Arme like to the Arme divine ?
Or is thy Voice as Thunder-like as Mine ?
　　Put-on thy Robes of Majestie and Might :
Deck thee with Glory, and with Beauty bright :
Dart forth the Lightnings of thy wrathfull Frown,
Against the proud, and bring them tumbling down :
Behold thou all, and every one that's proud,
And down with them, and all the wicked Croud :　　560
Trample upon them, in their very place :
Hide them in Dust at once ; there bind their Face :
Then will I grant (what thou hast urg'd so brave)
That thine own Self thine own right hand can save.
　　But now behold (thy fellow) BEHEMOTH,
Thy fellow Creature ; for I made you Both.
Hee, like an Oxe amid the Field doth graze :
In's Loynes and Navell, his most strength hee ha's :
Hee whisks his sinnewie Taile, stiffe as a Ceder ;
His stones (within) with nerves are wreath'd together,　570
His Bones and Ribs be strong as Brazen Bars,
And as unyeelding as the Yron-Spars :
Hee's of the Master-pieces of the Lord,
Who also arm'd him with a ready Sword.
The Mountains yeeld him meat ; where night and day,
All other Beasts doe fear-lesse feed and play.
Beneath the broad-leav'd shady Trees hee lodges
Amid the Fens, among the Reeds and Sedges,
Compast with Willowes of the Brook about :
Where, when hee enters (in the time of Drought)　　580
The massie bulk of his huge body bayes
The Torrent's course, and even the Current stayes :
There, yer hee go, the River dry hee drinks ;
And in his Thirst to swallow *Jordan* thinks.
Dare any come, before him, him to take,
Or bore his Snout, of him a Slave to make ?

CHAP. 41.

C Anst thou hale up the huge LEVIATHAN,
　　With hook and Line amid the Ocean ?

Canst thou his tongue with steely Crotchets thrill ;
Or with a Thorn his snuffing Nose, or Guill ?　　590
Will hee come sue, by Supplications, to-thee ?
Will hee with smooth and soothing speeches woo-
　　thee ?
Will he by Covenant, serve thee, at thy beck ;
Or be thy Slave, for ever at thy Check ?
Wilt thou with him, as with a Sparrow, play ?
And give him, ty'd, unto thy Girles, away ?
Shall Fisher-men of him a feast prepare ?
Shall they his flesh among the Merchants share ?
Canst thou his skin with barbed *Pheons* pierce ?
Or plant his head with groves of Otter-spears ?　　600
　　Lay hold on him : set on him : but, before
Think on the Battell, and come there no more.
For 'tis so far from hope of Victory,
That even his sight would rather make thee fly.
There's none so fierce that dares him rouze or hunt.
　　[Then, Who shall safely Mee my selfe affront ?
Who hath prevented mee ? To whom have I
Been first beholding for a Curtesie,
Or bound at all for any Benefit
Bestow'd on mee, that I should guerdon it ?　　610
Why ? is not All earth's ample arms' confine,
All under Heav'n, All in the Ocean Mine ?]
　　I will not hide his Parts and Properties ;
Neither his Strength, nor seemly Symmetries.
Who shall unhood him ? Who with double Rain
Shall bridle him, with Snaffle, Trench, or Chain ?
Or put the Bit between his Jawes (his Portall)
Impal'd with Terror of his Teeth so mortall ?
His shield-like Scales, hee chiefly glories in,
So close compact, glew'd, sealed ; that, between,　620
No Aire can enter, nor no Engin pierce,
Nor any Point dis-joyne them or disperse.
　　His Neesings cause a Light, as brightly burning ;
His Eyes are like the Eye-lids of the Morning ;
Out of his Mouth flow blazing Lamps, and flye
Quick sparks of fire, ascending swift and hie :
Out of his Nostrils, smoak, as from a Pot,
Kettle or Caldron when it boyleth hot :
His Breath doth kindle coals, when with the same
Hee whirleth out a storm of Fume and Flame :　　630
Strength dwelleth in his Neck ; so that hee joyes
In saddest storms, and triumphs of Annoyes :
His Flakes of Flesh as solid to his bone ;
His Heart's as hard as Wind-mils neather-stone.
　　To see him rise, and how hee breaks withall ;
The stoutest stoop, and to their Prayers fall.
No Weapons of defence, or of offence,
Can him offend, or from him be defence :
Iron and Brasse Hee waighs as Sticks and Straw :
Sling-stones and Arrowes, Him do never aw :　　640
Darts daunt him not, more then they Stubble were :
He laugheth at the shaking of a Speare :
Sharp ragged Stones, keen pointed Sherds & Shels,
Hee resteth on, amid his muddy Cels.
Hee makes the deep sea like a pot to boyl,
A pot of Oyntment (casting scummy Soyl :

Where hee hath past, hee leaves upon the streams
A shining Path, and th' Ocean hoary seems.
　In earth is nothing like him to be seen ;
So fear-lesse made, so full of haughty spleen ;　　650
Despising all high things, Himselfe beside.
Hee is the King of all the Sons of Pride.

CHAP. 42.

JOB, prostrate then, thus to the Lord profest :
　　Drad God, I know, and I acknowledge prest,
That All Thou *canst;* and all Thou *kennest* too :
Our thoughts not hid ; Thine own not hard to do.
I am the Man, who (to my selfe too-holy
Darkned thy Counsels, with Contentious Folly.
For, I have spoken what I understood not,
Of wondrous things which comprehend I could not. 660
　Yet, Lord, vouchsafe, vouchsafe, I thee beseech,
An eare, and answer to my humble speech.
Till now, mine eare had onely heard of thee :
But now, mine Eye thy gracious Selfe doth see.
Therefore, My self I loath, as too-too-bad ;
And here repent in Dust and Ashes sad.
　Now, after this with JOB ; it came to passe,
The Lord did also speak to *Eliphaz*
The *Themanite ;* and thus to him said hee :
My wrath is kindled with thy Friends and thee :　　670
For none of you have spoken of my Path,
So right and Just as JOB my Servant hath.
　Therefore go take you Rams and Bullocks faire ;
Seven of a sort ; and to my JOB repaire ;
Bring for your selves your burnt Oblations due,
And JOB my Servant hee shall pray for you,
(For him will I accept) lest, justly strict,
After your Folly, I revenge inflict ;
Because you have not spoken of my Path,
So right and just as JOB my Servant hath.　　680
　So *Eliphaz,* the ancient *Themanite,*
Bildad the *Shuhite,* the *Naamathite*
Zophar (together) them prepar'd and went,
And did according God's Commandement.
　Also the Lord accepted JOB, and staid
His Thrall-full State (when for his friends he praid)
And turned it to Solace-full, from sad ;
And gave him double all the goods hee had.
　Then all his Brethren, Sisters all, and Kin ;
And all that had of his acquaintance bin,　　690
Came flocking to his House, with him to feast ;
To waile his Woes, and comfort him their best,

For all the Evill which the Lord (of late)
Had brought upon his Person and his State.
And each man gave him (as best beare they could)
A piece of Money, and Ear-ring of Gold.
　So, that the Lord blessed JOB's latter Time,
With more abundance then his flowry Prime.
For, fourteen Thousand Sheep were now his flock ;
Camels six Thousand ; Steers a Thousand yoak ;　　700
Shee-Asses twice five Hundred ; Familie
Just as before : Seven Sons and Daughters Three.
　Th' Eldest *Jemima, Kezia* the next :
And *Keren-Happuch* (saith my sacred Text)
The Third hee named (Names of goodly Sense,
Alluding to some gracefull Excellence :
The first, as much as *Lustre of the Morn ;*
Cassia, the next ; last, *Alabastrine Horn*).
　In all the Countrey were no Women found
So faire as these. JOB, of his goods and ground,　　710,
Among their Brethren gave them Heritage.
　Yet, after This, JOB liv'd a goodly age.
Twice Seventy years, and saw his Sons Sons Sons,
Successively, Foure Generations :
And then Hee dy'd Ancient and full of Dayes.
　To GOD, for him, and all his Saints be Praise,
　And for his Succour in these sacred Layes.

AMEN.

EPITAPHIUM JOBI.

Qui Se, qui Sêclum vicit ; qui sæva Suorum
　Funera, Amicorum jurgia, Pauperiem ;
Ulcera carnis, qui Conjugis impia verba ;
　Qui Cœlum iratum, mente tulit placidâ :
Invictum virtute *Jobum, Patientia* Virgo,
　Nunc Vidua, hoc Sponsum condidit in Tumulo.

*	*	*	*
* *	* *	* *	* *
Who,	*Who,*	*Who,*	*Heav'ns*
SELF,	*Wealth's*	*Friends'*	*Frowne,*
The World,	*& Health's*	*Rebuke,*	*Earth's Force,*
&	*&*	*Foes'*	*Hels*
Satan,	*Children's*	*Rage, Wife's*	*Fury,*
triumpht-	*ruefull,*	*cursing*	*calmely*
o're ;	*Losse ;*	*Crosse ;*	*bore :*

Th' Invincible *in Vertue,* JOB, *Her* Pheere,
The Virgin Patience (*Widow now*) *toomb'd Here.*

FINIS.

NOTES AND ILLUSTRATIONS.

PAGE 144, col. 1, DEDICATION-VERSES, ARCHBISHOP ABBOT—see our Memorial-Introduction ; and so in pp. 145-6, on Ellesmere and Pembroke and Coke : P. 144, col. 2, l. 7 from bottom, 'Daliladies' = Delilah.

P. 147, THE PROEM, l. 8, 'Stower'—see under Glossarial Index : l. 31, 'disease' = distress, suffering : ll. 64, 747, 'Hussian'—from Uz : ibid., 'Jessean' = David, son of Jesse : l. 122, 'pointed' = appointed : l. 128, 'Hared' = timid as a hare ; or qu. = hurried? l. 184, 'winch' = wince : l. 233, 'thrill'—see Glossarial Index for other examples : l. 238, 'rac't' = razed : l. 288, 'dight' = indite : l. 291, 'Disease'—see on l. 31 : l. 391, 'momes' = blockheads : l. 407, 'poize' = weight : l. 445, 'ill appay'd'—see Glossarial Index, s.v. : l. 515, 'white' = centre of the 'mark' : l. 821, 'con you thank' —see Glossarial Index, s.v.

P. 156, SECOND BOOK, l. 13, 'convince' = convict : l. 34, 'Stock-stained' = in Adam or The Fall : l. 60, 'lardy' = fat ? l. 71, 'haut' = haughty : l. 95, 'raught'

= reached : l. 116, 'white'—see on Proem, l. 515 : l. 184, 'besides' = beside, beyond. So 'sometimes' for 'sometime' : l. 195, 'jet' = strut : l. 260, 'Intime-most' = most intimate : l. 287, 'doom' = adjudge : l. 350, 'than' = then—see Glossarial Index, s.v.

P. 161, THIRD BOOK, l. 118, 'ramp'—see Glossarial Index, s.v. : l. 130, 'poule' = poll : l. 200, 'sad' = solid—see Glossarial Index, s.v. : l. 205, 'List' = boundary : l. 287, 'Quars' = quarries : l. 383, 'Puisnés' little children, punies : l. 386, 'cure' = be curates of.

P. 167, FOURTH BOOK, l. 52, 'slent' = slit, burst : l. 127, 're-reduce' = re-lead back : l. 301, 'reak' = reckon : l. 316, 'brim'—see Glossarial Index, s.v. : l. 321, 'strouting'—see full note in Glossarial Index, s.v. : l. 419, 'discry'd'—ibid. : l. 494, 'Mow' = heap : l. 528, 'Clew'—see Glossarial Index, s.v. : l. 599, 'Pheons'—see Glossarial Index, s.v. : l. 654, ibid. for other examples : penultimate line, 'Pleere,' ibid.

G.

BETHULIA'S
RESCUE.

THE

{ *Wonder of Widowes;* }
{ *Honour of Wives;* }
{ *Mirrour of Maids.* }

Translated; and Dedicated

TO

The Soveraign of Women,

ANNE

Queene of Great Britaine.

BY

JOSUAH SYLVESTER.

TO THE Rɪɢʜᴛ-RIGHT

HONOURABLE *LADIES*,

Lucie, *Marchioness* of Winchester.

Lucie, Anne, Frances,	} Countess	{ of Bedford. of Dorset. of Exceter.	Frances, Katherin, Susan,	} Countess	{ of Hartford. of Salisbury. of Montgom.
		Barbara, Elizabeth, Elizabeth, } *Vi-Countess*	{ Lisle. Haddington. Fenton.		
Sara, Margaret, Honoria,	} *Baroness*	{ Zouch. Wotton. Hay.	Elizab. Elizab. Jane, } *Baroness*	{ Knowles. Cavendish. Roxborough.	

M*irrours of* HONOR, *Models of Perfection,*
    Low to You all, bowes the BETHULIAN *Dame ;*
    Beseeching All, but chiefly You, *by Name,*
    To daign her grace and place in your Affection.
You Noblest Lights, *whose* Vertues *bright reflection*
    Rare-richly sparkles every way some flame
    (*Divers in Form ; in Vertue* still the Same)
    On Objects worthy of your Worth's *Election :*
Your kinde Address *Shee craves, your sweet* Direction
    Towards the Presence of your Soveraign DAME :
    Whose High Endowments by the Trump of Fame,
Invite All Vertuous *under Her* Protection ;
    Which JUDITH *humbly prayes You, pray for Her :*
    And milde interpret Her Interpreter.

BETHULIA'S
RESCUE.

THE FIRST BOOK.

I Sing the *Vertues* and the valiant Deed
Of th' *Hebrew Widow*, that so bravely freed
Bethulian-Doores from *Babylonian*-Dread,
And with just Fauchin did behead their Head.
Thou, that to save, from *Pagan's* servile Rigor,
Thine *Isaac's* Heirs, didst steel with manly Vigor
Weak JUDITH's heart, my feeble heart advance ;
Raise, raise my thoughts in high and holy transe ;
Upon my Spirit, O ! let thy Spirit reflect :
Grant I may handle in a stile select   10
So sacred stuffe ; that whoso reads this *Story*,
May Profit reap, I Comfort, and Thou Glory.

And You, *great* Comfort *of* Great-Britain's King,
Whose Vertues *here I under* JUDITH *sing ;*
Thrice-royall ANNE, *vouchsafe auspicious Rayes*
Of Princely Favour *on These Pious Layes*
(*Composed first upon a* Queen's *Command*
Disposed next into a Queen's *own hand,*
Transposed now to a more Queen's *Protection :*
As most peculiar to all Queens *Perfection*).   20
Great-gracious Lady, let it not distaste,
That JUDITH *made not* (*as shee ought*) *more haste*
To kisse Your *Hands ; nor deem, nor doubt, the worst,*
Though Shee *have seen* Your *royall Spouse the first :*
It was her Truch-man, *much against her minde,*
Betray'd her so to goe against her Kinde.
For which Offence, *with other mo, to Her,*
Sh' hath got her now a new Interpreter ;
Shee hopes more faithfull (*wishes, more discreet*)
To say and lay Her *Service at* Your *Feet :*   30
To give DU BARTAS (*at the last*) *His Due,*
In her behalfe ; and in Her, *honour* You.

While *Israel* a happy *Peace* injoy'd,
And, dangerlesse, with diligence imploy'd
The fruitfull Soile, which seventy years unsow'n,
Had ly'n before, with Thistles overgrow'n ;
The Lord, Who often, by some Stroke severe
Of just Correction, *wakes* his Own (for fear
Lest too-long resting make them like the Horse,
Which standing still too-long, doth lose his Force,   40
Forgets to manage ; and, too-pamper'd, growes
Unruly, restive, and his Rider throwes)
Covers their Country with so huge an Hoast,
That clouds of *Arrows* darkned all the Coast,

Pikes, Bills and *Darts,* seem'd as they stirr'd, or stood,
A moving Forrest, or a mighty Wood :
And, of all sorts of souldiers, rankly-rude,
Under their Ensignes marcht such multitude,
As even drew dry the Rivers where they past
Through rich *Judea ;* so that, at the last,   50
Cleer *Jordan's* Selfe, in his dry oazie Bed,
Blushing for shame, was faine to hide his head ;
Because (flat Bankrupt) hee no more could pay
One Tribute-stream, of all hee ought the Sea.

The Sun-burnt Reaper had yet scarcely rid
The ridged Acres of their richest Weed :
The needy Gleaner scarce had gath'red clean
The scatter'd Ears the Binder left, to glean :
And scarce, as yet the Flayls upon the Floores
Began to groan ; when *Jacob* at his Doores,   60
Sees HOLOPHERNES his weak Frontiers spoile :
In bloudy Rivers drown his fertile Soile ;
Not sparing fell the tender Female-kinde,
Nor hoary hairs (already short confin'd)
Nor Sucklings, swaddled in their Mothers' arms,
From insolence of his insulting Arms.

Then, as a flock of Sheep, which sees their Foe
Come forth a Wood (who oft hath scar'd them so)
Minds no Defence ; but scudding to be gone,
Makes, in an instant, hundred Flocks of one :   70
Th' *Isa'cians* seized with a sudden fear,
Thinking his Hoast behinde them every where,
Disperst and scatter'd (like those silly Sheep)
Fly into Woods ; in Rocks and Caves they creep.

Th' affrighted Swains neglecting fields and flocks,
To save their lives, climb steepest Hills and Rocks :
Artificers, leaving their Tools to play,
Gain-greedy Chap-men, laying Trades away,
Hie them to hide them, in securer sort
In mossie Caves, then in a martiall Fort.   80
And greatest Lords hold Dens of Wolves and Bears
A safer Hold then Gold-lyn'd Walls of theirs.

Fear, lending wings to th' Aged, makes them ply
With lusty speed up to the Mountains nigh :
Fear makes the Mothers, all forlorn and lost,
Lug their dear Cradles to the Clouds almost :
Fear makes the Children (like so many Lambs)
Craule on all foure after their dabbled Dams :

There's nothing heard but hideous cryes and
  plaints,
Sad Lamentations, pitifull Complaints. 90
  O Lord! (say they) wilt thou for ever, thus
Thrill down the Darts of thy fierce Wrath on us?
Shall the *Chaldéan Idolists* again
Thy Chosen Flock in servile Yoak enchain?
Shall our sad Houses, turn'd to Heaps of stone,
With weeds and thorns again be over-grow'n?
Shall sacrilegious Fire again presume
Thy sacred House, thine Altar to consume?
  But *Joachim,* High-Priest of God, that tide,
And of the *Hebrews* then the chiefest Guide; 100
Follows the stout and expert Pilot's guise,
Who, when hee sees a sudden Storm arise,
Adds not more Fear, with his Fear, to his fellows,
Nor leaves his Ship to mercy of the Billows;
But, hiding his distrust, opposes brave
His Arm and Art against the Winde and Wave:
For, quick dispatching (hourely) Post on Post,
To all the Coverts of the Able-most
For Pate, Prowess, Purse; commands, prayes, presses
  them
To come with speed unto JERUSALEM. 110
  Since first th' *Eternall* gave his sacred Law,
Upon Mount *Sinai* (in so dreadfull Awe)
Th' *Ark,* which contained, in *Two leaves of stone,*
Much more sound *Wisdome,* in it selfe alone
Then subtile *Greece,* or *Rome* (renown'd for *Wise*)
In Worlds of Volumes ever could comprise;
Wandred from Tribe to Tribe, from Race to Race,
Throughout all *Jury,* without resting-place;
Yea, sometimes too (O too audacious Theft!)
The sacrilegious *Philistins* it reft; 120
Till th' happy day when *Jesse's* holy Stem
Lodg'd it for ever, in JERUSALEM.
  But, sith as yet, great *David's* hands were red
With bloud of Thousands hee had slaughtered;
The King of *Peace* would have a peacefull Prince
In Peacefull dayes, with all magnificence
To build his TEMPLE; whose high Battlement
Seem'd Earth to scorn, and threat the Firmament;
Till th' haplesse Day wherein a hatefull King
(In name and nature, just resembling 130
This *Tyrant's* Lord) with execrable Blaze,
Did burn it down, and the foundation raze.
A long-while after, *Abr'am's* sacred Stems,
Return'd from Shores of Tyrant *Tigris'* streams;
Beset with Fears, with Perill, and with Pain,
Re-builded Here God's glorious house again.
Which, though (alas!) that first no more it matcht,
Then a King's *Palace* a poor *Cottage* thatcht;
In Bignesse yet, Beauty, and Height, obscur'd
All Pagan *Wonders* which most Fame procur'd; 140
Th' *Assyrian Queen-kings,* (somtime) sumptuous
  Bowers,
Th' *Ephesian Temple,* the *Egyptian Towers,*
The *Pharians Pharus, Carian's* costly *Toomb,*
Rhodes' high *Colossus,* the huge *Heaps of Rome.*

For, for admired *Art,* This glorious TEMPLE
Serv'd *Ctesiphon* for *Model* and Example;
Lent rare *Apelles'* curious pensill Light,
And led *Lycippus'* cunning Chizel right.
  Thither by troups, th' *Isaacian* Tribes devout,
Return'd to *Salem,* flockt from all about: 150
As, when the Heav'ns, opening their Sluces wide,
Poure sudden Showers, surrounding every side;
The gurgling Rills with rapid Course descend
From sundry Hills, and to some River tend.
  But sad-sweet JUDITH in the mid'st (almost)
Shined as *Cynthia* 'mid the *Nightly* Hoast:
For, God (it seem'd) her Beautie's form had cast
In rarest Mould of Nature (first or last).
  Th' *High Primate* then, assisted with the Ligne
Of *Eleazer* (Priests, whose sacred Crine 160
Felt never Razor) on his oyled head
A pearly Mitre sadly setteled:
His sacred Body also soon hee heals
With sacred Vesture, fring'd with golden Bells.
Then burns for *Offring,* slayes for *Sacrifice,*
Kids, Lambs, Calves, Heifers, in abundant wise;
Th' horns of the Altar with their bloud bedying,
And lowly loud, thus to th' Almighty crying:
  Wee come not heer, O dreadfull Lord of Hoasts,
To plead a Roule of *Meritorious Boasts;* 170
Nor to protest, that in these Punishments,
Thou wrong'st thy *Justice,* and our *Innocence;*
No; wee confesse, our foule and frequent Crimes
Worthy worse Plagues then these, a thousand
  times;
Could'st thou forget thy dear authentick *Pact*
With *Abraham,* or would'st thou (so exact)
Forcing thy *Mercy* in thy *Justice* Scale,
Our waight of Sins with Judgements countervaile?
  Remove our Cause, wee therefore (Lord) intreat,
From *Justice* Bar, unto thy *Mercy*-Seat: 180
O! holy Father, pardon us (wee pray)
And turn from us this fearfull Storm away.
  Alas! what boots us, that thy mighty hand
Hath brought us home from *Tigris* hatefull strand,
Free from the Yoke, which wee so long (before)
Under th' *Assyrian* cruell Tyrants bore;
If these fat Fields, wee have but now re-tild,
If these fair Frames, wee doe but now re-build,
If these (O Dolour!) our dear loving Wives,
Our Babes, Sons, Daughters (deerer than our lives) 190
Must serve the *Chaldees, Ammonites* for *Pay,*
And be the *Persians'* and fell *Parthians'* Prey;
If this thine Altar, if these hallowed rooms,
Be re-profan'd with Heathen *Hecatombs?*
  O! if thou wilt not pity Us, abhor'd;
At least, be Jealous of thy *Glory,* Lord:
At least, have pity on this *Holy Place,*
Where to no God, but to JEHOVAH's *Grace*
Is *Incense* burnt, nor any *Sacrifice,*
But to thy Selfe, of all the Deities. 200
Lord! therefore turn, O turn the *Chaldean* Torches
From these rich Cedar *Roofs,* these stately Porches:

Preserve these *Plates*, this pretious *Furniture*,
From sacrilegious Pilferers impure :
And let our Sorrow, and our Sacrifice,
Unto thy *Justice* for our Sins suffice.
   The Service done, Each doth his way depart,
And *Joachim* instantly calls apart
The States of *Juda ;* and thus sadly sweet,
Consults with them how with this Storm to meet.   210
   Grave *Peers* (said hee) if your brave Zeal, of old,
Be not quite quenched, be not yet key-cold :
If Care of Wives, if tender Children's Love,
Had ever power your Soules dear Soules, to move :
If in your Breasts rests any noble Worth,
Now, now or never bring it bravely forth :
For, but God aid, and your auspicious Speed,
Wee are undone, Wee and our wretched Seed :
And never more shall the Immortall see
This Altar *Smoaking* to his *Majestie.*   220
   While th' Aire is mute, so that it scarce can make,
In Summer dayes, an Aspen leaf to shake :
While Seas be calm, so that, with Streamers brave,
A thousand Sail slide on the sleeping Wave :
While all the Winds be mew'd up in their Cell,
'Tis hard to say, which Pilot doth excell,
But, when a Tempest, one-while sinks a Ship
Down to the Bottom of th' infernall Deep ;
Another-while, with swelling Fury driven,
Tilts with her Tops against the Stars of Heav'n ;   230
Raking a Shelfe now, and a Rock anon ;
Then, and but then, is a good Master know'n.
   Therefore (alas !) let now no carnall Care
Of goods, lives, honours (for your private Share)
Make you forget your common-Countrey's Love,
This *Sacred Place,* th' Honour of GOD above :
But humbly all into His hands resigning
Your soule's whole sway, and all your spirits refining
In sacred Flame, from Drosse and Mists impure,
Which too-too-oft the cleerest Eyes obscure ;   240
Advise (I pray) the best, in likely-hood,
Most pleasing God, most for the Publick Good.
   An aged Traytor then, whose breath distill'd
Sweet hony words, whose brest with gall was fill'd,
Wringing false Tears from his dissembling Eyes,
His cursed Drift did in these Tearms disguise :
   My Spirit 's faint, my Speech doth fail me quite,
My frostie hairs for horror stand upright,
When I consider how this Tyrant fell,
With bloud-flouds drowning where hee comes to
    quell,   250
Draws neer Us ; threatning to our Houses Flames,
Death to our Selves, dishonour to our Dames ;
But, when (on th' other side) to minde I call
This mighty Prince's milde Receit of All
(Not onely such, as, rude and Reason-less,
Serve (like himselfe, dumb Idols) Blocks and Beasts :
But such, as matching our *Zeal's* holy Heighth,
Are *Abraham's* Seed, both in their flesh and faith ;
Which wisely have (and timely) turn'd (submisse)
The deadly Edge of his drad Vengeances)   260

I praise the Lord for such a Foe ; so meek
To yeelding Lambs, to Lyons Lyon-like ;
As flexible to humble Tears, as fell
To resolutions that (in vain) rebell.
   Sith therefore, yet we may have choise (for *Jury*)
Of War, or Peace ; his favour, or his furie ;
Winking in dangers, let's not wilfully
Follow our father's stubborn Sur-cuidry :
But, striking Sail in such Storm's violence,
Let 's live secure under so good a Prince.   270
   Yet, *None* mis-take that I this Counsell give,
To save my Stake, as one too-fain to live :
Alas ! my Years are of themselves of age
To *dye* alone, without *Assyrians'* Rage ;
Without the help of their keen Dart or Pole,
To launce my Heart, or to let out my Soule :
Where, were my Youth's Spring now re-flowr'd
    again,
And heatfull bloud boiling in every vein,
My *Zeal* to *GOD,* and to my Country's Good
Should shew mee well no Niggard of my bloud ;   280
Might (*Sampson*-like) my Death bring Death to all
The *Pagan* Hoast, and their proud Generall.
But, more I fear, lest, with a Zeal too-young,
Wee, fighting for the Law, the Law impugne ;
Inciting so the Souldiers' Insolence,
Incensing so the Fury of the Prince,
That they by conquest of one Day undoe
Dear *Israel,* and drown *GOD's* Glory too.
For, *Wee* bereft, What People, in *This Place,*
Truly-religious shall implore his grace?   290
Who, of all Nations that dispersed Wun
From Shores of *Indus,* to the *Setting Sun ;*
And from the farthest *Hyperborean* Coasts,
To those whose Clime continuall Summer roasts,
Hath chosen onely *Jacob* for his Own,
And on *This Mount* his drad-deer *Glory* shown?
   But, good old *Cambris* (else the mildest Prince)
Groans, griev'd and pale with Passion's vehemence ;
And, interrupting That, with this Discourse
Heartens the heartlesse Peers and Counsellors :   300
   Rather, O Earth (for which our Earthlings strive)
Gape under mee, and swallow mee alive :
Rather just Heav'ns, with sulphury Fire and Fume
(As *Sodom* yerst) Mee suddenly consume,
Then I should (Saint-without, within Malitious)
Give *Israel* a Counsell so pernitious.
   Were it, the Head of this inhumane Band
Meant but our Bodies onely to command,
Tho with our Birth, to this fair Light wee brought
Sweet *Liberty* (so sweet and dear, that nought,   310
No Hopes, no Heaps may be compar'd to it) :
The TEMPLE sav'd, I might perhaps submit.
But, sith this Tyrant, puft with foolish Pride,
With heavier Gyves to load our Soules (beside)
Which (onely Vassals of the *Thunder-Thrower*)
Nor know, nor owe, to any Scepters lower ;
Would that (forgetting him who made us all,
And of all People chose us principall,

And fatherly provides us every thing,
And shields us ay with Shadow of his wing)   320
Wee take for *GOD*, his proud ambitious Prince,
Who, *Nimrod*-like, with hellish Insolence,
Would climb to Heav'n, although his life be such,
As merits not the name of Man, by much ;
Let 's beard him boldly, bravely stand wee to 't,
Arms against Arms, Man to Man, Foot to Foot.
Victory lies not in vain-glorious hearts,
Number of Horses, nor of Pikes, and Darts :
These be but Instruments th' Eternall moves,
To crown with conquest whom his Goodness loves.   330
Yet, should the Lord now suffer Heathen's rage
To over-run his sacred Heritage ;
Because in life his Name wee so dishonour ;
In Death, at least, in Death, let 's doe him Honour :
And, if wee cannot *Assur* overcome,
Let 's win, by *Patience*, Crowns of *Martyrdom*.
   And, could our Foes (as fell as *Lestrigons*)
From off the Earth extirp our Tribes at-once ;
They could not tho *GOD's* glorious Name interr
(As these Apostates falsly would inferr).   340
For, Hee that with so sundry Nations stor'd
Th' unpeopled World, from one Man ; and restor'd
(Long after that) by one small Bark, the waste
The *Floud* had made, when it had All defac't ;
Is not Hee able even of stones to raise
A People Zealous of his glorious Praise ?
Is not Hee able once again to ope
Old *Sara's* Womb, and give her Spouse (past hope)
More Sons, than Sands on *Lybian* shores be cast,
By ruffling *Boreas*, loud Cloud-chasing Blast ;   350
Or twinkling Spangles nightly brightly roule
On sabled Circles of the whirling Pole ?
Which with more sacred voice, more humble aw,
Shall sound his Praises, and observe his Law ?
   Then rather, Fathers (foule befall You else)
Let us dye *Hebrews*, then live *Infidels*.
Let 's not prefer, too-base and too-too-blame,
Profit to Duty, idle Fear to Shame.
   Cambris' Oration was no sooner done,
But all th' Assembly (as all joyn'd in one)   360
Confirm'd his Counsell both with voice and gest :
And *Joachim*, (Joy-rapt, above the rest)
Lifting his Hand-in-ward reverent hands and face,
Said, Lord wee thank thee, that thy speciall grace
Hath steel'd our hearts, and linkt our wills no lesse :
A hopefull Signe of happy good Successe.
   Then, to the Princes hee the Charge commits
Of Towns and Provinces, as Each befits :
Lest any, spurr'd by Envy or Ambition,
In *Israel* should kindle new Sedition.   370

So, Each with-draws, and bravely-bold prepares
To front the worst that martiall Fury dares.
   Who th' *Aristæan* busie Swarms hath seen
On *Hybla's* Top ; Whether with Launcets keen,
Charging the Drones wch over-neer their homes
Come humming out to rob their fragrant Combs :
Whether, collecting their delicious Deaw
From various *Thyme*, and other Flowers not few :
Whether, extending, in rare *Symmetrie*,
With wondrous Art, their *Waxen* Canapey ;   380
And arching even, so many Thousand Cells,
So quick, so thick ; so like, as nothing else :
Whether conducting their too-full Supplies
Else-where to plant their goodly *Colonies ;*
Which keep, still constant, in their new Plantation :
Their Mother-Citie's Manners, Laws, and Fashion :
Hath seen the *Jews* as busie Diligence.
And quick Desire to put them in Defence.
   Some stop the Breaches made by Art or Age ;
By the Heav'n's anger, or the Heathen's rage :   390
Some, lest the Ram, butting with boisterous Fals,
Should pash to powder their too-feeble Walls,
With Bastions, Bulwarks, Rampiers, Rav'lins, Forts,
Flank on all sides their Cities where imports :
So me to and fro trudging with Baskets fill'd,
In places needfull, sudden Sconces build :
Some wanting time, or means their Town to wall,
With broad deep Trenches soon begirt it all :
And from a River neer they cut a Rill
The hollow bosom of their Dike to fill.   400
   While Armorers, in order, beating quick
Hot sparkling Steel on Anvils hard and thick,
Transform it soon to Corslets, Curtellaxes,
Helms, Gorgets, Gantlets, Bills and Battail-axes ;
And some, for need (to furnish and set out
Th' untrained Shepheard, Neat-heard, and the Lowt)
Ground the ground-slycing Coultar to a Blade,
And of the Sickle a streight Weapon made :
None Young and healthy took Repast or Rest :
One on his back, another on his Beast,   410
Others in waggons carryed-in apace
Corn, wine, and food to some importing Place :
   Even so, in Summer (as the *Wise-man* tels)
Th' Emmets by troupes haste from their hollow Cels
To get-in Harvest, graving where they gone
Their Diligence, even in a path of Stone :
The lustiest Swarms for their Provision range,
The sick and old wait at their thrifty Grange
T' unload the Burthens, and lay-up their Store
In their great Garner, byting yet before   420
Of every Grain, lest kept so warm below
Amid the mold, it after sprout and grow.

The End of the First Booke.

BETHULIA'S
RESCUE.

THE SECOND BOOK.

Now *Holophernes* in the *Scythick* Fort
Had pight his Standards ; and in various Sport
His Youthfull *Pagans* did them still delight ;
Nought lesse expecting then Affront, or Fight :
When hee had news, The *Jews* stood bravely out,
Defy'd his Pride, and fortifi'd about.
  Shall then (said Hee) shall then a sort of Slaves,
A sort of Clowns and Shepheards, arm'd with Staves,
With Slings and Stones, presume to stop the Course
Of mine exploits : which, nor the roaring source   10
Of rapid *Tigris* and swift *Euphrates*,
Nor snowie Tops of *Taure* and *Niphates*,
Conspir'd, could stay? You Chiefs of *Moabites*,
Of valiant *Ephraim*, and fierce *Ammonites ;*
You that as Neighbours (having long converst)
Know all the Nations on these Hills disperst,
Say, from what People had they their Descent?
What lies their Strength in? What 's their Government?
For, he that wisely knows his foe (they say)
Hath, in a manner gotten halfe the Day.   20
  Then *Ammon's* Prince, bending his humble knee,
Thus to the *Duke* reply'd right prudently ;
(For, though in heart a *Pagan*, born and bred ;
Against his minde, his Tongue, divinely led
By that same Spirit which did the See'r compell,
Which came to curse, to blesse his *Israel ;*
Of th' *Hebrews'* State did such Relation make,
As if in Him *Moses* and *Ezdras* spake) :
  My Lord, I shall, sith You so please, recite
Th' *Isa'cians'* Story ; and will follow right   30
Th' ingenious Bees, which wont not to devoure
All Sweet they meet, nor suck of every Flower ;
But even of those they chuse, take but the Crops.
This People (Sir) upon the Mountain Tops
Encamped here, originally came
From forth the loynes of famous ABRAHAM,
Who, to obey the GOD of gods, most High,
Maker of All ; of All Support, Supply ;
Came to *This Countrey* (then, in Occupation
Of *Cananites*, the rich and native Nation)   40
Where that same GOD not onely heaps with Gold,
And Goods, his House ; but also (though Hee old

An hundred years ; a third part lesse, his Wife ;
And, till that season, barren all her life)
Sent him a Son ; swearing, His seed should sway,
Triumphant Scepters many, many a-day :
But, when good *Abraham's* old-old Age expects
This happy Promise in the sweet effects,
Th' Immortall Voice (O piteous Mysteries !)
Commands that Hee his ISAAC sacrifice.   50
  Even as a Ship, upon the raging Sea,
Between two Winds Cross-tossed every-way,
Uncertain knows not in what Course to set-her,
Till one of them, striving to get the better,
Doubles his billows, and with boisterous blast
Drives her (at random) where hee list, at last :
So, th' *Hebrew* feeling in-ward War (that season)
'Twixt Love and Duty, betwixt Faith and Reason,
Doubts what to doe ; and his Perplexities
Lean now to that hand, and anon to this :   60
Till th' heav'nly love hee ought his GOD, had won
The earthly love hee bore his onely Son.
Then, having ready Fire and Fagot laid,
And on the Altar his dear Son displaid ;
The knife hee draws with trembling hand, and had
Even heav'd his arm about to strike the Lad,
When GOD, in th' instant staies the Instrument
Ready to fall on th' humble innocent :
As satisfi'd with so sufficient Triall
Of *Abraham's* Faith ; to Him his GOD so loyall.   70
  From ISAAC, JACOB ; and from JACOB sprung
Twelve sturdy *Sons ;* who with sore Famine wrung,
Forsaking *Canaan*, for a great-good-while
Had happy Biding by the Banks of *Nile :*
Where their blest Issue multiply'd so fast,
That they became th' *Egyptians'* Fear, at last :
Yea, though (alas !) their bodies had no rest,
And tho their backs with burthens were opprest ;
Like noble Palm-Trees, mounting stifly-straight,
The more, the more they be surcharg'd wth waight.   80
  Therefore the Tyrant which then held the Reins
Of that rich Soile where sad Heav'n never rains,
Commands that all male *Hebrew* Infants found
(Poor Innocents) be quickly kill'd, or drown'd,

As soon as Wombs had them delivered ;
That one same day might see them born and dead.
   O *Tyger* ! thinkst thou ? thinks that Rage of
     thine
To cut-off quite *Isaac's* Immortall Ligne ?
Well may it reave the scarce-born Life of those
New-hatched Babes, and them of Light fore-close : 90
But notwithstanding, *Jacob's* swarming Race
Within few Years shall cover *Canaan's* Face ;
And thine own Issue even the first shall be
To break (and justly) thine unjust Decree.
   Pharao's fair Daughter, with a noble Train,
For Bloud and Beauty rarely matcht again,
One Evening, bathing in the Crystall Brook
Which thorough *Gossen* crawls with many a crook,
Hears in the reeds a rueful Infant's voyce ;
But thinking it some of the *Hebrews'* Boyes 100
(As 't was indeed) her Father's Bloudy Law
Stopt for a while her tender ears with Awe.
But, at the last, marking the Infant's face
(I wot not what unusuall Tracts of Grace
And Types of Greatnesse, sweetly shining there)
Love vanquisht Duty, Pity conquer'd Fear :
For, Shee not onely takes him up from thence,
But brings him up, and breeds him as a Prince,
Yea, as her own. O Babe belov'd of God !
O Babe ordain'd to lighten th' *Hebrews* Load ! 110
To lead their Bodies, to direct their Mindes :
First, best, most Writer, in all sacred Kindes :
Thou hadst but now no Mother, (to be seen)
And now for Mother, thou hast found a Queen.
   Lo, thus (My Lord) could their wise *God* extract
Good out of Evill, and convert the act
Of Persecution (bent against the bloud
And Life of His) unto their greater good.
So *Joseph's* Brethren, by their Envious Drift
To over-throw him, to a Throne him lift : 120
So did proud *Haman's* deadly Hatred lend
Sad *Mordecay* a Ladder to ascend
To honour's Top, and trimm'd his neck (past hope)
With gracefull Chain, in stead of shamefull Rope.
   One day, this *Hebrew*, driving *Jethro's* Sheep
Upon Mount *Horeb* (where hee us'd to keep)
Saw on the sudden a bright blazing Flame
Burn in a Bush, and yet not burn the same ;
From whence, anon he heard (with fear and wonder)
A voice might shake both heav'n and earth in sunder.
   I, I that (onely) AM-WAS-SHAL-BE, Who 131
Made All of Nothing ; and can All un-doe,
When pleaseth Mee : I-AM, *The Holy-One*,
The Great, The Good, The Just ; Whose hand alone
Sustains, maintains, and rules the World : I-AM,
Th' Omni-potent, The GOD of Abraham ;
Fierce to my Foes, with my *Revenging* Rod :
But unto Those that worship Mee for God,
Mee sole, and whole in Thought, in Word, and Deed,
Most *Mercifull ;* to Them and all their Seed. 140
Then doe my Will : dispatch thee speedy hence ;
Goe, say from *Mee*, to that unhallowed Prince,

Which ruleth *Memphis*, and the fertile Plain
Where swelling *Nilus* serves in stead of Rain,
That hee dismisse my People : and lest Hee,
Incredulous, distrust thine Embassie ;
Cast-down thy Rod, thy Message to confirm :
It to a Serpent shall eft-soons transform.
   Hee throws it down, and instantly withall
Sees it begin to live, to move, to craul, 150
With hideous head before, and tail behinde,
And body wriggling (after Creepers' kinde).
Re-take it up, his *GOD* commands him then ;
Which, taken, takes the former Form agen :
And, past Man's Reason (by the power of *GOD*)
Of Rod turns Serpent, and of Serpent Rod.
   Arm'd with this Wand, wherewith hee was to
     quell
The sceptred Pride of many an Infidel,
Hee many a time importunes *Pharao*,
In *GOD'S* great Name, to let the *Hebrews* goe 160
Into the Desart, at their liberties
To serve the Lord, and offer Sacrifice.
   But *Pharao*, deafe unto his sacred Word,
Stifly withstands the Message of the Lord :
Who then by *Moses* working many Miracles,
Authorized His Orator and Oracles.
   First, Hee not onely turned into *Bloud*
Nile's seaven-fold Waves, and every other Floud
That fattens *Egypt ;* but even every Spring,
Whose captive Crystall, golden Pipes doe bring 170
To serve the Court : so that the King is forc't
With that *red liquor* to allay his thirst.
   Then, from the Fens, from puddly Ponds and Lakes
Millions of Millions of foule *Frogs* hee makes
To cover *Memphis* with their ougly Frie,
And not forbear the King's own Canapy.
   Then, of all Ages, of all sorts, and sexes,
With burning *Ulcers*, and hot *Biles* hee vexes ;
So that th' *Egyptians*, in uncessant anguish
Of unknown Poyson, on their Couches languish : 180
Nor can their Leaches their own Leaches be,
In their unheard-of, hidden Malady.
   Then on their cattle ; Flocks, and Heards, and Droves
In Downs and Dales, Fens, Forrests, Fields and Groves,
A strong *Contagion* suddenly hee spred ;
Which took so quickly both their heart and head,
That silly Shepheards neer the River's side,
Their Cattle dead, sooner then sick, espy'd.
   Then turns the earth's dust into swarms of *Lice :*
Then dims the Air with duskie Clouds of *Flies*, 190
Of Drones, Wasps, Hornets humming day and night
In every place, with every face to fight,
And fixing deep in every *Pagan's* skin
Th' unusuall anger of their steeled Pin.
   Then (when appear'd no Threat of troubled Air,
No signe of Tempest) at his Servant's Prayer
Th' Eternall thundred down such Storms of *Hail*,
As with the noyse and stroak did stoutest quail :
Here fals a Bull, brain'd with a Hail-stone's rap ;
There sprawls a Child, split with a Thunder-Clap : 200

Here a huge Forrest, lately all a Cloud
Of tufted Arms, hath neither Shade nor Shrowd :
And, if the native sap again re-suit
The naked Trees with comely Leaves and Fruit,
Again (alas !) the *Caterpiller* crops,
Within few hours, the Husband's yearly hopes.

Then with gross *Darkness* vailing close the Skies,
Hee so sield-up stubborn *Egyptians'* eyes,
That for three dayes with fearfull foot and hand
They groapt their way (except in *Gossen*-land) :   210
And *Titan*, tir'd in his long Course, for ease,
Seem'd then to rest him with th' *Antipodes*.

But as the same Sun, the same instant, makes
The Mud to harden and to melt, the Wax ;
So had these works, so full of admiration,
On diverse Subjects, diverse Operation.
The humble *Hebrews*, GOD's great hand adore ;
But wilfull *Pharao* spurns it more and more :
Even as a Corselet, when 'tis cold enough,
The more 'tis beaten growes the harder Proof.   220

Yet, at the sad newes of the Prince, his Son,
And all their Heires, all in one night undone ;
He was so daunted, that he early bod
The *Hebrews* go to serve the Lord their GOD :
Who, in a *Pillar of a Cloud* by Day,
Of *Fire* by Night, directed right their Way.

But, soon retracting his extorted Grant,
The stubborn Tyrant strangely arrogant,
Arms all his *Egypt*, and in post pursues
The Arm-less Legions of the harm-less *Jews*,   230
Then lodg'd secure along the sandy shore,
Where th' *Erythræan* ruddy Billows rore.

Was not such Noise, when, tearing *Gibraltar*,
Th' *Herculean* Sea came first to spred so far
Twixt *Calpe* and *Abile ;* nor when *Oenotrie*
Sad-sighing lost her dear neer *Trinacrie ;*
As in both Armies : Th' one insulting proud ;
Th' other in skrieches, and sad cryes, as loud,
Deafned the shores : while fifes, horns, furious horse,
With noise and neighs, did even the Welkin force.   240

Cursed Seducer (cry'd the *Jews*) what spight
Mov'd thee to alter our Live's happy plight?
What? are wee Fishes, that wee here should swim
Through these deep Seas? Or, are wee Fouls to skim
Over the steepest of these Mountains tall?
Were there not graves in *Egypt* for us all?
In our dear *Gossen ?* but wee needs must come
In this *Red-Sea* to seek our ruefull Tombe?

Yet mildest *Moses*, with his dead-live Wand,
Strikes th' awfull Streames : which, yeelding to his
          hand,   250
Discover Sands the Sun had never spy'd,
And wall'd the same with waves on either side :
Between the which (drad-lesse and danger-lesse)
The *Hebrews* dry-shod past the *Crimsin Seas.*
But, when the Tyrant rashly them pursues,
Marching the way was made but for the *Jews*,
The Sea returns, and over-turns his Force,
Himselfe, his Men, his Chariots and his Horse.

O happy People, for whom GOD (so kinde)
Arms, fire and aire, and clouds and waves and winde !   260
Whom all things serve : which hast all things in pay,
O ! never let Time's File to fret away
So rare a Favour? rather let the tongue
Of all thine aged tell it to their young ;
They to their seed, and they to theirs again ;
Eternally these wonders to retain.
Them, forty years, GOD in the Desert fed
With Angels' Food, with a celestiall Bread ;
And from a Rock (as dry as Pumice first)
Made Rivers gush, to satisfie their Thirst :   270
Kept (even) their Shooes, and all their Garments
          there
As good, the last, as the first day they were :
And sith our Soules will faint for want of Food,
Most liberall in all, for all their good,
Gave (on Mount *Sinai*) in his *Sacred Law*,
Soule to their Soules, through sharp-sweet filiall Awe ;
Teaching them all (as duty all doth binde)
To love Him, first, and next to Him, Mankinde ;
That wee might never break that sacred Twine
Which Man to Man, and Man to GOD doth joyn.   280

Grave *Moses* dead, brave *Josuah's* rule began ;
Whose happy Sword soon conquered *Canaan ;*
And in few years into subjection brings
The Lives and States of one and thirty Kings.
At his command, more powerfull than the Thunder,
The firmest Rocks and Rampires fall in sunder ;
Without the Shock of Tortoise or of Ram,
To batter Breaches where his Armie came :
For, but with bellowing of hoarse Trumps of horn,
As with an Engine, proudest Towers are torn :   290
As at his beck, the Heav'ns obey his will ;
The Fire-foot Coursers of the Sun stand still,
To lengthen Day, lest under wings of Night,
His *Heathen* Foes should save themselves by flight.

This scourge of *Pagans*, in a good old age
(To live in Heav'n) leaving this Earthly Stage,
Israel had many Magistrates of Name,
Whose Memories live ever fresh in fame.
Who knows not *Ehud, Sangar, Samuel,
Debora, Barac*, and *Othoniel ?*   300
Who hath not heard of mighty *Sampson's* Coile,
Who, sole, and Arm-lesse, did an Army foile?
What praise wᵗʰ *Jepthe's* might have well compar'd
Had but his rashnesse his dear Daughter spar'd?
What Clime, what Time, what River, dale or down
But rings of *Gedeon*, and his high Renown?

After the *Judges ; Kings*, (some good, some bad)
The sacred Helm of th' *Hebrew* Vessell had :
Had I their *David's* holy Harp and Skill,
Nothing but *David* would I warble still :   310
But as (my Lord) great *David's* Deeds, could none
(Yer-while) atchieve, but *David's* Selfe alone ;
Can none but *David's* Harp, and *David's* Hymne
Resound aright the Honours due to Him :
I will not therefore, with unworthy Layes,
Seeming to Praise him, derogate his Praise.

But, shall I balk his Son, whom Heav'ns adorn
With health, wealth, wisdome, and all-plentie's horn.
Whose prudent *Problems,* touching every Theam,
Draw thousand *Sophists* to JERUSALEM,   320
Arabians, Indians, Africans among ;
Chain'd by the Charms of his all-ṣkilfull Tongue ?
Or him, whose *Zeal* the Idols so defac't ;
Re-purg'd GOD'S TEMPLE, and his *Rites* re-plac't ?
Or him, that saw a Heav'nly hoast descend
To succour *Sion,* and his Foes offend ?
Or him, whose Army, neer to *Gerar,* yerst,
Proud *Ethiopian's* swarming Troops disperst ?
Or him, who praying for Heav'n's aid, to fight
'Gainst *Ammon, Moab,* and *Mount-Sëirite ;*   330
Saw, by themselves, his sad request ful-fill'd,
When, Self-incenst, Themselves they enter-kill'd ?
    But *Chaldei's* King, by their's *Captivity,*
Put (late) an end unto that *Monarchy.*
Yet did Great *Cyrus* Them again restore
To Liberty : and gave them furthermore
Leave to elect Two *Rulers* of their Race :
Whereof the One (who yet supplies the place)
Was *Joachim ;* who, for his holy Life,
Prowess, and Prudence, is respected rife,   340
Not sole in *Sion ;* but with *Ammonites,*
Syrians, Sydonians, Madians, Moabites.
    Thus was (my Lord) the *Prime,* this the *Progression,*
Of ISRAEL, through every Time's succession :
And thus the Lord hath lift them (nigh) to Heav'n
Som-times ; som-times, them (even) to hell hath driv'n.
    But, whether *Princely-priest,* or *Judge,* or *King,*
Of th' *Hebrew Tribes* have had the Governing ;
So long as they observ'd the sacred *Pact*
GOD with their Fathers did by Oath contract ;   350
Ay prosperous, triumphantly they troad
On proudest Foes : and all the World abroad,
Conspir'd in Spight, could nothing them annoy,
Much less distract them ; least of all, destroy :
On th' other side, soon as they have infring'd
His Ordinance, their GOD (to be aveng'd)
Hath thrall'd them, now, to cruell *Moabites,*
Anon to *Edom,* then to *Ammonites,*
Then *Philistins :* and ay his Wrath hath bin
Heavie upon them, when they hap to sin.   360
    If so be therefore, ay their *Offence*
The jealous *Justice* of their GOD incense ;
Mine not their Mounts, nor undermine their Bowers,
Nor bring thy Rams against their rampir'd Towers,
Nor scale their Wals, nor lead thy warlike Legions
(With Resolution) to assault them once :
For, let them heap, on *Carmel Libanus ;*
On *Liban, Niphate,* there-on *Emmaus :*
Yea, in one Chanel let them muster hither
Indus and *Rhone, Nilus* and *Rhine* together, 370
Tiber and *Iber* too, to fence their Coast :
They cannot scape from thy victorious Hoast.
    But, if they have not broke the *Covenant*
Which GOD to *Abram* and his Seed did grant :

Beware (my Lord) beware how you come neer
This *Holy Nation,* to their GOD so dear.
For should swart *Auster* him dispeople quite
To furnish Thee with all his, fit to fight :
Should swarming *Boreas* from his utmost end
All his tall Souldiers to Thy service send :   380
Should *Zephyrus* add to Thy dreadfull power
His martiall *Legions,* all *Hesperian's* Flower :
Should (lastly) *Eurus* send Thee for Supplies
His Troops which first see *Phœbus'* Rayes arise :
All These, all-daring, all-devouring Swarms,
This armed World, or all This World of Arms
Could never conquer (in a thousand year)
The least, worst, weakest, of these Cities here ;
Because Their GOD will be their sure *Defence :*
That GOD Almighty, whose Omnipotence   390
Can with a breath confound all Kings that dare
(As Thou dost now) 'gainst Him make open War.
    As th' Ocean's Billowes swell not by and by,
When (first) the Winds begin to bellow high ;
But, first begin to foam, and then to fume
Higher, and higher, till their Rage presume
To chide the Earth, and check the Welkin's Front,
And bandy Hills against the Heav'nly Mount :
Even so, the Princes of this *Pagan* rout,
Hearing GOD'S prayses, forth-with break not out   400
In rageful Furie ; but as th' *Ammonite*
Grows in Discourse, so grew they in Despight ;
Till at the last, with loud, proud murmurings,
They even blaspheme the glorious King of Kings.
    Kill (cry they) kill ; let 's hew and hale in peeces
The subtile Traytor, that with wylie Speeches,
To save his *Hebrews* from *Rhamnusius'* Rod,
Would fright us with a false and idle God.
    Renowned *Generall,* send but out a score
Of all thy Troops, and they shall soon run-o'r   410
Those rascall Rebels ; and reduce them all
Prostrate and humble at Thy feet to fall :
Ah Coward ! Villain ! But the Vice-Roy then,
Stopping their loud outrageous Storms again,
Began himselfe *Thus* to the *Ammonite ;*
    O impudent Impostor ! Tell Mee (right)
What Fiend, what Fury hath inspir'd these Spels :
What *Trevet* told thee, or what *Sibyl* else
Made thee beleeve that *Syrians* shall not quell
Th' *Isaacian* Troop, but stoop to *Israel,*   420
Whose GOD is but their *Dream,* or *Fansie* vain,
Or meer *Device* of MOSES' subtile brain ;
Neither, of power to give them Victorie,
Nor from Our hands to rescue Them nor Thee.
What God have wee, but the great King of Kings,
NABUCHADNEZZAR ? whose drad puissance rings
O'r all the Earth : who covering far and nigh,
The Plains with Horse, Hills with Infanterie,
Shall raze these Runnagates ; which, fled from *Nile,*
Have here usurped Others' Right yer-while :   430
Die therefore, Villain, die ; take the desert
Of thy false Tongue, and of thy treacherous heart.

What said I, fond? No, Dastard, I disdain
My valiant Blade in thy base bloud to stain :
Thou shalt so quickly not receive the meed
Of thy disloyall and detested Deed,
(For, a quick death is Wretches' blisse, wee know ;
Them quickly ridding both of Life and Woe)
But, with thy Dayes thy Dolours to protrack,
Thou shalt from hence unto *Bethulia* pack ;   440
Where still thou shalt, through infinite dismay,
Undying, die a thousand times a day ;
Untill, with those *Invincible* (thou saist)
With thousand wounds a wretched End thou hast.
Why tremblest Thou ? why doth thy colour faile ?
Why seems thy heart for horrour so to quaile ?
If so their GOD be GOD (as thou hast vaunted)
Now, by thy Face witnesse thy faith undaunted.

Then, the Lord Marshall, in Authoritie
Under the Vice-Roy, not in cruelty,   450
Transporteth speedy, neer *Bethulia's* side
Th' un-*pagan Pagan*, hand and foot fast ty'd ;
Leaving his Troops wounded with wondrous grief
To be deprived of so brave a Chief ;
Even so the Puttock in his crooked Serrs
The peeping Chicken through the Welkin bears ;
While the poor Dam below, cluck-cluking thick,
Cryes, but in vain, and calls her rapted Chick.

The Citizens, seeing th' approach of Foes,
Soon in *alarm* them all to Arm dispose ;   460
And, with meet Number of their Men of worth,
And choice Commanders, bravely sally forth ;
Faster than Torrents gushing from the Hills,
Run hopping down into the lower Fields.
The Foe, retiring to their mightier Bands,
Leaves captive *Ammon* in the *Hebrews'* hands ;
Whom with a forced foot, though free in thought,
And will right willing, to their town they brought.
Where, round-environ'd with a curious Crowd,
Lifting hee began : O thou great GOD, the Guide   470
Thus hee began : O thou great GOD, the Guide
Of Heav'n and Earth, and All that is beside ;
Whose living Spirit (spred in, and over All)
Gives All things Life, Breath, Growth, Originall,
I give thee, Lord, a thousand Thanks devout,
That thou hast daign'd, yer death, to take mee out
Of my wilde Stock, to graft mee in the Stem
Of th' happy Tree, deaw'd with thy *Gracious* stream ;
Which (maugre Blasts, and Blastings, rough and rife)
Of all the Trees, bears onely Fruit of Life.   480

And, good *Is'acians*, for GOD'S sake, I pray
Mis-doubt mee not, as comming to betray,
Or under-mine by wylie Stratagem,
Your Strength, or State ; or wrong JERUSALEM :
No : GOD doth know, I suffer This, for You,
For witnessing before yon wicked Crew,
GOD'S mighty Arm for your Fore-Fathers shown ;
As ready still, to save and shield his Own.

Fear not therefore Their mighty multitude,
Whose sight (almost) so many hath subdu'd,   490
Nor let their Boasts, nor braving Menaces,
Kill, quail, or cool, your holy Courages :
For, should the whole earth send her sons in
    swarms,
Against you onely, all to carrie Arms ;
So that your Trust be fixt in GOD alone,
Not in an Arm of Flesh, not in your Own ;
You shall, no doubt, make ruddy *Mocmur's* Floud,
With Idolist *Assyrian* Armies bloud :
You shall, no doubt, of Fearfull, Fierce become,
Your strong Assailants stoutly over-come.   500
Th' Almightie's hand, so ready bent to smite,
Is but to humble, not destroy you quite ;
And, but to shew you, that in all Distresse,
Hee, onely Hee, can give you quick Redresse,
As from a Bramble springs the sweetest Rose ;
As from a Weed the whitest Lilly grows :
Even so, divinest Sighes, devoutest Tears,
Demurest Life, are Fruits Affliction bears.
For, here the Faithfull are much like the Earth,
Which of it selfe (alas !) brings nothing forth   510
But Thorns and Thistles, if the Plough shee lack,
With daily wounds to launce her bunchy back.
But yet the Lord (who alwayes doth relent,
So soon as Sinners earnestly repent,
And in his time, his sharp hand doth retire,
And cast, at last, his Rods into the Fire)
Will rid your dangers, and restore you rest,
Even in an houre, when you can hope it least.
Then, courage, friends : let's vanquish God with
    tears ;
And then Our Arms shall quickly conquer Theirs,   520
Their World of Men. And, if as yet in Mee
Rest any Strength ; if any Courage bee ;
If mine Experience may in ought avail :
If with mine Age, all be not old and frail :
I vow it all, and all that else is Mine,
To your Defence, and for the *Law divine.*

The End of the Second Booke.

BETHULIA'S
RESCUE.

Flame-snorting *Phlegon's* ruddy breath began
   Reducing Day, to gild the *Indian ;*
   When early wakened with their ratling Drums,
Each *Heathen* Souldier from his Cabin comes,
Takes-up his Arms ; and marching in Array,
Towards *Bethulia* tends the ready way.
  In May, the Meads are not so py'd with Flowers
Of sundry Figures, Colours, Savours, Powers ;
As was this Hoast with Squadrons, different
In Language, Maners, Arms, and Ornament :   10
So that th' old *Châos* (wombe of th' UNIVERSE)
Was never made of Members more diverse.
Yet, here-in all agreed, for all their Ods,
To war against th' Eternall God of Gods ;
Whose breath, whose beck, makes both the Poles to
   shake,
And *Caucasus* and *Libanus* to quake.
  Here, cold *Hyrcania's* bold and braving Seed,
Mixt with (their neighbours) both *Armenia's* breed,
Wave wanton Crests : There, *Parthian* Archers try
Backward to shoot, the while they forward fly.   20
The *Persian*, there, proud of th' Imperiall state,
With golden scales scalops his Armed plate :
Here would the *Mede* shew, that for want of Hap,
Not heart, Hee lost his (late) *Imperiall Cap.*
And that, nor Pomp of his too sumptuous Suits ;
His painted Cheeks, his *Phrygick* Layes and Lutes ;
His crisped Bush, not his long borrowed Lock,
Had ever power his Manly mind to smock :
Happy-Arabians, who their Fern-thatcht Towns
Tumble in Tumbrels up and down the Downs :   30
The subtle *Tyrians*, who did first invent,
Our winged words, in Barks of Trees to print :
The men of *Moab*, and the *Ammonites*,
The *Idumèans*, and the *Elamites*,
Learned *Ægyptians :* those that neer confine
The swelting Coasts of swartest *Abyssine :*
In brief ; All ASIA was immur'd almost
Within the Trenches of this mighty Hoast ;
Wherein, well-neer as many Nations clustred,
As th' *Hebrews'* Army single Souldiers mustred.   40
  But, of all these, none plagu'd the *Israelites*,
More then their owne Apostate *Ephraimites ;*

Who not to seem of kin to *Israel*,
Rag'd with more fury, fought more deadly fell.
As, in the Spring time, while a Poole is still,
And smooth aloft, the Frogs lye croaking shrill ;
But if the least stone that a Child can fling
But stir the water, streight they cease to sing :
So, while a happy *Peace* JUDEA blest,
The Constancy of These stood with the best,   50
Among the Saints ; and the Lord's sacred Praise
Was in their mouthes daily and many waies ;
So that they seem'd like burning Lamps to shine
Amid the Flock, devoutly-most-divine :
But at the Noyse of *Holophernes'* Name,
Their famous Faith nothing but aire became ;
Their Mouth is stopt, the *Zeal* they did presume
So highly hot, is vanisht into Fume.
Nay, turned *Pagans* (for some Profits' sake)
They, worse then *Pagans*, their poor Brethren
   rake.   60
  O ! what a Number of such *Ephraimites*
Are now-adayes (Deceitfull Hypocrites !)
With-in the *Church*, the while a prosperous wind,
With gentle Gales, blows fair and full behinde ;
Which seem with *Zeal* the *Gospel* to imbrace,
While that it yeelds them either gaine, or grace :
But, if the Chance change ; if it hap to puffe
But halfe afront ; if *Shee* be fain to luffe ;
Faint-hearted, then forth-with they cast about :
And, with th' Almighty playing banque-rout,   70
With greater Rage his Law they persecute,
Then yerst with *Zeal* they did it prosecute ;
And in their Malice grow more fierce and furious,
Then *Julian* yerst, or *Celsus*, or *Porphirius.*
  Soon as the *Hebrews* from their Turrets spy
So many Ensignes waving in the Sky ;
And such an Hoast, marching in such Array,
Begirt afar their Citie every way :
They faint for dread ; not having where to run,
Save to the GOD their Grandsires trusted on.   80
  O Father (cry they) Father of Compassion,
Whose wing is wont to be our strong Salvation ;
Sith now against us all the World doth swarm,
O ! Cover us with thine Almighty arm.

Thus having pray'd, the carefull Governour
To Charge his Watches doth him quick bestir ;
And when the Sun in his moist Cabin dives,
With hundred Fires the Day again revives ;
Watches himselfe amid the *Court of Guard ;*
Walks oft the *Round :* and weens, that over-hard   90
Phœbe's black Coachman drives his sable Steeds,
Hebrews neer Ruine hasting more then needs ;
While, opposite, the *Pagans* think her fast
With her *Endymion*, in a slumber cast :
But, Men's frail wishes have (alas !) no force,
To hold, or hasten, th' Heaven's settled Course.
    Soon as they saw *Aurora's* saffron ray
On their *Horizon* to renew the Day,
The *Vice-roy* makes a thousand Trumpets sound,
T' assemble all his scatter'd Troups around ;   100
Which from all parts with speedy pases went
Environing their Chief-Commander's Tent :
As round about a Huntsman, in a morn,
The Hounds doe throng when once they hear his
    horn.
    Having in vain summon'd the Town ; hee tries
A hundred wayes it (wrathfull) to surprise :
Here, th' Enginer begins his *Ram* to rear ;
Here mounts his *Trepan*, and his *Scorpion* there ;
Bends here his *Bricol*, there his boysterous *Bow ;*
Brings here his *Fly-Bridge*, there his batt'ring *Crow :* 110
Besides high *Timber-Towers*, on rowling Feet
Mov'd and remov'd ; controlling every Street.
    Here, Pioners are put the Ditch to fill ;
To levell Mounts, to make a Hole a Hill :
To play the Moles, to dig a secret way,
Into the Town their Souldiers to convay.
    Here, others must their Ladders raise the while,
And quick surprise the Sentinels, by wile :
Others must under-mine : others aspire,
With matter fitting, every Gate to fire.   120
    But the most part stand ready in Array
To give Assault, soon as they see their way
Made meet and easie, by the battering Thunder
Of all their Engines, pashing Walls in sunder.
    Tower-tearing *Mars, Bellona* thirsting-bloud,
Fill there the faintest with their Furious-mood :
There fiery Steeds, stamping and neighing loud ;
There *Pagans* fell, braving and raving proud,
W^th hideous noise make th' heavenly Vault resound, 130
The Earth to eccho ; and even Hell astound.
    But Hee that keeps eternall *Sentinell*
On Heav'n's high Watch-Tower, for his *Israel*
Pitying his People, alters, in a trice,
The Tyrant's purpose, by a new Advice ;
Causing the Captains of brave *Moabites*,
Strong *Idumèans*, and stout *Ammonites*,
Thus to advise : Most noble *Generall*,
Terrour of Kings, redoubted Scourge of all ;
Wee would not wish (my Lord) in any sort,
You bring your brave Bands to assault this Fort :   140
For, neither pike, dart, sling, bow, sword, nor shield,
So back the Foe, or make them slac   to yeeld ;

As these proud rocks, which, by wise nature's
    grace,
Rampire the Rampires of this wretched Place :
Which yer you scale undoubtedly will cost
Ladders of Bodies ; and even Tythe your Hoast.
The Victor is no Victor, if his Gaine
Pass not his Loss ; nor th' Honour drown the Stain.
Wise-valiant Prince, that Fisher, Fool wee hold,
Who for a Gull, venters a Line of Gold :   150
And, ill doth th' honour of a Crown beseem
Th' inhumane, bloudy, barbarous Head of him
Who rather would the death of many Foes,
Then life and safety of one Friend, to chose.
    You may (my Lord) you may, without assault,
Or losse of Man, reduce them all to nought,
If in yon Hillocks you but seize the Springs,
Whence hollow Lead the *Hebrews* water brings ;
Who, so by Thirst distrest, and so put to 't,
Will come and cast them haltred at your Foot.   160
    The noble Lion never sets-upon
Base fearfull beasts, but on the no blest one :
Jove's sulphury Darts Hee seld or never thrils
But on Mount *Atlas*, or the *Ryphean* Hills :
And stormfull *Auster*, ever rather smote
Cloud-cleaving Turrets then a lowly Cote :
No more, no more let your drad Arms assail
So faint a Foe as of himselfe will quail.
    It is not Fear (my Lord) and much lesse Pitie ;
(Fear of our Selves, or Favour to the Citie)   170
Makes us oppose us to thy Purpose yet :
For yer that wee thy happy Standards quit,
For thee will wee defie th' immortall Gods :
For thee wee 'll break their Altars all to Clods :
For thee will wee march with unweary soles,
Beyond the *Arctick* and *Antarctick Poles :*
For thee will wee with winged Arms goe fetch
Jove's Aigle down ; and *Neptune's* Trident snatch :
For thee the Son shall not his Sire forbear,
Nor Sire the Son ; nor Brother, Brother spare.   180
    The *Generall*, who for avail revolves,
Peizes this Counsell ; and re-peiz'd, resolves,
Dispatching speedy a selected Force,
To seize the waters, and divert their Course.
    Th' *Hebrews*, their drift, and their owne danger see
In that Attempt : so sally instantly
To stop the Foe from stopping of the Stream
Which should derive Liquour and Life to them.
    Then *Pagans* fighting for ambitious Fame ;
Jews, not to dye with un-revenged Shame,   190
Bravely incounter with so fell Disdain,
That now the *Pagan* flyes, now fights again ;
Follows his flying Foe, and now the *Jew*,
Nigh foiled, faints ; now doth the Fight renew :
So that fair *Victory* seems long to waver,
As it were doubtfull whether side to favour :
Till (at the last) th' *Hebrews*, all over spred
With Clouds of Shot, back to their Bulwark fled :
Even as a Pilgrim in the naked Plain
Meeting a Storm of mighty Hail or Rain,   200

Runs dropping wet some hollow Rock to finde,
Or other Covert built by Nature kinde.
Pagans pursue them, and pel-mel among
Enter almost the City in the Throng.
Then every where did dreadfull Noise arise :
From street to street th' amazed Vulgar flyes ;
Tearing their hair, beating their breast and face :
As if the Foe had even possest the Place.
 Why flie yee Cowards? whither? do you know?
What Fortresse have you, if you this forgoe?   210
Or, in this City seek you for a stronger,
To guard you better, or preserve you longer?
If now (alas !) you dare not bear you stout
Against the Foe, while hee is yet without ;
How will you dare resist his violence,
Were hee once Master of your weak defence?
 The People, chid thus by their prudent Chief,
Som-what re-heartned, rescue with relief
Cambris and *Carmis ;* who, the while like Towers,
Had in the Gate withstood th' Assaulting Stowers   220
Of almost all the furious Infidels.
For Lance, a long Mast, either strongly welds,
For Arms an Anvile ; each a massie Targe
Of steel about his neck, as long as large :
Adown their shoulders from their Helms did wave
Thick Plumie Clouds of Colours-brightly brave ;
Both like, in Age, in Courage, Name and Nature ;
Both like in Bulk, both like in Strength and Stature
Both, like two Popplars which (on either side
Some silver Brook) their tressie Tops doe hide   230
Amid the Clouds ; and shaken by the winde,
Oft kisse each other, like Two Brethren kinde.
 The *Heathen*, seeing still fresh Troups descend
From every side, the City to defend ;
Leave-off their On-set : and welnigh disbanded,
Gladly retreat whither their Heads commanded.
 When I consider the extreme distresse
Which thirty dayes did the *Bethulian* presse ;
Song sad enough I hardly can invent,
So deadly Plight lively to represent :   240
My hand for horrour shakes, and can no more
Guide on this page my Pen as heretofore :
Yet doe mine Eyes with Tears bedeaw it so
It well appears a subject full of Woe.
 Thou Spirit which dost all Spirits vivifie ;
Which didst unloose the Tongue of *Zacharie ;*
And through the world thy sacred *Name* to
    preach,
Thy Messengers so sundry Tongues didst teach :
Direct my weary Quill, my Courage raise,
That I, This Work may finish to Thy Praise.   250
 Tho th' *Hebrews* saw their Town, on every part ;
Not with an Hoast, but with a World begirt,
Yet had they hope the long siege would no lesse
Consume th' *Assyrians*, then themselves' distresse :
But when the Foe had all the Pipes depriv'd,
Whence, water yerst the sacred Town deriv'd,
Alas ! their hope and even their heart did shrink,
As-quite cut-off, and dry'd up with their Drink.

 The Rulers though (yer Bondage, Death to take)
Give to the People what themselves did lack :   260
To wit, a hope, water enough to keep
In private Troughs, and publick Cisterns deep ;
Both Citizens and Souldiers to suffice,
So that they would be moderate and wise.
 So : th' Officers divide in silver measures,
To all, of all sorts, of these liquid Treasures,
This welcom Liquor ; which might serve (at first)
To keep their life a while, not quench their Thirst.
 Their Cisterns dry'd, they seek in every sink :
Of every Gutter greedily they drink ;   270
T' appease their thirst a while, not please their
    taste,
With Drink whose stink was oft the Drinker's last.
O wretched Men ! O wondrous Misery !
Little, or much ; drink, or not drink ; they dye.
Plenty and Lack of Liquor, in extreme,
Though Contraries, concur to murder them :
With-in whose Bodies warreth Thirst, as fell
As outwardly th' outrageous Infidell.
 Street, Lane, nor Alley had this wofull City,
Where-in the *Sisters*, Enemies to Pitie,   280
Invented not some new and uncouth guise
To murder *Hebrews*, and from firmest eyes
(In signe of Sorrow) showers to extract
Of pearly Tears, of bitter brine compact ;
'Mid all Degrees ; if rested any-where
But so much moisture as could make a Tear.
 There, an Old man complaineth that a Lad
Hath new snatcht from him all the Drink hee had :
But thirst contracts his throat, his voice and veins ;
And ends at once his Life, his Plaint, and Pains : 290
A Souldier here re-swils again (and gladder)
Th' unsavoury water which had sweld his bladder :
There th' wofull Mother, on her Couching-Settle,
Her half-dead Childe reviveth with her Spettle :
Here the sad Lover sighes her latest breath
With the last Sighes of her dear Love, in Death ;
For cruell *Thirst*, comn from *Cyrenian* Strand
(Where ay Shee lives amid the burning Sand,
Perpetuall panting for continuall Drouth,
Hanging her Tongue a foot without her Mouth ;   300
Her face all wrinkled, both her Eyes deep sunk ;
Her Body lean and light, her Bowels shrunk ;
Her Brest transparent, and her Veins repleat
With Brimstone, all, in steed of Bloud's moist heat)
Blows from her rotten Lungs a loathsome breath
Through all the Town ; infusing Fumes of Death
In th' *Hebrews*' Art'ries ; causing every Porch
Obscurely shine with some Funereall Torch.
So that the Heav'ns, seeing so many woes,
Could hold no longer ; but would fain with those   310
Sad-weeping *Hebrews* Their sad Tears have meld,
Save that their Tears the Lord of Hoasts with-held.
And I, my Selfe, that drown mine Eyes with theirs,
Unable though well to expresse those Tears,
Will with my Silence vail their Countenance ;
Following that Painter's learned Ignorance,

Who well conceiving that his live-lesse Colours
Could not to life expresse the deadly Dolours
Of *Agamemnon* at his Daughter's End,
Cover'd his sad Face with a sable Bend.   320

Mean-while, the few that of this Wrack remain,
Against their sad Chiefs murmur and complain :
The Lord, say they, in Justice recompence
Your wilfull Malice, and our Innocence :
The Lord, look down upon the wretched Teen
Your wicked Counsells have here plung'd us in :
For, had you yeelded to the Foe's demand,
Yer hee had entred on the *Holy Land*,
Wee, happy wee, had never seen our Friends
So hap-lesse brought to so untimely Ends.   330
Alas ! what Comfort rests ? O wretched City !
Those that besiege thee round would shew thee pity ;
Thine own are cruel : foes would fain preserve-thee :
Thy friends destroy thee : those would fain reserve-
thee,
Would save thy children : thine own children rather
Run headlong all on wilfull death together.

Lord, well we know, our wicked deeds have made
Thee (just displeas'd) to draw the keenest blade
Of thy fierce-kindled ire, which justly sheads
Thy deadliest darts on our disloyall heads.   340
Yet, thou, which dost not long thy wrath retain,
(Against thine owne) O turne to us againe :
Lord, change the purpose of our willfull Lords,
Who 'gainst our bosomes whet the *Pagan* Swords :
Or grant (at least) with thousand Arrows thrill'd,
Wee rather may by *Heathen* hands be kill'd ;
Than longer langour of this banefull Thirst
To linger us in living death accurst.

Dear Brethren, 'tis our onely duty bindes,
Their Rulers said (not our sinister mindes   350
Of undermining, or of pyning Ours)
Thus to hold out against these *Heathen* Pow'rs.
If you have pain, wee have our portion too ;
Wee are imbarkt in the same Ship with you ;
On the same Deep wee the same danger run ;
Our Crosse is common, and our Losse is one :
As common shall our comfort be, when God
Shall please to ease us of th' *Assyrian* Rod :
As sure he will, if your impatiency
Stop not the course of his kinde Clemency.   360

Then, strive not with th' All-perfect ; but depend
On God alone : whose actions all do tend
To profit His : Who, in his season, ever
(Almighty) can and will *His Church* deliver.
Sometime the Archer lets his bow, unbent,
Hang idly by ; that, when it is re-bent
With boystrous Arms it may the farther cast
His winged shafts, and fix them far more fast :
So, oft the Lord seems, in his bosom, long
To hold his hand ; and after (as more strong)   370
To hammer those whose impious impudence
Mis-spends the Treasure of his Patience,
Which (at first sight) gives all Impunity
(As think the lewd) to all Iniquitie.

But, at the last, his heavie Vengeance paies
Them home, for all his *Justice* long Delaies :
As th' Vsurer, forbearing of his poor
And needy Debtors, makes his debt the more.

What tho' th' high Thundrer, in his Fury dread,
Strike not in th' instant this proud *Vice-Roy* dead ?   380
Can all th' Amass of waters which he pent
Above and under th' ample Firmament,
Seditious, so shake off his Soveraigne pow'r,
As not to send the thirstie Earth a Shower ?
No, no : though Heav'ns, on every side so cleer,
Boad nothing less than Rain, or Moysture neer :
They with their Tears shall shortly soak the Plain,
As on the day when *Saul* began to raign ;
For, all the Heav'ns, the Starres, and Elements,
Must Execute his high Commandements.   390

But still the Plebe, with thirst and fury prest,
Thus roaring, raving, 'gainst their Chief's contest :
O, holy Nation ! shall wee, shall wee die,
Their Eldership's grave Sights to satisfie ?
O ! shall wee die to please These foolish-wise,
Who make themselves rich by our Miseries ?
And with our blouds would purchase them a Name,
To live for ever in the Roll of Fame ;
No, no : let 's rather break their servile bands
Which hold us in : let 's take into our hands   400
Our Citie's Helm ; that freeing it from Sack,
Wee wisely so may free our selves from wrack.

As the Physician, by the Patient Prest,
Who on his bed (unruly) will not rest ;
Permits sometimes what Art prohibiteth :
Osias so, importun'd, promiseth
To yeeld the Town, if in five dayes appear
No certain Signe of divine Succour neer.

The people then, their wofull past estate,
Their present pain, and future feares forgate :   410
Sith though it should not hap as most they thirst ;
At least, they should of Evils scape the worst.
But JUDITH (who the while incessant Showers
From her sad eyes, in signe of sorrow poures)
With mournfull voice now calls upon the Lord ;
Anon, her sad soule comforts in his word :
Prayers were her stairs, the highest Heav'ns to
clime ;
God's *Word*, a Garden, where (in needfull time)
Shee found her Simples (in Examples pure)
The Carefull *Passion* of her *Heart* to cure.   420

There, JUDITH reading (then not casually,
But by God's will, which still works certainly)
Light on the place where the left-handed Prince,
Who griev'd for Israel's grievous Languishments
Under the *Heathen ;* to deliver them
Slew *Moab's Eglon*, by a Stratagem.
The more shee reads, shee marks it, and admires
That Act of *Ehud*, and in zeale desires
To imitate his valour.   But frail flesh
With thousand Reasons would her purpose dash ;   430
Proposing now, the Fact's foule odiousness ;
Then, fear of death ; then dangers numberless,

Where-to shee puts her Honour : and that (though,
For *Israel's* sake, God should the Act allow)
Behooves a man's hand, not a woman's (there)
Much fitter for a Spindle than a Speare.

    While JUDITH thus with JUDITH doubts doth
        wage,
A sudden puffe turneth over that same *Page :*
And, that which followes showes how *Jahel* yerst
Couragiously the sleeping temples pierc't   440
Of that fell *Pagan*, who from th' *Hebrews* flying,
Accursed found in his defence his dying :
'To teach all Tyrants in all times to-come,
That they may fly, but not out-fly their Doome.
This last Example did so fortifie
The fearfull widow, that even by and by
Shee would with Engine of Revenge endeavour
So wicked Soules' and Bodies' knot to sever.

    But while apart Shee plots, and plots anew
Some wily way her purpose to pursue ;   450
Shee hears reported by a neighbour Dame,
The Town's decree, much grieved at the same :
So ; to prevent mischiefs so neer at hand,
She sends forth-with, for those of chief Command,
Whom sharply sweet shee thus begins to chide :

    Why ! how-now, Lordlings, shall the Lord be ty'd
Unto your Terms ? Will you th' Almightie's Arms
Chaine with your Counsells ? limit with your Charms ?
O ! unjudicious Judges, will you thus
Give Law to God, who gives it Heav'n and us ?   460
Will you subject, to time's confined stayes,
Th' Author of times, months, moments, years, and
    daies ?
Be not deceived ; The sacred Pow'r Divine
No Circumstance can compass or confine :
God can doe, what hee will ; will, what hee ought :
Ought love his righteous (whom his love hath bought)
This (Fathers) This my dead Hopes most revives,
That in our City not a man survives

Who lifts his hands (after the *Heathen* fashions)
Unto the dumb, dead Idols of the Nations.   470
All Sins are Sins ; but That foule sin, alone
Exceeds all blinde or bold transgression
That wee have heapt 'gainst sacred Heav'n : for that,
Seems to degrade God of his Soveraign State ;
To give his *Glory* to a Wedge of Gold,
Or block, or stock, or stone of curious mold.

    Sith then that sin doth not our Conscience taint,
Of God's dear succour let us never faint :
Let 's think, (alas !) how now all *Juda's* Eyes,
Agast, are cast upon our Constancies :   480
Let 's think, that all will (over all the Land)
By our Example either stoop or stand :
Let 's think, that all these Altars, Houses, Goods,
Stand (after God) on our couragious Moods :
Let 's think, Wee keep the Gate of *Israel ;*
And that, so soon opening to th' Infidell
(Who hates so deadly all our *Abramides*)
Wee shall be held Traytors and Paricides.

    Wee cannot, neither will wee now deny
But that our counsell (thus the Chief reply)   490
Was foolish and offensive to the Lord :
But now (alas !) wee cannot break our word.
But, if thou rew our common miseries ;
And canst not see our tears with tear-lesse Eyes ;
Weep night and day : O ! weep and sigh so much,
That thy sad sighs and tears with Ruth may touch
Th' Eternall Judge ; whose gentle ear is ay
Open to all that to him humbly pray.

    I shall, said shee, and (if God say *Amen*)
Dis-siege this City, yer wee meet again.   500
Sound mee no farther, but expect th' event
Of mine (I hope) happy as high Intent :
And, soon as night hath spread her dusky Damp,
Let mee go forth into the *Heathen Camp.*

    Go on, in God's Name : and where-ere thou art,
God guide (said they) thy foot, thy hand, thy heart.

The End of the Third Booke.

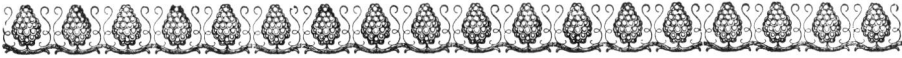

BETHULIA'S

RESCUE.

The Fourth Book.

Judith the while, trils Rivers from her eyes,
    Atters her knees, tends toward th' arched Skyes
    Her harmless hands : then Thus with voyce devout,
Her very Soule to God shee poureth out :
  Lord ! that didst once my Grandsire *Simeon* arm
With *Justice* sword, t' avenge his Sister's harm ;
Daign me that sword, that I may punish (just)
This Tyrant fell, far passing *Sichem's* Lust :
Who, not suffic'd with Virgins' ravishment,
And Rape of Wives ; is execrably bent   10
To root thy Name out from the Earth around ;
And raze thy Temple, levell with the ground.
Presumptuous Prince ! whose whole Affiance stands
In hundred thousand Souldiers hee commands,
In hundred thousand Horse, which (thirsting-fight)
With lofty Bounds the lowly earth do smite :
Without Belief, that thou alone (O Lord)
Bin'dst Heads and Hands ; with either *Crown* or *Cord:*
Strengthenst the Feeble, quickly foyl'st the Strong ;
And lay'st the Pow'r of proudest Kings along.   20
  Grant therefore, grant, good God, his charmed brain
The curious tramels of my Tress may chain :
Let every look of mine be as a dart
With Amorous Breach to wound his willing heart :
O ! let the little grace of Face and Form
Thou hast vouchsaft mee, calm his furious storm :
Let the smooth cunning of my soothing lips
Surprise the fell Fox in his Suttlships :
But chiefly, Lord, let my victorious hand
Be scourge and hammer of this *Heathen* Band :   30
That all this All may know, that *Abram's* Race
Is ever covered with thy Shield of *Grace ;*
And that no Tyrant ever toucht thy *Jury*,
But felt in fine the rigour of thy Fury.
Let not, good Lord, O let not one of These
Return to taste *Hitane* or *Euphrates.*
  Thus Judith prayes : and in the steed of stops,
With thousand Sighs her words shee interrupts,
Then from her sad sole Chamber late shee packs,
Adorn'd with *Ophir*-Gold, and *Serean* knacks.   40
  O ! silver-browd *Diana*, Queen of Night,
Dar'st thou appear, while here below, so bright

Shines such a sacred Star, whose radiant flame
Would even at Noon thy Brothers' splendor shame ?
Though, as unknown, to pass unshown shee ween,
Her Odors made her smelt, her Jewels seen ;
Musk, Ambergris, and Civet, where shee went,
Left all along an odoriferous sent :
A Carbuncle shin'd on her brow so bright,
That with the Rayes it clarifi'd the Night :   50
A silver Tincel waving in the winde,
Down from her head hung light and loose behind :
Gold bound her golden Tress ; her Ivory Neck
Rubies and Saphirs counter-chang'd in check :
At either Eare, a richer Pearle then yerst
Ægypt's proud *Princesse* in her cup disperst :
Her soft white Bosome (as with Curtains drawn)
Transparent cover'd under Cob-web Lawne :
Her Robe, Sky-colour'd Silk, with curious Caul
Of golden Twist, benetted over all.   60
The rest shee wore, might have beseem'd for Tires
The stately Foundress of th' *Euphratean* Spires.
  For, though her selfe were *Modesty* it selfe ;
T' intice this *Pagan* to the wrackfull Shelfe,
Besides her owne, sh' had borrowed Ornaments
Of other Ladies of most Eminence.
  Achior, watching in the *Court of Guard*,
Seeing her passe so late, and well-prepar'd ;
Enquires of *Carmis* (who then watched too)
What, Whence shee was, and what shee went to do :   70
So brave a Gallant, trickt and trimmed so ;
In such a time, in such a Place of wo.
  Yer while, said *Carmis*, in our City dwell'd
Merari ; a man here high in honour held :
To whom for Seed, God but this Daughter sent :
His House's Joy, this Citie's Ornament.
  Gain-greedy Fathers now-adayes turmoyle
Bodyes and Soules, Heap upon heap to pile :
But, have no care with the Mind's goods to grace
Th' heirs of their goods (which after melt apace) :   80
Much like a man that keepeth in his Chest
His costly Garment, folded fair and prest,
But lets his body, it was made to serve,
Naked the while, in Wet and Cold to starve.

But, as the Farmer spares no pains, nor cost,
In husbanding his Land ; but carefull most,
Now rids the stones, anon rips-up the ridges,
Here casts a ditch, there plants, there plashes hedges ;
And never is his hand or toole there-fro :
But chiefly careth there good seed to sow,   90
That when the Summer shall have ty'pt his Plains,
His Crop may pay him for his Cost and Pains :
Or as som Damsell, having speciall Care
Of some fair Flower, which puts-out early-rare
Th' *Incarnate* Bud ; weeds, waters every-houre
The fertill Plot that feeds her *Gilli-flower ;*
That, one-day blown, it may some Sunday-morn
Her lily Bosom, or her head adorn :
So wise *Merari* did endeavour fair
To form the Manners of his tender Heir ;   100
That, in his Age, hee thence again might gather
Th' Honour and Comfort worthy such a Father.
For soon as ever, stutting yet and weak,
Her tender tongue did but begin to speak ;
Hee taught her not (as many Fathers doe :
Too-many now) vain words, and wanton too,
But some good *Prayer*, or God's *Ten-fold Law ;*
That, with her Milk, shee might even suck the Aw
Of the Almighty : which not vain appears ;
For that the Damsell brought forth in few years,   110
Fruits worthy of such seed : whence did ensew,
That this her Nurture to a Nature grew.
So doth a Vessell long retain the Sent
Of the first Liquor wee have settled in't :
So doth a Bough bend ever (when 'tis big)
To the same side that it was bent, a twig :
So, Bears, Wolves, Lions ; and our wildest Game,
Bred tame with us, with us continue tame.
    When as twelve times, shee twelve new Moons had
        past,
This vertuous Pattern all Perfection grac't.   120
For, th' expert Pylot is not more precise
To shun, in Sayling, all the Jeopardies
Of *Cyane* Streight, of hatefull *Syrtes* Sand,
Charybdis Gulf, and of *Capharean* Strand,
Then was wise JUDITH to avoyd the Dames
Never so little spotted in their Names :
Knowing that long conversing with the light,
Corrupts the sobrest ; or at least, though right,
Right safe th' Honour be sav'd ; the Names not so,
From common Bruit (though often false) we know   130
For, haunting *Good, good* are wee holden ay :
Bad, with the Bad : *Like will to like*, wee say.
    Shee, ever modest, never us'd to stay
Abroad till midnight at a Mask or Play :
Nor trip from feast to feast, nor Street-webs span,
To see, and to be seen of every man.
But rather, knowing that such fond desire
To gaze and to be gaz'd-on (*Flax and Fire*)
Undid light *Dina*, and such gadding Dames
A thousand more ; their Noble houses shames ;   140
Shee wisely kept at home ; where, Morn and Even,
Daily shee call'd upon the God of heav'n.

The rest of every day in duteous course
Shee serv'd her Nursers for a tender Nurse :
As wont the Storks kinde and officious Brood
For their old Parents to go gather Food ;
And on some high Firre (far-off having flow'n)
Bring life to those from whom they had their own.
    If in the day, from Houswifes' needfull care,
Shee had perhaps an houre or two to spare,   150
Shee spent them reading in the *Sacred Book*,
Where faithfull Soules for sp'rituall *Manna* look.
Sometimes on Cloth sh' imbroydred cunningly
Some Beast, or Bird, or Fish, or Worm, or Fly.
Sometime shee wrought with silver needle fine
On Canvas-web some *History* divine.
    Here *Lot*, escapt from that drad Flame from high
Which burnt his town, with winged feet doth fly
To little *Zoar :* while his Wife (alack !)
Incredulous, and curious, looking back ;   160
God in the instant smiting for that fault,
Transforms her body to a Bulk of salt.
    Here, *chaste Susanna* (slandred of dishonour)
Seems led to Death, People seem prest to stone
        her :
But truth appearing, soon they seem at once
To turn on th' Elders all their storm of stones.
    Here, loyall *Joseph* rather leaves behinde
His cloak then heart with his too-*Lady-kinde :*
And rather chooseth (by her false disgrace)
His Irons, then her Arms, him to imbrace.   170
    Here, rash, rough *Jephthe* in unsacred slaughter
Imbrews his owne blade in his onely Daughter ;
By private and improvident Annoy,
Troubling the publike and the generall Joy.
    Weary of work, on her sweet Lute shee playes,
And sings withall som holy *Psalm of Praise ;*
Not following such as by lascivious dances,
Lavish expences, light and wanton Glances,
Seek to be sought, courted, and lov'd of most :
But as the Fisher-man that baits the Coast   180
With poys'ny Pastes, may have a greater draught,
And (tho lesse wholesom) hath more Fishes caught
Then those that onely use their hook or net :
So may these Gallants them more Lovers get,
Then *modest* Maids ; but their immodest flame
Fires none but Fools, Frantiks, or Voids of shame.
    Vertue alone begins, begets, conceives,
A perfect Love ; which though it slow receives,
His Form and Life, nor is so soon afire :
So, neither doth it half so soon expire.   190
Straw kindles quickly, and is quickly past :
Iron heats slowly, and its heat doth last.
    Now JUDITH'S fair Renown through *Juda* rings
In every City ; and great Suters brings
(From all-form *Fashions*, from fair *painted Faces*,
From *Powdred Tresses*, from *forc't Apish Graces*,
From *Prince-fit Pompe ;* from *Peacocks* strutting by
With *Bosoms* naked to the Navel nigh)
To woo Her Vertue.   But, Love's burning dart
Could neither harm nor warm her Ycie heart.   200

For, as hard Hammers, harder Diamant ;
Shee harder did resist love's grace to grant ;
Having resolv'd, sole and single, rather
To spend her dayes with her dear loved Father.
But at the Last, importun'd long, and prest
By her dear Parents, carefull of her Rest ;
Shee took MANASSES, one of Noble bloud ;
Rich in the Mind's, Nature's, and Fortune's good.
    Their *Marriage* then was neither stoln, nor packt,
Nor posted ; to prevent some *Pre-contract,*   210
To cheat some Heire, some Avarice to choak,
To cover Others, or their own sin cloak :
But duly past, modest, and reverent,
With either's Parents' knowledge and consent.
Dina's Disasters to this day doe prove
The sad successes of prepost'rous Love ;
Of privy Choyce, close Matches, and unkend ;
Which seldom bring Lovers to happy end ;
And that our selves ought not our selves bestow,
But those from whom our birth and breeding grow. 220
    This happy Match begun thus holily,
And holy carried ; did so firmly tie
This chaste young Couple, in so mutuall love,
That both their bodies seems one soule to move.
Th' one never wisht but what the other would :
Both by one Organ their own minde unfold ;
And, as a Hurt on the Right side (wee see)
Reacheth the Left ; even so, by sympathy,
Her Husband's Sorrows did sad JUDITH share,
And JUDITH's Sorrows her sad Husband bare.   230
    The Husband did not his dear Wife controule,
As Tyrants rule : but, as the tender Soule
Commands the Body ; not the same to grieve,
But comfort rather, cherish and relieve.
Him JUDITH lov'd as Brother (or more, rather)
Fear'd as her Lord, and honour'd as her Father.
    Their House, for Order so religious,
Seem'd more a *Temple* then a private House :
There, did no Mayd, with *merry-tricks,* intice
The bashfull Strippling to lascivious vice :   240
There, did no drunken Groom sick healths disgorge,
Nor against Heav'n blasphemous Oathes re-forge :
There, no broad Jester, no bold common Lyer,
No Gamester, Thief, Rogue, Ruffin, Apple-squire,
Had ever Harbour : but all Servants, there,
To their grave Ruler's Rules conformed were.
MANASSES, knowing what a Floud of Crimes
Surrounded all, in his enormous Times ;
Especially, what evils Confluence
Had even corrupted sacret *Governments*   250
(So that, for favour, or for Mony (more)
Fools, Knaves, Boyes, Basest, highest burthens
    bore)
Hee modestly refus'd all Publick Charge :
Holding him happy so, free and at large,
Far from the Courts of *State* and *Justice* too,
Quiet at Home, his *Houshold* dues to doe.
    Yet notwithstanding, knowing too that none
Was ever born so for himselfe alone,

But that the best part of our dayes (though few)
T' our Country, Kindred, and our Friends is due ;   260
No Magistrate, Hee daily serv'd the State
More then a hundred that in Office sate.
For, in his House did sacred *Justice* live,
And from his Lips would Shee her Sentence give.
    Hee ever was th' afflicted Poor's Protector,
Widow's Supporter, Silly-one's Director,
Orphan's kinde Father : every Age, Sex, Sort,
Had from his hand some kinde of kinde Support.
    Never vain thirst of the 'curs't Earth of *Inde*
Made Him wound Water, neither woe the Wind :   270
Never did *Avarice* his life endanger,
With mercenary Sword to serve the Stranger :
Never did Hee, to Adverse-Clyents, sell
A double Breath, blowing to Heav'n and Hell ;
But, strife-lesse, using harmlesse Husbandry,
Took of his Land both Stock and Usury
Of his lent labours. For, sometimes, by Line,
Hee plants an Orchard ; which hee orders fine,
With equi-distant Trees, in Rowes direct,
Of Plums, of Pears, and Apples most select :   280
Here-there, He Crab-stocks sets, then grafts theron
Some stranger Slip : inocculates anon :
Anon with keen Share the kinde Earth hee shreds :
Anon the Vine unto the Elm hee weds :
Anon hee prunes-off the superfluous shoots :
Anon the Bodies pares, then bares the Roots.
For, neither *Dog-Dayes,* nor *December's* yce,
Could keep him Pris'ner in his Chamber, nice.
    But, as one-day, his Reapers hee beheld,
Who, swelting, swift the yellow handfulls feld ;   290
Sol, from his head, caus'd a *Catarrh* descend,
Which shortly after caus'd MANASSES' End.
    Hee that can number, in *November,* All
The withered leaves that in the Forrests fall ·
Hee that can number all the Drops, in Showers,
Which *Hyades, Pleiades,* and moist *Orion* poures
Upon the Plains : may tell the Tears Shee shed,
For her dear Husband so untimely dead.
The Wealth and Treasure hee had left her, kinde,
In stead of easing, more afflicts her minde :   300
Th' use of his Goods still sets before her eyes
Their good old Owner's sweet and gracefull guise.
Had Shee had all the Gold was gather'd ever
On all the shoal-sands of the *Lydian* River ;
Sh' had not been rich, being bereft of Him,
Without whom, wealth, doubled her woes extreme :
And, wth whom, glad she would have born the
    crosses
Of wretched JOB's sad, sudden, many Losses.
    Phœbus had thrice through all the *Zodiack* past,
Since his Decease : Yet time, which all doth waste 310
And cures all Cares, could not her Griefs recover,
For losse of Him, her dearest Lord and Lover.
Still therefore, cover'd with a sable Shrowd
Hath Shee kept home ; as all to sorrow vow'd :
For, for the most part, solitary sad,
Tears in her eyes, sack on her back shee had,

Grief in her heart : so, on the wither'd Spray
The Widow-*Turtle* sighes her mournfull Lay ;
Sole, and exil'd from all Delights, that move ;
Chastly resolv'd t' accept no Second Love.   320
   If any time JUDITH went out of Doore
(As Duty bindes) it was to see some poore :
Some woefull woman in deep passions toyl'd
For sudden Losse of her deare onely Childe :
Some long-Sick body, or some needy soule,
With needfull Comforts of her Bag, or Boule :
Or else to goe (as GOD commanded Them)
To Pray and Offer at JERUSALEM.
   Thus, dear Companion, have I briefly shown
Fair JUDITH'S Story : on whose Worth alone   330
All eyes are cast, but cannot tell you out
Whither shee goes ; lesse, what shee goes about.
But, if wee may, from *former* things infer
A ghesse of *future ;* Wee may hope from Her
Some Happinesse : and sure, mee thinks, her cheer,
So pleasant chang'd, boads some good fortune neer.
With this Discourse, the wakefull *Hebrew* Knight,
Walking between, wore-out the weary Night.
   JUDITH the while, her Handmaid with her, hies
Towards the Trenches of the Enemies.   340
Yer from the Fort Shee had a furlong gon,
The *Heathen* Scouts descry'd her, and anon
Bespake her thus : O ! more then humane Beauty,
Whence ? What are you ? What cause hath hither
      brought ye
Into th' *Assyrian* Camp ? Alas ! I am
(Sighing, quoth shee) a wofull *Hebrew* Dame,
Who, to escape so many Deaths, or Thrall,
Come here to yeeld mee to your *Generall.*
   Then to the Duke they lead her. Who-so-e're
Hath seen, in Cities, how they flock, to hear   350
Som prating *Mountebank ;* or see som *Monster*
New brought from *Africk,* or from *Inde ;* may conster
What press of Souldiers from all parts did throng,
About his Tent ; and even prest in among
To see that compleat Shee, so comly deem'd ;
Who, the more lookt on, the more lovely seem'd.
   Her waved Locks, som dangling loose, som part
In thousand rings curl'd-up, with art-lesse art ;
With gracefull Shadows sweetly did set-out
Her broad high Fore-head, smooth as yce, about :   360
Two slender Bowes of *Ebene,* equall bent
Over two Stars (bright as the Firmament)
Two twinkling Sparks, Two sprightfull Jetty eyes
(Where subtle *Cupid* in close Ambush lyes,
To shoot the choicest of his golden Darts
Into the chariest of the chastest hearts) :
'Twixt these two Suns, down from this liberal front,
Descendingly ascends a pretty Mount ;
Which, by Degrees, doth neer those Lips extend,
Where *Momus'* Lips could nothing discommend :   370
Her ruddy round Cheeks seem'd to be composed
Of *Roses Lillied,* or of *Lillies Rosed :*
Her muskie Mouth (for shape and size so meet,
Excelling *Saba's* pretious breath, for sweet)

A swelling Welt of *Corall* round behems,
Which smiling shows two rows of orient Gems :
Her Ivory Neck, and Alabaster Brest
Ravish the *Pagans* more then all the rest :
Her soft, sleek, slender hands, in snow bedipt,
With purest Pearl-shell had each finger tipt.   380
In briefe, so passing her Perfections were,
That if rare *Zeuxis* had but found her there,
Or such another ; when from curious Cull
Of *Croton Dames* so choicely Beautifull,
By many Beauties (severally met)
His cunning Pencill drew the Counterfeit
Of her for whom *Europe* and *Asia* fought ;
This onely Piece had hee sufficient thought.
JUDITH no sooner came within the Tent,
But both her Cheeks a bashfull Blush besprent,   390
Trembling for fear : untill, inviting neerer,
The courteous *General's* gentle words re-cheer-her.
   Sweet-heart, I am not, I am not so fell
As false Report hath told fond *Israel :*
Who mee for father, I for children take ;
I love whom love my Lord their God to make :
And who doe both, may be assur'd to have
What ever good man's heart can hope or crave :
Which *Israel* well should find, would they give
      eare
To that King's favour, whose drad Power they fear : 400
Then fear not thou, my Love ; but tell mee free
The happy Cause that hither bringeth thee.
   O Prince ! said shee (with then, firm countenance)
Supreme, for Fortune, Wisdome, Valiance,
Of all that ever had command in Field,
Or ever manag'd martiall Sword or Shield :
Although my frail Sex and weake bodie's state,
No longer could endure the wretched fate ;
Wants, labours, dangers, and the deep affright
My fellow Towns-folk suffer day and night :   410
Yet is not that the Cause that drives mee thence,
Nor that which draws mee to your excellence :
But, 'tis a never-never-dying Worm
Which gnawes my Conscience ; a continuall Storm,
A holy Fear, lest I be forc't to eat
(Among my People) some unlawfull meat.
For, I fore-see (Sir) that our Folk, yer long,
With cruell Famine so extremely wrung,
Will be constrain'd to fill, and 'file them too
With unclean Flesh, which God forbids us doe :   420
And that the Lord (who strikes, with just revenge
Whom-ever dare his drad just Lawes infringe)
Will then without Fight, give Thee up their place ;
And one of thine thousands of them shall chase.
Therefore (my Lord) God's wrath and yours to fly,
Out of BETHULIA, to your Camp come I ;
Beseeching humbly, for your honour's sake,
That here no Rigour, neither Wrong I take.
Hee's more then Wit-lesse that him wilfull throws
(Winking) in dangers that hee well fore-knows ;   430
And when hee may live, pain-lesse, and secure ;
In Toil-full Fears will his own death procure.

Now : please thee grant mee, in this Vale (away
From noise and number) nightly to goe pray ;
Hebrews no sooner shall God's Wrath incense,
But I, inspir'd, shall shew thine Excellence :
And then shall I thy valiant Legions lead
Over all *Juda ;* and thy Standards spread
Shall swell in SION ; where not one shall dare
Lift Lance against thee, nor defence prepare :   440
No, not a Dog so much as bark at Thine
Arms-clashing Army, not their Armor's Shine.
Thy Name alone shall tame the stoutest Troup :
To thee the Hills their proudest Tops shall stoup :
Rivers, for thee, their rapid Course shall stay,
To yeeld thine Hoast a new un-wonted way.
  The Prince replies : O, World's sole Ornament !
Lady, as fair as wise and eloquent ;
Right-*Welcome are You :* and wee wish you ever
In all Contentment with us to persever.   450
And, if you prove in Truth and Loyaltie,
As you are pleasing to mine Ear and Eye ;
I shall from henceforth worship evermore
The mighty God you *Hebrews* doe adore :
You shall from henceforth onely *Lady* be
Both of my Scepter, of my Soule, and Mee :
Henceforth your name with high Renown shal ring
Where *Heber, Istir, Nile,* and *Ganges* spring.
  With Licence then, soon as the *Moon* with light
Of silver Rayes began to cleer the night,   460

The Widow hies to a dark Vale apart ;
Where first shee bathes her hands, and then her
    heart :
Then, from her eyes a luke-warm Rill she showrs :
Then, from her Soule this fervent Prayer she
    pours :
  Lord God, no longer now thine Aid deny
To those that onely on thine Aid rely.
Lord rescue those that ready are to spend
Their blouds and goods, thine honour to defend.
Lord, let our Infants' sad and cease-lesse Mones,
Our wofull Elders' deep and dismall Grones,   470
Our Matron's Scrieches, Cries of Virgins fair,
Our sacred *Levit's* Day-and-Nightly Prayer,
Pierce to thy Throne, to wake thy slumbring Eye.
Drad God of *Justice,* glorious Father ; Why
Doe sulph'ry Bolts of thy best Thunder light
On *Carmel's* Top, and little *Hermon* smite :
And let th' Heav'n-threatning Sons of Earth alone ;
On proudest *Ossa,* prouder *Pelion ?*
  Alas ! What said I ? Ah ! forgive mee, Lord,
This idle, rash, and unadvised Word ;   480
Which, in frail Passion, my fond Lips did borrow
From fervent *Zeal* of mine unfeined Sorrow.
No : O, Our Lignes sole Pillar dearly dread,
I know, Thou shortly wilt their Head behead :
I know, This hand, by Thy right hand led out,
Shall at one Blow, This *Heathen* Army rout.

The End of the Fourth Booke.

BETHULIA'S RESCUE.

THE FIFTH BOOK.

FOr bloud and marrow, in his veins and bones,
  The *Vice-Roy* feels new Pains, new Passions ;
W^{ch}, while he shuns, he seeks ; feels, yet not knows,
A dead-live Fire, which of Selfe's Cinders grows.
For th' *Hebrew Lady's* rapting rarities
Being now sole Object of his Soule's dim Eyes ;
Sad, peevish, pale, soft, drowsie, dream-awake,
Care of his Hoast hee doth no longer take :
Goes no more out, a-nights, to set his Watches,
And *Courts of Guard* about, on all Approches :   10
Comes not to Counsell, neither gives *The Word* :
Nor viewes the Quarters of his Camp : nor stirr'd.
  As sheep, that miss their wonted guard and guide,
Dispersed stray : now, by some River's side,
Or gurgling Brook ; now, up and down the douns ;
Now, in the Groves ; now, on the Fallow grounds :
So th' *Ethnik* Army, without Rule or Rein,
Pursue their Pleasures, violent, or vain :
None will obey ; None but will now command ;
Each, as him listeth, dares him now dis-band.   20
  Hebrews, Why stay you now mew'd in your city ?
Now, now or never, doth the Time befit-yee
To sally on the Foe ; whose rank Disorder
Among themselves, themselves (in fight) will murder.
  Nay ; bouge not though : of such a Victory
God will the Honour have and Author be.
  Yer that blinde *Cupid* did this Tyrant blinde,
To take the Town was Day and Night his minde ;
Now, Day and Night hee minds but how to gain
A Lady's grace ; Who, taken, is not ta'n   30
(Her soule being temper'd more then Fancy-proof) :
Yer-while, th' undaunted mighty *Theban* rough
Could not have fear'd Him, with his massie Mace ;
Now, but a glance of a weak Woman's grace
Dismaies him, daunts him, nay even wounds him deep,
Past care of Cure ; and doth him Captive keep :
Yer-while *Ambition*, with Drums rattling Din,
Awakt him early yer the Day peept-in ;
Now *Love* awakes him ; and with his Alarms
Makes him neglect the *Hebrews* and their Arms :   40
Yer-while, hee had Princes and Kings at bay ;
Now, of Himselfe hath neither Power nor Sway.

  Alas ! alas ! Unhappy Change, said Hee :
Must I live Captive to my Captive-Shee ?
Is This (alas !) to live : the Body bas't ;
The minde as brute ; and both their Powers defac't !
This is not Life : or is worse Life to feel,
Then sad *Ixion's*, on the brazen *Wheel*
Eternall turning : or a life (in briefe)
Most like the Life of that celestiall Thief,   50
Whose ever-never-dying heart and liver
On *Scythian* Rocks feed a fell Vulture ever.
  What boots mee t' have subdu'd so many Lands ?
What to have tam'd with my victorious hands
All Nations lodg'd betwixt *Hydaspes* large,
And th' Haven where *Cydnus* dote in Sea discharge ?
Sith I am vanquisht, by the feeble Might
Of Captive *Judith's* glance.   What boots my bright
Strong steeled Targe ? my brazen Burguinet ?
My martiall Guard about my Body set ?   60
Sith the keen Shot which her quick eye doth dart,
Through steel, and brass, and gard doth wound my hart.
What boots my Courser swifter then the winde,
Leaving the Swallows in his speed behind ?
Sith, on his back flying, I cannot flie
The willing Chains of my Captivity.
Change, change then *Hebrews*, into smiles our tears ;
Triumph of me, mine hoast, arms, swords and spears :
I am no more the *Duke*, whose Name alone
Yer-while with Terror shook you every-one :   70
No : I am Hee whose Courage, late so brave,
Is now become but Slave unto my Slave :
I am not come, to War with *Israel*,
To burn your Cities, or your Selves to quell :
But to intreat you, to intreat (For Mee)
Your match-lesse JUDITH that shee milder be.
  But whither, Wit-lesse, whither am I born
By Love's fond Fury ; wilfully forlorn ?
Have I not Her here in my Patronage,
That can the Anguish of my Soule asswage ?   80
And yet with idle Plaints I pierce the Skyes ;
And thus un-Manly melt mee at mine Eyes.
  Unhappy Mee ! my wretched Case is such
As His, who wants most what hee hath too-much ;

A Crystall River flowing to his Lip ;
Yet dies for Thirst, and cannot drink a sip :
For, so doe I respect her excellence :
Her Heav'n-given *Graces ;* that, for Reverence
Mine eyes dare scarce behold her, and my Tongue,
In stead of suing, to my roofe is clung.   90
O that my Breast transparent Crystall were,
That Shee might see my heart's dire Torment there ;
And there read plainly, what my Love's excesse
(Alas !) permits not my sad voice t' expresse !
    Since JUDITH first came to th' *Assyrian's* Camp,
Thrice had the heav'ns light put out their
        Lamp ;
And now *Aurora*, with a saffron Ray,
Began, in *Inde*, to kindle the *fourth* Day :
When as the *Duke*, who Food and Rest forsakes,
This heavie Moan, to 's *Eunuch* BAGOS, makes :   100
    BAGOS, my Sonne, adopted, not by Chance ;
BAGOS, whom I, still studying to advance,
Have made, of Meanest and neglected most,
First in my heart, and Second in mine Hoste ;
BAGOS, I burn, I rave, I rage, I dye,
Of wounds receiv'd from that fair Stranger's Eye.
Goe, seek her out : goe quickly : tell her Thou
My loving Languor : tell her, that I vow
To make her equall, nay above the best
Of greatest *Dames* whom royall Crowns invest :   110
Especially, insinuate so, that Shee
Be pleas'd this night to come and sup with Mee.
Were 't not a Folly, nay a Madnesse meer,
In Mee, to have the rarest Beauty here
This Age hath bred ; and yet, too-faint a Foole,
I should not dare my heart's hot Thirst to coole?
Would not my Souldiers laugh at it apace ?
Nay : would not JUDITH blush at my Disgrace ?
    BAGOS, too-apt, too-us'd to such a Turn ;
Thus oyles the Fire, which but too-fast did burn :   120
My Lord, if Private men (whose otious Care
Scarce passe the Threshold of their own Door dare ;
Whose Mindes, content with their unhappy Hap,
For other *Grace* or greatnesse never gape)
Live not content (alas !) unlesse some-while
Venus' warme Comforts their chill Cares beguile :
How-more unhappy then, are those that bear
An *Atlas* Burthen : those that rest forbear,
For Others' Rest : those that (like *Argus*) wake
While Others, fear-lesse, their full Naps doe take :   130
If, among all their Gall, their Toil, their Teen,
Some (*Cupid's*) Hony be not mixt between ?
    Then, Sir, pursue your Love : lose not the Game,
Which of it selfe comes to your Net, so tame.
And, if in like Imployments, heretofore
Y' have found Mee fit and faithfull evermore ;
In this new Trust, you shall by speedy triall,
Finde mee more secret, diligent, and loyall.
    Alas ! How-many BAGOS's, in our Time
In Princes' *Courts*, to highest Honours climbe,   140
More, for their cunning in such Embassies,
Then for Repute of *learned, stout,* or *wise ?*

Whilom, great *Courts* were *Vertue's Academs ;*
Now Schools of *Vice :* now (rather) *Sinks of Realms.*
    You, who, *Great-minded*, cannot be content
To be close-Brokers for th' Incontinent :
Who cannot brew (with too-too-dangerous Skill)
Both a *Love-Potion*, and a *Cup* to *kill :*
Who cannot, noble, your free Natures strain,
With flattering pencill on your Face to fain   150
A face of *Frownes*, or *Smiles ;* of *Wrath*, or *Ruth ;*
To please the *Great* (rather with *Tales* then *Truth*) :
Come not at *Court ;* if I may counsell you.
For, there, in stead of *Grace* and *Honour*, due,
Unto your *Vertues ;* you shall nothing gain,
But, that which *There* still haunts the *Good ;* disdain.
    You, *Noble Ladies*, in whose heart is graven
A filiall Feare of th' All-see GOD of Heav'n :
You that more prize your *Honour's* pure Report,
Then *Love* of *Princes :* keep you from the *Court.*   160
    But You, who, having neither Land nor Mony,
Out-brave the bravest : who with words of Hony,
And Friend-like Face, Dissemblers, humbly greet
Whom your false harts wish in their winding sheet :
Who lavish, sell your Wives for Offices :
Who make you Noble, by base Services :
Who, serving Time, can set your Faith to sale ;
Shift your *Religion ;* saile with every Gale :
Who, Parasites, can put more faces on
Then ever *Proteus* in the Seas hath show'n :   170
Who, forcing Nature, can your Maners fit
To my *Lord's* Humour ; and so humour it ;
Like a *Chameleon*, which, here blue, there black,
Here gray, there green, doth with his Object take :
Who can invent new Toules, new Taxes finde,
To charge the People : and the Poore to grinde :
Who, faining to possesse your Prince's Eare,
Make Suiters crouch, and court you every-where ;
And, subtle *Shifters*, sell them dear your Smoake,
Blinding the wretches with a wylie cloake.   180
    You, warbling *Sirens*, whose delicious Charms
Draw wariest youth into your wrackfull Arms :
You *Circe's*, you whose powerfull Spells transmute
Your Loves to Stones, Hogs, Dogs, and every Brute :
You *Stymphalides*, whose Avarice devoures
The richest Treasure of *Youth's* freshest Flowers :
You, you, whose *Painting*, and *Pearl-golden*-glister,
Of *Priam's* old Wife, make young *Castor's* Sister :
You *Myrrah's*, you *Canaces, Semiram's :*
And, if there be any more odious *Dames :*   190
Come You to *Court :* come quickly : there, on You
A hundred Honours shall be heapt, undue ;
You, there shall sell *Justice*, Preferments, Places :
Yea, you shall sell mis-govern'd Princes' Graces.
    But *Muse*, it boots not : Hadst Thou thousand-fold
The Strength and Stomack of *Alcides* bold,
Thou couldst not cleanse These *Sin-proud* shining
        Halls,
Fouler by far then foule *Augea's* Stalls.
    Let 's back to JUDITH ; who to bring about
Her hard designe, surveyes her, sets her out,   200

Be-curles her Tresses ; makes her Crystall cleer
Her Beautie's Judge, which had in Earth no peer.
  Then comes shee to the Tent, rich hanged round
With curious Arras, from the top to ground ;
Where Art-full fingers, for a Web of glory,
Had wov'n *Medes, Persians, Syrian* Prince's Story.
  There *Ninus* first, pusht by vain Prides amisse,
Usurps the *East :* here comes *Semiramis,*
Who, faining Her a Man, th' *Assyrian* swaies,
And to the Clouds her BABYLON doth raise.   210
  See, see a Prince, with soft white fingers fine,
Effeminate sits spinning flaxen Twine :
And, for a Launce, bearing a Distaffe, showes
That more to Female then to Male hee owes.
See, how hee poats, paints, frizzles, fashions him ;
Bathes, basks, annoints, views, and re-views his Trim,
Within his *Glass,* which for a *Glaive* hee wears.
See, how hee shifts to hide his Shame and Fears :
From Vardingale to Vardingale, hee flyes
His brave Lievtenant, lest Hee him surprise.   220
Yet, see, at last (to act one Manly thing)
Hee burns himselfe, not to out-live a King.
  See, here an Infant sucking of a Bitch
Under a Hedge and in a shallow Ditch ;
Who, grown a Man, here musters in his Train
Both bond and free, the Souldier and the Swain ;
Subdues the *East,* and into *Persia* draws
The *Medes'* proud Scepter ; and he gives them Laws.
  But who 's That marches so dis-figured there,
Before an Army, without Nose and Eare ?   230
'Tis that good Servant, who reduc't, alone,
Under *Darius,* Rebell *Babylon.*
  While, with these shows sad JUDITH entertain'd
Her Eyes, but not her heart (too-inly pain'd)
In comes the *Duke :* and with right curteous cheer
Kindely salutes her, hands her hand ; and neer
Causing her sit in a rich easie Chaire,
Himselfe, at ease, views and re-views her Faire.
Then, seeing him so nigh his wished Pleasure,
His heart's a-fire : nor hath hee longer leasure   240
To stay for *Venus,* till, Star-crowned bright,
On their *Horizon* Shee bring back the Night.
  The Widow, knowing Time and Place, as yet,
For God's Decree, and her Design, unfit ;
Findes still Delayes : and to delude his Love,
Shee (wylie) still Speech upon Speech doth move.
  My Lord, pray tell mee, What so great Offence
So grievously your Fury could incense ;
What ? when ? where ? why ? how ? and by whom our
    Folk
Could so the Wrath of such a Prince provoke,   250
So separate, in Language, Land, and Law ;
Who never Us ; and Whom wee never saw ?
  Uncivill were Hee (*Sweet*) replyes the Prince,
Could ought deny to such an Excellence.
Then ; as the Heav'ns cannot Two Suns sustain :
No more can Earth Two Kings at once contain,
Of equall Power and State : for, *Soveraigntie*
Brooks no Co-partner, no *Equality.*

  Witnesse my *Soveraign :* who offended at
The Power and Pomp of mighty *Arphaxat,*   260
Who, high aspire, and far to spred began,
And to the Clouds had built his *Ecbatane,*
Ninive's Shame, and dread of *Babylon :*
Bravely endevours to supplant his Throne,
Bereave his Scepter, sack, raze, ruinate,
His goodly Cities, and himselfe dis-State.
  But *Arphaxat,* as valorous as sage
(And both, right worthy of his Crown and Age)
Would rather venture *Media's* Royall Rings,
Then vaile to any. So between two Kings,   270
Two stout, and stirring spirits (whereof th' one
Could brook no Peer, th' other, Superior none)
Began a dreadfull and right deadly War,
Lasting (alas !) too-long, spreading too-far.
  Arphaxat arms those, where the Flower of *Greece*
Fetcht, not the Locks of an old *Golden Fleece,*
But massie *Ingots,* which doe richly pave
The happy Plains great *Phasis* Streams belave :
The *Harmastans,* th' *Albanians,* wont to mowe
Three times a year, where onely once they sow :   280
Whom *Oxus* boundeth with his swelling Tide ;
Whom *Anti-Taurus* double Horns divide :
Those on the Mountaine, whose high-lowly back
Bow'd to the Vessell which preserv'd from wrack
The World's Abridgement : Those along the Shores
Where proud *Jaxarte's* rapid Current rores :
In short, besides his *Medes* hee had in pay,
All neer the *Pontike* and the *Caspian* Sea.
So that, already, This great King-Commander,
Had Hopes as high as ever ALEXANDER.   290
  My Prince, resolv'd to conquer, or to die,
Omits no point of Opportunitie
For his Affaires : Hee armeth *Sittacen,*
Levies the Archers of all *Osrohen :*
Those, whose rich Plains hundred for one repay,
From *Euphrates* and *Tygris* march away :
Fish-fed *Carmanians* (who with *Seal-skin* Jacks,
In stead of Iron arm their warlike Backs)
Gold sanded *Hytan's* native Shores forgoe :
You *Parthians, Cossians,* and *Arabians* too,   300
By your sad *Magi's* deep prophetike Charms
Sacredly counsell'd, take you all to Arms :
And Thou *Chaldéa,* turn'st to Swords, and Spears,
And shields, thy *Rules, Squires, Compasses* and
    Sphears.
For, of his Subjects spares hee not a man
That beare a Launce, or Pike, or Crosbow can :
Wives, Beldams, Babes, Gray-heads (and Sickly som)
Through all his Countries onely kept at home.
  Hee also sends for *Persians* and *Phœnicians ;*
For soft *Egyptians, Hebrews* and *Cilicians,*   310
Quickly to come, and kindely take his Part :
But *Neuters,* They (more friends in face then heart)
Reject his earnest Sute, Himselfe neglect ;
And use his Legats but with small respect.
  My Lord dissembles for a while This wrong,
Till having triumpht of a Foe more strong,

Hee may with more ease, and with danger lesse,
Their sacrilege and surly Pride represse.

In *Raugau's* ample Plain, one Morning, met
These Royall Armies, of two Kings, as great   320
As ever *Mars* with steel and Furie arm'd,
Fury and Pride so Either's Souldiers warm'd,
That hardly could they stay till Trumpets shrill
Denounce the Battaile and give leave to kill :
But with stern looks, and braving Threats, afar ;
At hand, with blowes ; they had begun to war ;
Exchanging wounds.   Two thousand *Perduz* first
Give bravely th' Onset : and not much disperst :
From sudden whirle-winde of their nimble Slings,
So thick a Storm of humming Pebbles sings   330
So-sad a *Dirge* of Deaths, that they suppose,
That not one Troup, but All, had bin at Blowes,
To second Those ; then, in good ordinance,
With waving Ensignes, thousand Troups advance :
Both Armies joyn.   Now fiercely fall they to 't,
Mede upon *Chaldé*, pressing foot to foot :
Incount'ring felly with a furious noise
Of clashing Arms, and Angry-braving Voice,
Louder then *Nile*, rushing from Rocky-Coomb ;
Or then *Encélade*, when hee shakes his Toomb.   340
Here lyes one head-lesse ; foot-lesse there (alas !)
Another craules among the gorie Grasse :
One's shoulder hangs ; another hangs his Bowels
About his neck (but new bound up in Towels)
This, in the Face, that in the Flank is hurt :
This, as hee dyes, a Floud of Bloud doth spurt :
That, neither lives nor dyes ; but seems at once
Both upper *Jove's* and neather 's diverse Thrones ;
Because, some little spirit (too-stubborn-stout)
Still in the Body, will not yet come out.   350
     Yer-while the ground was yellow, green, and
          blue ;
Now onely cover'd with a Crimsin hue :
While one doth (here) another deadly thrill,
Another him, another him doth kill :
Still Rage increases : still doth Fury spread,
Till all the field be but a heap of Dead.

One-while the *Syrians* by the *Medes* are chas't ;
Anon the *Medes* by *Syrians* are re-chas't :
As one-while, from the Sea unto the Shore,
Surge after Surge, Wave after Wave doth rore.   360
Another-while from Shore to sea they ply
Wave after Wave, Surge after Surge to fly :
Or as (wee see) the Flowery Ears, in May
(When *Zephyrus* with gentle Puffs doth play)
Sway to and fro ; forward and backward bend ;
Now, stoop a little ; and now, stand an end.

Both Kings the-while, whose force and fortitude
Far past their Subjects, so their Blades imbru'd
In Bloud and Slaughter, that an open Glade
Where-e'r they came, in either Camp they made :   370
So that, nor Casks, Currets, nor Shields could save
From mighty Strokes their massie Weapons gave
Much like two Torrents, which with headlong fall
From two opposed Hils, down-bearing all,

Banks, Bridges, Trees, Corn, Cattell ; seem to vie
Whether of either shall most damnifie.
Especially, the *Medes'* King thundred so
Upon our Battails, that our Bravest, tho
Began to shrink, and with that shamefull sight,
Our Hoast dis-ord'red, fell to shamefull flight :   380
The Foe pursues, slayes, slashes (swift as wind)
Millions of wounds, and every one behind.

In briefe, that Day had *Ninivé* bin down,
Her King undone (dead, and depriv'd of Crown)
Had not I (full of Force and Furie) quick
Like Lightning, rusht where deadly blowes were
     thick.
Mails, Murrions, Corselets, Iron, Steel, and Brasse,
Before my Sword were brittle all, as Glasse.
And onely I, My hand alone, which lent
More deaths then blowes, brought more astonishment 390
Unto their Camp, then all our Camp beside.
Their Foot no longer could my Brunt abide :
Their Horsemen, fainting, in their Saddles shake ;
Arms on their Backs, hearts in their bellies quake.
Here, with a down-right Blow, from top to twist,
I cleave in sunder one that dar'd resist :
There, I so deep dive in another's minde,
That neer two handfulls 'pears my Sword, behinde ;
So that the *Medes*, now more then wavering,
In th' heat of Fight, abandon All their King.   400
Who, seeing him so betray'd, his Tresses tore,
Retir'd to *Ragau*, all besmear'd with gore :
There over-ta'n by Ours, Hee bravely fought ;
'Mid thickest Darts a glorious Death hee sought ;
Heaws, thunders, thrills, and of his Manly blows :
Not one in vain, not one amisse bestows.
But, yer Hee die, with quick, keen, Fauchin fell,
Hee sends before, thousand stout Soules to Hell :
So the fierce Tygre, compast every where
With Men and Dogs, to Fury turns his Fear ;   410
Fights where hee finds the greatest danger lie ;
Tears, tosses, kills ; not unreveng'd to die.

But, at the last, the vainly Valiant King,
Weary of killing, and of conquering,
Thrill'd with a thousand Darts, and wounded rife,
Ended at once his lofty Rage and Life :
And, falling, fares as doth a mighty Oake,
Which, planted high upon a massie Rock,
A thousand times hath felt the windes to beat,
And thousand Axes, it a Fall to threat ;   420
So that the Root groan'd, and the Valley nigh
Eccho'd the noise unto the steepest Sky,
While that the Top still reeling to and fro,
Now These, now Those, threatens with overthrow :
Yet, still it stands in spight of all their spite,
Till at the last, all under-mined quite
With million strokes, it falls ; and, with the Fall,
Bears to the ground Trees, Rocks, Corn, Cattle, all.

For, *Arphaxat* extinct, extinct with-all
Was *Median's* glory : and, My Lord of All   430
Raz'd *Ecbatane ;* and now grow Weeds and Grasse
Where, late, his lofty, rare-rich Palace was :

Where, late the Lute, and the loud Cornet's noise
In curious Consort warbled sweet their voice ;
The voice of Scrich-Owls, and Night-Ravens heard,
And every fatall and affrighting Bird.

My King-God, weary of War's tedious toile,
In NINIVE the great, for four months' while
Made Publique Feasts : and when the Feast was done,
Commands mee levie a huge Hoast anon,   440
Of chiefest men ; to goe and chastise those
That had disdain'd him Aid against his Foes :
And that, on all that dar'd his Hests infringe,
With Fire and Sword his Honour I avenge :
And that with speed. But *Madame*, see (alas !)
How far I am from bringing this to passe :
For comming here, your Nation to subdue,
My selfe am conquer'd and subdu'd by You :
So that (alas !) Death's draddest Tyrannies
In endlesse Night will soon siel-up mine eyes,   450
Except the powerfull sole Preservative
Of thy sweet Kisses keep mee yet alive.

Nay : good my Lord, said Shee, tell-on (I pray)
Your good Successe and Service by the way.

Then HOLOPHERNES, where hee left, began
A long Narration how hee playd the man ;
Halfe truth, halfe tales : For, 'tis great souldiers'
        guise
To bombast oft their Own Exploits with Lyes.

Mine Hoast all mustered and together brought,
T' inflame their hearts with martiall Heat I sought : 460
Fellows (said I) If ever Your Desires
Have thirsted Fame, to live when life expires ;
Let 's now goe punish that presumptuous Crew
Which rudely (late) our sacred Legats slew :
Let 's goe t' avenge our drad-dear Soveraign Liege
Of that fell Outrage, nay, foule Sacrilege
Against the greatest GOD came ever down
From Heav'nly Sphears to sway an Earthly Crown :
Arm, arm you, brave Blouds, arm your either hand,
This, with a Blade ; That, with a Fier-brand,   470
With Fire and Sword to over-run the *West*,
To lay it waste ; to bear away the best :
To sink it all under a Crimsin Floud ;
Or make (at least) your Horses swim in bloud :
Goe, take possession of Your Valours' due,
The whole World's crown, wch yeelds it all to you :
Take you this Honour : which in Time-to-come,
Shall keep your brave Names from th' oblivious tomb :
Take, take your pleasures of the richest spoils
Of richest Cities in a hundred Soils   480
Which you shall sack. So, may you once in health
Come laden home with Honour and with Wealth.

I ceast : and soon they second, all, my voice
With Caps cast up, with clapped hands, and noyse
Of gen'rall Joy, to have Mee GENERALL.

Some six-score Thousand was mine Hoast in all,
Or som-what more : with which from NINIVE,
But three-dayes' march I made to *Bectileh ;*
Thence past I forward by *Hierapolis,*
Then by *Amida,* then by *Nisibis.*   490

And thence to *Charan* (at the length) I came,
Once happy seat of your great *Abraham.*
Then wan I th' Hill, whose oblique Horns divide
All *Asia* neer, and limite far and wide
Many large Empires : Where, I sack, I slay,
I burn, I raze, what-ever in my way ;
My Souldiers seem so many Mowers, right,
Which in a Mead leave not a blade upright ;
But, by long Swathes of their degraded Grasse,
Well show the way their sweeping Scithes did pass : 500
This, *Phul,* and *Tharsis,* and all *Lydia* knows,
In whose waste Fields now onely bramble grows.

Comn neer the Streight which serves for wall and Fort
To soft *Phœnicians,* and Thief *Issian's* Port :
The *Rosians, Soleans, Mopsians, Tharsians, Issia,
Anchials, Ægæans :* briefly, all *Cilicia,*
Take-up this Gate, with all their Power ; in hope
To stay my Passage, and my Course to stop.

Should I here tell the dangerous Enterprises,
Brave Charges, Rescues, Sallyes, Shocks, Surprises, 510
Which there befell, the day would fail (I fear)
Before my Speech : for, the *Cilicians* were
So fortifi'd by favour of the Place,
That little could wee there prevail, a space :
Nay, all mine Hoast, which had so often chast
So many greater Hoasts ; now stood agast ;
Till in despight, and full of desperate rage,
In thickest dangers, I my Selfe ingage ;
Where, round assail'd, and wounded all in parts,
My Shield thick bristled with a grove of Darts,   520
I never shrunk : but so bestirr'd mee round,
That I alone made all their Hoast give ground.

Mine Army then, follows the way amain
Mine Arm had made, and paved thick with Slain :
Now our most Cowards (late) for Fear, adying ;
Wound most, kill most, and most pursue them flying.
Cydanus, yer while for 's pure silver Floud,
Call'd King of waters, wallows now in bloud ;
And rapid *Pyram* (past his wonted Toule)
To *Neptune,* Shields, Helms, Horse and Men doth
        roule.   530
In brief, as here your *Mocmur* stopt a while
By some new Bridge, or some unusuall Pile ;
Roars, rises, fomes, fumes, threats, beats, rages, raves,
Against his new bank ; with Waighty Waves
Waighty and strong, bears down at last the Bay,
And for a time, out-lashing every-way.
Tears, over-turns, and undermines, much worse
Then when hee freely hath his native Course :
Even so my Force, having the Force repell'd,
Which in these streights the struggling passage held : 540
Burns, kills, confounds, what meets it most and least.

ASIA, laid waste : returning to the *East,*
I conquer'd *Cælè,* spoyling, pitylesse,
The fruitfull Verge of famous *Euphrates :*
Rapsis I raz'd and *Agræa,* overthrow'n,
The Vertue of my mighty Arm hath know'n.

Thence, keeping still by the Sea coast, I spoile
The *Madianites :* then, marching *North* a-while,

Tow'rds double *Liban,* I *Damascus* race,
With her neer Towns, *Gaane, Abile, Hypæpas:*   550
Thence came I (curious) to that Hill, from whence
The Sun, by Night, is seen : and seen from thence
Also to Rise : Thence, tow'rds the *Western* Realms
Continuall beaten with *Phænician* Streams.

    Then, Those of *Gaze, Tyre, Sydon, Ascalon,*
Azotus, Byblus, Joppa, every-one,
Fear'd with my Fame ; in greatest humblenesse,
Dispatch their Legats to my Mightinesse.
Wee come not here with Force and Arms (say they)
To bid thee Battail, or to bar thy Way :   560
But rather, Mightiest Prince, in humblest awe,
To yeeld us Thine, t' accept Thy Will for Law ;
Of Life, or Death.   Thine are our Fields and Forts ;
Thine are our Cities ; Thine our Ships, our Ports,
Our Lands, our Goods, our Cattell, Corn, and Wine ;
Thine are our Children, and our Selves are Thine :
Onely be pleas'd (Sir) to accept us so,
And so esteem us : and right happy tho
Shall wee esteem our Selves, to have a Lord
Can wield so well the Scepter and the Sword,   570
The Lance and Balance ; and, besides, excels
Men, equalls Gods in every Vertue else.

    Nor did their People, nor their States disprove
Their Embassies ; but by all signes of Love
Both young and old, crown'd all with *Flora's* favours,
Of hundred colours and of hundred Savours ;
Came Dancing out with *Musick's* cheerfull Moods,
To offer Mee their Bodies and their Goods.

    Nor did I then a *Victor's* Right abuse ;
But with all Kindnesse them as Friends I use :   580
Leave them their Land : but first, their Forts I man'd
With some of Mine ; with some of theirs, my Band.
For (*Madame*) still the farther that I goe,
My Camp in Bands ; my Bands in Souldiers grow :
Even as *Danubius,* first beginning small
Through *Raurak* Plains wth shallow course to craul,
Still swelling more and more, with threescore rivers,
To th' *Euxin* Sea his Sea-like Selfe delivers.

    I hop't, as These, so also *Israel*
Would yeeld themselves ; and not at all compell   590
My just Revenge to threat Extremities :
But, when I came here to *Scythopolis*
(The *Tomb* of Her whose happy Milk had yerst
The twice-born *Dennis* in his Cradle nour'ct)
I was advertis'd of this stubborn Folly ;
Which will, no doubt, undoe the *Hebrews* wholly.

The End of the Fift Booke.

BETHULIA'S
RESCUE.

THE SIXTH BOOK.

YEr that the *Pagan* could his Story end,
From highest Hils did dusky Night descend :
And now the Steward full the Table fraights
With all, most pretious, most delicious Meats ;
As if the *Vice-Roy*, to This *Joviall* Feast,
Had bid the Kings both of the *West* and *East*.
O greedy-guts ! O Gulphs insatiate !
A thousand Worlds, with all their delicate
And various Cates devis'd by th' *Abderite*,
Cannot suffice your bound-lesse Appetite.   10
O Belly-gods ! for You (at any price)
To the *Moluques*, must wee trudge for Spice ;
To the *Canaries*, for your Sugars fine ;
To (*Joves Crete*) *Candy* for your choysest Wine,
To please your Tastes, your Palats to content,
Sea's sacred Bosome is profanely rent ;
Aire is dis-peopled ; yea right hardly can
The onely *Phœnix* scape the Jawes of Man.
O Poison ! worse then Plague to Martiall states,
Which bravest mindes basely effeminates :   20
While *Rome*, for Heads, had *Curio's* and *Fabricio's*,
Whom Roots suffic'd for dainties most delicious :
While *Persia* was with Sallets sole content ;
They flourisht Both, admir'd and eminent ;
And Either's Arms, tryumphing every-where,
Fill'd all the Earth with Tropheis and with Fear :
But, since that this, from soft *Assyrians* took
His vast excesse of Kitchin and of Cook ;
And, since that That fell under the Dispose
Of *Galba's*, *Nero's* and *Vitellio's*,   30
(More glorying to exceed Others' Excesse
Then conquer *Pyrrhus* or *Mithridates*)
Both have been oft and justly sackt and spoil'd
By petty Nations, whom they oft had foil'd.
Nature 's suffic'd with Little : Over-full
Deadeth the Courage, and the Wits doth dull.
Each being set ; anon, full filled-out
In massie Boules the *Malmsey* walks about :
One drinks devoutly in an Estridge Egge ;
One in a Lute, another in a Legge ;   40
One in a Ship, another in a Shell ;
Another takes a broad deep silver Bell,

To ring his Peal : but so his hand doth sway
And shake, that halfe hee sheds it by the way.
But, above all, the Prince him so behav'd,
That, now, the more hee drank the more hee crav'd :
Much like the Sea ; which, though it take this-while
Twin-nam'd *Ister*, and Seaven-mouthed *Nile ;*
Never increases, nor is full therefore ;
But ever ready for as many more.   50
Cup calls for Cup ; and when the Skinker weens
T' have done his Service, hee afresh begins
To fill them Liquor ; for, till Midnight past,
Among the Guests this Tippling game did last.
And then away, with much adoe, they went
(Feeling and reeling) Each unto his Tent ;
By th' amorous Tyrant often urg'd before,
Who thought each minute now a yeare and more.
When they were gone, Hee 'gan embrace and busse
The trembling Lady ; who besoothes him Thus :   60
Nay : leave (my Lord) such haste what need you make
To reap the Fruit which from you none can take ?
Get you to bed : and, if you leave mee room,
I will not fail you by and by to come,
So soon as I have but disburthened
My Load of Cloathes, and made mee fit for bed.
If suttled Wits, and if the sobred Brains,
Have hardly scaped Woman's wylie Trains,
Marvail not, Reader, if One, fool'd at-once
By *Semele's* and *Cytherea's* Sons,   70
Be thus beguil'd : sith either of the Two
Bereaves the bodie's and the minde's Force, too.
Then, letting her slide from his arms away,
Hee goes about himself to dis-aray :
Now hee unbuttons, now puls-off his hose ;
But, his heat hinders, and his haste foreslowes ;
For (sleep-awake, blinde-seeing) while hee plyes
T' untrusse his Points, them (fumbling) faster tyes :
Till, overcome with Rage, and Longing, more,
Hee cuts his knots, and off his Clothes hee tore ;   80
And then to Bed. Where (as the Crosse-bow-man,
Who, for his pleasure, watcheth now and than,
By some Crosse-path, some Coney, or some Hare ;
At every Noise, on every side doth stare

Where stirs a leafe ; and levels thither-ward,
At the least Wren, or the least Worm that stird
Neer where hee stands, still in a Hopefull-Doubt
Turning his Body and his Bow about)
The lustfull Tyrant, if hee hear a Mouse
Never so little stir about the house ;   90
Shivering for Joy, hee thinks his Mistresse there :
Nay, though hee nothing heare, his flattering Eare
Thinks it hears something, which can nothing be
But his admired most desired Shee :
Lifts-up, layes-down, and up again re-lifts
His heavie Noule ; from side to side hee shifts ;
Casting the Distance, counting in his head,
How many steps will bring her to his Bed,
The which the while hee full of thorns doth think.
But now the Fume of his abundant Drink,   100
Drouzing his Brain, beginneth to deface
The sweet remembrance of her lovely Face :
Already wheels his Bed, already shine
A thousand Rayes before his slumbring Eyne :
Already in his Ears (now waxen num)
A thousand Drones with buzzing noise doe hum :
He sees *Chimeras, Gorgons, Mino-Taures,*
Medusas, Haggs, Alectos, Semi-Taures.
But JUDITH's heart still beating thick with-in,
Felt a fell Combat in it selfe begin ;   110
Now, causing Fear her sacred Fervour quash ;
Anon, her Fervour her faint Fear to dash.
JUDITH, said Shee, Thy *Jacob* to deliver,
Now, is the Time ; Now to-it. *Doe-it never.*
O ! Yes.   O ! *No.*   I will : *I will not, I :*
Shall I profane kinde Hospitality ?
Nay, rather shall I sanctifie 't the more,
When by the same I shall the *Saints* restore.
But, Traytors ever bear Dishonour's brand.
Traytors be those betray, not save, their Land.   120
But Murderers Heav'n's Righteous Judge abhors.
Why ? all Man-killers are not Murderers.
But Hee's a Murderer who his Prince hath slain.
This is a Tyrant ; not My *Soveraign.*
But, GOD hath now bequeath'd him us for Lord.
Hee's not of GOD that warrs against his *Word.*
Why, then may All their Tyrants kill and rid ?
So *Ehud Jael,* and so *Jehu,* did.
Yea, but from Heav'n they had authentike Warrant.
So hath my Soule approved and apparant.   130
But, ah ! how weake art Thou this Work to act !
Whom God assisted, never strength hath lackt.
But, hadst thou done ; the Sequel's more to doubt.
God brought mee in ; and God will bring mee out.
What, if Hee please leave thee in the Heathen's
   hands ?
Their Chieftain dead, I fear nor Death, nor Bands.
But to their Lust thou shalt be left a Prey.
Never my Mind ; my Body force they may.
Then, in this point thus sacredly confirm'd ;
With hands heav'd up, her eys on heav'n she firm'd ; 140
And softly, Thus poures to the Lord her prayer :
   O gracious God, who with paternall Care

Hast ever kept thine *Israel,* strengthen Thou
Mine Arm with Thine, that it may nimbly now
Cut-off this Tyrant, who thus dares presume,
To scale the Heav'ns ; Thy Scepter to assume.
And, sith thy grace, through thousand storms and more,
Hath brought my Bark in sight of wished shore,
O, let it land : with *Poppie's* sleepiest sap
This Tyrant's sense benum in end-lesse Nap ;   150
That I may raise this Siege, Thy Thralls release,
Return Thee *Praise ;* and to Thy SION, *Peace.*
Her Prayer done, the Drunken Prince she hears
Snorting aloud.   Then fair and soft Shee neers
His Pallet's side, and quickly takes the Sword
Which had so oft the groaning Earth begor'd.
But, even about the fatall Blow to give ;
Fear, from her hand did the fell Weapon reave :
Her heart did faint, her strength did fail her quite.
O God (then said Shee) strengthen by Thy Might,   160
My timorous heart's and trembling hand's consent.
Then on the *Duke* so stiffe a stroke shee lent,
As happily, *tri-parted* (at the poule)
Th' Head from the Body, Body from the Soule.
His Soule to Hell : his Body on the Bed :
In JUDITH's hand his grim and ghastly Head ;
Which soon her Handmaid in her Night-bag hid.
Then speeding thence, suspect-lesse, or unspi'd ;
Without Impeach the *Pagan* Hoste they past.
For if that any saw them trip so fast,   170
Heav'n-blinde, they thought Shee went but (as before)
Into the Vale, bright *Diane* to adore.
Now, when chaste JUDITH came to th' *Hebrews'*
   Tower,
Ope, open (said Shee) : for the God of Power,
Th' *Assyrian* Forces hath this Night forlorn,
And lifted up his chosen *Jacob's* Horn.
The town amaz'd at her return un-hop't,
Presse to the Port ; which instantly they op't,
Thronging about her : who a Tarras mounts,
And her Exploit from point to point recounts.   180
Then, from her Bag, for Proofe of what shee said,
Shee pulls the-while the dreadfull *Pagan's* Head.
The Citizens, when in her hand they saw
Th' *Assyrian's* Head's Head : full of ample Awe,
Extoll th' Almighty, who so mighty Foe
By a weak Woman had subdued so.
But, most of all did *Ammon's* Prince admire
GOD's dreadfull Judgement : and to scape his ire,
Who *Israel* thus, of vanquisht, *victoriz'd ;*
His Flesh and Heart hee sudden *circumciz'd.*   190
How sweetly, Lord, Thy sacred *Providence,*
Men's suttlest Wisdome, in their Plots, prevents !
For, thine *Elected* unto life, to guide
Into thy Fold (when most they seem beside)
Good out of *Ill* thou draw'st : making their Sin,
Means ('gainst their minds) their goodness to begin.
Lord ! foule desire of murther and of spoile
Brought this (late) *Pagan* to th' *Is'acian* Soile ;
Where, meaning (first) thy people's bloud to spill,
Now, spend his Own for their dear sakes hee will : 200

Thy mercy so from his maligne Affect,
(Maugre his minde) brought forth a good Effect.
  So neer *Damascus*, mad'st thou, by thy Call,
Of Wolfe a Shepheard, of a *Saul* a *Paul ;*
Of Persecutor, an Apostle ; (briefe)
Of Chief of Sinners among Saints the Chiefe :
So suddenly, that all the Saints about
Admir'd his *Doctrine ;* Yet his *Deeds* did doubt.
So, the *Saint*-Thief, which suffered with our Saviour
Was led to Life by his Death-due Behaviour :   210
And, when no longer Earth could beare his Sin,
Was, in a Moment, made Heav'n's Citizen.
(*O fearfull-hopefull Precedent of Grace!*
Such as, but One, GOD'S holy bookes embrace :
One, that None (humbled) should despaire of Pardon :
But one, that None presume in Sin to harden.)
  So, turn, good Lord, O turn the hearts of Princes,
Whose rage their realms with Saints' dear bloud be-
    rinses,
O ! let the sword, thou in their hands hast put,
None but Thy foes, none but those Tyrants cut,   220
Who cursedly *Thee* or *Thy* CHRIST blaspheme
(Usurping JUDA and JERUSALEM,
And all Thy *Golden Candlesticks* beside ;
Threating the *West*, too, with their power and pride) :
Not those, who humbly, onely, evermore,
Thee, TRINITY in UNITY, adore.
  Then, as the brave *Virago* ordered,
A Souldier takes th' *Assyrian* Tyrant's Head ;
And, for the *Hebrews'* more Encouragement,
Glad sets it up upon the Battlement.   230
  There, Parents, Children, Maids, and Widows sad,
Who *Pagan* Swords but new bereaved had
Of Children, Parents, Lovers, Husbands dear,
Twixt Griefe and Anger, as distracted neer,
Pull-off his Beard, pull out his hatefull Tongue,
(Which had blasphemed Heav'n and Earth so long)
Spet in his Face, scratch and poach-out his Eyes ;
And all, that Hate and Fury can devise.
For, lyve Remembrings of their wrongs, them make,
On his dead Head, this dead Revenge to take.   240
  Aurora, weary of the cold Embrace
Of her old Spouse, began in *Inde* apace
To paint her portall of an *Opal* hue ;
When, of *Bethulians* all the bravest Crue
Issue in Arms : and such a Noise withall,
(Such Shouts and Cries) as if, in th' antike Braule,
All th' Elements, breaking the bands of Order,
Were by the Eares ; and in their old Disorder.
  The *Court* of *Guard* (that night unusuall strong,
Towards the Town) hearing such Noise so long,   250
Start from their Sleep ; and crying *Arm, arm, arm,*
Give suddenly to all their Host *Alarm.*
  One, for his own, his Fellow's Helm puts-on :
One, his right *Vantbras* on left arm doth don :
One, on his neck, for Launce, a Libbet takes :
One speeds him quick, another scarce awakes :
One mounts his Horse, yer hee be curb'd, or girt ;
And, without Spurs : Others, to shew more heart,

Would make a Stand : some neither wake nor sleep :
Some, brave in Word, in Deed, as faint as Sheep.   260
  Now, by degrees, this Noise comes to the Ears
Of *Holophernes'* Houshold Officers ;
So that sad BAGOS hies him in all hast
Unto the Tent where th' *Ethnick* slept his last.
W^{th} trembling hand, once, twice, or thrice he knockt :
But an eternall Sleep the Doors had lockt
Of his Lord's eares ; who had already crost
The *Stygian Ferry*, not to be re-crost.
  Then, hearing still th' *Is'acians'* louder shout,
Hee makes the Doore fly-open with his Foot ;   270
And, entring, findes, in gorie Bed, low shrunk,
Not *Holopherné*, but his head-lesse Trunk.
Then did hee teare his haire, and rent his Clothes,
And to the Clouds roars out in yelling Oathes :
Especially, when JUDITH there hee mist,
Whom now the Murdress of his Lord hee wist.
Then, ragefull rushing from the bloudy Tent,
This hideous Cry through all the Camp hee sent ;
  Woe, woe to us ! Alas ! this cursed Night,
A cursed Captive hath confounded quite   280
Our awefull Army, and undone us All,
By treacherous slaughter of our GENERALL.
  This new affright, redoubled on the first,
The stoutest hearts doe so dis-heart and burst,
That all, (at once abandoning their Arms,
Pikes, Swords, and Shields, Darts Arrowes, all) by
    swarms
Betake them to their heels ; o'r Hill and Dale,
Flying from one death, on a worse to fall.
  Then the Besieged in great Troups descend,
And on their backs revenging Bowes they bend.   290
Both run apace ; Those fly ; these follow fast :
But those that fly, make lesse good speed then haste.
For, without losse of Man, th' *Hebrews*, at will,
The flying *Pagans* slaughter, thresh and thrill :
Even as a Lyon, in *Getulian* Lawnes,
Bestreawes the soile with fearfull Kids and Fawnes ;
Where, not a beast his Furie dares abide,
Nor lift a horne against his awefull pride.
  One, from a Rock himselfe doth headlong dash,
And all to peeces all his parts doth pash ;   300
Other, forgetting that in deepest depth
Fate findes us out, into a River leap'th.
But, if by speed, or some good hap, perhaps
This Morning's first fell Fury any scapes,
Hee scapes not through those *Hebrews'* outrages,
Who kept (about) the Straits and Passages :
So that scarce one of such a Rout could bring,
To *Ninivé*, the News unto the King.
  The Battaile (rather, th' execution) done,
Out of the Citie flocked every one   310
Whom Sex or Age had hitherto restrain'd ;
To see the drad Revenge the Lord had rain'd
So suddenly, and past all Expectation,
On those fell Foes of His dear *Holy Nation.*
  One full of wounds, yet gasping, calls in vaine
On lazy Death, to end his lingering paine :

One, grinning ghastly, in his visage grim,
Shewes, dead, the Rage that living sweld in him :
Some mangled here, some there, some round about :
And every Soule a sundry way went out :   320
Accordingly as Valour, Sleight, or Chance,
Led the dead-doing Sword, or Dart, or Launce.
In short, This fight so truly *tragick* was,
That even the Victors would have sigh'd, alas !
Had the so vanquisht any Foe but This.
  But rifling long, among the Carcases,
At last the Body of the *Duke* they found
(Tho head-less, known best, by that only wound).
Thither they throng ; that, every blade must thrill,
And every one that Corps again would kill :   330
A hundred Swords, a hundred Pikes, and Darts,
Are every moment goring all his parts ;
And every Nerve, Vein, Muscle, Joynt they hack ;
Till room (at last) their Vulgar Rage doth lack.
For, were his Bulk as big as *Atlasse's*,
His Limbes as many as *Encélades*,
And strong *Briareus ;* yet, yet think I, all,
Their dire Revenge would still, still think too small.
For of the *Jews*, none so base Clown there is
But would a Gobbet of that Flesh of His.   340
  Give, Tyrant, give thy right hand to *Cilicians*,
Thy left to *Medes :* give one Arm to *Phœnicians*,
Th' other to *Ismael :* and divide thy Feet
Between th' *Egyptian* and the *Cœlianite ;*
That every Nation, whom Thine Arms offenc't,
May, by some Part, be partly recompenc't.
Alas ! I erre : for all in Atomies
Wert thou divided, all would not suffice.
  But JUDITH, nor forgetfull, nor ingrate,
Would neither bury, nor Selfe-arrogate   350
The sacred honour for Assistance given
In this great work, by th' all-work hand of Heav'n :
But, timing meet her Feet to Timbrel's noise,
This *Hymn* shee sings with glad-sad warbling voice ;

Follow'd by all the Flower of *Hebrew* Dames
(Maids, widows, wives) of faultlesse forms and fames.

  Laud, laud, we, lowd, with verse, with voice and
    strings,
The GOD of GODs, the Glorious King of kings :
Whose Power, alone, pulls Tyrants down, and reareth
Meek in their Room, who HIM ay-faithfull feareth. 360

  For, who would thinke, one City, in one Day,
So suddenly could such an Hoast dismay ;
Whose high exploits had all the world astounded,
And, from the Indes, *to* Japhet's *Inns resounded ?*

  Lord who would thinke, that Holophernes, *late*
Proud Conqueror of many a Potentate,
Should lose his Life (for all his Selfe-affiance)
By one weake Woman, not a Troup of Giants ?

  Who, who would thinke, that HE, who late possest
(At least, had Power) from farthest East to West, 370
From Pole to Pole stretching his arms all-over,
Should not have, left, one Inch of Turfe, for Cover ?

  That stately Prince, so thick attended-on,
Now dead (alas !) lyes, above ground, alone ;
Yet, not alone : for, Those that serv'd him, living ;
Consort him, dead ; proofe of their Duties giving :

  Nor yet, above ground ; for, the Rav'ns become
His mangled Bodie's better-worthy Tombe,
Then pretious Marble, Jet, and Jacinth gilded ;
Which, for his Bones Himselfe had proudly builded. 380

  So, so (good Lord) from Hence-forth, let us finde
Thee, not our Judge, but as our father kind ;
And so, Hence-forth, the Foes of SION rather
Feele Thee their Judge, then their propitious Father.

Here JUDITH ends : Here also end will I,
With thanks to *GOD ;* and to your Majestie.
To *GOD*, for bringing This my Work about :
To *You*, for daigning to have read it out.

FINIS.

NOTES AND ILLUSTRATIONS.

PAGE 176, '*Honourable Ladies*'—see our Introduction and Index of Names on these various 'fair ladies.'

BOOK I. l. 4, '*Fauchin*' = falchion : l. 15, '*Anne*' = queen of James I. : l. 25, '*Truch-man*' = interpreter : l. 27, '*mo*' = more : l. 51, '*oazie*' = oosy : l. 54, '*ought*' = owed : l. 63, '*fell*' = fierce, cruel : l. 93. '*Idolists*' = idolaters : l. 150, '*Ligne*' = line : l. 160, '*crine*' = hair : l. 162, '*sadly*' = solidly, weightily : l. 163, '*heals*' = hulls or encloses : l. 209, '*States*' = tribes : l. 212, '*Key-cold*'—see Glossarial Index *s.v.* : l. 268, '*Surcuidry*' = surquedry.

BOOK II. l. 2, '*pight*' = pitched : l. 61, '*ought*' = owed : l. 88, '*Ligne*' = line : l. 98, '*Gossen*' = Goshen : l. 99, '*rueful*' = pitiful : l. 181, '*Leaches*' = physicians : l. 301, '*Coile*' = tumult, difficulty : l. 337, '*Lestrigons*' —see Index of Names, *s.n.* : l. 361, '*gest*' = gesture : l. 392, '*pash*' = dash, beat : l. 396, '*Sconces*' = see Glossarial Index, *s.v.* : l. 398, '*bandy*' = toss to and fro : l. 404, '*Gantlets*' = gauntlets : l. 418, '*Trevet*'—see Index of Names, *s.n.* : l. 455, '*Puttock*' = kite : *ib.* '*Serrs*'—see Glossarial Index, *s.v.* : l. 512, '*bunchy*' = heaped-up as the camel's hunches or bunches.

BOOK III. l. 22, '*scalops*'—see Glossarial Index, *s.v.* : l. 27, '*Bush*' = hair : l. 68, '*luffe*' = love? l. 95, '*alas*' —an interjection not = sorrow or lamentation : l. 108, '*Trepan*,' l. 109, '*Bricol*,' l. 110, '*Crow*,'—see Glossarial Index, *s.v.* : l. 163, *ibid. frequenter* : l. 178, '*Aigle*' = eagle : l. 182, '*Peizes*' = ponders, weighs : l. 188, '*derive*' = communicate : l. 220, '*Stowers*'—see Glossarial Index, *s.v.* : l. 311, '*meld*' = mingled : l. 325, '*Teen*'—see Glossarial Index, *s.v.* : l. 381. '*Amass*' =

great mass : l. 391, '*Plebe*' = mob : l. 493, '*rew*' = pity.

BOOK IV. l. 1, '*trils*' = distills : l. 2, '*Atters*'—see Glossarial Index, *s.v.* : *ib.* '*tends*' = stretches : l. 22, '*tramels*' = net-work : l. 51, '*Tincel*' = tinsel : l. 103, '*stutting*' = stuttering : l. 186, '*Voids*' = those void of shame : l. 244, '*Ruffin*' = ruffian : *ib.* '*Apple-squire*'— see Glossarial Index, *s.v.* : l. 266, '*Silly-one's*' = innocents : l. 270, '*woe*' = woo : l. 316, '*sack*' = sackcloth : l. 352, '*conster*' = construe : l. 375, '*Welt*' = fringe? l. 381, '*passing*' = surpassing : l. 394, '*fond*' = foolish : l. 419, '*file*' = defile : l. 483, '*Lignes*' = lines.

BOOK V. l. 17, '*Ethnik*' = heathen : l. 25, '*bouge*' = budge : l. 45, '*bas't*' = debased : l. 121, '*otious*'—see Glossarial Index, *s.v.* : l. 131, '*Teen*,' as before : l. 175, '*Toules*' = tolls : l. 215, '*poats*' = pouts : l. 217, '*Glaive*'—see Glossarial Index, *s.v.* : l. 270, '*vaile*' = uncover, stoop : l. 304, '*Squires*' = squares : l. 339, '*Coomb*' = comb—see Glossarial Index, *s.v.* : l. 371, '*Currets,*' *ibid :* l. 387, '*Murrions*' = morions : l. 457, '*Bombast*' = stuff out : l. 531, '*Mocmur*'—see Glossarial Index, *s.v.*

BOOK VI. l. 39, '*Estridge*' = ostridge : l. 59, '*busse*' = press and kiss : l. 67, '*suttled*' = subtle : l. 78, '*points*' = tagged laces : l. 96, '*Noule*' = noll, head : l. 163, '*poule*' = poll : l. 169, '*Impeach*'—see Glossarial Index, *s.v.* : l. 175. '*forlorn*' = forsaken : l. 178, '*Port*' = gate : l. 179, '*Tarras*' = terrace : l. 218, '*berinses*'— see Glossarial Index, *s.v.* : l. 239, '*lyve*' = living : l. 254, '*Vantbras*'—see Glossarial Index, *s.v.* : l. 255, '*Libbet*' = club : l. 347, '*Atomies*' = atoms.—G.

A HYMN
OF ALMES:
OR
THE BEGGERS BELL;
HEARD FROM BEYOND
THE
CHARTER-HOUSE,
To ring all-in,
TO
The Temple of
CHARITIE.

In an Eccho
Iterated,
AND
Consecrated
To the Right-*right Reverend*
AND
Double honourable Father,
GEORGE ABBOT,
Lord Arch-Bifhop of Canterbury
&c.
By JOSUAH SYLVESTER.

TO
MY LORD
OF
CANTERBURY
HIS GRACE.

M*Y Wit, weak* Orphan, weaned *too-too-young*
  From PALLAS' *Brest, and too-too-Truant-bred*
  (*Not, as too*-wanton *but too*-wanting) *led*
From Arts, *to* Marts (*and Miseries among*)

Had else perhaps (*besides du* BARTAS) *sung*
  Some native Strains *the gravest might have read;*
  And to your Grace *now grately tendered*
  Some fitter Sound *than* This *rude* Bell *hath rung;*
Yet; sith it tends to drown *th' Heav'n reaching* Cry
Of Bloud *here shed by* Luxe *and* Avarice ;
  And to awake the World *to* CHARITIE
(*Whereof* Your Life *so lively* Pattern *is*)
Propitious, pardon *mine officious* Zeale,
In this loud Eccho *of a louder Peale.*

———————————Your Grace's most bounden

—————————————And humble Bead-man

————————————————JOSUAH SYLVESTER

AD EUNDEM
PRAESULEM
PRAEOPTIMUM
EPIGRAMMA
Ex lat. I. O. 1611.

S*Oon*, Oxford's *Head; Soon*, Winton's *Deane* Thou
  wert :
  Soon, Lichfield had thee Her *Diocesan*,
Soon, London had thee Her's, by Thy Desert :
Soon, England joyes thee *Metropolitan :*
Soon, by the King, call'd to His *Counsails* High :
What shall I wish thee *late?* but, *late* to die,

EJUSDEM AMPLISSIMI

Anagramma duplex.

Georgius Abbot.

Gregis Tuba böo :

Subito gregabo.

Ad Reverendissimum Dominum Episco-

pum LONDINENSEM

EPIGRAMMA.

T*Hee*, learned KING, the learnedst King elected
  Great LONDON's *Pastor;* which thee glad-ex-
  pected :
Others are wont, that hunt for such Reward
Of Wit and Art, sue in the SEE's *Vacation :*
Thee KING, the King, th' Arch-Bishop *call'd* preferr'd ;
The *Citie*, too ; *Thou* had'st thy SEE's *Vocation.*

Ejusdem Præconis disertissimi
ANAGRAMMA,

Johannes King.

Oh, Igni-Canens !

A HYMN OF ALMS.

ALMS (*holy Gift*, vouchsafed from above)
   Is a sure Pledge and Symbole of that *Love*,
   Which GOD, just Steward, as a Deaw pours-out
On Earth, expos'd to empty *Air* about :
For, from his *Union*, from this constant League,
From time to time Mankinde doth duely beg
All that the Sun imparts his powers unto,
Of living Creatures, and un-living too :
So that, our *Beeing, Begging* may wee call ;
Sith, of her Maker, Nature borrows all :   10
'Gainst *Usurers*, and Churles' *Unthankefulness*,
Who to CHRIST's Members shew them mercy-less.

   Hee that, for GOD, but a good motion hath,
Guiding his Minde up to the *Milkie Path*,
T' admire there (*Namelesse*) what hee cannot know
By th' eye of *Reason* (where yet shineth though
The Sun of Righteousnesse ; as th' usuall Sun
Through Crannies shines into a Dungeon) :
Hee, Hee (I say) that hath but Nature's Sense,
For *Faith ;* for *Law*, but native Innocence ;   20
In his simplicity hath alwayes care
To practise ALMS, ALMS to receive and share :
So common't is with sociable man
To give and take the mutuall ALMS hee can ;
Yea, in our Cradles, yer our Tongues can crave,
Wee beg with Cryes what wee had need to have.

   The Heav'ns, dispensing sacred Influences,
Predominant in Birth of Poor and Princes,
Aboundantly (with bounteous over-plus)
Pour th' *Hebrews' Manna*, many wayes, on Us ;   30
To teach, that wee, by sundry Charities,
Should mildely ease each other's Miseries.

   Even as the *Opal*, in his orient lustre,
Where various colours of all stones doe muster,
Shewes the rare Riches of the Pearly *East :*
Alms is *the Glasse* of wel-bred soules and blest,
Shewing each other *Vertue's* sacred Quality,
In th' Heav'n-allied Man of *Liberality*.

   ALMS, are the Cement of this round Theater :
Where, in a differing kinde, Earth, Air and Water,   40
Intend the same thing ; *liberally to give*
Their ALMS to Rocks, Plants, Creatures, all that live ;
Conducing Fire withall, whose Force unseen
Gives frankly, too, his helpfull Heat between.

   ALMS, in our bodies worketh all in all :
Th' *Eyes* lend it Light ; the *Hands*, most *liberall*

Laborious ALM'NERS, bring home to the Head
All needfull Store wherewith the Whole is fed :
The feet supply it with their meet Support ;
And each, each other, as their Parts comport :   50
The *Liver*, Nurse of Naturall Faculties,
First warms, then feeds, the Nerves, Veins, Arteries,
Causing the *Stomach* (as His *Alms*) receive
The heat which first his vertue doth conceive :
The spongy *Lungs* with gentle Sighes inspire
The vitall Air our *Little-Worlds* require :
Th' *Heart*, quick and ready, with *Alms*-vowed
    vigor,
Draws to it selfe (against extremest Rigor,
For utmost Refuge) all our liveliest Heat,
To succour Nature, when death seems to threat :   60
The *Soule* (solely divine) Life's motion brings
To all the Members of This *Thing of Things*
(*Alms* Heir-apparent) to Whom supream Sage,
Heav'n's *Alm'ner* gave the Earth for heritage ;
That, having *free* receiv'd so various Store,
Hee should be *frank* to th' Needy, Naked, Poor.

   Be bounteous *Alm'ners*, said All *Bountie's* Father ;
Y' are not here *Owners*, but meer *Stewards* rather :
I have ordain'd you to provide and care
For th' *Orphan* Poor, that unprovided are.   70
If, narrow-hearted, You shrink-in your hands
From th' humble *Begger* that your *Alms* demands,
I;'ll make your Goods (like water) leak away ;
Your Lands a Stranger shall inherit ay :
Your Gold (your god) before you be aware,
Som barbarous Souldiers in your sight shall share :
Your stately houses (stiled by your Names)
War's rage shall ruine, or some sudden Flames,
Which I shall kindle (in my just displeasure)
Against your selves, your seed, your trust, your
    treasure.   80
The *Mercy-lesse* with *Mee*, shall *Mercy* miss :
That *Vice* alone all *Vertue's* Poison is.

   Abram, Lot, Joseph, Job, were *Alm'ners* all
(To Strangers kinde, to Neighbours *liberall*)
By sacred record, which renowns them more
For this rare Vertue, then all else of yore ;
As if, with GOD (the Author of all Good)
Their chief perfection in this Function stood ;
Sole *Soule of vertues*, second *Life* of all
This various vast Orb, which the World wee call.   90

Calling to record the Rein-searching Eye,
Here I protest, that in my Poverty
(*Though these* dear *Times* daign *me so scant a* Scope,
That having *nothing, I can nothing* hope)
Next my Home-charge (*where* Charity *begins*)
My deepest Sighes (*save for my* Debts *and* Sins)
Rise from Compassion *and* Desire *to* steed
Others with Helps *which yet my Selfe I* need :
To succour *Others : to be* (*like the* Sun)
Extending *Light and Heat to* Every-one :   100
To be to all, in some sort, necessary
(*For* Vertue's Meed, *and not as* mercenary) :
Rather to give, *then* take ; *to* lend, *then* borrow ;
A pound to-Night, then but a Crown to-Morrow :
But th' Heav'nly Wisdome (*best, it Selfe knowes why*)
Doth still th' Effect of This Affect deny,
Denying Means and Matter to expresse
Mine inward Zeal *to* ALMS *and* Thankfulnesse ;
Which oft breaks out (*without a Trumpet blowne*)
To give (GOD knowes) *more then I know mine*
            Own.   110
(*The more my Griefe*) *the lesse my Thought of* Merit,
Or Thirst of Praise, *though here I thus aver-it,*
By th' humble Proffer of so Poor *a* Mite,
Th' aboundant Rich *to* Bounty *to incite.*

Vain-glorious ALM'NERS are effeminate,
Affecting *Works,* but to be wondred-at ;
Whose *Vertue* is meer *Vanity* (indeed)
And here receives their momentary *Meed :*
The *Meritorious* (such as ween them so)
Indebting GOD *to* Them for what they doe ;   120
In stead of *Heav'n,* where *Humble Soules* abide,
Shall purchase *Hell,* the Portion of their *Pride.*

O ! thrice, thrice *Happy* Hee, whose free Desires
To *Charity* a holy fervour fires :
Who onely mindes GOD'S glory, by his Gift,
And *Neighbour's Good,* without sinister Drift :
Famine (familiar unto Rogues that range)
Shall not come neer his Garner, nor his Grange :
His Fields, with Corn, aboundant Crop shall cover
His Vines with Grapes, his Hedg with Roses over ; 130
His douns with Sheep, his daery-grounds wth Neat ;
His Mounts with Kids, his Moors with Oxen great ;
His Groves with Droves (increasing night and day) ;
His Hills with Heards, his smiling Meads with Hay ;
His Fens with Fowl, his Pils and Poles with Fish ;
His Trees with Fruits, with Plenty every Dish :
Content and *Health* (the Best of Earthly Blisse)
Shall evermore remain with Him and His :
Him, *Pride* or *Envy* never shall molest ;
Or Cor'sive *Care,* Foe to Repast or Rest.   140
For, th' All-see Eye still carefully respects
The ALM'NER's House, and ever it protects ;
Till finally, when *Justice* endeth All,
Sweet *Mercie's* voice him to heav'n's kingdom call.

But, th' *Usurer* (how-ever here hee thrive
In Heards and Hoords) already dead-*alive*
(No heat of love, no heart to give a Mite,
Except to *gain* and *gather-double* by 't)

Him, in that Day (To Him a Day of Woe)
The *Holy-one,* th' All-Knower, will not know.   150
Shame and Confusion shall be-spread him over,
Wishing the Holes to hide, and Hills to cover :
Eternall Fire shall fry his thirsty Veins ;
Immortall dying in eternall Pains.
His Eyes, so nice to look on *Laz'rus'* Sore,
Shall swim in sulph'ry Tears (tortur'd the more,
To see above, in *Blisse* and *Glory* rife,
Whom, Ruth-lesse, here hee would not see, in life) :
His Ears, here deaf unto distressed-ones,
Shall there hear Horrour of the *Damned Grones :*   160
Nor shall the voice of *Mercy* him salute,
Who in Effect, to Needy Mones was mute :
Millions of *Masses* cannot him redeem,
Nor all *Church-Treasure* ever ransom him
From all-thought-passing Pangs of *Wretchednesse ;*
As, End-lesse, Ease-lesse, and Remedy-lesse.

ALMS are so usuall in the *Eastern* parts,
Where heav'n, and earth, and air, improve their
        parts,
That every Village there, in Winter's Need,
Is wont the Flocks of *Wildest Fowles* to feed,   170
And breake the yce (of purpose) for their drink,
When crystal Crusts have glas'd the Water's brink :
A *Charity* of *Infidels* to Fowles ;
Shaming some *Christians,* towards *Christian* Soules.

Rich *Anatolia,* and her happy Coast
(Th' abbridged Glass of all the World, almost)
In her huge Cities (rather Shires wall'd in)
These hundred years hath not a *Begger* seen ;
(GOD's strict *Edict* they there observe so well,
Forbidding Beggars in his ISRAEL)   180
Sith 'tis *misprision* of the Law of Nature,
Nay, impious Pride against our All-*Creator,*
To suffer Man (GOD's Image, and our Own)
Whom wee may succour, to be overthrown ;
To stark for Cold, to starve for Food, to perish
In *Penury,* when we have power to cherish
For, in such Cases, where (wee know) wee can,
There not to *Comfort,* is to *Kill* a Man.
Yet, sole the *Christian* (Each a Wolfe to other)
Disdains to look on his *Distressed* Brother :   190
And here, in LONDON [Coaching *swiftly by ;*
Or stalking on, with selfe-surveying eye ;
Or strutting out, to view his Purls or Lace ;
Or stepping-in, to see some painted face,
Or Fire-new Fashion in a Sleeve or slop ;
Or to some Tavern, or Tobacco-*Shop ;*
Or towards Burn-*Bull* (*if not* Turnbull) *street ;*
Or to Black-Fryers *some* White Nuns *to meet*]
At Doors, on Dunghils, under every stall,
Lets pined, sick, poor, naked Christians fall,   200
Faint, starve and dy, *for lack but of the price*
Of the least Crosse of his last Cast at Dice :
Or of the Tythe but of his Shooe-tie's Cost :
Or of the spangles from his Garters lost :
Or of his jetting the Canarie's *Jigg :*
Or of the puffing of his Periwig.

O Times ! O Manners ! *O mad, murd'rous* Vanity,
In either Sex, of equall Inhumanity !
   The hideous Cries of the Afflicted, fright
The sable Horrors of the silent Night :   210
So that Shee, pierced with their piteous Case,
Cloathes them with clouds, and lends them ease a space :
The Hollow Rocks, and hardest Marble Stones
Weepe when they weepe, and eccho with their grones :
Their Shivering fits, their fears, their feavers make
The Firmament, the fixed Poles, to shake :
Yet here (alas !) th' aboundant Riotous
Are never mov'd : much lesse the Covetous,
Rich, *raking Wretch ; the needy-greedy Chuff*
Whose (Hel-*like*) *heart can never have enough :* 220
Who rather grindes, *then gives, and* beggers *many,*
Yer to a begger hee afford a Penny,
Or penny-worth of all his plenteous store,
When Bags, and Banks, and Barns, can hold no
   more.
O Times ! O Manners ! *O mad murd'rous* Vanity,
In Young *and* Old *of equall* Inhumanity !
   But, Pardon, LONDON ; *I have over-slipt :*
I must recant, lest I be stript *and* whipt.
Christ-church, S. Thomas, Bartholmew (my friend)
Bride-well *and* Bedlam, *better* Thee *commend :* 230
Besides a many of peculiar Charges
Of Companies ; *and more of private Largess :*
And above all, that black Swan (SUTTON)'s Nest,
(From One, alone almost worth all the rest)
That new Zaccheus, *who* restored *free*
Th' old Charter-house *to better* CHARITY.
Are not these, ALMS ? *are not these,* Monuments
Of pious Zeal ? *of kinde* Beneficence ?
I grant they are (give GOD *and* Men *their due) :*
But, reverend Green-Staves, *what 's all this to you ?* 240
(Unlesse, as Romists *by implicite* Creed,
You hope for Heav'n, by Right of other's Deed ;
Or swell with glory of your Elders' Good :
As selfe-Ignobles boast their fathers' Blood)
That These few, *dead, here a few Hundreds cherish ;*
If living, you let many Thousands perish ;
For want, perhaps, not of your Gift, *but* Gain ;
Which some, perhaps from others' Gifts restrain ;
Which (if time serve) when they can hold no more,
They will (perhaps the tenth-tenth-part) *restore* 250
When they are dead to build a Front for Five
Of those five hundred they have starv'd, alive.
O Times ! O Manners ! *O mad murd'rous* Vanity,
In every sort, of equall Inhumanity !
Æthiops and *Turks* against *Our Rich* shall rise,
That can behold with unrelenting Eyes
Poor, Aged, Sick, Soules gasping out their last ;
As little moved, and no more agast
Than is the Hunts-man, when a Deer at Bay
Doubles, in vain, and windes to get away.   260
   During th' old *Golden,* happy, harmlesse *Age,*
When *Saturn* ruled (without *Satan's* rage) ;
When *Reason* sate as Judge on every Throne :
When *Justice* shar'd justly to each his Owne :

When *Innocence* was *Cities'* Citadell :
When *Charity* sole swaid the *Common-weale:*
Then had the Heav'ns nothing but ALMS for Eye :
Then had the Earth (which now the Heav'ns defie)
No other Heav'n than th' onely Mantle fair
Of ALMS, bestow'd by *Water, Earth,* and *Air,* 270
And *Fire* withall ; from whose fell Nature, ALMS
Extracts the fiercenesse, and the fury calms.
   ALMS was the *Word* th' All-perfect *Artist* said,
When, out of ALMS, he bade, *A Heav'n be made :*
A fruitfull Earth : a Lightfull, Heatfull Fire :
A sighfull Air (though Soule-less) to respire :
A moistfull Water, waving Changefully :
A World (in brief) full of all Quality.
So that (in fine) of all This All-*Theater,*
ALMS is the *Form,* ALMS is the *primer Matter,* 280
So necessary for our Lively-hood,
That after GOD, it is Man's *Soveraign-Good.*
   Martha's and *Marie's Alms* (in Bounty rife)
Restor'd their Brother to a second life :
Shee, who so free the *Fire-Coacht Prophet* fed,
Found happy *Guerdon :* for (her Darling dead)
Her *Faithfull Alms,* wing'd with her fervent praier,
Re-brought the Breath of her death-seized Heir.
   Alms is the Glue of *Friendship's* permanence :
'Tis of all *Vertues* th' onely *Quintessence ;* 290
Against Heav'n's Anger, 'tis an Anchor sure :
Against Earth's Rage, a Rampire to endure :
A Rock of Honour, against Slander's Arms :
A Shield of Safety, against hurtfull Charms.
   For, on the Man where *pious Pity* dwels,
Malice can nothing with *Thessalian* Spels,
Nor Traitor's Poignard, nor his *Powder-*Wit :
Nor cunning mixture of a murd'rous Bit.
Nor secret Wiles of cheating Hypocrites :
Nor privie Theeves, nor proud *Monopolites :* 300
Nor ought, nor All, that Mischief can revolve
To dare the Heav'ns, or Nature to dissolve.
   Alms calms the Windes, and gives them gentle
   breath :
The War of Waves it quickly quieteth :
From Shoals and Shelves, from where the *Siren* sings,
The ALM'NER'S Ship it swift and safely brings :
When need requires, it Oars and Sails supplies ;
And, past the *Pole,* another *Pole* espies
To steer his Course ; if, what his heart doth *vow*
Abroad, at home, his loyall hand allow   310
In liberall *Almes* unto the needy sort,
At his Return into his wished Port.
   The *Golden Table :* that Great *Pompey* pill'd
From *Salem,* served (as sacred *Vengeance* will'd)
For Sword to *Cæsar ;* GOD so *jealous* is
(Though nought he needs) of what is *vowed* His.
   Th' High Treasurer of ASIA'S *impious Rapt*
Within the *Temple* was with horror wrapt :
And, but th' High-Priest by prayer succoured,
The *Sacrilegious* had there perished..   320
   So may they speed, or worse than so, that spoil
GOD'S *living* TEMPLES (by or Gripe, or Guile),

That from their *Pastor*, or their PRINCE, detain
The *Tithe*, or *Tribute*, sacred Lawes ordain :
That from the *Poor* their *ancient Rights* conceal ;
Or, in their *new*, with them unjustly deal :
That have, by secret *sacrilegious* Theft,
Robb'd *Church*, or *State*, or holy *Alms* bereft :
O ! may they once, as high as *Haman*, mount ;
And from *Mount Faulcon* give a sad Account   330
Of all the Wrongs (as conscience them convinces)
Done to their God, their *Country*, *Peers* and *Princes* ;
While *Great*-ones, blinded, or as loth to spy,
Had oft their Fingers in the *Golden Py ;*
For private *Profit*, or peculiar *Pleasure*,
Neglecting *Poor*, *Publick's* and *Prince's Treasure*.
O Times ! O Manners ! most to be deplor'd :
O ! sudden mend them, or soon end them, Lord.

    For, if poor *France* fall in an *All-Consumption*,
Her Death's sad *Crisis* will be *This Presumption*,   340
Of *Private Lucre*, without *Publike Care ;*
While Each, Selfe-serving, winks at Other's share.

    GOD, for his Mercy, grant my fears be vain ;
Or rid me soon out of the *Carefull pain*
I suffer daily, while so few I see
From this Corruption's foule Contagion free :
Or, would I had been bred in humblest Thatch,
Borne of the loines of one that Sprats did catch ;
So poor in Wit, as not of power to know
The impious Traines that Empires overthrow :   350
So, happily, more dull of head and heart,
Lesse should I feele un-feeling *France's* smart ;
Who slaies her Selfe by Self's-*Disloyalties,*
Having no Foe but her owne *Avarice,*
With *Pride* her Partner, and *Impunity,*
Their strong Abettor : Which *Triumviri*
Are able, sole and soon, to ruinate
And raze the Glory of the greatest State ;
Or bury 't quick i' th' Toomb of carelesse Princes
That wink, or shrink, under their *Insolences,*   360
Robbing themselves of th' Honour and Renown
Which Heav'ns entail unto a happy *Crown.*

    But, if I can be willing not to dy,
'Tis out of hope, to see the Company
Of *Sacrilegious* roundly go-to-pot,
Expos'd in publike to some shamefull Lot ;
When our great *Hercules* (all Monsters dread)
Shall have cut-off the *Golden Hydra's* head ;
For an eternall *Trophey* of his Glory,
An Argument of an Immortall Story.   370

    But, now return we to our Theam, from whence
Our *Charity* (through *Zeal's* too-Vehemence)
Seems to have straid. Yet 'twas meer *Alms* did
    move
My grieved Verse These *Guilty* to reprove ;
To turn their hearts to GOD, and to their King ;
Their private heaps for publike helps to bring,
Against th' Ambition of some Foxy Foe,
That by our Selves, our Selves would overthrow ;
Not by his Arms, but by his *Alms*, to some ;
For, *Golden Launces* oft have overcome.   380

    Dear *Patriots*, that *Spitefull Alms* disdain,
Which brings your *Crowns ;* but 'tis our *Crowne* to gain :
Wᵗʰ groves of honours seems your brows t' imboss ;
But 'tis to grace her Profit and your Loss :
Which decks the *Church*, and doth the *Mass* adorn ;
But, by the *Mass*, 'tis but to serve her Turn :
Adores (in shew) both PETER's *Chair* and *Keyes*
But, if they *Ope* and *Shut* not as shee please,
Her *Charity* and her *Devotion* dy :
For, her *Religion* is but *Policy ;*   390
Her *Soule*, but *State ;* her *Life*, but *Rule's-Desire ;*
Whose Heat hath set all *Europe* on a Fire.

    Nilus (that serves for Rain to th' *Abyssine,*
The light-foot *Memphite*, and the *Canopine*)
Cools with his ALMS the Choler's fervency
In Earth and Air, which there the Sun doth fry :
Waters the Plains, which *Orion* parcheth ay
With twinkling Sparkles of his heatfull Ray :
Tempers the torrid *Æthiopian Zone :*
Seems to have Life, though it indeed have none,   400
Save that of ALMS ; sole Cause efficient
Of his fat Liquour, *Affrick's* Nourishment.

    The Heav'ns, as jealous of so *Bounteous Gifts,*
Would shut-up *Nile* within *Godonian* Clifts :
And Nature, envious of this *Affrick Prince*
His lavish Largess and Magnificence,
Fronts him with Hils that seem to threat the Stars,
(As if renewing the old *Titans'* Wars)
That one would think, amid the Mountains thick,
Nilus were bay'd-up, if not buried quick :   410
But, by the power which makes him charitable,
He findes that ALMS to force the Heav'ns are able.
Hee therefore, rushing, and out-roaring Thunder,
Surrounds the rocks that ween to keep him under ;
And with his swift Course breakes the *Cataracts,*
Deaf'ning withall the *Parthians* and the *Bacts.*

    Pactolus, Ganges, and the golden *Tay,*
Not onely steept their Stronds, enamell'd gay
With various Tinge of thousand Flowers and more
Sow'n on the surface of their winding Shore :   420
But for a richer ALMS, they *Gold* bestow,
As needfull now, as *Reason* (well wee know)
In *This Gold-Iron Age*, where, who so wants
All-mighty *Gold*, but *Scorn* and *Scandall* hants.

    When *Androde* fled his cruell *Master's Fist,*
And cause-less *Fury* (but for had-I-wist)
Amid the horror of the Woods hee meets
More ALMS and *Mercy*, than in *Rome's* proud
    streets :
There found he Man, to Man of brute Immanity ;
Here findes he *Brutes* of mildeness and humanity : 430
His Lord there paid his Service but with blowes ;
A *Lion* here him double gratefull showes :
Hee to the Beast had shown him serviceable ;
The Beast to him seems much more charitable.
For, having long wᵗʰ his best Preyes maintain 'd him
And in his Den, as dear Guest, entertain'd him,
Hee (two years after) also saves his Life,
Expos'd (in sport) to Fight and Fury rife

Of Man, and Beast, whom (forced) hunger, there,
Could never force, *The Slave* to touch or tear :⠀⠀440
But th' awfull Lion (which such Men may shame)
Him safely rescues from *Rome's* bloudy Game.

O noble *Lion !* thou hast brought to passe,
I almost yeeld to old *Pythagoras,*
In his Opinion of *Metempsychosis,*
Trans-animation (so the Word composes)
Of Soules deceast, to Bodies, good or bad,
As here, Delight in *Good* or *Ill* they had.
And durst I freely in his Doctrine wander,
I should suppose thee second *Alexander ;*⠀⠀450
And that, a Beast, his habits still are one
As when a Man and King of *Macedon.*

But, leaving Forrests, Floods, Fields, Earth, and Air,
Whose *Almes* already have appeared fair ;
Shall wee yet mount among the *Wandring Seaven,*
And see how constant they to *Alms* are given ?
There shall we find Man's monstrous Self-resisting,
Being made of *Alms,* all by meer ALMS subsisting.
Beasts, birds, and plants, roots, reptiles, daies and nights,
Have second *Being* from these Heav'nly Lights ;⠀⠀460
From whom our Selves, flat *Beggers,* borrowed have
The best that makes our worser part so brave :
The Sea 's their subject, and th' All-bearing Earth
Without their ALMS can bring us nothing forth.

Saturn is kind to Merchants, Mariners,
Storm-wonted Fishers, stooping Labourers,
Carefull House-holders, curious *Architects ;*
And every one that Gain with pain respects.

Milde *Jupiter* (more bounteous) *Beauty* gives,
Sweet gracefull Port, fresh health (that happy lives) : 470
ALM'NER of *Vertues,* storing Man with *Graces*
Most Angel-like, and meet for highest places :
Kings, Counsellors, Lords, Princes, Magistrates,
Hold after GOD, of him their high estates.

Mars, surest Patron of *Sarmatians* stout,
Of part of *Affrick,* and the *Southern* rout ;
Nights dayly give, them millions of delights,
And makes them naked make a thousand Fights.
All *Arts* wherein are Fire or Iron requir'd,
Of his sole *Alms* are to our Life acquir'd.⠀⠀480

Sol's Soule of *Alms ;* who richly *liberall,*
Gives him to All, yet cannot give him All :
Great *Season*-Bounder, artificiall Dresser
Of Years, and Daies, the even and onely Sessor
Of Time's rich *Alms,* which by his heat hee varies,
After the Innes wherein hee Monthly tarries :
His *Bounty* most is bent unto *Musicians,*
Bards, Poets, Leaches, Herbarists, Physicians.

Venus, each Morning, with a gentle Ray
Ushers the Sun, and summons us away⠀⠀490
From lazy Beds (our Bodies' living Graves)
When Day begins to issue from the Waves.
Her *Alms* goes chiefly to the preservation
Of Nature's Powers, and Parts of Generation :
Smooth smiles she gives ; sweet, cheerfull charming
⠀⠀Ein :
Love is Her *Gift ;* a Gift indeed divine.

Quick *Mercury,* great *Atlas's* Daughter's Son,
Wit's Treasurer, Well of *Invention,*
Hee gives us *Arts, Knowledge,* and *Eloquence,*
Which steals us oft from *Reason* and from *Sense,*⠀⠀500
A bounteous ALM'NER of *Astronomy,*
Rare (for the most) unto Man's feeble Eye ;
Who, yet, unseen feels (almost every houre)
Hundred Effects of its admired power ;
A Power which cannot be sufficient shown
By Verse or Voice (unlesse by *Hermes'* own)
For All that at this Day makes hunger fly
(*Gold, Silver, Brasse*) is drawn from *Mercury.*

Cynthia, ador'd with hundred fumes and flames ;
Honour'd (abroad) by more then hundred Names ;⠀⠀510
Shee gives us *Humours,* more or lesse abounding,
As in her Course her *Fall* or *Full* is rounding ;
Shee fashions Time ; which Shee again defaces
With constant Turns of her inconstant Faces :
Shee swaies the Flouds, and shews (by Evidence)
Her Selfe sole Law of liquid Elements :
Shee forms, by Night, the fresh and fruitfull Deaw,
Which every morning *Flora's* Buds doth streaw ;
Whose purled Pearls are ever bigger found
And more, the more *Lucina* waxeth round.⠀⠀520

In brief, All, given to ALMS and *Liberality,*
They all teach Man the same supernall Quality
Towards the Needy that doth nought possesse,
And from his Cradle brought but wretchednesse,
But *Sin* and *Death ;* had not Heav'n's ALMES beene
⠀⠀shed
In *Bloudy Bath,* to *White* This Monster's *Red ;*
A monster, made of Earth, for Earth still burning,
Although to Earth hee see him hourly turning.

Yea, proudest Kings have had no other Birth
Then poorest Beggers ; Both begin of Earth :⠀⠀530
Both like in Cries, in Perils, and in Pain :
Both alike *Guilty* in their *Grand-Sire's Stain :*
Both, as in Birth, so in their Death, alike :
Both Kings and Beggers one same Dart doth strike :
Both passe together, in one selfe-same Boat,
From th' arched *Palace* and the thatched *Cote.*
So that, in Life what-ever Ods there be ;
In Birth is none : none in their Death, wee see.

Onely, the *Good* (of what Degree soever)
Are free from *Death ;* and, though they dy, dy never ; 540
Save to the Grief of *Vertuous* Soules (their friends)
Whom, to survive the *Good,* it here offends :
I mean, in Body, which a Death they hold,
Or Toomb, or Prison, that doth Them with-hold
From th' *Happy Hav'n ;* and makes them less inclin'd
To seek their GOD, and his strait Wayes to find.

The *Good* are they, who not alone not wring ;
Who not alone not wrong, in any thing ;
Who not alone *not hurt ;* but (from their heart)
Doe Good to Others ; and their *Own* impart⠀⠀550
In liberall *Almes* unto the *Poor's* Reliefe,
After their power ; as grieved with their Griefe.

Such shall not dye, but to live ever *Blessed :*
Such shall not live, but to dye here *possessed*

Of *Grace*, and *Glory* with th' ETERNALL GOD,
Author of *Almes ;* and ever-scourging *Rod*
Of *Such* Gold-heaped, Iron-hearted Wretches
As to the *Poor* impart no part of *Riches ;*
Nor lend, *Nor lodge, nor cloathe, nor free, nor feed*

Distressed CHRIST, in *His* dear *Saints*, that need.   560
  Such shall not live, but to dye double-martyr'd :
Such shall not dye, but to live ever tortur'd
In Hell and Horrour, without End, or Ease.
  Now, Worldlings, chuse You which you will of these.

Sine fine fines.

NOTES AND ILLUSTRATIONS.

PAGE 207, '*Abbot*'—see our Introduction and Index of Names, *s.n.*

P. 208, col. 2, l. 6, '*Luxe*' = luxury.

Line 131, '*douns*' = downs : l. 135, '*Pils*' = pools ? l. 185, '*stark*' = stiff : l. 195, '*Fire-new*—see Glos- sarial Index, *s.v.* : *ibid.* '*slop*' = breeches : l. 300, '*Monopolites*' = monopolists : l. 313, '*pill'd*' = de- spoiled or plundered : l. 429, '*Immanity*'—see Glos- sarial Index, *s.v.* : l. 488, '*Leaches*' = physicians.

G.

MEMORIALS
OF MORTALITIE
Written in Tablets, or Quatrains,

By Pierre Mathieu.

The Second Centurie.

Translated; and *Dedicated*

To the Right Honourable, Henry
Wriothesley, *Earle of*
South-hampton, *&c.*

Shall it be said (*I shame it should be thought*)
    When After-Ages shall record Thy Worth;
    My sacred Muse *hath left* South-hampton *forth,*
    Of Her Record; to Whom so Much shee ought?
Sith *from* Thy Town (*where my* Saravia *taught*)
    Her slender Pinions had her tender Birth:
    And all, the little all shee hath of worth,
    Under Heav'n's Blessing, onely thence shee brought.
For *lack, therefore, of fitter Argument;*
    And lother Now, it longer to delay;
    (*Here while the Part of* Philip's *Page I play*)
I *consecrate This little Monument*
    Of gratefull Homage, to Thy noble-Bounty;
    And Thankefull love to (*My dear Nurse*) Thy County.

———————— Humbly devoted
————————Josuah Sylvester.

MEMORIALS
OF
MORTALITIE.

1.

Let who so list, think *Death* a dreadfull thing,
  And hold *The Grave* in horror and in hate :
I think them, I, most worth the *wel-comming ;*
Where, end our Woes ; our Joyes initiate.

2.

Man, *Death* abhors, repines, and murmurs at-her,
Blinde in that Law which made her, *good* for Him :
Both *Birth* and *Death* the daughters are of *Nature ;*
In whom is nought imperfect, strange, or grim.

3.

Death's ouglinesse is but imagined ;
Under foule Vizard a faire Face shee wears :
Her Vizard off, there is no more to dread ;
Wee laugh at Children whom a Vizard fears.

4.

Death, in strange Postures daily is disguised,
With Darts and Scythes in hand, Beers on her back :
As *Angels* are with wings and locks devised ;
So, Her a Body of bare bones they make.

5.

Who fears this *Death* is more then deadly sick ;
In midst of Life hee seems even dead for dread ;
Death in his breast hee bears, as buried Quick :
For, feare of *Death* is worse then *Death* indeed.

6.

Each fears this *Death ;* and with an equall dread,
The *Young*, as from a hideous monster, hie-them.
Th' *Old*, at her sight, shrink down into their Bed ;
All shun her ay, the more shee draweth nigh-them.

7.

What *Good*, or *Bad*, boads *Life* or *Death* to give ;
To be so fond of that, and this so flying ?
Thou would'st not *die*, yet know'st not how to *live ;*
Not knowing, *Life* to be a *living-dying.*

8.

One loves *This Life*, Another loathes it wholly :
Some look for Ease, Promotion some, some Profit :
To love it for the Pleasures here, is Folly ;
Weakenesse to hate it, for the troubles of it.

9.

The Storm at Sea under a Calm is bred :
Within Good-hap, Ill-hap hath life included ;
Begun in Tears, in Toils continued ;
And without Dolour cannot be concluded.

10.

Life, like a Taper, with the weakest Blasts
Is waved, wasted, melted, puffed out :
In some, somtimes, even to the Snuffe it lasts ;
In others hardly to the halfe holds-out.

11.

Fruit on the trees first blooms, then buds, then grows,
Then ripes, then rots : such our condition just ;
Begot, born, bred, live, dye ; so roundly goes
Time's wheel, to whirle our Bodies back to Dust.

12.

This Life 's a tree, whose goodly *Fruits* are men ;
One falls, himselfe ; Another 's beaten down :
It 's stript at last of *Leaves* and *Apples* then,
By *Time's* same hand wch had them first bestow'n.

13.

This Life 's a *Table*, where in earnest-jest
Foure *Gamesters* play : *Time*, eldest, vantage takes,
And biddeth Passe : *Love* fondly sets his Rest :
Man needs will see it ; but, *Death* sweeps the stakes.

14.

This Life (indeed) is but a *Comædie*,
Where this, the *Kaisar* playes ; and that, the *Clown :*
But, *Death* still ends it in a *Tragædie*,
Without distinction of the Lord from Lown.

15.

This Life's a *Warre*, civill, and forrain too ;
Within, without, Man hath his *Enemies :*
To keep the *Fort, Death* doth the *Towne* undoe ;
To save the Soule, the Body Shee destroyes.

16.

The World 's a Sea, the *Galley* is the life,
The *Master*, Time ; the *Pole*, Hope promiseth ;
Fortune the *Winde ;* the stormy *Tempest*, Strife ;
And man the *Row-Slave*, to the *Port* of Death.

17.

The World (mee thinks) is like our Parliaments,
Where Right too oft is over-born by Wrong ;
Where Quirks and Quiddits are of Consequence ;
Where lastly nought *Death's* Sentence can prolong.

18.

The World is much of a faire *Mistresse'* mood,
Which, wylie, makes more Fooles then Favourits ;
Hugs These, hates Those ; yet will of all be woo'd ;
But never keeps the Promise that shee plights.

19.

Life's smoothest glosse is like the *Sphear of Glasse
Archimedes* framed, and fill'd with Stars ;
As fraile as faire : for, the least storm (alas !)
That raps it, snaps it ; and the Pleasure mars.

20.

Th' Honour thou thirstest (as one dropsie-sick)
Weening to quaffe it, often stops thy winde :
'T 's a swelling Bladder ; which when *Death* shall prick
(Thou wilt confesse) thou but a puffe didst finde.

21.

And that *Ambition*, which affords thee Wings
To seek new Seas beyond Our Ocean's Arms
For mounts of Gold and Pearle, and precious things ;
Shall not preserve thy Carcass from the Worms.

22.

That *Pleasure* too, which stops thy *Reason's* ears,
Besots thy Soule, intoxicates thy Sense ;
And sad *Repentance* still behinde it bears ;
For moment Joyes, leaves Sorrow's Monuments :

23.

Pleasure which tires thee, but contents thee never,
Thy Body wearing more then wearying :
Like *Danaides* Sieve-like Tub, a-filling ever,
But never full for all their bucketing.

24.

Beauty, wch makes the proudest Kings to crouch,
Which serves the Soule as Letters in her favour ;
To see, delightfull ; dangerous to touch ;
From *Death's* drad Fury, may not, cannot save her.

25.

But, *Beauty, Grace-lesse*, is a Saile-lesse Bark,
A green-lesse Spring, a goodly light-lesse Room,
A Sun-lesse Day, a Star-lesse Night and Dark ;
And yet this *Grace* cannot escape the Toomb.

26.

When bodie's *Beauty* with soule's *Beauty* dwels,
There 's a Perfection passing all the rest :
Without This ; *Beauty* seems a Blemish else :
Without That, *Vertue* seems not seemly drest.

27.

That *Beauty*, which the Aire, Age, Ague quailes ;
Which busies so our eyes, tongues, hands, and hearts ;
At fifteen, buds ; at twenty, flowers ; and failes,
Or falls at thirty, and to dust reverts.

28.

Gold, the World's *God*, the Sun of *Pluto's* Sons ;
Whom Fire and Sword incessant serve so fell ;
Gold *Vertue's* Friend, and Vice's Fort at-once,
Serves oft for Bridge to passe in post to Hell.

29.

Man's *Knowledge* here, is but meer Ignorance :
Wee see the wisest foulely stumble oft ;
Learning is puft with doubtfull Arrogance,
And *Truth* is lost while it is too-much sought.

30.

With *Mysteries* the *Idiot* meddles most ;
Peeps into Heaven, into King's Counsels pryes ;
In Pulpit, *Phormio* doth dare an Host :
Thersites prates of Arms and Policies.

31.

Th' *Assyrian's* Empire is now seene no more ;
The *Medes* and *Persians* did the *Greeks* intombe ;
Great *Alexander's Kingdome* kinged foure ;
Whose Crowns, in fine, stoopt to the State of *Rome.*

32.

Where are those *Monarchs*, mighty Conquerors,
Whose brows ere-while the whole worlde's laurell drest,
When sea and land could shew no land but theirs?
Now, of it All, onely *Seaven Hills* do rest.

33.

Where are those Cities (great and goodly States)
Of *Ninivè*, with thrice five hundred Towers?
Great *Babylon ? Thebes*, with a hundred Gates?
Carthage (*Rome's* Rivall) *Dido's* dearest Bowers?

34.

All these huge buildings, these proud piles (alas !)
Which seem'd to threaten Heav'n it selfe to scale ;
Have now given place to Forrests, Groves, and Grass ;
And time hath chang'd their names and place withal.

35.

Nay, wilt thou see, how-far great Kings are foil'd?
See how sometime in Gold they swallow Poyson :
See *Ptolomeus* Cross't, *Bolestaus* boild,
Bajazeth in a Cage, *Richard* in Prison.

36.

See, see a Prince, neer *Cairo* flayed quick :
See *Sapores* by his proud Victor trod :
See Monk-like shav'n our cloistred *Childerick :*
See *Denis* beare, for Scepter, Pedant's Rod.

37.

See *Gordian* there in his owne Girdle hung :
See *Phocas'* bones broken with furious bats ;
See *Diomede* to his own Horses flung :
To Wolves *Lycâon, Popiel* to Rats.

38.

See, see proud *Salmon* sudden Thunder-slaine :
See *Theôderick* with horrid Terrour thrill'd :
See *Longuemare* hang'd in a golden Chain :
See a fierce Courser dragging *Brunechild.*

39.

See *Attalus*, having for Court a Forge :
See *Phalaris* burnt in *Perillus* Bull :
See *Memprice* left the greedy Wolves to gorge :
Cambyses' Sword sheath'd in Himselfe to th' full.

40.

Who but will feare amid the Frights of *France ;*
Seeing how *Death* Two *Henries* reft of Life ?
The Sire, in *Paris*, with a splinter'd Lance ;
The Son, before *it* with a pois'ned Knife.

41.

That *Queen*, whose Court was in a Castle coopt,
(A *Pris'ner* here ; above a Princesse hop't.)
Whose royall Throne t' a *Tragick-Scaffold* stoopt,
Her head shee felt with whiffing steel off-chopt.

42.

That *King*, who could within his Kingdoms drad,
See *Sol* still shine, when hence hee vanisheth ;
Who past our Seas, another Empire had,
For All hee had, had but a *louzie* death.

43.

Who more his Garden of *Salona* priz'd
Then *Rome's* great *Empire*, and the World's Command,
Knew well the *Cares* from *Crowns* insepariz'd ;
And *Scepter's* sad weight in the strongest hand.

44.

Towards our End insensible wee slip :
For, speaking, sporting, laughing, snoring deep,
Death still draws on-wards : as at Sea the Ship
Sails to her Hav'n-ward, though the Master sleep.

45.

Death each-where kils : in hunting, *Carloman ;*
In's Cave, *Caligula ; Aristobulus,*
In Bath ; by th' Altar, *Philip ; Julian,*
In Camp ; in Councell, conquering *Julius.*

46.

Death seeks the *Æmathian ;* and from *Nero* flies ;
One in a Shallow drownes, who Seas did scape :
An *Emperour* in eating *Mushroms*, dies :
A *Holy-Father* in a *Harlot's* lap.

47.

No hand but serves *Death's* turn, *Edric* by 's Mother ;
Albion by 's Wife, *Aristo* by his Friends ;
By 's own Son *Bajazeth, Conrad* by 's Brother ;
Mustapha, by his Sire, Self, *Cato* ends.

48.

Death diversly makes him familiar here,
Henry the Black, a bit of bread could fine ;
A King of *Goths* died in a Tub of Beer,
Thalis, of thirst, of hunger *Antonine.*

49.

Death, every-where, in every thing distils
Her fell Despite ; Fire, Air, Earth, Ocean :
Drusus, a Peare ; a Fig, *Terpander* kills,
A Fly (in drinking) choaketh *Adrian.*

50.

As soon a *Soveraign*, as a *Shepheard's* gone :
Men dying here have but one equall Quality :
By *Birth* and *Death* is Their Condition one :
Their Stay, and State, between, make th' Inequality.

51.

There's no *Death Sudden* to the godly-*Wise :*
His heart goes out to meet all haps before :
When hee embarks, hee casts Wracks Jeopardies ;
And when Wind serves not, he will rowe no more,

52.

Not knowing then, when, where thy *death* will snatch ;
At Sea, or Land ; Young, Old ; Morn, Noon, or Night :
Look for it ever, every-where keep watch :
For, what wee look-for little can affright.

53.

If Infants oft no sooner breathe then dye ;
If good men little last, and wicked long :
Be not too curious in that Secret's *Why ?*
Th' are stroaks of that hand which strook never wrong.

54.

Why good men goe, and why th' ungodly stay,
Dispute it not, God hath permitted so.
Those *dye*, to *live :* These *live* to *dye* for aye :
These *live* at ease, Those in a world of woe.

55.

If from thy Dayes thou but thy Nights subtract ;
Thy sleep's, thy care's, thy maw's, thy *Muse's* waste,
What thy Wife weareth, what thy Friends exact,
Thy Griefs, thy Suits : how short a Life thou hast !

56.

The Head-ach, Tooth-ach, Gout, or Fever rife,
Or Ulcer in the Leg, Stone in the Reins,
By ling'ring Drops strains out the tedious Life ;
Yet art thou loth that *Death* should rid thy Paines.

57.

Thy Term expir'd, thou put'st off payment yet,
And weenst to win much by som Months' delay.
Sith pay thou must, wer't not as good be quit ?
For, *Death* will be no gentler any day.

58.

Th' affaires of *Parting* poast not to to-Morn.
For, on *Delay, Repentance* waits with Woe :
The Winde and Tide will in a moment turn ;
All houres are good for those *resolv'd* to goe.

59.

Grudging to dye in flower of thine age,
Thou griev'st to be too-soon discharg'd from prison :
Repin'st too-soon t' have done thy Pilgrimage,
Loth to have-in thy Harvest in due Season,

60.

Make of thy Deeds, not of thy Dayes account :
Think not how far, but think how fair thou passest :
See to what Summe thy *Vertues* will amount ;
For, Life and Gold are chose by weight, the massi'st.

61.

Life's valued by th' effect, not by the age ;
The labour, not the lasting praise it most :
Long hath he liv'd that liveth to be sage ;
Good life (too-often) in long life is lost.

62.

Long *Acts* commend not most a *Comædy*,
'Tis still esteemed as the *Parts* are plaid :
So, in our Lives, not *Years* considered be ;
But, worthy *Actions* by the Wise are weigh'd.

63.

Who grieves because hee liv'd not here, yer born,
A hundred years, is double worthy laughter :
But, trebble hee who at his Death doth mourn ;
Sure not to live a hundred years here-after.

64.

Man 's not more *Happy* for *long living* here.
Number of Dayes doe not more Blisses bring ;
More Compass makes not a more complete Sphere.
As round 's a little, as a larger Ring.

65.

And if that *Death* wait on thee, and protract ;
With *Usurie*, shee 'll make thee pay it double ;
Thy Joyes in Dream, thy Dolors still in act,
To make long Life a long Repenting Trouble.

66.

If Hee that here, thee in his Vine-yard hir'd,
Pay thee at *Noon* thy Wages full as much
As Those that there all the whole Day have tir'd ;
Why murmur'st thou ? why dost thou grieve and grutch ?

67.

He casts his Work well, well his Workmen kens ;
Thy Slackness, Slowness, Weakness to hold out :
Therefore, yer weary, hee thy Way-fare ends ;
Lest staying longer, thou marre all 'tis doubt.

68.

Hee gives our Task, and hee again will take it ;
Who Him, unwilling ; Him, unworthy serves ;
Before hee call, 'tis folly to forsake it ;
And who-so leaves it, to be left deserves.

69.

Or first or last, on All this stamp is set :
Early or late, into this Port must Wee.
Who gave the Charge, ordained the Retrait ;
One self-same Law did life and death decree.

70.

The more the Body dures, Soule more indures ;
Never too-soon can shee from thence exile :
Pure, in shee came ; there living, shee impures ;
And suffers there a thousand Woes the while.

71.

The Soule is forc't within the Flesh to dwell ;
In danger there shee lives, and sleeps in fear :
To hatch her Bird, shee needs must break her Shell,
And think it never can too-soon appear.

72.

Soule blames the Body, Body blames the Soule ;
But *Death* surprising, ends their Quarrell prest :
Down goes the Body, in the Dust to roule ;
The faithfull Soule, up to th' eternall Rest.

73.

Death frees the Soul from Bodie's wilfull Errors ;
From the Soule's Vices, Shee the Body saves :
The Soule's Annoyes, are to the Body Terrors ;
The Bodie's Torments, to the Soule are Graves.

74.

This Body is not Man : His Stuff 's more fine ;
His Beauty, with Heav'n's beauty hath Affinitie :
The Body dead, That ever-lives, divine ;
Even as a Beam from the supreme *Divinity*.

75.

If then the Soule, so long here languishing
Within the Body, doe not gladly part ;
Shee hath forgotten her owne Source or Spring ;
And that She must, from whence shee came, revert.

76.

But, more then death, death's pain appalleth thee ;
That's but a Stream which swiftly vanisheth :
There's, as no Pain, in that extremity :
For, th' Body, down, doth nothing feele in death.

77.

Then quit those Fears that in thy phant'sie stick :
For, violent Evils have no permanence :
If that death's Pain be keen, 'tis also quick ;
And by the quicknesse takes away the Sense.

78.

To leave thy Babes behinde, thy heart it gripes ;
In Whom, Thou shalt revive, from lap to lap :
Happy who hath them ; for they are our Types :
And oft Who hath None, 's happy by mis-hap.

79.

To leave thy Wife thou wail'st, well worth excusing ;
'T's a necessary Ill, Good stranger-like ;
Which, cleerest Eyes (Selfe-wise) too-oft mischusing,
In little Flesh find many Bones to pick.

80.

Th' art loth to leave the *Court's* delights, devices,
Where None lives long unbrav'd, or unabhorred :
Where treason's prudence ; where the *vertues vices :*
Where som no eyes, and where som have no forehead.

81.

The Mariner, that runs from Rock to Rock,
From Wrack to Wrack, dwelling in dangers rife,
Wave's ball, wind's thrall, and tempest's shuttle-cock ;
Would not exchange His for the Courtier's life.

82.

The Court beguiles thee as black-Angel-Bands,
In giving Leaves for Fruits to *Circe's* Sisters :
Their brightest Torches are but funerall Brands :
And, in the *Court, All is not Gold that glisters.*

83.

Thou would'st in Death *revenge* thy wronged Worth,
Make known thy love, have shown thy brave ambition :
Why fram'st thou not thy *death* unto thy *birth,*
W^ch brought thee naked forth, and void of passion ?

84.

Fain would'st thou see thy *Learning's fruit* (perhaps)
Ripe, yer thou rot ; that's but a vain Desire :
Art, now a-dayes, may starve, while *Ignorance*
Hath Shades for Summer ; and for Winter, Fire.

85.

All day thou trudgest thorow thick and thin,
For that dull Bulk which doth thee daily brave :
Phinice wreaths Ropes, which ay his Ass-winds-in :
The soule that serves the Body is a Slave.

86.

As many steps in Death as Life wee tread :
Esteem for Deaths, all daies since thou hadst breath ;
To come's not Thine ; *Present,* is instant fled :
And *Time,* in time, is over comn by *Death.*

87.

When Man's imbarkt on th' *Universall* Deck,
Hee neither swiften can his Course, nor slack it :
Tide, Wind and Weather are not at his beck ;
And, To put back, hath many often wracked.

88.

Som, sometimes grieve for one that gladly dyes :
Socrates joyes sith wrong hee *suffereth :*
Xantippa melts in Tears ; Hee laughs, Shee cryes
Diversly judging of these Darts of *Death.*

89.

To run unto this *Death,* is *Desp'rate* rage :
Wise-*Patience* onely waits it every-where :
Who scorns it, showes a *Resolution* sage :
For, Cowards fly it, and the Idiots feare.

90.

When the last Sand of our last Glasse goes out,
Without recoyling, wee must step our last :
As, without grudge or noise, dislodge the Stout ;
And when they must goe, stay not to be chac't.

91.

The *Pilgrim* longs to have his Journey done ;
The Mariner would fain be off the Seas :
The Work-man joyes to end his Work begun ;
And yet man mournes to finish his Disease.

92.

For a short time Thy Sun is over-cast :
But, thou shalt once re-see 't more bright then ever :
And that same Day, wch here thou think'st thy last,
Is a New-birth Day, to be ended never.

93.

What wrong doth *Death,* I pre-thee Worldling say,
When, loosing (under hope of happier matches),
Curting thy Life, hee takes thy Card away ;
And when, to save thy Life, thy Light he snatches ?

94.

Fear'st thou, Faint heart, that narrow Plank to pass
Which God himself hath gon ; which all men must ?
That like a Child, held by the sleeve (alas !)
With Eye still glancing on the brim thou go'st ?

95.

Beyond it, thou shalt see those pleasant Plains,
Whose boundles Beauty all discourse transcendeth :
Where Kings' and Subjects' souls have fellow Raigns,
On blessed Thrones, whose Glory never endeth.

96.

What shalt thou see more, for more living Here ?
This Heav'n, this Sun, thou oft before hast seen :
And should'st thou live another *Plato's* Year,
This World would be the same that it hath been.

97.

Death's end of Ills, and onely Sanctuary
Of him that cannot scape the Grudge, the Gall
Of a severe Judge and proud adversary :
It is a point which Heav'n appoints to All.

98.

At that Divorce sigh Bodies, Soules do solace :
Th' Exile exulteth at his home-Retrait :
This Bodie's but the Inne, 'tis not the Palace :
Th' immortall Soule hath an immortall Seat.

99.

Death's as the Dawning of that happy day,
Where without Setting shines th' Eternall Sun,
Where-in who walk, can never, never stray :
Nor fear they Night who to the Day-ward run.

100.

There's Rest eternall for thy *Labours* rife :
There's for thy *Bondage* boundlesse *Liberty :*
There when *Death* endeth, she begins thy life.
And where's no more Time, there's *Eternity.*

FINIS.

MEMORIALS

OF

MORTALITIE.

Written in Tablets, or Quatrains,

By PIERRE MATHIEU.

The Second Centurie.

Tranſlated; and *Dedicated*

To the Right Honourable, ROBERT

DE'UREUX, *Earle of Eſſex and Ew, &c.*

*Y*Our double *Title to* My single *heart*
    Both by your Purchase, *and your Parents'* Right ;
Claims *both a better and a greater Part*
Of gratefull Service, *then this slender* Mite.
Yet, sith (to profit *more then* please) *I write,*
    More sighs then songs (lesse us'd to smiles then smart)
    Disdain not These Restrainers of delight ;
    Though bitter, fitter, then the Smoothing *Art,*
To keep *the* Minde *and* Bodie *both in* Health ;
    To coole *the Fits of* Lust, Ambition, Pride
    (Surfaits of Ease, Youth, Liberty, and Wealth)
And cure *all sicknesse of the Soule, beside.*
    Whence, Ever free ; and full of every Good
    From GOD and Men, be ESSEX Noble Bud.

Ex Animo exoptat

JOSUAH SYLVESTER

MEMORIALS

OF

MORTALITIE.

1.

THat height of Kings, Crowns, Honour, *Worthies* wonder,
  Is now but winde, dust, shade. Hee, whose Approach
Appall'd the Proudest, whom all trembled under,
A cursed base hand butcherd in his *Coach*.

2.

All Triumph, yesterday ; to-day, all Terror :
Nay ; the fair Morning over-cast yer Even ;
Nay ; one short Hour saw, live and dead, War's mirror,
Having *Death's* speed-stroak undiscerned given.

3.

In all this World, all 's fickle ; nought is firm :
It is a Sea *sans* Safety, Calm, or Port :
Lawes, Cities, Empires, have but here their Term :
What ever 's born must under death resort.

4.

Time flits as Winde, and as a Torrent swifteth :
It passeth quick, and nought can stop it flying :
Who knowes what ills it every moment drifteth,
Deems, that to leave to live, is to leave dying.

5.

Man in the Womb knowes nothing of his State :
(A wile of *Nature*) for, there, had he Reason,
Hee should fore-know this World's too-wretched Fate ;
And rather would intomb him in that Prison.

6.

Our birth begins our beer ; our death, our breath :
On that Condition here aboord wee come :
To be 's as not to be : Birth is but Death :
There 's but a Sigh from Table to the Tomb.

7.

Life 's but a Flash, a Fume, a Froth, a Fable,
A Puffe, a Picture, in the Water seeming ;
A waking dream, dream's shadow, shadowe's Table,
Troubling the Brain with idle Vapours steeming.

8.

Life, to the life, The *Chess-boord* lineats ;
Where *pawns* and *kings* have equal portion :
This leaps, that limps, this checks, that necks, that mates :
Their Names are diverse ; but their Wood is one.

9.

Death, Exile, Sorrow, Fear, Distraction, Strife,
And all those evils, seen before suspected ;
Are not the Pains, but Tributes of this Life ;
Whence, Kings no more than Carters are protected

10.

No : *Sacraments* have been no *Sanctuary*
From *Death ;* Nor *Altars*, for Kings *offring-up :*
Th' Hell-*hallow'd Host* poysons *Imperiall Harry :*
Pope Victor dies drinking th' *immortall Cup*.

11.

Thou ow'st thy Soul to Heav'n : to pay that *Debt*
Be not compell'd ; *Christians* are willing Payers :
But, yet, thy Soul as a good Guest intreat ;
Whom no good Host will tumble down the stairs.

12.

'Tis better fall, than still to fear a fall :
'Tis better die, than to be still a dying :
The end of Pain, ends the Complaint withall :
And nothing grieves that comes but once, and flying.

13.

This Life 's a Web, wov'n fine for som, som gross ;
Som Hemp, som Flax, som longer, shorter som :
Good and Ill haps are but the Threds a-crosse :
And first or last, *Death* cuts it from the Loom.

14.

These Names, which make some blubber, som so brave,
(Names sprung from injury, or from ambition)
In *Death* are equall : *Earle*, and *Sir*, and *Slave*,
Under *His* Empire, are in one condition.

15.

For Friends deceast, cease not repast nor sleep ;
Such sorrow Suits not th' *Intellectuall* part :
Who wails man's *death*, that he was man doth weep :
And, that he promis'd, comming, to depart.

16.

The young and old goe not as equall pac't :
Th' one ambles swift, the other gallopeth :
'Tis good to die, yer wee our life distaste,
A valiant Man should dare to feel his Death.

17.

Happy who leave the world when first they com ;
Th' Air, at the best, is here contagious thick :
Happy that Child, who issuing from the Wombe
Of 's *Spanish* Mother, there returned quick.

18.

The Bodie's Torments are but twigs to beat
And brush the Dust from *Vertue's* pleights about ;
And make the passions of the soule more neat :
As th' air is purest when the winds roare out.

19.

Grieving that *death* shuts not thine eyes at home,
And where the heav'ns vouchsaf't them first to ope ;
Thou fear'st the earth too little for thy Tombe,
And heav'n too narrow for thy Corpse's cope.

20.

Heav'ns no lesse Order have, than at their Birth,
Nor influence : Sun, Moon, and Stars, as bright ;
All hold their owne ; Fire, Water, Air, and Earth ;
Man, man alone 's fall'n from his *pristine* plight.

21.

Worldling, thou saist, 'Tis yet not time to mend ;
But, God hates sinners that in sin delight :
To grossest sinners doth he mercy send ;
But not to sinners sinning in despight.

22.

Who, Morn and Even doth of himselfe demand
Account of all that he hath *done, said, thought ;*
Shall finde him much eas'd, when he comes to stand
To that Account where all shall once be brought.

23.

For bitter Checks that make thy Cheeks to flame,
And to thy teeth tell Truths, thou hast no action :
To do the Evill, sith thou hadst no shame,
Be not asham'd to suffer thy correction.

24.

Perhaps this Child shall rich or poor become :
Perhaps a wretch, perhaps a liberall :
Perhaps a Wise-man, and perhaps a Mome :
But, past perhaps, assured, die he shall.

25.

When wine runs low, it is not worth the sparing ;
The worst and least doth to the bottome dive :
Wrong not thy leasure (years vouchsafe) in daring :
But some-times look into thy Grave, alive.

26.

Sinner, thy God is not inexorable ;
No *Radamanth, Returning* hearts to hate :
There is no sin, in heav'n *unpardonable ;*
Nor no *Repentance* in this life too late.

27.

The eye that fixtly the Sun-beams beholds,
Is sudden daz'd : So, in God's judgements high,
Men's cleerest judgements are as blind as Moules,
None, none but Eagles can the Lightning eye.

28.

O wretched *Vertue !* wretched is thy state ;
For, Fortune hath the fruit, Thou scarce the flower :
Thou art a Stranger at thy proper Gate,
Thy friends thence banisht and thy foes in bower.

29.

Man, *Knowledge* still, to the last gaspe affecteth ;
In learning *Socrates* lives, grayes, and dyes,
Free from *death's* process *knowledge* none protecteth :
But, to learn well *to die*, is to be *Wise.*

30.

To live, is to begin One-work, and end it ;
Life hath, with All, not same Repute, Report ;
'T;'s an exile, to the Sot ; Sage, Journey ween'd it :
Wherein he walks, not as the common-sort.

31.

For, having a good Prince, Peers just and wise,
Obedient people, Peace concluded fast,
A State 's not sure : Storms after Calms arise ;
And fairest dayes have foulest over-cast.

32.

Man, though thou be from heav'n Originary,
Presume not yet to peer thee with thy God :
Hee 's Soveraign King ; thou but his Tributary :
Hee 's every where, thou but in one poor clod.

33.

Of Elephants the biggest leads the Band ;
The strongest Bull over the Heard doth raign :
But, him behooves who will mankind command,
Not ablest body, but the aptest brain.

34.

Kings' Majesty seems as eclipsed much,
Unless great Servants in great Troops attend :
'Tis sure an honour to be serv'd by such ;
But on their Faith 'tis fearfull to depend.

35.

To build a Palace, rarest stones are sought :
To build a Ship, best timber is selected :
But to instruct young Princes (as they ought)
Ought all the *Vertues* to be there collected.

36.

Art's now-adayes a *Desart* desolate :
Kings' gracious Raies are there no more discern'd :
Philosophers wait at the Wealthie's Gate,
And rarely rich men do regard the learn'd.

37.

Th' hand bindeth not except the heart with-go :
What comes not thence, nor thank, nor thought deserves.
Hee giveth All that doth Himself bestow ;
He nothing gives who but his heart reserves.

38.

That curious thirst of Travaile to and fro,
Yeelds not the fruit it promis'd men in mind :
Changing their Air, their humours change not tho ;
But, many Lodgings, and few Friends they find.

39.

In vain the Soule hath Reason's attribute,
Which unto *Reason* cannot Sense submit :
For, Man (alas !) is bruter than a Brute,
Unlesse that *Reason* bridle *Appetite*.

40.

Self-swelling *Knowledge*, wit's own Overbearer,
Proves *Ignorance*, and finds it nothing knowes :
It flyes the Truth to follow Lyes and Error,
And when most right it weens, most wry it goes.

41.

The Vicious trembles, alwayes in Alarms ;
Th' eye of the Vertuous keeps him as at bay :
When all the World fear'd *Rome's* All-reaching arms,
One vertuous *Cato* did all *Rome* dismay.

42.

Vice blinds the soule, and understanding clogs,
Makes good of ill, takes foule for fairest look,
Yea, Dirt for Dainties : so live loathsome Frogs,
Rather in puddles, than in purest Brook.

43.

In greatest Houses Vice hath battered,
Whose honours though no less have shined bright :
What are the Graceless to the Good ? Not dead,
But living branches, in the tree have right.

44.

If Men might freely take Essay of Court ;
None, having tasted, would return so neer :
The happiest there meets many a Spight in Sport,
And knowes too-well he buyes his Weal too-dear.

45.

To love None, All to doubt ; to fain, to flatter ;
To form new faces, and transform true hearts ;
To offer Service, and flie-off in Matter ;
Are *Courtiers'* Lessons, and their ground of *Arts*.

46.

Set not thy Rest on *Court*, Sea's barren sand ;
There grows no goodness ; good, there evill grows :
Rest's Temple yerst did forth the *Citie* stand :
No Sent's so sweet as is the *Countrey* Rose.

47.

Who weens in *Court* to thrive, will finde him weak,
Without two Aiders ; *Impudence, Immunity :*
For first behooves him his own brows to break,
Yer Others' heads hee break with *Importunity*.

48.

Who is not sorry for Time's loss, in stay
For Kings' slow Favours, seems to have no sense :
The losse of Goods, a Prince may well repay,
But losse of Time Kings cannot recompence.

49.

Is't not the Top of Follie's Top, to note
An old *Sir Tame-ass* gallanting in Court,
To play the Yonker ; and Swan-white to dote
On *Venus'* Dovelings, in despight of Sport ?

50.

A mean man hardly scapes the mightie's claws ;
Hee's as a Mouse play'ng by a sleeping Cat ;
Who lets it run, then locks it in her paws :
And all her sports boad but the death of That.

51.

World's *Vanitie* is rife in every place,
(Alas !) that good Wits should be 'witched so !)
Maskt in the Church, in Court with open Face ;
For there's the place her perfectly to know.

52.

By evill Manners is good-Nature marr'd ;
None falls at once, all *Vertue* to defie.
Vice, in the Soule is a strange plant transferr'd :
And wer't not dressed, it would quickly die.

53.

With By-respects Impietie wee cover :
Earth more than Heav'n is priz'd among us now :
At God's great *Name* we scarce our heads uncover ;
When Kings are named, every knee doth bow.

54.

Disorder Order breeds : good lawes have sprung
From evill lives : Would All keep *Justice'* line,
In *Westminster* there woud be soon lesse Throng,
Less work, less wrack, less words for *Mine* and *Thine*.

47

55.

Law-tricks now stript the People to their shirt :
Shift is their Shield, Gold is their onely god :
Wasps break the Web, Flies are held fast and hurt :
The Guilty quit, the Guiltlesse under-trod.

56.

There 's now no trust : Brother betraies his Brother :
Faith 's but a phant'sie, but by fooles esteem'd :
Friend's false to Friend ; and all deceive each-other ;
Th' Ivie puls down the Wall by which it clim'd.

57.

Treasons be Trifles : Man 's a Wolfe to Man :
Crimes be but Crums ; Vice is for Vertue vanted ;
Sodom's and *Cypris'* sinnes wee suffer can :
And Impious Tricks in all their tracks are hanted.

58.

In perfect'st men some imperfection 's found,
Some-what amiss among their *good* is seen :
Gold, and pure Gold we dig not from the ground ;
There 's Dust and Drosse, and grosser stuffe between.

59.

Merit, of old did *Friendship* feed and fix ;
Where now-adayes 'tis founded all on profit,
With deep-dissembling and deceitfull-tricks,
And evermore the Poor is frustrate of it.

60.

Th' Earth cannot fill thy heart's unequall Angles,
Thy heart 's a Triangle, the earth 's a Round :
A Triangle is fill'd but with Triangles :
And th' infinite the finite cannot bound.

61.

'T 's a *Death* to die far from one's Native Citie :
Yet *Death's* not milder there, than else about :
Death, without ROME, did not *Rutilius* pitie ;
Neither, within ROME, Him that nere went out.

62.

When Man is com'n to th' old last cast of Age,
When Nature can no longer lend nor borrow ;
Hee thinks not yet to pack and leave the Stage ;
But still, still hopes to live untill to-morrow.

63.

Fain, would'st thou flie *Love's* wanton *Luxury ?*
Cut off occasions : speak far-off : flie Fitnesse :
Shun Solitude : live still in Company :
They fall alone that would not fall with witnesse.

64.

Muse not to see the wicked prosper faire :
The Sun his Shine even unto Theeves doth give :
When of their Patients Leaches do despaire,
They give them over as they list to live.

65.

Slander is worser than Hel's burning Torture,
The force more fierce, the heat more vehement :
Hell after Death, doth but the guilty martyr ;
Slander, alive, torments the Innocent.

66.

Affliction razes, and then raises hearts :
As, under weight, victorious Palms are wont :
As, under seales the Wax doth swell (in part) :
Under the Cross the Soule to Heav'n doth mount.

67.

Envie, in vain pure *Vertue's* Anvill bites,
Breaking her Teeth : as on a stone the Cur,
That barks of Custom, rather than Despight,
At every poor and harmelesse passenger.

68.

Envie's a Torture which doth men molest ;
Even from their birth ; yer they ought else can do :
Behold two Infants nursed at one Brest ;
They cannot brook their Teat for Meat to Two.

69.

This is the Ods twixt Honest men and Knaves :
Th' one tels his Neighbour, All mine owne is mine,
And all thine too : The other (voyd of Braves)
Saith, Thine 's not Mine ; but what I have is Thine.

70.

What *Envie* likes not, that shee makes a Fault :
Joseph with *Ismael*, for his Dream was barter'd :
Abel's pure Offring to his End him brought :
And for the *Truth* the Innocent are martyr'd.

71.

Flat-Cap, for whom hoord'st thou thy heaped Trea-
           sures ?
Thy bodie's Sweat, thy Soul's dear Price (poor Sot !) ?
Sir Prodige-all (thine Heir) in *Protean* pleasures,
Will waste in one day, All thine Age hath got.

72.

True *Liberalitie* would bee intire :
Yet not at-once, at all times, and to all.
One may mis-give, to give yer once require :
Yet Gifts un-asked sweetest Gifts I call.

73.

Content with Fruits from thine owne Labour grow'n,
A fore-hand still, a set Revenue save :
For, hee 's a Foole in more respects than one,
That spends his Store, or more, before hee have.

74.

Their is no Goodnesse in a groveling heart,
Bent on the World, bound to this Rock below :
Were not the Moone so neer his Neather part,
Shee would not, could not, be *Eclipsed* so.

75.

Goods are great Ils to those that cannot use them :
Misers mis-keep, and Prodigals mis-spend them :
Hel-hounds, to hasten toward hell, abuse them :
As wings to heav'n-ward, heav'n-bent-souls extend them.

76.

Presumptuous spirits spring not from right *nobility :*
Courage, that comes from *Pride*, proves never true :
Pride ruines hearts, whose Raiser is Humility,
The humble Shepheard the proud Gyant slew.

77.

Pride glitters oft under an humble Weed :
Oft lovely Names are given to loath'd Effects ;
Men sooth them in the Cause, to 'scuse th' ill deed :
And blame Light, rather than their Sight's defects.

78.

A *Prudent* man is, for himselfe, sought-forth :
He 's more admir'd than what the world most vants :
Praises are due unto one's proper Worth :
Not purest Gold adds price to *Diamants*.

79.

Th' *Humble*, doth Others prize ; Himself depress :
Save against *Pride* hee never bends his Browes :
The more his *Vertue* mounts-him, counts-him less :
God th' *humble Sinner*, not *Proud Just*, allowes.

80.

O ! *Hypocrite*, which hast but *Vertue's* Vaile,
Seem what thou art, and what thou seemest bee :
To hide thy filth, all thy Fig-leaves will faile :
Thou canst not hide thee from thy God, nor Thee.

81.

Mock-*Saints*, whose Soul-weal on your Works you lay,
With eyes and hands to Heav'n, while heart 's elsewhere :
For shame ye durst not to the least man say,
What you (profane) dare whisper in God's eare.

82.

Gold's fin'd in fire : Soules in *Affliction* better :
Moths gnaw the Garment locked in the Chest :
Still water stinks, unwholsome, black and bitter :
Swords rust in Sheathes, and so do Soules in Rest :

83.

Op'ning thy Soule to God, close Mouth from men ;
Nor let thy Thoughts roame from thy due Intent.
God sees the hearts, his judgement soundeth them,
And Them confounds whose Words and Deeds dissent.

84.

Gamesters may well All to to-morrow post ;
To see or to be seen, th' have never leasure :
With adverse Windes their minds are ever tost ;
Loss bringing griefe, more than the Gain brings pleasure.

85.

To Shun Affaires, behooves exceeding heed :
Troubles unsent-for, and unlookt-for, haste ;
Un-set, un-sow'n, too-early growes the Weed :
Wee meet too-soon the Care we hoped past.

86.

All *Idelness* dis-natures Wit, dis-nerves-it ;
A mod'rate Travell makes it quick, addrest :
Sloath quels and kils it ; Exercise preserves it :
But hee's not free that hath no time to rest.

87.

Who seeketh Rest in troublous Managings,
Thinks to find Calm amid Tempestuous Seas :
The World and Rest are two, two adverse things :
Thick streams re-cleer when storms and stirrings cease.

88.

Fortune in *Court* is fickle, apt to vary :
Favours sort seldome to the Suiter's minde :
They many times even in the port mis-carry :
The hotter Sun, the blacker shade they finde.

89.

Gifts, honours, office, greatness, grace of Kings,
Are but the Ushers of Adversitie :
For their last mischief have the *Emmet's* Wings :
And height of Health betokens sicknesse nie.

90.

Youth hath more lures, more traps, more trains to ill,
Than Fowler Gins, or Baits the Fisher-man :
Age would, but cannot what it would, fulfill :
Senex, thou leav'st not sin : sin leaves thee than.

91.

Th' Eye tends to beauty as the Center of-it :
After the Eyes, Heart and Affections draw :
'Tis hard to keep safe what so-many covet :
For, men's Desires Kings cannot keep in Awe.

92.

All Good or Ill-hap, that here happens thee,
Comes from *Opinion* (which all ruling seems).
Opinion makes us other than wee be :
Hee's not *unhappy*, who him *happy* deems.

93.

From contrary Effects is formed sadnesse :
Both Smoak and Smiles have made the eys to water.
Who sow in Tears, shall one day reap in Gladnesse :
Who sow in Joyes, shall reap Annoyes hereafter.

94.

Let 's leave out I, and No, in Conversation :
Words now transposed, and *wax-nosed*, Both,
By ROME's *new* Doctrine of *Equivocation*,
Which gives a Lye the credit of an Oath.

95.

Friends, now-adayes, wake at the noise of Gain,
As Bees to flow'rs, as Crowes to Carion haste,
As Flies to Flesh, as Birds and Ants to Grain :
So Friends to profit thickly flock and fast.

96.

Who reaves thine honour, scoffs, if hee presume
T' have done thee favour, that thy life hee left :
Why should the Bird live, having lost her Plume ?
The rest is nothing when the Honour's reft.

97.

Little sufficeth Life in th' un-delicious ;
The Sun for need may somtimes dress our victuall :
I blame, alike, the *Cynick* and *Apicius ;*
This, for his too-too-much ; That 's, too-too-little.

98.

Too-oft is made too-ill Interpretation
Of words and deeds best meant and built on reason :
All 's evill to the Evill, by Selfe-flation :
Whence Bees their Honey, Spiders suck their Poyson.

99.

Happy the People where *Just-Gentle Prince*-is :
Whose Sword is *Justice*, and whose Shield is *Love*.
For These, *Augustus Deified* long-since-is :
And without These, Kings' Scepters maimed prove.

100.

Good-hap, Good-heart, Favour, and Labour met,
Bring men to Riches and to Honors heer ;
But that 's the Way about : To be born *Great*,
Is great Advantage ; Not to buy so deer.

FINIS.

NOTES AND ILLUSTRATIONS.

FIRST CENTURY.—Stanza 4, l. 2, '*Beers*' = biers :
st. 14, l. 4, '*Lown*' = loon, rustic or clown : st. 17, l. 3,
'*Quiddits*' = subtleties, equivocations : st. 22, l. 4,
'*moment*' = momentary : st. 36, l. 1, '*quick*' = alive :
st. 41, l. 1, '*A Queen*' = Mary Queen of Scots : st. 93,
l. 3, '*Curting*' = shortening.

SECOND CENTURY.—Stanza 6, l. 1, '*beer*' = bier :
st. 18, l. 2, '*pleights*' = plaits : st. 29, l. 2, '*grayes*' =
grows grey : st. 32, l. 1, '*Originary*' = originally : *ib.*
l. 2, '*peer*' = equal : st. 64, l. 3, '*Leaches*' = physicians :
st. 94, l. 1, '*I*' = ay or yes : st. 98, l. 3. '*Selfe-flation*'
= self-flattery ? *ibid.* l. 4, '*Spiders*'—utterly false.

G.

Erratum.—P. 215, l. 5, *for* Second *read* First.

St. *LEWIS*, THE KING;

OR

A LAMP OF GRACE,
LIGHTNING THE

GREAT (*in the right way*)

TO GLORY.

Translated; and *Dedicated*

To My gracious Lord, Prince CHARLES.

NOt that your Highnesse *needs My mean* Direction
(*Having, within, a* Princely spirit *for Guide ;*
Without, your Parent ; *round about, beside,*
Precepts *and* Patterns *of Divine* Perfection)
Presume I thus to bring (*in dim reflection*)
This forrain LAMP (*admired farre and wide*) :
But as an humble Gift *this* New-year's-Tide,
To intimate my Faith, *and my* Affection.
Your gracious *hand thus bindes my* gratefull *heart*
To Offer *Heav'n my* Vowes ; *and You my* Verse,
For that Deliverance *You have daign'd, in part,*
To my poor Hopes *wrackt in your* Brother's *Herse.*
You have begun : *Vouchsafe mee,* Sacred Pow'rs,
You may go-on, *and make mee* wholly yours

In Effect

as

In Affection

——————*To* Your Highness' *Service*

— — — —*humbly devoted,*

——————JOSUAH SYLVESTER.

AD

EUNDEM PRINCIPEM
OPT. MAX.
EPIGRAMMA;
Ex Lat. I. O. *convers.*

WIll, Reason, Sense, the Brain, the Head, the
  Heart ;
  Each, in his Office, in Thee acts his Part :
Thy Will, thy Wit ; Thy Sense, thy Reason swayes ;
Thy Heart, thy Head, in every point obayes.
Thy WALES hath had GREAT-stiled Princes *Three :*
HENRY was *Fourth :* CHARLES the *Fifth* GREAT shall be.

Ejusdem

Auguſtiſsimi
ANAGRAMMA

Quadruplex.

CAROLUS STUARTUS, Princeps.

1. Tu, *Cyrus :* pulcra Spes nostra

CHARLES STUART.

2. *Arthur's Castle.*

3. *Heart's Last Cure.*

4. *Art's Chast Lure.*

In ARTHUR'S CASTLE, lies my HEART'S LAST
CURE :

To which I hasten, draw'n by ART'S
CHAST LURE.

A HYMN OF

St. LEWIS

(The Ninth of that Name)

KING OF FRANCE.

OF all the KINGS, admired over All,
  Whose *Prudence* swai'd this Crown Imperiall,
  Whose *Prowesse* most our *Lillies'* Bounds inlarg'd,
Whose *Justice* best their charge in *Peace* discharg'd,
Whom most the raies of glorious greatness crown'd,
Who brightest shin'd, who was the most renown'd,
Most magnifi'd for Manly Conquering
Within the World the World : was th' *Holy King*,
From whose chaste loins, from out whose loyall bloud
Th' *Heroick* Stems of Royall BOURBONS bud ;   10
Famous St. LEWIS ; GOOD KING'S *President*,
Who, for his CHRIST, and for his *Cross*, him spent :
Who by his Valour so renown'd his Name,
That all the Earth hath trembled at the same :
And Who, to free, from captive Fury fell,
The Fields where yerst our *Captain* conquer'd Hell
(Courageous *Zeal* setting his Soule on fire)
Led armed FRANCE against the *Asians'* ire.

  When I his *Vertues* read, and *Acts* so great,
Which him so high among the *Saints* have set ;   20
And here below so lasting glory wan,
I judge them scarce Works of a meerly Man ;
But, of an Angell in Man's shape bedight,
To shew the World the Way of *Vertue* right ;
Amaz'd to see, among so many Sins
As (fatally) the *Court* breeds and begins,
Among so many Pleasures, whose sweet Baits
Intrap the wariest with their wily Sleights ;
A KING to curb him so in Power supreme,
To *watch* himself so with such care extreme,   30
As not to taste *Delight* (of any kinde)
Which *Reason* bars a brave and noble Minde :
But, so *upright* in VERTUE's track to tread,
That even in Earth a Heav'nly Life hee led.

  For, never was there more accomplisht KING,
Whose royall heart had more replenishing
Of *Princely Vertues*, fit for Powerfull hand,
Or to be wisht in Mindes of High command.
Nay ; would the Heav'ns, their Treasures all producing,
All Gifts of Body and of Minde conducing,   40
Mould for Mankinde a *Prince* or *Potentate*
Worthy to govern th' UNIVERSALL State ;
They could not give the *World* (and Wee, much less,
Wish) *One* more worthy ; with more due Addresse
To take into his Royall hand the *Helm*,
In stormfull Times so apt to over-whelm.
So much the *Star*, which rules in *Birth of Kings*,
When hee was destin'd to *These* Managings,
Milde and propitious, in his heart connext,
First *fear* of GOD, and *love* of JUSTICE next :   50
VERTUES, whose *habit Happinesse* doth nourish :
Makes *Common-wealth* flow, and the *Church* to flourish :
Serves best for *Base* to each illustrious *State :*
Gives mightiest KINGS calme *Crowns*, and fortunate :
Causeth their Subjects *fear* them *lovingly :*
Keeps them, *in Dangers*, ever danger-free.
For, the *Almighty* printing in their Face
Milde-*Majesty*, sweet *Terrour*, dreadfull-*Grace*,
And heaping *Hap* upon them every-where :
The *Good* fear for them ; Them, the *Evill* fear,   60
  How many brave Marks left his noble Minde
Of th' Happinesse these *Vertues* bring Mankinde ;
When, full of Constancy, hee durst maintain,
That, raigning for Him, Who made him to raign,
These sacred *Twins*, nigh from the world dispell'd,
As in their *Temple*, in his Bosom dwell'd,
Guided his Person, govern'd his Affairs,
Counsell'd his Counsells, qualifi'd his Cares,
Steer'd all his Course through all his *Voyage* here,
As men their Ships by Card and Compasse steer !   70
  These making him with rarest spirits compeer,
In holy pride, Hee even despised here

The Kings, that, puft with glory of a Throne,
Commanded all, except themselves alone.
By th' one, hee happied his own Soule with Rest :
By th' other also, hee his People blest.
By th' one, becomming to himselfe severe,
Hee rul'd himself, kept his own Power in feare :
By th' other giving free Course to the Law,
Hee kept his Subjects in ; and happy, saw   80
Through all his kingdome *Peace* and *Plenty* flowr
In basest Grange, as well as golden Bowr.
    But twelve times *Sol* through the 12, Signes had
        gone,
When Heav'ns assign'd him to his Father's Throne ;
And to the hands of his Man-Childehood left
The glorious Burthen of This Scepter's heft :
    But, as in th' Orchards at *Monceaux* or *Blois*,
The Gardner's Care over some Graftlings choice,
The second year of their adoption there,
Makes them as good and goodly fruits to bear,   90
As Trees whose Trunk and branched Top bewraies
Their Months as many as the Other's daies ;
Through the Heav'n's favour, and Earth's fruitfulness,
Shewing that God their yong first-fruits doth bless :
His forward *Vertue* in his *Pupillage*
Brought forth th' effects of a man's perfect age ;
Disproving quite his feeble signes of youth,
And proving him invincible (in truth)
Against vain *Pleasures*, all their Baits condemning :
Against all *Perills*, *Death* it Selfe contemning :   100
Against all *Passions*, ever them resisting :
Against all *Crosses*, constant aye persisting.
    For, look how low, his heart in humble Awe
Hee bow'd to God, and bended to the Law ;
As high hee mounts it, in Praise-worthy Pride,
Above the World, Fortune, and All (beside)
Whose Vanity, with false glosse gilded o'r,
Fond Mortals most desire, admire, adore :
Desiring onely, with that holy *Mary*
(For his degree) That *One thing necessary ;*   110
Admiring solely th' holy Works, wherein
Th' Almighty Worker's wondrous hand is seen :
Adoring none but th' Everlasting *One ;*
Him loving best ; fearing but HIM alone.
Then, bearing aye *This Oracle* imprest
Within the Center of his royall brest,
That, *A sincere and true-Religious* KING,
Feared of all, needs fear at all no-Thing ;
Where Hee whose Soule hath not This Fear in-laid,
Of none is feared, but of All affraid.   120
    Arm'd with *this Brest-plate*, as with stronger arms
Then those (of old) blest with inchanting charms,
Hee brav'd all Perils that his Prowesse met :
And his calm Spirit, amid a Storm so great
As would have cast Youth in a swoun insensible,
Shew'd *Resolution* of a heart invincible ;
Appearing such, indeed, as Painters fain
Great *Hercules*, when, *Juno's* fell disdain
Pursuing him, hee Monsters quail'd and kill'd ;
A man in Courage, though in Age a Childe.   130

Which well hee prov'd to those *Rebellious Peers*,
Who, making light of his then-tender yeers,
And measuring his in-side by his age,
Troubled his State with storms of *Civill Rage ;*
Armed against him many a Tower and Town,
Aimed by Ambush to surprise his *Crown.*
When hee, to heal, by necessary Ill,
This Ill, before th' Imposthume over fill,
With Sword in hand their first Assault prevents ;
And, as his Subjects, bravely them convents,   140
To come and cast them arm-lesse at his feet :
Or else, as Foes, his armed Force to meet ;
From him, their true *Liege* (if true *French* they be)
Arm'd in the Field, to take This Offer free,
Revenge, or *Pardon*, of their past Mis-deeds,
And all the Mischief which the same succeeds.
The one, his Power should presse them to, perforce ;
Th' other their Duties, urged with Remorse :
If their blinde Fury did the one contemn,
Th' other should pour death and disgrace on them. 150
    O ! how the words of a brave *Prince* prevail !
This daring speech did so their Courage quail,
That though the cold yce of a prudent fear
Did not forth-with put-out there frenzy there ;
Yet did it daily from thence-forth decline,
And all their flame turn'd but to fume, in fine.
Yea, those, whose Fury dream't a *Diadem*,
Their Side abandon ; and, dis-banding them,
Reject their vain Hopes ; and, in season, fly
To the King's Mercy for their Remedy.   160
Others, more dreading Rigor of the Law,
Under protection of the *English* draw :
Gilding their Guilt with frivolous pretences,
Arming their weak Cause with as weak defences ;
Till, but increasing their dishonour by 't
Wanting as well good Fortune as good Right,
They 're also fain to beg his Bounty royall,
Ill worthy them, so obstinate-Disloyall.
    What proofs of *Prowess*, what contempt of danger,
Exprest this Prince upon the envious Stranger,   170
On crystall *Charant*, in *Xantognian* Coast,
When false *la-March*, backt with a forrain Host,
Mustred against him, from so many parts,
So many Groves of Lances, Pikes and Darts !
    There *France* and *England*, fully bent to fight,
Had both their Armies in their Order pight ;
From Either side mount winged clouds amain ;
On Either side they poure their Showers again :
While Silver *Charant*, to have barr'd their Teen,
Her swelling shoulders did oppose between.   180
    This River makes the Reed-crown'd banks to
        kiss,
By th' arched favour of a Bridge there is :
Whose gain or loss (besides the honour) boads,
Or bars, the Prize of *Victory* by ods :
The *English*, friended by a Fort at hand,
Which proudly did the neighbour Plains command,
Had won this Passage, and were passing on
Cheerly to end their *Victory* begun :

When *Lewis*, rushing to the Bridge, the first,
Repels the Foe, and puts him to the worst ;   190
With dead and wounded all the place hee paves,
And, then *Horatius*, braver him behaves :
Re-heartens His : re-haleth from the Foe
Fair *Victory*, ready with them to goe :
Standing alone, as a firm rock, a-front,
Almost alone, to bear the Battel's brunt ;
As th' onely mark of many thousand Darts
At him alone still aimed from all parts :
Till at the last, by his example prest,
Hee winning all, his Army won the rest ;   200
When, if his *Courage* shin'd in Conquering,
More did his *Mildnesse* in the Managing.
    Who can recount, and yet who would conceal,
Th' illustrious *Vertues*, whose industrious zeal
O'r all the World his honours blazed yerst,
After these mists, these first clouds, were disperst,
And scatter'd all by the bright-shining Rayes
Of this new Sun, in Summer of his dayes,
When (*Europe's* Umpire) making *Peace* with
    men,
Hee *War* proclaim'd against their *Vices* then ?   210
    The glorious Works his Royall *Vertues* did,
Cannot, without impietie, be hid ;
Although, without diminishing their Worth,
My *Muse* (alas !) can never set them forth :
For, of all *Vertue's* sacred Tracts (least rife)
His *Life*'s a Picture, limned to the life,
And such a Pattern, as to match again,
The wish is vertuous, but the Hope is vain :
Sith, the more wondrous 'tis, and worthy Table
To imitate, 'tis more inimitable.   220
So that, His *Worth*, weening to-life to limne,
I over-reach, in stead of reaching Him :
And, like bad singers (as too-bold, too-blame)
Sounding his Praise, rather my Selfe I shame.
    In heav'nly *Annals* are his *Acts* enroll'd ;
His Royall *Gests* are yet in *Asia* told ;
In *Afrike*, yet his *Valour* is renown'd :
Through *Europe* ever shall his *Vertues* sound ;
And every-where *Ninth* LEWIS (*Great* in Fame)
Seems, not a Man's but very VERTUE'S Name.   230
    Never did *Faith, Honour, Uprightnesse*, raign,
With *Constancy*, in SOULE of SOVERAIN
More pious-given, more fearing-God, more Foe
To Idol-Rites (Religion's overthrow) ;
Nor more desirous *Vertue* to prefer,
To propagate CHRIST'S *Kingdome* every-where,
To root-out *Vice*, to raze *Idolatry*,
And raise the *Tropheis* of TRUTH'S *Victory*.
    Burning with this Desire (his best Delight)
In *Africk*, twice, Hee *Crossed* Standards pight,   240
Expos'd his Life unto the chance of War ;
By Sea and Land adventur'd oft, and far :
Where, seeking Death, at last, hee *Durance* fand
Within a faith-lesse, love-lesse, law-lesse Land ;
Where Hee, as Gain, and as to raign, did take,
To serve and suffer for his *Saviour's* sake.

    But, all the Battels, won and lost, to sing,
Abroad atchieved by this Valiant King :
The Sack of *Damiete*, and the bloudy Spoil
Of *Saracens*, both on the shores of *Nile*,   250
And of the Sea, thrice strewed (as it were)
With Carcases of *Pagans* slaughtered there :
The Siege of *Cairo*, when brave Victory
Mourn'd all in black for his Captivity :
The sacred Terror and Majestike Grace,
Which (from above) shin'd in his Eyes and Face,
When two *Turk*-traitors (wth their swords, in grain
Dy'd with the bloud of their late *Souldan* slain)
Comming to kill him, felt, with strange remorse,
Their fury feebled by a secret force ;   260
From murd'rous fists letting their weapons fall
When they beheld his face majesticall.
His *Lybian* journey, when to *Carthage* tho
This Champion seem'd another *Scipio :*
Th' honour hee won at *Tunis*, where hee crown'd
His Life and Fortunes, evermore renown'd.
    In briefe, to undertake to tell at large
All his Exploits, were a more waighty Charge
Then can the powers of my weake Soule support :
And such a Web to weave in worthy sort,   270
Behoves the hand of a more happy Wit,
Both warp and woof with golden Threeds to fit.
I therefore, quitting th' hopefull Arrogance
Sprung from ignoring of our Ignorance
Shall think my Labour crown'd sufficient,
If this my speaking *Pencil, Phœbus* lent
To colour Verses, can but duely lim
Least-glittering raies that shin'd with Praise in
    him.
    Leaving therefore his Wars' discourse to those
Whose buskind Muse *Bellona's* march out-goes ;   280
Whose numbers thunder, and whose stile distils
Fresh drops of Death from their Heroïck Quils,
In lofty strains, as gravely, bravely-bold :
I'll lowly sound his *Laurels* lesse extoll'd,
Which hee (at Peace) won in his War with *Vices*,
And happy Toil in holy Exercises.
For, as I cannot his high *Prowesse* expresse ;
Much-lesse can I with silent Slothfulnesse,
Under *Oblivion's* rusty keyes conceal
The wondrous Care, the right religious Zeal,   290
Which from his Youth aye in his heart had burn'd,
To see *The seen House of the Lord* adorn'd :
For, in this Vertue, none hath neer him com
Of all the Kings have raign'd in *Christendom*.
Not, for, wee owe to him the Monuments
Which with his bloud *Our Saviour's* Patience
Bath'd in his *Passion*, and whose Sight, as yet,
Shakes godly Soules in glad-sad sacred Fit :
But, for (abhorring Shepheards bad and blinde)
A studious Care boil'd in his zealous Minde,   300
Yea, burn'd his Soule's soul with a hot desire,
That, in the *Church-ship*, none to Charge aspire,
But, skilfull, faithfull, carefull Mariners,
Able and apt for all Affaires of Hers ;

Whose holy Labours, in courageous sort,
Maugre all Storms, may steer into the Port.
  Devoured of this Zeal, and dreading aye
Lest hee be charged at the later Day
By th' *onely Judge*, with *Vice* and *Ignorance*
Of those hee chose, through all the folds of *France*, 310
To feed the Flocks under his Power alli'd :
When 's royall office bound him to provide,
With wondrous Care did hee their lives explore,
Who ever had commended them before :
And never gave hee the supreme Degrees,
Th' *Ecclesiastick* sacred *Dignities*,
But unto those whose *Life* and *Learning* too
Were eminent, both to *direct* and *doe ;*
To feed, as Shepheards ; as a Watch to ward ;
To heal the Sick, Sound from the Wolf to guard ;   320
And carefull Stewards, in due time to break
The *Bread of Life* both to the strong and weak :
Not those whose Eyes deep-vail'd with *Ignorance*,
Or *Knowledge* stain'd with Sinne's *Exorbitance ;*
Made like th' old woodden *Mercuries*, erect
In publike *Waies*, the Passage to direct,
Who with their *finger* the Right Path did point,
But, with their *foot* could never move a joynt.
  How, how should Those for Guide and Lanthorn
    serve
To th' Ignorance of People prone to swerve ;   330
Whose Ignorance, devoid of *Learning's Light*,
Cannot discern from crooked *Wayes* the right?
Or, How can Those, foule, Sin-sicke Soules recure
(Whom Patterns more then Precepts would allure)
Whose Eloquence, whose Excellence of Wit,
Marres their *Well-saying* by *Ill-doing* it :
While, what they *Preach*, in *Practice* they deny,
And by their *Deeds* give their owne *Words* the Ly.
  Neither the *Learned*, of true *Vertue* void ;
Neither the *Vertuous*, without *Learning's* aid ;   340
Can, in the Flock of CHRIST'S *Redeemed dear*,
Bear th' holy *Sheep-hook's* sacred burthen here,
With that Success which should be wisht by them
That seek the glory of *Jerusalem*.
Learning and *Vertue* must together match,
Those sacred Flocks duely to *Weeld* and *Watch :*
In vain's their Pain, who doe not *lead*, but *drive*,
Preaching like *shepheards*, while like *wolves* they *live ;*
Said this good Prince : and that same very thought
W^ch from his heart this holy speech had brought,   350
Brought forth th' effect : hee did so thirst to see,
Religion flourish ; and, through th' industry
Of *Labourers*, divinely *Will'd* and *Skill'd*,
GOD'S holy *Vineyard*, truely, duely till'd.
  Nor was his Care lesse, nor, much lesse, his Zeal
Of *Lawes*' support (Props of the Publike-Weal)
So strict hee was, and so precise in Choice
Of those (not waigh'd but by their Merits' poiz)
Whom, arming with his sword, as Delegates,
Hee sent amid the Rank of *Magistrates ;*   360
Garnisht with *Vertues*, grac't with *Learning*, fit
On bright *Astræa's* sacred Thrones to sit.

  His *Predecessors*, winking at the Crimes,
Or else constrain'd with mischiefe of their Times
(All given to gain, greedy of Gold) had made
Of *Offices* a miserable Trade :
Never regarding, that they set (withall)
Both Innocence, Honour, and Right to-sale :
Sold, to th' insatiate, *Licence* (as they please)
To pill the People under Shewes of Ease ;   370
And let the Knave, with his full *Purse*, prevent
The knowne long *Merit* of the Excellent.
  Hee, seeing this Abuse to ope the Gate
To all *Injustice*, to confound a State :
The Guilty quit, the Innocent condemn'd ;
Wrong countenanc't, Right rated, or contemn'd ;
And onely *Favour* (under fained Gown)
O'r-ruling Judgements, *Equity* put-down :
Justice, in Courts using her *Balance* bright,
To weigh the Parties' Money not their Right :   380
Bold *Ignorance*, in Dignities supreme,
Soiling their sacred Chairs with Wrongs extreme ;
Selling too-shame-lesse, too-unconscionable,
What Shee, unworthy, bought unreasonable :
Seeing, in brief, his Realms neer Jeopardy :
The strength of Lawes turn'd to meer Robbery :
Apparent Thefts, with Warrant under-handed,
Not onely not condemned, but commanded :
Soon as his Valour, quelling all his Foen,
Had set him quiet on his Father's Throne,   390
Hee banisht quite This sad *Confusion's* Cause,
This fatall Death of *Letters*, and of *Lawes ;*
According to our *Saviour's* blest Example,
Who, angry, chas't the *Chapmen* forth his Temple.
  Then, where hee met a well-disposed Wit,
Whose *Knowledge* and whose *Carriage*, matching fit,
Gave him good hope, that, being (free) preferr'd,
He would be th' Orphan's and the Widow's Guard :
The Poore's Protector, in their Right to stand :
No eye for *Favour ;* and for *Bribes*, no hand :   400
No awe of Threats, and for Intreats no Ear :
Laying aside, *Love*, *Hatred*, *Hope* and *Fear*,
When hee shall sit as Oracle, to doom ;
Where Man is unto Man, as in God's Room :
Him would this Noble Prince freely *create*
A *Chancelour*, a *Judge*, a *Magistrate*,
A *Dean*, a *Bishop*, without busie Suit
Of bribed Minions basely to pursue 't.
  O ever-wished, never-hoped, Dayes,
Which Gold's-contempt so guilt with golden Raies,   410
How calm you past ! how was the People blest,
Under the Lawes of such a Prince's Hest !
And O ! how worthy hee, in spite of Time,
To be renowned over every Clime !
Through whom *Integrity* reviv'd again,
And *Sentences*, ceasing to passe for Gain
(As now, God wot, too-many witnesse can)
Where God's owne *Sentence* in the Mouth of
    Man,
  For neither spar'd hee Rigor nor Reward,
Where hee had hope, by gentle hand or hard   420

To conquer *Vice*, and that same *servile Vein*,
Which loves not *Goodnesse*, but for Goods and
Gain ;
And with a heart whose Gold-Thirst never *sat* is,
Will never Till the Field of VERTUE *gratis*.
Knowing therefore, that in a Season vitious,
Wee sooner find a *Pyrrhus*, then *Fabricius ;*
And wisely fearing, lest the fear of Want,
Or love of Wealth, should worldly minds supplant,
And make them pass their duties' bounds perchance,
Whom hee to place of Honour should advance :   430
To keep their Port, with People venerable ;
To bear their Charge of needfull Train and Table :
Hee arm'd their *Vertue* against Poverty
(The secret Foe to sound *Integrity*)
With ample Stipends able to repell
The law-lesse Lawes of those two Tyrants fell,
Whose Iron Scepter too-too-often forces
Right honest Natures to dis-honest Courses.
And then, if Favour, Feud, or Avarice,
To grosse *Injustice* did their hands intice ;   440
Hee punisht aye their Trespass with such Rigor,
That Lawes, recovering then their ancient Vigor,
Seem'd that severe Example to revive,
Which in the *Skin* of Father flaid alive
(For wrong *Decrees*) his Son succeeding thrust :
A bloudy *Doom ;* yet, for *Injustice*, just :
That after-*Judges*, by their *Judg-skin* Chair,
From *Bribes*, and *Brokeage* might be warned fair.
Above all Crimes, his heart's just Jealousy
Abhorred most *Murder* and *Blasphemy :*   450
Nor ever did the first escape with life ;
Unlesse by Proofs it were apparent rife,
That, *Self-defending*, 'twas unwilling done :
Forc't, deadly Stroke, by deadly Stroke, to shun :
Th' other was punisht where hee sinned, just :
A red-hot Iron thorow his tongue was thrust :
To teach blasphemous Mouthes no more to blame
That holy, high, un-utterable Name ;
Ador'd in Heav'n and Earth, and every-where :
Which, even the Angels speak not but with fear.   460
O ! how hee hated Those light, lothsome places,
Where *Venus* sells her to all lewd Embraces !
The Shepheard, finding, under Stacks or Stones,
A Nest of Hornets, or a Swarm of Drones,
Or Knot of Vipers, is not bent more fierce
Their Cels to spoil, Themselves dispatch, disperse,
Than Hee was eager, and against Them bent
Severest Lawes, with sharpest punishments ;
Clensing with Fire those foule *Augean* Stalls,
And, to the ground, razing their filthy Walls ;   470
Lacing with lashes their un-pitied Skin,
Whom *Lust* or *Lucre* had bestow'd therein.
Himself so chaste of Body, and of Minde
(If *Fame* say true : who seldome soothes behinde)
That never Hee (Rare in a Prince's Life !)
Knew other *Venus*, than his *Queen* and *Wife.*
What Prince was ever, to the silly Poor,
More tender-hearted, either helpfull more ?

A many Kings have, by high Feats in War,
Renown'd their Names and spred their Glories far : 480
By wholsome Lawes Licentious Rage represt :
By many proofs their *Prudence* well exprest :
By all the parts of *Policie* and *Prowess*,
Won all the Honours earthly State allowes :
But, few vouchsafe to stoop their stately eyes
To th' humble Poore that on the dunghill lyes :
And little think, that, in those Little ones,
Christ, *Christ* Himself unto their Greatnesse grones ;
Begs at their Feet, in rags, and hunger-driven ;
And promiseth, for *Bread* to give Them *Heav'n.*   490
O hearts of Adamant ! This piteous King
From Your fell Natures was far differing ;
For oftentimes from his high Throne descending,
To sow and reap the Fruits on *Alms* attending,
All, all that could from ordinary rate
In Royall Charge of Kingdome, House, and State,
Be safely spar'd with honourable Thrift,
From such a heart and hand so apt to Gift ;
Would Hee bestow in building *sacred Cells*,
For th' *Aged, Poore, Sick, Sightlesse* (*Helplesse els*) 500
In ayding *Widowes*, whom the bliss of *Bearing*
Made wretched, wanting for their children's *rearing :*
Redeeming Captives, raising Doweries
For honest Maydens apt for Marriages,
(Whose *Banes* (unaskt) still *Povertie* forbad)
Passing their Flower in Feares and Langours sad :
In breeding Orphans, and in feeding Those
Whose bashfull Silence, biting-in their woes,
Smother'd the Sighes within their swelling brest,
Which from their Mouthes meer hunger often
prest.   510
In briefe, in pouring on all *Poore*, no lesse
Streams of Reliefe, than Fortune of Distresse ;
Approving plain, that, in most *Pompe* of *State*,
Himselfe a Man hee ay did meditate.
His People Hee so lov'd, and their Prosperitie,
That, easing them of former Kings' severitie
In Imposts, Tributes, Taxes, and the rest,
Where-with his Kingdome had been sore opprest :
Hee wont with tears to bathe his Cheeks (they say)
When urging Cause compelled him to lay   520
On his poor Subjects any new Excise,
Never so needfull, just, or light to prize :
Which yet his Pitie rarely did permit ;
And onely when *Bellona* (pressing it)
Against our *Lillies* some such Storm had blowne,
As hath too-often *Empires* overthrown.
For, for the Charge of needfull Dignity,
And royall State beseeming Majesty,
He never sought from other Source to drain,
Than th' ever-springs of his own just *Demain ;*   530
Detesting th' use of other Potentates,
Who, but to gild their Pride in pompous States,
Pill'd all their Subjects with extreame Excesse ;
And then consuming it in Showes and Feasts,
And scorning those whom they had eaten-up
(Without Compassion) in a golden Cup

Caroused deep their wretched People's bloud,
Whom God had given Them to protect, in good.
 What Lawes-Oblivion, what Contempt of GOD
(Thus this good Prince, Then, shrill and sharply
  chod)   540
Deaffens your Eares against so many a Plaint !
Inhumane soules, who, toucht with bloudy Taint,
Ill Shepheards, sheare not but even flay your fold,
To turn the Skins to Cassakins of Gold ;
Thinke you, the Heav'ns, which hate all Tyrannie,
Will wink at yours, and let you scape so free ?
No, no : they 'll ruine your unrighteous Power :
And, causing soon your Subjects rise in Stower,
The just Revenger, who all Realms transfers,
Of mightiest Kings shall make you School-masters : 550
Shall break your proud *Tax*-puffed Scepters so,
That, for th' abuse, you shall the use forgoe :
Or shall so curse the cruell Policies
Your *Minions* finde to feed their Vanities,
That in your hands your Gold shall melt away,
And still the more you pill, the more you may :
(Like *Dropsie-sick*, the more they drink the dryer)
The more you shall devour, the more desire :
New *Erisichthons*, through insatiate heat,
Forced in fine your selves to teare and eate : 560
Branding with shame of Marks so mercilesse,
So impious Pride of hearts so Pity-less,
Who burd'ning Subjects more than bear they can,
Hold neither God for God ; nor Man from Man.
 But, whether run I, on so harsh a string,
Out of my tune? to tell how this good King
Reprov'd bad Princes of his Time, for pressing
Their People cause-lesse with un-cessant Sessing !
Let's re-assume our Song, our proper Theam :
Let's passe by *Vice :* and rather covering them, 570
Than them recounting in eternall Story,
Let us return to sing of *Vertue's* Glory.
 How happy is the Prince, who squaring right
By sacred Lawes the limits of his Might ;
Joyes in *Well*-doing, and as *Just* as *Wise*,
Thinks not himselfe to raign ; save Noblewise,
When hee his People heeds, and hearing aye
Their just Complaints, doth in due time repay
What every Monarch (with devotion) vowes
To GOD and Men, when first his royall Browes 580
(Under so many solemne Mysteries,
With hopefull subjects wishfull, joyfull Cryes)
Put-on the glad-sad sacred *Diadem*,
Which instantly from thence-forth puts on Him
That *Robe of Power*, which those doth much mis-suit
Who have not on rare *Vertue's* richest Suit.
 Among such Kings, who ay, as right directs,
Measure their Greatness by their Good-effects ;
Not by their Fortunes, or their force of hand ;
Or many Nations under their command ; 590
Was that illustrious Prince to whom wee pay
Heroick Duties in this *Hymnik* Lay.
For, while, at home, hee happy Peace injoy'd,
Hee never suffer'd day to vanish voyd

Of giving Audience, and extending free
Fruits of his *Justice* unto each Degree ;
Grieving in minde, grudging at those, as lost,
Less worthy spent, although unwilling most ;
Perswaded sure, that with what eye or eare
His People's Case a Prince doth heed and heare, 600
With like, the Lord, in his extreme Affaires,
Will look on him, and listen to his Pray'rs :
That that same pompous, glitt'ring, glorious Slav'ry
Improperly call'd *Royall* (for the Brav'ry)
In proper speech (by due experience scann'd)
'T's an *Onerous-Honour*, a *Confin'd Command :*
That Kings were made for subjects ; and not they,
Not they for Kings : that though both Land and
  Sea
Adore their Greatnesse (Lawes' support alone)
Yet Princes Eares are not indeed their own ; 610
But their own Peoples that do humbly live
Under th' obedience of the Lawes they give :
That, to be briefe, of mightiest Kings that are,
Labour's the Glory, and their Greatnesse Care.
 Such sound Instructions, from his Cradle us'd,
His vertuous Mother wisely had infus'd ;
Which in his Princely brest digesting milde,
A Man, hee practis'd what hee learn'd, a Childe :
Ready to heare the meanest that complaine ;
Preferring wisely such a sacred paine 620
Before the pleasure of the choicest Sport
Could be devis'd in Countrey or in Court :
Whence in his People such Affection spreads,
They blesse his Birth-day, and the ground he treads ;
Call him their Father and with Vowes amain
Frequent the Altars for his long-long Raign :
As if that Wish (the Sum of their Desire)
Contained All all Prayers could require,
Or us'd to beg of Heav'n's eternall Bountie,
In asking *Peace, Riches, Religion, Plentie*, 630
And all the blessings which ASTRÆA's hand
Can plant or poure upon a happy land.
 What Tracts of Art, what Tropes of *Eloquences*
Can lively represent to modern Princes
(So as even *Envie's* Selfe shall nought controule)
That Self-severe *Integritie* of Soule,
Whose humble, patient, constant Temperance,
Hath no Successor as yet had in *France*,
Nor yet els-where : How-ever every State
Can yet admire it, none can imitate. 40
 EUROPE (where ever *Vice* and *Vertue* most
Have striven for Empire, best and worst to boast)
Hath whilom seen Kings treading in the Path
Of noted'st Tyrants, who with Threatfull Wrath,
And all the 'Terrors, which Man's cruell Rage,
To fright Mankind had found in former age,
Restrain'd their subjects from their Death's conspiring :
Who, so, lesse-daring, had the more desiring.
But, this right generous Prince, still walking fit,
Within the path which Tyrants never hit, 650
Onely restrain'd all Publique Insolence,
By th' even-born Reanes of his own Innocence :

Giving so little hold to *Mal-contents*,
Taking, at sharp Reproofs, so small offence,
That by effect his Royall Soule did show,
That in the same no livelier Flame did glow,
Than a desire, so Temperate to frame-him,
That all might boldly, none might justly, blame-
   him.
   Smooth Soothers, pois'ning by the eare the heart,
Pernicious Weeds, who (Ivie-like) subvert,   660
Distort, destroy the Trees you Climbe upon ;
Still feeding Vice with such Contagion,
That seldome, Soules who with Applause approve
Your *praising* them, do ought *Praise-worthy* love :
Vizards of Homage, Vertue's Pestilence,
Right ill-come were you to this Vertuous Prince ;
Who, shunning aye your banefull Whisperings,
As common pois'ners of the publique Springs,
Abhorr'd your presence, and could better brook
A miss-Fault-finder, than a *Fawner's* looke.   670
So much a Noble Minde, remote from Vice,
Loving true Honour, loatheth *Flatteries.*
   What pleasure took hee, how extreme Delight,
In Histories, how many times he might
Review himselfe ; amaz'd, to read the things
There said *of Kings ;* which none dare say *to Kings!*
How was he rapt ! how sweetly extas'ed,
When that Divine *Eternall Will* he read,
Where, with so liberall, just, and loving hand,
God shares to his the *Heav'nly-Holy-Land !*   680
   That which is said of *Alexander's* love
To *Homer's* Works (whose graces all approve)
May well of him, for honouring the Miracles
Of th' *Heav'nly Author*, speaking in his Oracles :
Which as a pretious Treasure, richly cas't
In Gold and Cedar, had hee neer him plac't :
Calling it aye his joy of Exercises,
The Spur of *Vertues*, and the Curb of *Vices.*
If happily his *Publike Cares* lent leasure,
He spends it not in more contenting pleasure ;   690
Than what so sacred Studie's Fruit imparts
To th' healthy Taste of true *God-fearing* hearts.
   And well appeared, by rare, rich Effects
Of *Vertues* shining over all his Acts,
That that divine *Seed* (happy sow'n the while)
Fell in no *Thorny, Stony, Sandy*, Soile.
For, if that ever Soule did Vice avoid,
If ever hee meer humane Spirit injoy'd
Prowess, Pietie, Prudence, and *Justice*, mixt,
Without the foil of follies' dross betwixt   700
(From proudest wrong, the poorest right defending :
Disdaining pleasures towards Vice but tending :
Milde to the Meeke ; to Malapert austere ;
To good men bounteous ; to the bad, severe)
'Twas this brave Prince, whom they, do best resemble,
In whom *These Vertues* most of all assemble.
   Kings of his time, raigning in *East* and *West*,
Revering him for such, his Greatness blest :
The Afflicted Princes chose him for Refuge :   709
The Strong, for Friend ; and Those at Strife, for Judg,

When they grew weary to dispute their Cause
By th' old sharp Argument Kings' Furie drawes,
When, *Mars* usurping milde *Astræa's* room,
In sted of words, their swords must give the doom ;
When Injury with Injury repelling,
And strength of Lawes by stronger Lawes refelling
(To back their Own, or Others, *Claim* to bar)
They seek their right, in might ; their Peace in War.
   Such was Saint LEWIS : *and such was, wel-neer,*
Our own Saint EDWARD *(and* ELIZA *dear ;*   720
Save for her Sex, the Salique *Law perchance,*
Bars her Succession to the Saints *of* France)
For all prime Vertues of a compleat Prince
To make a Saint-King. *And, if ever, since,*
EUROPE *hath seen, or any kingdome know'n*
A living Shrine of both these Saints in One
(*Though, som,* suspect *of the smooth* Soothing-
   Crime ;
Some grosse Neglect *of this* Ingratefull *Time,*
*Too-*Envie-*prone, permit not* so to say)
It will be said *and* sworne *another-day*   730
(*When swelling* Clouds, *that dare* Eclipse *our Sun,*
Shall, by his Rayes dispersed, be undone ;
And HEE *Himselfe in his Own splendor shine*)
'*T was our* JUST-MASTER, *learned and divine.*
   And if that ever (for the Time to come)
There have been Hope of like *in* CHRISTENDOM ;
There was a Prince, and is a Prince with GOD,
Whose Name is dear, and dear the Dust he trod
(*Whose* Memory *my* Tears *must ever mix*)
On Whom all Eyes, in Whom all Hearts did fix :   740
Whose Vertue's Harvest ripened in his Spring :
HENRY *was made a* Saint, *before a* King,
Leaving his Brother (where His best re-flowers)
Sole Heire-apparent to His Hopes and Ours.
   And, if yet, under Heav'n's gilt-azure Cope,
There now remaine Another *living* Hope
Of new Saint LEWIS, *or His* like *again,*
For godly, goodly, gracious, glorious Raign,
With Bliss to BRITAIN, *and the Sacred Flock,*
Not built on Peter's ROME, *but* Peter's Rock ;   750
This : this is Hee : My Patrone *and my Prince,*
PANARETUS ; *Whose* Pupill-Excellence
Boads, in his Age, to make This Poëm *seem*
No Poëm, *but a* Prophecie *of* HIM.
   For, never was there Sonne more like to Sire,
In face, or grace, or ought that wee admire ;
Then is our CHARLES *in his young* Vertue's Spring,
Like th' happy Non-Age of that Holy King
(*Like his Owne Father ; like his Onely Brother,*
So as hee seems rather the same, then Other)   760
For Gracious Gifts, and Native Goodnesse till'd,
By like grave Tutors, in their Function *skill'd.*
   O Thou All-Giver ! Fountain of all Good !
Poure daily down upon this Hopefull Bud
Thy Deawes of Grace : *shine on it from above*
In mildest Rayes of Mercie *and of* Love :
In stead of Suckers, *send it* Succours *still*
To feed the Root, that That the rest may fill

With lively Verdure of a fruitfull Sap,
To load with Plenty *every* Vertuous *Lap.* 770
Breathe on it Blessings : *leave no* Weed *with-out,*
Nor Worme *with-in it : hedge it round-about*
From Bores, *and* Beasts, *domesticall and stranger ;*
Both wild and Wily (*Where least dread, most*
danger.)
That it may kindely spring, and timely spred,
In bulk and Branch, *with leaves that never shed :*
Under whose Shade *mine aged* Muse *may warble*)
Some Monument (*out-lasting Brasse, and Marble*)
In Swan-like notes, to my Mecœnas' *Honour,*
When hee bestowes some Nest *of rest upon her.* 780
Nor may my Vowes *ingratefully forget*
Our Other Branch (*in other Soile new-set*)
Whose tender leaves shaken with Sighs of ours,
In stead of Tears, have dropped Silver showers
To cool my Thirst, my Cares to cure, or calm,
With timely Use of Bounties *princely Balm.*
O Sea of Bounties *never-dryed Source!*
So water it with thy rich Favours' *Course,*
That happy thriving by her PALATINE,

The Royall Issue of their Rosie-Vine, 790
From Rhine *and* Ister, *may to Tibur spred ;*
And, over-topping ROME'S *usurping* Head,
From Bramble-*Kings recover* CESAR'S *Seat,*
With greater Sway *then* CONSTANTINE *the great.*
Great Arbitrer, *whose Counsels none can sound ;*
Who canst all Thrones confirm, and all confound :
Conferring Kingdoms, and transferring them,
How, when, and where thou wilt, from Stem to Stem :
Establish, Lord, in Royall JAMES *his Race,*
These Kingdoms' *greatnesse, and thy* Kingdom's
grace : 800
Prosper our DAVID, *bless his* SALOMON,
That after them, upon GREAT BRITAIN'S *Throne*
(*Maugre* Hell's *malice, and the Rage of* ROME,
Their roaring Buls, *their charms, their arms to-come,*
Their Powder-*Plots, their Pistols, Poysons, Knives :*
And all their Jesuits *murd'rous* Art *contrives*)
Their Seed may sit, and never Other hand
Then STUART'S *sway the* Scepter *of This Land :*
Wise, Great, Good, STUARTS, *that may shine as cleer*
As This Saint LEWIS, *both in* Heav'n *and* Here. 810

NOTES AND ILLUSTRATIONS.

PAGE 229, col. 1, ' *Prince Charles* ' = Charles I : col. 2, ' *Ex Lat. I. O.* ' = John Owen.

HYMN.—l. 22, ' *a meerly* ' = merely a : l. 86, ' *heft* ' = haft, handle : l. 176, ' *pight* ' = pitched : l. 179, ' *Teen* ' = rage : l. 219, ' *Table* ' = portrait ? l. 226, ' *Gests* ' = actions, *frequenter :* l. 243, ' *fand* ' = found—*Scoticè* still : l. 394, ' *Chapmen* '= traders : l. 410, ' *guilt* ' = gilded : l. 423, ' *sat* ' = satiated : l. 477, ' *silly* ' = innocent : l. 479, ' *a many* '—a provincialism (Lancashire) still : l. 505, ' *Banes* ' = bans : l. 533, ' *pill'd* ' = spoiled, preyed on : l. 544, ' *Cassakins* '—see Glossarial Index, *s.v.* : l. 548, ' *Stower,* ' *ibid.* : l. 568, ' *Sessing* ' = assessing. G.

HENRIE
THE GREAT
(The Fourth of that Name)
LATE KING OF
FRANCE
AND *NAVARRE;*
His *Tropheis* and
Tragedie.

Written in French by Pierre Mathieu.

To the right honourable William Cecill,
Earle of Salisbury.

*B*Esides the Bonds which did most vowes engage
    To your dear Elders ; and besides the Due
    Which to your selfe might justly thence accrew ;
Th' apparent Vertues of your April-Age
Challeng'd of right This Poëm's *Patronage :*
    The rather, sith we first receiv'd from you,
    The speedy Notice (no lesse quick then true)
Of Henry's *Death through Hell's dis-chained Rage.*
You saw this Sunne, at his High-Noone-shine Set
    In sudden Clowd of his owne Royall Bloud.
    O Horrid Hap ! Who ever can forget
Such Fate, such Hate ; of one so Great, so Good :
    O ! just revenge, rout out th' Ignatian *Pack,*
    The Moules that mov'd in Faux *and* Ravillac.

—Josuah Sylvester.

THE
TROPHEIS OF
THE VERTUES AND
FORTUNE OF
HENRIE the Great.

S Ince first *Apollo* lent the World his light,
And Earth impregned with his heatfull might ;
Europe hath seen no Potentate, no Prince,
To Parallel Great HENRY's excellence.
No Terme, no Time, his fresh Renown shall shed :
Never was King more deare, never more dread.

Phœnix of Kings, wonder of Christendome,
Passing all past, and without Peere to come ;
His Courage onely matcht his Clemencie,
And, should his Tombe to these two equall be,   10
Both Spain and France, could not contain the same,
Which have so often seen his Feates of Fame.

His Life's a lamp to Princes, and a line ;
A Trophey rear'd by miracle divine ;
A Theater to all the Vertues built ;
A goodly Garden, with such plenty fill'd
Of choicest fruits and flowers, that chusing, there
Aboundance troubles more then want else-where.

The year that EDWARD in *Great Britain* dy'd :
That *France* (beyond the Mountains) *Spain* defi'd :   20
That *Therwin* walls were thundred to the ground :
That a fair flower our Royall *Hymen* Crown'd :
I' th' winter *Solstice* (when the yeare is worne)
Within *Pau* Castle This young MARS was born :

Born for the World's Good : as his Enterance
Presag'd him then the HERCULES of *France ;*
To re-advance her *Lillies* long decayd :
For as (by chance) bare-head abroad he playd,
At foure years old, a Snake hee finds and kills ;
At fourty, foiles the *Hydra* of our Ills.   30

Nor was hee bred in soft delicious wise
(Which forms young spirits into the form of vice :)
His Grandsire us'd him to all Weather's Ire,
His Sauce was Labour, Excercise his Fire ;
His noble heart did never ought inflame,
Save Heav'n's desire, and th' Honour of the same.

Scarce fourteen times had hee beheld the birth
Of th' happy Planet (which presag'd his Worth)
Predominant in his Natitiall ;
When hee became an Armie's Generall,   40
Whose hottest flame, without him was but fume ;
Nor, but by Him, durst any good presume.

Hee purchast Peace, the wch eft soons was staind
With his friend's bloud, and his young soul constraind
To faine som Change of his Religion :
At *Vinseine* Castle Hee was seiz'd upon,
And to the Court confin'd ; where, discontent,
His Spirit droopes, out of his Element.

Escaped thence : with restlesse toile, hee tends
To save the side of his Afflicted Friends ;   50
By peace again hee bringeth all in ure :
And *Mounsieur's* death doth well his Hopes assure
Of th' after Crowne, who but between him stood ;
So, now was hee the first Prince of the Bloud.

Then from afarre hee doth new Stormes descry :
To threat his fortune, and his force to try :
Hee meets the danger with undaunted front,
And in foure years bears ten brave Armies' brunt,
All with the might of a great Monarch grac't ;
Whereof, at *Coutras* hee defeats the last.   60

At last, the King to extreme Streights reduc't,
In doubt of all, and daring none to trust,
Implores this Prince, who rescues him from *Tours,*
With just revenge ; and had, yer many houres,
Re-humbled *Paris* to her Prince's yoake,
But for *Saint Clement's* Paricidiall stroake.

After which stroake (which all true French-men hate)
France sadly falls in a most wretched state :
Who hath least Reason, hath most Insolence ;
Who hath most Power, hath least Obedience.   70
Nor Awe, nor Law ; Disorder every-where ;
Good without hope, and Wicked without feare.

Rebellion spawnes as fast as (in the Spring)
Fruit-fretting vermine ; it doth Discord bring
In Families, Dearth in Townes, Death in Field :
O ! happy you who never daign'd to yeeld
Unto that Hagge ; but, loyall to the Crowne,
Have left your Heires, Heires of a true renowne.
   Who counts the Cares that on a Crown do wait,
As well may number *Autumne's* fruitfull fraight,   80
And *Flora's* too. Yet this great Spirit of man,
Mid th' ebbs and flouds of this vast Ocean,
Seems a still Ship, which, maugre Winds and Waves,
In wished Hav'n her and her burthen saves.
   Hee's never idle, nor his Excercise
Other than stands with Princely Offices :
MARS and DIANA, and CUPID wait on him :
Maugre his Losse, hee alwayes gaines by Time,
Unto Affaires his ears are open aye,
Nor waits hee lazying on his bed for day.   90
Shafts, Tigers, Torrents : no, nor lightning flies
More swift about, than this bold Eagle plies
(Amid all perils) to preserve his State,
With heed and speed, from Rebels' pride and hate.
In Battels first, last in Retreats : in briefe,
In Action, Souldier ; in Direction Chiefe.
   Diepe saw his Fortunes on a desperate Dye ;
The league presum'd hee needs must yeeld, or fly :
But, as a Brook, the more wee stop his Course,
Breaks down his Bay, and runs with swifter force ;   100
He foiles his foes at *Arques*, and shews them plain,
That Heav'n's just hand doth his dear right sustain.
   'Tis buzz'd in *Paris*, and beleev'd in part,
That he is taken ; or constrain'd to start
From *Diepe* to *Dover*, to seeke *England's* Aide :
And, while Him coming Prisoner-wise, they said,
To the *Bastile ;* Hee came and over-came
Their Suburbs soon, to their Suborner's shame.
   Conquests attends him, whether he encamps,
Or marches on : again he takes *Estampes :*   110
Lizieux, Eureux, Mans, Meulan, Vandosme, Perch,
And *Honfleur*, formost, in his *Trophie* march ;
As earnest-pence of his recover'd State,
And Crowne of *France*, which well admits no Mate.
   Tiber and *Iber* then together flow
(Too-strong in wrong) his Right to over-throw.
There proudeth Pow'r, here Prowesse brighter
   shines ;
And dayly shewes us by a thousand signes,
How great advantage a true Birth-right brings
(Against Usurpers) unto lawfull Kings.   120
   In JURY Fields, hee seems a blazing Star ;
Seen in the Front of all his Hoast, a-far :
Majestic Fury in his Martiall Face,
The bravest Troops doth in an instant Chase :
And boldest Rebels, which the rest had led,
Came Charging one way, and by fourty fled.
Melun surrenders to his War-like Lot,
Chartres is chastiz'd with his thundring Shot,
Louviers lies humbled at His Conquering Foot,
Noyon lamenteth her three Succours' rout,   130

Espernay yeelds her wholly to his hest,
Dreux twice besieged, opens as the rest.
   The *League*, that late so violently burn'd,
To a cold Fever now her Frenzie turn'd :
And trusting still in strange Physicians' aid,
Neglects her Cure till all her strength decaid :
In dread of all, in doubt her owne will quaile ;
As a weak Ship affraid of every Saile.
   That (late) *Achilles* of the *Spanish-Dutch,*
Farnezean Parma that atchiev'd so much   140
In *Anwerp's* Siege, by matchlesse Stratagem ;
And weend the World had had no Peer to Him :
Had here the heart, twice, to refuse to fight ;
And twice departed, and bad none *Good-Night.*
   Fortune, for him, no longer us'd her Wheel ;
But kinde, and constant, followes at his heel ;
Hee's happy every where, and over all
Spring Palms and Lawrels : onely neer *Aumale*
A mur'drous Bullet put him to some paine,
Yet hindred not his Rescue of his Train.   150
Who weens to vanquish him, makes him invict ;
Milde to the Meek, to Proudlings stern and strict :
He loves the Lawrels without blood be-sprent.
A Cruell Conquest hee doth even lament.
His thunder Batters but rebellious Walls :
And who least fear him, on them first hee falls.
   France Self to slay, and her own Throat to cut,
Arms her own hands ; and (in strange rage) doth put
The Knife to whet, in *Spaine's* ambitious pawes ;
Spain that would Spoile her Crownes primordiall
   lawes,   160
And would a Scepter with a Distaffe blin :
But all in vain : the *Lillies* cannot Spin.
Re-Romaniz'd, so (say they) Heav'n conjures ;
His errours at Saint *Denis* hee abjures :
This Change, in Court yet chang'd not one nor other ;
For, though his Subjects have not all one Mother,
Hee holds them all his Sons, They him their Sire ;
And Christians all, all to one Heav'n aspire.
   Within the Temple of the *Mother-Maid,*
That bore her Son, her Sire, her God, her Ayd,   170
With Heav'n-sent Oyle hee is annointed King,
Dons th' *Order Collar ;* and by every thing,
To prove in him Saint *Lewis'* Faith and Zeale,
The sick he touches, and his touch doth heale.
   By law of Arms, a Citie tane by force,
Should feel the Victor's rage, with small remorse.
Paris so taken, is not treated so :
Though well his Justice might have razed lowe
Those Rebell Wals, which bred and fed These Wars ;
To save the guilt-lesse, hee the guilty spares.   180
   There, there 's the Hope and Safety of his Side
If there hee faile, then farewell all beside :
The *Spaniard* therefore thither speedy sends,
A great strong Convoy to confirm his Friends.
Which soon defeated, There began the end
Of Civill Wars, and all to Union tend.
   Th' Honour of saving and restoring *France*,
Is not alone due to his *Valiance :*

His *Clemencie* hath part ; which lets him in
The stronger Holds, than all his Arms could win :   190
That, satisfied with Tears, makes from all parts,
Repentant Rebels yeeld him up their Hearts.
Lyons, the Porter of one part of *France*,
Rou'n, that sees none like strong in Ordinance,
Orleans, which *England* did undaunted prove,
Marseillis, jealous of old *Neptune's* love,
Aix, Bourges, Sens, Meaux, Poictiers, Troy, Tholouse,
And *Reins ;* of these, each to his *Bounty* bowes.
    This gracious Prince excus'd the simpler sort,
Whom (Malice-lesse) blind passions did transport   200
Against the Lawes, with fury of the Time ;
Who self-affraid to sail in fouler Crime,
Seduc'd by other's slie seditious Lore,
Follow'd (like Sheep) their Fellowes straid before.
    This heav'nly humane *Clemency* of his,
Yet cannot shield him from some Treacheries.
One wounds him in the Mouth, and breaks withall
One of his Teeth, (O Act unnaturall !)
And had not God in part put-by the blow,
Even then in *Paris* had hee perisht so.   210
    But having quencht the Civill Fires in *France*,
'Gainst his ill Neighbours now his Arms advance ;
In *Piedmont* Fields, his Lilly-flowers hee plants,
Pills *Bourgoignie*, and all *Artois* hee dants,
And makes the Great *Castalian* MARS to fly,
With Fear, within ; without, with Infamy.
    Then, those great Warriours that had disobey'd
(Whom not their courage but their cause betrai'd)
Which came with shame and sorrow (as was meet)
To cast their Swords at his victorious feet,   220
Fearing his Rigour : hee receives them (rather)
With King-like grace, and kindnesse like a Father.
    Heav'n daily works for him, som speciall Miracle :
His Faith 's an Altar, and his Word an Oracle :
His greatest foes have never found him faile.
And should Sincerity in all men quaile,
Exiled the World (as *Moors from Spain*)
In This King's soule shee had been found again.
    Spain by a Train of many Wiles well laid,
Surpriseth *Amiens : France* is all affraid :   230
The Spaniard, hence prouder then ever, swells :
Undanted *Henry* Thence him soon repells,
Regains his City, and constrains his foes,
To beg their Peace, or to abide his blowes.
    The Stormes that long disturb'd the State are
        val'd,
Th' ill Vapours now are from all hearts exhal'd,
And *France* is now all *French*, even all about :
Onely the *Breton* stifly yet, stood out.
But, those white *Ermines* at the last must need,
Of th' onely Sent of the fair *Lillie's* seed.   240
    Old PHILIP longs to see the Waters calme,
Finds all designes vain to supplant this Palme ;
Sith the more shaken, it more fast doth grow :
Hee seeketh Peace, the *Pope* solicits so,
Vervins doth treat it, *Bruxells* swears it done,
And PHILIP pleas'd departs the World anon.

France still retains one sensible Offence,
For which shee vowes Revenge or Recompence :
Among the Alps her thundring Canons roare,
Proud-brow'd *Mont-meilan* flaunts and vaunts the
    more   250
To stop her fury, but in fine is fain
To rue her rashnesse and repent in vain.
    God hastens his own work : this Monarch marries
In *Lyons* Church, the choice, the Chief of *Maries ;*
The Heav'ns delight, our *Lillie's* ornament :
Love, in one heart two lovely Souls hath blent :
Whence Peace is more confirm'd, and Discord dasht.
For, by this knot many great Plots are quasht.
    At *Fountain-bleau* (a Paradise for site)
Shee brought him forth his *Dolphin*, his delight,   260
Whose tender youth gives happy hopes of Worth :
One Daughter also did shee there bring forth,
And two Sons more (Supporters of the Crown :)
Two Daughters more, *Paris* for birth doth owne.
    His Clemency hath conquered Rebels' rage,
Made of dis-loyall, loyall Vassalage,
Yea forced Wils by Pardons and by Grace ;
The proof whereof is writ in every place,
Through all the Towns of *France* both great and small ;
Where, for Revenge, Reward was daign'd to all.   270
    Once, onely once, his Mercy admirable,
Was deafe to *Biron*, and inexorable ;
Sith when hee might, his hault despite would none.
I wonder not to see that *Myridon*,
In the *Bastile*, a shamefull death to beare :
But this I wonder, that hee would come there.
    O factious sp'rits, of close deep hearts and double
(Whose Life is strife, whose Rest is best in trouble)
He knowes the drifts, and known dissolves the same,
As fast as fire melts Lead within the flame.   280
His voice alone, as Dust cast up aloft,
Breakes Hornets' buzzing, and their swarming, oft.
    Discord, disturbing holy Churches' rest,
'Twixt *Rome* and *Venice* did debates suggest :
Ambition set-in foot, sore-sweld with hope,
To bridle both the Senat and the *Pope :*
Both prest to fight : his Prudence reconcil'd
Their Difference, and did their minds re-mild.
    Hee relisht now the harmlesse Sweets of Peace,
Willing his People should partake no lesse :   290
But yet some-where hee feels a Thorne to prick :
To pluck it out, hee armes and marches quick,
Even to the Frontier : There attains his will,
Wisdome (so) fitly takes her Season still.
    You nations, that for fourty years have seen
Bellona's Tempests, and felt *Mars* his Teen :
That for your Liberties have pawn'd your Lives :
If freely now you joy your Wealth, your Wives :
If now your Trades into the East you bring,
(Under Heav'n's Kingdom) onely thank this King.   300
    Thus heapt with honors, this brave King is loth
That his brave Knights effeminiz'd by Sloth,
'Mid Games and Dames, during so long a Peace,
Should still lie still in Cities pomp and ease :

47

Therefore hee rears an Army, strongly dight,
In *Gulich's* Claim, his wronged friends to right.

A noble Prince, whose Prow's and Prudence, late
Buda admir'd, and *Rome* hath wondred-at
(The Honour of his Time) was Generall;
So stor'd with gold, with Guns, with Arms, with all,   310
That neighbour Princes all were in alarm :
Yet Them this Thunder brought more feare then harm.

Fearlesse it marches ; and respectlesse, threats
What-ever Log its ready Passage lets ;
Gesture and voice already skirmishing,
And under conduct of so brave a King,
Great-Britains, Germans, Switzers, Belgians,
Serve all the Greatnesse of the Crown of *France.*

Els-where, the while, the Duke that rules the *Alps,*
Seem'd t' have his heart no more beyond the *Calps :*   320
Brave noble heart, *Saxonically-French.*
Fuentes affraid, with shoulder-shrinking wrench,
Doubts lest that *Milan* stoop to *France* again :
And *Charles* provoked prove the Scourge of *Spain.*

Heav'ns now, to crown his *Tropheis,* had set down,
That at Saint *Denis* hee his Queen should Crown
With royall Diadem : and in one Day
The State, the Majesty of *France* display.
Nothing but Great ; but great Magnificence ;
But, *Marie's* Grace excell'd all Excellence.   330

H Ence, hence false Pleasures, momentary Joyes ;
       Mock us no more with your illuding Toyes :
A strange Mis-hap, hatched in Hell below,
Hath plung'd us all in deepest Gulfe of Woe.
Taught us that all World's-hopes as dreams do flye,
And made us all, Cry *All is Vanity.*

Four houres from Noone, forth from the *Louvre* rode
This mighty Prince (without his Gard) abroad,
To see his Arcenall : To his Caroche,
In a strait Lane, a Hell-hound durst approach ;   340
And with a knife, twice stabbing kill'd him quite,
Turning that fairest Day to foulest Night.

Twice did the Monster stab : for else, the first
Had not been mortall, but the knife, accurst,
Thrilling his Lungs, cut at the second stroake
Th' *arterial vein,* whose bloud-floud soon did choak
The peerlesse Prince ; His dying Eyes and Heart
Imploring Heav'n, soon did his Soule depart.

Fell Tyger, tell us, tell us why, or whence,
Thou durst (accurst) assault so great a Prince ?   350
Wherein had hee to thee or thine done wrong,
When once (yer this) thou didst too neer him throng,
His Gard rebuk't thee ; but, hee them, for that,
Caus'd that *Thy Malice,* and his Murd'rous fate ?
Fate's ruthlesse Law allots his royall brest
To dye the death that CÆSAR thought the best ;
Death without sense of death, a death so quick,
It seldome leaves Kings leasure to be sick ;
Nor gives him leave for his fixt *Decad's* date
To fill the Roule ; but seven six months did bate.   360

Hee, hee that was the hope, the prop of his,
Hee that restored *France* to what it is,

Hee that confin'd the Pow'r of Princes still,
Hee that commanded *Victory* at will,
That was the World's delight, Kings' glory sheen,
Hee, hee receives Death's treacherous stroak unseen.

Th' unhappy street where this fell Hap fell-out,
Where wofull *Paris* saw her light put-out,
Where cursed Iron pierc't her Prince's heart,
It shall no more be clept *The Iron-mart :*   370
It shall be call'd *The cursed Corner* still ;
The Hag-street, or *the Hell-street :* which you will.

Lord ! where wert thou, when that disloyall wretch
With cruell hand did thine Annointed reach ;
Quenching the Rayes of royall Majesty ?
No heart is hid from thine All-piercing Eye ;
It sees the center, knows the thoughts, yer thought ;
Could it see this, and suffer it be wrought ?

Hell oft before, out of his black *Abyss,*
Had spew'd up Monsters to have acted this :   380
But, still thy hand from former wounds did ward.
And had hee not still trusted to thy Gard,
His owne had waited round about his Coach,
And this fell Tyger never should approach.

These words, these rasher words escapt my tong ;
When I beheld that Monarch laid along
Dead on his Bed ; so dead, so butchered :
I blamed Heav'ns, and Whispering soft, I said,
Because they stopt not this strange Hap before,
Their slumbring eies now watch the world no more. 390

But, are mine eyes mine own ? Is this that Prince
Which might have made all *Europe* his, long
              since,
Had hee not thought th' Empire of *France* enough ?
That Lion-heart, that courage Cannon-proofe,
Which did so oft impossibles atchieve ?
I see 'tis hee : yet scarce my sight beleeve.

Is this that mighty King, God's lively Image,
To whom the greatest in the World did Homage ?
In Peace a Dove, in War an Eagle quick,
NESTOR in Court, in Camp ACHILLES-like ;   400
That with an hundred horse, a thousand foil'd :
That from most dangers never yet recoil'd.

Great *Rome* was strangely maz'd and all a-mort,
When Shee beheld her CÆSAR's bloudy shirt :
And say, Great City, how wert thou dismaid,
When first thou saw'st thine HENRY sadly laid
Along his Coach, and covered with a Cloak ?
"*I thought the prop of all my Fortunes broke.*

Those that have seen in Towns surpriz'd (while-yer)
When to the Churches All have fled for feare,   410
May well imagine *Paris'* deep affright.
Nothing but shivering Nobles armed bright,
Clergie at Prayers, Peeple weep and howle :
And HENRY's wound hath wounded every Soule.

Paris in honour of her Peerlesse Queen,
Had plotted Showes (more Pompous never seen)
As, rich to th' outward, rare to th' inward sense ;
But, all those Arks (Marks of magnificence),
Those *Tropheis, Terms, Statues, Colosses* all,
Make but more Mourners at the Funerall.   420

I yeeld My Pensill : help *Apelles*, here,
To Limn (to life) Her dying-living Cheere ;
Beliefe is hardly in Man's heart imprest,
Her Griefe more hard to be by Art exprest.
Therfore O Queen ! great Stay, great Star of *France*,
This Vaile I draw before thy Countenance.
Heav'n steel'd thy heart with fortitude that Day,
Thy Courage kept the Kingdome from Decay ;
And to the Throne thy Son our Soveraign heft :
Though angry Fates of Father him bereft, 430
Yet mercifull, they left him such a Mother,
That *France* could hardly have been rul'd by other.

The sudden Clap of this drad Thunder sounds,
From *Alexander's* to *Alcides'* bounds :
The Kings and Princes stand amazed all,
With horror of an Act so Tragicall.
Some, Rest forsake : Others, Repast forbeare :
And Each, like Fortune to himselfe doth feare.

So suddenly to see Day turn'd to Night,
Triumphant Palmes into *Funereall* Plight, 440
The Royall Crown to a deep mourning Vale,
A living King, to a dead Corps and pale,
Our Flow'rs to Thornes ; seem Tricks of Sorcery,
Wherein, Conceit consents not with our Eye.

Yes, hee is dead : and his eye-lids no more
To view this Light shall open (as before) ;
Those lovely eyes, the Load-stars of the Court,
Whose gracious glances, on the Worthy sort,
Gave Vertue vigour ; and whose awfull frowne
Dis-dared Vice ; are now Eclipst and downe. 450

Where are those ready Battell-ranging Hands?
Those lightning eyes whose wrath no wall with-
stands?
That voice so dreadful to the stoutest harts?
That heart wch wrought so many wondrous parts?
That piercing Wit, dispersing Clouds of Doubt?
Where is that mighty King, so Fam'd about?

Inexorable *Death !* inhumane, cruell,
Thou shalt no more reave us so rare a Jewell ;
Nature hath broke the Mould shee made him in.
In all thy *Triumph* (trayling every Kin) 460
Shall never march his Match, nor worthier Prince
T' have been exempted from thine Insolence.

Ah ! poor, weak *Vertue ;* zealous Love of Thee,
Prolongs not Life, protracts not Death (I see).
This Prince that gave Thee even his heart for Temple,
This Prince, whose reign shal serve for rare exemple
To future Kings, in future things dis-maid,
Should have come sooner, or have later stay'd.

His piety, was neither fond, nor fain'd ;
His Prowesse, neither feare nor rashnesse stain'd ; 470
His Prudence cleer'd his Counsels, steer'd his State ;
His Temperance his Wrath did temperate ;
His Justice with his Clemency did yoake :
Yet could not all free him from fatall stroake.

Invincible in all : onely, the Darts,
Which have not spar'd the Gods' immortall hearts,
Have often battered His : but (by your leaves,
O fairest beauties ! *Beauty it selfe deceives*).

You never were the Soveraigns of his brest ;
Hee You (perhaps) You never him possest. 480

In *Arms-Art*, what he knew not, none can know't,
Neither attempt what hee attempted not.
Reason was aye the Aime of his designes ;
His brave exploits (worthy immortall lines)
Shall furnish Theam to Thousand learned Clarks,
Whose Works shall honour him, hee more their
works.

His *Royall Gests* are every-where extold
Graven, Carv'd, Cast, in Marble, Wood, and Gold ;
His Life alone 's an History admired,
Wherin all Pens, all Pencills shall be tired, 490
In pourtraying all his valued Feats to-forn,
Whose Tables ever shall all Courts adorn.

His *Bountie's* Temple had a hard Accesse,
Not known to any, but to *Worthinesse :*
That Gate (indeed) did seldome open quick.
His *Liberality* (coy beauty-like)
Lov'd to be woo'd, prest and importun'd still ;
Yea, forc't to give, what glad and fain shee will.

Yet, by th' effects to weigh his Clemency,
Mee thinks his heart must more than humane be ; 500
Mee thinks therein some higher Power did shine,
It surely seem'd celestiall and divine :
And, but I saw him dying, pale and wan,
I could have scarce beleev'd this Prince a Man.

Hee ever lov'd rather to save than spill,
Not cementing his Throne with Bloud, with Ill ;
Nor ween'd, by Feare, his Diadem assur'd ;
With mildnesse rather grieved minds hee cur'd :
His memory did never wrongs retein ;
Beloved Kings, Hee thought, securest reign. 510

Praise you his bounty, you that past the Poles,
Beare Heav'n's Embassage to Belief-less Soules :
Henry restor'd your Countrey and your Credit,
Hee gave you leave over all *France* to spread it ;
Restor'd your *Byzance*, and each pleasant part,
Left you his Court, bequeath'd to you his heart.

If *France* now flourish, proyning, round about,
Olives within, and Lawrels all without,
If now, Shee give the Law to other States,
If Peace and Plenty raigne within her Gates, 520
If now Shee feare no Civill storms again,
These are the fruits of this Great *Henry's* raign.

If now her Schooles with learned men abound,
If her rare Wits be through the World renownd,
If doubts of Faith be cleered and explor'd,
If Learning be to her due Place restor'd,
If now Desert the Charge in Church attain,
These are the fruits of this Great *Henry's* raign.

If now her Buildings passe for beauty far
The world's old Wonders (which so famous are) 530
If *Paris* Thou be peerlesse to behold,
For State, for Store, for People, Goods and Gold,
If in thy Citie, Cities sprout again,
These are the fruits of this Great *Henry's* raign.

If the *French* Scepter be now Self-entire,
Fearlesse of Forein or Domestick fire :

If *France* have Fellowes of *Achilles'* Fame ;
If now in *France* be nothing out of frame,
If now the *Indies* her *Bastile* containe ;
These are the fruits of this Great *Henry's* raign.   540
    If now wee joy to see our Countrey free
From Theeves and Rebels (which exiled be)
If Justice now do keep the lewd in awe,
If Desperate Duels be now curb'd by Law,
If now the weak waigh not the Strong's disdain,
These are the fruits of this Great *Henry's* raign.
    If Merchants rich, if Magistrates be sound,
If Officers like Emperours abound,
If Pursie Lawyers live Prince-like at home,
If now inventions to their height be come,   550
If now good Wits finde where them to sustain,
These are the fruits of this Great *Henry's* raign.
    Who lov'd not Him, never beheld his browes ;
Who knew his fortunes, must admire his Prowes ;
Who fear'd him not, His Greatnesse did offend ;
Who weend him to beguile, his Wisedome kend ;
Who durst displease him, knew his mercies' store ;
Who durst not speake, his mildnesse did ignore.
    Who waileth not his Death, knew not his Life,
Glory of his, and others' envie rife,   560
Incomparable, Admirable Prince,
Excelling all th' old *Heroes'* excellence.
For his true Story shall their fables shame :
Inimitable Life, Illimitable Fame.
    O *French-men,* stop not yet your weeping flood :
This Prince for you hath lavisht oft his blood.
O ! be not niggards of your Tears' expence.
(Vaile here, my Verse, do ANNE a reverence.
Rare ANNE that shames the rarest wits of Ours,
Her divine Stances furnish mee these Flowers).   570
    The Heav'ns may give us all Prosperities,
Sustain our State, remove our miseries ;
But cannot dry up our Tears' bitter streame :
In extreme evils remedies extreme.
Restore our King, quick shall our joyes recover :
Else, never look our Sorrowes shall give-over.
    Each where our grief finds matter to augment it,
His Name's remembrance doth each-where present it,
His famous Gests doe busie every sort ;
Some tell his Warres, others his Works report.   580
Others his Favours past, glad-sad deplore ;
Then, not to mourn, is not to minde him more.
    Ah ! must wee live, and see so sudden dead
The Life that late our lives inspirited ?
Strike saile my soule, let 's put into thy Port,
While HENRY liv'd 'twas good to live (in sort) :
But let us after : sith hee 's reft of breath,
Desire of Life is now far worse than Death.
    Sorrow, with us doth both lye down and rise,
Wrinkles our Brows, withers our Cheeks and Eyes :   590

Wee shun what ever might our Griefs allay,
Wee wish the Night, w' are weary of the Day ;
Night brings sad silence with her horrid shade,
And even her colour seems for mourning made.
    Extremest Woes yet are with Time ore-past,
Rivers of Tears are dryed-up at last :
But never ours : Ours ever fresh shall flow :
Wee defie Comforts, Wee 'll admit no moe,
Nor seek them, but as *Alchimy* profound
Seeks that which is not, or which is not found.   600
    Who, from the Ocean, Motion can recall,
Heat from Fire, Void from Air, Order from All,
From Lines their Points, from IRIS all her Dyes,
Perils from Seas, from Numbers Unities,
Shadowes from Bodies, Angles from the Square,
May free our hearts from grief, our minds from care.
    Hee must be heart-less that is smart-less found :
The Soule that is not wounded with this wound,
Most brutish, hath no humane Reason in't :
There is no brest of Steel, no heart of Flint,   610
But must be-moan so great a King, so slain.
Who would not waile a Gally-slave so ta'n ?
    Let us no more name HENRIES, Kings of *France.*
Death wth two knives, and with one shiver'd Lance,
Hath kill'd three HENRY'S : one at Jousts (in jest) :
Th' other in 's Closet : in 's Caroche, the best :
So, Three King RICHARDS, and five Other, cry,
Some fatall Secret in some Names doth lye.
    What worse Disastre can you have behind,
To threaten *France* O Destinies unkinde ?   620
What greater Mischief can your Malice bring ?
So good a Father rest, so great a King ;
What will you more ? sith wee no more can hope
For any Good that with this Ill may cope.
    This noble Spirit doth to his Spring re-mount,
This bountie's Flood retireth to his Fount,
This Atomie to 's Unity unites,
This star returns to the first Light of Lights,
This Ray reverts where first it light did take :
And mortall wounds, this Prince immortall make.   630

    Fare-well sole Honour of all earthly Kings,
Fare-well rare Prince for all kind Managings,
Fare-well Great HENRY, Heav'n's and Nature's Gem,
Fare-well bright Star of Kings, glorie's great Beam,
Fare-well sole Mortall that I keep in mind :
Fare-well false Hope, Fortune and Court unkinde.

Here, lest Oblivion should usurpe her roome,
FAME writes in Gold, these Lines upon thy Toomb.

This Prince, un-peerd for Clemency and Courage,
Justly Sur-nam'd the Great, the Good, the Wise,   640
Mirour of Future, Miracle of Fore-Age ;
One short Mis-hap for ever Happifies.

FINIS.

THE BATTAIL

OF YVRY

OR

THE BREAK-NECK

OF

The Hellish-Holy League;

IN

That famous Victory

Wonne

By HENRY the Great;

Written

By Du *BARTAS*

Translated; & Dedicated

TO

The Right Honourable

RICHARD

EARLE OF DORSET,

By Josuah Sylvester.

TO THE RIGHT HONOURABLE
EARLE OF DORSET.

A S th' *awefull* Child, *that long hath* truanted,
 Dares not returne unto the Schoole, *alone;*
For Shame *and* Feare *to be there discipled*
With many stripes for many Faults in One :
So fares (my Lord) *My long* Omission
 Of th' humble Thanks *I ought have* tendered
 For kinde Endeavours *You bestow'd upon*
 My Right, *my* Wrong *to have* recovered.
And, (*as in fine*) *Hee brings his* Mother *forth*
 To beg Forgivnesse, *or his Fault to 'scuse :*
 So bring I here my dear Du BARTAS' *Worth,*
To mediate for my too-faulty Muse ;
 Whom daign to pardon : *and in gentle Part*
 Accept *This last of* His, *not least in* Art.

Your Lordship's

most Obliged,

JOSUAH SYLVESTER.

Ad eundem

Comitem Illustrissimum

(*Nuper ex Galliis reducem*)

EPIGRAMMA

Ex. Lat. I. O.

A Yr's *Change* hath changed (which but rare doth chance)
 Your *good* to *best :* in *Science* and in *Sense.*
Wiser and *better,* both ; and *Both,* from FRANCE :
Welcom, Great Earle : few are so *Well com* Thence.

Ejusdem

Clarissimi

ANAGRMMATA:

Clarus, Divis Charus;

Richardus Sacvilus :

Is Clarus, diu Charus.

Exoptat. J. S.

THE BATTAIL

OF

YVRY.

O! What a Sun-shine gilds us round-about!
    O! What a *Hymn* of *Triumph* troule they
        out,
In all our *Temples!* O! what cheerfull noyse!
What *Bels!* What *Bonfires!* O! What *Publike Joyes!*
The day is Ours: and on the *Leaguers*' head,
The angry Heav'ns have their just *Vengeance* shed.
    Be smooth, my *Browes;* and You my throbbing
        thoughts
(Long, deeply sunk in *sorrow's* sable vaults)
Soar-up to Heav'n : You *Sisters Three-fold-Three*,
Who of late Years have scarce vouchsafed Mee   10
To wet my lips : Now sweetly steep my Tongue
In your best Syrups : poure upon *This Song*,
A deaw of Gold ; a May of learned Flowers.
Let not mine eies, blubber'd with private Showers,
Cross publike Glee : nor (silent) mee conceale,
While others sing *These Tropheis* of our Weale.
    Ah! now begins my rapted Brain to boyle
With brave Invention : Now's the fittest while
For my Career.   Others may hold their tongue ;
But hardly can great Joyes be hidden long.   20
    But now ; How, Where, of What shall I begin
This gold-grownd Web to weave, to warp, to spin?
For, here I list not, in these leaves, my Lord,
The famous Facts of thy first Arms record :
So many, and so numb'ry Armies scatter'd
So many Towns defenc't, so many batter'd
By thy young Valour.   Neither shall my Pen
Re-purple *Lisle ;* nor with dead Grease agen
Re-soile the Soile at *Courtras :* neither (dread)
Here reave againe thy ragefull Foes of Head.   30
Nor shall my Muse relate, how that yer-while
(Abusing *King's* and *Churche's* sacred stile)
All *Europe* nigh (all sorts of *Rights* reneg'd)
Against the *Truth* and *Thee, un-holy Leagu'd ;*
While thou (a Prince, not having Men, nor Treasure
But poor, in All ; save rich in Hope past measure)
Resemblest right one of thy Hils in *Foix,*
Which stands all Storms, firm'd by it self's sad poiz ;

Boldly beholds the frowning Upper-Stage,
Disdaining Winds, deriding Weather's rage :   40
And with his brows cleaving the proudest thunder,
With knobbed knees still keeps it bravely under.
Nor may I now our thoughts cleer Heav'n ore-cast
With Cloudy Theam of miseries fore-past :
Nor cruelly begin again to launce
New-skinned wounds, to the new griefe of *France.*
    Sing others those : Me shall suffice to sing,
That in few Months, since Thou wert here *Our King,*
Thy valiant hand hath more strong places won
Then Both the Sides in thirty yeers have done.   50
Though Swarms besieg'd, in number did surmount
Besieging Troups, in so unequall count,
That oft there seem'd of foes more troups (almost)
Then single Souldiers in thy Royall Host.
Thou seem'st a lightning, and thy nimble Bands,
Follow thy Will rather with wings, then hands ;
And impt with plumes of Honour-thirsting minds,
Are bravely born with thy *good-fortune's* winds :
Thou cam'st, saw'st, overcam'st, as swift well-neer
As these swift Words I have digested here.   60
    Onely, neer *Arques,* for few dayes the Foe
Thine Expeditions som-what doth fore-slowe :
But as a Torrent, whose proud stream for stop,
Hath the thick height of som new Causwaie's top ;
The Bottom undermines, beats on the shore,
And still (in vain) adds Forces more and more,
Till, at the last, aided with Showers and Snowes,
Fell, foaming, lowd, his Prison over-throwes,
Tears bridges down, bears away Mounds and Mills,
And having won the Valleys, threats the Hils ;   70
Swels as a Sea, and in his furious Pother
Takes Land from som, and giveth more to other :
So thou re-camp'st, runn'st, rushest, ruinest
Holds, Houses, Towns, and never dost thou rest,
Till rebell *Paris,* pale for guilty feare,
Behold thy Face with too-just Fury there,
In her vast Suburbs ; Suburbs flanked strong ;
Suburbs, whose streets wth souldiers thickly throng :

Thou tak'st *Estamps :* and losing scarce a man,
Thy martiall Troups ingratefull *Vandosme* wan.   80
Mans is assail'd, and ta'n ; *Falaise Eureux :*
Maine followes those ; and after that *Lizieux,*
And *Honfleur* too, stoop to thy *Sacred Flowers.*
And now began thy Sulphury Thunder-stowers
To batter *Dreux :* whenas the *Leaguer's* Chief,
Puft with som new Supplies, and fresh Relief,
From fatall *Philip* (who right Foxy-wise,
Wide yawning still after so rich a prize ;
Ambitious waits, nor wishes nothing more,
Then that our *Great* each other enter-gore,   90
In Civill Rage ; that at the easier rate,
Himselfe may snatch the Price of their debate)
Drawes neer thine Host.   Then thou, whose fear was
          great
Lest Hee too-fear'd thee, fained'st a Retreat,
Seem'st loth to fight, seem'st thy hault heat to slack
And to leap further, stepst a little back.
Thou stopst, He flies : Thou follow'st, then he stands :
And now, both Sides for Battell range their Bands :
They seem two Forrests : every Chief, apart,
Darrains his Troups with order, speed and art.   100
The Lightning-flash from swords, casks, courtilaces,
W^{th} quiv'ring beams begilds the neighbour grasses ;
As th' Host of Stars, which shine above so bright,
Bespangles rich the Mantle of the Night.
The Souldier now looks sterner then of long ;
Rage in his eyes, fell out-rage on his tongue,
Iron on his back, Steel in his hand : and fell
Erynnis makes in *Yvry* Fields her Hell.
    There's nothing heard but Drums, Fifes, Trumpets'
          noise,
But sharp shril neighs, but dreadful Tempests' voice. 110
Terror and Horror over all are spread ;
Horror's there lovely, and their sweet is Dread :
Already fight they with their voice and gest :
Already Horsemen couch their staves in rest ;
Much like a Lyon, meeting hand to hand,
Some Savage Bull upon the Desart sand ;
Th' one with wide nostrils, foming wrathfull heat,
With lowd proud bellows, with a thundrous threat
Defies his Foe ; tosses his head on high,
Wounds with his hooves the Earth, with horns the
          sky :   120
Th' other, as furious from as fiery Throat
Roaring, replies him with more hideous note ;
Under his horrid Front, in ghastly-wise
Hee roules the Brands of his fierce flashing Eyes ;
Rearing his Crest, hee rears his courage stout,
And whets his rage, whisking his train about.
The Canon 's primed, discharg'd, hand stroaks begin :
Friends, fellows, neighbours, brothers, cosins, kin,
Lose all respects ; save onely where they may,
Deep, deadly Wounds, worthy their rage, repay.   130
    But, North-west winde, under the weeping *Kid,*
Never so thick his volleys racqueted,
Of bounding Balls of Ice-pearl slippery shining,
On those high hils my *Gascony* confining,

As here rain Bodies, here haile lumps of Lead,
Making a Floud of Bloud ; a mount of dead.
Torn Limbs, tost truncheons, Shiver, Fire, and smoak,
As with thick clouds, both Armies round becloak :
Th' Earth quakes for fear, the Air recoyleth quick,
And *Plutoe's* selfe seems to look pale and sick.   140
This side advances now, and now retreats :
That lost but now ; and now the better gets.
    For, yet (JOVE's issue) *Victory* (begirt
With Sword by side, and Trump behind, athwart ;
Her head wth crowns, her hands wth scepters fraught
Her costly Robe with many Conquests wrought,
Flourisht with Palms, figur'd with Towns about,
Embost with Ensignes, with Assaults set-out)
Flyes to and fro ; from Camp to Camp she plies,
And in her hand shee leads triumphant-wise   150
Sweet-rapting *Glory,* full of Cheerefull grace,
To either side shewing her lovely Face.
    O Sons of *Mars !* which, which of you this day,
As worthy Spouse, shall beare, for Bride, away
This Beauteous Love? Who by her side shall lye?
Who, of her kisse the balmie Bliss shall try?
Thrice happy hee : him shall the Kings adore :
Him shall the Nobles humbly bow before :
Him shall the Vulgar (as a Sea it were)
Follow, and flock about : and every-where   160
His famous Face shall set a-work the chiefe
Of Pensils, Gravers, Chisels, Moulds : in briefe,
Hee shall be *Summe* of an admired Story ;
And every Age shall celebrate his glory :
His high renowne shall onely bounded be
With the World's bounds, and with Eternity.
    Thus having said, into their breasts shee blew
No common Heat, but Fits of Fury new :
Here number wins, there Courage, and there Art :
And yet *Good-fortune* falls to Either part :   170
As when the spitefull sullen Earth hath meant
War with the Flouds, war with the Firmament,
Sh' incites, inflames, sets-on, in new-found-Duel,
Ice-bearded *Boreas,* Storm-arm'd *Auster* cruell ;
Flouds float uncertain, and the Clouds doe vary
Whither it pleases either Blast to carry :
Till th' one at last, the other conquering,
Become Air's Tyrant, and the Water's King.
    But, lo My Liege : O Courage ! there he comes :
What Ray of Honour round about him looms ?   180
O ! what new beams from his bright eyes do glance !
O Princely Port ! Presagefull Countenance
Of Hap at hand ! Hee doth not nicely prank
In clinquant Pomp (as som of meanest Rank)
But arm'd in Steel ; that bright abiliment
Is his rich *Valour's* sole rich Ornament.
Steel was his Cradle, under steel hee dight
His Chin with Doun, in steel begins it white :
And yet by steel he conquers, bravely-bold,
Towns, Cities, States, Crowns, Scepters, goods and
          gold.   190
    Yet void of Mark, Hee doth not hide him quite
Amid the Throng : a plume dread-dancing light

Beclowds his Cask, and like a Willow showes ;
Which, prun'd below, close by a River growes ;
And hath no sooner Heav'n's calm favour lost,
But instantly his Top's green Tuft is tost,
Now up now down, and waves (as please the Wind)
Now to, now fro ; now forward, now behind.
   Thus (to be known) invincible by Force,
Hee, with six hundred, charg'd six thousand Horse. 200
The first that felt his Arm and Fauchin keen,
Was blindly bold, a Warriour that did ween
Himselfe as stout, as strong ; as strong, as great ;
And, daring so, undaunted *Henry* met ;
Who offers prest his Pistol in his Face,
Which would not off, although it fir'd a space.
Whence somwhat mov'd, with angry voice, quoth He,
Hence, guilefull Arms ; the glittring Sword for Me :
And draws withall ; then nimbly tossing light
The flashing Horror of his Fauchin bright   210
(Like an *Autumnal* ruddy streaming Star
Presaging Famine, Pestilence and War)
Copes with his Foe ; th' Assailant hee assaults,
And resolute observes his Arme's defaults :
At last, betwixt his Brest-plate and his Bases
Seekes for his soule ; there findes, and thence it chases.
   Goe, happy Soule, goe tell the news beneath,
How thou wert honour'd to have had thy death
By th' onely hand of th' *Hercules* of *France*,
Th' invincible ; (for, such a death, perchance,   220
Shall more extoll thy famous Memory,
Then to have won some other *Victory*) :
Say, here revives a *Martel*, Foes to maul ;
And that *Orlando* rules again in *Gaul*.
   But, Thou go'st not alone : this deadly Fray
Thou but beginn'st, as Prologue of his play.
Hee deales about as many Deaths as Blowes :
Hee hacks, heaws, hurts all, all hee overthrowes ;
Swifter then winde, or Cannon-shot, or Thunder,
Trees, towns, and towers, turns up, beats down, brings
    under.   230
One place, one push, one deed, one death, one wound,
Cannot suffice, nor his brave Fury bound :
Hee layes on all ; and fiery-fierce and stout,
A hundred wayes cross-carves the Field about ;
All fall, in fine, but fall not all alike :
Some did hee thrill, some thwart, some down-right
    strike.
   But, as a Lion in *Numidian* Field,
Feeding a while on trembling Heards that yeeld ;
If so hee heare a Bear's noyse neer about,
Rearing his Eares and Crest, hee roareth-out ;   240
Leaves lambs, kids, kine ; glad hee incountred hath
An Object worthier of his noble Wrath :
My match-less Prince, discrying *Duke de Mayne*,
Spares vulgar bloud, and speeds to him amain ;
Through thickest troups of stoutest men at-arms,
Through horse and foot, through shot, pikes, ensignes,
    arms,
Incounters him : on him his load hee layes ;
And round about on every side assayes,

Under his arms, to seek in every part
The heart which onely gave the *Leaguer's* heart.   250
   But, dreading his disdain, *De-Mayne* with-drew :
And all his Hopes, so sudden dasht, did rue :
Blusht at his past Bliss, full of carefull toile,
Loathing the Field, new witnesse of his Foile.
Now *Yury* out of sight, hee *Mante* approaches :
His weary horse, his weary rowell broches :
Untill, broak-winded, crest-faln, sweaty-swelted,
And all his grease in and without him melted,
Lolling his eares, hanging his head and neck,
For spur he stirs no more, then stock or stick.   260
   O, noble *Duke!* O wherefore flyest thou?
What *Panik* Terror daunts thy Valour now ?
Thy constant Face what paints with pale affright ?
Alas ! thou lack'st not Courage here, but Right.
The cause confounds thee : *Charles*, yet stay and stand
To *Henry's* mercy ; humbly kiss his hand.
If red Revenge, for thy dead Brethren's chance,
Make thee take Arms : what 's that (alas !) to *France ?*
What, to this King? whose heart and hands are
    known
From both their blouds as cleer as are thine own.   270
   If 'twere Ambition, mought'st thou not expect
From him, that knowes how Vertue to respect,
And can, as King, magnifikly advance
His faithfull Servants : and the Friends of *France*,
More honour and reward, then from the rude
Poore, giddy, grosse, ingratefull Multitude ;
Of many Heads, of more then many Mindes,
Leaking in every Storm, led with all Winds ;
Who pay with Death, or Exile (at the best)
Their *Dions, Phocions, Camils*, and the rest :   280
Whose rule is Rage ; Who (Ivie-like) in time
Decay the Tower whereby themselves did clime ?
   If it were Feare to finde his favour's gate
Now barr'd too-fast for thee to enter at ;
O ! was there ever known more gracious King,
Forgetting Ill-turnes ; Good remembring !
Hee rather would, by Benefits then Blowes,
Reduce his Rebels. When his fury glowes,
'Tis but as Straw-fire ; while hee strikes, he sighs ;
And (for the most part) from his Enemies   290
Drawes not more bloud, then tender tears withall
From his owne Eyes : His Spirit 's voyd of Gall
(Peculiar Gift, hereditary Grace,
The heavn's have given unto the *Bourbons'* Race) :
And never did the all-discerning Sun,
Which daily once about the World doth run,
Behold a Prince religiously more loth
To shake, for ought, his honour-binding Oath.
Offer my Liege the *Germain* Emperie,
Spain's Diadem, the *Turk's Grand-Signiorie*,   300
Yea, make him *Monarch* of the World, by wile ;
Hee 'll spurn all Scepters yer his faith hee file.
   But, 'tis (saist thou) for the *Faith Catholike*.
Why ? who commands in matters Politike?
Who in his Camp ? but such as more then thou
With Tooth and Naile, *Rome's Vatican* avow ?

Serves not his Name for Refuge, every-where
Securing Priesthood from all Force and Fear?
No *Atheisme*, Hee, nor *Superstition* sents,
Hee's a right *Christian* and Religious Prince.   310
Hee firm beleeves, that God's *reformed* Awe,
Hee from his Cradle, with his milk did draw:
Yet, is not partiall, nor prejudicate.

And, if the *Church*, now neerly ruinate,
By our profane hands, our strife-strirring Quils,
May ever look for a Redresse of Ills;
If it may ever hope to reprocure
A holy and a happy *Peace*, to dure;
It shall be, doubtlesse, under such a Prince,
So free from Passion's blinded Vehemence.   320

Back to the Battell, *Muse*, now cast about:
Ah! there they flee, there all are in a Rout:
All's full of Horrour, full of Ruth and Fear,
Full of disorder, and Confusion, there:
There, none obey; there, none at all command;
There, every Souldier makes apart his Band.
The ample Plain is cover'd all about
With casks, swords, muskets, pikes; and the most stout
To darkest Groves carry their Deaths conceiv'd,
In deepest Holes bury their deaths receiv'd.   330

The Victor follows, over-takes anon:
Fears not the way the Flyers fear'd t' have gone.
The most hee fears, is, lest Som's shiftfull fear,
Other's despair, finde out for saf'ty there,
Som flat, som foord, som bank, som bridge, som way
To passe the *Eure*: but, pressed with dismay,
All, breath-lesse panting in a desperate haste,
Them here and there into the River cast.

The immortall *Nymph* NAVONDA, azure-ey'd,
Queen of that crystall, and that Current's Guide;   340
Scar'd with their noise, above the water pushes
Her dropping head, in Caul of weeping Rushes.
O! whence, quoth she, whence coms this iron spawn?
These metal-men? from what mount *Gibel* drawn?
What *Vulcan* gave, what *Myron* lent (I pray)
Steel life, to stir; to Iron breath, to neigh?
Hence, Monsters, hence (war's dreadfull workman-ship):
With bloudy deaws your Mother-Earth be-dip;
And let us gently, without stop or stain,
To meet our *Tritons*, roule into the Main.   350

Her voice doth vanish in so various noise:
This with his own; That, with his armour's poiz
Sinks instantly: Som have in stead of graves,
Nought but their Steeds; their Steeds, no tombs but
waves:
Some, more dismai'd, for Skiff their Targets take;
For oars, their arms; their sail, their plumes they make:
But, greedy whirle-pooles, ever-wheeling round,
Suck-in at-once, Oars, Sails, and Ships to ground.

Those that, by chance, scape to the other Shore,
Changing their place, change not their case the more.   360
Dikes, Bridges broken, Cities, Rampires cast
Cannot secure their more then headlong haste.
Did any Squadrons dare thy Conquest crosse,
They but increast thine Honour, and their Losse.

Witnesse the Band of *Spanish Belgian* Foes,
Under three Ensignes marching strongly close:
Whom thou the fifteenth, chargest; beatest down
That mighty Body, sudden overthrown;
Even as a Galley, in smooth Sea subdues
The tallest Ship that in *The Streights* doth use: 370
Or as a Jennet in his nimble Speed
Oft over-turns the strongest German Steed.
Thou heaw'st, beat'st, breakest down: thou conquer'st
ay,
Till dusky Night have robb'd thee quite of Day;
And death, of Foes. Th' *Helvetian* Bands alone,
Loth to disgrace their ancient Valour known,
Against the Victor their steel Staves addresse;
As most courageous in the most distresse;
But, soon the Lightning of thy Martiall eyes
Their Diamantine hearts dissolves to yce;   380
That yce to water; that to Vapour vain:
And those whom death rather then fear could strain,
Those, those that never turn'd their backs at all,
But to war's-*Phœnix*, conquerour of *Gaul*;
Those King-correcting, Tyrant-scourging Braves,
Cast at thy feet their Bodyes and their Staves.

Thou, then, as loth perpetually to brand
People so loyall to the *Lillies'* Land,
Calming the rage of thy just heart's disdain,
Their Colours to their Comets giv'st again.   390

O! proudest *Trophey*, which all *Tropheys* passes!
O Browes, whom *Bayes'* eternall tresse imbraces!
Invincible! O more then royall breast,
Who, of thy selfe, and *Triumph*, triumphest!
Who pleasest all: with Victory thine Host,
Thy Foes with Grace: both with thy Glory, most.

Earth's Ornament, thou honour of our Times,
Ay on the wings of mine Heroik Rimes,
So brave Exploit be bravely born about:
May all our Commons (commonly too-stout)   400
Who bred in braules, in Broils, and Insolence,
Stood, as at gaze, distracted in suspence,
Expecting th' Issue of this dreadfull Fight,
Make their due profit, and apply it right.
May now the *Nobles* freely grant, for true,
That the World's Empire to thy worth is due:
That, now they have Wise happy Prince for head:
That by this Battail thou hast rendered
To them their Rank, reveng'd the King deceast,
Restor'd the State, and captive *France* releast;   410
May now the *Clergie* ingeniously confesse,
God on thy side, giving thy Right Successe,
Crowning thy Vertues, and with sacred Oyle
Of his own spirit annoynting thee the while.
May now (in briefe) all *Frenchmen* say and sing,
Thou art, Thou ought'st, Thou onely canst be King.

But, O! some Gangreene, Plague, or Leprosie,
O'r-spreads us all: a Brand of Mutinie
Burns *France* to ashes. And but thou (unidle)
Bear'st-up so hard this stumbling Kingdom's Bridle;   420
Our State (yerst honour'd where the Sun doth rise)
Would fly in Sparks, or die in Atomies.

Priests strike the fire, the *Nobles* blow the coale
Of this consumption : *People* (peevish whole)
Pleas'd wth the blaze, do, wretched-witched Elves,
For fuell (fooles) cast-in their willing Selves.

O *Clergie* (mindlesse of your Cure and Coat)
Becoms it you to cut your Prince's throat?
To kill your King? who, in the Wombe (of kin
To thousand Kings) that Office did begin :   430
Who, for your law, your altars, and your honours,
Hath ventur'd oft his bloud in many maners :
Who as devout to *Rome*, as any man,
Fear'd most your roaring Buls of *Vatican :*
And canonize amid the sacred Roule
Of glorious Saints, a Parricidiall Soule ;
Whose bloudy hand had stabb'd with baneful knife
The Lord's Annoynted, and Him reft of life?

Ignoble *Nobles* see you not (alas !)
Your King supplanting, you your selves abass?   440
And, while you raze this royall *Monarchie*,
You madly raise a monstrous *Anarchie*,
A *Chaos* rude ; still whetting, day and night,
Against your Selves, the people's proud Despite ;
Who hate the Vertuous, and have onely hope
T' ensue the *Switzer's* too-rebellious Scope?

And thou fond *People*, Who (before a Father,
A wise, just King ; a valiant *Monarch*) rather
Tak'st hundred Tyrants ; who, with tushes fell,
Will suck thy marrow out, and crack thy shell :   450
To whom the Gold, from *India's* bowels brought,
Or 'mid the Sands of shining *Tagus* sought,
Seems not so good, as doth the gold they set
From out thy Womb, or what thy tears shall wet.

No, no : the *French*, or Deafe, or Lethargick,
Feele not their danger, though thus deadly sick :
Or if they live and feele ; they, frantik, arm
Against their Leach that fain would cure their harm
Applying many sound-sweet Med'cines fit :
But they the more increase their furious Fit.   460

Yet, courage *Henry*, fix thy thoughts hereon,
Pursue (brave Prince) thy Cure so well begun :
And sith so little, gentle Plaisters thrive,
Let it be lanc't, lay-on the Corrosive :
Choke me this *Hydra* whence such Monsters sprout,
And with thy Fame fill mee the World about.
Follow thy Fortune : Hills most lofty-browd,
Stoop to thy Steps : swift Rivers, swelling proud,
Dry-up before thee : Armies, full of Boast,
Like Vapours vanish at thy sight, almost.   470
Yea, at thy Name alone, the strongest Wall,
And massiest Towers shake (as affraid) and fall.

But yet, my Liege, beware how thou expose
Thy blood so oft among thy bloody Foes :

Be not too-lavish of thy Life ; but waigh,
That Our *Good-hap* on thine dependeth aye.

But, if thou light regard this low Request
Of *Thy Fame's Trumpet ;* list how *France* (at least)
Presents her to thee : not as once shee was
(When *Baltik* Seas within her bounds did pass :   480
When *Nile* and *Euphrate*, as her under-Realms,
Through fruitfull Plains roul'd tributary streams :
When to proud *Spanyards* Shee did Kings allow ;
And to her lawes imperiall *Rome* did bow)
But lean, and lank, bleak, weak, and all too-torn,
And in a Gulfe of miseries forlorne.

Dear Son (saith shee) nay, My Defender rather,
My Staff, my Stay, my Second-founding Father ;
For, Grief, and Fury, I should desperate die,
I should Selfe stab-mee, I should shamefully   490
Stop mine own breath, to stint these Cares of mine
Wert thou not mine (my Liege) were I not thine.
Therefore, deare Spouse, be of thy Life less lavish ;
Let not, my Lord, Fame's greedy thirst so ravish
Thy daunt-less Courage into Dangers need-lesse,
Nor, too-too-hardy hazzard thee so heed-lesse.

A brave great *Monarch* in Youth's heat behoves,
Once, twice, or thrice, to shew Courageous proves :
For Prowess is bright *Honour's* bravest Gate ;
Yea, the first Step, whereby the Fortunate   500
Climbe *Glory's* Mount : and nothing more (in brief)
Fires Souldiers' Valour, than a Valiant Chief :
But, afterward, hee must more warie war ;
And with his Wit, ofter then Weapon, far :
His spirits contenting with the pleasing-paine,
Not of a Souldier but a Soverain.

My Son, too-often hath thine owne hand dealt
Too-many blowes, which thousands yerst have felt :
My Liege, too-often hast thou toiled thee
For Honour's Prize : brave Prince, My Victory   510
Not in thine arm's strength, but thy years' length lies ;
Thy life, my life ; thy death, my death implies.
If thou thy selfe neglect, respect mee though,
At least some pitie to thy Countrey show.
Weigh, weigh my sad plight, if untimely Death
Should (O, untimely !) reave My *Henry's* breath :
Even like a widow-Ship, her Pilot lost,
Her Rudder broke, in ragefull Tempest tost
Against the horned Rocks, or horrid Banks,
Hoaring the Shore with her dispersed Planks.   520

But, if too-much-Heart, of thy life too care-less,
Too-soon expose thee not, to *Sisters*-spareless,
I hope to flourish more than e'r in *Arts*,
Wealth, Honours, Maners, Vertues, Valiant hearts,
Religion, Lawes ; and the just *Raign* (at rest)
In *Happinesse* shall match *Augustus* best.

F I N I S.

NOTES AND ILLUSTRATIONS.

DEDICATION . . . DORSET. See Memorial-Introduction : l. 1, '*awe-full*' = full of awe, terrified.
Line 2, '*troule*' = troll : l. 9, '*Sisters*' = Nine Muses : l. 25, '*numb'ry*'—see Glossarial Index, *s.v. :* l. 33,
'*reneg'd,*' *ibid. :* l. 38, '*sad*' = solid : l. 57, '*impt*'—see Glossarial Index, *s.v. :* l. 59, '*cam'st,*' etc. = veni, vidi,
vici of Cæsar : l. 100, '*Darrains*'—see Glossarial Index, *s.v. :* l. 280, '*Camils,*' *ibid. :* l. 294, '*Bourbons*'—alas !
what a different story the facts tell in our own times ! Witness Naples and Spain : l. 309, '*sents*' = scents, but a
false rhyme for ' Prince :' l. 339, '*Navonda*'—see Glossarial Index, *s.v. :* l. 344, '*Gibel,*' *ibid. :* l. 380, '*Diamantine,*'
ibid. : l. 449, '*tushes*' = tusks—now in nursery language applied to our infants' first teeth : l. 520, '*Hoaring*'—see
Glossarial Index, *s.v.*

G.

SIMILE NON
EST IDEM:
Seeming is not the-Same.
OR,
All's not Gold that glisters.

A CHARACTER of This Corrupted Time,
Which makes RELIGION but a Cover-Crime.

TO THE WORTHILY-HONO-
red Sir HENRIE BAKER,

Knight-Baronet.

*T*Is better late *than* never, *to repay* :
    Better a little, *than* no Part *at all* :
    Take therefore, in good-part, This Part (*though small*)
Of your great Debt : *and pardon my Delay,*
Till (more mine owne) with more Respect, *I may*
    In better Measure (*as I hope, I shall*)
    Answer your Merit ; *though not answer all*
Your Bountie's *Bonds, renewed Day by Day.*
You minde your MAKER in your Dayes of Youth :
    You shew us, by your Works, your Faith's *sincerity* :
    You are so friendly *to the* Friends *of* Truth,
Your vertuous *Life so proves your Love* to Verity,
    That None *I thought, could, with more patient Eye,*
    Abide to look on this ANATOMIE.

——————————————— Your Vertues' Humble Honourer,

—————JOSUAH SYLVESTER.

S I M I L E   N O N

E S T   I D E M :

Seeming is not the-Same.

O R,

All's not Gold that glisters.

1.

How Times are *chang'd!* and wee *with* Times,
  In new, nefarious, various Crimes !
    Exceeding all that have preceded,
In *Pride, in Fraud, in Filth, in Force,*
Rape, Treason, Poyson, past Remorse :
    Such, as (in Time) will scarce be creeded.

2.

O Mindes ! O Manners ! most absurd !
When (to the Scandall of *The Word*)
    The more our Light, the worse our Works :
When *seeming* SAINTS *be* nothing lesse ;
And more Profane, who most Professe,
    Than *Infidels,* or *Jewes,* or *Turks.*

3.

And when, between our *roaring* GIANTS,
That openly, bid Heav'n Defiance,
    Heaping-up Hills of wickednesse ;
And th' undermining close despights
Of double-hearted *Hypocrites,*
    Masking in Hollow-*Holiness.*

4.

From Earth are FAITH and TRUTH exil'd ;
False *Error* hath all hearts beguil'd.
    All-over All ABUSES raign.
Vertue is Vice, Vice Vertue growne,
Justice is justled from her owne :
    Honour and *Right* are in disdain.

5.

'Tis, to be *Foolish* To be *Wise :*
With Reason, is against the Guise :

Read they that can my Riddle right.
Christ, Son of Man ; and God of *Hoasts,*
How-many of Thy *Baptisme,* boasts,
    Whose life doth to the death defi't !

6.

For, thy Disciples Thee beleeve ;
And in thee onely double live ;
    According to thy GOSPEL'S *veritie ;*
But, dare wee say, that wee are such,
When now-adayes in Poor or Rich,
    Is found nor *Faith,* nor *Hope,* nor *Charitie.*

7.

God hath ingrav'n in every Soule
A native Law, on *Nature's* Roule ;
    Whereby (alas) Wee stand convict :
And *Precedents* of pious *Zeale,*
Who by their blouds, their hopes did seal,
    To double Death condemn us, strict.

8.

Wee ought infringe That *Statute* never,
From everlasting firm'd for-ever :
    Doe, as Thou would'st be done unto :
Doe not, what Thou would'st not accept :
O Pure, plain, gentle, just *Precept !*
    Yet This (alas !) Who looks to do ?

9.

When all Degrees so tender bin
Towards themselves, without, with-in,
    They neither Wrong, nor Right can suffer ?
But towards Others (made as they,
By the same hand, of the same clay)
    Against all Rights all Wrongs doe offer.

10.

LORD, Thou hast said, and shew'n it cleer
When (in thy Flesh) Thou sojourn'dst here
  Thy Kingdome is not of This World:
So shall I ever more suspect,
While here I see, with such neglect,
  Thy holy Statutes after-hurld.

11.

All those (*O Lord*) that cry, *Lord, Lord;*
With shadow of thy *Sacred Word*,
  To cloak their *Wickednesse*, with-in ;
Are none of *Thine:* but of Thy *Name*
Profanely make a mocking-Game,
  To countenance their cursed Sin.

12.

Like that IGNATIAN-*Latian Colledge*,
Where, under shew of *Sacred Knowledge*,
  They study *State* and *Stratagems;*
Making a Staple-Trafick of it
After their Pleasure, or their Profit)
  To murther *Kings*, and mangle Realms :

13.

Thee JESUS (Mercifull and Meek)
They make a Tyrant (*Nero*-like)
  Bloody and brute, to kill and quell :
Thee, SAVIOUR, Source of *innocence;*
Thee, *Prince of Peace and Patience;*
  They make a *Fury* fierce and fell.

14.

Thee, *Justice*-Fountaine, *Order's* Author,
They make *Wrong's* Fort, *Confusion's* Fautor :
  Immortal Spring immaculate
Of *Love*, of *Concord*, and of UNION,
They make Thee Trumpet of *Dis-Union*,
  And Tinder of immortall *Hate*.

15.

Such *Canons* roare from *Trent* and *Tiber*,
From *Powder-Traitors'* bloody *Briber*,
  Whose HOLYNESS is *Hollownesse;*
Whose *Synagogue* is Sinners' Wrack ;
Whose *Faith* is FAUX and RAVILLAC ;
  Whose *Deeds* and *Doctrine*, Wickednesse.

16.

O, where is then *The Holy Flock!*
Call'd in one *Hope*, built on one *Rock*,
  Into one *Faith* incorporing ;
Thorough one *Baptisme*, by one *Word*,
Under one *Father* (*God* and *Lord*)
  One onely *Prophet, Priest* and *King*.

17.

There, there (as *Children* of one *Mother*)
They succour and support each other,

In *Union*, and in mutuall *Charitie';*
All making but one Body, being
All of *One Minde*, in One agreeing :
  Bound by *One Bond of Peace, and Verity*.

18.

O, can Wee (wretched, witched Elves)
Can Wee, Wee Many, boast our Selves
  One Bread, one Body (*mystick-wise*) ;
And say that wee are daily fed
In common with one *Drink* and *Bread*,
  Amid our many Enmities?

19.

Alas ! Where are those *Saints* become,
Worthy the stile of *Christendome;*
  From Sin's *Dominion* inly freed ;
Vessels of Honour, full of *Grace*,
Abounding in *good-works* apace ?
  None now good Thought hath ; less good *Deed*.

20.

Nothing but false *Equivocation:*
Nothing but wilfull *Obduration:*
  Nothing but *Errour* and *Disorder;*
Nothing but *Pride* and *Insolence:*
Nothing but impious *Impudence:*
  Nothing but *Treason, Theft*, and *Murder*.

21.

Contempt of God and of all *Good*,
Rape, Riot, Incest, Brib'ry, Blood,
  Perjury, Plotting, all Impiety,
With more than brutest *Brutishness*,
This more-than-*Iron-Age* possesse :
  No *Love*, no *Friendship*, no *Society*.

22.

Court, Citie, Countrey, Every sort
Of either Sex, make Sin a Sport
  (*Pride, Painting, Poys'ning, Cous'ning, Whoring*) ;
In *Sloth*, or *Surfeit*, ever-drownd ;
To *Bacchus*, or *Tobacco* bound ;
  With *swearing, staring, stabbing, roaring*.

23.

Wrath, Envie, Slander, and Suspition,
Fraud, Rancour, Rapine, and Ambition,
  With *Blasphemies*, all over-spread :
Th' old *Christian's* Badge, bright *Charitie*,
(Most frequent then ; now raritie)
  Is now-adayes, not down but dead.

24.

Wee are so Punctuall and Precise
In *Doctrine* (*Pharasaik-wise*)
  To seem (at least) the most RELIGIOUS,
That true RELIGION wee deforme
While to our Phant'sies wee reforme
  Shadowes, and not *our Selves*, litigious.

25.

RELIGION ! O, Thou Life of Life !
How Worldings, that profane thee rife,
  Can wrest thee to their Appetites !
How Princes, who thy Power defie,
Pretend thee, for their *Tyranny ;*
  And People, for their false *Delights !*

26.

Under Thy sacred Name, all-over,
All Vicious all their Vices Cover :
  The *Violent*, their *Violence :*
The *Proud*, their *Pride :* the *False*, their *Fraud :*
The *Theefe*, his *Theft :* her *Filth*, the *Baud :*
  The *Impudent*, their *Impudence.*

27.

Ambition, under Thee, aspires :
Avarice, under Thee, desires :
  Sloth, under Thee, her Ease assumes :
Lux', under Thee, all over-flowes :
Wrath, under Thee, outrageous growes :
  All Evill, under Thee, presumes.

28.

RELIGION, yerst so venerable,
Th' art now-adayes but made a Fable ;
  A holy Mask on *Follie's* Brow,
Where-under lyes *Dissimulation*,
Lined with all *Abhomination :*
  Sacred RELIGION, where art thou ?

29.

Not in the *Church*, with *Simonie :*
Nor on the *Bench*, with *Briberie :*
  Nor in the *Court*, with *Machiavell :*
Nor in the *Citie*, with *Deceits :*
Nor in the *Country*, with *Debates :*
  For, What hath *Heav'n* to do with *Hell ?*

30.

Sith whatsoever Show wee make
(For Profit or Promotion's sake)
  What-ever Colour wee put-on ;
Where, *Faith* no other Fruits affords,
But evill-*Works* (though civill words)
  Indeed is no RELIGION.

31.

Reverend RELIGION, where 's the heart
That entertains thee as thou art,
  Sincerely, for thine owne respect ?
Where is the Minde, where is the Man,
May right be call'd a *Christian ;*
  Not formall, but in true effect ?

32.

Who, fixing all his *Faith* and *Hope*
On God alone, from sacred Scope

Of his pure Statutes will not stray :
Who comes in *Zeal* and *Humblenesse*,
With true and hearty *Singlenesse*,
  Willing to walk the perfect Way :

33.

Who loves, with all his Soule and Minde,
Almighty God, All-wise, All-kinde,
  All-whole, All-holy, All-sufficing :
Who but One onely God adores
(Though *Tyrants* rage, and *Satan* rores)
  Without digressing, or disguising :

34.

Who God's due *Honour* hath not given
To Other things, in Earth or Heav'n ;
  But bow'd and vow'd to Him alone ;
Him onely serv'd with filiall Awe,
Pleas'd and delighted in his Law,
  Discoursing Day and Night thereon ;

35.

Not, not for Form, or Fashion sake ;
Or for a Time, a Show to make,
  Others the better to beguile :
Nor it, in Jest, to wrest or cite ;
But in his heart it deep to write,
  And work it with his hands the while ;

36.

Loving his neighbour as himselfe,
Sharing to him his Power, his Pelfe,
  His Counsels, Comforts, Coats, and Cates :
Doing in all things to his Brother,
But as Himself would wish from Other,
  Not Offring Other what he hates :

37.

Whose Heart, inclin'd as doth behoove-it,
Unlawfully doth nothing covet
  (To Any an offence to offer) :
But just and gentle towards all,
Would rather (unto great, or small)
  Than do one wrong, an hundred suffer :

38.

Not thirsting Others' Land or Life ;
Nor neighing after Maid or Wife ;
  Nor ayming any Injury ;
Neither of polling, nor of pilling,
Neither of cursing, nor of killing,
  Neither of Fraud, nor Forgerie :

39.

But will confesse, if hee offend,
Relent, *Repent*, and soon amend,
  And timely render Satisfaction.
Sure, his RELIGION is not fained,
Who doth and hath him thus demeaned ;
  Ay deadly hating *Evill-action.*

40.

Therefore, O ! Vassals of the Divell,
That cannot, will not cease from Evill,
   Vessels of *Wrath* and *Reprobation ;*
Presume no longer Now to shrowd
Under RELIGION'S sacred Clowd
   Your Manifold *Abhomination.*

41.

If, but to *seem good*, goodly seem :
To *bee good*, better farre esteem :
   Why *seem* you what *to be* you care not ?
If to *seem evill*, be amiss ;
Sure *to be evill*, worse it is :
   Why *be you* what *To seem* you dare not ?
Be, as you *seem ;* or *seem* the Same
You *be :* to free RELIGION'S Blame.

FINIS.

NOTES AND ILLUSTRATIONS.

DEDICATION—SIR HENRIE BAKER.—Eldest son of John Baker, Esq. of Sisinghurst, Kent. He was knighted 15th July 1606, and created a baronet 29th June 1611. He married Catharine, d. of Sir John Smith of Ostenhanger. Kt. He died in 1623, and the title expired at the death of his grandson in 1661.

Stanza 14, ' *Fautor* ' = abettor : st. 15, ' *Faux* ' = Guy Faux : ' *Ravillac* ' = Ravaillac, assassin of Henry IV. st. 16, ' *incorporing* ' = incorporating.   G.

A

GLIMPSE OF

HEAVENLY

JOYES:

OR NEW

HIERUSALEM.

IN AN OLD HYMN

EXTRACTED FROM THE

moſt Divine St. *Auguſtine.*

TO THE WORTHY FRIEND OF

Worthineſſe, Sʳ PETER MANWOOD,

Knight of the Honourable Order

Of the BATH.

TO register, to After-Times,
  Your noble Favour to my Rimes;
  Your love to Vertue, Learning, Arts;
Your Bounty towards Worthy Parts;
Your Pitie; and your pious Zeale
To GOD, to Church, to Common-weale;
Your Loyalty, in every kinde:
The honour of your humble Minde:
All, all my MANWOOD to rehearse,
Merits a Volumne, not a Verse.
  But poor divided I (that owe,
To many, Much, as many know;

And fain would give Content to Each,
So far-forth as my Stock will reach)
Unable (after your Desert)
To render All, must render Part,
To testifie my Thankfull Thought,
(But as I could, not as I ought)
And what my Weaknesse cannot pay,
Th' AL-MIGHTIE-most I humbly pray
To guerdon with a Diadem.
Within His NEW-JERUSALEM.
                Yours much Obliged,
                JOSUAH SYLVESTER.

NEW

HIERUSALEM.

MY Heart (as *Hart* for Water) thirsts
    For Life's eternall Fount :
My Soule, my Bodie's Pris'ner, longs,
    From Prison free, to mount ;
Sighes, sues, pursues, poor exile here,
    Her Countrey to recover ;
Too-abject, subject to disgrace,
    And too-too-triumpht-over.
¶ Shee seems to see the glory now,
    Which, when shee sinn'd, shee lost :   10
An instant Ill, of Good for-gone
    Augments the mem'ry most.
¶ But of celestiall *Soveraign Bliss*,
    Who can set-forth the Solace !
Where stands of ever-living Stones,
    An ever-lasting Palace ;
The lofty Roofes and stately Roomes,
    Reflecting golden beams :
The gates and goodly walls about,
    Of rich and orient Gemms :   20
The Streets, all pav'd with purest Gold,
    As smooth as any Glass-is :
No Foile, no Soile, no Sorrow there ;
    No Sicknesse thither passes.
No Winter's Frost, no Summer's Toast,
    Doth there distemper bring :
But Flow'rs, perpetuall flowring there,
    Make there perpetuall Spring.
There, *Balsam, Saffron, Lilly, Rose,*
    Doe sweat, sent, shine, and blush :   30
There, Mead and Field, spring, spire, and yeeld ;
    Rills, Milke and Hony gush :
There *Aromaticks* breathe-about
    Their odoriferous Aire :
There, ever dangle dainty Fruits,
    On trees still blooming faire :
There, never Moon doth wax or wane,
    Nor Sun, nor Stars decline ;
But there, the LAMB (the Light of Lights)
    Eternally doth shine.   40
There Time hath no alternate Term ;
    No Night, but ever Day ;
For, There, the *Saints* are (as the Sun)
    Most bright, in white Aray ;

Triumphant ; after Conquest *crown'd*,
    In mutuall Joy they greet :
Recounting safe the Battells fought,
    Their Foes now under-feet ;
Pure, purifi'd from dregs and dross ;
    From fleshly Combats freed :   50
Their flesh, made spirituall, with the Spirit,
    In one selfe-same agreed :
In perfect and perpetuall *Peace ;*
    Subject no more to sinning :
Obnoxious nor to Change, nor Chance ;
    Return'd to their *Beginning ;*
And Face to Face for ever see
    All *Beautie's Glory* bright,
Possessing sempiternall Joyes,
    In that supernall Sight   60
(The Sight of *GOD*, the *Soveraign Good*,
    The Sun of *Happinesse,*
Such as no heart can here comprise,
    Nor any *Art* expresse).
Installed in a *Bliss-full* State
    Of Glory, still *The same ;*
As sure, as pure, from Faile or Fall,
    From Sorrow, Sinne, and Shame.
All joyous, lively, lovely, bright,
    To no Mis-hap exposed :   70
No Danger, Death, Disease, nor Age ;
    In Health and Youth reposed.
Henceforth, for all *Eternity*,
    They flourish fresh and green :
For, *Death* is dead, *Time* termined,
    Corruption conquer'd clean.
Now know they him, that knoweth all,
    And in beholding him
They all behold (as in a Glass)
    Before them bright and brim.   80
In Unity of minde combin'd,
    One very thing they Will ;
And ever constant, never cross,
    One and the same they Nill.
As here in *Grace*, in *Glory* there,
    Though diversly, they shine :
Love equall's All ; Each loving All
    With mutuall Love divine,

So that the Good of every-one
    Becoms of all the Good. 90
Where is the Body, thither right
    Right Eagle-shoales doe scud ;
Where-with, with Angels, *Saincted-Soules*
    Are aye refresht and fed,
(For, Either Countrie's Burgesses
    Are nourisht with One Bread)
And ever fain, though ever full ;
    Wishing but What they have :
Not sated with Satietie ;
    Nor needing more to crave : 100
Desiring still, their fill they eate ;
    And eating, still desire.
Still new melodious Songs they sound
    With Heav'n's harmonious Quire ;
And Organs Worthy (for His Worth
    Through Whom they overcame)
Sing *Holy, Holy, Holy, Praise*
    To HIS most HOLY *Name.*

¶ O happy, happy, happy, Soules,
    That see Heav'n's *King,* above ; 110
And underneath-them Sun and Moon,
    And all the World to move !
¶ *O Christ, victorious Lord of Hoasts,*
    So lead my soule and Heart,
That having fought, as here I ought,
    I may have there a Part,
Among that Blessed Hierarchie,
    In Happinesse supreme ;
A free and fellow-Citizen
    Of NEW JERUSALEM. 120
Vouchsafe mee Grace, to run my race,
    And strenuously to strive
Unto the End, that in the End
    I may the Crowne atchieve :
Not for My Worke, but for Thy Worth :
    Thy Mercy, not My Merit :
So Laud and Praise be sung alwayes,
    To FATHER, SON, and SPIRIT.

TRIN-UNI DEO,

Creatori, Redemptori, Directori Meo,

GLORIA In Secula-Seculorum. AMEN.

NOTES AND ILLUSTRATIONS.

DEDICATION—SIR PETER MANWOOD. —Only surviving son of Sir Roger Manwood, chief baron of the Exchequer. He was created a Knight of the Bath at the coronation of James I., 25th July 1603. He was of St. Stephen's, Canterbury. Died 1625.

LINE 75, ' *termined* ' = terminated ; l. 80, ' *brim* '—See Glossarial Index, *s.v.,* for other examples.—G.

AUTO-MACHIA:

OR THE

SELFE-CONFLICT

OF A CHRISTIAN.

From the Latin of Master

George Goodwin.

Translated ; and Dedicated to the truely-
honorable *Mistris Cecilie Nevil.*

Anagramma Italiano.

Cecilia Nevila.

E Vicina al Ciel.

Heav'n's Neighbour *is your Anagram.*

Your Noble Graces prove the same.

FAir *Heir* of all Your MOTHER'S *good*
(Wit, Vertue, Beauty, Bounty, Blood)
Among the *Honours* that accrue,
By her decease divolv'd to You ;
Mine humble *Service* and *This Song*
(How little) doth not least belong
(In *Little* lies a *Mickle* Right ;
As in a *Million*, in a *Mite*)
To her *Memoriall*, and Your *Merit*,
True *Mirrour* of MINERVA'S *Spirit.*
Accept it therefore *double* Yours ;
By Her Donation, and by Ours.

——————————*Humbly devoted,*

(as most bound)

———————— *To both your noble Families,*

——————————— JOSUAH SYLVESTER.

TO

THE RIGHT

NOBLE, VERTUOUS

AND LEARNED LADY,

The Lady MARIE

Nevil.

Maria Nevila.

Alia Minerva.

MAdame, Your love to Learning, and the Learned
(*In such a time so full of Art's neglect*)
Right worthily to Your rare Self hath earned
The love of Learning, and the learned Sect :
Whereby, Your Name already is eterned
In MEMORY'S *fair* Temple, *high erect :*
And there devoutly at Your Vertue's Shrine,
I humbly offer this poor MITE *of Mine.*

Too small a Present *to so great a* GRACE ;
And too un-worthy of your Worthinesse :
Save that the Matter *so exceeds the Masse,*
That oft (perhaps) a greater may be lesse :
For, you may see, within This *little glasse,*
The Little-World's *great-little-Mindednesse :*
Man's strife with Man ; *Our Flesh and Spirit in*
Duell :
Courageous Cowards, too-self-kindly cruell.

Vouchsafe t' accept then this small New-year's-Gift,
With humble vowes of a disastred Muse ;
Which lavishly hath sown her Seeds *of Thrift*
So high and dry, that yet no Fruit *ensues.*
Else need Shee not have made so hard a Shift ;
Nor this small Gift so greatly to excuse.
But sith, as yet, Shee cannot what Shee would ;
Madame, *accept her Zeal, and what Shee could.*

——————— To Your Honourable Vertues,

——————————————*most devoted,*

———————————————JOSUAH SYLVESTER.

AUTO-MACHIA:

OR

SELFE-CIVIL-WAR.

I *Sing not* Priam, *nor the Siege of* Troy :
  Nor Agamemnon's *Jarre with* Thetis' *Joy :*
  I sing not here Æneas' *stormfull Fate ;*
Queen Dido's *love, nor Goddesse* Juno's *hate :*
I sing not Cæsar, *nor his Son-in-law ;*
Whose Civill Rage, Rome *and* Pharsalia *saw.*
I sing my Self ; *my* Civill-Wars *within ;*
The Victories *I hourely lose and win ;*
The daily Duel, *the continuall Strife,*
The War *that ends not, till I end my Life.*   10
And yet, not Mine alone, not onely Mine ;
But every One's that under th' honour'd Signe
Of Christ *his Standard, shall his Name enroule,*
With holy vowes of Body and of Soule.
  Vouchsafe, O Father, *succour from above ;*
Courage of Soule, comfort of heavn'ly Love :
Triumphant Captaine, Glorious Generall,
Furnish mee Armes from thine owne Arcenall :
O Sacred Sp'rit, my sp'rit's assistant be ;
And in This Conflict, *make Mee conquer* Mee.   20
VERTUE I love, I leane to *Vice :* I blame
This wicked World, yet I embrace the same.
I climb to Heav'n, I cleave to Earth : I both
Too-love my Selfe, and yet my-selfe I loath.
Peace-less I peace pursue ; in *Civill War,*
With and against my self, I joyne, I jar :
I burn, I freeze ; I fall down, I stand fast :
Well-ill I fare ; I glory though disgrac't :
I die alive : I triumph, put to flight ;
I feed on Cares, in tears I take delight :   30
My Slave (base-brave) I serve, I roame at large,
In libertie, yet lye in Gaoler's Charge :
I strike, and stroake my selfe : I, kindly-keen,
Work mine own woe, rub my gall, rouz my spleen.
Oft in my Sleep, to see rare Dreams I dreame ;
Waking, mine Eye doth scarce discerne a Beame.
My mind's strange *Megrim,* whirling to and fro,
Now thrusts mee hither, thither then doth throw.
In diverse *Factions* I my Self divide ;
And All I try, and fly to every Side.   40

What I but now desir'd, I now disdain :
What (late) I waigh'd not, now I wish again :
To-Day, to-Morrow ; this, that, Now, Anon,
All, Nothing, crave I ; Ever Never-one.
  Dull Combatant, unready for the Field,
Too-tardy take I (after wounds) my Shield.
Still hurried headlong to unlawfull things,
Down-dragging *Vice* mee eas'ly downward dings ;
But, sacred *Vertue* climbs so hard and high,
That hardly can I her steep steps descry.   50
  Both *Right* and *Wrong* with mee indifferent are :
My *Lust* is *Law :* what I desire, I dare,
(Is there so foule a *Fault,* so fond a Fact,
Which, Folly asking, Fury dares not act ?)
But, art-lesse, heart-lesse, in *Religion's* Cause
(To do her Lessons, and defend her Lawes)
The All-proof Armour of my God I lose,
Flee from my Charge, and yeeld it to his Foes.
  Guilty of Sin, Sin's punishment I shun,
But not the Guilt, before th' Offence be done : 60
(For, how could shunning of a Sin ensew
To be occasion of another New ?)
Oft and again at the same stone I trip,
As if I learn'd, by falling, not to slip.
Alive I perish, and my Self undo ;
Mine eyes (Self-wise) witting and willing too.
  Sick to my Self I run for my reliefe :
So, Sicker of my *Physicke* than my *Griefe :*
For, while I seek my swelting Thirst to swage,
Another Thirst more ragingly doth rage :   70
While burnt to death, to coole mee I desire ;
With flames, my flames, with Sulphur quench I fire :
While that I strive my swelling waves to stop,
More stormily they toss above my top.
Thus am I cur'd, this is my common ease ;
My *Med'cine* still worse than my worst Disease :
My Sores with Sores, my wounds with wounds I heal,
While to my Self, my Self I still conceale.
  O what lewd Leagues ! what Truces make I still
With sin, with Satan, and my wanton Will !   80

What sleight occasions do I take to sin !
What silly Trains am I intrapped in !
What idle Cloaks for Crimes ! what Nets to hide
Notorious Sins, already long descri'd !
I write in Ice (Winds witness, sign'd with Show'rs)
I will redeem my *foul Life's* former houres :
But, soon the swinge of custome (whirl-wind-like)
Rapting my Passion (ever Fashion-sick)
Transports mee to the Contrary ; alone,
Faint Guard of *Goodnesse ;* Arm-lesse Champion.   90
    My *Green-sicke* Taste doth nothing sweeter finde
Than what is bitter to a *gracious* Minde :
Egypt's fat Flesh-pots I am longing-for :
Th' eternall *Manna* I do even abhorre.
World's Monarch *Mammon* (dropsie mysticall)
Crown'd round-fac't Goddesse, coined *Beliall :*
Midas' Desire, the Miser's onely Trust ;
The sacred hunger of *Pactolian* Dust,
Gold, Gold bewitches mee, and frets accurst
My greedy Throat with more than *Dipsian* Thirst.   100
My mind 's a Gulfe, whose gaping nought can stuff ;
My heart a Hell, that never hath enough :
The more I have I crave, and lesse content ;
In Store, most Poor ; in Plenty Indigent.
For, of these Cates how-much so-ere I cram,
It doth not stop my mouth, but stretch the same.
    Sweet *Vsurie's* incestuous *Interest,*
For Dallers, Dolours hoordeth in my Chest.
The world's slave, *profit,* and the mind's slut, *pleasure*
(Insatiate both, both bound-less, both past measure :   110
This *Cleopatra,* That *Sardanapale*)
For huge Annoies, brings Joyes but short and small.
    O Miracle ! begot by Heav'n in Earth
(My Minde divine, My Body brute by Birth)
O ! what a Monster am I, to depaint !
Half-Friend, half-Fiend, half-Savage, half a Saint ;
High'r than my Fire doth my gross Earth aspire :
My raging Flesh my retch-less Force doth tire,
And (drunk wth worlds-must, and deep sunk in sleep)
My spirit (the spy, that wary watch should keep)   120
Betraies, alas ! (Wo that I trust it so)
My soule's deer Kingdom to her deadly Fo.
    Through Care's *Charybdis,* and through Gulfs of grief,
Star-lar-boord run I, sailing all my Life
On merry-sorry Seas ; my Wind, my Will ;
My Ship, my Flesh ; my Sense, my Pilot still.
    As in a most seditious *Common-weal,*
Within my Brest I feel my Best rebell :
Against their Prince my furious People rise ;
Their Aw-less Prince dares his owne Law despise.   130
Mine *Eve's* an Out-law : And my struggling twins,
Jacob and *Esau,* never can be friends :
Such deadly feud, such discord, such despight
(Even between Brethren) such continuall fight.
    What 's done in Mee, Another doth, not I ;
Yet both (alas !) my Guest and Enemy :
My mind, unkind (suborned by my Foe)
Indeed within mee, but not with mee tho ;

Neer, yet far off, in fleshly Lees bee soil'd,
And with the World's contagious Filth defil'd.   140
    I am too-narrow for mine owne Desires ;
My selfe denies mee, what my self requires :
Fearfull I hope : carefull-secure I languish :
Hungry too-full ; Dry-Drunken ; sugred Angish ,
Weary of Life, merry in Death ; I suck
Wine from the Pumice, Hony from the Rock.
On Thorns my Grapes, on Garlick grows my Rose :
From crums my sums ; from flint my fountain flowes
In showrs of Tears, mine hours of Fears I mourn :
My Looks to Brooks, my Beams to Streames, I turn : 150
Yet, in this Torrent of my Torments rife,
I sink Annoies, and drink the Joyes of Life.
    Dim light, brim night, Beams waving cloudy-cleer :
Unstable State, void Hope, vain help, far-neer :
False-true Perswasion, law-less Lawfullnesse :
Confused Method, Milde-wilde War-like Peace :
Disord'red Order, Mournfull Meriments :
Dark Day, Wrong Way, Dull-double Diligence :
Infamous Fame, known Error, skill-less Skill,
Mad Minde, rude Reason, an unwilling Will :   160
A healthy Plague, a wealthy Want, poor Treasure :
A pleasing Torment, a tormenting Pleasure :
An odious Love, an ugly Beauty ; base
Reproachfull Honour, a disgracefull Grace :
A fruitless Fruit, a dry dis-flowered Flower :
A feeble Force, a conquered Conquerour :
A sickly Health, dead Life, and restlesse Rest :
These are the Comforts of my soule distrest.
O ! how I like, dis-like, desire, disdain ;
Repell, repeal, loath, and delight again !   170
O ! what, whom, whether (neither Flesh nor Fish)
How, weary of, the same again I wish !
I will, I nill ; I nill, I will ; my Minde
Perswading This, my Mood to That inclin'd.
My loose Affection (*Proteus*-like) appears
In every Form ; at once it frowns and fleers.
Mine ill-good will is vain and variable :
My (*Hydra*) Flesh buds heads innumerable :
My Mind 's a Maze ; a Labyrinth, my Reason :
Mine Eye (false Spy) the door to Phant'sie's Treason : 180
My rebell Sense (self-soothing) still affects
What it should flee ; what it should ply, neglects :
My flitting Hope with Passion's Storms is tost
But now to Heav'n, anon to Hell almost :
Concording Discord kils mee ; and again,
Discording Concord doth my Life sustain.
    My Self at once I both displease and please :
Without my Self, my Self I fain would seaze :
For my too much of mee, mee much annoyes ;
And my Self's Plenty, my poor Self destroyes :   190
Who seeks mee in mee, in mee shall not finde
Mee as my Self : *Hermaphrodite* in minde,
I am (at once) Male, Female, Neuter : yet
What-e'r I am, I am not mine, I weet :
I am not with my Self as I conceive :
Wretch that I am, my Self my Self deceive :

Unto my Self, my Self my Self betray ;
I from my Self, banish my Self away :
My Self agrees not with my Self a jot,
Knowes not my Self : I have my Self forgot :   200
Against my Self, my Self moves jarres unjust :
I trust my Self, and I my Self distrust :

My Self I follow, and my Self I fly :
Besides my Self, and in my Selfe, am I :
My Self am not my Self, another same ;
Unlike my Self, and like my Self I am :
Self-fond, Self-furious ; and thus, Wayward Elf,
I cannot live with, nor without my Self.

FINIS.

A

CUP OF CONSOLATION

FOR THE CHRISTIAN

In his Conflict.

WHy, silly Man, sick of exceeding grief,
      What boots it thee, uncertain of thy Life,
Of thy disease to make so much adoe ?
Thou coward Souldier, and untoward too,
Away with Fear : defie both Death and Hell :
Meet Arms with Arms, and Darts with Darts repell :
So, the first On-set, in this furious Fray,
Shall towards Heav'n make thee an easie Way ;
And open wide those Gates so hardly won,
Where Snowie-winged *Victory* doth wun :   10
Thou must be valiant, and with daunt-lesse brest
Rush through the thickest, run upon the best
Of braving Foes : and on their Flight and Foil,
Reare noble Tropheis of triumphant Spoil.
For, this world's Prince, dark *Limbo's* Potentate,
Drifts Man's destruction, and with deadly hate
(Still strife-full) labours, and by all means seeks
To trouble All, and Heav'n with Hell to mix.
   Great war Within there is, great War without ;
With Flesh and Bloud, and with the World about.   20
On this Side, smiling *Hope* (with smoothest brow)
False-promiseth long Peace and plenty too :
On that Side, sallow *Fear* (with fainting breath)
Checks those proud thoughts wth threats of War and
      Death ;
And (weary of it Selfe) it Self distrusts,
It selfe destroyes, and to Confusion thrusts :
And, ignorant of its Selfe's Good (yer Triall)
In jealous Rage it even betrayes the loyall.
   Here, Cloud-brow'd *Sorrow*, Whirle-winde like, it hies
Th' amated Minde to tosse and tyrannize :   30

There, dimpled joy nimbly enringeth round
Her gawdy Troups that stand upon no ground ;
Whose brittle glosse and glory lasts and shines
As Stubble-Fire, and Dust before the Windes.
   What should I speak of all the snarefull Wiles,
And cunning Colours of mysterious Guiles,
Wherewith Death's Founder, and thy Life's drad foe,
Improvident mankind doth over-throw ?
   Yet be Courageous, yeeld not unto Evill :
Resist Beginnings, and defie the Divell.   40
For sure defence amid these fell Alarms,
Quick buckle-on these ay-victorious Arms :
   First gird thy Loins with *Truth*, thy Bosom dress
In the sure Brest-plate of pure *Righteousnesse* :
Put, on thy Head, the Helmet of *Salvation* :
Upon thy feet, Shooes of the Preparation
Of *Heav'n's Glad-tidings* : Bear upon thine Arm
The Shield of *Faith* (Shot-free from every harm).
Hel's fiery Darts repell thou with the same ;
And, through its splendor, quench their flame with
      flame :   50
Take in thy hand the bright two-edged Sword
Of God's Soule-parting, Marrow-pearcing, *Word*.
   Thus compleat arm'd from God's own *Arcenal*,
And watching duely for his aid to call,
Thou without doubt shalt quickly overcom
The world, the flesh, sin, death, and hell (in summe).
And so (through Christ, thy Captain and thy King)
Of Sin, thy Self, and *Satan*, triumphing,
Thou shalt (in fine) the *Happy Crown* obtain,
And in th' Eternall promis'd *Kingdom* raign.

FINIS.

NOTES AND ILLUSTRATIONS.

DEDICATION—Of the NEVIL 'fair ladies' see Memorial-Introduction : and the same for notice of GEORGE GOODWIN, whose Latin poem is herein translated or paraphrased.

AUTOMACHIA, etc.   Line 48, '*dings*' = casts down, so still *Scoticè :* l. 53, '*fond*' = foolish : *ibid.* '*Fact*' = deed or act (not a truth) : l. 82, '*Trains*' = snares : l. 153, '*brim*'—see Glossarial Index, *s.v.*, for other examples l. 176, '*fleers*' = fawns, flatters.

A CUP, etc., l. 10, '*wun*' = dwell.   G.

T O B A C C O

B A T T E R E D,

AND

THE PIPES SHATTERED

(about their Ears that idlely

Idolize ſo baſe and barbarous
a *W E E D*;

O R

AT LEAST-WISE OVER-LOVE

ſo loathſome Vanitie :)

B Y

A Volley of Holy Shot

Thundered

From *Mount* HELICON.

Fide ivstvs vivet : *Devs providebit.*

TO THE RIGHT HONOURABLE

Sir *GEORGE VILIERS*, Knight, Baron

of Whaddon: L. Vicount VILIERS: Earle of

Buckingham: Mr. of the Horse to his Majesty,

and Knight of the most Noble Order of

the Garter, &c.

YOur Noble *Order* and your hallowed *Name*,
Your *Soveraign's* Favour, and your owne *Profes-*
sion *;*
Promise your *Valour* towards the *Suppression*
Of *Heathen* foes, that *Christian* FAITH defame:
Hence, here *presume* wee (by the Trump of Fame)
To call your *Aid* against the proud *Oppression*
Of th' *Infidel*, usurping FAITH'S Possession ;
That *Indian* Tyrant, onely *England's* Shame.
Thousands of *Ours* here hath Hee Captive taken,
Of all Degrees, kept under slavish Yoak.
Their *God*, their Good, *King*, Countrey, Friends for-
saken,
To follow *Folly*, and to feed on *Smoak.*
Bee GOD our *Guide*, S^t. GEORGE our *Generall;*
Wee shall *repell* Him, and *redeem* Them All.

At Your Lordship's Command,
J. S.
The humble Eccho of the Muses.

A double Anagram.

George Viliers : Sir George Viliers.

Re-give glories : Glorie-givers rise.

S*Ir:* Re-give glories : Glory-givers rise.

How fits your happy Fate, *your happy* Name !

Wherein a Precept *with a* Promise *lies,*

Presaging Good to gracefull BUCKINGHAM ;

For, be you Gratefull for your Dignities ;

GOD *and the* KING *will still* increase *the same.*

GOD, while you honour him, *will* honour *You :*

The KING *will* favour, *while you* serve *Him* true.

TO MY REVEREND AND WORTHY

Friend, Mr. William Loe, *Batchelor of Divinity.*

LO, what your Love and this *Chimera's* hate,
Care of my Friends, Compassion of my Kin ;
Zeal of God's Glory, Horror of this Sin ;
My Soveraign's Service, Honour of our State :
Lo, What all these had pow'r to propagate
(Perhaps, more hardy then my Hope had bin,
When first this Theam you gave mee to begin)
Besides my Way, beyond my Waining Date.
Lo, therefore, whether Well or Ill, I fare ;
Whether the doubtfull field I win or lose ;
In Fame, or Shame, you needs must have a Share,
Who on my Weakness did this weight impose.
Like *Moses* therefore lift your hands on hie,
That *Josuah's* hand may have the Victory.

A Warning-Piece.

R*Ight noble* Nobles, *Generous* Gentlemen,
Lovers of Honour, *and your* Countrey's *Weal;*
You 'll need no Warning *to avoid our* Peal ;
Nor are in Level *of our* Poudred *Pen :*
Nor those *that yet will* yeeld, *and turn agen*
From th' Idol-Service *of their* Smoakie Zeal,
To serve their GOD, *their* KING, *their* Common-weal :
Wee Shoot at Manners, *Wee would save the* Men.
But, Those rebellious *that will still* stand out
Under the Standard *of our Heathen Foe,*
With Pipe *and* Pudding *rampir'd round about,*
Puffing *and* Snuffing *at their threatned* Woe ;
At such, our Canon *shall Here thunder thick :*
Gunner, *your Lin-Stock ;* Come, *give fier quick.*
'Tis best Praise-worthy, to have pleas'd the Best :
This Wee indeavour ; and *defie the Rest,*

TOBACCO

BATTERED.

WHat-ever God *created*, first, was *good*,
    And good for Man, while Man uprightly
        stood :
But, falling Angels causing Man to fall,
His foule *Contagion* con-corrupted All
His fellow-Creatures, for his Sin accurst,
And for his sake transformed from their first ;
Till God and Man, Man's Leprie to re-cure,
By Death kill'd *Death*, re-making *All things* pure :
    But, *To the pure ;* not to the still-Profane,
Who (Spider-like) turne Blessings into Bane ;   10
Usurping (right-lesse, thank-lesse, need-lesse) here,
In wanton, willfull, wastefull, lustfull Cheer,
Earth's plenteous Crop ; which God hath onely giv'n
Unto his owne (Heires both of Earth and Heav'n)
Who onely (rightly) may with *Praise* and *Prayer*,
Enjoy th' increase of Earth, of Sea, and Ayre,
Fowle, Fish, & Flesh, Gems, Mettals, Cattel, Plants,
And namely (That which now no *Ingle* wants)
Indian TOBACCO, when due cause requires ;
Not the dry *Dropsie*, of *Phantastick* Squires.   20
    None therefore deem that I am now to learn
(How ever dim I many things discern)
Reason and Season to distinguish fit,
Th' *Use* of a thing, from the *Abuse* of it ;
Drinking from *drunking*, *Saccharum cum Sacco ;*
And *taking of*, from *taking all TOBACCO.*
    Yet out of high disdain and indignation,
Of that stern Tyrant's strangest Usurpation,
Once demi-Captive to his *puffing Pride*
(As millions are, too-wilfull foolifi'd)   30
Needs must I band against the *need-lesse Use*
Of Don TOBACCO, and his *foule Abuse :*
Which (though in *Inde* it be an Herbe indeed)
In *Europe* is no better then a Weed :
Which, to their *Idols*, *Pagans* sacrifize,
And *Christians* (here) doe well-nigh *Idolize :*
Which taking, *Heathens* to the Divels bow
Their Bodies, *Christians* even their Soules do vow.
Yet th' *Heathen* have, with th' *ill*, som *good* withall ;
Sith, Their *con-native*, 'tis *con-naturall.*   40
But, see the nature of abounding Sin,
Which more abounding Punishment doth win

For *knowing* Servants' wilfull Arrogance,
Than *silly* Strangers' savage Ignorance.
For, what to them is Meat and Med'cinable,
Is turn'd to us a Plague intolerable.
    Two smoakie Engines, in this latter Age
(*Satan's* short Circuit ; the more sharp his rage.)
Have been invented by too-wanted Wit,
Or, rather, vented from th' *Infernall Pit ;*   50
Guns and *Tobacco-pipes*, with *Fire* and *Smoak*,
(At least) a third part of Mankind to *choak :*
(Which happely, * th' *Apocalyps* fore-told)   Apoc. 3. 17.
Yet of the *Two*, Wee may (think I) be bold,
In some respects, to think the Last, the Worst,
(How-ever Both in their Effects accurst)
For, *Guns* shoot *from-ward*, onely at their Foen ;
Tobacco-pipes, *home-ward*, into their Owne
(When, for the Touch-hole, firing the wrong end,
Into our Selves the Poyson's force wee send) :   60
Those, in the Field, in brave and hostile manner ;
These, Cowardly, under a Covert Banner :
Those, with Defiance, in a threatfull Terror ;
These, with Affiance, in a wilfull Error :
Those, (though loud roaring, goaring-deep) quick-
        ridding ;
These, stilly stealing, longer Languours breeding :
Those, full of pain (perhaps) and fell despight ;
These, with false Pleasure, and a seem-delight
(As Cats with Mice, Spiders with Flies) full rife,
Pipe-playing, dallying, and deluding Life.   70
    Who would not wonder, in these Sunny-Dayes
(So bright illightned with the GOSPEL's Rayes)
Whence so much *Smoak*, and deadly Vapours come,
To dim and damne so much of *Christendome ?*
But, wee must ponder too, These dayes are Those
Wherein the Divell was to be let lose ;
And yawning broad Gate of that black *Abyss*
To be set ope, whose bottome bound-lesse is ;
That *Satan*, destin'd evermore to dwell
In *Smoakie* Fornace of that darksom Cell,   80
In *Smoak* and *darknesse*, might inure and train
His Own dear Minions, while they here remain ;
As roguing *Gypsies*, tanne their little Elves,
To make them tann'd and ugly like themselves.

Then in despight who-ever dare say Nay,
TOBACCONISTS, keep-on your course : you may,
If you continue in your *Smoakie* Ure,
The better far Hell's sulph'ry *Smoak* endure ;
And herein (as in All your other Evill)
Grow neerer still and liker to the Divell :   90
Save that the Divell (if hee could revoke)
Would flee from filthy and unhealthy *Smoak;*
Wherein (cast out of Heav'n for hellish pride)
Unwilling hee and forced, doth abide :
Which, herein worse then hee (the worst of Ill)
You long-for, lust-for, ly-for, dy-for still :
For, as the *Salamander* lives in Fire,
You live in *smoak*, and without *smoak* expire.

S Hould it be question'd (as right well it may)
    Whether Discovery of *AMERICA*,   100
That *New-found World*, have yeelded to our Old
More Hurt or Good : Till fuller Answer should
Decide the Doubt, and quite determine it,
Thus for the present might wee answer fit :
That, thereby Wee have (rightly understood)
Both giv'n and taken greater hurt then good :
And that on both sides, both for *Christians*
It had been better, and for *Indians*,
That onely good men to their Coast had com,
Or that the Evill had still staid at home.   110
    For, what our People have brought thence to us,
Is like the head-piece of a *Polipus*,
Wherein is (quoted by sage *Plutarch's* Quill)
A pest'lence great Good, and great Pest'lence Ill.
    We had from them, first, to augment our Stocks,
Two grand Diseases, *Scurvie* and the *Pocks :*
Then, *Two* great *Cordials* (for a Counterpeiz)
Gold and TOBACCO ; both which, many waies,
Have done more Mischief then the former twain ;
And all together brought more Losse then Gain.   120
    But true it is, wee had this Trash of Theirs,
Onely in Barter of our broken Wares.
Ours, for the most part, carried out but Sin ;
And, for the most part, brought but Vengeance in :
Their Fraight was *Sloth, Lust, Avarice, and Drink,*
(A Burthen able, with the Waight, to sink
The hugest Carrak ; yea, those hallowed *Twelve,*
Spain's great *Apostles*, even to over-whelve)
They carried *Sloth*, and brought home *Scurvie skin :*
They carried *Lust*, and brought home *Pocks* within : 130
They carried *Avarice*, and *Gold* they got :
They carried *Bacchus*, and *TOBACCO* brought.
Alas, poor *Indians !* that, but *English*, None
Could put them down in their owne Trade alone !
That None, but *English* (more alas ! more strange !)
Could justifie their pitifull Exchange !
    Of all the Plants that *Tellus'* bosom yeelds,
In groves, glades, gardens, marshes, mountains, fields,
None so pernicious to Man's Life is knowne,
As is TOBACCO, saving HEMP alone.   140
Betwixt which Two there seems great Sympathy
To ruinate poor *Adam's* Progeny :

For, in them Both, a *strangling* vertue note,
And both of them doe worke upon the Throte ;
The one, within it ; and without, the other ;
And th' one prepareth Work unto the tother;
For, There doe meet (I mean at *Gail* and *Gallowes*)
More of these beastly, base *Tobacco*-Fellowes,
Then else to any profane Haunt doe use
(Excepting still *The Play-house* and *The Stewes*)   150
Sith 'tis their common Lot (so double-choaked)
Just Bacon-like, to be *hang'd up* and *smoaked :*
A Destiny, as proper to befall
To morall Swine, as to Swine naturall.
    If there be any *Herb*, in any place,
Most opposite to GOD's good *Herb of grace*,
'Tis doubt-lesse This : and this doth plainly prove-it ;
That, for the most, most *grace-less* men doe love-it,
Or rather, doat most on this *wither'd Weed*,
Themselves as *wither'd* in all *gracious Deed.*   160
'Tis strange to see (and unto mee a Wonder)
When the prodigious strange abuse wee ponder
Of this unruly, rusty *Vegetall ;*
From modern *Symmists Jesu-Criticall*,
(Carping at us, and casting in our Dish,
Not Crimes, but ⌐Crums : as eating Flesh for
    Fish :)
W'heare, in this case, no Conscience-cases holier,
But, *like to like ; The Divel with the Collier.*
    For, a TOBACCONIST (I dare aver)
Is, first of all, a rank *Idolater*,   170
As any of th' *Ignatian Hierarchie :*
Next, as conformed to their Foppery,
Of burning Day-light, and Good-night, at Noon,
Setting up *Candles* to enlight the Sun :
And last, the Kingdom of NEW-BABYLON
Stands in a *Dark* and *Smoakie* Region,
So full of such variety of *Smoaks*,
That there-with-all all *Piety* it choaks.
    For, There is, first the *smoak* of Ignorance,
The *smoak* of Error, *smoak* of Arrogance,   180
The *smoak* of Merit super-er'gatory,
The *smoak* of *Pardon*, *smoak* of PURGATORY,
The *smoak* of Censing, *smoak* of *Thurifying*
Of Images, of *Satan's Fury-flying*,
The *smoak* of Stewes (for *smoaking* thence they com,
As horrid hot as torrid *Sodom*, som) :
Then, *smoak* of *Powder-Treason, Pistols, Knives*,
To blow-up Kingdoms, and blow-out Kings' lives ;
And lastly, too, TOBACCO's *smoakie*-Mists,
Which (comming from *Iberian* BAALISTS)   190
No small addition of Adustion fit
Bring to the *smoak* of the *Unbottom'd* Pit,
Yerst opened, first (*as openeth Saint* John)
By their ABADDON and APOLLYON.
    But, sith they are contented to admire
What they dislike not, if they not desire
(For, with good reason may wee ghess, that they
Who swallow Camels, swallow Gnatlings may) ;
'Tis ground enough for us, in this Dispute,
Their *Vanities*, thus obvious to refute   200

(Their *Vanities, Mysterious Mists* of *Rome*,
Which have so long be-*smoaked Christendome*).
And for the rest, it shall suffice to say,
Tobacconing is but a *smoakie* Play.
Strong Arguments against so weak a thing
Were needlesse, or unsuitable, to bring.
In this behalfe there needs no more be done,
Sith of it Selfe the same will vanish soon :
T' evaporate *This smoak*, it is enough,
But with a Breath the same aside to puff.   210

N Ow, my first puff shall but repell th' ill savour
    Of Place and Persons (of debaucht behaviour)
Where 'tis most frequent : Second, shew you will,
How little *Good* it doth : Third, how great *Ill*.
'Tis vented most in Taverns, Tippling-cots,
To Ruffians, Roarers, Tipsie-Tostie-pots,
Whose Custom is, between the *Pipe* and *Pot ;*
(Th' one Cold and Moist, the other dry and Hot)
To skirmish so (like Sword and Dagger-fight)
That 'tis not easie to determine right,   220
Which of their Weapons hath the Conquest got
Over their Wits ; the *Pipe*, or else the *Pot.*
Yet 'tis apparent, and by proof express,
Both stab and wound the Brain with *Drunkenness :*
For even the *Derivation* of the *Name*
Seems to allude and to include the same :
TOBACCO, as Τω Βακχω, one would say ;
To (Cup-god) *Bacchus dedicated ay.*
    And, for Conclusion of this Point, observe
The places which to these *Abuses* serve ;   230
How-ever, of them-selves noysom enough,
Are much more loathsom with the stench and Stuff
Extracted from their *limbeckt* Lips and Nose.
So that, the Houses, common Haunts of Those,
Are liker Hell then Heav'n : for, Hell hath *Smoak,*
Impenitent TOBACCONISTS to choak,
Though never dead : There shall they have their fill :
In Heav'n is none, but Light and Glory still.
    Next : Multitudes them daily hourly drown
In this black Sea of *Smoak*, tost up and down   240
In this vast *Ocean*, of such *Latitude*,
That *Europe* onely cannot all include,
But out it rushes, over-runs the Whole,
And reaches, wel-nigh round, from *Pole* to *Pole ;*
Among the *Moors, Turks, Tartars, Persians,*
And other *Ethnicks* (full of Ignorance
Of GOD and *Good :*) and, if wee shall look home
To view (and rew) the State of CHRISTENDOM ;
Upon this Point, wee may This *Riddle* bring ;
The Subject hath more Subjects then the King :   250
For, Don TOBACCO hath an ampler Raign
Then Don PHILIPPO, the Great *King of Spain*
(In whose Dominions, for the most, it growes).
Nay, shall I say (O Horror to suppose !)
Heathnish TOBACCO (almost every where)
In *Christendom* (CHRIST'S *outward Kingdom* here)
Hath more *Disciples* then CHRIST hath (I fear) ;

More Suit, more Service (Bodies, Souls, and Good)
Then *Christ* that bought us wth his precious bloud.
O Great TOBACCO ! greater then Great *Can,*   260
Great *Turke*, Great *Tartar*, or Great *Tamberlan !*
With Vulturs' wings Thou hast (and swifter yet
Then an *Hungarian Ague, English Sweat*)
Through all Degrees flown far, nigh, up and down ;
From court to cart ; from *Count* to country Clown,
Not scorning *Scullions, Coblers, Colliers,*
Jakes-farmers, Fidlers, Ostlers, Oysterers,
Roagues, Gypsies, Players, Pandars, Punks, and All
What *common Scums*, in *common-Sewers* fall.
For, all, as *Vassals*, at thy beck are bent,   270
And breathe by Thee, as their *new Element.*
Which well may prove thy *Monarchy* the Greater ;
Yet prove not Thee to be a whit the better ;
But rather Worse : for, *Hell's* wide-open Road
Is easiest found, and by the most still trod.
Which, even the *Heathen* had the Light to know
By Arguments, as many times they show.
    Here may wee also gather (for a need)
Whether TOBACCO be an *Herb* or *Weed :*
And whether the excessive Use be fit,   280
Or good or bad ; by those that favour it :
Weeds, wilde and wicked, mostly entertain it ;
Herbs, holesome *Herbs*, and holy mindes disdain it.
    If then *Tobacconing* be good ; How is't,
That lewdest, loosest, basest, foolishest,
The most unthrifty, most intemperate,
Most vitious, most debaucht, most desperate,
Pursue it most ? The Wisest and the Best
Abhor it, shun it, flee it, as the Pest,
Or piercing Poyson of a Dragon's Whisk,   290
Or deadly Ey-shot of a Basilisk.
    If *Wisdome* baulk it, must it not be *Folly ?*
If *Vertue* hate it, is it not unholy ?
If Men of Worth, and Mindes right *generous,*
Discard it, scorn it ; is 't not *scandalous ?*
And (to conclude) is it not to the Divell
Most pleasing ; pleasing so (most) the most Evill ?

M Y second *Puff*, is Proof *How Little Good*
    This *Smoak* hath don (that ever hear I cou'd).
For, first, there 's none that takes *Tobacco* most,   300
Most usually, most earnestly can boast
That the excessive and continuall use
Of this *dry Suck-at* ever did produce
Him any Good, Civill, or Naturall,
Or Morall Good, or Artificiall :
Unless perhaps they will alledge, It drawes
Away the Ill which still it Self doth cause.
Which course (mee thinks) I cannot liken better
Then to an *Vsurer's* kindness to his *Debter ;*
Who under show *of lending*, still subtracts   310
The *Debter's* Owne, and then his own exacts ;
Till at the last hee utterly confound-him,
Or leave him worse and weaker then he found-him.
    Next, if the Custome of *Tobacconing*
Yeeld th' Users any *Good* in any thing ;

Either they *have* it, or they *hope* it prest
(By proof and practise, taking still the best) :
For, none but Fools will them to Ought beslave,
Whence Benefit they neither *hope* nor *have.*

   Therefore, yet farther (as a *Questionist*)   320
I must enquire of my TOBACCONIST,
Why, if a *Christian* (as some somtimes seem)
Beleeving GOD, waiting all *Good* from Him,
And unto Him all *Good* again referring ;
Why (to eschew th' Ungodly's *Grace-less* erring)
Why pray they not ? Why praise they not his Name
For *hoped Good*, and *Good* had by this Same ?
As all men doe, or ought to doe for All
The Gifts and *Goods* that from his *Goodnesse* fall.
Is 't not, because they neither *hope*, nor *have*,   330
Good (hence) to thank God for, nor farther *crave :*
But, as they had it from the *Heathen*, first ;
So, *Heathnishly* they use it still, accurst :
And (as som jest of *Oysters*) This is more
Vngodly Meat, both *After* and *Before.*

   Lastly, if all Delights of all Mankind
Be *Vanity, Vexation* of the Minde ;
All under Sun : must not TOBACCO be,
Of Vanities, the vainest *Vanity ?*
If *Solomon*, the wisest earthly Prince   340
That ever was before, or hath bin since ;
Knowing all Plants, and them perusing All,
From *Cedar* to the *Hyssop* on the Wall ;
In none of all professeth, that hee found
A firm content, or Consolation sound :
Can wee suppose, that any Shallowling
Can find *much Good*, in oft *Tobacconing ?*

M Y Third and last *Puff* points at the *great Evill*
   This noisom *Vapour* works through wily divell.
If wee may judge ; if knowledge may be had   350
By their Effects, how things be *good* or *bad ;*
Doubtlesse, th' Effects of this pernicious *Weed*
Be many *bad*, scarce any *good*, indeed :
Nor doth a man scarce any *Good* contain,
But of this *Evill* justly may complain ;
As thereby, made in every Part the worse,
In Body, Soule, in Credit, and in Purse.

F Or, first of all, it falls on his *Good-Name ;*
   And so be-smears, and so *be-smoaks* the same,
That never after scarce discerned is 't.   360
Rare *good Report* of a TOBACCONIST :
Where, if to take it, were a vertuous thing,
'Twould to the Takers Commendation bring ;
And som-what grace them (tho they else were bad)
Or hide a little, the Defects they had :
But from their Credit rather it abates,
And their Disgraces rather aggravates :
And how-much better that they were before,
It stinks the worse, and stains their name the more.

   For, if a Swearer or a Swaggerer,   370
A Drunkard, Dicer, or Adulterer,

Prove a TOBACCONIST, it is not much :
'T is suitable, 'tis well-beseeming Such
(No lesse then flaring, garish, whorish Tire,
Which now-adayes most *Mad-dames* most desire :
Owl-fac't *Chaprones*, Cheeks *painted*, *Izland* Tress,
Bum *Bosse*-about, with *broad deep-naked* Brests ;
Borrow'd and brought from loose *Venetians*,
Becoms *Pickt-hatch*, and *Shoreditch Courtizans*).
Not that *Tobacconing* is not amisse ;   380
But that the bright Noon of their better Vice,
Spred far and wide, doth darken and put down
TOBACCO-*taking*, and its Twilight drown.

   But, let it be of any truly said,
Hee 's *great, religious, learned, wise*, or *staid ;*
But hee is lately turn'd TOBACCONIST :
O ! what a Blur ! what an Abatement is 't
'T is like a handfull from *Augæus'* Stable,
Cast in the Face of *Beautie's* fairest Table.
Whence it appears, This too-too to frequent,   390
It is not *good ;* no, not *indifferent.*

   It best becomes a *Stage*, or else a *Stewes*,
Or *Dicing-house*, where All Disorders use.
It ill beseems a *Church, Colledge*, or *Court*,
Or any place of any civill sort :
It fits Blasphemers, Ruffians, Atheists,
Damn'd *Libertines*, to be TOBACCONISTS :
Not *Magistrates*, not *Ministers*, not *Schollers*,
(Who are, or should be, Sin's severe Comptrollers)
Nor any wise and sober personage,   400
Of Gravity, of *Honesty*, of Age.

   It were the fittest Furniture (that may)
For Divell, in a Picture or a Play,
To represent him with a fiery Face,
His Mouth and Nostrils puffing *Smoak* apace,
With staring Eyes, and in his grizely Gripe
An over-growne, great, long TOBACCO-*Pipe.*
Which sure (me thinks) the most TOBACCONIST
Must needs approve, and even applaud the Jest ;
But much more *Christians* hence observe how evill 410
It them becoms, that so becoms the Divell.
And therefore, think this *Weed*, a *Drug* for *Jews*
More fit by far [who did so foule abuse
(Base rheumy Rascals) with their Spawlings base,
Our loving SAVIOUR's lovely-reverend Face,
Whom (wilfull-blinde, stiff-necked stupefi'd)
They spet on, scorned, scourged, *Crucifi'd*]
Then for us *Christians*, who his Name adore :
Whom by his *Death* hee doth to *Life* restore.

   If, notwithstanding all that hath been said,   420
TOBACCONISTS will still hold on their Trade,
And by their practice still hold up their Name,
Though *Jews*, though *Divels* better suit the
    same ;
I 'll say no more but onely This, of This :
Henceforth let none whose meaner Lot it is
To live in *Smoak ; Lime-burners, Alchimists,*
Brick-makers, Brewers, Colliers, Kitchinists ;
Let *Salamanders, Swallows, Bacon-flitches,*
Red-Sprats, red-Herings, and like *Chimny*-wretches,

Think no Disparagement, nor hold them base :   430
TOBACCONISTS their Company will grace,
And teach them make a Vertue of Necessity,
Turning their *Smoak* into a *grace*-fool-*Assity*.

NExt the *Good-name*, now let the *Body* show
    What wrongs to it from out TOBACCO flow :
For, as That is Man's baser Part indeed,
It is most basely handled by this *Weed*.
    And first (as was significantly said
Before our *Soveraign*, by an *Oxford* Head)
TOBACCO *Smoak* into the *Parlour* puts,   440
And basest Office in the best Room shuts,
While to the Head it doth exhale and hoist
The Bodie's filthy and superfluous Moist ;
Causing a moist Brain, by unceast supply
Of Rheums still drawn to th' bodie's *Stillary :*
Which in experience, and in Reason, make
Men most unapt deep things to undertake.
For, for the most part, shallow are the Wits,
Conceits and Counsels of TOBACCONISTS.
Sith *Wisdome dwels in Dry :* Her proper Seat   450
Is a dry Brain, embatteld well with Heat.
    Also, it fries and dries away the Bloud
(As did that *Persian* the *Euphratean* Floud,
To conquer *Babylon*) by whose *incrasion*,
The *Vitall Spirits*, in an unwonted fashion,
Are bay'd, and barred of their Passage due
Through all the veins, their vigour to renue :
So that the Humours (as all out of frame)
Tending to putrefie and to inflame,
Fire the whole house ; from whence there follows ever   460
A dangerous, if not a deadly *Fever*.
    Lastly, this boyling, broyling of the Bloud,
Breeds much adusted *Melancholy*-Mood
(*Satan's* fit Saddle, from their sullen Cell,
To ride in poste, his wretched Slaves to Hell,
With two keen spurres (too-quick in their Effect)
Th' one of Excesse, the other of Defect ;
A violent *Passion*, pushing *Reason* back,
Or fell *Despaire* when *Conscience* is awake.)
For, as of all *Insensibles*, hath none   470
More *Melancholy* and *Adustion*,
Then *Chimnies* have ; What kind of *Chimny* is 't
Lesse *Sensible* then a TOBACCONIST ?
And in receiving *Smoake*, sith th' are so equall ;
Can their *Adustion* then be much unequall ?
Thus then the Habit of TOBACCONING,
Makes one more *Chimny-like* then any thing.
    Som also think it causeth exsiccation
(As of the Bloud) of Seed of generation ;
By th' acrimony stirring more to covet,   480
Then fruitfully producing Issue of-it ;
Whence, wee may learn to marvell so much lesse,
That (for the most) our *Gentles*, that professe
TOBACCONISME, love *Lemman*-Sauce so well ;
Or that such Legions of the Base *pel-mel*,
Under the Standard of TOBACCO, use
To *Turn-bull* first, then to *Our Bartholmews*.

And where there have been many great inquests
To finde the Cause Why Bodies still grow less,
And daily neerer to the *Pigmie's* Size ;   490
This, among many Probabilities,
May pass for one : that their *Progenitours*
Did gladly foment their Interiours
With wholesome food, unmixed, moderate,
And timely Liquors duely temperate :
But, now-adayes, Their Issue inly choak
And dry them up (like Herrings) with This *smoake :*
For, Herrings, in the Sea, are large and full,
But shrink in bloating and together pull :
Whence, in effect, Smoak unto Smoak referring,   500
TOBACCONISTS are not unlike Red Herring.
    Undoubtedly beyond all Moderation
It dries the Body, robs of irrigation
The thirsty parts ; so that the bowels cry
For Moist and Cold, to temper Hot and Dry :
Whence, th' Elementall Qualities of Theirs,
In faction, fall together by the Eares.
For, in the Herb excesse of Dry and Hot
Drawes-in excesse of Cold-Moist from the Pot ;
For which they troup to th' Ale-house shortly after,   510
As rats-ban'd Rats doe hie them to the water.
And yet, their liquid Cooler cures them not,
No more then water doth the baned Rat :
For th' Heat and Drought of th' *Herb American*
Being intensive (fitter call'd Man-bane)
The one dries-up the *Humour Radicall*,
The other drowns the *Calor Naturall*.
    But the most certain and apparent Ill
Is an Ill Habit which doth haunt them still ;
Transforming *Nature* from her native Mould :   520
For, *Custom* wee another *Nature* hold.
And this vile *Custom* is so violent,
And holds his *Customers* at such a Bent,
That tho thereby more hurt then good they doubt :
To dye for it, they cannot live without.
Which doubtlesse, is a miserable State :
For, Men are surely the more fortunate,
Of fewer Creatures that they stand in need :
More, but more Bondage, and lesse freedom breed.
A House, that must have many props and staies,   530
Is neerer Fall, and faster it decayes :
Variety and surfeit feed the *Spittle*,
And fill the Grave. *Nature's content with little.*
    Why then should Man, *living* and *rationall*,
Beslave himselfe to a dead *Vegetall ?*
Why demi-heav'nly, and most free by Birth,
Should hee be bound unto this *Childe* of Earth ?
Why, Lord of Creatures, should Hee serve : at least
Why such a Creature, baser then a Beast ?

OFt had I seen *Fools* of all sorts frequent it,   540
    Fooles of all Size, *Fooles* of all Sexes haunt it,
Fooles of all Colours, *Fooles* of all Complexions,
Fooles of all Fashions, *Fooles* of all Affections,
Fooles naturall, *Fooles* artificiall,
Fooles rich and poor, young *Fools*, old *Fools*, and all ;

Whom, *Foole*, I pitied, for their wilfull folly ;
Supposing, none discreetly Wise (or Holy)
Could be entangled with so fond a thing,
As is the habit of *Tobacconing.*
For, what Discretion, or what Wisedome can   550
Think *Physick* Food, or *Med'cine* Meat for Man?
  I rather thought *Ulysses* rather would
Have stopt his ears, eyes, hands, and mouth with-hold
From such a *Cyrcean* Drug ; whose working strange,
Would soon his best into a Beast exchange.
But when I saw some wise ones snared-in
This *Spanish Cobweb* (Satan's speciall Gin)
And that so fast, they cannot when they would
Get out again ; or will not if they could :
Wisdome, mee thought, must vary much ; or else   560
This *Ware* is *spiced* with som forrain Spels,
So to bewitch the Wise (needlesse, and nilling)
To take and love ; and not to leave it, willing.
For, those that say and sweare they even abhor it,
Cannot abandon, but thus bandy for it :
  'Tis good (say they) 'tis speciall good for Rheums ;
  Exhales grosse humours, their excesse consumes ;
  And voids withall, all Inconvenience
  There-on depending, or descending Thence.
Which should I grant, it must be yet with Clauses   570
Of needfull Caution, suitable to Causes ;
When time requireth Preparation fit
To rarifie congealed Rags of it ;
Which by the Heat and Drynesse, probably,
This Plant performes in mediocrity :
Or else where the aboundant Quantity,
Dangerous Effect, Malignant Quality,
Of over-moistures, aske *Evacuation,*
To free the parts from totall Inundation.
  How-be-it, many safer Meanes there are,   580
Better and fitter in themselves by farre ;
More certaine, more direct ; with lesse adoe,
Lesse Cost, lesse Damage, and lesse Danger too
Then *Don* TOBACCO's damnable Infection,
Slutting the Body, slaving the Affection.
  'T were therefore better somwhat else to seek,
Then rest in this so worthy of dis-like ;
Sith, curing thus one small Infirmity,
It doth create a greater Malady,
When ther-by freed (perhaps) from *Rheumes*, we fal 590
In Bondage of this *Custom* capitall ;
For they that *Physick* to a *Custom* bring,
Bring their *Disease* too, to accustoming.
Perpetuall *Physick* must of force imply
Perpetuall *Sicknesse ;* or deepe Foolerie
Compos'd of *Antick* and of *Phrantick* too :
For, where's no *Sickness*, what should *Med'cine* do ?

THus for the *Body :* Now, the *Soule* divine
  With this wilde *Goose-grasse* of the *Perusine,*
Hath foure great Quarrels, in foure-fold respect 600
Of her foure Faculties ; the *Intellect,*
The *Memory*, the *Will*, the *Conscience ;*
All which are wronged, if not wounded, Thence.

  First, in th' *Intellect*, it d' outs the Light,
Darkens the House, th' understanding's Sight ;
Through never-ceast succession of *Humidity*
The Dam of dulnesse, Mother of *Stupidity ;*
Making Man's generous Brain (best, dry and hot)
Lie drown'd and driveling like a Changeling Sot.
Why then should Man, to put out *Reason's* Eye,   610
Suffer his Soule in *Smoakie* Lodge to lye?
For, though some others, and my Selfe by proofe
(When scornefully I tooke it but in *Snuffe*) ;
Have thereby somtimes found some benefit ;
Superfluous humors from the Brain to quit,
To cleer the Voyce and cheer the *Phantasie*,
Which for the present, it did seem supply :
Yet doth the *Custom* (as wee likewise finde)
Dis-nerve the Body, and dis-apt the Minde.
  Next, It decayes and marres the *Memory*,   620
And brings it to strange Imbecillity,
By still attraction of continuall *Moist,*
Which from the lower parts it wonts to hoist :
For, though best *Memory* dwell in a Brain
Moist-moderate ; Yet over-*moist*, againe
Makes it so laxe, so diffluent and thin,
That nothing can be firmly fixt there-in ;
But instantly it slides and slips away,
As weary heels on wet and slippery Clay.
For proofe whereof : None more forgetfull is   630
Of GOD and *Good*, then are *Tobacconists.*
  Touching th' *Affections*, they are tyr'd no lesse
By This fell Tyrant's insolent Excesse :
For the *Adustion* of th' inherent *Heat,*
Drought, Acrimony (Tartar-like) doth fret ;
Makes men more sudden and more heed-less heady
More sullen sowr, more stubbornely-unsteady,
More apt to wrath, to wrangle, and to braule ;
To give and take a Great offence for Small ;
Cause-less Rejoycing, and as cause-lesse Sory,   640
Exceeding-Mournefull, and excessive-Merry :
Whence growes, in fine, excessive Griefe and
    Fear ;
For Dumpier none then the *Tobacconer :*
None sadder then the gladdest of their Host ;
None hating more then hee that loved most ;
None fearing more, none daunted more then such
As, in a *Passion*, rather dar'd too-much.
For, *Relatives inseparable dwell :*
And Contraries their Contraries expell.
And (with th' *old Poet*) *'Tis the Cox-comb Course,* 650
Flying a Fault, to fall into a Worse.
  But, if they say, that sometimes, taking it,
The Minde is freed from some instant Fit
Of Anger, Griefe, or Feare ; Experience tells
It is but like some of our Tooth-ake Spells,
Which for the present seem to ease the Pain,
But after, double it with more Rage again ;
Because a little, for the time, it drawes,
But leaves behinde the very Root and Cause.
  Lastly, the *Conscience* (as it is the best)   660
This *Indian* Weed doth most of all molest ;

Loading it dayly with such Weight of Sin,
Whereof the least shall at the last com-in
To strict Account : the Losse of precious hours,
Neglect of GOD, of *Good*, of Us, of Ours :
Our ill Example, prodigall Excess,
Vain Words, vain Oaths, Dice, Daring, Drunkenness,
Sloath, Jesting, Scoffing, turning Night to Day,
And Day to Night ; Disorder, Disaray ;
Places of Scorn and publick Scandall hanting ;   670
Persons of base and beastly life frequenting ;
Theeves, Unthrifts, Ruffians, Robbers, Roarers, Drab-
     bers,
Bibbers, Blasphemers, Shifters, Sharkers, Stabbers,
This is the *Rendez-vous*, These are the Lists,
Where doe incounter most TOBACCONISTS ;
Wherein they walk, like a blinde Mill-horse round
In the same Circle, on the selfe same ground ;
Forgetting how daies, months, and yeers do passe ;
No more regarding, then an Ox or Asse,
How *Age* growes on, how *Death* attendeth them,   680
GOD knowes how neer ; (*Whom* on each side behem
A late *Repentance*, or a flat *Despair*)
And after *That*, a noisom stinking Air
Of their infamous rotten *Memory*
With Men on Earth ; in Heav'n with GOD on hye
A Fearfull *Doom ;* and finally in Hell,
Infinity of Fiery *Torments* fell.
     The Last and least of all TOBACCO-harms,
Is to the *Purse :* which yet it so becharms,
That, Juggler-like, it jests-out all the Pelf,   690
And makes a Man a *Pick-purse* to himselfe.
For, as by This, th' *Iberian Argonauts*
May be suppos'd (even among serious Thoughts)
T' have kill'd more Men then by their Martyrdom,
Or *Massacre* (which yet to Millions com)
So, by the Same they have undone more Men,
Then *Vsury* (which takes from Hundred, Ten,)
And no-where more then in *This witched Isle :*
Woe to their Frauds, Woe to us Fools, the-while.

Ow-many *Gentles*, not of meanest Sort   700
H   (Whose Fathers liv'd in honourable Port,
For Table, Stable, and Attendance fit ;
Loving their Country, and belov'd of it,)
Leaving their Neighbours, flee from their Approach ;
And, for the most, keep House in a *Caroach*
(Hell's new-found Cradles ! where are rockt asleep
Mischiefs that make our Common-weal to weep).
Or in som *Play-house*, or some *Ordinary*,
Or in som piece of som *Vn-sanctuary ;*
Where, through his *Pipe-puft Nose* more *Smoake* they
     wave,   710
Then all the *Chimnies* their great Houses have ;
Consuming more, in their *Obscure Obscænity*,
On *Smoak* and *Smock*, with their *appendent Vanity*,
Then their brave Elders did, when they maintain'd
Honour at home, and forrain Glory gain'd.
     How do they rack, and wrack, and grate, and grinde,
Shuffle and cut, wrangle, and turn, and winde,

Borrow and beg (under a Courtly Cloak)
And all too-little for this liquorish *Smoak !*
     Alas the while ! that men thus needs will be   720
Begger'd, undone (of no *Necessity*)
In Body, Minde, and Meanes ; unapt, unable
For any *Good*, through this so needlesse Bable.
     For, What a Folly, through the Nose to puff
Th' whole Bodie's Portion in this idle stuff ?
Or, what need any with TOBACCO, more
Now meddle, then his Ancestors before ?
Who knew it not, but had, without it, Health,
Liv'd long and lusty, in aboundant Wealth.
Or, what is any, when he all hath spent,   730
The better for This dear Experiment ?
Which now-adayes a number daily finde
Like *Alchimie* (though in another Kinde)
To circulate, and calcinate (at length)
Insensibly (TOBACCO hath such strength)
Manours, Demains, Goods, Cattell, Elm and Oak,
Gold, Silver, All, to *Ashes* and to *Smoak ;*
While all, too busie blowing at the Coal,
Deject their Body, and neglect their Soule.
     For, O ! What place is left to *Christianity*   740
'Mongst such a Crew (nay, almost to *Humanity*)
Where Oaths, Puf-snuffing, Spauling-Excrement,
Are *reall Parts* of GENTLES' Complement ?
     And, for our *Vulgar*, by whose bold Abuse
TOBACCONING hath got so generall Use ;
How mightily have They since multiply'd
Taverns, Tap-houses ! where, on every side,
Most sinfully hath Mault been sunken heer
In nappy *Ale*, and *double-double-Beer ;*
Invincible in a Threefold Excesse ;   750
Strong *Drink*, strong *Drinking*, and strange *Drunken-
     nesse :*
Which on the Land hath brought so visibly
So great a Mischief, so past Remedy,
That Thousands daily into Beggery sink
Through *Idlenesse ;* in wilfull *Debt* for *Drink*.
Nor can the Law's severest curb keep-in
This coltish, common, priviledged Sin.
     Then (shallow Reptile, superficiall Gnat)
Why doe I humme ? why doe I hisse there-at ?

Ut, awefull *Justice* will with keener Edge   760
B   Clip short (I hope) this sawcy Priviledge ;
And at one blow cut-off this *Over-Drinking*,
And ever *Dropsie*, of TOBACCO-*stinking*,
When *Our* ALCIDES (though at *Peace* with men,
At war with Vices) as His *armed Pen*
[Among the LABOURS of his *Royall* hand,
Where *Piety* and *Prudence* (joyntly) stand
Eternall PILLERS to His glorious *Name ;*
Unto all Times to testifie the same,
BRITAIN'S right *Beau-Clerk*, both for *Word and*
     Writ :   770
The Miracle, The ORACLE *of Wit :*
For Knowledge, Judgement, Method, Memory,
Divine and Morall ENCYCLOPÆDIE]

Hath, as with Arrowes, from His sacred Sides,
All-ready chac't These *stinking Stymphalides;*
Shall, with the *Trident* of some sharp *Edict,*
Severe enacted, executed strict,
Clense all the Staules of This *Augæan* Dung,
Which hath so long corrupted Old and Young :
Or, at the least, impose so deep a *Taxe*   780
On all these *Ball, Leafe, Cane,* and *Pudding-packs :*
On Seller, or on Buyer, or on Both,
That from Henceforth the *Commons* shall be loath
(Unwilling-wise) with that *grave Greek* to *buy*
Smoak and *Repentance at a Price so high.*
    If, notwithstanding, yet some Wealthy will,
Needs poyson, and undoe them with it, still ;
It shall be onely some of Those profane
Loose *Prodigals* (their Countrie's Blot and Bane)
Best to be spar'd, least to be mist ; whose Lands   790
(If any left) will come to Wiser hands
Then such weake *Ninnies,* needing *Wardship* yet ;
Not for their want of *Age,* but want of *Wit.*
    Avidius Cassius (as *Lampridius* showes)
Did first invent, and first of all impose
That uncouth Maner of tormenting Folk
On a high beame to smother them with *Smoak :*
Where, had TOBACCO bin then known, he need
But have enjoyn'd them to have ta'n the Weed.   800
    But, with more Reason and more Equity,
Severus Cæsar when hee did discry
The double-dealing of *Vetronius*
[A Cousening Courtier (Such are none with Us)
A Jack-of-both-sides, with both hands to play
(As now-adayes some Lawyers doe, they say)
Faining great Favour with his Soveraign,
To take great Bribes of many, to obtaine

Great Suits ; for whom his Prince he never mov'd]
Aloud complain'd of, and apparent prov'd ;
Caus'd his false *Minion* with this *Doom* to choak,   810
Let the Smoak-seller suffocate with Smoak :
Which our *Smoak*-Merchants would no lesse befit ;
TOBACCO-*Mungers,* Bringers-in of it :
Which yeerly costs (they say, by *Audit* found)
Of better Wares an hundred Thousand pound.
    And, if the *Sentence* of this *Heathen Prince,*
On that *Impostor,* for his *Impudence,*
Were just : How juster will the Heav'nly GOD,
Th' *Eternall,* punish with infernall Rod :
In Hel's dark Fornace (with black *Fumes,* to choak)   820
Those, that on Earth will still *offend in Smoak ?*
Offend their Friends, with a most *un-Respect :*
Offend their Wives and Children, with Neglect :
Offend the Eyes, with foul and loathsom spawlings :
Offend the Nose, with filthy Fumes' exhalings :
Offend the Eares, with loud lewd *Execrations :*
Offend the Mouth, with ugly Excreations :
Offend the *Sense,* with stupefying *Sense :*
Offend the Weake, to follow their *Offence :*
Offend the Body, and offend the Minde :   830
Offend the *Conscience* in a fearefull knide :
Offend their *Baptisme,* and their *Second Birth :*
Offend the *Majesty* of Heav'n and Earth.
    Woe to the World because of such *Offences ;*
So voluntaire, so voyd of all pretences
Of all *Excuse* (save *Fashion, Custom, Will*)
In so apparent, proved, granted, *Ill.*
Woe, woe, to them by Whom *Offences* come ;
So scandalous to All our CHRISTENDOM.

F I N I S.

NOTES AND ILLUSTRATIONS.

DEDICATION-SONNETS . . . '*Earle of Buckingham*'—*the* historic Buckingham, killed by Felton : '*William Loe*' —see a full Memoir of him prefixed to his Poems in Fuller Worthies' Library Miscellanies ; also our Introduction.

Line 7, '*Leprie*' = leprosy : l. 18, '*Ingle*' = fireside, *e.g.* Fergusson's 'Farmer's *Ingle,*' prototype of Burns's Cottar's Saturday Night : l. 87, '*Ure*' = use : l. 128, '*over-whelve*'—odd spelling, *r.g. :* l. 164, '*Symmists*'—see Glossarial Index, *s.v. :* l. 260, '*Can*' = Cam ? or Khan ? l. 454, '*incrasion*'—see Glossarial Index, *s.v. :* l. 499, '*bloating*' = bloaters : l. 643, '*Dumpier*' = given to dumps or despondency : l. 705, '*Caroach*'—see Glossarial Index on this odd bit : l. 824, '*Spawlings :*' cf. l. 742, = foul spittle.   G.

L A C R Y M Æ

L A C R Y M A R U M :

O R

The Spirit of Teares,

DISTILLED

FOR THE UNTIMELY DEATH

OF

The Incomparable Prince,

H E N R I E

(L A T E)

Prince of Wales.

BY

Josuah Sylvester.

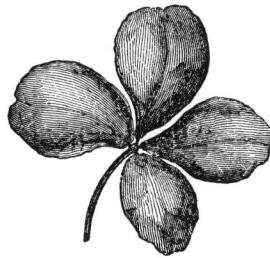

Fide ivstvs vivet: Deus providebit.

LACRYMAE
LACRYMARUM.
A Funerall Elegie.

The Argument, in an EPITAPH.

H Ere lies (Drie Eyes read not this EPITAPH.)
   Here lies Great-Britain's *Stay, Great* Jacob's
Staffe :
The stately Top-bough of Imperiall Stemme,
World's richest Jewell, Nature's *rarest Gemme,*
Mirrour of Princes, *Miracle of Youth,*
All Vertues' Pattern, Patron of all Truth ;
Refuge of Armes, ample Reward of Arts,
Worth's *Comforter, milde Conquerour of Hearts :*
The Churche's *Tower, the Terrour of the Pope,*
Herbick HENRY, *Atlas of our Hope.*   10

H Ow-ever, short of Others' *Art* and *Wit,*
   I know my powers for such a Part unfit ;
And shall but light my Candle in the *Sun,*
To doe a work shall be so better *Done :*
Could *Tears* and *Fears* give my Distractions leave,
Of sobbing words a *sable Web* to weave ;
Could *Sorrow's Fulness* give my voice a vent ;
How would, how should, my saddest *Verse* lament,
In deepest Sighes (in stead of sweetest Songs)
This loss (alas !) which unto All belongs !   20
To All, alas ! though chiefly to the Chief ;
His *royall Parents,* Principals in grief :
To All the *Peers,* to all *Confederate,*
To All the *Church,* to all the *Christian State :*
To all the Godly *now,* and *future* far :
To all the *World ;* except S. P. Q. R.
To all together, and to Each a-part,
That lives, and loves *Religion, Armes,* or *Art :*
To all abroad ; but, to Us most of all
That neerest stood to my *High Cedar's* fall :   30
But, more then most, to *Mee,* that had no *Prop*
But *Henry's Hand,* and but in *Him,* no *Hope :*
In Whom, with *Nature, Grace,* and *Fortune* met,
To consummate a *Prince,* as *Good* as *Great :*
In Whom, the Heav'ns were pleas'd to shew the Earth
A richer *Jewell* then the World was worth,
Or worthy of : therefore, no more to make
So rare a *Piece,* His precious Mould they brake.

O sudden Change ! O sad *Vicissitude !*
O ! how the Heav'ns our Earthly Hopes delude !   40
O ! what is firm beneath the Firmament !
O ! what is constant here that gives Content !
What Trust in Princes ! O ! what Help in Man,
Whose *dying* life is but in length a span !
Melting, as Snow, before the Mid-day Sun ;
Past, as a Poste, that speedy by doth run ;
Swift, as the Current of the quickest Stream ;
Vain, as a Thought ; forgotten, as a Dream.
   O Dearest *Henry,* Heav'n and Earth's *Delight !*
O clearest Beam of *Vertues,* Rising bright !   50
O purest Spark of *Pious* Princely *Zeal !*
O surest Ark of *Justice'* sacred Weal !
O gravest Presage of a *Prudent* Kinde !
O bravest Message of a *Valiant* Minde !
O All-admir'd, *Benign* and *Bounteous !*
O All-desir'd (right) *Panaretus !*
Panaretus (*All-vertuous*) was thy Name ;
Thy Nature such : such ever be thy Fame.
   O Dearest ! Cleerest ! Purest ! Surest *Prop !*
O Gravest ! Bravest ! Highest ! Nighest *Hope !*   60
O ! how untimely is this Sun gone down !
This *Spark* put out ! This *Ark* (as) overthrown !
This Presage crost ! This Message lost and left !
This Prop displac't ! This Hope of all, bereft !
O ! how, unkinde ! how, graceless ! how, ingrate !
Have *Wee* cut-off Thy likely longer Date !
   For, were *this stroak* from Heav'n's immediat hand,
Or (by Heav'n's leave) from Hell's suborned Band
Of *Romulides* (what dare not they presume,
If this, that Sea a sulph'ry Sea consume ?)   70
How-e'r it were, *Wee* were the *Moving Cause*
That sweet *Prince Henry* breath no longer draws.
Wee all (alas !) have had our hands herein :
And each of us hath, by some *cord of sin,*
Hal'd down from Heav'n from *Justice'* awfull Seat,
This *Heavy Judgement* (wᶜʰ yet more doth threat.)
   Wee Clergy first, who too-too-oft have stood
More for the Church-goods, then the Churche's good :
   Wee Nobles next, whose Title, ever strong,
Can hardly offer Right, or Suffer Wrong :   80

Wee Magistrates, who, mostly, weak of sight,
Are rather fain to feel then see the Right :
   Wee Officers, whose *Price* of every *Place*
Keeps *Vertue* out, and bringeth *Vice* in grace :
   Wee Gentry then, who rack, and sack, and sell,
To swim, like *Sea-crabs* in a *foure-wheel'd Shell :*
   Wee Courtiers next, who *French-Italianate*,
Change (with the *Moon*) our *Fashion, Faith,* and
   Fate :
   Wee Lawyers then, who *Dedalizing* Law,
And deadly *Conscience*, like the Horse-leach draw : 90
   Wee Citizens, who, seeming *Pure* and Plain,
Beguile our Brother, make our *god* our GAIN :
   Wee Countrymen, who slander Heav'n and Earth
As Authors of our *Artificiall Dearth :*
   Wee Purveyours, last, who, taking ten for two,
Rob both, at once, our *Prince* and *People* too :
   All, briefly all, all Ages, Sexes, Sorts,
In *Countries, Cities, Benches, Churches, Courts,*
(All *Epicures, Wit-wantons, Athëists,*
Mach'-Aretines, Momes, Tap-To-Bacconists, 100
Bats, Harpies, Syrens, Centaurs, Bib-all-nights,
Sice-sink-ap-Asses, Hags, Hermaphrodites)
And *Wee*, poor *Nothings* (fixed in no Spheare,
Right *wandring* Tapers, *Erring* every where)
Scorn of the *Vulgar*, Scandall of the *Gown*,
Have pull'd this waight of *Wrath ;* this *Vengeance*
   down.
All, All are *guilty* in a high Degree,
Of this *High-Treason* and *Conspiracy ;*
More brute then *Brutus*, stabbing more then *Cæsar*,
With Two-hand SINS of *Profit* and of *Pleasure ;* 110
And (th' odious *Jngine*, which doth all include)
Our many-pointed proud *Ingratitude*,
   For, for the *People's* Sins for *Subjects'* Crimes,
God takes-away good *Princes* oftentimes.
So, good *Josiah* (*Henry's parallel*)
Was soon bereft from Sin-full *Israel :*
So, our good *Edward* (*Henry's Precedent*)
For *England's Sins* was hence untimely hent.
So, here, good *Henry* is new taken hence,
For now Great-*Britain's* great *Sins'* Confluence. 120
   Wee see th' Effect : wee have the Cause confest :
O ! Turn wee then, with speed to *save the Rest :*
O ! Turn us, *Lord*, turn to us, turn away
Thy *Frowns*, our *Fears*, with humblest tears, wee
   pray.
O save our *Soveraign ;* save his *Royall seed ;*
That still his *Own* may on his *Throne* succeed.
   Let Each of us make privie Search within ;
And having found, bring forth the *Traitor* SIN

To *Execution*, with all *Execration*
Henceforth renouncing such *In-Sin-newation.* 130
   Let Each of us (as Each hath throw'n a *Dart*,
A *Dart* of Sinne, at *Henry's* princely heart)
Send-up in Sighes our *Soules'* devoutest breath,
To Shield our *James, Anne, Charles, Elizabeth*,
And *Him* whose *Love* shall render *Her* her *Brother*,
And make Her soon a happy *Prince's* Mother.
   Let Each of us cease to lament (in vain)
Prince Henry's Loss : Death is to *Him* a Gain.
For *Savoy's* Dukelings, or the *Florentine*,
Hee wedds his *Saviour* of a Regall *Line ;* 140
Glory, for *Gold ;* for *Hope, Possession* (*there*)
Of *Crownes* so Rich as never entred Eare,
Eye never saw, nor ever Heart conceiv'd ;
So strong *Assur'd* as cannot be bereav'd.
   Waile not his death : His *Vertues* cannot *Dye ;*
Immortall Issue of *Eternity*.
His *Soule* in Blisse beholds her Maker's Eyes :
His goodly Body shall more glorious *Rise*.
   Weep not for *Him :* weep for our selves, alas !
(Not for our *Private*, or *Peculiar* case : 150
As, for our *Sonn's, Brother's*, or *Master's* lack,
Or *Prince's* losse (our *Expectations* wrack)
Our *Places, Graces, Profits, Pensions* lost,
Our *present Fortunes* cast, our *future* crost).
   Weep for our *Sins*, our *Wicked*-Provocations,
Our haynous, horrid, high *Abominations ;*
Both *seen* and *secret ;* both in High and Low :
Weep, weep for *These ;* and stript, from Top to Toe,
Of *giddie Gaudes*, Top-gallant *Tires* and *Towers*,
Of *Face-pride, Case-pride, Shin-pride, Shoo-pride*,
   ours 160
(*Like Ninivites* so neer Their *threatned Fall*)
In blackest *Sack* and *Cinders* shrouded All :
Not like a *Bul-rush*, for a day or two,
To stoop and droop, and *seem* as others *doe*
(As *Achab* yerst, and *Pharao*, in Distresse)
And then return unto our old excesse
(As Dogs unto their Mewt, Hogs to their Mire)
But day by day, untill our last expire,
With bended Knees, but more with broken hearts,
And th' *inward* rest of right *Repentant* Parts, 170
Prostrate our Soules in *Fasting* and in *Prayer*,
Before the Foot-stool of th' *Empyreall Chaire :*
That So, What-ever bloudy *Deluge* float
From th' old *Red Dragon's* wide-wide-yawning *Throat*,
Wee *Humbled Mourners* may be Heav'nly *Markt*,
In *Mercie's Vessell* to be All inBARKT.

               F I N I S.

NOTES AND ILLUSTRATIONS.

   See Memorial-Introduction on Sylvester's relations to Prince Henry : line 2, *Jacob's Staffe'* = Jacobus, James I. :
l. 26, 'S. P. Q. R'—see Glossarial Index : l. 89, *Dedalizing'—ibid.* : l. 100, '*Mach'-Aretines*' = Machiavelli-Aretine
—anticipation of Carlyle's compound names : l. 118, '*hent*' = withdrawn, taken : l. 161, '*Sack*' = sackcloth : l. 167,
'*Mewt*' = vomit, filth.
                                                    G.

AN EPITAPH.

WHen *Great* French-HENRY *Fates bereft,*
His Name and Fame to OURS *Hee left;*
As ablest ATLAS *then to* proppe
The Waight of WORTH, *the World of* HOPE :
But, ENGLAND'S Sinnes (*a heavier Load*)
So over-laid *His Shoulders broad,*
That, crushed-*down,* Here lyes HEE dead,
So HOPE *is fall'n, and* WORTH *is fled.*

ANOTHER.

WHom *All admir'd, whom All* (almost) *ador'd,*
For all the Parts of all PANDORA'S *Treasure;*
The Hope of all, to have all Good *restor'd;*
HIM, *All our* Ills *have slain, by Heav'n's Displeasure.*

By HIS (late) HIGHNES'S

First   Worst

&

Poet   Pension[r]

JOSUAH SYLVESTER.

A N
E L E G I A C
EPISTLE

CONSOLATORIE.

AGAINST

IMMODERATE SORROW

FOR THE

IMMATURE DECEASE

OF

Sir WILLIAM SIDNEY

Knight,

Sonne and Heire apparent

To the Right

HONOURABLE

ROBERT, LORD SIDNEY

Lord Vi-Count Lisle;

Lord Chamberlaine to the Queene

AND

Lord Governour of His

MAJESTIES

Cautionarie Towne of

ULUSHING.

BY

JOSUAH SYLVESTER.

TO
THE RIGHT
HONOURABLE
THE LORD VI-COUNT
LISLE, and his most

vertuous Lady.

To Sir ROBERT SIDNEY, Knight, their
Hopefull SONNE.

To the most Worthy Lady WROTH, with the
rest of their right vertuous Daughters :

and

To all the Noble SIDNEYS

and

SEMI-SIDNEYS.

A Lthough I know none, but a Sidney's *Muse,*
    Worthy to sing a Sidney's *Worthinesse :*
None but Your Own Al-*WORTH, Sidniëdes
In whom, her Uncle's *noble Veine renewes :*
And though I know (sad Nobles) *to infuse*
   My fore-spent Drops into the bound-lesse Seas
   Of your deepe griefes, for your dear Joy's Decease ;
   To your full Ocean *nought at-all accrues :*
Yet, as (the Flouds' Queen) Amphitrite *daignes*
   To take the Tribute of small Brooks and Bournes ;
   Which to her Bounty (that their Streams maintains)
The humble Homage of their Thanks returnes :
   Accept these Sighs and these few Tears of ours,
   Which have their Course but from the Sourse of yours.

* Anagram. LA. WROTH.

———————————Your Noble Name's and Vertue's

————————————most Observant,

—————————————— JOSUAH SYLVESTER.

AN ELEGIAC

EPISTLE.

W Hat object less then our *great Henry's Herse*,
    Could so have seiz'd the voice of every *verse ?*
    What Subject else could have ingrossed so
    The *publike* Store and *private* Stock of *Woe ?*
What Sea, but th' *Ocean* of His *Vertue's* Fame,
Could drink all *Tears*, or drown a *Sidney's Name*
(As buried quick) so quickly (though so young)
So un-bewailed, so un-sight, un-sung?
   O, glorious *Henry !* though alone to *Thee*,
I owe my all, and more then all of *Mee ;*   10
And though (alas !) the best and most of *mine*
Reach not the least, the lowest dues of *Thine :*
Yet, wouldst thou, couldst thou hear (as heer-to-fore)
And grant a *Boon ;* I onely would implore
Thy *leave* a little, for a *Sidney's* Death
To sigh a little of my mournfull breath :
The rather, that, as *Yerst* Hee serv'd you here,
And, in his *End* attended Yours so neer ;
Through-out all *Ages*, subsequent to *Ours*,
His *Name* and *Fame* may ever wait on YOURS :   20
Sith All the MUSES owe that *Name* alone,
A *Dia-pason* of each *sad-sweet* Groan :
But more peculiar, and precisely mine ;
Lineally bound unto that Noble Line.
   Arcadians know no Other, for *Apollo*,
No other *Mars* (in *Arms* or *Arts* to follow
As *Demi-Gods*, as well of War as Wit)
Then *Sidneys yerst*, or *Semi-Sidneys*, yet.
Yet, fit I said : for, of *This* dear *Descent*,
Nature (of late) too-lavishly hath spent,   30
(Like *My Ill-huswifes* which at once do burn
Two or three lights, where one would serve the turn)
Not her Owne only, but more orient Gemms,
More rich, more rare ; more fitting *Diadems*.
   As, first, th' old Father, famous-fortunate,
The prime firm Founder of our *Irish State :*
Next, His Son PHILIP (more then PHILIP'S Son)
Whose World of *Worth*, a World of *Honour* won :
Then, His sole *Heire* (sole *Venus-Juno-Pallas*)
All *Beauties' Pattern*, and All *Vertues'* Palace ;   40
(Whose memory, on *Muses' fairest Hill*
Is *Canonized*, by a *Phœnix* Quill).

These *Three*, the which *Three Ages* might have grac't,
All *These* and moe in my short Age have past :
Besides *This* new *Sweet-William* now deceast
(Th' *Epitomè* and *Summe* of All the rest)
The Flower of *Youth*, of *Honour, Beauty, Bloud*,
Th' Apparent *Heir* of All the SIDNEYS *Good ;*
For mind, for mould, for sp'rit, for strength, and stature
A Miracle, a Master piece of *Nature*.   50
   Alas ! How grossely doe our Painters erre
In drawing *Death's* grim Visage (every-where)
With hollow holes, as wholly dark and blinde !
Ah ! See wee not, how still hee sees to finde
The fairest mark, the rarest and the best
Of *Vertue's* buds, and lets alone the rest?
Ravens, Brambles, Bandogs, *Sirens*, here he leaves ;
Swans, Roses, Lions, *Dians*, hence hee reaves :
Nay ; th' *onely Phœnix* hath hee newly slain
(But, maugre *Death*, That *Bird* revives again).   60
No marvaile then, if SIDNEYS fall so fast,
So early ripe are seldome apt to last :
So *Eminent* are imminent to *die ;*
Malicious *Death* doth *such* so eas'ly spy.
   But, why of *Death* and *Nature* rave I thus ;
Another *Stile* (My LISLE) befitteth us.
Another *Hand*, another *Eye*, directs
Both *Death* and *Nature* in these high Effects ;
The *Eye* of *Providence*, the *Hand* of *Power*,
Disposing All in *Order* and in *Hower ;*   70
So *Working* in, so *Waking* over All,
That but by *Those* doth nothing here befall.
   Then, not (as Currs) the stone or staffe to bite,
Un-heeding *why*, or *who* doth *hurle* or *smite ;*
Unto that *Eye* let us erect our owne ;
And humble us under That *Hand* alone,
Which (as the Potter his owne Work controules)
Dissolveth Bodies, and *absolveth* Soules :
Un-partiall ever, Un-preposterous ;
How-ever Other it may seem to us.   80
   For, ever since *first Woman* teemed *Twin*,
And at a *Birth* brought forth both *Death* and *sin*,
(*Sin*, as her *Heir : Death*, as an *Heritage*
Justly derived down from Age to Age)

It is *Decreed* (by a more Change-lesse *Law*
Then ever yet the *Medes* and *Persians* saw)
That *All men once* (as well as Low, the High,
Of either *sex*, of every *sort*) *must dye.*
Yea, th' INNOCENT, for *Our imputed Ill*
(Who *came*, not *Lawes* to break, but to *ful-fill*)   90
The *Son* of GOD (The *Son* of MAN become)
Th' *Immortall* yeelded to This *mortall Doome.*
So that (*for Sin*) no *Son* of MAN hath breath
But once must dye ; *Wages of* SIN *is Death.*

   As for the reason, Why it comes to passe
Somtimes, that *Age* seems to have turn'd his *glass ;*
While oftentimes *Youth's*, yer it seem *begun*,
Is crakt, or broken, or already run :
Why *Lillies, Roses, Gilli-flowers* be reft ;
When *Nettles, Thistles, Hemlocks* here be left :   100
Why *Cedars, Okes, Vines, Olives* rather fall,
Then *Brush* and *Bryars* (good for nought at all)
Let Flesh and Bloud, let *Dust*, be rather mute,
Then with *His* MAKER sawcily dispute.

   Yet here (mee thinks) but little Question needs ;
Doe not Wee rather gather Herbs then Weeds?
Doe not Wee take the timber for our turn,
And leave the Dotrells, in their time to burn?
And in the Shambles, who is it but would
Be rather sped of young Flesh then of old ?   110
And yet in Season, when wee see it good,
Wee weed our Gardens, fell our Under-wood :
And kill old Cattell, lest they goare the young,
Or fall away, or mize som Mange among.

   Much like, the Lord, who knoweth best all season,
And best observes.   But will wee urge his Reason?
His Reason is his WILL : His *Will* is *just*,
Or rather *Justice ;* Which his *Power* must
In *Wisdome execute* (right understood)
To his *Owne Glory*, and His *Children's Good ;*   120
Wherein His *Goodness* through his *Mercy* shines,
To cleer and cheer devout and humble mindes.
For to the *Godly*, (in despight of Hell)
Heav'n maketh all things to re-issue *well.*

   Here here 's a Harbour ; here 's a quiet Shore
From *Sorrowe's* Surges, and all Storms that rore.

This is *Cap Comfort* (a high *Promontory*
Of *richer* Store then here is room to storie).
Here let us bide, and ride-out all Events,
With Anchor *Hope*, and Cable *Patience ;*   130
Untill our Bark some happy Gale shall drive
Home to the *Hav'n* where wee would All arrive.

   Come, Noble *Vi-Count*, put into *This Bay*,
Where with a Light our A'M'RAL leads the way,
Though deepest laden, and the most distrest,
The greatest *Ship* of Burthen, and the best.
HIM boldly follow : and though here, as CHIEF
In *Grief*, as *Greatnesse*, His must drown your *Grief :*
Count it an Honour, to be call'd to try
Your *Vertue's* Valour, in your *Soveraign's* eye.   140
Wee all partake his *Cross ;* his *Losse* is *Ours :*
But his *Affections* (to the life) are *Yours.*
The neerer then You match his *mournfull* fate,
His *royall Patience* neerer imitate.
And *you*, sad *Lady*, Mother of Annoy
For having lost the *prime* Son of your Joy ;
Ah ! see the *Soveraigne* of your *sex* hath so.
Some think it ease, to have some peer in *Woe :*
But such a PEER, and *such* a *Pattern* too,
Should much (mee thinks) confirm and comfort
   You   150
To beare-up hard into this happy *Road*,
And lighten somwhat of Your heavy Load :
   The rather, sith besides the *Happinesse*,
Which now, *above*, your *Darling* doth possesse ;
(The *Crown*, the *Kingdome*, and the *Company*
Of All the *holy, heav'nly* HIERARCHIE)
Besides your mess of goodly GRACES left
(Whose WORTH from All, the *Price* of *Worth* hath
   reft ;
Foure lovely *Nimphs*, foure *Rivers*, as it were,
Your veins of *Vertue* through the Land to bear)   160
You have another *Model* of *The same*,
To propagate *renowned* SIDNEY'S *Name ;*
Another, like in every part to prove
As worthy of our Honour, and your Love ;
In whom (if now, You, JOB-like, bear this *Crosse*)
Heav'n may restore you, manifold, your Losse.

FINIS.

NOTES AND ILLUSTRATIONS.

OF the Sidneys here celebrated, see our Memorial-Introduction : page 282, SONNET, l. 10, '*Bournes*' = burns,
streams : EPISTLE, line 8, '*un-sight*' = unsighed, unlamented : l. 57, '*Ban-dogs*' = bound-dogs : but see Glossarial
Index to Dr. Joseph Beaumont, *s.v.* : l. 79, '*un-preposterous*' = not premature? l. 108, '*Dotrells*'—see Nares, *s.v.*,
for a full note and references : l. 114, '*mize*' = mix or infect'with : l. 157, '*mess*' = a set.   Cf. Love's Labour Lost,
iv. 3 ; 3 Henry VI. l. 4.   G.

HONOUR'S
FARE-WELL
TO
HER HONOURABLE FRIENDS:
OR
THE LADY HAY'S
Last Will:

TO
THE RIGHT HONOURABLE
Executors and *Overſeers,*

EDWARD,   *JAMES,*
Lord Denny;   *Lord Hay;*

&

MARY,
Lady Denny.

From Gratitude, *From Duty, From Affection,*
   To You (my Lords) Your *Honour, and Your Name*
   (Without Offence, Without Mis-sense, *or Blame*)
Receive, conceive, *consider This* Direction
Against th' Excesse, the Rage, *The Insurrection*
Of Tears, of Sighs, *of Sorrowes* for This Dame
As Dead, Who Lives (in Soule, in Seed, *in Fame*)
Inspiring Breath, Life, *Strength* To This Collection
Made, aimed, *meant,* For quick, kind, *Keen* Correction
Of Men, of Minds, *of Manners,* (Out of Frame)
In Citie, Court, *and Countrey* (All too-Blame)
Through Sin's, through Satan's, *Through our Selves'* Infection.
   Som Vow, Som Verse, *Som Monument* To Honour
   I thought, I ought, *and Thus I* Dreamed on-Her.

      Josuah Sylvester.

HONOUR'S
FARE-WELL.

*F*Rom Man-God's birth (*the Scale of earth to heav'n*)
  Th' Yeer *twice eight hundred and twice single*
    sev'n ;
Amidst the Month *which Second* Cæsar *names ;*
Upon the Day *which* Diane *weekely claimes :*
About the Hower *that golden* Morpheus *uses*
Fantastickly to feast perplexed Muses
(*While* Phœbus' *Coach-man scarce awake, did seem*
Hying to harnesse all his fiery Teem)
Being, me thought (*ith'* Ward-robe, *or at* Waltham)
Among the Chief, where Grief did so assault 'em   10
(*On either side*) *that neither Great nor small*
Had one dry Eye to see My sight *withall :*
Me thought I saw a White bright-shining Creature
(*Just in the Forme of* HONOUR'S *Wonted Feature*)
Approaching softly to a Sable Bed
Where weeping Sorrow *layd his sleeplesse head ;*
And with a Voice like one devoutly praying,
Shrill-softly, Thus (*me thought*) *I heard it saying :*

  Sweet Love, my Lord, *Loadstar* of my Desire,
Whose purest flame had onely power to fire   20
The Icie Fort of HONOUR'S chaste Affection,
Wonne by thy love ; but more by thy Perfection :
Deare Soule, which draw'st (by unseen vertue) so,
My Soule to greet thee once yet yer I goe ;
Cease, cease to weep, give-over Sighs and sobbing,
Thine eyes of Rest, thy brest of Comforts robbing :
For, though soft Water hardest Marble weares,
Flint-hearted *Death* is never pierc't with *Teares.*
Use therefore other Arms against his Rages :
And, of thy Love, give more authentick Gages.   30
  Whom yerst I chose among the choisest Worth
Of *Brittish Gallants* (over *South* and *North*)
For *Parts* and *Port ;* for mild and Martiall manner,
In brave *Designes* to doe their Countrey honour :
Who, in mine eye, seem'd to excell the rest,
And Whom my Mind esteem'd above the best ;
Must not expresse His love to Mee *departed,*
With vulgar Showes of the most-vulgar-hearted.
  No : light me Lamps that may thy love become ;
Such as may shine, about, above my Tombe,   40
To all beholders, as a holy Mirrour,
Reducing Nobles, from Ignobles' Errour :

Or as a *Pharus* to direct the Court,
From Rocks and Wracks, into the *Happy Port.*
For, though my love seek but my HAY and DENNY,
My *Charity* is here-in meant to many.
As from the *Dead,* I come, the *Quick* to call
From *Sin's* deep *Sleep :* and *Thee* (*Deer*) first of all.
  Dear, if thou yet hold-dear a Soule devested
Of worldly Pomp (wch hath the World impested)   50
Sweet heart, put-off ; sweet *Hay,* now leave thou quick,
What (O !) I left not, till nigh deadly Sick :
Forsake the World yer it have thee forsaken ;
And yer thy Youth with Ruth be over-taken,
Regard thy Soule, thy Body lesse respect :
Kill *Vanity,* curbe every fond Affect,
Whereby the World still striveth to imprison
The purest Rayes of Man's divinest Reason ;
Creep here no longer with thy mortall Dust :
Climbe with thy fiery Soule up to the Just ;   60
Exhale thee so, in heav'nly things admiring,
As to the place of thy first Birth aspiring.
  Few are thy Dayes with many Dolours fill'd,
With *Hoping* tired, with *Desiring* kill'd,
Yer thou attain what thou wouldst fain and merry :
Or, if thou dost, anon it makes thee weary.
For, what *Delight* that ever Earth thee lent,
Hast thou aye found *pleasing* and *permanent ?*
Honour's faire Mask, for all the Pomp and Bravery,
In *golden Gyves* is chain'd to *Silken Slavery.*   70
Wealth, which the World holds *super-Soveraign,*
With use, doth vanish ; without use, is vaine :
And Both, too often (as *Coat-Cards* may cotten)
Unworthily, as well are lost, as gotten.
  Few Objects here (my *Dear*) but subject be
To Labour more then unto Liberty :
Youth's health and strength are quickly quasht, or
    dated :
Pleasure and Love as soon are crost, or sated :
Affront still drives the Weakest to the Wall :
The Mightiest ay are under Envie's Maule ;   80
A lowly Fortune is of all despised :
A lofty one, oft, of it selfe, nullized.
  In Brief, *Dear Soule,* thou seest how *Certain Fate*
Conduces all things to their *finall Date.*

As on the Shore a rouling Billow splitteth,
When foaming high, and roaming home, it hitteth
Against the keen Knees of a horned Cliff,
Ending his course in an Incounter stiff ;
Then swels another, which yet higher wallowes,
In the same course : whom the same fortune follows : 90
So, Wee (*O World's-Waves!*) as soon dead as born,
With divers Shock, on the same Rock are torn.

This age hath show'n great *fortune's* greedy Minions
(By hook or crook) above the world's opinions ;
Above their owne Hopes : nay, above (wel-nigh)
The clouded Aime of their insatiate eye :
But, now where are they ? where's their grace ? their
     glory ?
Rotten in Dust ; forgotten all their Story
(Unlesse, perhaps, what here so goodly shin'd,
Went out in Snuffe ; and left ill sent behinde)   100
And all their vaine Fume, turn'd to violent Fire,
For ever burns (such is *Ambition's* Hire) :
Where, too-too late, they finde unto their Cost,
Such Favours, so found, had bin better lost.

Soul's sad Repenting, and Heart's heavy Throeing,
Are surest Fruits that in the World are growing :
Here's nothing firmer, nothing frequent more,
Then *Death :* Which (living) not to mind before
Makes men run headlong to the Gulf infernall ;
And, for howrs' Joyes, to lose the Joyes eternall :   110
Drawn diversly by divers Appetites,
After the Humors of their vain Delights.

Some *Apish*, acting every *Fashion's* Model :
Some *Swinish*, wallowing in their Surfeit's Puddle :
Some *Goatish*, haunting Fillies with their Dams :
Some *Wolvish*, worrying innocentest Lambs :
Some *Currish*, snarling at all good men's Good :
Some *Monkish*, hollow under *Holy-Hood :*
Some *Brutish*, Monsters in all kind of Evill :
Some *Hellish*, Actors, Factors for the Divell.   120

Deare, tread not Thou in *Error's* common Track :
But in thy *Life sure thine Election* make.
Feare, love, beleeve, serve, sorrow, sue, contemple ;
And rather walk by *Precept*, then *Exemple.*

'Tis utterly to be of judgement voyd,
'Tis wilfully to have one's Selfe destroyd ;
To trust our Soule with such whose Stipulation
Cannot repaire, cannot reprive, *Damnation.*

Who, curious, cares but for the things below,
Shall finde in fine, that hee shall Both forgoe ;   130
But Hope of things above (with due progression)
Is far more sure, then th' other's full Possession.

Labour thou therefore for the *certain Gain :*
And if thou lov'st mee, higher, higher strain.
In *Holy-Pride*, hence-forth disdain the Creature,
And mount thy thoughts up to the Lord of Nature :
Love, free thy love from this dark Dungeon here,
And hence-forth fix it in th' *Empyreall* cleer :
Whither no sooner shall thy mind be rais'd,
But all thy Mournings will be soon appeas'd,   140
With other comforts then the World affords
In bitter Deeds candied in sugar Words.

The World it selfe is dying and decaying :
The earth more steril, heav'nly Stars more straying :
The Sphears distun'd.   These are the last, last Times :
Where *Vertue* fails, where *Vice* prevailes and climes ;
Where good men melt away ; ungodly harden.

How many flow'rs (the choise of all our Garden)
Of either Sex, of every Age and Rank :
From every Quarter, Border, Bed, and Bank   150
[Besides that paire of *Royall Sister-Buds*,
Whose life had promis'd *Europe* many Goods :
Beside that *Prime*-ROSE, Miracle of Princes,
Whose Herse as yet a Sea of Tears berinses :
Besides that *knot of Noblest* HARRINGTONS,
Th' old Father's Honours doubling in the Sons :
Besides GODOLPHIN, BODLEY, *Muses'* Father ;
Rare SACVIL'S-*Nevill* (new *Minerva* rather) :
Besides Saint *Drury*, *Sydney's-Rutland*, *Cheiney*,
Mirrour of *Dames*, and other Worthies many]   160
Hath our *Great Husband* lately snatched hence,
Before his Wrath's approaching storm commence ?

Why wail'st thou then my happy *Dissolution*,
By Nature's Current, and Heav'n's Constitution ?
Repell thy Sorrowes : and repeale to Thee
All active Vertues.   Mourn no more for Mee.

I lived long enough ; sith while I lived
Thou lovedst mee : but (so should I have grieved)
Hadst thou appear'd unkind unto thy Wife,
My longer Date had bin a shorter Life.   170

I leave thee Babes enow : A Son and Daughter :
Enow to crave thy care, and cause thee laughter :
Enow for Thee ; enow for Mee to beare :
Which oft I wisht ; and the Almightie's Eare
(Who hears his Owne, and on them ay bestoweth
Their owne desires ; or what Hee better knoweth)
Heard mee in this ; and one Petition more ;
That, when wee parted, I might passe before.

So, fare thou well (Dear Heart) fare-wel : my leasure
Serves now no longer for this last best pleasure.   180
Fare-wel, dear Pheer : Fare-well, dear Father too !
This is my last Will, which I leave with *You.*
You, joynt *Executors* I have ordained :
And for an *Helpe*, My Mother's love unfained
As *Over-seer* I beseech you call :
And for your *Counsell* use our heav'nly *HALL.*

So, in the heav'ns, among my Joyes supernall ;
So, in my Glass, the *Vision* of th' *Eternall ;*
If I shall see *You*, in your Pilgrimage,
O ! be it happy, as my Hope's presage.   190

So, in our Children, as their yeers be growing,
May Nature's Gifts and Heav'nly Grace bestowing.
One have I heer ; two have you there below ;
Wee here have peace, you there have Wars (wee
     know)
With-out, with-in : the more therefore behoves you
Defence from Hence.   So wishes She that loves you.

So, grant mee God (if it be lawfull here)
I never lose remembrance of my Dear : !
So, calmed be the Tempest of your mourning
For My *Decease* (according to my warning),   200

So, casting off this Load of Heavinesse,
Our Love unceasing, may *Your* Sorrow cease.
So ceast the Voyce, *and so the* Shadow *Vanisht,*
The Mourners *then, more ravisht then astonisht,*
Did still, still listen with a longing Eare
For more such Musick : *which then missing there*
(*Mee thought*) *the* Sable Curtains *back they haled.*
And, looking round, *were ready to have called ;*

When instantly their Passions *so abound,*
That down they sink ; and as they sink they swound : 210
Whereat, I (griev'd *to see such Friends bereft mee*)
Starting *to help, disturbed* Morpheus *left mee :*
But, as hee rouz'd, *by chance hee* cast a Quill,
For present Pen *to copie HONOUR'S* Will.

NOTES AND ILLUSTRATIONS.

PAGE 285—SIR EDWARD DENNY (youngest son of Henry Denny, Dean of Chester) was summoned to Parliament as Baron Denny, 27th October 1604, and created Earl of Norwich 24th October 1626. He married Lady Mary Cecil, d. of Thomas, Earl of Exeter, and had an only daughter Honora, who married Sir James Hay, afterwards Viscount Doncaster and Earl of Carlisle. He was created Lord Hay 29th June 1615. His first wife (above Honora) must have died soon after, as he married a second wife in 1617. See the Peerages. Line 3, '*Second Cæsar*' = Augustus, August : l. 73, '*cotten*'—see Glossarial Index, *s.v.* : l. 82, '*nullized*' = nullified : l. 84, '*conduces*' = conducts : l. 94, '*hook or crook*'—see Glossarial Index, *s.v.* : l. 123, '*contemple*' = contemplate : l. 160, '*other Worthies*'—see our Memorial-Introduction on the names enumerated : l. 181, '*Pheer*' = mate, husband. See Introduction on Bp. Hall, in reference to next page.   G.

Honour's Epitaph.

Here-under, lies
The wonder of her kinde :
The rarest Work
Of Nature and of Grace :
A beauteous TEMPLE
Of a bounteous Minde ;
Where *Venus, Juno,*
Pallas, had their Place.
Nay ; Heav'n's and Nature's
Gift singled to Many,
Here All concurr'd
TO HONOUR HAY AND DENNY.

TO MY REVEREND FRIEND,

Mr. Doctor HALL.

None should, *but* Thou, *This* Ladie's death *be grieving;*
None knew so well, the Vertues *of her life:*
Death*'s rob'd of her Death, by* Thy labours *rife:*
By Thee, *is* Shee *in Heav'n and Earth still living:*
In Heav'n, by hearing, *and (through thee)* beleeving
Th*' eternall Word ; which taught her* holy Strife
'Gainst Hell *and* Sin ; *and (as becoms a* Wife)
Peace *with her* Spouse, *him due* Obedience *giving:*
In Earth, for acting (*in so gracious measure*)
*The twice-*preacht Lectures *of thy Life and Tongue;*
Alms, Meeknesse, Mildnesse, (*towards Old and Young*)
Forgiving *Wrongs,* forgetting *all Displeasure.*
O happy Seed *that fell in such a ground!*
And happy Soil *that such a* Seed-*man found.*

JOSUAH SYLVESTER.

A FUNERALL
E L E G I E.

TO

MY REVEREND FRIEND, M.D. HILL:

In pious memory of that worthy Matrone, his right

vertuous and religious Wife, MARGARITE

WYTS (late Widow of the reverend Dr.

HADRIANUS SARAVIA)

Deceased.

ALL, that in this wide *World* is inclos'd,
  Is of *Two kinds* (and divers, too) compos'd :
Mortall, the one ; *Immortall*, th' other sort,
Exempt from *Death* (wch spilleth worldlings' sport)
And unto each a diverse place is giv'n,
Th' one droops on earth : the other dwels in heav'n.
  For, all, above bright *Cynthia's* silver Car,
Live out of fear, from *Death* and danger far :
Far from corruption, and as free from *Change*,
Selfe-stable ever, never selfly-strange :   10
Never transformed, not trans-substantiate :
Sith neither subject to the power of *Fate*,
Neither obnoxious to those cumbers rife,
Cares, snares, and surfaits, that doe combat Life :
  And, all, beneath her many-formed *flame*,
That sojourns here amid this fickle *Frame*
(Whether, the winged *Myriades* of the Sky,
Whether, the *Millions* of the *Ocean's* fry,
Whether, the *Legions* in the woods and groves,
Of savage herds, or of domestick droves)   20
All, all, doe dy : All are to *Death* inthrall'd :
And, for their *dying*, are here *Mortall* call'd.
  But, chiefly *Man*, though in his better part
Most like to *God*, in This, most like to smart :
So that his *Reason* (though *divine* inspir'd)
Seems over-rated, or too dear acquir'd.
  Yet, if kind *Nature* nobly had decreed,
By certain and irrevocable Deed,

None but the vitious and the lewd to dy
(The *Vertuous* living here eternally)   30
There were some comfort in Man's wretched case ;
And *Nature then* might hold a Mother's place :
  But when wee see the *Wicked* (for the most)
Live long and lusty, ruling all the roast,
Though ever *turning*, and *returning* quick
(As Swine, or Dogs) their vomit to re-lick :
While (for the most) the godly soon are gon,
Or daily going, deadly laid upon
By humane malice, or from hand divine :
O ! flesh and bloud, how can it not repine ?   40
  Alas ! To see a goodly field of *Wheat*
All burnt with *lightning*, or with *hail*-stones beat
(When the full Ears, humbling their flowry top,
Were even as ready, with a gratefull crop,
To thank the Husband for his taken toill,
His cost and care, his sweat, his seed, and soil ;
While safe the *Tares, Cockle* and *Darnell* rest,
With *Thorns* and *Thistles* that the *Corn* opprest :
O ! Who so constant, but would grieve and grudge
(*If not a Christian*) at th' All-ordering Judge ;   50
And wag his head at Heav'n,—weak earthly worm !—
Against the Author of that angry storm ?)
  Such is thy case : Such was thy heavy Crosse,
To lose thy *gold*, when others kept their *drosse :*
To have thy vessell, *full of Vertues*, split ;
Where *lighter* Keels, and *empty*, never hit :

To be bereft so sweet, so *sainct a Wife;*
While here be left Harpies, and *Hels of Life.*
  But, I have *learn'd;* and *thou* hast *taught* (my *Hill*)
Wee must content us with our Maker's will: 60
The Rule of right, disposing all that is:
And ordering all things to the good of his.
  So, for her *good* (thy *good*) was his good pleasure,
To snatch so soon, thy *Marg'rite,* hence, thy treasure;
Thy *Pearl* (indeed, the *Jewell* of her kinde,
For worth and wealth of body and of minde)
Tri'd in her cradle, train'd from tendrest youth
Under the *Cross,* for CHRIST's eternall *Truth:*
Forsaking *Gaunt* for th' holy Gospel's sake;
Lands, good and air, which Nature dear doth make: 70
Fleeing from *Antwerp* (in poor *Begger's* weed)
The *Spanish fury,* in a fearfull need;
With her dear Parents, tossed to and fro,—
Right noble Parents, partners in her wo.
  Her *April* past, her *Summer-Age* prepares,
If much lesse dangers, not much lesser cares;
In House-hold charge, under her *Virgin*-sway,
Her puisne *Orphan-sisters* to defray.
  For, her owne Father, *Nature* had unhous'd:
And *Metkerk* had her Mother re-espous'd   80
(Renown'd *Sir Adolph,* of whose noble stuff,
Little is nothing; and much, not enough,
To be recorded: But, his stile and state,
Learn of *S. Butolph,* neerest *Aldersgate*)
And, hee releast, and shee deceast soon after,
Most worthy Mother of so worthy Daughter.
Religious Lady, leaving by her Will,
Charge to her children, to persever still
In *Truth's* profession; and here rather rest,
Though poor and mean; then to be re-possest, 90
Return to *Flanders* (on the best condition)
To be replung'd in *Romish* superstition.
  And well her *Will* her valiant Sons observ'd,
Both *Serjant Majors* (as both well deserv'd,
In *Faith's Defence,* by wounds yet healed scarce)
To both those brave *Nassauvian Sons of Mars:*
So did the rest: but rest my *Margarite,*
Executrix (her years and vertues right)
All which shee past; and with so pure report
Fitting the mirrour of her sex and sort: 100
  Such exercise of every *Hous-wife's part,*
Such honest *shift,* such *thrift,* such *use,* such *art:*
Such *modesty,* such *gravity,* such *grace,*
Such *speech,* such *silence* (suiting time and place):
Such due *devotion,* such *discretion* seen,
As seemed neerer *sixty* then *sixteen.*
  How well, and worthy of her former fames,
Shee did demean her with two *noble Dames,*
In *honour'd service,* (many years with Each :)
With praise and love, without the least impeach: 110
Palavicine, and *Hastings* will avouch
(Though now new-nam'd: that *Cromwel,* and this
    Zouch)
So *vertuous* both, that (for so long together)
None but so *vertuous* could have *served* Either.

Such was her *Minor-age: such Maiden-life:*
Such-*Woman-state:* and such shee was a *Wife*
To (*My*) SARAVIA; to whose *reverend Name*
Mine owes the honour of *du*-BARTAS' fame.
For (*as our London* (else for drought undon)
Sucks from the Paps (the Pipes) *of Middleton,* 120
(*Whose memory mine never shall forget,*
But to Hugh's *name adde the surname of Great,*
For his great Work abundant *streams to drench,*
Cool cleanse and clear: and fearfull flames to
    quench.)
From th' ample *Cisterns* of his Sea of *skill,*
Suckt I (*my Succour*) my short shallow *Rill:*
The little *All* I can and all I could
In *three poor years,* at three times three years old.
His love and labour apted so my wit,
That when *Urania* after rapted it, 130
Through⁋ Heav'n's strong working, weaknesse did
    produce
Leaves of delight, and *fruits of sacred use:*
Which, had my *Muse* t' our either *Athens* flowne,
Or follow'd him, had been much *more mine owne,*
Then was the fault that so it fell not out.
(*But prais'd be God, who pleas'd to bring about*
His better will, to better mine; lest I,
Too-puft with knowledge, should be huft too-hie.)
  Howbeit, Him needs must I honour much:
And Her for him, and for Herself: sith *such* 140
(When *such* so *few,* in such an Age as this:
So foul, so false, so full of *vanities*)
So milde a Childe, so meek a Servant, rather:
So loving Nurse to one, less *Pheer* then *Father*
(So weak and wayward thorough Ache and Age,
As still in *Patience* steept her *Pilgrimage* :)
O, happy Hee! so, happy Shee, the while:
Till Hee, more happy, left Her *Widowe's* stile.
  Whenceforth, sequestred from all publike sight,
From all occasions that might move Delight: 150
As hearty sorry as in habite sad,
Tears in her eyes, Sighs in her brest shee had
(As grieved Turtle on the green-lesse Spray
Groanes, and bemoanes her, in a mournfull Lay)
Lamenting many Months in heavy Cheer
Her losse (alas!) Her loving *Father-Pheer:*
Resolved chastly, not to change her Life,
Her Widow-state, to be a stately Wife:
Still keeping home; still tasked, sober-wise,
In Hus-wife's Use, or holy exercise. 160
Or, if at length shee looked out of Door,
'Twas but to visit some weake, aged Poor;
Some wofull Woman, or som wretched wight,
Through som disaster in som wofull plight:
Som long-Sick Neighbour, or som needy Soule,
With timely comforts of her Bag or Boule:
Or, on the *Sabbaths,* or the *Lecture-dayes,*
To *hear,* and *learn,* to *read,* and *pray,* and *praise:*
Such was thy *Marg'rite, morally divine;*
Maid, Widow, Wife (*Hill*) till thou hadst her
    thine. 170

This, I record : to *Thee* belongs the rest :
If here I ly, doe thou deny my *Test,*
Or testifie under thy hand with Mee,
That *Such* shee was, and *Such* shee was to Thee ;
And, to that end, insert thy *Paragraph*
Before, or after her sad *Epitaph.*
  Or, if thy *Grief* as yet permit thee not,
Make mee thy *Proxie :* for, right well I wot,
Will-nill thou *Hill,* Thou canst not but aver,
That *Such* shee was, as I have vouched Her :   180

And *Such* to Thee, well witnest by her *Will,*
Bequeathing all to her dear Dr. *Hill :*
And more then so, by a deer *Mother's* Smart,
Thy glad-sad Partner in a *dead-live Part*
(Her first and last) unhappy-happy Boy,
Which cost her life, and thee thy Life's best Joy.
Such then Shee liv'd and dy'd : for such must *dy :*
Yet such shall live here, and *eternally.*
So Shee ; so Shee (though sudden from thee took)
Shall *live,* with *Thee,* in *this* thy living *Book.*   190

NOTES AND ILLUSTRATIONS.

OF SAVARIA—husband and wife—HILL and other names introduced in this ' Elegie,' and on next page—see our Introduction : l. 78, '*puisne*' = puny, small (Fr.)—see Nares, *s.* 'puny :' l. 138, '*huft*' = heaved. So 'huff' = swagger : in the Epitaph on next page, col. 1, l. 20 is misprinted in the original, ' To parents' troubles ; and to me did fall.'   G.

TO GOD'S GLORY.

IN PIOUS MEMORY OF THE

Nobly Vertuous and Religious Matrone,

MARGARITE, Wife of ROBERT

HILL, Dr. of Divinity, and

Pastor of this Parish.

Here lies a Margarite, *that the most excell'd,*
(*Her Father* Wyts, *her Mother* Litchterveld,
Rematcht *with* Metkerk) *of* remark *for birth,*
But much more gentle *for her* genuine *worth :*
Wyt's (*rarest*) Jewell (*so her name bespeaks*)
Vertue's brave Load-starre, *to enlight her* Sex
In pious, prudent, peacefull, praise-full life,
Fitting a SARA, *and a* Sacred's *Wife.*
Such as SARAVIA *and* (*her Second*) HIL,
Whose joy of life Death *in her Death did kill.*

Quàm piè Obiit, Puerpera, { *Salutis,* 1615.
Die 29. Junii,   Anno { *Ætatis,* 39.

Pignus Amoris } *ac Mœroris* { *Posuit*   Rob. Hill.
Signum Honoris } { *Composuit* Jos. Syl.

Uxor Felix.

Loquitur post funera virtus.

From my sad Cradle to my sable chest,
Poor Pilgrim, I did find few months of rest.
In Flanders, Holland, Zeland, England, *all.*
To parents and to mee did troubles fall.
These made mee pious, patient, modest, wise :
And though well born, to shun the Gallant's guise.

But now I rest : my soule where rest is found ;
My body here in a small piece of ground.
And from my Hill, *that Hill I have ascended,*
From whence for mee my Saviour *once descended.*
Live yee to learne, that dye you must,
And after come to judgement just.

AN EPITAPH.

Maritus mœstissimus.
Thy rest gives mee a restlesse life,
Because thou wert a matchlesse Wife :
But yet I rest in hope to see
That day of Christ, and then see Thee.

Margarita a Jewell.
I, like a jewell tost by Sea, and Land,
Am bought by him who wears mee on his hand.

Margarita, Margareta.
Margarita beat, sed Margareta beavit :
O utinam posset dicier, ista beat.
One night, two dreams made two propheticals :
Thine, of thy Coffin ; mine, of thy Funerals.
If Women all were like to Thee,
Wee men, for wives should happy bee.

R. H.

Margarita surrept' est, mons exaruit.

FINIS.

A BRIEFE
CATECHISME.
THE PREFACE.

Q. Now'st thou, my child, wherfore thou wast
created?
A. Sir, to serve God, who mee and all created.
Q. How ought wee him to serve and to adore?
A. The Summe thereof consisteth in these foure.
Q. Which foure be they? *A.* Faith, and obedient living
After God's law, wth prayer and thanksgiving.
Q. Of each of these apart, and (orderly)
First, of the first let mee examine thee.

1. *Of Faith.*

Q. In whom hast thou thy faith's affiance founded?
A. In God alone my trust is wholly grounded.
Q. Why? *A.* God the Father made me first of nought;
And God the Son redeem'd me worse than nought;
God th' Holy Ghost (my Guide and Consolation)
Instructs, conducts mee to Sanctification.
Q. Are th' Holy Ghost, the Father and the Son
Three gods? *A.* No; Persons three, God only one.

2. *Of Obedience.*

Q. Will God be served after the Commission
Of his owne word, or after Man's tradition?
A. Doubtlesse according to his owne behest,
And not the motions of man's brain or brest.
Q. But, of thy self canst thou accomplish fully
The Law of God? canst thou perform it wholly?
A. No, God doth know. *Q.* Who doth it then in thee?
A. The Holy Ghost begetting faith in mee.
Q. Having (within) the Spirit for thy direction,
Canst thou performe obedience, in perfection?
A. No, neither yet. *Q.* Yet God rejecteth all
That perfectly keep not his Law in all.
A. 'Tis very true. *Q.* How then, or by what action
Canst thou please God, give the law satisfaction,
Or scape that death which to damnation brings?
A. By Jesus Christ, and by his sufferings.
Q. How so? *A.* Why thus: Christ our High-priest
for ever,
Self-offring once to be re-offred never,
Hath pleas'd his Father, hath appeas'd our strife,
And by his Death purchast us endlesse life;

So that, by lively faith to us applying
Th' one Sacrifice of Christ our Saviour dying,
By imputation w' have his righteousnesse
As Ours, with God; and thereby life and peace.

3. *Of Prayer.*

Q. Whom prai'st thou to? *A.* To the true God (of pow'r
And will to help) who hears us every hour.
Q. But in whose name will hee be call'd upon?
A. Onely in Christ's, our Saviour and his Son,
Our Price, our Peace, Our Reconciliation,
Our Advocate of much commiseration,
Sole Mediatour of mankind; who needs
No Aid of Saints, or any that succeeds.

4. *Of Thanksgiving.*

Q. While Christ, our King, our Prophet, Priest, and
Preacher,
Convert with his Disciples as a Teacher;
Tell mee, I pray, how many Sacraments
Did hee ordain his Church for evidence?
A. Two. *Q.* W^ch are they? *A.* Baptism, and the
Supper
Which hee assign'd the night yer hee did suffer.
Q. Of Sacraments what end, what use have wee?
A. Signes to our Sense, seals to our Faith they be.

Of Baptism.

Q. What is it that is signifi'd unto us
In sacred Baptism? *A.* It betokens to us
Full pardon and remission of our sins,
And a new birth, where better life begins.
Q. But in whose name is Baptism to be giv'n?
A. In th' only name of th' one-three God of Heav'n;
The Father, Son, and Holy Ghost: to whom
Be praise alwayes beyond all time to come.

Of the Lord's Supper.

Q. What's signifi'd unto us and presented
In th' holy Supper? *A.* There is represented
The true Communion of Christ's body and bloud
Giv'n for, and to us, for immortall food:
Whereby our soules are fed in expectation
Of Life eternall purchast by his passion.

Q. When wee receive these Mysteries Divine,
  What's showne unto us by the Bread and wine?
A. These Elements before us lively figure
  Of Christ his Death the vertue and the vigor.
  For, as our bodies by the staff of Bread,
  And cheer-heart Wine, are strengthned here, and fed :
  Even so his Body and his bloud doe nourish
  Our Faith-mouth'd Soules, that they may never perish.
Q. But, is Christ present in the Sacrament?
A. Yea : and his Flesh hee doth us there present.
Q. How meanest thou, that the substantiall Essence
  (After a reall and a carnall presence)
  Of Christ his Body, in the Bread is closed :
  And, of his Bloud within the Wine inclosed?
A. No ; nothing less. *Q.* Then plainly let mee know
  Where wee may find him. *A.* Not in Earth below ;
  But, in Heav'n's glory, with his glorious Sire :
  Whence hee shall come, to judge the World, in fire.

Q. But to climb Heav'n, what Ladder can suffice us?
A. Faith. *Q.* Then we must beleeve, ere ye advise us
  Unto this Feast for faithfull ones ordain'd?
A. So it behoves. *Q.* But, how is Faith attain'd?
A. Faith comes by hearing ; when the Holy Spirit
  Works with the word, and in us doth aver-it ;
  Confirming us in all the promises
  Which in his Gospell, Christ hath made to his.

The Prayer.

Q. O Gracious GOD, that grant'st the just desires
  Of Soules whose zeal to thee by Faith aspires :
  Sith only those doe worthily receive
  The Sacred Supper which thy Son did leave ;
  Who first by Faith, with strict examination,
  Doe sound themselves by upright conversation :
  Give us the grace, so to examine (then)
  Our Faith and Life as appertains. *A.* AMEN.

FINIS.

S P E C T A C L E S.

New-New-Polished

Perspectiue	*To discern*
SPECTACLES	*THE WORLD'S*
of	*Vanitie,*
Efpecial Vse,	*Leuitie, and Breuitie.*

These Glaſſes in indifferent Lights,
Serue Old, and yong, and midle Sights.

---

1   *Sol, Annus, Stellæ.*

WHen wee can stop th' accustomed Career
   Of heav'n's bright champion, mounted on the
     Dawn :
When we can cease the circuit of the Yeer,   [=seize
Whose winged car, by months, daies, hours, is drawn :
When wee can stint the wandring Armies cleer,
Which march above (in Blew-Gold-tinseld Lawn)
Tilting at ours their many-pointed Eyes :
Then may wee stay the WORLD'S Inconstancies.

2   *Orbis Cœli & Terræ.*

Who will not wonder, looking up, to see
The moving Heav'n's set, certain, Constancy ;
When, looking-down, in Earth unmov'd and stable,
Hee nothing findes but vainly variable ?
What lives on Earth, what-so partakes of Clay
Is frail and mortall ; hath no rest nor Stay :
Heav'n's rest-less roul ; yet in the Heav'n's there dwels
An end-less Rest, and Life that life excels.

3   *Quatuor Elementa.*

Fire, Air, Earth, Water, warring Each with Other,
Turn and return them one into another ;
As pleas'd th' All-Maker in This All-dispose
Th' accorded Discords of these friendly-Foes,
  To shew, that wee should for our blisse repair
Else-where then where is Earth, Fire, water, Air ;
And that Our Rest rests in a Place far higher
Then Earth, or Water, or the Air, or th' Fier.

4   *Mare.*

Is ought more fierce, more furious to withstand,
Then stormy Billows of the raging Sea ?
Is Ought more feeble then the flitting Sand ?
Yet doth the Sand the swelling Ocean stay.

O ! then, how fiercer ! O ! how furious more
Is th' aw-less Storm of Man's Concupiscence !
Which so transports him, that no Sand, no Shore,
No Bank, no Bound, can stop his Violence.

5   *Fontes & Flumina.*

You silver Brooks, cleer Rivers, crystall Fountains,
  Whose smooth swift-sliding pase
  Still, still roules down apace ;
Say, why so long you drive through Vales and Mountains?
To shew Thee, that thy Life (in This Theater)
  Flees from thee as the Water :
  And, that thy Soveraign Blisse
Abides not Here ; where nought abiding is.

6   *Dies.*

When the Day (the Sun's bright Son)
  New-awake, begins discover
  Mountain-Tops new-gilded-over,
With his ruddy Raies thereon :
That (mee thinks) should make us think
  On that true eternall Morning,
  When no Night shall be returning,
When both Heav'n and Earth shall shrink.

7   *Nox.*

When the Night's black Curtain, spread,
  Hides the Day, and Light bereaveth ;
  Then, my wakening Thought conceaveth
Other Night, more dark, more dread :
There where Worldlings, wilfull-blinde,
  Loath Instruction, leave Light's Mirrour,
  Double-nighted in dark Errour ;
Selfely put-out Light of Minde.

8   *Ver.*

When youthful spring the earth in green hath drest,
When Trees with Leaves and Blossoms them re-vest ;
  Their Flowers (white, red, blew, yellow)
  Betoken Fruit to follow.
But Worldlings, though they flourish in their prime,
Nor bud, nor bear, nor bring forth Fruit, in time :
  Their Health, Wealth, Wit, mis-wasted,
  Are but as blossoms blasted.

9   *Æstas.*

When Summer's Heat hath done his Part,
The Husband hath a gladsom heart ;   [=husbandman
Sith golden Treasures of the Plains
Make large Amends for all his Pains.
  But, th' idle Lubber, labour-loathing,
Walking, talking, wishing Store ;
Sowing Nought, but Winde, before ;
Shall, but Winde behinde, reap Nothing.

10   *Autumnus.*

When the Leaves in Autumn wither,
With a tawny-tanned Face
Warpt and wrinkled-up together,
Th' Year's late Beauty to disgrace :
There thy Life 's Glass maist thou finde-thee.
  Green now, gray now, gone anon ;
  Leaving (Worldling) of thine Own,
Neither Fruit, nor Leaf behind-thee.

11   *Hyems.*

When chill Winter's cheer wee see
Shrinking, shaking, shivering, cold
See Our Selves : for, such are wee
After Youth, if ever Old.
  After Winter, Spring (in order)
Coms again : but, Earthly Thing,
  Rotting here, not rooting further,
Can Thy Winter hope a spring.

12   *Quinque Sensus.*

How swift is Beauty vanisht from thine Eye !
How sudden Musick drowned in thine Eare !
How soon doe Odours from thy Nostrils fly !
How short, touch-Pleasures (tipt with pain and fear) !
How sower, tast-sweetest, in small time's expense-is !
Then, Epicure, well may wee blame thee, since
All under Sense thus vain, Thou hast no sense
Of Vanity, which so besots thy Senses.

13   *Vita & Mors.*

Worldlings that live in State and dye in strife,
Wretched their Death, and wretched is their Life.
For, their Life kills them, keeps them fetter'd in
The Chains of Death, the Cage and Wage of Sin.
Their death is double ; termin'd and eternall :
So much more deadly as it dyeth not.
For Errors, Terrors here ; there Torments hot :
Their Life, a Death ; their Death, a Life infernall.

14   *Eccho.*

What is the World, but a vain *Eccho's* Sounding,
From Woods, and Caves, and hollow Rocks rebounding?
A new No-noise, a dead-live Voice, to summon
Deluded Ears to listen to a Dumb-one :
A speaking Fiction of a mocking Faëry :
A formall Answer, in Effect but aëry?
  Hence, hence, vain *Eccho*, with thine idle Mocks ;
  Keep in thy Woods, sleep in thy Caves and Rocks.

15   *Incarceratus & Mendicus.*

As a close Pris'ner, in dark Durance chained,
Dreams that hee walks, runs, ranges at his will :
As a poor Begger, with sharp hunger pained,
Dreams that hee eats, and yet is empty still :
  So, the world's Captives, sleeping here securely,
Dream them the freest in their deepest Thrall,
Dream them abounding, seeming Lords of all :
Yet still are Beggers, and still Pris'ners surely.

16   *Fumus & Aura, convivium.*

The Worldling feeds his greedy Minde
With golden Hopes of high Conceits
(As vain and voyd as Smoak and Winde)
Which prove in fine but fine Deceits ;
Yet keenly set his Teeth on Edge.
  No Marvail though : for, he must needs
  Be ever light, that ever feeds
On winde and Smoak (and Chaff and Sedge).

17   *Cupido & Timor, constitutum.*

Desire and Fear cheer the Worldling ever martyrs,
Still double-racked with two divers Tortures :
  Desire's a Fire, running through all his bones,
  Which dries him, fries him, and his rest bereaves :
  His Fear's a Frost, chilling his heart at-once,
  Killing his Hopes, spilling the Webs he weaves :
So that, distract with Fear and with Desire,
In Frost hee fries, and freezes in the Fire.

18   *Ambitio, Luxus, Avaritia.*

Ambition, Luxe, and Avarice three witches
(Ladies, I should say) whom the world doth wooe
With suit and service (and that slavish too)
For their three Daughters, honour, pleasure, riches,
Serve All alike : the Ambitious, but with Winde :
With Woes, the Wanton (after Shews of Mirth) :
The Avaricious, with som Crums of Earth ;
Ever the lesse, the more hee sets his Minde.

19   *Avis & Navis.*

As in the Air, th' high-soaring Ægle scuds :
  As on the water slides the winged Ship :
So flees, so flits the wealth of worldly goods ;
  So swift away doth wanton Pleasure slip.
And, as wee cannot, in the air or water,
  See the Ship's furrow, nor the Ægle's footing :
When Wealth is past, and Pleasures posted after ;
  To track their trace, nor is, nor can be booting.

20 *Fratres in Malo.*

Th' Ambitious alwayes doth aloft aspire ;
  Honour on Honour striving still to heap :
The Avaricious stoopeth his Desire,
  From under ground his Golden Crop to reap.
Th' one tendeth upward, th' other downward tends ;
  As if at Ods, and utterly Contrary :
  Yet, though they seem, indeed they do not vary ;
But mean to meet together in their Ends.

21 *Væ Vobis.*

Who but hath heard Both bitterly deplore
  Their dismall Fortune, and disastrous Fates ?
O ! cryes th' Ambitious, I have lost my State :
O ! th' Avaricious, I have lost my Store :
Why cry you out on *Wracks*, and *Rocks*, and *Shelves*,
  And *Wars* and *Wiles*, that have your States undon ?
Rather complain, rather cry-out, upon
  Your *goods* and *greatness*, where you lost your selves.

22 *Punctus non dividendus.*

Is Heav'n a Circle, and is Earth the Centre
  So small a point (as Sages oft have Showne) ?
Why then fond mortals dare you Battell venture,
  Who the most part of so small Point shall owne ?
Why, silly worldlings, do you toil you so,
Train'd with false hopes of your too-fond Ambition ?
O ! dangerous Error is it, not to know
  'Tis vain to strain about a Point's partition.

23 *Onus cuique suum.*

Sure, Avarice is an extreme Disease ;
  So is Ambition an extreme Vexation :
Yet shall wee finde, survaying Both of These,
  That Either's Self bears his Own severall Passion.
But, th' eagre Fit, the Force, the Frenzy (rather)
  Mis-called Love (dead-Living, merry-Sadnesse)
Of one same Sicknesse makes Two sick together ;
  And Two at-once mad of One very Madnesse.

24 *Dulce Venenum, vel sibi lædens.*

Why wail'st Thou, Fondling ? and why weep you, Fair ?
Sighing your souls into the senseless Air ?
  Blame but your Selves : Desire is your Disease :
  Your Pain proceeds from what your Selves doth
    please.
Your chief content is in our torment's top :
  Your most delight is in you most Diseasing :
You drink you drunk in the sweet-bitter Cup,
W^{ch} sowrs your *joyes*, and makes *annoyes* as pleasing.

25 *Aquæ, Sagittæ, Venti.*

Swiftly Water sweepeth by :
Swifter winged Arrowes fly :
Swiftest yet, the Winde that passes,
When the neather clouds it chases.
  But, the Joyes of Earthly Mindes,
Worldly Pleasures, vain Delights,
Far out-swift far sudden flights,
Waters, Arrowes, and the Windes.

26 *Inconstantia.*

Inconstant Countrey, Thou maist witnesse be,
The world hath nought but vain *Inconstancy*.
Thy peace for war, thy war for peace thou takest :
  Thou doubtfull floatest on uncertain Waves :
  Thou ween'st, the slaughter thee from shambles saves :
Thy most Despight thy most Delight thou makest.
Th' hast nothing fixed, nothing firm, in Thee :
Nor constant Ought, but thine *Inconstancy*.

27 *Mundus qualis.*

What is the *World ?* tell, Worldling (if thou know it)
  If it be good, why do all Ils ore-flow-it ?
If it be bad, why dost thou like it so ?
  If it be sweet, how coms it bitter then ?
  If it be bitter, what bewitcheth men ?
If it be Friend, why kils it (as a Foe)
  Vain-minded Men that over-love and lust it ?
  If it be Foe, Fondling, how dar'st thou trust-it ?

28 *Aura, Flos, Vnda.*

World's best Beauty Self-defaces,
Sooner then the Puff that passes :
  Sooner then the fragrant Flow'r,
Blowne and mowne within an how'r :
Sooner then a Wave (that follows)
His owne Predecessor swallows.
  O ! what is then the World wee have ?
  Alas ! a Blast, a Bloom, a Wave.

29 *Quam malè conveniunt !*

More eas'ly far may wee
  Make black and white,
  And Day and Night,
In one same Terme agree :
And rather (rarely-od)
  Wed fire and water ;
  Death and Nature :
Then with the world match GOD.

30 *Emblema.*

Friend *Faber*, cast mee a round hollow Ball
Blown full of winde (for Emblem of this All) :
  Adorn it fair, and flourish every part
  With Flow'rs and Fruits, wth Brooks, Beasts, Fish,
    and Fowl ;
  With rarest cunning of thy curious Art :
  And grave in Gold, about my silver Bowl,
Thus roules the World (*the Idol of Mankinde*)
Whose Fruit is Fiction ; whose Foundation, Winde.

31 *Glacies.*

Ice is fair and shines externall ;
  Fair and shining th' All-Theater :
  From the ice they fall in water ;
From the World to Death eternall.
Both at last shall vanish : ice
  Into Water shall re-solve ;
All the World (and all his Vice)
  Into Nothing shall dissolve.

32   Rome (*Conquerer*) *conquered.*

The Stranger, wondring, stalks, and stares-upon
  Rome's antique Glories, in her Ruines seen :
Hee sees high Arches, huge shining Heaps of Stone,
  Maim'd, mutil'd, murder'd, by years wasteful teen :
Hee sees a rugged, ragged, rocky Quar
  Hang in the Air, with Ivie lac't about.
  O ! what can last, alas ! (then cries hee out)
Sith Time hath conquer'd the world's *Conquerer ?*

33   *Arbor.*

The World's a Tree (in my Conceit)
The Arms wide-spread, the body great,
The Root deep-reaching, nie to Hell :
The Leaves fresh varnisht lively green,
The Blossoms various to be seen ;
The Fruit doth suit the rest right well :
The Flow'r it bears, Som Beauty call ;
Hony the Fruit ; indeed, but Gall.

34   *Hortus.*

The World's a Garden ; Pleasures are the Flowers,
  Of fairest hues, in form and number many :
  The Lily (first) pure-whitest Flow'r of any,
Rose sweetest rare, with Pinked-Gillie-Flow'rs :
The Violet, and double Mari-gold,
  And Pansie too : but, after all Mischances,
Death's Winter comes ; and kills with sudden cold,
  Rose, Lily, Violet, Mari-Gold, Pink, Panses.

35   *Avaritia, Invidia.*

Never have, and never crave,
  Are the Worldling's thoughts intire :
Honour, Wealth ; the more they have,
  More they covet, more aspire.
They never doe enjoy their Own,
  But Other's wish, like, love, admire :
And having all, yet have they None ;
  For, after all, they more desire.

36   *Scientia, & Ignorantia.*

In Heav'n's sweet Language have I learn'd yer This,
  That to the wise the world's as night to morning,
As Deaw to Sun ; as Cloud to Noon-sted is :
  For vertuous knowledge, in his brest bright burning,
Is Morning, Sun and Noon : but, Ignorance
Is th' ugly Night ; Pleasures, the vading Deaw ;
Cloud Vanity, which doth our soules pursue,
Till Vertue's Raies infuse their Radiance.

37   *Bona cur Mala.*

Antiquity, O ! why didst thou devise
  This name of Goods unto these worldly Riches !
  Sith th' are (alas !) but Evils (Pains or Pitches)
To silly men that doe them over-prize,
  Rather ô worldling, why dost thou mis-use them ?
Why dost thou wrong Vertue's good Instruments ?
  Goods (Ills to those that doe them ill dispense)
Sith goods are goods to those that rightly use them.

38   *Quatuor Monarchia.*

The *Babylonian*, with ambitious fist,
  First the grand Scepter of the World possest :
The *Persian*, Him ; the *Grecian*, Him dismist :
  Him, th' awfull *Roman* after dispossest :
And Him, his Own Waight let not long subsist ;
  Him, his Own Greatness ruin'd with the rest.
Who then (alas !) this Fall of *Monarchs* seeing,
  Can hope on Earth for an eternall Being ?

39   *Glacies.*

Hee that makes the World his Nest,
Settling here his onely Rest ;
  Never craving other Scope,
  Never having higher hope :
What thinks (think you) such a One ?
Thus : to sit secure upon
  A Ball of Ice, a slippery Bowl,
  Which on the Seas doth ever roul.

40   *Diruit Edificans.*

When-as the worldling moils, and toyles, and tires,
  Incessantly to heave-up Wealth on Wealth,
  Pleasure on Pleasure, Stile on Stile ; by stealth,
To reach the top of his too-vain Desires :
When, the moor loaden, the less Waight he feeleth,
  Plotting his Ease i'th Pain hee doth pursue-in :
When hoord on hoord, when heap on heap he hilleth,
  What doth hee else but build himself his Ruine ?

41   *Bellum cum vitiis.*

One-Day I saw the World in furious Fight
  With lovely Vertue, his most loathed Foe ;
It dared her, shee bravely did defie 't :
It entred Lists (She first had entred through).
It traverses, it toils, it heaws, it hacks ;
  But all in vain, his blowes come never nigh-her :
For the World's Weapons were but lythie Wax ;
And Vertue's Shield is of celestiall Fier.

42   *Naufragium.*

Thou, thou, whose heart dives in the world so deep,
  Seest thou thy case ? know'st thou thine own condi-
    tion ?
  Like head-less bark tost 'twixt the opposition
Of blustring Storms which every way doe sweep.
Reason, Thy Rudder, is already lacking :
  The Gales of Pleasure, and the Gusts of Passion,
  Hurry thee headlong in the Gulf of Fashion,
On rocks of death thy wretched life soon wracking.

43   *Mors in Olla.*

Where's *death ?* i'th' *world.* Where is the *world ?* In
  death :
  Death to it Self : for, nothing in the *world*
  Kils and confounds the *world*, more then the *world ;*
Which breeds and feeds, and giveth life to *death.*
But, from the *world* could God's love wean the *world,*
  Killing the *world's* Love, and his Issue, *death ;*
  Then happy wee should triumph over *death ;*
The *world* not worldly ; *death* dead in the *world.*

44 *Somnium.*

I saw, I saw, the World was but a dream,
When heav'n's shrill voice had rouz'd and rais'd my
eyes :
For, in the World I found but Lies ;
Eyes clos'd, Ears stopt, mindes inly toil'd extreme ;
All dark, all night : Man out of Man (in Cumber)
Himselfe with Fumes and Phant'sies feeding,
Not feeling Pains, nor Passions heeding ;
Loth to be waked from so sweet a Slumber.

45 *Quasi non utens.*

O ! happy hee can be so highly wise,
As not to know the vain and vicious pleasures
The vicious take (when they will take their leasures)
Which so besot their Soules, and blinde their eyes.
O ! happy Hee that can disdain and deem
Those Pleasures, Poisons ; and that Hony, Gall.
But, who can so ? Hee that contemning All,
Lives in the World, and not the World in Him.

46 *Monstrum horrendum.*

What Monster's that which hath so many heads ;
So many Ears, so many Eyes between ;
So lively clad before in lusty Green ;
So black behinde, in cloudy Cloak of Shreds ;
His feet so sliding down a round steep Hill :
Rouled by Time, which turns it swift away ;
Death running after, shooteth at it still ?
Ah ! now I see. What is 't ? The World, I say.

47 *Sordescit & Surdescit.*

Stay, Worldling stay : Whither-away so fast ?
Hark, hark a while to Vertue's Counsels Current.
No, no : alas ! after the World in haste,
Hee hies, flies, follows : as a rapid Torrent
Too-proudly swelling with some fresh Supply
Of liquid Silver from the Welkin gushing,
My warning (as a Rock) he rouleth by
With roaring Murmur, sudden over-rushing.

48 *Sufficit Vnum.*

'Twas a loud Lie (think I) a very Slander,
Th' Ancients ascrib t' ambitious *Alexander*,
Weeping for wo there were no mo worlds made.
Suffic'd not One, so busie and so bad ;
If true it were, Great Monarch, cease to mourn ;
And give mee leave, O let mee weep my Turn ;
Who strain and strive ; yet cannot all my Care
All Vanities of this One World declare.

49 *Variable.*

Vary, re-vary ; tune, and tune againe
(Anon to this String, and anon to That ;
Base, Treble, Tenor ; swift, slow, sharp, and flat)
Thy One same Subject in a sundry Strain :
To represent, by thy so divers Ditties,
The dying World's so divers Alterations :
Yet will the World have still mo Variations ;
And, past thy Verse, thy various Subject yet-is.

50

'Tis but Vanity and Folly,
On the World to settle wholy.
All the Joyes of all this Life
Are but Toyes, Annoyes and Strife.
O God ! onely wise and stable,
To establish Mee in Thee,
Give mee, Thou that art All-able,
Wisedome with true Constancy.

FINIS.

MOTTOES.

Fulmina montes.

LE Rocher orgueilleux
  Sent tomber sur sa teste
  La plus rude Tempeste :
Le fouldre perilleux
  Au groz Arbres s'attache :
Ainsi Dieu de ses mains
  Des lieux plus hauts arrache
Les superbes humains.
The highest Rocks and Hils,
  Which seem the Clouds to threaten,   10
  With roughest Storms are beaten :
The lofty Cedar feels
The Lightning's Flash and Thunder :
  So God's Almighty hand
Soon from aloft brings under
  The proudest that withstand.

Omnia Christus.

Que sont les Conseils humains?
Que sont les Œuvres des mains?
  Qu'est l'Excellence des hommes?
  Qu'est tout l'Estat ou nous sommes   20
Si CHRIST en est separé?
Ce n'est qu'un Cachot pavé
  De vents, d'ombres, de fumées,
  D'un Feu de Mort allumées.
  What's the wisdome of Mankinde?
  What the works of hand or minde?
  What the Vertues of the Rarest?
  What is all our Best and Fairest,
    Void of Christ? Alas! a Grave,
    Dungeon, Den, or dreadfull Cave,   30
  Lin'd with wind, with shades, with vapors,
  Set on fire with deadly Tapers.

Fuimus fumus.

Mon Ame, ou sont les grands Discours
De ces hautains filz de la Terre?
Ou sont les magnifiques Tours
  Des Roys qui en Ciel ont fait Guerre?
Je cuide voir en y pensant,
  Une Fumée s'amassant
  Au Feu d'un Bois sec que l'haleine
  Du Vent escarte par la Plaine.   40
  Where, where are now the great Reports
Of those huge haughty earth-born Giants?
  Where are the lofty Towrs and Forts
Of those proud Kings bade Heav'n defiance?
  When Them I to my Minde revoke,
  Mee thinks I see a mighty Smoake
Thick mounting from quick-burning Matter
Which in an instant Windes doe scatter.

Omnia Somnia.

Pauure Ver, travaille, tracasse,
  Sans te lasser,   50
  Pour amasser
Les Honneurs, ou d'Or quelque Masse :
Mais la Mort qui ta force ronge,
  En t'abatant
  Tout a l'instant,
Prouvera que tu n'es qu'un Songe.
Goe, silly Worm, drudge, trudge, and travell,
  Despising Pain ;
  So thou maist gain
Some Honour, or some Golden Gravell :   60
But Death the while (to fill his number)
  With sudden Call
  Takes thee from All,
To prove thy Daies but Dream and Slumber,

Quorum meminisse pudebit.

  As tu miz en Oubliance,
  Homme, ta brutale Enfance?
Riant, ozes tu chanter
  Les Erreurs de ta Jeunesse?
  En courant vers ta viellesse
Voudrois Tu bien plaisanter?   70
  Pleure donc, puis que ta Vie
  Est a touts maux asservie.
Art thou, Man, no more now mindefull
Of thy Child-hood, brute and blindefull?
  Dost thou laugh, and dost thou sing
Th' Errors of thy Youth and folly?
Canst thou be so blithe and jolly,
  Towards Age now galloping?
Rather wail thy Life's Condition,
Thrall to Sin, Death and Perdition.   80

Quasi Bulla.

I'apperceus un Enfant qui d'un tuyau de Paille
  Trempé dans la Savon, avecques Eau meslé,
Des Ampoules souffloit encontre une Muraille,
  Dont l'œil de maint passant estoit esmervillé :
Riches, Elles sembloit, fermes, de forme ronde :
  Mais les voyant crever en leur lustre plus beau,
  Voire soudainement ; voy-la (di-je) un Tableau
De la fraile splendeur et vanité du Monde.
I saw a child with slender pipe of stubble
(From hollow shell with Soap and Water mixt)   90
Against a Wall to blow-up many a Bubble ;
  Where many an Eye of many by was fixt :
For, rich they seem'd, and firm round Form did render.
  But, when I saw them (and that suddenly)
  Break at the best ; behold a Type, said I,
Of World's vain glory, and soon-vading splendor.

Rosa non sine
pina.

Quand je lis, quand je contemple
L'estat de cest heureux Temple
   Que *Christ* en Terre a planté,
   Courant par le Monde, enté   100
Sur l'Ordure et la Malice ;
   Je devien triste et joyeux,
   J'embrasse et chasse le vice
   Je quitte et cherche les Cieux.
When I read, when I contemple,
Th' estate of that happy Temple
   Christ hath planted here below
   Amid this World ; and grafted so
On Dirt, in danger of the Divell ;
   Sad and glad at-once I am :   110
I imbrace and chase the Evill :
   Heav'n I shun, yet seeke the same.

Deteriora sequor.

Le monde est outrageux, et si est bien servi :
   C'est un Tyran cruel, et si est bien suyvi :
C'est un infame Monstre, et tandiz se contente :
Il gist au lict de Mort, et de viure se vante :
   Il n'est rien que malheur, et si est trop aimé :
   C'est Dueil, Honte, et Dommage, et si est estimé :
Il cerche son Repos en se faisant la Guerre :
Il abhorre les Cieux et perit en la Terre.   120
The World is full of Wrong, and yet is serv'd too-well :
   'Tis too-well follow'd too, and yet a Tyrant fell :
'T's an ugly Monster-most, and yet the most contenteth :
'Tis on the Death-bed laid, and yet of life it vanteth :
   'Tis sorrow, shame, and losse, and yet is most approved :
   'Tis nothing but a Crosse, and yet is best beloved :
'Tis seeking peace in war ; choaks whom it seems to
   cherish :
'Tis hating heav'n for earth ; and it in hell shall perish.

Ce Monde est une Galere
Equipée de Misere ;   130
   Cinglant en Mer de Douleurs :
   Ses Forçats, ce sont les Pleurs :
Son Pilote, Coeur rebelle :
   Ses Vents, funeuz Desires :
   Ses Routes, tristes Plaisirs :
Son Havre, Mort eternelle.
This World is a Galley fraightea
With mis-haps (or Haps mis-treated)
   Sliding on a sea of Care.
   Tears and Fears her Sailers are :   140
Will, her Pilot (still at Stern, all) :
   Strong Desires, her Windes (for most) :
   Bitter-sweet, her Course and Coast :
And her Hav'n is Death eternall.

Qu'est ce du Cours et de l'arrest du Monde ?
   C'est un Chemin rabotteux, ennuyeux :
   Un Cocher sol, desloyal, dangereux,
Trainant son Coche en la boüie profonde.
Un Logie fumeux, sale puant :
   Un hoste avare, infame, remuant :   150
Un lict pierreux : un faschcux et vain Songe :
Un Resueiller d'Orgueil et de Mensonge.
What the World's Progress ? what our Gifts here living ?
   But a foul way, all full of Baulks and Sloughs :

   (A follish Coach-man, false and dangerous,
Through thick and thin our old weak Chariot driving)
   A smoakie Lodging, stinking, nastie-most :
   A greedy, needy, churlish, filthy Hoste :
A stony Bed, a strange unquiet Slumber :
Awakt with Lies, Pride, Perill, and Incumber.   160

Des Monarques la grandeur,
De tant de Nobles la Race,
   De tant de Preux la Splendeur,
   Des bons Esprits le grand-heur,
Le Temps et la Mort Efface.
   N'arrestons donques les Yeux
A ceste lueur qui passe,
   Ains les eslevons aux Cieux.
   Monarch's greatest Greatnesse here,
Nobles noblest Ranks and Races,   170
   Worthies' Tropheis, passing peer,
   Sages Worth for Wisdome cleer,
Time (alas !) and death defaces.
   Why then fix wee here our Eyes,
On this glimpse that sudden passes ?
   Rather rear them to the Skies.

Mais que feroy-je plus au Monde
Que en Monde de Maux abonde ?
   Adieu Monde, adieu tes debats,
   Tes Cris, tes Assaults, tes Combats :   180
Verité Retraitte sonne.
   L' Eternel tire a Soy mon Coeur
   (Par foy de ta force Vainqueur)
Et de sa Gloire me couronne.
Why, why should I the World be minding,
Therein a World of evils finding ?
   Then farewel World : farewel thy Jars,
   Thy joyes, thy toyes, thy wiles, thy wars.
Truth sounds Retrait : I am not for-yee.
   Th' Eternall drawes to him my heart   190
   By faith (which can thy force subvert)
To crown mee (after Grace) with Glory.

Inveni portum
Spei, etc.

Quelle est ceste Beauté que je voy tant extreme,
   Qui avec ses Cheveux, et sa voix, et ses yeux,
D'un lieu, & d'un Charm, & d'un Traict amoreux,
Et s'enchaine, et s'enchante, et s'aveugle soy mesme ?
C'est la monde changé en Courtisanne infame,
   Qui se va desguizant de mille fards le Corps ;
   Mais, ce'est une Beauté seulement par dehors,
Qui ne peut effacer les Laideurs de son Ame.   200
What Beautie's This, so brave bedeckt in Riches ?
   Whose wanton Looks, whose waving Looks and
   Song,
   As with a Dart, a Chaine, a Charm (too-strong)
Self-blinds, self-bindes, and self it self bewitches ?
O ! 'tis the World 't's a Courtisan transformed,
   Who pranks and paints her body round about :
   But all this Beauty onely is without,
And cannot hide the Soule within deformed.

Mundus immun-
dus.

Le Peché, et la Mort, et le Monde, et la Chair,
Conspirerent un Jour contre l'Ame immortelle :   210
   Le traistre Corps des ja les laissoit approcher,
Si la Foy n'eust esté pours lors en Sentinelle :

Qui du Peché, du monde, et de la Chair l'effort
Surmonta par sa croix, de quoy l'Ame enhardie,
Fit se bien qu'en plain champelle vint mettre a Mort
La Mort qui s' attendoit de luy oster la Vie.

The World and Flesh, combin'd with death and
    sinne,
Against th' immortall Soule were privie-banding;
    Selfe Traitor Nature had even let them in;
Had not the Faith for Sentinell bin standing;   220
    Who by the Cross, did Sin, Flesh, World subdue:
Whereby, the Soule re-heartned and revived,
    Led by her Head, pursu'd the Fight and slew,
Slew Death, which sought Her Life to have deprived.

Morte est la Mort, et non le Monde,
Qui au Monde donner la loy;
    N'ayant plus Crainte que la Foy
    Quelque autre Querelle luy fonde.
Dautant qu'au Ciel la Foy demeure,
Hors du Monde; ne pouvant voir   230
    Que dans son siege on vienne assoir
    Toute Inconstance et tout Pariure.

Death's dead indeed, the World yet is not;
    But yet, yet rules the World about;
    Of Faith's Affront no more in doubt:
Sith her here fighting more it sees not.
For, Faith hath now in Heav'n her Station,
    Forth of the World; disdaining here
    To see her Seat usurpt so neer
By Error and Equivocation.   240

Pourquoy mets tu ton Esperance,
Monde, en la Mondaine Inconstance?
    Veu que du Monde les Delices
    Ne sont qu'une grand Mer de Vices:
Ne sont qu'un miserable sort:
    Qu'un vain Espoir, et qu'un pur Songe:
    Et qu'un Orage qui de plonge
En fin au Goufre de la Mort.

Why? why build World's their Hopes Assurance
    On this vain World's enduring Durance?   250
Sith all the Sweet of worldly Pleasures,
Worldly Honours, worldly Treasures,
    Is nothing but a Blast, a breath,
    An addle Hope, an idle Dreaming,
    A sudden Storm with fury streaming.
    And drowning all in Gulf of Death.

Tout ce Monde est un Tabourin qui sonne
L'alarme au Monde, et cruel espoinçonne
    Filz contre Pere: et scavez vous comment?
    Par un Moyen qui n'est fait que de vent.   260
Monde, dis moy, d'ou vient qu'un simple Son
    Qui sort de peaux qu'on bat sur un escorce,
Peut esmouvoir d'une telle fason
    Encontre Toy la force de ta force?

The World's a Drum, with loud Alarum stirring
The World to war; and too-too-cruel spurring
    Son against Sire. The Means if you would finde,
    '*Tis by a Mean that is but made of Winde.*
But tell mee, World, how coms a simple Sound
    Sent but from Skins, upon a Skin but beating,   270

T' incite thee so, so to bestir thee round
To face thy Force, thy Face's force so threating?

Monde, pourquoy fuis tu? Pour chercher assurance,
    Et, si ce n'est en Toy, ou la trouveras Tu?
    Ou le Monde n'est pas du Monde combattu.
Le Monde se faict il a soy mesmes offense?
Ouy trop; car en la Terre, au Feu, en l'Air, en l'Onde
    Le Monde s'occit, s'ard, et se noye et se pend.
Monde, fuy donc au ciel: car fol est qui s'attend
D'Anchrer sa Nef flotante en l'*Euripe* du Monde.   280

Why fleest thou, world? Alas! to seek Assurance.
    Where to be found, if in the world it fail?
    There where the world doth not the world assail.
Why? doth the world cause to it self Ill-durance?
Yes; too-too-much: for in Fire, Air, Earth, Water,
    The world self-drowns, self-burns, self-hangs, self-
    slaies.
Flee then to heav'n. Fond he that Anchor layes
In th' Euripus of this vain World's Theater.

Peintre, si tu tires le Monde,
Ne le pein pas de Forme ronde: 290
    Car, ce qui en Rond est pourtraict
    Est estimé du tout parfaict:
Et le Monde ne le peut estre
    Ou defaut le Soveraign Bien;
    Et ou tant seulement le Rien
Et l'Inconstance prennent estre.

Friend Larkin, if the world you figure,
You must not draw it round of Figure:
    For, Sages hold the compleat Round
    In every part is perfect found.   300
So never can this world be; seeing
    There wants the Chief, The chiefest Good:
    And Nothing there (right understood)
But Nothing hath (inconstant) Beeing.

Plustost les Yeux du Firmament
Seront sanz reglé Mouvement;
    Et Vagabonde
    Ne sera l'Onde:
Plustost qu'on voye desplacée
    Des vains Appats   310
    De ces lieux baz
Du Mondain la folle pensée.

Sooner shall all the Heav'n's bright Eyes
Cease their set courses in the Skies:
    Sooner shall the Ocean
    Have no more Motion:
Sooner then worldly mindes removed
    From vain Deceits
    Of Earthly Baits,
By Worldlings here too-dear beloved.   320

Et le Monde et la Mort entr' Eux se desguiserent
    Un Jour pour pouvoir mieux l'Homme Mondain
    surprendre
L'adjournent pour ce faict, et puis l'interroguerent
    Qu'il dist, au quel des deux pour serf se vouloit
    rendre.
L'homme mondain cuidant ne s'addonner qu'au monde,
    Par le Monde trompeur s'asservit a la Mort.

Mais se voyant deceu, Il appella du Tort,
A Un qui par sa Mort chassa la Mort du Monde.
The world and Death one day them cross-disguised
To cosen Man (when sin had once beguil'd him) 330
Both call'd him forth ; and questioning advised
To say, whose servant he would fainly yeeld him.
Man, weening then but to the world t' have giv'n-him,
By the false world became the Slave of Death :
But, from their fraud hee did appeal by Faith
To Him, whose death kild death, and hence hath driv'n-
him.

Le Monde est un grand Parlement :
Son Avocat, est l'Arrogance :
Son Soliciteur, est l'Offense :
Son Procureur, vain Pensement : 340
L'Huissier, qui les Causes appelle
Est le Remords : Juge, la Mort
Qui prononce en dernier Resort
L'Arrest de la Peine eternelle.
The World's a Sessions, or Assize ;
The Counsellor is Arrogancy :
Sin the Sollicitor (fee'd by Fancy)
Th' Attourney is but vain Surmise :
Remorse is Marshall : Conscience, Crier :
Death sits as Judge in dreadfull room ; 350
Pronouncing, for a finall Doom,
The sentence of eternall fire.

Vous Pleuples bazanez les quels le Gain attire
Ores a recercher une incognue Mer ;
Ores de vers la Tane, et vers l'Inde ramer
Fondans tout vostre Appuy sur le vol d'on Navire.
Pour Patron, qu'avez vous que vaine passion ?
Pour Timon, qu'Avarice ? et pour Voles, que Rage ?
Et poussez par le vent de toute Ambition,
Que pensez vous gaigner qu'un asseuré Naufrace ? 360
You tanned Tiphys, whom Gain's love bewitches,
From Inde to Inde, and from the North to Nile,
To sound new seas, to seek new shores, the While
Your Life's best hope but in a Plank and Pitch-is.
What Pilot have you but your Passion, still ?
Your Rudder, Avarice ; and your Mast, Ambition ;
Your Sails, but Pride ; which Furies puffs' doe fill :
What think you then to gain, but deep Perdition ?
Ce Monde est un Pelerinage
Les Meschants forcenez de rage 370

Y sont les devots Pelerins,
Qui four voyes des droits Chemins,
Tombent en la fosse profonde
De la Mort : Mais O Toy Mon DIEU,
Guidant mes paz in autre lieu,
Tire Moy du Chemin du Monde.
This World is but a Pilgrimaging,
Where wicked men, most felly-raging,
Doe trudge and travell most devout :
But, from the right way wandring out, 380
They headlong fall in Pit of Terror,
The Gulf of Death. But, O my God,
Guiding my steps in better Road,
Draw mee to Thee, from worldlings' Error.

FINIS.

AN APPENDIX.

ALthough thou canst not write so rare a Ditty.
Nor sing so sweetly, be thou vertuous though :
For, doing well is more then saying so :
And, to be Wise, is more then to be Witty.
The Vertuous, reading and recording sweet 390
The sacred Song, is cheered in his Courses :
The vicious, reading, singing, rather worse-is ;
Rapt with the Sound, not with the Sense, awhit,
Surcease thy Musick, lay aside thy Muses :
Paschal and *Pibrac*, you have toil'd too-long :
Seing that vertue serves but for a Song
To this vain World, that on all Mischief muses :
Lo, here in Paper is poor Vertue painted :
Alas, dead Vertue ! Thus these times do use-thee :
Yet, if all hands, yet if all hearts refuse-thee, 400
Remaine Thou ever in these Songs imprinted.
As fiercest Lion, fretting in his Cage,
Is somtimes calmed with harmonious sounding
Of Lyrike strings, and made to leave his rage,
Let go his Prey, and fall to Dance-like bounding :
So, the vain World, in Pangs and Passions flinging,
Charm'd (as it were) and bound with sev'nty chains,
It's Fits and Phant'sies, for a while, refrains ;
Here, to it Selfe, it Selfe's Inconstance singing.

FINIS.

THE WOOD-
MANS BEAR.
A Poeme:

By JOSUAH SYLVESTER.

Semèl infanivimus Omnes.

TO THE WORSHIPFUL, HIS MOST
approved Friend, Mr. ROBERT
NICOLSON.

S Ir, the kind Welcom that you alwayes daign
   To the faire Muses, and their Favorites ;
And chiefly mee, the meanest of their train,
   (Too mean to meddle with their sacred rites)
My willing heart with thankfull hand invites
   To offer you my busie-idle pain,
Ill-shapen shadows of my young delights,
   Till better fruits my better Fates ordain.

Yet (pray-you) private let this Jigg bee kept,
   Unworthy Object for judicious Eyes :
Which, but for you, eternally had slept ;
   And, but to you, from hence-forth ever dyes :
      But, lack of better forc't mee, for a shift,
      To bring you now this old-new New-yeers Gift.

Semper Arcto-philos.

TO HIS
DIVINE ARCTO
HER DEVOUT
ARCTOPHILOS.

B Ecause I count a promise debt (*my Dear*)
   Especially unto a speciall friend,
      This promis'd pledge to your sweet Self I send ;
         A gloomy glasse of your perfections cleer :
A pourtraiture resembling nothing neer
   Your heav'nly Features that in worth extend
Beyond the reach of my poor rymes' Commend,
   As in this plot I make too plain appeare.

Yet since for you amid my dumps I drew-it,
   And since your selfe have since desir'd to see-it ;
With milde aspect vouchsafe (bright-Star) to view-it,
   To doom whereof, in your discretion be-it :
      But deem withall, that in this bitter story
      I grave my griefs, and not your beautie's glory.

Vicenti gloria Victi.

THE WOOD-
MANS BEAR.

1.

Seventy nine-score years and sev'n
  Were expired from the birth
  Of a Babe begot by Heav'n,
To bring Peace unto the Earth ;
  Peace that passeth all esteeming,
  Sin-bound soules from Hell redeeming.

Ver. 2.

Phœbus in his yearly race
(Having past the *Ram* and *Steer*)
Now began to post apace
Through the *Twins*' fair houses cleer,
  Pranking in perfumed robes
  All these goodly neather Globes,

Aurora. 3.

And *Aurora*, richly dight
In an azure mantle fair,
Freng'd about with silver bright,
Pearl-deaws dropping through the air,
  Hung the gate with golden tissues,
  Where *Hiperion's* Chariot issues.

4.

At which sight (that all rejoyces)
All the cunning Forrest Quier,
Tuning loud their little voyces,
Warbled who should warble higher :
  Striving all to beare the Bell
  (All in vain) from *Philomel.*

5.

When my joylesse senses, dulled
With the busie toil of Cities,
Mee from pensive fancies pulled,
To goe hear, their heav'nly Ditties :
  To goe hear, and see, and sent,
  Sounds, sighs, savours excellent.

6.

Wending then through Lawns and Thickets,
Where the fearfull Deer doe brouz,
Where the wanton Fawns and Prickets
Crop the top of springing boughs :

Where the Stag and light-foot Hinde
Scud, and skip, and turn, and winde ;

7.

While I led my wandring feet
Through a silent shady Grove,
Paved thick with Primrose sweet :
As mine eyes about did rove,
  Neer a spring I chanc't to spy,
  Where a wretched man did ly.

8.

Like a *Wood-man* was his weed :
Groveling on the ground hee lay,
Mourning so as doth exceed
All that ever I can say.
  Beasts to bellow, birds to sing,
  Ceast, to see so strange a thing.

9.

Wringing hands, and weeping eyes,
Heavy sighs, and hollow groans,
Wailing words, and wofull cries,
Were the witnesse of his moans ;
  Moans that might with bitter passion
  Move a flinty heart's compassion.

10.

Fain would I the cause have kend,
That could cause him so complain :
But I fear'd him to offend
With repeating of his pain :
  Therefore I expected rather,
  From himselfe the same to gather.

11.

Sitting then in shelter shady,
To observe and mark his mone,
Suddenly I saw a *Lady*
Hasting to him all alone,
  Clad in Maiden-white and green :
  Whom I judg'd the Forrest Queen.

12.

Who the eager game pursuing,
Lost her Ladies in the chase,

Till shee heard the wretche's ruing :
Unto whom shee hied apace ;
   Moving him, with milde intreat,
   To unfold his grief so great.

13.

When the Queen of Continence,
With the musick of her words,
Had by sacred influence
Charm'd the edge of sorrow's words :
   (Swords that deeper wounds have made
   Then the keen *Toledo* blade.)

14.

Fain hee would, and yet hee fainted
To unfold his fatall grief :
Passions in his face depainted,
Striving whether should be chiefe :
   Thus at last, though loath and sorry,
   Sigh't hee out his mournfull story.

15.

Madam, quoth hee (yet hee knew not
What shee was) that you may see,
That I cursed causelesse rue not,
Lend awhile your eare to mee ;
   And you shall perceive the source
   Whence my cares have had their course.

16.

Whence my cares and sad incumbers
Have arisen and proceeded :
Whose account of countlesse numbers
Hath the *Ocean's* sand exceeded ;
   Whose extreme tormenting smart
   Passeth all conceit of heart.

17.

Thrice-sev'n Summers I had seen
Deckt in *Flora's* rich array ;
And as many Winters keen
Wrapt in suits of silver gray :
   Yer the *Cyprian* Queen's blinde Boy
   Grudged at my grief-less joy.

18.

But when on my maiden chin
Mother *Nature* 'gan ingender
Smooth, soft, golden Doun, and thin
Blades of Bever, silk-like slender ;
   Then hee, finding fuell fit,
   Sought for coales to kindle it.

19.

Coals hee found, but found no fire :
For, th' East *Frisian* Icy sky
Made the sparks of love's desire
Sudden born, as soon to dy.
   Thus so long as there I bid,
   All was vain that *Venus* did.

20.

Seeing then that nought might boot,
Shee (consulting with her bastard)
Bid the busie wanton shoot :
But alas hee durst not, dastard :
   In that quarter well hee wist
   Armes to meet with mee, hee mist.

21.

Therefore weary of his toile,
Hopelesse still of better hap,
In that so unhappy soile,
Where few *Brutes* hee could entrap ;
   Hee forsooke the frozen *Ems*
   Soaring towards silver *Thames.*

22.

On whose lilie-paved banks,
Where faire water-Nymphs resorted,
Plaid hee many wanton pranks,
While the silly Damsels sported ;
   Wounding with his cruell darts,
   Their unwary tender hearts.

23.

Chiefly in my Mother-Towne,
Where the Paragon of honour,
Vertue's praise, and beautie's crowne,
With sweet Ladies tending on her,
   Kept her Court in Palace royall,
   Guarded by Attendants loyall.

24.

There the *Paphian* Prince (perceiving
Lords and Ladies, young and old,
Apt (through ease) for Love's deceiving)
Sends about his shafts of gold,
   Striking all, save her hee dares not,
   Dian's selfe : the rest hee spares not.

25.

Having triumpht there a season
Over all degrees and sexes,
Planting love, supplanting reason,
Where his darts dire venome vexes :
   Suddenly hee crost the floud,
   To the famous Seat of *Lud.*

26.

Finding there sufficient fuell,
To maintaine his wanton fires,
By and by begins hee cruell
To inflame both Sonnes and Sires,
   Maid and Mistris, Man and Master,
   Dame and Daughter, light or chaster.

27.

Thus hee tortures, voide of pitie,
Rich and poor, and fond and wise,

Through the streets of all the Citie ;
Causing by his cruelties,
  Sighing-singing, freezing-frying,
  Laughing,-weeping, living-dying.

28.

Fates by this time had contrived
Causes that mee thither drew.
Which, ere ever I arrived,
This detested Tyrant knew :
  Wily waiting time and place,
  To revenge his old disgrace.

29.

Oftentimes hee did attempt
Even in streets of second *Troy*,
To have punisht my contempt,
By bereaving freedome's joy :
  But unable there to match mee,
  Else-where yet hee thought to catch mee.

30.

I was wont (for my disport)
Often in the Summer season,
To a Village to resort,
Famous for the rathe ripe Peason ;
  Where, beneath a *Plumm*-tree shade,
  Many pleasant walks I made.

31.

Till a grasse-born-kricket, mounted
On that goodly Tree's fair top,
Made his fore fruit (rare accounted)
Over-soon to fall and drop ;
  Loading every branch and bough
  With her brood of krickets now.

32.

Hither while I us'd to haunt,
Cupid seeking change of harbour,
Leaving stately *Troy-novant*,
Lighted under this fresh Arbour,
  Neere the houre when *Titan* wondrous,
  Hides our shadowes wholly und'r-us.

33.

When the Dwarfling did perceive mee,
Mee, *Love's* most rebellious scorner ;
By some cautell to deceive mee,
Skipt hee soone into a corner
  Where, lest I should spie the Elfe,
  In a *Bear* hee hid himselfe.

34.

Many Beasts, and Birds beside,
Adorned with the pride of nature ;
Faire of feather, rich of hide,
Trim of forme, and tall of stature,
  Us'd this Orchard to frequent,
  Till the Summer's heat was spent.

35.

But the *Bear* was my Betrayer ;
Nay, she was my life's defender :
But shee was my freedome's slayer ;
Nay, shee was my thraldome's ender :
  But shee fill'd my soule with sadnesse ;
  Nay, shee turn'd my griefe to gladnesse.

36.

Blessed *Bear*, that bears the bell
From the fairest of her kind :
Such a *Bear* as doth excell
Those to either *Pole* assign'd :
  Such a *Bear*, as 'twould not grieve mee,
  To be Bear-ward made : beleeve mee.

37.

In a *Crofte* where *Musick's* King
(Making mends for *Daphne's* wrong
Made out of the ground to spring
Trees transform'd to *Daphne's* young :
  In the *Crofte* so faire and pleasant,
  Harbour of the Prince-dish Pheasant.

38.

Southward was this white *Bear* bred,
Yet not scorcht with *Affrick* heate ;
For her Dam had dipt her head
In the Crystall waters neat
  Of a Spring call'd *Hamberwell*,
  Which can Sun-burnt spots expell :

39.

And besides, while young shee was,
Shee was carried from that coast,
To be taught such practice, as
Makes such Beasts beloved most :
  Beast am I to call her beast :
  Yet indeed a *Bear's* a beast.

40.

Bear in name, but not in nature,
Was this much admired creature,
Peerlesse piece of perfect stature,
Full of all desired feature :
  Feature such, as all too-faint,
  My dull pen presumes to paint.

41.

Lovely Lilly-white shee was
Strait proportion'd, stately-pased,
Coy, or kind (as came to passe)
Courteous-spoken, comely-graced :
  Graces seem'd of graces lavish,
  Eyes that gaz'd on her to ravish.

42.

Locks like streams of liquid Amber,
Smooth down dangling, seem'd to spred

Hangings fit for Beautie's chamber,
Curtains fit for Beautie's bed :
Of which slender golden sleave,
Love his wanton nets did weave.

43.

Fore-head fair as Summer's face,
Built upon two *Ebene* Arch's :
Under which in equall space
Stood two bright resplendent sparks :
Sparks excelling in their shine,
Fairest beams of *Ericyne*.

44.

From these Arch's between these eyes,
(Eyes that arme Love's Arches tillar)
Even descending did arise,
Like a pale *Pyramid* pillar,
That faire double-doored port,
Where sweet *Zephir* loves to sport.

45.

On each side whereof extended
Fields, wherein did ever grow
Roses, Lilies, Violets blended,
Steept in streams of sanguine snow :
Red-white hils, and white-red plaines,
Azure vales, and azure veines :

46.

Veines, whose saphir Seas do slide
(Branch-wise winding in and out)
With a gentle flowing tide
All that *Little World* about,
Up and downe, aloft and under,
To fill all this world with wonder.

47.

With her mouth I meddle not,
Nor with *Ecchoe's* dainty mazes :
Lest these hearing any jot
Mis-reported of her prayses
In their form, might them incense
To reprove my proud offence.

48.

But fond hee that over-skips
(Fearing fancie's had I wist)
Those smooth smiling lovely lips,
Which each other alwayes kist :
Sweetly swelling round like Cherries,
Fragrant as our garden-berries.

49.

Lips like leaves of Damaske-Rose
Joyned just in equall measure,
Which in their sweet folds inclose
Plenteous store of pleasant treasure :
Treasures more then may be told ;
Balme, and Pearles, and purest gold.

50.

Balme her breath, for so it smelt ;
Pearles, those pales about the Parke,
Where that golden Image dwelt,
Her pure tongue that most I marke :
Such a tongue, as with my tongue
Never can enough be sung.

51.

Now remaines of all this *Ile*
Onely that white *Ivory* Ball,
Dimpled with a cheerfull smile,
Which the *Cape* of *Love* I call.
Eden was this Iland, Madam :
While I gaz'd, mine eye was *Adam.*

52.

Next her Swan-like neck I saw :
Then those spotlesse snowie mountaines,
Which, when Love's warme Sun shall thaw,
Shall resolve in *Nectar* fountaines :
'Twixt which mountaines lies a valley,
Like *Jove's* heav'nly milken alley.

53.

What my song should further say,
Art envying my delight
(As the night conceales the day)
Shrowdes in shadowes from my sight :
Art, that adds so much to others,
Here a world of beauties smothers.

54.

Yet not so, but that I saw,
As the Sunne shines through the rack,
Smalling down by measure's law,
Her straight comely shapen back :
Which, though well it liked mee,
Lest of all I long'd to see.

55.

But her slender virgin Waste
Made mee beare her girdle spight,
Which the same by day imbrac't,
Though it were cast off at night ;
That I wisht, I dare not say
To be girdle night and day ;

56.

Lest those hands that here I kisse,
As offended there-withall,
Rise to chastise mine amisse,
Though their rage be rare and small ;
Yet God shield, her prayses' singer
Should offend her little finger.

57.

Yet I feare in much I shall :
For, to say her hands are white,

Slike and slender, fingers small,
Straight and long, her knuckles dight
  With curled Roses, and her nailes
  With pearle-muscles' shining scales :

58.

These are praises great I grant ;
But full oft heard I before,
Many may like honours vant,
Such as these have many more :
  Hers are such, as such are none,
  Save that hers are such alone.

59.

For, if shee had lived, when
Proud *Arachne* was alive,
Pallas had not needed then
To come downe with her to strive :
  Her faire fingers, finely fast,
  Had *Arachne's* cunning past.

60.

But when to the musick, choice
Of those nimble joynts shee marries
Th' *Eccho* of her Angel-voice,
Then the praise and prize shee carries
  Both from *Orpheus* and *Amphion*,
  Shaming *Linus* and *Arion*.

61.

Here before her nimble feet
Fall wee flat (mine humble Muse)
To endevour (as is meete)
All our errours to excuse :
  For, these are the beautious bases
  That support this frame of graces.

62.

Now, like as a Princely building,
Rare for Model, rich for matter,
Beautified without with guilding,
Fond beholders' eyes to flatter,
  Inwardly, containeth most
  Both of cunning and of cost :

63.

So this frame, in framing which
Nature her owne selfe excelled,
Though the outward walles were rich,
Yet within the same there dwelled
  Rarest beauties, richest treasures,
  Chief delights, and choicest pleasures.

64.

For, within this curious Palace,
'Mongst the *Muses* and the *Graces*,
Phebe chaste, and charming *Pallas*
Kept their Courts in sundry places,
  Lawes of Vertue to enactize,
  There proclaim'd in daily practice.

65.

Here the Foster waxing faint,
Looked on the lovely Dame,
Sighing-saying, Gracious Saint,
Here-hence all my sorrowes came.
  Lady, pardon, if my song
  Have detain'd you over-long.

66.

Not your song : your sorrowes seem
Longer then I would (quoth shee)
Yet, as yet I cannot deeme
How your griefes with this agree :
  For did this faire sight intrap yee,
  This fair sight might make yee happy.

67.

Happy (mee unhappy most)
(Then repli'd hee) had I been,
Had my life or light been lost
Ere my sight that sight had seen :
  Then had I not liv'd to languish
  In this ease-lesse end-lesse anguish.

68.

But because you doubt (faire Dame)
How from such a heav'n as this,
Full of every beautie's flame,
Full of bounty, full of blisse,
  Full of each delightfull joy,
  Could descend the least annoy :

69.

If you daigne attend, I 'll tell
(As my feeble tongue will let mee)
All mis-fortune that befell,
Though the thought thereof doe fret mee :
  Madam, so your kindnesse moves mee,
  That to shew you all behoves mee.

70.

Therefore think upon (I pray)
What, when first my tale begun,
Was fore-spoken to bewray
Shifts of *Cytherea's* sonne :
  How, for feare I should have spi'd him,
  In a *Bear* the Urchin hid him.

71.

Thence-from crafty *Cupid* shot
All the Arrows of his quiver :
But my heart that yeelded not,
Made them all in sunder shiver ;
  Till hee, full of shame and sorrow,
  Better bowes and shafts did borrow.

72.

Borrow did hee of that *Bear*,
Arms more apt to work my woe.

Stringing with her golden haire
Her faire brows, hee made his bow :
　　Whence for shafts hee shot likewise
　　Beames of her keene piercing eyes.

73.

Of which Diamond-headed darts
(Beating hard my bosom's Center,
Whence resisting pow'r departs,
Where, but these, none else could enter)
　　Some abiding, some rebounded,
　　Wherewith-all the *Beare* was wounded.

74.

Wounded was the gentle *Bear*,
With the weapons that shee lent ;
That shee lent (alas) for feare
Lest your *Love-God* should her shent :
　　So wee see, who lend their Armes,
　　Oft procure their proper harmes.

75.

So did harmlesse shee (alas)
That I ever must bemoan :
Moan I must for never was
Marble-hearted *Mermidon*
　　But would moan, and mourne, and melt
　　To have seene the paine shee felt.

76.

To have seen her piteous plaining,
To have heard her loud lamenting,
To have thought on her complaining,
To imagine her tormenting ;
　　Eyes would weepe, and ears would wonder,
　　Hardest heart would break in sunder.

77.

So mine eyes, mine eares and heart,
Fild with waters, wonders, woes,
Drowned, deafned, dead in part,
Wel-nigh all their vertues lose :
　　Every sense, and all my reason
　　Fled, and fail'd mee for a season.

78.

Here when this hee had rehearsed,
Ere the ruefull rest could follow ;
So the fresh remembrance pierced,
That his voice waxt weake and hollow :
　　Bitter teares aboundant dropping,
　　Drowned words their passage stopping.

79.

Words were turn'd to sighs and sobbing,
Inward griefes did inly groan :
Hopelesse heart with heavie throbbing,
Shew'd all signes of saddest moan.
　　Signes made moan, but voice was mum :
　　Small griefes speake, but great are dumb.

80.

Wo-begon, and wondrous sorry
Was the *Goddesse* to behold him,
Through repeating of his story
In so sad a fit to hold him ;
　　Fearing further to provoke him,
　　Lest new Seas of sorrow choak him.

81.

For, as Sea-coales flame the faster,
When wee cast cold water on them :
Or as Children under Master,
Mourne the more, the more wee moan them :
　　So the more shee spake, her speeches
　　More increast his cries and screeches.

82.

Yet shee would not so forsake him,
Lest some savage hungry beast
In this tragick transe should take him,
Of his flesh to make a feast :
　　Danger of which dire event,
　　Thus her pity did prevent.

83.

Lowd her bugle Horne shee blew,
Babbling *Eccho* voice of vallies,
Airy Elf, exempt from view,
With the Forrest musick dallies :
　　Doubling so the curled Winde,
　　That the first was hard to finde :

84.

Yet her nimble Nymphs, inured
Often to the Fairies' guile,
Could not be so soon allured
To ensue her subtle wile :
　　For where first they heard the blast,
　　Thither-ward they trip it fast.

85.

But because these maids had follow'd
Eagerly their game together ;
They, when first the Lady halloo'd,
Could not by and by be with her :
　　For, before shee found the Foster,
　　All her traine (I told you) lost her.

86.

In came these bright beauties than,
Where as they their Lady found
Standing by this wretched man,
That lay there upon the ground :
　　With which wofull sight amaz'd,
　　Each on him with wonder gazed.

87.

To whom their Goddesse did relate
All before that hee had told her,

All his miserable state :
Who did all the while behold her
  With a heavy halfe-shut eye,
  As a man at point to dye.

88.

At which the Nymphs with pity moved,
Somewhat to asswage his woe
For the *Beare's* sake whom hee loved,
And that him had loved so ;
  Bade him of their helpe assure him,
  For they could the Art to cure him.

89.

For in a Grove thereby, there grew
An herbe which could Love's power expell :
Which (but they) none ever knew,
As how it prosper'd neer a Well ;
  Where *Diana* us'd to bathe her
  When the scorching heat did scathe her.

90.

Which the *Sylvans* of those Groves
Held in every high account :

For therewith they cur'd their loves.
It was call'd *Dianae's* Fount :
  And that Herb, the pride of Summer,
  Took that speciall vertue from her.

91.

And the swiftest of the traine,
Away to fetch the same was sent.
Which her nimble joynts did straine,
And return'd incontinent ;
  And the Simple with her brought,
  By which the cure was strangely wrought.

92.

Which unto the sense apply'd,
As the juyce thereof hee tasted,
Hee might feele even in that tide
How his old remembrance wasted.
  By the med'cine thus revealed,
  Was the Wofull Wood-man healed.

NOTES AND ILLUSTRATIONS.

DEDICATORY-SONNET—see Memorial-Introduction on this ROBERT NICOLSON and Mrs. MARTHA NICOLSON of p. 314. In the latter, 'Soon calm in heart' is an anagram of her name. Stanza 21, '*Ems*'—see Glossarial Index : st. 30, '*rathe*' = early : st. 32, '*Troy-novant*' = London : st. 33, '*cautell*' = caution : st. 43, '*Ebene*' = ebony : st. 52, '*resolve*' = dissolve : st. 57, '*pearle-muscles*' = mussels or shell-fish so named : st. 74, '*shent*' = reprimand, but see Glossarial Index, *s.v.* On the biographical significance of this poem see Memoir. G.

EPITHALAMION.

O You that on the double-mountaine dwell,
   And daily drink of the *Castalian* Well,
If any Muse among your sacred number,
Have power to waken from a dying slumber,
A dull conceit, drown'd in a gulfe of griefe,
In haplesse ruine, hopelesse of reliefe :
Vouchsafe (sweet sisters) to assist me so,
That for a time I may forget my woe,
Or (at the least) my sad thoughts so beguile,
That sighes may sing, and tears themselves may smile,
While I in honour of a happy choice,   11
To cheerefull Layes tune my lamenting voice ;
Making the Mountains and the vallies ring,
And all the young-men and the maidens sing,
All earthly joyes, and all heav'n's blisse betide
Our joyfull Bridegrom, and his gentle Bride.
   Then, peace complaint, and pack thee hence, proud
     sorrow,
I must goe bid my merry Greeks *good morrow :*
Good morrow, Gallants : thus begins our game :
What ? fast asleep ? fie sluggards, fie for shame,   20
For shame shake off this humour from your eyes.
You have ore-slept : 'tis more then time to rise.
   Behold, already in the ruddy East
Bright *Erycina*, with the beaming crest
Cals up *Aurora :* and shee rose-like blushing,
From aged *Tython's* cold armes, quickly rushing,
Opens the wide gates of the welcome day,
And with a beck summons the Sun away :
Who quickly mounting on his glist'ring chaire,
Courseth his nimble Coursers through the aire,   30
With swifter pase then when hee did pursue
The Laurel-changed Nymph that from him flew ;
Fearing perhaps (as well hee might) to misse
A rarer object, then those loves of his.
Such, as at sight (but for the kinde respect
Of loyall friendship, to a deare elect
Child of the Muses) had with hotter fire
Inflam'd the wanton *Delphian* god's desire,
Altars adorn'd with blisse-presaging lights
In saffron robes, and all his solemne rites   40
Thrice-sacred *Hymen* shall with smiling cheere
Unite, in one, two Turtles loving deare.

And chaine with holy charmes their willing hands,
Whose hearts are linkt in love's eternall bands.

M *ilde vertues mirrour, Beautie's monument,*
A *dorned with Heav'n's praise, and Earth's perfection :*
R *eceive (I pray you) with a brow unbent,*
T *his petty pledge of my poore pure affection :*
H *ad I the Indian's golden heaps and hoords,*
A *richer present would I then present you.*   50
N *ow such poore fruits as my bare field affords*
 I *nstead of those, here have I rudely sent you.*
C *ount not the gift's worth but the giver's will :*
O *ft mighty Princes have accepted small things ;*
L *ike as the aire all empty parts doe fill,*
S *o perfect friendship doth supply for all things.*
O *be it ever so : so never smart*
N *or teene shall trouble the* Soon calm in hart. [=*wrath*

M *ind first your Maker in your dayes of youth :*
A *ske grace of him to govern well your wayes :*   60
R *everence your Husband with unspotted truth :*
T *ake heed of pride, the poison of our daies :*
H *aunt not with those that are of light report :*
A *void the vile charmes of unchaste temptation.*
N *ever lend look to the lascivious sort :*
 I *mpeach not any's honest reputation :*
C *omfort the poore, but not beyond your power :*
O *ver your houshold have a needfull care :*
L *ay hold on Time's lock, lose not any hower :*
S *pend, but in season ; and in season spare :*   70
O *ff-spring, if any heav'n vouchsafe to send you,*
N *urture them godly ; and good end attend you.*

So shall your life in blessings still abound,   [=*defend*
So from all harme th' almighty hand shall shend you,
So with cleere honour shall your head be crown'd,
So for your vertue shall the wise commend you,
So shall you shun vile slander's blasting voice,
So shall you long enjoy your loving Pheare,
So shall you both be blessed in your choice,
So to each other be you ever deare.   80
   O ! be it ever so in every part,
   That nought may trouble the Soon calm in hart.

FINIS.

A HOLY
PREPARATION
TO A JOYFULL
RESURRECTION.

2

Deare, deare Soule, Awake, awake.
  Ah ! What Answer wilt thou make,
  When *Christ* in glory shall appear ?
When Hee comes to take Account
Of thy Sins that hourely mount,
By acting or neglecting here ?

3

Of that irefull Day to come
(That red dreadfull Day of Doome)
Th' affrighting Terrour to prevent,
  Bleeding tears let heart distill ;
  Right reform thy crooked will ;
And speedily Repent, Repent.

1

That, That dreaded Day of Ire,
Shall dissolve the World in Fire ;
As holy Prophets have foretold.
  O ! What horrour will be then,
  When the Lord shall come agen,
Our deeds of Darknesse to unfold !

4

Shrillest Trumpet's thundring sound
Through earth's entrails shall rebound,
To summon all before the Throne.
  Nature, Death shall stand amaz'd,
  When the Dead (alive) be raised,
To heare their Judgement, every one.

5

Open shall the Bookes be laid,
  Wherein what wee have mis-said,
Mis-done, mis-deem'd, is registred :
  So that when the Judge is set,
  Closest crimes (conceal'd as yet)
Reveal'd, shall all be punished.

12

(Then alas !) what shall I say ?
To what Patron should I pray,

Sith the Justest are not cleer ?
  King of awfull Majestie,
  Health of All that hope on thee,
My saving Health as then appear.

14

Jesu, Lord, my Sute attend :
Oppose thee to th' accusing Fiend ;
Remembring, once thou cams't for mee,
  Weary seeking wilfull Losse ;
  Mockt, torn, tortur'd on the Crosse,
In vain these Suffrings may not be.

15

O ! Just Judge of each Condition,
Gracious, grant mee free Remission :
Let not my Works receive their Meed.
  Sighing, I lament my Sin :
  Teares without, and Feares within :
Break not, dear God, this bruised Reed.

16

Marie's Sin thou didst remit :
Theefe on Crosse Thou didst acquit.
Like Hope in mee thou dost inspire ;
  For this glorious Grace of Thine,
  (For no worth or work of mine)
Lord save mee from th' infernall fire.

37

'Point my place among the Sheep :
  Sundred from the Goats mee keep ;
Disposing mee, on thy Right-side ;
  That (the *Cursed* being cast
  Into Flames that ever last)
I with the *Blessed* may abide,

Full of Joy, Blisse, endlesse Glory,
  (Free'd of Feare, Grief, sin-full Folly)
Loud-singing *Holy*, *Holy*, *Holy*.   Amen.

FINIS.

THE MYSTERIE OF MYSTERIES.

THREE beare Recorde in Heauen, & Thefe THREE are ONE. 1. Iohn. 5. 7.

Math. 19. 28.   Luke. 22. 30.

PATER   NON EST   FILIVS

EST   EST

D E V S

EST

NON EST SPIRITVS NON EST

THE FATHER.

ALPHA and OMEGA, GOD alone :
  ELOI, My GOD, the HOLY-ONE ;
Whose Power is Omnipotence :
Whose Wisedome is Omni-science :
Whose BEEING is All Soveraigne Blisse :
Whose Worke Perfection's Fulnesse is :
  Under All things, not under-cast :
Over All things, not over-plac't :
Within All things, not there included ;
Without All things, not thence excluded :
  Above All, over All things raigning :
Beneath All, All things aye sustayning :
Without All, All conteyning sole :
Within All, filling-full the Whole :
  Within All, no where comprehended :
Without All, no where more extended :
Under, by nothing over-topped :
Over, by nothing under-propped.

  Unmov'd, Thou mov'st the World about ;
Unplac't, Within it, or Without :
Unchanged, time-lesse, Time Thou changest :
Th' unstable, Thou, still stable rangest.
No outward Force, nor inward Fate,
Can Thy drad ESSENCE alterate :

  To-day, To-morrow, yester-day,
With Thee are One, and instant aye ;
Aye undivided, ended never :
To-day, With Thee, indures for-ever.

  Thou, FATHER, mad'st this mighty Ball :
Of nothing thou created'st All,
After th' *Idea* of thy Minde,
Conferring Forme to every kinde.
Thou wert, Thou art, Thou wilt be ever :
And thine *Elect*, rejectest never.

THE SONNE.

WIth FATHER co-eternall LORD,
  Co-equall, consubstantiall WORD,
His Wisdome, Glory, graven Feature,
Thou MAKER, made (for Us) a Creature,
Took'st humane Flesh and Servant's Forme,
Man-kinde to ransome and re-forme :
  ETERNITIE (in time) began ;
Immortall Mortall : GOD and MAN,
MAN, God-head's bodily Aboad :
ONE, unconfounded MAN and GOD ;
  Not God-head into Flesh converting :
Nor by the flesh subverting :
Nor by the God-head, Flesh consuming ;
But, to the God-head Flesh assuming.
  As GOD, co-equall with the Father :
As very MAN, inferiour rather :
GOD onely Father, but of God-head :
Maid onely mother, but of Man-head.

  In this so sacred secret Band,
So Joynt-distinct Both Natures stand,
That Either 's What it was before ;
And both together Somewhat more :
One CHRIST, our onely *Advocate*
(Prince, Prophet, Priest) to mediate ;
True GOD, true MAN (excepting Sin)
Like us in all, without, within.

  Borne, circumciz'd, baptiz'd, contemn'd,
Tempted, tormented, mockt, condemn'd,
CROSSE-fixed, dead, buried, descended,
Arose againe, and then ascended
To his bright Throne of Majestie,
At the right hand of GOD on high :
From whence Hee shall returne afresh,
Judge to his Judge, and to all Flesh.

THE HOLY-GHOST.

THe COMFORTER, ay Uncreate,
  Unmade, Unborne, Ungenerate,
The FATHER'S Equall and the SON'S,
Proceedeth so from Both at-once,
That Neither is in Power greater ;
Neither, in their Condition better :
  For, What, How-great, How-Aye They be
As Great, as Lasting, Such, is Hee :
Save (past conceit) all time beforne ;
FATHER begat, and SON was borne :
The HOLY-GHOST from both proceeding :
All THREE in ONE, ONE THREE abiding.
Each of the THREE is perfect GOD :
Yet not THREE GODS, but ONE sole GOD.
  In this true Onely GOD alone,
True faith beleeveth THREE and ONE :
Ascribing, to the ESSENCE, *Unitie* :
And to the PERSONS onely *Trinitie* :
Whereof (indeed) is none Before
Or After Other ; lesse, or more :
But Each remaines the Same, unmixt ;
So constant and so ever fixt,
That Neither, in it Selfe, Selfe-changes,
Nor into Other it exchanges.

  This is the Orthodoxall Creed,
From Heresie *and* Errour *free'd :*
This is the Faith *that I professe,*
Without declining more or lesse.
No Worke I plead, nor worth of mine,
But Faith *in this* Eternall TRINE.

  Lord, I beleeve : relieve (*my GOD*)
Mine unbeliefe, remove my Load :
And let thy Mercie's Soveraigne Balme
Salve all my Sinnes, my conscience calme.

THE LAW, THE GOSPEL; MOSES, CHRIST;
IN BRIEF COMPAR'D; IN CHIEF COMPRIS'D.

The LAW.   *The GOSPEL.*   The LAW.   *The GOSPEL.*

PReceeds, *Succeeds;* Retaines the Right of bitter Death, *Of life:*
  Promiseth, *Giveth;* Hopeth, *Hath,* CHRIST (*Rock of Comforts rife*):
But to the JEWES, *To all the World;* But for a Time, *For aye:*
Standeth aloof, *Approacheth NEER;* Dismay'd, *Without dismay:*
As darke as Night, *As cleere as Noone;* All shadie, *Shadow-lesse:*
Discovers Faults, *Recovers Falls;* Threats Judgement, *Gives Release:*
Accuseth Sinnes, *Excuseth SONNES;* Depresseth Soules, *Assureth:*
Dejects, *Erects;* Gives grievous wounds, *The bleeding Conscience cureth:*
Condemnes, *Absolves;* Retaineth SINNES, *Remitteth all Amisse:*
Damnes, *Justifies;* Enjayleth deep, *Entaileth CROWNES of Blisse:*
Destroyeth, *Buildeth;* Curseth All, *All BLESSING* (*onely*) *brings:*
Confounds, *Confirmes;* Ter-terrifies, *Sweet CONSOLATION sings:*
Strippeth, *Cloatheth;* Calls for Works, *A working FAITH imposes:*
Bindes, *Breaks the Bands;* Layes heavie Loads, *Our weary Burdens loses:*
Dishonours, *Honours;* Reaveth Grace, *Adds Grace to Graces given:*
Takes away Riches, *Makes us Rich;* Gives earthly Goods, *Gives Heav'n:*
Makes scorners sad, *Makes mourners glad;* Brings Sorrow, *Sorrow ceases:*
Kils, *Quickens;* Spoyles of Vertue's Show, *True Vertue's Seed increases:*
Weighs downe to Hell, *Lifts up to Heav'n;* Would punish, *Will remit:*
Solicits Wrath, *Appeaseth Rage;* Calls Vengeance, *Cryeth Quit:*
Makes bloudy wars, *Wins battels glorious;* Still fights, *Still triumphs still*
  Victorious.

To the Right Reverend, Learned and Religious,
The L. BISHOP; Deane and Chapter,
CHURCH and COLLEDGE
Sacred
To the HOLY TRINITIE,
in GLOUCESTER:

And
To the Right Worshipfull
The MAYOR, & SENATE There.

PRostrate before *This ONELY-TRINE,*
  For pardon of Defects of mine
In This Mysterious *serious* Song,
To your grave Censures *I submit,*
And dedicate *My Part of it.*
  For, to Whom fitter doth belong
Discussion of so Deep Divinity,
Then to a Colledge *of the TRINITIE?*
  And to Whom rather than to YOU
(*Most kinde, though most unkinde in view*)
  Should I with Love *these Layes address;*
To signe, and (*in a sort*) *to* seale
A Counterpane *of gratefull* Zeale
  To your Love-worthy Lovingnesse?
Therefore, as Rills *to th'* Ocean *render;*
This Thus resend *I to the* Sender.

Cæruleo conspersa solo, rosa, lilia, cruces,
  Præ se Virtutis stemmata sacra ferunt.
Effigies Veri, campus ; sunt lilia, luces :
  Imminet his Cœlum, dimidiata rosa.
Aurea per cruces via fit prælata Salutis :
  Lactea sic Nobis sit via strata Poli.

G. L.

Humbly Devoted
JOSUAH SYLVESTER.

P O S T H U M I.

OR

S Y L V E S T E R S R E M A I N S:

CONTAYNING

Divers Sonnets, Epiſtles,

Elegies, Epitaphs, Epigrams,

AND OTHER

Delightfull Deviſes,

REVIVED

OUT OF THE ASHES

OF

THAT SILVER-TONGUED

TRANSLATOUR

AND

DIVINE POET-LAUREAT,

MASTER

Josuah Sylvester,

NEVER,

Till Now, IMPRINTED.

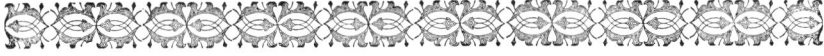

SONNETS.

AN ACROSTICK SONNET TO MASTER HENRY

PARVIS *deceased*.

M^r.alignant Death our ever dreadfull Foe,
H ow hast thou robb'd us of our Countrie's praise?
E ngland lament that thou hast lost him so,
N ow in the sun-shine of his Summer-Dayes :
R ich *Asian* Merchants, and the men of *Nile*,
Y our wonted travell and your traffick cease
P eople of *Greece* and you of *Candi-Ile ;*
A h, henceforth, who shall have the brave increase ?
R enowned PARVIS famous far and neere,
V ntimely dyes ; so short is Earthly glorie ;
I n vainee wee weepe, in vaine wee waile him here,
S orrow prevailes not, death is peremptorie.

R are Paragon (therefore) restrain your plaints,
N ow lives your dear-love 'mong the blessed Saints.

2 AN ACROSTICK SONNET ON HIS

Owne NAME.

J n paine, 'tis paine, past pleasures to record ;
O how it grieves, in griefe to think of gladnesse !
S mart after Smiles ingenders treble sadnesse :
U se of delight makes dolour more abhorr'd.
A h, what availes mee (then) thy wonted favour?
H igh hopes dejected, double in despaire ;
S o, ev'ry smile-beame of thy sun-shine faire,
Y f now thou frowne, makes ev'ry torment graver :
L ove, think not (then) ah think not it sufficeth,
V nto thy Merit, that thou didst affect mee ;
E ven that remembrance, if you now neglect mee,
STings more then all-else sorrow that ariseth.

E asie 's his paine, who never pleasure proved,
R ougher, disdaine, to him that hath beene loved.

3 AN ACROSTICK, TO THE RARE PATRON AND

right PATTERN of vertuous

GENTRIE, R. N.

R eviv'd afresh by your Muse-friending favour,
O ur griefe-starv'd-Muse begins again to stirre,
B reathing againe, the Breath your Bounty gave-her,
E ven when despaire had hope to burie her.
R estored (thus) by your kinde love, to life,
T hese thankfull lines shall tell the Times that follow,
N o niggard praises of your vertues rife,
I t shall be said you were our *Pen's-Apollo*.
C ount it no blemish to be so accounted ;
O ur humble notes, though little-noted now,
L auriz'd (hereafter) 'mong the loftie-mounted ;
S hall sing a part that Princes shall allow :
O ur numbers (then) with Time-contemning breath
N ow rais'd by You, shall raise your Name from death.

4 AN ACROSTICK ON HIS OWNE NAME, TO

His afore-said Friend.

J mping his broken wings with better plumes,
O ur ill-mew'd Muse shall (one-day) mount your merit
S o high, that cankred Time which all consumes,
U ertue except, shall have no power to wear-it.
A nd this, our little World-divided Ile,
H opefull already of your rising Fame,
S hall grow too narrow for so great a Name ;
Y n baptisme noted, *BORN TO CROS the NILE.
L et not the meaning of that Motto daunt-yee :
V nder that Fate-spell only are fore-showne

* Anagr. on Robert Nicolson.

E ternall praises which our pens shall chaunt-yee,
ST retching beyond the *Sultan's Babylon ;*
E lse, if our *Thames-tunes* cannot sound so loud ;
R hone, Rhyne and Po, shall lend their Numbers proud.

---

5 SONNET.

Puis qu'assiegé des ondeux Exercites
L'humble parler des Escrivains Anglois,
Confiné court dans ce coing Britanois,
N'ose franchir ses fatales limites.
    Pour ne borner de bornes si petites,
De vos vertuz la loing volante voix
Du Loyre et Po : os'emprunterai par fois
Mots pelerins, pour chanter vos merites.
    Si que l'amour qu'aux Muses vous portez,
Aislé du vent de mes errantes rimes,
S'oyra sonner outre les blanches cimes,
Des Apenins, de megé enfarinez.
    Mers, Monts, et Vaux, rauiz de vostre nom,
    Retentiront le loz de NICOLSON.

---

6 SONNET.

ACROSTITELIOSTICHON.

J f patience true could termine passion's war R——
O ur thankefull Harpe had tendred long-a g O——
S ave that, our Griefs, whose deep-gulfs never eb B——
U nto you sacred, by the which you se E——
A h, muse not, then, if all our Muse-work favou R——
H eart sad, Art bad ; yet pray you read the res T——
S o deare *Mecœnas,* if your patience daig N——
Y our praises due to publish farre and n I——
L ifting your Name, the glory of your Sto C——
V nthrall to Time, for, Time that tryeth s O——
E lse had th' old Hebrews and brave Worthies al L——·
ST ones wear, steel wasts, too weak to bear their glorie S——
E ven so devout as wee are found to do O——
R ecording loftie though wee low begu N——

---

7 SONNET TO

MASTER *R. N.*

S Ith round beleaguer'd by rough *Neptune's* legions,
    Within the straite-nookes of this narrow Ile ;
The noblest volumes of our vulgar style
Cannot escape unto more scopefull Regions ;
Resolv'd to rescue from death-threatning dangers
Arctoa's Name, pride of her sex and soyle,
* Anagr. on And yours kind Patrone, *BORN TO CROS the NILE,
Robert Nicolson. Our friend-strong Muse shall use the helpe of Strangers.
Sweet *Petrarch's* Po, and swan-proud *Sein* shall lend

Their Syren-voyces, loud-resounding Layes
To sing her wonders and your worthie praise,
Till English victors having Heaven to friend,
Pouling the *Pyrés,* with their valiant swords,
Through Spayne make passage for our English words.

---

6 SONNET.

ACROSTITELIOSTICHON.

——R are type of gentrie, and true Vertue's Sta R
——O ne entire payment of the Zeale wee O
——B reake still the best threades of our busie we B
——E vill the Muses with griev'd mindes agre E
——R uth, more then Youth, and rather cry then quave R
——T is said of somethings, that the last is bes T
——N o praise, but pardon to our new-found strai N
——I will enforce my leaden Thoughts to fl I
——C loude-high, to grave it, in a Diamond Ro C
——O n every thing, forbeares the Muses th O
——L ost with their lives, their Lives memorial L
——S weet learning, yet, keeps fresh their famous storie S
——O ur verse, your Vertues shall eternize to O
——N othing a whit more cleare then radiant Su N

---

8 SONNET.

W Ilt thou not, yet, beleeve how deare I love thee ?
    O ! thou unjust, how thy distrust doth grieve
    me !
What shall I say to make thee to beleeve mee ?
What shall I doe that may suffice to move thee ?
Have I not made my voyce all hoarse with moaning ?
Are not mine eyes growne blinde with ever weeping ?
Are not my wits growne wild with never sleeping ?
Is not my heart halfe dead and more, with groaning ?
All eares but Thine, doe pity my complaining ;
All eyes but Thine, my weeping makes to water ;
All wits but thine, doe blame my wits' abater ;
All hearts and Thine conceive not my heart's paining :
    And yet my love exceeds my Sorrow fell,
    For, still the Cause doth its Effect excell.

---

9 SONNET.

TO MY SOVERAIGNE LORD THE KING.

JAMES STUART.

Anagram.

A JUST MASTER.

S Ick of the evill which you onely heale,
    Onely to you my prostrate Sighes appeale,

From long delayes of Others' doubtfull Art,
Assur'd of pitie in your princely heart.
Should, None-beside, second mine humble suit,
Du BARTAS, yet, I hope will not be mute,
Nor you disdaine, what, for his sake, I seek,
Of a JUST-MASTER, mercifull and meeke.
Mine, is no swelling, but a sinking Sore,
Which, but you salve, will daily gangrene more :
More needfull patient to lesse-carefull cure,
Did never, yet, your royall Hand procure ;
Your word and sword is all that it requires
To grace with Knighthood two sufficient Squires.

10 SONNET.

O Eyes, more beauteous then those blazing eyes,
Whose wanton sparks did fire the town of Troy !
O Tongue, more tunefull then those melodies,
Of him that *Daphné* lov'd, the Damsell coy !
O Wit, more wondrous then that wondrous-wise,
Jove's braine-borne Daughters, or *Latona's* Boy !
O Eyes ! O Tongue ! O Wit, all words exceeding !
See, say, suppose, whence is my pain proceeding.

11 SONNET.

IF these mine eyes were ever sent to seek,
In sumptuous shewes, for better-Beauties' choice ;
If these mine Eares were ever lent to like
Of any sound above the Heav'nly-Voice ;
If this my heart did ever meane mislike,
Of thee, or did in Other-Love rejoyce ;
Blind be these Eyes, deafe be these Ears for ever,
Sad be this Heart conceiving comfort never.

12 SONNET. TO HIS BELOVED.

FArewell my Hope, adieu,
My chaste remembrance sweet ;
Farewell my Trust to you,
Untill againe wee meet.

You have forsaken mee,
And yet I know not why ;
If ought I have offended yee
For pardon here I cry.

The sweet delightfull Flowers
Are pleasant to the Eye ;
So are those spotted bowers
Which in thy Cheeks doe lye

The orient Colours fine
Will fall and fade away ;
But let that sweetest love of thine
Still live and ne'r decay.

The margaritall-gem
For praise deserves thy name ;
So like you are to them,
As nature shewes the same.

Sweet Love remember this
That though thy beauties shine
And hath resplendent beames amisse,
Yet, alwayes I 'll be thine.

The Sunne shall cease to shine,
The Moone shall lose her light ;
Before these constant eyes of mine
Choose any new delight.

In token of my Love,
I here protest and vow,
And by all sacred sense approve
I will love none but you.

The highest ardent powers,
The fiery Strall of *Jove,*
Shall lighten brightly upon yours
And still increase my love.

Sweet Earth, sweet Water, Ayre,
And Fire in your Degree ;
Be meanes unto this Orb so faire
That Shee likewise love mee.

13 SONNET.

EVen as the timely sweet heat-temp'ring showers
Feed the faint Earth and fill it all with flowers green ;
Green, grain, and grasse, and plants, and fruits, and flowers
Whereby the beauty of the world is seene :
Even so my tears temp'ring mine inward fire,
Doe feed my Love and foster my Desire.
And as a sudden and a stormy raine,
Makes *Flora's* children hang their painted heads,
And beateth downe the pride of *Ceres'* plaine,
Drowning the Pastures and the flow'ry Meades :
Even so my teares that overflow my fire,
Drowne my Delight but not my Love's desire.
And as a little Water, cast upon
A Forge, doth force the flame to mount the more ;
Which being by the panting bellows blowne,
It glowes, and growes much hotter then before :
Even so my teares cast on mine inward fire,
Blown by my sighs augment my high desire.
And as a Brooke that Meadowes undermines,
Doth make them seem more green, more fresh more fair :
And as the deaw before bright *Phœbus* shines,
Gives the sweet Rose a more delightfull aire :
Even so my teares wat'ring mine inward fire,
Adorn my love, and garnish my desire.
Thus, then, though weeping waste my life away
And drench my Soule in ever-flouds of care,

Yet by my teares I doe my faith display,
Whereby my merits (still) recorded are :
　　So that my teares refresh mine inward fire,
　　And yet my tears quench not my high desire.

14 A MASKE SONNET, TO QUEEN *ANNE.*

Hye wee,
　　Hye wee, Sisters, Fairies,
Dead our comfort, deep our Care-is
　　　　While wee misse our Mistresse' grace :
　　　　In the mirrour of whose Face,
Majesty and mildnesse meet
Stately shining, smiling sweet :
　　　　In whose bosome
　　　　Aye repose-em
All the Honours of Diana ;
Say, who saw our Glorie-Anna ?

This way,
This way Grace did guide-her,
Could so rich a Jewell hide her ?
　　　　So unseene that none can say,
　　　　Whither Shee is gone this way.
Or doth envie make you mum ?
Or hath Wonder strook you dumb ?
　　　　Iô Sisters,
　　　　Here 's our mistresse.
Iô, Fairies, have wee found her ?
Daunce wee rapt with joy and wonder.
　　　　　　After the Daunce.

Haile,
All haile ; O Queen of Graces,
Whose aspect, auspicious, chaces
　　　　All our cares and feares away,
　　　　Cleering all with cheerfull ray :

Whom, who-ever never saw,
Knowes not Vertue's Love nor Law ;
　　　　Bountie's presence,
　　　　Beautie's pleasance ;
Modell and divine Idea,
Both of Pallas and Astrea.

Welcome,
Welcome Phœnix royall,
Wils and Wals her eccho loyall ;
　　　　In all Fairie is not found
　　　　A more happy piece of ground,
Then your presence maketh here,
Where, together with your Pheere,
　　　　All I wish-you
　　　　And your Issue,
With all joyes of grace internall,
Outward glory and eternall.

15 SONNET.

Looke crueller, you lovely eyes, yee kill mee
　　With pleasing poyson of your sweet aspects :
Yet doe not so, for cruelty dejects
My mounting hopes, and with despaire doth fill-mee.

Doe but a little vaile your beames divine,
Whose over-brightnesse dimmes my tender sight ;
Yet, vaile them not, for then eternall night
In ever darknesse drowns this soule of mine.

Alas, faire eyes, how will yee stint this strife ?
Favour or frowne, love ever makes mee languish
In living deaths and in delightfull anguish,
How ere you looke, I looke to lose my life :
　　Ah looke no more (then) if you doe, ye spill mee,
　　Yes, looke (alas) unlesse yee looke yee kill mee.

16 SONNET.

They say that shadowes of deceased ghosts
　　Doe haunt the houses and the graves about,
Of such whose lives'-lamp went untimely out,
Delighting still in their forsaken hostes :

So, in the place where cruell love doth shoote
The fatall shaft that slue my love's delight,
I stalke and walke and wander day and night,
Even like a ghost with unperceived foote.

But those light ghosts are happier far then I,
For, at their pleasure, they can come and goe
Unto the place that hides their treasure, so,
And see the same with their fantastick eye.

Where I (alas) dare not approach the cruell
Proud Monument, that doth inclose my Jewell.

17 SONNET.

Love, doe thy worst, use all thy tyrannies,
　　And as thou list torment and torture mee :
I'll ne'r relent, nor shalt thou ever see
Mee cease to serve her ever-sacred eyes.

I know my fault, and knowing I confesse it ;
Like th' Argive Lad, I tooke my flight too high :
But what of that ? there 's now no remedy,
Unlesse, perhaps, propitious death redresse it.

Back reason (then) thou dost in vaine advise mee ;
If death prevent mee, then my paine expires,
And honour'd death doth waite on high desires ;
I must proceed what ever end arise mee :
　　If it were pride, at first, to undertake it,
　　'Twere cowardize, now, faintly to forsake it.

18 SONNET.

BReak heart and cease in sorrowes thus to swell,
  Or shrink thy veines that vanities may end ;
Or else record the cause why thoughts rebell,
Or else forget thou serv'st so faire a friend :
  Or if thou meane to feed on fancy still,
  Break heart ; for bloud best fits to blaze thine ill.

For, blubber'd eyes doe but in water write,
And sighes are signes of dolour, not of death ;
And pale is but a change from red to white,
And plaints are pangs but of a strained breath :
  But bloud bewrayes the bitter ruefull state ;
  Then write in bloud, thy love, thy hope, thy hate.

Then, starting-up, forthwith I took a knife,
As one resolv'd, and yet in doubt, to kill ;
'Twixt feare of death and loathing of my life,
'Twixt hope of good and greedinesse of ill,
  I so remain'd, doubting the stroak to give,
  Because I dare not dye, yet cannot live.

19 SONNET.

MY prayers have turn'd my Mistresse to a stone,
  A virgin have they chang'd into a Beare :
Ah yet some hope remains unto my mone,
For thousands write, Raine drops hard flints doe wear,
And savage Beares on no dead corps will prey.
No savage, but cœlestiall Beare art thou,
Spare mee that am a Corse cleane fall'n away ;
Doe not, ah doe not ay my death avow :
Flint though thou beest, yet thou art full of fire ;
Kindle my hopes, burn not my waxen wings :
Bear though thou be, yet will rough Beares retire
From humane bloud, if one them hony brings.
Oh let the hony of my words appease thee,
Still must I love, though I can never please thee.

Oh that her heart were but a heart of stone,
(As, often raine the rocky Marble weares)
Yer this, the oft fall of my fraudlesse teares,
Had pierced it, and made her feele my mone.
Were shee no fiercer then a forrest Beare,
(As from dead bodies that foule Beast abstaines,
And pleas'd with hony humane bloud refraines)
My hony words had wrought remorse in her :
But shee 's a Beare of that cœlestiall breed,
That in the Poles imperious *Jove* did plant.
Her heart is stone, but it is Diamant,
Whose hardnesse doth the hardest things exceed ;
Therefore it is, that teares'-raine cannot pierce her,
And hony words doe make her seem the fiercer.

20 SONNET.

THrice tosse these oaken ashes in the aire,
  And thrice three times tie-up this true Love's knot ;

Thrice sit thee downe in this enchanted chaire,
And murmure soft, shee will or shee will not.
Goe burn these poys'ned weeds in that blew fire,
This Cipresse gath'red at a dead man's grave ;
These Scriech-owles' feathers, and this pricking bryer,
That all thy thorny Cares an end may have.
Then come you Fairies, dance with mee a round :
Dance in this circle, let my love be center,
Melodiously breath out a charming sound ;
Melt her hard heart, that some remorse may enter :
  In vain are all the charmes I can devise,
  Shee hath an Art to breake them with her eyes.

21 SONNET.

FRom thy faire lookes I count my Kalender,
  For, viewing them mine eyes make holy day ;
Depriv'd of them, my soule through jealous feare,
In restlesse labour weares the time away.
Thy smile foretels a solemne feast is neer ;
But most of all it doth my minde dismay
To finde no certain seasons in my yeare :
Spring, Winter, Summer, Harvest finde I not,
Nor day nor night, th' are all confounded there :
No grasse can grow, thy beauty shines so hot ;
Thy beautie's Sun which no Eclipse can beare.
  Therefore by guesse I make my times agree ;
  Alas, that Kalenders so uncertaine be.

22 SONNET.

THou art not faire for all thy red and white,
  For all those rosie temp'ratures in thee ;
Thou art not sweet, though made of meer delight ;
Nor faire, nor sweet, unlesse thou pity mee :
Thine eyes are black, and yet their glistring brightnesse
Can night illumine in her darkest denne :
Thy hands are bloudy, yet compact of whitenesse,
Both black and bloudy, if they murther men ;
Thy brow whereon my fortune doth depend,
Fairer then snow, or the most lilly thing ;
Thy tongue which saves at every sweet word's end,
That hard as marble, This a mortall sting.
  I will not sooth thy follies : thou shalt prove,
  That beauty is no beauty without love.

23 SONNET.

MIght bashfull shame put on a paper maske
  And whisper passion in his mistresse' eares :
Then should my Verse his numbers overtaske
To lead thee to the storehouse of my teares.
Oh, I have seen content in thy faire eyes,
My soule's content, if thou be so content :
Faire eyes, bright skies, what praise may I devise,
To paint the pleasure of your blandishment ?

Onely this will I speake with pleasing anguish,
Those Lamps are cause that make my life to languish.

24 SONNET.

THese lines you reade as his who never knew
    What beauty meant, save that which shines in you.
For should'st thou please to dwell in desert Grove,
Thy eyes would teach the senselesse trees to love,
Thy sight (one sight) made mee that scorn'd before,
Feare fraile effects, and trust mine eyes no more :
So from thy sight these my sad passions grew,
And therefore read them if thou wilt not rue ;
Read them and see how my coy heart came thrall,
And then goe sweare thou wilt not love at all.
Oft had I seene men sigh and weepe and mourne,
And curse desire, and looke with eyes forlorne :
Oft had I heard them ban their bitter fate,
As they of all had beene unfortunate :
Then would I smile and count their outcryes vain,
And say when they did weepe, they did but faine :
Fond thoughts too simple to conceive the force,
Of Love's desire, that kils without remorse.
Weepe wayward eyes, then let my soule complain,
For it hath tasted love's immortall paine.
When first false fortune, to betray my heart,
Had slily brought and left mee where thou wert.
When I beheld thine amiable face,
Thy lovely hair which seem'd thy brow t' imbrace ;
Then I envi'd thy curious locks arow,
And wisht to twine about thy forehead so :
But when I view'd thy lips, thy cheeks, thine eyes,
So red, so white, so full of delicacies ;
Mee thought that I their beauty long had knowne,
And therefore would have kist you (as mine owne).
But feare and jealousie stept 'twixt us two,
And told mee I had nothing there to doe :
Henceforth I found my Liberty was fled ;
My heart's ease, and Soule's comfort banished,
Alone I went ; alone was my delight,
Tedious the day, and wearisome the night :

No soft repose or delicate repast
Could ease my limbs or please my froward taste ;
Onely I fed upon that pleasure store
Which mine eyes suckt from thy sweet face before.

25 SONNET.

AS in the deadnesse of the silent night,
    A dreame doth forge strange shadows of delight :
So thy faire image in my fancy wrought,
Presenting wonders to my troubled thought.
For, still (mee thinks) that I doe either heare,
Thy voyce, as any challeng'd Eccho, cleere,
Thy voyce that makes the silver strings contend,
How they may best thy most fine fingers bend :
Or that I see thy feet in measures fall,
And then I start, as one distract withall :
I dye, revive mee, that it may be sed
Your beauty can put life into the dead.

26 SONNET.

YOur sweet behaviour makes mee bold to write,
    More then my tongue durst utter in your sight,
Unlesse before I spake I could surprize
My pardon, written in your gracious eyes :
But, wherefore should'st thou judge amisse of me ?
If I offend it is in loving thee.
How hard and haplesse were our wretched state,
If for true love wee purchase unkinde hate ?
I doe not seek as others Lovers doe,
Who doe attempt to win before they wooe :
Sufficeth I may live a thrall to thee
(Grant that of favour which of force must be).
None but thee must I honour day and night ;
Thee I must love, though in mine owne despight :
Fortune and Fates have chain'd my fancie so,
And thou maist free them, which none else can doe.
If thou be piteous, shew it now or never,
Save me but once, and I will serve thee ever.

NOTES AND ILLUSTRATIONS.

PAGE 321, 1 Acrostick—Of HENRY PARVIS, the Nicolsons, etc., see our Memorial-Introduction.

,,   ,,   4   ,,   line 1, '*Imping*' = inserting feathers.

,,   322, the second Acrostiteliostichon (2d col.) is numbered 6, as = companion for the first (1st col.).

,,   323, col. 2, l. 18 (12th Sonnet) '*Strall*' = *sagitta ;* but see Glossarial Index, *s.v.*   G.

ELEGIES,

EPISTLES AND

EPITAPHS,

Written by

JOSUAH SYLVESTER.

AN ELEGIE, IN
REMEMBRANCE OF THE
WORSHIPFULL AND WOR-
thy Merchant, Master *Henry Parvis*,
Deceased August the twentie
fifth, 1593.

HOw frail is flesh ! how worldly bliss is brittle !
 How in our birth begin wee all to die !
Youth, beauty, bloud, wealth, worship, last but little !
All these like Shadowes of the night doe flye ;
Vertue alone gives men eternity.
　Vertue, which drawes mine over-tasked Verses,
　Sadly to sing these tragick Tombs and Herses.
Alas how far fond Painters erre, in drawing
Death's ghastly visage, void of eyes and dark !
Ah, see wee not That-Archer all-men awing?
How sure hee shoots still at the fairest mark !
Foule Rav'ns hee leaves, and reaves the dainty Lark ;
　Nettles forsakes, and takes the fragrant Roses ;
　Contemnes the Cockle, and the Corn hee choses.
Else had not *London* lost her lamp of glory,
The pride of Merchants and the prime of men,
Milde-portly PARVIS, whose live's worthy story
Merits the praise of an immortal Pen :
　Whose death not only our own Thames tormenteth,
　But Arne, and Po, and Rhine and Maine lamenteth.
The man that Europe in his life admir'd :
Enricht with all that heav'n and nature could ;
With inward gifts and outward grace attir'd ;
Gallant and grave ; nor bashfull nor too bold :
Mirrour to Youth, amazement to the Old :
　A Personage of comely limbs and stature :
　Of vertuous Nurture joyn'd with gentle nature.
What might be wisht for that this worthy wanted ?
Wit, wealth and worship did adorn his life ;

And more, to glad him, gracious *Hymen* granted
A choice, chaste, vertuous, faire and fruitfull wife :
A pleasant Vine, whose branches spreading rife
　Inviron'd round his Table with her treasure,
　Eight lively pledges of their love and pleasure.
Into his travaile I forbeare to enter,
To tell the profit and the praise hee got
In forrain Countries, where hee us'd to venter :
Where never blemish did his Credit blot ;
Where PARVIS' Name shall never be forgot.
　'Mid the stern *Germans* and *Italians* stately,
　That mourne his death (still) most affectionately.
But, where (alas) shall I sad phrases borrow ?
To shew his Countrie's sighs for his decease ;
Court, Citie, Countrie, all are fill'd with sorrow,
The rich lament, the poore complaints increase ;
But, his deare Turtle's teares that never cease,
　Exceed the number of the pearl-drops-rainy ;
　Sad *Niobè* did never shed so many.
Alas it boots not, therefore leave lamenting ;
For ruthlesse death doth no complaints regard :
In his stone-breast no pitie moves relenting,
Rough and remorselesse, more then marble-hard.
Rejoyce in this, your PARVIS is preferr'd
　From world's delights, which wise-men oft bewitches
　To the possession of eternall riches.

Flumina de Parvis *oriuntur fontibus alta,*
　Et sæpe ex Parvis *grandis acervus erit.*

MONODIA.

AN ELEGIE, IN COMMEMO-
RATION OF THE VERTUOUS LIFE,

And godly death of the right worshipfull and most
religious Lady, Dame Hellen BRANCH Widow (late
Wife to the right worshipfull Sir *John Branch* knight, somtimes L. Maior of this honourable City, and daughter of *M.*
W. Nicolson somtimes of London Draper) who deceased the 10. of *April* last, and lieth interred in
Saint *Mary Abchurch* in London, the twentie
ninth of the same, 1594.

SIth unto mee, unworthy, you commit
    This worthy taske (for better Muses fit)
To sing (nay rather sadly to deplore)
This common losse, that nothing can restore :
You sacred brood, borne of celestiall race,
You virgin-Ladies which poure downe the grace
Of Arts and Learning on your servants deare,
Vouchsafe assistance to my mournings here.
Teach mee sad accents and a weeping measure,
To straine forth pitie, not to stir-up pleasure.

    And you my private cares (although the cause
Of your dispaires doe never, never pawse)
Pawse you a little, and give leave a-while,
'Mid publike griefs my private to beguile ;
Give leave I pray you ; for a private case
Unto a publike ever must give place.

    Alas, how fitly is this life of ours
Compar'd to field-grasse and to fading flowers,
Fresh, greene and gallant, in the morning sun,
Wither'd and dead before the day be done !
Did ever yet the world's bright eye behold
(Since first th' Eternall earthly slime en-soul'd)
A frame of flesh so glorious here beneath,
But hath been ruin'd by the rage of Death ?
Of Death, dread victor of all earthy things,
Who in a moment equals clownes with Kings.
For majestie can nothing him dismay,
No strength nor courage can his comming stay,
No wealth can wage him, nor no wit prevent him,
No lovely beauty can at all relent him ;

Nay (which is more) no vertue can availe ;
Ay mee, that death on vertue should prevaile.
But 'tis decree'd, death is the meed for sin ;
This by ambition did our grand-sire win ;
And wee the heires both of his work and wages
Must all dye once, throughout all after ages.

    ' And here for instance see this sable hearse
' Shrowding the subject of my mournefull verse,
' The breathlesse body of a worthy Dame,
' The Lady *Branch* a *Nicolson* by name :
' A godly, vertuous and religious Matron,
' For maids, and wives, and widows, all, a pattern.
' Worship and wealth adorn'd her parentage,
' Favour and beauty grac't her personage,
' But vertuous manners, by good education,
' Brought to her youth the greatest commendation ;
' Wherein so well shee spent her virgin-dayes
' That envie's selfe saw nothing to dispraise.'

    Now when her age had made her apt to marry,
With friends' advise, that of her choice were chary,
Shee was espous'd to one of speciall sort,
Wealthy in purse, and worshipfull in port,
Master *John Minors ;* prais'd for zeale and pietie,
One of the Drapers' worshipfull societie :
To him shee bare foure children, one a boy,
The rest all daughters ; all, their parents' joy.
But all these joyes (alas) but little lasted,
All these faire blossoms were untimely blasted.
All dyed young ; for what drawes lively breath
But young or old must yeeld at last to death ?

47

But they, long mourning for their mutuall losse,
Frame mutuall comforts to each other's crosse,
Till time, that all things weares, had worn away
Their sorrowe's edge, uneasie to allay.
Then happily many faire dayes they spent,
To other's comfort and their owne content,
In all the practise of a Christian life,
And mutuall duties meet for man and wife :
Hee happy in his chance, shee in her choice,
Both joyntly blessed in themselves, rejoyce.
But ah, these earth-joyes doe not ever last.
' After long cleernesse clouds will over-cast :
' After long calmes still followes stormy weather.'
When they had liv'd full fortie yeares together,
Hee dyed, alas ! for what drawes lively breath,
But, young or old, must yeeld at last to death ?
  Then desolate and comfortlesse alone,
Like to the Turtle when her mate is gone,
With sigh-swoln heart and sorrow-clouded eyes,
Shee wailes her lost Love in a woefull wise,
Till time, that all things weares, had worne away
Her sorrowe's edge, uneasie to allay.
  Then after modest and meet intermission,
Becomming well her years and her condition,
In second wedlock shee was linkt again
Unto another wealthy Citizen ;
To master *Branch*, who afterwards became
Lord Mayor of London, worthy well the same :
In which high office hee him so acquighted,
That for his service hee was after knighted.
Hee was her husband twentie years, and more,
And much increast her stile, her state, and store.
But boughs and branches, shrubs and Cedars tall
Wither and dye, and into ashes fall :
So fell this *Branch*, for what drawes lively breath
But old or young must yeeld at last to death.
  Then all forlorn, thus having lost her knight,
This dolefull Lady left all world's delight,
All shewes of pleasure, and all pomp forsaking,
Her selfe to sadnesse and to solenesse taking ;
With inward sighes and outward teares lamenting
His death, whose life was all her live's contenting.
Even like unto the sad and wofull Winter,
Who (soon as ever the bright season-stinter
Hath left her widow of his wonted raies,
Whil'st to another world hee takes his wayes)
Casting aside her rich enamell'd crownes,
Flower-poudred mantles, and embroidered gowns
Of grass-green silk-shag, and the gawdie pride
Of all her Jewels and her Jems beside ;
Her mirth-lesse selfe in mournefull manner shrouds
Down to the ground in robe of sable clouds :

And from her swoln-heart sighs a thousand stowers,
And from her drown'd eies weeps a thousand showers.
  But now becom her self, her self's commander
To shield her life safe from all shot of slander,
(As 't were) sequestred from much conversation,
Shee past her time in holy meditation,
In thanks and prayer unto Christ our Lord,
And often hearing of his sacred Word ;
In godly almes and liberall pensions rife,
And all the duties of a Christian life ;
Laying up treasure with the joyfull just,
Safe from the force of theeves, and fret of rust.
So that her three-fold godly life alludeth
To virgin *Ruth*, wife *Sara*, widow *Judith*.
This life shee led ; but this life will away,
Wee are but Pilgrims, here wee may not stay :
No more might shee ; for when thrice thirty yeere
(A goodly age) shee had expired here,
' Shee also dyed ; for what drawes lively breath,
' But, young or old, must yeeld at last to death ?
  ' Such life, such death : well ends the well begun,
' And by the Even the faire Daye's praise is won.
' Well shee began, and wondrous well shee ended,
' Faire rose this sun, and fairely it descended
' To rise againe to glory at the last,
' At that great Angel's all-awaking blast.'
  And therefore (deare friends) doe not waile nor weep,
For her that is so happy fall'n asleep ;
But waile our losse, our common cause of griefe,
' The riche's load-star, and the poore's reliefe :
For to the rich in life shee gave example,
And to the poore in life and death was ample.
Weep rich, weep poore, let high and low lament ;
But most you poore, let your salt tears be spent,
For you alas have lost your liberall Ladie,
Your nurse, your mother : but alas, why wade I
' With my poore stile in so profound a streame ?
' You springs of Arts, eyes of this noble Realme,
' *Cambridge* and *Oxford*, lend your learned teares,
' To waile your owne losse, and to witnesse theirs :
' Tell, you that have the voice of eloquence,
' This bounteous Ladie's large beneficence,
' First to your selves, for love unto your lore,
' Then severally to every kinde of poore
' Within this Citie : To the Drapers' Hall,
' To every Prison, every Hospitall,
' To Lunatikes, and poore Maides' marriages,
' And many other worthy Legacies ;
' And when you have drawn all your teare-springs drie
' For her decease, here let your comfort lie,
' That of this Phœnix' ashes there revives
' Another, where her vertue still survives.'

FINIS.

NOTES AND ILLUSTRATIONS.

SEE our Memorial-Introduction for more than the poem tells of the Branch Family, etc. : Page 329, col. 1, l. 29,
' *wage* ' = give sufficient wages or bribe : p. 330, col. 2, l. 1, ' *stowers* '—see Glossarial Index, *s.v.*

G.

ARCTOPHILOS'S
EPISTLE TO HIS
Dearest *ARCTOA.*

A *Rctophilos* to his *Arctoa* sends
　　Such salutations as beseeme such friends.
　　Let not my sweet Love take the matter ill,
That at this season, sore against my will,
I parley thus in paper to my deare,
Being my selfe in person now so neere :
Sith by the malice of so many spies
That watch us still with more then *Argus* eyes,
Wee are debarr'd of every time and place
Wherein wee wont to commune face to face :
So that, alas, as seldome as wee meet,
Wee dare not speake and one another greet.
　For, whil'st with other, arme in arme you walk,
That tyr'd your eares with toyes and idle talke ;
Courting you quaintly with continuall sute,
I march among you like a shadow mute :
In hollow silence, sighing to my selfe
To see my roome usurped by an Elfe.
So fares the Merchant that hath lost his goods,
Among false Pirats on the raging flouds ;
Where too too cheape hee chanceth to behold
Before his face his substance bought and sold :
And lavish waste made of the finest ware,
That hee had got with mickle cost and care :
Whil'st hee, poore soule, as partner of their sinne,
Must hold his peace and bite his sorrow in.
　But you perhaps may Muse, and not amisse,
Unlesse mistaking what my purpose is,
How I can brooke and put up such disgrace,
To see his dwarfship court you to my face :
Sith neither love nor Lordship can allow
Competitors, as wee have proofs enough.
Now, that I love you needs not now be scann'd,
You know too well my life lyes in your hand :
You know your frowne turns all my mirth to sadnesse :
You know your smile turns all my grief to gladnes :
You know so well that I doe love so much,
That you admire my patience can be such.

For some say patience is the Cowardly's badge ;
But ill, mee seems, that Cognizance doth fadge
To such a Coate , sith wiser men conclude,
That Patience is the Crest of Fortitude :
And they are fooles that doe forget this sentence,
That rash Revenges never want Repentance.
But leaving this, that I may let you know
Why I refraine from my corriving foe :
You doe not think (I think) that I doe feare him ;
And that the cause wherefore I doe forbeare him,
Not that I dare not, but that I disdaine
On such a dwarf my stronger hands to staine.
Have I forborne ? for valiant minds despise
A victory wherein no glory lyes ;
But most of all (which most concerns the cause)
For that this strife your name in question drawes.
I strive the more to master my desire,
Lest stirr'd, our ashes doe bewray their fire :
' For fondly loves, how ere hee fawne upon her,
' Who tenders not his Ladie's dearest honour.
Besides, considering calmely of the matter,
Unlesse wee list selfe-wounding wrath to flatter,
I see no cause why I should draw my weapon :
For who forbids gaine-thirsty Chapmen cheapen
Another's ware, unlesse it beare some token
Of him that hath the same before bespoken :
If at the leastwise, being at the best,
It lye in sight no lesse then all the rest.
　For, like as when some Gentleman hath bought *Simile.*
Some rare rich Jewell, passing curious wrought ;
And, giving earnest, leaves the same a season,
With the knowne Artist for some speciall reason :
Hee, glorying in his work and glad to shew it,
Still sets it forth, as if hee still did owe it :
While other Gallants gazing and admiring
Th' ingenious Gemme, the costly price inquiring,
Carelesse of cost doe inly presse and pray him,
Offring, perhaps, more then the first shall pay him.

But th' honest workman, to conclude, doth tell them
Tis gone already, 'tis not his to sell them.
So when a Lover, by desert and duty,
Hath purchased a Paragon of Beauty,
Binding the bargaine with sufficient pledge
Till the conclusions' feathers may be fledge.
Nature as proud of forming such a Creature,
Adorns her shop still with the matchlesse feature,
While other blouds, beholding such a baite,
Doe inly sigh, and sue, and presse, and waite ;
Swearing to passe more perils for her sake,
Then *Juno* made *Alcides* undertake.
But then, what then ? sweet, I referre the rest
To your deare selfe, that may apply it best.
But thus small quarrell can arise of this,
Sith commonly a Lover's custome is
To love his choice the more, and more to like it,
The more hee sees that other suitors seek it :

Although some drown'd in that detested humour,
Which bred of love, becommeth love's-consumer,
Like wretched *Procris*, work their owne destruction
Through fond surmises, and a false construction.
' But I am none of that mistrustfull crew
' That pout and pine in peevish jealousie,
If they but see another man come nigh,
To the deare Saint whereto themselves doe sue.
For thee I know so faithfull and so true,
That though I see fresh rivals daily plye
To purchase favour to thy peerlesse eye :
I never feare that thou wilt change for new.
If any wise and worthy Suitors seeke thee,
The more I love thee, and the more rejoyce
To see the prudent to approve my choice.
If any foole or franklin Lob doe like thee,
It grieves mee not, no, I am glad therefore,
For such a foile shall grace my grace the more.

EPIST. II.

TO ARCTOA.

NO doubt you deem that I have done you wrong,
  To make you waite for my reply so long ;
But pardon that, that I may pardon you
The treble trouble you have put mee too,
In over-racking my unready wit,
To make my words to march in measure fit.
For though the Patrons of *Pernassus'* Mount,
Be virgins all, as verses doe recount :
Yet every virgin cannot verse it well ;
Nay, few or none, can tuned numbers tell.
Then marvaile not to see my Rimes so rough,
For even my prose is hard and harsh enough ;
And both too base, even at their best, to be
Matcht with the meanest of your melodie.
But setting what might more be said aside,
You crave (forsooth) my Censure, to decide
A controversie 'twixt a loving Lad
And his sweet Love, that seem'd to use him bad :
And also aske my judgement of the Dame,
And which of both was worthy greatest blame.
But, for because you doe not there discover
The qualities of her, nor him, the Lover,
'Tis hard for mee to censure of the cause ;
And that was chiefe occasion of my pause.
But now at last, and better late then never,
I have employ'd my uttermost endevour
To satisfie your doubtfull, darke demand,
As farre, at least, as I can understand :

For, to the depth I cannot duely enter,
But must reply to all by peradventure :
By peradventure I must needs discusse
Th' ambiguous Theam, that you propound me, thus :
Perhaps the man was worthy that did wooe her ;
If so, some fault may be imputed to her :
Perhaps his judgement, and his gesture too
Were quick and comely, fitting for to wooe :
Perhaps his person, and his parentage
Did answer well his birth and personage :
Perhaps his Lands and wealthy Livings wai'd
Her Dowrie down ; If so, perhaps the maid
Wronging her selfe, did with her selfe abuse him ;
And yet perhaps had reason to refuse him :
Perhaps her eye had seene a man before,
A better man, that had deserved more :
Perhaps her heart had made a firme election,
Of such a man for manifold perfection :
Perhaps her hand had giv'n the trusty token
Of stedfast Faith, that never must be broken :
Perhaps her soule was joyn'd to *Juno's* state,
And then perhaps this Lover came too late :
If so it were, as so perhaps it was :
I blame not her, but his hard hap, alas :
Perhaps this Suitor was some simple patch :
Why should she grant with such a Mome to match ?
Perhaps his maners were mis-seeming men ;
Why should I blame her for misliking then ?

Perhaps his Parents were but basely bred ;
Why should shee yeeld to make her foot her head ?
Perhaps his person did not please her eye ;
Why should shee not in such a case deny ;
Perhaps his purse was lesser then his pride ;
Is any bound to be a begger's Bride ?
If so it were, as so perhaps it was,
I blame not her, but beg him for an Asse :

Blame him, or her, or both, or chuse you whether ;
For I can judge but by perhaps of neither.
Perhaps (I say) for till I know the storie,
I can pronounce no sentence peremptorie :
But thus conclude ; No woman's bound to marrie
With every Lout that loves her, by St. *Marie :*
For, granting that, succeeds by consequent,
That Queens belov'd of Carters, must consent.

EPIST. III.

Phileremus to his kinde friend *Philopolites* in due com-
mendation of this his first ESSAIES.

THy worke it selfe, it selfe, enough commends,
    And well approves thy busie labour such,
As of thy Countrey seemes to merit much
And promise more, as well thy name portends :
For, good beginnings seldome have bad ends.
These short Essayes, but as it were, a touch
Of ampler Tomes that in thy store doe couch,

Shew thy wit's worth, which worthiest things attends.
If any *Critick* at thy Tables carp,
Apelles, bid him meddle with his last ;
Let th' Asse crop Thistles, keep him from the Harp,
Whose learned Sound sound judgments only taste :
And such can take and make right use of these,
With praisefull thanks to *Philopolites.*

EPIST. IIII.

To his very friend Master *Robert Nicolson.*

THere needs no praising of a perfect Creature,
    There needs no signe to help good wine away,
There needs no Candle to commend the day,
There needs no foile to grace a faultlesse feature ;
Nor needs our friend my fameless pen's obscureness
To give a luster to his lightsome glasse ;
Sith the bright substance of the same doth passe

The cleerest Crystall farre, for price and purenesse.
Who list to looke in his faire glasse, shall finde
Faire *Albion*, full of life-prolonging smiles,
Choice Queen of beauties and the chiefe of Iles,
World's wonder, and the maze of every minde :
Then who can see such beauties, and refrain
To praise the hand that tooke such happy pain ?

EPIST. V.

To his friend Master *John Norden.*

YEt lives *Apelles* in despight of time,
    Though time long since hath worne his tables out

For the rare Pourtrait of that Monarch stout,
That in young yeares the world's high throne did climb

But *Norden* here, that doth so lively limne
The blisfull beauties that the heav'ns doe wooe ;
Makes th' elder ages, and *Apelles* too,
Resigne the praises and the prize to him :
The wealth, the worth, the beauty and the state,

That hee depaints, excels *Olympia's* Sonne ;
His matchlesse Art, that never age shall date,
Hath from the *Greeke* the goale and glory won :
Then give it him, for hee that doth deny it,
Is envie's Sonne, and shames not to descrie it.

EPIST. VI.

To the worshipfull my most assured loving Friend

Master Robert Nicolson.

THe rowling Stone that never gathers Mosse,
   The restlesse Ball that Fortune still doth tosse,
The hopeless Barke that findes no certaine Port,
The hapless man, whose heart is all amort ;
To you deare paire of chiefe-approved friends,
The joyes hee wants in zealous wishes sends ;
To shunne suspect of grosse ingratefulnesse,
To both your vertue's gentle gentlenesse.
I stole the leasure of these hasty lines
From out a *Chaos* of confus'd designes ;
Wherein incumbred with a thousand cares,
Inviron'd round with infinite Affaires,
I pine my body and impair my wit ;
Not for mine owne, but others' benefit :
As Bees, and Birds, and Sheepe, and other Beasts,
To others' uses, yeeld their rich increase.
Pardon therefore, although I ill deserve,
A time will come (though yet it doe not serve)

When thankful thoughts shall prove and publish better
Then these dull rimes, how deeply I am debter
To both your favours ; and for both your sakes,
To whomsoever in your love pertakes :
Which, one day, *Tangley* (if I live) shall tell,
Where thrift and bounty in aboundance dwell.
I blush to be so briefe, because so rare ;
But my occasions so importune are,
That I protest, by all your friendships past,
I am so pressed, by the bearer's haste,
And instant causes that this while attend mee ;
That in despight I here must recommend mee,
And end abruptly ere I had begun,
The strange Career my Muse had meant t' have run.
But take in worth, this fragment, and, I hope,
Another time will lend mee longer scope :
Till then farewell, and still immortall *Jove*
Maintaine you both, in plenty, peace, and love.

EPIST. VII.

TO MY VERY LOVING AND MOST

Constant friend Master *Robert Nicolson*

at his house at BRAMLEY.

I Am in doubt you have mee oft indighted,
   Cast and condemn'd, unheard, though not uncited,
And stil'd mee still, forgetfull and ingrate :
But if confession faults can expiate,
You blame mee not, more then my selfe I blame,
For th' oft omission which mee ill became,
Of timely answer, to those new, true signes,
Of old good will, your ever welcome lines.

Spurre mee, therefore, and spare not, I confesse,
At sight, I seem'd to have deserv'd no lesse.
But, by your leave, 'tis errour to esteeme
Or censure all things, alwayes as they seeme ;
When every thing now Tuskanizeth so,
That nothing is the same it is in show :
When neither vice dares like it selfe appeare,
Nor vertue's selfe dare show her selfe too clear

Lest th' one (too ougly) be of all condemn'd,
Th' other (too honest) be of all contemn'd.
For 'tis a question whether excellence,
Be now a dayes more loath'd, or impudence :
And therefore now our skilfull Neuters hold,
The best complection neither hot nor cold ;
But such a temper as can temporize
With fate and state, whence health and wealth arise :
So that both reason and religion too,
In spight of both, may doe as others doe :
And even the Soules deare Soule divinest zeale,
May take, like wax, the print of every Seale,
Such are our dayes, such are our deeds in Court,
Such is our Citie, such is every sort
Of every Science and of every Sex ;
O griefe of griefes, a righteous Soule to vex.
Then doome not rashly, lest you may misdeem ;
Ah, few or none, are found the same they seeme.
So though I seeme, as yet, to be ungrate ;
Because, alas, my yet too niggard fate
Cannot acquit, nor yet requite, in kinde,
Old courtesies, that have beene long behinde :
And though I seeme to have forgot my part,
* Anagr. of Martha Nicolson. Both to your selfe, and your * *Soon calm in Hart ;*
It was not so, it is not so, nor shall,
Till I in death forget my selfe and all.
No, no defect of true affection's fire
Dims your desert, nor dampeth my desire :
No scant of leasure, nor no want of love,
No distant absence, no remote remove,
No change of fortune, either mine or yours,
No smiles of Sun-shine, neither frowning showr's :
No, none of these, nor all of these, in one,
Shall ever taint mee with oblivion
Of your deserts ; nor of the mutuall dues,
Whence Phœnix-like our ancient love renewes.
And therefore faine I would not have you think,

That I from *Lethé* fetch my frozen inke ;
Or that from thence such a *Torpedo* comes,
As fetters letters, or my Pen benums.
No, I assure you, though for just excuse
Some serious causes I could well produce,
Besides attendance on my tender * *Lord,*   * *Henry* Prince of
And taske impos'd mee by his princely word ;   Wales.
Perhaps so large, and of such consequence,
As may command my utmost diligence.
Yet neither these, nor those, nor both together,
Have held my hand, but hope of comming thither ;
And not alone bare hope, which boads delay,
But present purpose, almost every day ;
To come my selfe, and in my mouth to beare
And bring my letters, to your longing eare ;
Which yet in hope yer many dayes is meant,
If gracious heav'ns be pleased to consent :
Till then I pray, let this, though short, suffice,
To wipe my seeming faults from your surmise :
So, for your fishes, shall my wishes be,
That on your store you may such blessings see,
As Christ our Saviour on those fishes shed,
When with so few, so many folk hee fed :
That like the Widowe's little Tub and Cruse,
You may have more, daily the more you use.
Besides your Carps I must in fine avow
I have receiv'd a Pig of mine owne Sow :
A timelesse birth, *Minerva* like, begot
Without a mother, of I wot not what :
A Beare indeed, a Seed without a shape ;
Th' upbraiding blurr of my young Muse's rape.
For these I thank you ; but my chiefe desire,
Was for the Damme to damne her to the fire ;
Lest, if shee should out-live mee, shee defame
My lineall heires, and scandalize my name.
Fare ever well, so ever wishes hee,
Who is more yours then hee can seeme to be.

***

EPIST. VIII.

TO THE WORSHIPFULL HIS AP-
proved friend Master *Robert Nicolson* Merchant, *Josuah*
Sylvester wisheth ever all true content.

TO you youth's Load-star, London's Ornament ;
    Friend to the Muses, and the well-inclin'd ;
Loving and lov'd of every vertuous minde ;
To you these tunelesse accents I present,
Of humble stile, and uncouth ornament :
Not to requite, but to record your kinde
And gentle favours, by the which you binde

My best endevours to acknowledgement.
Accept I pray This Present in good part,
This simple pledge of my sincere affection ;
Weigh not the worth, but weigh my willing heart
Perfect Goodwill supplies all imperfection :
    So may I one day write your worthy name,
    By better pen, upon a bigger frame.

EPIST. IX.

TO MY RIGHT WORTHY DEARE

Affected, most respected Friend Master

Robert Nicolson Gentleman.

THough providence all-prudent have decreed,
  To hold mee still under the Tyrant need :
So hard and scant, that, scarce a breathing while,
My carefull life hath had just cause to smile.
Of all the wants I feele, of all the woes,
(Witnesse hearts'-searcher which all secrets knows)
None woundeth deeper my distrestfull breast,
Then want of power to parallel the least
Of thousand favours, of a thousand kindes,
Vouchsafed mee from many noble mindes :
Among which number, neither least, nor last
In my memoriall, is your merit plac't.
The constant kindnesse of whose Cordiall love,
From my best thought shall never ought remove.
For though, alas, my fates no meanes afford,
To quit good turnes ; my Faith shall them record,
And sue with sighs, unto th' Eternall Throne,
My friends may reap what they have kindly sow'n :
So, as for one, they may have seaven times seaven,
In Earth of Grace, of Glory more in Heav'n.
Hereby in part, you may perceive, report
Hath bruited false my fortunes in the Court :
The King indeed (whose bounty is renown'd)
Now five years since, gave me five hundred pound,
Of debts long due to our late royall Maid ;
Which never were, nor never will be paid :
Because Sir * *Cæsar* who devis'd my plot,
Dy'd suddenly ere any thing was got :
Nor could I since have light of any thing,
Wherein to seek the favour of the King.
My gracious Prince, O how his name doth pierce
My grieved Soule, and sables all my verse.
Henry my whole, and sole *Mecænas* late,
With Princely pension did releeve my state,
With Princely purpose to have daign'd mee room,
Of grace and gaine, his privie Chamber-groome.
But hee is dead, alas, and with him dy'd
My present helpe, and future hope beside :
So that with *Job* I murmure not, but mourne,
Naked I came, and naked shall returne.
His will be done, that can doe what hee will ;
Hee to us all is All-sufficient still :
For at all times, in all extremest streights,
His sacred Arm, our secret armie, waits

* Prince *Henry*.

To succour us ; and in all various sort,
Our wants, our weakenesse, to supply, support :
Whereof mine own proofs pass mine own account,
And past examples past all numbers mount.
What shall I then repay his providence,
His goodnesse, bounty, and beneficence,
For all his mercies, and for every one ?
Besides, beyond, yea, against hope bestowne
On me, whose sins mought more his wrath incense.
What can I give my friends for recompence
Of all their favours severally showne ;
Unsought, unthought, unknowing, some unknown,
To mee the least in my most indigence ?
But laud the Author, love his instruments :
Praise him for all, and pray for all their weale
Whose hearts heé moves by faith, with hope and
      zeal
To succour Art's poore humble Innocents ;
As you on mee and mine heap sweet contents :
So, manifold be multipli'd to you,
All earthly goods, heav'n's grace, and glorie too.
To you and yours, so ever I beseech
Th' Eternall grant his treasure truly rich.
And so I rest as ever by desert,
Much bound to you and your **Soon calm in*
      Hart,
In hearty love, though lacking helpfull powers,
Unfained, faithfull, and as thankfull yours.
This messenger, your Brother and our friend,
Gave first occasion these few lines to send,
With these few teares that have been lately shed,
For two great *Henries*, too untimely dead :
A sigh for *Sidney* and the map of man,
These if you please mildely a while to scan,
Yer many months (or weeks I hope) expire,
Except the heav'ns still envie my desire ;
I'll send or shew you, ere the presse prevent,
My *Little Bartas*, and my *Parliament
Of royall vertues*, summoned long since,
And now assembled to create a Prince :
Such as was *Henry* while hee was with us,
And *Charles* will be (wee hope) *Panaretus ;*
Of whom no more, till face to face wee meet,
To view avie our papers sheet for sheet.

* Anagr. of Martha Nicolson.

TRANSLATED OUT OF

THE LATINE VERSES
Of George Dicher.

SEeking some luckie Starre, whereby to steer
  Our wandring Pinnace to her wished Peer ;
First *Venus* bright-star in the welkin blazes,
And quiet Seas, the Sea-borne *Venus* raises :
But yet I fear'd shee favour'd more our foe,
For commonly like will to like yee know.
In *Venus* pranks this Priest hath *Venus* past,
Therefore mine eyes on other Stars I cast.
Then *Lædas Twins* perceiving in the skie,
These shall be guides unto our saile said I.
Yet these, I fear'd, might more our foe befriend,
For such, to such, doe rightly band and bend ;
Like unto like, and still fowles of a feather,
Are wont, they say, to flock and fly together.
Those Bastard Cignets Godhead did assume,
This base-sprung Shaveling doth as much presume.
For, scarce a man, for God this Priest is plac't :
Therefore mine eyes on other Stars I cast.
Then both the bright-Beares I began to mark,
These thought I then, will better guide our bark :
Yet fear'd I these our foe might rather minde,
For like to like are ever most inclin'd.
The cruell'st Beares this cruell Priest exceeds,
For on the flesh of his owne flock hee feeds.

Alas what loadstar shall I then implore,
To lead my poor ship to th' appointed shore ?
Why fly'st thou fondling to the shadowie night-signs !
No doubt yᵉ day wil yeeld thee happier bright-signs.
The Sun wil serve ; when nightly Lamps shall faile,
Be sure the Sun will safely guide thy saile.
The Sun joyes all things, and without his light,
The world were *Chaos*, and the day were night.
The Sun first gave men knowledge of the Arts ;
A noble name knowledge to men imparts.
Darts, Musicke, Physicke first of all he found ;
And those sweet numbers, sacred verses sound.
O thou that art the Laureat's liberall Fautor !
O wittie thou, that lov'st a wittie Author !
Sith nothing cleerer then the Sunne doth shine,
Guide thou, *Apollo*, this first course of mine.
Now fear no more my boat the boy'strous billows
Of swolne-fac't *Auster*, nor his stormy fellows ;
Neither *Charibdis'* rage, nor *Scilla's* rore :
The Sun, be sure, will bring thee safe to Shore.
Goe, and the Golden Sun propitious stand.
Now take wee (Muse) our new-found taske in hand.

F I N I S.

A devise sent to is good friend Iistris Martha icolson.

* *To her that is* Soon calm in hart
A Winter's Posie made by Art.

Arctophilos.

NOt to requite, but to record
  Thy worth and kindnesse in a word,
I kindly here present to thee,
This little brittle peece of mee.
A *Larke* they say is worth a *Kite ;*
Till more my might accept this mite.
Some greater, greater things present,
Of lesser worth, or worser meant.
God measures not our work but will ;
Doe thou the like and love mee still.

Phileremus.

BEtween two hearts by love made one,
  Let this be shar'd, or else to none.

47

ON THE BACK SIDE
Of the Deux of hearts,
THUS :

ALthough the flowers I here present,
  Fresh to the view, but void of sent,
Like th' Apples on the sulph'ry floud,
Where *Sodome* and her Sisters stood,
Be like this World's deluding show,
Where vertue seemes, but is not though :
Yet mark them neer and you shall finde
Some pleasant Posie for the minde,
Of wholsome savour, holy use,
Delightfull taste, and sprightfull juice :
To cleer the soule, or cleer the sight,
Or breed a better appetite.
For in the nature even of flowers,
Are remedies and rules for ours.

The Lilly, Rose, and Marigold,
Within their leaves these Lessons fold :
First spotlesse, though on stinking stalke,
How pure among th' impure to walke :
The next, which from a bramble springs,
That Grace more grace then nature brings :
The third, which with the Sunne doth ope,
To th' onely Sonne directs our hope ;
And richer clad then *Salomon*,
They altogether cheer us on,

With hearts'-ease, thrift and patience.
To trust th' Eternall providence.
Now add but Time to these, my friend,
And learne thy last, respect thy end :
For even the fading life of flowers,
Is but a lively type of ours :
Fresh in the morning, fall'n at noone ;
Wither'd yer night, and vanisht soone.

F I N I S.

Canzone delle : 3. Grazie.

OMNES CHARITES.

To the most faire and vertuous President of all female perfection, the *Soon calm in Hart*.

THE GRACES ALL TOGETHER.

ALl her good children Nature hath inclin'd,
    T' aspire to full perfection in their kinde :
Therefore shee makes each thing som good to love,
That being had, that good may better prove :
Yet in their choice of good they often erre ;
And seeming good before true good preferre.
But let us see if wee can choose the thing
That to our Sex doth most perfection bring.

1   *Aglaia sola*, Beauty.

Our perfect'st Crown is made of beautie's flowers,
Which of it selfe supplies all other dowers :
Women excell the perfect'st men in this,
And therefore herein their perfection is.
Wee for the beauty heav'n it selfe admire,
Faire fields, faire houses, gold and pearles desire ;
Beauty doth alwaies health and youth imply ;
Beauty delights the noblest sense, the Eye.

2   *Sola Thalia*, Wit.

Beauty delights the sense, but Wit the reason ;
Wit lasts an age, and beauty but a season ;
The sense is quickly cloy'd with beautie's taste ;
But wit's delight still quick and fresh doth last.
Beauty, weake eyes with her illusion blindes ;
Wit conquers spirits and triumphs over minds :

Dead things have beauty, onely men have wit ;
And man's perfection doth consist in it.

3   *Euphrosyne sola*, Wealth.

Wit will want matter, beauty ornament,
If wealth doe want which is omnipotent :
Wealth is a power which passeth nature farre ;
Wealth makes a goose, a swan ; a spark, a starre :
Wealth, on a Cottage, can a Palace build,
New-paint old walls, and rotten timber guild.
Not a faire face, but fortunes faire I crave ;
Let mee want wit, so I fooles' fortune have.

4   *Omnes Charites*, Vertue.

Yet these perfections most imperfect be,
If there be wanting vertue's modestie :
Vertue's aspect would have the sweetest grace,
If wee could see, as wee conceive her face :
Vertue guides wit, with well-affected will,
Which if wit want, it proves a dangerous ill :
Vertue gets wealth, with her good government,
If not, shee 's rich, because shee is content.

F I N I S.

Epitaphium *Helenæ Nicolson,* *Dominæ Branch.*

Quam, tér fœlicem, Pietas, Opulentia, Forma,
  Fecêre in terris, modò suffragante Popello :
Suffragante Deo, fidei constantia vivæ
Æternùm in cœlis te nunc jubet esse beatam.

J. H.

Anglicè.

Whom Piety, Plenty, and Beauty made
Thrice happy, here, on earth among the best :
Her lively faith, whose true fruits never fade,
Makes now with God, in heav'n for ever blest.

J. S.

An Epitaph on the death of the *right vertuous and universally beloved* BENJAMIN NICOLSON Gent.

Who deceased at *Bramly* in *Surrey,*

January the 4. 1599.

UNkindly kind, why mourn we, friends, in vain ?
  Whose bitter death is better Life's beginning ;
Whose flesh-freed Souls are henceforth free from sin-
  ning ;
Whose earthly loss redoubles heav'nly gain.
For meed of sinne, th' All-maker did ordaine
All (once) to dye, all flesh returnes to dust ;
But, deare is the memoriall of the just
In his remembrance ; and they blest remaine
That dye in him ; for, from their carefull paine
They ever rest : so ever blest and deare,
Ben. Nicolson's old Body resteth, here :
His Soule in Heav'n among the Saints doth raigne.
  Borne gentle, gently bred, nobly ally'd ;
  Liv'd vertuously, and christianly hee dy'd.

An Epitaph, on ever-blessed *Queene Elizabeth.*

IF ever royall vertues crown'd a Crowne,
  If ever mildnesse shin'd in Majestie,
If ever Honour honoured Renowne,
If ever Courage dwelt with Courtesie,
If ever Princesse put all Princes downe,
For Temp'rance, Prowesse, Prudence, Equity ;
  This, this was Shee, that in despite of death,
  Lives (still) ador'd, admir'd *Elizabeth.*

Idem ad Eandem.

ZEalous of God, Jealous of ev'ry Ill ;
  Devout to God, and to the Godly deare ;
Whose vertues (like a Candle on a Hill)
Shin'd to her Sex for conduct farre and neere.

For, all the Graces, else-where, single-sowne,
Met all, at once, in her chaste Breast alone.

Idem.

SPaine's Rod, Rome's Ruine, Netherlands' Reliefe,
  Heav'n's gem, earth's joy, world's wonder, nature's
  chiefe.

An Epitaph on the Lady *Maney.*

MAny religious, many be discreet ;
  Many officious, many faithfull wives ;
Many severe, many sincerely sweet ;
Many be meeke, kinde, constant all their lives.
  But, all these Gifts in many single-set,
  In *Jeff'ryes Maney,* All-together met.
Mirrour of Nature, miracle of Grace ;
Pattern of Women, Paragon of Wives :
In whom Affection had perfection's place ;
With whom deceast more Good then ill survives.
  For, all heav'n's Gifts in Many single set,
  In *Jeff'ries-Maney,* All-together met.
Devout to God, officious to her Pheere ;
Zealous of Good, jealous of every Ill :
Wise, milde, and more then can be mention'd here ;
Her Many-vertues would whole volumes fill.
  For, All Heav'n's Gifts in many single-set,
  In *Jeff'ryes Maney,* All-together met.

Epig. I. Of Nobility.

WHat are the badges of Heroike Bloud,
  But blots to those that have their birth bely'd ?
What 's outward Greatnesse without inward good,
But glorious painting of a gracelesse Pride?
But where with Banners, vertuous Maners bud ;
Where honours are with honesty ally'd,
  With Pity, Prowesse, Prudence, Right, Humility,
  Faith, Justice, Bounty ; there 's the true Nobility.

Epig. II. To his most deare friend *Mistresse* E.

YOur humble servant most sincerely wishes
  More happy joyes then in the Sea be Fishes ;
Fowles in the Aire, or on the Earth be Flowers ;
Or then be drops in twenty thousand Showers :
Heav'n's peace, earth's plenty, soule's and bodie's bliss ;
And all true Comforts incident to this.

Epig. III. The twelve Signs.

MAn's head and face Heav'n's Ram obey :
  Our neck the neck-strong Bull doth sway :

Th' arm-twining Twins guide hands and armes :
Breast, Sides and Stomach, Cancer charmes ;
The Lion rules our back and heart :
Bowels' and belly's Virgo's part :
Reines, Hanches, Navill, Libra friends :
Bladder and secrets Scorpio tends :
The halfe horse Bow-man claimes our thighs :
Unto the Kid our knees suffice :
Our leggs are but the Butler's fees :
The Fish our foot-steps over-sees.

Epig. IV. Pallas & Astræa.

PRowesse and Prudence are my double part,
    Either alone is as a headlesse Dart :
Or if not headlesse, heedlesse, throwne (as ill)
From feeble arme without or aime or skill.
But both united by their mutuall worth,
Begin estates, beget and bring them forth ;
And in the joynt, and the just use of them,
Consists, subsists, persists a Diadem.

Epig. V. Astræa.

BOth temperance and Justice I containe,
    As well as Pallas, my one part is twain ;
And, in this presence, many proofes there bee,
I may as justly vaunt my parts as shee.
For, but my Balance counterpoize her Lance,
And, but I steepe her wit in temperance,
Spee[d] failes her course, and fals in her discourse ;
Yea too-too oft brings things from bad to worse :
And (by her leave) in all shee arrogates,
My share is most in th' happy state of States.

Epig. VI. The true honour of the *truely Honourable.*

NEither the birth drawn though in long descent
    From noble, royall, or imperiall Race :
Neither the match (with houses eminent)
When heirs with heirs, their arms with arms they grace :
Neither possession of a princely Rent,
With sumptuous service in a stately place ;
  Are honours reall (being right defin'd)
  But reall vertues and a royall minde.

Epig. VII. To the Noble Captain *and Commander in the* Barke *Care,* the honourable Baronet Sr. *Henry Baker* and to his right vertu-ous Lady *Katherine Baker,* ANAGRAMS.

HEre is thy *Bark* Care, *Anker* be
    (Sir, so your names bid, so beg wee)

Well-grounded Hope ; your Cable, Love ;
Your Compasse, Wisedome, from above ;
Your Helm, Discretion, steering faire ;
Your Maine-Mast, Faith ; your Fore-saile, Prayer ;
Your tackling, sure ; your reck'ning, just ;
Your Pilot, Truth ; your Purser, Trust ;
Your Trafficke, Grace ; your Profit, Glory ;
Your Hav'n, in Heav'n (prepared for-yee) ;
That whiles you crosse the tossing Seas,
'Twixt Rocks of Ill, and Wracks of Ease ;
If Stormes arise, you safe may ride,
Though *Nereus* chafe, and *Boreas* chide.
So prayes the heart, whose love, whose zeale,
Would worke as well as wish your weale ;
Had it the power as well as will,
To serve and to deserve you still.

A contented Minde.

I Waigh not Fortune's frowne or smile,
    I joy not much in earthly Joyes,
I seeke not state, I reake not stile,
I am not fond of fancie's Toyes :
  I rest so pleas'd with what I have,
  I wish no more, no more I crave.
I quake not at the Thunder's crack,
I tremble not at noise of warre,
I swound not at the newes of wrack,
I shrink not at a Blazing-Starre ;
  I feare not losse, I hope not gaine,
  I envie none, I none disdaine.
I see Ambition never pleas'd,
I see some *Tantals* starv'd in store,
I see gold's dropsie seldome eas'd,
I see even *Midas* gape for more ;
  I neither want, nor yet abound,
  Enough 's a Feast, content is crown'd.
I faine not friendship where I hate,
I fawne not on the great (in show),
I prize, I praise a meane estate,
Neither too lofty nor too low :
  This, this is all my choice, my cheere,
  A minde content, a conscience cleere.

The Fruites of a cleere *Conscience.*

TO shine in silke, and glister all in gold,
    To flow in wealth, and feed on dainty fare,
To have thy houses stately to behold,
Thy Prince's favour, and the people's care :
  The groaning Gout, the Collick or the Stone,
  Will marre thy mirth, and turne it all to moane.
But, be it, that thy body subject be
To no such sicknesse, or the like annoy :
Yet, if thy Conscience be not firme and free,
Riches are Trash, and Honours but a Toy.

This peace of Conscience is the perfect joy,
  Wherewith God's Children in the world be blest ;
  Wanting the which, as good want all the rest.
The want thereof made *Adam* hide his head ;
The want of this made *Cain* to waile and weep :
This want (alas) makes many goe to bed,
When they (God wot) have little list to sleep.
Strive, O then strive to entertaine and keepe
  So rich a Jewell, and so rare a Guest,
  Which being had, a rush for all the rest.

Of Crosses or Afflictions.

UNhappy is the life feeles no mishap ;
  For, Crosses in this easie erring way,
Are guides that teach us how to shun decay,
In all the tempting Paths of pleasure's Map.

When such as prosp'rous-Chance lulls in her lap,
Forget their maker God, their substance Clay :
And by their faults, their heav'n-born soules betray
Into Sin's Iron Cave, old Sathan's Trap :

Then suffer not thy need, shame, death, or others
Falsly accounted Ils, thy spirit to grieve ;
For small affliction great offences smothers ;
And, as it touches, teaches to beleeve.
  Then, thanking God, cease to be vainely sorry ;
  For, Crosses come for Our good and His glory.

Wise advise, fond mistrust.

IN serious matters to make sober speed,
  In doubts to looke before one leape in danger ;
In waighty cases to take wary heed,
In briefe, to try, before you trust a Stranger,
  Argues great wisdome, and such circumspection
  Doubles your vertue, trebles my affection.
But to be still casting beyond the Moone,
Still to be sounding in a channell knowne,
Still to be looking for the light at Noone,
Still to suspect a heart, so much your owne,
  Implies a weakenesse which doth still bewray
  Irresolution, Mother of delay,
And that delay, deluding (for the most)
But selfe and others with some maske of reason,
The fairest fortunes hath as foulely lost,
By overslipping their peculiar season :
  Delay breeds danger, every day doth prove ;
  It quencheth hottest, killeth hearty love.
Let wisedome (therefore) first at large explore,
Thereby resolve, and then revolve no more.

A Caution for Courtly Damsels.

BEware faire maid of mighty Courtiers' oaths,
  Take heed what gifts or favours you receive ;
Let not the fading glosse of silken cloaths
Dazle your vertues, or your fame bereave :
  For once but leave the hold you have of Grace,
  Who will regard your fortune or your face ?
Each greedy hand will strive to catch the flower,
When none regard the stalke it growes upon ;
Basenesse desires the fruit still to devoure,
And leave the tree to fall or stand alone :
  But this advise, faire Creature, take of mee,
  Let none take fruit unlesse hee 'll have the tree.

Beleeve not oaths, nor much protesting men,
Credit no vowes, nor a bewailing song ;
Let Courtiers sweare, forsweare, and sweare agen,
The heart doth live ten Regions from the tongue :
  For when with oaths and vows they make ye tremble,
  Beleeve them least, for then they most dissemble.
Beware lest *Cræsus* doe corrupt thy minde,
Or fond Ambition sell thy modesty ;
Say, though a King thou even courteous finde,
Hee cannot pardon thine impurity.
  Begin with Kings, to subjects you will fall,
  From Lord to Lackey, and at last to all.

Natalis Christi.

WHo made al time, this time was made a man,
  Bred after time, but being ay beforne,
Th' All-Father's Sonne, of his own Daughter born ;
Eternity now (as it were) began :
Clouts swaddle him, whom no Clouds circle can :
Hee cries for milke, who giveth all things meat :
Th' Almighty, feeble ; little, th' onely-Great ;
Christ in a Cratch, who all the world doth span :
The Lord of all lies in an humble Lapp ;
Who cloths the Fields with green, the Sphears with gold,
Hath not a ragge, his naked Limbs to wrap :
Heav'n's Majesty, Earth's Misery doth fold.
The King of glory comes with shame to dwell,
To open Heav'n (for his) and shut up Hell.

Passio Christi.

DEare Lord, who did'st (to open heav'n for us)
  Endure thine owne side to be opened so ;
And wert thy selfe shut in the grave below,
To shut the gates of gaping *Erebus :*
Who, to exalt us, did'st thy selfe abase ;
Who, thine to loose, did'st bind thy selfe for them ;
Who, to acquit us, did'st thy Selfe condemne :
Who, us to heale, thy selfe wert hurt, alas ;
Who bar'st thy selfe, our Curse, to bring us blisse ;
Who, to enrich us, mad'st thy selfe so poore ;
Who dyd'st thy selfe, that wee might dye no more.
Lord with thy merit cover mine amisse,
In bloud and water, thy deare bosome's bath,
O drench my sins, O quench thy righteous wrath !

The Soule's Errand.

GOe Soule, the bodie's guest,
  Upon a thankelesse Errand,
Feare not to touch the best,
The truth shall be thy warrant :
  Goe thou, since I must dye,
  And give the world the lye.

Goe tell the Court it glowes,
And shines like rotten wood ;
Say to the Church it showes
What 's good, but doth not good.

Tell Potentates they live,
Acting by others' Action,
Not lov'd unlesse they give,
Not strong, but by a faction.

Tell men of high condition,
That in Affaires of State,
Their purpose is ambition,
Their practice onely hate.

Goe tell the young Nobility
They doe degenerate,
Wasting their large ability
In things effeminate.

Tell those that brave it most,
They beg for more by spending ;
And, in their greatest cost,
Seeke but a selfe-commending.

Tell Zeale it wants Devotion,
Tell Love it is but Lust,
Tell Priests they hunt Promotion,
Tell Flesh it is but dust.

Say Souldiers are the Sink
Of Sinne to all the Realme ;
Given all to whores and drink,
To quarrell and blaspheme.

Tell Townesmen, that because that
They pranck their Brides so proud,
Too many times it drawes-that
Which makes them beetle-brow'd.

Goe tell the Palace-Dames
They paint their parboil'd faces,

Seeking by greater shames
To cover lesse disgraces.

Say to the City-wives,
Through their excessive brav'ry,
Their Husband hardly thrives,
But rather lives in Slav'ry.

Tell London Youths that Dice,
Faire Queanes, fine Clothes, full Bouls,
Consume the cursed price
Of their dead-Fathers' Soules.

Say Maidens are too coy
To them that chastely seeke them,
And yet are apt to toy
With baser Jacks that like them.

Tell poets of our dayes
They doe profane the Muses,
In soothing Sin with praises,
That all the world abuses.

Tell Tradesmen waight and measure
They craftily abuse,
Thereby to heap-up treasure,
Though Heav'n thereby they lose.

Goe tell the vitious rich,
By usury to gaine,
Their fingers alwayes itch,
To Soule's and Bodie's paine.

Yea tell the wretched poore
That they the wealthy hate,
And grudge to see at doore
Another in their state.

Tell all the world throughout
That all 's but vanity,
Her pleasures doe but flout
With sly security.

Tell Kings and Beggers base,
Yea tell both young and old,
They all are in one case,
And must all to the mould.

And now kinde Host adieu,
Rest thou in earthly Tombe,
Till Christ shall all renew,
And then I 'll thee resume.

FINIS.

NOTES AND ILLUSTRATIONS.

PAGE, 331, col. 2, l. 2, '*fadge*' = agree, fit : l. 8, '*corriving*' = corrival : p. 332, col. 1, l. 8, '*feature*' = person —see Glossarial Index. *s.v. :* col. 2, l. 16, '*franklin Lob*' see *ibid. :* Epistle II., p. 332, col. 2, l. 25, '*patch*' = foolish, rude fellow : l. 26, '*Mome*' = blockhead : Epistle IV., col. 2, l. 5, '*maze*' = puzzle : p. 336, Epistle IX., col. 2, last line, '*avie*'—see Glossarial Index, *s.v. :* p. 337, *George Dicher*—see our Memorial-Introduction : col. 2, l, 13, '*Fautor*' = patron, favourer. Of the names and places occurring in the preceding poems see our Memorial Introduction ; also the same for critical notice of Raleigh's 'Soule's Errand," as erroneously assigned to Sylvester, *supra* (p. 342). G.

PANTHEA:

OR

DIVINE WISHES

AND

MEDITATIONS.

THE AUTHORS INVOCA-
TION AND IMPRECATION

Againſt his Infernall Enemies.

Supreme Commander of the Crystall Sky,
    That ALL of NOTHING powerfully didst frame,
Be 't not offence against thy Deity,
With humble Accents to adore thy Name :
    Though in this teare-composed terrene Globe,
    I weare Mortalitie's Sin-stained Robe.

Let mee behold with Contemplation's Eye,
The Beauty of thine Angell-guarded Throne ;
And let my soule with humble boldnesse fly,
Above the Starry Constellation :

And there with that most holy Hierarchie,
Sing Hymns and Anthems to thy Deitie.

Let my sad soule, long pierc't with swords of Griefe
By *Fiends*, *Alastors*, *Harpies*, *Furies* fell,
Receive (my God) from thee Divine Reliefe,
Which may their Pride and canker'd Malice quell :
    Make those *pure Hell-Dogs* in their Dens to couch,
    And *Belzebub* himselfe at last to crouch.

JOS. SYL.

PANTHEA.

The Induction.

WHat should I wish for on the Earth?
   Goodnesse is grown to such a dearth;
While want of Grace doth make abuse
Of that which might be for good Use:
That who observes what most men wish,
Shall finde how fond and vaine it is.
  Some wish for Wealth, to pamper Pride;
The Med'cine's good, but ill appli'd.
Some wish for Honour, in high thought;
Honour is good, Ambition nought.
Some wish for Health, to live at ease;
Health may be good, Ease breeds Disease.
Some wish for Power, to wrong at will;
Power oft is good, Oppression ill.
Some wish for Youth, to nourish Folly;
Youth may be good, the Wish unholy.
Some wish for Love, to answer Lust;
Love may be good, the Wish unjust.
Some wish for Strength, to crush and kill;
Strength may be good, but Murther ill.
  Thus still th' Abuse which Will brings forth
Doth make the Wishes nothing worth.
Yet since that Wishes may be good,
When Worth is truely understood,
Let mee set downe my Heart's desire,
And what hath set my soule on fire.
  It is not Earth, nor earthly Treasure,
Nor worldly Honour, fleshly Pleasure,
Nor Power, nor Place, nor Youth, nor Strength,
Nor drawing out this Life at length,
Nor idle pleasing Nature's Eye,
With fond Affection's Vanity.
Not one of these comes neer the White
Of my Heart's Wish and Soule's Delight.
The Course of my true Care's content
Extends above the Firmament.
The levell of my Soule's chiefe Love
Is onely in the Heav'ns above;
Where I shall see my Saviour sweet,
And how his Saints and Angels meet
With such an Harmony of Voyces,
As shewes how every Soule rejoyces
In the beholding his sweet Face,
That is the glory of all Grace.
This, this, my Wish shall onely be,
To live where I may ever see

My Saviour sweet, and in his sight
Have all my Heart's and Soule's Delight.
  Daigne then (my God) this Boone to give
Whiles here upon this Earth I live,
That neither Wealth, nor Poverty,
Nor Comfort, nor Calamity,
Nor Health, nor Sicknesse, Ease, nor Paine,
Nor Hope, nor Feare, nor Losse, nor Gaine,
May ever take such hold on mee,
But still my Joy in CHRIST may be.

I. Wish or Meditation.

OH! had I of his Love but part,
   That chosen was by God's owne heart,
That Princely Prophet, David, hee,
Whom in the Word of Truth I see
The King of Heav'n so dearely lov'd,
As mercy beyond measure prov'd:
Then should I neither Gyant feare,
Nor Lion, that my soule would teare;
Nor the Philistims, nor such Fiends,
As never were true Christians' friends:
No Passions should my spirit vex,
Nor Sorrow so my minde perplex,
But I should still all glory give
Unto my God by whom I live.
Then Health nor Sicknesse, Griefe nor Ease,
Should so my minde disease or please;
But Want, or Woe, what-ere I prove,
The Lord of Life should be my Love.
To him I should my minde impart,
And to him onely give my heart,
And to his mercy onely pray,
To put my secret sinnes away:
To heale my sinfull wounded Soule,
And put my Name in Mercie's Roll:
In all my Cares and Crosses still
To comfort mee with his good Will:
And when I cry and roar in Griefe,
In deepe despaire of Hope's Reliefe,
My Faith should yet in Mercy find
The Comfort of a constant Minde;
And I should ever joy to see
How Mercie's Eye did looke on mee;
Then should my Heart tune every string,
That to his glory I might sing

A *Song* of ever-lasting Praise,
To end in never-ending daies.
Then should I *play*, and *sing*, and *dance*,
And to the Heav'ns mine Eyes advance,
With joy to see in Triumph so
The *Arke* of God in Glory goe :
And whatsoever I possesse
In *Power* or *Honour*, more or lesse,
Nor Earth nor Heaven should mee move,
But still my Lord should be my love.
If I were *sicke*, Hee were my *Health* ;
If I were *poore*, Hee were my *Wealth* ;
If I were *weake*, Hee were my *Strength* ;
If *dead*, Hee were my *Life* at length ;
If *scorn'd*, Hee onely were my *Grace* ;
If *banisht*, Hee my *Resting place* ;
If *wrong'd*, Hee onely were my *Right* ;
If *sad*, Hee were my Soule's *Delight* ;
In summe, and all, All-onely Hee
Should be All, above All, to mee.
His *Hand* shall wipe away my *Teares*,
His *Favour* free mee from all *Feares*,
His *Mercy* pardon all my *Sinne*,
His *Grace* my life *anew* begin,
His *Love* my *Light* to Heav'n should be,
His *Glory*, thus to comfort mee.
   Thus was the Kingly Prophet blest,
To live in Love's eternall Rest.
And since I see his Grace so great,
To all that Mercy doe intreat :
And how the faithfull Soule doth prove
An heav'nly blessing in his Love ;
Let mee but onely *This* request,
To be but *thus* with *David* blest,
That *Joy*, or *Griefe*, what-ere I prove,
The Lord of Life may be my Love.

II. *Wish* or *Meditation.*

O H ! that I were as *Wise* as * Hee
   That did by Observation see
What all things are, with all their Worth,
That under Heav'n the Earth brings forth ;
How *vaine* they are, and how they vex
The Soule whom *Passion* doth perplex.
Then should I neither *carke* nor *care*
For things that so uncertain are ;
Nor toile nor labour for a Life
So full of falshood, feare and strife.
Nor ayme at Title, Power, or Place,
Nor Favour, Wealth, or Wordly Grace ;
Nor trouble Patience with a hope
Of ought beyond my onely Scope ;
Nor sooth, nor flatter, lye, nor sweare,
Nor stand in Danger, nor in Feare
Of him, of her ; of this, of that,
Nor hunt I know not after what :

47

But love the measure and the meane,
That keepes the Soule and Body cleane.
Then should I finde this Life but Breath
That Sinne hath subject made to Death :
For from the greatest to the least,
No Soule but lives at some unrest :
The soundest and the deepest *Wit*
Sometimes in idle Thoughts doth sit ;
The fairest and the sweetest *Face*
Is sometime subject to disgrace.
The noblest and the valiant'st *Minde*,
Sometime may hap goe downe the Winde.
The richest *Hand*, and proudest *Heart*,
May chance to play the Begger's part.
The valiant'st Arme, and strongest Hand,
Sometime at *Mercie's* Gate may stand.
The purest *Soule* that would not sinne,
May chance to fall in Satan's Ginne.
   Then since I see there is no state,
But that sometime, or soone, or late,
Is subject to so hard a course
As leaves the *Better* for the *Worse*,
Though I be not so wise as *Hee*
That made mee *This* to know and see,
Yet will I joyne with him in this,
Upon *this Earth* to build no *Blisse* ;
But with the Wings of *Faith* to flye
Unto my Glorious God on high :
And in his *Mercy* onely prove
The Blessings for my *Soule's* behoofe ;
From *Sorrow*, *Sinne*, and *Satan* free ;
And love the *World* that list (for mee).

III. *Wish* or *Meditation.*

O H ! that I had that *Patience*
   That is the Spirit's Excellence,
That *Job* in all his paines did prove,
Unto the Lord to shew his Love :
Then should no *Losse* of *Lands* or *Goods*,
Bring in such Flotes of Sorrowe's Floods ;
Nor *Children's* death, nor dogged *Wife*
Nor wounded Heart, nor weary Life,
Nor Scoffs of Friends, nor words of griefe,
Nor Heart's *Despaire* of Hope's Reliefe,
Should make mee once (which God forbid)
Offend his Grace, what ere hee did :
But say with *Job, if hee will kill
My heart, yet will I love him still;*
And in his sight, my Waies reprove,
That is the God of gracious Love.
That then, when *All* were at the worst,
And that my Heart were almost burst,
My Soule might feele, that Comfort sweet
Did tread all sorrow under Feet.
But *Job* was just, so am not I,
His God did but his *Patience* try ;

And made his *Faith* in Mercy finde
The comfort of a *constant* Minde :
But my Soule hath so wicked bin,
That I am scourged for my Sinne,
In *Justice :* but with *Mercy* such,
As I can never praise too much.
For had not mercy heal'd my Sore,
I had beene slaine for evermore.
But my good God is ever *One ;*
His Hand is not to *mee* alone,
But unto *All* that in distresse
Doe in his Mercy seeke redresse ;
And whose true *Patience, Faith,* and *Love,*
Doe in his *Justice, Mercy* prove.

IV. *Wish* or *Meditation.*

OH ! that I had that *Gracious Call*
      That from the Heav'ns had blessed *Paul ;*
That chosen Saint of sacred Blisse,
Where onely Saints' true blessing is :
Who from the way of wicked Thought,
Unto the gates of *Grace* was brought ;
And when his *Eyes* were stricken blinde,
Had such an insight of the *Minde,*
As made him see through *Mercie's* light,
(That is the Soule's eternall sight)
How blinde is *Reason's* ruthfull Eye,
Where Errour leads the Heart awry ;
Whil'st *Conscience* thinking to doe well,
Doth carry *Misconceit* to Hell ;
Till *Mercy* meeting on the way,
Brings home the Sheepe that went astray :
Then should no *Office, Power,* nor *Place*
Make mee to seek my Soule's Disgrace,
To take a Tyrant's powerfull Rod,
To persecute the Saints of God.
But I should more in soule rejoyce
In Mercie's Gracious-Glorious Choice,
All *Persecutions* to abide,
Where *Patience, Faith,* and *Love is try'd*
Of the sweet Lord of Heaven's Blisse,
Then persecute one Saint of his :
But all my *Love,* and Love's *Delight,*
My *Meditation* day and night,
Should onely, all, and ever be
Of *Mercy* that so called mee.
No *Griefe,* no *Paine,* no *Want,* nor *Woe,*
That I should ever live to know,
But I should thinke too little all,
In Love to answer Mercie's Call :
For all the World I would not care,
Nor K[ing] nor *Kesar* would I feare ;
No *threats,* nor *thraldom, scourge* nor *death ;*
To speake his Praise, should stop my breath ;
But I should plainely speake and write
My knowledge of the Lord of Light :

And to the Glory of his Name,
Throughout the World divulge the same.
My *Walke* should be but in his Waies ;
My *Talke* but onely in his Praise ;
My *Life* a Death, but in his Love ;
My *Death* a Life, for him to prove :
My *Care* to keepe a Conscience cleane ;
My *Will* from wicked thoughts to weane ;
My *Prayers* for the Good of all,
That Mercy unto Grace doth call :
My *Labour* for the Love of Truth
To leade the life of Age and Youth :
My *Comfort* truely to convert
The Soules which Sathan did pervert :
My *Health,* to labour for their Love,
That seeke their blessing from above :
My greatest *Ease,* to worke for those
Whom Mercy to Salvation chose :
My *Paine,* and pleasure, Travell, Ease,
My God *thus* in his Saints to please.
Then should I this base *World* despise,
With all Earth's *idle Vanities ;*
And governe mine *Affections* so,
That Sin should never overthrow
This wounded wofull Soule of mine,
But still in Mercie's love divine,
My Soule should finde that *life* of Grace,
As should all *Earthly love* deface :
And I should onely wish to live,
All *Glory* to my God to give ;
And all in all my *Joy* to be
His *servant* that so *called* mee.

V. *Wish* or *Meditation.*

OH ! that my Soule might live to prove
      Some part of that sweet blessed Love,
Which *John* th' Evangelist possest,
When hee lean'd on our Saviour's brest :
When *Wisedome, Vertue, Grace* and *Truth,*
Embrac'd the blessed dayes of Youth !
Then should I fly with *Eagles'* wings
Unto the Glorious King of Kings ;
And see that *Heav'nly Court* of his
The Beauty of the Angels' Blisse ;
Where *Goodnesse, Grace,* and *Glory* dwels,
And *Love,* and *Life,* and nothing else
But *Holinesse* and Heav'nly *Light,*
All, onely in my Saviour's sight :
Then should I *loath* this World of Woe,
That doth *bewitch* the Worldling so ;
And seeke (but at my Saviour's *feet*)
To finde my Soule's eternall *Sweet ;*
Till Mercy will vouchsafe mee grace
To have a glimpse of his sweet *Face,*
In whose least sweetest *Looke* of Love,
A *Sea* of Joy the *Heart* doth prove ;

And swimming in the Soule's Delight,
Is *ravisht* with that Glorious *Sight.*
But though I cannot be so blest,
To leane upon my Saviour's *Brest ;*
As all unworthy of such Grace,
To looke on his Cœlestiall *Face :*

Yet let mee beg at *Mercie's* Feet,
That I may but receive this Sweet,
That when his Saints and Angels sing
Their *Haleluiahs* to their King,
My Soule in Joy all-sounding then,
May have but leave to sing *AMEN.*

FINIS.

NOTES AND ILLUSTRATIONS.

PAGE 343, col. 2, l. 4, '*Alastors*'—see Glossarial Index, *s.v. :* p. 344, col. 1, l. 33, ' *White* ' = mark shot at.

G.

UPON THE
SEVERALL PETITIONS
OF THE
LORD'S PRAYER:

LETANIE I.

Hallowed be thy name.

1.

O God the Father, who on high
  In Heaven hast thy dwelling place ;
Yet dost thy Soveraigne Majestie
So far beneath it selfe debase,
Out of thy great abundant grace,
Us wormes on earth, here earthly bred
Thence to behold, man's mortall race ;
  Thy Name be ever hallowed.

2.

O Son of God, of like degree,
God with the Father, who didst make
Thy selfe of no repute to be ;
But didst man's nature undertake,
Made flesh and bloud for mankind's sake,
With servants' rags apparelled ;
Who heav'n and earth dost make to shake ;
  Thy Name be ever hallowed.

3.

O God, the holy Ghost, who when
Our Saviour us departed from,
Returning back to heav'n agen,
Didst streight descend to take his roome,
And daily still on us dost come,
To visit us in his blest steed,
Till hee shall come all flesh to doome ;
  Thy Name be ever hallowed.

4.

O holy, glorious, ever blest,
Eternall individuall Trine,
Who every one, as do the rest,
With equall lustre forth do shine,
One God in endlesse sacred Twine
Of persons three distinguished ;
O Father, Son, ô Spirit divine ;
  Thy Name be ever hallowed.

5.

For our Creation by thee made
After thine owne similitude,
With righteousnesse as garment clad,
With judgement, wit and grace endew'd,
And power over creatures rude,
Ordein'd to be their Soveraigne dread ;
Next to the Angels none so good ;
  Thy Name be ever hallowed.

6.

For our Redemption, by thee freed
And ransom'd at a costly price,
Thy life-bloud, costly price indeed,
O Christ, no meaner sacrifice ;
When our first parents by advice
Of cursed Serpent altered
Thy service for thine enemies ;
  Thy Name be ever hallowed.

7.

For that proportion of thy Spirit,
Whereby, when wee thine image faire

Defaced had beyond our merit
Thou of thy goodnesse debonaire
Didst freely it againe repaire,
Wee will abroad thy glory spread,
And make it be our daily prayer ;
   Thy Name be ever hallowed.

8.

For hope of glory to us giv'n
By assurance of thy promise true
Of everlasting blisse in heaven,
Made us hereafter to ensue,
When thou our bodies shalt renew,
And them againe raise from the dead,
Wee give thee praise and honour due ;
   Thy Name be ever hallowed.

9.

Such glory whereto Virgin chast
Thou glorious Lord, above the rest
Of womankind advanced hast,
Whom thou, ô Father, thoughtest best
With so great honour to invest,
To make thy Son of her be bred ;
For *Marie* virgin-mother blest,
   Thy Name be ever hallowed.

10.

That blisse, whereof those heavenly ones,
Of Angels' sacred Hierarchie
Partakers are Archangels, Thrones,
And all that blessed companie :
Who though thy visage heavenly
They still behold, are destined
Our 'tendants ; for whose minist'ry
   Thy Name be ever hallowed.

11.

That joy, which soules enjoy departed,
That are in booke of life enroll'd,
Of pious men and humble-hearted,
Of Patriarkes and Prophets old,
Apostles and of Martyrs bold,
Who have the way before us led ;
For whose examples manifold
   Thy Name be ever hallowed.

12.

And for that speciall benefit,
Their lives and thine owne lawes record,
Which some of them themselves have writ,
The pen-men of thy holy Word,
Whereby thou dost us light afford,
Where wee ought after them to tread
Step after step ; for this ô Lord,
   Thy Name be ever hallowed.

13.

And for that blessed, heavenly food,
Thy Sacraments given to sustaine

Our soules' deare life and livelyhood,
Which thou as pledges didst ordaine
Of thy great love still to remaine ;
For which in forme administred,
As thou, ô Christ, commandedst plaine,
   Thy Name be ever hallowed.

14.

And for that holy Discipline,
Which makes vice starve and vertue spring,
For exercise of things divine
Through a religious, gratious King,
Under the shadow of whose wing
Wee may in godly quiet lead
And spend our daies ; wee to thee sing,
   Thy Name be ever hallowed.

15.

For other blessings severall
Concerning this life's present state,
Of which wee, Lord, do more then all
The world beside participate,
(Which to thy praise wee now relate ;)
For what wee have not merited,
Beyond last ages' utmost date,
   Thy Name be ever hallowed.

16.

For our prosperity and peace,
Our maintenance's competence,
Our cattel's and our lands' encrease ;
Thy watchfull care and providence
To help our want and indigence,
Comfort of friends in time of need,
Wee have but this for recompence,
   Thy Name be ever hallowed.

17.

For many great deliverances
From enemies against us bent ;
From sundry mischiefes and mischances
Open and private by them meant
With full ill purpose and intent,
Which not our strength or subtle head,
But thy sole goodnesse did prevent ;
   Thy Name be ever hallowed.

18.

For thousand things beside and more
Unto us thy poore servants done,
Of thine abundant mercie's store,
Thy name, ô Father ; thine, ô Son ;
Thine, holy Ghost ; who three in one ;
Of like degree, like honoured,
Doe sit above in heavenly throne ;
   Thy Name be ever hallowed.

The end of the first

L E T A N I E.

LETANIE 2.

Thy kingdome come.

1.

O God, chiefe Soveraigne Lord and King
   Of all the world, who dost command
The heav'n and earth and every thing
By thy Almighty-pow'rfull hand ;
   O Father whom
No mortall creature can withstand ;
   Thy Kingdome come.

2.

And thou, ô Son, his onely Birth,
Who with like pow'r dost all things sway,
To whom the things in heav'n and earth,
And under earth, doe all obey ;
   O Saviour, from
Thy lips it came, what wee now pray,
   Thy Kingdome come.

3.

O holy Ghost, whose power doth
With like authority entire
For managing their kingdome both
All faithfull hearts with grace inspire ;
   Thy Halydome
Infuse into us this desire,
   Thy kingdome come.

4.

O God, the Father, God the Son,
O God the holy Spirit, three
In person, yet but monarch one,
Of the same power and degree,
   Unto whose doome
Both men and Angels subject be ;
   Thy kingdome come.

5.

Let all the heavenly hoast above
Of Saints and Angels glorifi'd,
Which stand assured of thy love,
In such possession, ne'er to slide
   Or fall there-from,
Sing this to thee, who dost them guide :
   Thy kingdome come.

6.

Let *Michaël, Gabriel, Raphaël,*
Angels, Archangels' royall band,
And all the powers in heav'n that dwell,
In order howsoe're they stand ;
   Let all resume
This song, that are at thy command,
   Thy kingdome come.

7.

Let *Abr'am, Isaac, Jacob* sing,
Let Patriarchs, Priests, and Prophets sound

Unto the praise of thee their King ;
Apostles, virgins, victors crown'd
   With martyrdome ;
Let every one this forth rebound,
   Thy kingdome come.

8.

Kings upon earth and magistrates,
Subjects, men, women, old and young,
Of all degrees, of all estates,
Sing forth aloud, with heart and tongue ;
   Let none be dumb ;
But every one joyne to this song,
   Thy kingdome come.

9.

The divell now comes up and downe,
Like rampant lyon to devoure,
Searching through countrie, court and towne,
To make men thrall each day and hower ;
   But though hee come,
Yet keepe us, Lord, in thine owne power ;
   Thy kingdome come.

10.

His whole intent, thy people is
To draw from their allegiance,
To make thy servants to be his,
To bring them to his governance
   And masterdome ;
But thou thy selfe, ô Lord, advance,
   Thy kingdome come.

11.

His time, he knowes, is short ; his wrath
Is by so much the fiercer growne ;
Finding how little space he hath,
Ere his proud state be overthrowne :
   But save us whom
Thou hast made subjects of thine owne,
   Thy kingdome come.

12.

The Flesh against the Spirit rebels,
Our members are our enemies :
Our foe within our castle dwels
In readinesse us to surprise
   In our owne home :
But to our help, ô Lord arise ;
   Thy kingdome come.

13.

What stirs doth foule Concupiscence
Raise in our hearts, within the bars
Of our owne troubled Conscience ?
O what tumultuous fearefull jars
   Thence issue from ?
But hasten thou to end these wars ;
   Thy kingdome come.

14.

Ambition, lust and avarice,
The eye's desire, the pride of life,
The fleshe's sin and every vice,
O Lord, be in us too too rife ;
    Not few, nor some,
But every one ; to part which strife,
    Thy kingdome come.

15.

The world and worldly men abroad
What squadrons, troupes, what armies they
Against us muster up, ô God,
By their example's wicked sway ?
    To conquer whom,
We have, ô Lord, but this to pray,
    Thy kingdome come.

16.

The Nations doe themselves combine,
The Heathen rage, as once they did,
Like to wilde boares they spoile thy vine ;
They fome their shame and vent amid
    Their filthy scum :
But, Lord, for their conversion, bid
    Thy kingdome come.

17.

Great *Cham*, that seekes to disposesse
Thy Son of all his majestie,
And daily doth thy Saints oppresse,
Curse him once more, sore enemy
    To Christendome :
Let, maugre all his tyrannie,
    Thy kingdome come.

18.

Thou blessed, onely Potentate,
Thou King eternall, King of kings,
Whose principality and state
Blisse everlasting to us brings,
    And doth us from
Drive far away all hurtfull things ;
    Thy kingdome come.

19.

Thy scepter is a scepter right
Of vengeance fierce, an Iron rod,
To such as use thee with despite,
To breake and bruise them like a clod
    Of earth or cloome :
So let thy power be seene, ô God ;
    Thy kingdome come.

20.

To them that in thy favour stand,
Thy Scepter is a golden one,
Like Persian King's when he his hand
To *Esther* stretcht, that fairely shone
    In *Vashtie's* roome :

So give us leave t' approach thy throne,
    Thy kingdome come.

21.

Thy hand shall heavie light on those,
Who thy displeasure do provoke,
Upon all such as be thy foes ;
Who breake thy lawes and think thy yoke
    Too burdensome :
But rule thou us with gentle stroke,
    Thy kingdome come.

22.

Thine, Lord, whose kingdom doth exceed
All kingdomes else without compare,
Like Sun and Moon established ;
Whose dayes more firme and lasting are,
    Beyond the summe,
Beyond the dayes of heaven far ;
    Thy kingdome come.

23.

By Salem's King, *Melchisedech*,
The King of Peace prefigured,
Who King and Priest and Prophet eke,
To make us such hast promised :
    Unto us, whom
Thou hast the same determined ;
    Thy kingdome come.

24.

By Prophets anciently fore-told,
That thine should the dominion be,
And that all nations worship should,
Bow and do service unto thee ;
    May we hence-from
So happy be, ô Lord, to see
    Thy kingdome come.

25.

By Angel's mouth King *David's* son
And heire declar'd, for evermore
To sit upon his royall throne,
So to thy mother, ere she bore
    Thee in her womb,
Did *Gabriel*, Lord, make knowne before :
    Thy kingdome come.

26.

Sought for by name King of the Jewes
By Kings themselves, who did not spare
To come at thy birth's blessed newes
Unto Jerusalem from far,
    From Easterne home,
By guid and conduct of a star :
    Thy kingdome come.

27.

The same by *Pilate* at thy death
In Hebrew, Greeke and Latine writ

Of thee, JESUS *of Nazareth,*
King of the Jewes : God thought it fit
 That other some
Beside the Jewes should 'knowledge it ;
 Thy kingdome come.

28.

Then having by thy death subdu'd
The pow'rs of hell, and them bereaven
Of all their strength, thy grant renew'd
Of Soveraigne pow'r in earth and heav'n,
 Streight from the tomb
By thee declar'd to be thee given :
 Thy kingdome come.

29.

Then after thine Ascension high
Placed above at God's right hand,
Invested in thy majestie.
With pow'r Imperiall and command,
 All men to doome,
When we before thy seat shall stand ;
 Thy kingdome come.

30.

O be thou mindfull of us then,
When thou shalt come at later day
To sentence us poore, sinfull men :
Meane while our faults wipe cleane away,
 And purge us from
All drosse of sin, that we may pray,
 Thy kingdome come.

The end of the second
LETANIE.

LETANIE 3.

Thy will be done in earth, &c.

I.

O Father, God omnipotent,
 Who sitt'st above in heavenly seat ;
By whose alone arbitrement
Things stand dispos'd in order sweet ;
 Thy will be done here in earth, even
 As it is done above in heaven.

2.

And thou, ô Saviour, blessed Lord,
His deare beloved Son, whose will
Doth with thy Father's will accord,
To will the same, the same to nill ;
 Thy will be done here in earth, even
 As it is done above in heaven.

3.

And thou, ô holy Sp'rit of both,
Who of God's will revealer art,

Whose sacred inspiration doth
The knowledge of the same impart ;
 Thy will be done here in earth, even
 As it is done above in heaven.

4.

O glorious Soveraine majestie,
Who three in one, and one in three,
In one divine Oeconomie
To governe all things do agree ;
 Thy will be done here in earth, even
 As it is done above in heaven.

5.

The heavenly quire Angelicall
Thy servants and attendants are ;
To do thy errands severall
Is their whole study, all their care :
 Thy will be done here in earth, even
 As it is done by them in heaven !

6.

They stop, they move, they come, they go,
They run, they flie, at thy command ;
They streight, with all observance, do
What e're thou bid them take in hand ;
 Thy will be done here in earth, even
 As it is done by them in heaven !

7.

The Sun, the Moon, the Stars above
In all their great variety,
How in their severall orbs they move
Each one distinct and orderly :
 O could we doe thy will, but even
 As these do it above in heaven !

8.

The fixed Stars, that to their spheares
Above the stars fast linked be,
There is not one but true him beares,
As fast and faithfull unto thee :
 O could we doe thy will, but even
 As do the Stars above in heaven !

9.

The Planets, every wandring star,
Though in their various courses they
And in their motions differ far,
Yet all concurre thee to obey ;
 O could we doe thy will, but even
 As do the Planets there in heaven !

10.

The Sun doth know his rise and fall,
Yet yeelds himselfe at thy command ;
Back to returne when thou dost call,
To stand when thou dost bid him stand :
 O could we do thy will, but even
 As doth the Sun above in heaven !

11.

The Moon, that in her habit strange
Twice like her selfe was never seene,
Constant in her inconstant change,
To thy command hath ever beene ;
  O could we doe thy will but even
  As doth the Moon above in heaven !

12.

The Meteors in the aier below,
Fire, haile, ice, lightning, frost and cold,
The fierce and stormy winds that blow,
Yeeld thee their service manifold :
  O could we do thy will but even
  As these do in the neather heaven !

13.

Nought more uncertain then the weather,
Yet this keepes certainty with thee,
To be at thy appointment, whether
It calme or yet tempestuous be :
  O could we do thy will, but even
  As doth the weather under heaven !

14.

The severall seasons of the yeare,
Spring, Summer, Harvest, Winter dead,
Do still continue as they were
By thee at first established :
  O could we do thy will, but even
  As these here do it under heaven !

15.

Nought more unruly then the Sea,
A most unquiet element ;
Yet he yeelds service unto thee ;
Man onely is contrary bent :
  O could we do thy will, but even
  As doth the Sea here under heaven !

16.

Beasts, foules and fishes, oxen, sheepe,
Thou hast subjected to our hand,
That we should them in order keepe ;
And they be all at our command :
  O could we do thy will, but even
  As these do ours here under heaven !

17.

The Oxe his owner knowes full well,
And yeelds himselfe unto the yoke ;
The Asse his master's crib can tell,
And patiently receives his stroke :
  O could we do thy will, but even
  As these do ours here under heaven !

18.

Unruly creatures, horse and mule
With bit and bridle's gentle straine

We manage and their bodies rule,
Which way our selves them please to raine :
  O could we do thy will, but even
  As these do ours here under heaven !

19.

O could we be contented too,
Since thus we cannot do thy will,
To suffer what thy selfe doth doe,
And patiently to beare it still,
  To yeeld to thy correction,
  And say at least, *Thy will be done.*

20.

And that we cannot do nor suffer,
Thy blessed will in any case,
If thou unto us do not offer
Thy helping hand and speciall grace ;
  When thou shalt lay us ought upon,
  To make us say, *Thy will be done.*

21.

And may we still be of this mind,
To lay it alwayes unto heart,
If we thy hand do heavie find,
To think, all is but our desert ;
  What ever be th' affliction,
  Let us still say, *Thy will be done.*

22.

From suff'ring yet for foule offence,
Keepe us, that we deserve it not ;
But for a guiltlesse conscience
To suffer if so be our lot ;
  Welcome such persecution,
  When ere it comes, *Thy will be done.*

23.

If *Shimei* curse and raile for spite,
And call us sons of *Belial* too ;
If thou do think it for us fit,
And hast him bidden so to do,
  So let him ; let him still raile on,
  And spare not, Lord, *Thy will be done.*

24.

If either of thy judgements sore
Thou please to send upon our Land,
O let us not repine therefore,
But with all patience at thy hand
  Accept thy visitation,
  And alwaies say, *Thy will be done.*

25.

From plague, from famine, and the sword
We pray thee to deliver us ;
Yet if it be thy pleasure, Lord,
Thy people's sins to punish thus,
  We have no way of help but one,
  Thou, Lord, hast done 't : *Thy will be done.*

26.

Amidst our cares, amidst our crosses,
What ever ill shall us befall,
In time of our most heavie losses,
Of wealth, of health, of life and all ;
     This let our mind be set upon,
     To think and say, *Thy will be done.*

27.

If thou 'gainst us give Satan leave,
As 'gainst thy servant *Job* thou didst,
Us of our substance to bereave,
Servants or children ; this amidst
     Be still our Resolution,
     Thy name be blest, *Thy will be done.*

28.

If he us smite with botch or blaine,
And some there be that bid us curse,
O, God forbid ! shall w' entertaine
The better, Lord, and not the worse ?
     Nay, but with all submission
     Make us still say, *Thy will be done.*

29.

If bitter cup of death we see
Approach us neere before our face,
And that it is thy pleasure, we
Should drink it ('twas our Saviour's case,)
     Let him be our instruction,
     Not ours, ô Lord, *Thy will be done.*

30.

Betide us then, what may betide,
(A thousand troubles more then are :)
Make us thy pleasure to abide ;
So thou our soules hereafter spare,
     Our bodies launce, bruise flesh and bone,
     Do what thou please ; *Thy will be done.*

The end of the third
LETANIE.

LETANIE 4.

Give us this day our daily bread.

I.

O Blessed God, who Father art
     To every creature severall,
And dost the meanes to them impart,
To keepe them in their being all,
Regard thou thy poore servant's need,
And heare us now who to thee call ;
     Give us this day our daily bread.

2.

O Son of God, who dost denie
Thy servants nothing that is good,
For whose behoofe thou wouldest die,
And shed forth thy most precious bloud ;
Who dost both soule and body feed,
True-living bread, our heav'nly food ;
     Give us this day our daily bread.

3.

And thou, ô holy Sp'rit of both,
Life of our soules, whose sacred breath
Our hearts with grace enliven doth ;
Whose bounteous mercy cherisheth
The poore for hunger almost dead,
And them againe recomforteth ;
     Give us this day our daily bread.

4.

O holy, blessed, glorious Trine,
Three persons, all in Godhead one
By sacred mysterie divine,
O God the Father, God the Son,
And Sp'rit who dost from both proceed,
Behold us from thy heavenly throne,
     Give us this day our daily bread.

5.

No sooner thou the world hadst made,
Man, beast, foule, fish, and creeping thing,
But they from thee prepared had
Each one his sev'rall victualling,
After his kind, herb, fruit and seed :
Grant still our fields with corne may spring,
     Give us this day our daily bread.

6.

Thou that didst *Jacob* once preserve
From jawes of cruell griping dearth,
When he and his were like to sterve
Through famine that did all the earth
At that time strangely over-spread ;
As thou hast hither from our birth,
     Give us this day our daily bread.

7.

Thou fed'st his seed in desert wild,
When out of Egypt they were driven,
With fruit of garden, nor of field,
But Manna, Angels' food from heaven :
O let our wants be furnished,
Continue still what thou hast given ;
     Give us this day our daily bread.

8.

Thou which the ravens didst command
To bring *Elias* bread and meat
At Morne and Evening, from thy hand,
Give us our food what we shall eat ;
That beeing by it strengthened
We in thy service be not let :
     Give us this day our daily bread.

9.

Thou giv'st the ravens' selves their food,
The foules which in the ai'r do flie ;
The old ones' and the younger brood
Are by thee succour'd when they cry :
O may we still by thee be sped ;
O Lord, our hunger satisfie ;
Give us this day our daily bread.

10.

Nor oyle did waste within the cruise,
Nor meale in barrell that remain'd
In widow's house, for both their use,
Whil'st she the Prophet entertain'd :
O let us not be minished
Or of our needfull fare restrain'd ;
Give us this day our daily bread.

11.

Thou with five loaves and fishes twaine
Who did'st five thousand soules and more,
And by like miracle againe
With a few fishes, as before,
And seven loaves, foure thousand feed,
O grant us of thy bountie's store ;
Give us this day our daily bread.

12.

Thy bountie 's such, if bread we beg,
Thou wilt not give us, Lord, a stone ;
If we thy children aske an egge,
Thou wilt not give a Scorpion :
Nay thou art better purposed,
To give us what to feed upon ;
So give us still our daily bread.

13.

It is the thing thy selfe did'st teach
Thy servants, Lord, upon that day,
When thou upon the Mount did'st preach,
And shew the people what to say,
In thine owne words delivered ;
That in this manner we should pray,
Give us this day our daily bread.

14.

Thy meaning was not, we should vex
Or eat our hearts with cark and care,
That we our selves should ought perplexe
Concerning this, our bodie's fare,
With what we should be nourished,
That we to pray thus bidden are,
Give us this day our daily bread.

15.

Thy purpose was and thine intent,
That we should wholly trust in thee,
And of thy goodnesse confident

Without all jealous doubting be :
And to assure us, we shall speed,
When we to thee alone do flee,
To give to us our daily bread.

16.

It is but labour spent in vaine
To rise betimes and breake our sleepe,
To spend our selves in toile and paine,
To sit up late, long watch to keepe :
Without such trouble of the head
Thy blessing 'tis, makes all things cheape ;
To give to us our daily bread.

17.

No costly dainties deerely bought,
No artificiall cates devis'd,
From forraigne coasts or countries brought,
By curious palates highly priz'd :
We beg things lower valued,
By high-fed stomachs quite despis'd,
Give us this day our daily bread.

18.

What *Jacob* did content afford,
When he was on his journie bent
To *Padan Aram*, shall, ô Lord,
Afford to us the same content :
With food and clothing us bestead,
And it shall be sufficient ;
Give us this day our daily bread.

19.

Our prayer is what *Agur's* was :
O give us neither poverty,
That we should steale for need, alas ;
Nor wealth, that we grow proud thereby :
But us with food convenient feed,
That wee may not forget to cry,
Give us this day our daily bread.

20.

Bread is the staffe that doth support
Man's life that else would faint and fall,
It is the cement in a sort,
That holds our bodie's tottering wall,
Soone else to be demolished :
This then so needfull to us all,
Give us this day our daily bread.

21.

In bread all things comprised are,
That our necessities require,
Not onely of the bodie's fare,
Our meat, our drink, and our attire,
But all things 'longing to our need :
O grant us then, what wee desire,
Give us this day our daily bread.

22.

In bread more yet contained is,
Thy selfe, ô Christ ; thy body blest,
True bread of life, substantiall, this,
Wherewith our soules thou nourishest
In Sacrament exhibited :
O give us this above the rest,
Give us this day our daily bread.

23.

This day and every day : so we
Our vowes and offerings shall pay,
And render praise and thankes to thee,
Not onely this, but every day ;
Untill this life be finished,
That we no more shall need to pray,
Give us this day our daily bread.

The end of the Fourth
LETANIE.

LETANIE 5.

Forgive us our trespasses, &c.

1.

O Gracious God, who downe didst send
 Thy deare-beloved Son from heaven,
To pay our debts, and to this end,
That we might them be, Lord, forgiven ;
 O God the Father, *may 't thee please,*
 To pardon all our trespasses!

2.

O thou the Father's onely Son,
Who undertook'st to be the price,
The sole propitiation,
Oblation and sacrifice
 For all our sins, *O may 't thee please,*
 To pardon all our trespasses!

3.

And thou, ô holy Spirit blest,
Who dost all faithfull hearts inspire,
Whose power, right and interest
Is with them both the same entire
 To pardon sin ; *O may 't thee please*
 To pardon all our trespasses!

4.

O blessed, glorious Trinitie,
The Father, Son, and holy Spirit,
Whose mercy is abundantly
To sinners showne beyond all merit,
 Their sins to pardon ; *may 't thee please*
 To pardon all our trespasses!

5.

Our Senses five, sight, hearing, smell,
Our taste and touch, which should have bin
Each one a several cittadell
To keepe out sin, have let it in :
 Our sins, Lord, pardon, caus'd by these,
 And all our other trespasses.

6.

Our Wits, which should have bin the womb
For to conceive more heavenly birth,
Of all good things hath been the tomb,
Fit to bring forth but thoughts of earth :
 Our sins, Lord, pardon, caus'd by these,
 And all our other trespasses.

7.

Into our traitour Memories
The thiefe by night, ô Lord, hath crept,
And stollen thence such rarities,
They should more faithfully have kept :
 Our sins, Lord, pardon, caus'd by these,
 And all our other trespasses.

8.

Our Wils and our Affections both,
Which were to thee affianced,
Have prov'd unchaste and broke their troth,
And have defil'd thy marriage-bed :
 Our sins, Lord, pardon, caus'd by these,
 And all our other trespasses.

9.

Our parts and members corporall,
Hands, heart, tongue, feet, each severall lim,
Have to thy foe them yeelded thrall,
And done their service unto him :
 Our sins, Lord, pardon, caus'd by these,
 And all our other trespasses.

10.

The sins and trespasse of our youth,
Our childhood and our pupillage,
Our manhood and our elder growth,
Our trespasses of every age ;
 Lord, of thy goodnesse, pardon these,
 And all our other trespasses.

11.

All our misdeeds which we have done
Or witing or unwittingly ;
Of boldnesse and presumption,
Of weaknesse and infirmitie ;
 Lord, of thy goodnesse, pardon these,
 And all our other trespasses.

12.

Sins secret, open, present, past,
Remembred and remembred not,
So long conceal'd, that we at last
Have them our selves now quite forgot :
 Lord, of thy goodnesse, pardon these,
 And all our other trespasses.

13.

Our greater and our lesse offences,
Jealous mistakes, grosse ignorances,
Our many carelesse negligences,
With their attending circumstances :
   Lord, of thy goodnesse, pardon these,
   And all our other trespasses.

14.

The things by us omitted, which
We should have done, and yet we would not,
The things by us committed, such
As we have done, and yet we should not ;
   Lord, of thy goodnesse, pardon these,
   And all our other trespasses.

15.

Each sev'rall sin, each sev'rall fault,
Whether in thought, in word or deed,
Through flesh, or world or divel's assault,
Conceiv'd, spoke or practis'd ;
   Lord, of thy goodnesse, pardon these,
   And all our other trespasses.

16.

Our pride, vaine-glory, avarice,
Rash anger, envie and despite,
Our idlenesse, lust's filthy vice,
And our intemp'rate appetite :
   Lord, of thy goodnesse, pardon these,
   And all our other trespasses.

17.

That we have beene unto the poore
Hard-hearted, too too pitilesse,
When they stood hungry at our doore,
To succour them in their distresse ;
   Lord, of thy goodnesse, pardon these,
   And all our other trespasses.

18.

Though of good workes we empty be,
As be their bellies we should fill ;
Yet let not us be so by thee
Dealt with according to the ill :
   But, of thy goodnesse, pardon these,
   And all our other trespasses.

19.

The sick we have not visited,
Nor cloath'd the naked and the bare,
Nor to the hungrie dealt our bread,
Nor stranger entertain'd from far :
   Lord, of thy goodnesse, pardon these,
   And all our other trespasses.

20.

The simple wee have not advised,
The froward we have not corrected ;

To comfort those that were despised,
We have too carelessly neglected ;
   Lord, of thy goodnesse, pardon these,
   And all our other trespasses.

21.

Our pettie wrongs and injuries
We have not taken in good part,
Nor pray'd thee for our enemies,
To pardon them and turne their heart ;
   Lord, of thy goodnesse, pardon these,
   And all our other trespasses.

22.

And of thy goodnesse grant this too,
What for our selves of thee we crave,
The same that wee for them may doe :
That like as we desire to have
   Our debts forgiven, so may wee
   Forgive them that our debters be.

23.

It is the Covenant, as it were,
We stand bound in each unto other ;
That thou wilt us alike forbeare,
As we our selves forbeare our brother ;
   Forgive then, Lord, our debts, as we
   Do them, or should our debters be.

24.

The measure wee to others make,
Shall back to us be measur'd even ;
Vengeance, if we do vengeance take ;
If we forgive, to be forgiven :
   Forgive then, Lord, our debts, as we
   Forgive them that our debters be.

25.

O what is all that trifling score,
All the offences done to us,
If they a thousand times were more,
To hinder us from praying thus ?
   Forgive us, Lord, our debts, as we
   Forgive them that our debters be.

26.

What be their debts to ours compar'd
Not mites to talents, pence to pounds :
Why doe we then so light regard,
To pray on such uneven grounds ?
   Forgive us, Lord, our debts, as we
   Forgive them that our debters be.

27.

O may it please thy heavenly grace,
The leaven of our hearts to purge,
All malice from them to displace,
That we may pray without all urge ;
   Forgive us, Lord, our debts, as we
   Forgive them that our debters be.

28.

So henceforth by thy grace we will,
And here that promise we renew,
To pardon our blasphemours still,
And all that do our soules pursue :
Forgive us, Lord, our debts, as wee
Forgive them that our debters be.

The end of the fifth

LETANIE.

LETANIE 6.

Lead us not into temptation.

I.

O God, whose sacred providence
    Doth even unto sin extend,
On whom the first beginnings, whence
It issueth, alone depend ;
From all occasions ministred
Thy children, Father, still defend,
   Ne them into temptation lead.

2.

And thou by everlasting birth
The onely Son of God, begot
Before all worlds, who borne on earth
Of Virgin blest without all spot,
Wast by the Tempter visited ;
Without thy help us suffer not
   Into temptation to be led.

3.

O God the Holy Ghost, who didst
Our Saviour lead into the vast
And desert wildernesse, amidst
The thornie brakes and wood-lands wast,
To Satan's tempting offered ;
Do not us on such dangers cast,
   Ne us into temptation lead.

4.

O thou who reign'st eternally
In one consent and sweet accord ;
O blessed, glorious Trinitie,
By Divels' slight suffer not, Lord,
Our soules to be endangered,
(Unlesse thou help withall afford,)
   Ne us into temptation lead.

5.

With armed troupes of cruell foes
We are encompast round about :
O do not thou us weake expose
To enemies so strong and stout,
As have us now environed :
But set thy hand to help us out,
   When we be' into temptation led.

6.

Among those troupes the Divell first
His standard 'gainst us doth advance,
Accompanied with Fiends accurst
All under his ill governance :
But let not us be vanquished
By them, if so it be our chance
   Into temptation to be led.

7.

The world is up in armes abroade,
And is confederate combin'd,
Unto the Div'll in league, ô God,
Of hellish partnership conjoyn'd :
But let not their intent be sped
Which they against us have design'd,
   Into temptation to be led.

8.

The Flesh as bad, false traiteresse,
As either of the other twaine,
More mischiefe, greater wickednesse,
Is like to worke us by her traine,
In our owne fort and castle bred :
But, Lord, help thou us out againe,
   When wee be' into temptation led.

9.

The Serpent when by subtle wile
To tempt our parents hee began,
The woman first hee did beguile,
And shee did after tempt the man :
So deales he still ; his subtle head
Contrives by all the meanes he can,
   Into temptation us to lead.

10.

The Divell is that serpent base,
The Flesh is as our mother *Eve*,
And *Adam* stands in Reason's place :
The Fiend our flesh doth first deceive,
The flesh doth then with reason plead,
Then reason yeelds to give her leave,
   Into temptation us to lead.

11.

Temptation is the sowing tares,
The Divell is the seeds-man skill'd ;
He sowes them close and unawares,
Which if they fall in fruitfull field,
They grow apace, unhappy weed :
But let not us beare fruit so wild,
   Nor be into temptation led.

12.

The Divell, parent is to get,
The Flesh, the mother is to beare,
And these two when they both are met,
What goodly off-spring do they reare !

What but foule sin can thence proceed ?
A bastard brat, because we were
By them into temptation led.

13.

And this is Sin's accursed brood,
Which if it were observed well,
And rightly by us understood,
Like Cockatrices in the shell,
Or rather in their spawne and seed,
We would them crush like Imps of hell,
Which us into temptation lead.

14.

Against each sev'rall enemie
Thou of thy goodnesse dost provide
A sev'rall sundry remedie,
Their sharp encounters to abide ;
Wherewith if we were furnished,
Lesse might we feare to be thus tri'd,
Into temptation to be led.

15.

And specially against the Divell,
As specially thou hast prepar'd,
This precious good against his evill,
Of Angels and Archangels gard ;
To be against him strengthened,
That he to hurt us be debar'd,
When we be' into temptation led.

16.

Against the world's lewd practises,
The profits false and honours vaine,
We have the Saints' examples, these,
And many precepts Soveraigne ;
By them to be encouraged,
'Gainst it defiance to maintaine,
If we be' into temptation led.

17.

Against the flesh, when she grows proud
Through lust and foule concupiscence,
Fasting to tame and coole the bloud,
And keepe it in obedience :
Which if it be well practised,
A weapon proves for our defence,
When we be' into temptation led.

18.

Against them all in generall
We have those weapons Christian,
That complete armour, which *St. *Paul*
Adviseth every faithfull man,
Therewith to get him furnished :
We shall it feare the lesse, if than
We be into temptation led.

phes. 6. 13.

19.

Truth, for our girdle ; righteousnesse,
For breast-plate ; faith, to be our shield,

Shoes on our feet, the Gospel's peace ;
The word of God, our sword to wield ;
Salvation, helmet for our head ;
Thus sped wee shall not need to yeeld,
If we be' into temptation led.

20.

If unto these we Prayer adde
So much the stronger we shall be
To make resistance in the bad
And evill day, if we to thee
Devoutly pray, who canst us speed :
Thou, Saviour, bid'st us so, that we
Be not into temptation led.

21.

Returne we to our prayers then,
And having prayed ten times o're,
Still we will pray, and pray agen,
Ten thousand times to that and more :
We have already trespassed
Too much : ô adde not to our score,
Into temptation us to lead.

22.

Wee guiltie stand of grievous crimes,
Of many foule offences past,
O give us grace for future times,
That we amend our lives at last,
And be no more endangered,
To doe what thou forbidden hast,
If we be' into temptation led.

23.

Diseases prove most dangerous,
When men to them againe relapse :
Let not the case stand so with us,
Who mind to leave our former scapes :
As men to health recovered,
So keepe us, Lord, from like mishaps,
Ne us into temptation lead.

24.

To our owne power doe not leave us,
Withdraw not, Lord, thy helping hand :
For of thy grace if thou bereave us,
By our owne strength wee cannot stand.
'Tis thou alone, that canst us steed :
So steed us then, and give command,
Wee be not to temptation led.

The end of the sixth
L E T A N I E.

L E T A N I E 7.
But deliver us from evill.

1.

O God the Father, heavenly King,
Fountaine of light invisible,

Of goodnesse everlasting spring ;
Be to thy servants mercifull,
To keepe us from all hurtfull thing :
   Be thou our helper now and ever,
   Us from all evill to deliver.

2.

O God the Son, heav'n's Prince and heire,
Of Father's light the glorious beame,
His countenance's mirrour faire,
His goodnesse' ever-flowing streame ;
Be to thy servants debonaire,
   And be our helper now and ever,
   Us from all evill to deliver.

3.

And thou, ô holy Ghost, above
Who raign'st with them in heav'nly seat,
In equall glory, spirit of love,
Light's influence and quickening heat,
Conduit through whom life's waters move :
   Be thou our helper now and ever,
   Us from all evill to deliver.

4.

O holy, individuall, blest,
Eternall, glorious Trinitie,
Who by thy wisedome orderest
Things good and evill severally ;
The worst keep from us, send the best,
   And be our helper now and ever,
   Us from all evill to deliver.

5.

Against the Fiend, the wicked one,
Man's enemie profest, the Divell,
Whose minde is wholly set upon
To work our woe and doe us evill.
To thee wee pray and make our mone ;
   Be thou our helper now and ever,
   Us from the Divell to deliver.

6.

Against him and his 'complices,
Companions and his fellow-mates,
The world and flesh ; 'gainst both of these,
That be his sworne confederates,
To worke us mischiefe, as they please ;
   Be thou our helper now and ever,
   Us from their evill to deliver.

7.

Against their wicked, lewd intents,
Which toward us they harbour still,
To bring us to their sinfull bents,
That wee may do after their will,
And breake all thy commandements ;
   Be thou our helper now and ever,
   Us from their evill to deliver.

8.

Against all actuall forfeiture
Of our obedience to thy lawes,
That wee should carelesse and secure
Sin against any point or clause,
Or others thereunto allure ;
   Be thou our helper now and ever,
   Us from this evill to deliver.

9.

'Gainst taking of offence at other
Through rash mis-apprehension,
Or giving it to our weake brother,
By what in us lies to be done,
'Gainst doing this, or one or t' other ;
   Be thou our helper now and ever,
   Us from this evill to deliver.

10.

'Gainst turning back to any thing,
Whereof wee have repentant beene,
Like sow unto her wallowing
Back to the mire when shee was cleene,
Or dog unto his vomiting ;
   Be thou our helper now and ever,
   Us from this evill to deliver.

11.

Against those sins the rest among
Especially whereto wee find
Our selves by use and custome long,
Or else by nature more inclin'd,
That they are now growne in us strong ;
   Be thou our helper now and ever,
   Us from these evils to deliver.

12.

'Gainst Idlenesse and Luxurie,
Pride, Anger, Malice, Envie, Spite,
Oppressing any wrongfully ;
Against foule, greedie Appetite,
Both Covetise and gluttonie ;
   Be thou our helper now and ever,
   Us from these evils to deliver.

13.

'Gainst sects and factions too too rife
Both in the State and in the Church,
Which cut more keene then sharpest knife,
From living traitor-like at lurch,
'Gainst our King's honour, state or life ;
   Be thou our helper now and ever,
   Us from these evils to deliver.

14.

Against presumption, confidence,
All boldnesse to commit lewd sin,

Hardnesse of heart, impenitence,
With purpose to remaine therein
With cauterized conscience ;
   Be thou our helper now and ever,
   Us from these evils to deliver.

15.

Against Despaire, no one more foule,
More ougly or more hainous crime,
To bring thy wrath upon us whole ;
Downe unto hell before the time
Without all hope to plunge the soule ;
   Be thou our helper now and ever,
   Us from this evill to deliver.

16.

'Gainst sland'ring and back-biting tongues,
Which seek our credits to deface ;
'Gainst all the like enormous wrongs,
That wee should other men disgrace,
Or credit ought thereto belongs ;
   Be thou our helper now and ever,
   Us from these evils to deliver.

17.

'Gainst thy great plagues and judgements, Lord,
Which our offences have deserv'd,
By pestilence to be devour'd,

Or pinch through famine hunger-starv'd,
Or fall by adversarie's sword ;
   Be thou our helper now and ever,
   Us from these evils to deliver.

18.

'Gainst utter want and begger's ease,
'Gainst bondage and our freedome's losse,
'Gainst lothsome, foule, uncleane disease,
Crazing our wits, and every crosse
Too heavie for us ; 'may'st thee please,
   To be our helper now and ever,
   Us from these evils to deliver.

19.

'Gainst all thy curses temporall,
The fierce effects of thy displeasure,
Those curses more especiall,
Which doe thy wrath in greater measure
Declare, when they upon us fall ;
   Be thou our helper now and ever,
   Us from such evils to deliver.

20.

'Gainst sudden death, that we should dye
And meet our judgement unprepar'd ;
'Gainst fire that burnes eternally
Of wicked men the just reward,
'Gainst everlasting miserie ;
   Be thou our helper now and ever,
   Us from these evils to deliver.

FINIS.

ADDITIONAL MINOR POEM.

From 'The English Usurer, or Usury Condemned, by The most Learned, and famous Divines of the Church *of England*, and Dedicated to all his *Majestie's* Subiects, for the stay of further increase *of the same.* Collected by Iohn Blaxton Preacher of God's Word, at Osmington, in Dorcetshire. The Second Impression, Corrected by the Author. London, Printed by Iohn Norton, and are to be sold by Francis Bovvman, in Oxford. 1634.' (4to.)

The *Charitable* happy, the *usurer* accursed.

Blessed are the mercifull.
Math. 5. 7.
Psalm 37. 19.

O ! Thrice, thrice happy he, whose free desires
　　To charity a holy fervor fires :
Who onely minds God's glory, by his gift,
And neighbour's good without sinister drift ;
Famine (familiar unto rogues that range)
Shall not come neere his Garner, nor his Grange :
His Fields with Corne, abundant crop shall cover,
His Vines with Grapes, his Hedge with Roses over ;
His Downes with Sheepe, his Moors with Oxen great ;
His Groves with Droves (encreasing night and day ;)
His Hils with Heards, his smiling Meads with Hay ;
His Fens with Foule, his Rils and Pooles with fish ;
His Trees with Fruits, with plenty every Dish ;
Content, and health (the best of earthly blisse)
Shall evermore remaine with him, and his :
Him, pride or envy never shall molest,
Or corsive care, foe to repast and rest.

Phil. 4. 11, 12.
1 Tim. 6. 6.

For th' all-see Eye still carefully respects
The Almner's house, and ever it protects ;
Til finally, when justice endeth all,
Sweet mercie's voyce him to heav'n's kingdome call.
But th' usurer (how ever here he thrive,
In Heards and Hoords) already dead alive,
(No heat of love, no heart to give a mite,
Except to gaine and gather double by 't)
Him, on that day (to him a day of woe)
The Holy-one, the All-knower will not know.
Shame and confusion shall be-spread him over,
Wishing the holes to hide, and hils to cover :
Immortall dying in eternall paines.
His eyes so nice to looke on Lazarus sore
Shall swim in sulphury teares (tortur'd the more,
To see above in blisse, and glory rife,
Whom ruthlesse here, he would not see, in life)
His eares here deafe unto distressed ones ;
Shall there heare horrour of the damned grones :
Nor shall the voyce of mercy him salute,
Who, in effect, to needy moans was mute :
Millions of mones cannot him redeeme,
Nor all Church-treasure ever ransome him,
From all thought-passing pangs of wretchednes ;
As, endlesse, easelesse, and remedilesse.

Esay 58. 8, 9, 11. &c.

Cursed are the usurers.
Psalm 15. 5.

Ezek. 18. 13.

Iames 2. 13.
Revel. 6. 15. 1

IOSHVA SYLVESTER.

See our Memorial-Introduction for notices of the various names, etc., introduced in these minor poems, including Blaxton of the closing one—hitherto overlooked. See also the same for a further overlooked little poem in French by Sylvester.—G.

NOTE.

IN the Glossarial Index, etc., of SYLVESTER—as with the others of the Series—my endeavour has been to record every noticeable word; albeit, spite of all care, it is possible that even with the special lists, birds, fishes, plants, diseases, and the like, may have, in some cases, escaped me. Considerable additions—in the aggregate—will be found to the Notes and Illustrations. As before, these occasionally correct earlier explanations in the places. From the number of words enrolled, the utmost compression has been exercised throughout, even where fuller notes were promised. The student-reader will profit by consulting Nares's inestimable Glossary (2 vols. 8vo, 1876, edited by Halliwell-Phillipps and Wright), and the references to Shakespeare, etc. The Errata and Corrigenda, it will be well to put right in the places. They are (relatively) few and unimportant. For more on these Glossarial Indices, etc., see our Introduction (II. Critical). As in Breton and Davies, the toil has been very great in preparing these matterful lists; and I could scarcely have borne it, had not my dear friend, George H. White, Esq. of Glenthorne, done me yeoman co-operative service once more. The references are simple :—

I. = Vol. I.   II. = Vol. II.

3/7 = page 3, line 7.

Others are self-explanatory.   A. B. G.

I.—GLOSSARIAL INDEX.

A

ABASS, v., II. 251/440.

Abater, sb., II. 322. Son. 8.

Abates, v. = to cast down. So *Coriolanus*, iii. 3. I. 158/570. From the French *abbatre*, to beat down.

Abbreviates, v., I. 151/746.

Abbridged, *adj.*, II. 210/176.

Abderian, I. 58/655.

Abhomination, I. 255/504 ; II. 108/375. Shakespeare ridicules the affectation of more correct spelling in this word, based on a false derivation from *ab homine* instead of *abominor*, through the pedant Holofernes—'This is *abhominable* which he [Don Armado] would call abominable' (L. L. L. v. 1). See Nares, *s.v.*

Abid, v., I. 30/297, 40/37.

Abiliment—sometimes spelled abibliament = habiliment, II. 248/185.

Abject, *sb.*, I. 93/2, 17. 'Yea, the very *abjects* came against me unawares,' Ps. xxxv. 15 (Prayer-book).

Able-most, II. 178/108.

Abod, v., I. 182/429.

Abortives, *sb.*, I. 195/1321. '*abortives* and presages' (K. John iii. 4).

Aboundance, II. 67/45.

Aboundant, *adj.*, I. 30/345, 84/73 ; II. 93/999, etc.

Aboundantly, II. 209/29.

Abramide, *sb.*, I. 224/1244 ; II. 190/487.

Abramites, *sb.*, I. 205/801, 232/647.

Abrave = a defiance—printed in earlier texts as two words, I. 201/363.

Abscission—sometimes 'abscession' = abscess, I. 200/181.

Absented, v., I. 260/1071.

Absolute, II. 85/68, 81, 86/163, 94/1114, etc.

Academs, *sb.*, II. 197/143. 'Our court shall be a little academe' (L. Lab. Lost, i. 1).

Accompt, *sb.*, I. 220/833.

Accompter, I. 220/833.

Accustoming, *sb.*, II. 272/593.

Acquight, v., acquighted = requite, I. 189/559 ; II. 94/1091, 330, col. 1, l. 29. 'Palme or cypress should his paines *acquite*,' Carew's *Tasso*. See 'Acquite.'

Acquite, v., II. 171/496.

Acquittance, I. 169/622.

Acrimony, II. 271/480, 272/635.

Act-simple-pure, I. 113/652.

Adamant, I. 48/944, 54/195, 88/580, 230/445 ; II. p. 39, Son. 18, etc. See Nares, *s.v.*, for a full article.

Addle, *adj.*, I. 157/89, 256/566 ; II. 98/215, etc.

Addresse, *sb.* = skill, II. 230/44.

Addresse, v., II. 250/377.

Addrest, v., II. 227, st. 86.

Adjourn'd, v., I. 135/309.

Admirables, *sb.*, I. 42/279.

Admiration = wonder, II. 183/215.

Admire, v., I. 180/204.

Adons, I. 233/833, 255/434.

A-doo, *sb.*, I. 231/582.

Adoptive, I. 22/335.

Adultering, v., I. 252/146. 'He *adulters* stills' (Ben Jonson's Epigram xxvi.).

Adust, II. 116/1324, 171/502.

Adusted, *adj.*, II. 271/463.

Adustion, II. 268/191, 272/634, 271/471, 475. See Nares, *s.v.*, for other examples.

Adverse-Clyents, II. 193/272.

Advertis'd, v., II. 201/595.

Adying, v., II. 200/525.

Aeglets, I. 12/17.

Aeolian, *adj.* = windy, I. 37/1180, 38/1212.

Aeolian Crowd = winds, I. 135/356.

Afear'd, v., II. 135/1318.

Affect, v., I. 208/1173, 225/1338 ; II. 67/46, etc.

Affects, *sb.*, I. 160/667, 227/142.

Affectioning, *sb.*, II. 88/344.

Affection-less, II., p. 30, st. 85.

Affiance, I. 256/535 ; II. 191/13, 267/64.

Affie, v., II. 92/849.

Affray, v. = to affright, II. 154/827. So Spenser, 'Or when the flying heav'ns he would *affray*.'

Affoord, v., I. 123/129.

Affright = affraid, I. 116/277.

Affront, v., affronting, I. 167/333, 212/8, 217/516.

Affront, *sb.* = encounter, II. 181/4. 'Only, Sir, this I must caution you of, in your *affront* or salute, never to move your hat.' Greene's Tu Quoq.

A-filling, II. 217/23.

A-fire, II. 198/240.

Afront, v., a-front, I. 167/307, 194/1153 ; II. 130/746 etc. Cf. Hamlet, iii. 1.

Afront = in front, II. 186/68.

Afrunt, II. 57/267.

After-claps, II. p. 42, Son. 35, 100/383.

After-comming, I. 119/560.

After-friends, I. 213/44.
After-hurl'd, II. 254, st. 10.
After-kin, I. 155/70.
After-king, I. 257/734.
After-power, I. 138/53.
After-worlds, I. 185/129.
Age-chill'd, I. 68/817.
Age-worn, I. 144/62.
Agnize, *v.*, agniz'd = acknowledge, I. 7/8, 101/277, 137/597 ; II. 129/603. Othello, i. 3.
Agon (a year agon), II. p. 13, st. 50.
Agonize, *v.*, II. 112/826.
A-good (laughs a-good), II. 100/421. Two Gent. iv. 3. 'This merry answer made them all laugh *a-good*, so downe the hill they came laughing.' (North's Plutarch, 200, E.)
Agrising, *v.*, I. 246/726. See Spenser's F. Q., v. 10, 28 ; ii. 6, 46.
Ague-sick, I. 53/146, 118/426.
Aigle = Eagle, II. 187/178.
Aire-engendring, I. 46/719.
Alabaster, I. 176/1405 ; II. 194/377.
Alabastrine, I. 222/1081 ; II. 173/708.
A-land, I. 249/1029.
Alastors, ἀλάστωρ = the avenging deity, and so generally a plague ; also one who suffers from such, one who is accursed, II. 343, col. 2, l. 4.
Alchimie, *sb.*, alchimy, II. 244/599, 273/733.
Alchimists, II. 270/426.
Alchymist, I. 35/979.
Alcides (our Alcides), II. 273/764.
Alcides-griefe, I. 119/542.
Al-circumference, I. 135/301.
Aldars = alders, I. 45/564. Slice-sea. Alders were used in ship-building ; so Sylvester calls them also 'adventurous alders,' Babylon. Cf. Georgics, i. 136.
Alhidade, I. 159/638.
All, *sb.* (this ample All), II. 85/83. 'Then did the arch-work master of this *all*' (Taylor's Workes, 1630) = the Universe.
All, *sb.* (All this All), I. 249/1069.
All-able, II. 301, st. 50.
All-ball, I. 196/1382.
All-bearing, I. 245/577.
All-break, I. 246/727.
All-changing, I. 184/36.
All-cindring, I. 260/1062. See Nares, *s.v.* 'Cindering.'
All-circling, I. 246/692.
All-circumference, I. 23/457.
All-clasping, I. 100/99 ; II. 87/260.
All-coloured, I. 103/513.
All-compassing, I. 36/1054.
All-comprizing, I. 237/1230.
All-consuming, I. 257/657.
All-creator, I. 20/74, 28/169, 30/311, etc.
All-danting, I. 176/1376.
All-differing, I. 140/212.
All-dispose, I. 297, st. 3.

All-divine, I. 143/594.
All-drowning, I. 165/112.
All-enlightning, I. 158/428.
All-faining, I. 102/394.
All-fair, al-fair, I. 120/650, 128/720, 157/364.
All-filling, I. 174/1107.
All-flaming, I. 193/1083.
All-form, II. 192/195.
All-forming, I. 142/440 ; II. 85/53.
All-foreseeing, I. 102/300, 255/427.
All-gnawing, II. 60/605.
All-guiding, I. 199/164.
All-guiltlesse, II. 88/441.
All-heale, II. p. 37, Son. 3.
All-healing, I. 246/95.
All-hiding, I. 203/553.
All-inflaming, I. 188/512.
All-inspiring, I. 161/771.
All-knower, II. 88/391.
All-knowing, II. 88/442.
All-loved, I. 14/26.
All-maker, II. 297, st. 3.
All-monarch, I. 40/38, 249/1057.
All-onely, II. 345, col. 1, l. 19.
All-pierce, II. 41, Son. 31.
All-plentie, II. 184/318.
All-powerfull, II. 228/248.
All-proof, I. 180/190, 204/703 ; II. 261/57.
All-prudent, I. 20/75, 157/370.
All-quickning, I. 114/22, 160/738, 203/576.
All-regency, II. p. 141, col. 1, l. 19.
All-sacred, I. 202/485.
All-scient, II. 91/751.
All-seas, I. 135/327.
All-see, II. 197/158, 210/141, 362, col. 2, l. 1.
All-seeing, I. 110/383, 203/549.
All-seer, I. 238/1334.
All-skilfull, II. 184/322.
All-sundring, I. 260/1062.
All-taming, II. p. 19, Son. 23.
All-theater, I. 44/487, 76/448, 134/283 ; II. 211/279.
All-thought-passing, II. 210/165.
All-to-fore, I. 191/784. Cf. Nares under 'All to' = entirely.
All-work, II. 205/352.
All-working, I. 158/422.
Allom = alum, I. 43/321.
Allow, *v.*, II. 321, Son. 3.
Almadarats, I. 159/629.
Almain, *adj.* = German (Allemagne), I. 80/899, 193/1019.
Almightiest, I. 80/975, 84/126.
Almighty-most, I. 209/1287.
Almners, almner—sometimes spelled 'amners' as in Henry Smith's Sermons (1609), 'The rich are but God's *amners*,' II. 209/47, 64, 210/115, 362, col. 2, l. 2.
Alms-vowed, II. 209/57.
Almycantharats—an astrological term for a circle drawn paralled to horizon, I. 159/628. See Halliwell, *s.v.* 'Almicantaratte,' with quotations from Albumazar.

Alonely, I. 46/730, 68/807, 218/636, etc.

Alongst, I. 24/579.

Aloose, I. 48/947.

Al-regency, II. 141, col. 1, l. 19.

Altar-spoyling, I. 249/985.

Alterable, II, 29, st. 67.

Alterate, *v.* = altered, II. 316, col. 1, l. 24. Chaucer, Tert. of Cressid.

Amafrose = amaurosis, *gutta serena*, I. 117/377.

Amalthean Horn, Cf. Paradise Regained, II. 356 ; Ovid, Fasti, v. 115. I. 27/52.

Amass, *sb.* = a heap, II. 189/381. 'This pillar is nothing in effect but a medlie or an *amasse* of all the precedent ornaments, making a new kinde by stealth.' Wotton's Elements of Architecture, 1624, p. 38.

Amasst, I. 173/1097.

Amated, II. 263/29. See Nares, *s. v.*, for several examples.

Amazefull, I. 238/1398.

Ambage, *sb.* II. 112/793.

Amber Bush—bush = beard, I. 238/1416. See Halliwell *s. v.*, 'K. James had a gray-beard's wisdom though a young man, whose beard was not gray but amber coloured.'

Amber-greece, I. 229/404, 235/1081.

Ambligon = an obtuse-angled triangle, *ἀμβλύς γωνία*, I. 156/198.

Ambrosiall, I. 192/882, 229/353, 233/867.

Amiss, *sb.*, amisse, I. 48/918, 181/311, II. 60/565.

Ammell = enamelling, I. 45/613, 142/504. 'Set in *amel* white,' Fletcher's P. I. x. 33.

Amost, (all amost), II. 334, Ep. 6, l. 4.

A-most, II. 242/403.

Amphitrite = the Sea, I. 108/181.

Amramide, *sb.* = Moses, 'wild Amramide,' Numbers xii. 3. I. 206/953.

Anagram, I. 141/380.

Anathem = a curse, I. 200/261.

Anatomie, *sb.* = skeleton, I. 192/911, 194/1108 ; II. 116/1274, 168/100.

Anatomize, I. 230/477.

Angelliz'd, *v.* angeliz'd, I. 180/268, 213/39.

Angell-guarded, II. 343, col. 1, l. 5.

Angerfull, I. 134/205.

Anger-lesse, I. 134/222.

Angine, *sb.*, I. 101/285.

Angish, *sb.*, II. 262/144.

Angled, *v. tr.*, I. 259, 938.

Angles, *sb.* = baits, I. 25/666.

Angles, *sb.* = corners, I. 156/285.

Angors, *sb.*, I. 119/607.

Angry-braving, *adj.*, II. 199/338.

A-nights, II. 196/9.

Animadversion = warning, II. 141, col. 2, l. 5.

Ann'let, I. 48/965.

Anorexie, I. 118/450.

Another-where, I. 248/915.

Ante-date, *v.*, I. 43/325.

Antichrists, I. 48/938.

Anticks, *sb.*, I. 104/549 ; II. 272/596.

Antick, *adj.*, I. 115/81.

Antientest, II. 154/773.

Antik, antike = ancient, I. 147/218, II. 40, Son. 21, 105/5, 204/247.

Antiperistasis, I. 31/475, note the context on the use of the term here = opposition of a contrary quality of which the quality opposed acquires strength. See Richardson, *s.v.*

Antipodes, I. 84/87 ; II. 56, col. 1, l. 8, 183/212.

Antique-fram'd, II. 126/323.

Ape-like, I. 109/264.

Apelleses, I. 120/734.

Apian-way, I. 120/679.

Apoplexe, I. 117/356.

Appaid, *v.*, appayd, II. 59/407, 151/445.

Appels, *sb.*, II. 126/211.

Apple-squire, II. 193/244. See Nares, *s.v.*

Appose, *v.* = to puzzle, I. 237/1306.

Approches, *sb.*, II. 196/10.

Approve, I. 56/486, 194/1212.

Apricock. See Special Lists, under 'Plants.'

April age, II. 238, Son., l. 4.

April of mine age = spring-time, II. 3, st. 1. See our Introduction.

Apted, *v.*, II. 292/129. See Nares under 'Apt.'

Arbiter, II. 161/72, 166/539.

Arbitrement, II. 352, st. 1.

Arbourd, *v.*, I. 201/343.

Arcenall, arcenels, I. 72/17, 205/859, 215/236, etc.

Arch-archer, I. 136/496.

Arch-architect, I. 56/442 ; II. 38, Son. 10.

Arch-colonel, I. 202/419.

Arch-essence, I. 128/711.

Arch-foe, I. 143/600.

Arch-master, II. 64/967.

Arch-mover, I. 21/206.

Arch-tyrants, I. 111/469.

Argentine (heraldic) I. 69/972.

Argolian, I. 228/275.

A-rightly, II. 60/600.

Aristæan, II. 180/371.

Arks, *sb.* = arches, II. 50, Son. 1.

Armados, I. 112/637.

Arm-arming, I. 184/12.

Arm-lesse = unarmed, I. 172/902 ; II. 183/230, etc.

Arm-twining, II. 340, col. 1, l. 1.

Armi-potent—'the armipotent soldier' (All's Well that Ends Well, IV. 3), I. 216/390, 242/214.

Arms-art, II. 243/481.

Arms-clashing, II. 195/442.

Army-shaving, I. 257/656.

A-row = in a row, I. 251/5 ; II. 326, Son. 24.

Arrands, I. 174/1119 ; II. 125/136.

Artemisian. See Index of Names, *s.n.*

Art-full = skilful, I. 69/920, 73/176 ; II. 198/205.

Art-lesse = unskilled, I. 55/307, 84/102, 99/32, etc.

Art-passing, II. 124/81.

Art-ship, I. 165/118.

Art-various, I. 143/649.

Artirs, *sb.* = arteries, I. 244/497 ; II. 60/549.
A-shoare, II. 61/732.
Ash-pale, I. 179/104.
Ashy, I. 170/667.
Asp = aspen, I. 169/608.
Aspes, *sb.* = aspens, I. 213/30.
Aspic, aspick, aspik, I. 74/273, 185/110, 197/1463, 218/584.
Asp-tree = aspen, I. 120/689.
Aspire, *v. tr.*, aspired, II. 37, Son. 1, 126/319.
Assay, *v.* = to tempt, I. 108/82.
Assever, *v.*, II. 158/268.
Assize, I. 201/330 ; II. 20, st. 41.
Ass-shees, II. 148/78.
Astound, *v.* = astounded, I. 73/168 ; II. 187/131.
Astronomer, I. 69/897.
Astund, *v.*, astuns, I. 116/264, 124/231.
Atlas, I. 139/113.
Atomies, II. 31, st. 86, 205/347, 250/422.
Attents, I. 261/1137.
Atters, *v.* = casts to earth, I. 191/2 ; II. 191/2.
Attonement, I. 181/371 ; II. 91/745.
Auls, *sb.*, I. 75/325.
Authenticall, I. 142/477.
Authentikily, I. 254/405.
Authorize, *v.* = to invest with authority, I. 186/278 ; II. 182/166.
Avail, *sb.*, II. 187/181.
A-vie, avie = wager, challenge, I. 194/1151 ; II. 336, col. 2, l. 42. See Nares under ' Vie.'
Avoid, *v.* = quit, I. 112/619.
Avoyd, *v.* = begone, I. 234/980.
Avoydes, *v.* = to withdraw, I. 218/575.
Awefull, II. 246, Son., l. 1.
Aw-lesse, aw-less, I. 182/490 ; II. 297, st. 4.
Awook, *v.* = awoke, I. 137/596.
Ax-less, II. 87/264.
Ay-poor, II. 98/116.
Ay-turning, I. 85/262, 109/182.
Azimyuths, I. 159/629.
Azure (heraldic), I. 235/1036.
Azure, I. 66/609, 69/971, 2.
Azure-gilded, I. 128/657.
Azure-spangled, I. 103/451.

B

BAALISTS, *sb.*, II. 268/190. Jeremiah Warton, in a letter dated 1642, applies this term to Cathedral Clergy :—' We went to the Minster, when the pipes played and the puppets sang so sweetly that some of our souldiers could not forbear dauncing in the quire, whereat the Baalists were sore displeased.'
Babble, *v.*, I. 140/272, 141/357.
Babbling, *adj.*, I. 37/1121 ; II. 312, st. 83.
Babel-building, *adj.*, I. 147/264.
Babel-wonder, I. 145/44.
Babies, I. 21/190.
Bable, *sb.*, bables, II. 29, st. 74, 273/723.
Baboone, I. 215/265.

Baby-fearing bugs, II. 57/216.
Back, *v. tr.* = to drive back, II. 187/142.
Backs, *v.*, to back a horse, I. 126/417, 233/777.
Back-blow, I. 204/735.
Badgerd, *sb.* = badger, I. 259/932.
Baen, *sb.* = bane, I. 46/697, 745, 47/792, etc.
Baen'd, *v.*, I. 112/571, 133/167.
Baen-baening, I. 255/424.
Baen-full, I. 172/944, 233/759.
Bag-pipe, I. 39/340. Singular how this musical instrument has become associated with Scotland only. It is frequent in Sidney and contemporaries.
Bait, *v.*, baits = to feed, I. 36/1030, 158/462.
B'al-blinded, II. 92/907.
Balde-pate, I. 124/187.
Baldrick = a belt, I. 54/226, 61/18, 234/906, 235/1050. Much Ado, I. 1. Spenser, F. Q. I. vii. 29. *Frequenter* in Scott.
Balk, *v.*, II. 165/510, 184/317.
Ball (Tobacco Ball), II. 274/781.
Balloons, I. 248/941.
Bal'nites, I. 235/1016.
Balsamum, I. 151/686.
Band, *v.* = to league, II. 131/904.
Bandelier, I. 158/520, 193/1068.
Bands, *sb.* = bonds, I. 149/506 ; II. 61/669, 65/1175, etc.
Bands (to bring in bands), II. 16, st. 7.
Bandogs, II. 283/57.
Bandy, *v.*, II. 184/398, 272/565.
Bandying, *sb.*, II. 45, col. 2. l. 22.
Bane, *sb.*, I. 12/15, 67/739, 74/258, etc.
Bane, *v.*, baning, I. 119/551, 120/728.
Baned, *adj.*, II. 271/573.
Bane-breath'd, I. 152/790.
Banefull, I. 46/708, 62/89, 63/274, etc.
Baner, *sb.*, I. 74/258.
Banes, *sb.* = bans, II. 234/505.
Bannaret, I. 200/198, 214/92.
Bann'd, *v.*, banning, I. 244/508, 253/201, 259/920 ; II. 126/237.
Banque-rout, II. 186/70. Cf. Comedy of Errors, iv. 2.
Barbarian, *adj.*, I. 141/393.
Barbarian, *sb.*, I. 159/633.
Barbarie (Barbary horse), I. 64/349.
Barbarisme, I. 159/632, 185/154.
Barb'd, *v.* = shaved, I. 116/1248. 'The stooping scytheman that doth *barb* the field' (Marston's Malecontent). So our 'barber' = shaver.
Barded, *adj.*, I. 63/279.
Bards, *sb.*, I. 171/801.
Bar-geese, I. 222/1048. See Nares, *s.v.* ' Barnacle.'
Barkingly, I. 109/248.
Barnacles, I. 82/1129.
Bartholmew, I. 45/629 ; II. 271/487.
Barton, II. 116/1311. Florio, Sherwood, Holyoke's Rider, Minsheu, Miege, Cooper (Th.), and Coles give it as = a hen-house or hen-roost. The ' English Expositor,' by J. B. says it is a corn-farm ; but extended to such lands as the Lord of a Mannour

keeps in his own hands, as it were in Demesn, not let out. Cocker gives both significations, 'A Corn farm ; also a place to keep poultry in.' In Sylvester = outhouses generally.

Base, *adj.* = lowly, I. 87/525, 159/629.

Base, *adj.* = low (base centre, *e.g.*), I. 87/477 ; II. 39, Son. 17.

Base, *sb.* = (the base = the low), I. 115/62.

Base, *sb.* = basis, foundation, II. 67/8.

Base, *sb.*, in music, I. 160/745, 170/685.

Base-brave, II. 261/31.

Base-court, I. 228/202.

Basens, I. 54/265.

Bashfull-boldness, I. 232/680.

Basilisk, I. 74/192, 242/239, 244/504 ; II. 269/291.

Basks, *v.*, II. 198/216.

Bassus, I. 52/33.

Bas't, *v.* = abased, II. 196/45.

Baste, *v.*, I. 246/701.

Bat, *sb.* = cudgel bats, I. 89, 724 ; II. 218, st. 37.

Bat, *sb.*, batt (animal), I. 251/7, 253/265, 272.

Bate, *v.* = to abate, I. 58/692, 191/777 ; II. 109/476.

Bate, *sb.*, II. 58/395, 62/816.

Bated, *v.* = abated, I. 29/199.

Battails, *sb.* = troops, battalions, II. 199/378.

Battell ranging, II. 243/451.

Battle-ray, II. 11, st. 13.

Batten, *v.*, I. 246/701.

Batter, *v.* = to beat down, II. 92/232.

Batter, *v.* = to force, II. 183/288.

Baulk, *v.*, I. 48/944, 135/321.

Baulks, *sb.* = hindrances, I. 208/102 ; II. 303/154.

Bawling, *adj.*, I. 245/542.

Bay, *sb.* = bound, II. 240/100.

Bay, *v.*, bayes = to bound, II. 172/581, 200/535.

Bay'd, *v.* (bay'd and barred), II. 271/456.

Bayd-up, *v.*, I. 37/1169 ; II. 212/410.

Bay, *v.*, bayd = to keep at bay, I. 189/610, 190/649, 720.

Beadman, II. 138/1652.

Beak-less-bird = Bat, I. 253/276.

Beam-brow'd, I. 244/428.

Beamling, *sb.*, II. 24, st. 13.

Beam-pasht, II. 15, st. 36.

Bear, I. 23/458. See our Introduction on this long-lived myth.

Beardless, I. 46/688.

Beardy, I. 46/688.

Bear-ward, II. 309, st. 36. See 2 Henry VI. v. i.

Beastly-brute, *adj.*, I. 128/741.

Beau-clerk, II. 273/770.

Beaugle-beard = shaggy beard, like that of a bugle or buffalo, I. 58/708. Nares has 'bugle-browed.'

Beauty-mock, *sb.*, I. 251/2.

Beblest, *v.*, II. 165/499.

Be-cedered, I. 167/318.

Becharms, II. 273/689.

Be-checkt, *v.*, I. 133/103.

Beck, *sb.*, I. 74/211, 84/179, 103/484, etc.

Becked, *v.*, II. 97/80.

Becloak, II. 248/138.

Becloud, *v.*, beclowded, I. 189/545, 261/1165 ; II. 114/1081, etc.

Becomn, *v.*, I. 232/647 ; II. 165/430.

Be-curles, *v.*, II. 198/201.

Bedeaw, *v.* = bedew, II. 188/243.

Bedight, I. 171/771, 215/217, 253/1017, etc.

Bedims, *v.*, I. 110/406, 149/485.

Bedipt, bedip, II. 194/379, 250/348.

Bedlam, *adj.*, I. 127/629.

Bed-rid, I. 68/817.

Bedy'd, II. 109/514.

Bedying, II. 178/167.

Been, *v.* (to been), I. 197/1486.

Beer, *sb.* = bier, I. 224/1267, 244/494 ; II. 216, st. 4.

Beetles, *sb.* = wooden hammers, I. 236/1105.

Beetle-blind, II. 11, st. 3.

Beetle-brow'd, II. 342, col. 1, l. 38.

Befoams, I. 126/463.

Before-un-sorrow-drained, I. 123/86.

Beforn = before, I. 76/474.

Befum'd, II. 106/141.

Begilds, II. 248/102.

Begor'd, II. 203/156.

Behem, *v.*, behems, II. 153/688, 194/375, 273/681.

Behight, I. 15, col. 2. l. 26, 101/260, 121/789, etc.

Beholding, I. 15, col. 2, l. 35.

Behoofe, *sb.*, II. 62/826, 64/984.

Behoove, *v.*, II. 30, st. 81, 57/322, etc.

Behoove, *v.*, I. 215/223.

Be-known, II. 151/486.

Bel, etc.—see our Introduction on Sylvester's use of Italian. I. 46/658/9.

Belave = to wash, I. 194/1112, 199/147 ; II. 198/278.

Belay'd, I. 224/1256.

Belch, *v.*, I. 34/852, 109/247, 208/1214, etc.

Beldam, *sb.*, I. 45/626, 218/624, 219/733 ; II. 112/803, etc.

Beleguer, *v.*, II. 158/247.

Belief-less, II. 243/512.

Bell (hadst won the bell, bear the bell), I. 171/851 ; II. 307, st. 4, 309, st. 36.

Belly-gods = gluttons, II. 202/11.

Be-moateth, I. 83/31.

Bend, *sb.*, I. 54/228.

Benetted, II. 191/60.

Benum, I. 218/600, 223/1115.

Benumming, I. 63/249.

Be-pitch, *v.*, I. 136/479.

Beraid, *v.* = defiled, I. 252/89, 155.

Bereave, *v. tr.*, II. 198/265.

Bereaven, I. 36/1072 ; II. 352, st. 28.

Berinses = washes, II. 188/154, 204/218.

Berrie, *sb.* = burrow, I. 259/930, 952.

Bescramble, I. 123/119.

Beseek, *v.* = to beseech, II. 110/614.

Beseem'd, II. 191/61.

Be-seen, *v.*, I. 235/1065.

Beshade, I. 234/975.

Beside (beside their little wits), I. 205/764.
Beslave, I. 213/47 ; II. 270/318, 271/535.
Besmear, I. 115/190 ; II. 270/359, 199/402.
Besmoaked, *v.*, besmoaks, II. 269/202, 270/359.
Besoothes, *v.*, II. 202/60.
Besott, *v.*, besotted, I. 27/23, 237/1231 ; II. 50, Son. 1.
Bespangles, II. 248/104.
Be-spred, *v.*, be-spread, I. 108/162 ; II. 210/151.
Besprent, II. 194/390, 240/153.
Be-star, I. 215/275.
Besteads, *v. tr.*, I. 205/772.
Bested, *v.*, I. 64/318 ; II. 149/294.
Bestreawes, II. 204/296.
Beswarms, *v.*, I. 148/356.
Betake, I. 89/714.
Betideth, I. 85/215 ; II. 65/1193.
Betonie, I. 46/740.
Betterment, *sb.* = improvement ; used still in the United
     States, *e.g.*, ‘ The betterments of the city of Boston.’
     —(But query only in official documents ?) ‘ There
     is no betterment twixt him and myself,’ *i.e.* nothing
     to choose (*Pilgrim's Progress*, pt. i. p. 35, fac-
     simile of first edition). II. 57/243.
Better-worthy, II. 205/378.
Bever, *sb.* = beaver, *i.e.*, moss soft as—a somewhat
     artificial comparison, I. 50/1106 ; ‘ blades of bever ’
     = down or hair, II. 308, Son. 18.
Bever, *sb.* = armour, I. 216/292.
Bever-supple, I. 105/680.
Bewray, *v.*, bewraies, I. 14/5, 121/785.
Bias-like, II. 57/204.
Biaz = cross-ways, diagonally ; ‘ biaz and thwart,’
     Troil. and Cress., i. 3.
Biaz-wise, I. 54/229.
Bib, *v.* = drink, I. 192/964.
Bib-all-nights, *sb.*, II. 278/101.
Bibbers, *sb.*, II. 273/673.
Bibbing, *sb.* = drinking, tippling, I. 120/746.
Bi-corn'd, *adj.*, I. 157/379.
Biding, *sb.* = residence, II. 181/74.
Bi-front, I. 31/492, 122/49.
Big-looking, I. 214/168.
Bigger-bellied, I. 249/1017.
Biles, *s.* = boils, I. 188/511, 224/1256 ; II. 182/178.
Bill, *v.*, billing, I. 69/970, 70/1070.
Bills, *sb.*, bils weapons, I. 205/787 ; II. 177/45, 180/
     404.
Bill-men, *sb.* = wood-cutters, I. 200/242.
Billited, *v.*, I. 159/643.
Bin, *v.* = are, I. 87/499, 95/226, 204/696, etc.
Binder, *sb.* (of sheaves), II. 177/58.
Bird-lime, I. 120/709.
Birds—See Special Lists of, that occur in Sylvester.
Bi-sexed, I. 145/22.
Bissextile, II. 86/194.
Bitch, *sb.*, I. 253/182, 217.
Blab, *sb.*, I. 100/133, 137/611.
Black-art, I. 218/631.
Black-artists, II. 88/408.

Black-band, II. 92/907.
Black-blew, I. 244/421.
Black-day, II. 156/52.
Black-red, I. 151/689.
Black-sant, I. 116/278. See Nares, *s.v.*, and under
     ‘ Sanctus black.’
Blades, *sb.* = swords, I. 49/1054, 72/87, 89/724.
Blain, *sb.*, blaine, I. 121/766 ; II. 354, st. 28.
Blanch, *v.*, blancht, I. 42/254, 43/319, 74/211.
Blandishment, I. 123/78 ; II. 325, Son. 23.
Blasphemous, II. 193/242.
Blazing-stars, I. 79/852, 194/1168, 244/402 ; II. 340,
     col. 2, l. 26.
Bleak, *adj.* = pale, bleached (*e.g.*, bleak for fear), I.
     192/906 ; II. 125/110.
Bleaking, *v.* = bleaching, whitening, I. 127/634, 224/
     1272. ‘ Scythian sands *bleakt* with continuall
     freezing ’ (Nabbes's Hannibal and Scipio, 1637).
Blear, *v.*, I. 108/155.
Blear-ey'd, I. 169/553, 174/1183.
Blent, *v.*, I. 36/1005.
Blew, *adj.* = blue, I. 46/702, 67/717, 136/493.
Blew'd, *v.* = made blue, I. 236/1175.
Blew-gold-tinseld, II. 297, st. 1.
Blew-golden-green, I. 136/494.
Blew-green-gilt, I. 34/773.
Blin, *v.* = cease, II. 240/161.
Blinde-burning, I. 254/296.
Blind-fold, I. 242/260.
Blindefull, II. 302/74.
Blind-led, II. 120/1784.
Blindled, *v.* = blind-led, *i.e.*, without the lamp, or
     query = blended ? I. 23/527.
Blindely-black, I. 258/768.
Blisse-presaging, II. 314, l. 39.
Blist, *v.*, II. 135/1338.
Bloating, *v.*, II. 271/499.
Blocks, *sb.* = fools, blockheads, I. 197/1452.
Block, *sb.* = idol, II. 190/476.
Blood-gain'd, I. 251/43.
Blood-shedding, *adj.*, I. 48/917.
Blood-soil'd, II. 92/907.
Blood-thirsty, I. 56/471.
Bloody-flix, I. 46/725.
Blouds, *sb.*, I. 258/830 ; II. 200/469.
Bloud-boyling, I. 116/180, 119/557.
Bloud-drowned, I. 170/705.
Bloud-flouds, I. 209/1222.
Bloud-less, I. 120/688.
Bloud-sweating, I. 117/329.
Bloudy, *v. tr.*, II. 41, Son. 28.
Bloudy-bright, I. 214/84.
Bloudy-fluxes, I. 119/534. Acts xxviii., 8th edition,
     1611 : in modern Bibles altered to ‘ flux.’
Blubber, *v.*, II. 223, st. 14, 247/14.
Blubbered, *adj.*, I. 120/665 ; II. 325, Son. 18.
Blub-cheekt, I. 193/1004.
Blurr, *sb.*, II. 232, col. 2. l. 31.
Boads, *v.* = bodes, II. 88/360, 189/386, 194/336.

Boading = boding, I. 135/376.

Boan, *sb.*, I. 77/573.

Boany, I. 78/684 ; II. 39, Son. 14.

Boaul, *sb.*, I. 49/1078.

Boawls, *sb.*, I. 46/714.

Boaws, I. 167/403.

Bocconi (Italian) = grovelling on ground, mouth downward—a boar running a-muck puts its head close to the ground, I. 120/726.

Bod, *v.* = bade, I. 200/194 ; II. 183/222.

Bodkins, I. 75/325, 261/1176.

Body-toomb, I. 257/717.

Boer, *sb.* = peasant, I. 102/350.

Boldens, *v.*, I. 34/794, 126/431 ; II. 84/10.

Bold-fabling, I. 158/448.

Bole, *sb.* = bowl, I. 34/779.

Boln, *v.*, I. 248/965.

Bolt, *sb.*, I. 252/66.

Bombace, *sb.* = cotton, I. 47/815. See Nares, *s.v.* ' Bombase.'

Bombards, *sb.*, I. 200/232.

Bombast, *v.*, II. 200/458. See Nares, *s.v.*

Bonarets, I. 104/570.

Bond-led, II. 120/1784.

Bone, *sb.*, bones (to make no bones)=make no difficulty, don't hesitate, I. 251/22 ; II. 108/317. See Nares under ' Bone.'

Bones, *sb.* = dice, I. 231/567.

Bon-fire, I. 22/408, 122/30 ; II. 247/4.

Bon-jours, I. 140/214.

Book-cases (legal expression), I. 237/1311.

Book-skill, II. 100/413.

Boord, *sb.*=board, table, I. 33/744, 76/470 ; II. 26, st. 38.

Boores, *sb.*, II. 127/422.

Boot, *sb.* = booty, II. 162/119, 171/472.

Boot, *sb.* (to no boot), I. 119/601.

Boots, *v.*, booted, I. 35/925, 70/1088, 74/234, 172/976, etc.

Boot-less, I. 74/278, 140/229 ; II. 27, st. 51.

Booth, I. 104/543.

Bosoming, *v.*, I. 84/142.

Bosse, *sb.*, bosses, boss, I. 55/388, 83/26, 228/204.

Bosse-about (Bum bosse-about), II. 270/377.

Boss-work, I. 205/812.

Botches, *sb.*, botch, I. 188/511 ; II. 354, st. 28.

Bottomlesse, I. 105/641.

Bouge, *v.* bougeth, I. 56/421, 65/437, 125/337, etc.

Boule, *sb.* = bowl, II. 194/326.

Boulime, *sb.*, I. 118/450.

Boult, *v.*, I. 47/862.

Boundifi'd, *v.* = bounded, confined, I. 164/13.

Bout, *sb.*, I. 37/1113.

Bouze, *v.*, bouz = drink over-much, I. 192/964 ; II. 100/401. See Nares, *s.v.*

Bow'd, *adj.* = bent, I. 77/639, 87/466.

Bows, *v.*, bow'd, bow = to bend, I. 44/451, 49/1035, 88/565, 236/1136, etc.

Bow-boy, I. 27/18.

Bowles, *sb.* = balls, globes, I. 157/351.

Bow-man, I. 75/328, 216/347.

Box'd, *v.* = stored up, I. 136/523.

Boy-stragglers (of a camp), II. 57/285.

Brackie, *adj.*, II. 171/486.

Bradypepsie = slow or imperfect digestion, I. 118/451.

Brain, *v.*, I. 122/7, 188/516, 205/863 ; II. 92/882, etc.

Braine-borne, II. 323, Son. 10.

Brain-sick, *adj.*, I. 146/134 ; II. 126/233.

Brain-sicks, *sb.*, I. 53/150.

Brakes, *sb.*, I. 259/964.

Brall, *sb.* = brawl, I. 30/317, 32/607, 48/927.

Bramble-kings, II. 237/793. Cf. Judges ix. 14.

Branchy, I. 44/451, 139/159.

Brand, *sb.* = a torch, I. 69/990, 80/973, 214/77, 228/282, etc.

Brandisht, *v. tr.*, lit up, illumined, ' Brandisht with a sun-like fire,' I. 128/644, 258/757.

Brandish, *v. int.*, 'a friendly Sun to brandish bright,' I. 128/729, 135/393.

Brangle, *v.*, I. 111/484.

Brasil, *sb.*—a very hard wood, I. 220/839. Quarles, Emblems, I. x. 41 ; III. v. 51.

Brass (Corinthian), I. 86/387.

Brat, *sb.*, I. 230/494.

Braule, *v.*, II. 272/638.

Braule, *sb.*, braul, II. 149/263, 204/246.

Bravados, I. 112/636.

Brave, *sb.* = boaster, I. 188/493, 206/983, 214/113, etc.

Brave, *adj.* = bold, courageous, I. 40/18, 57/599, 66/619, etc.

Brave, *v.* = to bully, II. 32, st. 107.

Braves, *sb.* = boasts, I. 26/790 ; II. 226, st. 69.

Braves, *v.* = to boast, braved, I. 190/745, 253/201.

Brave-ambitious, II. 24, st. 14.

Bravely, *adv.*, I. 57/613.

Bravely-bold, I. 128/638 ; II. 183/371.

Bravely-bright, I. 158/457, 215/216.

Brave-minded, I. 55/390.

Braver, *adj.*, I. 66/603.

Brave-resolved, I. 68/850.

Braving, *adj.* = boasting, I. 112/626, 120/685, 140/190 ; II. 107/269, etc.

Brazell, *sb.*, I. 75/335.

Brazen-face, *sb.*, II. 32, st. 106.

Brazen-headed, I. 260/993.

Brent, *v.*, I. 139/139.

Brethren, foure = the four elements, Earth, Water, Air, Fire, I. 84/82.

Brew'd, *adj.*, I. 32/540.

Bribe-blinded, II. 152/621.

Briber, II. 254, st. 15.

Bricol, II. 187/109.

Bride-belt, I. 195/1344.

Bridge (London),—famous for its shops, etc., as now in Florence, Venice, and elsewhere, I. 102/372.

Brigandin, I. 168/463.

Bright-bespect, I. 108/135.

Bright-brown, I. 145/18.

Bright-eyed, I. 235/1072.

Bright-flaming, I. 35/977.
Bright-light, *adj.*, I. 233/847.
Bright-keen, I. 170/746.
Bright-winged, I. 242/231.
Brim, *adj.* = publicly, and so clearly, I. 55/325, 184/22 ;
　　II. 118/1481, 119/1766, 138/1615, 170/316, 258/80,
　　262/153. See Nares, *s.v.*, but in first reference *not*
　　= fierce, but probably as in note = brimfull. ' Bale-
　　ful shrieks of ghosts are heard most brim.' (Sack-
　　ville's Induction.)
Brimmer, *adj.*, I. 160/742.
Brine-quar = brine-quarry or salt-pit, I. 48/898.
Brinie-ball, I. 41/179.
Bristled, *adj.*, I. 58/708.
Bristly, I. 123/155.
Britain, *adj.*, I. 93, col. 2, l. 16.
Britaine Kings, I. 262/1210.
Brizes, *sb.*, II. 127/423.
Broach, *v.*, broacht, broacheth, I. 139/140, 243/296,
　　261/1176, etc.
Broachers, I. 73/95.
Broaching, *adj.*, I. 206/909.
Broad-length, I. 27/58.
Broak, *v.* = broken, I. 135/322, 152/753.
Broakers, I. 44/524.
Broak-winded, II. 249/257.
Broath, *sb.* = broth, I. 246/672.
Brocheth, *v.*, I. 74/277.
Broke, *v.* (have not broke), II. 184/373.
Brokeage, II. 234/448.
Brokery, II. 141, col. 1, l. 29.
Bronts, *sb.*, I. 127/537.
Brood-bed, I. 68/789.
Brooks, *v.*, I. 12/14, 78/73, 138/34, etc.
Brothell, I. 121/787.
Brother-slaughter'd, I. 242/247.
Bruit, *sb.*, bruite, I. 117/347, 238/1407 ; II. 133/1092,
　　etc.
Bruited, *v.*, bruits, I. 254/384 ; II. 117/1466, 336, col. 1,
　　l. 22.
Brunt, *sb.*, I. 212/8 ; II. 57/268, 60/526, etc.
Brush, *sb.* = brushwood, II. 284/102.
Brute, *adj.* = brutal, I. 179/148 ; II. 91/749, 196/46, etc.
Brutely, I. 137/582, 145/54, 116/211.
Brutenesse, II. 60/591.
Bruter, *adj.*, II. 225, st. 39.
Brutest, *adj.*, I. 49/1044, 246/706 ; II. 254, st. 21.
Brutish, I. 147/177.
Brutus, I. 100/69.
Bubastick, *adj.*, I. 185/91. Bubustis was the Egyptian
　　Diana : there was also a city in Egypt of the name.
Bucketing, *sb.*, II. 217, st. 23.
Buckled, *v.*, I. 54/228.
Buckling, *v.*, I. 72/58, 216/576.
Buff, *sb.*, I. 171/795.
Buffon, II. 32, st. 106.
Buffs, *sb.* = oxen, II. 89/484.
Bug, *sb.*, buggs = bug-bears, which see, I. 206/917 ; II.
　　57/216, 137/1532. So used in an early English

Bible, it has given the name of the ' Bug ' Bible
　　to it.
Bug-bears, I. 200/209.
Bulk, *sb.*, bulks, I. 28/84, 101/235, 230/414 ; II. 192/162.
Bull, Denis (see under ' Denis ').
Bullion, I. 142/499.
Buls, *sb.* (of Vatican), II. 251/434.
Bulwark, *v.*, bulwarkt, I. 77/557 ; II. 39, Son. 15.
Bumbards, *sb.* = a kind of cannon ; but see Nares, *s.v.*,
　　I. 184/13.
Bunch-backed = camel-like, I. 149/453.
Bunchy, *adj.*, II. 185/512.
Bung, *sb.*, I. 180/294.
Burgages, I. 147/282.
Burgers, I. 65/421, 76/515.
Burgesses, II. 259/95.
Burguinet, II. 196/59.
Burly, II. 18, st. 17.
Burn, *v.*, to burn daylight, II. 113/789, 268/173.
Burn-bull, II. 210/197.
Burn-grain, I. 115/165.
Burning-bold, I. 243/378.
Bush-beard, *sb.*, I. 214/73.
Busie-bold, II. 88/379.
Busie-buzzing, I. 102/364, 201/365.
Busie-idle, I. 53/115, 195/647, 253/197.
Busie-swarming, I. 107/48.
Buskind, *adj.*, II. 232/280.
Buskins, I. 58/706, 155/156, 192/969.
Buss, *v.*, busse, I. 58/676, 143/543, 230/499 ; II. 202/59.
But, *sb.*, a cask, I. 100/62.
But = unless, I. 203/604 ; II. 179/217.
But = only, I. 204/749.
Butt, *sb.*, but, I. 182/422, 193/1076, 205/804, etc.
Butt, *v.*, I. 157/379.
Butter (bath'd in butter), II. 164/345.
Button'th, *v.* = to cover with buttons or blotches, I.
　　119/53.
Buttrest, *v.*, I. 44/448.
Buttry, *sb.*, II. 120/1766.
Buzzards, II. 107/231.
Buzzard kites, I. 12/3.
Buzzers, *sb.* = bees, I. 117/338, 167/332.
By and by = immediately, I. 134/271, 207/1086 ; II.
　　58/348, 59/446, etc.
By-designs, I. 209/1269.
By-paths, I. 242/201.
By-respects, II. 225, st. 53.
Byles, *sb.*, I. 118/487.

C

Cabalistik, I. 155/66.
Cabins, *sb.*, I. 68/863.
Cackling, *adj.*, I. 88/627.
Cæsars, *sb.*, Cæsar, I. 34/804 ; II. 336, col. 1, l. 27.
Cake, *sb.* (payd with cake for bread), I. 204/659.
Cake, *sb.* (his cake is dough), I. 252/138. ' An obsolete
　　proverb, implying the loss of hope or expectation ;

a cake which comes out of the oven in the state of dough being considered as utterly spoiled.' Nares, *s.v.* Cf. Tam. of Shrew, v. 1.

Cakes, *sb.*, I. 73/163. Qy. misprint for cares?

Calamary = a case for keeping pens (calami), but here apparently a man who carries such, and is a scribe, I. 62/72. But see Sylvester's own ' Briefe Index,' *s.v.*

Calcinate, *v.* = calcine, reduce to calx, burnt ashes, II. 273/734. It is used by Bacon (Nat. and Exp. Hist.).

Calcinize, I. 223/1200.

Calm-pride, *sb.*, I. 140/249.

Calm-rage, *adj.*

Calmly-cleer, I. 134/210.

Calor, *sb.* (natural) = heat—word adopted for the nonce, II. 271/517.

Cals, *sb.*, call, bird-calls, I. 139/93, 161/767.

Camils, II. 249/280.

Camosh, *sb.* = Chemosh, II. 111/672.

Camp, *sb.*, the watery camp, I. 49/993.

Can, *v.* (which no knowledge *can*), I. 105/694. Cf. Hamlet, iv. 7, and Spenser's Shep. Cal. Feb. 77.

Can, *sb.*, the great Can, II. 269/260.

Canapie, *sb.*, canapey, canapy, I. 55/374, 138/63, 169/580, etc.

Canaries Jigg, II. 210/205. Cf. All's Well, ii. 1. See Sir John Hawkins's Hist. of Music, iv. 391.

Candid, *adj.*, I. 190/684.

Candied, *v.*, candies, I. 32/580 ; II. 288/142.

Candle-flames, I. 36/990.

Cane, *sb.* (tobacco), II. 274/781. See Nares, *s.v.* ' Cane-tobacco.'

Canele, *sb.* = Cannell (Fr. Canelle)=cinnamon, I. 146/65.

Canes, *sb.*, hollow canes = telescopes, I. 77/545.

Cangeant, I. 252/107. Nares, *s.v.*, queries ' changing ' ? Query = the French *changeant* with ' h ' dropped ?

Canicular, I. 244/411.

Cankers, *sb.* = cancers, I. 118/487, 176/1398, 248/867. See Eastwood and Wright's Bible Word-Book, *s.v.*

Cankred, *adj.*, II. 321, st. 4.

Cank'red, *v.*, II. 106/134.

Canon, *sb.* = cannon, I. 128/667.

Canonized, *v.*, I. 283/42.

Cantonize, *v.*, I. 240/20.

Cap-case, ' a small travelling case or band-box ; originally, doubtless, to hold caps,' I. 248/886. Nares, *s.v.*, which see for good illustrations.

Cape-comfort = simply ' comfort,' but preserving the metaphor of a voyage, I. 93, col. 1, l. 4. A friend at Southampton asking a sailor after his brother, who was from home and also a sailor, received for answer that he was in ' Sick-bay,' *i.e.* on the sick-list.

Caper, *v.*, I. 102/327.

Caps, *sb.*, bows, salutations, II. 115/1171.

Captivate, *v.*, I. 64/322.

Captive-Shee, II. 196/44.

Carack, carak = a large ship of burden, a galleon, I. 64/344.

Caraques, I. 49/991, 216/309. See Nares, *s.v.*

Card, *sb.*, I. 159/628 ; II. 220, st. 93, 230/70.

Card, *sb.*, card and compasse, II. 19, st. 40.

Cardinall, *adj.*, I. 155/121.

Cardon, I. 176/1409.

Care-charming, I. 69/882, 133/68, 235/1070. See our Introduction on this compound word.

Care-clog'd, I. 94, col. 2, l. 11.

Care-free, I. 154/19.

Care-full, I. 179/96, 208/1107 ; II. 147/66, etc.

Carion, *sb.*, I. 230/495.

Cark, *sb.*, II. 355, st. 14.

Carkanets, I. 189/623.

Carke, *v.*, II. 345 ; M., l. 7.

Car-nails = nails used for a carriage—here those that fasten the tire on the wheel, I. 53/144.

Caroach = coach, II. 273/705. See Nares, *s.v.*, for a full note.

Caroche, I. 203/554 ; II. 243/339.

Carouse, I. 112/801. See Johnson and Richardson, *s.v.*

Carp, *v.*, II. 333, Ep. III.

Carpese, *sb.*, a plant, I. 115/172.

Carpet-knights, I. 167/341, 253/199. See Nares, *s.v.*, for a full note. Cf. Twelfth Night, iii. 4.

Carrak, carrack, I. 135/369 ; II. 268/127.

Carrion, *adj.*, I. 241/121.

Carry-castle = elephant, I. 72/65.

Carry-tale, *sb.*, II. 26, st. 41.

Cart, *sb.* (from Court to cart), II. 269/265.

Carters, *sb.*, II. 333, col. 2. l. 8.

Carvels, *sb.*, small ships—spelled usually ' caravel,' I. 149/443, 498.

Case, *sb.* = carcass, II. 125/193.

Case, *v.* = to cover, II. 159/411.

Case-pride, II. 278/160.

Cask, *sb.* = casque, I. 121/805, 166/288, 169/625 ; II. 199/371.

Cashier, *v.* = to dismiss, I. 212/14 ; II. 51, col. 2, l. 24.

Casquet, I. 254/363.

Cassakins = little cassock, II. 235/544. Though now rather an ecclesiastical garment, ' cassock' was formerly applied to dress of all sorts of people, including women.

Cast, *v.* = to condemn, I. 48/937, II. 334, Ep. VII. But see Nares under ' Casse.'

Cast, *v.* = to calculate, I. 155/93 ; II. 90/644, 203/97.

Casting, *v.*, casting up = vomiting, I. 86/376. So in Ben Jonson's Poetaster, i. 1.

Casteth, *v.* (casteth the first foundations), I. 117/338.

Cast, *sb.* (cast of Falcons) = a flight, I. 171/870.

Cast, *sb.* (last cast of age), II. 226, st. 62.

Casts, *v.* (casts a ditch), II. 192/88.

Caster, *sb.*, II. 130/786.

Cataract, *sb.*, disease of the eyes, I. 117/377.

Cates, *sb.*, I. 64/369, 122/2, 139/66, etc.

Caters, *sb.* = caterers, I. 244/458.

Cat-fac'd, I. 75/308.

Caul, *sb.* (caul of weeping rushes), II. 250/342.

Caul, *sb.*, cauls = spider's webs, I. 123/91, 228/219.

Caul, *sb.* (cleaves their skulls and cauls), I. 203/533.
Caul, *sb.* (curious caul of golden twist), II. 191/59.
Causwaie, *sb.*, II. 247/64.
Cautell, *sb.*, II. 309, st. 33.
Cauter, *sb.* = cautery, II. 58/305,
Cautere, *sb.* = cautery (Reason's cautere), I. 121/767.
Cauterized, *adj.*, II. 361, st. 14.
Cautionarie, Towne, II. 281, title page.
Caveats, *sb.*, II. 112/880.
Cease, *sb.*, II. 63/933.
Cease, *v. tr.*, I. 241/68, 69 ; II. 297, st. 1.
Ceasures, *sb.*, I. 15, col. 2, l. 33.
Cecropian, I. 192/983.
Cell, I. 65/418. See our Introduction for Holmes's poem referred to in the note.
Cellers, *sb.* = cellars, I. 42/267.
Censing, *sb.*, II. 268/183. See Nares under ' Censer.'
Censor, I. 58/652, 133/110.
Censure, *sb.*, I. 96, col. 2, l. 15 ; II. 167/48.
Censure, *v. tr.*, I. 77/593, 138/22, 244/540, etc.
Censurers, I. 77/630.
Censuring, *adj.*, I. 140/293.
Cephus, *sb.*, I. 75/313.
Cerastes, I. 74/200.
Ceruses, *sb.*, I. 252/166.
Cest, *sb.*, I. 234/949.
Chaffie, I. 47/844, 87/531 ; II. 116/1284.
Chaire, *sb.*, II. 314/29.
Chaldee wife = a diviner, I. 159/585.
Cham (the Great Cham), II. 351, st. 17.
Chamber-groome, I. 233/851 ; II. 336, col. 1, l. 36.
Chamæleons, chamelion, I. 141/346, 254/308.
Chamelion-like, II. 40, Son. 24.
Chamfred, *adj.* = furrowed, I. 228/204. So Spenser, Shep. Cal. Feb. 43.
Chamlet—stick originally made of camel's hair, I. 160/538, 222/991. See Richardson, *s.v.*
Champain, I. 61/43, 118/491, 123/107.
Champian, *adj.* (Champian War), I. 150/563.
Champing, *v.*, II. 137/1528.
Championize, *v.*, I. 167/359.
Change-colour'd, II. 111/678.
Change-full, I. 29/224.
Change-inthralled, II. 56, col. 2, l. 52.
Changeling, I. 50/1133 ; II. 272/609.
Chante-cleer = cock, *i.e.* chanticleer, Fr. clair, I. 169/548. ' Sweet' applies to the bird, not to its ' crow.'
Chape, *sb.* (Chape of massy gold), II. 125/103. Fr. *chappe*, catch of anything by which it is held in its place, as the hook of a scabbard by which it sticks in the belt—' *chape* of his dagger ' (All 's Well that Ends Well, iv. 3).
Chap-men, I. 44/523 ; II. 177/78, 233/394.
Chaps, *sb.* = jaws, I. 74/289, 253/173.
Chapt, *v.*, I. 149/412.
Chaprones, *sb.*, II. 270/376.
Character, *sb.* = letter, I. 20/186, 141/389.
Character, *sb.* = image, I. 81/1001, 110/368.
Charge-full, I. 93, col. 2, l. 5.

Charie, I. 12/20 ; II. 112/849.
Chariest, II. 194/366.
Charles his Wain, II. 171/458.
Charm-care, *adj.*, I. 527/562.
Charm-charming, I. 219/735.
Charm-chasing, I. 169/590.
Charming, *adj.*, I. 169/615.
Charrets, I. 206/916 ; II. 11, st. 6, 18, st. 14.
Charvel, *sb.*, a plant, I. 184/43.
Chaste-sweet, I. 234/958.
Chat, *sb.*, II. 156/8.
Chats, *v.*, II. 12, st. 19.
Chawes, *v.*, I. 185/83.
Check, *v.*, checkt, I. 27/1 ; II. 184/397.
Check, *sb.*, I. 236/1186'; II. 172/594.
Checkers, *sb.*, I. 123/109, 236/1102, 241/57.
Checquer, *sb.*, II. 117/1457.
Cheek by joule = proximity, closeness, as is the cheek to the jaw, I. 23/432, 52/18. ' They cheeke by *jowle* may with each other goe.' (Rowland's Knave of Sp. and Di.).
Cheer-cheek, *adj.*, I. 246/696.
Cheer-heart, *adj.* (cheer-heart wine), II. 295, col. 1, l. 6.
Cheerly = cheerfully, I. 166/220.
Cherishment, II. 68/138.
Chermes, I. 104/600.
Cherries, *v.* = to make red like a cherry, I. 252/122.
Cherrylets = paps, II. 50, col. 1, l. 8.
Chest, *sb.* = coffin, II. 294, col. 1, l. 17. Cf. ' chested in heading of Genesis. See Davies's Bibl. Engl.
Cheveris, *sb.*, Fr. *chevesne*—' Chevan and chub are one, (Lawson's Comments on Secrets of Angling, 1653 ; Arber's Engl. Garner, i. 197.) I. 62/142.
Chevron, in heraldry, I. 69/973.
Chief-chief-justice, I. 22/406.
Chieftie, I. 69/974.
Childe-age, II. 90/657.
Childe-great, I. 118/452, 192/896.
Child-world, I. 139/99.
Childre-spel, I. 200/203.
Chill-heat, I. 232/681.
Chill-shivering, I. 58/702.
Chimæras, II. 106/146.
Chimick-Juice, II. 112/790.
Chimney-like, II. 270/477.
Chimney-wretches, II. 270/429.
Chine, *sb.*, I. 73/124.
Chiromancy, II. 88/405.
Chit-chit-chat, I. 253/273.
Choak-pard, I. 46/736.
Chod, *v.*, I. 235/540.
Choice-full, I. 151/681.
Choice-planted, I. 35/920.
Choice-tearm'd = well-languaged, I. 143/613.
Choler, *sb.*, cholers, I. 28/93, 46/755, 102/398.
Chops, *sb.* = chaps, jaws, I. 133/65.
Chopt, *v.* (chopt and chang'd), I. 193/1055.
Chrisocholle = a carbonate of copper (χρυσός, gold ;

κόλλα, glue ; from being found with gold as a sort of solder to it), I. 231/601.
Christian-Israelites, I. 10/16.
Christianize, *v. int.*, I. 148/379.
Christianly, I. 159/599.
Christ-kin, I. 164/8.
Christ-typing, I. 184/9.
Chuff, *sb.*, II. 211/219.
Church-chaffering, *sb.*, I. 120/747 ; II. 15, st. 35.
Church-ship = Ship of the Church, II. 232/302.
Church-thief, I. 201/235.
Churlish, I. 220/848.
Churn'd, *v.*, II. 67/29.

> 'Hee that churn'd the cream of Poetry
> To honied Butter.'

Chymick, *adj.*, I. 78/753.
Cieling, *sb.*, I. 30/306.
Cifer, I. 105/720.
Cignets, *sb.*, II. 337, col. 1, l. 15.
Cimmerian, I. 22/313, 147/234 ; II. 4, st. 21.
Cindred, *adj.*, I. 176/1340.
Cindrous, I. 230/436.
Cipres, *adj.*, I. 89/669, 167/336.
Cipres, *sb.*, I. 233/841.
Circlets, II. 49, col. 1, l. 18.
Circuiting, *v.*, 1 Samuel vii. 16 (margin), I. 66/600.
Circularly, I. 89/666.
Circumcised, *adj.*, I. 31/473.
Cirque = arch or circumference of heaven, I. 30/399, 72/18, 150/610. Hudibras, II. iii. 434 ; Hall Satires, II. vii. 31, 34.
Cite, *v.*, I. 70/1045.
Citterns, I. 228/177.
City-vipers, I. 44/520.
City-wives, II. 342, col. 2, l. 3.
Civilize, *v. int.* = to behave civilly, I. 193/1100.
Civill, *adj.* = domestic, II. 92/892.
Clamber, *v.*, I. 47/807, 56/454, 70/999, etc.
Claps, *sb.* = applause, II. 115/1171.
Clarifi'd, *v.*, II. 191/50.
Clarks, I. 49/1047, 53/155, 78/662, 225/1359, etc.
Clash, *sb.*, I. 173/1061, 193/1011 ; II. 170/341.
Clavers, *sb.*, in music, I. 160/732.
Clawing = flattering, Much Ado, i. 3. See Nares, *s.v.* 'Claw' and 'Clawback.'
Clayie, *adj.*, I. 125/374.
Cleapt, *v.* = called, I. 122/42.
Clear-sighted, I. 49/998.
Clear-styl'd, I. 143/598.
Clerks, I. 37/1173.
Clew, *sb.*, clews = guiding thread, I. 69/956, 218/622, 111/487, etc.
Clift, *sb.* = Cliff, I. 110/352 ; II. 162/126, 164/396.
Clift, *sb.* (in music), I. 114/29.
Clinquant, *adj.* = shining, I. 234/895 ; II. 248/184. So K. Henry VIII. i. 1.
Clip, *v.*, clips, I. 22/352, 110/354, 190/758 ; II. 130/744, etc.

Cloake, *sb.* = pretext, II. 197/180.
Cloase, *sb.* = close, I. 147/259.
Clock-less, I. 43/379.
Clods, *sb.* (break all to Clods), II. 187/174.
Cloome, *sb.*, II. 351, st. 19.
Close-brokers, II. 197/146.
Close-clasped, I. 23/423.
Clotted, *adj.*, II. 171/467.
Cloud-bounding, I. 128/650.
Cloud-brow'd, I. 189/625 ; II. 263/29.
Cloud-chasing, I. 38/1213 ; II. 180/350.
Cloud-cleaving, II. 187/166.
Cloud-climbing, I. 142/452.
Cloud-crown'd, I. 200/224.
Cloud-kissing, II. 18, st. 33.
Cloud-lesse, I. 189/528.
Cloud-sundring, I. 193/997.
Cloud-threatning, II. 9/21.
Cloudy-clear, II. 50, Son. 1, 262/153.
Clout, clowts, I. 55/334, 75/356, 192/900, etc.
Clov'n-foot, I. 260/993.
Clowds-prop, *adj.*, I. 256/615.
Cluck-clucking, II. 185/457.
Clue, *sb.*, II. 90/596.
Clung, *v.* (closely clung), II. 116/1284, 197/90.
Clutted, *adj.* = clotted, I. 28/89.
Coach-man = the Sun, Phoebus, I. 57/548 ; II. 287/7.
Coaly-brow'd, I. 243/399.
Coat, *sb.*, coate, II. 251/427, 331, col. 2, l. 3.
Coat, *sb.* (of one coat), I. 242/262.
Coat-armour, I. 235/1037.
Coat-cards, II. 287/73.
Coat-changing, I. 45/561.
Cob-web-Lawne, II. 191/58.
Cob-web (this Spanish Cob-web), II. 272/557.
Cochenel, I. 104/599.
Cockatrice, I. 197/1461.
Cockle, *sb.*, plant, I. 89/721.
Cockles, *sb.* (cockles of her head = curls), I. 252/97, 'Cockle' = to twist or wrinkle, 'the camblet's cockled grain.' So the Latin *cocklea* = anything twisted like a cockle, a screw.
Cock-pit, I. 216/321.
Cocos = cocoa-nut, not cacao, I. 47/853.
Codlings, *sb.*, I. 73/151.
Cods, *sb.*, I. 33/644, 47/844.
Cofers, *sb.*, I. 33/744, 50/1146.
Cogitations, I. 178/57.
Cognizance, II. 331, col. 2, l. 2.
Cohabitation, I. 10/12.
Coign, *sb.*, Coin, Coins = corner-stone, I. 147/251, 206/872, 236/1119. Coriolanus, v. 4.
Coile, *sb.*, II. 183/301.
Coile, *sb.* (to keep a coile), II. 100/398.
Coins. See under 'Coign.'
Coition, II. 87/223.
Cold-burning, I. 117/325.
Cold-distilling, I. 118/413.
Cold-dry, I. 29/261, 30/334.

Cold-lym'd, I. 31/519.

Cold-moist, I. 29/260, 36/1049 ; II. 271/509.

Cold-raw, I. 207/1011.

Cole, *sb.*, a mere generic name for the cabbage tribe : colewort = young cabbage, I. 115/98.

Cole-wort, *sb.*, I. 115/98.

Collations, I. 127/586.

Collier, *sb.* (the Divel with the Collier), II. 268/168.

Colliers, II. 269/266, 270/427.

Collops, *sb.*, II. 156/60.

Collow'd *v.* = blackened or dirtied, I. 176/1352. Nashe (Lenten Stuffe) has 'becollow.'

Colls, *v.*, I. 247/777.

Colosses, I. 72/18, 228/205.

Colossus-like, I. 214/71.

Coltish, II. 273/757.

Columb = Columbus, I. 44/427.

Colure, I. 157/322, 328. Cf. Paradise Lost, ix. 66.

Comb, *v.* = to smooth, to polish, I. 132/32.

Combrous, II. 137/1518.

Comburgess, I. 64/384.

Com-Bungership, I. 174/1194.

Comely-grave, I. 228/289.

Comet-like, I. 207/1001.

Comitial-Ill = epilepsy—so-called because if any one was seized with it during the comitia, the meeting was broken up on account of bad omen, I. 119/583.

Commandements, II. 189/390.

Commixation, I. 105/700.

Commixing, *v.*, I. 219/753.

Commixtions, II. 6. st. 67.

Commons, *sb.*, provisions, fare, I. 192/890.

Commotive, *adj.* (misprinted in Notes and Illustrations 'commutive '), I. 40/47.

Commotive = adjective of substantive *commotion*. We should say commotional = tumultuous, boisterous, unruly. ' David's thoughts here were anxious commotive thoughts' (Adams, III. 283). I. 40/47.

Commutation = exchange, I. 142/483.

Comœdies, I. 84/137.

Comn, *v.* = come, II. 188/297, 226, st. 52.

Compack, *v.*, compackt, I. 80/888, 147/221, 252/72.

Compact, *v.*, II. 188/284.

Compassly, I. 189/540.

Compile, *v.*, I. 165/67 ; II. 138/1640.

Complete, I. 23/430.

Complexion, *sb.* = constitution, I. 229/374 ; II. 271/542.

Complexions, *sb.* = paints and cosmetics for the face, I. 252/120.

Complot, *v.*, I. 261/1131.

Composure, *sb.*, in Art. = composition, II. 90/568.

Comprehended, *v.*, II. 316, col. 1. l. 15.

Comprise, *v.*, comprisd, comprising, I. 100/160, 186/258; II. 171/429, 178/116.

Compriz'd, *v.*, I. 142/520 ; II. 133/1125.

Compt-lesse, I. 229/358.

Comptrollers, II. 270/399.

Con, *v.* (con you thank) = study expressions of gratitude, II. 154/821. Cf. Timon of Athens, iv. 3.

Conceipts, *sb.*, I. 12/10, 109/192.

Conceipt-full, I. 221/979.

Conceit, *v.*, I. 140/216.

Conceited, *adj.*, I. 95, col. 2, l. 4.

Conceits, *sb.*, I. 78/662, 141/366, 173/1043 ; II. 58/348. etc.

Conceive, *v.*, I. 108/104, 111/484, 141/359.

Con-citizens, I. 213/45.

Concoct, *v.*, concocted, I. 78/694, 713.

Concoctions, I. 77/597.

Con-corrupted, II. 267/4.

Condignitie, I. 6, col. 2, l. 10.

Condole, *v. tr.*, II. 97/12.

Conduces, *v.* = leads, II. 287/84.

Conduct, *sb.* (in conduct = in leading), I. 120/682.

Conduct-pipes = conduit-pipes, I. 230/410.

Conduit, *sb.*, II. 360, st. 3.

Cones, *sb.* = wedges ? I. 236/1110.

Confederate, *sb.*, I. 255/510.

Confedered, *v.*, I. 67/662.

Confer, *v.*, I. 13, 6. Ep.

Confer, *v.* (to confer to), I. 78/751.

Confine, *sb.*, II. 172/611.

Confines, *sb.* = neighbours, I. 140/260.

Confine, *v.* = to border on confining, II. 186/35, 248/134.

Confluence, II. 193/249.

Conform, *adj.*, II. 86/200, 87/280.

Congratulate, *v. int.*, I. 96, col. 1, l. 22.

Congratulates, *v. tr.*, I. 164/5.

Congratuling, *v.*, II. 84/6.

Conjecturals, *sb.*, I. 220/791.

Conjure-lover, *sb.*, I. 140/249.

Con-native, II. 267/40.

Con-naturall, II. 267/40.

Conned, *v.*, I. 67/695, II. 31, st. 87.

Connex, *v.*, connext, I. 226/52 ; II. 230/49.

Conney, I. 73/117.

Consacring, *v.*, consacred, II. 16, st. 5, 111/672.

Consequent, *sb.*, II. 31, st. 92, 115/1178.

Conserve, *sb.*, I. 104/619.

Consolate, II. 19, st. 38.

Consort, *v. tr.*, I. 14, col. 2. l. 2 ; II. 91/680, 169/270.

Consort, *v. int.*, I. 21/219, 29/292, 55/410 ; II. 62/821.

Consort, *sb.*, consorts = companion, I. 65/434, 84/101, 185/69.

Consort, *sb.*, in music, II. 38, Son. 12, 147/36, 200/434

Consorter, I. 258/752.

Conspire, *v.*, conspiring, I. 65/475, 212/16, 252/73. etc

Conster, *v.*, II. 194/352.

Consubstantiall, I. 79/773.

Consumate, *v.*, II. 22/10.

Contemnedly, II. 61/664.

Contemple, *v.*, I. 154/26, 173/1034, 165/118, etc

Contre-changes, *v.*, II. 86/142.

Contribute, *v.* = to pay tribute, I. 41/155.

Contriven, *v.*, 155/143.

Conveigh, *v.*, I. 40/60, 78/649.

Convent, *v. tr.*, convented, I. 111/444 ; II. 127/230, 231/140.

Conversing, *v.*, II. 127/410.
Convert, *v. int.*, I. 28/75, 76/420, 176/1404.
Convert, *v. tr.*, I. 42/252, 66/564, 86/379.
Convince, *v.* I. 134/259, 182/512 ; II. 38, Son. 9, 156/13, etc.
Convoy, *v.* I. 160/690.
Coombs, *sb.* = valleys between mountains, I. 193/1002, 216/300 ; II. 199/339.
Coop, *v.*, II. 88/411.
Cope, *sb.*, I. 34/797, 38/1228 ; II. 224, st. 19.
Cope, *v.*, I. 204/749, 214/113, 216/309 ; II. 249/213.
Coperass, I. 48/901.
Copers, *sb.* = coopers, I. 151/676.
Cops, *sb.* = copse wood, I. 124/229, 168/480, 200/243.
Copy-holder, I. 50/1155.
Cordial, *adj.*, I. 84/123.
Corduban, *sb.* (The Corduban's), II. 122, col. 1, l. 16.
Cores, *sb.*, I. 188/510.
Corianders, I. 191/818.
Coriers, I. 151/676.
Corinthian Brass—a famous amalgam (mythically) traced to the burning of the treasures at a temple at Corinth, I. 86/387 ; II. 9/14.
Cormorants, II. 32, st. 106.
Cornaline, *sb.* = cornelian or kind of onyx, I. 234/919.
Corn-cumbring, I. 115/166.
Corn-ears, I. 73/114.
Corn-fit, I. 157/385.
Corne-master, II. 118/1480.
Corner-lesse, I. 156/207.
Cornet, *sb.*, I. 61/69, 184/19, 191/789.
Cornish, cornich, *sb.* = cornice, I. 21/224, 103/518, 143/548, 236/1123.
Corps, I. 70/1054, 65/508, 152/762, etc.
Corps de gard = the place where the guard musters, I. 26/808. Breton, Pilgr. to Paradise (p. 19), has court de garde.
Correspond, *v. tr.*, II. 124/43.
Corriving, *adj.*, II. 331, col. 2, l. 8.
Corrosive, *sb.*, II. 251/464.
Corses, *sb.*, corse, I. 104/567 ; II. 325, Son. 19.
Cor'sie, *adj.* = corrosive, I. 117/399.
Corsive, *adj.*, II. 361, col. 1, last line.
Corsive, *sb.*, II. 42, Son. 38, 210/140.
Corslets, I. 173/1014.
Corvet, *v.*, I. 73/111, 164/24.
Corvet, *sb.*, I. 126/455.
Corvine, I. 118/439.
Cor'zive, *adj.*, I. 150/551.
Cosen, *sb.* = cousin, I. 242/271.
Cosmopolite, *sb.*, I. 10/13.
Cotes, *sb.* = cottages, cote, I. 50/1158, 125/365 ; II. 109/535, 187/166, etc.
Cotten, *v.*, II. 287/73. See Nares, *s.v.* 'cotton.'
Couch, *v.*, I. 78/687, 231/631 ; II. 248/114, 333, Ep. III.
Couchant, II. 171/471.
Couching-settle, II. 188/293.
Could, *v.*, II. 313, st. 88.
Coulter, *sb.*, coultar, I. 35/867, 49/1058, 157/385, etc.

Counsail-man, I. 94, col. 1, l. 4.
Count, *sb.*, I. 111/500.
Counter-baen, I. 46/721.
Counter-bane, *sb.*, I. 101/228.
Counter-bufft, II. 136/1377.
Counter-change, *sb.*, I. 145/11.
Counter-chang'd, *v.*, II. 191/54.
Counter-conquest, I. 182/484.
Counter-fait, *v.*, I. 28/152, 150/618 ; II. 151/463.
Counter-faited, *adj.*, I. 104/567.
Counterfeit, *sb.* = a picture or representation of anything, a portrait, I. 79/875, 233/769, 252/163 ; II. 194/386.
Counterfeit, *sb.* = counterfeiter (of coin), I. 175/1326.
Counterfeited, *v.*, counterfeit, I. 23/495, 69/943.
Countermine, *v.*, I. 209/1272 ; II. 41, Son. 32.
Counter-muse, *sb.*, I. 220/762.
Counterpane, I. 12/8 ; II. 317, col. 2, l. 22.
Counterpeiz, II. 268/117.
Counterplead, I. 253/261.
Counterplots, *sb.*, I. 259/961.
Counterpoyson, I. 47/791.
Counterpoyseth, *v.*, I. 259/913.
Counterpoiz, *v.*, I. 44/415 ; II. 88/378.
Counterpuff, *sb.*, I. 180/246.
Counterpush, *v.*, I. 259/961.
Counterscarfs, I. 140/179.
Counterservice, I. 219/716.
Countertunes, I. 160/743.
Countervaile, *v.*, II. 178/178.
Coupled points, I. 127/614. ' Tying the points [*i.e.* the tag or latchet] was another fascination, illustrations of which may be found in Reginald Scot's Discourse concerning Devils and Spirits (p. 71) ; the ' Fifteen Comforts of Marriage' (p. 225), and ' British Apollo' II. No. 35 (Brand's Pop. Antiq. ii. 170, Bohn's edition). In Sylvester, however, ' tying the points' seems to have been used as a charm to deprive a bridegroom of his vigour. In Gervase Markham's ' Famous [Italian] Whore,' etc., 1609, in speaking of means of divination, he names ' cursed points.'
Courser, *adj.* = coarser, course, I. 222/993, 995.
Court of guard, II. 187/89, 191/67, 196/10.
Court-eclipses, I. 49/1061.
Courtilaces = cutlass, Fr. coutelas, II. 248/101. See ' Curtilace.'
Courtin, *sb.*, I. 259/957, 260/999.
Courtly-cart, I. 252/87.
Cousening, *adj.*, II. 274/804.
Cousin, *sb.*, I. 30/314.
Couvies, *sb.*, I. 232/695.
Couzenage, II. 141, col. 2, l. 17.
Covent, *sb.* = convent, II. 127/382.
Covetize, *sb.*, I. 86/405, 145/56, 232/677, etc.
Cow-heard = coward, I. 204/748.
Cox-comb, II. 272/650.
Cozen-swords, I. 205/829.
Crabs, *sb.*, fruit of crab-tree, I. 35/922.

Crab-like, I. 157/392, 158/526.
Crackling, *adj.*, I. 193/1011.
Cracks, *sb.* = sound of cracking, I. 193/998, 195/1336, 7.
Cradle toom'd, I. 142/511.
Crafts-men, I. 122/28, 155/159 ; II. 136/1441.
Craggy-forked, I. 124/247.
Craking, *adj.*, II. 18/53.
Cramp-fish, I. 63/246.
Crannies, *sb.*, cranny, I. 30/302, 169/572 ; II. 15, st. 30, 209/18.
Cratch, *sb.*, II. 341, col. 2, l. 30.
Craze, *v.*, I. 121/763.
Creases, *sb.* = groves, I. 126/514.
Creeded, *v.*, II. 253, st. 1.
Creeds, *v. int.*, II. 42, Son. 36.
Cressets, I. 53/116, 54/236. See a full note in Nares, *s.v.*
Crest, *sb.*, II. 331, col. 2, l. 4.
Crest-faln, II. 249/257.
Crest-peoples king = cock, I. 69/895.
Crevish, *sb.*, Fr. écrevisse, I. 56/479.
Crie, *sb.*, of hounds, I. 234/968.
Crick-crakling, *v.*, I. 257/635.
Crimsin, I. 42/264-5, 45/625.
Crimsin-colour'd, I. 104/603.
Crimsin seas, II. 183/254.
Crine, *sb.* = hair, II. 178/160.
Crisis, *sb.*, I. 220/794.
Crisped, *adj.*, I. 83/27.
Crisped bush = hair, II. 186/27.
Crispy, I. 168/466, 234/975.
Crock, *sb.* = an earthenware pitcher, I. 192/971, 261/1158.
Crofte, *sb.*, II. 309, st. 37.
Crook, *v.*, croking, I. 78/650, 158/433, 157/320.
Crooks, *sb.*, I. 48/948, 78/723 ; II. 182/98.
Crook-bild, I. 158/519.
Crooked, *adj.*, I. 88/603.
Crook-horn, I. 54/236.
Crooking, *adj.*, I. 78/734.
Crook-tooth'd, I. 65/515.
Cross-bow-man, II. 202/81.
Cross-carves, *v.*, II. 249/234.
Cross-disguised, II. 305/329.
Crosse, *adj.*, I. 101/223.
Crosse, *sb.*, a coin, II. 210/202.
Crosse-bow-shot, I. 216/403.
Crosse-fix'd, II. 316, col. 2, l. 29.
Crosse-presse, I. 192/879.
Cross-stars, I. 58/689.
Cross-toss'd, II. 181/52.
Crossly-crost, I. 140/226.
Crost, *v.*, I. 48/878.
Crost out, II. 51, col. 2, l. 24.
Crost (crost for crown), II. 68/142.
Crotchets, *sb.*, II. 172/589.
Crow, *sb.*, warlike weapon = crow bar, II. 187/110.
Crown-demain, I. 228/226.
Cruciates, *v.*, cruciate = torment, I. 75/395, 110/321, 116/251, 134/233, 252/141.

Cruci-fixt, I. 128/675.
Crud, *sb.*, II. 153/670.
Crudie-cold, II. 135/1302.
Crudity, I. 119/528.
Crump, *adj.*, I. 40/36.
Cruse, *sb.*, I. 246/684.
Crusible, I. 202/469.
Crusts, *sb.*, of crystall = ice, II. 170/356.
Crutiate, *v.*, II. 148/186.
Crystall-crusted, I. 258/813.
Crystall-flowing, II. 49, col. 2, l. 23.
Cubit-thick, I. 192/889.
Cud-chewing, I. 64/314.
Cucuio, a bird, I. 68/794.
Cuirace, I. 171/857.
Cuirets, I. 74/227.
Cukoos, used contemptuously, I. 252/144.
Cull, *sb.* = choice, selection, II. 194/383.
Culvers = pigeons or turtle-doves, I. 83/35, 232/711. So Spenser, Sonnet 88, Tears of the Muses, v. 245.
Cumber, *v.* I. 36/1077, 55/313, 64/342 ; II. 16, st. 46.
Cumber, *sb.* (in cumber), II. 301, st. 44.
Cumbers, *sb.*, I. 165/165, 229/328 ; II. 90/589, etc.
Cunning, *sb.* = skill, I. 21/219, 108/95, 123/168.
Cunning, *adj.*, I. 83/12, 102/326, 187/392.
Cunning-cost, I. 260/1075.
Cunningly, I. 149/460, 234/943, 236/1126.
Cup-fume, II. 125/183.
Cup-god, II. 269/228.
Cure, *sb.* = cure of souls, II. 251/427.
Cure, *v.* = to take care of, II. 164/386.
Cure-less, I. 81/1031 ; II. 38, Son. 7, 63/536, 569.
Curious-witty, I. 150/611.
Curiousing, *v.*, I. 234/920.
Curled-purled, II. 50, col. 1, l. 8.
Currets, II. 199/371.
Currish, I. 184/38.
Curst, *adj.*, I. 173/999 ; II. 136/1378.
Curstest, *adj.*, I. 230/421.
Curstly, II. 97/69.
Curtall, *v.*, II. 130/744.
Curtelace, I. 104/595.
Curtellaxes, II. 180/403.
Curteous, I. 186/186.
Curting, *v.*, II. 220, st. 93.
Curtsy-capping, *sb.*, I. 49/1060.
Customed, I. 15/38.
Customers, *sb.*, II. 271/523.
Cymmerian, I. 222/1098.
Cynosure, I. 88/584.
Cynthian, I. 5/18.
Cyrcean, *adj.*, II. 272/554.

D

Dabbled, *adj.*, II. 178/88.
Daery-grounds = pastures, II. 210/131.
Daign, *v.*, I. 94, col. 2, l. 28 ; II. 118/1143.

Daliladies = either Dalila ladies, *i.e.*, ladies like Delilah, or Dalilades = daughters of Dalila, II. 144, col. 2, l. 29.

Dallers = dollars, II. 262/108. Shakespeare has 'dollars,' Tempest, ii. 1 ; Measure for Measure, i. 2 ; Macbeth, i. 2.

Dallies, *v.*, II. 312, st. 83.

Dam, *sb.*, II. 272/607.

Dam-devouring = devourers of their parents—common to all creatures, I. 189/547.

Dam-murdering, I. 209/1237.

Damn, *v.* = to condemn, I. 142/499.

Damnifie, *v.*, I. 187/401, 216/313 ; II. 15, st. 32, 199/376.

Dampish, I. 33/698.

Dance-guide, *adj.*, I. 234/957.

Dance-lover, I. 37/1110.

Dandiprat = dwarf or child, I. 215/263. See Nares, *s.v.*

Dandled, *v.*, I. 62/154.

Danger-dreadlesse, I. 109/279.

Danger-lesse, II. 56, col. 2, l. 54, 177/34, 183/253.

Dangle, *v.*, dangled, dangling, I. 100/104, 104/523 ; II. 309, st. 42.

Daniell, I. 99/48.

Dant, *v.*, I. 48/945.

Dare-full—' we might have met them darefull ' (Macbeth, v. 2), II. 132/994.

Darkes, *v.*, I. 219/670.

Darks, *sb.*, II. 163/280.

Darnell, I. 255/423.

Darrains, *v.*, II. 248/100. '*Darrain* your battle ' (3 Henry VI. ii. 2.)

Dart-darting, I. 200/275.

Dart-man, I. 167/304.

Dash, *v.*, dasht, I. 105/700 ; II. 189/430, 241/257, etc.

Dated, *v.* = ended date, II. 287/77, 334, col. 2, l. 2.

Date-lesse = unending, I. 115/102.

Daunt-earth, I. 143/566.

Day-bred, I. 102/405.

Day-reducing, I. 203/558.

Day-star = sun, I. 143/577. So Milton in Lycidas.

Daze, *v.*, I. 117/369.

Dead-alive, I. 69/953.

Dead-doing, *adj.*, II. 205/322.

Dead-laughing, I. 116/174.

Dead-live, I. 12/6, 48/945, 100/139, 261/1184, etc.

Dead-living, I. 190/693.

Dead-seeming, I. 109/260.

Dead-speaking, I. 160/717.

Deaf-dead, I. 169/583.

Deafly-deep, I. 203/620.

Deale, *sb.* (some little deale), II. 55, col. 2, l. 36.

Deale, *sb.* (by any deale), II. 59/430.

Dear-drad, I. 87/425, 228/248.

Death-due, II. 204/210.

Death-like, I. 169/616.

Death-prest, I. 100/63.

Death-summon'd, I. 226/1.

Deathlings—applied to Adam and Eve as having incurred the penalty of death, I. 110/374. Swift (Death and Daphne) writes, ' Death should get a numerous brood, young-deathlings.'

Deaths-man = executioner, I. 125/395. So 3 Henry VI. v. 5, and Rape of Lucrece.

Deaw, *sb.* = dew, I. 143/527, 195/1293, 196/1359.

Deaws, *v.*, deaw'd, II. 38, Son. 11, 185/478.

Deawlesse, II. 116/1322.

Debility, II. 91/776.

Debonaire, II. 349, st. 7, 360, st. 2.

Decay, *v. tr.*, II. 249/282, 272/620.

Deceases, *v.*, deceasing, I. 36/1033, 133/126.

Deceipts, *sb.*, deceipt, I. 44/524, 48/881, 150/594, 227/154.

De-creets, *sb.*, II. 85/8.

Dedalian, I. 136/425.

Dedalizing, *adj.* = dedalous, *i.e.* various turnings and windings, II. 278/89. See Richardson *s.v.* ' Dedalous.'

Deep-affected, I. 110/305.

Deep-affrighted, I. 119/581.

Deep-deep, II. 38, Son. 9, 41, Son. 28.

Deep-fet, II. 128/465.

Deep-naked, II. 270/377.

Deep-piercing, I. 229/385.

Deep-reaching, I. 55/417.

Deep-wide, I. 194/1157.

Deeply-frienged, *v.*, I. 235/1005.

Defected, *adj.*, I. 112/573.

Defenc'd, *v.*, II. 134/1230, 247/26.

Defendants, I. 57/617, 74/270.

Defies, *sb.*, I. 46/743.

Deform = deformed, *r. g.*, I. 21/259. Sylvester never hesitates thus to snip off an inconvenient syllable or ending ; nor did his contemporaries. Paradise Lost, ii. 740.

Degeneriz'd, *v.*, I. 165/104.

Degraded, *adj.*, degraded grasse = cast down, laid low, II. 200/499.

Deject, *v.*, dejected = to cast down, I. 19/10, 207/1037, II. 13, st. 48, etc.

Delates, *v.*, I. 199/56.

Delectation, I. 102/386.

Delian Princess, I. 181/325. See Index of Names, = Diana.

Delicates, *sb.*, I. 58/693, 76/473.

Delve, *v.*, I. 136/525, 137/532.

Demains, *sb.*, I. 103/457, II. 234/530.

Demean, *v.*, demeaned, II. 225, st. 39, 292/108.

Demi-captive, II. 267/29.

Demi-heav'nly, II. 271/536.

Demi-moores, II. 125/108.

Denay, *v.*, I. 107/44.

Denies, *sb.*, I. 241/73.

Denis Bull, II. 30, st. 80,—the Calcraft or Marwood of his day. He is mentioned in Nashe's Pierce's Super-erogation (1593). Cf. Index of Names, *s.n.* Dennis.

Depaint, *v.*, depainteth, I. 102/405 ; II. 262/115, 334, col. 2, l. 1.

Depend, *v.* = to hang, depended, I. 84/93, 245/533

Depopulate, *v.*, I. 243/346, II. 156/62.

Deposited, *v.*, deposited to, I. 142/471.

Deprave, *v.*, depraving, I. 24/642, II. 30, st. 82, 32, st. 1107, 142, col. 1, l. 4. See my edition of Dr. Sibbes's Works for a historically-noticeable use of the word 'deprave' = depreciate, under-value. Queen Elizabeth's Act of Uniformity provides penalties against those who 'speak anything in the derogation, depraving or despising of the Prayer-book.'

Deprive, *v. tr.*, I. 167/65.

Deprive, *v.*, to deprive from, I. 202/476.

Deputi'd, *v.*, I. 194/1126.

Derogate, *v. tr.*, II. 183/316.

Derrain'd, *v.*, II. 89/472.

Descants, *v.*, I. 67/696.

Descry = detect or discover, *i.e.* point out clearly = to cause one to descry or detect the difference. 'Yourself your counsail may descrie,' Chaucer (quoted in Richardson, *s.v.*). I. 24/551.

Desist, *v.* = to cease, II. 163/206.

Despight, *v.*, I. 128/692 , II. 164/403.

Devested, *v.*, II. 287/49.

Devise, *v. int.* = to consider, to meditate, I. 128/692.

Devise, *v. int.* = to communicate, I. 194/1114.

Diamant, *sb.* = diamond, I. 200/286, 230/444 ; II. 193/201, 227/78, 325, Son. 19.

Diamantine = adamantine, I. 56/515, 134/237, 176/1338 ; II. 250/380.

Diamond-headed, II. 312, st. 7.

Diapason, I. 49/1091 ; II. 283/22.

Diapry, di'pry, I. 128/654, 149/428.

Dicing-house, II. 270/393.

Di'd, *v.* = dyed, I. 165/122.

Di-dapper, I. 68/775.

Dies, *sb.* = dyes, colours, I. 100/89, 102/385.

Diffidence, I. 237/1285.

Diffluent, II. 272/626.

Digest, *v.*, I. 37/1186.

Dight, *v.*, I. 76/471, 79/765, 169/598, etc.

Dikes, *sb.*, II. 250/361.

Dild (God dild you) = God shield you, I. 252/138. See Nares, *s.v.*

Dilicious = delicate, self-indulgent, I. 102/314.

Dimpled, *adj.*, II. 263/31.

Ding, *v.*, I. 111/456 ; II. 32, st. 111, 62, 764, 65/1082, 261/48.

Dipsas, I. 74/202.

Dirge, *sb.* = dirge, I. 252/84.

Dipsian, *adj.*, II. 262/100.

Dirtlesse, II. 110/577.

Dis-abbridge, II. 16, st. 11.

Disannuls, *v.*, I. 238/1337.

Dis-apt, II. 272/619.

Dis-armed, *adj.*, I. 171/769.

Disarray, II. 273/669.

Disastred, *adj.*, II. 260, col. 1, l. 26.

Dis-band, *v.*, II. 196/20.

Dis-chained, II. 238, Son., l. 8.

Discipher, I. 231/570.

Discipled, II. 246, Son., l. 3.

Discommodate, II. 147/14.

Discourse, *sb.* = reason, I. 111/512.

Discreated, *v.*, I. 30/318.

Dis-custom'd, I. 132/13.

Dis-dared, *v.*, II. 243/450.

Disease, *sb.*, I. 48/881 ; II. 90/651, 147/31, etc.

Diseasing, *sb.*, II. 299, st. 24.

Dis-fertileth, *v.*, I. 176/1347.

Dis-flowred, *adj.*, I. 237/1238 ; II. 262/165.

Dis-grace, *v.*, I. 32/584 ; I. 187/346.

Disgorge, II. 193/241.

Dis-heart, II. 204/284.

Dis-ingage, II. 150/390.

Dis-know, *v.*, I. 191/851.

Dis-leav'd, *v.*, dis-leaves, I. 132/15, 232/666.

Dis-lodg'd, I. 169/582, 180/273.

Dis-mantled, I. 257/643.

Dis-matches, *v.*, I. 69/907.

Dis-mount, *v.*, dismounted, I. 100/155 ; II. 154/786.

Dis-natur'd, *v.*, dis-natures, I. 209/1238, 223/1210 ; II. 227, st. 86.

Dis-nerves, II. 272/619.

Dis-newes, *v.*, II. 227, st. 86.

Dis-order, *v. tr.*, I. 258/765.

Dispackt = unpacked, opened out, I. 23/578.

Dispatron'd, II. 156/62.

Dis-payer'd, I. 145/41.

Dis-pense, *sb.*, II. 99/300.

Dis-pense, *v.*, I. 78/668.

Dis-people, *v.*, dispeopled, II. 184/377, 202/17.

Dis-pight, *sb.*, I. 118/427.

Dis-plume, *v.*, I. 225/1347.

Dis-pointed, I. 259/905.

Disports, *v.*, I. 258/821.

Dis-rank, *v.*, disrankt, I. 67/325 ; II. 68/115.

Dis-ray'd, *v.* = dis-array'd, I. 261/1124.

Dis-robe, I. 139/156, 229/313.

Dis-sceptre, I. 77/615.

Dis-seize, *v.*, II. 190/500.

Dis-self, *v.*, I. 223/1116.

Dis-seysin, *v.*, I. 35/974.

Dis-sheveled, *adj.*, I. 247/750.

Dis-siped, II. 130/771.

Dis-state, II. 198/266.

Dis-sunder, I. 141/340.

Distain, I. 128/694 ; II. 12, st. 25.

Distaste, *v.*, I. 191/867, 192/903, 206/967.

Distasting, *sb.*, I. 86/377.

Distemper, *sb.*, I. 30/396, 57/623.

Dis-throne, I. 77/615, 133/99, 257/655.

Distraught, *v.*, I. 109/235, 111/418.

Distuned, *v.*, I. 114/3 ; II. 188/145.

Dithyrambik, *adj.*, I. 245/547.

Dittanie, I. 47/774.

Ditty, II. 305/385, 307, st. 15.

Divell-Owle = devil in form of an owl, II. 113/905.

Divers-branch'd, I. 41/100.

Diverse-floured, II. 86/129.

Divin'd, *v.* = made divine, II. 117/1415.

Divolv'd, *v.*, II. 260, col. 1, l. 17.

Dizzie, I. 255/423.

Document, I. 178/29.

Doft, *v.*, I. 23/535.

Dogged, *adj.*, II. 345, III. l. 7.

Dog-hunger, I. 118/451.

Doit, I. 43/392.

Dole, *sb.* = lot, I. 253/278.

Dolor, *sb.*, dolours, I. 192/940-1 ; II. 57/269, 133/1075, 165/427, etc.

Dolphin = Dauphin, II. 124/19, 241/260.

Domage, *sb.*, I. 168/469.

Domberton = Dumbarton, I. 222/1044.

Domesticall, II. 20, st. 41, 237/773.

Doms, *sb.* = dooms, I. 33/660.

Don, *v.* = done (don to death), I. 253/237.

Don, donns, *sb.* (Spanish), II. 125/116, 267/32.

Donns, dons, *v.*, donn'd, I. 243/340, 247/858 ; II. 117/1371.

Doom, *v.*, II. 306, col. 2, l. 4, Son. 2, 335, col. 1, l. 17.

Doom, *sb.*, I. 19/7, 23/451, 107/32, etc.

Dor-mouse, II. 19, st. 33.

Dottrells, II. 184/108. See Nares, under 'dotterel' for a full note.

Double-bunched, II. 109/490.

Double-chin'd, I. 125/403.

Double-dented, I. 232/738.

Double-doored, II. 310, st. 44.

Double-double-beer, II. 273/749.

Double-meaning, *adj.*, I. 79/824.

Double-named, I. 146/161.

Double-nighted, II. 297, st. 7.

Double-racked, II. 298, st. 17.

Double-sexed, I. 155/130.

Double-source, I. 41/78. As stated in note, Jordan has at least three sources, all of which I have traced, *i.e.* three fountain-heads, which contribute to it. Indeed there are strictly four.

Double-topped, II. 4, st. 26.

Doublely, *adv.*, I. 223/1212.

Doubles, *v.*, hunting term, II. 211/260.

Doublest, I. 85/192.

Doubling, *adj.*, I. 109/209.

Doubling, *v.*, II. 312, st. 83.

Doubt, *v.* = fears, I. 248/947.

Doubts, *v.* = suspects, I. 108/75.

Douns, *sb.* = hills, II. 210/131.

Douny-clad, I. 232/698.

D'outs, *v.*, II. 272/604.

Dovelings, II. 225, st. 49.

Dowland (a famous fiddler), I. 109/219.

Down-dragging, II. 261/48.

Down-hanging, I. 70/1012.

Down-hills, *sb.*, I. 27/39.

Down-treading, *v.*, I. 86/408.

Down-trod, I. 221/887.

Down'd, *v.* = depressed, I. 244/433.

Downie-feathered, I. 145/42.

Downing, *v.*, I. 190/735.

Drad, I. 5/18, 73/173, 75/359, etc.

Drad-dear, II. 97/7, 179/296, 200/465.

Drad-desired, II. 20, st. 42.

Drad-lesse, II. 183/253.

Drad-sweet, I. 103/429.

Drader, *adj.*, I. 193/1020.

Dradest, draddest, *adj.*, I. 199/76 ; II. 200/449.

Dradly, I. 224/1277.

Dradly-deep, I. 228/196.

Dradly-glorious, II. 162/172.

Dradly-sad, I. 188/519.

Dradly-wonderfull, I. 176/1344.

Draff, *sb.*, I. 246/733.

Dragons, I. 107/49, 109/199, 117/391, 187/406, etc.

Draught, *sb.* = picture, I. 233/787.

Draught, *sb.* = sewer ? I. 253/227.

Drave, *v.*, I. 116/244.

Dread, *sb.* = thing dreaded, I. 216/365.

Dread-spread = alarming, I. 235/991.

Dreadlesse, dreadless, I. 35/928, 89/726.

Dream-awake, *adj.*, II. 196/7.

Driery, *adj.* = dreary, I. 219/700.

Drifts, *sb.* = purposes, I. 25/733, 34/793, 58/662, etc.

Drifts, *v. tr.*, drifteth, II. 223, st. 4, 263/16.

Drinesse, I. 33/740.

Drips, *v. tr.*, I. 230/448.

Driveling, *adj.*, I. 253/175.

Driveling, *v.*, II. 272/609.

Drop-ling, *sb.*, II. 24, st. 13.

Dropping-wet, II. 158/201.

Dropsie, I. 136/523.

Dropsie-breeding, I. 116/176.

Dropsie-sick, II. 217, st. 20, 235/557.

Dross-full, I. 95, col. 2, l. 14.

Drouth, *sb.*, I. 244/435, 253/193.

Drouzing, *v.*, II. 203/101.

Drunking, *v.*, II. 267/25.

Dry, a-dry = thirsty, I. 151/745.

Dry-fat, *sb.*, II. 259/944.

Dry-drunken, II. 262/144.

Drynas, a serpent, I. 74/201.

Duck, *v.*, ducks, I. 36/1000, 192/965.

Duck, *sb.* = salutation, II. 111/737.

Due-devis'd, *v.*, I. 238/1342.

Due-timely, *adv.*, I. 173/1002.

Duer = more due, II. 105/60.

Duke, *sb.*, last : Dux = leader, I. 22/346, 192/916, 194/1114, 1?00, 201/348, etc. See Eastwood and Wright's Bible Word Book, *s.v.*

Dukelings, II. 278/139.

Dulls, *v. int.*, I. 74/230.

Dull-double, II. 262/158.

Dumb-speaking, I. 232/681.

Dumbing, *v.*, II. 40, Son. 25.

Dumpier, *adj.*, II. 272/643.

Dung, *v.* = to manure, I. 242/213.

Dunker, *adj.* (the dunker mole on Venus dainty cheek) = dark, I. 227/67.

Durance = duration, II. 304/250.
Durance, *sb.* = prison, II. 63/894, 65/1188, 91/737, etc.
Dure, *v.*, dures, I. 173/1096 ; II. 250/318.
During, *adj.*, I. 143/549.
Dust-born, I. 111/483.
Dust-bred, II. 137/1547.
Dustlesse, II. 110/577.
Dust-spawn, I. 140/178.
Dusty, *adj.* = made of dust, I. 111/498.
Dwarfling, II. 309, st. 33.
Dwarfship, II. 331, col. 1, l. 40.
Dying-living, I. 124/287 ; II. 243/422.

E

EACH-WHERE, I. 58/662, 159/619 ; II. 86/142.
Eagle-brood, I. 50/1162.
Eagle-like, I. 107/43.
Eagle-shoales = flocks of eagles, II. 259/92.　The
　　reference is to St. Luke xviii. 37.
Eagre, II. 299, st. 23.
Eagrest, *adj.*, I. 100/106.
Eare-charming, I. 15, col. 2, l. 22.
Ears, *sb.* (were by the ears), II. 204/248.
Ear-tickling, I. 141/328.
Early-rare, II. 192/94.
Earned, *adj.*, I. 105/654.
Earnest-pence = deposit money in a bargain or engage-
　　ment : sometimes ' God's penny,' II. 240/113.
Earth-desires, II. 64/1019.
Earth-Heav'n, I. 109/295.
Earth-worms, II. 64/140.
Earthen, *adj.*, I. 110/404.
Earthlings, *sb.*, II. 179/301.
Ease-full, II. 107/221, 113/1001, 141, col. 1, l. 27.
Ease-less, ease-lesse, I. 181/399, 207/1051 ; II. 210/166.
Eas-lessly, II. 60/530.
Easie-yielding, I. 94, col. 2, l. 19.
Eath = easy, I. 226/42.
Eaws, *sb.* = ewes, I. 195/1284.
Ebbe-flowing, *v.* II. 40, Son. 24.
Ebbing-flowing, I. 43/363, 233/820.
Ebene, *sb.* = ebony, II. 50, Son. 1, 194/361.
Ebene, *adj.*, II. 310, st. 43.
Ebony, I. 151/689.
Effected, *adj.*, II. 45, col. 1, l. 18.
Effect-less, I. 38/1255.
Effeminiz'd, *v.*, II. 241/302.
Efficace, *sb.*, I. 173/1026, 174/1116.
Eft-soons, I. 63/235, 158/482, 170/650, etc.
Egge, *v.*, egg'd, I. 218/547 ; II. 107/277.
Egre, *sb.*, II. 158/246.
Eigh me ! I. 233/757.
Eke, II. 62/840.
Eld, *sb.*, I. 26/800, 32/628, 68/823, 88/644, etc.
Eldership, I. 142/419 ; II. 107/296, 189/394.
Elect, *v.* = elected, I. 166/252.
Electrum, II. 3, st. 11.

Elixir, II. 6, st. 59.
Elf, *sb.*, elfe, I. 62/76, 81/1109, 84/129, 120/670.
Ells, *sb.*, I. 157/338.
Elphine = Elfin? I. 99/46.
Else-comparisons, II. 49, col. 1, l. 8.
Else-what, II. 56, col. 2, l. 46.
Els-pains, I. 101/286.
Elves, *sb.*, II. 110/357, 267/83.
Elvish, I. 147/175.
Elvish-envie, I. 10, col. 2, l. 24.
Embas't, *v.*, I. 45/543.
Embassador, embassader, I. 79/822, 202/424.
Embassage, I. 77/633, 96, col. 1, l. 6, 243/376 ; II. 243/
　　512.
Embatteld, *v.*, II. 271/451.
Emboss, *v.*, embossed, I. 48/900 ; II. 117/1372.
Embost, *v.*, I. 45/543, 49/1022, 123/135, etc.　See Nares,
　　s.v., for a full note.
Embow'd, *v.*, I. 236/1150.
Embrew, *v.*, I. 73/87, 167/313.
Embright, *v.*, I. 58/730.
Embrodered, II. 85/23.
Embrodery, II. 110/626.
Embryon, I. 21/298, 158/423.
Emmet, *sb.*, emets, I. 50/1129, 63/230, 89/683 ; II. 180/
　　414.
Empal'd, *v.* = made pale, I. 81/1036.
Emperesse, emperesse, I. 27/16, 49/1030, 56/424, etc.
Emperiall, *adj.*, I. 20/158, 161/772, 220/848, etc.
Empery, emperies, I. 40/39, 80/923, 133/139, 151/722,
　　etc.

　　　　　　　　　　　' A lady
　　So fair, and fasten'd to an *empery*
　　Would make the greatest King double.'
　　　　　　(Cymb. i. 7, and cf. Henry v. i. 2).
　　' No bounds but Heaven shall bound his empery.'
　　　　　　　　Marlowe's Dido. i. 1.

Empiem, *sb.*, a disease, I. 117/402.
Em-pill, *v.* = to give a pill—as people slip medicine
　　under cover of sugar to children, I. 220/767.
Empyreall, *adj.*, I. 36/1093, 55/371, 88/572, 156/292,
　　etc.
Empyreall, *sb.*, II. 288/138.
Ems, II. 308, st. 21.
En-agd, *v.*, I. 100/154.
Enactize, *v.*, II. 311, st. 64.
Enamel, *v.*, enammel, I. 79/798, 142/505, 236/1177,
　　etc.
Enameld, *adj.*, enamelld, I. 143/546 ; II. 330, col. 1,
　　l. 47.
Enbow'd, *v.*　See ' Embow'd,' I. 37/1161.
Enchanteresse, I. 219/745.
Encheck, *v.*, I. 252/106.
Encheere, *v.*, II. 105/28.
Encomion, I. 49, col. 1, margin.
En-commond, *v.*, I. 237/1317.
Encyclopedie, encyclopedy, encyclopædie = whole circle
　　of learning, I. 140/768 ; II. 14, st. 15, 94/1066,
　　273/773.

Endite, *v.*, = to indict, II. 154/860.
Enduements, II. 56, col. 2, l. 24.
Enfeoff, *v.*, I. 40/39.
Enfire, *v.* I. 84/89.
Enforceth, II. 34, st. 121.
Engastromith = ventriloquist, and so magician, I. 109/
    230. See Davies's Bibl. English, p. 24.
Engin, *sb.*, engins, I. 65/450 ; II. 40, Son. 25.
Enginer, I. 43/316 ; II. 187/107.
Enion, and see Enyon, I. 121/807.
Enjayleth, *v.*, II. 317, col. 1, l. 13.
Enlight, *v.*, I. 59/855 ; II. 268/174.
Enormous, II. 193/248.
Enring, *v.*, enringeth, II. 159/334, 263/31.
Enrowled, *v.*, I. 141/399.
Ens, *sb.*, II. 91/741.
Enseal'd, *v.*, I. 102/290.
Ensew, *v. int.*, II., 192/111.
Ensoul'd, *v.*, I. 118/444 ; II. 329, col. 1, l. 22.
Enstile, *v.*, I. 5/7, 149/425.
Enstock, *v.*, I. 56/514.
Ensue, *v. tr.*, I. 10, col. 2, l. 31, 25/703, 45/640, etc.
Entail, *v.*, I. 195/1263.
Enter, *v.* = inter, I. 73/93.
Enter-bathe, *v.*, I. 122/21.
Enter-blinning = intermingling, I. 30/402.
Enter-braid, I. 124/209.
Enter-changed, I. 167/310.
Enter-course, II. 3, st. 14.
Enter-crusht, I. 133/152.
Enter-deal, *sb.*, enter-deale = dealing together, or inter-
    course, I. 207/1013 ; II. 36/7. So Spenser, ' learn
    the enterdeale of princes ' (M. Hub. Tale).
Enter-glancing, *v.*, I. 233/828.
Enter-gore, II. 248/90.
Enter-kill'd, II. 184/332.
Enter-kissing, *adj.*, I. 36/1050.
Enter-laced, *v.*, I. 55/326.
Enter-mine, I. 259/949.
Enter-split, I. 167/301.
Enthousiasmos, I. 118/431.
Envaporeth, *v.*, I. 169/555.
Envie-vext, II. 99/302.
Envious-idle, I. 237/1318.
Enyon, I. 115/80, and see Enion.
Eolian, I. 19/15.
Ephemerides, I. 22/411.
Epicures, *sb.*, I. 34/847, 84/128, 109/251 ; II. 7, st. 75,
    25, st. 20, etc.
Epithalamie, epithalamy, I. 57/607, 174/1136, 237/1214.
Equi-poiz'd, *v.*, poizing, I. 156/189, 157/405.
Equivocation, II. 227, st. 94.
Erisipiles, I. 118/486.
Erithræan (erithræan deep, or seas), I. 41/77, 158/501 ;
    II. 183/232.
Ermin (in heraldry), I. 69/973.
Erring, *adj.* = wandering, I. 35/972, 159/617 ; II. 278/
    104.
Erroneous (th' erroneous Prince of Lies), II. 88/418.

Errors, *sb.*, wanderings, windings, I. 104/563, 143/614,
    229/389.
Escuage, I. 150/521.
Eschew, *v.* eschew'd, I. 115/93 ; II. 29, st. 72, 148/131.
Essay, *sb*, I. 77/589 ; II. 33, st. 108.
Estate, *sb.* = condition, II. 189/409.
Estridge, estrich, I. 69/901, 123/157 ; II. 202/39.
Etern, *adj.*, I. 140/269 ; II. 124/7.
Eterned, *v.*, I. 144/697, 221/977.
Eternal-moving, I. 150/613.
Eternall-taming, I. 173/1053.
Eternall-Trine, I. 189/540.
Eternise, *v.*, eternizeth, I. 176/1425 ; II. 67/79.
Etesian, I. 189/538.
Ethnick, *sb.*, I. 192/916, 715/290, 204/264 ; II. 269/246.
Ethnik, *adj.*, ethnick, I. 171/799 ; II. 196/17.
Ev'n-halved = equally divided, I. 160/660.
Even-slated (roofs), I. 43/351.
Ever-base, II. 98/110.
Ever-blisses, *sb.*, II. 61/643.
Ever-bowes, I. 228/287.
Ever-flouds, II. 323, col. 2, Son. 13.
Ever-keep, *v.*, I. 209/1288.
Ever-king, I. 218/562.
Ever-maiden, I. 158/532.
Ever-memory, I. 100/91.
Ever-never, II. 58/319.
Ever-never-dying, II. 196/51.
Ever-one, I. 189/566.
Ever-radiant, I. 157/351.
Ever-rage, *v.*, II. 92/876.
Ever-selfe-resembling, I. 134/218.
Ever-tilting, *adj.* (tide), I. 165/123.
Ever-trembling (field = sea), I. 128/646.
Ever-want, II. 98/113.
Ever-wicked, I. 213/17.
Ever-witnesse, *v.*, I. 213/44.
Ever-word, I. 191/875.
Every-while, I. 77/581.
Evince, *v.*, II. 167/40.
Eviternall-One = Everlasting, II. 90/565.
Eviternall-vast, *sb.*, II. 90/596.
Exceedlng (in exceeding = excessively), II. 61/691.
Excelling, *adj.*, I. 49/1023.
Excellently-rare, II. 85/67, 94/1113.
Exchange—predecessor of the more famous ' Royal
    Exchange' of Gresham, I. 102/369.
Excreation, II. 274/827.
Excrements, I. 187/352.
Exercitation, II. 63/877.
Exhalates, *v. tr.*, I. 151/747.
Exhaling, *sb.* = exhalation, I. 194/1167.
Exorbitance, II. 233/324.
Exorcist-like, I. 217/454.
Expir'd, *v.* = breathed out, I. 155/88 ; II. 330, col. 2,
    l. 18.
Exploiting, *sb.*, I. 255/451.
Expulst, *v.*, I. 112/630, 193/1072.
Exsiccation, II. 271/478.

Extased, *v.*, II. 4, st. 29, 236/677.
Extasie, I. 102/380, 150/612, 237/1215.
Extense, *sb.*, II. 90/583.
Extenuate, *v.* = extenuated, I. 208/1153.
Externly, I. 48/882.
Extirp, *v.*, I. 221/887, 251/3 ; II. 180/338.
Extorters, I. 44/516.
Eye-bold, *adj.*, I. 230/424.
Ey-shot, II. 269/291.
Eyne, I. 216/405.

F

FABLE-FORGERS, I. 53/114.
Face-pride, II. 278/160.
Fact, *sb.* = deed, I. 112/571, 182/460, 487, 206/888, etc.
Factors, II. 288/120.
Faded. See under 'Vaded.'
Fadge, *v.* = suet, fat, II. 331, col. 2, l. 2.
Fadome, I. 65/438.
Fag, *v.* = to wag? but qu. misprint for 'sag'? = to shake or swing. I. 44/417.
Fain, *adj.*, faine, I. 57/556 ; II. 66/1205.
Fain, *v.*, faining, I. 117/354, 133/122, 204/638.
Fain'd, *adj.*, fained, I. 49/1060, 1086, 94, col. 1, l. 21.
Fainer, *sb.* = lover, I. 67/715, 143/614.
Faint-breath'd, I. 141/301.
Fainted, *adj.*, I. 110/408.
Faint-hearts, II. 57/290.
Faintless, II. 58/323.
Faintly-bold, I. 110/343.
Faintly-vile, I. 215/281.
Fair, *sb.*, faire, I. 37/1139 ; II. 198/238.
Fair-built, I. 102/372.
Faith-famous, II. 120/1780.
Faith-mouth'd, II. 295, col. 1, l. 8.
Fallacians, *sb.*, I. 56/458.
Falling-sickness, I. 119/567, 609.
Fallow, I. 201/352.
False, *v.*, falsed, I. 142/473, 168/513.
False-contracting, *v.* I. 120/746.
False-promiseth, II. 263/22.
False-suspect, I. 96, col. 1, l. 17.
False-true, II. 262/155.
Fame-full'st, I. 43/377.
Fame-less, I. 96, col. 2, l. 20 ; II. 333, Ep. 4.
Fame-thirsting, I. 142/486.
Fames-foe monster = envy, II. 7, st. 81.
Fames-thirst, *sb.*, I. 213/46.
Famin-while (the), I. 244/472.
Fancie-pleasing, I. 14, col. 2, l. 1.
Fancy-proof, II. 196/31.
Fan'd, *v.* = fanned? I. 84/181.
Fand, *v.* = found, I. 154/34 ; II. 232/243.
Fane, *sb.*, I. 197/1479 ; II. 129/656.
Fantasticall, I. 101/190 ; II. 15, st. 39.
Fantastickly, I. 28/151, 57/596, 117/354 ; II. 287/6.
Fantastick-wise, I. 101/186.
Farcels—misprint for 'sarcels,' I. 31/412.

Farfalla, I. 229/362. Florio (1598) has = 'a gnat, a moth, a flie that houering about a candle burnes itselfe, called a bishop,' = fire-fly.
Far-feard, I. 221/918.
Far-flown, I. 222/1049.
Far-spread, I. 123/136.
Farm, to give in farm, I. 102/309.
Fat, *s.* = vat, I. 32/554, 236/1136.
Fat, *v.*, I. 34/840, 167/389.
Fatall, *adj.*, I. 56/519.
Fate-spell, II. 321, Son. 4.
Father, *v.* = to become father of, I. 173/997.
Father-stock, I. 150/526.
Father-tree, I. 165/139.
Fatlings, *sb.*, I. 223/1159.
Fatted, *v.*, I. 29/200.
Fauchin = falchion, I. 168/448, 170/746, 191/769, etc.
Fault, *v.* = to fail, I. 258/826.
Fauter, II. 254, st. 14, 337, col. 2, l. 13.
Faux, II. 254, st. 15.
Fealty, II. 150/334.
Fear, *v.*, fears, I. 116/254 ; II. 216, st. 3.
Fear'd, *v.*, II. 196/33.
Fear-fled, I. 248/901.
Fearfull = timid, I. 214/106 ; II. 190/446.
Fearfull-sounding, I. 249/1065.
Feast-famous, I. 62/143.
Feather-clouded, I. 204/747.
Feather-tongued, II. 149/205.
Feature = making, II. 316, col. 2, l. 3, 332, col. 1, l. 8. See my edition of Sir Robert Chester's 'Love's Martyr,' etc., etc.
Fee, *sb.* = reward, I. 179/91.
Fee, *sb.*, to hold in fee, II. 92/843.
Fee-simple, I. 172/936.
Feebled, *v.*, II. 232/260.
Feebly-faint, I. 244/441.
Feined, *adj.*, I. 109/193.
Feld, *v.* = felled, I. 256/629.
Fell, *adj.*, I. 38/1251, 56/469, 68/846, etc.
Fell, *sb.* = a husk, I. 159/625.
Fellest, *adj.*, I. 46/733, 86/369 ; II. 33, st. 116, etc.
Felly, *adv.*, I. 74/249 ; II. 13, st. 2, 199/337.
Fellow-fals, *sb.*, I. 261/1188.
Fellow'd, *v.*, II. 89/454.
Fels, *sb.* (with Fels of Feathers clad), I. 77/604.
Fels, *sb.* = skins, I. 260/991 ; II. 89/496.
Felters, *sb.*, dealers in Fels or skins, I. 151/677.
Fern-thatcht, *adj.*, II. 186/29.
Ferret, *v.* = to search out, I. 228/198 ; II. 127/373.
Ferret, *sb.*, I. 259/953.
Fertiler, *adj.* (more fertiler), I. 246/683.
Fet, *v.*, I. 141/372.
Fetches, *sb.*, I. 109/241.
Fewell, *sb.* = fuel, I. 45/567.
Fibrous, I. 166/255.
Fickle-founded, I. 261/1199.
Fieldy, *adj.*, I. 126/451.
Fier-brand, I. 33/668.

Fiercely-fell, I. 132/38, 245/536.

Fierize, *v.* = to become fiery, I. 29/264.

Fiery-flaming, I. 158/469.

Fift = fifth, I. 22/385, 127/534.

Fifty (lend for fifty fifty = 50, etc., etc.), I. 121/793.

Fight-field, I. 259/931.

Fight-lesse, I. 130/782.

Figs, *v.*, I. 126/505.

Figure-flowing Pen, I. 143/623.

Filberd, *sb.*, filberds, I. 45/573, 123/128, 252/117.

File, *v.* = to defile, I. 215/280, 243/357 ; II. 194/419, 249/302.

Fillies, II. 288/115.

Finall cause, II. 86/157.

Fine (in fine), I. 47/759, 22/318, 106/756, etc.

Fine, *sb.* = fee, penalty, I. 172/885 ; II. 59/481.

Fine, *sb.* = end, II. 38, Son. 8, 89/558.

Fine, *v.* = to end, II. 218, st. 48.

Fines, *v.* = to refine, fineth, I. 24/576, 245/622.

Fingers, *sb.* (Had oft their fingers in the Golden Py), II. 212/334.

Finger-ferne, I. 47/758.

Finials, I. 21/223, 69/985.

Finn-less, I. 62/89.

Fire, *v.* = to inflame, I. 231/625.

Fire-arm'd, I. 101/249.

Fire-breathing, I. 52/22.

Fire-coacht (prophet), II. 211/285.

Firefoot, *adj.*, II. 210/195.

Fire-new = newly come from the fire, said originally of manufactures in metal, II. 210/195. Twelfth Night, iii. 2 ; Richard III. i. 3 ; Love's Lab. i. 1.

Fire-snort, *adj.*, I. 245/629.

Fire-wing'd, I. 33/656, I. 108/114, 248/961.

Fires, village of a hundred fires, I. 150/538.

Firm'd, *v.* = fixed firmly, II. 203/140, 247/38, 253, st. 8.

Firm-less = unsettled, I. 160/667, 192/926.

First matter, I. 28/168.

First-mov'd (heaven), I. 115/114.

First-moving, I. 31/430, 156/291.

First moving sphear, I. 87/481.

Firstling, *sb.*, I. 135/382.

Fishes—see Special Lists for fishes, etc., that occur in Sylvester.

Fish-fed, II. 198/297.

Fish-full, I. 42/231.

Fish-mariner, I. 64/381.

Fisk, *sb.* = Treasury, I. 231/609.

Fisketh, *v.*, I. 108/110.

Fisking, *adj.*, I. 119/600.

Fit-forked, I. 124/214.

Five-double, I. 37/1103.

Fixly, I. 69/983.

Fixtly, I. 120/722, 128/643, 134/224, etc.

Fixtly-fair, I. 157/375.

Flag-shaggie = shaggy with flags, I. 199/123.

Flaggy, *adj.*, flaggy fens = overgrown with flags, I. 68/771.

Flakes (tatter'd in flakes), I. 242/236.

Flame-bred-flie, I. 229/361.

Flame-darting, I. 244/403.

Flame-feathered, *adj.*, I. 54/272.

Flame-full, I. 102/401.

Flame-snorting, II. 186/1.

Flameless, I. 213/55.

Flamer, *sb.*, I. 36/996.

Flaring, *adj.*, II. 270/374.

Flaskets = kind of baskets, I. 236/1135.

Flat-cap, *sb.*, II. 226, st. 71.

Flatling, I. 157/325.

Flatter, *sb.* = flattery, II. 59/437.

Flaw, *sb.* = gust of wind, I. 176/1435, 249/989.

Flayed, *adj.*, I. 118/467.

Fleame, I. 118/459.

Flea-work, I. 116/177.

Fledger, *adj.*, I. 232/698.

Flee, *v.* = to fly, flees, I. 30/350, 132/43, 140/221, etc.

Fleers, *v.*, fleering, II. 128/445, 262/176.

Flerk, *sb.*, I. 216/348.

Flesh, *v.*, flesht, I. 109/244, 167/213, 259/953 ; II. 40, Son. 25.

Flesh-burden, II. 60/627.

Flesh-delights, II. 57/218.

Flesh-freed, II. 339, col. 1, Ep. II.

Fleshly, I. 108/82.

Flight, *sb.*, of pigeons, I. 171/871.

Fling, *sb.* (to have a fling), II. 159/335.

Flings, *v. int.*, I. 164/23, 247/844.

Flinger, *sb.*, I. 216/380.

Flint-hearted, I. 75/386 ; II. 287/28.

Flitting, *adj.* = fleeting, I. 36/1059 ; II. 56, col. 2, l. 34.

Flix, *sb.*, I. 119/540 ; II. 18, st. 11.

Floar = floor, I. 145/55.

Floating Inns = ships, I. 135/328.

Flock-lesse, I. 129/809.

Flood-nymphs, I. 234/871.

Florentizing, I. 35/943.

Flotes, *sb.*, II. 345 ; III. 66.

Floud-lesse, I. 190/702, 194/1197.

Flourisht = flowred, adorned, I. 156/272, 235/1007, 252/115 ; II. 248/147.

Flout, *v.*, I. 188/474 ; II. 342, col. 2, l. 33.

Flowr, *v.* (to flowr a field with dead), II. 133, 1051.

Flowr-crown'd, I. 233/808.

Flower-poudred, II. 330, col. 1. l. 48.

Flowry, *adj.* = floury (flowry grain), I. 33/649.

Flowry-mantled, I. 40/69.

Fluent, *adj.*, II. 134/1151.

Fly-bridge (warlike apparatus), II. 187, 110.

Fo ! I. 252/167.

Fodder, I. 54/241.

Foils, *sb.*, foile, I. 246/720 ; II. 249/254.

Folk, *sb.*, I. 238/821.

Fond, I. 22/351, 27/34, 34/791, etc.

Fondlings, *sb.*, I. 70/1022, 111/471, 182/479, etc.

Fondly, I. 105/643, 140/293, 245/573, etc.

Fondly-false, II. 55, col. 1, l. 1.

Food-fit, I. 53/132, 255/423.

47

Foolifi'd, *v.*, II. 127/369, 267/30.
Foole-fat-feeding, II. 60/638.
Foord, *sb.* = ford, I. 190/702.
Foot, *v.*, to foot it = to dance, I. 234/893 ; II. 67/13.
Foot-less, I. 62/89.
Foppery, II. 268/172.
Forbidden-bit-lost, *adj.*, I. 107/27.
Forbod, *v.*, I. 182/450.
Forcefull, I. 31/380, 78/735, 222/1038.
Forcelesse, I. 24/649 ; II. 15, st. 26.
Fore-acted, II. 155/865.
Forebode, *v.*, II. 135/1286.
Fore-close, *v.*, II. 182/90.
Fore-conceited, *adj.*, I. 21/213.
Fore-conceiv'd, I. 158/424.
Fore-decrees, II. 124/20.
Fore-friends, II. 167/11.
Fore-named, II. 167/1.
Fore-passed, II. 164/337.
Fore-possest, I. 47/800.
Fore-promised, II. 108/410.
Fore-sent, II. 105/20.
Fore-sentence, I. 137/599.
Foreslowes, *v.*, foreslowe, II. 202/76, 247/62.
Fore-spoke, I. 35/903.
Fore-top, I. 191/768.
Fore-typ'd, II. 108/409.
Fore-ward, *sb.* (in our fore-ward stands), I. 212/2.
Fore-ward (to foreward = in front), II. 57/268.
Forgate, *v.*, II. 189/410.
Forgeries, I. 101/256.
Forked, *adj.*, I. 56/476, 84/79, 119/600, 187/377.
Forking, *v.*, I. 134/243.
Forlorn, *v.*, I. 44/461 ; II. 203/175.
Form, *sb.*, seat of a hare, I. 126/510.
Form, *sb.* (alms in the Form), II. 211/280.
Formlesse, I. 109/191.
Fornace = furnace, II. 267/80, 274/820.
Forrain = foreign, I. 194/1165.
Forrest-haunting, I. 142/429.
Fortifies, *v.* = strengthens, I. 171/774.
Forth set, *v.*, I. 78/688.
Fortun'd, *v.*, I. 184/62.
Fortune-lesse, I. 189/650.
Foster, II. 311, st. 65, 312, st. 85.
Fould, *v.* = defiled, II. 4, st. 19.
Foule-squinting, I. 120/670.
Foul-mouth'd, I. 256/593.
Fountains, see under Index of Names, I. 42/246 *seqq.*
Foure-wheel'd (like crabs in a foure-wheel'd shell), II. 278/86.
Fourm, *sb.* = seat, II. 132/965.
Foxy, *adj.*, II. 212/377.
Foyls, *v.*, foyld, I. 139/80, 178/44, 204/673, etc.
Foyns, *sb.*, I. 171/769.
Fraight, *sb.*, I. 233/867 ; II. 240/80.
Fraighted, *adj.*, I. 232/692.
Fraighting, *v.*, fraights, fraighted, II. 4, st. 34, 202/3, 303/137.

Frails, *sb.* = slight baskets, I. 236/1135. See Nares, *s.v.*
Franklin Lob, II. 332, col. 2, l. 16.
Franticks, *sb.*, frantiks, I. 208/1194 ; II. 192/186.
Frantick-wise, I. 245/562.
Fraught, *v.*, I. 79/777.
Free-booters, II. 162/119.
Freeze, *sb.*, a sort of cloth, I. 58/705 ; II. 107/216.
Freez-clad, I. 124/191.
Fregat, I. 64/345, 65/476.
French-italianate, II. 278/87.
French-sick, I. 121/776.
Frenges, *sb.* = fringes, I. 142/450.
Frenging, *v.*, freng'd, I. 50/1107 ; II. 307, st. 3.
Frequented = frequent, I. 23/424.
Frequenting, *v.*, I. 141/313.
Fresh-declare, *v.*, II. 42, Son. 38.
Freshed, *v.*, freshing, I. 175/1280, 216/325.
Freshly-fine, I. 232/657.
Fret, *sb.*, II. 330, col. 2, l. 12.
Fret, *v.*, fret away, II. 60/605.
Frets, *v.*, II. 262/99.
Fret-work, I. 34/782.
Frie, *sb.* = progeny fry, I. 158/502, 185/78 ; II. 118/1495.
Frie, *v.*, frying fries, I. 217/427 ; II. 58/370, 271/452.
Friend, *v.*, II. 113/967.
Friend-foe, II. 42, Son. 40.
Friend-strong, II. 322, Son. 7.
Friendge, *sb.* = fringe, I. 235/1037.
Friezing-frying, *sb.*, I. 233/756.
Frise, *sb.* = frieze, cloth, I. 21/224.
Frizadv'd, I. 127/591.
Frize, *sb.* (in architecture), I. 103/518, 236/1122.
Frizzle, *v.*, frizzles, I. 232/742 ; II. 198/215.
Froathy, I. 87/509.
Frockt, *v.* = clad, I. 169/559.
Frolick, *adj.*, frolike, I. 151/651 ; II. 98/211, 216.
From-ward, I. 55/354 ; II. 267/57.
Front, *sb.* = face, I. 47/822, 58/731, 249/995.
Frontispice, *sb.* (of a building), I. 236/1121.
Fror'n, *v.*, I. 176/1417.
Frost-firmed, I. 68/875.
Frostie, *adj.*, frostie hairs = hoary, II. 179/248.
Fruit-fretting, II. 240/73.
Fruitfull-spawning, I. 81/1096.
Fruitfull-swarming, I. 137/605.
Frump, *v.*, I. 137/572.
Frustred, *v.*, I. 261/1127 ; II. 162/119.
Fry—see 'Frie.'
Frying, *adj.* (frying zones), II. 86/134.
Full-ear'd, I. 10, col. 2, l. 15.
Full-fill, *v.*, full-fild = to fill full, I. 59/813, 221/961.
Fumbling, *v.*, II. 202/78.
Fume, *sb.* = smoke, I. 27/23, 33/654, 697, 38/1297, etc.
Fume, *v.*, to smoke, I. 30/307, 83/54, 159/569, etc.
Fume-blind, II. 130/791.
Fumie, *adj.*, I. 36/1006.
Fuming, *adj.*, I. 32/553, 589, 46/714 ; II. 88/404.
Fumosities, I. 104/620.
Funambulant, *sb.*, I. 259/911.

Funerals, *sb.*, I. 41/129.
Furbish, *v.*, furbisht, I. 157/385, 256/598.
Furie-storm, I. 261/1106.
Furious-curious, II. 88/407.
Furls, *v.*, I. 232/742.
Furning = smoaking, *v.*
Furnisht, *v.*, I. 256/578.
Furniture = supply, II. 61/688.
Furrows-up, *v.*, I. 147/223.
Furrs, *v.* (furrs our Palate), I. 28/149.
Fury-flying, II. 268/184.
Fusty, *adj.*, I. 48/940, 244/450.

G

GAD, *v.*, I. 245/519.
Gadding, *adj.*, II. 192/139.
Gads, *sb.*, I. 69/904.
Gage, to hold in gage, I. 172/989.
Gages, II. 287/30.
Gail, *sb.* = jail, I. 141/350 ; II. 63/955, 961.
Gain-greedy, I. 44/523 ; II. 177/78, 191/77.
Gain-spurred, I. 42/282.
Gaine-thirsty, II. 331, col. 2, l. 24.
Gainlesse, II. 85/48.
Galactite, *sb.*, I. 226/51. A fossil substance which when immersed in water makes it the colour of milk.
Galenite, *sb.*, I. 220/793.
Gallantize, *sb.*, I. 80/906.
Gall'd, *v.*, I. 133/162.
Gall'd, *adj.*, I. 240/41.
Galliard, *sb.*, galiard, I. 143/579, 234/933.
Gallein, *sb.*, ship, I. 136/438.
Galley-fish, I. 64/381.
Gantlet, I. 259/866 ; II. 180/404.
Gaping-fish, I. 63/225.
Garish, II. 270/374.
Garter-knight, I. 57/610.
Gastly-grim, I. 73/166.
Gaudes, *sb.*, II. 278/159.
Gaulian, I. 43/338.
Gays, *sb.*, usually = pictures, I. 49/1040. See Nares ; but here = gaiety or showy things. Breton says 'each youth . . . to follow every *gaye*.' Toyes of an Idle Head (p. 28).
Geare, *sb.*, gear, I. 214/114 ; II. 106/160, 156/4.
Gelt, *adj.* = gelded, short-dayed ? I. 119/549.
Gentle-gentle, I. 148/310.
Gentles, *sb.*, I. 234/982 ; II. 273/700, 743.
Gentilize, *v.* = to make gentle, *i.e.* gentleman, I. 44/527.
Geomancy = divination by means of earth, as by figures drawn on it, etc., II. 115/1189.
Geometer, II. 87/305.
Germaniz'd, *v.*, I. 143/624.
Gests, *sb.* = deeds, I. 99/21, 104/613 ; II. 3, st. 4, 105/4, etc.
Gests, *sb.* = gestures, gest, I. 102/363, 215/251 ; II. 180/361.

Gesture, I. 173/126 ; II. 332, Ep. 11. l. 7.
Ghastly-glowing, I. 120/721.
Ghess, *v.*, ghest, I. 58/723, 59/810, 101/196, etc.
Ghesse, *sb.*, I. 127/613 ; II. 194/334.
Ghost-like grim, I. 219/668.
Ghostly, II. 105/33.
Gibbrish, *sb.*, gibb'rish, I. 21/197, 140/207, 287.
Giddie, *adj.*, II. 278/159.
Giddy-brain'd, I. 150/596.
Gilden, *adj.*, I. 45/611, 64/330, 208/1180.
Gilli-flower, II. 192/96, 284/99.
Gingling, *adj.*, I. 189/638.
Ginne, *sb.*, gin, I. 194/1178 ; II. 46, col. 1, l. 4, 157/195, etc.
Gird, *v.* = to jeer, II. 106/113.
Gird, *sb.*, II. 158/291.
Girl-boy, I. 125/315, 215/280.
Glade, *sb.*, of a wood, I. 168/470.
Glads, *v.*, I. 20/152.
Glad-sad, II. 61/630, 205/354, 232/298, etc.
Gladly-sad, I. 66/624, 233/793, 259/885.
Glaive, *sb.* = broad-sword, II. 198/217, and see Nares, *s.v.* 'Glass,' for a most interesting note.
Glased, *v.* = frozen, I. 258/814.
Glass, *sb.*, glasse, II. 42, Son. 37, 209/36, 210/176.
Glasse, *v.*, II. 138/1615.
Glasse-dust, I. 140/264.
Glead, I. 38/1256.
Glew, *sb.* = cement, I. 202/491.
Glews, *sb.* = bird-lime, I. 139/93.
Glib-gliding, I. 84/90.
Glistering, *adj.*, glistring, I. 23/430, 40/13, 156/273, etc.
Glisters, *sb.* (in medicine), I. 120/646.
Glistring, *v.*, I. 48/877.
Globy, *adj.*, I. 31/444.
Glorie-Anna, II. 324, Son. 14.
Glorious, *adj.* = vain, I. 48/878.
Glory-beaming, I. 55/413.
Glory-winged, I. 143/582.
Gloze, *sb.*, I. 110/312, 158/420, 192/923 ; II. 15, st. 27.
Glozing, *adj.*, I. 109/224, 121/765.
Glue, *sb.* = cement, II. 211/289.
Glue-in, *v.*, II. 126/297.
Gnatlings, II. 268/198.
Gnat-snap, a bird so called, I. 67/714.
Gnidian Idols, II. 5, st. 46.
Goad-man, I. 175/1277, 204/710.
Goad-groom, II. 92/877.
Goaring, *adj.*, I. 116/243, 135/361.
Goaring-deep, II. 267/65.
Goary, *adj.*, I. 254/348.
Gobbets, I. 247/783 ; II. 205/340.
God-directed, I. 157/307.
God-wise, II. 145, Son. 1, l. 1.
Godded, *adj.*, I. 240/14.
Godding, *v.*, I. 240/3 ; II. 41, Son. 30.
Godling, *sb.*, I. 227/149, 256/597, 237/1325, 255/460 ; II. 111/697. 'Yet did no god, nor godling, intervene,' Peter Pindar.

Godly-most, II. 119/1671.
Godly-wise, I. 255/473.
Goggle-eyes, I. 215/290.
Gold-azure-crimsin, I. 232/730.
Gold-ground, I. 50/1144, 155/100, 226/33 ; II. 247/22.
Gold-grounded, I. 235/1022.
Gold-head, I. 232/722.
Gold-heaped, II. 214/557
Gold-iron, II. 212/423.
Gold-like, I. 170/655.
Gold-lyn'd, II. 177/82.
Gold-mouthed, I. 143/599.
Gold-sanded, I. 41/122 ; II. 198/299.
Gold seel'd, I. 227/99, 232/736.
Gold-shod, I. 258/760.
Gold-thirst, II. 234/423.
Gold-thirsty, I. 41/125, 67/760.
Gold-winged, I. 143/536.
Golden-brow'd, II. 87/238.
Golden-eye, I. 64/313.
Golden-fleeced, I. 73/118.
Golden Guls, I. 56/455.
Golden Py (fingers in the), II. 212/334.
Goldy-locks, I. 55/400.
Gone, v., II. 180/415.
Gonorrhé, I. 118/479.
Good-cheap, I. 64/404 ; II. 109/477. See Nares s.v.
Good-great, II. 135/1324.
Good-natur'd = well-disposed, I. 224/1270.
Goose-grasse, II. 272/599.
Gordian-knots, I. 237/1312.
Gore-pond, I. 221/920.
Gorget, sb., gorgets, I. 235/1035 ; II. 180/404.
Gossen = Goshen, II. 182/98, 183/210.
Gouge, sb., a tool, II. 90/572.
Gourmandize, v., I. 247/793.
Governance, II. 105/36, 131/816.
Governings, sb., I. 160/699.
Grace-followed, I. 143/589.
Grace-fool-Assity—assity = asininity or stupidity ; grace-fool, pun on grace-ful, II. 271/433.
Grace-lesse, II. 217, st. 25.
Graftlings, II. 231/91.
Grailed (heraldic), I. 69/973.
Grain, sb. (died in graine), I. 104/604 ; II. 124/88, 232/257.
Grandam, I. 31/444, 109/217, 110/334.
Grand-captaine, II. 57/267.
Grand-signiorie, II. 249/300.
Grand-sire = ancestor, I. 100/171, 112/594, 124/188, 128/696, etc.
Grange, sb. granges, I. 49/1064 ; II. 28, st. 55, 86/141, etc.
Grapple, sb., I. 127/521.
Grass, sb. (seaven years old at the next grass), I. 126/415.
Grassie, I. 40/24, 47/762.
Grasse-born, II. 309, st. 31.
Grasse-green, II. 330, col. 1, l. 41.

Grass-less, I. 32/574.
Grately = gratefully, II. 92/841.
Grave, sb. = Earl, I. 201, l. 362.
Grave-brave, I. 212/6.
Grave-gracefull, I. 199/42.
Grave-mild, I. 166/240 ; II. 50. Son. 2.
Grave-sweet, I. 107/31 ; II. 5, st. 43, 39, Son. 14.
Grave-sweetly, I. 217/437.
Grav'd, v. = buried, I. 135/327.
Grav'd, v. = inscribed, grave, I. 158/451, 233/787 ; II 93/980.
Graving, v., II. 180/415.
Graven feature, II. 316, col. 2, l. 3.
Graver, sb., I. 205/852.
Gray-beard, I. 66/633.
Gray-headed, I. 80/906.
Grayes, v. = grows gray, II. 224, st. 29.
Great, v., I. 190/639.
Great-grand-sire, I. 128/696.
Great-great-grand-sires, I. 207/1021.
Great-little, II. 135/1338.
Great-world, I. 37/1203 ; II. 89/528.
Greatest, I. 80/957.
Greaze, v., I. 43/399.
Greaze, v., to greaze the paws = bribe, I. 93, col. 2, l. 21.
Greedy-gaping, II. 171/474.
Greedy-guts, I. 117/328, 247/807 ; II. 202/7.
Greedy-wise, II. 138/1602.
Greekish, I. 53/93 ; II. 3, st. 4, 13, st. 40.
Green-dry, I. 143/567.
Green-ever, I. 36/1041.
Green-gold, I. 187/373.
Green-gown'd, II. 18, st. 13.
Green-lesse, II. 217, st. 25, 262/91.
Green-mantled, I. 147/269.
Green-sick, I. 12/5 ; II. 292/153.
Green-staves, II. 211/240.
Green-yellow, I. 235/1040.
Green'd, v., I. 236/1175.
Greft, v., I. 54/220.
Griefe full, II. 59/420.
Griefe-guiding, I. 157/403.
Grief-less, I. 81/1034.
Griefe-starved, II. 321, Son. 3.
Grievers, I. 119/603.
Grievous-guilty, I. 133/117.
Griezly, II. 114/1019.
Griffin, griphin, I. 7, col. 1, l. 23, 67/720.
Grim-fac't, I. 116/240.
Gripe, sb., II. 211/232, 270/406.
Grissell, I. 145/40.
Grizel, adj., I. 67/713.
Grizly, grizely, I. 219/688 ; II. 270/406.
Grizly-grim, I. 127/632.
Groaping, v., II. 27, st. 50.
Groapingly, I. 22/417.
Groom, sb., grooms, I. 112/569, 139/114, 166/238, etc.
Groonland, I. 169/532.
Grosse (in grosse), I. 141/382, 199/34 ; II. 10/10.

Ground-less = bottomless, I. 167/393, 226/40 ; II. 152/582.

Ground-slycing, II. 180/407.

Grounsill, I. 128/689.

Grove-haunting, I. 253/259.

Grovie, I. 233/813.

Grub, *v.* = to uproot, I. 227/115.

Grutch, *v.*, II. 219, st. 66.

Gryphins, I. 108/129.

Guarded, *v.* = adorned, II. 110/626.

Guerdon, *sb.*, I. 45/536, 52/35, 192/417, etc.

Guerdon, *v.*, I. 174/1173, 195/1269, 197/1491, etc.

Guest-wise, I. 223/1292.

Guilefull, I. 108/160, 231/567.

Guill, *sb.*, II. 172/590.

Guilt, *adj.* = gilt, I. 253/177 ; II. 233/410.

Guilt-head, a fish, l. 64, col. 1, margin.

Guise, *sb.* = manner, II. 178/101, 193/302.

Guise, *sb.* = fashion, II. 253, st. 5.

Guittern, I. 237/1298.

Guize, *v.*, I. 166/192.

Guize, *sb.*, I. 166/193.

Gull, *sb.*, guls, I. 56/455, 220/848.

Gull, *v.*, I. 202/456.

Guns, *sb.*, II. 267/51, 57.

Gurgling, *adj.*, II. 196/15.

Gush, *v.*, I. 31/550.

Gut-less, I. 189/643.

Gutter, *v.*, II. 164/346.

Gutter-gorging, I. 100/116.

Gyant-stooping, I. 232/703.

Gyngling, I. 169/539.

Gyves, *sb.*, I. 63/277, 88/644, 204/653, etc.

H

HABILLIMENTS, I. 176/1389.

Habit, *sb.*, habite = dress, I. 148/301 ; II. 292/151.

Habitacle, II. 158/211.

Hackneys, *sb.*, I. 102/335.

Hackneys-Jades, I. 260/1059.

Hacksters, II. 40, Son. 25.

Had-I-wist—see Breton, Glossarial Index, *s.v.* There is an old English proverb, 'Had I wist comes always too late,' *i.e.* men find out too late ill results of their conduct, which had they known they would not have so behaved = an accident—some offence not intended. II. 212/426, 310, st. 48.

Haft, *sb.*, hafts, I. 127/534 ; II. 89/504.

Haggards, I. 7, col. 1, l. 23, 135/315.

Hail-fellow, II. 137/1575.

Hail-shot, I. 170/738.

Hail-torn, I. 237/1238.

Haily, I. 203/535.

Hainous, I. 220/769, 223/1151.

Hair (to shrink a hair from), I. 87/515.

Hair (differs not a hair), I. 156/197.

Hairs-breadth, I. 44/509.

Hair-strong, *adj.*, I. 159/530.

Hairy-clad, I. 249/1039.

Halcyon, I. 68/699.

Hale, *v.*, hales, I. 20/115, 110/358, 133/163, 190/737, etc.

Hale, *v.*, to hale in pieces, II. 184/405.

Half-bent, I. 58/744.

Half-broild, I. 259/977.

Half-dead, I. 32/570.

Half-globe, I. 58/740.

Halfe-horse, I. 54/270 ; II. 340, col. 1, l. 7.

Half-living, I. 32/570.

Half-made, I. 32/569.

Half-men-horses, I. 104/566.

Half-mud, I. 32/570.

Half-naked, I. 127/537.

Half-selfe, *adj.*, I. 242/275.

Half-tadpoles, I. 32/568.

Half-toomb'd, I. 66/553.

Half-unmade, I. 32/569.

Halfly-hanging, I. 258/858.

Halters, *sb.*, halting irresolute persons, I. 254/315.

Haltred, *v.* = bound, II. 187/160.

Halydome, II. 350, st. 3.

Hammer, *sb.*, a smiter, avenger, I. 204/705, 243/384 ; II. 191/30.

Hammer, *v.* = to smiter, II. 189/371.

Hammer-ill, *sb.*, I. 139/86.

Hammering, *v.* = considering, II. 109/500—*frequenter* contemporaneously.

Hammonian, I. 42/246.

Hanches, *sb.*, hanch = haunch, I. 129/778, 171/839.

Handeled, *v.*, I. 46/726.

Handler, *sb.*, I. 46/727.

Hand-gripe, II. 135/1258.

Handsome, I. 50/1153, 64/410, 150/595.

Hands-thirsting, II. 61/672.

Handy-crafts, I. 102/367, 127/535.

Hang-man, hang-men = executioner, I. 115/145, 116/225, 179/140 ; II. 13, st. 37, etc.

Hangman-like, I. 119/632.

Hant, *v.* = to haunt, I. 148/391, 172/964 ; II. 212/424.

Haplesse-hopefull, II. 5, st. 52.

Happied, *v.*, II. 231/75.

Happifies, *v.*, II. 244/642.

Happy-arabians, II. 186/29.

Happy-most, II. 104, Son. 1, l. 6.

Harbenger, harbinger, I. 26/779, 834, 135/346, 158/543.

Hard, *v.*, II. 153/723.

Hard-besieged, I. 204/101.

Hard-bested, II. 159/344.

Hard-rack-rented, I. 50/1154.

Hard-ruled, I. 165/81.

Hard-wracked, II. 136/1441.

Hard-wrought, I. 205/786.

Hardy-witted, I. 144/650.

Hared, II. 148/128.

Hare-like, I. 203/552, 214/121 ; II. 99/323, 129/671.

Harmfull, I. 74/197, 214/90.

Harp-skill, I. 213/8.

Hart-like = stag-like, I. 125/402.

High-lowly, II. 198/283.
High-noon-shine, II. 238, Son., l. 9.
High-thundring, I. 193/1066.
High-topped, high-topt, I. 10, col. 2, l. 16, 62/119.
High-warbling, I. 160/751.
Higher-house, I. 226/21.
Hight, *v.*, I. 23/493 ; II. 11, st. 2, 14, st. 17, etc.
Hilleth, *v.* = heaps up, II. 300, st. 40.
Hind, *sb.*, hinde = servant, II. 100/434, 107/213.
Hindges, *sb.*, I. 157/313, 334, etc.
Hinge-less, II. 87/264.
Hippocrass, *sb.*, hippocras, I. 49/1079, 123/99.
Hip-gout, I. 119/540.
Hirable, I. 73/104.
Hist, *v.* = hissed, I. 56/459.
Hoar, *adj.* = mouldy, I. 202/431. 'Age like frost has
    hoar'd his hairs,' Feltham. In the song in Romeo
    and Juliet, ii. 4, hoar is = grow musty, white being
    the colour of musty or mildewed things.
Hoaring = whitening, II. 251/520.
Hoar-headed, I. 199/113.
Hoard, *v.*, hoars, hoaring = to whiten, to make hoary,
    I. 43/344, 115/86, 249/1044 ; II. 251/520.
Hoarie, I. 246/634.
Hoast, *sb.*, I. 81/999, 172/935.
Hoast, *v.* = to be a guest, I. 61/22.
Hobby = horse ; also a species of hawk, I. 215/224.
Hoist, *v.*, I. 33/694.
Hollow canes = telescopes, I. 77/545.
Hollow-ground, I. 256/537.
Hollow-vein, I. 78/719.
Holmen, *adj.*, made of holm-tree, II. 109/541, 120/1782.
Holp, *v.*, holpen, I. 32/594, 65/430 ; II. 67/8, etc.
Holsom, II. 18, st. 19.
Holy-counterfait, *sb.*, II. 152/546.
Holy-hood, II. 288/118.
Holy-tricks, *sb.*, II. 127/359.
Home-haven, I. 61/725.
Home-plotted, I. 123/66.
Home-retrait, II. 221, st. 98.
Home-revoake, *v.*, I. 48/974.
Homicidiall, I. 253/251.
Honey-makers, I. 201/365.
Honey-sweeter, II. 50, col. 2, l. 8, 63/930.
Honied butter, II. 67/30—

> 'Hee that churn'd the cream of Poetry
> 'To honied Butter.'

Honor-giver, I. 55/400.
Honor-wing'd, I. 57/609.
Honour-binding, II. 247/57.
Honour-thirsting, II. 249/298.
Hony, *adj.*, I. 147/257, 235/1086.
Hony-birds = bees, I. 208/1143.
Hony-dropping, I. 260/1052.
Hony-flies = bees, I. 88/591, 248/897.
Hony-gall, I. 137/542.
Hony-people = bees, I. 117/336.
Hony-steeped, I. 89/652.

Hony-words, II. 179/244.
Hood, *sb.* ('Hast thou onely wisdome in thy Hood'), II.
    156/18.
Hooded up, *v.*, hoodeth up, I. 105/697, 112/576.
Hook or crook, II. 98/189, 288/94. See Nares *s.v.*, and
    Breton *s.v.* (Glossarial Index).
Hook-crookt, I. 259/883.
Hooking, *adj.*, I. 120/688.
Hoop, *v.*, II. 88/412.
Hoord, *v.*, I. 33/743, 89/687, 123/128.
Hoorded, *adj.*, I. 134/280 ; II. 88/410.
Hoove, *sb.*, II. 6, st. 62.
Hop, *v.* = his hope shall hop = depart, II. 158/206.
Hope-cheer'd, I. 135/362.
Hope-full, I. 262/1212.
Horn, *v.*, I. 63/211.
Horned, *adj.*, I. 36/1036, 40/34, 83/29, 136/499, 201/342;
    II. 288/87.
Horned-bird, I. 232/716.
Horners, *sb.*, workers in horn, I. 151/676.
Horn-god, I. 194/1206.
Horn-trumpets, I. 200/197.
Horny, *adj.* = made of horn, I. 200/215.
Horny-gate, II. 11, st. 1.
Horror-boading, I. 116/234.
Horse-leach, I. 253/192.
Horse-like, I. 149/453.
Hoste, *sb.* = Lat. hostia, 180/287.
Hot-breathed, I. 54/301.
Hot-cold, I. 214/103 ; II. 89/456.
Hot-dry, I. 29/260, 194/1167.
Hot-fuming, I. 126/412.
Hot-humid, I. 160/748 ; II. 135/1284.
Hot-moist, I. 29/261.
Hotch-potch, I. 192/895.
Howlet, I. 100/128.
How-much-much, II. 6, st. 66.
Hucking, *v.*, II. 109/476.
Huddling, *v.*, I. 164/31.
Hue and cry, II. 27, st. 44, 114/1054, 164/394.
Hu-on-cries, I. 110/345.
Huff'd, *adj.*, I. 35/949.
Huffing, *adj.* = smelling, I. 62/109 ; II. 130/703.
Huff-puft, *adj.*, I. 257/12.
Huft, *v.*, II. 292/139.
Huft = participle of huff, and not = heaved, as in note
    (p. 293), but = vaunted, etc., II. 292/138.
Huge-armed, I. 62/119.
Hugenesse, I. 249/1016.
Hugie, *adj.*, hugy, I. 68/792 ; II. 63/902.
Hulk, I. 171/797.
Hull, *sb.*, II. 136/1370.
Hulling, *v.* = to float, I. 164/29. Twelfth Night, i. 5 ;
    Henry VIII. ii. 4.
Humber, *sb.* = hummer, 169/606.
Humblenesse, humblenes, I. 20/131, 225/1347 ; II. 39,
    Son. 13.
Humbly-sacred, I. 125/298.
Humming, *adj.*, I. 216/349 ; II. 199/330.

Humors, *sb.*, I. 56/423.

Humor-brethren, II. 59/465.

Humour, *sb.*, humor = moisture, I. 40/55, 41/136, 180, 42/233, etc.

Hunder = hundred, I. 155/179.

Hundred-pointed, I. 187/321.

Hunger-driven, II. 234/489.

Hunger-starved, II. 150/355, 361, st. 17.

Hunt is up—see Nares, *s.v.*, for a full note = runes up, I. 50/1114.

Hurle, *v.*, II. 283/74.

Hurly-burly, I. 37/1180.

Husbands, *v.*, II. 40, Son. 25.

Husbands, *sb.* = husbandmen, I. 189/549, 227/115, 232/665, etc.

Hussian, II. 147/64.

Huswife, I. 89/655, 187/394 ; II. 292/160.

Hy, *v.* = hie, I. 43/202.

Hyanthean, I. 72/30.

Hydrautic, I. 104/556.

Hydrargire = Hydrargyrum (ὑδράργυρος) quick-silver, I. 115/67. The poet is referring to the ease with which gold forms an amalgam with it, not that mercury does not amalgamate as readily with other metals, but because gold is not so amenable to other and ordinary means. Just after, he speaks of amber, which, when its electric power is excited, attracts a light thing like a straw.

Hye wee, II. 324, Son. 14.

Hymnik, *adj.*, II. 235/592.

Hyper-borean, I. 66/635.

Hypocrism, I. 35/938.

Hypocritely-coy, I. 188/473.

Hyrens = seductive (hireling) women, I. 114/35.

Hyve, *v.* = to hive, to dwell. II. 62/759.

I

I = aye, I. 106/769 ; II. 227, st. 94.

Iberian-argonauts, II. 273/692.

Ice-bearded, II. 248/174.

Ice-pearles, ice-pearl, I. 166/293 ; II. 248/133.

Idea, Idæa, I. 123/63, 128/714, 158/424 ; II. 50, Son. 2, etc.

Idiocy = ignorance, I. 110/323.

Idiom, *sb.*, I. 140/283.

Idiots, *sb.* = ignorant persons, I. 12, col. 1, l. 6, 101/193, 221/976 ; II. 93/955, etc.

Idiot, *adj.*, II. 55, col. 1, l. 14.

Idle (in idle), I. 237/1319.

Idlely, I. 102/311.

Idol, *v.*, I. 138/20.

Idol-clergy, I. 253/226.

Idol-gods, I. 255/481.

Idol-like, I. 248/968.

Idol-ocean, I. 243/371.

Idol-prone, I. 194/1121.

Idol-puddle, I. 204/637.

Idol-service, I. 35/938.

Idol-serving, I. 232/645.

Idol-shepheards, I. 35/941.

Idol-sin, I. 253/184.

Idol-wedded, I. 200/217.

Idolants = idolaters, II. 18, st. 3.

Idolism, I. 255/502, 256/518.

Idolist, II. 165/577, 178/93, 185/498.

Idolize, *v.*, I. 161/763.

Ignatian (allusion to Ignatius Loyola), II. 268/170.

Ignatian-Latian (allusion to Ignatius Loyola), II. 254, st. 12.

Ignatian Pack (allusion to Ignatius Loyola) = Jesuits, II. 238, Son., l. 13.

Ignobles, *sb.*, II. 287/42.

Ignore, *v.*, ignoring, II. 232/274, 244/551.

Ill'd, *v.*, II. 128/454.

Ill-appaid = ill-satisfied, II. 14, st. 12. See Nares under ' Apay.'

Ill-advising, *v.*, I. 246/727.

Ill-bestid, II. 98/101.

Ill-chasing, I. 55/384.

Ill-come, II. 236/666.

Ill-good, II. 262/177.

Ill-habitude (Il-habitude), I. 119/582.

Ill-huswife, huswives, I. 187/394 ; II. 283/31.

Illightned, *v.*, I. 262/1218 ; II. 267/72.

Ill-intreat, *v.* = to ill-treat, I. 186/212.

Il-levell'd, *adj.*, I. 44/416.

Ill-mew'd, *adj.*, II. 321, Son. 4.

Ill-polisht, I. 226/53.

Ill-savory, I. 100/102.

Ill-stated, *adj.*, I. 207/1010.

Illuders, I. 146/121.

Illuding, *adj.*, I. 180/267 ; II. 242/332.

Illustre, *v.*, illuster, illustring, I. 23/534, 69/985, 222/997, etc.

Imager, I. 78/750.

Imbarks, I. 65/472.

Imbattle, I. 147/183.

Imbellished, *v.*, I. 29/273.

Imbold, II. 141, col. 1, l. 3.

Imboss, II. 212/383.

Imbost, *v.*, I. 54/227, 156/273, 193/1069, etc.

Imbrace, *v.*, imbrac't, I. 79/877, 160/674 ; II. 4, st. 22, 186/65, 192/170. From the Fr. *embraser*, to set on fire.

Imbrew, II. 3, st. 4, 199/368.

Imbrodered, *adj.*, I. 156/271.

Imbroydred, *v.*, imbrodred, I. 49/1021 ; II. 192/153.

Immanity = barbarity, savagery, II. 212/429.

Immature = premature, II. 281, Title page.

Immense = infinite, I. 237/1216 ; II. 85/25, 86/97, 163, 90/584.

Immounds, *v.*, I. 42/218.

Immure, *v.*, immures, I. 101/279, 125/374, 386, 134/237.

Imp, *v.*, impt, imping, I. 31/412 ; II. 247/57, 321, Son. 4.

Imp, *sb.*, I. 122/12, 254/360; II. 29, st. 72, 40, Son. 20. See Nares *s.v.* for various examples and illustrations—curious to trace its odd changes of meaning on to its diabolic one.

Impaire, *v. int.* = to become worse, I. 165/101, 242/198.

Impal'd = paled in, enclosed, I. 103/520.

Impatiency, II. 189/359.

Impawn'd, II. 134/1239.

Impeach, *v.* = hinder, I. 25/710; II. 314/66

Impeach, *sb.* = challenge or hindrance, II. 62/853, 203/169, 292/110. Spenser, F. Q. I. viii. 34.

Impeachment = hindrance, I. 30/379; II. 163/284.

Impearle, *v.*, impearl'd, I. 50/1117; II. 39, Son. 18.

Imperiall maids = The Fates, I. 38/1277.

Imperible = imperishable? II. 91/761.

Impertinent, I. 134/267; II. 162/184.

Impested, II. 287/50.

Impested = infected as with a pest, II. 287/50. In Cotgrave this: Empes*tré* Empestered; but under Empesté-er only other English synonyms; but a verb in *im-* could readily be made in those days. Richardson quotes from Pitt (Epistles, Imitation of Spenser):—

'So may . . . . . No bitter dole *impest* the passing gale.'

Impetrate, *v.* = impute, I. 227/151.

Implicit Creed, II. 211/241.

Imploy, *v.*, II. 6, st. 59, 57/259, 131/797, 177/34.

Imployments, II. 197/135.

Impoisoning, *adj.*, II. 18, st. 4.

Importing, *adj.* = suitable, II. 180/412.

Importunates, I. 173/1088.

Impostume, impostumes, I. 75/375, 117/40; II. 165/426.

Impoysoned, *v.*, I. 232/643.

Impoysoning, *sb.*, I. 254/357.

Impregned, *v.*, II. 239/2.

Impugne, *v.*, impugn, I. 243/361; II. 92/816.

Impures, II. 219, st. 70.

Inables, *v.*, I. 203/607.

Inameld, I. 100/79.

Inammeld (imammeld), I. 74/199, 117/332, 233/761.

Inamoured on, I. 58/738.

Inbarkt, II. 278/176.

Inbow'd, *v.*, II. 163/203.

Incamped, I. 125/384.

Incapable, I. 20/162.

Incarnadine = make red, I. 66/609. See Macbeth, ii. 2.

Incarnate, II. 192/95.

In-cast, I. 159/625.

Incensed, *v.* = enraged, II. 125/158.

Incestious, I. 44/520, 46/691, 128/734.

Incestiously, I. 176/1447, 223/1211.

Inchace, *v.*, I. 144/703, 226/29.

Inchain'd, I. 107/61.

Inchanting, inchaunting, I. 232/691; II. 16, st. 46.

Inclines, *v.* = bends, I. 34/819.

47

Incomb'rance, II. 63/941.

Incomprehensible, I. 19/57.

Incontinent, I. 86/378, 123/168, 150/525, etc.

Incorporing, II. 254, st. 16.

Incounter, *sb.*, II. 130/746, 288/88.

Incounter, *v.*, incountring, I. 151/574, 249/241, 7, 187/191, 199/337.

Incoup, *v.*, I. 246/665.

Incrasion, II. 271/454.

Increments, II. 113/976.

Incroach, *v.*, I. 199/124.

Incubus, I. 118/406.

Incumbers, *sb.*, I. 27/55, 132/28; II. 134/1141, etc.

Incumbred, *v.*, II. 334, Ep. VI.

Indecencies = defects, I. 137/567.

Indent, *v.*, indented, I. 41/126, 137/544, 250/1053; II. 89/481.

Indents, *v.* indents a saw = makes indentations, I. 127/524.

Indentings, *sb.*, I. 226/59.

Indian (Tobacco), II. 267/19.

Indifferent, I. 86/367; II. 131/805.

Indighted, II. 334, Ep. VII.

Indignitie, I. 6, col. 2, l. 1.

Individuall, *adj.*, II. 360, st. 4.

Individuum—the human race, remains though the individuals comprising it are continually changing, its individuality fluctuates but the *genus* endures, I. 68/843.

Indow, I. 112/598.

Induce, *v.* = to lead, I. 35/878.

Indu'd, *v.*, II. 56, col. 1, l. 10.

Indures, *v.*, indurs't, I. 104/619, 217/472; II. 58/373, etc.

Induring, *v.*, I. 135/388, 165/72.

Infamize, *v.*, I. 137/577.

Infãmous, I. 67/763.

Infamousest = most infamous, 'the lowest of the people, I. 207/1082.

Infanterie, II. 184/428.

Infidell, *sb.* = unbeliever, I. 247/853.

Infinite, finite, I. 37/1109.

Inflam'd, *v.* = set on fire, II. 133/1067.

Influent, I. 72/29.

Influing, II. 171/451.

Infold, II. 24, st. 9.

Inforc't, *v.*, inforced, I. 110/371, 149/439; II. 64/987.

Infract, II, 17, st. 23, 57/206.

Infranchised, II. 16, st. 8.

Ingage, *v.*, II. 200/518.

Ingeniously, II. 250/411.

Ingines, *sb.*, ingine, II. 149/268, 278/111.

Ingle, II. 267/18.

Ingrain, *v.*, I. 128/695.

Ingrate, I. 152/825, 184/7, 185/103.

Ingratefull, I. 35/915, 74/250, 75/343, etc.

Ingratefullnesse, II. 334, Ep. VI.

Ingrately, I. 80/954, 125/289, 137/569.

Ingrave, *v.* = to inscribe, I. 194/1113, 249/1076.

Ingraven, I. 115/135 ; II. 120/1772.
Ingross, v., ingross'd, I. 5, col. 1, l. 20, 194/1184 ; II. 283/3.
Ingulf, v., I. 181/315.
Inhance, I. 142/489.
Initiate, II. 216, st. 1.
Injoy'd, II. 177/33.
Ink-like, I. 189/552.
Inkling, sb., I. 252/96.
Inky, I. 62/87.
Inlarge, v., II. 116/1245.
In large, II. 85/12.
In the large, II. 85/54.
Inlighten, I. 23/531.
In little, II. 85/12, 43.
Inly, I. 150/556 ; II. 56, col. 1, ll. 37, 48.
Inns, v., I. 199/150.
Inns, sb., innes, I. 201/369 ; II. 205/364, 213/486.
Innammel'd, I. 151/710.
Innoble, v., innobling, I. 214/162 ; II. 90/625.
Innovate, I. 193/1057.
In-one-Christ-baptised, II. 42, Son. 36.
In-reflecting, adj., II. 90/645.
Inrowld, v., inrould, II. 7, st. 86 ; 16, st. 5.
Insensible, adj., II. 86/161.
Insensibles, sb., II. 271/470.
Insepariz'd, II. 218, st. 43.
In-side (in-side = abilities), II. 231/133.
In-sight, sb. = inspection, II. 115/1187.
In-sin-newation (a pun), II. 278/130.
Insisted, v. = stood firm, I. 187/301.
Insnar'd, I. 63/299.
Insoul'd, I. 46/661.
Inspired, v. = breathed, I. 109/291.
Inspirited, v., II. 244/584.
Instant = present, II. 148/111.
Institute, v. = to instruct, I. 86/307.
Insulted on, II. 157/94.
Intangles, v., I. 25/667.
Intemperate (intemperate zones), I. 44/502.
Intemperous = intemperate, violent, I. 126/269.
Intend, v. = to endeavour, to act—not merely as with us to 'mean.' See Davies's Bibl. Engl. I. 25/736 ; II. 98/193.
Intensive, II. 271/515.
Inter-blend, I. 59/774.
Interess'd, II. 125/185.
Inter-gerning = to mutually growl at each other— 'gern' = grin, 'grin like a dog.' I. 259/938.
Inter-sect, v., I. 157/356.
Inter-justling, sb., I. 22/359.
Inter-medling, sb., I. 43, col. 2, margin.
Inter-mingle, I. 37/1202.
Internex, v., II. 130/725.
Inter-wound, I. 205/823.
Intestine, I. 36/1032.
Inthrall'd, II. 291/21.
In-throniz'd, I. 139/104.
Intice, v., I. 29/278 ; II. 191/64.

Intime-most, II. 158/260.
In-train'd, I. 201/379.
Intrap, v., intrapped, II. 230/28, 262/82.
Intreat, sb., intreats, I. 139/96, 171/851 ; II. 308, st. 12.
Inure, II. 267/81.
Inventions, I. 13, col. 1, l. 11, Ep.
Invict, v., II. 240/151.
Inviron'd, II. 62/781.
Invocate, I. 202/407.
Involuble, II. 86/161.
Inwards, sb., II. 88/433.
In-yoated, yoat = to pour, II. 158/271. " His [Selden's] grave was . . . walled about two feet high with grey marble coarsely polished, each piece being yoated (that is, fastened with lead melted in) with iron champ." (Wood, Ath. Ox. s.n.)
Irefull, I. 49/1093, 62/151, 81/109, etc.
Irks, v., irketh, I. 245/616 ; II. 65/1160, 98/115.
Iron-footed, I. 166/277.
Iron-hard, I. 49/1045.
Iron-hearted, II. 214/557.
Ir-religion, I. 231/639.
Irrigation, II. 271/503.
Isacian, I. 201/306, 202/498.
Ishean, sb., I. 240/15.
Island = Iceland, I. 79/871.
Issue-blest, I. 150/539.
Italian Judge = Pontius Pilate, I. 23/451.
Italian Priest = Pope—as Indian Pluto refers to Spain, I. 122/54.
Iterate, v. = to repeat, I. 127/544.
Izland Tress, II. 270/376.

J

Jacks, sb., armour, I. 173/1014.
Jacks, sb. = jackets, II. 198/297.
Jacks, sb., contemptuous epithet, II. 342, col. 2, l. 14.
Jack of both sides, II. 274/805.
Jacob's-staffe, an astronomical instrument, called like-wise a cross-staffe. See Nares, s.v. I. 156/238.
Jacquet, I. 123/148.
Jades, sb., I. 35/893, 252/76, 259/893.
Jakes, sb., I. 118/465.
Jakes-farmers, II. 269/267.
Jakes-like, I. 224/1251.
Jambe, sb. (in architecture), I. 236/1123.
Jangle, v., I. 140/217.
Jangling, adj., I. 140/202.
Jangling, sb., I. 174/1152.
Jar, v., I. 261/26.
Jarre, sb., II. 154/751, 261/2, 263/201.
Jasper-stones, I. 230/441.
Jaundize, I. 118/454.
Jaunts, v., I. 126/466.
Jealous-phrenzy-sick, I. 167/306.
Jeering, adj., II. 32, st. 106.
Jemmes, I. 93, col. 1, l. 4.

Jennet, I. 64/349, 126/416 ; II. 250/371.
Jerkin, I. 171/794.
Jerks, *v.*, I. 252/76.
Jessean, II. 4, st. 17.
Jesu-criticall, I. 268/164.
Jet, *v.*, jetting, I. 121/768, 151/648 ; II. 210/205, etc.
Jet-like, I. 222/1078.
Jetty, *adj.* = black as jet, I. 125/399 ; II. 194/363.
Jew-gentiles, I. 253/257.
Jig, *sb.*, jigg, I. 42/256, 157/361 ; II. 210/205, 306, col. 2, l. 1.
Jocund, I. 110/313.
Joint-losing, I. 41/166.
Joint-proceed, I. 208/1146.
Jot, *sb.*, II. 154/751.
Joule, I. 126/410.
Joust, *v.*, jousting, I. 166/285, 259/941 ; II. 39, Son. 15.
Joustling, *v.*, I. 32/534.
Jousts, *sb.*, I. 139/65, 150/553.
Joynt-distinct, II. 316, col. 2, l. 20.
Joy-rapt, II. 180/362.
Judaize, *v. int.*, I. 148/378.
Judge-skin (chair), II. 234/447.
Judge-turned-father, I. 114/23.
July-flower, I. 164/18.
Jumble, *v.*, I. 116/271.
Jumps, *v.*, II. 168/150.
Jumping together, I. 240/50—more commonly 'jump' alone, as in Twelfth Night, v. i. or in the common saying 'great wits *jump*,' where the persons without concert make the same remark at the same time.
Junkets, I. 191/818.
Jury = Judea, I. 246/704, 253/250 ; II. 178/118.
Jury-land, I. 231/611.
Just-duked, I. 199/1.
Just-gentle, I. 122/24, 133/94.
Just-just, I. 188/440.
Just-kindled, I. 135/350.
Justing, I. 23/515.
Justles, *v.*, I. 126/466.

K

KAISAR, II. 216, st. 14.
Kaking, *v.* = note of a crow, I. 175/1276.
Karos, I. 117/356.
Keel, *sb.* = a vessel, II. 291/56.
Keen-cold, I. 33/698.
Keen-piercing, II. 56, col. 1, l. 24.
Keep, *v.*, to take, keep, II. 114/1106.
Keep, *v.*, to remain, II. 182/126.
Kend, *v.*, kennest, II. 107/288, 156/19, 158/251, etc.
Kesar, II. 346, IV. l. 34.
Key-cold, II. 179/212.
Kiff nor kin, I. 138/37.
Kil-men = kiln-men, I. 139/164.
Kind, *sb.*, kinde, I. 84/103, 102/391, 112/572, etc.
Kinde-blinde = born blind, blind by nature, I. 259/923.

Kinde-cruell, I. 72/48, 157/387, 176/1385.
Kindled-coldness, I. 232/681.
Kindly, *adj.*, I. 149/515.
Kine, *sb.*, I. 102/351.
King-correcting, II. 250/385.
King-favour'd, II. 128/543.
King-god, II. 200/437.
King-killers, II. 123, col. 2.
King-killing, I. 251/4.
King-maiming, I. 209/1262.
King-upholding, II. 68/134.
Kingdoms it, *v.*, II. 45, col. 2, l. 24.
Kinged, *v.*, II. 217, st. 31.
Kingling, I. 125/381, 192/981, 207/1078, etc.
Kings'-evill, evils, I. 118/486, 254/297.
Kings-bench, I. 93, col. 2, l. 19.
Kinreds-tree, I. 150/543.
Kisse-cloud, *adj.*, I. 186/234.
Kit = a fiddle, I. 109/218.
Kit will after kinde, II. 100/342.
Kitchinists, II. 270/427.
Kix, *sb.*, I. 124/270,
Kixey, *adj.*, I. 254/396. See Nares *s.v.* 'Kex.'
Knobbed, *adj.*, II. 247/42.
Knobby, *adj.*, I. 124/251.
Knot, *sb.*, a company, II. 288/155.
Knotty, I. 204/727.
Knowledge, *v.*, II. 109/442, 352, st. 27.
Knurry, *adj.*, I. 53/103. 'Now I am like the knurrie-bulked oak.'—Drayton's Shep. Garland.
Kons, *v.*, I. 230/447.
Krickets, II. 309, st. 31.

L

LABOUR-LESSE, II. 89/459.
Labour-loathing, II. 298, st. 9.
Laboursom, I. 83/41.
Laced, *v.*, lac't, lacing, I. 49/1020, 84/81 ; II. 234/471, 300, st. 32.
Lack, *sb.*, I. 112/559.
Lackey, *sb.*, I. 341, col. 2, l. 22.
Lad-age = youth, I. 165/170.
Lade, *v.* = to load, II. 60/556.
Lady-cow (contemptuous), I. 215/274.

> 'A pair of buskins they did bring
> of the cow-ladie's currall wing.'—Herrick

See my edn. *s.v.* Glossarial Index.
Lady-misterisse, II. 110/640.
Lamb-lyn'd (lamb-lyn'd buskins) = wool of lamb, I. 58/706.
Lambling, I. 28/181.
Lampfull, I. 136/500, 149/424.
Lanar, I. 67/720. See our Introduction for separate list of birds, etc., that occur in Sylvester.
Lanching, *v.* = launching, I. 179/67.
Land-bred, I. 53/160.
Land-less, I. 194/1197.
Lands-men, I. 121/806.

Langa, a bird, I. 68/790.

Lanthorn, I. 81/1003, 102/297, 109/211.

Lardar, I. 151/740.

Lardeth, v., larded, I. 171/805 ; II. 126/217.

Large = wide, I. 136/410.

Largess = gift, charity, II. 211/232, 212/406.

Lash-out, v., I. 199/141.

Laske, v. = to suffer from diarrhœa (flux), or a substantive *frequenter*, I. 119/529.

Last-past, I. 241/127.

Latonian, I. 57/538, 61/12.

Latton, *adj.*, latton is an alloyed metal, I. 261/1143.

Lauds, *sb.*, I. 104/613.

Launce, v., II. 172/179.

Launch, v., II. 185/512.

Launches, *sb.* = lances, II. 110/597.

Laureat, *sb.* I. 9, col. 2, l. 1, 55/401 ; II. 337, col. 2, l. 13.

Laurel-chang'd, II. 314/32.

Lauriz'd, v., II. 321, Son. 3.

Laver, *sb.*, II. 109/444.

Laveth, v., I. 149/470.

Law-learn'd, I. 237/1308.

Law-loving, I. 149/424.

Lawfull-loved, I. 261/1143.

Lawn, *sb.*, I. 89/667.

Laxative, *adj.*, I. 120/646.

Laxe, *adj.*, II. 272/626.

Lay, *adj.* = fallow (lea), I. 86/392.

Layd'st about thee, II. 39, Son. 16, 105/66.

Lay'st along, I. 191/20.

Lazy-pait, I. 73/106.

Lazying, II. 240/90.

Leach, *sb.* = physician, I. 121/754, 209/1226, 257/690, etc.

Leach-man, I. 55/401.

Leachers, I. 158/482.

Leaden-heeld, II. 89/534.

Leaf (tobacco), II. 274/81.

Leaguer, leaguers, = camp or cordon of the besieging cloud, I. 33/700 ; II. 247/5, 249/250.

Lean-fac't, I. 56/470.

Leap (leap-year), II. 86/192.

Leareth, v., I. 70/1012.

Leashes, *sb.*, I. 62/140.

Leasings, *sb.*, I. 137/568.

Leasure, II. 85/46.

Leaver = rudder, I. 156/233.

Leav'n = levin, lightning—' the flashing leavin (Spenser's F. Q., v. vi. 40), I. 194/1223.

Leavy, *adj.*, leavie, I. 104/522, 124/218.

Lee, *sb.* = lea, I. 42/240.

Lee, *sb.* = shelter, II. 91/736.

Leek, *sb.*, I. 44/575.

Leek—somewhat obscure. Does he mean ' leaue sorrow (the leek like the onion causing tears), the sins of the fathers being visited on the children ?' or does this French proverb given by Cotgrave at all explain it : *Bourse liée avec feuilles de porreaux*—A purse that is ready, or easy, to be opened ? or query

= something worthless. Cf. trash = money—' not worth a leek,' etc. I. 44/515.

Leese, v. = to lose, I. 28/167, 101/195, 179/131, 207/1029.

Legats, *sb.*, I. 173/1092, 186/294, 249/1055, etc.

Leman, I. 149/425.

Lemman-sauce (play on word) II. 271/484.

Len = to lend, I. 143/532.

Length, v., I. 37/1122.

Leperize, v. *tr.*, II. 18, st. 7.

Lepry, *sb.*, leprie, I. 119/557 ; II. 267/7.

Lesbian-squire, I. 236/1117.

Less-Ex, I. 69/968.

Lesse-Asia = Asia Minor, I. 158/490.

Lestrigon, lestrigons—ancient inhabitants of Sicily, and reputed very fierce cannibals ; Ovid, Metam. xiv. 233 ; I. 75/388, 261/1150 ; II. 179/337.

Let, *sb.* = hindrance, I. 50/1170, 128/712, 140/196.

Let, v. = to hinder, I. 142/433, 227/100 ; II. 63/895, etc.

Let, v., to be let blood, I. 160/693.

Letanies, II. 348, Title.

Letharge, I. 169/616.

Lethargie, a disease, I. 117/356.

Lethargie, *sb.*, lethargy, a metal, I. 48/903, 116/188.

Letter-lesse, II. 32, st. 97.

Level Sice, I. 251/45.

Levell, *sb.*, I. 164/55.

Lew, *sb.* = the part or side sheltered of the wind, I. 58/656. Halliwell and Wright, *s.v.*

Lewd, *adj.* = ignorant, I. 194/1213, 256/565 ; II. 40, Son. 23, etc.

Lewdly-lavish, I. 114/33.

Lezards, I. 188/450, 200/282.

Libbet, II. 204/255.

Liege, *sb.*, I. 103/460.

Lievtenancie, I. 203/593.

Life-lengthened, I. 251/10.

Lift, v. = lifted, I. 85/233.

Light, v. = lit, I. 42/246.

Light-brain'd, I. 89/703.

Light-bringer, I. 55/401.

Light-crediting, *sb.*, I. 31, st. 94.

Light-foot, I. 73/119, 75/310 ; II. 149/205, 307, st. 6, etc.

Light-full, I. 200/199 ; II. 148/91, 211/275, 164/339.

Light-less, I. 59/779 ; II. 217, st. 25.

Light-winged, I. 258/760.

Lightning, II. 50, col. 2, l. 5.

Light-some, I. 36/1048, 53/139, 55/411, 234/888.

Lightsomness, I. 23/508.

Ligne = line, lineage, II. 178/159, 182/88, 195/483.

Like, v. = to please, II. 67/14.

Like, v., to like well of, II. 56, col. 1, l. 15.

Likely, *adj.* = similar, I. 37/1160.

Likely-hood, II. 179/241.

Like-wisely, I. 157/327.

Lill, v., I. 63/228.

Lillied, II. 194/372.

Lillie-white, lilly-white, I. 81/1052 ; II. 309, st. 41.

Lilly, *adj.*, I. 31/415 ; II. 325, Son. 22.

Lilly-paved, lillie-paved, I. 104/531 ; II. 308, st. 22.
Limbeck, I. 41/136, 103/438.
Limbeckt, *adj.*, II. 269/233.
Limber, *adj.*, I. 63/233, 144/711, 166/207.
Limb-numming, I. 115/173.
Limbo, II. 263/15.
Lim'd, *v.*, lime = bird-lime, I. 144/711.
Lime, *sb.* = bird-lime, II. 56, col. 1, l. 51.
Lime-burners, I. 270/426.
Lime-twigs, I. 232/704.
Limne, *v.*, limns, I. 9, col. 2, l. 6, 11, col. 2, l. 16, 34/ 77, 40/32.
Limner, *sb.*, II. 85/42.
Limon, I. 103/521.
Lin, *v.*, I. 171/868 ; II. 100/456.
Linage, *sb.* = lineage, I. 80/976.
Line, *sb.* = lineage, posterity, I. 111/514, 112/601.
Lineats, *v.*, II. 223, st. 8.
Linger, *v. tr.*, lingring, I. 101/234 ; II. 189/348.
Linots = linnets, I. 234/970. See Special Lists for notes of birds, etc., that occur in Sylvester.
Lin-stock, II. 266, col. 2, Son. l. 14.
Linzie-woolzie-wise, I. 226/32.
Liquor-god = Bacchus, I. 55/396.
Liquorish, II. 273/719.
List, *v.*, listeth, I. 43/374, 89/682, 111/501 ; II. 196/20.
List, *v.* = to listen, I. 223/1151.
List, *sb.* = inclination, II. 341, col. 1, l. 7.
Lists, *sb.* = bounds, list, I. 43/407, 142/509, 164/13, 150/ 627, etc.
Little-beaten way, I. 243/337.
Little-ease, *sb.* = pillory or stocks, but see Nares *s.v.*, II. 114/1068.
Little-world, I. 21/305, 37/1197, 57/576, 72/8, etc.
Live-less, I. 82/1115, 88/586, 114/59, etc.
Lively, *adj.* = living, I. 22/336, 45/642, 78/754, 79/879, etc.
Lively, *adv.*, I. 65/431.
Lively-breathing, II. 58/332.
Lively-flaming, I. 126/411.
Lively-light, I. 235/1049.
Live-ning, *adj.*, I. 149/410.
Living-dumb, I. 160/717.
Living-dying, I. 233/757.
Livings, *sb.*, I. 62/183.
Loaden, *v.*, I. 119/606.
Load-star, starre, I. 205/800 ; II. 243/447, 287/19, 294, col. 1, l. 6, etc.
Load-stone, I. 40/10, 48/946, 980, 50/1175, 63/200, 165/138.
Load-stone-like, II. 22/14.
Load-stone-touched, I. 48/965.
Lob, *sb.*, II. 332, col. 2, l. 16.
Lob-like, I. 169/589.
Lobstarize, *v.* = to go backwards, I. 203/621.
Lock, *sb.* (Time's-lock), II. 314/69.
Lofty-brave, I. 234/881.
Lofty-staring, I. 120/684.
Lome, *sb.* = earth, I. 206/880.

Long (of long), II. 248/105.
Long-breath'd, I. 184/19.
Long-broad, I. 27/58.
Long-Home, II. 85/33.
Long-long, I. 5, col. 2, l. 29 ; II. 28, st. 61, 235/626.
Long-long-lived, I. 152/858.
Long-long wished, II. 124/2.
Long-seeming, I. 221/950.
Long-streaming, I. 35/881.
Long-tail'd, I. 229/395.
Longst = along, I. 149/478.
Loom-beam, I. 214/88.
Looms, *v.*, I. 83/55 ; II. 248/180.
Loose, *v.*, I. 48/980.
Lord Paramount, I. 103/460.
Lordlings, II. 190/456.
Loud-crackling, I. 200/252.
Loud-roaring, I. 33/733.
Loud-rowling, I. 230/465.
Loud-proud, I. 166/281.
Loud-thundring, I. 80/905.
Lout, II. 233, col. 2, l. 6.
Louver = pigeon-house, I. 171/182.
Love-betraying, I. 178/34.
Love-blind, I. 69/989.
Love-bred, II. 92/837.
Love-burning, I. 29/203.
Love-darting, I. 205/849.
Love-full, I. 149/505.
Lovely, *adj.* = loving, I. 233/786.
Loving-silence, *adj.*, I. 157/403.
Lowd-buzzing, II. 127/435.
Low-rooft, I. 123/90.
Lowly-loud, I. 192/960.
Lown, *sb.*, II. 216, st. 14.
Lowt, *sb.*, II. 180/406.
Lowting, *v.*, II. 118/1480.
Lozenge-wise, I. 41/94.
Lubber, *sb.*, II. 298, st. 9.
Lud, II. 308, st. 25.
Luffe, *v.*, II. 186/68.
Lug, *v.*, lugs, I. 119/592 ; II. 177/86.
Luke-warm, I. 112/643.
Lummond-lake = lomond, I. 222/1046.
Lun, name of dog, I. 201/386.
Lung-lesse, I. 220/760.
Lupercals = feast in honour of Pan observed at Rome, I. 86/416. Two naked youths ran striking with special whips those whom they passed. Women believed that a blow from the whip was efficacious in barrenness. Cf. Julius Cæsar, I. 1, III. 2.
Lurch (living at lurch), II. 360, st. 13.
Lure, *sb.*, II. 56, col. 2, l. 1.
Lusks, *v.* = idle, be indolent, I. 58/714, 84/115.
Lust, *sb.* = pleasure, II. 60/560.
Lust-burning, I. 81/1108.
Lust-full, I. 204/714, 223/1212.
Lust-greedy, I. 121/786.
Lust-less, I. 104/583, 118/481.

Moons, *sb.* = crescents, I. 35/876.
Moon-wort, I. 47/763, 6, 235/1006.
Mooned-standards, II. 42, Son. 38.
Moony, *adj.* = crescent-shaped, I. 31/467.
More = root or stump, still in use in Hampshire.
Mores, *sb.*, I. 46/676.
Morisko, I. 234/873.
Morning-sted = place of the morning or sun-rise? II. 115/1176. See Davies's Bible Engl. (p. 135) :—

'And pale Cynthia with her borrowed light
Beginning to supply her brother's place
Was past the noon-stead.' (Sackville, Induction, st. 7.)

Mornly, *adv.* = in the morning, I. 141/327.
Morrell, *sb.*, morell, a plant, I. 112/591, 115/170.
Mortalizing, *v.*, I. 99/18.
Most-humour-poys'ning, II. 135/1302.
Most-most, I. 63/190 ; II. 41, Son. 31, 172/542.
Mot, *sb.*, I. 158/506.
Mote, *sb.* = a trifle, I. 45/537.
Motes, *sb.*, I. 19/44, 33/649.
Moted, *v.* = moated, I. 184/42.
Motly, *adj.*, I. 24/585, 141/309.
Motleys, *v.*, I. 100/89.
Mother-citie, II. 180/386.
Mother-voyce, I. 144/682.
Mought, *v.*, I. 54/282, 177/1468, 260/1051, etc.
Moule, *sb.* = mole, I. 206/882.
Mould, *sb.*, I. 205/852.
Moulten, I. 41/84.
Mound, *v.*, I. 140/257.
Moundlesse, I. 27/59.
Mounsieur, I. 122/40.
Mount, *v. tr.* = to raise up, to elevate, I. 86/409 ; II. 93/947, 152/577, 158/298.
Mountain-siler, I. 119/621.
Mountibanks, II. 88/416.
Moveless, I. 134/180 ; II. 113/901.
Mow, *sb.*, I. 174/1171, 171/494 ; II. 150/402.
Moyls, *sb.*, I. 260/1088.
Moystfull, I. 136/481.
Much-fold, I. 193/1051.
Much-much-labour, I. 89/707.
Much-much-less, I. 53/83.
Much-much-more, I. 54/196.
Muck, *sb.*, I. 246/701.
Muddled, *v.*, I. 11, col. 2, l. 28.
Mud-mixt, I. 124/222.
Mues, *v.*, II. 136/1372.
Muffled, *v.*, I. 120/661.
Muffles-up, *v.*, I. 248/922.
Mufflers, I. 57/542, 112/576.
Mug-work, I. 255/423.
Mum, II. 312, st. 79, 324, Son. 14.
Mumbling, *adj.*, I. 219/733.
Mummerie, II. 45, col. 1. l. 23.
Mummy, I. 151/689, 249/1049.
Mundane, I. 156/279.
Mur'd, *v.*, II. 130/773.

Murdred, *sb.*, I. 205/843.
Murdrer, *sb.*, I. 205/843.
Murrain, I. 119/542, 610.
Murrions = morions, II. 199/387.
Musaick, *adj.*, I. 222/1091.
Musaicks, *sb.*, I. 227/60.
Muse-friending, II. 321, Son. 3.
Musefull, I. 9, col. 2, l. 3 ; II. 106/185.
Muse-work, II. 322, st. 6.
Musket-shot, II, 65/1077.
Muskie, *adj.* = perfumed, II. 194/373.
Muskie-rosed, II. 50, Son. 1.
Must, *sb.* = wine, I. 28/109, 137/618, 236/1138.
Must-mouth, I. 157/404.
Mustachios, mustachoes, I. 47/811, 167/352. Florio (1598) has mustacho and Cotgrave mustachoe and —oes, and the Italian original is mostacchio. 'Dally with my mustachio' (Love's Labour Lost, v. i.). We speak of bearded grain.
Muster-roule, I. 203/625.
Mutil'd, *v.*, II. 300, st. 32.
Mutiner, mutiners, I. 24/625, 194/1209.
Mutining, *sb.*, II. 241/139.
Muttons = sheep, I. 124/190.
Myching, *adj.*, II. 18, st. 5.
Myrabolan, I. 246/696.
Mystick-wise, II. 254, st. 18.

N

NACRE, *sb.*, I. 64/372.
Nacre, *adj.*, I. 199/117.
Nacre, I. 64/572, 199/117, 190/699. Cotgrave under Nacre has 'A Naker ; a great and long shell-fish, the outside of whose shell is rugged, and brown of colour ; the inside smooth, and of a shining hue ; the form (broad at the one end, and narrow at the other) somewhat like a smith's bellows ; (it is but seldome, or never found on our coast).' Under *Nacre de perles*, 'Mother of Pearle ; the beautifull shell of another fish, wherein the best, and most pearles be found.' While Sylvester speaks of the oyster as the pearl-fish, he would seem to use *nacre* as we would use mother-of-pearl for the oyster or any shell with a similar pearly hue inside.
Nacre-shels, I. 190/699.
Namely, *adv.* = specially, notably, II. 267/18.
Napell (a plant), I. 116/179.
Nappy ale, II. 273/749.
Nard, *sb.*, I. 229/353, 249/1049, 258/821.
Narrow-streamed, I. 42/217.
Naso (our new Naso), I. 99/50.
Nastie-most, II. 303/157.
Natitial, *sb.*, II. 239/39.
Nature-grac'd, II. 105/73.
Nature-drowning, I. 101/197.
Nature-shaking, I. 219/674.
Nature-taught, I. 43/378.
Natur'd-ill, I. 251/8.

47

O

Oase, I. 125/367, 249/1003.
Oazie, II. 177/51.
Obdur'd, *v.*, II. 113/997.
Obscænity, II. 273/712.
Odiousness, II. 189/431.
Ods (by ods), II. 57/284, 58/404.
Oeconomick, *adj.*, I. 236/1200.
Oeconomie, II. 352/4.
Oedems, a disease, I. 118/486.
Oe'r-fly, I. 137/556.
Oe'r-topping, II. 67/3.
Oe'r-reached, I. 115/77.
Off-chopt, II. 218, st. 41.
Off-cutting, II. 130/779.
Off-scums, I. 187/328.
Off-shaken, II. 156/76.
Offenc't, *v.*, II. 205/345.
Oft-quickned, *adj.*, I. 195/1235.
Often-breathed = often-pursued and so made ' often ' to
  'breathe' hardly, I. 102/331.
Often-while, I. 202/457.
Old-old-age, II. 181/47.
Old-wives-tales, II. 6, st. 74.
One-Eternall-Three, I. 34/851.
One-eyd Champion = Hannibal, I. 150/574.
One-Trine, I. 127/611, 128/733.
One-while, I. 118/444, 451.
Onely-being, I. 113/652.
Onely-Trine (onely not = only, but one-ly = Trine in
  one?), I. 237/1224 ; II. 85/53, 317, col. 2, l. 10.
Opal-colour'd, I. 140/210.
Opal-like, I. 136/495.
Ophir-gold, II. 191/40.
Oppone, *v.*, I. 245/522.
Oppugn, *v.*, I. 243/360.
Opthalmy, I. 117/374.
Or, heraldic, I. 69/973, 235/1036.
Oracler, I. 79/823.
Order-lesse, I. 157/354.
Ordinance = ordnance, II. 18, st. 3.
Ordinance = discipline, II. 199/333.
Ordinary, *sb.*, II. 273/708.
Ordure, I. 25/71.
Orenge, I. 45/569.
Orient, I. 66/609, 77/594, 136/493, 164/57, etc.
Orient-pearly, II. 50, col. 2, l. 5.
Original, *sb.*, I. 79/851, 237/1329 ; II. 185/474, etc.
Originary, II. 224, st. 32.
Orion, qy. should be Ocean? I. 105/714.
Orizons = horizons, I. 136/489.
Ork, I. 62/109. See Nares *s.v.* for a full note.
Orpiment, I. 116/188.
Orpine, I. 48/903.
Orque, I. 117/292, 169/602.
Orthodoxall, II. 316, col. 3, l. 25.
Osiars, *sb.*, osier, I. 64/316, 125/294, 214/89.
Ostlers, II. 269/267.
Ostridge, II. 171/498.
Other-some, som = some other—Sylvester affects such

reverse-forms. I. 20/142, 162/120, 93, col. 1, l. 27,
  etc.
Other-where, I. 259/954 ; II. 86/137.
Otious, *adj.* = leisurely, easy, II. 197/121.
Ouches, I. 189/622.
Ought, *v.*, II. 86/197, 126/248, 177/54, etc.
Ouglinesse, II. 216, st. 3.
Ougly, I. 219/730 ; II. 182/175, etc.
Out alas ! I. 110/350.
Out-brave, II. 197/162.
Out-fly, II. 190/444.
Out-goe, out-goes, I. 166/275 ; II. 232/280.
Out-lashing, II. 200/536.
Out-shrills, I. 184/20.
Out-swifts, *v.*, II. 299, st. 25.
Out-swifted, *v.*, I. 171/855.
Out-swim, II. 110/595.
Out-wear, I. 11, col. 1, l. 25.
Out-went, I. 171/855.
Outly, I. 28/167.
Ovals, II. 130/768. Query—(1) Is *ovals* a misprint for
  orats, and this used for oration, a triumph for a
  bloodless victory? or (2) Is it a misprint for *olives*
  which he speaks of again, l. 880? or (3) As it re-
  occurs elsewhere, is it = a medal?
Over-baked, II. 171/468.
Over-balanceth, I. 241/117.
Overbearer, II. 225, st. 40.
Over-borne, I. 256/600.
Over-burthen, *sb.*, II. 171/440.
Over-cast, I. 249/1045.
Over-climbs, I. 149/496.
Over-cooled, I. 106/756.
Over-counts, II. 58/350.
Over-creeds, *v. int.*, II. 42, Son. 36.
Over-dainty, I. 227/173.
Over-daring, II. 38, Son. 12.
Over-deep, I. 102/404.
Over-drinesse, I. 30/396.
Over-drinking, II. 273/762.
Over-drunk, I. 137/541.
Over-dull, *v.*, I. 228/192.
Over-fitted, I. 233/867.
Over-full, II. 202/35.
Over-give, I. 47/804.
Over-gliding, I. 121/761,
Over-grow, I. 147/262.
Over-jumps, I. 258/798.
Over-lay, II. 58/326.
Over-pass, passe, I. 56/474, 236/1164.
Over-peers, *v.*, I. 139/69.
Over-plac't, II. 316, col. 1, l. 8.
Over-plus, *sb.*, II. 86/189.
Over-prest, I. 236/1145.
Over-racked, I. 102/293.
Over-read, I. 49/1000.
Over-run, I. 164/48.
Over-seer of Will, II. 288/185.
Over-shone, II. 162/176.

Over-skips, II. 310, st. 48.
Over-slip, over-slipt, II. 38, Son. 12, 211/227.
Over-sloap, I. 258/843.
Over-soar, I. 88/623.
Over-sow'n, II. 125/125.
Over-swaies, II. 85/26.
Over-thinks, II. 168/147.
Over-thwart, I. 66/538, 104/536, 140/287, etc.
Over-thwarts, v., I. 235/1051.
Over-topt, over-topped, I. 165/106 ; II. 316, col. 1, l. 17.
Over-waid, II. 165/484.
Over-warming, I. 117/352.
Over-weigh, I. 74/299.
Over-whelve, II. 268/128.
Over-whurld, I. 49/1094.
Ow, owe, v. = to own, I. 40/3, 243/286 ; II. 59/413, etc.
Owl-fac't, adj., II. 270/376.
Owl-like, II. 114/1063.
Owlie, adj., I. 112/535.
Owne-grown, I. 50/1148.
Owres, sb. = oars, I. 54/251, 61/68, 65/430, 447, etc.
Oxigon = a triangle having three acute angles, I. 156/199.
Ox-teem, I. 204/711.
Oyl, v. (to oyl the Jawes), I. 93, col. 2, l. 22.
Oyl, v. (oyles the fire), II. 197/120.
Oyled, adj. = anointed, I. 194/1170, 243/345 ; II. 178/161.
Oynt, v. = to anoint, I. 194/1214.
Oysterers, II. 269/267.
Oziar, I. 58/694.

P

PACE, v., I. 69/933.
Pack, v., pachs, I. 145/49 ; II. 185/440, 191/39, 226, st. 62, 314/17.
Packt, v., sent away, II. 161/17.
Packt, v. (marriage neither stolen nor packt) = arranged or continued (in an evil sense) as we speak of packing a jury, II. 193/209. See Nares s.v.
Pact, sb., I. 219/716, 247/762, 838 ; II. 178/175, etc.
Pactolian, I. 228/275 ; II. 262/98.
Pain, sb., paine = labour, I. 145/16 ; II. 24, st. 17, 57/230, 213/468.
Paine, sb. (a paine of wall)—query = a square of wall, I. 206/876. 'The knyght shewed me a pane of the wall, and said, Sir, you see yonder parte of the wall which is newer than all the remnant.' (Berners' Froissart, vol. ii., c. 22.) Nares quotes from a 'Journey through England' (1724), thus :—' And one wall particularly I observ'd of a churchyard, which took up the whole length of a street, built of pains of this stone about a foot square, look very particular and handsome.'
Painfull, I. 73/133, 86/306, 102/310.
Pain-lesse, I. 24/590, 83/62, 102/340, 169/630 ; II. 87/313. etc.
Pain-pleasing, I. 232/688.
Paisants, II. 127/422.

Palace-mice, I. 253/197.
Paladines, II. 129/596, 130/690.
Pale-fac't, I. 244/429.
Pale-green, I. 195/1303.
Pales, sb., II. 310, st. 50.
Palfraies (of the Sun), I. 219/696.
Palfreys, II. 117/1433.
Pall, sb., I. 110/330.
Pallet, sb., I. 24/581, 53/146 ; II. 203/155.
Palmfull, II. 147/66.
Palsie-shaken, I. 43/330.
Palsie-sick, II. 18, st. 11.
Palted = pelted, I. 215/263.
Pampelon, I. 7, col. 1, l. 22.
Pamprednesse, II. 113/1002.
Panaretus, II. 236/752, 277/56-57 336, col. 2, l. 40.
Panch, I. 67/730 ; II. 89/492.
Panchaian, I. 38/1297.
Pandar, I. 108/85.
Pandects, I. 21/209.
Pandora-like, II. 135/1349.
Panegyres, sb., II. 104, Son. 1, l. 4.
Panik, adj., II. 249/262.
Pantofles, I. 151/701.
Paper-tables, I. 69/908.
Paragon, I. 94, col. 2, l. 21 ; II. 92/896, 308, st. 23, etc.
Paralitique, II. 93/952.
Parallel, v., II. 136/1462, 336, col. 2, l. 8.
Paramour (in good sense), Fr. par, L. per, and amour ; Norman paraimer, to love affectionately—a lover or wooer—a mistress : now a loose liver, I. 115/82.

'A lovely bevy of fair ladies sate
Courted of many a jolly Paramoure.'   (F. Q. II. ix. 34.)

Even as late as Smollett—at end of Humphrey Clinker—we read of ' my aunt and her paramour,' where ' paramour ' is simply = bridegroom. Milton designates the sun as Nature's 'lusty paramour' (Ode on Nativity). The bad sense is as old as Chaucer's Canterbury Tales, 6954.
Para-nimphs, I. 167/351.
Parboild, adj., II. 342, col. 1, l. 40.
Parbreak, v., I. 116/253 ; II. 5, st. 35.
Parcas, I. 117/361.
Parcelliz'd, I. 208/1154.
Parent-tribute, I. 41/172.
Parget, sb. = plaster-work, I. 236/1162. So Spenser, (Visions of Bellay, 23) :—

'Golde was the parget ; and the seeling bright
Did shine all scaly with great plates of gold.'

Park, sb. = Paradise, I. 113/647.
Parley, sb., I. 110/334.
Parley, v., I. 48/963 ; II. 331, col. 1, l. 5.
Paricidiall, parricidiall, I. 121/797, 218/532 ; II. 239/66, 257/436.
Parlour, sb., met = the head, i.e. the best room, II. 271/440. There may be allusion also to the parlour

being the room for conversation—as the name implies—so the head or brain is that whence this
originates.

Partializing, *adj.*, II. 42, Son. 36.

Participates, *v. tr.* = apportions, I. 172/914 ; II. 28,
st. 54.

Partie = person, I. 185/115.

Partition, II. 299, st. 22.

Partlet, I. 151/701.

Part-sympathize, I. 76/517.

Pase, *v.* = to pace, I. 73/111.

Pase, *sb.* = pace, I. 76/416.

Pash, *v.*, pashes, pasht, I. 117/311, 156/226, 171/835,
188/489, 190/665, 206,876, 255/480 ; II. 62/744,
165/508, etc.

Pasports, *sb.*, I. 128/700.

Passados, I. 171/768.

Passant, *adj.*, II. 171/472.

Passe, *v.*, passing = to excell, I. 236/1165, 249/1066 ; II.
61/698, 91/725, etc.

Passe-lamb, I. 189/583.

Passe-man, *adj.* = superhuman, I. 237/1254.

Passing-keen, I. 188/503.

Passing lamely, II. 67/18.

Passing-pleasant, I. 246/680.

Passing-pleasing, I. 170/681.

Passing-poore, II. 61/691.

Passing-price, II. 39, Son. 18.

Passing-strange, I. 68/803.

Passion, *sb.* = intent, I. 216/336.

Passion-stirred, I. 230/510.

Passion-toss'd, I. 207/1070.

Passionates, *v.*, I. 99/50.

Past-humane, II, 135/1257.

Pastors, *sb.*, I. 89/696.

Past-port *sb.*, I. 95/27.

Pat (to come so pat), II. 107/233.

> ' Pat he comes like the catastrophe of the old comedie.'
> (Lear, i. 2.)

> ' Now I might do it pat while he is praying.'
> (Hamlet, III. 3.)

Patagon, I. 186/211.

Patch, *sb.*, II. 332, Ep. II. col. 1, l. 25.

Pate, *sb.*, II. 178/109.

Paten, I. 142/517.

Pavane, *sb.*, a dance, I. 235/1048.

Peace-loving, I. 58/719.

Peace-plant, *adj.*, I. 195/1314.

Peacock-like, I. 124/179.

Peal, *sb.*, II. 266, col. 2, Son. l. 3.

Pearled, *adj.*, I. 43/300, 149/427.

Pearled, *v.*, I. 135/373.

Pearl-golden, II. 197/187.

Pearl-muscles, II. 311, st. 57.

Pearl-shell, II. 194/380.

Pearl-shell helmets = finger nails, II. 50, col. 2, l. 20.
See our Memorial Introduction on this.

Pearly, I. 137/601, 138/20, 176/1374.

Pearly-purled, I. 243/401.

Pears, *v.* = appears, I. 112/586.

Peart, *adj.*, II. 42, Son. 35.

Peason, II. 309, st. 30.

Pedestall, I. 49/1027.

Pedestall (on his conduct's pedestall), I. 227/93.

Peece, *sb.*, I. 232/642.

Peece-meal (by peece-meal), I. 143/528.

Peeping, *adj.* (cry of bird), II. 185/456.

Peer, *sb.* = pier, I. 99/27, 260/1002 ; II. 337, col. 1,
l. 2.

Peer, *v.* = to match with, II. 224, st. 32.

Peize, *v.*, peiz, II. 90/641, 187/182.

Peizelesse, *adj.* = light, without weight, I. 248/978.

Pelfe, *sb.*, pelf, II. 255, st. 36, 273/690.

Pel-mel, I. 139/106, 167/327, 171/849, 224/1269 ; II. 188/
203, 271/485.

Pelusian foord, I. 186/227.

Pend, *v.* = pent, confined, I. 164/14 ; II. 170/412.

Pen-man, men, I. 55/416 ; II. 349, st. 12.

Penny-less, *sb.*, I. 93, col. 2, l. 19.

Penny-worth, II. 211/223.

Pension, I. 77/585.

Pensiveness, I. 93, col. 2, l. 23.

Pent, *v.* = enclosed, confined, I. 37/1126.

Pent-house, I. 77/562.

Peonie, I. 46/712.

People-state = democracy, I. 208/1200.

Percers, *sb.*, I. 61/67.

Perduz, *sb.*, II. 199/327.

Perewigs, *sb.*, periwig, and see Perriwig, I. 37/1145,
58/704 ; II. 210/206.

Perfect-less, I. 84/133.

Peril-lesse, II. 87/313.

Peril-proof, I. 179/75.

Peripneumony, I. 117/400.

Perish, *v. tr.* = to destroy, I. 33/750.

Perjure, *sb.*, I. 237/1236.

Perking, *v.*, II. 40, Son. 21.

Pern, *v.*, I. 254/293.

Perpend, *v.*, perpending, II. 99/301, 114/1110.

Perriwig, *v.*, I. 124/187.

Perséver, *v.*, I. 83/3, 208/1188, 242/197, etc.

Persian fruit = produce, *i.e.*, opium from the poppy,
much of which then came from Persia, II. 135/1303.

Persian state, II. 123, col.1.

Perusine = Peruvian—' The American, the Perusine, and
the very canniball do sing and also say their highest
and holiest matters in certaine riming versicles.'
(Puttenham's Arte of Eng. Poesie, bk. i. c. 5). II.
272/599.

Pest-full, I. 243/401.

Pestiferous, I. 116/217.

Pest'lence (a pest'lence, great good), II. 268/114.

Petti-foggers, I. 49/1084.

Pettrall, I. 206/906.

Phalariks, *sb.*, I. 259/964.

Phansies, I. 196/1415.

Phantasmas, I. 148/339.

Pompous. Glanville (Pre-existence of Souls, c. 14) eulogises the 'copious and pompous eloquence of Henry More.'

Poop (blows not in the poop), I. 221/898.

Poor-daiery-renter, I. 50/1156.

Pope-powder'd, I. 209/1304.

Pope-prompted, I. 209/1234.

Popinjayes, I. 208/1181.

Po-poysoned, *adj.* = (I suppose) Italian, from the Po, and so papal, I. 138/44.

Poppy, *sb.* = narcotic, I. 63/248.

Porie, *adj.* = porous, I. 246/673.

Pork-porking = cry of raven, I. 242/285.

Port, *sb.* = bearing, I. 45/555, 79/866, 102/297, 110/410, etc.

Port, *sb.* = gate, I. 55/411, 86/317, 125/375, etc.

Portall, *sb.* (Zeno's Portall), I. 159/582.

Portly, I. 126/469.

Portly-stronting, I. 69/891.

Portugals, *sb.*, I. 64/385.

Port-vein, I. 68/717.

Posted, *v.* = hastened, II. 193/210.

Post-hume, I. 69/953.

Post-humes, I. 93, col. 1. l. 14.

Posthumiall, I. 7, col. 1, l. 11.

Post-like = swiftly-passing, II. 62/758.

Pothecaries, I. 151/675.

Pother, II. 247/71.

Poudred, *v.* = sprinkled, I. 55/376.

Poudred, *adj.*, ' in level of our poudred Pen ' = charged with gun-powder, II. 266, col. 2, Son., l. 4.

Pouldrons, pouldros, Fr. épaule, armour for the shoulder : ' réfulgent pouldrons ' (Sandys, Ovid, Met. bk. III.) I. 167/384.

Poule, *sb.* = poll, head, I. 76/427 ; II. 203/163.

Poule, *v.*, II. 162/130.

Poulpy, *adj.* = pulpy, I. 47/860.

Poulse, *sb.*, I. 33/644.

Pounc'd, I. 50/1143.

Pourtraid, *v.*, II. 5, st. 41.

Pout, *v.*, II. 232, col. 2, l. 6.

Povrisht, I. 100/156.

Powder-plots, II. 237/805.

Powder-traitor, traitors, II. 123, col. 2, 254, st. 15.

Powder-treason, II. 268/187.

Powder-wit, II. 211/297.

Powl'd, *v.*, powle = polled, I. 102/345, 139/159, 141/309, 223/1155.

Poyzing, *v.*, I. 26/797.

Poysonie, *adj.*, poysony, I. 46/709, 49/1072, 74/284, 218/584, etc.

Practive, II. 63/947.

Præoccupate, I. 6, col. 2, l. 24.

Præsage, *sb.*, II. 135/1350.

Praise-full, I. 136/520, 143/638 ; II. 60/548.

Praise-winning, II. 63/947.

Prance, *v.*, prancest, I. 59/833, 88/536 ; II. 86/212.

Prank, *v.*, pranck, prankt, I. 37/1141, 56/446, 58/664, 674, 142/488, etc.

Prank, *sb.*, II. 154/822.

Prate, *v.*, I. 140/226.

Prater, *sb.*, I. 259/893.

Pratling, *sb.*, II. 19, st. 32.

Prattle, *v.*, I. 141/328.

Prattling, *adj.*, I. 230/453, 238/1399.

Prattling, *sb.*, I. 230/500.

Preasse, *v.*, I. 234/983.

Preasse, *sb.*, I. 234/983.

Pre-appointed, II. 38, Son. 9.

Pre-aver = to prophesy, I. 26/778.

Precinct, *sb.*, I. 87/510.

Precise, I. 254/294 ; II. 254, st. 24.

Pre-contract, II. 193/210.

Predomining, I. 28/104.

Prefer, *v.* = to display, I. 15, col. 1, l. 11.

Prefer, *v.* = to place before, I. 15, col. 1, l. 23.

Prefer, *v.* = to promote, II. 38, Son. 10.

Prefixtly, I. 189/561.

Prejudicate, *adj.*, II. 250/313.

Prentice-Princedome, I. 138/55.

Prentice-ship, II. 120/1793.

Prentiship, I. 186/232 ; II. 28, st. 63.

Pre-ordinance, I. 186/209.

Prepostrously, I. 34/822.

Presaged, II. 138/1625.

Presagefull, I. 185/179 ; II. 248/182.

Pre-scæne, I. 81/1072.

Prescript, *sb.*, I. 255/492.

Presently = now, II. 65/1167.

Presidents, *sb.* = precedents, I. 61/9, 86/357, 88/586 ; II. 230/11, etc.

Prest = ready, I. 57/628, 63/219, 67/727, 185/200, etc.

Prest, *v.* = induced, II. 122, col. 2, l. 16.

Prester-Jans = Prester-Johns. See Nares *s.v.* II. 136/1389.

Prevent, *v.*, preventing, I. 35/932, 85/208, 190/673, 191/809, etc.

Preventing, *adj.*, I. 176/1431.

Prevention, II. 91/784.

Prickets, II. 307, st. 6.

Prime-church, I. 87/421.

Prime-rose, II. 288/153.

Primes, *sb.* = Spring, I. 66/605.

Primer, *adj.*, I. 40/55, 101/270, 111/527, 145/20, 235/989.

Primer Mater, II. 211/280.

Primero-rest, I. 121/778.

Primordiall, II. 240/160.

Prince-Catholiks, I. 254/294.

Prince-dish Pheasant, II. 309, st. 37.

Prince-fit, I. 213/12 ; II. 192/197.

Prince-grac't, I. 78/655.

Prince-humour-pleaser, I. 56/418.

Prince-loyal, II. 42, Son. 34.

Prince-protestants, I. 254/294.

Prince-proud, I. 115/161.

Prince-treachers, II. 42, Son. 34.

Prince-worthy, II. 122, col. 1, l. 12.

Princeling, II. 124/4.

Princely-loyal, I. 209/1268.

Principals, *sb.* = originals, I. 158/441.
Princox, I. 254/395.
Prison'd, *v.*, I. 261/1104.
Prisoned, *adj.*, I. 118/462.
Prisonment, II. 57/209, 269, 64/1063.
Pristin, *adj.*, I. 105/725.
Privation, II. 91/741.
Privie-banding, II. 304/218.
Privie-dyet, I. 188/453.
Privie-groom, II. 104, Son. 2, l. 13.
Probablest, I. 231/576.
Probation = proof, I. 44/422.
Prodige-all (Sir Prodige-all), II. 226, st. 71.
Prodigious, I. 34/819, 35/880, 115/149.
Produce, *v.* = to extend, II. 135/1351.
Proems, II. 110/604.
Prognosticall, *sb.*, II. 115/1180.
Proin'd, *v.* = pruned, I. 112/588, 137/533, 208/1117.
Promise-full, I. 139/96.
Prone, *adj.*, I. 94, col. 2, l. 20.
Prooves, *v.*, II. 30, st. 81.
Propheticalls, *sb.*, II. 294, col. 2, l. 19.
Prophetize, *v.*, I. 245/563.
Prophetizing, *adj.*, I. 129/785.
Prophet-wise, I. 222/1052.
Prop-less, I. 84/94 ; II. 87/265, 287.
Propriety, II. 86/175.
Protean, II. 226, st. 71.
Proto-Bartas, I. 96, col. 2, Son., l. 4.
Proto-martyr, I. 158/494 ; II. 17, st. 28.
Protrack, *v.*, II. 185/439.
Proudeth, *v.*, prouds, I. 224/1303 ; II. 240/117.
Proudling, *sb.*, II. 240/152.
Proud-trampling, I. 58/678.
Proudly-brave, I. 252/157.
Proudly-rude, I. 256/596.
Prowesse, prowess, I. 152/822, 172/918, 215/213 ; II. 178/109, 184/340.
Prowes, prow's, I. 117/389 ; II. 244/553.
Prows-full, I. 138/3, 258/839.
Proxie, II. 293/178.
Proyning, *v.*, and see 'Proin,' II. 243/517.
Prysing, II. 40, Son. 24.
Psalmograph, I. 128/669 ; II. 16, st. 10.
Psylly, a plant, I. 116/176.
Pudder, *v.*, I. 62/172.
Puddle, *sb.*, II. 111/728, 225, st. 42, 288//114.
Puddle-water, II. 114/1076.
Pudding-packs (of tobacco), II. 274/781.
Puddly, *adj.*, I. 164/56 ; II. 182/173.
Pudefitan, I. 104/624.
Puff, *sb.*, puffs, I. 78/706.
Puffe, *v.*, puft, pufft, I. 50/1143, 229/336, 256/613 ; II. 170/371, 136/1376, etc.
Puff'd, *adj.*, I. 35/949.
Puffing, *adj.*, I. 147/174 ; II. 130/707, 267/29.
Puffing, *sb.*, II. 210/206.
Puf-snuffing, *sb.*, II. 273/742.
Puisne, *adj.*, II. 292/78.

Puisnes, *sb.*, II. 164/383.
Puling, *v.*, I. 119/529.
Pullein, *sb.* = poultry, I. 115/94.
Pulse-beating, *sb.*, I. 118/413.
Pulveriz'd, *v.*, I. 194/1142.
Pumy-stone, I. 115/153.
Pun, *v.* = to pound? I. 47/826.
Punctual, II. 254, st. 24.
Punks, II. 269/268.
Puntilios, II. 125/227.
Pupill = infant, II. 162/127.
Pupillage, I. 14, col. 1, l. 21, 36/1042 ; II. 12, st. 26, 91/686, 231/95.
Purchase-profanation, II. 97/46.
Pure-whitest, II. 300, st. 34.
Purfled, *v.*, I. 104/552,—ornamented with trimmings, flowers or embroidery. See Nares *s.v.*
Purge-humours, *adj.*, I. 249/1053.
Puritan, I. 174/1202.
Puritanisme, II. 141, col. 1. l. 25.
Purld, *v.*, purleth, I. 41/81, 72/31, 192/880.
Purl'd, *adj.*, purled, I. 35/949 ; II. 213/519. See Nares *s.v.* for interesting notes.
Purling, *adj.*, I. 166/254.
Purls, *sb.* (dress), II. 210/193.
Purse-leaches, I. 49/1085.
Pursie, *adj.*, II. 244/549.
Pursuivants, pursuivan, I. 26/831, 101/250.
Pushes, *sb.* I. 117/398.
Puttock, I. 115/94 ; II. 185/455.
Py'd, *v.*, II. 186/7.
Py'd-mantled, II. 18, st. 13.
Pyed, *adj.*, I. 83/46.
Pyn'd, *v.*, I. 96, col. 1, l. 11.
Pyning, *adj.*, II. 189/307.
Pyramid, II. 310, st. 44.
Pyramid-wise, I. 214/81.
Pyrausta, I. 82/1121.
Pyrés = Pyrenees, II. 322, Son. 7.

Q

Quadran, I. 124/206.
Quadrat, *adj.*, II. 26, st. 39.
Quail, *v. tr.*, quail'd, I. 221/892 ; II. 13, st. 44, 38, Son. 8, etc.
Quail, *v. int.*, quail, II. 185/446, 187/168.
Quantiti'd, *v.*, I. 174/1115.
Quar, quarr, *sb.* = quarry. Sylvester also uses the word as applied to stone = quarry, and speaks of quar-men. I. 176/1408, 236/1149, 1157 ; II. 89/513, etc. So Jonson,

> ' The very agate
> Of state and policy, cut from the *quar*
> Of Machiavel.' (Magnetic Lady, i. 1.)

Quar, *sb.* = quarry, prey—or qu. a fish so named? I. 189/643.
Quar-man, I. 236/1110.

Quash, *v.*, quasht, II. 203/111, 241/258, 287/77.
Quavers, *v.*, I. 159/579, 160/733, 170/683.
Quaver-skild, I. 220/841.
Queans, *sb.*, I. 230/481, 5 ; II. 342, col. 2, l. 8.
Queasie, II. 122, col. 2, l. 2.
Queen-Kings, II. 178/141.
Queint, I. 21/221, 232/684 ; II. 127/347.
Queintly, I. 232/734.
Quel-pride, *sb.*, I. 140/249.
Quern-like, I. 77/595.
Questionist, II. 270/320.
Quests, *sb.*, I. 137/92.
Quick, I. 31/514, 109/260, 141/346, 171/846, etc.
Quick, to press to the quick, I. 110/392.
Quick-nos'd, I. 227/132.
Quick-silver, I. 234/965.
Quick-trembling, I. 77/564.
Quick-thick, I. 232/728.
Quick-whirled, I. 170/733.
Quickly-rowling, I. 126/411.
Quiddle-quirk, II. 128/510.
Quiddits, *sb.*, II. 217, st. 17.
Quills, *sb.* = stalks of corn, I. 73/114.
Quils, *sb.* = narrow tubes or passages? I. 133/154.
Quincy = quinzy, I. 117/383, 119/611.
Quint-essence, *sb.*, I. 36/1020, 78/753 ; II. 6, st. 61, 85/43.
Quint-essence, *v.*, I. 103/441, 154/18, 237/1217 ; II. 4, st. 15.
Quipt, *v.*, I. 19/5.
Quirks, *sb.*, II. 217, st. 17.
Quirry, *sb.* = Equery, I. 85/302.
Quit (to cry quit), II. 317, col. 1, l. 23.
Quit (to declare quit), II. 115/1163, 152/634.
Quites, *v.*, I. 68/814.
Quittance, *v.*, quittanceth, I. 195/1268, 253/239.
Quittance (to cry quittance), II. 13, st. 42.
Quoist, *sb.*, a bird, I. 67/713.
Quote, *v.*, I. 160/683.

R

RABBIES, I. 205/794.
Rabican, I. 57/613.
Race, *v.*, I. 197/1445.
Rackers, II. 141, col. 2, l. 13
Rackets, *sb.*, I. 203/527.
Racqueted, *v.*, II. 248/132.
Radicall (radicall humour), II. 271/526.
Rage-blinded, I. 168/413.
Ragefull, I. 81/1020, 168/493, 179/95, 219/669, etc.
Ragingly, II. 261/70.
Rail, *sb.*, article of dress, I. 151/700.
Rain, *sb.* = rein, II. 106/174, 132/959, etc.
Rain-lesse, I. 189/528.
Rake, *v.* (let him rake Hell), I. 214/126.
Rake, *v.* (rake their poor Brethren), II. 180/60.
Raking, *adj.*, II. 211/219.
Ramp, *v.*, ramping, rampeth = romp in a bad sense, I. 33/706, 75/412 ; II. 162/118. See Davies's Bible

English (p. 242). 'Yonder is your punk of Turn-bull, *ramping* Alice has fallen upon the poor gentle-woman within, and pulled her hood over her ears, and her hair through it.' (Jonson's Bart. Fair, IV. 4.)
Ramping, *adj.*, I. 75/353, 79/878.
Ramping, *sb.*, I. 235/1031.
Rampire, *sb.*, rampiers, I. 125/371, 200/234, 248/959 ; II. 180/393, etc.
Rampire, *v.*, rampired, II. 187/144, 266, col. 2, Son. l. 11.
Rampir'd, *adj.*, II. 184/364.
Rampyr'd, *v.*, II. 98/149.
Rams, *v.*, I. 168/413.
Rams, *sb.* = battering rams, I. 200/191, 261/1127 ; II. 180/391, 183/387, etc.
Rance, *sb.*, I. 223/1110 ; II. 9/15. Nares, *s.v.*, states this to be peculiar to Sylvester ; but he is mistaken. It occurs frequently as = a kind of marble. Du Bartas' word is '*marbre.*'

> 'The spark-engendring flint
> Shall sooner melt, and hardest *rance* shall first
> Dissolve, and quench thy thirst.'
> (Quarles, Emblem II., x. 12.)

Randon, I. 72/58, 146/139 ; II. 60/560.
Rangle, *v.*, I. 63/261.
Rankly-rude, II. 177/47.
Rape, *sb.*, I. 70/1005, 103/434, 245/626, 246/651.
Rapid-rowling, I. 219/653.
Raps, *v.*, II. 38, Son. 12, 217, st. 19.
Rapt, *v.*, rapting, rapts, I. 46/663, 52/12, 103/430, 115/115, 158/459, etc.
Rapt, *sb.*, II. 211/317.
Rapted, *adj.*, I. 161/775 ; II. 185/458, 247/17.
Rapting, *adj.*, I. 81/1017, 161/775, 223/1110, 233/856, etc.
Rapt up, II. 7, st. 84.
Rare, *adj.* = excellent, I. 42/244, 69/943.
Rare, *adj.* = rarefied, I. 33/671.
Rare, *adj.* = seldom, I. 85/300.
Rare-builder, II. 19, st. 32.
Rare-precious, I. 5, col. 2, l. 24.
Rare-rich, I. 140/248 ; II. 87/261, 199/432.
Rare-richly, I. 260/1075 ; II. 176, Son., l. 6.
Rare-skilfull, I. 78/674.
Rarely, *adv.* = excellently, I. 81/1042, 161/774, 179/146 ; II. 182/96.
Rarely-od, II. 296, st. 29.
Rarely-sweet, I. 222/1041, 233/857.
Rarely-wise, I. 206/964.
Rarest, *adj.*, I. 143/603, 164/43 ; II. 4, st. 33, 7, st. 79, 25, st. 27.
Rarifie, *v.*, II. 272/573.
Rarities, *sb.* = perfections, II. 196/5.
Rascall, *adj.*, II. 184/411.
Rashers, *sb.*, I. 192/899.
Rashlings, II. 65/1161.
Rated, *v.* = estimated, II. 58/351.
Rathe, *adj.*, II. 95/135, 135/1328.
Rather, *adj.* = earlier, II. 50, col. 1, l. 11.

47

Rather = sooner, II. 38, Son. 11.
Rathe-ripe, II. 309, st. 30.
Rats-baned, *adj.*, II. 271/511.
Raught, *v.*, I. 24/619, 32/589, 221/890 ; II. 114/1123, etc.
Raveld, *adj.*, I. 235/1037.
Ravillac, II. 254, st. 15.
Ravishment = rape, II. 191/9.
Ravisht, *v.*, I. 143/632.
Rav'lins, II. 180/393.
Ray, *sb.* = array, I. 242/222 ; II. 167/68.
Razor = sickle, I. 58/685.
Re-advance, *v.*, re-advanceth, I. 128/702, 133/71.
Reak, *v.*, reake, I. 219/642, 230/452, 254/351 ; II. 100/410, etc.
Reanes, *sb.*, reans = reins, I. 165/125, 181/396, 217/430, 240/40, etc.
Reaning, *v.*, I. 126/460.
Reason-less, II. 179/255.
Reason-scanners, I. 48/970.
Reave, *v.*, I. 24/644, 29/202, 108/105, 111/517, etc.
Reav'n, *v.*, I. 185/161.
Rebate, I. 235/990.
Rebecks, I. 127/566.
Re-behold, I. 191/808.
Re-bemires, I. 258/786.
Re-blest, I. 149/505.
Re-blew'st = to make blue again, I. 122/13.
Re-blooms, I. 195/1236.
Re-bought, II. 211/288.
Re-boyl = to ferment, I. 137/618.
Re-breeding, I. 247/788.
Re-bring-back, I. 219/667.
Re-buds, I. 195/1226 ; II. 155/888.
Re-chanting, *adj.*, I. 122/31.
Re-chast, *v.*, II. 199/358.
Re-cheer, II. 161/63, 194/392.
Re-childing, I. 231/526.
Re-cleers, *v.*, re-cleering, I. 188/469, 170/752, 188/469, 222/1100 ; II. 22, st. 87.
Re-comfort, recomforteth, II. 161/62, 354, st. 3.
Re-conjoyning, I. 190/722.
Re-courst, *v.*, I. 188/432.
Re-crush, II. 153/668.
Receits, *sb.*, II. 67/52, 179/254.
Recipes, I. 86/326.
Reck, *v.*, II. 134/1206.
Reclus'd, I. 157/400.
Recollect, *v.* = to re-collect, collect again, I. 86/402.
Recoyl, *v.*, I. 62/157, 137/581, 619, 171/802 ; II. 7, st. 79, etc.

'Ye both forewearied be ; therefore a while
  I read you rest, and to your bowres recoyle.'
    (Spenser, F. Q., I. x. 17.)

Recure, *v.*, II. 58/309.
Re-darkned, I. 23/522.
Re-descend, I. 36/1071.
Re-dissolves, II. 24, st. 17.

Red-herrings, I. 199/899 ; II. 270/429, 271/501.
Red-gums, I. 119/531.
Red letters, I. 23/424.
Red-sprats, II. 270/429.
Red-white, II. 310, st. 45.
Red-yellow, I. 252/101.
Reducing, *v.* = to bring back, II. 186/2.
Re-espous'd, *v.*, II. 292/80.
Re-entoyl, *v.*, I. 220/777.
Reed, *v.*, II. 115/1230.
Reed-crowned, *adj.*, II. 231/181.
Reed-like, I. 167/358.
Re-fand, II. 107/308.
Re-fled, I. 160/672.
Re-flour'n = flowered again, I. 258/793.
Re-flowred, *v. tr.*, re-flowers, I. 133/66, 233/805 ; II. 179/277, 236/743.
Re-forge, II. 193/242.
Re-forme, II. 316, col. 2, l. 6.
Re-found, I. 195/1260.
Refell'd, *v.*, refels, I. 132/7, 178/5 ; II. 93/970, 236/716.
Reft, *v.*, I. 134/267 ; II. 158/240.
Reflect, *v.*, to reflect on, I. 31/494.
Re-gilt, *v.*, II. 156/63.
Re-glas'd, *v.*, II. 156/63.
Re-glost, *v.*, II. 156/63.
Re-greens, *v.*, I. 133/66.
Regals, *sb.* (musical instrument), I. 160/737.
Regiment, I. 28/95, 118/446, 228/187, 240/15.
Re-haleth, II. 232/193.
Re-hardened, *v.*, I. 188/472.
Rehartned, II. 188/218, 232/193, 304/222.
Re-hope, II. 152/632.
Re-incenst, II. 106/132.
Re-inspire, I. 180/188.
Re-issue, *v.*, II. 284/124.
Rein-searching, II. 210/91.
Rein-sounding, I. 125/304.
Re-jerk, *v.*, I. 203/527.
Re-knit, *v.*, I. 220/774.
Re-lick, II. 291/36.
Re-lifts, II. 203/95.
Re-live, *v. tr.* = bring to life again, II. 18, st. 12.
Re-madest, II. 93/936.
Re-making, *v.*, II. 267/8.
Re-mild, *v.*, II. 241/288.
Remedilesse, II. 362, col. 2, l. 25.
Remembrings, *sb.*, II. 204/239.
Remises, *v.*, I. 28/164.
Remnant, I. 102/349.
Remora, I. 65/432.

'All sodainly there clove unto her keele
  A little fish that men called Remora
  Which stopt her course, and held her by the heele
  That winde nor tide could move her thence away.'
    (Spenser's World's Vanitie, IX.)

'Like remoras
  Hanging upon her keel to stay her flight.'
    (Massinger's Renegado, II. 8.)

'What mighty and invisible remora is this in matrimony, able to demur and to contemn all the divorcive engines in heaven or earth?'
(Milton's Divorce, bk. i. c. 8.)

Remorse, I. 46/747, 65/530, 196/1439.
Remorselesse, I. 133/128 ; II. 108/310.
Remunerate, I. 64/368 ; II. 67/44.
Re-named, II. 156/64.
Rendered, *v.* = given up, II. 130/772.
Rendez-vous, I. 27/57, 41/173 ; II. 127/407, 273/674.
Renegate, *sb.*, I. 111/424.
Reneg'd, *v.*, II. 247/33.
Renown'd, *v.*, II. 230/13.
Rent, *v. int.*, renting, I. 22/394, 33/734, 115/107 ; II. 151/476.
Re-offred, II. 295, col. 1, l. 34.
Re-peiz'd, II. 187/182.
Re-percussion, I. 187/402.
Re-perriwig'd, I. 258/815.
Re-pilgrimage, I. 95, col. 2, l. 6.
Re-plac't, II. 184/324.
Re-plants, I. 147/234.
Re-possest, II. 292/90.
Re-prise, II. 56, col. 2, ll. 14, 17
Re-profan'd, II. 179/254.
Re-promise, II. 157/175.
Re-purg'd, II. 184/324.
Re-purple, II. 247/28.
Re-puts-on, II. 113/907.
Repeale, *v.* = to call back, Fr. *rappeler*, I. 101/252, 245/598 ; II. 288/165.
Repell'd, *v.*, I. 215/263.
Repine, *v. tr.*, II. 33, st. 117.
Replunged, II. 292/92.
Repolishing, I. 148/318.
Reprinteth, I. 157/393.
Reprive, *v.*, repriv'd, I. 182/525 ; II. 93/954, 159/419.
Reprocure, II. 250/317.
Repugne, II. 92/815, 97/92, 99/322.
Re-recording, II. 154/861.
Re-re-delves, I. 137/532.
Re-reduce, II. 167/127.
Re-relapse, II. 42, Son. 35.
Re-repeat, I. 89/746.
Re-romaniz'd, II. 240/163.
Re-salute, I. 65/471, 96, col. 2, l. 26.
Re-see't, II. 220, st. 92.
Re-seize, I. 125/327.
Re-send, II. 317, col. 2, l. 25.
Re-shoot, II. 155/884.
Re-shut, II. 118/1569.
Re-sobering, II. 6, st. 70.
Re-soile, II. 247/29.
Re-spews, I. 168/412.
Re-spins, I. 244/490.
Re-spire, II. 167/53.
Re-stablish, I. 240/30.
Re-suit, *v.* = to re-clothe, II. 183/203.
Re-swils, II. 188/291.

Resolve, II. 310, st. 52.
Respect-lesse, I. 120/712, 251/16.
Respire, II. 211/276.
Resplendencies, II. 131/830.
Restauration, II. 38, Son. 11.
Resting-day = Sabbath, I. 128/678.
Restlesse stars, II. 88/364.
Rest-nest, II. 58/296.
Rest-ordained, I. 43/313.
Resty, I. 187/339.
Re-take, II. 172/548, 182/153.
Re-tild, II. 178/187.
Re-tomb, I. 75/319.
Re-treading, I. 160/740.
Retchless, II. 262/118.
Retire, *v. tr.* = to withdraw, I. 110/341, 133/72, 181/336 ; II. 185/575.
Retiredness, II. 122, col. 1.
Retorting, *v.*, II. 131/873.
Retortions, I. 41/100.
Retrait, *sb.*, I. 123/58, 139/118 ; II. 219, st. 69, 303/189.
Retreat, *v. tr.* = to draw back, I. 41/79.
Retrive, I. 34/792.
Retrograde, *v. tr.*, I. 103/502, 157/391.
Retuneth, *v.*, I. 222/1040.
Re-vary, II. 301, st. 49.
Reverst, *v.* = overturned, II. 86/207, 132/972.
Revert, *v.*, reverted, I. 253/243 ; II. 106/181, 163/283 220, st. 75, etc.
Revest, *v.*, I. 23/440 ; II. 37, Son. 4, 298, st. 8.
Revise, *v.* = to see again, II. 158/305.
Reviser, *sb.*, I. 23/487.
Reviving, *sb.*, II. 6, st. 70.
Revoke, II. 302/45.
Re-whelps, *v.*, I. 75/318.
Re-win, I. 167/339.
Rews, *v.*, rew, I. 66/674, 261/1103 ; II. 92/903.
Rewfull, II. 147/39.
Rex (plays the rex), I. 255/412.
Re-young, *v.*, I. 192/955.
Rheums, *sb.*, I. 252/166 ; II. 271/445.
Rheumy, I. 28/158, 137/602 ; II. 270/414.
Rhinocerot, I. 72/53, 125/295, 136/414, 148/341
Rich-bedight, I. 228/270.
Rich-fraighted, II. 17, st. 35.
Rich-perfumed, I. 253/213.
Richess, I. 69/974.
Richly-divers, I. 141/316.
Richly-grave, I. 236/1198.
Richly-neat, I. 235/1018.
Richly-rare, I. 165/118, 226/9, 252/111.
Rick, *sb.*, I. 236/1147.
Rife, I. 85/300 ; II. 134/1193, 159/368, 184/340.
Rife-full, II. 133/1035.
Right-descerning, *sb.*, II. 31, st. 94.
Right-lesse, I. 199/37 ; II. 166/555, 267/11.
Right-participate, I. 43/397.
Right-reverend, I. 254/307.
Right-wrong, I. 104/563.

Rine, *sb.* = rind, I. 47/857.
Ring-worms, I. 118/488.
Rinse, *v.*, I. 147/199.
Rivaling, *sb.*, I. 227/76.
Riverlings, I. 41/133, 78/755.
Rivers, *sb.* = rivets, part of armour?—and so in early texts. I. 173/1014.
Roabes, *sb.* = robes, I. 61/700.
Roarers, II. 269/216, 273/672.
Roaring Boyes, II. 123, col. 1.
Robe-spinning (worms), I. 123/131.
Rock-battering, I. 184/13.
Rock-faln, I. 104/548.
Rock-razing, I. 257/656.
Rock-rushing, I. 203/623.
Rock-waters, I. 184/9.
Rocky-coomb, II. 199/339.
Rodomont, I. 253/201.
Roguing, I. 190/750 ; II. 267/83.
Romists, *sb.*, II. 211/241.
Rommidged, *v.*, I. 118/422. Properly a sea-term = to pack the hold or roomage of the ship, then to search this. ' Our greedy seamen rummage every hold ' (Dryden's Annus Mir. 208).
Romulides, II. 279/69.
Rose-crowned, I. 143/542.
Rose-mixt, I. 70/1029.
Rosed, *v.*, II. 194/372.
Rosiall—a favourite word with the after-school of Crashaw and compeers, I. 31/442, 229/353 ; II. 49, col. 1, l. 10. ' The *rosial* colour whiche was wonte to be in his visage towrned into salowe' (Sir T. Elyot's Governour, bk. II).
Rosie-blushing, I. 158/449.
Rosie-red, I. 252/159.
Rost, roast, to rule the rost, II. 152/620, 164/379, 291/34.
Rough-blust'ring, I. 193/1003.
Rough-cast, I. 237/1266.
Rough-skin'd, I. 136/412.
Roule, *v.*, rouls = to roll, I. 33/712 ; II. 180/350.
Roules, *sb.* = roll, I. 62/72, 79/837, 256/580 ; II. 178/170.
Roules-arbiter, I. 99/46.
Round, *sb.* = circle, II. 226, st. 60.
Round, *sb.* (to dance the round), I. 233/857.
Round-about, *sb.* = circuit, I. 80/911.
Round-arched, I. 234/887.
Round-blazing, I. 53/130.
Round-bow'd, I. 44/436.
Round-fenc'd, *v.*, I. 138/38.
Round-flat, I. 33/648.
Round-front, I. 67/666.
Round-round-round, I. 33/712.
Round-rumbling, I. 116/264.
Round-winding, I. 77/629, 104/561, 222/1001.
Roundels, roundles, I. 55/328 ; II. 114/1099.
Roundly (roundly go to pot), II. 212/365. See Davies's Bible English for 'go to pot' (p. 53), and for 'roundly' (p. 57).
Rover-shooting, I. 146/118.

Rowels, *sb.*, I. 156/275.
Rowle on, *v.*, I. 116/268.
Rowles, *sb.* = rolls, I. 158/454.
Rowlers, *sb.* = rollers, I. 236/1148.
Rowling, *adj.*, I. 22/387, 41/70.
Row-slave, II. 217, st. 16.
Royalize, I. 227/79.
Rozen, I. 116/259.
Rozen-weeping, I. 259/970.
Rub, *sb.*, rubs, I. 55/395, 255/425.
Rubble, *sb.*, II. 129/621.
Rubites = rubies, I. 235/1016.
Rubrick, *sb.*, I. 194/1118.
Ruck, *v.*, II. 172/535.
Rudder-lesse, I. 185/168.
Rue, *sb.*, I. 255/425.
Rue, *v.*, I. 171/867, 216/307.
Ruff, *sb.*, ruffe, I. 227/64, 235/1018 ; II. 159/332.
Ruff, *sb.* (in their insulting ruff), I. 260/1091.
Ruff, *sb.*, a fish, I. 249/1010.
Ruffin, *sb.*, II. 193/244.
Ruffon, *sb.*, I. 260/1077.
Ruffling, *adj.*, II. 180/350.
Ruinate, *v.*, I. 22/319 ; II. 14, st. 7, 86/101, 198/265.
Ruing, *sb.*, II. 308, st. 12.
Rule-unworthy, I. 57/643.
Rumble, *v.*, rumbles, I. 33/712, 116/271.
Rumining, *v.*, II. 108/421.
Rumor = murmur, I. 244/436.
Runnagate, *sb.*, runagate, I. 75/405, 166/181 ; II. 184/429.
Rush (a rush for all the rest), II. 341, col. 1, l. 10.
Rustred, *v.*, I. 242/186.
Rut, *sb.*, I. 245/624.
Ruth, *sb.*, II. 41, Son. 29, 190/496, 197/151, etc.
Ruthless, I. 88/562, 111/482, etc.
Ryne, *sb.* = rind, I. 101/229.

S

SA, sa, a term in fencing, used as an exclamation indicating readiness to encounter, I. 167/398, 201/395, 242/224.
Sabbaoths, I. 35/940, 155/132.
Sable, *adj.*, II. 193/313.
Sable Bend, II. 189/320.
Sabled, *adj.*, II. 180/352.
Sables, *v.*, II. 336, col. 1, l. 32.
Sacks, *sb.*, wines, I. 151/692, 152/805.
Sack, *sb.* = sack cloth, I. 201/308, 278/162 ; II. 193/316.
Sacre, *v.*, sacring = to consecrate, I. 6, col. 1, l. 2, 66/558, 94, col. 1, l. 26, 99/44 ; II. 132/936, etc. Tyndale says the bishop ' sacreth the oil of confirmation.'
Sacred, *adj.*, II. 38, Son. 12, 262/98.
Sad = heavy? I. 215/227.
Sad = solid, I. 30/555, 44/440 ; II. 87/290. Wiclif (St. Luke vi. 48) translates ' rock '—' a *sad* stone,' *i.e.* set or fixed.

Sad = serious, II. 198/302. 'My father and the gentle-
men are on sad talk' (Wint. Tale, iv. 3) : 'good
sadde studdie' (Ascham's Schoolmaster).
Sad-glad, I. 5, col. 2, l. 19.
Sad-sweet, I. 178/155 ; II. 283/22.
Sad-sweetly-most, I. 94, col, 1, l. 20.
Sad-weeping, II. 188/311.
Safe-guard, *sb.*, II. 25, st. 24.
Safe-guarded, I. 155/103.
Safe-keeping, *v.*, I. 155/70.
Safe-shelter, *v.*, I. 33/728.
Saffran'd, *adj.*, I. 235/1018.
Saffron-colour'd, I. 102/398, 149/427.
Sagapen = a resinous gum—something of the assafœtida
kind, I. 47/786.
Sagbut, I. 77/641, 108/136, 160/713.
Sage-sweet, I. 234/879.
Sa-haw, hunting cry = so-ho? I. 202/410.

> PROT. Run, boy, run, and seek him out.
> LAUNCE. Soho ! soho !
> PROT. What seest thou ?
> LAUNCE. Him we go to find.
> (Two Gent. of Verona, III. 1.)

The word was used when the game was found or
sighted.
Sail-lesse, II. 217, st. 25.
Sainct, *adj.*, II. 292/57.
Saincted, I. 156/292.
Saint-descent, *sb.*, I. 112/595.
Saint-poor, I. 109/245.
Saint-thief, II. 204/209.
Saints-firstling, I. 173/1020.
Saker = a species of hawk, I. 67/721. See Nares *s.v.*
Puttenham (Eng. Poesie, bk. III. c. 19) says that
Queen Elizabeth is as superior to all other princes

> ' As eagles eyes to owlates sight
> As fierce *saker* to coward kite.'

Salamander, I. 82/1116 ; II. 270/428.
Sale-tongued, I. 48/936.
Salique, II. 236/721.
Sallets, II. 202/23.
Sallow-fac't, I. 155/148.
Salmon-like, I. 150/618.
Sal-peetry, I. 246/674.
Salt-blew, I. 148/305.
Salt-mount, I. 48/897.
Salty-blend, I. 248/937.
Salve, *v.*, I. 53/184, 68/835, 851, 101/237.
Salved, *v.* = healed, II. 39, Son. 17, 42, Son. 40, 133/
1094, 316, col. 3, l. 34.
Salve-serpent, I. 238/1386.
Same-kind, II. 87/295.
Sampler, *sb.*, I. 233/769.
Sand-cast, I. 260/1003.
Sanguine, *adj.* = red, I. 28/89, 67/726.
Sans, I. 20/100, 28/98, 84/188, 101/237, etc.
Sant (black sant), I. 116/278.

Sapience, I. 80/986.
Sappy-bloud, I. 258/814.
Sarcell, *sb.*, sarcels = pinion of a hawk's wing, I. 31/412
(misprinted 'farcels '), 67/721, 232/7290. See Nares
s.v.
Sargous—a fish, I. 115/70. See Nares *s.v,*
Sargus=Sargous (which see), I. 63/206. Pliny describes
this as a fish which attends closely on the mullet
when the latter routs up the mud and is ready for
any food that may emerge. Pliny makes no mention
of its adulterous character.
Satan-taming, I. 158/509.
Saturnals, *sb.*, I. 86/417.
Sauced, *v.*, II. 65/1084.
Sawes, *sb.*, I. 236/1201 ; II. 65/1095.
Sawcily, II. 284/104.
Saxonically-French, II. 242/321.
Sayes, *v.* = essays, I. 123/⟨
Scævolize, *v.*, II. 10/20.
Scaine, II. 62/751.
Scala Cæli, II. 68/89.
Scallop = to mark or shape like the edge of a scallop
shell, II. 186/22,

> ' The wooden heel may raise the dancer's bound
> And with the *scalloped* top his step be crowned.'
> (Gay's Trivia, I. 32.)

Scalps, I. 251/39,
Scammony, I. 234/942.
Scant, *sb.*, II. 335, col. 1, l. 29.
Scapheth, *v.*, I. 117/361.
Scar-crows, I. 200/207 ; II. 57/216.
Scar-fac't, I. 146/162.
Scarlet-robe, II. 18, st. 13.
Scarre, *v.*, scarrd, *v.*, I. 125/350, 245/558.
Scathe, *sb.*, I. 247/846.
Scene-servers, I. 254/298.
Sceptred, *v.*, sceptereth, I. 145/7, 179/85.
Sceptre-grac't, I. 204/664.
Sceptre-rods, I. 260/1089.
Scions, *sb.*, scions of plant, I. 134/247, 233/810.
Schismick, *adj.* = schismatic, I. 245/525 ; II. 94/1047.
School-lesse, II. 93/1009.
Schyrrhes, I. 118/486.
Sconce, *sb.*, of paper = a small fort, I. 229/337. 'I
spend too much time to pull down a sconce of sand,'
Hacket's Life of Abp. Williams, II. 166.
Sconces, *sb.*, II. 180/396.
Scopefull, II. 322, Son. 7.
Scourge-Turk, II. 13, st. 41.
Scout, *v.*, II. 3, st. 2.
Scraping, *adj.*, I. 93, col. 2. l. 21.
Screech, *sb.*, I. 204/854.
Screeches, *sb.*, II. 312, st. 81.
Scrieches, II. 195/471.
Scriech-owles, II. 325, Son. 21.
Scritch-owls, II. 200/435.
Scud, *v.*, skudding, I. 36/1082, 116/188, 205/864 ; II.
177/69, 258/92, etc.

Scullions, II. 269/266.
Scums, *sb.*, II. 164/400.
Scummy, I. 32/554, 137/621 ; II. 172/646.
Scuse, *v.* = to excuse, I. 94, col. 2, l. 27, 185/131.
Scyons, *sb.*, and see scions, I. 137/531.
Sea-borne, II. 337, col. 1, l. 3.
Sea-citizens, I. 61/3.
Sea-coales, II. 312, st. 81.
Sea-crabs, II. 278/86.
Sea-drying, I. 201/294.
Sea-gate = sea-ford, I. 115/134. See Davies's Bibl.
    Eng. p. 120.
Sea-gibb'rish, I. 248/929.
Sea-man's-diall, I. 49/986.
Sea-oak, I. 104/598.
Sea-theives, I. 64/340.
Seal-fit, *adj.*, I. 48/907.
Sealskin Jacks—' jack,' properly a coat of mail, II. 198/
    297. ' An helmette and a Jacke or plate coate
    bindeth all partes of a manne sauying the legges.'
    Udal's Erasmus, Apop. p. 308.
Seam-rent, II. 135/1286.
Season-stinter, II. 330, col. 1, l. 34.
Seav'n-fold, I. 43/363.
Seav'n-horn'd, I. 186/321.
Seaze, *v.* = to seize, II. 114/1067.
Secret-burning, I. 120/702.
Secret-spreading, I. 63/264.
Securenesse, I. 35/895.
Security, I. 35/928.
Seed-less, I. 111/479, 129/770.
Seed-man, men, I. 47/833, 209/1282 ; II. 290, last line.
Seed-pair, I. 37/1210.
Seed-remnant, I. 150/559.
Seed-wheat-kernel, I. 115/164.
Seeded, *v.*, II. 59/467.
Seedfull, I. 66/626.
Seedster, I. 159/606.
Seel, *v.*, to ceil = roof, I. 76/440.
Seeled, *v.* = ceiled, I. 104/549 ; II. 129/639.
Seeling, *sb.*, = ceiling, I. 124/211, 165/119, 199/114,
    236/1160.
Seem-beautie, I. 252/134.
Seem-deeds = forged deeds, II. 127/418.
Seem-delight, *sb.*, II. 267/68.
Seem-flee, II. 130/750.
Seem-rights, I. 253/263.
Seem-Samuel, I. 213/5.
Seeming-serpents, I. 188/416.
Seeming-sowr's, II. 62/765.
Seignory, I. 29/286.
Seiz'd of, *v.* = possessed of, I. 231/555 ; II. 60/642.
Seizelesse, I. 148/346.
Seld, I. 58/328 ; II. 67/15.
Selder = seldomes, I. 258/806.
Seldom-times, I. 119/536.
Self-affiance, II. 205/367.
Self-affraid, II. 241/202.
Self-amisse, II. 60/582.

Self-angerless, I. 134/222.
Self-arched, I. 104/537.
Self-arching, I. 100/123.
Self-arrogate, II. 205/350.
Self-aw'd, I. 110/330.
Self-bald, I. 58/703.
Self-beside, I. 203/627.
Self-bindes, II. 303/204.
Self-blinde, I. 189/574.
Self-blinds, II. 303/204.
Self-blamed, I. 258/775.
Self-burning, I. 167/399.
Self-burns, II. 304/286.
Self-cleer, II. 28, st. 53.
Self-commanders, I. 138/16.
Self-conceal'd, I. 121/758.
Self-conceit, *sb.*, I. 94, col. 2, l. 15, 133/166.
Self-consuming, I. 120/666.
Self-content, II. 58/398.
Self-corruption, II. 60/564.
Self-counter-poiz'd, II. 87/266.
Self-cruell, I. 34/866, 121/799.
Self-debates, II. 59/425.
Self-defaces, II. 299, st. 28.
Self-deserving, *sb.*, I. 125/301.
Self-devis'd, I. 241/169.
Self-distrusting, II. 94/1062.
Self-divides, I. 199/2.
Self-doomed, I. 96, col. 2, l. 4, 110/393.
Self-drowns, II. 304/286.
Self-dumb, I. 109/224.
Self-eating, I. 120/670.
Self-entire, II. 243/535.
Self-eternall, I. 146/142.
Self-eternitie, I. 237/1327.
Self-examples, I. 138/17.
Self-father, II. 61/682.
Self-flation, II. 228, st. 98.
Self-furnish, I. 75/332.
Self-gaine, II. 63/876.
Self-gazing, I. 194/1210.
Self-good, II. 56, col. 1, l. 11, 58/398.
Self-guiltless, I. 68/834.
Self-guilty, II. 108/389.
Self-hangs, II. 304/286.
Self-ignobles, II. 211/244.
Self-ill, II. 58/397.
Self-incenst, II. 184/332.
Self-ingendred, II. 60/596.
Self-invention, I. 99/54.
Self-jarring, I. 27/60.
Self-kill, II. 41, Son. 32.
Self-lame (self-lame Sloath), II. 26, st. 34
Self-like, I. 261/1144.
Self-like-sunnes, II. 49, col. 1, l. 7.
Self-liv'd, I. 116/197.
Self-magnifi'd, I. 230/453.
Self-meriting, II. 60/616.
Self-obedient, I. 74/213.

Self-obstin'd, I. 237/1274.
Self-offring, *v.*, II. 294, col. 1, l. 34.
Self-paine, II. 58/397.
Self-parricides, I. 111/451.
Self-partiall, I. 89/702.
Self-pined, I. 169/559.
Self-pining, I. 102/295.
Self-powring, I. 101/245.
Self-privacy, I. 233/762.
Self-private, I. 50/1136.
Self-presumption, I. 215/192.
Self-proud, I. 171/820.
Self-resisting, *sb.*, II. 213/457.
Self-return'd, I. 179/110.
Self-rumineth, I. 72/44.
Self-sadly, II. 112/879.
Self-sedition, II. 94/1055.
Self-severe, II. 235/636.
Self-shav'n, I. 138/26.
Self-shine, I. 229/392.
Self-simple, I. 186/266.
Self-slaies, II. 304/286.
Self-soathing, I. 121/764.
Self-spending, I. 93, col. 2, l. 14.
Self-spirit, II. 11, st. 6.
Self-stable, II. 291/10.
Self-substance, I. 77/583, 79/768.
Self-surnam'd, I. 255/441.
Self-swelling, II. 225, st. 40.
Self-swoln, I. 108/72.
Self-sway, I. 227/143.
Self-tasked, I. 220/864.
Self-thirstless, I. 88/648.
Self-triumphing, *sb.*, I. 204/693
Self-uned, I. 103/408.
Self-unstable, I. 258/770.
Self-usurp, I. 133/99.
Self-wanting, I. 100/60.
Self-weale-wounding, II. 42, Son. 39.
Self-wind, II. 11, st. 6.
Self-wise, II. 220, st. 79.
Self-wounding, II. 331, col. 2, l. 22.
Self-wounds, I. 245/559.
Self-yielders, I. 261/1113.
Selfly, *adj.* = by one's-self, I. 245/561.
Selfly, *adv.*, I. 37/1176, 43/402, 58/731, 101/261, etc.
Selfly-blam'd, II. 27, st. 52.
Selfly-foes, II. 37, Son. 5.
Selfly-innocent, I. 128/676.
Selfly-rear'd, I. 15, col. 2, l. 16.
Selfly-slain, I. 213/5.
Selfly-strange, II. 291/10.
Selfly-turning, II. 87/301.
Selfs-disloyalties, II. 212/353.
Selfs-essence, I. 78/758, 79/786.
Selfs expence, I. 78/760.
Selfs-furie, II. 29, st. 64.
Selfs-kindred, I. 75/331.

Selves-errors, II. 100/360.
Semi-circle, *adj.*, I. 67/671.
Semi-ray, II. 87/217.
Semi-taures, II. 203/108.
Sempiternall, I. 142/420.
Sense-contrarie, II. 60/592.
Sense-full, I. 81/997.
Sense-lesse, I. 115/97.
Sent, *v.*, senting = smelling, I. 227/132 ; II. 258/30.
Sents, *sb.* = scents, I. 62/148, 77/589, 79/805, etc.
Sent-lesse = without sense of smelling, I. 197/1473.
Sent-lesse = without scent, II. 18, st. 15.
Sent-strong, I. 67/660.
Serean, *adj.* = Syrian, I. 47/813.
Sereans, *sb.*, I. 229/316.
Serean knacks, II. 191/40.
Serely, *adv.*, II. 117/1439.
Seres, *sb.* = claws, talons, I. 214/136. See Nares, *s.v.*
Serjant, I. 26/780, 50/1122.
Serpenter, *sb.*, I. 155/170.
Serpenting, *v.*, I. 222/1038.
Serpent-slayer, I. 158/508.
Serr or sere, serrs, *sb.* = talons (Tropheis 136), II. 185/455. See Nares *s.v.*, who seems to think it peculiar to Chapman. French, *serre, serson.* 'Sers' is used both as verb and noun : 'As you are *sersed* in the river's books so are you in God's books.' (Bp. Andrewes, Sermons, v. 38.)
Servily, II. 150/360.
Sessions, I. 23/453.
Ses, ses, dog-call, I. 253/216. See our Memorial-Introduction, II. Critical, on this.
Sessing, *sb.*, II. 235/268.
Sessor = assessor ? II. 213/484.
Sets by, *v.* = estimates, I. 57/267.
Setteled, *v.*, I. 126/487 ; II. 63/858, 178/162.
Seven-double-folded, II. 3, st. 10.
Sex-changing, I. 230/420.
Sex-less, I. 104/583.
Shaft-never-wanting, I. 75/328.
Shag, *sb.*, Silken shag, I. 146/71.
Shak't, *v.*, I. 81/11011.
Shallow-brain'd, I. 135/408.
Shallowling, *sb.*, II. 270/346.
Shambles, I. 254/329 ; II. 284/109, 299, st. 26.
Shamfac'd, *adj.*, shamefac't, I. 27/43, 233/841.
Shamefac't, The shamefac't = Sensitive Plant, I. 104/625.
Shape-depriving, *sb.*, II. 6, st. 70.
Share, plough-share, I. 35/867.
Share, *v.* = to shear, cut, I. 240/18 ; II. 31, st. 86.
Sharkers, II. 273/673.
Sharp-conceited, I. 99/48, 143/618.
Sharp-green, I. 28/108.
Sharp-sounding, I. 179/100.
Sharp-sweet, I. 103/521, 110/365, 235/1079 ; II. 57/240, 60/561, etc.
Sharpling, *sb.*, I. 115/69.
Sharply-sweet, I. 86/331.

Sky-like, I. 48/912.

Slasht, v., I. 190/664.

Slat, sb. = slate, I. 48/896, 154/43, 175/1297.

Slaughter-feast, I. 215/201.

Sleads, sb., I. 59/808.

Sleaves, sb., sleave (silk) = soft floss silk, I. 69/955, 244/487 ; II. 310, st. 42. Herrick speaks of Venus' paps that feele like slevied silke ' (see my edition s.v.). See Nares s.v. for examples.

Sleds, sb., I. 139/160.

Sleep-awake, II. 202/77.

Sleep-bringer, I. 58/718.

Sleep-sick, I. 84/129.

Sleep-swoln, I. 169/563.

Sleepiest, II. 203/149.

Slent, v., slenteth, I. 26/813, 171/857, 236/1111, 242/188 ; II. 163/295, 167/52.

Slice, v., I. 189/537.

Slice-sea, adj. = keel-cleaving of the sea, I. 45/564. See ' Alder.'

Slicing nimbleness, I. 173/1019. Cf. ' cutting along :' also ' clip ' = to fly—clipper, a fast ship.

Slide, v., I. 85/255.

Sling-men, I. 171/825.

Slippery-sleeke, II. 97/78.

Slips, sb., of plants, I. 112/613.

Sloaping, v., sloaps, I. 66/538, 157/319.

Sloath, sb., II. 57/225.

Sloath-lov'd, I. 143/530.

Sloath-shunning, I. 79/868.

Slops, sb., slop, clothes, I. 124/199, 202/426 ; II. 210/195.

Sloth, adj., I. 185/138.

Slouch, sb., I. 260/1077.

Slow-growing, I. 29/186.

Slow-pac't, I. 157/383.

Slowly-swiftly, I. 28/136.

Slugging, v., slug, I. 86/340, 414. ' Episcopacy . . . worsens and slugs the most learned and seeming religious of our ministers' (Milton's ' Of Reformation in England '). Quarles (Emblems, IV. iii. 6) has it as neuter verb.

Slut, sb., I. 117/329.

Slutling, v., II. 272/585.

Slyc't, v. (slyc't with scourges), I. 187/343.

Smacks, v., I. 246/744.

Smalling, v., II. 310, st. 54.

Smartlesse, II. 56, col. 1, l. 32, 244/607.

Smell-strong, I. 63/238.

Smile-frowning, II. 50, Son. 1.

Smiling-sweet, I. 160/710.

Smoak, v., I. 158/437.

Smoak, sb., I. 49/1097, 152/752.

Smoak, sb., to sell smoak, II. 197/179.

Smoak-seller, II. 274/811.

Smoakie, adj., II. 267/47, 80.

Smoakie-mists, II. 268/189.

Smoaking, adj., I. 157/383.

Smoaky-waving, I. 139/133.

Smock, v., II. 186/28.

Smoke-merchants, II. 274/812.

Smooth, v. int., I. 207/1007 ; II. 154/823.

Smooth-sliding, I. 100/117.

Smooth-slie, I. 218/584.

Smooth-soothing, I. 232/682.

Smother, sb., II. 7, st. 82.

Snaffle, sb., II. 40, Son. 21, 172/616.

Snail-like, I. 129/602.

Snailling, v. = winding like a snail, protracting, I. 77/637. ' Draw in your horns, and resolve to snail on as we did before, in a track we are acquainted with.' (Richardson's Cl. Harlowe, IV. 124.)

Snake-girdle, I. 234/912.

Snake-trest, I. 116/250.

Snake-wanded, I. 188/428.

Snaking, adj. = serpentine, I. 84/81.

Snarefull, II. 263/35.

Snarled, adj., I. 105/723, 196/1377.

Snib, v. = snub, snibbing, I. 241/92, 256/532. Often used by Thomas Adams, I. 12, 47, as a verb ; and III. 113 as a noun (Nichol's edition) ; also Ward, pp. 8, 99 ; it occurs also in Pilgrim's Progress.

Snight, a bird, I. 68/775.

Snips, sb., I. 222/1103.

Sniveling, adj., I. 253/175.

Snorted, v., snorting, I. 26/809, 35/928, 169/554 ; II. 203/154.

Snorting, adj. = snoring, I. 137/553.

Snow, v. tr. = to whiten, I. 152/761.

Snow-white, I. 142/495.

Snow-whiter, I. 222/1077.

Snow-winged, I. 235/1073.

Snowie-winged, II. 263/10.

Snuffe (broke in snuffe), II. 272/613.

Snuffe (went out in snuffe), II. 288/100.

Snuffing, adj., II. 172/590.

Snuffing, v., II. 266, col. 2, Son., l. 12.

Sober-wise, II. 94/1053.

Sod, sb. (sod and roast), II. 107/218.

Sodain, sodaine, I. 65/448, 76/417, 77/646.

Sod-away = seethed or boiled to rags, I. 157/397. See Bibl. Eng., p. 18.

Softlings, I. 139/64, 206/983.

Soft-pantingly, I. 232/701.

Soft-skind, I. 59/807.

Sol, I. 55/400.

Solace-full, II. 172/687.

Sole-happy, I. 235/987.

Sole-seated, I. 50/1123.

Sole-selfly, I. 174/1114.

Solenesse, I. 233/762 ; II. 330, col. 1, l. 40.

Somers, sb. = sommers, beams, I. 236/1108.

Sommon'd, adj., I. 126/443.

Som-while, whiles, I. 87/454, 185/124, 260/1000.

Soon-depart, sb., I. 85/247.

Soon-vading, II. 302/96.

Soothers, sb., II. 236/659.

Sooth-sin, adj., II. 65/1110.

Sophister, II. 156/12.

Sophisticate, *v.*, I. 133/173.
Sophistick, I. 22/390, 119/623.
Sophists, II. 184/320.
Sophy, sophies, I. 227/106 ; II. 136/1390.
Sops in tar—instead of in wine, I. 192/899. See Nares *s.v.*, sops in wine.
Sops in wine, I. 164/18. See Nares *s.v.* for a full and valuable note.
Sorrow-bringing, I. 116/176.
Sorrow-clouded, II. 330, col. 1, l. 19.
Sorrow-daunted, I. 133/71.
Sorrow-torn, I. 257/725.
Sort, *sb.* (a sort of = many), II. 181/7, 8.
Sot, *sb.*, sots, I. 66/591, 139/172, 200/209 ; II. 272/609.
Sottish, I. 35/906, 197/1452.
Soule-adorning, II. 131/839.
Soule-boyling, I. 226/19.
Soul-charm, *adj.*, I. 143/560.
Soule-health, II. 60/587.
Soule-idlenesse, II. 65/1089.
Soul-rapting, II. 29, st. 72.
Soule-ravishments, II. 67/62.
Soule-sick, I. 121/759.
Soule-subduing, I. 14, col. 2, l. 3.
Soul-tainting, I. 86/333.
Soul-weal, II. 227, st. 81.
Soul-wise, II. 56, col. 1, l. 30.
Soule-wounded, II. 93/960.
Soultry, I. 31/440, 33/642 ; II. 171/455.
Sound-stated, I. 102/302.
Sound-sweet, II. 251/459.
Sour-sweet, I. 63/297.
Souse, *sb.*, I. 189/641 ; II. 108/342.
Soust, *v.*, soused, I. 70/1087, 249/999.
South-bounded, I. 146/83.
Southren, I. 68/877, 100/145.
Soverainlesse, I. 58/718.
Sowr, *adj.*, I. 165/107.
Soyl (to take soyl), I. 73/123.
S. P. Q. R. = Sanctus Populusque Romanus, *i.e.* Prince Henry's death was a blow to all except the Roman or Papal Court—which hated England as heretical, II. 277/26.
Space-lesse space, II. 90/564.
Spangled, I. 53/79.
Spangles, *sb.* = stars, I. 24/603, 52/1, 54/207 ; II. 180/357.
Spare-lesse, I. 179/140 ; II. 251/522.
Sparlengs, I. 64/330.
Spauling, *adj.*, I. 252/1666.
Spauling-excrement, II. 273/742.
Spawling, *adj.*, I. 117/402.
Spawlings, *sb.* = spittle, II. 270/414, 274/824.
Specked, *v.*, I. 54/208.
Speckled, *adj.*, I. 116/217.
Speckle-starr'd, I. 64/143.
Speed-praise, I. 171/861.
Speed-stroke, *sb.*, II. 223, st. 2.
Speights, birds, I. 123/157.
Sperage, a fish, I. 115/70.

Sperm, *sb.*, I. 119/551.
Sperst, *v.*, I. 103/407.
Spet, *v.*, spets, I. 34/853, 46/741, 54/269, 256/616 ; II. 114/1032, etc.
Spet-at, *v.*, I. 33/702.
Spettle, *sb.*, I. 256/617 ; II. 151/510, 188/294.
Spew'd, *v.*, I. 156/224, 256/585, 259/880.
Spewing, *adj.*, I. 175/1306.
Spiall, *sb.*, I. 203/551.
Spid, *v.* = spied, II. 127/346.
Spider-like, II. 5, st. 36, 267/10.
Spight, *sb.*, I. 107/54, 108/72 ; II. 57/284, 61/673.
Spightfull, I. 117/391 ; II. 30. st. 83.
Spike, *sb.*, a plant, I. 78/725.
Spill, *v.*, I. 179/167 ; II. 137/1546.
Spin, *v.* (to spin good hap), I. 221/932.
Spink = a sort of finch, I. 67/676. 'The spink chaunts sweetest in a hedge of thorns' (Harte, quoted in Latham *s.v.*).
Spire, *v.*, II. 258/31.
Spirit-full, I. 261/1155.
Spirit-imping, I. 184/26.
Spittle, *sb.* = hospital, II. 271/532.
Spoaks, *sb.* = spokes, I. 30/375, 61/66, 127/521.
Sponge-fly, I. 64/378.
Spongy, I. 77/573.
Sportfull, I. 42/259.
Spotty-spangled, I. 117/391.
Sprawling, *v.*, I. 259/882.
Sprenges, *sb.*, I. 139/93.
Sprent, *v.*, II. 109/516, 148/150.
Sprigs, *sb.*, I. 66/605.
Sprightfull, I. 42/226, 46/742, 196/1407, etc.
Sprightlesse, I. 79/782, 86/350, 134/184.
Sprinkle, *sb.*, I. 219/683.
Sprinkled, *v.*, I. 54/208.
Spritefull, I. 235/1053.
Spritely, *adv.*, I. 234/924.
Sprung, *adj.* (a sprung Partridge), I. 149/431.
Spumy, *adj.*, II. 114/1122.
Spungy, spungie, I. 31/490, 129/759, 170/754, 224/1254.
Spur, royals = stars, II. 90/616.
Squarenesse, I. 126/213.
Squaring, *v.*, II. 235/573.
Squire, *sb.*, squire = square, I. 164/55, 236/1117 ; II. 198/304.
Squires, *sb.*, term of contempt (Phantastick squires), II. 267/20.
Stabbers, II. 273/673.
Stabbling, *v.* = stabling, I. 158/461.
Stablisht, *v.*, II. 164/329.
Stagyrian, I. 43/360, 88/651 ; II. 122, col. 1, l. 15.
Stain, *v.*, I. 233/825.
Stallion-like, I. 174/1155.
Stall, *sb.*, II. 135/1306.
Stall, *v.*, stall'd, I. 199/54.
Stammell, I. 45/612.
Stance, *sb.* = position, stand-point, II. 128/473, 135/1294, 244/570. 'He failed not to carry his body

perfectly round, just into its former *stance*.' (Urquhart's Rabelais, bk. i. c. 35.) 'The boy . . . danced down from his *stance*' (Scott's Kenilworth, i. 184). In Blackburn it is in current use, as 'a *stance* in the market,' or a place for the stall.

Stand of pikes, I. 171/826.

Staple traffick, II. 254, st. 12.

Stares, *sb.*, bird, I. 47/788, 61/49, 67/711, 166/235.

Star-beasts, I. 235/1051.

Star-boord, I. 114/43.

Star-bright, I. 221/982, 233/840.

Star-clarks, I. 44/494.

Star-crowned, II. 198/241.

Star-divines, I. 53/134.

Star-doctors, I. 19/7.

Star-full, I. 172/889.

Star-gazing, *sb.*, II. 88/381.

Star-glistring, I. 19/12.

Star-lar-board, II. 262/124.

Star-like, I. 234/933.

Star-kings, I. 58/738.

Star-seeled, I. 157/343.

Star-ship, I. 215/216.

Star-spangled, I. 37/1172, 88/199 ; II. 91/690.

Star-wise, I. 220/796.

Stark, *v.*, II. 210/185.

Stark-blinded, *v. tr.*, II. 18, st. 9.

Starriest, I. 36/1089.

Starrifi'd, *adj.*, I. 126/413.

Starrs-doctrine, I. 160/680.

Starrs-guide, I. 238/1334.

Starry-flowers, I. 232/662.

Starry-golden, I. 54/201.

Startups, *sb.* = up-starts, high shoes, I. 252/114. 'That young start-up hath all the glory of my overthrow.' (Much Ado, i. 3.) See Halliwell *s.v.*

Starvelings, I. 31/487.

State-clothes, I. 76/472.

Statefull, I. 75/342.

State-stabling, II. 40, Son. 24.

Stately-grave, I. 69/891.

Stately-pased, II. 309, st. 41.

States-friend, I. 55/400.

Staules, *sb.* = stales, decays, II. 274/778.

Staves, I. 202/413.

Steans, *sb.* = stones, I. 228/274, 261/1159.

Sted, *v.*, I. 66/638, 94, col. 1, l. 9.

Steddy, I. 84/95.

Steed, *v.*, I. 156/236 ; II. 94/1030, 210/97.

Steed, *sb.*, in the steed of, I. 216/297 ; II. 168/190, 191/37.

Steel, *v.* = to strengthen, II. 161/80.

Steel-headed, I. 236/1110.

Steel-pointed, I. 75/324, 216/315.

Steeled, *adj.*, II. 196/59.

Steely, I. 116/268, 9, 117/390, 171/775 ; II. 39, Son. 14, 172/589.

Steely-gads, I. 69/904.

Steep-hanging, I. 83/26.

Steep-rising, I. 190/659.

Steep-full, I. 171/828.

Steepy, I. 110/353.

Steer, *s.*, steers, I. 159/553, 175/1276 ; II. 173/700.

Steer-man, I. 20/117.

Stentorian, *adj.*, I. 184/20, 228/264.

Step-dame, dam, I. 11, col. 2. l. 1, 230/491, 231/592.

Stept, *v.* (stept in hoary haires), II. 104, Son. 2, l. 3.

Stern, *sb.*, I. 85/233.

Stern-less, I. 66/555.

Sternly-valiant, I. 261/1114.

Sterops, I. 127/537. See Aeneid VIII. 425.

Sterve, *v.*, II. 3108/39, 354, st. 6.

Stibium = antimony, I. 48/903.

'Ceruse nor stibium can prevail,
No art repair where age makes fail.'
(Collop's Poesie Revived, 1656.)

Sticht, *v.*, 119/604.

Sties, *sb.*, I. 125/363.

Stiff-rustling, I. 169/538.

Stiff-thrown, I. 258/795.

Stifly-straight and stiffly, I. 214/90 ; II. 181/79.

Still, *sb.*, I. 111/518.

Still, *v.* = to distil, I. 160/703.

Stillary, II. 271/445.

Still-green = evergreen, I. 48/981 ; II. 6, st. 60.

Still-rocking, I. 169/553.

Still still (reduplication), I. 166/235.

Stinger, *sb.*, II. 16, st. 2.

Stinter, *sb.*, I. 100/140.

Stint, *v.*, stinteth, I. 157/392, 226/13 ; II. 251/491, 297, st. 1, 324, Son. 15.

Stipulation, II. 288/127.

Stoccados, I. 171/769.

Stock, *sb.* = idol, II. 190/476.

Stock-stained, *adj.* (stock-stained man), II. 156/34.

Stocked, *v.*, I. 73/77 ; II. 159/333.

Stomack, *sb.* = courage, I. 116/275, 139/77, 189/602, 242/278, etc.

Stone-rowling, I. 222/1045.

Stone-still, I. 65/434.

Stoap, *v. tr.*, stoopt = to abase, I. 160/753, 215/234 ; II. 130/777.

Stop-ship, I. 65/444.

Store-seed-world, I. 136/524.

Storie, *v.*, II. 784/128.

Storing = filling with store, I. 56/507.

Storm-armed, II. 248/174.

Storm-breed, *adj.*, I. 245/577.

Stormfull, I. 66/576, 170/736, 214/102, 199/88 ; II. 230/46, etc.

Stormless, I. 69/918.

Storm-wonted, II. 213/466.

Stormy-calm, II. 50, Son. 1.

Story-wrought, I. 228/267.

Stound, *sb.* = a moment, I. 32/609, 47/866, 59/812, 219/659. F. Q., III. i. 24. See Halliwell *s.v.*

Stour, *sb.* stours, I. 75/364, 100/154, 118/446. 'impetuous stoure,' Hall's Satires, II. iii. 35.

Swallow-like, I. 232/747.
Swallow-swifter, I. 149/429.
Swan-like, I. 67/727, 144/665 ; II. 17, st. 17, 310, st. 52.
Swan-poorer, I. 55/364.
Swan-proud, II. 322, 7on. 7.
Swan-white, II. 225/49.
Swart, *adj.*, I. 14, col. 2, l. 2, 24/550, 253/173.
Swartest, *adj.*, II. 186/36.
Swarthy-hew'd, I. 127/537.
Swarty, I. 59/796.
Swath-band, II. 170/408.
Swath'd, *v.*, II. 149/250.
Swathes, *sb.*, II. 200/499.
Sweat-full, II. 150/361.
Sweat-lesse, I. 191/839.
Sweat-sweet, I. 73/148.
Sweaty-swelted, II. 249/257.
Sweet, *v.*, II. 85/57, 128/530.
Sweet-bitter, I. 73/133.
Sweet-bright-lightning, I. 144/671.
Sweet-charming, I. 160/742, 249/1039.
Sweet-distilling, I. 133/64.
Sweet-furious, II. 38, Son. 12.
Sweet-heart, I. 124/172 ; II. 194/393.
Sweet-numbred (Homer), I. 143/590.
Sweet-piercing, I. 237/1218.
Sweet-rapting, II. 248/151.
Sweet-sacred, I. 114/29.
Sweet-smelling, I. 77/574, 78/729.
Sweet-smiling, I. 215/279.
Sweet-sweating, I. 229/400.
Sweet-sweet, I. 173/1019.
Sweet-tuned, I. 100/129.
Sweet-warbling, *adj.*, I. 217/440.
Sweet-William, II. 283/45.
Sweetly-rapt, I. 237/1216.
Sweetly-shrill, I. 114/56.
Swelt, *v.*, swelting, I. 24/576, 63/271, 83/44, 118/473, 244/413 ; II. 167/5.
Swelting, *adj.*, I. 192/963 ; II. 186/36, 193/290, 261/69.
Sweltring, *adj.*, I. 42/182, 149/410.
Swift-flying, I. 184/62.
Swift-foot, I. 152/792.
Swift-rebounding, I. 139/72.
Swift-sliding, II. 279, st. 5.
Swift-slow, I. 101/226.
Swift-turning, I. 158/505.
Swift-winged, I. 58/677, 228/194.
Swifteth, *v.*, II. 223, st. 4.
Swiftly-light, I. 147/184.
Swill, *v.*, swils, swilling, I. 117/307, 249/1008, 261/1175.
Swill'd, *v.* = swallowed up, I. 23/438.
Swim-brethren, I. 62/187.
Swindging, *v.*, swinged, I. 75/410, 87/507.
Swines-bread, a plant, I. 46/704, 115/98.
Swinge, *v.*, II. 262/87.
Swolne-fac't, II. 337, col. 2. l. 18.
Swom, *v.* = swam, I. 244/431 ; II. 157/124.

Swoun, *sb.*, swoune, I. 111/466, 133/126, 206/874, 219/659, etc.
Swoun, *v.*, swouning, I. 127/634, 248/867.
Swound, *v.*, II. 289/210, 340, col. 2, l. 25.
Swouning-passion, I. 119/567.
Swown, *sb.*, I. 75/365.
Symbolize, *v.* = to agree together, I. 29/265, 157/377.
Symmists, *sb.*, II. 268/164.
Sympathiz'd, *v. tr.*, I. 238/1343.
Symphonize, *v. int.*, II. 42, Son. 35.
Synonimas, I. 141/368.
Syrbonian, II. 120/1713.
Syrups, *sb.*, II. 247/12.
Sythe, I. 24/584.

T

TABLE, *sb.* = picture, Fr. *tableau*, I. 14, col. 1, l. 6, 79/818, 81/1014, 83/63, and I. p. 83, col. 1, margin ; 158/431, 159/631, 5, etc.
Table-book, I. 155/101.
Table-peer, I. 191/843.
Table-pure, I. 191/844.
Tablets, I. 233/785 ; II. 85/27.
Tables = tablets, I. 102/400.
Tadpals = tadpoles, I. 149/411.
Talk-full, I. 137/611.
Tallies, *sb.*, II. 136/1408.
Tamarice, I. 47/756.
Tame-Ass (an old Sir Tame Ass), II. 225, st. 49.
Tame-griefe, I. 165/151.
Tane, *v.* = taken, II. 41, Son. 30.
Tang'd, *v.* = made stinging ? or leaving a tang behind ? I. 241/122.
Tangle, *v. int.*, I. 104/522, 180/278.
Tanne, *v.*, tann'd, II. 267/83, 4.
Tanned, *adj.*, II. 305/361.
Tantara, I. 193/1009.
Tap-houses, II. 273/743.
Tap-tobacconists, II. 278/100.
Tapers, *sb.* (heavenly tapers = stars), I. 136/522.
Tapistry, I. 100/79.
Targe, *sb.*, II. 196/59.
Tarras, I. 222/1095 ; II. 203/179.
Task-lords, I. 185/137.
Taskers, II. 151/468.
Taste-changing, *sb.*, I. 191/842.
Taste-curious, I. 100/109.
Taste-less = deprived of taste, I. 53/148.
Tast-sweetest, II. 298, st. 12.
Tatter'd, *v. tr.* = torn to pieces, I. 254/342.
Tattle, *v.*, I. 141/329.
Taxation = accusation, I. 40/6.
Taxations, I. 75/397.
Taxe-less, II. 166/555.
Taxe-puffed, *adj.*, II. 235/551.
Taxeth, *v.*, taxt, taxes, I. 111/492, 134/207, 138/40, 218/626.

Tawny, I. 169/566.
Tawny-tanned, II. 298, st. 10.
Tay = Tagus, II. 212/417.
Tear-bridge, I. 149/429.
Teare-composed, II. 343, col. 1, l. 5.
Tear-drown'd, I. 110/406.
Tears-wiping, I. 165/151.
Tearm, *sb.* = designation, II. 90/577.
Teen, *sb.* = sorrow, I. 117/323, 186/242 ; II. 89/454, 189/325, 197/131.
Teen, *sb.* = sorrow, II. 60/544, 231/179, 241/296, 300, st. 32, 314/58.

    ' How well they couch'd in forest green,
    Frolic and lively withouten *teen.*
                 (Peele's Edward I.)

Teen, *sb.* = anger, II. 60/544, 231/179, 241/296, 300, st. 32, 314/58. ' How strange when men grieve us, to turn our teen upon God, and rend him to pieces.' (Adams, i. 320.)
Teen'd, *v.* = kindle ? I. 128/707, 181/306.
Temeritie, temerity, I. 6, col. 2, l. 3, 147/231.
Temperate, *v.*, I. 235/991 ; II. 243/472.
Temper-lesse, II. 136/1374.
Tempest-beaten, I. 65/433, 152/757.
Tempestious, I. 149/438.
Temple-sacred, I. 189/553.
Temporize, *v.*, II. 335, col. 1, l. 7.
Temp'raments, I. 32/619.
Tender, *v.*, I. 138/13, 139/86, 150/591, etc.
Tender-bearded, I. 43/296.
Tender-imped, *adj.*, I. 95, col. 2, l. 12.
Tenters, *sb.* (hooking tenters), I. 120/708.
Tercell, I. 67/720, 214/135.
Tercell-gentle, I. 70/1048.
Term, *sb.* = period, II. 90/578, 675, 169/271.
Termined, *v.*, II. 258/75, 298, st. 13, 322, Son. 6.
Terrene, *adj.*, I. 236/1171 ; II. 19, st. 24, 63/866, 67/73.
Terrestrial, II. 56, col. 1, l. 47.
Terriblize, *v.*, I. 166/271.
Terryes, *sb.*, dogs, I. 259/939.
Ter-terrifies, II. 317, col. 1, l. 15.
Test, *sb.*, II. 111/667, 118/1515, 119/1596, 293/172.
Tester, *sb.*, I. 53/78.
Tethers, *v.*, I. 30/329.
Tetters, *sb.*, I. 118/488.
Thames-tunes, II. 322, Son. 4.
Thankly, I. 47/809.
Theam, I. 27/53, 95, col. 2, l. 26.
Theater, I. 30/382, 392, etc.
Thence-from, II. 311, st. 71.
Then-time, I. 186/198.
Therms, *sb.* = baths ? I. 223/112.
There-fro, II. 192/89.
Thick-round, I. 34/760.
Thinckling—misprint for ' twinckling,' *adj.*, I. 176/1417.
Thin-thicknesse, I. 36/1080.
Thirst-panting, I. 31/454.
Thistly, *adj.* = prickly, I. 159/625.
Tho = then, I. 37/1206, 171/865, 206/898, etc.

Thorn-bristled, I. 115/141.
Thorn'd, *v.* = pinned, I. 123/140.
Thorny-thrummed, I. 70/998.
Thorough, thorow, I. 166/182, 218/598 ; II. 89/485, 109/443.
Thorough-lin'd, I. 193/1006.
Thorough-reformation, I. 255/505.
Thorough-seasoned, I. 100/62.
Thought, *sb.* = anxiety, I. 120/667.
Thoughtfull, I. 111/465.
Thought-shaming, I. 167/373.
Thought-sounding, I. 125/304.
Thousand-headed, II. 40, Son. 24.
Thrall, *sb.* = thraldom, I. 126/420, 256/575 ; II. 28, st. 58, 38, Son. 6, etc.
Thrall, *v.*, I. 112/610.
Thrall, *sb.* = a slave, I. 152/751, 204/685 ; II. 61/669.
Thrall'd, *v.*, II. 184/357.
Thrall-full, II. 173/686.
Threat, *v.*, threating, I. 56/531 ; II. 204/224.
Threatfull, I. 173/999, 214/85, 102, 247/841, etc.
Threatfully, I. 114/42.
Threat-lesse, I. 200/201.
Threeds, *sb.*, II. 232/272.
Three-fold, I. 127/618.
Three-fold-three, II. 247/9.
Three-forked, I. 35/883.
Thrice-Eternall, I. 142/518.
Thrice-One, I. 158/507.
Thrice-sacred, I. 172/938, 189/554.
Thrill, *v.*, thrild, thrilling, I. 145/35, 171/860, 190/666, 217/497 ; II. 159/338. See Halliwell ; also F. Q., III. ii. 32, III. v. 20.
Thrilled, *adj.*, II. 168/145.
Throeing, *sb.*, II. 288/105.
Throughly, I. 70/1014.
Through-thilled, I. 167/375, 254/322.
Throws, *sb.* = throes, I. 116/235.
Thrumd, *v.*, thrumm'd, I. 50/1106, 83/27, 104/552. ' There 's her thrumm'd hat.' Merry Wives of Windsor, IV. 2.
Thunder, *sb.* (new-found earthly thunder), II. 62/743.
Thunder-clash, I. 230/425.
Thunder-darter, I. 21/272, 101/184.
Thunder-scar'd, I. 62/142.
Thunder-shot, I. 175/1304.
Thunder-stowers, *sb.*, II. 248/84.
Thunder-thrower, II. 179/315.
Thunder-throwing, I. 206/920.
Thunder'd, *v.*, II. 239/21.
Thundred-down, *v. tr.*, I. 122/27.
Thundrous, I. 216/370.
Thundry, I. 161/779, 257/648.
Thurifying, *sb.*, II. 268/183.
Tiars, I. 151/679.
Ticing, *adj.* = enticing, I. 108/84.
Tickles, *v. int.*, I. 120/679.
Tickle, *adj.*, I. 253/196 ; II. 119/1636.
Tide, *sb.* = time, II. 178/99.

Tillar, II. 310, st. 44.

Tilting, *adj.*, I. 165/123.

Timbers, *v.*, I. 233/1034.

Timber-towers, warlike implements, II. 187/111.

Timb'ring, *v.*, II. 40, Son. 21.

Time-contemning, II. 321, Son. 3.

Time-grace-ordered, I. 126/478.

Time-less, I. 219/681 ; II. 335, col. 2, l. 28.

Time-proof Poems, II. 4, st. 29.

Time-suiting, I. 251/6.

Time-torn, I. 143/640.

Times-child Truth, I. 158/481.

Tincel, *sb.*, II. 191/51.

Tin-colour'd, I. 234/926.

Tinder, *sb.*, I. 206/891, 259/895 ; II. 40, Son. 24, 254, st. 14.

Tinder-box, I. 33/738, 222/1018.

Tinding, *adj.* (tinding fume), I. 33/654.

Tinkling, *adj.*, I. 161/769.

Tinnhé (= tinnen ?), I. 55/388.

Tiphyes, II. 305/361.

Tippling-cots, II. 269/215.

Tippling-game, II. 202/54.

Tipsie-tostie-pots, II. 269/216.

Tires, *sb.* (dress), II. 191/61, 270/374, 278/159.

Titan, II. 183/211.

Tithe-lesse, II. 166/555.

Toad-like, I. 120/673.

Toad-stools, I. 149/419.

Toast, *sb.*, II. 258/25.

Tobacco (Don Tobacco), II. 269/251.

Tobacco (Τω Βακχω), II. 269/267.

Tobacconer, II. 272/643.

Tobacco-fellowes, II. 268/148.

Tobacco-harms, II. 273/688.

Tobacco-mungers, II. 274/813.

Tobacconing, *sb.*, II. 269/204, 284, 314, 270/347, 380.

Tobacconists, II. 268/86, 169/270, 386, 408, 269/236.

Tobacco-pipes, II. 267/51, 58, 270/407.

Tobacco-shop, II. 210/196.

Tobacco-stinking, *sb.*, II. 273/763.

Tobacco-taking, *sb.*, II. 270/383.

To-fore, II. 116/1307.

To-forn, II. 243/491.

Togh, *v.*, toghes = to tow, to tug, I. 24/578, 114/51.

Togethers, I. 30/330.

Toil-full, II. 194/432.

Toledo blade, II. 308, st. 13.

Toll-free, I. 89/708.

To-morn, II. 219, st. 58.

Tongue-lesse, I. 220/760.

Tonnies, *sb.*, fish, I. 222/1085.

Too-craking, II. 98/184.

Too-fear'd, *v.*, II. 248/94.

Too-greazy, I. 43/399.

Too-love, II. 261/24.

Too-mew'd, II. 133/1133.

Too-mickle, II. 25, st. 26.

Too-pyned, II. 101/485.

Too-self-humouring, I. 228/208.

Too-vehemence, II. 212/372.

Too-wanted, *adj.*, II. 267/49.

Too, too, I. 81/1000, 114/52, 119/559, 152/824, 251/47, etc.

Too-too-blame, II. 180/357.

Too-too-foolishly, I. 223/1189.

Too-too-happy, I. 213/18.

Too-too-light, I. 208/1192.

Too-too-malapert, I. 241/94.

Too-too-much, I. 6, col. 1, l. 30, 28/164.

Too-too-self-rapt, I. 228/208.

Too-too-soon, I. 222/1100.

Too-too-tired, I. 167/325.

Tooth and nail (with), I. 29/263.

Tooth-ake-spells, II. 272/655.

Tooth-full, I. 47/834.

Top, *sb.*, II. 29, st. 69, 67/23, 164/370, 182/123, etc.

Top to toe, I. 34/834.

Top-bough, II. 277/3.

Top-full, I. 175/1324, 252/52.

Top-gallant (tires), II. 278/159.

Top-leaves, I. 6, col. 2, l. 30.

Top-lesse, I. 102/359, 133/161.

Topsie-turvie, I. 137/549, 167/408, 191/763.

Topsi-turneth, turned, turning, I. 170/744, 248/993 ; II. 133/1086.

Torch-like, I. 127/631.

Torch-man, II. 108/364.

Torpedo, II. 335, col. 2, l. 2.

Torrid, II. 268/186.

Tortoise, warlike implement, II. 183/287.

Touch, *sb.*, I. 178/4.

Touch (by the touch), I. 86/321.

Touch-pan, I. 83/36.

Touch-pleasures, II. 298, st. 12.

Touch-stone, I. 249/1064.

Toules, *sb.* = tolls, I. 195/1297 ; II. 197/175, 200/529.

Touze, *v.*, touz'd, I. 169/584, 230/501.

Tow'r-back't, I. 244/437.

Tow'r-full, I. 149/424.

Tower-razing, I. 216/401.

Tower-tearing, tow'r-tearing, I. 34/805 ; II. 187/125.

Towers, *sb.*—dress, II. 278/159.

Towred, *adj.*, I. 72/41, 186/228.

Toyes, *sb.*, I. 12, col. 1, l. 4, 101/257, 151/680, 232/684, etc.

Toying, *v.*, I. 20/188.

Toyl, *v.*, toyl'd, I. 217/416, 227/164 ; II. 194/323.

Trace, *sb.*—beaten trace, I. 160/740, 253/232 ; II. 25, st. 29, 298, st. 19.

Trace, *v.*, I. 222/1031, 229/344, 234/969, 235/1047.

Track, *v.*, I. 253/232.

Tracts, *sb.* = traits, I. 222/1101, 252/153 ; II. 182/104, 232/215.

Trade, *v. int.*, I. 23/473, 128/654.

Trade, *v. tr.*, I. 151/725.

Trade, *sb.* (free trade), I. 62/133.

Tradefull, I. 102/373, 122/23, 208/1158.

Train, *v.*, train'd, I. 164/32, 168/417.

Trains, *sb.*, II. 158/199, 212/350, 262/82.
Tra-lucent, II. 39, Son. 14.
Tralucing, *adj.*, I. 30/380.
Tramels, II. 191/22.
Trammels, I. 234/948.
Transanimation, II. 213/446.
Transform, *v. int.*, I. 128/719.
Transmutation, I. 58/754.
Transmute, II. 197/183.
Transoms, I. 236/1108.
Transpierce, *v.*, transpiercing, I. 77/544, 110/380.
Trans-ported, I. 253/242.
Tran-substantiate, II. 291/11.
Trans-villag'd, *v.*, I. 253/242.
Trapezunce, I. 118/440.
Travaile, *v.* = to travel, II. 159/416.
Travaile, *sb.* = travel, II. 225, st. 38.
Travailers = travellers, I. 26/842.
Travell, *sb.* = travail, I. 86/347, 102/316, 170/744, etc.
Travell, *v.* = travail, I. 86/323, 89/706, 230/505, etc.
Traverses, *v.*, traverse, I. 74/269 ; II. 300, st. 41.
Trayles, *sb.*, II. 42, col. 2, l. 10.
Trayling, *v.*, trayled, I. 155/153 ; II. 243/460.
Treason-trove, I. 67/737.
Treen, *sb.*, I. 29/188, 62/119, 100/104, 165/121.
Trees-brood, I. 222/1048.
Tree-turn'd Lady, II. 6/60.
Trench, *sb.*, II. 172/616.
Trendle, *sb.*, I. 55/336.
Trepane, *sb.*, I. 260/994.
Tresse, *sb.* = hair, tresses, II. 92/880, 191/22, 250/392.
Tressels, I. 142/451.
Tress-full, I. 232/734.
Tressie, *adj.*, II. 188/230.
Trevet, *sb.*, II. 184/418.
Trewants, *sb.*, I. 20/188.
Triacle, II. 89/498.
Triangle, II. 226, st. 60.
Tribute, *adj.*, I. 199/119.
Trice (in a trice), I. 32/525, 171/788 ; II. 187/134.
Trice (with a trice), II. 68/86.
Trickt, *v.*, II. 191/71.
Trident, II. 274/776.
Trils, *v.*, trileth, trils, II. 191/1. 'As wise as he who carried the coach-wheel upon his back, when he might have *trilled* it before him all along ' (Howell's Forraine Travell, p. 5).
Trilleth, *v.*, I. 68/825, 174/1173, 196/1358, 216/355.
Trim, *adj.*, trimme, I. 10, col. 2, i. 12, 40/33, 105/700, 152/781, etc.
Trim, *sb.*, I. 219/669, 236/1162 ; II. 198/216.
Trimbled, *v.*, I. 116/204.
Trimmed, *v.*, I. 114/19 ; II. 191/71.
Trine, *sb.*, I. 44/427 ; II. 94/1108, 316, col. 2, l. 30, 354, st. 4.
Trine, *adj.*, I. 188/413.
Trine-One, I. 158/427, 246/647.
Trine-One-Selfe, II. 90/566.
Trinely-odde, I. 238/1341.

Trines, *sb.*, I. 20/383.
Trip, *v.*, I. 172/943 ; II. 312, st. 84.
Tri-parted, II. 203/163.
Tri-pointed, I. 188/487.
Tripes, *sb.* = entrails, I. 47/761, 230/411 ; II. 106/152.
Triple-di'd, I. 232/729.
Triple-formed, I. 234/921.
Triple-Trine, I. 14, col. 1, l. 18, 155/135.
Triple-Unity, I. 78/759.
Triumphals, II. 11, st. 1.
Triumphing of, II. 105/17.
Triumvirs, II. 212/356.
Troad, *v.*, II. 184/351.
Troglodite, I. 160/657, 260/1022.
Troth, *sb.*, II. 356, st. 8.
Trouble-rest, I. 117/328.
Trouble-tares, *sb.*, I. 244/506.
Troublous, I. 253/240.
Trough, *sb.*, I. 38/1268.
Troule, *v.*, II. 247/1.
Trowt-famous, I. 78/653.
Troy-novant, II. 309, st. 32.
Truanted, *v.*, II. 246, Son., l. 1.
Truce-hating, I. 29/251.
Truck-man, I. 49/992, 140/256, 222/1042 ; II. 135/1255, 177/25.
Truck, *v.*, I. 142/485, 151/664.
Trudge, *v.*, II. 162/133 ; II. 302/57, 305/379.
True-heart-tuned, I. 123/60.
True-repent, I. 209/1290.
True-strong, I. 114/55.
True-sweets, II. 62/776.
Trunk, *sb.* = body, I. 176/1425.
Tuffs, *sb.*, I. 78/707.
Tuft, *sb.*, I. 199/124.
Tuft, *v.*, I. 219/683.
Tufting, *adj.*, I. 110/397.
Tug, *v.*, I. 230/501.
Tumbrels, II. 186/30.
Tun, I. 40/52.
Tuneless, I. 109/218.
Tune-skill'd, I. 234/898.
Tup, *sb.*, II. 120/1785.
Turbands, II. 115/1194.
Turk-traitors, II. 232/257.
Turmoils, *v.*, I. 115/80.
Turmoyle, *v.*, II. 191/77.
Turn-about, *sb.* = vertigo ? I. 119/610.
Turn-bull, II. 271/487.
Turn-coat, *adj.*, I. 49/1083.
Turn'd tail, I. 114/53.
Turn-sols, I. 235/1015.
Turves, *sb.*, II. 102, col. 2, l. 16.
Tushes, *sb.*, I. 74/226 ; II. 251/449.
Tuskanizeth, *v.*, II. 334, Ep. VII.
Tutelage, I. 95, col. 2, l. 7.
Tutor, tutors, I. 26/830, 251/9, 255/417.
Twice-born, I. 248/909 ; II. 201/594.
Twice-childish, I. 101/224.

Twice-foul, I. 55/304.
Twin-balled, I. 261/1165.
Twin-named, II. 202/48.
Twin-Princes = Sun and Moon, II. 90/617.
Twin-twins, I, 27/64.
Twine, *sb.* (the twine—opposed to uniform), I. 238/1338.
Twine, *sb.*, II. 183/279.
Twinklers, I. 57/574.
Twinkling, *adj.*, I. 154/63.
Twist, *sb.*, I. 125/293, 141/381 ; II. 191/60.
Twist, *sb.* (from top to twist), II. 199/395.
Two-hand, *adj.*, II. 278/110.
Tyer-less, I. 57/597.
Tygre, II. 199/409.
Tympany, I. 34/770.
Typhon-like, I. 112/637.
Typt, *v.*, II. 6, st. 62, 192/91.
Tyrant-scourging, II. 250/385.
Tyrant-tamer, I. 204/704.
Tyring, *v.*, I. 107/50.
Tythe, *v.*, = to decimate, II. 187/146.

U

UMPEER, I. 62/182.
Unacquainted, *adj.* = unknown, I. 63/199. 'To her paine Una brought this *unacquainted* guest.' (F. Q., I. x. 29.)
Un-bare, II. 158/204.
Unbeginning, I. 22/343.
Un-benums, *v.*, I. 124/237.
Un-blest-full, I. 244/417.
Un-bloody, I. 233/868.
Un-bore = unborn, I. 179/133.
Unbottom'd, *adj.*, II. 268/192.
Un-bound, *v.*, I. 147/178.
Un-brac't, I. 205/834.
Unbridledly, I. 85/211.
Un-cast, I. 93, col. 2, l. 8.
Uncasuall, II. 130/781.
Unceast = continuous, I. 147/244.
Un-censur'd, I. 222/1055.
Uncertain-certain, I. 86/381.
Uncessant, II. 182/179, 235/568.
Un-chang'd, I. 21/290.
Unchanted = unpeopled, I. 145/12.
Unchauk, *v.* = uncaulk, I. 248/949.
Uncharitie, II. 141, col. 2, l. 21.
Uncircumcised, *adj.*, I. 37/1185.
Uncited, II. 334, Ep. VII.
Un-close, *adj.* = unreserved, I. 207/1075.
Uncocted, *adj.*, I. 118/481.
Unconceived, I. 48/949.
Unconcoct, I. 28/132.
Unconfounded, II. 316, col. 2, l. 10.
Unconvict, II. 167/12.
Un-couth, II. 106/189, 107/273, 108/401, 188/281, 246/661.
Un-crowneth, *v.*, I. 179/85.

Un-curious, I. 122/2.
Undelicious, II. 235/568.
Under-cast, II. 316, col. 1. l. 7.
Under-earthly, I. 134/281.
Under-folds, *sb.*, II. 163/286.
Under-go, *v.* = to undertake, I. 93, col. 2, l. 7, 186/291. 'I have moved certain Romans to *undergo* with me an enterprize.' (Julius Cæsar, I. 3.)
Under-grinde, I. 120/731, 258/847.
Under-ground, *sb.*, II. 163/278.
Under-orbs, I. 55/349.
Under-propped, II. 316, col. 1, l. 18.
Under-realms, II. 251/481.
Under-trod, II. 226/55.
Under-tub, I. 236/1139.
Undisputable, I. 156/210.
Uneasie, II. 330, col, 1. l. 22.
Un-eath, I. 241/165.
Unfeltly, I. 185/107.
Unfixed, I. 155/131.
Unforced, I. 149/573.
Un-french, *v.*, I. 14, col. 1, l. 25.
Un-full, I. 127/540.
Unfurnisht, unfurnished, I. 243/298, 252/61.
Un-garnished, I. 21/291.
Ungenerate, II. 316, col. 3, l. 2.
Un-gilt, I. 21/291.
Un-goard, I. 166/288.
Ungraced, I. 94, col. 2, l. 28.
Un-graft, I. 104/525.
Ungrate, II. 335, col. 1, l. 19.
Unhallow, *v.*, unhallowed, I. 11, col. 2, l. 22, 214/159.
Un-hallow-washt, II. 125/196.
Un-happieth, *v.*, II. 59/410.
Unhappy-happy, II. 293/185.
Un-hideable, I. 237/1256.
Unholsome, II. 135/1274, 1306, 156/6.
Unhonest, II. 112/888.
Unhood, *v.*, II. 172/615.
Unhorse, *v. tr.*, I. 253/233.
Un-housed, *v.*, I. 146/154 ; II. 292/79.
Unicall, I. 113/651.
Unicorns, I. 206/904.
Unidle, II. 250/419.
Uni-form, *sb.* (the uniform), I. 238/1335.
Universitie, university = universe, I. 23/471 ; II. 15, st. 4.
Unjudecious, II. 190/459.
Unjustice, II. 169/210.
Unkemb'd, *v.*, I. 205/835.
Unkend, *v.*, I. 50/1160 ; II. 111/748, 193/217.
Unkinde, *adj.*, I. 224/1232.
Unkindely, *adj.*, unkindly, I. 67/765 ; II. 37, Son. 4, 92/905.
Unkindly, *adv.*, I. 122/7, 205/833.
Unkindly-kinde, I. 182/480.
Un-kinged, I. 57/643.
Unkingly, I. 241/139.
Un-kinsman, I. 223/1216.
Unlearnednesse, I. 100/159.

Unleav'd (un-leav'd), I. 100/122.
Un-leave, *v.* = deprive of leaves, I. 123/136.
Unlight = unlit, I. 33/670.
Un-mastering, II. 56, col. 2, l. 10.
Unmew'd, *v.*, II. 96, col. 1, Son, l. 8.
Un-moving, I. 103/440.
Un-niggard, I. 55/375.
Un-old, *v.*, I. 246/697.
Un-pagan, II. 185/452.
Unpalpable, I. 79/811.
Unpartiall, II. 134/1167, 283/79.
Un-peer'd, *v.*, II. 244/639.
Unplac'd, I. 23/529.
Un-plumed, I. 167/319.
Un-preposterous, II. 283/79.
Unpuddled, *v.*, II. 117/1437.
Unpuff, *v.*, I. 56/526.
Un-puft = un-elated, I. 255/452.
Un-ready, I. 114/30.
Un-reel, *v.*, I. 196/1377.
Un-respect, II. 274/822.
Un-right, *sb.*, I. 247/803.
Un-rip, I. 248/949.
Unsacred, I. 242/188 ; II. 192/171.
Un-sanctuary, II. 273/709.
Unschooled, *adj.*, II. 147/54.
Unseamed, II. 16, st. 49.
Un-self-changing, I. 29/212.
Un-self-delicious, I. 49/1057.
Un-self-like, I. 156/195.
Un-selfly, I. 186/253.
Unsettled, *adj*, = turbulent, I. 31/404.
Unshoos't, *v.*, I. 47/767.
Unshown, II. 191/45.
Unsiege, II. 16, st. 11.
Un-sight (= sighed), II. 283/8.　Dr. Johnson calls
　　this a low word only used in the phrase, ' unsight,
　　unseen,' as in Hudibras (I. ii. 635).　In this he was
　　mistaken : ' unsight, unseen,' occurs also in
　　Spectator, No. 511.
Un-skill, *sb.*, I. 101/277.
Un-slave, *v.*, II. 119/1641.
Un-soule-clog'd, I. 207/1022.
Unspiable, II. 150/367.
Unspid, *v.*, I. 54/277.
Un-suspect, *v.*, I. 222/1055.
Unthankfull = unthanked, I. 119/626.
Unthrifts, I. 48/878 ; II. 273/672.
Un-toyld, I. 140/262.
Un-transparent, I. 21/290.
Untrusse, II. 202/78.　Word later rendered notorious
　　in the Dekker-Jonson quarrel.
Un-turning, I. 21/290.
Un-tutor'd, I. 140/262.
Untwist, I. 237/1314.
Un-venter'd, I. 169/631.
Unvictual'd = unfed, I. 141/351.
Un-vulgar, I. 99/40, 166/209.
Un-weary, I. 102/355.

Unweeting, *v.*, I. 248/527.
Unwildes, *v.*, I. 124/277.
Unwinde, *v.*, I. 166/203, 196/1376.
Un-wrap, *v.*, II. 30, st. 83.
Upbraiding, *adj.*, II. 335, col. 2, l. 31.
Up-down-bending, I. 156/180.
Up-holsters, I. 151/674.　' We will not set up for
　　upholsters, and stuff cushions and pillows to lay
　　them under their elbows.'　(Bp. Andrewes, Sermons,
　　v. 7).
Up-tane, I. 12, col. 1, l. 4.
Urchin, I. 89/683 ; II. 311, st. 70.
Ure (in use), I. 81/1031 ; II. 40, Son. 25, 239/51, 268/87.
Urge, *sb.*, II. 357, st. 27.
Use, *v.*, II. 250/370, 287/5.
Use and principall, I. 188/501.
Use upon use, I. 44/521.
Usher-lesse, I. 123/88.
Usury, II. 193/276.
Utter, *adj.* = outer, I. 236/1192 ; II. 88/432.

V

VADE, *v.*, I. 106/769, 127/559, 132/15, 202/478 ; II.
　　58/301.　See Glossarial Index : in my edition of
　　Vaughan, Donne, Southwell, etc.　I add these
　　examples :—

> ' I blindfold walked, disdaining to behold
> 　　That life doth *vade*, and young men must be old.'
> 　　　　　　(Greene's Never too late to Mend.)

> ' Fair Narcissus tooting in his shade
> 　　Reproves disdain, and tells how form doth *vade*.'
> 　　　　　　(Peele's Arrainment of Paris, i. 2.)

Cf. F. Queene, ix. 20.
Vading, *adj.*, II. 300, st. 36.
Vail, *v.*, vaile = to bow to abase, I. 15, col. 1, l. 22,
　　42/204, 233/840, 248/927, etc.
Vail, *sb.* = a veil, I. 54/200, 59/793, 81/1005, etc.
Vail, *v.* = to veil, I. 90/570, 188/315.
Vaileth bonnets, I. 114, col. 2, margin.
Vain, *sb.* = vein, I. 41/89, 126/492.
Vaine-glorious, I. 86/418, 120/682.
Vain-proud, II. 61/667.
Vain of vains = vanity of vanities, I. 236/1208.
Vale, *v.* = to bend, II. 124/49.
Val'd, *v.* = abated, II. 241/235.
Vales, *v.* (vales a valley), I. 83/53.
Valiance, II. 132/944, 194/404.
Valiancie, I. 167/345.
Valour-murdering, I. 184/13.
Valour-softning, I. 114/35.
Vant-guard, I. 72/39.
Vantbras, II. 204/254.　(See ' Vaunt-brace.')
Vantage, *sb.*, I. 246/648.
Vantage, *v.*, II. 169/227.
Vaporie, vapoury, I. 115/165, 116/262.
Vardingale, II. 198/219.
Variance, I. 240/17.

Variate, *v.*, I. 31/435.
Varifi'd, *v.*, I. 232/661.
Varlets, I. 241/116.
Varnish, *sb.*, I. 37/1150, 144/649.
Varnisht, *v.*, II. 300, st. 32.
Vate, *sb.* = vat, I. 204/745.
Vaunt-brace (see 'Vantbras '), I. 167/384.
Vaunt-full, I. 256/532.
Vegetal, *sb.*, II. 268/163, 271/535.
Vegetive, I. 176/1354.
Veinlings, II. 163/273.
Venerian, *adj.*, I. 136/419.
Venetians, *sb.*, II. 270/378.
Vengeance-sword, I. 249/1061.
Venge, *v.*, venging, venged, I. 22/406, 74/189, 136/467, 254/377, etc.
Vengers, I. 116/222.
Venging, *adj.*, I. 111/495 ; II. 40, Son. 26.
Venice glass, I. 28/72. 'The first making of Venice glasses in England began at the Crotched Friars in London about the beginning of the reign of Queen Elizabeth by one Jacob Venclise, an Italian.'— Stow's Chron.
Vennies, *sb.*, I. 204/727.
Vent, *v.*, I. 108/76, 151/665 ; II. 267/50, 269/215, etc.
Vent, *sb.*, I. 137/620, 180/293 ; II. 167/51.
Venter, *v.*, ventred, I. 20/112, 72/54 ; II. 187/150, etc.
Vent'rous, I. 99/27.
Veny, *sb.*, I. 26/813.
Venzon = stags, II. 89/484.
Ver, *sb.* = spring, I. 100/79, 142, 119/543, 123/126.
Verdict, *sb.*, I. 231/516 ; II. 88/373, 400, 115/1138, 163/219.
Verdue, *sb.*,—misprint for 'verdure,' I. 125/334.
Verge, *sb.*, I. 223/1157.
Verity, veritie, I. 37/1150, 127/572 ; II. 65/1129, etc.
Vestiments, I. 194/1171.
Vices, *sb.*, tools, I. 127/523.
Vice-loathing, I. 111/506.
Vice-upbraiding, I. 138/35.
Victoriz'd = made victors, II. 203/189.
Victualling, *sb.*, II. 354, st. 5.
Vie, *sb.*, I. 199/10.
Vies, *v.* (vies sighs from her heart), I. 120/664.
Violon, I. 217/436.
Viper-war, warre, I. 73/95 ; II. 41, Son. 28.
Viper-worm, I. 74/199 ; II. 18, st. 5.
Viperous, II. 12, st. 31.
Viragos, *sb.* = heroines, II. 17, st. 30, 204/227.
Virginals, I. 127/567, 228/177 ; II. 65/1140.
Vittle, *sb.*, II. 108/355.
Vizard, *sb.*, I. 252/165 ; II. 12, st. 18, 41. Son. 31, 216, st. 3, 236/665.
Vizor = mask, I. 231/590.
Void, *sb.* = vacuum, II. 244/602.
Voluntaire, *adj.*, II. 274/835.
Voyce-match'd, I. 143/575.
Voyce-ordering, I. 160/715.
Voyds, *v.*, voided, voyding = to empty, I. 117/296, 146/62, 234/884, 246/677.

Voyds, *v.* (voyds our dangers), II. 42, Son. 40.
Voyds, *sb.*, II. 192/186.
Vulgars, *sb.*, vulgar, I. 133/105, 142/507 ; II. 32, st. 97, 188/206.
Vulter-rented (Prometheus), I. 148/298.

W

WAG, *v.*, wagg'd, I. 123/149 ; II. 291/51.
Wag, *sb.*, I. 203/520, 232/718.
Wag-son, II. 3, st. 7.
Wag-tayling, *v.*, I. 214/137.
Wage, *v.* = to hire, I. 329, col. 1, l. 29.
Wage-lesse, II. 166/555.
Wagging, *adj.*, I. 195/1336.
Wagging, *sb.* (wagging of a straw), II. 13. st. 49.
Waigh, *v.* = to esteem, II. 340, col. 2, l. 17.
Waight, *sb.*, II. 178/178, 181/80.
Waighty, *adj.*, II. 200/534, 5.
Wain, *v.* = to wean, I. 99/41.
Walken, *v.*, I. 13, col. 2, l. 35.
Wall, *sb.*, to take the wall, II. 164/409.
Wall-break, *adj.*, I. 246/727.
Wall-ward, I. 257/724.
Wallet, I. 166/190.
Wallowes, *v.*, II. 288/89.
Wan, *v.* = won, I. 94, col. 1, l. 2 ; II. 200/493, 230/21.
Wanderers = planets, II. 86/211.
Wanderment, I. 159/614.
Wane, *v.*, II. 87/216.
Wane-less, II. 87/216.
Wanly, 1. 70/1028.
Want, *v.*, II. 12, st. 16, 25, st. 26, 68/135.
Want-less, I. 43/393.
Wantoniz'd, I. 166/236.
Wanton-pampering, II. 61/683.
War-eloquent, I. 189/589.
War-thirst, I. 121/806.
War-worthie, I. 94, col. 1, l. 14.
Ward, *sb.* = prison, I. 33/710.
Ward, *v. int.*, I. 72/41, 160/677 ; II. 169/224.
Ward-robe (the ward-robe), II. 287/9.
Wariefide, *v.*, II. 131/801.
Warmly-wet, I. 47/836.
Warm-temp'red, I. 31/437.
Waste-full, I. 75/306.
Watch-births, I. 236/1197.
Watch-clock, I. 123/105.
Watchet, *adj.*, I. 156/271.
Water-gates, I. 237/1241.
Water-guests = sea-fowl, I. 142/429.
Water-loaden, I. 129/776, 136/478.
Water-mixed, I. 189/589.
Water-rills, *sb.*, I. 219/751.
Water-rover, I. 64/337.
Water-want, *adj.*, I. 136/413.
Water-wracks, I. 102/401.
Wat'rish, I. 34/768, 9.

Watt, *sb.*, a hare, I. 201/391.
Wattled, *adj.*, I. 38/1218.
Waved, *adj.*, I. 199/114.
Wave-laced, I. 234/965.
Waves, *v.*, I. 204/645.
Waves-mother, I. 64/362.
Waving, *adj.*, II. 7, st. 82.
Wax, *v.*, waxen, I. 123/152 ; II. 87/216.
Wax-less, *adj.*, II. 87/216.
Wax-nosed (wax-nosed words), II. 227, st. 94.
Waxen, *adj.*, made of wax, I. 117/339 ; II. 39, Son. 14, 180/380.
Waxen, *adj.*, of wax = impressionable, I. 29/211, 254/288.
Waxen-wings, II. 12, st. 20.
Way-fare, II. 91/714, 97/44.
Way-less wayes, I. 64/389, 77/603.
Wayns, *sb.*, winged wayns = ships, I. 116/194.
Weed, *sb.*, weeds = clothes, I. 23/535, 45/545, 256/586 ; II. 227, st. 77.
Weed, *sb.* = corn, II. 177/56.
Weed, *sb.*—distinction between herbs and weeds, II. 267/34, 269/279.
Weed-full, II. 141, col. 1, l. 7.
Ween, *v.*, II. 91/731, 125/185, 126/275, etc.
Weening, *v.*, I. 256/532, 561.
Weer, *sb.* = weir, I. 249/1011.
Weet, *v.*, II. 135/1259, 262/194.
Weight-lesse, I. 36/1029.
Welds, *v.*, II. 188/222.
Welkin, I. 31/414, 575, 34/789, 66/563, 67/672, etc.
Well-breath'd, *adj.*, I. 186/182.
Well-fresh'd, I. 192/970.
Well-ill, II. 261/27.
Well-manned, I. 29/191.
Well-tempered (climate), I. 146/65.
Well-will'd, II. 111/688.
Welling, *adj.*, I. 41/181.
Welt, *sb.*, II. 194/375.
Weltred, *v.*, I. 224/1293.
Wend, *v.*, wends, I. 116/201, 160/750, 214/132 ; II. 86/117.
Wex, *v.*, wexen, wexing, I. 56/523, 58/760, 127/560, 135/306, 137/612, etc.
Weyre, *sb.* = weir, I. 64/315.
Whale-like, I. 249/1016.
Whay, *sb.* = whey, I. 50/1157.
Wheezes, *v.*, I. 28/79.
Whelpings, II. 56, col. 1, l. 24.
Whence-from, I. 135/306.
Whereas = where, I. 104/559.
Where-under, I. 149/432.
Whether = whither, II. 86/117.
Whiff, *sb.*, I. 55/334.
Whiffing, *adj.*, I. 32/545, 245/620, 257/652 ; II. 218, st. 41.
Whift, *v.*, II. 159/395.
While-yer, I. 247/769 ; II. 242/409.
Whilom, I. 40/19, 66/547, 79/879, etc.

Whilom-beauties, I. 192/94.
Whirl-about (whale), I. 62/98.
Whirl-fires, I. 193/1011.
Whirl-poole (whale), I. 62/109.
Whirl-whale, I. 190/732.
Whirl-wind-like, I. 126/448 ; II. 263/29.
Whirlers, I. 229/396.
Whirli-gig, I. 42/191.
Whirr'd, *v.*, I. 202/516.
Whirring, *sb.*, I. 115/115.
Whisk, *sb.*, II. 269/290.
Whisking, *adj.*, I. 26/817, 33/637, 145/39.
Whisteling, I. 248/932.
White, *v.*, II. 213/526.
White, *sb.*, I. 105/709, 127/585, 167/293, 188/505, etc.
White-blew, I. 248/935.
White-bread, I. 191/836.
White-exceeding, II. 50, col. 2, l. 11.
Whitely, *adj.*, I. 176/1392.
White-red, II. 310, st. 45.
Whittls, *sb.*, I. 127/521.
Whoods, *sb.* = hoods, II. 115/1195.
Whurld, *v.*, I. 48/494, 79/795.
Whurre, *v.*, I. 191/779.
Wicked-walking, I. 253/236.
Wide-side, I. 228/266.
Wide-spreading, I. 42/222.
Wide-staring, I. 247/863.
Wide-straddling, I. 206/945.
Wide-yawning, I. 63/241, 159/591.
Wide-wide-yawning, II. 278/174.
Widenesse, I. 156/289.
Widow, *adj.*, II. 330, col. 1, l. 45.
Widow-curst, II. 130/767.
Widow-turtle, II. 194/318.
Wiery, *adj.*, I. 127/566, 254/397.
Wight, *sb.*, I. 230/467 ; II. 55, col. 2, l. 2, 162/185, etc.
Wight, *adj.*, I. 232/726.
Wild-ash-tree, II. 134/1177.
Wilde-age, II. 9/657.
Wilfullings, *sb.*, I. 189/610.
Will-he-nill-he, II. 97/21.
Will-it, II. 98/200.
Will-nill, II. 38, Son. 12, 293/179.
Will-nill-they, I. 85/209.
Will-they-nill-they, I. 53/143.
Will-thou-nill, II. 169/212.
Will-we-nill-we, I. 260/1056.
Winch, *v.*, II. 148/184.
Winde (down the winde), II. 345, col. 2, l. 12.
Winde, *sb.* (to have the winde at will), II. 91/756.
Wind-less, I. 44/480.
Winds-but, I. 133/155.
Wine-driv'n, II. 68/85.
Wine-hurdles, I. 204/743.
Wine-stuft, I. 137/548.
Wing-footed, I. 101/251.
Wing-lim'd, I. 230/428.
Winged-beast = bat, I. 253/276.

Winkt, *v.*, I. 33/665.

Winter-chill, I. 202/482.

Winter-feed, I. 206/947.

Winter-shaken, I. 15, col. 1, l. 24, 168/483.

Wist, *v.*, I. 102/377 ; II. 204/276.

Witched, *adj.*, II. 254, st. 18.

Witches, *v.*, witching, I. 25/664 ; II. 15, st. 42.

With, *sb.*, I. 124/224. It is told by his Biographers that the first gleam of intellect shown by Sir Walter Scott—*the* stupid boy of his school—was his defence of his definition of 'with' as a noun by appeal to the Bible that they tied Sampson with 'green withes.'

With-child, *v.*, with-childes, I. 30/390, 144/666, 157/355 ; II. 99/223.

With-go, *v.* = to go with, II. 225, st. 37.

Within-boord, I. 53/170.

Withouten, I. 21/234.

Wit-gracing, I. 52/34.

Wit-less, II. 194/429, 196/77.

Wit-pride, I. 37/1151.

Wit-wantons, II. 278/99.

Wit-wondrous, I. 143/584.

Wits, *sb.* = witty persons, I. 61/66. See Memorial-Introduction (II. Critical).

Witts-worthie, I. 94, col. 1, l. 13.

Witty = wise, I. 49/485, 76/438, 110/363, 117/338, etc.

Witty-fained, I. 78/746.

Witty-pretty, I. 232/684.

Wittily, I. 184/54.

Wizzard (in a bad sense), I. 218/631.

Woad, I. 151/694.

Wolfs-drum, I. 115/107.

Women-men, I. 167/344.

Won, *v.*, wonnes, wonn, I. 87/498, 151/674, 169/526 ; II. 17/21, 118/1490.

Wonder-smit, II. 162/99.

Wonder-strook, I. 137/597.

Wonts, *v.*, he wonts = he is wont, II. 89/501, 125/156, 135/1305.

Wood, *adj.* = mad, I. 179/154, 190/723 ; II. 91/781.

Wood-sale-time, I. 200/243.

Wooden-bridle = helm, II. 130/705.

Wooll, *sb.* (harsh hard wool = ice), I. 219/751.

Woont, *v.*, I. 103/461.

Work, *sb.* (to set a-work), II. 248/161.

Work-fit, I. 43/313.

Workmanships, I. 20/144, 69/912, 83/60, 84/113, 114/17.

World, *sb.*, *pron.* as dissyllable, II. 291/1.

World-adorning, I. 101/231.

World-devouring, I. 136/449.

World-divided, I. 122/50 ; II. 321, Son. 4.

World-mourned (Sidney), I. 143/664.

World-shaking, I. 136/444.

World-tossing, I. 257/657.

Worlds-drad, I. 217/433.

Worlds-must, II. 262/119.

Worlds-re-colonizing Boat = the Ark, I. 132/60.

Worlds-weale, II. 67/52.

Worm-clasp, *sb.*, I. 63/289.

Worm-gnawn (worm-gnawn words), ·I. 142/491.

Wormeth, *v.*, I. 127/523.

Wormling, *sb.*, I. 111/498.

Wormly (wormly brave), I. 171/852.

Worse-apply'd, I. 31/418.

Worship, *sb.*, II. 328, col. 1, l. 29, 329, col. 2, l. 13.

Worshipfull, II. 329, col. 2, ll. 22-24.

Worth (to take in worth), II. 334, Ep. VI.

Worthy-sing, *v.*, I. 213/34.

Wot, *v.*, wote, I. 21/251, 37/1158, 58/721, 105/742 ; II. 165/438.

Woundless, II. 108/338.

Wound-soule, I. 111/513.

Wo-worth, I. 108/152, 112/632-3.

Wrack, *sb.*, I. 20/111, 93/10, 129/781, 134/257.

Wrack, *v.*, I. 28/128, 66/546, 136/477.

Wracked, *adj.*, I. 220/823, 243/371 ; II. 139, Son. 1, l. 10.

Wrackfull, I. 30/353, 66/576, 151/706, 249/991, etc.

Wrangling, *sb.*, I. 174/1152.

Wrastle, *v.*, wrastling, I. 215/268 ; II. 61/659, 110/593.

Wrathfull, I. 35/902, 44/474.

Wrathlesse, I. 127/635.

Wreakfull, I. 101/197, 116/187, 180/193.

Wrench, *v.*, I. 63/258.

Wrench, *sb.*, II. 67/15.

Wrest, *sb.*, I. 84/176.

Wrested, *v.*, wrests, I. 84/187 ; II. 106/151.

Wretched-witched, II. 251/425.

Wriggle, *v.*, wriggelled, wriggling, I. 63/258, 187/407 ; II. 182/152.

Wriggling, *adj.*, I. 185/83, 259/887.

Wring, *v.*, II. 166/537, 169/204, 213/547.

Wringers, *sb.*, II. 141, col. 2, l. 10.

Wringling, *adj.*, I. 118/462.

Wrinkle-faced, I. 55/380.

Wrinkle-full, I. 252/121.

Wrong-vext, I. 93, col. 2, l. 18.

Wry, I. 36/1070 ; II. 130/706, 225, st. 40.

Wrythed, *adj.*, I. 185/96.

Wun, *v.*, wuns = won, dwell, I. 184/46, 205/767 ; II. 55/10, 179/291, etc.

Wyer, *sb.* = wire, I. 214/74.

Wyerie, *adj.* = wiry, I. 141/350.

Wylie-guiles, I. 232/684.

Y

Y, The forked Y, crane's flight, I. 68/871.

Yarn, *sb.*, I. 37/1122.

Yarnes, *sb.*, I. 220/870.

> 'So many yarnes I still am faine to strike,
> Into this web'. . . .

Yauld, *v.*, II. 128/441.

Yawling, *sb.*, I. 140/228.

Yawning, *adj.* (thirsty yawning plain), I. 243/392.

II.—INDEX OF NAMES.

. Persons, places, and (occasionally) things, are herein included. Besides, the Reader will find a considerable number of these in Sylvester's own 'Briefe Index Explaining Most of the hardest words scattered through the whole Worke' (Vol. II. pp. 69-81). It has not been attempted to record the numerous Scriptural and Classical and commonly-used proper names, etc., etc.— trite and easily found if by chance not known. Neither are technical terms of the creation, etc., fully registered.

III.—SPECIAL LISTS.

₊ These would have so swollen the Glossarial Index as to make it cumbrous. By classifying them thus it is relieved, and quaint and curious references and folk-lore and the like guided to.

(a) Trees, plants, flowers, etc.

ACONITE, I. 46/736, 47/793, 116/174.
Aldars, I. 45/564.
Angelica, I. 46/721.
Apium, I. 116/174.
Apple, I. 45/572.
Apricock, I. 45/568.
Artemisian stem, I. 46/711.
Artificial garden, I. 104/560.
Ash, I. 45/560.

Balm, I. 45/584.
Bandans, I. 45/581.
Bay, I. 119/619.
Betonie, I. 46/740, 752.
Box, I. 45/558.

Carpese, I. 115/172.
Cedar, I. 45/558.
Cherry, I. 45/573.
Citrons, etc., I. 235, l. 1013.
Cinamon, I. 45/579.
Cocos, I. 47/853.
Colchis, banefull Lilly, I. 116/177.
Cole-wort, I. 115/98.
Cork, I. 45/561.

Damson, I. 45/574.
Date, I. 45/575.
Dittanie, I. 47/774.

Elm, I. 45/561, 115/71.

Fig, I. 45/574.
Filberd, I. 45/573.
Finger-ferne, I. 47/758.
Flax, I. 45/611.
Flea-wort, I. 116/177.
'Fleece of Flowers,' I. 157/380.
Flowers, I. 45/670.
Flowers, herbs, I. 84/90.
Fruits, apricocks, peaches, etc., I. 45/568.

Garden of Eden, I. 100/76.
Gardens, meadows, I. 151/710.

Helleborus, I. 46/738.
Hemlock, I. 47/788, 115/172, 119/617.
Hemp, I. 47/818.
Henbane, I. 115/170.
Holly, II. 116/1273.
Holm, I. 45/560.

Larch, I. 45/557.
Laurel, I. 48/981.
Lillie, I. 45/613.
Lotas (Lotos), I. 46/649.
Love's Grove, I. 232/660.

Madder, I. 46/726.
Maiz, I. 47/824.
Mandrake, I. 116/181, 119/620.
Maple, I. 45/561.
Marigold, I. 45/611.
Meddeler, I. 45/573.
Misseltoe, I. 116/180.
Moon-wort, I. 47/763, 766.
Morell, I. 115/170.
Mountain-Siler, I. 119/621.
Myrtle-bush, I. 115/71.

Napell, I. 116/179.
Nepenthe-moly, I. 101/250, 234/914, Mandrake, etc.
Nutmegs, I. 45/580.

Oke, oake, I. 45/560, 115/100.
Oleander, I. 47/790.
Olive, I. 45/575, 115/71, 100.
Orenge, I. 45/569.
Osiars, I. 45/564.
Ox-lip, II. 116/1267.

Pansey, I. 45/613.
Pastures in Eden, I. 103/512.
Peach, I. 45/569.

Pear, I. 45/572.
Pebbly Bush, I. 104/530.
Peonie, I. 46/712.
Pepper, I. 45/578.
Pimpernell, I. 46/724.
Pine, I. 45/556.
Plants, I. 255/422.
Poplars, I. 45/565.
Popy, I. 115/171.
Psylly, I. 116/176.

Quince, I. 45/569.

Reeds, I. 115/99.
Rose, I. 45/612.
Rose-daffodil, II. 109/470.
Rue, I. 119/616.
Rush, I. 115/70.

Saffron, I. 46/716, 116/178.
Sagapen, I. 47/786.
Sops-in-wine, I. 164/18.
Sperage, I. 115/70.
Succorie, I. 46/702.
Swines'-bread, I. 46/704, 115/98.

Tamarice, I. 47/756.

Vine, I. 45/586, 115/71, 98.
Violet, I. 45/612.

Wal-nut, I. 45/573.
Weeds, I. 115/164.
Willo-wort, I. 46/753.
Willows, I. 45/565.
Woad, I. 46/728.
Wolf's-bane, I. 116/175.

Yew, I. 116/180.

(b) Beasts.

Adder, I. 74/201.
Amphisbæna, I. 74/207.

IV.—ERRATA ET CORRIGENDA.

VOL. I. p. 49, l. 1074, add 'sups.'
,, 51, note, l. 67, read *commotive* not *commutive.*
,, 51, note, 985 (not 983), read *witty* for witly.
,, 71, note, l. 856—query masty = mastiff?
,, 73, l. 163, 'chill cold *cakes*'—query read *cares?*
,, 78, l. 736, for *lift* read *list.*
,, 79, l. 792, add *blasts.*
,, 80, l. 937, add *should.*
,, 90, l. 317, note, read *port,* not *post.*
,, 105, l. 728, for 'dull' of our text (1641 folio), earlier editions, read 'hull,' and perhaps the nautical context suits 'hull' = to float, drive without sails or rudder (Par. Lost, xi. 840).
,, 105, l. 714, *Orion*—query read *Ocean?*
,, 127, l. 588, insert *as* after *craves.*
,, 136, l. 488, add *Thrones.*
,, 146, l. 83, add *streams.*
,, 149, l. 466, for *thench* read *thence.*
,, 161, lines mis-numbered : for 660, etc., read 760, etc.
,, 161, notes for 772, 777, read 762, 767.

VOL. I. p. 165, l. 78, for *the* read *thee.*
,, 165, l. 173, for *Eire* read *Fire.*
,, 171, l. 868, for *Tor* read *For.*
,, 176, l. 1338, for *Diamant in* read *Diamantin.*
,, 196, l. 1383, insert *a* after *thee.*
,, 197, notes, l. 91, *Bubastic* = Egyptian.
,, 201, l. 363, for *abrave* read *a brave?*
,, 212, a stanza, l. 5, for *happy* read *happily?*
,, 222. l. 1060, for *Song* read *Song's?*
,, 234, l. 875, for *surgred* read *sugred.*
,, 239, note, l. 609, *Fisk* = *Treasury?*
,, 241, l. 69, for *cease* read *ease?*
,, 245, l. 627, *though* = then.
,, 251, l. 16, for *Age* read *Rage?*
VOL. II. p. 41. Son. 31. The two concluding lines of this Sonnet have been tacked on to Son. 32.
,, 149, l. 279, for *resell* read *refell.*
,, 180, l. 395, for *So me* read *Some.*
,, 183, l. 214, place comma after *harden,* and omit after *melt.*
,, 196, l. 56, for *dote* read *doth.*
,, 219, st. 19. l. 2, imperfect—query read 'which Archimedes,' etc.

END OF VOL. II.

FINIS.

Edinburgh University Press:
THOMAS AND ARCHIBALD CONSTABLE, PRINTERS TO HER MAJESTY.